WESTERN EUROPE

WAYNE C. THOMPSON

THE WORLD TODAY SERIES®

2020-2022

39TH EDITION

Graphic Materials Acknowledgments

For their generosity in providing certain visual material for use in this book, and in order of their appearance, special thanks to the following:

European Community Information Services
Delegation of the European Union in Washington
North Atlantic Treaty Organization
The Swiss National Tourist Office
The Government of Liechtenstein
The Government of Andorra
French Cultural Services, New York
The Royal Netherlands Embassy
The Embassy of Belgium

The Embassy of Ireland
The British Embassy
The Embassy of Italy
The Embassy of Malta
The Sovereign Military Order of Malta
The Government of Monaco
The Embassy of Spain
The Embassy of Portugal

First appearing as *Western Europe 1982*, this annually revised book is published by:

Rowman & Littlefield
An imprint of The Rowman & Littlefield Publishing Group, Inc.
4501 Forbes Blvd., Suite 200, Lanham, MD 20706
www.rowman.com

Copyright © 2021 by The Rowman & Littlefield Publishing

Group, Inc.

Library of Congress Control Number Available

ISBN 978-1-4758-5623-1 (pbk.)

ISBN 978-1-4758-5624-8 (electronic)

Cover design by Sarah Marizan

Cartographer: William L. Nelson

Typography by Barton Matheson Willse & Worthington
Baltimore, MD 21244

The World Today Series has thousands of subscribers across the US and Canada. A sample list of users who annually rely on this most up-to-date material includes:

Public library systems
Universities and colleges
High schools
Federal and state agencies
All branches of the armed forces and war colleges
National Geographic Society
National Democratic Institute
Agricultural Education Foundation
ExxonMobil Corporation
Chevron Corporation
CNN

DEDICATION

To the memory of my mother and father

ACKNOWLEDGMENTS

I am especially grateful to the Alexander von Humboldt Foundation, a farsighted German organization which, since 1869, has persistently nurtured the spirit of intellectual discovery and has sought to tighten the links between Europe and the rest of the world, for having granted me a two-year research fellowship at the University of Freiburg in Germany. Without its aid, I would have been unable to complete the first edition of this book.

No author could possibly write a book with the breadth of this one without the assistance of numerous persons and organizations. Mark H. Mullin, a Harvard graduate who earned an MA as a Marshall Scholar, Oxford University, wrote the first drafts of all but the political and economic sections of the chapters on the United Kingdom and the Republic of Ireland. I have updated them over the years. I thank my fellow author, Malcolm B. Russell, whose chapter on Cyprus we have moved to this volume after its accession to EU membership in 2004. We have also moved Greece to this book from our Nordic, central and southeastern Europe volume in order to group Mediterranean Europe together.

I wish also to thank my colleagues and acquaintances throughout western Europe and the US who took the time to read or to comment upon various chapters dealing with their own countries or specialties. They include Peter Strohm, David M. Keithly, Richard Laurijssen, Jacky Paris, Philippe Vidal, and Maureen and Peter Ward. I am grateful to my students at the College of Europe who critiqued the chapters on their native countries. They are Andres Arnaldos Montaner (Spain), Ritienne Bonavia (Malta), Nuno Borges (Portugal), Diego Calatayud (Spain), Núria Carrasco Comes (Spain), Isabelle Costa (Monaco), Laurence Deglain (France), Yannis Couniniotis (Greece), Francisco Bossa Dionisio (Portugal), Elena Donnari (Italy), Sylvain Dufeu (France), Javier Fernandez Gonzalez (Spain), Maaike Göbel (Netherlands), Gregory Gosp (France), James Hughes (UK), Vincent Imperiali (Belgium), Eelco Keij (Netherlands), José Maria Lanzarote (Spain), Koen Lenssen (Netherlands), Antoine Kopp, Jean Micallef Grimaud (Malta), Bérénice Orban de Xivry (Belgium), Nuno Queirós (Portugal), Laura Requejo (Spain), Alejandro Ribo Labastida (Spain), Emmanuel Lenaerts (Belgium), Panagiotis Papadopoulos (Greece), Chryso Ritsou (Greece), Hélène Stergiou (Netherlands), Sabine Tomordy (Liechtenstein), Tim Van Broeckhoven (Belgium), Edwin Van Os (Netherlands), Stijn Van Wesemael (Belgium), and Giuseppe Zaffuto (Italy). Renée Maeyaert and Anne Heber-Suffrin, librarians at the College of Europe, Bruges, consistently gave me important assistance in obtaining European newspapers and visuals for this book. Sonja Fernandez (France) kindly collected for me French newspapers reporting on the 2008 US election. Jean-Michel Cassiers and Monika Sapilak provided me in Brussels with information and materials on Belgium's language laws and practices. Michael Nix did a wonderful job in 2006 of reading every word of this book and making copious editorial changes based on his decades of experience as a Canadian government editor. I am deeply grateful for the generous gift of his time and talent. The late Catherine L. Lowe thoroughly read the entire manuscript in order to comb out style, spelling, and typographical errors. My wife, Susan L. Thompson, took some of the photographs and carefully proofread some of the manuscript. My daughter, Juliet Bunch, also provided photos for this book.

I am grateful to Pro Helvetia, which arranged and financed a week-long study tour of Switzerland, as well as to numerous embassy and foreign ministry officials who provided information and arranged visits to western European capitals to speak with representatives of parties, parliaments, universities, research institutes, and news media about this book. A Fulbright Teaching Fellowship to Estonia in 1995–1996 enabled me to become more familiar with Nordic Europe. A second Fulbright professorship in the spring semester of 2001 at the College of Europe in Bruges provided me with intellectual stimulation by top graduate students from all over Europe, in addition to an in-depth look at the BENELUX countries and EU and NATO institutions. My dear friend, the late Philip F. Stryker, was without doubt one of the most competent, encouraging, and congenial publishers with whom an author could work. Finally I would like to thank David T. Wilt, who supports my work in countless ways.

W.C.T.

Lexington, Virginia, June 2021

iii

Wayne C. Thompson . . .

Professor Thompson taught politics at Washington and Lee University in Lexington, Virginia. He is also an emeritus professor at the Virginia Military Institute in Lexington. He attended Ohio State University (BA in government) and Claremont Graduate University (MA and PhD, with distinction). He did further graduate study at the Universities of Göttingen, Paris/Sorbonne, and Freiburg im Breisgau, where he was subsequently a guest professor. He studied and researched many years in Germany as a Woodrow Wilson, Fulbright, Deutscher Akademischer Austauschdienst (DAAD), Earhart, and Alexander von Humboldt Fellow. He served as scholar-in-residence at the Bundestag and as a Fulbright professor in Estonia. During the 1999–2000 academic year, he was a visiting professor at the Air War College in Montgomery, Alabama. In the spring semester of 2001, he had a second Fulbright professorship at the College of Europe in Bruges and continued for seven years to teach at the Bruges and Warsaw campuses of that graduate institution. In the fall semester of 2003, he was a visiting professor of politics at the American University of Bulgaria. He is the author of *In the Eye of the Storm: Kurt Riezler and the Crises of Modern Germany* (Iowa City: University of Iowa Press, 1980), *The Political Odyssey of Herbert Wehner* (Boulder, CO: Westview Press, 1993), and *Historical Dictionary of Germany* (Metuchen, NJ: Scarecrow, 1994) and coauthor of *Redefining Transatlantic Security Relations: The Challenge of Change* (Manchester University Press, 2004). He has written two other books in the World Today Series: *Canada*, as well as *Nordic, Central, and Southeastern Europe*. He also coedited *Perspectives on Strategic Defense and Space: National Programs and International Cooperation* and *Margaret Thatcher: Prime Minister Indomitable* (Boulder, CO: Westview Press, 1987, 1989, 1994). He has written many articles on European politics, philosophy, and history which have appeared in such periodicals as *The American Political Science Review, Western Political Quarterly, East European Quarterly, Journal of Politics, Central European History, The American Review of Canadian Studies, German Studies Review, Das Parlament, Current History, The Yearbook on International Communist Affairs, The History Teacher, Armed Forces and Society, Freedom at Issue, Communist and Post-Communist Studies, Contemporary French Civilization, Europe-Asia Studies,* and *Virginia Social Science Journal*. He has published a book about George C. Marshall as secretary of defense.

CONTENTS

A new president and First Lady meet the queen.

IRELAND
UNITED KINGDOM
NETHERLANDS
BELGIUM
LUXEMBOURG
LIECHTENSTEIN
SWITZERLAND
FRANCE
MONACO
SAN MARINO
ITALY
ANDORRA
VATICAN
PORTUGAL
SPAIN
GREECE
MALTA
CYPRUS

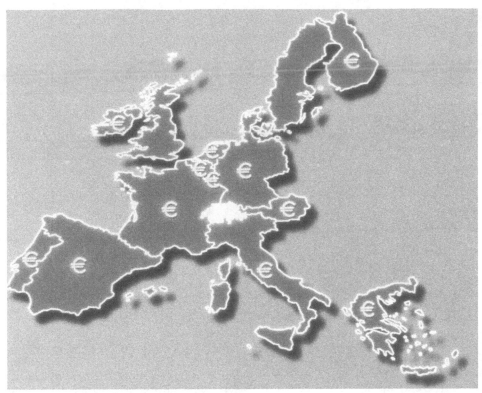

First countries to adopt the euro

"McDonald's? Me? Always!!!"

In 1945 much of Europe lay in ruins, its peoples destitute and demoralized following a war on its own soil more destructive than any conflict in history. Two world wars in the 20th century (World War I from 1914 until 1918 and World War II from 1939 until 1945) had brought Europe's dominance over world affairs to an end and had led to a rise of the United States of America and the Soviet Union as the world's most powerful nations. These wars also ended Europe's colonial hold on much of the world, a hold which, despite some negative effects, had spread European civilization to the Western Hemisphere, Africa, the Middle East, and the Far East.

Western Europe is a region rich in diversity, with a population of 262 million

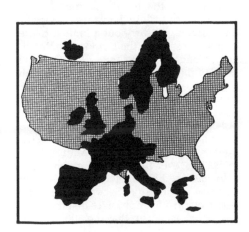

persons (382 million if one adds Germany, Austria, and the Nordic countries and over 500 million if one considers the entire European Union). This compares to over 311 million in the US.

Geographically, western Europe is much smaller than the US. The entire region is scarcely more than twice the size of Alaska and would easily fit into the continental US west of the Mississippi with much room to spare. Like the US, western Europe offers a very rich diversity of climates and landscapes, from the permafrost and midnight sun of northern Norway to the hot, dry, sunny Mediterranean; from the fog and rain of northern Germany to the warm blue skies of the Azores and to the snows and arctic winds of Iceland; and from the Alpine peaks of Austria and Switzerland to the flat and sub-sea level terrain of the Netherlands.

With the collapse of communism in Europe, the unification of Germany, and the dissolution of the Soviet Union, Europeans are faced with the most significant alteration of their continent's political map since World War II. Because two hostile Europes no longer face each other, Europe has doubled its size. From Moscow to Lisbon and Dublin to Budapest, democracies exist in which free elections provide the only legitimate claim to power and which are basically committed to freedom, individual rights, and some variant of capitalism.

Looking eastward, western Europeans see more than a dozen newly independent nations and a few more emerging, all in difficult economic circumstances and some with ethnic scores to settle and millions of discontented and frightened citizens who may decide to seek a better future in the west. Most are clamoring for admission to the plentiful western European table and a place under the Atlantic alliance's security umbrella. The December 1991 collapse of the former Soviet Union temporarily destroyed central authority and dispersed power among its various republics.

Western Europe still has many cultures and many lands and regions with characters and appearances of their own. However, there are many things which make much of modern western Europe and the US look similar: large shopping centers, fast-food restaurants, freeways, modern cities with skyscrapers and much concrete, many automobiles, and everywhere signs of prosperity.

Americans and western Europeans face many of the same problems and have many of the same concerns, though in differing degrees: the role and rights of women in modern society, illegal immigration, the integration of racial and religious minorities, a steady stream of political refugees, urban violence, the protection of the environment and the quality of life, the defense of their homeland and values in an age of terrorism and weapons of mass destruction, the provision of adequate supplies of energy and raw materials, and the maintenance of prosperity and generous social security programs in an age of globalization.

The reader will confront numerous abbreviations and acronyms, and one must understand not only what the letters signify but also what function the indicated institutions serve. Therefore, in the following pages, these acronyms will be presented in the context of a more general discussion of some of the more important European bodies and organizations.

Today, western Europe is a region that is, on the whole, highly prosperous, though it is relatively poor in natural resources. It has a large industrial base, much capital

Western Europe Today

and know-how and a highly educated and skilled workforce. It is also secure militarily. Such prosperity and security are partly due to the countries' high degree of voluntary cooperation, formalized in numerous international organizations. All major western European countries are full members of the United Nations (UN), and all participate in the many organizations linked to the UN, such as the UN Educational, Scientific, and Cultural Organization (UNESCO); the UN Conference on Trade and Development (UNCTAD); the World Court, which sits in the stately Peace Palace built with funds contributed by Andrew Carnegie in The Hague, Netherlands; the International Labor Organization (ILO); the UN Industrial Development Organization (UNIDO); the World Health Organization (WHO); the Food and Agriculture Organization (FAO); and a number of others.

Defense

Most western European countries would be unable to defend themselves alone. Therefore, the majority has chosen to join the North Atlantic Treaty Organization (NATO), also known as the Atlantic Alliance. It is housed outside of Brussels in a steel and glass structure that symbolizes the transparent modern NATO. In 2016 it moved into a new headquarters nearby. Created in 1949, NATO links the power of the United States and Canada and the geographic position of Iceland (which has no military) with the military resources of Belgium-Netherlands-Luxembourg (BENELUX), Great Britain, Norway, Denmark, the Federal Republic of Germany (FRG or Germany), Italy, Portugal, Turkey, Greece, France, and Spain and, since 1999, Poland, Hungary, and the Czech Republic. At its 2002 Prague summit, NATO invited seven more countries to join in April 2004: the three Baltic states (Estonia, Latvia, and Lithuania), Slovakia, Slovenia, Romania, and Bulgaria. At its April 2008 summit in

NATO headquarters, Brussels, Belgium, commemorating 9-11 victims

Bucharest, NATO leaders invited Albania and Croatia to join, which they did the following April. The alliance has 29 members. The only major western or Nordic European countries that remain neutral or nonaligned are Ireland, Switzerland, Austria, Sweden, and Finland.

When the question arose concerning the organization of a European military combination, France, Italy, and West Germany initiated in 1952 a treaty creating a European Defense Community (EDC). It was intended to bring into being an integrated European army under a unified command structure, which would ultimately include troops from West Germany and the BENELUX countries. However, in 1954 the French National Assembly rejected this plan, fearing the possible loss of its sovereignty if it relinquished command over its army.

As a compromise, Great Britain proposed a Western European Union (WEU),

composed of the BENELUX countries, France, Italy, Germany, Great Britain, Greece, Spain, and Portugal, with headquarters in Brussels. Turkey, Norway, and Iceland became associate members. It conducted contingency planning, organized and controlled small all-European military operations (with the possibility of using NATO units and equipment), and attempted to coordinate the defense policies and armaments programs of its members.

At the 1991 EU summit meeting in Maastricht, it was agreed that the WEU would be Europe's own defense system, albeit "linked to" NATO. It largely ceased to exist, the end of 2000, and most of its staff and activities were folded into the EU. At its Helsinki summit in 1999, the EU decided to create a 60,000-strong rapid-reaction corps, officially operational in 2003, to act in crises when the US and NATO choose not to get involved.

It also began the creation of about a dozen "battle groups" of 1,500 soldiers for rapid deployment anywhere in the world. In July 2003 the French formed such a group, which included Swedish troops for the first time, to carry out a limited peacekeeping mission in the Democratic Republic of Congo. This was the EU's first solo military mission outside of Europe. In July 2006 the Germans commanded a similar battle group to the Congo to oversee elections, and in the spring of 2008, the French organized a battle group to deal with violence in Chad. By 2013 the EU had active military missions in Bosnia, Mali, and Somalia. However, there is no European army.

In 2003 the EU adopted its first security doctrine, entitled "A Secure Europe in a Better World." It emphasizes that the union is a global actor and that the alliance with

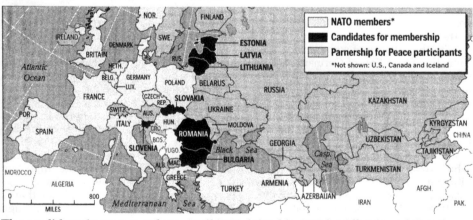

The candidates become members, April 2004, joined in 2009 by Albania and Croatia.

Source: *The Washington Post*

Jens Stoltenberg

the United States is indispensable. An informal organization within NATO known as the "Eurogroup," composed of all European members of NATO except France, Portugal, and Iceland, serves as a forum for some European states within NATO to discuss their special defense needs.

NATO itself has both political and military components. The highest political organ and decision-making body is the North Atlantic Council (NAC). It selects the secretary-general of NATO, who chairs all meetings and seeks consensus among members. By tradition he is always a European. In 2014, former Norwegian prime minister Jens Stoltenberg replaced Denmark's ex-prime minister Anders Fogh Rasmussen. Each member country sends a permanent ambassador to the NATO headquarters

in Brussels, and these ambassadors meet once a week. Less frequently, the member countries' heads of government or foreign, defense, or finance ministers meet to iron out higher-level political problems. All decisions are reached by consensus, not by majority vote. In other words, each member has an actual veto power, although such vetoes are seldom cast.

The ambassadors or ministers of all but those nations that do not participate in the integrated defense system (France and Iceland) also take part in the Defense Planning Committee (DPC), which is assisted by a variety of committees and working groups. A staff of about 1,000, divided into divisions of political affairs, defense planning and policy, defense support, and scientific affairs, are in Brussels to assist in the NATO effort.

The highest NATO military authority is the Military Committee, made up of the chiefs of defense from all states participating in the NATO military command, plus France (since 1995). By tradition it is chaired by a European officer, but in 2006 a Canadian general, Ray Henault, occupied the post. Although the chiefs-of-defense meet infrequently, their permanent representatives meet regularly in their absence. The Military Committee's primary role is to advise the DPC.

NATO has an integrated system of commands. The Supreme Allied Commander Europe (SACEUR), who by tradition is always an American, heads the Allied Command Europe (ACE). He also commands all US forces in Europe, and his European command encompasses Russia and all of Africa except the Horn. The position of deputy SACEUR alternates between a British and German officer.

ACE is based outside Mons, Belgium, at the Supreme Headquarters Allied Powers Europe (SHAPE). In case of war, ACE is responsible for military operations in the entire European area and wherever in the world NATO forces are deployed. Since the 2002 Prague summit, this strategic command for operations, which remains in Belgium, was made leaner, more efficient, more effective, and more deployable. A British or a German general alternate in commanding one of its two top regional subcommands in Europe, the Regional Command North, in Brunssum, Netherlands. The Regional Command South in Naples, Italy, is always entrusted to an American admiral. The US Sixth Fleet provides the most potent naval forces in the Mediterranean area.

Before the 2002 Prague summit, the other major NATO strategic command was the Allied Command Atlantic (ACLANT), commanded by an American admiral or general and headquartered in Norfolk, Virginia. A strategic command is based in Norfolk, Virginia, with a presence in Europe. It is responsible for continuing transformation of military capabilities and interoperability of allied forces. After reentering NATO's integrated command structure in 2009, France provides the commander for this transformation effort, as well as the top commander of NATO's regional headquarters in Lisbon, Portugal, which organizes the alliance's rapid-reaction force.

Only the US engages in negotiations with Russia aimed at limiting nuclear forces in Europe. But western European members are consulted about any American negotiating positions which might affect European interests. Europeans have developed bodies, such as the NATO Nuclear Planning Group (NPG) and the less formal Special Consultative Group, which serve as channels to inform the US of its allies' views and to keep the latter informed of US objectives.

In 1989 the Conventional Forces in Europe (CFE) negotiations in Vienna replaced the moribund Mutual Balanced Force Reduction (MBFR) talks. This culminated in an agreement between NATO and the now-defunct Warsaw Pact in 1990 to thin out their military equipment in the center of Europe. It did not apply to troops. Several years after the Warsaw Pact collapsed, the terms of the CFE Treaty began to be reexamined, at Russia's insistence, to take account of the fact that Moscow no longer has allies and has potentially serious internal instability.

In 1991 President George H. W. Bush announced unilateral nuclear cuts that went far beyond the Strategic Arms Reductions Talks (START) Agreement reached in July. European allies and Soviet president Mikhail Gorbachev gave Bush's plan

President Obama and Secretary of State Clinton at a NATO summit

Western Europe Today

The European Council and European Commission, Brussels

Courtesy: Central Audiovisual Library, European Commision

unanimous backing. The greatest impact was on Europe, where the only targets for NATO's tactical nuclear weapons were in areas that are no longer enemies, such as Poland and eastern Germany. Officially endorsed by NATO, the cuts did not make Europe nuclear-free: NATO still has some atomic bombs on dual-capacity aircraft to provide a measure of nuclear deterrence against unknown threats. NATO declared in May 2010 that it would retain its tactical nuclear weapons to protect its total population of 900 million "as long as nuclear weapons exist." Also, Britain and France retain some of their nuclear systems. But European defense has become almost entirely nonnuclear.

The sweeping American disarmament proposals, following the disappearance of a clearly identifiable foe, prompted Europeans to develop a distinct European Security and Defence Policy (ESDP), now called Common Security and Defence Policy (CSDP). A consensus exists that such a European identity is necessary, while preserving NATO in one form or the other.

In 1999 the EU created a new post of "high representative" to breathe life into its Common Foreign and Security Policy (CFSP) and named Javier Solana Madariaga to occupy it. In 2010 he handed the reins to Lady Catherine Ashton of the UK, who in 2014 was succeeded by Federica Mogherini of Italy. To give CFSP a military arm, the EU created ESDP with a rapid-reaction force. This enabled the EU to take command of the small peacekeeping force in North Macedonia in 2003 and in Bosnia in December 2004. By 2008 the EU was running more than a dozen foreign operations, and there were nearly 200 admirals and generals based in EU institutions in Brussels. They are increasingly engaged in planning, an activity always dominated by

NATO. By 2010 there was a "Director General of the European Union Military Staff."

No European country wants the total withdrawal of American troops, which had already been drawn down from 320,000 to under barely 30,000 (plus 14,000 in the Sixth Fleet) by 2013. Americans have called on Europeans to bear a greater responsibility for their own defense and but not in competition with NATO, which remains the major pillar for American influence in Europe. One American diplomat said, "Sure, we want the Europeans to do more, but we're always going to be wary of anything that looks like it could push the U.S. out of Europe."

In order to facilitate greater European security independence, NATO in 1998 reduced the number of its command headquarters from 65 to 20, emphasized a multinational approach to the manning of these headquarters, and arranged them in a way that they can support both regular NATO tasks as well as combined joint task forces (CJTF), authorized in 1994. If certain members, such as the US, do not wish to participate in a certain military operation, a coalition of those that do can use NATO units and assets under EU leadership. This is called "Berlin Plus." Non-NATO countries can also be included in such combined joint task forces.

International military groupings have proliferated in Europe since the end of the Cold War. Within NATO, a Dutch-German corps under alternate command has been formed; its troops use English. British, German, Dutch, and Belgian troops constitute a multinational division with an airmobile brigade. It is part of the ACE rapid-reaction force. The Dutch navy has merged its naval headquarters with those of Belgium. A corps has been created with headquarters in Szczecin, Poland, that comprises Polish,

German, and Danish troops and is commanded by a Polish officer.

This unit was modeled on the French-German Eurocorps in Strasbourg, France, created in 1992. The Eurocorps now includes BENELUX and Spanish troops and uses English as its common language. In the summer of 2000, this Eurocorps took temporary charge of the NATO-led peacekeeping operation in Kosovo (KFOR); in 2003–2004 it fielded peacekeeping forces in Afghanistan. In 2009 it was announced that German troops would be stationed permanently on French soil for the first time since the Second World War; a battalion is located in Alsace-Lorraine.

A US combat division serves in a German-led corps, while a German division is part of a US-led corps. Outside NATO, Italy, Austria, and Slovenia created a joint land-based force, and the Spanish, French, Portuguese, and Italians formed a rapid operational force called EUROFOR based in Florence. Many NATO troops served alongside other European and non-European soldiers in the Stabilization Force (SFOR) to guard the peace in Bosnia and Herzegovina, as well as in KFOR.

In 1991 NATO was transformed into a more political organization seeking to reach out to its former enemies. It created a North Atlantic Cooperation Council (NACC, renamed in 1997 the Euro-Atlantic Partnership Council—EAPC) comprising 44 countries at century's end to provide for regular consultations between NATO and the former Soviet republics and eastern European nations on such subjects as security issues, arms control, and the conversion of defense industries. In 1994 NATO initiated the Partnership for Peace (PfP), which links a dozen and a half nonmember countries, including Russia, in bilateral treaties with NATO. The purpose is to expand and intensify political and military cooperation and to strengthen stability and peace, primarily through training forces for peacekeeping operations. A special NATO-Ukraine Commission was

EU members

established to deepen cooperation with that important country.

These nations are also linked in the 55-member Organization for Security and Cooperation in Europe (OSCE, known until 1994 as the CSCE), to which all European states, former Soviet republics, and the United States and Canada belong. It meets irregularly to consider how to defuse threats to peace through mediation, crisis management, and the dispatch of observers during elections.

Many countries regard PfP as a stepping-stone to full NATO membership. In principle, the alliance is prepared gradually to accept new members on the condition that they have solid democratic credentials, including a firm civilian grip on the armed forces, and can make a genuine military contribution to the common defense. The door remains open to European democracies.

Russia opposes such enlargement, especially insofar as former Soviet republics, such as the Baltics, are concerned. To assuage Moscow's fears, the Atlantic allies signed with Moscow in 1997 a NATO-Russia Founding Act. This is not a legally binding treaty, but it states that NATO has no need, intentions, or plans to create additional capabilities or permanently station troops or nuclear weapons in the new member states. Agreements in 2006 permit such stationing of small numbers of American forces in Romania, Bulgaria, the Baltics, and Poland. NATO gets around objections about permanent stationing of troops there by rotating them. NATO also created a Permanent Joint Council (PJC) at its headquarters, in which Russian officials could discuss, though not veto, NATO policies and decisions.

In the wake of close Russian-US cooperation in the war against terrorism after the September 11 terrorist attacks in New York and Washington, the PJC was upgraded and renamed in 2002 the NATO-Russia Council. The spirit of cooperation was severely damaged by Russia's 2008 invasion of Georgia and its February 2014 military takeover of the Crimea, which is a part of Ukraine. NATO cooperation with Russia was temporarily suspended. The NATO-Russia Council did not convene for two years.

NATO's outdated doctrine of containing Soviet power through "forward defense" and "flexible response" was replaced by one that gives NATO a reason to exist in the changed European environment. Smaller, highly mobile, conventional, and multilateral forces are being created which can be deployed on short notice anywhere in the world and which can help manage unpredictable crises and instability in eastern Europe, the Balkans, the Mediterranean area, and beyond. To remain relevant, NATO must provide security beyond just Europe. The allies benefited from the experience of fighting together for more than a dozen years in Afghanistan, temporarily ending in late 2014. It improved its multinational rapid deployment capability by creating a NATO Response Force (NRF), with a headquarters and 13,000 highly ready and technologically advanced troops on a rotating basis by members. It can be used against enemies in or out of Europe and is intended to be "the tip of the spear" for future alliance deployments.

European Integration

No region in the world has been so successful in creating voluntary economic unions of sovereign states as western Europe. In 1922 the Belgium and Luxembourg Economic Union (BLEU) was created, which made the two countries a single unit for importing and exporting purposes and established a unified currency. In 1944 the Netherlands joined to form BENELUX, which was later extended to include even noncustoms matters.

In order to help the devastated countries of Europe recover economically, the United States offered Marshall Plan aid in 1947 but insisted that all countries receiving such aid sit down together and decide as a group how the money should be spent. Thus, the US provided an important initial impetus for a unified Europe. In response, the Europeans created in 1948 the Organization for European Economic Cooperation (OEEC) for making the decisions and the European Payments Union (EPU) for administering US funds.

In 1960, the US and Canada joined the OEEC, which was renamed the Organization for Economic Cooperation and Development (OECD), with headquarters in Paris. Later other western industrialized nations and Japan, Australia, and New Zealand joined OECD, making a total of 30 members by 2007. It does economic analysis and forecasting for industrialized countries, including estimates of future growth, inflation, unemployment, and gross domestic product (GDP, a measurement of an economy's total production of goods and services. A related and less used term, gross national product— GNP—adds to this value citizens' foreign earnings and subtracts foreigners' income within the country). The OECD also attempts to coordinate members' economic and development aid, and it provided a forum for member states to hammer out an antibribery convention in international commerce. All western European countries belong. Wanting closer contact with the world's industrial leaders, the Czech Republic, Hungary, Poland, and Slovakia joined, and Russia decided to enter. With only 16% of the world's population, its 30 members produce two-thirds of the world's economic output.

The Council of Europe was created in Strasbourg in 1949. Its 40 members include all western European countries and most newly independent countries in eastern Europe. Its assemblies of parliamentarians from the member states serve as a forum for discussing political, economic, social, and cultural issues of interest to all European countries. Perhaps its main contribution has been its various conventions, especially its Convention for the Protection of Human Rights and Fundamental Freedoms (known as the European Convention on Human Rights—ECHR), adopted in 1950. Acceptance of all the convention's principles is a precondition for EU membership. Since 1991 it has been particularly active in trying to strengthen democracy and human rights in eastern Europe. The

European Parliament building, Strasbourg, France

Western Europe Today

United States requested and was granted observer status in 1996 in order to be able to promote democracy more effectively in eastern Europe.

The BENELUX countries, together with France, West Germany, and Italy, made in 1951 the first significant move toward transferring a portion of their national sovereignty to a supranational organization by creating the European Coal and Steel Community (ECSC). Many persons could scarcely believe at the time that six countries that had been locked only six years earlier in a bloody struggle would be willing to transfer sovereignty over questions relating to these commodities, which are so crucial for heavy industry. Not only was it bold and farsighted to share these important goods rather than to fight wars over them, but also the ECSC gave these nations the practice in economic cooperation needed to convince the six that a move to create a unified Europe could succeed.

The same six nations signed the Treaties of Rome in 1957, which created both the European Economic Community (EEC), frequently called the "Common Market") and EURATOM, which seeks to coordinate the six countries' atomic research and policy. Both came into existence the following year and merged with the ECSC under the same overall organization. This union provided for the elimination of tariffs and customs among themselves, common tariff and customs barriers toward nonmembers, the free movement of labor and capital within the union and equal agricultural price levels through the establishment of the Common Agricultural Program (CAP). To avoid giving the impression that the three communities were only economic in nature and to express the fact that they are managed by common institutions, they were referred to in the singular as the European Community (EC). On January 1, 2002, when its 50-year mandate came to an end, the ECSC was fully absorbed into the EU.

The 27 member states (with over 500 million citizens, almost two-thirds more than the US) now include the BENELUX countries, France, Germany, Italy, Great Britain, the Republic of Ireland, Denmark, Greece, Spain, and Portugal. In 1995 Austria, Finland, and Sweden joined. In 2002, 10 more countries were invited: Estonia, Latvia, Lithuania, Poland, Hungary, the Czech Republic, Slovakia, Slovenia, Malta, and Cyprus (the Greek section); they entered on May 1, 2004. Romania and Bulgaria joined on January 1, 2007, with Croatia following on July 1, 2013. In 2016 the UK voted to leave the EU, and negotiations for a "Brexit" commenced in March 2017. This raises the question about the role of English as the dominant language, as English would be the primary tongue spoken only in tiny Ireland and Malta!

Because of its questionable human rights record, constitutional grant of political power to the military, continued Greek wariness, and fear by some western European countries that a flood of Turkish immigrants would arrive at their doorstep, Turkish consideration for entry was postponed until 2006. The Turkish part of Cyprus must also await unification of the island before becoming part of the EU. The irresistible logic of European unity has affected countries all over the continent. Norway was offered membership in 1972 and 1994, but its voters rejected it both times.

The issue of immigrants and refugees is a very sensitive one. Some western Europeans fear that they bring in crime and terrorism and overburden their generous welfare states at a difficult time when their economies are suffering under the challenges of the global economy.

Controlling the movement of outsiders who have entered the EU area has been made more difficult by the Schengen Agreements of 1985 and 1990 that eliminated many of Europe's internal border controls. The idea is that one need only go through border formalities when entering one of the membership states; then one can pass freely into the others, submitting only to occasional spot checks. All of the earlier 15 EU members except the UK and Ireland have joined. Since the Nordic countries long since abolished internal border controls among themselves, Norway and Iceland are automatically included. In 2005 Swiss voters chose to take part starting 2007. On December 21, 2007,

**Jean-Claude Juncker,
ex-president of European commission**

nine more countries joined the Schengen Zone: Estonia, Latvia, Lithuania, Poland, the Czech Republic, Slovakia, Hungary, Slovenia, and Malta.

On November 1, 1993, the Maastricht Treaty came into force, bringing with it terminological confusion. It created a European Union (EU), which added common foreign and security policy and cooperation in justice and police matters to the EC. But unlike the EC, the EU has neither a single decision-making process nor a legal persona; it cannot conclude international agreements. Although the EC and EU are technically not exactly the same entities, most scholars and journalists now employ the term EU instead of EC. The term "EU" is used throughout this book.

It is this political element that had prevented some other European states, such as Switzerland, from joining the EU. But the EU has successfully dealt with this problem by granting associate membership (which generally excludes agricultural aspects only) to most non-full-member states in western Europe. Regular contacts are also maintained with 70 African, Caribbean, and Pacific (ACP) countries linked to the EU through the Lomé Convention of 1975. Since 2002 the EU has a European Neighborhood Policy (ENP) to facilitate ties with former Soviet Republics in Europe and with Middle Eastern countries from Morocco to Turkey. In 2009 another multilateral grouping of nations not in the EU was formed: the Eastern Partnership Initiative, which links Armenia, Azerbaijan, Belarus, Georgia, Moldova, and Ukraine to the EU.

Most of the success the EU can claim has been in the economic field. The record

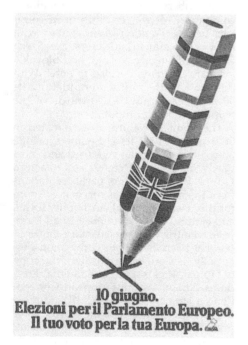

**10 giugno.
Elezioni per il Parlamento Europeo.
Il tuo voto per la tua Europa.**

Italian election poster for the European Parliament: "Your vote for your Europe"

is most impressive. With only 7% of the world's population, the EU accounts for 22% of the world's economic output, making it the world's top commercial power. It provides almost half (47%) of the development aid.

Together, the US and the EU states account for over half of the world's GDP and a third of global trade. They exchange $2.6 billion in goods and services each day. Their annual commercial relationship, including investments, amounted in 2005 to $2.5 trillion, the equivalent of 20%–25% of each side's GDP. They are working on an ambitious transatlantic free-trade deal called the Transatlantic Trade and Investment Partnership (TTIP). EU officials speak of creating "something approaching a transatlantic single market in goods." Big business wants this, and labor unions and Greens no longer oppose it. Tariffs are low (below 3%), but the hard part is the numerous nontariff barriers and reaching "regulatory convergence" (common rules).

In terms of foreign direct investment (FDI), they are each other's favorite targets. Two-thirds of America's FDI flow to Europe, while three-fourths of Europe's are directed to the United States, with Texas as the favorite state. America's preferred investment site is the UK, where total US investment is roughly equivalent to that in Asia, Latin America, Africa, and the Middle East combined. It invests 10 times more in the Netherlands (and 2.5 times more in Ireland) than in China. No wonder many observers claim that economics is the stabilizer of the European-American relationship.

Having cornered a fourth of global trade, the EU is the world's largest trading power. Politically, western Europe is and will probably remain a region of sovereign states, which ultimately make their own decisions about the vital matters that affect them. For example, in May and June 2005, French and Dutch voters decisively rejected an EU constitution that would have strengthened Europe's political union. About 90% of lengthy document's contents were salvaged two and a half years later in the EU treaty signed in Lisbon.

European Union

The EU has a well-developed institutional apparatus. It has a dual executive: The European Council is the major decision-making body and is composed of the heads of state or government; it is called the Council of Ministers when member state ministers with responsibilities for finance, agriculture, etc., depending upon the specific matter which is pending, meet.

The second part of the executive that directs the day-to-day business of the EU is the European Commission, which meets in Brussels. The commission is composed of 28 members, 1 from each member state. The 2000 Nice Treaty stipulates that there be fewer by 2009. The Lisbon Treaty, which went into effect in 2010, calls ultimately for each member to lose the right to send a commissioner. The total number will instead be capped at a rotating two-thirds of the number of member states. In the meantime, up to three members are proposed by the government of his or her country for five-year renewable terms. The EC

EU president Herman Van Rompuy and High Representative Catherine Ashton (until autumn 2014)

Western Europe Today

Old currencies go . . .

president selects one and assigns that commissioner a specific portfolio. After joining the College of Commissioners, each commissioner is expected to make decisions based not upon the interests of his or her home country but upon the interests of the EU as a whole. The commissioners decide issues by a simple majority vote; none has the power of veto.

The Lisbon Treaty created a confusing structure, with lines of responsibility blurred. It partially fixed the problem of the rotating six-month presidency of the all-powerful European Council (which is composed of the chiefs of government) by creating a standing president elected by the council for a two-and-a-half-year term, renewable once. The idea is to give the EU political prominence in the world that matches its economic weight.

Taking office in January 2010 as the first EU president was Herman Van Rompuy (ROM-pow). He is a multilingual economist and was Belgium's prime minister for almost a year. He is a skilled negotiator who reduced the influence of the European Commission. His term ended in 2014, and he was replaced by former Polish prime minister Donald Tusk. He was reelected in 2017. He was followed by former Belgian prime minister Charles Michel. The six-month rotating presidency still exists, but the country's leaders do not chair meetings of the European Council (done by the EU president) or gatherings of foreign ministers (done by the high representative).

The council gained a simplified voting system relying more on majority voting as long as 55% of the states containing 65% of the total EU population say yes to a measure. Vetoes are more difficult to cast. Members try to make as many decisions as possible by consensus.

The high representative is like a foreign minister in all but name, combining the former posts of commissioner for external affairs and foreign policy spokesman for the council. The first to be elected by the council was Lady Catherine Ashton, a former Labour leader in the UK House of Lords and EU trade commissioner. She had almost no foreign policy experience. However, she proved to be effective in sealing a peace agreement between Serbia and Kosovo, in chairing the six powers negotiating with Iran over its nuclear program, and in dealing with the chaos in Ukraine in 2014. She was succeded by Federica Mogherini of Italy, who was in turn followed by Josep Borrell.

One of her main tasks was to create a European External Action Service (EEAS), a future 6,000-strong diplomatic corps that one day would coordinate and supplement but not replace the national diplomats and foreign offices. Former French ambassador to the US, Pierre Vimont, was named head of this diplomatic organization. The EU has its own intelligence analysis unit, Intcen.

A total of 34,000 persons work in the EU institutions. Two-thirds of them are at the commission, and most are in Brussels, with a minority working in Luxembourg

and Strasbourg. This amounts to fewer civil servants (dubbed "Eurocrats") than work in medium-sized city governments in Europe.

The highest EU official is the European Commission president, selected by member countries and confirmed by the European Parliament for a five-year renewable term. In 2004 President José Manuel Barroso, former Portuguese prime minister, became president. He was reelected in 2009 by a secret ballot in the European Parliament and served until 2014. In 2019, the post was occupied by Germany's Ursula von Leyen. An example of unclear authority stemming from the Lisbon Treaty was Barroso's appointment in 2010 of his former chief of staff and countryman Joao Vale de Almeida as the new EU ambassador in Washington. He was criticized for not consulting the member states, the EU president, or the high representative.

The 751-seat European Parliament is the world's only directly elected international legislature. The formula for seats is based roughly on the population size of the member states, but larger states are under-represented and smaller ones overrepresented. It meets seven to eight times a year for one-week sessions. Formerly, the parliament met in both Strasbourg and Luxembourg. However, in 1981 the parliament voted to hold all its sessions in Strasbourg, leaving only the administrative headquarters in Luxembourg. Parliamentary committees meet in Brussels. Since most of the real bargaining and revising takes place in the committees and since "additional" plenaries can be held in Brussels, most members of the European Parliament (MEPs) do all of their work in Brussels. In a 2011 poll, 91% of MEPs and their staffs preferred to stay full time in Brussels.

Since 1979 its members, who work in 24 languages, have been elected directly in their home countries according to each country's own preferred method of election. Its members do not sit in national delegations but in party groupings, such as the Communists and Allies, Socialist European People's Party (Christian Democratic), European Progressive Democratic,

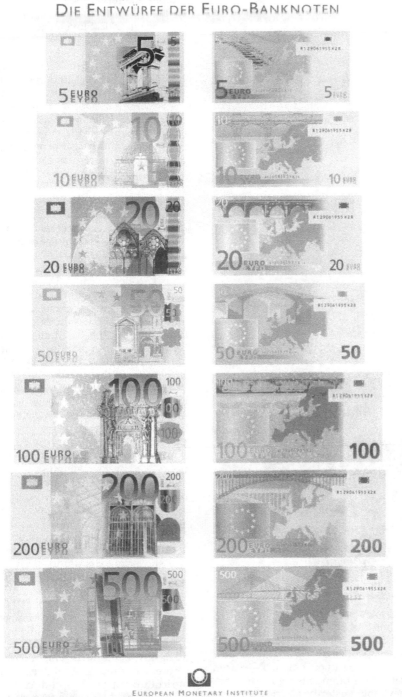

THE EURO BANKNOTE DESIGNS
LES MAQUETTES DES BILLETS EN EURO
DIE ENTWÜRFE DER EURO-BANKNOTEN

EUROPEAN MONETARY INSTITUTE

. . . and a new one arrives.

Courtesy: Central Audiovisual Library, European Commision

in 1987, the parliament's power and influence have grown, and it got another boost from the Lisbon Treaty. It has a say over almost 90% of all legislation, but it does not have a veto over most of it. Some legislation, most importantly that covering measures to bring into effect a unified European market, can be altered or amended by the parliament. It must approve the budget. It can veto the accession of new member states to the EU, as well as new trade agreements with non-EU countries. It can launch investigations. Finally, it oversees the commission, a power that was dramatically demonstrated in 1999 and 2004.

For years it had been asking questions about waste and mismanagement, but the commission responded with arrogance and indifference. In January 1999 the parliament threatened a vote of censure; a two-thirds majority could have removed all the commissioners. This threat was averted when a panel of five independent experts was appointed to investigate financial impropriety. In March the panel published a devastating report accusing the well-paid commissioners ($200,000 salary and expenses in 1999) of tolerating widespread fraud, corruption, nepotism, favoritism, and mismanagement. All commissioners felt compelled to resign.

The consequence of this scandal was not only more democratic accountability but also a dramatic alteration of the political balance of power in favor of the elected European Parliament. It showed its muscle again in 2004, when it questioned the competence of five of the proposed commissioners. This forced EC president Barroso to reshuffle his lineup of commissioners in order to win parliamentary approval. This was the first time this had ever happened.

Finally, there is a European Court of Justice, with its seat in Luxembourg and composed of 28 justices, each chosen by member states for six-year renewable terms; they are assisted by eight advocates general. The court judges violations of three major documents, the ECSC and the EU and Euratom Treaties, as well as all subsequent EU treaties that are collectively called the Treaty of the European Union (TEU). This includes the Nice Treaty of 2000. It redistributed national votes, restricted vetoes, revamped certain institutions, limited the number of commissioners, and granted the European Parliament more power and seats. The court rules on whether national laws are in accordance with European laws in those fields within the EU's competence (jurisdiction). It is the final arbiter of the Lisbon Treaty, which gave the Charter of Fundamental Rights legal force.

The Single European Act (SEA) amends the European treaties by spelling out certain EU objectives: completion of the European

and Liberal and Democratic Groups. There are a few unaffiliated members.

The Lisbon Treaty requires that the European Council "proposes" a candidate who is then "elected" by parliament. But it also stipulates that EU leaders must "take into account" the EP election results when selecting the EC president. Nobody knows exactly what that means. In a departure from past practice, these parties entered

the May 2014 EP elections with "top candidates" selected to lead them. Their expectation is that the leader of the party that does best would be the EC president, not a politician chosen by the member governments.

The European Parliament is officially entitled to oversee the work of the European Commission and to approve or reject the EU's budget. Since the SEA was introduced

Western Europe Today

help us *unite* Europe!

JEF

Jeunes Européens Fédéralistes
Young European Federalists
Junge Europäische Föderalisten

www.jef-europe.net
info@jef-europe.net

a September 2000 referendum. Greece enthusiastically entered on January 1, 2001. Despite the fervent support by their government, Swedish voters rejected the new currency in 2003. Slovenia joined on January 1, 2007, and Malta and Cyprus joined a year later, making 15 EU member states in the eurozone. Slovakia joined in 2009, and Estonia was admitted in January 2011.

In order not to hurt national feelings, the new euro bills bear generic European designs: Gothic arches, bridges, windows, and a map of Europe. No scene from a particular country is recognizable. The only national concession for paper money was made to Greece, which does not use Roman letters. The word for the currency appears both as "EURO" and "EYPO." Bulgaria became the first EU member to use the Cyrillic alphabet, and that may be added, as well. The coins are uniform on one side, but each participating country made its own design for the reverse side. Thus 17 different coins circulate but are legal tender throughout the eurozone.

The new EU members were expected to join the eurozone within four to five years after entering the EU in 2004 and 2007, but most had to postpone adoption. The euro is a qualified success: By 2007 there were more of them in circulation around the globe than US dollars, although the dollar remained the favorite reserve currency for central banks. However, the 2010 euro crisis and the need for an emergency EU and IMF standby rescue fund raised doubts in the world's first currency that is not backed by a sovereign state.

A few countries that are not full members of the EU belong to the European Free Trade Association (EFTA), which was created in 1959 and whose headquarters are located in Geneva. Whereas the EU has a huge bureaucracy and budget, EFTA is a shoestring operation, with about 60 full-time staff. English is the working language, even though no member nation uses it as its mother tongue. EFTA has no political objectives, and its members have not relinquished a shred of sovereignty.

EFTA eliminated tariffs and customs on all industrial products bought or sold from all member nations, but it does not include agricultural or fishing products. All EFTA members have separate free-trade agreements with the EU. EFTA's economic importance declined after Great Britain, Ireland, and Denmark left to join the EU in 1972, and Finland, Sweden, and Austria, in 1995. To restore EFTA's significance, its members—Switzerland, Liechtenstein, Norway, and Iceland—concluded cooperation agreements with Egypt, Morocco, and Tunisia.

In 1991 the EU and EFTA countries agreed to form a European Economic Area (EEA), which creates a market of

internal market, creation of a great area without frontiers, technological development, progress toward economic and monetary union, improvement of the environment and working conditions, creation of more effective and democratic institutions, and institutionalization of cooperation among member states in the field of foreign policy. The target year of 1992 was chosen for its symbolic importance: 500 years after the discovery of the New World.

From 1979 the European Monetary System (EMS) attempted, not always successfully, to coordinate the monetary affairs of certain western European countries by trying to link their currencies. At their 1991 Maastricht summit, EU leaders agreed to create a single European currency (called the "euro") and a European Central Bank

(ECB) located in Frankfurt. The criteria for joining this Economic and Monetary Union (EMU)—a budget deficit of not more than 3% of GDP and a total national debt not in excess of 60% of GDP—placed political strains on member governments. The inevitable austerity policies were resented by many of their voters. Many Europeans thought that the price to be paid for the euro was not worth it. However, the euro crisis that emanated from Greece in 2010 showed that many eurozone members had disregarded the criteria.

In 1998 the governments of 11 members (known unofficially as the "eurozone") decided to adopt the euro as of January 1, 1999, with Britain, Sweden, Denmark, and Greece waiting until later to join. Danish voters rejected the euro again in

500 million customers extending from the Mediterranean to the Arctic and accounting for over 40% of world trade. Within the EEA, EFTA members enjoy the EU's "four freedoms"—of goods, services, capital, and people—but EEA does not include agriculture, fish, energy, coal, and steel. EFTA members live under many EU rules, although they have no voice in their writing; this lack of representation gives them added incentive to join the EU as full members.

All Scandinavian countries are in the Nordic Council, which meets regularly to discuss nonmilitary problems that they have in common. Eleven nations belong to the European Space Agency (ESA) which, with American assistance, launched the first European Spacelab into orbit at the end of 1983. Onboard this Spacelab was the first European astronaut to travel into space with Americans—Dr. Ulf Merbold, a German physicist. In 1988 ESA also joined with the US and Japan to begin construction of the Space Station Freedom.

Western European countries are active in such international economic treaties or organizations as the General Agreement on Trade and Tariffs (GATT); the World Trade Organization (WTO), which since 1995 attempts to resolve disputes relating to the GATT Treaty; the International Monetary Fund (IMF), which provides funds for countries with balance-of-payments problems; the International Bank for Reconstruction and Development (World Bank); and the European Bank for Reconstruction and Development (EBRD). Headquartered in London, the EBRD was created after the collapse of communism to help central and eastern European countries make successful transitions to free-market economies.

The International Energy Agency (IEA) exists to ensure that all industrialized nations have minimally sufficient energy supplies in times of crisis. No European country belongs to the Organization of Petroleum Exporting Countries (OPEC), whose headquarters is in Vienna. Nevertheless, those western European countries which export large quantities of oil, such as Great Britain and Norway (from the North Sea), note what is charged by the OPEC countries before setting their own prices.

Interpol, headquartered in Paris, provides some coordination in fighting international crime. Europol, based in The Hague, shares information among national police forces and cooperates in a limited way with the US. SitCen exists for intelligence sharing among EU countries. Eurojust coordinates the EU countries' prosecuting authorities. Following the September 11 attacks in the US, EU governments rapidly accepted a single European arrest warrant to facilitate the struggle against terrorism.

This high degree of cooperation and organization explains in great measure the tremendous growth of the economy of western Europe. In a sense it may be likened to the United States, which, after discarding the Articles of Confederation and creating the present Constitution two centuries ago, abolished tariffs on goods shipped between the states and laid the groundwork for ever-closer cooperation among formerly sovereign entities. Through the many organizations they have formed and joined, western European nations are better equipped and prepared to face the complicated problems of today.

September 11, 2001

For the United States, the world changed dramatically on September 11, 2001, when fanatical Islamic al-Qaeda terrorists, trained and financed by Osama Bin Laden and sheltered in Taliban-ruled Afghanistan, hijacked four American commercial airliners and crashed three of them into the Twin Towers of the World Trade Center in New York and the Pentagon in Washington, killing more than 3,000 persons from 81 different countries. More British and French citizens perished that day than in any previous terrorist attack.

Americans' feeling of invulnerability from outside threats went up with the noxious smoke from the buildings' rubble. Any temptations to pursue an isolationist, North America–focused policy disappeared, at least temporarily. A shaken America looked for help from its friends, and the most steadfast of them were Europeans and Canadians. They responded with emotion and resolve. Within 36 hours of the attack, NATO offered to invoke the mutual-defense clause, article 5, for the first time in its half-century history.

Former EC president Romano Prodi called an emergency session the next morning. After a moment of silence for the victims of the attacks, he decided to send "the strongest possible signal of European solidarity with the American people" and to "call for a common European approach to all aspects of this tragedy." In moving language he announced, "this barbaric attack was directed against the free world and our common values. It is a watershed event, and life will never be quite the same again. . . . In the darkest hours of European history, the Americans stood by us. We stand by them now."

In a poll taken a week after the attack, Europeans showed a strong willingness to support a US military assault: 80% in Denmark, 79% in Britain, 73% in France, 58% in Norway and Spain, and half in Germany. The EU called for a three-minute silence on September 14, and from Finland to Italy and Berlin to Paris, businesses and stock exchanges, buses and shoppers stopped to honor the dead and reflect upon their world that had changed so suddenly.

The Complexity of US-European Cooperation

The transatlantic relationship is intense, multilayered, exceedingly complex, increasingly interdependent, and fraught with fluctuations and frictions. It takes place within several interrelated channels. The United States and all European states conduct bilateral relations with each other. In times of crisis, Washington tends to prefer these bilateral contacts because they bring action and cooperation more quickly than does a complicated evolving structure like the EU. The same applies to European governments. The German daily Die Welt called the antiterrorist crisis "the moment of the nation-states, the time in which individual European governments turn to the American partner after consulting among themselves."

The allies interact closely within NATO. The highest political leader within the

Western Europe Today

alliance, the secretary-general, is always a European. But American military leadership is institutionalized through the permanent appointment of an American general as the SACEUR. Decisions are reached on the basis of consensus. However, not all European countries belong to this organization, and not all members participate in the integrated command structure, such as France and Iceland, although they have a part in NATO's political structure. The partners collaborate in a wide variety of international fora, such as the OSCE, the G8 (which includes Japan, Canada, and Russia), the G20 (which includes the G-8 and major developing countries, especially China, India, and Brazil), and most importantly the United Nations. Finally and of ever-increasing importance, the US has had to adapt to and work intensively with an evolving EU. This was symbolized in February 2005 by the first visit by an American president to the EU institutions in Brussels.

The transatlantic partnership involves the meshing of many different systems of government—the US central government and individual American states; the EU; its member states; and, in some federations such as Germany, states or "Länder." Thus political authority is dispersed, and there are many points where one or more of the numerous players can veto policies. On both sides of the Atlantic, domestic politics is of vital importance. Negotiators often need to make domestic tradeoffs that adversely affect the foreign policies they are trying to pursue. Since all the states involved in this thick network of links are democracies, electoral cycles strongly affect the effort to reach agreements. On the American side, it is often pointed out that presidents and Congress find it especially harrowing to make bold, potentially unpopular moves within a year of reelection. It is no different in the EU.

The American political system divides power both geographically (between the central government and the states) and within the governing institutions inside Washington and the 50 state capitals. This can create diplomatic nightmares for both American and European leaders. For instance, American states have become more and more assertive in global politics and conduct their own foreign policies, particularly in economic and trade matters. Ignoring Washington, the Massachusetts legislature passed a "Burma Law" in 1996 forbidding the state and its agencies from buying anything from companies or individuals that invest in or trade with Myanmar (Burma), which is under military rule. The same can happen in Europe. Germany's Länder have supremacy over certain aspects of immigration policy. Thus they can impede both the policy of the German central government in Berlin and that of the EU itself.

Europeans must deal with America's large, highly decentralized institutions, which wield power of their own and often seem to be hostile to each other. Separation of powers is particularly troublesome for foreign policy: It is often impossible for a president to produce what he promises to foreign leaders. An American president occupies a central position in the making of effective foreign policy. If he is not personally involved or committed to achieving important foreign policy goals, little gets done. The political system enables persons who are largely unknown in Europe to rise to the highest national political office through a painfully long and complicated electoral system. The unique American selection procedure permits a person to arrive in the White House who had pursued a nonpolitical career as a soldier (Eisenhower), farmer (Carter), actor (Reagan), or governor of a state (Carter, Reagan, Clinton, George W. Bush). It almost always brings to the White House a neophyte in foreign policy; Eisenhower and the first George Bush were the exceptions. Most presidents learn diplomacy as on-the-job training, learning by doing.

When that president seems to overlook the multilateral dimension of America's dealings with the outside world and the need to engage former adversaries, Europeans react negatively. Although many of the red-letter issues—such as the Comprehensive Test Ban Treaty, the Kyoto Protocol, and the International Criminal Court—had gained prominence during the Clinton administration, Bush's predecessor was able to give the appearance in public that he supported these issues and to put the blame on the Republican Congress for not ratifying them.

A newly elected president may have little or no experience in foreign affairs and yet have the power to select a multitude of foreign policy advisers, secretaries, and agency chiefs, many with little or no foreign or defense policy background themselves. Such a presidential "team" appears often to operate in an uncoordinated way, frequently sending off widely differing signals. This inevitably creates and fuels doubts about American leadership capabilities and the continuity of US foreign policy. The complicated and extensive interagency bargaining in Washington confuses many people, European and American alike.

The powerful US Congress can also be frustrating. In the last two decades of the 20th century, Congress underwent significant changes: The seniority system in committees had weakened, and the number of committees and subcommittees proliferated. Also, the workload became so demanding that congressmen and senators are retiring earlier. Therefore, an increasingly high percentage of the legislators are new in Congress. For example, by the mid-1990s, half the members of the House of Representatives had entered the chamber after the fall of the Berlin Wall. What these changes did was to take much of the power that used to be concentrated in a few key figures and dispersed it within Congress. In this more decentralized (or, more positively, "democratized") Congress, legislative work has become much more complicated. For instance, more than 40 congressional committees and subcommittees deal with the defense budget alone.

In the absence of the kind of strong party discipline that exists in most European parliaments, American congressmen and senators are more protective of their constituents' interests and can safely vote against their party leaders or the president if an issue of great interest in their districts or states is at stake. Thus there is no stable coalition on foreign policy matters. Nevertheless, the Congress is not as obstructionist and isolationist as it might sometimes seem from across the Atlantic. For example, in the 1990s and the first half-decade of the 21st century, it supported the United States' entry into the North America Free Trade Association (NAFTA), the World Trade Organization (WTO), and two enlargements of NATO. Its unflagging and vigorous support of President Bush's antiterrorist measures after September 11 revealed yet again that presidential-congressional unity is the norm in times of crisis.

President George W. Bush took more straightforward opposition to policies he thought would damage American interests, and he suffered for it in European public opinion. Most Europeans were convinced that he knew less about Europe than did his predecessor, even though Clinton's opinions did not substantially differ from Bush's on many key issues. The sole Bush policy favored by Europeans was his decision not to withdraw American troops from Bosnia and Kosovo. Bush's gestures to patch up the transatlantic relationship after his reelection in 2004 were unprecedented, but they had only limited effect.

The election of Barack Obama as president of the United States in November 2008 satisfied a European longing for the return of an America that could again be a source of hope, not of fear. He made a triumphant tour of Europe, attending G20, NATO, and EU summits in April 2009. European leaders vied to be photographed at his side, and his charismatic wife, Michelle, helped underscore what a dramatic historic change had occurred in America. French commentator Dominique Moïse wrote, "America, thanks to Mr. Obama, has returned to be the emotional center of gravity of the world." Many Europeans believed that President Obama, who grew up in the Pacific, no longer focused as much on Europe as did his predecessors. Most Europeans have a negative opinion of his successor, Donald Trump.

Complexity on the European Side of the Atlantic

One exasperated American official during the Nixon administration described the European Community to be "as mystifying as the Tibetan theocracy." William Wallace was more subdued, calling the EU institutional structure "complex and opaque." Desmond Dinan attributes this to the "incremental, often untidy nature of European integration." The European Union is in the process of steady evolution; it is a polity in the making. The American ambassador to the EU, Richard Morningstar, put it this way: "If we look 20 years into the future, we know what the U.S. will look like. But Europe? It is hard to predict what the relationship will be when we do not know what one part will be."

Those who deal with Europe must constantly adapt to its changing institutions. It is therefore not simple for Europeans and Americans alike to know precisely who has the authority to make decisions on what, what exactly is the division of labor among many bodies of the community, or where the line is between EU competence and that of the member states. The Lisbon Treaty merely added to this confusion. This is one reason the United States still prefers to utilize its bilateral ties with European allies in times of emergency.

European countries all have variations of parliamentary systems, which simplify the conduct of foreign policy. Responsibility is clearer than one finds either in the EU or the US, and once policy is established by the central government, there are fewer obstacles to its implementation. Given party discipline and the fact that a prime minister or chancellor is in office precisely because his party or coalition has a parliamentary majority, it is not easy for its foreign policy to be thwarted by legislative action. Nor does a European government need to worry as much about ratification after having negotiated a treaty as does an American president.

One of the difficulties of EU foreign policy is created by the presidency of the European Council. Until the Lisbon Treaty became operative in 2010, it revolved every six months. The member states still rotate, but they now do this alongside an elected EU president. Each brings its own perspectives and priorities to its presidency. For instance, the Spanish presidency brought a redirection of attention to Latin America, something in which Finland would have only mild interest. But the Finnish presidency heralded the "Northern Dimension," with which Spain would not share a strong affinity.

The member states have differing opinions on how the community's relations with the US should be, and this can affect the transatlantic relationship. A country can assume the presidency with a firm agenda but find it hijacked by international events. The presidency is so important for setting the EU agenda that the US and other nonmembers cannot ignore it. But such a short presidency inevitably create discontinuity and could disrupt or complicate ongoing negotiations. It is the job of the newly elected EU president to provide stability, continuity, and predictability; it is unknown if he will succeed.

In determining who really makes decisions in EU external policy, the outsider must decide now among a variety of powerful figures: the EU president, the EC president, the European Council's high representative, the trade commissioner or the prime minister or foreign minister of the current presidency country. A prestigious German daily wrote what many people already know: "Neither the European public nor Europe's partners understand the distribution of competencies (if there is one)." All travel around the world speaking in the name of Europe. It continues, "The same applies to operative politics. The EU has countless commissioners and representatives for special regions or issues, but outside the EU apparatus, nobody knows what powers they have and in whose name they speak."

Despite the many-headed EU leadership that still exists, this stable of influential EU leaders represents considerable progress toward enhancing the community's ability to conduct foreign policy. Former secretary of state Henry Kissinger was mistakenly reported to have asked what number he should dial when he wanted to call Europe. He denied ever having said that. But former senior director for European affairs on the US National Security Council Antony J. Blinken argued that there is now a number to call at the EU, depending on the problem. "It is true, however, that while each has the receiver in one ear, he also has 15 [now 28] European ministers whispering in the other. As a result, Brussels' executive decision-making authority is circumscribed." In an interview with the German weekly Die Zeit, ex–commissioner for external affairs Chris Patten admitted: "I don't claim for a minute that there will be one single telephone number in the near future, which a Secretary of State Kissinger could dial."

LE FIGARO

« Sans la liberté de blâmer, il n'est point d'éloge flatteur » Beaumarchais

4€

Vins
Le projet de réforme des AOC en France. Exclusivité

Aujourd'hui, Le Figaro et ses magazines avec le DVD "Ridicule"

7€

L'ESSENTIEL

Les chefs d'État et de gouvernement seront demain à Dublin pour célébrer l'élargissement de l'Union

Les défis de l'Europe à 25

The United Kingdom
of Great Britain and Northern Ireland

Political power's most coveted address: 10 Downing Street, residence of the prime minister

Area: 89,038 sq. mi. (230,609 sq. km., slightly smaller than Oregon).

Population: 68.2 million.

Capital City: London (pop. 8.1 million, including the city's sprawling suburbs).

Climate: Mild and temperate, rarely above 86°F (30°C) or below 41°F (5°C).

Neighboring Countries: Ireland (a short distance across the Irish Sea to the west); France, Belgium, and the Netherlands (a short distance across the English Channel or North Sea to the east).

Official Language: English.

Other Principal Tongues: About a fourth of the population of Wales speaks Welsh, and about 60,000 Scottish speak a form of Gaelic. Both are Celtic dialects.

Ethnic Background: Angle, Saxon, Celtic, and Nordic.

Principal Religions: Christian 90%. In England, Church of England (Anglican) 49%; Roman Catholic 7%; in Scotland, Church of Scotland (Presbyterian) 19%; in Wales, Church of Wales; Muslim 3%; Sikh and Hindu 2%; Jewish 1%; other 4%.

Main Exports: Finished and semifinished manufactured products, oil and gas, foodstuffs, chemicals, motor vehicles.

Main Imports: Manufactured goods, foodstuffs, fuels.

Major Trading Partners: EU (50.5% of exports and 48.6% of imports), Germany (10.6% of exports and 12.5% of imports), US (9.6% of exports and 5.8% of imports), Netherlands (7.6% of exports and 7% of imports), France (7.1% of exports and 5.7% of imports), Ireland (5.8% of exports), China (8.2% of imports).

Currency: Pound sterling.

National Holiday: Celebration of the birthday of the queen is in June, although she was actually born on April 21.

Head of State: Her Majesty Queen Elizabeth II, b. 1926. Married Lieutenant Philip Mountbatten (Prince of Greece and Denmark) on November 20, 1947; he had been created Duke of Edinburgh on the preceding day and (in 1957) Prince of Great Britain. Queen Elizabeth II succeeded to the throne on the death of her father, George VI, on February 6, 1952; her coronation took place on June 2, 1953.

Heir Apparent: His Royal Highness Prince Charles (b. November 14, 1948), Prince of Wales. His son, Prince William of Wales (b. June 21, 1982), is second in succession to the throne.

Head of Government: Boris Johnson (since July 2019).

National Flag: The Union Flag—a dark blue charged with the white cross of St. Andrew (for Scotland), the red cross of St. Patrick (for Ireland), surmounted by the red cross of St. George (for England) bordered in white. Sometimes called the Union Jack.

No country in the world has closer ties with the United States in language, history, shared assumptions, and emotion than does the United Kingdom. In the capital of each country, there stands a prominent statue of one of the greatest leaders of the other. Abraham Lincoln gazes at the Houses of Parliament in London, and in a prominent section of Washington, Winston Churchill (himself half American) stands giving his famous "V" for victory salute. Although the British influence on

The United Kingdom

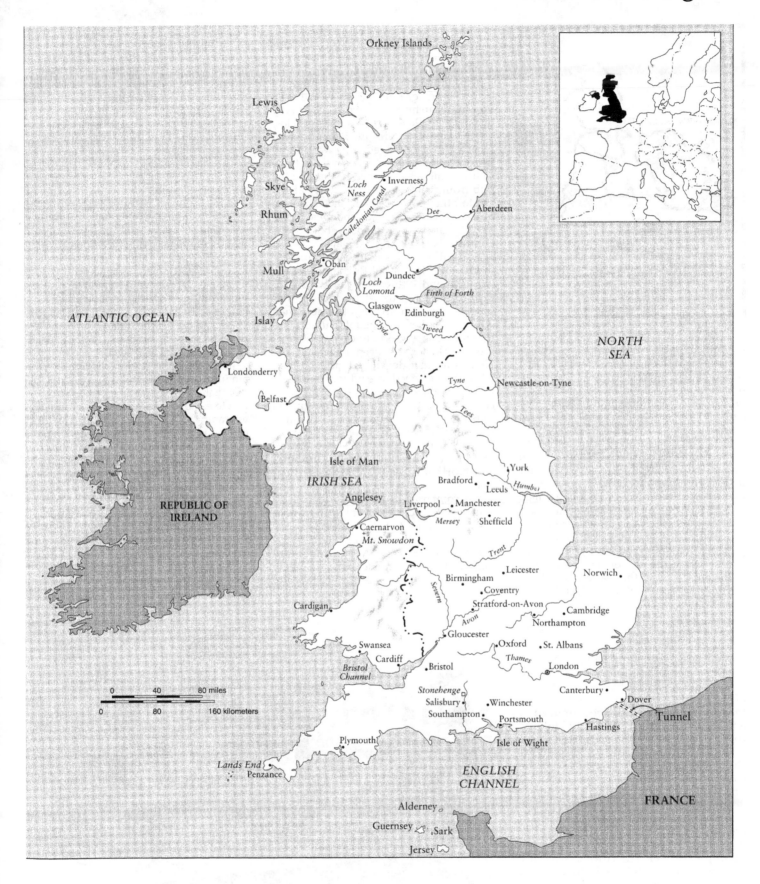

The United Kingdom

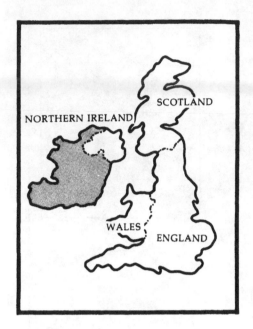

the United States is not surprising, what is remarkable is the influence that the United Kingdom has had on the rest of the world. It is striking that a moderate-sized island off the coast of Europe should achieve first a pivotal role in European affairs and then domination of much of the entire globe.

Britain is blessed with a moderate climate, despite its northerly location, due to the warmth of the Gulf Stream, which after originating in the Caribbean Sea crosses the Atlantic. Its waters provide a warmer, albeit moister, climate than would otherwise be the case. Rain is frequent but not overabundant. The sun shines in most parts for one out of four to eight daylight hours during the winter. The mountains of the west modify this pattern, condensing the clouds into rainfall, which is more abundant there.

The climate is not suited to plant life needing heat, but it is ideal for water-seeking crops, particularly grasses. With a population density of about 640 persons per square mile, much of Britain is urbanized. In spite of the fertile soil, it is an importer of foodstuffs. The Industrial Revolution, for which Britain is renowned, resulted in a particularly dense type of city building construction. Wales is a mixture of industry, agriculture, and herding. Virtually all sheep and cattle are consumed within the country; the sheep support production of fine woolens, few of which are exported. Scotland, about one-quarter the size of England and Wales, consists of a small area of lowlands and the larger highlands, which actually reach a maximum height of only 4,400 feet. The cities of Glasgow on the Clyde River and Edinburgh on the Firth (Bay) of Forth are seats of heavy industry and are highly urbanized. The mountains are widely interspersed with valleys, where intensive sheep raising supports the production of world-famous Scotch tweeds and plaids, treasured by tailors throughout the world.

While Roman remains can be found in various parts of England today, the most important architectural work is virtually invisible. London, located at the spot closest to the sea where the Thames could most easily be bridged, was walled and became a Roman center, even though the Celtic name was retained. It became the hub from which spokes of roads headed out to other parts of the island. This pattern still shapes the roads and rails of Britain. The city today extends far beyond the boundaries of the original wall.

Natural resources that were important in the early Industrial Revolution in the late 18th and 19th centuries have been a second blessing. Its island location has protected it from invasion for more than 900 years and encouraged it to use the sea for commercial and political gain. But its greatest blessing has been a relatively stable history that developed quite early in a tradition of freedom and representative government. Americans are sometimes confused by the various names applied to Britain. Its official name is the United Kingdom of Great Britain and Northern Ireland. Four areas combine to make up the country: England, Wales, Scotland, and Northern Ireland. The word "Britain" encompasses the first three. The last is composed of the six northern Irish counties. Because England is the site of the capital and over the centuries came to control the other areas, the term "England" or "the English" is sometimes (but inaccurately) used to describe the whole country. Residents of Wales, Scotland, and Northern Ireland prefer to use the term "Great Britain" or "British."

The growth toward world leadership and representative democracy in Britain has not been smooth or steady, but the history of Britain has been a stage on which royal pageantry has combined with remarkable commercial, industrial, and political success of more humble citizens.

HISTORY

The Early Period

It must have been quite a shock for the Roman legionnaires who left the brilliant sunshine of Italy, marched across Gaul, and then made the short but perilous crossing of the English Channel. They arrived in a land of soft greens, frequent rains, and fearsome warriors who painted themselves blue and drove chariots armed with sharp blades at the axles. These Celts had come to the island during the Iron Age and spoke a dialect known as Brythonic, and thus their land was known as Britain.

Julius Caesar led two expeditions to Britain in 55 and 54 BC, but it was not until 43 AD that the Roman emperor Claudius began to establish settlements. The campaign to stamp out Celtic Druid beliefs, with all of their mysticism, that have faded into the mists of time, produced the first of the great British queens, Boadicea, who managed to kill several thousand Romanizing Britons before finally being captured and committing suicide. While the popular image has always seen the British as chauvinists in their men's clubs, the fact that in the 1980s both the throne and the office of prime minister were occupied by women is less surprising when one remembers that the first resistance leader and the monarchs with two of the greatest reigns in English

The prehistoric ruins of Stonehenge on the Salisbury Plain, which scholars date from 1800 to 1400 BC

history, Elizabeth I (1558–1603) and Victoria (1837–1901), were women, however different they were. The first was an astute monarch, who is reported to have utilized amorous affairs to advance the affairs of state. The latter was conservative, conventional, prudish, and astute, devoted only to her husband, Albert. Indeed, rightfully or wrongfully, an entire age is known by the name of each in the English-speaking world.

Celtic tribalism continued in the mountains of Wales and Scotland. Hadrian's Wall ran for miles to seal off the northern borders of the Roman area, since the people in the mountains there were beyond conquest. No attempt was made to invade Ireland.

The Early Christian Era

Roman soldiers and merchants brought Christianity with them to the island. Their persecution by Emperor Diocletian produced the first Christian martyr of the island, St. Alban. But after Emperor Constantine legalized Christianity in the empire, the church began to flourish in Britain.

The Romans occupied England for about 400 years, but as the empire collapsed inward, barbarian pressure on England increased. Angles, Saxons, and Jutes, Teutonic tribes from what is now northern Germany and Denmark, filled the vacuum left by the Romans. Now it was the Celts leading their tribal lives in Wales, Scotland, Ireland, and Cornwall, who kept alive the light of western civilization and Christian culture.

King Arthur may be more legendary than historical, but his story represents the urge to restore Christian order during the dark period that lasted for two centuries. In 597 the monk Augustine (named for the more famous St. Augustine of Hippo) was sent from Rome to convert the English. He established Canterbury as his see and became its first archbishop. As Roman Christianity spread, it came into contact and then into conflict with Celtic Christianity. The synod of Whitby, meeting in 664, decided that Roman Christianity would prevail. This proved to be a most significant decision, for England was thus brought once more under the influence of Rome; its culture, politics, and religion would be shaped by events on the Continent. Nearly 900 years later, when England turned away from Roman Christianity, the effects would be even more important. During the 8th century, English culture flourished. The first English historian, Venerable (later Saint) Bede, wrote his Ecclesiastical History of the English People; the great Anglo-Saxon epic Beowulf was written; and the Saxon monk Alcuin of York was a leading intellectual of Charlemagne's court.

A castle in Wales

Viking Invasion and Expulsion

By the 9th century, Vikings (Norsemen, Northmen, Normans) from Norway and Denmark attacked and then conquered much of the British Isle. In response, the only English king to be known as "the Great," Alfred of Wessex, whose capital was at Winchester, organized an army, developed a navy, founded schools, and stopped the growth of Norse-Danish power. It is ironic that the Norsemen then invaded France, where their region became known as Normandy. Almost two centuries later, one of their leaders would head the last successful conquest of England. Although Alfred died in 899, his son Edward the Elder conquered the remaining Danish-controlled areas and thus became the first king of a united England.

For the next 100 years, Anglo-Saxons and Norsemen merged during a golden age of relative peace. As the English historian Trevelyan said, "Had it not been for the Scandinavian blood infused into our race by the catastrophes of the 9th century, less would have been heard in days to come of British maritime and commercial enterprise." Again ironically, at about the same time, the Scandinavians were invited to Russia to establish order among the belligerent, disorganized Slav warlords.

By the start of the 11th century, a weak king, Ethelred the Unready, allowed his kingdom to fall into confusion. The Danish king Canute invaded the island in 1016, and England became part of an empire that included Denmark and Norway. Canute was followed by his two sons, each of whom died shortly after ascending the throne. Ethelred's son Edward the Confessor, who was half Norman and had lived in Normandy during the reign of Canute and his sons, was placed on the throne. He made two decisions with far-reaching consequences. He founded Westminster Abbey outside of London, starting the separation of the government from the city. Because he was childless, he promised his cousin, William Duke of Normandy, that the throne would one day be his.

The Final Conquest and the First Plantagenets

The year 1066 is to the English school children what 1492 is to Americans. In that year, Edward the Confessor died. The Witan (national council) elected his brother-in-law Harold as his successor. A Norwegian invasion in Yorkshire called Harold to the north. Seizing the opportunity, William landed a Norman force in the south of England. Harold raced south to meet his death—at the Battle of Hastings, he was killed by a sword blow, and William established himself and his Norman lords as rulers of England.

William chose to rule by a rigorous system of feudalism. He established Normans

The United Kingdom

loyal to himself as lords of all the great manors. But they were tenants on the land; ownership was the king's right. The most important lords made up the Great Council, the forerunner of parliament. William also placed Normans in the most important positions in the church hierarchy and ruled that clergy would be tried in ecclesiastical rather than secular courts.

All over England, Norman buildings characterized by massive rectangular towers showed that the conquerors had come to stay. The most notable were the Tower of London and Westminster Hall. Scores of parish churches, castles, and monasteries dotted the landscape. William dispatched Norman legal scholars to go among the people and inquire by what laws (including customs which were virtually laws) they lived. These were organized into the Common Law—the law of the people, which were to be used in secular courts. Whenever William's judges determined the law, that would be uniform law for the entire realm. This greatly pacified the conquered people, since they corresponded with what had prevailed before the Norman conquest. Writs were established which were an intriguing combination of Latin, Anglo-Saxon, and French—Assumpsit, Trespass Quare Clausum Fregit, Indebitatus, etc.

William's great-grandson Henry II (the first of the Plantagenets) came to the throne in 1154. He asserted the power of the king at the expense of the barons by tearing down unlicensed castles and creating a militia instead of depending upon the nobility for armed troops and created traveling judges. The decisions of these judges were based on the Common Law, which operated by establishing written precedents rather than a codified law. Henry II also invaded Ireland and, with the permission of the pope, established himself as king of England's western neighbor. No one could possibly foresee what enormous consequences this would have for England in the years to come—consequences that affect Britain to this day.

Henry might have foreseen the consequences for which he is most remembered. He got into a dispute with his archbishop Thomas Becket over the issue of whether the clergy should be tried in church courts or civil courts. Whether Henry ordered that Becket be killed or merely hinted that it would please him will never be known. But Becket's murder turned him into a martyr and Canterbury into a shrine. Henry's two sons, Richard and John, were low points in the history of the English monarchy. Richard (who came to be known as the Lion-Hearted) spent most of his reign out of the country as a crusader, trying to wrest Jerusalem and Israel from the Arabs. His absence did

Mark H. and Mrs. Martha Mullin chat with Prince Charles.

England little good, but it did provide that great scene in stories and movies where, when he returns to England, he reveals himself to Robin Hood.

John was not only ineffective but also very unpopular. He lost English possessions on the Continent, including Normandy, and ran up such a debt that the barons were able to force him to sign the Magna Carta in 1215. This document was not the forward-looking cornerstone of freedom that it is sometimes portrayed to be, but rather it guaranteed the rights that the nobility and the church expected. At the same time, it established the principle that there are limits on the powers of the monarch, and thus it was a first step toward the largely unwritten constitutional monarchy of today.

The 13th century was a time of intellectual growth. Groups of scholars gathered at Oxford, and a splinter group later moved to Cambridge. Roger Bacon was a leading teacher stressing scientific experimentation. The King's Council was expanded to include representatives of shires and boroughs; thus the way was prepared for a representative House of Commons. At the end of the century, Edward I epitomized the medieval monarch. Physically imposing, he aided the growing spirit of nationalism by checking the power of the barons and the church and by increasing English power in Wales and Ireland. However, unsuccessful attempts to invade Scotland led Edward into financial difficulties, and in 1297 he was forced to sign a confirmation of the Magna Carta. He agreed that the king could not impose taxes without the consent of the newborn parliament.

Edward's grandson Edward III attempted to reassert English power on the Continent. In 1337 the Hundred Years, War began. At first, success came to the English, and the war strengthened the

nation. However, in 1348 the Black Death (Bubonic Plague) swept the country, and nearly half the population died. The country sank into economic depression, and by the time the king died in 1377, all the lands he had conquered in France had been lost, except for a small area around Calais.

The period produced the first great work of literature in primitive English, Chaucer's Canterbury Tales. For centuries, Latin had been spoken by the church and French by the nobility, but now the nation was uniting with the use of the English language.

The War of the Roses and the House of Tudor

Among Edward's sons were John of Gaunt, Duke of Lancaster, and Edmund, Duke of York. During the first half of the 15th century, the Lancaster branch held the throne, but in 1455 the Wars of the Roses, symbolized by the red rose of Lancaster and the white rose of York, subjected the country to a brutal civil war. Shakespeare puts the words "Uneasy lies the head that wears a crown" in the mouth of Henry IV, the first of the Lancastrian kings.

The instability of a monarch's life continued throughout the 15th century. Perhaps the best example was Richard III of the House of York, who usurped the throne by allegedly having two of his nephews, young princes, murdered in the Tower of London. He was brutally assassinated at age 32 in the aftermath of the Battle of Bosworth Field against Henry Tudor of the House of Lancaster in 1485.

The most reviled of English monarchs, Richard III was hastily buried by friars. More than five centuries later, in 2012, he burst into the public eye again when his unmarked skeleton was discovered beneath a city parking lot in Leicester. DNA evidence confirmed the authenticity. In March 2015 he was given a quasi-state funeral. His coffin was marched to Bosworth and back, escorted by people in period dress and suits of armor and greeted by "Long live the king!" He was interred in Leicester Cathedral.

Despite the battles for the throne, the 15th century was one of growing prosperity for England, especially in wool and foreign trade. To this day, the lord chancellor's seat in the House of Lords is a woolsack.

With the arrival of the Tudors, the medieval world drew to a close. During the first Tudor reign (Henry VII), Columbus sailed for the New World. The wealth that Spain acquired there provided constant problems for the Tudors, and it was not until their successors, the Stuarts, that English colonies were firmly established. Soon the winds of the Reformation would bring even greater changes to England.

King Henry VIII

Anne Boleyn

Henry arranged for his eldest son, Arthur, to marry Catherine of Aragon, daughter of the king of Spain. This was a particularly important match for diplomatic reasons, because Spain controlled the Netherlands through which much of English trade entered the Continent.

Arthur died in 1502 before his father. Despite both scriptural and canon law injunctions against marrying one's brother's widow, the pope granted a dispensation allowing Arthur's brother Henry to marry the young widow. Henry's sister Margaret married the king of Scotland, thus providing England with marital allies on several sides. When Henry VIII assumed the throne after his father's death, he realized the importance of a male heir. But his union with Catherine only produced a daughter, Mary. It is important to note that Henry was initially loyal to Roman Catholicism, and because of a work he authored attacking the doctrines of Martin Luther, the pope granted him the title "Defender of the Faith." It is ironic that his non–Roman Catholic descendants still carry that title.

Because Henry realized that Catherine would not produce a son, and because he was lusting after the attractive, dark-haired Anne Boleyn, he asked the pope to grant him an annulment of his marriage to Catherine, claiming that it had been illegal in the first place. Unfortunately for Henry, Catherine's uncle Charles V of the Holy Roman Empire had his troops in Rome at the time. When the pope refused to grant Henry's request, in an unprecedented

move, Henry had himself declared head of the church in England. His marriage to Anne Boleyn, however, produced only a daughter, Elizabeth, and Henry then proceeded through four more wives, making six in all, only one of whom produced a son, Edward. Pupils learn to keep track of Henry's wives by the saying "Divorced, beheaded, died, divorced, beheaded, survived."

Edward VI followed his father to the throne in 1547 at 11 years of age. His guardians moved the country rapidly in the direction of Protestantism. But the sickness-prone boy died six years later (he was possibly murdered), and the first of Henry's daughters, Mary Tudor, assumed the throne. Had Mary wanted to move England back to the religious position of her father, she probably would have lasted. But she felt a calling to return the nation to full Roman Catholicism and further alienated her subjects by taking Philip of Spain as her husband.

Although the number of resisting Protestants who were burned at the stake was actually quite small, there were enough prominent bishops ignited to earn the queen the historical title of "Bloody Mary." The words of one of these bishops—"Be of good cheer, Master Ridley, we shall today light such a candle as will by God's grace never be extinguished in England"—proved to be prophetic. On Mary's death after only five years on the throne, her half-sister, Elizabeth I, became queen, and with her, one of the great ages in English history began.

The Elizabethan Period

Since the Catholic Church considered Elizabeth illegitimate, she moved the country back toward Protestantism. It was a moderate protestant position, with the old forms of worship retained in English and no vigorous attempt to be overly scrupulous in matters of doctrine. As Elizabeth put it, "We shall make no window into any man's soul." Elizabeth's cousin Mary Stuart abdicated the throne of Scotland in favor of her son James and fled to England. For years, Roman Catholic attempts to oust Elizabeth flurried around Mary, who was Catholic. Despite "that divinity that doth hedge a king" (or queen), Elizabeth finally yielded to the advice of her court and had Mary beheaded in 1587.

That same year, Sir Francis Drake, having already stolen Spanish gold from the New World, raided the port of Cadiz. In reprisal, the next year Spain sent a Great Armada to invade and conquer England. But a "Protestant wind" and English naval tactics carried the day; less than half of the armada managed to limp back to Spain. England had established itself as a ruler of the seas, a position it would continue to enjoy for almost 400 years.

The Elizabethan Age was a flowering of English culture, and the brightest blooms were uses of the language that still affect our thought and speech. Although William Shakespeare was the most magnificent of the blossoms, others, such as Spenser, Drayton, Donne, and Marlowe, bloomed in the sunshine.

The United Kingdom

Thomas Cranmer produced a *Book of Common Prayer* in 1549 whose magnificent collects shaped the way the English-speaking world addressed God and whose words start the most important ceremony in most people's lives: "Dearly beloved, we are gathered here together in the sight of God and in the face of this company to join together this man and this woman in holy matrimony: which is an honorable estate instituted of God, signifying unto us the mystical union that is betwixt Christ and His church." The musical liturgy of the book was done with assistance from Lutherans, who had retained Catholic plainsong chant traditions in German; they were adapted to English. Further, harmonized Anglican chant was first produced. All of this is preserved with little change in many churches to this day.

In the last part of Elizabeth's reign, William Shakespeare began to write his plays. Their plots shape our view of history, or romance, and humor, and his phrases fill our speaking and our reading, even when we do not know the source of the words. Finally, shortly after Elizabeth's death, the language of the *Book of Common Prayer* and the language of Shakespeare came together in the most influential of all English books, the King James Bible. Until recently, it was read by more people than any other book in the English language, and for many Americans on the frontier, it was their only book in the English language. It has been only in the past five decades that serious attention was paid to any of the "modern" English translations.

The Tudor monarchs were able to dominate England by their political skill and by the force of their personality. All except Edward and Mary enjoyed considerable popularity, and if those who followed them had enjoyed similar success, the Parliament might have melted out of British life. But the Stuarts, of whom it could be said, "They learned nothing and forgot nothing," tried to push the doctrine of the divine right of kings farther than the English wished to have it carried. When Elizabeth died unmarried in 1603, James Stuart, king of Scotland, became James I of England, and the whole island was united under one monarch.

The Stuarts' Brief Tenure

The second of the Stuarts, Charles I, came to the throne in 1625. He soon began to have trouble with Parliament over taxation, and his inflexibility and demands for royal absolutism only angered the democratic movement within the country. Moreover, Charles was a "high" churchman, with Roman Catholic leanings, and most members of Parliament were Puritan Protestant in inclination (i.e., a full, chanted Eucharistic service with all ceremonial acts, including incense, holy water, etc., versus three hymns, a psalm, lessons, and sermon). For 11 years Charles managed to rule without Parliament, and his persecution of Puritans led to the founding of the colonies in New England. In order to raise revenues, Charles reconvened Parliament in 1640, and soon civil war broke out in England. Catholics, high churchmen, the nobility, and the rural people of the north and west supported the king; Puritans, people of trade and commerce, and most important, Londoners, supported Parliament.

Religious and Civil Turmoil

Unlike the Wars of the Roses, the civil war of the 17th century was not simply a fight over who should occupy the throne but also an ideological struggle to determine the very nature of English society. Oliver Cromwell emerged as leader of the parliamentary forces after Charles had been captured. Cromwell purged Parliament of all but his loyal supporters, abolished the House of Lords, and in 1649 had Charles beheaded. He was the only English monarch to die for religious reasons and the last to be killed for political reasons. Whether Charles was a martyr for the causes of royal stability and the Anglican Church or whether he justly died for opposing the representatives of the people depends on one's viewpoint—and perhaps both views are true.

The Commonwealth Period and Return of Monarchy

Cromwell had hoped to rule in a liberal and democratic way, but continued factionalism and the threatening anarchy in English society caused him to assume absolute power as Lord Protector. This

Queen Mary I

Queen Elizabeth I

period was known as the Commonwealth. When Cromwell died in 1658 and the monarchy was restored in 1660, Charles II, the son of the dead king, returned from the Continent, to which he had escaped, and was greeted by a joyful people.

During Charles' reign, English culture extricated itself from the heavy burden of Puritanism and flourished again; Bunyan, Milton, and Pepys were the most famous writers. The Great Fire of 1666 destroyed much of London but allowed such master architects as Christopher Wren to rebuild a new and even more glorious city. On another continent, the Dutch were driven out of North America, and New Amsterdam became New York.

James II followed his brother to the throne but did not renounce his faith in Roman Catholicism. The English then turned to William of Orange, a grandson of Charles I, who came to England and later defeated James in the July 1690 Battle of the Boyne in Ireland. From then on, the fact that England was Anglican (not Roman Catholic or Puritan) was settled. But both William of Orange and his wife were childless. The

most logical successor was Queen Anne, daughter of James II, but she died childless in 1714. What was the answer for a people accustomed to a monarchy?

The House of Hanover (Later Windsor) and Parliament Power

Britain turned to George of Hanover (a great-grandson of James I and a Protestant) to become king. The fact that he could speak no English (only German) was of immense importance. It meant that the king had to leave many of his powers in the hands of the chairmanship of his council, and that person was the leader of the Whig Party, with a majority in the House of Commons. Thus, England developed the tradition of having a prime minister preside over a cabinet that grew out of Parliament.

During the middle part of the 18th century, the first British Empire took shape. English forces defeated the French for control of much of India, and the defeat of the French forces at Quebec in 1759 meant that Canada and the area west of the 13 colonies were brought under British

rule. In 1760, George III succeeded to the throne. Since he believed a king should rule the country, he suspended the cabinet government, intending that the king and the "king's friends" would rule.

As the British Empire expanded with Captain Cook's discovery of Australia, relations with the 13 American colonies deteriorated. By 1782 they had been victorious in their revolution, and the period of the First British Empire was largely over. With the disaster in North America came the return of the cabinet system to England, as William Pitt the Younger became the new prime minister. For the next 50 years, the Tories would lead the country and maintain a steady and conservative posture while the French Revolution and then the armies of Napoleon forced Britain once again to demonstrate its mastery of the seas.

19th-Century Change

At the turn of the century, the Act of Union dissolved the Irish parliament and incorporated Catholic Ireland into the United Kingdom. Tragically, religious persecution of the Catholics kept the Irish from full integration into British society, and thus, the union was doomed from the start.

But change was occurring in England. The Industrial Revolution, gradual at first, gathered momentum. Early machines made of wood were replaced by stronger and more efficient ones of iron. James Watt's inventions harnessed the power of steam. Reforms in agriculture improved food production but caused many farmers to leave the land. Thus, as industry and commerce were growing, along with the wealth and power of those who controlled them, so, too, there was a growing urban class kept in degrading poverty. As populations shifted, Parliament became less representative.

In so-called rotten boroughs, a few voters could control who was elected to Parliament. In one district in Cornwall, a single voter could elect two members! It is coincidental but symbolic that in 1830 the Reforming Whigs Party obtained a majority in Parliament and the first railroad line on which the Rocket whizzed along at 35 miles an hour was opened.

The Whigs were able to get their Reform Bill through Parliament in 1832. This most important piece of legislation abolished many "rotten" boroughs, gave representation to the new towns, and significantly lowered the property qualifications necessary to be a voter. Many observers think that this Reform Bill saved the country from revolution, which had become so popular in the rest of Europe. Certainly, it gave new power to the middle classes and was an important step toward mass democracy.

George III (1738–1820)

The United Kingdom

John Constable's *Hay Wain* (1821)

Victoria

In 1837 the 18-year-old Victoria began the longest reign in British history. As the last half of the 17th century had belonged to Elizabeth, so the 19th century belonged to Victoria. During Victoria's reign, reform acts gradually increased the number of people enfranchised and gave protection to the lower classes. The repeal of the "Corn Laws" and free trade not only stimulated industry but also reduced the cost of living for the poor. Thus, under the leadership of such greats as Palmerston, Gladstone, and Disraeli, Parliament found a course that kept England moving toward democracy without being caught up in the excesses that racked so much of the Continent. By 1846 Canada had been made self-governing, and within a few years, Australia and New Zealand were given internal self-rule. Thus, the concept of the empire of free countries bound to the mother country by loyalty to the queen was born.

Two great events marked the reign of Victoria. The Great Exhibition of 1851 demonstrated British industrial might and middle-class prosperity, whereas the Golden Jubilee of the queen in 1887 marked the high point of the empire. The claim that the sun never set on the British Empire was indeed true. Its members included Canada in North America, British Guiana in South America; the United Kingdom in Europe; South Africa, Kenya, and Somaliland in Africa; India and Ceylon in Asia; and Australia and New Zealand in the Pacific. The greatest problem, however, was closest to home, and various attempts to solve the Irish problem through home rule were unsuccessful.

Until 1900 the roar of the British lion could be heard throughout the world. Britain controlled over one-fifth of the earth's land surface and ruled a quarter of the world's population. Its flag flew on every continent, and the largest and most powerful navy in the world protected its magnificent empire. At the same time,

Britain was invulnerable to foreign invasion. This meant that, unlike many other nations with frontiers instead of shorelines, it could leisurely develop a democratic form of government. Nations under the constant threat of attack often could not afford the luxury of a relatively inefficient and cumbersome governmental order that involved parliamentary meetings, long debates, votes, press coverage, and criticism. As a nation equally invulnerable, the Americans shared this advantage with their English forebears.

Also, Britain did not need to maintain a large standing army. As the history of many countries indicates, ambitious soldiers led by prestigious officers close to the political heart of the country sometimes cannot resist meddling in the political affairs of a nation. The British never had difficulty in maintaining control over their military; a military putsch is unthinkable in the British context. Fortunately, the tradition of civilian supremacy over the military was passed on to many (though not all) of its former colonies, including the United States.

Political Power Struggles and Social Change

A watershed year in the growth of power of the House of Commons was 1911. The Liberal Party government had proposed a land tax, and although tradition had it that only Commons controlled finances, the House of Lords rejected the bill. The Parliament bill of 1911 deprived the Lords of any control of finance and limited their power over other bills to a two-year delay. In a move to make the Commons more responsive to the popular will, the maximum life of a Parliament was reduced from seven to five years. When it appeared that the Lords would veto this bill, George V threatened to increase the number of Lords and pack the Upper House with those favorable to the bill. The Lords yielded to the threat, and thereafter the House of Commons gained virtual total control of legislation. In the same year, members of the House of Commons began to receive pay, and thus, those without independent incomes could be in Parliament.

World War I, known then as the "Great War," devastated a generation of Englishmen. In 2009 the last survivor among the millions of British soldiers who fought in the trenches, Harry Patch, died at age 111. But the bloody conflict helped to produce changes in society. As recognition for their part in the war effort, women received the vote in 1918. Because they involved so much of the population, both world wars did much to further popular democracy and reduce the differences between social classes. Shortly after World War I, the

THE
BRITISH NAVY
guards the freedom of us all

southern part of Ireland left the United Kingdom and achieved dominion status as the Irish Free State. Protestants living in the north clung tenaciously to their membership in the United Kingdom and their loyalty to the Crown, but their conflict with Catholics living alongside them has not been solved to this day.

Following World War I, trade unions grew in power and were able to call a general strike in 1926. But the Great Depression of the 1930s significantly reduced the power of the Labour government, and the conservatives led the country in the years before World War II. The last crisis to affect the monarchy occurred in 1936. Edward VIII ascended the throne, but within months he abdicated so that he could marry the divorced Wallis Simpson, an American.

The Hitler Threat and World War II

As Hitler began to threaten more and more of Europe, Prime Minister Neville Chamberlain practiced a policy of appeasement. This only whetted the German appetite; after an attack on Poland in September 1939, Britain joined France as allies in World War II. In May of the next year, Winston Churchill became prime minister. His courage and his words epitomized the best of the British spirit. They inspired the nation to rescue 340,000 British and French soldiers from the beaches of Dunkirk and to withstand withering aerial attacks from bombers and rockets in the Battle of Britain, launched in 1940. Germany's Operation Sealion was the first invasion of England since 1066. With tremendous but belated assistance from the US, Britain and its allies were victorious. But the United Kingdom was prostrated and devastated by the end of the conflict in 1945.

The Postwar 1940s and 1950s

Two world wars in the 20th century brought enormous changes. These included revolutions in many European countries; the rise of the United States and the Soviet Union as the most powerful countries in the world; and the relative decline of the traditional global powers, including the United Kingdom, in terms of political and military significance. As a victorious ally, Britain gained a veto right in the United Nations Security Council, but it had to liquidate most of its foreign investments to finance its own recovery; these foreign investments had once paid for a third of British imports. The merchant marine was depleted, and factories and equipment were either destroyed or obsolete.

The negative economic consequences of the wars reduced Britain's ability to be a global power and stimulated in many British colonies the desire for independence. By proclaiming the Truman Doctrine, the US assumed from Britain the burden of economic and military aid to Greece and Turkey and relieved the UK of its responsibility for supporting the struggle against communist forces in the Greek civil war. The British also found themselves in the crossfire between Jews and Arabs in Palestine and Hindus and Muslims in India and were forced in 1947 to abandon both important regions. In 1952 it lost control of Egypt. When Egypt seized the Suez Canal in 1956, Britain, supported by France and Israel, attempted to reconquer that important waterway. However, stiff joint United Nations, US and Soviet opposition to this move, which seemed like the last gasp of colonialism, forced the British, French, and Israelis to back down.

In 1959 Britain still ruled over 53 countries with a population of 81 million, and 86,000 British troops were deployed around the world outside of Europe. But the floodgates opened, and by the 1960s a tidal wave of separations swept through Africa, the Middle East, and Asia. Having lost most of its Asian empire in the late 1940s, the British recognized the inevitability of African independence. Fortunately, Britain had trained many Africans as capable administrators and had established there a relatively efficient system of local administration. Therefore, when they gradually relinquished their hold, well-trained Africans were usually able to take their places. An exception was Rhodesia, whose tiny white minority took power in 1965 and held it for years before finally handing the reins of power to the new black-ruled state of Zimbabwe. Britain spearheaded the international UN boycott of Rhodesia. But the UK was in the throes of such economic distress that it was not only unable to steer

events in Africa but it was also forced in 1971 to terminate most of its military and political responsibilities "east of Suez." This withdrawal was unfortunate for the US, which was trapped at the time in the quagmire of Vietnam. The US felt compelled to assume Britain's prior responsibility for maintaining "stability" in the Middle East. It thereby became embroiled in one of the world's least stable regions. This untimely responsibility prompted American administrations in the 1970s to help build up the shah's power. The hope was that a modernized and well-armed Iran could maintain order in the oil-rich Persian Gulf region and keep the Soviet Union's power and influence out of the area. The Americans paid heavily in the 1980s for this gamble.

Elizabeth II succeeded her father, George VI, on the British throne in 1952. Thirty generations separated her from her ancestor William the Conqueror, and she began her reign in a nation struggling to find a new role in the modern world. The empire became a commonwealth of independent nations, bound together by language, democratic principles, and a residue of loyalty to the person (but not the power) of the British monarch. Decolonization had a serious negative economic impact on Britain by depriving it of many protected markets, sources of raw materials at low prices, and cheap food. The resulting economic difficulties harassed the United Kingdom for a quarter-century following the Second World War.

Domestic Politics before Thatcher

On July 5, 1945, voters delivered a dramatic blow to the Tories by electing the first Labour prime minister with a clear majority of 145 seats in the House of Commons, Clement Attlee. Although the British deeply admired Churchill as a great wartime leader, they associated his Conservative Party with the soup lines and unemployment of the prewar Depression. Labour had ably guided the home ministries in the national government during the war. It had impressed the British as being the best team for creating full employment, housing, and better social security and health care for a people who had just sacrificed so much in the war effort.

Although ideologically divided, as always, between more pragmatic and radical wings, the Labour Party moved boldly to make many sweeping economic changes, including the nationalization of the Bank of England, hospitals, railways, aviation, and public transport and the gas, electrical, coal, and steel industries. Unlike France and Italy, though, the newly nationalized industries were placed under the direction of autonomous corporations (subsidized from the state treasury)

The United Kingdom

Horse guardsmen leaving their barracks for duty at Buckingham Palace

rather than government agencies and ministries. In 1946 the National Insurance Act and National Health Service Act were the prime examples of popular social welfare legislation which strengthened or created old-age pensions, unemployment compensation, education, social insurance, and free health service. No sooner were these innovations in place, though, than the Labour government began losing popularity. It was badly divided, British influence abroad was noticeably eroding, the pound was losing its value, and economic recovery was painfully slow.

At age 77 Winston Churchill was returned to power in 1951, and his Tories ruled until 1964, the longest period of continuous party government in modern British history until Margaret Thatcher and John Major ruled 18 years from 1979 to 1997. His government returned the iron and steel industries and road transport to private ownership, although Labour renationalized iron and steel in 1967. However, accurately sensing the sentiments of the British nation, the Tories did not make a radical U-turn. It accepted the national welfare and health services, as well as the commitment to full employment.

Following a stroke, Churchill was finally persuaded to step down in 1955. His successor was his longtime foreign minister Anthony Eden. After only a year, Eden had

to resign in the aftermath of the Suez crisis of 1956. He was followed by Harold Macmillan, who, like Churchill, had an American mother. He optimistically predicted a turnaround in Britain's economic fortunes (for which reason he was dubbed "Supermac"). There was a short-lived economic boom in the late 1950s, and the living standards of some British rose. But inequalities of wealth remained which the government could not alleviate because of a rising imbalance of payments and a serious sterling crisis. Britain was obviously not keeping up with its international trade competitors,

Winston S. Churchill, surrounded by the royal family

24

and management and trade unions were not inclined to introduce more efficient and modern methods of production. In an attempt to protect the value of the pound, the government had to introduce an unpopular wage freeze and raise the bank rate. Macmillan sought to halt the growing economic malaise and increase British industry's competitiveness by leading Britain into the EU, but French president Charles de Gaulle vetoed its entry in 1963.

Following this humiliation came the coup de grace for the Macmillan government: a lurid sex scandal involving Secretary of War John Profumo. He was alleged to be involved with a call girl who had been asked by the Soviet naval attaché to gather information from him on the UK's nuclear weapons. No government could possibly benefit from such a spicy and embarrassing affair. But what forced Macmillan to demand Profumo's resignation was not so much the illicit activity itself as the fact that he had insulted Parliament by lying to it about his involvement. He thereby dragged both himself and the prime minister down.

The colorless Sir Alec Douglas-Home replaced Macmillan in the fall of 1963. Home (pronounced Hume) was a rare example of a prime minister being drawn from the House of Lords, even though he scrambled to win a by-election seat to the Commons. He had sat in the Commons earlier, but when his father died, he was obligated to become a Lord. Parliament passed a law permitting Lords to renounce their title. Home could not quiet the growing desire for a change, and with only a razor-thin majority, he could not prevent Harold Wilson's Labour Party from winning power in October 1964.

A former Oxford University economics don (lecturer), Wilson was from the more conservative, reformist wing of the Labour Party. Faced with daunting economic problems, he not only pared down the UK's military commitments abroad, but he also applied the traditional conservative policies of increasing taxes and reducing government spending. These unpopular economic policies widened ideological divisions within his own party, sparked industrial unrest and strikes and brought Wilson into a head-on collision with the trade unions. Widening trade imbalances, another devaluation of the pound, and a renewal of strife between Catholics and Protestants in Northern Ireland all spelled disaster for Wilson in the June 1970 elections, when the Tories, led by Edward Heath, returned to power.

Heath's government knew little happiness, aside from Britain's entry into the EU in 1973. His bitter confrontations with the assertive coal miners brought serious economic disruptions and forced the prime minister to declare states of emergency five times. The crippling coal strike in the winter of 1973–1974 destroyed what credibility remained for the cabinet. Voters brought Wilson's Labour Party back to power in February 1974 on the assumption that they would have better relations with the powerful unions.

Wilson had only a miniscule majority, which he widened in a snap election in October 1974. He expended precious energy and patience fending off an ambitious radical left wing within his own party which sniped at him constantly and openly advocated such unpopular policies as a "socialist transformation" of British society, massive nationalizations of large companies, the abolition of such elite institutions as the House of Lords and private schools, withdrawal from NATO and the EU, and unilateral disarmament. These leftist antics ultimately drove some moderates out of the party and led to the formation in 1981 of the now-defunct Social Democratic Party (SDP).

It is hardly surprising that Wilson was unable to improve the economic situation. The skyrocketing price of oil resulting from the 1973 OPEC embargo hit the struggling British economy hard, despite the discovery of oil in Britain's own sectors of the North Sea. Inflation rose to a dizzying level, and for the first time since the war, unemployment reared its ugly head. These problems made hopes for harmonious labor relations a pipe dream, as the spate of disruptive strikes indicated. In 1976 an exasperated and tired Harold Wilson turned the keys to Number 10 Downing Street over to his foreign minister, James Callaghan. The new prime minister was no more successful than Wilson had been in controlling the unions, improving the overall economy, and coping with rising violence in Northern Ireland and growing separatist movements in Scotland and Wales.

It has been said that the world stands aside for a man who knows where he is going. By the spring of 1979, the British voters were prepared to do just that, with one historical twist: They brought to power the first woman prime minister in British politics, Margaret Thatcher. She acted with such determination and decisiveness that, by January 3, 1988, she had become the longest continuously serving British prime minister in the 20th century. Ruling over a country with the highest economic growth of any major economy, low inflation, declining unemployment, a rising pound, and tamed unions, she had every reason to believe that she would remain at the helm into the 21st century and perhaps even overtake the record of Sir Robert Walpole, whose 21 consecutive years of service as prime minister began in 1721.

Attitude and Political Change

Terrorism related to the unsolved problem of Northern Ireland, along with rising crime in Britain, helped shift British voters' view of the world in an important way. It helped many of them shape a tough-minded attitude and become more receptive to political appeals based on "law and order," replacing the compromise politics of the 1960s.

The parliamentary elections of 1979 and 1983 took many foreign observers by surprise because they revealed that the political landscape in Britain had dramatically changed. Upon closer scrutiny, it can be seen that these changes are the consequence of important changes in Britain's economy and society in the course of the 1970s. Those changes broke down much of the class structure of Britain, which traditionally had shaped British politics to such a large extent.

Public opinion polls and election analyses continually confirm that fewer and fewer British spontaneously identify with a particular class and that class-consciousness has and is declining markedly. Class itself has become only one of many factors shaping individual attitudes and preferences. It has become harder to classify Britons by class, which has increasingly become more a matter of taste and culture rather than of income and occupation. With less than a quarter of workers in manufacturing jobs, fewer than two workers in five belong to a labor union. Two thirds of all British own or are buying their homes; even one of three unskilled manual laborers is a homeowner. Also, leisure is no longer the privilege of a few; instead, almost all full-time workers receive four weeks of leave. In short, more workers have become middle class. Young people from all economic strata mingle more easily and are more likely to intermarry than they used to. Since Britons have become more individualistic, their social attitudes and political behavior have become less predictable. These changes are bound to have a negative effect on political parties whose appeals have traditionally been heavily class-based, especially the Labour Party.

Since 1979, Britain's population has barely grown, but the size of the electorate increased from 39.3 million in 1970 to 42.2 million in 1983. The voting age was dropped to 18 in 1970, but the number of pensioners has grown, so the average voter today is actually older than in 1970. He or she is also more highly educated; more likely to be divorced and live alone or in small households; own his own home; and, despite high unemployment, have a higher standard of living than in the 1970s. Disenchantment with unions and changes in social patterns (see "Culture") that were

The United Kingdom

occurring in the 1970s set the stage for dramatic political shifts in Britain. After 1979 these effectively altered much of the conventional wisdom about British politics and realigned the structure.

Although the diminishing numbers of unionized workers in the mines and factories retained their traditional loyalty to the Labour Party and the managers remained steadfast to the Conservative Party, their diminishing numbers hoisted the flag of change on the pole in the 1970s. Soaring inflation and rising unemployment, accompanied by increasingly strident union demands, alienated the people. Their revulsion at the excessive "unelected power" which union bosses wielded boiled to the surface in "the winter of discontent," 1978–1979, when coal and transportation strikes threatened to paralyze the entire nation.

These changes led to conditions whereby a party leader would advocate a policy based on the notions that the best help was self-help; that initiative deserved rewards; that an economic pie must be baked before it is divided; that welfare could not produce prosperity; that private business is better than nationalized industries; that the problem of inflation is more important than the problem of unemployment; and, finally, that the government cannot control the economy. In other words, traditional Keynesian economics was no cure for British problems but was part of the disease. That leader was Margaret Thatcher, leader of the Conservative Party (Tory) since 1975, who was elected prime minister in 1979. Leading a changed party, she captured the mood of an altered society and spoke for the new social realities.

Return to the Conservative Party

When she moved into the prime minister's office, she promised "three years of unparalleled austerity," and for three years the pain of Thatcherism was far more evident than the benefits. Unemployment rose, and economic conditions worsened. She was unable to cut government spending significantly because of greater numbers on welfare and pay raises for government workers to bring them into equity with the private sector. Nevertheless, the "Iron Lady," as she began to be called, held firm to her monetarist policies (restricting the money supply) and vowed, "I will not stagger from expedient to expedient." By 1982 her party was well behind the Labour Party in the polls, and she seemed to be heading for sure defeat in the next elections, when the unexpected occurred.

The Falklands War

Argentine troops invaded and captured a small group of offshore islands that had long been settled and ruled by the British.

Mrs. Thatcher galvanized the nation with her firmness and resolution in organizing the recapture of the Falklands Islands. The British basked again briefly in imperial glory, and an overwhelming majority of them applauded their leader for her ability to deal with a crisis, winning back control of the islands, albeit at a tremendous financial cost. The Falklands War boosted her party's popularity, and the economy fortuitously began to revive at the same time, with inflation shrinking to the lowest level in 15 years. The electorate became convinced that her economic medicine had been a harsh necessity and that she was a true leader. Sensing the political winds blowing briskly at her back, she took advantage of the prime minister's privilege to set an election whenever it suits his or her party. It was called for June 1983 and demonstrated beyond doubt that the party landscape had greatly changed and that a new Conservative Party had become the dominant force in British politics by the mid-1980s.

Her astonishing electoral triumph in June 1983, which made her the first Conservative prime minister in the 20th century to be reelected to a second term, revealed both her leadership image, established in the Falklands War, and the extent to which most social and economic groups in Britain accepted her diagnosis of the nation's problems. Most voters did not even blame her for the country's most pressing problem: continuing unemployment, which shot up from 5.4% to 13.3% during her four years of rule. They clearly patted her on the back for bringing inflation down.

"The Iron Lady"

She was a fundamentally cautious politician, whose bark was often more powerful than her bite. She did take modest steps to return some of the nationalized industries to private hands, but she did not precipitously withdraw the public from the economy; in 1988 government spending

amounted to 42% of GNP, about the same as in 1979. Nor did she dramatically reduce public employment, welfare assistance, or taxes; she disliked spending what she did not have. Therefore, most voters did not see in her a fanatic ideologue who wished to turn the clock backward.

She never enjoyed "popularity," as her many nicknames reveal: "Leaderene," "Attila the Hen," "Rhoda the Rhino," and "Nanny," to mention only a few of the "kinder" ones. Many saw her as uncaring, cold, and obsessed. But she had authority and respect because of what she accomplished and what she represents. She strode firmly forward to remake her country in her own self-image: brisk, hardworking, frugal, and self-sufficient. She combined some of the best 19th-century values with 20th-century energy. She was a strong leader who entered office with a sense of mission: to make Britain great again. Of course, she benefited from an opposition that was in disarray.

Part of Thatcher's appeal was that she represented a new kind of Conservative Party that had emerged. The image of the party as the preserve of the landed gentry, bankers, or high-level civil servants, which could display charity when needed toward the lower classes and which assembled in prayer in the Church of England, has changed.

The attitude of most citizens, an overwhelming majority of whom are baptized Protestant, is now indifference toward religion—its traditional role in politics has all but vanished. Tory leaders cannot count on the support of the Church of England, containing many clergy bitterly opposed to its policies.

Thatcher was an example of the "new" kind of Tory, who worked her way up in the world. The daughter of a dressmaker and grocer from Grantham, Lincolnshire, she lived with her family in an apartment above the shop and worked all her childhood in her father's store. She studied

Mr. Denis Thatcher and former prime minister Thatcher

Hyde Park Corner, London

chemistry at Oxford, where she led the Conservative student organization and held off-campus jobs. She later acquired a law degree after marrying a successful businessman, Denis Thatcher, who served as the nation's "First Gentleman," staying a discreet half-pace behind the prime minister. She was never an insider in "the establishment," and she harbored a bias against the party elite. She served only four years in the early 1970s as education secretary before gaining the party leadership in 1975.

Having emerged from the middle class herself, she was well able to forge an alliance between skilled workers and the middle class in a society which is becoming more and more middle class. She capitalized on the dream of owning one's home by giving residents of government-built houses the opportunity to buy them at bargain prices. About a half-million gratefully did so. This was the greatest transfer of wealth to the British working class in history. By the time her Tory Party was voted out of power in 1997, 68% of all housing units were owner-occupied, a higher percentage than in the United States or elsewhere in Europe.

She benefited from a transformation within the party, which extends from the grassroots all the way up to Parliament. Its seats are no longer occupied primarily by traditional local notables but increasingly by insurance agents, housewives, teachers, salesmen, and self-made middle-management types. Perhaps as good an example of the new kind of Tory as Thatcher herself was a speaker of the House, Bruce Bernard Weatherill, a former tailor who always carried in his pocket a thimble to remind himself of his humble background. It is said that, when he entered Parliament, one aristocratic Conservative MP was overheard saying to another, "I don't know what this place is coming

to, Tom: they've got my tailor in here now!" The point is that the tailor to whom they were referring was a Tory.

In April 2013 Lady Thatcher died of a stroke in a suite in London's Ritz Hotel. There was an outpouring of sympathy, reverence, and respect. She was hailed as Britain's greatest peacetime prime minister and "the great transformer." A special session of Parliament debated for seven hours her importance for Britain. The queen granted her a funeral with military honors in St. Paul's Cathedral costing £10 million ($16 million). She agreed to attend, the first time since Winston Churchill's death in 1965 that she was present at a former prime minister's funeral. However, there were many reminders of how divisive and hated she had been. "Death parties" were held in major cities with banners reading "Rejoice, Rejoice!" The song, "Ding Dong: The Witch Is Dead," shot up to number 1 in the pop music charts. A coal miners' unionist proclaimed, "It's a great day. She did more damage to us than Hitler did." Another unemployed coal miner added, "Mrs. Thatcher? She should rot in hell for what she did to us."

GOVERNMENT

Simplicity and Flexibility

Speaking of his country, the great Victorian prime minister Benjamin Disraeli stated, "In a progressive country, change is constant, and the great question is not whether you should resist change which is inevitable, but whether that change should be carried out in deference to the manners, the customs, the laws and the traditions of the people." Americans often imagine the British as a conservative nation. In fact, Britain has skillfully adjusted to change for centuries, and today it confronts fundamental shifts in its society,

economy, political system, and place in the world. The British genius is to combine astonishing continuity with necessary change; they excel in pouring "new wine into old bottles."

Great Britain remains a monarchy with a noble class that still enjoys certain privileges. However, Britain is the birthplace for the most durable democratic model of government in the world. Unlike the complicated American democratic system, which has almost never been successfully adapted to other societies, the "Westminster model" not only fits the British people and circumstances, but it can quite easily be made to fit other nations, as well. Its secret lies in its simplicity and its flexibility. It can be modified and tailored to other peoples' needs and circumstances without losing its essentially democratic character.

British politics operates according to an unwritten constitution that prescribes the "rules of the game" and places limits on the rulers. In the UK voters elect 650 members of the House of Commons, the lower house of Parliament. The leader of the party that wins a majority of the seats (or has more seats than any other party) becomes the prime minister, the most powerful political figure in the land. The monarch is the head of state, but her role is largely symbolic; she makes no important political decisions. The prime minister selects other ministers, who are also parliamentary leaders in the party, to sit in the cabinet.

Contrasts with the US

Unlike the United States, where both houses of Congress are equally powerful, the British upper house, the House of Lords, has far less power than the House of Commons. Also, unlike in the United States, there is neither "separation of power" among the executive, legislative, or judicial branches nor a distribution of political powers among the national government and many state governments. Executive and legislative powers are fused, and the prime minister is both the chief executive and the chief legislator. Through party discipline the prime minister controls the House of Commons. Further, political power is concentrated in the central government. Britain is a unitary, not a federal, state, so he/she does not have to contend with separate states that wield constitutionally granted powers of their own. No court in the country can judge a law unconstitutional. Parliamentary supremacy is the fundamental principle of British government.

This setup is the basic model for most democracies in the world. Even the founders of the American government, whose political views had been shaped by British political ideas but who had consciously sought

The United Kingdom

to depart from that model, adopted more from the British system than many Americans care to remember. After all, what the founders had deemed to be so unjust and tyrannical was the fact that Americans had been "denied their rights as Englishmen." Even the arguments and wording of the Declaration of Independence bear striking resemblance to the work by the 17th-century English philosopher John Locke, entitled *The Second Treatise of Government*, an important blueprint and philosophical foundation for British government.

The American Founding Fathers were certainly aware of their debt to Westminster when they included in the American Constitution such provisions as the necessity of senatorial confirmation of cabinet ministers, congressional election of the president in the event that no candidate wins a majority in the electoral college, and the possibility for the national legislature to impeach and remove a president. It is indeed fitting that the statue on the top of the Capitol faces toward London, symbolic of the extent to which the American government, the political habits, and the thinking of its people have been shaped by Great Britain.

The Unwritten Constitution

As the British political system is more closely examined, perhaps the first striking aspect is the fact that the country's constitution is unwritten; that is, there is no single document, as in the United States. One must refer to one or all of five sources to know what is constitutional: First are particularly important documents, such as the Magna Charta (1215); the Habeas Corpus Act (1679); the Bill of Rights (1689), which, unlike the American Bill of Rights, defines rights of Parliament, not rights of individual citizens; the Parliament Act of 1911; and the Statute of Westminster (1931). Then there are interpretations of courts of law and principles of common law (which has itself been in a constant state of change). For example, basic individual liberties, such as the freedom of assembly, speech, and religion, are all derived from common law. There is the Law and Custom of Parliament, which deals with the special privileges which Parliament and each member of Parliament (known as MP) enjoy.

Finally there are wholly unwritten elements, known as conventions. These include such practices as: Parliament must meet at least once a year, the government must resign if it loses a vote of confidence, and the monarch cannot attend cabinet meetings or enter Parliament without permission. On the occasion of her Diamond Jubilee on December 18, 2012, the cabinet invited her attend one of its meetings. This was the first time in more than a century that this honor had been extended. On the same day, a large expanse of Britain's Antarctic territory was christened Queen Elizabeth Land.

The monarch always opens Parliament with a speech from the throne in the House of Lords. She is there in all her finery, displaying the majesty and royal tradition that stretch back continuously over so many centuries. Yet, she is surrounded by members of Parliament, freely elected by the people and operating within the context of an effective multiparty system. Her speech does not contain her own ideas but puts forward the program of the prime minister and the government which holds a majority in the lower house of Parliament. Members of the opposition party, often called the "Loyal Opposition," listen to it. Because the monarch delivers the speech, tradition requires that even critics refer to it as "the gracious speech." For example, opposition leader John Major responded to Prime Minister Tony Blair's text read by the queen in May 1997 as follows: "The road to hell is paved with good intentions, and this gracious speech is very full of good intentions."

Perhaps no other idea has been a more important gift of the British to the growth of free government than the concept of the "Loyal Opposition." That someone may be opposed to the present government's policies and yet still be loyal to the country and not subject to political punishment is incomprehensible in totalitarian or one-party states.

No politician could violate these conventions without touching off a serious political crisis. The well-informed and respected Economist described Britain's constitution as a "contraption, stuck together from old laws, bits of precedent, scraps of custom and practice and blind faith in the steering ability of its driver, the prime minister of the day. The machine is notoriously short on brakes: the checks and balances which are a feature of written constitutions." A Constitutional reform advocate Peter Facey said in 2010 that it is "like a wet bar of soap. You try and catch it and it slips out of your hands." A favorite joke is that, "if you got rid of three or four elderly commentators on our constitution, there would be no one around to tell us what it is."

Why does a nation of 61.9 million persons have no written constitution? One reason is that Britain is one of the few democracies in the world to enter the democratic age without a revolution. After successful revolutions, winners are far more inclined to put in writing the kind of guarantees and rights that had been denied them by the former rulers. The outlines of the British regime were established before the Industrial Revolution in the 19th century. Therefore, the economic and social conflicts which that revolution sparked could ultimately be reconciled within the system. Also, the British aristocracy had the foresight to make concessions to the middle and working classes, prompting the latter to realize that they could achieve change and satisfaction through reform rather than rebellion. This is one reason Marxism was never as potent a political force in Britain as it was on the European continent. Further, Britain is not a federal state, so there is no need for a careful delineation of jurisdictions between various governments, as in the US.

Most important, however, is the kind of political culture one finds in Britain. There is widespread agreement on basic political values, and the population broadly supports the leading institutions. This consensus has meant that disagreements over policies have (except under Cromwell) never led to fundamental challenges to the regime and constitution. The British have changed their political system only gradually. Important changes usually only occur after much dialogue and after the major parties have reached general agreement on them. The British also are a law-abiding people, a fact that makes it especially shocking to read about bombings or racial riots in that country. They tend to be moderate and pragmatic and are remarkable for their unwillingness to mount the barricades over abstract or idealistic principles.

They are inclined to boil political disputes down to conflicting interests rather than to conflicting morals or ideas, and this makes compromise much easier. Finally, there is a widespread acceptance of democracy and pluralism. Any foreigner who needs a reminder of the fact that there are many different groups or viewpoints which have a right to exist and be heard in Britain can go to Hyde Park on any Sunday morning to hear the soapbox speeches of dozens of advocates.

The Monarchy

Britain is a monarchy, and in theory the queen or king has sweeping powers. She theoretically appoints the prime minister, assembles or dissolves Parliament, approves of all laws, makes foreign policy, commands the "Armed Forces of the Crown," and appoints officers who hold their rank by "Royal Commission." The trappings of political power would seem to confirm this. The "Queen's government" contains "Ministers of the Crown," who propose laws which always begin with the following words: "Be it enacted by the Queen's Most Excellent Majesty, by and with the consent of the Lords Spiritual and Temporal and Commons in this present Parliament assembled." She is the

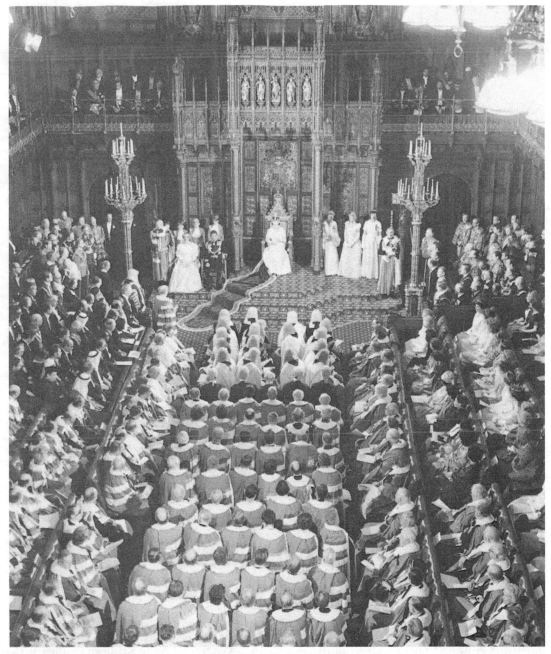

Her Majesty Queen Elizabeth II opens Parliament in the House of Lords.

temporal head of the Church of England, the country's official religion, and she appoints the leading priests. Also, in theory, sovereignty resides not in the people but in the "Crown," which is not the person of the monarch but rather the symbol of supreme executive power.

Actually, she no longer exercises any of the above powers. She "reigns but does not rule." The "Glorious Revolution" in 1688 established parliamentary supremacy and spelled the end of any monarchical pretense to rule absolutely. The last exercise of royal veto power was in 1707. Walter Bagehot wrote in 1867, "the

greatest wisdom of a constitutional king would show itself in well-considered inaction," and Queen Elizabeth II has obeyed this dictum.

By the 21st century, the real reason "the Queen can do no wrong" is that the government never permits her to make any important decisions. In the case of Elizabeth, she does not even express her opinions publicly. In 2012 it was considered to be a shocking breach of etiquette when a BBC correspondent declared in a radio interview that the queen had once told him she was "pretty upset" about a radical Islamic cleric in North London. Prince Charles is

more willing to express his opinions on such things as the environment, architecture, farmers' burdens, Britain's military, helicopters, or the aspects of Russian foreign policy that resemble Hitler's.

This does not mean that the monarch does not perform any important functions whatsoever. She retains the right "to be informed, to advise and to warn." This right confers no power, but it does provide influence. As constitutional expert Ivor Jennings notes, "she can be as helpful or as obstreperous as she pleases: and she is the only member of the Cabinet who cannot

The United Kingdom

The Order of Succession to the Throne

Her Majesty Queen Elizabeth II with her successors Charles (left) and William (right)

The heir apparent, eldest son of the queen:
1. His Royal Highness the **Prince CHARLES Philip Arthur George**, Prince of Wales and Earl of Chester, Duke of Cornwall and Rothesay, Earl of Carrick, Baron of Renfrew, Lord of the Isles and Great Steward of Scotland, b. November 14, 1948. Married Lady Diana Frances Spencer (third daughter of the Eighth Earl Spencer) July 29, 1981. Divorced August 28, 1996. Married Camilla Parker Bowles April 9, 2005. Parker Bowles was granted the title Duchess of Cornwall.

The first son of Prince Charles:
2. His Royal Highness **Prince WILLIAM Arthur Philip Louis of Wales**, b. June 21, 1982. Married Catherine (Kate) Middleton April 29, 2011, and were granted the titles Duke and Duchess of Cambridge. In addition, William also became the Earl of Strathearn and Baron Carrickfergus. Thus, Middleton became the Countess of Strathearn and Baroness Carrickfergus.

The children of the union:
3. His Royal Highness **Prince GEORGE Alexander Louis**, b. July 22, 2013. Known as Prince George of Cambridge, he will one day become King George VII.
4. Her Royal Highness **Princess CHARLOTTE Elizabeth Diana**, b. May 2, 2015. Known as Princess Charlotte of Cambridge.
5. His Royal Highness **Prince LOUIS Arthur Charles**, b. April 23, 2018. Known as Prince Louis of Cambridge.

The second son of Prince Charles:
6. His Royal Highness **Prince HENRY Charles Albert David of Wales,** b. September 15, 1984. Known as Prince Harry, Duke of Sussex. Married Meghan Markle May 19, 2018, and were granted the titles Duke and Duchess of Sussex. In addition, Harry also became the Earl of Dumbarton and Baron Kilkeel. Thus, Markle became the Countess of Dumbarton and Baroness Kilkeel.

The son of the union:
7. **ARCHIE Harrison Mountbatten-Windsor**, b. May 6, 2019.

The second son of the queen:
8. His Royal Highness the **Prince ANDREW Albert Christian Edward**, Duke of York, b. February 19, 1960. Married Sarah Margaret Ferguson July 23, 1986. They separated in 1992 and were divorced in 1996.

The daughters of that union:
9. Her Royal Highness **Princess BEATRICE Elizabeth Mary of York**, b. August 8, 1988.
10. Her Royal Highness **Princess EUGENIE Victoria Helena of York**, b. March 23, 1990. Married Jack Brooksbank October 12, 2018.

The third son of the queen:
11. His Royal Highness the **Prince EDWARD Antony Richard Louis**, Earl of Wessex, b. March 10, 1964. Earl of Wessex. Married Miss Sophie Rhys-Jones June 19, 1999.

The son and daughter of that union:
12. **JAMES Alexander Philip Theo Mountbatten-Windsor**, Viscount Severn, b. December 17, 2007.
13. **Lady LOUISE Alice Elizabeth Mary Mountbatten-Windsor**, b. November 8, 2003.

The daughter of the queen:
14. Her Royal Highness the **Princess ANNE Elizabeth Alice Louise**, Princess Royal, b. August 15, 1950. Married Captain Mark Anthony Peter Phillips, November 14, 1973. The marriage was dissolved April 23, 1992. Married Commander Timothy James Hamilton Laurence, RN, December 12, 1992.

The son of the first union of Princess Anne:
15. **PETER Mark Andrew Phillips**, b. November 15, 1977. Married Autumn Kelly May 17, 2008.

The daughters of that union:
16. **SAVANNAH Anne Kathleen Phillips**, b. December 29, 2010.
17. **ISLA Elizabeth Phillips**, b. March 29, 2012.

The daughter of the first union of Princess Anne:
18. **ZARA Anne Elizabeth Tindall** (née Phillips), b. May 15, 1981. Married Michael James Tindall July 30, 2011.

The daughters of that union:
19. **MIA Grace Tindall**, b. January 17, 2014.
20. **LENA Elizabeth Tindall**, b. June 18, 2018.

The sister of the queen:
Princess **MARGARET Rose**, Countess of Snowdon, b. August 21, 1930. Married Anthony Armstrong-Jones, First Earl of Snowdon, May 6, 1960. They divorced July 11, 1978. She died February 9, 2002.

The son of Princess Margaret:
21. **DAVID Albert Charles Armstrong-Jones**, Second Earl of Snowdon, Viscount Linley, b. November 3, 1961. Married Hon. Serena Alleyne Stanhope (only daughter of Viscount Petersham, son and heir of the 11th Earl of Harrington) October 8, 1993.

Buckingham Palace

The son and daughter of that union:

22. **CHARLES Patrick Inigo Armstrong-Jones**, Viscount Linley, b. July 1, 1999.
23. **Lady MARGARITA Elizabeth Rose Alleyne Armstrong-Jones**, b. May 14, 2002.

The daughter of Princess Margaret:

24. **Lady SARAH Frances Elizabeth Chatto** (née Armstrong-Jones), b. May 1, 1964. Married Daniel Chatto July 14, 1994.

The sons of that union:

25. **SAMUEL David Benedict Chatto**, b. July 28, 1996.
26. **ARTHUR Robert Nathaniel Chatto**, b. February 5, 1999.

The first cousin of the queen, the son of the Prince Henry, Duke of Gloucester:

27. His Royal Highness **Prince RICHARD Alexander Walter George**, Duke of Gloucester, b. August 26, 1944. Married Birgitte Eva Van Deurs (of Denmark) July 8, 1972.

The son of Prince Richard:

28. **ALEXANDER Patrick Gregers Richard Windsor**, Earl of Ulster, b. October 24, 1974. Married Claire Alexandra Booth June 22, 2002.

The son and daughter of that union:

29. **XAN Richard Anders Windsor**, Lord Culloden, b. March 12, 2007.
30. **Lady COSIMA Rose Alexandra Windsor**, b. May 20, 2010.

The eldest daughter of Prince Richard:

31. **Lady DAVINA Elizabeth Alice Benedikte Windsor**, b. November 19, 1977. Married Gary Christie Lewis July 31, 2004. They divorced in 2018.

The daughter and son of that union:

32. **SENNA Kowhai Lewis**, b. June 22, 2010.
33. **TĀNE Mahuta Lewis**, b. May 25, 2012.

The youngest daughter of Prince Richard:

34. **Lady ROSE Victoria Birgitte Louise Gilman** (née Windsor), b. March 1, 1980. Married George Gilman July 19, 2008.

The daughter and son of that union:

35. **LYLA Gilman**, b. 2010.
36. **RUFUS Gilman**, b. 2012.

The first cousin of the queen, the first son of the Prince George, Duke of Kent:

37. His Royal Highness **Prince EDWARD George Nicholas Paul Patrick**, Duke of Kent, b. October 9, 1935. Married Katharine Lucy Mary Worsley, June 8, 1961.

The first son of Prince Edward:

38. **GEORGE Philip Nicholas Windsor**, Earl of St. Andrews, b. June 26, 1962, was excluded from the line of succession upon his marriage to Sylvana Palma Tomaselli, a Roman Catholic, January 9, 1988. He was restored to the line of succession March 26, 2015, with the Succession to the Crown Act 2013.

The son and daughters of that union:

EDWARD Edmund Maximilian George Windsor, Baron Downpatrick, b. December 2, 1988. He became Roman Catholic in 2003, excluding himself from the line of succession.

Lady MARINA Charlotte Alexandra Katharine Helen Windsor, b. September 30, 1992. She became Roman Catholic in 2008, excluding herself from the line of succession.

39. **Lady AMELIA Sophia Theodora Mary Margaret Windsor**, b. August 24, 1995.

The second son of Prince Edward:

Lord NICHOLAS Charles Edward Jonathan Windsor, b. July 25, 1970. He became Roman Catholic in 2001, excluding himself from the line of succession. Married Paola Doimi de Lupis Frankopan Šubić Zrinski November 4, 2006.

The sons of that union:

40. **ALBERT Louis Philip Edward Windsor**, b. September 22, 2007.
41. **LEOPOLD Ernest Augustus Guelph Windsor**, b. September 8, 2009.
42. **LOUIS Arthur Nicholas Felix Windsor**, b. May 27, 2014.

The daughter of the Prince Edward:

43. **Lady HELEN Marina Lucy Taylor** (née Windsor), b. April 28, 1964. Married Timothy Verner Taylor July 18, 1992.

The sons of that union:

44. **COLUMBUS George Donald Taylor**, b. August 6, 1994.
45. **CASSIUS Edward Taylor**, b. December 26, 1996.
46. **ELOISE Olivia Katherine Taylor**, b. March 2, 2003.
47. **ESTELLA Olga Elizabeth Taylor**, b. December 21, 2004.

The first cousin of the queen, the second son of the Prince George, Duke of Kent:

48. His Royal Highness **Prince MICHAEL George Charles Franklin of Kent**, b. July 4, 1942, was excluded from the line of succession upon his marriage to Baroness Marie Christine von Reibnitz, a Roman Catholic, June 30, 1978. He was restored to the line of succession March 26, 2015, with the Succession to the Crown Act 2013.

The son of Prince Michael:

49. **Lord FREDERICK Michael George David Louis Windsor**, b. April 6, 1979. Married Sophie Winkleman September 12, 2009.

The daughters of that union:

50. **MAUD Elizabeth Daphne Marina Windsor**, b. August 15, 2013.
51. **ISABELLA Alexandra May Windsor**, b. January 16, 2016.

The daughter of Prince Michael:

52. **Lady GABRIELLA Marina Alexandra Ophelia Kingston** (née Windsor), b. April 21, 1981. Known as Lady Ella. Married Thomas Henry Robin Kingston May 18, 2019.

The first cousin of the queen, the daughter of the Prince George, Duke of Kent:

53. Her Royal Highness **Princess ALEXANDRA Helen Elizabeth Olga Christabel**, the Honourable Lady Ogilvy, b. December 25, 1936. Married the Honourable Sir Angus James Bruce Ogilvy (second son of the 12th Earl of Airlie) April 24, 1963.

The son of Princess Alexandra:

54. **JAMES Robert Bruce Ogilvy**, b. February 29, 1964. Married Julia Caroline Rawlinson July 30, 1988.

The son and daughter of that union:

55. **ALEXANDER Charles Ogilvy**, b. November 12, 1996.
56. **FLORA Alexandra Ogilvy**, b. December 15, 1994.

The daughter of Princess Alexandra:

57. **MARINA Victoria Alexandra Ogilvy**, b. July 31, 1966. Married Paul Julian Mowatt February 2, 1990. They divorced October 15, 1997.

The son and daughter of that union:

58. **CHRISTIAN Alexander Mowatt**, b. June 4, 1993.
59. **ZENOUSKA May Mowatt**, b. May 26, 1990.

The United Kingdom

Charles, Prince of Wales, and Camilla, Duchess of Cornwall

be informed that her resignation would assist the speedy dispatch of business."

In unusual circumstances or in times of crisis, the monarch could actually exercise considerable influence. If a prime minister dies or resigns and a successor has to be appointed from the same party, or if an election yields no majority, the queen could wield authority, so long as she would not act according to personal preference. For instance, in 1963 Queen Elizabeth named a member of the House of Lords, Sir Alec Douglas Home, as prime minister, an exercise of her theoretical powers about which many Britons were unhappy. Home survived in office for one year when his party was defeated in elections.

The monarch holds other significant "prerogative powers," such as dissolving Parliament or rejecting requests for dissolution. The ultimate guarantee that the monarch will not overstep her bounds is the British people, who are sovereign in reality, if not in theory. Prince Charles, who turned 71 in November 2019 and is the oldest heir to the throne in history, admitted this fact frankly, saying, "something as curious as the monarchy won't survive unless you take account of people's attitudes. I think it can be a kind of elective institution. After all, if people don't want it, they won't have it."

Much more importantly, she symbolizes the unity of the nation and the continuous thread through a millennium of English history. She is thus the focus of national pride. Politics touches not only the mind but also the heart, and she helps to provide her subjects with an emotional

attachment to their country. She is therefore an important cornerstone for the kind of low-keyed but deep-rooted patriotism most Englishmen share. Finally, because of her dual position as head of state and defender of the faith, she helps to link governmental with religious authority in the minds of many Englishmen.

In his brilliant book published in 1867, The English Constitution, Walter Bagehot distinguished between the "dignified" and "efficient" parts of government. The "dignified" parts, especially the glittering monarch and nobility, were useful in securing authority and loyalty for the state from the citizenry, while the "efficient" parts actually used the power and resources of the state to rule. In his book The Body Politic, Sir Ian Gilmour argued that "legitimacy, the acceptance by the governed of the political system, is far better aided by an ancient monarchy set above the political battle than by a transient president, who has gained his position through that battle. . . . Modern societies still need myth and ritual. A monarch and his family supply it; there is no magic about a mud-stained politician."

Bagehot had written, "we must not let daylight in upon magic." But in an age of nondeferential journalists and citizens in Britain, royal indiscretions have completely exposed that "magic." In the wake of lurid reports in the tabloid press about marital breakdowns and infidelity within the royal family, which over the years have included Elizabeth and especially Philip themselves, the succession to the throne and the very future of the monarchy in Britain are being

questioned. The concept of a family monarchy, a Victorian-era notion that granted a symbolic and public role to royal offspring and consorts, as well as to the king or queen, has been severely shaken.

Three of Queen Elizabeth II's four children were unable to sustain a stable first marriage. The year 1992 saw the formal separation of Prince Charles from Diana, a superstar princess who overshadowed the estranged crown prince until her tragic death in Paris in 1997. In 1999 he began appearing in public with his longtime love, Camilla Parker Bowles. On April 9, 2005, he became the first heir to the throne to marry a divorcée. They were betrothed in a civil ceremony that the queen and her husband, Prince Philip, refused to attend. However, his parents were present at the church service that followed.

Polls indicated that most Britons either approved of or were indifferent to the wedding. However, a sizable majority did not want to see Camilla become queen. To assuage that sentiment, Charles emphasized that Camilla wants only to be called "princess consort" and will have the lower title of "Duchess of Cornwall," not "Princess of Wales," as Diana was called. Nevertheless, the Department for Constitutional Affairs confirmed that the marriage would not be "morganatic," meaning one in which the spouse of inferior status has no claim to the status of the other. Unless Parliament passes a law barring Camilla from becoming queen, she will assume that title the moment Charles becomes king. She has come a long way from the time the tabloids cast her as Britain's most hated woman. Thanks to her discretion and to her embracing Charles' two sons, polls reveal a sharply reduced level of animosity toward her.

Prince Andrew is divorced from Sarah Ferguson, whose nonregal antics embarrassed the royal family more than once. In 2010 she was videotaped by the tabloid

Prince William

32

The News of the World, which folded in July 2011, promising to introduce a fake "rich businessman" to her former husband for a price of about $717,000. She took $40,000 in cash on the spot. Until 2011 Prince Andrew served successive governments as an envoy to promote British exports. His royal status enabled him to entertain customers by sponsoring splendid business lunches and receptions at Buckingham Palace. His friendship with an American pedophile cost him his standing in the royal family.

In 1992 Princess Anne, who divorced her first husband, Mark Phillips, became the first top-ranking British royal since King Henry VIII to divorce and remarry. She wed a divorced naval commander, Timothy Laurence. The ceremony had to be held in Scotland because the Church of England does not condone second marriages. In 2002 she suffered the indignity of becoming the first member of the royal family to be convicted of a criminal offense since Charles I was beheaded for treason in 1649.

Edward announced his engagement to Sophie Rhys-Jones in 1999. They married and had their first child in 2003.

Personal revelations about the royals are dangerously corrosive because an unelected institution in a democracy depends on the popular will for its legitimacy. Despite the bad publicity, a MORI poll in 1996 confirmed that the royals still enjoy considerable trust: When voters were offered a choice among 13 candidates for an elected president, the clear favorite was Princess Anne. A 1997 poll taken September 7, the day after Diana's moving funeral and an outpouring of grief that saw 60 million bouquets placed around the royal palaces, revealed that the mood toward the monarchy had changed: 73% of respondents (82% if Diana's eldest son, William, were to be the next monarch) favored its retention (down from 85%–90% a decade earlier); fewer than half thought it would survive the next 50 years; and 39% thought less of the royal family. In 2012, 80% favored continuing the monarchy; only 13% preferred a republic. This was the strongest support for the monarchy in two decades.

A hostile mood was shown in the reaction to a fire that caused $90 million worth of damage to Windsor Castle in 1992. The royal family had invented its name Windsor after this favorite castle in 1917 in order to shed its German name (Saxe-Coburg-Gotha) during the war against Germany. Popular outrage greeted the government's decision to pay the costs of the repair, which were completed beautifully in 1998.

The flames reignited the debate over whether the monarch should pay taxes and whether the state should provide annual incomes to the members and staffs of a very wealthy royal family. To quiet the fury, Queen Elizabeth announced that she would pay income taxes amounting to about $4 million annually and about $1.9 million to most members of her family out of her own fortune, estimated by Forbes in 2010 to be worth £300 million ($500 million). She noted in 1997 that the cost of operating the monarchy had fallen by 39% since the beginning of the decade and that the royal yacht Britannia, had been decommissioned for financial reasons. It is understandable that, on the 40th anniversary of her coronation she publicly described 1992 as an annus horribilis.

In 2010 the Conservative government announced as a part of its austerity program a change in the financing of the Crown. Her income would fall 14% until the new system began in 2013. It would end the arrangement struck with George III in 1760 transferring income from the Crown lands to the government in return for the "Civil List," an annual payment voted for and scrutinized by Parliament. Instead the monarch will take an annual share of revenues from the Crown Estate, a sprawling £6.6 billion ($11 billion) property and land empire, whose assets range from Regent Street to 265,000 acres of agricultural land and to the British seabed extending to the 12-nautical-mile limit. This income is estimated to amount to £30 million ($48 million) per year from 2013 on. This freed the Crown from having to go to Parliament every time it needs more funding.

Prince Charles receives his own independent income from the Duchy of Cornwall, and that has been profitable. The family remains exempt from inheritance tax and from the more than £50 million ($80 million) price tag for police protection. The need for this was seen in December 2010, when an anarchic mob of young people purporting to be protesting a rise in university tuition fees attacked the car carrying Prince Charles and Camilla, broke windows, and appeared to threaten the frightened royal couple.

Princess Diana's death in 1997 was one of the few times the queen was ever personally criticized by the media; she felt obliged to share her grief publicly and to lower the flag at Buckingham Palace to half-mast. She made a rare gesture of humility by bowing her head when the princess's casket passed Buckingham Palace on the way to the funeral. Her predicament and the role played by the newly elected prime minister Tony Blair in helping point Elizabeth in the right direction were portrayed with insight and sympathy in the British film *The Queen*. Helen Mirren, herself an opponent of the monarchy until she immersed herself in the role of Elizabeth II, won an Oscar as best actress.

After Diana died the royals made a real effort to be more accessible and open. They hired pollsters to help them come closer to the people and to read the public's message. Elizabeth II admitted, "Read it we must." It appears to be working. In 1996 only 41% of Britons thought that Charles would make a good king; by 1998 that had risen to more than 60%.

House of Commons, view of the chamber showing the speaker's chair and seating for clerk of the House and assistants.

The United Kingdom

The year 2002 was the jubilee to celebrate Queen Elizabeth II's half-century on the throne. But it was also a year of death. On February 10 Princess Margaret died, and she was followed on March 30 by the most popular royal, the 101-year-old Queen Mother. The splendor of her burial showed that the British public still likes monarchical dignity and theater. But the funeral could not stifle the noisy national debate about the role of an inherited monarchy in a nation that champions democracy and meritocracy. One caller to the BBC said, "The Queen Mum had 40 people waiting on her, and we taxpayers had to cough up 600,000 quid [over $1 million] to support it. What did she do to deserve it, except marry the right bloke 80 years ago?"

On April 21, 2006, Elizabeth II celebrated her 80th birthday as a remarkably popular monarch after 54 years on the throne. By the end of 2007, she had become both the first reigning British monarch to celebrate a diamond (60 years) wedding anniversary and the oldest-ever monarch at 243 days after her 81st birthday. Her husband, Philip, who turned 90 in June 2011 and who is known for uttering rude, off-the-cuff remarks for which he never apologizes, is the longest-serving consort in British history. In 2019, at age 97, he was driving without his seatbelt fastened and crashed into another car, slightly injuring its passengers. He voluntarily surrendered his driver's license.

At age 86 in June 2012, Elizabeth celebrated a rare event: a Diamond Jubilee marking 60 years on the throne. Not since 1897 had such a celebration taken place. In September 2015 Elizabeth surpassed Queen Victoria's length of reign (63 years). She now elicits almost no criticism from politicians or press. Polls show there are only 15 million republicans in a kingdom of about 68.2 million. There is a steady rise in Britons who think the monarchy will exist 10 years into the future, even though only 10% of those between the ages of 16 and 24 think the monarchy is important to their lives.

On April 29, 2011, more than a third of the Earth's population watched the televised wedding of Prince William, the second in the line of succession, with commoner Catherine (Kate) Middleton. They met at St. Andrews University eight years earlier. She became the first royal bride with a university degree, and William would be the first monarch with a university diploma. They were also the first royals to live together before marriage. He was a Royal Air Force search-and-rescue helicopter pilot in northern Wales. He deployed to the Falkland Islands in 2012, his first overseas military tour. He was involved in the rescue of 149 people. After seven years of service, he retired from the military in 2013 to focus on his charitable and conservation work. Her

The funeral cortege of Diana, Princess of Wales, proceeds through Hyde Park toward Westminster Abbey.

Photo: Edward Jones

parents are self-made wealthy people who provided their three children with a stable family environment and an excellent modern education.

The Windsors desperately needed a marriage that works in order to have the stability and glamor necessary to save the monarchy in the long run. Kate is very attractive, and she is liked by the press and the public. Her middle-class origins and her maturity (age 28 at her marriage) are pluses.

In expectation of the royal couple's first child on July 22, 2013 (a boy, George Alexander Louis, Prince George of Cambridge), followed on May 2, 2015, by a sister, Princess Charlotte Elizabeth Diana, the government moved to change the law of succession in Britain and in all 16 of the queen's realms, such as Canada, New Zealand, and Australia. In a historic agreement at the Commonwealth heads-of-government meeting on October 28, 2011, it was agreed without dissent that the prince's children would succeed in order of seniority, regardless of sex. They also agreed to scrap an ancient law, rooted in earlier religious wars, forbidding the monarch's spouse from being a Roman Catholic. However, the monarch himself or herself still cannot be Catholic. All 16 sovereign governments had to pass the necessary legislation and then backdate it to the October 2011 agreement.

The popular couple quickly became disaffected with the press and the royal duties. They renounced their royal perks and left for an uncertain future in the United States. They ceased using their "royal highness" titles as well as Harry's military titles. They remain Duke and Duchess of Sussex, and Harry remains a prince, sixth in the line of succession.

In 2018 Prince Harry married American actress Meghan Markle, a divorced biracial American. Their marriage reflects the extent to which British society has changed. The popular couple quickly became disaffected with the press and their royal duties. They announced their royal ties and left for an uncertain future in the United States. They ceased using their "royal highness" titles, and Harry stopped using his military titles. They remain the Duke and Duchess of Sussex, however, and Harry remains a prince, sixth in the line of succession.

Parliamentary Government

The seat of power was once the House of Commons, which elected and controlled the prime minister and the cabinet. It debated the great issues of the day and shaped the laws of the land. It was supreme, and no political institution in the entire kingdom can block its will. A century later this was no longer true. The rise of powerful catchall parties firmly controlled by party leaders had largely converted the majority in the House of Commons into the tail wagged by the dog in Number 10 Downing Street, the residence of the prime minister. Observers gradually stopped speaking about parliamentary government and began talking first of cabinet government, then prime ministerial government.

The prime minister is not all-powerful. He must face a powerful civil service (collectively called Whitehall), sometimes count his votes carefully in the Commons, and deal with a multitude of quasi-governmental and interest groups. In theory, the British political process is simple; in practice, it is surprisingly haphazard. British governments do at least as much "muddling through" as they command.

The need to persuade, coax, beg, threaten, or compromise with so many groups and institutions, all with independent standing of some sort, changes the traditional picture of British government, which is centered on the prime minister and cabinet, who can do anything they want. In truth, British government has never been exactly as it appears to be on the surface. While clothed in basically the same institutional garb, the reality of British politics is always changing.

The House of Commons

Since 2010 the House of Commons has 650 members of Parliament (MPs, 646 in 2005 and 639 in 2007) elected at either general elections, which must be held at least every five years, or at by-elections, held when a seat falls vacant because of the death or resignation of a member. From the Great Reform Bill of 1832 until the electoral reform of 1970, the suffrage was gradually expanded until all men and women 18 years and older can vote. Also, all citizens of the Republic of Ireland who reside in the United Kingdom are allowed to vote. Compared with American elections, British campaigns are very short.

Usually only about four weeks elapse between the time the prime minister sets the date for new elections and the polling day. Many voters complained that the six-week campaign in 1997, the longest in 70 years, was much too long. The threat of sending MPs out on the hustings with very little notice is a powerful tool of persuasion in the hands of the prime minister. The MP does have certain advantages over the US congressman at election time: The parties pay the bulk of the campaign expenses. Also, since the MP's constituency has only one-seventh as many inhabitants as an American congressional district, he or she is able to canvass the voters at their doorstep and get the full blast of public opinion face to face.

MPs are elected by a system that is very simple and controversial: the single-member simple plurality. The candidate with the most votes in each of the 650 constituencies is elected, even if he or she won fewer than 50% of the votes. This electoral system has the advantage of preventing many parties from gaining seats in Parliament. By bolstering the two-party system, proponents say it enhances political stability. Since one or the other of the large parties usually has a majority in the House of Commons, there had never been the need for a formal coalition to rule. That changed in May 2010, when no party won a majority.

Opponents say that it is undemocratic and unfair because it favors the larger parties by enabling them to win a far higher proportion of parliamentary seats than the percentage of votes they won nationally.

For example, in the May 2015 elections, the Conservative Party climbed to 36.9% of the votes, among the lowest shares for a winner since the Reform Act of 1832. But it captured 331 seats or 51% of the total. The Labour Party won 30.4% of the total vote. Nevertheless, it received 232 seats, or 36% of the total.

The SNP won only 4.7% of the national vote, but got 56 seats, 8.6% of the total. In stark contrast, the Liberal Democrats, with 7.9% of the total vote, captured only 8 seats or a mere 1.2% of the total. No wonder they demanded a reform of the electoral system as the price for its entry into the governing coalition with the Conservatives. They have long been in favor of a proportional representation (PR) system, which would award seats in proportion to the total votes won. In two postwar elections (1951 and February 1974), the party with the largest number of votes only received the second-largest number of seats. In three others (1950, 1964 and October 1974), the winner's shaky parliamentary majority was in the single figures.

The questions are: Does the current system really produce more decisive majorities? Exactly how could elections be made fairer? Would the two large parties go along? It is increasingly common for MPs to be elected with the support of fewer than half the voters; in the House of Commons elected in 1997, 312 of 659 were in this situation. A Liberal Democrat, Sir Russell Johnston, won his Inverness constituency in 1992 with only 26% of the votes.

Virtually every other European democracy has some form of PR. But the British political system has needed an electoral method that offers voters a clear choice between the governing party or coalition, whose performance can be judged, and an opposition party, whose promises can be weighed and considered. This facilitates a change of government within an hour and a half after the votes have been counted, including visits to the queen. There is no 10-week transition period like a newly elected American president has before taking office. In some European democracies, it can take months to hammer together a coalition government. In May 2010 the Conservatives and Liberal Democrats did it in five high-drama days. In the past, the clear distinction between the two sides discouraged third parties from developing. It prevented the formation of coalition governments since 1940–1945, when Winston Churchill led a wartime coalition government of all three major parties.

In 1998 then–prime minister Blair appointed a commission under Lord Jenkins to examine the electoral system but with two stipulations: that the need for "stable government" should be kept in mind and that the link between MPs and their constituencies should be preserved. The conclusion was that a "lack of democracy" would have to be accepted at the national level in the interest of retaining a stable, one-party government, while proportional representation could be practiced at the regional and local level. That is exactly what is done in regional elections in Scotland, Wales, and Northern Ireland, as well as in elections to the European Parliament.

Desperately needing the Liberal Democrats as coalition partners, Prime Minister David Cameron agreed to a referendum May 5, 2011, on a new way of voting that is not proportional representation; it is called the alternative-vote (AV) system. This would change the "first-past-the-post" method. (Whoever gets the most

Queen Elizabeth II and six former prime ministers celebrate the 250th anniversary of 10 Downing Street as the official residence of the prime minister.

The United Kingdom

votes wins the seat, whether he wins a majority or not.) AV would allow voters to rank candidates on the ballot in order of preference instead of merely marking the one preferred candidate. If no candidate in the constituency receives 50% of the first-preference votes, then the second choices of those who voted for the last-placing candidate are redistributed until one candidate gets an absolute majority (50%). If this system had been used in the May 2010 elections, the Lib Dems would have won 22 more seats, all from the Conservative Party. It was defeated by 68% to 32%. Voters liked the old system because it is simple, and it usually produces a governing majority. They agree with Benjamin Disraeli, who once said, "England does not love coalitions."

The very organization and physical structure of the House of Commons depends upon a government and an opposition, without a wide spectrum of opinion. The House of Commons is arranged in rows of benches facing each other rather than in seats facing the podium. This arrangement encourages debate and questions because members of the opposing parties sit facing each other across an aisle. By ancient custom, and for good reason, the aisle is two sword-lengths wide so an MP may not reach across it with a sword and skewer his opponent during debate. The government sits on the front row to the right of the speaker's throne, and the leaders of the opposition (known also as the "shadow cabinet") sit on the first row to the speaker's left. MPs on the lower end of the pecking order in their respective parties sit higher up on the back rows and are therefore called "backbenchers."

The speaker from 2000 to 2009 was Michael Martin, a former sheet-metal worker; the speaker directs the debate. By tradition the speakership alternates between the two main parties, and the new speaker resigns from his party. But like his predecessor, Betty Boothroyd, Martin was a Labour MP. A former shop steward and son of a stoker, he grew up in poverty in Glasgow. He observed the tradition of feigning reluctance to assume the post and having to be tugged to the speaker's chair, a throwback to the days when speakers were occasionally beheaded because of their uncomfortable position between the Commons and the monarch. When he strides into the chamber, his aides call for the long-standing ritual of respect: "Hats off, strangers!" The speaker has little control of the Commons' business. The Leader of the House, who belongs to the cabinet, organizes this.

A skillful speaker can protect the prerogatives of the House against the government and the people, but Martin was not able to do this. In 2009 The Daily Telegraph published the names of more than 200 MPs who had padded their expense accounts at a time when the nation was being battered by economic recession. Citizens were furious, and he became the first speaker since 1695 to be ejected from office. He was replaced in June 2009 by Conservative MP John Bercow, who was reelected after the 2010 general election. His influence expanded in Parliament, passionately divided on the question of leaving the EU.

Unlike in the United States, the opposition party in Britain has an alternative cabinet that is preselected and ready to assume office at a moment's notice. Indeed, a major strength of British parliamentary democracy is that talented leaders in a government which loses an election still retain their front-row seats in Parliament and are therefore kept in reserve until a later date when the electorate's moods change and their services are again desired. This shadow government leads what is known in Britain as "Her Majesty's loyal opposition," a concept grounded in the notion that two persons of goodwill can disagree agreeably on an important issue. In contrast to the US, though, the "loyal opposition" has no means of delaying governmental action through filibuster in Parliament.

In theory, Parliament checks and controls the executive (the prime minister and the cabinet). In practice, it is normally the other way around. Parliament lacks the facilities to watch over the government competently, and MPs are underpaid, understaffed, and underinformed. Despite some recent pay increases, MPs still earn far less than their American counterparts. In 2014 their base salary was £66,396 ($106,234), plus more than $72,000 for secretarial and research assistance. MPs do receive expenses for travel, phoning, postage, and housing allowances (if they must maintain two homes). After the 2001 elections, the salary for a cabinet minister was raised to the equivalent of about $155,000 and that of the prime minister in 2010 to £197,000, or the equivalent of $315,000.

Two-thirds continue working at their normal jobs. For centuries until 2002 the hours of the parliamentary sessions had been set from 2:30 p.m. to 10:30 p.m. in order to accommodate that need. Now parliamentary business starts at 11:30 and must normally be concluded no later than 7:30 p.m. in order for MPs to have a more "family-friendly" schedule. Exceptions are sometimes approved. One-third even work for private lobbying firms and other businesses with interest in legislation, something forbidden for US congressmen. They have inadequate office space and receive only a modest sum for secretarial and research assistance, while the average American congressman has 16 aides, and the average senator, 36. With such minuscule staffs, ordinary MPs have great difficulty acquiring sufficient information to challenge the government, which has the entire civil service to provide it with facts.

Unlike the US Congress, the House of Commons does not have a well-developed committee system to do the detailed work which cannot be done on the floor of the House. The ad hoc "standing committees" have too little expertise and are too large to be truly effective. The smaller "select committees" have a relatively permanent membership, are often chaired by an opposition MP, and do play a more important role. In 1980, new committees were set up to oversee the work of specific ministries and to deal specifically with Scottish and Welsh affairs. There is considerable discussion of reforms to improve the committee structure in the House, but in the absence of successful reforms, it is likely to remain more a forum to debate the important issues of the day than a powerful lawmaking body. In 1988 the Commons voted to allow television to record its often-rowdy deliberations.

It remains the government's job to determine what will be the law of the land. All important legislation, including the budget, is drafted by the government and Whitehall. Since the government determines the order of parliamentary business, its proposals always take priority over those of private members or the opposition. Parliament can make amendments and must give its approval, but the government has numerous ways to ensure that its policies will be accepted. First, all MPs are almost always party members (after 2001 there were three independents, one of whom had been elected as such), and they can jeopardize their careers if they defy their party leaders. Renegades are seldom reelected. Second, as many as 110 MPs are actually members of the government, and all are expected to vote with the government.

Finally, since the very survival of the government depends upon maintaining a majority, MPs are under far greater pressure from the cabinet to support the government than is the case in the US. Rigid party discipline on most bills has always been essential in order to make the political system work. MPs are permitted to "vote their conscience" on moral issues, such as abortion and gun control (Britain has a near total ban on handguns.). In 2005–2006 it applied to votes to outlaw smoking in public places by 2007, to permit pubs to remain open after 11 p.m., and in 2013 to allow same-sex partnerships in England and Wales. The latter grants the same property and inheritance rights as married heterosexual couples and gives partners the same pension, immigration, and tax benefits.

Among the first takers was pop singer Sir Elton John, who formalized his relationship with David Furnish.

Control by the government is much less effective than it once was. From 1945 to 1970, no government lost a vote of the full House of Commons. The 1970s brought a significant change. The Conservative government of Edward Heath suffered defeat in Parliament six times. Before 1970 it would have been unthinkable for a government so defeated to remain in office, but he returned to the 19th-century practice of resigning only upon losing a declared vote of no confidence. The Labour government that ruled from 1974 until 1979 suffered 23 such defeats, and Thatcher was defeated twice. MPs can now often vote against the government without bringing it down. This encourages backbenchers to revolt without severely endangering their careers. The days are over when the backbenchers automatically vote as their leaders order.

The Blair government changed the raucous "prime minister's question time" in the House of Commons by converting it into a more serious, once-a-week, half-hour session every Wednesday in which more questions from opposition backbenchers are allowed. The leadership confrontations with the opposition leader remain the most entertaining and sometimes most embarrassing interchanges for the prime minister. In order to be able to prepare better for these weekly duels, Blair switched the day for his weekly half-hour audience with the queen in 2004 from Tuesdays to Wednesdays after question hour. It was switched back to Tuesdays.

Such audiences date back to 1739 and are a valuable opportunity for the head of government to tap the vast reservoir of knowledge Queen Elizabeth has accumulated in her more than half-century on the throne. David Cameron is her 12th prime minister since Churchill, and Barack Obama is the 11th president with whom she has dealt. By tradition, the opinions expressed at such audiences are strictly confidential. Even the prime minister's closest aides are kept in the dark. Harold Wilson (1964–1970) regarded the queen as the only person with whom he could confide without thinking a knife was being sharpened behind his back. John Major (1990–1997) said no notes were taken, and the sanctity of the event was preserved by the "total block" on the discussions. He remembered that he could talk to the monarch in a way he did to no one else. Tony Blair (1997–2007) initially viewed the meetings as "ancient etiquette." But he soon found them to be a great opportunity to talk to a very wise person in the knowledge that it would go no further. Only Margaret Thatcher

(1979–1990) is reported to have had an uncomfortable relationship with Elizabeth.

The House of Lords

Great Britain is a monarchy, and it should therefore not be surprising that its aristocracy continues to enjoy certain political privileges. These are institutionalized in the upper house of Parliament, the House of Lords. Before 1999, of the 1,164 members (known as the "peers"), 650 had hereditary titles. This meant that all the offspring of these peers who inherited the titles would automatically be entitled to a seat in the House of Lords. These titles, in order of precedence, are duke, marquess, earl, viscount, and baron, all except Dukes being commonly addressed as "lord." Some peerages have ancient origins, such as the Marquis of Salisbury or the Duke of Norfolk, but half the hereditary peerages were created in the 20th century "for services to the nation." No new hereditary peerages were created after 1964 until Prime Minister Thatcher ennobled senior minister William Whitelaw and retiring speaker of the Commons George Thomas.

A law of 1958 creating "life peers" set an irreversible trend. Such peers are appointed for their learning or their distinguished public service. However, after they die, their heirs cannot claim their seats. Among the life peers named in 1997 was composer (now baron) Andrew Lloyd Webber. Sir Paul McCartney (now a knight) and Dynasty star Joan Collins (now an officer of the Order of the British Empire) were not awarded peerages.

By 2014 there were only 781 active peers remaining in the reformed House of Lords, although that number can go up if the prime minister so decides. There are 92 are hereditary peers, whose tenure remains uncertain. Their heirs can assume their titles, but they no longer have the right to sit in Parliament. There are 23 Church of England lord bishops and archbishops. The rest are life peers, half of whom entered the House of Lords since Labour came to power in 1997; Tony Blair appointed 374, and David Cameron packed the chamber. Approximately 67 are peeresses, such as the late Margaret Thatcher. By 2006 the largest party was Labour (206 seats), followed by Tories (205) and Liberal Democrats (74). In 2012, 30.3% of the seats were Labour, 27.7% Tory, 8.8% Liberal Democrat, 23.6% crossbench (independent), and 6.9% other. In this new House of Lords, most peers attend regularly and are less inclined than earlier to do what the governments tells them. A 2006 poll revealed that 68% of respondents think it is all right for the lords to vote against government bills.

As the democratic wave caused a steady expansion of the franchise in the 19th and 20th centuries, the powers of the House of Lords came under increasing attack. In the Parliament Acts of 1911 and 1949, its veto right was taken away; now the only kind of bill it can veto is one to prolong the life of Parliament beyond five years. Also, its power to delay legislation was reduced; it can now hold up bills for 13 months at the most (only 30 days for a financial bill). Until the Thatcher era, it seldom exercised its power out of fear that, if it fully used its powers, it would ultimately lose them.

The Labour Party has long sought "to abolish the undemocratic House of Lords as quickly as possible." One of Labour's most influential leftists even renounced his title of Viscount Stansgate, giving up his right to sit in the House of Lords. He also shortened his name from Anthony Neil Wedgewood Benn III to the more proletarian Tony Benn. He married an American. His 2014 obituary called him a "dazzling orator" and "scion of a political family." His son, Hilary Benn, shared his father's aristocratic appearance and mannerisms. A state secretary for international development in Tony Blair's government and later shadow foreign minister, he emphasized that he is "a Benn, not a Bennite."

In normal times, opposition to the prime minister's policies is exercised in the House of Commons. But Thatcher so dominated that body until 1990 that another institution performed that function: the House of Lords. One Labour lord said in 1988, "It hurts to admit it, but on many issues we are the government's only real opposition." A Liberal baroness added, "As an unelected body, it would obviously be quite improper for us to try to kill a bill outright. But there is nothing to stop us from being an utter nuisance to the government. We call it playing Ping-Pong—holding up a bill for so long that the government is compelled to accept our amendments just to get the thing passed." In fact, by 1988 Thatcher had suffered 107 defeats in the House of Lords, compared with only 2 in the House of Commons. Between 1999 and 2007, the lords defeated more than 350 government bills.

Why is such a privileged house, to which no one is elected, retained in a democratic country? In fact, debates in the House of Lords are at least as well informed and much less partisan than in the lower house. In order to demonstrate this fact, debates in the upper house began to be televised in 1985. The lords' main job is to examine and to revise bills that have proceeded too hastily through the House of Commons. With such experienced peers, the most active of whom had already distinguished themselves in all walks of life outside Parliament, the lords perform an important function in improving legislation by applying their expertise.

The United Kingdom

Also, the fact that the most active lords are persons of great prestige and influence in British society means that no government systematically ignores the House of Lords.

Supported two to one in a 1997 MORI poll, Tony Blair's Labour government moved swiftly to enact its campaign promise to remove "the absurdity of the hereditary element." He appointed a royal commission that produced a white paper in 1999. It recommended that the hereditary peers' right to sit and vote be removed, that the nomination of life peers be accomplished through an independent appointments committee (not the prime minister), that some be indirectly elected by such bodies as the new regional assemblies, and that longer-term reform be considered.

To move this reform through the legislative process, Blair agreed to a temporary compromise with the Tory leader in the House of Lords: 92 hereditary peers were permitted to stay until a final second-stage reform of the house could be undertaken; over 600 life peers retained their seats. Two Labour peers were suspended in 2009 for offering to amend laws in exchange for cash payments. This was the first time any member had been removed from the House of Lords since 1642. In 2011 a lord was found guilty of falsely claiming more than £11,000 ($18,000) in travel expenses. He became the first member of the upper house to be convicted in a jury trial. Peers receive no salary, but they get £300 ($465) a day tax free for attending. They get a desk in Parliament and lifetime access to its parking lot, restaurants and bars.

After facing further opposition, in the upper house, the Blair government proposed additional constitutional reforms. It abolished the ancient and powerful position of lord chancellor, who was speaker of the lords, a cabinet minister, head of the country's judiciary, and titular member of the highest court, the now-abolished Law Lords. The position was broken into three posts. Since 2005 a speaker of the House of Lords presides over the upper house. In 2006 a Labour Party baroness, Helene Hayman, became the first elected lord speaker. The lord chancellor's other roles were assumed by a Department for Constitutional Affairs. In October 2009 the reform replaced the 12 Law Lords with a Supreme Court, which is the highest court in England and Wales.

The House of Lords had been doing a good job scrutinizing laws, producing quality reports, and challenging Commons; that is why the pressure to reshape the lords comes from politicians, not the voters. In 2007 a majority in the House of Commons voted in favor of an all-elected House of Lords. This was a nonbinding vote, but it will influence the government's future choices.

View of London across the Thames, with "Big Ben" (right)

It is unclear what will ultimately happen to the lords; its reform is a work in progress. The Tory-Liberal Democrat government that took power in May 2010 vowed to produce a wholly or partly elected House of Lords. It unveiled a set of proposals in May 2011 calling for the abolition of the present House of Lords. After a transition period, the 781 current members would be replaced by a semi-elected house that could be called a senate with as few as 300 members. Eighty percent of the members would be elected for a single 15-year term by a form of proportional representation to help smaller parties get seats. The remaining 20% would be appointed. The 92 hereditary peers would be removed, as would be half or more of the 23 Anglican lord bishops and archbishops who now have seats. It is too early to tell if these recommendations will be enacted, watered down, or dropped. Although the House of Commons approved the bill, many Tory MPs block progress because they fear that an elected upper house would challenge the primacy of the lower house.

Prime Ministerial Government

The nerve center of British politics is "the government," a collective term to describe the prime minister; the 16 to 23 cabinet ministers; and the parliamentary secretaries or junior ministers, a team which may total from 70 to 110 members.

In theory, the prime minister is the "first among equals" within the governing team. But as a senior Whitehall official noted at the end of the 20th century, "The idea that the prime minister is primus inter pares is wrong. The prime minister is not pares. He's way above that. Like Caesar he bestrides the world like a colossus."

The prime minister is the leader of the party that has a majority (or at least a plurality) in the House of Commons. Thus, the holder of this highest office is an MP who has worked his or her way upward through the legislative system. In earlier times, the average prime minister had served a quarter-century in the House of Commons and had occupied several cabinet posts. That is no longer the case. The prime ministry was Tony Blair's and David Cameron's first post, and the latter had been in Parliament only eight years before become prime minister. Nevertheless, it is unlikely that a stranger to the national capital, such as Jimmy Carter, Ronald Reagan, Bill Clinton, or George W. Bush, could become prime minister. The powers of the post are so great that the description "first among equals" is misleading.

The prime minister's powers, which are almost nowhere clearly spelled out in statute, strike the American as sweeping. As the nation's chief executive, chief legislator, and chief administrator, he is the primary focus of political attention. After the election, he is rather free to appoint and dismiss cabinet members, thereby largely determining the broad political direction the government will take. The convention of "collective responsibility" prevents his ministers from criticizing him in public, and the tradition of secrecy shields many of his decisions and actions from the public eye.

He decides on the agenda for cabinet meetings and appoints the cabinet committees, which prepare government policies or deal with crises and carry out most ministerial business. For example, in 1982 Thatcher formed a "war cabinet" to manage the Falklands crisis; she also had influential committees for economic, foreign and defense, domestic, and legislative policy. Such grand committees have subcommittees. There are no votes taken in cabinet meetings, and the prime minister interprets the sense of the cabinet. Cabinet minutes are sparse in detail and taken in long hand to keep them that way.

Given the tradition of cabinet secrecy, the Brown government was shocked in February 2008, when Britain's information commissioner, citing the "gravity and controversial nature" of the decision to go to war in Iraq in 2003, ordered the government to release the minutes of two cabinet meetings discussing the legality of the invasion. The government appealed the order, arguing that it set a "dangerous precedent" for releasing cabinet papers, which cannot normally be published for 30 years.

Regardless of how the debate in the secret cabinet meetings might have gone, he can always announce the meaning in a way which conforms to his own views. As ex-Labour cabinet member Richard Crossman revealed, any prime minister who is subordinate to the cabinet is "consciously refusing to make use of the powers which now constitutionally belong to the office." In practice, most issues are decided either in Whitehall or in cabinet committees and are not even discussed in full cabinet meetings, which are normally held twice a week, including each Thursday morning. The modern cabinet is increasingly a reporting and reviewing body and less and less an executive one. Crossman was correct. Collective decision making has been replaced by a system in which ministers have been reduced to agents of their leader, forced to deal with him bilaterally rather than as part of a collectively responsible group. The prime minister directs the nation's sizable civil service.

He determines the country's foreign and defense policies and at one time could commit Britain to a policy that the cabinet and Commons could do little to alter. Prime Minister Cameron suffered a spectacular defeat in August 2013, when a narrow parliamentary majority rejected his bid to use military force in Syria. The opponents included 30 members of his own Tory Party and 9 Liberal Democrats in his coalition. This was the first time since 1782 that a prime minister had been defeated in Parliament on a matter of war and peace. The vote reflected public opinion: Only 22% of the population favored such use of force.

He can enter treaties with foreign nations that need not be approved by Parliament; foreign policy was a "royal prerogative" which was never passed to Parliament, although a prime minister does customarily discuss with it treaties and declarations of war. The 2003 war in Iraq demonstrated that even a strong and activist prime minister like Tony Blair must be very attentive to both British law and popular and parliamentary sentiment when using the prime minister's war powers.

Finally, as leader and chief strategist for the national party, he alone can decide the date of the general election and thus determine when the entire government and Commons must face the voters. That power was clipped by the Fixed-Term Parliaments Act, which requires two-thirds disapproval by MPs to dissolve Parliament immediately. He is burdened neither by separation of powers nor by a federal structure. No American president wields such power.

Limitations on the Prime Minister

A closer look at the contemporary British political system reveals that the prime minister's power is more restricted that initially meets the eye. Although he appoints and dismisses the cabinet members, he can hardly lord over them. Unlike most American cabinet members, the British ones are often experienced and influential members of Parliament with whom the prime minister has worked for some years. He cannot scout the country for talented individuals whose main responsibility is to carry out the chief executive's policy; he can only choose from his colleagues in Parliament who have political bases of their own in the party and in the nation. He thus does not normally deal with minions but with somewhat-powerful political office holders who would be less afraid to stand up to him in private.

He must retain the confidence of the most important factions within the parliamentary majority party. He must inevitably take into the cabinet some persons who disagree with him on some fundamental issues. This has tended to weaken the convention of cabinet solidarity. Thatcher had to cope with scarcely concealed criticism from those within her own cabinet, whom she dubbed "wets."

John Major lost the 1997 elections in part because he never succeeded in silencing Tory colleagues who opposed his policy toward Europe. Finally, since 1999 the prime minister must deal with regionally elected parliaments in Scotland, Wales, Northern Ireland, and since 2000 a Greater London Assembly.

It is often argued that the prime minister enjoys the advantage of not having to direct huge ministries, as cabinet members do. Therefore, he is freer to deal with larger political questions. To some extent, this is true, but the other side of the coin is that he lacks manageable administrative backing. He has no department to provide him with independent analyses and advice. His "private office" at his residence, Number 10 Downing Street, is too small. More valuable to him is the "cabinet office," headed by a top civil servant, which organizes the agenda for cabinet discussions. Thatcher established a "policy unit" at Number 10 composed of some expert advisers. Yet these specialists were no match for the massed expertise available to departmental ministers. Thus, the quality of the prime minister's information is not generally better than that of his cabinet members.

He must deal with a complicated network of ministries and departments with diverse views and a good deal of autonomy in their own areas of responsibility. By American standards, there is virtually no "spoils system" in British politics. The prime minister is able to send to each ministry only one minister and one to three parliamentary secretaries. But when they arrive, often with little or no detailed experience in the particular areas of responsibilities and with no staffs of their own, they are faced with a permanent secretary, the senior civil servant of his department with several decades of experience. He and his subordinate civil servants have the facts at their fingertips and brief the minister.

Author's daughters feeding the pigeons, Trafalgar Square, London

The United Kingdom

Although it is his job merely to give technical advice and let the minister set the political direction, it is but a short step from persuasively "giving the facts" to actually determining departmental policy. Usually continuity, not change, wins out. New policies must be negotiated with these bodies, not simply imposed upon them. Nevertheless, if the minister comes to clear, firm decisions, then his officials will almost always carry them out.

Bureaucracy and the Civil Service

As in all advanced countries, much of the work which used to be done by leading politicians has now been delegated to the civil service, which numbers about 640,000 bureaucrats. Most do not actually work in Whitehall, that small area in London where the chief administrative buildings are located. Britain is fortunate to have civil servants who generally work efficiently, who are almost entirely uncorrupted, and whose decisions usually arise not from personal or political reasons but from good administrative ones.

Personnel are frequently criticized because they, the top people, come from too narrow a social background and because they operate under a blanket of secrecy. It remains essentially true that the top 3,500 administrators are drawn heavily from the "Oxbridge" (Oxford and Cambridge) Universities after having received a generalist's education, despite the fact that the three-class hierarchy was replaced in 1971 by a single, open structure. The recruitment system remains largely unchanged.

Not only the cabinet but also the top 3,500 or so civil servants must take oaths of secrecy. Among cabinet ministers, this convention is breaking down somewhat, as they leak information to the press or write revealing memoirs. The civil servants' oath makes it a crime to disclose any official information, whether it is classified or not; he is bound to remain silent for life.

A vigorous campaign was launched by a variety of groups to punch some holes in this screen of secrecy by adopting a law similar to the US Freedom of Information Act. One hole appeared in 1991, when for the first time the newly appointed chief of the MI5 Security Service (counterespionage) Stella Rimington (the first woman ever to occupy the post) was identified by name; now the chief speaks publicly. MI5 is the first British intelligence organization to advertise for recruits. Its head is known as "M."

Secret Intelligence Service (SIS, still widely referred to as MI6), deals with foreign intelligence. It provides intelligence on "requirements" from the field and is primarily a collection agency that relies heavily on human sources, agents who operate under cover and in dangerous situations. Its existence was only publicly admitted in 1994. In 2010 for the first time in MI6's 100-year history, the head, Sir John Sawers, made a public speech. This was a step toward greater transparency and improved public confidence. Like his predecessors, he is referred to as "C", after the service's first chief, Mansfield Cumming, and he signs his letters with green ink, as tradition dictates. Sir John noted that more than a third of MI6's resources were directed toward counterterrorism. He emphasized the importance of sharing intelligence with the US, "an especially powerful contributor to UK security." The communications intelligence service, GCHO, was completely unknown to the media. In November 2013 the three heads made history when they appeared live on TV before Parliament's Intelligence and Security Committee.

All three of these agencies have long inspired the imagination of thriller writers. When disgruntled former MI6 agent, Richard Tomlinson, put the names of more than 100 British secret agents on the World Wide Web in 1999, British security officials conceded that the Internet is so far-flung that no government can control the flow of information on it.

Despite the Official Secrets Act and tradition, the British news media have always been an important check on governmental power. Britain has more newspapers per capita than any other country. Nevertheless, the Blair government introduced in 2005 a Freedom of Information Act, a reform with the backing of three-fourths of the population. Unlike its equivalent in the US, where Americans have to take their government to court to force it to share its secrets, a British information commissioner does this job for Britons.

Acts of Parliament usually merely establish the basic principles of law, and the civil service fills in the details. Bureaucratic regulations now vastly outnumber actual laws, as is the case in the United States. Traditionally, the treasury, led by the chancellor of the exchequer (treasury minister), has been the main coordinator of the many departments and ministries. Since it was responsible for the budgets of the various departments, it gained the right to comment on any policy proposal from any department. There is some skepticism about the treasury's ability to oversee and review all policy effectively. But if anybody is master of Whitehall, it is the treasury and not the cabinet as a whole.

In addition to the huge bureaucracy, the prime minister must deal with a maze of so-called quasi-autonomous nongovernmental organizations, mercifully shortened to "quangos." Depending on how wide the net is thrown, these organizations number up to 5,521 and include such bodies as the Arts Council, the University Grants Committee, the Commission for Racial Equality, the BBC, Trustees of National Museums, and the nationalized industries. Many are purely advisory, but some dispense large sums of money. All consider themselves to be more or less autonomous, but most are financed, and most members are named by the central government, usually by a department of Whitehall. The government can sometimes force these "quangos" to comply with overall policies by giving or withholding grants, but it frequently faces stiff opposition and must often modify its policies in order to win compliance. They have taken over many services formerly performed by local authorities. The budget-conscious Cameron government announced in 2010 that 481 of these would be merged, reformed, or abolished in order to cut spending.

Alongside the "quangos" are especially important interest groups that have semi-official status with the government or with various ministries. They include the Church of England, the universities, and the umbrella organizations for the unions and industry—the Trades Union Congress (TUC, which has 6.2 million in 58 unions) and the Confederation of British Industry (CBI). The latter is the largest employers' association in the world, with a highly professional bureaucracy.

The Judiciary

Another limitation on the government's power, which has long been one of the chief cornerstones of British liberty, has been an independent judiciary. Political leaders are forbidden to obstruct the judicial process, even though judges make decisions that significantly influence politics. As with most other aspects of the British public life, the legal structure is fragmented and complicated. There are different court systems: one for England and Wales; one for Northern Ireland, and one for Scotland, which has always retained its own separate, Roman-based legal system. There are different layers of courts. At the pinnacle were the 10 to 12 Lords of Appeal (known as the "Law Lords"), who sat in the House of Lords and who, constituted as the Judicial Committee of the Privy Council, could even hear appeals from some parts of the British Commonwealth.

Usually the Law Lords' hearings were dry and poorly attended; they involved less pomp and ritual than does the US Supreme Court. But the eyes of the world were on them in 1998–1999, when former Chilean leader General Augusto Pinochet went to Britain for medical treatment. While there, Spain and other European countries demanded his extradition because of his alleged international human

Siambr y Tŷ

Dyluniwyd Siambr bresennol Tŷ'r Cyffredin gan y diweddar Syr Giles Gilbert Scott ac fe'i hagorwyd ym 1950. Cymerodd le'r Siambr a ddyluniwyd gan Syr Charles Barry, a ddefnyddiwyd gyntaf gan Dŷ'r Cyffredin ym 1852, ac a ddinistriwyd gan fomio'r Almaenwyr ym 1941. Cafodd aelodau Tŷ'r Cyffredin eu cartref parhaol cyntaf ym 1547, pan neilltuwyd Capel San Steffan ar eu cyfer. Fe'i defnyddiwyd gan y Tŷ tan 1834, pan gafodd ei ddinistrio gan y tân a ddifaodd Balas San Steffan bron yn llwyr. Gorosoedd rhan isaf capel San Steffan y tân, ac fe'i hadnabyddir bellach fel 'Capel y Crypt'. Ar yr union safle hwn y lleolir Neuadd San Steffan, y bydd ymwelwyr yn cael mynediad trwyddi i'r Cyntedd Canolog, ac mae hi'r un maint â'r hen Siambr.

O ran ei ffurf a'i maintioli mae'r Siambr bresennol bron yn atgynhyrchiad o Siambr Barry, er bod ei haddurniadau'n llai cywrain, a bod orielau mwy wedi'u darparu ar gyfer ymwelwyr. Ehangiad yw trefniadau eistedd cyffredinol y Tŷ mewn gwirionedd

ar y trefniadau eistedd a ddefnyddid bedwar can mlynedd a rhagor yn ôl yng Nghapel San Steffan, pan fyddai'r Aelodau'n eistedd yn eisteddleoedd y côr a phan safai Cadair y Llefarydd ar risiau'r allor. Mae 650 o Aelodau Seneddol; ond ceir eisteddleoedd (gan gynnwys yr orielau ochr) ar gyfer 437 yn unig. Mae'r cyfyngiad hwn yn fwriadol; nid fforwm ar gyfer areithiau gosod mo'r Tŷ; i raddau helaeth mae'r trafodaethau'n ymddiddanol yn eu hanfod; ac ar gyfer llawer ohonynt – rhai arbenigol dros ben o ran thema, neu o natur rigolaidd – ychydig o Aelodau a fydd yn bresennol, a llawer o'r lleill yn brysur â dyletswyddau Seneddol eraill ym Mhalas San Steffan. Gan hynny mae Siambr fach ac agos atoch yn fwy cyfleus. I'r gwrthwyneb, ar achlysuron o bwys, pan fydd y Tŷ yn llawn a phan fydd rhaid i'r Aelodau eistedd yn y rhodfeydd neu ymgasglu o amgylch Cadair y Llefarydd, ger y Bar ac yn yr orielau ochr, cryfheir drama'r Senedd ac yng ngeiriau Syr Winston Churchill, ceir 'ymdeimlad o dorf ac o frys'.

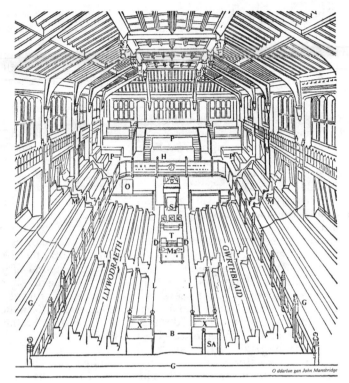

O ddarlun gan John Mansbridge

S	Mr Llefarydd	T	Bwrdd y Tŷ	SA	Rhingyll Arfau
P	Orielau'r Wasg	D	Blychau Gohebiaeth	M	Orielau'r Aelodau
H	Gohebwyr *Hansard*	Ma	Brysgyll †	G	Orielau'r Ymwelwyr
O	Blwch Swyddogion y Llywodraeth (ymgynghorwyr y Gweinidogion)	L	Llinellau ‡	
		B	Bar y Tŷ	
C	Clerod y Tŷ*	A	Meinciau Traws	

*Pan fydd y Tŷ'n Pwyllgora, bydd y Llefarydd yn ymadael â'r Gadair a'r Cadeirydd yn eistedd yng nghadair Clerc y Tŷ, sef yr un ar y chwith.   † Pan fydd y Tŷ'n Pwyllgora, rhoddir y Brysgyll "islaw'r Bwrdd" ar fraced.   ‡ Llinellau nad oes hawl gan Aelodau gamu drostynt tra byddant yn siarad o'r meinciau blaen.

Ymgorfforwyd mwyaduron yn y gwaith coed yng nghefn pob mainc. O bwyso yn ôl ychydig yn hytrach na phwyso ymlaen gall ymwelwyr glywed yn well.

Arddangosir gwybodaeth am yr hyn sy'n digwydd yn y Tŷ ar setiau monitor teledu yn ymyl y ffenestri yn yr Orielau ochr.

Gellir cael ffurflen archebu ar gyfer prynu Adroddiad Swyddogol (Hansard) eisteddiad y dydd drwy'r post oddi wrth y Porthorion neu o'r Swyddfa Archebion Mynediad.

Os oes arnoch angen rhagor o wybodaeth ynglŷn â'ch ymweliad, neu am waith y Tŷ'n gyffredinol, ffoniwch y Swyddfa Hysbysrwydd (01-219 4273).

Welsh description of House of Commons

rights violations. He claimed immunity as a former head of state and current member of the Chilean senate, so the Law Lords were asked for a ruling.

Normally the top British jurists do not have reputations for their political leanings, as do American Supreme Court justices, but their politics became an issue in the long legal battle. In the end, they rendered seven judgments that revealed differing interpretations on points of law. Nevertheless, they ruled that Pinochet could be extradited to Spain to face charges of torture but only for those acts committed after December 1988, when Britain implemented the 1984 Torture Convention.

They made another landmark decision in December 2004, when, sitting for only the second time since the Second World War in a panel of nine justices instead of the usual five, they struck down the government's practice of detaining terrorist suspects indefinitely without trial. They ruled in December 2005 that evidence obtained through torture in other countries could not be used in British courts. Four months later they struck down a key provision in the government's antiterrorism law allowing house arrest for suspects. In

2005 the House of Lords voted down the Blair government's antiterrorist package four times until the prime minister offered an acceptable concession: to allow Parliament to review it within a year.

In October 2009 the Law Lords gave way to a new Supreme Court of 12 judges appointed by the government. Parliament is not involved in the selection process. Its president, Lord Phillips, said this new court was "the last step in divorcing the law lords from any connection with the legislative business of the House of Lords." This enhances the court's image of independence. It cannot strike down statutes as unconstitutional since Parliament itself is supreme. But it can return to Parliament or refer to the European Court of Justice laws it deems to contravene the European Convention on Human Rights, incorporated into British law in 1998.

It has the same powers of the former Law Lords except that it can rule on devolution issues. It must be established to what extent Scotland, which possesses its own legal system, will defer to it. The Supreme Court shares its members and the Middlesex Guildhall in Parliament Square with the Judicial Committee of the Privy Council. The latter hears appeals from

some smaller Commonwealth countries and from private jurisdictions, such as professional or academic bodies. Among the Supreme Court's first decisions were that Jewish schools cannot favor applicants based on whether one's mother is Jewish and that LGBTQ asylum seekers cannot be deported if they face persecution in their home countries.

Much of criminal law and most civil law in Britain do not come from acts of Parliament but instead from "common law." Unlike "civil law," which most European democracies have, "common law" is based on tradition, a slow development of rules based on previous cases ("precedents") which are reported in writing, indexed, and published in an elaborate system for reference. It is law made by judge and jury. In order to make legal language more comprehensible for litigants, civil courts eliminated Latin legal terms from proceedings in 1999, replacing them with plain English.

Britain's tradition of parliamentary supremacy excludes the possibility of "judicial review," such as exists in the United States. This would permit the courts to overturn acts of Parliament on the ground that they were unconstitutional. This was theoretically impossible since nobody

The United Kingdom

could be superior to Parliament. That ended in 2000. A kind of individual bill of rights went into effect by incorporating into British law the European Convention for the Protection of Human Rights and Fundamental Freedoms (often referred to as the European Human Rights Charter or EHRC). This convention includes such protections as rights for criminal defendants and freedom of speech, religion, and assembly. These are rights that have been recognized for centuries under common law. To these freedoms is now added a defendable right of privacy.

A half-century earlier, British jurists had played a leading part in drafting the charter, and it has applied to British citizens since the UK entered the EU in 1973. But it was not enforceable in British courts. That has changed. Parliament should not make laws that violate the EHRC. Judges still do not have the right of judicial review, that is, the right to strike down legislation. However, they can now make a "declaration of incompatibility" when British laws conflict with the EHRC. Parliament or the government must determine whether the "incompatible" statute can remain. The government can bypass Parliament by amending the law by statutory instrument. Although the legislative and executive branches have the last say, political pressure is very strong to bring any law in line with the European charter.

Only a small part of the governing of Britain is carried out by parliamentary acts. Ministers, civil servants, local government authorities, and "quangos" must use discretion in applying general laws to concrete situations, and it is precisely this discretion that can be checked by the courts. In the 1970s a group of parents took the minister responsible for education to court on the charge that the way in which he had applied the school reform was illegal, and the court ruled in their favor. In order to deal with concrete cases, judges must decide what the laws mean. It is in such interpretation that judges have most of their power; the whole thrust of a law can be changed or bent by judges. When judges have this kind of power, one might ask, Who needs judicial review?

As in the United States, there is much controversy over the question of whether the courts have too much power and whether they are, in fact, political. There can be no question that judges' ability to assess the propriety of ministerial actions opens up another course of action to persons who oppose the government's policy. Of course, if Parliament does not like what the courts are doing, it could make new laws that are clearer and more specific, but Parliament has taken that step only once since 1945. It is far too busy to monitor the judges' use of their discretionary

power. Whether one likes it or not, the impact of judicial interpretations will remain political and will continue to place limits on governmental power. However, judicial restraint still prevails in Britain to a greater degree than in the United States.

Local Government

Largely because of historical circumstances, the United Kingdom is a unitary, not a federal, state. That is, it is not a collection of "united states." Unlike the United States of America, the UK was not consciously created by sovereign states that carefully retained important powers. The English conquered Wales militarily in the 12th century; it was politically integrated with England in 1536. The thrones of England and Scotland were united in 1603, and the process of union was completed in 1707. The question of succession to the throne led to Anglo-Scottish conflicts in 1715 and 1745, which culminated in the occupation of Scotland by English armies. Ireland was simply taken by force, and the 6 northern counties remained in the United Kingdom in 1922, when the southern 26 counties became independent.

Therefore, the British government is, in theory, freed from the problems of getting its policies accepted by powerful states or provinces. This centralization would seem to fit well with the land and its people—it is a small country, no bigger than the state of Oregon, with a population of almost 60 million. It is highly urbanized, with 40% of the population living in only seven urban centers that account for less than 4% of the total land area.

London, with a population of 8 million (over 15% of the United Kingdom's total), is seven times larger than the second-largest city, Birmingham. Only four other cities have more than a half-million inhabitants: Liverpool, Manchester, Sheffield, and Leeds. A massive migration into London is taking place. Only two-thirds of Londoners were born there. Unlike Washington, New York, Ottawa, or many national capitals, London is simultaneously the center of government, finance, the mass media, and the arts. Nearly three-quarters of the people who earned a place in Who's Who live within a 65-mile radius of London. Half the MPs never resided in their constituencies before their election, and many of them are from London. Further, most ambitious civil servants climb the career ladder in London.

Nevertheless, unitary government does not mean that orders from Number 10 Downing Street, Westminster, or Whitehall are automatically carried out in all corners of the UK. There are many institutions that give much scope for local resistance to central authority. Let us look first at local government.

It is not a surprise that, like most other British political and legal institutions, the structure of local government is diverse and highly complicated. In 1974 a reorganized structure of local government came into effect in an attempt to produce a fairly uniform pattern throughout the entire kingdom. This reform scarcely made the structure of local government easier for the foreigner to understand. To begin with, local government still differs in England, Wales, Scotland, and Northern Ireland. In the first three, there are two tiers of administration, each with elected councils, taxing authority, and its own powers. The top tier (composed generally in England of metropolitan or county councils and in Scotland of nine regional councils) and the lower tier (composed of borough, or district, councils) together provide schools; local roads; government-owned housing (known as "council housing"); and an array of services, such as buses, garbage pickup, libraries, swimming pools, and (except in London) police protection.

These two tiers often clash with each other, especially in metropolitan areas. To muddle things even more, there is usually even a third tier composed of parish or community councils with powers of their own. In all, there are more than 14,000 local governments in Britain. These local units account for a quarter of all government spending. Most is handed out by the central government rather than raised locally, but they do provide for close to half of their own expenses through local property taxes (known as "rates") and fees for services. They employ almost 3 million people (over 12% of the total workforce), far more than the central government.

Former prime ,inister Thatcher locked horns with local authorities. In 1988 she sought to abolish the existing system of local taxes based on the size and value of personal property and to replace it with a flat-rate levy, or community charge, which would spread the tax burden to residents of all incomes. Opponents said this was regressive and unfair, while she said that, by spreading taxes evenly, the new tax would bring pressure to bear on local councils, many of which are dominated by Labour politicians, to reduce their budgets. Thus, a motive to modernize the tax system was mingled with one to reduce the opposition's power even further. So unpopular was this flat-rate levy that it helped lead to her downfall in 1990.

She also moved to abolish the metropolitan councils, at least in part because some of them had become centers of leftist power. These included the Greater London Council (GLC) and what was sometimes derisively referred to in Tory circles as the "Socialist Republic of Yorkshire." While eliminating the GLC in her

1986 reform, the elected councils in London's 32 administrative areas, such as Kensington and Chelsea, Westminster, and Lambeth and Hackney, continued to exist. Within days of assuming office in May 1997, Prime Minister Blair proposed a referendum for Londoners to create an elected government and mayor.

In 1998, 72% voted in favor of a directly elected mayor, and in May 2000 self-proclaimed socialist Ken Livingstone, running as an independent, was elected London's mayor. He was known as "Red Ken" because of his outspoken opposition to Thatcher and his earlier policies as GLC head of declaring the capital a nuclear-free zone, making common cause with IRA supporters, and backing LGBTQ rights. He vowed to rid Trafalgar Square of pigeons, which he described as "rats with feathers."

In 2003 he launched a revolutionary program to diminish central London's traffic congestion, among the world's worst. Every private automobile and truck driving into an eight-square-mile area in the heart of the city on weekdays between 7 a.m. and 6:30 p.m. must pay the equivalent of $14 per day for the privilege. The proceeds are spent on public transport projects. When in 2006 the US embassy and other foreign embassies called this a tax (from which they should be exempt) and refused to pay it, Livingstone called the US ambassador "a chiseling little crook" and a "car salesman." The forthright mayor was also suspended from office for four weeks in 2006 for saying a Jewish reporter was "just like a concentration camp guard."

Even Blair had called him and his colleagues a "ragbag of Trotskyists" and threw him out of the Labour Party. In May 2008 Livingstone was voted out of power when the Conservatives won 44% of the popular votes in the London local elections. The flamboyant, eccentric ex-journalist and TV personality Boris Johnson became mayor. He was reelected in May 2012, narrowly defeating his predecessor, Ken Livingston.

Sometimes strong-armed measures toward local governments do work, depending largely on the skill and determination of the prime minister. Nevertheless, it would be more accurate to describe the overall relationship in terms of bargaining between interdependent levels of government.

Island Governments

The United Kingdom includes certain island groups, such as the Outer Hebrides, Orkney, and Shetland, which have more local authority than county, district, or metropolitan county councils on the mainland. For instance, Shetland controls oil developments in its own territory and has launched a strong movement toward total internal autonomy. The Isle of Man in the Irish Sea and the partly French-speaking bailiwicks of Guernsey and Jersey off the French coast already have autonomous legal status; Norman-based legal systems; their own parliaments; and governments which control domestic, fiscal, and economic policy. They are quaint anomalies in that they are not part of the UK but are Crown dependencies. They are also not in the European Union, so their citizens do not enjoy the freedom to move and work in its member states.

The Channel Islands had been occupied by 30,000 Germans during World War II. In 1993 embarrassing evidence was released that islanders had collaborated with, profited from, or slept with the German masters. In one notorious incident in 1942, local authorities helped the Germans identify 2,100 Jews and English-born residents to be deported to camps in Germany. These revelations reopened old wounds and prompted Britons to think about how they might have reacted if Hitler's forces had overrun the entire country.

Wales, Scotland, and Northern Ireland

The three large regions on the outer fringe of the United Kingdom comprise about a fifth of the UK's total population: Wales (2.9 million), Scotland (5.6 million), and Northern Ireland (1.9 million). These populations compare with 48.7 million in England. By 2004, however, the usual migration had been reversed, and Scotland and northern England were gaining people. Until 1999 all were, in varying degrees, Celtic in background and relatively poor economically. All three were ruled by departments of the central government: the Wales Office, the Scottish Office, and the Northern Ireland Office, each with a mini-Whitehall at its disposal. The prime minister appointed a secretary of state for each, and these politicians, who never come from the areas they control, sat in the cabinet.

Although these regions' relations with London have rarely been smooth, regionalism was seldom a major factor in British politics. The differences were masked by a common language, the facade of unitary government, and economic prosperity. This changed dramatically in the 1970s. Strapped with a disproportionate number of dying industries and unhappy with the remoteness of central government, nationalist parties in Wales and Scotland grew. At the end of the century, Westminster transferred important powers to these regions. "Devolution," which resulted in all three having their own elected parliaments in 1999, represents a historic shift in the way Britain is governed.

Wales

Wales is technically a principality whose titular ruler is the Prince of Wales, who is always the heir apparent to the English throne. It lost all traces of political identity through the Act of Union with England in 1535. However, its social integration with England proceeded much more slowly. English was the language of the government after 1535, but until the 19th century, the Welsh language, which is a Celtic dialect related to Irish, Scottish, and Breton, was spoken by a majority of the people. It is the strongest surviving Celtic language. Now only one-fifth of the Welsh population speaks it, mainly in rural areas and small towns in North Wales, but one-third claim to have "some understanding" of the language. Welsh speakers form a majority in outlying areas in the west, inhabited by only 10% of the population. All public-sector bodies give Welsh equal status with English.

Unlike Scotland, it was the preservation of the language more than independence from England which fired the Welsh nationalist movement in the 1970s. Lacking its own aristocracy, the Welsh always tended to be somewhat more egalitarian in their outlook. The coal mining and basic industry, especially in the more populous South Wales, have always made it a Labour Party stronghold. In 1978 London offered both Wales and Scotland regional assemblies whose powers would have fallen short of American state legislatures. But in a 1979 referendum, Welshmen rejected such an assembly by a margin of four to one, largely because of the revulsion English-speaking Welshmen felt toward the pretensions of the Welsh-speaking minority.

To help satisfy Welsh nationalist urges, Welsh-language schools were established. By 2006 they numbered 448 primary and 54 secondary schools that teach mostly or entirely in Welsh. Since they tend to be good schools, parents, even newcomers from nearby England, want their children to attend them. The result is that a new generation of articulate nationalists is graduating from Welsh-language schools. Welsh is a compulsory subject until age 16 in English-language schools. For the first time since reliable statistics have been taken, the proportion who claim to speak Welsh is rising: Between 1991 and 2001, the proportion grew from 19% to 21% (and from 5.8% two decades ago to 10.9% in the capital, Cardiff). Teenagers are more likely to speak than their parents. Since 1993, public agencies are obliged to provide service in both languages, and court cases can be heard in Welsh if the plaintiff or defendant wishes. Welsh speakers are favored in the job market and earn 6%–8% more than English-only rivals.

Second, a separate Welsh-language television channel was established (Sianel Pedwar Cymru—channel 4—S4C), which,

The United Kingdom

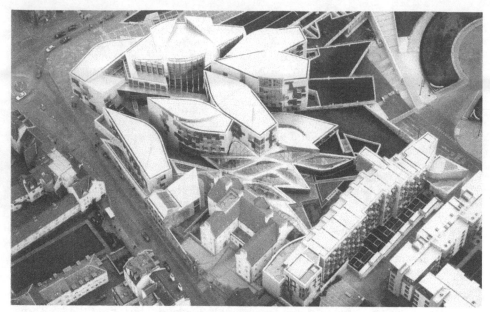

Holyrood, Scottish Parliament

due to the small viewing audience, is one of the most expensive television channels in the world. BBC Wales has a Welsh-language station, Radio Cymru. Whereas Scots have their own newspapers, most Welsh read the English press. Finally, the Welsh Language Act of 1993, which declared that Welsh and English were to be considered "on a basis of equality," enabled Welsh speakers to be more insistent that Welsh be spoken more. Language disputes are mild compared with Belgium or Quebec.

A colony of a few thousand Welsh speakers was found in Patagonia. Having emigrated to Argentina in the 19th century, they are being actively recruited to return to Wales to help keep the language alive, despite their noticeable Spanish accents. In 2004 one such Patagonian lady became the first person to take her naturalization oath in the Welsh language.

Welsh nationalism is alive though not robust. A nationalist party, Plaid Cymru (pronounced "Plide Cumry"), founded in the 1920s amid anti-English feeling, no longer talks much about an independent Wales with a seat in the United Nations, since most citizens do not want that. A pressure group, the Independent Wales Movement, was organized in 2000 outside Plaid's ranks. It is more exuberantly nationalist, forcing Plaid leader Ieuan Wyn Jones to speak of "full national status" for Wales. He explained that this meant the same standing as Ireland has within the EU.

It settled for the referendum leading to an elected Welsh Assembly. In 1997 a razor-thin majority in Wales, with only half the eligible voters participating, voted in favor of its first elected parliament in

nearly 600 years. This National Assembly has 60 members (AMs). Its powers are more limited than those of the new Scottish Parliament. It can amend certain acts of Westminster, but it cannot pass its own laws or raise taxes. It can decide how to spend the budget formerly administered by the Welsh Office, including for health, housing, and education, and scrutinize and alter the administration of Wales.

In 1999 the first elections were won by Labour. A new electoral system modeled on that of Germany was used: Each voter has two votes, one for his preferred representative (called member of the Welsh Parliament—MWP) in the 40 constituencies and one for the party of his choice. Thus it is a combination of Britain's "first-past-the-post" system and proportional representation. Secretary of State for Welsh Affairs Alun Michael of the Labour Party handed over his powers to himself in his new capacity as first secretary of the Welsh Assembly. In 2000 Labour's popular Rhodri Morgan was elected as first minister.

A 2007 survey revealed that a majority of Welsh believe devolution has improved the way Wales is governed and favor more powers to their own assembly, which will come. Though not as desirous of independence as are Scots, three-fifths of them prefer to call themselves "Welsh" rather than "British." That Welsh identity is more cultural than political. In the May 2010 British elections, Labour remained the largest party, winning 26 of Wales's 40 seats. The Conservatives snatched four of Labour's seats, climbing from three to eight. Only three went to Plaid Cymru. Labour performed strongly in the May 2011 local and regional elections, narrowly

failing to win an overall majority in the devolved parliament. Two months earlier, voters overwhelmingly supported proposals in a referendum for more devolution. From May 2011, the Welsh Assembly can initiate laws in 20 areas, including education. It is growing more independent from Westminster.

Scotland

Scotland, which is still a kingdom in its own right, joined England by agreement in 1707. Although the Scottish Parliament voted itself out of existence at that time, other institutions remained intact, such as the legal system, based on Roman law; a distinctive educational system; and a Presbyterian Church of Scotland. By long-standing custom, the queen worships as a Presbyterian in Scotland and as an Episcopalian in England. One should therefore not wonder at the fact that the Scots have a secure sense of separate national identity that has survived union with England.

Scottish nationalist feeling has simmered for two and a half centuries, but the intensity and strength surged furiously in the 1970s, when oil was discovered in the North Sea off Scotland's coasts. The Scottish Nationalist Party (SNP), founded in 1928, argued that "It's Scotland's Oil!" and that it would make this relatively poor region in the UK wealthy and capable of independence. In the 1974 parliamentary elections, its vote surged to 30%. In the face of such rising nationalism in their traditional party stronghold, the ruling Labour government offered to create a popularly elected Scottish assembly if such a move were approved by a majority in a referendum.

Such an instrument of "direct democracy" means that, between parliamentary elections, the people, not Parliament, decide. Because of the tradition of parliamentary supremacy, there were no referendums in Britain until the 1970s. Parliament did stipulate that at least 40% of the eligible Scottish voters had to approve the transfer of powers to the region (a process known as "devolution"). The referendum was held in March 1979, and 51.6% of the voters approved the assembly; however, only 33% of the eligible voters participated, so Parliament repealed the devolution act for Scotland. The Labour Party, which had always won most of the Scottish seats, reasserted itself in Scottish affairs and picked up the torch of devolution.

The 1990s witnessed a resurgence of Scottish nationalism and the SNP. Polls in 1992 indicated that 80% of Scots wanted either a Scottish parliament or outright independence. One native son, actor Sean Connery, compared Scotland to the independent Baltic states. This was quite a role reversal for "James Bond," who onscreen risked everything to serve the British Crown. He said he would permanently move from his adopted home in the Bahamas back to Scotland if it were ever to win its independence. The hit movie Braveheart in the mid-1990s also boosted the movement for greater Scottish independence. Even more Scotsmen began saying, "We're not free. We need a William Wallace."

This feeling helped fuel an upsurge of interest in learning Scotland's Gaelic language, which had declined to only 60,000 speakers, or about 3%–4% of Scotsmen, who may use it in the assembly if they choose. Still there is no language motive to Scottish nationalism, as in Wales. Nor are there religious ones, as in Northern Ireland, or ethnic motives, as in eastern Europe. Nor is cultural nationalism as strong as it is in Wales. SNP leader Alex Salmond remarked, "we are a mongrel nation."

In the 1997 elections the SNP, which captured six seats, for the first time in Scotland's history drove the Tories out completely. Scottish MPs in Westminster enjoy the privilege, known as the "West Lothian question," that they can vote on all matters that concern the entire UK, whereas English, Welsh, and Northern Irish MPs cannot vote on matters devolved to Scotland. This quirk helps stimulate "English nationalism." Some polls have shown that two-thirds of the English support an English-only Parliament, and the proportion who define themselves as "English, not British," had by 2005 risen to 40%.

While Labour dominated Westminster until May 2010, devolution of powers to Scotland and Wales came back on the agenda. A referendum in Scotland in 1997 paved the way to a democratically elected assembly in 1999. Voters overwhelmingly approved a 129-seat parliament, Scotland's first in 300 years, with wide powers over such local matters as health, education, municipal government, economic development, housing, criminal and civil law, fisheries and forestry. They also voted for the right to raise or lower income taxes by up to 3% and to levy charges, such as road tolls. Each Scot continues to receive about 1,000 pounds ($1,500) in subsidies from London.

The polling set the stage for the most important constitutional change in British government in modern times. It also signaled the peaceful rebirth of a nation in an extraordinary way: no guerrilla army, separatist terrorists, civil disobedience, or even mass demonstrations. Edinburgh has become Britain's second diplomatic capital, with 16 foreign missions established there by 2005. A couple of dozen Scotsmen work in "external relations," a

Scottish first minister Nicola Sturgeon

term carefully selected so as not to irritate British diplomats in the "foreign office." Half of those diplomats work in Brussels, Washington and Beijing.

On May 6, 1999, voters elected their first Members of the Scottish Parliament (MSP). Using the same mixed single-member constituency/PR electoral system as the Welsh, they favored Labour. This was a setback for the SNP's independence cause. In 2000, Labour's leader Donald Dewar slipped on his front porch and quickly died of a brain hemorrhage. This was a blow to those who advocated autonomy rather than separation from Britain.

The SNP, under John Swinney, had clearly failed to persuade voters in May 2003 that it would be a plausible government and that full independence would be a good thing. The party was divided between those who wanted to return to being a protest party and those who believed that a gradual accumulation of power by the Scottish Parliament is the best route to go.

SNP leader Alex Salmond, a former economist with the Royal Bank of Scotland, concluded that an election victory in Scotland would no longer be a sufficient mandate for independence. It would need to be followed by a referendum before an SNP government could enter negotiations to remove Scotland from Britain. Scots appeared to want to see how devolution worked before leaping into independence. Indeed it seemed that devolution, not independence, was still the preferred direction, even among some SNP voters. Although three-quarters of Scots prefer to be called "Scottish" than "British," only about a third favor independence, according to polls. But "independence" can mean

Gerry Adams, president, Sinn Fein

different things to different people. When they went to the polls in May 2007—the 300th anniversary of the Treaty of Union with England—to elect a Scottish Parliament, two-thirds voted for parties that favor union with Britain.

Although there was no mandate for independence in 2007, the results were still a sensation: For the first time since 1959, Labour came out in second place, winning only 46 to the SNP's 47 seats in the 129-seat assembly. The Tories got 17, and the Liberal Democrats, 16. This ended a half-century of Labour dominance of Scottish politics. It presents a real problem for Labour. It cannot win Britain without winning Scotland. An elated Salmond declared that "never again will the Labour Party think it has a divine right to govern." He became first minister in a minority government. With the SNP in power, the English can no longer be blamed for everything that goes wrong in Scotland.

By the standards of separatist movements around the world, Scottish nationalism has been a peaceful success story. The May 5, 2011, Scottish elections were nothing short of historic: The SNP gained 23 seats to win a majority of 69 out of 129 seats in the Scottish Parliament. Labour lost 8 seats to capture 37, and the Tories slipped from 20 to 15. This spectacular outcome does not mean that most voters would support independence in a referendum. More voters like the SNP and its leader, Nicola Sturgeon, more than they like the idea of severing from the UK. The SNP must define precisely what independence means in the modern age.

In October 2012 Salmond and Prime Minister Cameron signed a referendum deal to stage a Scottish vote on September 18, 2014. The ballot question was a simple in-or-out one: "Should Scotland be an independent country?" Sixteen- and seventeen-year-olds were permitted

The United Kingdom

to vote. All three major parties in Parliament opposed it.

Salmond confirmed that he would seek a currency union with the UK, but all three main parties flatly rejected this. EC president Barrosa stated that it would be almost impossible for Scotland to join the EU. Salmond promised to issue Scottish passports, create a separate defense force, and expel British nuclear submarines from Scottish bases. Scotland would remain in NATO, retain the monarchy, and claim 90% of the North Sea oil and gas revenues. Britain would lose 8% of its economy and population, along with a third (32%) of its territory. The "no" vote won by 55% to 45% in 2014. However, in the May 2015 parliamentary elections, the SNP scored a dramatic victory, capturing 56 of 59 Scottish seats, wiping out the previously dominant Labour Party. Nicola Sturgeon, a charismatic SNP member since age 16, triumphantly announced that "the political firmament, the tectonic plates of Scottish politics [have] shifted." Independence is back on the agenda, and polls in 2020 showed that a majority of Scots favored it. However, its citizens overwhelmingly favor remaining in the EU.

In 2004 the queen officially opened the new ultramodern Scottish Parliament, Holyrood, right across the street from her official Scottish residence. Housing 129 lawmakers, it was three years late and, at £431 million ($650 million), 10 times over budget. Sitting in its beautiful interior, MSPs can look out over the rugged hills that symbolize their land.

Northern Ireland

The UK's most serious regional problem by far was Northern Ireland. The Irish island can be said to be England's oldest colony, having been invaded by the English in the 12th century and ruled as a colony until 1800, when it received its own parliament. Ireland remained legally a part of the United Kingdom until 1922, when the 26 predominantly Catholic southern counties formed what is now the Republic of Ireland. The Protestant majority in the six northern counties rejected "home rule" (independence from Britain). The British at the time pledged that no change in the link between Northern Ireland and the United Kingdom would occur without the consent of the majority of the people. Every subsequent British government held firmly to this commitment.

The largely Presbyterian and Church of Ireland Protestants are descendants of Scottish immigrants who began arriving in the 17th century. Their loyalty to the English Crown is based upon the monarch's historical status set forth in the 1689 Bill of Rights as "the glorious instrument of delivering this kingdom from Popery

and arbitrary power." It is not surprising that this historical attitude, along with the Protestants' rejecting unification of the two parts of Ireland, has always antagonized the Catholic minority in Northern Ireland (who comprise 42% of the population of 1.6 million). Although Northern Ireland is officially a secular (i.e., nonreligious) state, in actual practice the friction between Catholics and Protestants dominates politics there.

Northern Ireland was in turmoil since 1968, when a Catholic civil rights movement organized internationally publicized street demonstrations to object Protestant discrimination in housing, jobs, and electoral representation. British governmental pressure on the Northern Irish parliament (which has existed since 1921 and is known as Stormont because it met in Stormont Castle) to meet many of the Catholic demands created a Protestant backlash. Peaceful street demonstrations in 1969 gave way to open violence, and British troops were sent to reestablish order.

The Irish Republican Army (IRA) sprang to life again and launched a modern terrorist campaign to remove the British from the territory and to reunify the entire island. It received money and arms from overseas sources ranging from Gadhafi in Libya to the Irish Northern Aid Committee—NORAID—in the United States. Due to bad publicity, IRA fundraising in the US became more difficult. It found a lucrative substitute: extortion and racketeering in Northern Ireland itself. Because it also seeks the overthrow of the Dublin government, it has been banned in the south since 1936.

In retaliation, some Protestants in the north organized illegal forces. The best-known illegal Protestant paramilitary group, known for its violence, is the Ulster Volunteer Force (UVF). This illegal unit should not be confused with the Ulster Defence Regiment (UDR—the British army in Northern Ireland), the Royal Ulster Constabulary (RUC—the mainly Protestant police force), or the Ulster Defence Association (UDA—a moderate and legal Protestant paramilitary group). In 1993 Protestant gunmen murdered more people than did the IRA.

The British disbanded Stormont in 1972 and resorted to the unpleasant task of ruling the region directly, through a secretary of state for Northern Ireland. Successive British governments sought earnestly for ways to devolve governmental power to the Northern Irish themselves. The problem was always how to protect the Catholic minority's interests against a perpetual Protestant majority. This difficulty revealed a major weakness of the English model of parliamentary democracy,

which presents great power to any political group that commands an electoral majority: The model does not work well in societies which are divided religiously, ethnically, or racially because minorities can be voted down so easily.

Realizing this, the British government had to reject in 1975 a proposal by the leaders of the Protestants that a constitution be drawn up for Northern Ireland that would copy British parliamentary practice. Instead, British governments sought some form of "power-sharing" arrangement that would guarantee the minority Catholic parties a place in any Northern Irish executive. This idea infuriated the two Protestant political parties, the Ulster Unionists and the Democratic Unionists.

The IRA, which became a dedicated and ruthless band of 400 to 500 paramilitaries operating in small cells called "active service units," was divided into two groups: The "official" IRA was formerly Marxist, but now it seeks power through elections; the "provisional" IRA (Provos) was strictly nationalist, but it shifted to armed struggle to convert Ireland into a Marxist state. This shift was one reason Irish Americans became less generous toward the IRA. Both these wings face some competition from the smaller but more radical Irish National Liberation Army (INLA, the paramilitary wing of the Marxist Irish Republican Worker's Party).

From 1976 to 1982, the IRA campaigned for special treatment as "political prisoners." After the failure of such tactics as refusing to wear prison garb and smearing the walls of the cells with their own excrement, they resorted to hunger strikes. The deaths of 10 IRA hunger strikers in Maze Prison in 1981 sparked renewed militant Catholic nationalism. Shortly before his death, one of the hunger strikers, Bobby Sands, even managed to win a seat in the House of Commons while he was still in prison.

In response, the British government tried again to restore a measure of devolved government by means of the 1982 Northern Ireland Act. Elections for a 78-seat Northern Ireland Assembly and an executive branch were held in 1982. This new body was to have the power to make proposals to the British government on how to return to self-government. It failed. Neither the mainly Catholic, moderate, and law-abiding Social Democratic and Labour Party nor the militant Sinn Fein (the political arm of the IRA, pronounced "Shin Fane," receiving only 10% of the total votes) took their seats in it. The Ulster Unionist Party also walked out and vowed that it would not return until security had been restored in Northern Ireland.

That is exactly what the British tried to do. In 1975 it ended the detention of both

Catholic and Protestant terrorist suspects without trial, and it refused to declare martial law in the violence-torn area. Because of the risk of intimidation against jurors, nonjury courts (known as "Diplock Courts") were created for those accused of terrorist-related offenses. The British have always contended that the fundamental principles of British justice—a fair trial, the onus on the prosecution to prove guilt, the right to be represented by a lawyer, the right of appeal if convicted—are maintained for all.

The most effective antiterrorist measure undertaken by the government in 1983 was the granting of pardon or lenience to onetime terrorists if they would tip off the police (in Northern Irish slang, "to grass") on the whereabouts of active terrorists. The testimony of such "supergrasses" led to a dramatic number of arrests in both the IRA and Protestant Ulster Volunteer Force. These organizations were so paralyzed that terrorist deaths in Northern Ireland dropped by half in one year, from 97 in 1982 to about 50 in 1983. IRA terrorists did give British Christmas shoppers a grisly indication they were alive in 1983, however, when they exploded a bomb outside of the bustling Harrods Department Store in London, claiming still more innocent lives (including an American teenager, a fact that hurt IRA fund-raising in the US) in their ruthless struggle.

The Brighton bombing of 1984 was another grim reminder of the IRA's intent to wreak as much havoc as possible, this time by assailing the highest levels of British government itself. Having organized into "cells," the IRA became more difficult for police to combat. The violence prompted the Irish Republic to ratify the European convention on terrorism, which requires the extradition of terrorists.

By 2003 the toll stood at over 3,600 since 1969. In doing its bloody work, the IRA had the tactical advantage over the 30,000 security forces, which were kept on the defensive by the IRA's meticulous planning and constant shifting of tactics. To minimize its own losses, it increasingly struck at "soft targets," such as bands, military hospitals, off-duty RUC officers, and civilian firms that supply goods and services to the security forces. It also acquires state-of-the-art equipment; for example, it has surface-to-air missiles to use against army helicopters.

Democracy still existed at the local level in Northern Ireland, and voters send 27 MPs to the House of Commons in London. Protestants win a majority of these seats. Catholics would take more if the competing SDLP and Sinn Fein would unify in constituencies with predominantly Catholic populations. In the 1997 elections, the two Catholic parties captured an unprecedented 40.2% of the votes.

The Protestant unionist parties also have trouble working together, with Ian Paisley's hard-line Democratic Unionists taking five seats and David Trimble's larger Ulster Unionist Party winning six. Sinn Fein traditionally refused to take any seat in the British Parliament, whose authority it does not recognize and which would require them to swear allegiance to the queen. In 2002 Adams and three other party members took a historic step by going to the House of Commons and signing up to use all of the facilities except actually occupying a seat. Adams emphasized, "There will never ever be Sinn Fein MPs sitting in the British houses of Parliament." In 2005 the party's parliamentary expenses of £400,000 ($6,400) were withheld to punish the party for IRA crimes.

In 1997 Sinn Fein won an all-time high of 16% of the votes in Northern Ireland. Two of its candidates, Gerry Adams and Martin McGuinness (an IRA leader who has served jail sentences), won seats, which remained vacant. Sinn Fein does occupy seats in local councils on both sides of the Irish border and in the Northern Ireland Assembly. In 2002 it decided to run for seats in the Irish Republic's elections, and it won five; there was general relief when it lost one of those seats in May 2007. In June 2002 Sinn Fein won control of Belfast, and Alec Maskey became lord mayor.

There was progress in addressing the problem of social and economic discrimination. For members of the growing Catholic middle class, life has never been better. They are upwardly mobile and increasingly move into middle-class Protestant neighborhoods, where they are tolerated. Catholics now outnumber Protestants at universities by four to three. The unemployment gap is shrinking. Three out of 10 persons are employed in the public sector, and hiring policies are scrupulously equal and fair. They have begun to intermarry; one-tenth of marriages are mixed. Tourists are returning to the province, which has the lowest rate of violent crime in the UK. Investment is entering from the Irish Republic, which has become Europe's third-richest country. Businesses on both sides of the border are working together. There would be even more cooperation if corporate taxes (30% in Northern Ireland and 12.5% in the Republic) were more equal. However, there is still mistrust. A quarter of respondents said in a 2004 poll that a close relative had died in the Troubles. That figure is probably higher in working-class areas.

In 1985 former Irish taoiseach (prime minister) Garrett FitzGerald and British prime minister Thatcher signed an Anglo-Irish agreement on Northern Ireland. This marked the first time the British government formally permitted the Irish Republic involvement in Northern Ireland's affairs, a concession many Northern Irish Protestants could not accept. It is regrettable but perhaps not surprising that all groups in Northern Ireland condemned this landmark act, despite the fact that its first article stated that no change in the province's status would come about without the consent of a majority of its people.

Peace Talks in Northern Ireland

In 1993 optimism was ignited by a joint declaration by the British and Irish prime ministers offering Sinn Fein a seat at the bargaining table to discuss Northern Ireland's future if the IRA renounced violence. Former prime minister John Major, who admitted that his government had conducted secret contacts with the IRA, promised that Britain would not stand in the way of a united Ireland if a majority of Northern Ireland residents supported such a step. His Irish counterpart pledged that there would be no change in the six counties' status without majority consent.

The following year President Bill Clinton, betting that the IRA wants peace in Northern Ireland, made a risky decision to grant a visa to Sinn Fein leader Gerry Adams to come to the US. Although the British government criticized him for this, it triggered a series of historic events. On August 31, 1994, the IRA declared a cease-fire, which prompted the Irish government to begin meeting with Sinn Fein leaders. Six weeks later Protestant loyalists also declared a truce. While paramilitaries on both sides continued to terrorize their own communities, intersectarian violence and IRA attacks on British forces stopped. As a result, the British government relaxed its security measures in Northern Ireland and began drawing down its 18,000 troops. In December London opened direct talks with Sinn Fein and, later, with the Protestant paramilitaries. In February 1995 the British and Irish governments issued a "Framework for Agreement," outlining their proposals for Northern Ireland's future.

The US government did its part to keep the momentum going by permitting Sinn Fein to open an office near Dupont Circle in Washington in 1995 and to raise money legally in the US. Much to London's displeasure, Clinton invited Gerry Adams to a St. Patrick's Day party in the White House honoring Ireland's taoiseach. In May the US also organized a Northern Ireland Investment Conference in Washington that brought together more people from more different Northern Irish parties under one roof than ever before. It was

The United Kingdom

also attended by top government officials from the UK and Ireland and was the venue for the first meeting between Gerry Adams and Britain's ex–secretary of state for Northern Ireland Patrick Mayhew. This was the highest-level meeting between British and IRA leaders in 75 years and a giant step toward Adams's goal of receiving the same recognition and treatment accorded to Northern Ireland's other political leaders.

Clinton gave another powerful boost to the peace process in November 1995 by paying the first visit to Belfast ever made by an American president. It was a triumph. The very approach of his historic visit helped dissolve a stalemate in the talks and revitalized cooperation. Hours before his arrival the Irish and British prime ministers met and agreed to a breakthrough: preliminary all-party talks, led by former US senator George Mitchell, would be held, while an international "decommissioning commission," led by former Canadian chief-of-staff and ambassador to Washington General John De Chastelain, sought a way around the weapons impasse.

John Major admitted that Clinton's coming helped "concentrate the mind." Greeted everywhere in Belfast by cheering crowds waving American flags, Clinton addressed over 100,000 people, the largest throng in memory to gather in the square of Belfast City Hall. He appealed to everyone to put aside "old habits and hard grudges" and to seek peace. One witness said, "I've never seen anything like this before. Everybody's come together." His American optimism reportedly made a deep impression. He met with all major leaders in the conflict and invited them to a reception at Queen's University; most came, which would have been unthinkable earlier. It was a very different Belfast that he saw: Gone are the soldiers on the hunt, the countless roadblocks, and the barbed wire. Although the ugly wall topped with razor wire separating Protestants and Catholics, inaptly called the "peace line," still stands, most of the blockaded streets have been reopened in Belfast.

There is little support in Northern Ireland or elsewhere for immediate reunification of Ireland. But not since 1969 had there been so many grounds for optimism that "the Troubles" can end and that the Northern Irish can discuss their future peacefully. As a symbol of returning normalcy with Britain in 1995, Prince Charles became the first member of the royal family to make an official visit to the Irish Republic since 1922. Also in 1995, David Trimble, leader of the Ulster Unionist Party, the main Protestant group, traveled to Dublin and met with the Irish taoiseach.

This was the first time since 1922 a Unionist leader was received in Dublin. In 1996 the IRA ended an 18-month cease-fire and launched a bombing campaign in Britain and Northern Ireland. Negotiations resumed in June 1997.

Since the Labour government is not dependent upon Unionist MPs from Northern Ireland to win important votes in Parliament, as John Major was, it had more political flexibility on Northern Irish issues. A couple weeks after becoming prime minister, Blair lifted the ban on official contacts with Sinn Fein in order to explain London's position and to assess whether the IRA was really prepared to renounce violence. Gerry Adams accepted the offer. Blair dropped London's insistence that terrorists disarm before joining peace talks. He visited Northern Ireland on May 16, 1997, in order to demonstrate that he is willing to take risks for peace in the six counties.

To continue the negotiation process, he invited Gerry Adams to a meeting in Downing Street in December. This was the first visit by an Irish Republican leader to the prime minister's private residence in 76 years. It was a richly symbolic encounter, with the meeting over tea held in the cabinet room, the target of an IRA mortar attack only six years earlier. A month later, in January 1998, Adams returned to Downing Street to hear from the prime minister that the peace process is an "absolute priority" and that "the status quo is not an option." To balance his gesture to Sinn Fein, Blair told Protestants that "none of us . . . , even the youngest, is likely to see Northern Ireland as anything but a part of the United Kingdom."

Talks involving eight Northern Ireland parties and the British and Irish governments continued, despite the outbreak of renewed violence following the assassination of a Protestant terrorist, Billy Wright, in Maze Prison just after Christmas. American George Mitchell emphasized the importance of the negotiations: "We're talking about, literally, people's lives, the possibility of the resumption of the terrible conflict that enveloped this society with fear and anxiety. So, frustrating and tedious as it seems—and it is—you have to be patient and recognize how tough it is for them to move."

Good Friday Agreement

In the early-morning hours of Good Friday 1998, after a series of marathon sessions, all parties at the table reached a historic agreement: A new 108-member Northern Ireland Assembly would be elected using the Irish Republic's system of proportional representation with the transferable vote. To protect Catholics from being permanently outvoted on

sensitive "cross-community" issues and to necessitate consensus, a majority of both Catholic and Protestant blocs or an overall "weighted majority" of 60% would be required for decisions. The cabinet would consist of 10 seats distributed proportionally to the 4 largest parties.

The assembly would share power with a new North-South Ministerial Council, composed of ministers from the republic and Northern Ireland. This gives the Irish Republic its first formal role in Northern Ireland's affairs. In return, Ireland's leaders agreed to give up the republic's claim to the north. All parties pledged to use their influence to persuade armed groups to turn in their weapons within two years, and imprisoned members of those armed groups would be released within two years, as well.

On May 22, 1998, referenda were held on both sides of the border, and 71% of Northern Irish and 94.4% in the republic approved of the Good Friday settlement. The following month, the first elections to the new assembly were held, and David Trimble's UUP came out on top with 28 seats. John Hume's SDLP (later led by Seamus Mallon) was second, with 24 seats. For their indispensable role in the entire peace process, Trimble and Hume shared the 1998 Nobel Prize for Peace. Hume had declared that "we finally decided that agreement for the whole community is more important than victory for one side." Other seats went to the DUP (20), Sinn Fein (18), the Alliance (6), the UKUP (5), Independent Unionists (3), and the Women's Coalition and PUP (2 each). The great number of parties winning seats demonstrated the effect of the proportional representation electoral system. Trimble became first minister, and the body met for the first time in the traditional Stormont building on July 4.

This being Ireland, an island with so much history and so many memories, things were not destined to go smoothly. In August 1998 a fringe Catholic organization calling itself the "Real IRA" exploded a car bomb in the Northern Irish city of Omagh, killing 29 people. The public was so repelled by this grisly act that the "Real IRA" apologized and announced a permanent cease-fire on September 12. This was soon broken, and the IRA was forbidden from raising money in the United States.

After the BBC named four men it said were involved in the attack, three were arrested in 2000. In 2002 the first was convicted and sentenced to 14 years in jail. Colm Murphy, a wealthy pub owner and building contractor, was found guilty by a three-judge panel in a special criminal court in Dublin. To the chagrin of the victims' families, Murphy's conviction was overturned by a Dublin appeals court.

He faced retrial and was acquitted again in February 2010 for lack of sufficient evidence. Another suspect, Sean Gerard Hoey, was charged in 2005 for participating in the bombing. But all convictions were subsequently overturned, including that of Hoey in December 2007. Nevertheless, the tragedy ultimately strengthened support for the peace process. In June 2009 the victims' relatives won a civil case against the "Real IRA" splinter group. They were awarded $2.6 million in damages.

The "Real IRA" was also the prime suspect in the September 2000 rocket attack against the London headquarters of MI6, Britain's foreign intelligence service. To maintain his credibility in the Protestant community, Trimble called for a beginning of "decommissioning" (turning in) of weapons even before the creation of a Northern Ireland cabinet. Noting that this precondition had not been in the agreement, Sinn Fein balked at completing the peace process.

Endless haggling over paramilitary groups laying down their arms threatened the peace deal. However, both sides began taking cautious steps to implement the agreement. On December 1, 1999, a new coalition government in Ulster was formed that shared power devolved from Westminster in London. It included both the party of hard-line Protestant Reverend Ian Paisley and former IRA commander, Martin McGuinnes as minister of education. However, this government was suspended in February 2000 after the IRA failed to meet the Unionists' deadline for starting turning in its arms.

Power sharing was reestablished in May 2000, when the Unionists accepted an IRA pledge to put its arsenal "beyond use" and to allow limited inspections by international observers to verify that that the promise is being kept. Such visits were conducted in June and October 2000, and the arms dumps were reported to have a substantial amount of military material that was safely stored. For a year and a half, the IRA dragged its heels. As a result David Trimble, leader of Northern Ireland's power-sharing government, quit in 2001, and things came to a standstill.

In November 2001 the IRA finally began destroying some of its weapons under international supervision. In quick response to this breakthrough, Britain began demolishing military installations, including army watchtowers overlooking regions with high IRA support. Trimble led his Ulster Unionist Party back into the assembly and was narrowly reelected first minister with the help of the Alliance Party, which had steered a middle road between unionists and republicans. Peace was back on track.

Genuine struggles remain on such emotional symbolic issues as flying flags over official buildings and reforming and renaming the Royal Ulster Constabulary (RUC), which is 93% Protestant. A top American law enforcement official, Tom Constantine, former head of the Drug Enforcement Administration (DEA), was appointed as "oversight commissioner" to scrutinize changes in the RUC. But progress is undeniable. The bloodletting has subsided, although armed dissidents abound. Maze Prison, just outside of Belfast, was emptied and closed in September 2000. Ex-prisoners had played a role in the peace process; they were crucial in the maintenance of their various organizations' cease-fires. The British closed 6 bases along the Irish border and looked forward to reducing the number of bases from 64 to no more than 20 and of troops from 13,500 to 10,500 in 2005 and ultimately to only 5,000.

In July 2002 the IRA stunned everybody with an expression of "sincere apologies and condolences" for all the persons it had killed in the Northern Irish sectarian violence. The "Troubles" appeared to be close to an end when a spy scandal at the heart of the Northern Irish government broke in October 2002. After raiding Sinn Fein homes and offices at the Northern Ireland Assembly, British authorities charged three members of gathering intelligence from Britain's Northern Ireland Office that could be used for terrorist operations. Police found sensitive political material, including minutes of conversations between Blair and his Northern Ireland secretary of state, and names, home addresses, and license plate numbers of many provincial police officers and British security personnel. It was feared that some of the information could be used for assassinations.

Sinn Fein leaders denied the allegations and claimed the police had orchestrated a frame-up. The British suspended the assembly, and Protestant leaders vowed that they would not resume participation unless the IRA renounces violence unmistakably. The IRA then broke off all contact with the independent panel established to oversee disarmament, which had already supervised the destruction of two caches of IRA weapons. One Sinn Fein leader, Martin McGuinness, announced that he had abandoned his fight with Britain and was committing himself to preventing the deaths of any more people: "My war is over." Nevertheless, the peace process had suffered its most serious blow since the Good Friday Agreement five years earlier.

In April 2003 President George W. Bush visited Blair and Irish prime minister Bertie Ahern in Belfast to lend his endorsement to the peace plan. The president had aroused the ire of the British government when Gerry Adams was invited to a White House St. Patrick's Day party in March, this when IRA operatives had been arrested while traveling undercover in the US. Although Blair sensed that breaking the stalemate was "frustratingly close," all his efforts to get the IRA to make a crystal-clear statement that it had given up paramilitary activities like gathering intelligence, threatening and attacking adversaries, and acquiring weapons failed. Adams's statement that there would be "no activities which will undermine in any way the peace process or the Good Friday Agreement" was not enough.

The atmosphere became even more strained when the head of London's Metropolitan Police released evidence in 2012 that agents working for the British army had worked with death squads in Northern Ireland. This included the 1989 murder of Belfast lawyer Patrick Finuncane, who had represented IRA terrorists. Two gunmen from the outlawed Ulster Defence Association broke into his home and shot him 14 times at point-blank range before the very eyes of his wife and three children. One of the gunmen left prison in 2006 under the terms of the 1998 peace accord. Nearly a quarter-century later, an official report detailed how British intelligence was implicated in the murder. Prime Minister Cameron immediately went to Parliament. There he condemned the murder as "an appalling crime" and apologized to the family.

Despite unprecedented direct talks in the fall of 2003 between David Trimble and Gerry Adams, the results of those elections, which were finally held in November 2003, brought a cruel surprise: The confrontational parties outpolled the conciliatory ones, which were the architects and supporters of the peace process. Ian Paisley's Democratic Unionists (DUP) won 30 seats in a 108-seat assembly that does not function, and David Trimble's Ulster Unionist Party (UUP) captured only 27. On the nationalist side, Sinn Fein got 24 seats, while the more moderate Social Democratic and Labour Party (SDLP) fell from 24 to 18. The nonsectarian Alliance Party held on to its six seats, and independents got three.

The same thing happened in the May 2005 British parliamentary elections, which delivered convincing victories to the hard-line parties and moved Northern Ireland closer toward a two-party system. David Trimble resigned his leadership of the Ulster Unionist Party after losing the seat he had held for 15 years. This capped a decade of steadily declining influence for the party. In June 2006 he was granted a life peerage in the House of Lords. Ian Paisley's Democratic Unionists captured

The United Kingdom

Former first minister Ian Paisley and Deputy First Minister Martin McGuinness enjoy their historical moment.

half of the 18 seats allotted to Northern Ireland. Sinn Fein took five, and Gerry Adams won easy reelection. The SDLP held on to its three seats. Blair noted in 2003 that "it is more than a little frustrating." Paisley's DUP must be included in any talks to restore devolved government. But Paisley's position as of May 2005 was that the Good Friday Agreement is "finished completely" and "only paper."

A hoped-for settlement ended in December 2004, when the IRA refused to permit photographic verification of its disarmament. Then the IRA was accused of masterminding a spectacular £26.5 million ($40 million) bank robbery in Belfast. A month later, a Catholic father of two, Robert McCartney, was beaten and stabbed to death by a dozen IRA thugs outside a Belfast pub. Seventy-two witnesses in the pub were intimidated in the usual IRA way from testifying. But the man's wife and five sisters decided to depart from the traditional code of silence and bring the matter to international attention.

With increasing publicity on both sides of the Atlantic, Sinn Fein found itself in the limelight as the incident galvanized public opinion against the IRA. It made one of its most extraordinary blunders ever: it offered to shoot all the IRA members involved in the killing, an offer McCartney's family rejected out of hand. Four of the sisters were invited to Sinn Fein's annual conference in 2005 and were seated in the front row to hear Gerry Adams call on the killers to turn themselves in and to confess. However, since Sinn Fein/IRA rejects

police authority, it advised witnesses to offer statements to lawyers, a policy widely criticized in Northern Ireland.

An even greater invitation was extended to the six women from the American president, who met with them on St. Patrick's Day while refusing to receive Adams, the first time in 10 years this had happened. Adams was also denied the kind of visa that would have permitted him to raise funds in the US. More and more families of persons murdered by Catholic and Protestant paramilitaries are coming forward with their stories and standing up to the terrorists they once feared. Adams appealed to the IRA, which British and Irish intelligence officials no longer believe is a separate entity from Sinn Fein, to use words, not guns, to end British rule in Northern Ireland. But he faced a stark choice: remain linked to an increasingly discredited IRA or break with it and lead his followers into modern democratic politics without the backing of a murderous paramilitary force.

In July 2005 the IRA formally declared an end to its armed struggle against British rule and pledged to pursue its aims of uniting Ireland through "exclusively peaceful means." In September General John de Chastelain certified that the IRA weapons dumps had been destroyed. Some Protestants, especially Ian Paisley, claim that the IRA had not, in fact, disarmed. A half-year later, a report by the Independent Monitoring Commission (IMC) stated that the IRA is moving in the right direction but that some IRA members are still armed and involved in

robbery, gasoline smuggling, and financial crime, perhaps without the knowledge of the leadership. The IRA admits that.

British intelligence reports also contend that the IRA kept some weapons, but Chastelain disagreed. Other reports say that the IRA's intelligence service, a formidable group, is still actively spying on public officials and providing information to organized crime networks. None of the reports contend that the IRA is still engaged in terrorist operations. However, there were suspicions of that in April 2006, when a senior official in Sinn Fein, Denis Donaldson, admitted to having been a British agent for 20 years and was soon thereafter shot dead after being tortured. The IRA denied responsibility. That Northern Ireland is more peaceful is beyond dispute. In 1972, 500 persons were killed; in 2005, the number was only 5.

A glimmer of hope was produced in May 2006, when the Stormont assembly met for a ceremonial hour. Sinn Fein proposed that the leader of the largest party, Ian Paisley, lead a power-sharing executive to revive the stalled peace effort. This was perhaps a ruse to portray itself as cooperative and Paisley as intransigent. In any case, Paisley, whose DUP had never accepted the 1998 peace agreement, declined, remarking that Sinn Fein had not done enough to disarm and distance itself from violence: "I am not saying I will never sit in Stormont with the IRA. I am saying I will not sit in Stormont until the IRA gives up its weapons. It's a conditional no, not a 'No, I'll never do it.'"

In the meantime, an impatient British government, which had funded the assembly and the members' $60,000 annual salaries for the previous three years, joined with the Irish government in setting a deadline of November 24, 2006, for the formation of a Northern Irish government that would take over from London such responsibilities as education, health care, and transport.

That got people's attention. The Royal Ulster Constabulary (RUC), which had once been 97% Protestant, was transformed into the Police Service of Northern Ireland, with one-fifth of the officers Catholic. In January 2007 Sinn Fein recognized that force. In March the voters went to the polls and confirmed that Paisley's DUP (with 30% of the votes) and Adams's Sinn Fein (with 26%) are the dominant groups. This enabled them both to claim a mandate to strike a deal, which they did. Both announced their willingness to share power.

On May 8, Paisley was sworn in as first minister, with Sinn Fein's Martin McGuinness as deputy first minister. The formerly recalcitrant Paisley said, "I believe Northern Ireland has come to a time of peace, when hate will no longer rule." After

Former Prime Minister Teresa May

more than 3,700 deaths, this was a very welcome message. Of those, 1,800 were killed by the IRA, and about 1,000 by extremist Protestant groups. The British army killed about 300. IRA fighters killed 1,000 members of the security forces. Half were regular soldiers, and half, locally recruited police and soldiers.

Bertie Ahern hailed Tony Blair as the driving force behind the peace effort and declared that "we can, and are, shaping our future in a new and better way." A few days later, Ahern became the first Irish leader to address a joint session of the British Parliament, and he got a standing ovation. Blair noted at the power-sharing ceremony that "these islands have at last escaped the heavy chains of history." The settlement may well be his most illustrious legacy after a decade in power.

In the end, Blair had high praise for Paisley, whose "contribution to peace, after all the years of division and difference, was decisive and determinative." Both prime ministers convinced him that only a man of his stature could bring peace. Paisley succeeded in bringing most of his community onboard, but the die-hards in his unionist movement felt betrayed and could not forgive him. Their loathing was only increased by the jovial photos in the press of him and McGuinness enjoying each other's company. This ultimately forced him to shed his leadership positions. Rather than risking ouster as head of the Free Presbyterian Church of Ulster, which he had founded 56 years earlier, he stepped down in January 2008. In May he quit as first minister and as leader of the Democratic Unionists, which he had created 37 years earlier. He became Lord Bannside, but his passionate life came to an end in September 2014. Reflecting on his 88 years, he said, "No one can justify

everything they've ever done. Things happen in the day when blood is flowing. It is a sad thing, but it is a fact. But we are rid of those days now."

His replacement for both was his long-standing number 2 in the party, Peter Robinson, a wealthy Belfast lawyer. Paisley remained only as an MP in London until May 2010 and member of the Stormont assembly. Power sharing continued.

Resistance to the agreement was softened by a generous hand extended by the central government. It amounted to a financial package of £50 billion ($75 billion) over 10 years to an area where one in three jobs and two-thirds of economic output come from the public sector. The central government spends over £2,000 more per capita than it does in Britain as a whole, and income is only about 80% of the British average. But this is important because getting the economy moving is not easy in a corner of Ireland where violence has discouraged both investors and local entrepreneurs. By 2008 more than $6 billion in foreign investments had poured into the north. One sign of the economic renaissance is the glittering, new Victoria Square in Belfast, an $800 million shopping center with a huge, glass dome hovering over the downtown skyline.

Securing the peace is the highest priority. Within days after the agreement, the oldest loyalist paramilitary group, the Ulster Volunteer Force (UVP), announced that it was going out of existence, although its weapons were merely put out of reach, not destroyed. Britain created a new Catholic-Protestant panel to oversee the police force, and for the first time, it includes Sinn Fein officials. However, policing remained a problem, even though crime by 2010 had gone down eight consecutive years, and overt sectarian violence became increasingly rare. The newly created Police Service of Northern Ireland (PSNI) is smaller and less experienced than the Royal Ulster Constabulary that it replaced. The British army officially ended Operation Banner, its longest continuous operation ever, in effect since 1969. But it left a garrison of 5,000 soldiers to offer support to the police. Few people are ready to remove the 50 "peace walls" that separate Catholic and Protestant housing, and a few more have been constructed.

More time is needed to build trust and complete the healing. That was demonstrated in March 2009, when two British soldiers, who had ordered a last pizza before deploying to Afghanistan, were gunned down when they stepped out of their Northern Irish base to take the delivery. Two days later a constable answering a call was shot in the head. These were the first murders of security forces since 1998, and four rejectionist groupings (the

Real and Continuity IRAs, ONH, and the Irish National Liberation Army), who may number no more than a few hundred, claimed responsibility.

The remarkable thing was the political leaders' and citizens' response: Thousands joined in silent marches and vigils all over the province to condemn the killings. Sinn Fein deputy first minister Martin McGuinness called the dissidents "traitors to the island of Ireland" and "Neanderthals." Breaking with tradition, then–first minister Peter Robinson, a Protestant, attended a funeral mass for a Catholic constable murdered near Omagh in April 2011. The hard-line factions who reject the peace agreement seem to have no clearer strategy than to get Britain out of Northern Ireland by plunging the province back into bloody strife. Their chances of success are nil, given the fact that 90% of nationalists are reconciled to the peace settlement. But security forces worry that the dissident splinter groups have recruited former IRA veterans to join them and lend their expertise in booby traps and car bombs. Since the settlement has brought little economic improvement to the island, authorities fear that bored unemployed young people could be drawn into the small violent groups.

The year 2010 saw major progress in the power-sharing and reconciliation process. In February, after almost two weeks of marathon negotiations overseen by the British and Irish governments and supported by ex–US secretary of state Hillary Clinton and former president George W. Bush, a landmark agreement was reached giving the Northern Irish government direct responsibility for policing and justice. This includes responsibility for police, prisons, and the prosecution service. This "devolution of policing" was the last missing piece of the Good Friday agreement that established power sharing.

In March all the nationalist members and most of the unionists (except the UUP) voted for the historic measure in Stormont. In accepting it, Sinn Fein agreed for the first time to recognize and cooperate with the British state. Winning the DUP's unanimous support for the deal was a personal triumph for then–first minister Peter Robinson and eliminated demands for his resignation. Despite a series of bomb attacks by deadly splinter groups attempting to undermine the agreement, it took effect on April 12. The same day, Northern Ireland's first justice minister in four decades was appointed, David Ford.

Power sharing has provided considerable political harmony and has ended most paramilitary violence, even though it has not eliminated the last die-hard bombers and gunmen. Nor are the Orange

€3.80 Albania US$2; Australia A$7.50 (inc GST); Bulgaria BGL7.30; Canada C$ 5.95 (Toronto C$ 5.50); Croatia KN30; Cyprus €3.80 C€ 2.22; Czech Rep CK106; Denmark DK33; Estonia K30; Gibraltar GE0.80; Hungary F780; Kenya KSH230; Latvia LVL 1.35; Malta €3.20; Morocco D33; Norway NK40; Poland Z€14.00; Romania €4.20; Russia US$2.79; Slovakia €3.80/Sk; 14.50; Sweden SK43; Switzerland SF7.20; Thailand B190; Turkey TL 6.00; Ukraine US$3.50; USA US$3.75

Election 2010

Latest news, comment and analysis on 24 hours of political drama in the UK

International edition
Saturday 08.05.10
guardian.co.uk

theguardian

weekend edition

- Tory and Labour leaders make rival offers to Lib Dems
- Brown remains in Downing Street after inconclusive result
- Markets suffer most frenetic day since bank crisis began

Clegg: deal or no deal?

Patrick Wintour
Nicholas Watt
Allegra Stratton

David Cameron was last night trying to form the first Tory government since 1997 by offering a deal to the Liberal Democrats, including the possibility of cabinet seats and a cross-party committee of inquiry into electoral reform.

After being thwarted in his bid to secure an overall Commons majority, leaving Britain with its first hung parliament in 36 years, Cameron reached out to Nick Clegg with what he described as a "big, open and comprehensive" offer.

But it left senior Liberal Democrats divided on how to respond, with Gordon Brown also pitching to secure Clegg's support with a more concrete offer of reform of the electoral system - one of the Liberal Democrats' most cherished and totemic policies.

In an extraordinary day of political horsetrading, held against the background of volatile markets, Cameron said he was open either to a full coalition with the Liberal Democrats or a formal agreement whereby a minority Tory government was guaranteed more than the passage of its budget and the Queen's speech.

The carefully crafted proposal was designed to trump a rival earlier offer made to Clegg by Brown, who made a statement outside Downing Street in which he insisted he was getting on with government while the Conservatives and Lib Dems began negotiating. Brown made clear he would continue as prime minister until a deal was done. He said it was his "constitutional duty to seek to resolve the situation for the good of the country".

Cameron then took the initiative after an unexpectedly resilient Labour campaign left the Conservatives with 307 seats, a net rise of 98, but 17 seats short of an overall majority. Cameron's setback was greeted with relief by Labour, which finished with 258 MPs, down 91. The Lib Dems were surprisingly down five seats on 57, with other parties on 28. The Conservatives got a 36.1% share of the vote (up 3.8%), Labour 29.1% (down 6.2%) and the Lib Dems 23% (up 1%).

Facing fierce internal party criticism over his campaign's effectiveness, Cameron had to tread carefully in making his offer to Clegg in order not to spark a rebel

Gordon Brown, 1.48pm
'I would be prepared to discuss with Mr Clegg the areas where there may be some measure of agreement ...'

David Cameron, 2.39pm
'I want to make a big, open and comprehensive offer to the Liberal Democrats ...'

WITH THE OUTCOME OF THE GENERAL ELECTION WE FIND OURSELVES IN A POSITION UNKNOWN TO THIS GENERATION OF POLITICAL LEADERS, WITH NO SINGLE PARTY ABLE TO WIN A COMMONS MAJORITY. THEREFORE HAVE A MAJORITY GOVERNMENT.

THEREFORE FELT I SHOULD GIVE YOU, AND THROUGH YOU THE COUNTRY, AN ASSESSMENT OF WHERE WE ARE.

I DO SO AS PRIME MINISTER WITH A CONSTITUTIONAL DUTY TO SEEK TO RESOLVE THE SITUATION FOR THE GOOD OF THE COUNTRY AT A TIME OF THE LEADER OF THE LABOUR PARTY FOR A DAY ACTING ...

Seats won

306
258

Share of vote

29%   36.5%

25%   23%

Key developments

- First hung parliament since 1974
- LibDems slump
- First Green MP
- First Muslim women MPs
- Legal challenges over ballots
- BNP routed
- Charles Clarke, Jacqui Smith among high-profile casualties

lion among his MPs, who are deeply worried electoral reform would leave them shut out of government for decades.

He admitted there were policy disagreements between the Tories and Lib Dems - including on the EU, immigration, spending cuts this year and defence. But he insisted there were also "many areas of common ground" such as a "pupil premium" in schools, a low-carbon economy, tax reform for the low paid and shared opposition to Labour's ID cards scheme. Crucially, he did not pledge a

2-11 »

Continued on page 2 »

Order marches free of violence yet. Only three months after the handover of police powers, hundreds of rioters in Belfast battled the police with gasoline bombs, bricks, metal bars, planks, and concrete slabs, leaving 82 police officers injured. The violence, reminiscent of earlier times, erupted when the Orange Order rejected a new system for mediating the routes and timing of the marches. Nevertheless, power sharing has enormously improved life in Northern Ireland. In the May 5, 2011, regional elections, the DUP and Sinn Fein consolidated their positions, and their leaders remained in power.

A flag debate showed how much passion can be whipped up. The Belfast city council voted in late 2012 to stop flying the Union Jack every day at city hall; instead, it would be flown only for 18 days a year, including on the birthdays of the British royals. For weeks Loyalist protesters took to the streets to protest the decision.

The year 2010 witnessed an electrifying apology by newly elected prime minister David Cameron. On June 15, a 10-volume, 5,000-page final report was issued on the events of January 30, 1972, a fateful day known as "Bloody Sunday." British paratroopers opened fire upon unarmed demonstrators during a civil rights march in the Bogside area of Londonderry, leaving 14 men dead and 13 injured. It was a deeply held nationalist grievance, and relatives' requests for an investigation went unanswered. In 1998 then–prime minister Blair ordered what became the longest and most expensive public inquiry in British history to be conducted.

After 12 years, more than 900 witnesses and a cost of $288 million, Cameron stood up in the House of Commons to announce the conclusions: The soldiers had shown a "widespread loss of fire discipline. Some members of our armed forces

acted wrongly." The demonstrators had not provoked the attacks. Even Martin McGuinness, who was present and probably armed with a submachine gun, did not "engage in any activity that provided any of the soldiers with any justification for opening fire. What happened should never, ever have happened." The shootings were "both unjustified and unjustifiable." And then the dramatic words: "On behalf of the government, I am deeply sorry."

In Londonderry, thousands gathered at the site of the shooting and cheered as the prime minister's speech was broadcast live on giant screens. The inquiry left some open questions. The main one is whether to prosecute any of the soldiers. However, few are in favor of such a move, especially given the fact that all IRA members accused and jailed for terrorist activities have been released as a part of the peace process.

The queen is also playing an important role in the reconciliation that is extending across the Irish Sea. In 2011 she went to Dublin. This was the first visit by a reigning British monarch to the Irish Republic. The following year she ended a visit to Northern Ireland by shaking hands with Martin McGuinness, who had belonged to the terrorist organization that murdered her cousin Lord Mountbatten in 1979. Elizabeth smiled but did not speak while McGuinness spoke to her in Irish, using words that translated to "goodbye and Godspeed." The brief meeting signified a new era. Prince Charles followed up in May 2015 by meeting with Gerry Adams in Galway. McGuinness died in 2017 without his dream of a united Ireland being fulfilled. He was replaced by Michelle O'Neill.

When clashes in the assembly and Belfast streets broke out in July 2013, former American diplomat Richard Haass was asked to help find a compromise on three issues: how violent crimes committed during the Troubles should be investigated, whether and when the union flag could fly from public buildings, and what rules should govern parades. Months of negotiations, seven position papers, and visits by both the British and Irish prime ministers failed to resolve the issues. But some progress was made in identifying areas of agreement and disagreement and on the issue of historical crimes.

The talks resumed. A gangland murder in Belfast with suspected IRA involvement in 2015 set off a political crisis that prompted Peter Robinson to step down as first minister. He was replaced in January 2016 by Arlene Foster, the first woman and also the youngest to occupy that post. When McGuinness resigned in January 2017 because of Foster's "arrogance" and "inflexibility," a snap election was called for March 2. The two unionist parties won only 38 seats in the assembly out of 90 (the new total number of seats). Foster stepped down as first minister, but she assumed that office again in January 2020. Sinn Fein surged. When Gerry Adams retired in 2018, he was replaced by Mary Lou Mc-Donald, who sought to soften Sinn Fein's image. (See Ireland chapter that follows.)

TODAY'S POLITICAL PARTIES

Like any modern democracy, the British system could not function without parties. They recruit and select candidates, define issues that are important, educate voters about them, finance and fight electoral campaigns, put up governments that rule at all political levels, and provide well-organized opposition that continually remind the electorate of the government's shortcomings. For the government, the party is an essential tool for maintaining a parliamentary majority, and for the individual politician, it is the ladder to power. For the political activist, it is an important means for putting his ideas into practice. For the voter, it is an indispensable label for a set of politicians, policies, sympathies, or interests.

British parties bear some similarities to those of America, but there is a striking difference that stems from a fundamental difference in the two political systems: The real power in American parties is at the bottom of the hierarchy; a national party in America is nothing more than a loose coalition of state and local parties. By contrast, in Britain the real power within the party is at the top.

Basically, all British parties have a similar organization. At the lowest level are party units in the wards, which are grouped together into 650 constituency parties, each of which struggles for a seat in the House of Commons. These ward or constituency parties raise funds (part of which must be passed up to the national party), recruit members, campaign at election time, and select candidates.

National parties rarely try to overrule constituent parties' choice of candidates, although the national parties clearly influence the selection. The most obvious evidence is that about half of all MPs do not reside in their constituencies before their election to Parliament. Unlike the US, there is no legal requirement for this. The national party leaders search all over Britain for "safe seats" for important MPs. Constituency party leaders often decide that national party interests override their own local desires. All constituency parties are grouped into regional organizations, which, except in Wales and Scotland, have little importance.

At the national level, each party organizes an annual conference, to which each constituency sends representatives. This large conference debates and adopts the party's overall policy (which is never binding on the party if it is in power) and, in the case of Labour, elects the party's leadership. At the national level, two other party organizations also exist. The central bureaucracy assists the party at all levels. The parliamentary party consists of the MPs and members of the House of Lords belonging to it.

All British parties are coalitions of differing interests and ideologies. It is often assumed that British parties are class parties. While this, to a diminishing extent, is true of the Labour Party, the Conservative Party has always had an appeal which cuts across class lines. In terms of policy, the major parties have normally been far closer together than is often assumed. From 1945 until the early 1970s, there was a large measure of consensus among the major parties. All were agreed on a welfare state, the mixed public-private economy which permitted much state intervention in the economy, and employer-union-government collaboration (sometimes referred to as "corporatism").

Some observers even spoke of the "end of ideology" in Britain. That broad consensus collapsed in the 1970s, and both the Conservative and Labour Parties became more ideologically oriented. By the 1983 elections, the major parties had become more polarized than they had been in a half-century. Margaret Thatcher's embrace of market-oriented economics and rejection of state intervention, of "welfarism," and of "corporatism" was matched by revived class-warfare rhetoric in the Labour Party. Its moderate wing found itself placed on the defensive by the left wing, which demanded radical changes in Britain's social, economic, and political power structures. Sir Winston Churchill's observation was no longer correct that "four-fifths of the two major British parties agree about four-fifths of the things that need to be done." But four defeats in a row from 1979 to 1992 prompted Labour to move toward the political center. The payoff—three general election victories in a row—exceeded its wildest expectations.

The first-past-the-post electoral system is designed to favor the two large parties. However, the Conservative and Labour Parties have been steadily losing both seats and members. In 1951, 97% of all voters chose one or the other of these two parties; by 2015 that had declined to only 67.3%. This increases the likelihood of governing coalitions, not one-party majorities. The 19th-century prime minister Benjamin Disraeli noted that England "does not love coalitions." Membership

is also going down. In the 1950s, with a smaller British population, 4 million voters were card-carrying party members; by the 2010 elections, only 500,000 belonged to one of the three main parties, with the governing Conservatives counting only 200,000. Members who remain are less active than earlier.

The Conservative Party

The Conservative Party (also known as the Tory Party) is conscious of its heritage, which it traces back to the 17th century. Its pragmatic approach has always enabled it to appeal to British from all classes, even though its strongest appeal could be found among those who were well-off economically. At the heart of the Tory Party, as it was formerly known, is the unity of the whole nation. It has always preferred voluntary effort to public assistance, and this stems from its insistence on free enterprise in industry, advocacy of the profit motive, and indirect (sales) taxes rather than direct (income) taxes.

It has never argued that the state has no role in the economy, and it even nationalized industries under certain circumstances, such as the Central Electricity Board in 1926 and Rolls-Royce in 1971. Nor has it ever rejected the notion that the state should provide social welfare services sensibly. In her 1987 campaign, Margaret Thatcher said that all decent people want to help the ill, the unemployed, and the aged but that a healthy economy is needed to provide the level of services which the British want.

There has, of course, always been division within Tory ranks between proponents of more state intervention and those who favor less regulation and a much freer market economy. Some of the differences in political orientation within the party are reflected in well-established pressure groups: They include the Bow Group, which presses for policies which benefit all classes; the Monday Club (the old right); the Tory Reform Group (progressives); and the Charter Movement, who want to democratize the party.

It was publicly known in 1975, when Thatcher defeated Edward Heath for the party leadership, that the new leader represented a different Toryism than Heath. After she became prime minister in 1979, those persons in her cabinet who loyally supported her views were dubbed "dries." Those who had doubts about her medicine, especially about how it would affect millions of citizens and their families, were dubbed "wets." In a cabinet reshuffle after the 1983 and 1987 elections, she dismissed the "wets" in her cabinet.

Thatcher's stunning victory in the 1987 elections revealed that, although she was an unpopular and unloved leader,

The United Kingdom

British voters respected her no-nonsense competence and will. They grudgingly accepted her bitter economic medicine of sound money, hard work, and standing on one's own two feet. She was the first prime minister to win a third consecutive term in modern British history and surpassed Winston Churchill and H. H. Asquith as Britain's longest-serving prime minister in the 20th century. Why did she win?

The first reason is that her opposition was severely divided. Second, the prime minister had won considerable stature and influence in the international arena. She could boast with justification that "we have put the Great back into Britain." The main reason for her victory was the undeniable economic success her government had achieved.

Post-Thatcher

The willingness of France and Germany to relinquish more sovereignty to Europe widened the chasm between the UK and its continental partners. Thatcher's cabinet had been rocked by high-level resignations stemming from disagreements over Europe. In 1986 Michael Heseltine stormed out because he wanted a European consortium, not one from the US, to purchase a British helicopter company. In 1989 Nigel Lawson left because he wanted to include the pound in the European Monetary System (EMS). The fatal resignation—and the catalyst for her downfall—was that of Sir Goeffrey Howe, the last surviving member of her original 1979 cabinet and an architect of "Thatcherism." He charged in Parliament that her obstruction in Europe carried "serious risks for our nation."

The devastating speech led to a successful challenge to her leadership in November 1990. After a historic 11-year rule, the longest prime-ministership since the Victorian era and the longest consecutive one since the Napoleonic age, Thatcher resigned. The events leading to her fall related to Europe, but the reason 45% of her parliamentary party colleagues voted against her was that she was guiding her party toward defeat in the next elections. For 18 months her party had trailed in the polls a Labour Party that had become more moderate, had overthrown its suicidal commitment to nuclear disarmament, and had embraced the EU. Her country was experiencing high inflation, a growing trade deficit, a slowdown in economic growth, and intense domestic opposition to her poll tax for local governments.

With her leaving, the UK entered a period under John Major, Britain's youngest prime minister in the last century, until Labour leader Tony Blair evicted him from Number 10 Downing Street. Major was a self-made man from a very humble background and with no university education. His father had been a circus performer and minor league baseball player in the US. Major was the Iron Lady's protégé and handpicked successor. Nevertheless, he backed away from strident Thatcherism, abolishing the hated poll tax in 1991. He buried the grudge Thatcher had borne against both the EU and Germany and became a more cooperative European. Like Thatcher, he benefited from an unexpected war, this time in the Gulf in 1991, which went very well for Britain and its allies.

He entered the 1992 elections with the highest popularity rating of any British prime minister in three decades, but nobody expected his stunning victory in the midst of Britain's worst recession in a half-century. He led his party to a 21-seat majority, based on 42% of the votes and 336 seats (down from 376).

The Tory Party was deeply divided, especially over Britain's role in the EU. Major's government was sometimes held hostage by several dozen vocal Euroskeptics in his own party, including Thatcher herself, who were determined to sabotage all moves to a closer European union. The government appeared to be at war with itself and was dogged by a succession of scandals and sleaze. Voters were tired of Tory rule after 18 years. Even the party's most significant achievement—a booming economy and unemployment half as high as when Major took office in 1992—played in the opposition's favor, since voters seemed to think they could afford the risk of voting Labour.

The 2001 elections brought the second devastating defeat in a row for the Conservative Party. It won only one constituency in Scotland and none in Wales. It has become a regional party confined to the southeastern English countryside. It failed to win a single seat in any major city outside London, where it captured only 13 out of 74. It was demoralized after its two worst election defeats since 1906. Party leader William Hague resigned immediately. His replacement, Iain Duncan Smith, was selected by a new kind of primary election: First, the parliamentary party voted on the contenders. The top two candidates then were submitted to a vote by all 250,000 registered party members in the UK (average age over 65).

The Tories were jolted in 2002 by stories of another sensational sex scandal, this time involving John Major. Miffed that he had not mentioned her in his autobiography and had not given her a cabinet post during his prime-ministership, former education minister Edwina Currie and later talk-show host revealed in her published diaries that she and Major had had a four-year affair from 1984 to 1988.

She had indirectly alluded to this in her 1997 novel, A Parliamentary Affair. This lapse of judgment blemished both Major's reputation for honesty and the wisdom of his 1993 campaign, "back to the basics," calling for strict moral values.

Most Tories supported Prime Minister Blair's decision to participate in the war against Iraq in 2003, but this did not help the party in the polls. It remained internally divided, and Duncan Smith was a poor manager of people, a bad communicator and debater, and an uninspired strategist. In October 2003 he was deposed, becoming the first Tory leader to be dismissed without having the opportunity to fight an election. He confided to his colleagues that "only a lunatic would want to lead the Conservative Party."

He was replaced by Michael Howard, who was unopposed. The son of a Romanian-born father and Russian-born mother, Howard was the first professing Jew to lead a major British party. (Benjamin Disraeli was baptized as a child into the Church of England.) He led his party to defeat in the May 2005 parliamentary elections. It has won only about a third of the votes for three elections in a row. It gained some ground in the southeast and in prosperous London suburbs. But its continued division over Britain's place in Europe and campaign focus on the problem of immigration, demanding annual limits, turned many voters off.

Part of its problem is that Tony Blair's Labour Party adopted Margaret Thatcher's market reforms and notions of

British students celebrate the special relationship.

Daily Mail

FRIDAY, MAY 8, 2015   www.dailymail.co.uk   £2.70

PRINTED IN
EUROPE
FRIDAY

■ **Exit poll puts Tories on course for over 300 seats**

■ **Red Ed faces disaster with 'worst result for 30 years'**

■ **Clegg is 'humbled' – but SNP sweep the board**

CAMERON 'HEADING BACK TO NUMBER 10'

Confident of victory: David Cameron

DAVID Cameron appears to be heading back to Number 10 today after 'shy Tories' delivered an extraordinary late surge for his party.

Voters took to the polls in massive

By James Chapman
Political Editor

numbers yesterday and, although Britain was heading for a second hung parliament, the Conservatives were expected to pick up 316 seats, according to exit polls.

In a triumph for the Tories, they

looked likely to be the first ruling party since 1983 to put on seats.

Labour leader Ed Miliband's career – and that of Deputy Prime Minister Nick Clegg – appeared to have been brought to a crashing end as both of their parties were smashed.

Labour was on course for its worst result since Neil Kinnock's defeat in 1987, with a forecast of 239 seats. If TV

exit polls are correct – and they were in 2010 – the Lib Dems face more turmoil and will be left with just ten seats.

The Scottish Nationalists appeared to have delivered an earthquake north of the border, winning all but one seat in Scotland. That leaves Nicola Sturgeon as the leader of what is likely the

Turn to Page 2

economic efficiency. By doing that, New Labour not only made itself electable, but it also made it very difficult for the Conservatives to define how they are different from Labour. In 1998 The Economist called Blair "the strangest Tory ever sold."

Howard announced immediately that he would step down. His surprise replacement in 2005 was his young (then 39) protégé, David Cameron, whose mantra was "change to win." Only in Parliament since 2001, Cameron was down-to-earth, pragmatic, flexible, decisive, unflappable, and cool under pressure. He quickly managed to make the Tories look human and approachable again. He was likable, quick-witted, informal, self-assured, and charming. He assembled around him a strong team of young modernizers who could give the party a new face by "detoxifying the brand." He sought to bring more women and minorities into the party and Parliament. The Tories' and his own image had to change if it wanted to rule. He went by "Dave," wore jeans and open-necked shirts, rode his bicycle to Parliament (sometimes his limo drove behind

him with his briefcase), and supported environmental causes and LGBTQ rights. He made his party more socially liberal.

He was born in 1966 into wealth and privilege and is distantly related to the queen, being a descendent of a mistress of King William IV. At age seven, he was sent to an exclusive "public" school, Heatherdown. This prepared him for Eton, the traditional finishing school for the ruling classes, which had produced 18 prime ministers before him. He finished his education at Oxford.

The Tories entered the May 7, 2015, general elections head to head with Labour. However, voters, especially Scotsmen, were afraid of Labour rule. The Conservatives ended up winning 36.9% of the votes and 331 seats, a gain of 24 and an absolute majority. However, it remained practically invisible in Scotland, where it got only 1 seat out of 59, and in Wales.

Cameron, age 43 when he became PM (the age of John F. Kennedy when he won the presidency), was the youngest prime minister since the Second Earl of Liverpool two centuries earlier. In 2010 he was

forced to enter the first coalition government in 65 years and the first-ever Conservative–Liberal Democrat government.

The Conservative Party remains ambivalent about Europe. The anti-EU UK Independence Party (UKIP), led by Nigel Farage, demands "we want our country back!" and Euroskeptics within his Conservative Party are nipping at his heels. In May 2015 UKIP captured 12.6% of the votes but only one seat.

Cameron wanted opt-outs from such things as the EU's social chapter, charter of fundamental rights, employment laws, environment, justice, security policy, and immigration. He and most of his party comrades wanted to remain in the EU, but they did not want the euro, and they wanted a new relationship that retains the trading advantages without the closer political union, the regulatory burdens, and the financial contributions.

Cameron said he would give "heart and soul" to win a vote to remain in the EU. If voters rejected it, the government would have to enter torturous negotiations for an exit from the EU. Surveys in 2015 had indicated that a majority wanted to stay in. The prime minister was caught between the strong anti-Europe faction in his Tory Party and powerful business groups who favored continuing close ties with Britain's most important trading partner. A referendum was held on June 23, 2016. The results were a disaster: 52% voted to leave.

Its relations with America are cordial for the most part, despite Cameron's statement that "we should be solid but not slavish in our friendship with America. I and my party are instinctive friends of America and passionate supporters of the Atlantic alliance." He is aware that "we are the junior partner." The first phone call from abroad to congratulate him after walking through the door at Number 10 Downing Street was from President Barack Obama. Both leaders rebranded their countries' ties as "the essential relationship."

Cameron created Britain's own National Security Council in 2010 with a staff of 200. It is a useful forum for senior politicians and meets with members of the American equivalent four times a year.

Cameron also announced that he would not run for a third term. However, events outpaced him after losing the Brexit vote in June 2016. He departed a few weeks later. He was replaced by Home Secretary Teresa May. She used her prerogative in 2017 to call new elections set for June 8. This decision backfired spectacularly: The Tories lost 43 seats and their majority and had to form a government with 10 demanding Northern Irish unionists. May was replaced as prime minister by former London mayor Boris Johnson.

The United Kingdom

The Labour Party

Although its roots extend far back into the 19th century, the Labour Party was officially founded in 1900. Under the influence of the small but well-connected Fabian Society, which sought to reform British society gradually from above rather than through violent revolution or labor union agitation from below, the party adopted in 1918 a new constitution which transformed it officially into a socialist party. It proclaimed that the goal of the party is to "secure for the producers by hand or by brain the full fruits of their industry and the most equitable distribution thereof that may be possible upon the basis of common ownership of the means of production and the best obtainable system of popular administration and control of each industry and service."

That purely Marxist objective helped prevent the Labour Party from sharing the fate of many socialist parties in Europe that split apart in the aftermath of the Russian Revolution. However, it became the source of continuous intraparty friction ever since. During most of its history, the party was in reality more moderate than its constitution might indicate. It sought to "democratize" the economy by nationalizing key industries and regulating others, to distribute wealth more equally, to expand social welfare services, and to eliminate class differences.

During the Thatcher government Labour took a leftward lurch and embarked upon an almost-suicidal political course. Grossly underestimating Britain's first woman prime minister and the public support for her economic austerity policies, the Labour Party committed itself to radical promises: unilateral nuclear disarmament, withdrawal from the EU, massive nationalization of industries, and huge increases in public spending.

This led to an electoral disaster, and in the 1983 elections, it suffered its worst defeat in 60 years. Its 27.6% was Labour's lowest popular vote since 1918 and was 20 percentage points lower than in 1966. Almost a quarter of those voters who had identified themselves consistently with the Labour Party abandoned it.

It failed to win a majority of the votes among the working class or among labor-union members. This was a severe setback for a party created by and organizationally linked to the unions; it seriously hollowed out the party's claim to be the party of the worker. Only the traditional working class remained more loyal: that segment who worked in nationalized or "smokestack" industries or who lived in council housing, Scotland, Wales, or the north of England. This represented the most significant basic shift in the social basis of British politics since World War II.

'New Labour has the vision – and the energy – to build a strong dynamic economy breathing new life into Britain'

Campaign brochure for Charlotte Atkins

Within hours after the polls had closed, the move to replace the ineffective Labour leader Michael Foot began. The choice was Neil Kinnock. He began immediately to mend the gaping, intraparty split between the left and right, which had led to electoral disaster and the massive drop in party membership between 1979 and 1983, to a level comparable to that of 1945. He moderated his party's views on the EU, defense, and the status of capitalism. With a sharp eye on the social changes which have occurred in Britain, Kinnock announced that Labour must appeal to the "newly well-off" and should be a party which appeals to the haves, as well as the have-nots. Foot passed away in 2010.

Going into the 1987 elections, the party shied away from extremism. Its platform purged the earlier pledges to abolish the House of Lords (which has been critical of some of Thatcher's policies), to nationalize much more industry, and to control the country's banking system. It accepted the principle of selling public-owned houses, and it no longer opposed the UK's membership in the EU. An enormous electoral liability was Kinnock's decision to stand by his party's unilateral nuclear disarmament position. The electoral effect was suicide. The party suffered its second-worst defeat in more than a half-century, capturing only 32% of the votes and 229 seats.

In the 1992 elections, it faced important social changes which worked against it: Its traditional support base—trade-union members, manual laborers, and tenants of state-owned housing—is shrinking. Party leaders conducted a thorough rethinking of its positions. In order to be able to present a credible challenge to the Conservatives, Labour had to develop a moderate, nonsocialist program. It unveiled its new policy, which scrapped unilateral nuclear disarmament, as well as vote-losing calls for withdrawal from NATO, removal of US military bases in Britain, scuttling the Trident nuclear submarine program, and state ownership of industry. It reconciled itself to the market system.

The year 1992 seemed ideal for a Labour victory, but voters handed Labour its fourth consecutive defeat, even though it climbed to 35% of the votes and 271 seats. Voters continued to associate it with crippling strikes, chaos, and economic decline. Kinnock had begun to introduce the kinds of changes that would ultimately lead his party to victory in 1997, but he had failed at the time to persuade his countrymen that Labour's transformation and pragmatism were genuine and lasting.

In 1994 another leader who could bring the party victory was chosen: Tony Blair. The son of a lifelong Conservative, Blair was educated at a private boys' school and studied law at Oxford. He took no interest in student politics and spent his spare time singing in a rock band called Ugly Rumours. He entered Parliament in 1983 representing a traditional Labour constituency in the north. He bore no scars of Labour's dismal rule in the 1970s, and he was its first leader with no roots in the labor movement and with no grounding in traditional socialism.

This made it easier for him to complete the process of modernizing his party. He lessened its dependency upon and identification with unpopular unions. In the 1960s, union money made up 80% of the party's budget; by 1995 that figure was 50% and then 30% by 1998. That began rising again to 57% in 2005, 78% in 2006, nearly 90% in 2007, and more than 90% in 2010, as donations from wealthy entrepreneurs dried up. He remained silent during a 13-week railway strike in 1994, breaking a long tradition of unfailing party support for the unions' actions. He curbed the voting power of union leaders, who had controlled large blocks within the party. In 2014 the party further weakened its institutional links to the unions by changing the selection of its leader to a simple one-person-one-vote system. Their power was diluted by changes in the complicated rules governing party voting and policy making.

He persuaded the powerful NEC to accept his revision of clause 4 of the party constitution, setting aside the party's 1918 commitment to public ownership of key industries. This had been a major obstacle to its return to power. Blair confessed later that scrapping clause 4 had "shown me what I intuitively thought but wasn't sure of: that the party was actually behind change." Since it was a democratic process every step of the way, he was sure that most of the party's rank and file had changed and were behind the reform.

Through his patience, charm, and power of persuasion, he reversed the radicalism within the party and opened it up to fresh ideas. He led Labour toward the political center. He ceased regarding Labour as a tribal party focusing on the working class. By enhancing its appeal among the middle class in the heavily populated south of Britain, he aimed directly at the bedrock of the Tories' support. He was highly confident, disciplined, focused, energetic, and quick to master a brief. He was also sometimes accused of being brutally autocratic when it came to bringing his party in line with his reforms, a quality Margaret Thatcher is said to have admired in him. Unlike Thatcher, though, who relished battering her opponents into submission, Blair preferred logical argument and persuasion.

In the 1997 elections, he demonstrated what a skillful campaigner he was. He could orchestrate a tightly organized campaign, present himself convincingly in two television debates with his opponent (an innovation in British campaigns), "work a crowd" very effectively, and inspire voters without promising too much. His main challenge was to convince voters that his party had indeed shed the heavy baggage of the past. He stuck to a single message: that his party was now "New Labour." "The old ideologies are dead. New Labour is offering a new and different form of politics. . . . There has been a revolution inside the Labour Party. We have rejected the worst of our past and rediscovered the best. . . . We have made ourselves fit to face the future."

He distanced his party from the "outdated ideology" of high taxes financing expensive government programs, from powerful unions, and from unilateral nuclear disarmament. He established friendly relations with business leaders. He vowed neither to renationalize industries nor raise income taxes. Instead, he pledged to keep inflation low, to spend no more than the Tories had already budgeted but nevertheless to improve the struggling National Health Service and the school system, to introduce a minimum wage, to combat crime, and to reform the constitution.

Seeing too little difference between his program and that of the Tories, some observers dubbed him "Tony Blur." He responded by arguing, "I do not think everything that has happened in the last 18 years has been bad. My attitude is: keep what is working and change what is not." Clearly Britain's economy was already working well. This fact persuaded even more voters that there was little danger in voting for a Labour Party that promised not to tamper with one of Europe's most robust economies. Blair assured his countrymen within hours after his victory, "We ran as New Labour and will govern as New Labour."

The electoral payoff for Labour was historic: It won 418 of 659 seats on the basis of 43.1% of the votes. Its majority of 179 seats was its best performance ever. It wiped the Tories out of Scotland and Wales altogether and made deep inroads into Tory strongholds in southern England and London, capturing even Thatcher's north London Finchley constituency. In a stunning turnaround, women flocked to Labour, which won 53% of their votes (compared with 30% who voted Tory). The number of women with seats in the House of Commons shot up from 63 to 120, and 101 of them were from Labour. Most of the nine ethnic minorities, including a wealthy Muslim man, elected to Parliament ran on the Labour ticket. Blair's cabinet also contained many firsts: five women; an openly gay man (Chris Smith,

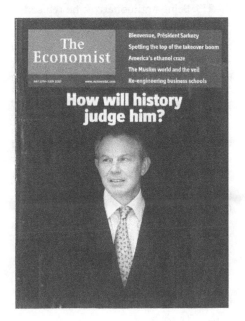

secretary of state for culture, media, and sport, who later admitted that he is HIV positive); and a blind man, David Plunkett, as education and employment secretary. Plunkett resigned in 2004 because of his affair with a married woman and his attempts to speed up the visa process for her nanny.

In the June 2001 elections, which saw a startling 12% drop in turnout to 59%, the lowest since 1918, Labour slipped to 42% and lost six seats. Nevertheless, with 413 seats, it still commanded two-thirds of the seats in the House of Commons. This was the first time in its century of existence that it had succeeded in being reelected to a second full term.

Turnout rose slightly to 61% in the May 2005 elections. Labour's share of the votes fell by 4.5% to 35.2% of the total votes, the lowest percentage ever recorded by a winning party since 1832. Hurt by the growing unpopularity of the Iraq War, new tuition charges at universities, foundation hospitals, and damaged credibility from a wide range of other domestic policies (more than half the voters surveyed a few days before the elections said he could not be trusted), Labour also suffered a loss of over half its majority in the House of Commons, falling to a nevertheless comfortable 67. As in the two earlier elections, it benefited from the division of the opposition.

Blair became the first Labour prime minister in British history to win a third straight term. Turning 52 the day after the elections, he said that this would be his last election as prime minister. This was an unprecedented declaration for such a relatively young leader to make.

On June 27, 2007, he passed on the leadership to his chancellor of the exchequer, Gordon Brown, the intellectual son of a Presbyterian minister, an admirer of the United States, and excellent manager of the economy. He had entered Edinburgh University at the age of 16 and was elected its rector at 21. Hardworking and extremely smart, he held strong views about poverty and injustice.

Brown's three-year tenure as prime minister was troubled. He was reported to be mean to his staff ("grumpy Gordon"), and his declining poll figures and electoral prospects sparked within his party mutterings that he should go. He had to suppress two open rebellions. He failed to connect with the public. During the 2010 campaign, he committed one of the most damaging gaffes in recent British electoral history. In an arranged sidewalk meeting, a Labour voter asked him about immigration, a major issue in the election. Back in his limousine, Brown called the encounter "a disaster" and the woman "bigoted." But he had forgotten to turn off his lapel

The United Kingdom

Prime Minister David Cameron and Deputy Prime Minister Nick Clegg form the government, 2010.

microphone, so his remarks were picked up by a TV station and broadcast. He never recovered.

Election day, May 6, 2010, was not a pleasant experience for the party that had ruled 13 years. It captured only 29% of the votes (down 6%) and 258 seats (a loss of 89). The only regions where it won big were Scotland (41 of 59 seats) and Wales (26 of 40). No party won a majority (this being the first "hung Parliament" since 1974).

The Liberal Democrats' price for a governing alliance with Labour was too high: that Brown step down as prime minister. According to Mandelson's memoir that appeared only two months after the election (*The Third Man: Life at the Heart of New Labour*), the embittered and exhausted leader moaned, "I have been humiliated enough."

Seeing his political future in ruins, Brown quickly resigned his leadership, and the jostling of contenders began. In the selection process, the unions have one-third of the votes, the Labour MPs another third, and rank-and-file Labour members also a third. Voters rank the candidates in order of preference. If no candidate garners 50% on the first round, the second choices of those who voted for the last-place finisher are distributed until one person has a majority.

The favorite was former foreign secretary David Miliband, a 44-year-old modernizer supported by the Blair wing in the party. He refused to repudiate New Labour's record and had the majority of support by the party's MPs and rank-and-file members. But his younger brother Ed Miliband (age 40) narrowly beat him 50.65% to 49.35% after four rounds of voting. "Red Ed" successfully tapped the unions, a segment of the party that had

long been ignored. David gave up his parliamentary seat in 2013 and accepted a job as chief executive of the International Rescue Committee in New York.

A 2012 poll for the *Sun* showed that only 19% of respondents thought Miliband looked fit to be prime minister. In May 2015, the British marked their ballots accordingly. The results were a disaster, Labour's worst since 1987. It won 30.4% of the votes (up 1.5%). But it fell to 232 seats (a loss of 26). It collapsed in Scotland, winning only 1 seat, while the SNP captured 56 of 59. Miliband resigned as leader.

He was replaced by a man of the hard left, Jeremy Corbyn. He wants to take the party back to its roots in the working class. He is stridently anti-American, anti-NATO, antinuclear deterrent, and anti-Israel. He opposes an EU trade deal with the US. Being antimonarchy, he refused to sing "God Save the Queen" during a commemoration of World War II veterans. He had little support among Labour MPs, and moderates left the party in droves. Labour entered the June 8, 2017, elections with its most leftist manifesto since 1983: renationalizing royal mail and some nail and energy companies, scrapping university tuition fees, and increasing spending on health and social services. It won 40% of the votes, a gain of 9.5%. Corbyn consolidated his position.

Corbyn's far-left policies and tolerance for anti-Semitism were electoral suicide. In the December 2019 elections, Labour suffered its worst defeat since 1935. He was replaced as party leader by Sir Keir Starmer.

Tony Blair's Legacy
It became increasingly difficult for Blair to find a parliamentary majority. His

party performed poorly in the May 2007 local and regional elections. Scandals involving questionable party donations, sexual misbehavior, and failure on the part of some of his ministers, along with the unpopularity of the Iraq War, beset Labour. These prompted irresistible calls for Blair to make way for his successor. An increasingly popular Tory Party with a dynamic new bike-riding green leader, David Cameron, was able to exploit this. On June 27, 2007, Blair handed the keys to the prime minister's office to Gordon Brown, his chancellor of the exchequer for a decade. What many analysts will discuss for years in the future is the legacy that this extraordinary politician and statesman will leave behind.

Leading his party to three straight electoral victories (something no Labour leader had ever done), Blair was Britain's most successful Labour prime minister ever. He moved his leftist party to the center, where elections can be won, and he eliminated Labour's reputation for incompetence in government. He made British politics competitive by making Labour electable again. He removed hereditary peers from the House of Lords and reformed that upper chamber irreversibly. He extended self-government to Scotland and Wales. He was also the driving force in achieving a power-sharing agreement in Northern Ireland, perhaps his greatest success.

He left Britain a better country. The average citizen is more prosperous, and Britain's openness to large numbers of immigrants boosted the economy without producing a serious backlash. The war in Iraq cost him his popularity. He persuaded a majority to allow universities to charge higher tuition fees, thereby beginning to solve higher education's chronic underfunding. Now 40% go to universities.

In his decade as prime minister, the challenges facing his country shifted from domestic to foreign policy, as he was forced to face terrorism, energy shortages, and climate change. He was Britain's most pro-EU leader ever. At the same time, he attempted to guard his country's traditionally close ties with the United States. More than any other leader, he built the coalition that ended genocide in Kosovo and terminated the murderous career of Serbian president Slobodan Milosevic. He was a key player in the successful war to end Taliban rule in Afghanistan. He brought peace to Sierra Leone, after murderous rebels kidnapped 500 UN peacekeepers and threatened to renew warfare.

Blair is still young and vigorous, and he remains an international star. The UN tapped his expertise on the Middle East by appointing him special Middle East envoy for the Quartet (UN, EU, US, Russia)

THE TIMES

Thursday November 6 2008 timesonline.co.uk No 69,454   80p

Inside 24-page souvenir

Ben Macintyre, Maya Angelou, an extract from his autobiography Dreams From My Father and a new poem by Derek Walcott

Plus the victory speech in full

Obama

Obama gets to work

President-elect starts to form his administration

Tom Baldwin Washington

62.5%
The highest turnout since 1960

Barack Obama, the President-elect, has appointed a chief of staff and an advisory board to set up his administration

---

it won only 57 seats in the House of Commons, less than 9% of the total.

Many analysts had believed that the precursors to the LDP could supplant the Labour Party and that the former Social Democrats and the traditionally independent, undisciplined Liberals could forge a partnership that could "break the mold of British politics." But they had failed to establish themselves as an electable nonsocialist alternative. That made their merger unavoidable.

It was led for 11 years by Paddy Ashdown. He stepped down as leader in 1999, having rescued the party from the splits and name changes of the 1980s and having moved it close to the center of power. Former journalist Charles Kennedy, a good-humored Scotsman, replaced him and led the party in the 2001 elections, in which it captured an impressive 18.8% of the votes and 52 seats. The party's opposition to the 2003 war in Iraq paid political dividends as enthusiasm for the war wore off. In 2006 Kennedy stepped down as leader after being forced to admit that he had sought medical treatment for a drinking problem. He was replaced by former Olympic sprinter Sir Menzies Campbell, who in December 2007 handed the leadership over to Nick Clegg (then age 40) after the party had been the big loser in the May local elections.

WORLD

The queen and First Lady embrace
Source: *Maclean's*

---

the day he left Number 10. Among other jobs, he was appointed a senior adviser at JP Morgan Chase; a consultant on international politics for Zurich Financial Services, Switzerland's largest insurer; and senior green technology adviser at Khosla Ventures in Silicon Valley.

He agreed to teach a course at Yale University during the 2008–2009 academic year on faith and globalization and to work with the divinity and management faculties as a Howland Distinguished Fellow. He runs the Faith Foundation on reconciling religions. He employs about 150 people around the world to administer a variety of good causes, and he spends at least two-thirds of his time on unpaid work. He lectures for astronomical honoraria and signed a lucrative deal for his top-selling memoirs, A Journey. It is ironic that the two most important prime ministers since World War II who changed Britain the most—Blair and Margaret Thatcher—are far more popular in the United States than in their own country.

The Liberal Democrats

In reaction to the Labour Party's earlier swing to the left, a group from the party bolted and in 1981 formed the Social Democratic Party (SDP). This new grouping sought to occupy the center ground of the British political spectrum, which had opened up because of the polarization between the two larger parties. Its strategy was to align with the older Liberal Party of the center.

The Liberals had been one of the two major parties during the 19th century, but it had not been in power since the Labour Party eclipsed it just after World War I. Their heaviest emphasis has been on individual freedom, and it speaks for decentralization of state power, for a greater focus of local political issues, and for workers' (not union) councils sharing control with management. Both the Liberals and the SDP strongly support European integration and reform of the electoral system in favor of proportional representation.

Just how important such a change would be for what is now named the Liberal Democratic Party (LDP or "Lib Dems," previously called the SDP-Liberal Alliance and the Social and Liberal Democrats) was demonstrated in the 2010 elections. It won 23% of the vote. Its even support across the entire class spectrum proved that it was not merely a fashionable "wine and cheese" grouping, as critics sometimes charge. But

The United Kingdom

Unlike most British politicians, Clegg, a former EU trade negotiator and member of the European Parliament for five years, is a Europhile through and through who spent his formative political years in Brussels. He was born to a half-Russian banker father and a Dutch mother. He speaks five languages.

His privileged background parallels that of his partner in government, Prime Minister David Cameron. He was schooled at the elite private Westminster School and then at Cambridge University. He spent a year at the prestigious College of Europe in Bruges, Belgium, establishing friendships all over the continent. Like Cameron, he was 43 years old, the age of John F. Kennedy when he became president. Elected to Parliament in 2005, he is tall, handsome, self-assured, and well-spoken, as one would expect from a person with such an educated and cosmopolitan background.

Like Cameron, he reoriented his party toward the center to win elections. This was not easy, given the complicated nature of the Liberal Democrat Party: On economic issues, many of its members are to the left of the Labour Party, but the wider public sees it as libertarian. For example, it wanted to end "the culture of spying on its citizens" by scrapping the nation-wide identity cards and the new biometric passports and by placing curbs on tens of thousands of closed-circuit cameras in public places.

His debating skills were demonstrated in Britain's first-ever televised election debates. He stamped himself as the candidate of change and touched off the campaign's biggest surprise: "Cleggmania." Before the debates, few Britons even knew what he looked like. Afterward he and his party appeared as a fresh departure from the agonizing parliamentary expenses scandal and the arrogance and abuse it symbolized. They tapped into the anger toward politics and politicians. Some observers called this the most "Americanized" election yet, with the candidates' wives traveling around, fulfilling their roles as potential first ladies.

Election day 2010 did not deliver the dramatic gains the Lib Dems had hoped for: They won 23% of the votes (up 1%) and 57 seats (a disappointing loss of 5). But because the Tories had fallen 20 votes short of a majority, they formed Britain's first governing coalition in 65 years with the LDP. Clegg became deputy prime minister, the most senior office any British Liberal has occupied since Lloyd George. Cameron and Clegg had not shown any previous liking to each other. Once asked what his favorite joke was, Cameron had answered, "Nick Clegg." But they were pragmatic partners determined to reform British politics in fundamental ways.

By entering the Tory-LDP coalition government in May 2010, the Liberal Democrats tasted power for the first time in almost a century. But "Cleggmania" disappeared, and the party suffered a frightful loss of popularity in the polls. Parties which choose to govern become more vulnerable to criticism; ridicule; and, in the case of the LDP, the sense that it is being marginalized. In the May 2011 elections and referendum on changing the electoral system, the LDP was doubly devastated. It had staked its future on electoral reform, but that was defeated in a referendum by 68% to 32%.

Liberal Democrats hoped they were not seeing a repeat of what happened to their party the last time it coalesced with the Conservatives in the 1930s: It split in two. The 2015 elections brought the party's worst nightmare. It lost half of its voters, plummeting from 15.2% to only 7.9%. Its 49 seats in 2010 shrank to only 8. Clegg won his seat, but he dutifully resigned as leader after this electoral catastrophe. After another electoral disaster in December 2019, winning only 11 seats, Sir Ed Davey assumed the party leadership.

RECENT FOREIGN AND POSTCOLONIAL POLICY

Today the sun technically does not set on the British Empire. Fourteen islands, rocks, and scarcely inhabited strips of land on the map are still ruled by Britain: They include Pitcairn in the south Pacific Ocean; Bermuda, British Virgin Islands, Caymans, Leeward Islands, Turks and Caicos in the Caribbean area; the Falkland Islands, St. Helena in the south Atlantic Ocean; Gibraltar in the Mediterranean; and Diego Garcia (where the US leases a military base) in the Indian Ocean. Yet it must still deal with many problems that stem from its colonialist legacy. They have included both foreign policy problems and domestic political difficulties, such as how to control and treat millions of immigrants from the former colonies (see "Culture").

The Commonwealth of Nations is a loose, voluntary association of the former ruler and the ruled, and the head is the British monarch, even though some of its members are republics. In 1995 it opened its doors to such states as ex-Portuguese Mozambique, formerly French Cameroon, and ex-Belgian Rwanda (which formally entered in 2009). It holds its members to the Commonwealth's declared values. Zimbabwe was suspended, and then it quit in 2003. In 2005 and again in 2009, Fiji was suspended for failing to return to democracy. After Gambia was criticized in 2013 for human rights violations, it quit, calling the organization "neocolonial."

Member states, which numbered 53, represent a fifth of the earth's land area and encompass 2 billion people (half of them Indians). They regularly confer at Commonwealth gatherings. Sometimes Britain must assume additional, unwanted responsibilities under the aegis of the Commonwealth, such as in helping to arrange a transition to democracy in the tiny Caribbean island of Grenada after four years of totalitarian rule and an invasion by the United States and six other Caribbean island states. Few people seem to know much about the Commonwealth. Only a third of respondents in a 2009 poll in seven member states could name something it did, and only a third in Australia or Canada would be "sorry" or "appalled" if their country quit the organization.

Britain and its wealthy Commonwealth allies bear over two-thirds of the running costs, but decisions are made on the basis of consensus. Britain shares its embassy in Myanmar with Canada, and Canada returns the favor in Haiti. Britain also shares an embassy with Germany in Iceland. More such deals are being negotiated.

Britain also faces terribly complicated problems with the smaller enclaves it rules because local inhabitants there fear their larger neighbors and look to Britain for protection. It has declared that the principle of self-determination must not be violated and that a neighboring land can absorb subject peoples only by their consent. The principle is an admirable one, but it has a high cost. The 3,000 inhabitants of the Falklands, located 300 miles (480 km) off Argentina's southern tip, called upon Britain to defend them when Argentina occupied what it calls the "Malvinas" islands for 73 days in April 1982. These islands had first been discovered by an Englishman in 1690. After the French and Spaniards had claimed them, the British established a naval garrison there in 1833. Sovereignty has been disputed ever since. It has never been tested in an international court. In 1984 a House of Commons committee decided it was "unable to reach a categorical conclusion" on the validity of the UK's claim.

Britain's military victory in 1982, costing 258 British and 649 Argentine lives, did not convince Argentina to renounce its claims to the islands. Buenos Aires also has its eye on the Falklands' potential offshore oil reserves of perhaps 500,000 barrels a day. As a deterrent, London stations 1,200 troops, only 150 of whom are combat soldiers; 3 ships; and 4 Typhoon fighter bombers in the area. Prince William was sent to the islands on his first overseas military tour, flying helicopters out of the new Mount Pleasant Air Base, which doubles as an international airport.

Although Britain still refuses to discuss its sovereignty over the islands unless the largely British inhabitants request it, it established friendly relations with Argentina. The two countries set up a "sovereignty umbrella," under which they cooperate on practical issues while maintaining their separate claims to ownership. They collaborate on fishing licenses worth $40 million each year. A memorial to the 649 Argentine war dead was constructed on the islands. President Carlos Menem received a warm welcome in London in 1998, where he laid a wreath to the Britons who died in the war. Prince Charles visited Argentina the following year.

Nevertheless, Argentine politicians, including presidents, still cannot resist whipping up support at election time by verbally attacking "illegal" British rule over the "Malvinas." Four out of five Argentines believe the islands belong to them. In 2007, on the 25th anniversary of the war, Argentine president Néstor Kirchner called again for an end to the "illegitimate" occupation, cancelled charter flights to the islands, pulled out of a 1995 agreement on oil and gas exploration, and banned energy companies that did business with the Falklands. His successor and wife continues the increasingly belligerent approach to the islands.

The dispute flared up again in 2010, when Desire Petroleum, a British company, began exploratory drilling off the Falklands' coast. Argentina countered by requiring ships sailing in Argentine waters between it and the Falklands to have a permit. The US government sat on the fence and offended London by suggesting that it negotiate with Argentina over the islands. In part because of these economic ties, Falklanders have a per-capita GDP of $50,000, one of the world's highest. In response to the resurgence of Argentine nationalism, the islanders conducted a referendum in March 2013 on remaining British: With a turnout of 92%, only three voters marked "no."

The 34,000 inhabitants of Gibraltar cling to their rock and are largely self-ruling. But they rely on the protection of 5,000 British troops stationed there because they are afraid of becoming a part of Spain. In 1985 the border between Gibraltar and Spain was reopened, and discussions over its sovereignty and eventual disposition continue. [See Spain chapter]

Painstaking negotiations with the People's Republic of China (PRC) over Hong Kong resulted in an agreement that gave the PRC sovereignty over the colony in July 1997. But it committed China to guaranteeing Hong Kong's capitalist economy and lifestyle for 50 years.

Essential Relationship with the United States

Britain's foreign policy involves close cooperation with the United States and a primary focus on Europe. As separate sovereign states with their own interests, the Americans and British sometimes have different views on issues, ranging from the British-French invasion of Suez in 1956 to the American invasion of Grenada in 1983. But many people on both sides of the Atlantic still talk of a "special relationship" between the two countries stemming from their common language and heritage, as well as from their alliance during two world wars. They cooperate closely on defense, intelligence gathering and nuclear technology.

This relationship never excluded disagreement. Ex–foreign minister Geoffrey Howe spoke in 1983 of the "special intimacy and a special mutual confidence that we're able to talk with each other with the candor which one would normally expect only between one's own advisers." But some Europeans suspected that Britain is a sort of Trojan Horse for American objectives on the Continent. This, among other things, influenced former French president Charles de Gaulle to reject Britain's first attempt to join the European Community.

No country's leader seized the moment more decisively after the September 11, 2001, terrorist attacks against the US than did Tony Blair. They claimed 100 British lives and thereby became the worst terrorist strike against British citizens in history. He flew to America immediately after the disaster; visited Ground Zero, where the World Trade Center once stood; listened to President Bush's speech to the nation from the gallery of the House of Representatives; and offered stirring words to the Americans and his own people: The terrorists "have no moral inhibition on the slaughter of the innocent. If they could have murdered not 7,000 but 70,000, does anyone doubt they would have done so and rejoiced in it? There is no compromise possible with such people, no meeting of minds, no point of understanding with such terror. Just a choice: Defeat it or be defeated by it. And defeat it we must. To the Americans, we were with you at the first. We will stay with you to the last." The queen awarded former New York mayor Rudolph Giuliani an honorary knighthood for his leadership in the aftermath of the crisis.

Blair put his country's money where its mouth was. Within two months Britain had sent 4,200 troops to the war zone in and around Afghanistan. In the opening salvos against the Taliban regime, British submarines fired cruise missiles at key targets and put special operations forces and Royal Marines on the ground to assist the opposition's push to rout Taliban forces. In 2002 its commandos joined the Americans and other allies on search-and-destroy operations aimed at remnants of al Qaeda and Taliban forces. For a half-year, it commanded the international peacekeeping forces in Kabul trying to stabilize the traumatized country.

The UK took command of NATO peacekeeping forces in Afghanistan in May 2006, under Leutenant General Sir David Richards. In July it announced an increase in its troop strength amid debates at home over whether the mission has been underresourced, misrepresented, or misconceived. In 2010 it had almost 10,000 troops in Afghanistan, mainly in the dangerous south, to deal with fierce Taliban raids and tribal complexities by means of challenging counterinsurgency tactics. By July 2010, 315 of its soldiers had died, a third of them in Helmand Province alone.

Between them, the US and UK contributed more troops to NATO's effort in Afghanistan than all other allies put together. Britain withdrew its soldiers in the face of a rejection by three-fourths of Britons to a continued commitment in Afghanistan.

The American president and people benefited greatly from Blair's support, and the two leaders developed a close personal relationship. The prime minister was mocked in left-leaning British media as the "president's poodle." He was criticized at home for getting too little in return. However, his position was always that it is difficult or impossible to do much good in the world without a powerful and engaged American partner.

The March–April 2003 war in Iraq offered a further opportunity for Britain to act as a transatlantic bridge; it provided 45,000 well-trained troops, 15% of the total. With a sensitivity to growing European concerns about the US role in the world, Blair stood up for a disliked and distrusted American president and repeatedly condemned anti-Americanism, reminded his countrymen of past American contributions to their security, and warned that opposing the US would merely reinforce American tendencies toward unilateralism. He did this at considerable temporary damage to his popularity at home, and even 139 of his own Labour MPs voted against the war, one of the largest rebellions in parliamentary history. He tirelessly argued the case for military action against Saddam Hussein's dictatorship and withstood merciless

The United Kingdom

heckling and a strange British form of disagreement toward speakers—slow hand clapping.

His eloquence and persuasiveness paid off; at the beginning of 2003, only 13% of Britons thought their country should go to war against Iraq; by the time war began, 56% were in favor, as was the majority of party leaders and MPs. He was able to demonstrate that America did not stand alone in the world and that the transatlantic divide ran down the middle of Europe rather than through the Atlantic. The result was a strengthening of the "special relationship" and an elevation of British influence in the world. One senior Bush official put it this way: "The special relationship had become a cliché which was being constantly trotted out, but all of a sudden it is very real. It is very deep and very operational." He continued: "This kind of partnership makes the United Kingdom a world player."

For his part, Blair reminded his party comrades at Labour's 2002 conference, "For all the resentment of America, remember one thing. The basic values of America are our values too. . . . My vision of Britain is not as the 51st state of anywhere, but I believe in this alliance, and I will fight long and hard to maintain it because alliance with America is in the interests of this country." Nevertheless, Blair was weakened politically by having led Britain into a war against Iraq that many British consider to have been unnecessary and for having gotten so little from the American president in return for his loyalty. "Bush's poodle" was a tag that hurt the prime minister.

The government was bruised by several inquiries into the political conduct of the Iraq War. In July 2004 the Butler Report argued that the government had oversold the case for war and that there had been intelligence failures. But it refrained from questioning Blair's "good faith," criticizing the prime minister individually, or saying that he or his government had distorted the evidence to build a case for war. "There was no deliberate attempt . . . to mislead."

Just days before the May 2005 elections, confidential documents from the attorney general's office at the time of the war seemed to indicate concerns about the legality of the war, even though the attorney general stated publicly that the war was legal, in his judgment. The documents did show some diplomatic discord between London and Washington. Both agreed that Saddam had weapons of mass destruction and had to be removed. But Blair wanted to work harder to "construct a coalition" and to "exhaust" efforts to deal with the problems within the UN. The British were also somewhat more concerned about what could go wrong once war began.

Britain's most famous lieutenants: Princes William and Harry

In November 2009 a fifth inquiry on Britain's role in the war opened. It was open to the public. Like the earlier inquiries, it provided no definitive proof that Blair had lied to start the war. The former prime minister gave a strong defense of his decision to send troops to Iraq.

Prince Harry, who had completed his officer's training, threatened to resign if he was prohibited from deploying to Iraq with his regiment. Military leaders decided against sending him on the grounds that his presence would make his unit an irresistible target for insurgents. However, in March 2008, he returned home from 10 weeks of combat duty in Afghanistan. His tour had to be cut short after American and other foreign news media reported his deployment, which British outlets had vowed to keep secret. He returned for a 20-week tour in 2013, flying an Apache attack helicopter. In 2015 he left full-time service with the armed forces.

Nothing tarnished the last stage of Blair's prime-ministership more than the bloody aftermath of the Iraq War. Gordon Brown's tricky task was to distance himself from Blair's Iraq commitment without being tagged as soft on defense. In April 2009 they relinquished the remainder of their command authority to the US, thereby ending a controversial six-year engagement that had cost 179 British lives. Winston Churchill's words in 1926 echoed in some British ears: "I hate Iraq. I wish we had never gone to the place." Staying there, he continued, was like "living on an ungrateful volcano."

Barack Obama enjoyed unprecedented popularity in Britain and elsewhere in Europe. Brown was the first to host Obama on the latter's maiden European tour as president. During that visit in April 2009, Queen Elizabeth departed from the usual protocol by wrapping her arm around Michelle Obama at the end of the first lady's courtesy call at Buckingham Palace. She almost never shows such affection in public.

As Britain reduces its military spending in an effort to reduce the budget deficit, some observers wonder if the special relationship with the US is over. The leaders of both countries deny it. Prime Minister Cameron said, "I and my party are instinctive friends of America and passionate supporters of the Atlantic alliance." His first foreign secretary, William Hague, affirmed in Washington three days after taking office that the US "is without doubt the most important ally" of Great Britain. Obama observed that "we see the world in a similar way."

Indeed the two countries' interests are aligned on the most pressing challenges they face: combatting violent terrorism, resolving the conflict in Afghanistan, dealing with a nuclear Iran, bringing the air war over Libya to a successful end, fighting the Islamic State in Iraq and Syria, and trying to persuade the Israelis and Palestinians to make peace. In any mix of core interests, Britain depends on close ties with America. Thus both countries can pursue their own interests in the context of a historic relationship. Both leaders agreed that the myths and emotion should be dropped, and the ties can be described as an "essential relationship."

In May 2011 the Obamas made a state visit to London, and the countries' leaders tried to give new meaning to the longstanding relationship. He became the first American invited to speak in Westminster Hall before a joint session of Parliament. He reminded his audience that his grandfather had been a cook in the Britsh army. When he finished, the dignitaries erupted in applause, and it took him a half-hour to leave the hall as they mobbed him for photos and handshakes. In January 2018 the US opened its gleaming new embassy, the most expensive ever built, in Nine Elms, a former industrial area along the south bank of the Thames.

Defense

For centuries Britain was a global power, whose interest in Europe was merely to prevent any one power or combination of powers from upsetting the military balance there and dominating the entire continent. After the Second World War, it shifted its primary focus to Europe. This is best seen in defense. It was a founding member of NATO, and until 1990 it organized its defense on the assumption that the chief threat was the Soviet Union. It therefore channeled the bulk of its resources into strengthening NATO rather than defending British outposts elsewhere. In 1971 it abandoned its defense commitments east of Suez.

The "NATO-first" policy necessitated fundamental changes in defense structure. Britain converted the once-mighty Royal Navy into a specialized force whose purpose was primarily to assist the American navy and to defend against submarines. In the 1970s it phased out its attack aircraft carriers. The Falkland Islands war in 1982 revealed how this change in force structure could affect Britain's commitments outside of Europe. It had to lease luxury liners and merchant vessels just to transport its troops and equipment to those faraway islands. The conflict prompted Britain to bolster its capabilities to project military power in the world by canceling the scheduled deactivation of an aircraft carrier and the Royal Navy's last two amphibious assault ships.

The heart of the British defense effort today is the army. It deploys a diminishing number of troops on the European continent, mainly in Germany. In 2010 it announced that, after 65 years of deployment on German soil, all of its 20,000 troops and the 23,000 dependents and British civilians working for the forces in that country would be withdrawn by 2020, a full 15 years earlier than expected. All 12 bases would be closed. The costs for this force are great, especially since Britain has a volunteer army. With the disappearance of the Soviet threat to Europe, NATO faces fundamental restructuring that affects the British military. In 1991 the allies decided to establish a sizable rapid-reaction force to confront unforeseen threats anywhere in Europe. This force is stationed mainly in Germany and is commanded by a British officer.

Within Britain itself, the most controversial aspect of British defense was its nuclear arsenal. Aside from France, the UK is the only European country to possess atomic weapons. The Thatcher government decided to replace the aging Polaris vessels (each carrying 16 missiles) with more modern submarines, capable of

firing ultramodern, American-made Trident missiles, each of which could attack eight separate targets.

The Labour Party, which took power in May 1997, dropped its long-standing opposition to Britain's nuclear force. But that was reintroduced in 2015. In post–Cold War Europe, nuclear weapons have become largely irrelevant. The UK decided in 1998 to halve the number of its nuclear weapons at sea to under 200 on 4 Trident submarines. This is its total number of nuclear warheads, since the Royal Air Force scrapped its in the same year.

The government debated what do about its four Vanguard-class Trident submarines that reach the end of their lives in 2024. Stationed in Scotland, at least one is at sea on constant patrol. The Blair government decided in 2007 to devote £20 billion ($32 billion) to build a new generation of nuclear submarines to carry a reduced number (ca. 160) of American-supplied Trident missiles. This makes Britain's nuclear arsenal the smallest among the five permanent UN Security Council members and the only one of them whose warheads are based on a single platform. Since it relies on American Trident missiles, it keeps the cost of its nuclear arsenal at half the level of France's.

Although nuclear targeting is coordinated with the United States, only the British prime minister can order the use of Britain's nuclear weapons. The willingness of the British government since the 1950s to permit the deployment of American nuclear weapons on British soil, which are not under the direct command of the British prime minister, reflects NATO's importance in British defense planning. "Dual-key" safeguards were considered unnecessary because the UK had a firm agreement with the US (which has never

been published) that no American nuclear weapons could ever be launched from Britain without the approval of the British government.

In 1991 Britain's participation in the war to drive Iraq out of Kuwait was solidly supported at home. The UK sent a powerful contingent of land, air, and naval forces serving under the overall command of American general Norman Schwarzkopf, whom the queen knighted after the successful campaign. In 1998 it dispatched an aircraft carrier back to the Persian Gulf to show its solidarity with the American and UN efforts to force Saddam Hussein to open his weapons facilities to international inspectors.

No sooner were the warriors home than the government began a steady reduction. In the two decades to 2010, it cut the army from 156,000 to 100,290; the navy from 63,000 to 35,650 and 6,840 Royal Marines; and the RAF from 89,000 to 39,750. Infantry battalions sank from 55 to 40, and front-line tanks, from 699 to 304. The British Army of the Rhine was halved to 20,000. However, Britain built up its special operations forces to 2,000–3,000. Its total active forces are 161,000, and its reserve forces, 199,280.

The Royal Navy has responsibilities in the south Atlantic, off west Africa, in the Caribbean, and around the Middle East. It retains its three aircraft carriers (to be replaced by two new ones from 2016 to 2018) and four ballistic-missile submarines (Tridents). But its fleet of 28 attack submarines was cut to 12, and its 49 frigates and destroyers, to 25. The RAF lost 9 of its 30 front-line combat squadrons; its total front-line fighters and bombers sank from 630 to 500, some of which are flown by women. Its ships must often put to sea without their full crew or equipment. The air force took control of the navy's Harrier jump jets, and in 2007 its carriers sailed without planes four-fifths of the time. To keep up the crews' training, the navy allowed allied aircraft to land and fly off its ships.

Britain sent 35 combat aircraft, 8 ships, and 6,600 troops to participate in the air war over Yugoslavia in 1999. The UK has increasingly assumed peacekeeping responsibilities. In 2010 it had 900 deployed in Kosovo, 2,791 in Cyprus, 9,000 in Afghanistan, and 320 in Gibraltar. For training, it had 700 soldiers in the US and 557 in Canada.

Defense spending was cut by over a fifth from 1990 to 2015, to below 2% of GDP, the lowest since 1930. Despite the reductions, defense spending is still among the highest in Europe, the fourth highest in the world after the US, China, and Russia.

The government shows interest in a European defense capability. Blair gave

Navy to cut its fleet by half

■ Six destroyers and frigates to be mothballed   ■ Retired First Sea Lord attacks 'outrageous' plans

The United Kingdom

his blessing to the European (now "Common") Security and Defence Policy (ESDP, now CSDP), which decided in 1999 to build a European rapid-reaction force that could act when NATO chooses not to do so. Britain's cooperation with France and Germany has tightened.

Faced with unmanageable defense costs, the British government signed a 50-year defense and security cooperation treaty with France in November 2010. The two countries account for half the defense spending in Europe and two-thirds of the military research and development. It was driven by the need to restrain their defense budgets while maintaining their willingness and capability to project power globally. The two countries had explored such defense cooperation before, most notably in the 1998 St. Malo Declaration following a meeting between French President Jacques Chirac and Tony Blair. But the Iraq War in 2003 prevented progress. This was one of the few times the two midsized nuclear powers found themselves on opposite sides in an international conflict.

The main items in the treaty are a joint expeditionary force, combined training, and maintenance for the new A400M transport airplane and shared A300 aerial tankers. France offered Britain access to its jet pilot school, and both will cooperate in developing armed drones and ways of combatting roadside bombs. They will jointly operate aircraft-carrier strike groups with the aim of ensuring a permanent carrier presence at sea. Perhaps most dramatically, they will cooperate on nuclear weapons while retaining their independent deterrents and means: Britain depends on American equipment, while France develops its own.

Immediately upon taking office in May 2010, the Cameron government ordered that a Strategic Defence and Security Review be made; its unveiling only five months later called for the largest defense cuts since the end of World War II: by 8% over four years. It described the forces as "overstretched, underequipped and ill-prepared" to meet the unconventional warfare challenges of the future. Military personnel were cut by 10% (7,000 from the army and 5,000 each from the navy and air force) and the army's artillery and tanks by 40%. The cuts left Britain with fewer readily deployable forces and reduced its ability to influence events. Its highly regarded special forces were left largely intact.

The aircraft carrier Ark Royal would immediately be scrapped, even though it is the only one in Britain's inventory that can launch fixed-wing jets; all 80 naval and air force Harrier jump jets would be taken out of service. Two new carriers are being built by 2020 at a cost of $9 billion, and

View of London from St. Paul's Cathedral

one of them would be sold or mothballed three years after completion. The operational carrier would be equipped by a naval version of the F-35 Joint Strike Fighter. Replacement or modernization of the four Trident subs would be delayed by up to five years. As the Afghanistan war wound down, the government produced in 2012 another defense review that called for the largest overhaul of the armed forces since the 1950s. Regular troops would decline by 20% to 82,000, the lowest level since the Napoleonic Wars.

The Conservative-LDP government that took office in May 2010 relegated foreign affairs to the backburner, as it focused on saving the country's financial health. There would be no more "wars of choice" or "humanitarian intervention." Any focus abroad would be on the pursuit of the nation's economic and commercial interests. It also pledged significantly to increase spending on overseas aid. Its diplomatic footprint would be shrunk as the Foreign Office faced a reduction of a fourth of its budget. Its diminished military force would be used less for moral causes. The aim would be to bring the domestic economy in order, not to maintain or enhance Britain's influence abroad.

Like so many good intentions, these priorities did not survive the first contact with reality. When revolution broke out in the Arab world, Britain did not hesitate to intervene diplomatically and militarily. Cameron was the first foreign leader to visit Egypt after Hosni Mubarak was toppled. Along with France, it led the international effort to enforce a UN- and Arab League–mandated no-fly zone over Libya, using its submarine-launched Tomahawk cruise missiles, fighter jets, and attack helicopters. It struck at Islamic State targets in both Iraq and Syria. These were precisely the kinds of assets that are slated for severe cuts.

The prime minister argued that Britain need not choose between its interests and its values, between stability and freedom. There is serious concern that the UK will no longer be able "to punch above its weight" both diplomatically and militarily. Thanks to unpleasant experiences in Iraq and Afghanistan, much of the public is opposed to armed engagements. In August 2013 Parliament rejected the Cameron government's participation in an American-led air strike on Syria. That was reversed two years later.

ECONOMY

Britain for two centuries has been a highly industrialized and developed nation. It led the Industrial Revolution in the 18th and 19th centuries, but after World War II, it enjoyed less efficiency than some of its newer rivals. Only 20% of the present gross domestic product now comes from industry and manufacturing (employing 18.9%, still the world's sixth-largest manufacturer), while service industries provide 79% of GDP and 79% of jobs, and agriculture, 1% of GDP and 1.2% of employment. British farmers produce more than half of the country's food requirements. Two-thirds of Britain's agricultural land is used for grazing; the main field crops are wheat, barley, oats, potatoes, and sugar beets.

Because of the extraction of oil and natural gas from the North Sea, Britain became self-sufficient in these sources of energy in the 1980s. It remains one of the dozen or so largest oil producers in the world. But the North Sea supplies are gradually running out, and British drivers pay the highest gasoline prices in the world (about $10 per gallon in 2013). It already gets a third of its electricity from gas and does not want a greater reliance on this one source. The UK is no longer the biggest coal producer in western Europe, but its coal supplies could last for another 300 years if needed. EU environmental rules and halts in government subsidies caused many coal plants to shut down. Although it gets 20% of its electricity from coal, it will close all of its coal-fired power plants by 2025. Along with Sweden and Germany, Britain was the only country in Europe that was meeting its Kyoto greenhouse gas emissions target, so it does not resist such closures. Unlike Germany, which gets 28% of its electricity from renewable sources, Britain gets only 1%.

Having calculated that world energy demand will increase by 50% in 2030, especially given the increased needs of China and India, and worried about climate change, the government declared in 2008 that investment into a new generation of nuclear reactors is needed. In 1996 the government had privatized its nuclear-power arm British Energy, but the upfront capital costs of atomic plants make long delays inevitable. However, nuclear energy produces little carbon dioxide, the technology is well developed, and uranium can be bought from stable countries like Australia and Canada.

No reactors have been built since 1994, and its two oldest commercial nuclear stations were closed in 2007. Nuclear power provides about a fifth of Britain's electricity, but its 10 plants are aging, with only 1 to be left running in 2023. This sudden turnabout is controversial, but voters are generally receptive to the idea that nuclear power should continue to make up a part of the nuclear mix. Polls show that more British favor it than oppose it. Waste is stored temporarily at the Sellafield site, and plans call for a long-term underground facility to be built.

Temporary Decline in Economic Performance

Economic and social shifts in Britain helped to bring important changes in some fundamental assumptions. From 1945 to 1970, it had generally been assumed (and was broadly the case) that, despite temporary ups and downs, the economy would always continue to improve; that inflation was unimportant; that full employment was normal; and that, if the economy got a little out of kilter, it could be put back on course by reducing or raising demand through taxes and public spending (classic economic methods of the late British economist John Maynard Keynes). It was therefore widely accepted that governments should regulate the economy in order to maintain employment while expanding the welfare state out of ever-increasing national prosperity. By 1975, state spending amounted to more than 60% of national income.

The Keynsian assumptions, which more or less enjoyed an acceptance by both major parties, were torn asunder in the 1970s. At the beginning of the decade, inflation began to rise, reaching the stratospheric level of 25% annually in the mid-1970s and 22% in 1980. Unemployment began to rise steadily, and the old cure did not seem to work anymore.

As economic growth slowed to a standstill, governments were faced with an unpleasant dilemma: Demand for welfare services continued to grow, while the national income to pay for them did not. British economic discussions began to be preoccupied with "managing decline." The nationalized industries (most of which had passed to public control in the immediate postwar years) were performing poorly and were becoming an increasing drain on the nation's productivity, thereby discrediting the very idea of public ownership. Everywhere people began talking about the "English disease."

The Thatcher Revolution

Margaret Thatcher brought dramatic economic changes during her prime ministership from 1979 to 1990. Neither the Tory government of John Major nor Tony Blair's Labour government, which took office in 1997, moved to undo her reforms in any fundamental way. She denationalized more than a third of Britain's nationalized industries, including Rolls-Royce, British Airways, and the British Gas Corporation. The sale of these brought more than $40 billion into the state treasury, eliminated the need for taxpayers to subsidize them, and reaped handsome annual tax revenues. In 1987 the government began selling shares of British Petroleum. In 1988 plans were announced to privatize the electric industry in England and Wales. British Telecom was sold, and in 1996 its merger with the American MCI was made public. Thatcher's large-scale privatization program included two dozen major companies. Nevertheless, state spending still accounts for 39% of GDP (compared with 30% in the US), roughly the same percentage as when she took office.

Thatcher had argued that the state was overspending, and the shortfalls were being covered by public borrowing and expanding the money supply rather than by taxes. These expedients stimulated inflation and absorbed the capital that was desperately needed to finance industrial innovation. The cure, she argued, was to restrict the money supply and cut public expenditures, which would both reduce inflation and free investment capital. To create economic incentives, income taxes should be cut. Finally, trade-union power had to be curbed.

Her pride and her optimism were borne out by the facts: Since the country began pulling out of recession in 1981, productivity increased at an annual rate of 3.5%. The economy grew at an annual rate of 3%. Inflation was down from a high of 24.2% to 3.3% in 1995. Taxes had been reduced slightly, and the average voter's real pretax income had increased by 25% since 1979. From 1971 to 1994, real disposable income grew by almost 50%, and spending on social benefits increased by 168%. Britons live more prosperous lives. Nevertheless, the UK is the only EU country in which working hours have increased, to 43.4 hours.

Unemployment was higher when she left than the 4.3% when she took office. Nevertheless, 1 million new jobs had been created under her rule, in part because of incentives to small enterprises. Also, the jobs of those who were employed seemed far less threatened than in the early 1980s. Interest rates were falling, and the pound was much stronger. Its stock market was booming, and the UK had again become a leading creditor nation. Public borrowing had fallen to 1% of national income. Most important, she had restored morale and seemed to have ended decades of relative economic decline.

After her 1987 victory, London's Sunday Times pronounced that Thatcher had brought about Britain's "biggest transformation since the Industrial Revolution." Indeed, her economic performance profoundly changed her country. She created what she called a "property-owning democracy," in which "every earner shall be an owner." Two-thirds of Britons now own their homes, compared to 50% in 1979, and car ownership has risen from 54% to 66%. In 1979 four times as many Britons belonged to trade unions as owned shares in the stock market. But by 1989 the number of stockholders had tripled from 7% to 21%. As a result of a fall in union membership by one-fourth to 9 million, the number of union members and stockholders are now equal.

Thatcher enormously reduced the power of the once-mighty labor unions, which had been able to topple the governments of her two predecessors. She introduced laws that limit unions' legal immunities. They restrict picketing rights, ban secondary picketing and political strikes, make national unions financially responsible for the actions of their members, and require unions to have a secret balloting of members before declaring a strike. She rooted out one of the main causes of the "English disease" by taking on the bosses of the most powerful unions and crushing them: the steel workers in 1980, the coal miners in 1985, and the teachers in 1986. By 1987 strikes were at a 50-year

The United Kingdom

low; workdays lost to union disputes declined from 29.5 million in 1979 to 1.9 million in 1986.

The reduction in the number and length of strikes was, in part, due to workers' and employees' fear of losing their jobs and to their realization that real earnings for those with work has risen almost 35% between 1980 and 1987. There has also been a change of attitudes: Many workers associate unions with strikes and therefore have increasingly turned their backs on the unions, whose membership has continued to decline. An important result for the overall economy is that the unions are no longer able to block the introduction of state-of-the-art technology in order to protect jobs. Thus, while from 1974–1980 output per worker in British manufacturing did not increase at all, from 1981 to 1987 it grew by 40%. So powerful had the unions been that many people wondered, "Who governs?" After she was finished, no one would suspect that it was the union bosses.

More and more workers became homeowners (43% by 1983 and one-third of even unskilled laborers by 1988), thanks in part to Margaret Thatcher's policy of selling many state-owned council houses to their occupants. By the time her party finally left power in 1997, 68% of all households owned their own homes. It is not surprising that the percentage of Britons who consider themselves to belong to the middle class increased from 30% of the population in 1979 to roughly 50% in 1987. Their lifestyles became more and more like those of the middle class; this was given added impetus by the education changes in the 1970s that largely did away with the several schooling tracks and brought most British schoolchildren together in one school. The massive occupational shifts and breakdown in elite structure in the educational system fostered increasing social mobility. It is no wonder that persons who lived in several classes in their own lifetime ceased to use class as a major political reference point. It is quite simply no longer accurate to speak of "two Britains," one a deprived working class and the other a traditional upper class.

Thatcher created a more prosperous and productive Britain that is still the basis for the country's exemplary economic performance. But her chief economic legacy was one of the mind. The pursuit of comfort and wealth had become marks of bad form. But she made prosperity an acceptable goal and free-market capitalism morally defensible. Tony Blair's Labour Party not only embraces both, but he also won the 1997 elections by promising that his government could manage Thatcher's economy even more competently. By the 1990s anybody

working in Britain's offices and factories could see that they were much better and more productively run than was the case two decades earlier. Industrial relations have improved dramatically.

Labor Unions

Public sympathy and enthusiasm for labor unions gradually eroded in the 1970s and early 1980s. In order to gain wage restraint from the powerful unions, Labour governments made so many concessions to them that many persons began to blame the unions for high prices and many of the economic problems. Their revulsion at the excessive "unelected power" which union bosses wielded boiled to the surface in the 1978–1979 "winter of discontent," when coal and transportation strikes threatened to paralyze the entire nation.

Both the economic recession and the Conservatives' broadside attacks against the Labour Party in general and the unions in particular greatly weakened the latter. Between 1979 and 2007, their membership dropped from 12 million to 7.5 million. In 1979 more than half the workforce (55%) was unionized; 38% was in 1990, and 27%, in 2010. In 2011, 14.2% of private-sector employees and 56.3% of public-sector employees were unionized. Union-negotiated settlements cover more than 70% of those public-sector workers. By election time in 1983, almost three-fourths of all Britons favored stricter laws to regulate unions; an astonishing three-fifths of all trade unionists also favored legal curbs on union power. Union popularity declined further as the result of a protracted coal miners' strike in 1984–1985. Union leader Arthur Scargill fanned the flames of anti-unionism with public pledges to bring down Thatcher's government. He failed, and her ability to break trade-union power is her most lasting legacy.

In the 1990s strikes were at their lowest level in more than a half-century. In 1979, 29.5 man-days were lost to strikes; in 1995 that figure had fallen to 4.15. In the 21st century, the figures are even more dramatic: Only 158,000 working days were lost to strikes in 2005, compared with 12.9 million in the 1970s and 7.2 million in the 1980s. This is fewer than in the US and Canada and about half the rate for the EU and OECD countries. Perhaps because of affluence and higher homeownership, strikes also tend to be much shorter. One expert noted, "It's much more risky to strike now. If you don't do it right according to the law, you end up in court."

Unions affiliated with the TUC lost a third of their members after the Tories came to power in 1979. Even within the Labour Party the unions' influence has been reduced though not eliminated. The support of the trade unions for the party

can still be helpful in a crunch. They provide more than half of its money.

The gap between the working and middle classes has also been narrowed by the changing composition of the labor unions. The increase in the number of civil-service employees, the growth of the service sector within the economy, and the rise of computer-related and other high-technology industries in the south of England and especially around London and Cambridge prompted the growth of so-called white-collar unionism. That is, union members were no longer exclusively manual workers in factories and mines, but they also could be teachers, engineers in a nationalized industry, secretaries in Whitehall, etc.

With talk of "paring down the public sector," these white-collar unions even became quite militant in pressing their demands. Thus, Britain began to experience a different breed of striker, from nurses and hospital personnel to civil servants. This militancy among the white-collar employees has helped even more to bridge the social gap between workers and employees and to break down class divisions.

There are still workers concentrated in large manufacturing or mining industries living in rented council housing in working-class sections and remaining in a largely isolated social environment. They confront employers and managers whose political attitudes are also traditional and are diametrically opposed to those of their workers. These groups are far more likely to retain a strong loyalty to either the Labour Party or the Conservative Party and a strong class-consciousness. However, these kinds of workers and managers are becoming a diminishing minority in Britain's more service-oriented economy. Union members in the service sectors work in an environment that brings them into contact with all other classes, a factor that reduces rather than sharpens class-consciousness. As a consequence, their voting behavior is far less class-bound. They can be attracted to parties that portray a new, nonclass image and seem capable of overcoming the old social divides.

Britain and Europe

In 1973 the UK entered the EU, a move that has had a dramatic impact on its economy. The EU now buys half of British exports, compared to a third in 1972. It provides half of its imports. Still, many British remain critical of their country's membership in the EU.

In practice, British governments have tended to put British interests ahead of European interests. They have been cool on a common EU energy policy, a directly

The United Kingdom

elected European Parliament, and European Monetary Union (EMU). Britain traditionally showed little interest in deepening European integration, and it tends to be opposed to political and supranational integration. But it supports enlargement, perhaps to water down the union, as some critics contend.

Margaret Thatcher tried hard to reduce the British contribution to the EU budget. Declaring that "I want my money back," she insisted on a "British rebate" of two-thirds the difference between what Britain paid into the EU and what it got back out. The Blair government declared in 2005 that it would not give this up until significant changes were made in the union's Common Agriculture Policy (CAP), which gobbles up 40% of all EU spending; about a quarter of CAP spending goes to France. By 2005 Britain had become the fourth-largest net contributor as a percentage of national income and the second-largest in total cash contribution, two and one-half times more than France pays in.

Thatcher signed the Single European Act in 1986 because it was an economic, not political, step toward integration. In 1989–1990 she remained suspicious of "deepening" EU unity on the grounds that it would undermine national sovereignty and that it was no time to create new bureaucracies and weaken national parliaments just when eastern European nations were digging themselves out from underneath their bureaucracies and breathing new life into their legislatures. Not all British, not even all Tories, agreed with her foot dragging, and this contributed to her fall.

At the historic 1991 summit in Maastricht, Britain agreed to greater economic and political union on the condition that the UK could "opt out" of an eventual single European currency, which it chose to do when the euro was introduced in 12 EU countries. It also rejected moves to make an EU "social policy" mandatory for all members, and the Euroskeptic Tories threatened to stop observing it. There was much resistance in all parties, especially the Conservative Party, to the Maastricht Treaty. However, Parliament finally accepted it in 1993.

The Labour governments were more supportive of British membership in a more united Europe, although Prime Ministers Blair and Brown promised to put British interests first. With Nick Clegg and the LDP playing key roles in the Cameron government, the Tories' Euroskepticism was restrained. The UK would have to worry about meeting the criteria for the euro, even if wanted to join. Its budget in 2021 had a deficit of 17.1% of GDP, and overall public debt stood at less than half of GDP.

One of Labour's first acts in 1997 was to transfer the power to set interest rates from the chancellor of exchequer to an unelected panel of the Bank of England. Its greater independence was demonstrated in July 2013, when it appointed Canadian central bank chief Mark Carney as governor of the Bank of England. He was the first foreigner in 318 years to assume this post, which is arguably the most influential unelected job in Britain. Blair found it publicly expedient to announce in 2000 that "people don't want Europe interfering in every aspect of people's national lives."

Britain has always had two chief aims in Europe: slow down the drive for political union and prevent Franco-German domination of European politics. The temporary death of the EU constitution in 2005 accomplished both.

In the campaign the French government had heaped criticism on what it saw as the "Anglo-Saxon" economic model. In supposed contrast to France's and Germany's shorter work week, higher welfare benefits and restrictions on the influx of low-wage workers from central Europe, Britain is an economic free-for-all that lacks all these amenities. This is a caricature.

The failed EU constitutional treaty was doctored up by getting rid of the most unpopular provisions (about 10% of the original text). The revised version, which was not labeled a "constitution," was adopted by the member states in Lisbon in December 2007. The Lisbon Treaty was unpopular in Britain. Then Prime Minister Brown had the treaty ratified by parliament. Prime Minister Cameron announced in 2015 that a referendum on British membership in the EU would be conducted by June 2016 following tough negotiations on new terms for Britain. The result was a catastrophe: 52% voted to leave the EU, and Cameron lost his job.

Current Economic Situation

Spending for social welfare and health care has been greatly increased. Child and pensioner poverty rates have declined to near average EU levels. Income distribution has widened. All this is paid for by tax levels on par with most continental countries; government spending is 52% of GDP, but the Cameron coalition vowed to bring it down to 41%.

The Blair government introduced new market and financial discipline to the National Health Service (NHS). A 2006 study concluded that middle-aged English are "much healthier" than their American counterparts, even though the healthcare system costs half as much ($5,635 versus $2,231) per capita than in the US Smoking and drinking rates are slightly higher in England, while there is greater

obesity in the US Life expectancy is 79.4 for men and 83.1 for women. The NHS universally covers all citizens, while 16% of Americans under age 65 were without health insurance until the 2009 health reform, which seeks to lower that figure to 6%. The NHS therefore provides important psychological reassurance. Healthcare costs, which have risen to 9% of GDP (faster than any other public service), or almost a fifth of government spending, were exempted from the budget cuts ordered by the Cameron government in 2010. The government tried to make the NHS more efficient, but the effort was chaotic, and a formidable array of critics called it "a mess." A pause to reflect on how to proceed was declared.

The British and French finally agreed to construct a twin-bore, 32-mile channel tunnel (dubbed "Chunnel") through which an auto-rail link between the two countries passes. Road vehicles are loaded on trains at terminals on both sides of the Channel and whisked at a speed of 100 miles per hour from one side to the other. The Channel became what Napoleon had described as "a ditch that will be leaped whenever one has the boldness to try." The two nations' leaders shared a bold vision of the future. In 1990 the burrowing French and British crews linked up under the channel, and the Chunnel opened in 1994.

It is mired in serious financial difficulties, having cost twice as much to build as projected. Repayment of the $11 2 billion debt had to be suspended while its finances were restructured, which was done in 2006 and 2007. The problem is that too few passengers are using this undersea link even to pay the interest on the construction costs. It was assumed that 10 million passengers would use the Chunnel each year, but in 2003 only 6.3 million did so. Also only 1.7 million tons of freight were shipped through in 2003, far short of the 5-million-ton estimate each year. The result was a severe cash crunch, although the tunnel operator, Groupe Eurotunnel, reported its first annual net profit in 2007. In 2013 the EU ruled that access charges were "excessive" and should be lowered.

In November 2007 Britain completed its $12 billion 109-kilometer (68-mile) high-speed railway linking the Channel Tunnel to the newly renovated terminal, St. Pancras Station. Its imposing ironwork train-shed had once been the world's largest enclosed space. The train journey to Paris now takes two and one-quarter hours going 186 mph, and passengers can also travel to Brussels. The Eurotunnel Group managed a small profit in 2009, despite a disastrous fire in September 2008 that disrupted traffic until February 2009. At Christmastime 2009 problems again

67

The United Kingdom

The 600-foot long boring machine which led others in clawing through 7.5 million cubic meters of chalk-marl one mile beneath the sea which divides Britain and France

struck when heavy snowstorms caused electrical outages inside the tunnel and interrupted service for about a week. Nearly 90,000 passengers were affected. A large illegal refugee camp on the Calais side of the Chunnel is the jumping-off point for thousands of men trying to make it to Britain through the tunnel. Their efforts are fraught with peril.

The United Kingdom has been heavily involved in overseas trade for many centuries, and the importance of that trade continues to grow. In the last 50 years, the export of goods and services has moved from being one-fifth of the gross domestic product to one-third. Of these exports, 9.1% go to the United States (which provides 5.8% of imports).

After the US, Britain is the world's largest investor abroad. After the U.S., it was also the favorite destination of foreign direct investment (FDI). Roughly a quarter of all foreign direct investment flowing into the western European EU nations goes to the UK. Many well-known "American" brands are now British: Brooks Brothers belongs to Marks and Spencer, and Diageo owns Burger King and Pillsbury. The Greyhound bus company is in British hands. The favorite candy in the UK, Cadbury, was acquired in 2010 by the American food giant Kraft. Foreigners own everything from London's water supply to its airports. Its steel industry has almost been entirely purchased.

In 1995 it surpassed Japan to become the largest source of foreign direct investment in the US. By 1999 the UK was directing 30% of its direct investment to America, while the US sends a fifth of its foreign direct investment to Britain. By 2003 the US had invested almost as much in the UK as it had in all of Asia, Latin America, the Middle East, and Africa. After the turn of the century, only the US and China attract more money from foreigners than does Britain. In part, this is due to the fact that Britain's labor costs are lower than in some major industrialized countries.

The City of London (a small area within greater metropolitan London) is of immense significance in international finance. It has the world's largest insurance market, the lengthiest listing of overseas securities, the highest proportion of the Eurodollar market, the biggest foreign exchange market, and the largest secondary market for Islamic bonds. It generates a fifth of all corporate-tax revenues in the UK. In 1986 a "big bang" occurred in the London financial world: The financial markets were largely deregulated, and foreign companies were permitted to trade in British financial markets for the first time. The overall effect was to make London the world's most important financial center, although it was hit hard by the 2008–2010 recession.

Each day, 600,000 people go to work in 580 banks; that is more than the total population of Frankfurt. Big American banks have their continental headquarters there, and London's traders have grown to control 30% of global foreign-exchange trading. Britain's financial institutions are fully competent in dealing with the euro, even though its political leaders are not yet ready for it. All this financial activity has helped make London the world's second-most-expensive city in the world for expatriate employers, after Moscow; New York was not even among the top 10.

Prime Minister Cameron inherited an economy in 2010 that was in a dire state. The recession had hurt it badly because of the country's overextended banks, the indebted private sector, and the excessively large public sector. Its growth rate was 2.7% per year from 1998 to 2006 and 6.9% in 2021. The earlier steady expansion pushed up per-capita GDP above that of Germany and France. Unemployment was 5% in 2021, while inflation was .5%. The budget deficit was 7.1% of GDP in 2021.

Given the seriousness of the public finance crisis, the Conservative-LDP government had no alternative to the most brutally austere budget since Thatcher's rule. It acted quickly so that it could pin the blame for the pain on the previous Labour government. As a beginning, the salaries of MPs and ministers were cut by 5%, and wider public sector pay decreases and layoffs would follow. The departments' budgets (except health and foreign aid) were cut an average of 25% over four years. The VAT was raised from 17.5% to 20%. It retained a 50% income tax rate on the wealthiest individuals.

In 2002, 400,000 rural Britons marched in London to dramatize what they called a "crisis in the countryside." It suffers from a depression in agriculture, made worse by the disastrous handling of the foot-and-mouth disease. Since the mid-1990s, farm incomes have halved, and weekenders and 100,000 Britons resettling in rural Britain each year have driven house prices so high (overall they trebled in the decade to 2007) that many locals can no longer afford to live where they grew up. The positive side of this real estate inflation is that the value of farmers' assets has risen by about 40% since 1992. Thus the average farmer possesses an net worth of £700,000 ($1.2 million).

In 2004 fox hunting that involves a pack of dogs sniffing out foxes and killing them was prohibited. Riding with hounds is still permitted, as is the shooting of foxes forced out of cover by a maximum of two dogs. Some judges have found the Hunting Act confusing and poorly written, and only a handful of hunters have been convicted of violating it. The Conservative-LDP government agreed in 2010 to allow a parliamentary vote whether to lift the ban. Since the abolishment went into effect, the 300 hunt clubs have seen their membership grow by

Globe Theatre

about 45,000. However, most Labour and LDP MPs oppose lifting the ban. A positive vote would be unlikely.

Britain is the fifth-most-popular tourist destination in the world, attracting 25 million foreign visitors annually; it is Americans' most popular destination. The 125,000 mostly small tourist businesses employ 1.75 million people, more than agriculture, food production, coal mining, steel, car and aircraft manufacturing, and textiles combined.

CULTURE

The impact and pervasiveness of British culture on the rest of the world has been out of all proportion to the size and population of the United Kingdom. While those who participated in the Beatlemania of the 1960s might disagree, two British gifts to world culture stand out as most important. First, the achievement of English writers in producing a magnificent body of literature has influenced the way people think around the world. Within English literature, certainly Shakespeare and the King James Bible have been most important. One-third of the world's most translated authors come from the UK.

Second, the development of constitutional, parliamentary democracy set an example to all the world of how men and women may live in freedom and guide their own destinies. It also shows how compromise and civility rather than coercion are the best ways to pull together the social fabric. In a world in which the majority of human beings do not enjoy political or individual freedoms and other countries that attempt democracy

are unable to achieve stability, the United Kingdom stands a worthy example of a free society living under laws.

The widespread knowledge of English as a first or second language throughout the world speaks for itself, be it the Americanized or British version. It has become the language of scientific expression almost worldwide. English is not spoken throughout England, Wales, Scotland, and Ireland in an identical fashion. Local expressions and local pronunciations vary widely. The urbanized lower classes of London traditionally speak Cockney English, which the average American can seldom understand. Language has traditionally been a key to identifying the social class of a British person. The reason lies partly in the educational system.

Education and Class in Britain

The traditional school system had been tracked in such a way that a child's educational program was more or less fixed at age 11. After the crucial "11-plus exam," some children went into trade or commercial schools. Others went into the more elite, state-supported grammar schools or the independent, privately endowed "public schools" (the most prestigious being Eton, Harrow, and Winchester). Technically only those schools that sent a delegate to a specific school conference in the 19th century have a right to call themselves "public schools." But the term is loosely used to refer to almost any private school. They were especially geared to preparing pupils for the few seats in universities, especially at Oxford and Cambridge (known collectively as "Oxbridge"), which held the keys to

success in politics, industry, and scholarship. A 2007 study concluded that the top 10 universities in the world were either American or British: Cambridge and Oxford placed second and third; Imperial College London, fifth; and University College London, ninth.

In a 1992 study of the top 100 persons in Britain's elite, The Economist found that two-thirds had attended public schools, and more than half had studied at Oxford and Cambridge. Only a decade later, in 2002, those percentages had fallen noticeably to 46% public-school and 35% Oxbridge graduates. However, 15 out of 23 cabinet members in the Cameron government studied at an Oxbridge university. The number of women had climbed from 4% to a mere 5%.

The loosening hold of public-school and Oxbridge alumni reflects the growth of competition, especially in business, which has resulted from deregulation and globalization. Life in Britain's larger and more multinational companies is no longer as cozy as it used to be. Ambitious products of the country's expanded university system have claimed top positions once reserved for the well-born and those from famous schools.

Critics had long charged that the traditional educational system actually hardened and perpetuated class lines in British society. That is a major reason the old grammar and secondary modern schools were fused into "comprehensive" secondary schools, in which all pupils learn under one roof. State-sponsored schools can no longer select for ability, and state scholarships to the coveted private schools were eliminated. About 7% of all pupils attend the fee-paying "public schools" that provide a good education for average tuition fees of $21,000 per year; those costs can be as high as £30,000 ($46,000).

A reform proposed in the Blair years to provide more choice and competition among the state schools has taken flight under the Conservative–Liberal Democrat coalition: independent "academies." They are funded by the state but have more freedom in their operation. Between May 2010 and May 2011, their numbers jumped from 203 to 629. They include one in six English secondary schools.

Some say that these reforms actually lowered educational standards, and the gap between rich and poor people's education has in fact widened, as has income. However, to make the testing easier, less intimidating, and fairer, the old A-levels taken in the pupil's final year of secondary school, which were crucial for university admission, were changed. They now take "Advanced Supplementary," or AS-level, exams in their second-to-last year in school, and they are permitted to

The United Kingdom

retake some of those tests to improve their grades. They then take the more difficult A2 exams at the end of their last year. Their final grades are based on the results of the two years combined.

British schools still reflect the social stratification of the country. A majority of pupils leave full-time education or training at age 16. As a result, less than half the workforce is classified as skilled, compared with 85% in Germany and 75% in France. According to an *Economist* survey in 2007, more than a third of adults left school with no formal qualifications. A sixth were judged functionally illiterate and a fifth innumerate. There is a strong feeling that British schools are not fully prepared for the challenges of the 21st century.

Two-fifths of university-age Britons (up from 5% in 1960 and one-eighth in 1980) study in 1 of the 87 universities or polytechnic schools. A funding boom for the universities occurred from 1997 to 2009, when their total income doubled, while student numbers increased by only 20%. Nevertheless, the dramatic increase in enrollment broke the budget and required that students contribute to the cost of their education.

Many of these students were distressed by the Labour government's decision to end tuition-free higher education and to levy in 2006 a flat-rate £3,000 ($4,500) yearly tuition charge. Adding the £5,000 ($7,500) the taxpayer provides, this falls well short of the $18,700 The Economist estimated it costs each year to educate a student at Oxford or Imperial College. This is on top of the more than $3,000 room and board costs, much of it borrowed or obtained through grants, including from local governments.

Although Britons with a university education earn 17% more over a lifetime, there is resentment over such tuition and over any talk of raising it to a level needed to cover the annual cost of a student. Oxford University chancellor Lord Chris Patten points out that universities charge half of what parents pay for a place at an average nursery.

Some enterprising British universities attract large numbers of non-EU foreign students and charge them American-level tuition. For example, Imperial College London charges overseas students £20,750 ($31,125) per year to study physics. Britain attracted 12% of the world's international students, second only to the US (20%). For instance, one-half of all undergraduate students at the London School of Economics (LSE) are non-EU foreigners. In 2005, some 9% of university students came from outside the EU; that is one-fourth more than in the preceding year. To improve its bottom line and be more able to compete

with top American universities, Oxford announced its decision to raise its number of non-EU students from 8% to 15% over a decade, deemphasize undergraduate teaching, get away from its hallmark tiny tutorial groups, and have graduate students teach undergraduates.

Despite the emotional resistance to higher tuition, the Blair government succeeded in winning a House of Commons vote in 2004 by a whisker-thin five-vote majority authorizing a rise in tuition in English universities to £3,000 ($4,500) from 2006. Wales and Scotland are different; Scotland charges no tuition for Scottish students. Only the most affluent paid the full amount. Those from lower-income families paid less, and the lowest 30% paid nothing. Although low by American standards, this rise reflected an important shift in thinking that is very controversial in Britain.

The Cameron government's austerity policy called for a substantial reduction in direct grants to universities. To make up the difference, universities are permitted to charge between £6,000 ($9,600) and £9,000 ($14,400) in yearly tuition. Through a state-managed loan system, students can borrow interest-free what they cannot pay. In some cases they could borrow as much as £40,000 ($63,000) for a three-year education. They begin paying it back after graduation. When their income reaches £21,000 ($38,000) per year, they pay 9% of their earnings over that amount to settle the debt. After 30 years, any remainder is forgiven. This change drove many students and other protesters onto the streets, and a few of the demonstrations turned violent. Universities are also taking a page from America's book and are soliciting donations from alumni and other benefactors. For example, J. K. Rowling, who became richer than the queen from her Harry Potter books, gave £10 million ($16 million) to the University of Edinburgh, and Oxford University had raised £1 billion ($1.6 billion) by 2011.

A product of this educational system is Kazuo Ishiguro, the 2017 recipient of the Nobel Prize in literature. He studied English at the University of Kent in Canterbury and wrote The Remains of the Day and Never Let Me Go.

While there is considerable dissatisfaction with the educational system, there is little doubt that Britain's establishment and class system have changed dramatically in the last decades. Intelligent and ambitious individuals have always been able to succeed in Britain, whose society has long been less rigid than in many other countries. But in the UK today, status is largely earned, not inherited. BBC producer Nick Guthrie spoke of a revolution in the class system and argued, "it's not so much your family that matters; it's

what you've achieved, and of course how much money you've got." Former prime minister Gordon Brown agreed, noting that on corporate boards "titles are out, for the most part. Today it's not who you are, but what you have done. . . . The old class system is not dead. But it is much weaker than ever before." It can even be a disadvantage to come from a privileged background. In 2010 David Cameron and Nick Clegg worked hard to master the common touch in order to increase their chances of electoral success.

An example of the new kind of establishment, based on money, athletic prowess, or celebrity, is the knighthood conferred in 2002 on Sir Michael Jagger. The musical superstar asked meekly, "does this mean I'm part of the establishment?" Considering his global reputation, massive wealth, and elegant country estate, the answer is yes.

Religion

Polls in 2012 revealed that only 59% call themselves Christian (down by 13 points in one decade). The Anglican Church of England (in Scotland the Presbyterian Church of Scotland) is the official state religion. The queen is its head, and Parliament approves its prayer book. Only in 2007 did the prime minister relinquish the right to select its bishops, 26 of whom have seats in the House of Lords, even though only 1 out of 6 Britons are Anglicans. The Archbishop of Canterbury, since 2013 former oil executive Justin Welby, is the spiritual leader of the world's 80 million Anglicans. It claims up to 30 million members on paper, but only a sixth of religiously active Britons belong. Church attendance has fallen dramatically in the Church of England. In 1960, 2.1 million attended on Easter Sunday, a figure that had fallen to 1.3 million by 1994. It is estimated that it lost about 1,000 church-goers every week during the 1990s. By 2012 around 3% attended an Anglican service at least once a month. In 2015 the Church of England consecrated its first female bishop, Libby Lane.

In 2005 only 3 in 10 Britons even belonged to a religion and attended services, down from nearly three-quarters in 1964. One study in 2007 showed that more people visit bingo clubs each week than go to church. The joke is that the C and E in the Church of England's abbreviation stand for "Christmas" and "Easter." Polls in 2002 indicated that barely 1 in 50 British families say grace regularly before meals, compared with close to half in the US.

Most worshipers are drawn to religions that are better able to satisfy the thirst for spirituality: immigrant religions (mainly Islam, Sikhism, and Hinduism); cults; Pentecostal or charismatic Christian churches, or new-age, nonmainstream faiths. In an attempt to lure worshipers back to the Church of England, its General Synod voted in 1992 to ordain women, a decision which had to be approved by Parliament and the queen in 1993. In protest, traditionalist Anglicans threaten to split away from the church, and some migrated to Catholicism. By 2012 a third of its clergy were women, some holding senior positions, such as canons and archdeacons. But until 2015 the church refused to appoint female bishops. The Anglican establishment is holding firm against ordaining LGBTQ people to the priesthood, as is practiced in some American dioceses. It also opposes same-sex marriages, although a bill allowing this sailed through the House of Commons, 400 to 175, in 2013. This issue has the potential of creating a schism in the church.

In 2008 then-archbishop Rowan Williams found himself in a furious tempest when he suggested that some aspects of the Muslim Sharia law, such as those regulating marriage, property, and inheritance, be recognized and formalized. He failed to anticipate the explosive effect of the very word "Sharia" in a public that has deep concerns about Islam in Britain. He was condemned by all political parties and even some Muslim leaders, and the prime minister himself phoned him to request that he calm the storm. The besieged archbishop publicly apologized and explained that he was not advocating that Islamic law be granted equal status with British law.

One can no longer call Britain's 6 million Catholics embattled. Catholics have gotten one top job after another, including Chris Patton (chancellor of Oxford University), Michael Martin (earlier speaker of the House of Commons), and Mark Thompson (head of the BBC). Almost the only thing a Catholic, or even the spouse of a Catholic, cannot be by law is king or queen. Former pope Benedict feared that many of Catholics were falling away and that Britain was drifting from Christianity. He made the first papal state visit to Britain in September 2010 (his predecessor, John Paul II, had made a pastoral visit in 1982) to meet the queen and political leaders and to beatify Cardinal John Henry Newman. Some Anglicans are not pleased about the Vatican's creation of a new structure enabling traditionalist Anglicans uneasy about the ordination of women and gay priests to convert to Catholicism.

Thanks to the influx of as many as 500,000 central Europeans since the 2004 EU enlargement, about two-thirds of them Poles, many Catholic churches are experiencing a boom. One London church had fallen to 20 members when it introduced masses in Portuguese. Suddenly its attendance soared to about 1,400 each Sunday.

The Media

Britain has nine countrywide newspapers with a circulation of over 200,000. London boasts both high-quality titles, such as the Guardian, the Times, and the Financial Times, as well as the more popular Daily Mirror and Sun, which launched a Sunday edition. After 168 years, the News of the World shut down on July 10, 2011, when evidence was discovered that it had hacked into voice-mail messages of celebrities, public figures, grieving families of dead soldiers, and a 13-year-old girl who was abducted and murdered. Two-thirds of the papers sold are conservative; in order of circulation, they are the Sun, Daily Mail, Daily Express, Daily Telegraph, Daily Star, and Times. Fewer than 10% are nonaligned: today the Independent, and Financial Times, which celebrated its 125th birthday in 2013. In 2005, the latter was judged the world's best newspaper by the Swiss-based consultant Internationale Medienhilfe. Only a fourth are left-leaning, chiefly the Guardian and the Daily Mirror.

The latter, with a circulation of about 2 million, was dealt a severe blow in 2004, when its editor was forced to resign after publishing shocking photos showing alleged British mistreatment of Iraqi

The United Kingdom

prisoners that were proven to be fakes. The following year similar photos appeared in the press, which were regrettably not fakes.

Britain has among the world's most competitive and irreverent presses. However, most newspapers face financial problems, and they are losing readers to digital news. Since 1990 overall national readership has fallen by a fifth. Most troubling is that young people are not buying newspapers as their parents did and have not developed the habit of reading a daily at the breakfast table. Instead they are getting their news from TV, radio, or online.

Russian tycoons Alexander and Evgeny Lebedev acquired the Independent, which is the first new national paper since 1985 and which they sell for only 20 pence, a fifth the price of most quality dailies, and the Evening Standard, whose circulation doubled to 700,000 when it was distributed free. Evgeny is optimistic: "People are hailing the death of newspapers. But if you go into the Tube, you'll see almost everybody is reading one." The Cameron government introduced a new system of press regulation to deal with phone-hacking and bullying of celebrities and crime victims. It involves a tougher press regulator scrutinized by a committee.

Reuters, the news wire service with particularly good international coverage, is renowned for its meticulous accuracy and avoidance of editorializing. In spite of the fact that ownership of these London dailies is concentrated in a few hands, they keep a sharp eye on Downing Street, Westminster, and Whitehall. Bringing the important political news to all corners of the country, they do not stifle the lively regional press. They are also reinforced by widely read weekly news magazines, such as the Economist and the Observer.

The written media is supplemented by radio and television, which are controlled by two public bodies, the British Broadcasting Corporation (BBC), created in 1932 and whose directors are nominated by the government, and the Independent Broadcasting Authority (IBA), which permits private advertising. Both receive revenues (in the case of BBC, over £2.5 billion annually) from licenses which everyone who owns a TV must pay. Both are expected to remain politically impartial, and both vigorously resist being used by the government in power.

In 2004 the world-famous BBC (popularly dubbed "Auntie Beebs") found itself implicated in the worst crisis in its 82-year history. It had carried a story from a government weapons expert, who later committed suicide, that the Blair government had "sexed up" a dossier on weapons of mass destruction (WMD) in order to strengthen the case for war against Iraq. The government was furious. An independent judicial inquiry in 2004 issued the Hutton Report that cleared the prime minister and his aides of charges, reported without scrutiny by the BBC, that they had exaggerated or falsified intelligence reports to bolster the case for war against Iraq. It argued that the BBC had broadcast "unfounded" allegations against the prime minister and his aides and had failed to investigate its source's charges and the government's complaints properly.

BBC's two most senior officials resigned. But a majority of Britons did not believe the report's findings. Soon afterward, the government felt obligated to launch a formal inquiry into the reasons Britain's (and America's) intelligence services apparently failed in their prewar assessments of Saddam's weaponry. His government was again found innocent of wrongdoing, despite some exaggeration of the threat. Nagging questions about his use of intelligence information to justify going to war weakened Blair and cost his party some seats in the past election.

Although a 2004 poll revealed that the BBC was still trusted by three times as many Britons as was the Blair government, it has to deal with the erosion of its viewership over the years. In 2010, BBC provided only 46% of the TV viewing by skilled and professional workers aged 55 and over and only 23% of that by working- and lower-middle-class viewers between the ages of 16 and 34. It is more popular among the wealthy and elderly than it is among the poor and young. Since multi-channel TV came to Britain in 1990 and is now received by 88% of homes, BBC faces stiff competition, and a flood of American shows have appeared. However, BBC has a range of offerings, from radio to websites, and an estimated 98% of British adults use a BBC service each week, if only a few minutes of radio.

The BBC finds itself torn between its responsibility as a neutral public service news broadcaster and its desire to compete for its viewership by taking a more aggressive and controversial approach to the stories it covers. It got into trouble in 2007, when it manipulated bits of footage in its documentary *A Year with the Queen*, to make it look like she had stormed out of a photo shoot when she had not. In addition to "Crowngate," the BBC had to admit that it had faked the winners of phone-in competitions on several programs. Auntie Beebs found herself in hot water again in 2012, when it was revealed that a popular eccentric TV presenter, Jimmy Savile, had been a serial pedophile, with hundreds of victims, and that BBC might have concealed this information. The director-general of BBC resigned, and other top news officials followed him out the door. An official report pointed to a culture of deference to untouchable stars above the law and a climate of fear at the BBC that allowed predators to commit sexual assaults.

These scandals left the BBC's reputation with the public tarnished. It launched a 24-hour news service, News 24, to compete against Sky News and CNN. It continues to produce high-quality films, which Americans like to watch on public television. In 2005 BBC secured its future with another decade of generous public funding. It remains popular, even though its audience share is dropping. The BBC had to play its part in the Cameron government's austerity policy. In 2011 it faced a funding freeze, the shedding of a third of its staff, amounting to 650 jobs, and the closure of 5 of its 32 language services.

The British film industry is far too small to compete with Hollywood. But those who go to the cinema found 2007 a very good year, with the British films The Last King of Scotland and The Queen winning Oscars. In 2008 Atonement was nominated for best picture. The King's Speech, starring Colin Firth, won the Oscar for best picture in 2011. In 2012 Daniel Day-Lewis took the best actor Oscar for his portrayal of Abraham Lincoln.

Ethnic Changes in Britain

A basic change in British society is ethnic. It had for 900 years experienced almost no immigration, except from Ireland. By the second decade of the 21st century, it was in the midst of the largest immigration in British history. From 2000 to 2009, more than 5 million foreigners moved to the country for 12 months or more, and 13.2% of the labor force was foreign-born, an increase of two-thirds since 2002.

It is no longer a racially homogeneous society. As a consequence of decolonization, Asians and blacks poured into Britain from India, Pakistan, Africa, and the Caribbean. The population is 19% non-white (half of them Asians of Indian, Pakistani, and Bangladeshi descent), a percentage that is likely to grow because of the declining birth rate of white Britons. Only 45% of persons residing in London is white. In 2006 the Muslim population constituted an estimated 1.8% of the total. Of these, 45% were of Pakistani origin, 19% from India, and 13%–16% from Bangladesh. Muslims have the youngest profile of any religious group in Britain. About a third is under age 16. Their unemployment rate is triple the national average.

Britain is faced with the difficult problem of integrating large groups of non-white minorities, who tend to be concentrated in the decaying inner cities (half are in London), even though there is less residential segregation by race in Britain than in the US. Such concentration gives the impression that the minority presence in the UK is far greater than it actually is. A fifth to a third of London's population belongs to an ethnic minority. They often speak little or no English; 22% of Londoners and 42% of children in London do not speak English as their first language. More than a third of Londoners were born abroad (up from 18% in 1987). They worship religions that are quite unfamiliar to most British and groom themselves or dress in very different fashion from the rest of the population. Critics disparage the city as "Londonistan."

Foreigners continue to pour into London at a faster rate than at any time in its history, while Britons are moving out. Other cities' populations are declining. For example, Manchester's population shrank by 10%; Liverpool's, by 8%; Newcastle's, by 6%; and Birmingham's, by 3% in the 1990s, while London's grew by 4.8% over that period. The mix has also changed: In the 1970s newcomers came mostly from India, Pakistan, and Bangladesh.

Today two-thirds of new immigrants come from high-income countries. Among the wealthiest are Russians, whose numbers in London are over 200,000 and climbing. Faced with the prospect of a flood of immigrants from the eight former communist countries (as many as 600,000 came) that entered the EU in May 2004, Britain declared that they would be permitted to seek work in Britain, but those without jobs are not permitted to claim most welfare benefits for two years after arrival. An estimated half-million persons live illegally in Britain.

This central European influx has been good for the economy, and they pay more in taxes than they take out in benefits. Arrivals are now at the top and the bottom of the economic ladder. The foreign-born are more likely to have a university education than the native population (61% to 30%). More of their kids are less likely to drop out of school and more likely to finish university degrees. They are less likely to claim welfare benefits. Nevertheless, some Britons feel overwhelmed. Many feel that they push up house prices, pour into schools without knowing English, and hold down wages. But thanks to immigration, the UK is one of the few developed countries that have a growing population. Foreign-born women are helping to stabilize the birth rate at 1.84 children. Polish women bear more children in Britain than those from any other foreign country. If this continues, Britain's population would rise to roughly 71 million by 2032 and 77 million by 2050.

Ethnic minorities suffer the most from any economic downturn, especially unemployment. British blacks have not penetrated the top levels of business, the professions, the judiciary, or the cabinet as the American black elite has. Only 1% of soldiers are minorities (compared with 27% black in the US), 2% of the police (3.3% in London), and 5% of civil servants. This may change as a result of an increase in non-white enrollment at British universities; 12% of students are from ethnic minorities, double their representation in the overall population. In London 29% of nurses, 31% of doctors, and more than 20% of civil servants are already from ethnic minorities.

In an effort to improve their public image, the London Metropolitan Police and other police forces in the country have recruited more black policemen. This is the kind of policy enacted to prevent black-white racial conflict that has proved successful. Ethnic minorities no longer have to deal with the earlier combined hostility of the police, the local government, and public opinion. Only seldom are there clashes with whites or the police; more common today are clashes between ethnic minorities themselves.

In some ways Britain is a more integrated society than is the US, at least if one observes only the Afro-Caribbean population. There is more dating and intermarriage between white and black men and women. According to a 2014 survey, almost half of Afro-Caribbean men have a white partner; the figure for women was about a third. This is lower among British-born Indians, but the figures still show change: 20% for men and 10% for women. Pakistanis and Bangladeshis mix more slowly: About 8% of men and fewer women are in mixed marriages. In the US only 4% of black men and 2% of black women have a white spouse.

Since 1999, more immigrants are coming from outside the Commonwealth and the EU than both of those sources combined. This means that there are more black Africans with large families. They intermarry far less. Tolerance for interracial marriage is strong: 74% of respondents said in a 1997 poll that they would not object to one of their close relatives marrying a black percent, and 70% said the same about Asians.

A glowing example of integration is Trinidad-born V. S. Naipaul, who won the 2001 Nobel Prize for literature. He graduated from University College at Oxford in 1953 and remained in England. An eternal outsider, he is a prickly critic of religious extremism. The panel praised him for transforming "rage into precision" in such books as *Among the Believers*. Another foreign-born British novelist, 88-year-old Doris Lessing, won the Nobel Prize for literature in 2007. Born in Iran, she moved with her parents at age six to southern Rhodesia (now Zimbabwe), where she grew up. Her writing draws heavily from her experiences in Africa. A school dropout at age 14, she moved to Britain in 1949, where she joined the Communist Party and became a fierce critic of the South African regime. She explored the divide between whites and blacks in her autobiographical *The Grass Is Singing* and in her series of novels entitled *Children of Violence*. She died in 2013 at age 94.

A combination of tough anti-immigration policies, unusually detailed laws against racial discrimination, and the fact that legal immigrants have always been treated not as migrant workers but as permanent settlers with automatic rights to vote, to run for office, and to claim social security benefits had prevented the spread of the kind of anti-immigrant sentiment and support for racist parties seen on the Continent. But this has changed, as more than a half-million immigrants pour into the country each year. There are fewer asylum seekers than before; most are workers and people entering as spouses or relatives of Britons. The government unveiled plans in 2005 to apply an Australian-style point system, ranking applicant workers according to their skills and occupations. Those with little or nothing to contribute to the British economy or who risk becoming a burden to the welfare system would be weeded out.

Anti-immigrant feelings are rising: 64% of respondents indicated in a 2010 poll that the current level of immigration is making their country "a worse place to live"; 63% thought it made the National Health System worse, and 66% said it degraded the state education system. Polls in 2007 showed that race and immigration have become main concern in the UK. In a 2005 poll, 54% had agreed that "parts of the country don't feel like Britain anymore because of immigration." At the same time, 62% of the general public (and 87% of Muslims) had favorable views of multiculturalism, and 48% believed that "immigration is generally good for Britain." Only a quarter of Britons worry about racial balance in their country. They tend to regard ethnic minorities and immigrants as one and the same, whereas in America they have always been viewed as two different things. The fact that immigration has less to do with race in Britain makes it easier to criticize immigrants.

That gave hope to those whites who want to exploit the rising tensions at election time, such as the neo-Nazi British National Party (BNP), which favors repatriation of nonwhites, and the anti-EU UK Independence Party (UKIP), which promises "freedom from overcrowding" and

The United Kingdom

Statue of Martin Luther King

an end to economic migration. As usual, these parties fell flat on their faces in the 2005 and 2010 parliamentary elections and failed to win a single seat.

Labour, which has always presented itself as the party of the underdog, receives the overwhelming majority of nonwhite votes. In the 1987 election, 27 nonwhites ran for office, and for the first time since 1922, nonwhites took seats in the House of Commons. In 2007, there were 15 members of Parliament from ethnic minorities, and there were even more in the House of Lords. The first Muslim women entered the House of Commons in 2010. Most black people in the UK are either British citizens or Commonwealth citizens who can vote in Britain. That is changing, though, as black Africans arrive in greater numbers.

It has been difficult to integrate black people and Asians into the political process, except in direct defense of their own interests. But there has been progress. Nonwhites in the UK have visible positive role models in sports, the arts, business-and the professions. There are grounds for optimism that the lauded English tolerance and gradualism will lead more British to accept the immigrants and their children as nonwhite Britons. It is symbolic that in 1998 a statue of Martin Luther King was placed in the last remaining niche above the Great West Door of Westminster Abbey. In 2007 a nine-foot bronze statue of Nelson Mandela was unveiled outside Parliament to honor his campaign to end apartheid in South Africa. It joins statues of Abraham Lincoln and Winston Churchill in Parliament Square.

British Muslims and Terrorism

Just as the celebrations over winning the 2012 Olympic Games were dying down, during the morning rush hour of July 7, 2005, death struck 52 commuters in the heart of London. Four young British Muslims, three of Pakistani origin and one convert from Jamaica, killed themselves and as many as they could take with them in three Tube (subway) stations and one double-decker bus in al-Qaeda-linked attacks. Not surprisingly for a multicultural city like London, half the victims were foreign-born, and one was an American. They included victims from all major religions. Two weeks later similar attacks were botched without fatalities.

The bloody attacks on July 7 seemed to have been planned to coincide with the G8 summit meeting in Scotland, hosted by Tony Blair. He rushed back to London, vowing that "our determination to defend our values and our way of life is greater than their determination to cause death and destruction to innocent people in a desire to impose extremism on the world." In their usual way, British citizens and parties rallied around their leader in such a time of crisis and sorrow to show that they will not be intimidated. Then–opposition leader Michael Howard extolled "the calm resolute and statesmanlike way in which the government has responded." Former London mayor Ken Livingstone assured the terrorists, "Even after your cowardly attacks, you will see people from around the world coming to London to achieve their dreams." He continued to go to work every day by subway.

Such attacks had been long feared and expected. London's antiterrorism precautions are among the most elaborate and well practiced in the world. Intelligence services in London said that many such attacks had been thwarted in recent years. After much experience with aerial and terrorist bombing, Londoners are very resilient people. The very next day, they returned to their daily routines.

But life was not the same for Britain's 1.8 million Muslims, more than a million of whom are of Pakistani ancestry. A generously defined tradition of free speech had allowed extreme clerics to preach hatred and violence, to the frustration of the majority Muslim moderates. It is not clear what motivates homegrown terrorists. Most are not poor, and they are no more likely to live in heavily Muslim neighborhoods than in mixed or white ones. Three of the bombers had been born and raised in Britain; all four were British citizens. However, a 2006 Pew Global Attitudes poll of Muslims found that 81% of British Muslims considered themselves Muslims first and Britons second. That is stunningly high when compared to France, where only 42% considered themselves Muslim before French.

Britons are looking for answers to the question of why young men who had grown up in Britain and seemed to be at least partly assimilated could become so alienated that they would commit such treacherous acts against ordinary citizens in their adopted country. Three had spent some time in Pakistan, receiving some schooling and training. Al-Qaeda's leadership, based in Pakistan, has easy access to thousands of Britons of Pakistani origin who visit their ancestral country easily and frequently.

But it is a disturbing thought that Britain now has homegrown suicide bombers who are difficult to catch. Police and intelligence agencies must contend with diffuse and overlapping jihadi groups, who are willing to die in an effort to kill as many people as possible. A *Times* poll showed that 86% of British respondents supported giving the police new powers to arrest people suspected of planning terrorist attacks. Yet the surge in recruits and supporters of radical Islamic networks continues.

The UK is faced with the task of persuading moderate, law-abiding Muslims, who constitute the large majority, to rally around the Muslim Council of Britain (MCB) to try to root out extremism on the fringes of mosque life. The government would like to draw Muslims into the policing of their own communities. The Sunni Council in the Birmingham area responded by issuing an edict condemning "all forms of terrorism, be it state terrorism or otherwise." A 2005 poll indicated that 86% of British Muslims believed the use of violence for political ends is unacceptable, even though four out of five considered the "war on terrorism" to be a war against Islam. In 2007, 79% answered that suicide bombings are rarely or never justified, while 15% thought they were often or sometimes justified.

Polls a couple of weeks after the 2005 bombings indicated that two-thirds of Britons believed their country's involvement in the Iraq War had something to do with their being targeted. Britain's prominence as America's ally in both Iraq and Afghanistan no doubt feeds some persons' rage. In February 2008 a Muslim man in Birmingham was sentenced to life in prison for plotting to kidnap and behead a British Muslim soldier and to record it all on video "to cause panic and fear within the British armed forces and wider public." In secret recordings played in court, the man was heard instructing his five-year-old son on how to behead a person.

Blair took another position, arguing that such people as the bombers can always find an excuse to persuade themselves to take other people's blood. But one thing is incontrovertible, he said: Nothing justifies such slaughter of innocent people. The attacks reinforced his case for achieving the long-term task: help establish stable democracy in Iraq, promote peace between Israel and Palestine, and support democratic reform elsewhere in the Middle East.

On August 10, 2006, police thwarted a huge terrorist plot to blow up in midair 10 American planes departing from Heathrow Airport, causing what was described as "mass murder on an unimaginable scale." Authorities arrested two dozen young Muslims, most of them British citizens of Pakistani origin; accomplices were also detained in Pakistan. In three trials from 2008 to 2010, the final one the longest and costliest terrorism trial in British history, 10 men were charged, and all but 2 were convicted of plotting to commit murder. Three were given life sentences with no possibility of bail for 20 years.

Fueled by disenchantment at home, poor educational achievement, high unemployment, discrimination, and rage about fighting in Iraq, Afghanistan, and Lebanon that they see as part of a western "war against Islam," the ranks of violent Islamic extremists are growing in Britain.

Many Britons are wondering whether their country has struck the right balance between encouraging cultural diversity and insisting on a shared national identity.

Immigration was an important campaign issue for all major parties, and it was a divisive issue in the Cameron-Clegg coalition government. Clegg and his LDP defend multiculturalism. But in a speech in Munich in February 2011, the prime minister said that, while Britain had benefited "immeasurably" from immigration, "state multiculturalism" had failed and had led many Britons to live segregated lives, without the desire to integrate. He said that somehow Britain must foster a stronger sense of national identity. The country's challenge is how such an open and liberal society that embraces diversity of all kinds can also create a sense of solidarity and belonging.

FUTURE

The Conservative government does not challenge the conventional wisdom of the foreign policy establishment that the alliance with the US is the UK's pivotal security relationship, despite the massive unpopularity of ex-President Donald Trump. The UK does not so much as hint that Europe might be an alternative pillar of Britain's security. There is less talk about a "special relationship," now rechristened

by both countries' leaders as an "essential relationship."

Prime Minister Cameron held a referendum on EU membership on June 23, 2016. The results stunned the world: 52% voted to leave the EU. Only Scotland (which threatened to leave the UK if this happened), Northern Ireland, Wales, and London voted to remain. The issues of immigration and "taking back control of the country" and its sovereignty swung the vote to leave. Cameron was replaced by Home Secretary Teresa May. As a woman politician, she had much female company: One-third of MPs and three of the four leaders who run the countries that make up the UK are women.

The first steps of separation required two years of difficult negotiations with Brussels and the 27 other EU member states until March 29, 2019. Not since World War II has Britain's future been so uncertain.

Only one out of four Tory members supported continued membership in the EU's single market, whereas 87% of Labour members did.

Hoping to strengthen her hand in the negotiations with the EU, Prime Minister May called an early snap election for June 8, 2017. The results were a disaster for her Conservative government. It lost 13 seats and its parliamentary majority despite capturing 42.4% of the votes, an increase of 5.5% over 2015. Labour won 40%, an improvement of 9.5% over 2015, but it was still 64 seats short of a majority. This was Labour's third general election loss in a row. To scrape together a feeble majority, the Tories turned to the small hard-right Democratic Unionist Party in Northern Ireland, led by Arlene Foster.

Although by the time negotiations concluded on January 1, 2021, most Britons thought Brexit was a bad idea, the House of Commons voted, 521 to 73, to approve the trade and cooperation agreement with the EU. Most Labour MPs supported it. Most Scots favor an independent Scotland and demand a second referendum.

Queen Elizabeth II, who turned 90 in April 2016, celebrated a rare event in June 2012: a Diamond Jubilee marking her 60th year as monarch. Not since 1897 had such a celebration taken place. In September 2015 Elizabeth surpassed Queen Victoria's length of reign. Her 95-year-old husband, Prince Philip, announced his retirement from public events in 2017.

Since July 2019 Britain faces the future with a new prime minister: Brexit hardliner Boris Johnson. Johnson and his Tory government continue to regard the Covid virus as its greatest future threat.

- I will lead a new government with new priorities
- A different type of politics, a more open dialogue
- My passion is education. My priority is the NHS

- I do not regret close relationship with Bush
- I would take the same position again
- There is still work to do for the common good

The Republic of Ireland

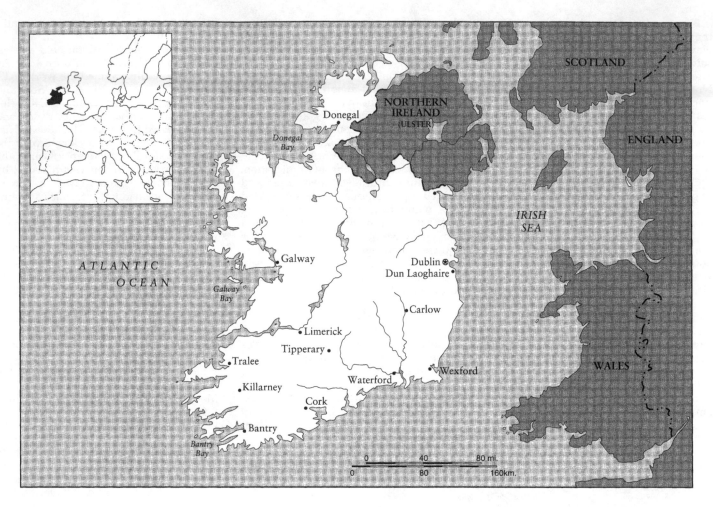

Area: 27,136 sq. mi. (70,262 sq. km, slightly larger than West Virginia).

Population: 5 million.

Capital City: Dublin (pop. 1 million, est.); a third live in or around Dublin.

Climate: Cool and damp (rarely above 65° or below 40° Fahrenheit).

Neighboring Countries: Great Britain lies a short distance eastward across the Irish Sea.

Official Languages: English, which is the first language of 98% of the population. Irish (Gaelic) is spoken as a native language by only 2% (ca. 70,000).

Ethnic Background: Celtic (some Norman and Norsemen).

Principal Religions: Roman Catholic 88.4%, Church of Ireland (Protestant) 5%, Presbyterian .4%, Muslims 19,000 and growing.

Main Exports and Imports: Machinery and transport equipment, chemicals, foodstuffs and tobacco, high-tech equipment, petroleum and other fuels.

Major Trading Partners: EU (57.7% of exports and 69.5% of imports), UK (15.6% of exports and 39.2% of imports), US (21.5% of exports and 12.8% of imports), Belgium (14.8% of exports), Germany (6.8% of exports and 7.7% of imports),

France (5.5% of exports and 3.8% of imports), Netherlands (5.7% of imports), Switzerland (4% of exports), China (3.7% of imports).

Currency: Euro.

Former Colonial Status: "Given" to England in 1155 by the pope; turbulent English control until 1922; its own parliament, diminishing control until independence.

Dates of Independence: December 6, 1921 (dominion status); April 18, 1949 (independent republic).

Chief of State: Michael Higgins, President (since November 2011).

Head of Government: Micheál Martin, Taoiseach (pronounced Tea-such), or Prime Minister (since July 2020).

National Flag: Three vertical stripes of green, white, and orange.

Green fields, white-washed thatched cottages, leprechauns, and men sitting in front of a peat fire spinning tales that are part fact and part fiction are images of Ireland that the first-time tourist seeks. This scene is also found on St. Patrick's Day cards, framed in green. While the tourist may miss much of what is new in Ireland, both the green fields and the confusion of

fact and fantasy are still there for him to find. And both are largely the result of Ireland's location—it lies at the spot where the warm air and water of the Gulf Stream confront their cold rivals of the northern latitudes. This produces a climate in which temperature variations are rare; it is an unusual day when the temperature is more than slightly warm or cold.

The confrontation of warm and cold produces air that is frequently moist—thus the lushness of the green, and skies that are always changing—gray and sad one minute, brilliant and joyful the next. If the sky is not constant, why should reality be constant? And, perhaps it is the soft, moist air that blurs fact and fantasy. George Bernard Shaw wrote of Ireland to an English friend, "You've no such colors in the sky, no such lines in the distance, no such sadness in the evenings. Oh the dreaming! The dreaming!"

If one may generalize about the people of a nation, the Irish people reflect their climate. There is a gentleness about the Irish, an essential sadness punctuated by flashes of sparkling wit. And there is a willingness to let the line between reality and dream be as indistinct as that between the distant mountains and the evening sky.

Ireland

If its location has shaped the green beauty of Ireland and the character of its people, its location has been more responsible for shaping its history. Ireland is not merely an island; it is an island off the coast of another island. While its contact with the Continent has usually been indirect, its subjugation to England has been of paramount influence. Being one step removed from the mainland has kept continental armies and the cultural influences that they brought out of Ireland. Roman legions never tramped across its fields. Although Norsemen settled on the east coast and raided many other areas, Irish culture achieved a flowering of learning and artistic brilliance while the rest of Europe slipped into the Dark Ages.

As nation-states developed on the Continent, Ireland was involved in European dynastic wars only when England had a stake in the contest. The last continental troops to be in Ireland made an unsuccessful attempt to export the French Revolution. Ireland even managed to be one of the few European countries to be neutral during World War II. As the English, century after century, negotiated and fought rivals on the continent, they did not want to have to worry about the island on their other side. The English always felt a domination of Ireland was essential to their security. The Irish Sea, after all, varies in width from 120 miles to only 11 miles, thus the fates of England and Ireland have been intertwined for the past 800 years.

Ireland is like a small bowl floating in the Atlantic. Its mountains ring the coastal region; they seldom reach more than 3,000 feet (914 km) into the sky. But the steepness with which they meet the sea gives them the appearance of considerable height. The center of the island is relatively flat, with the Shannon River flowing from north to south like a fine crack in the bottom of the bowl. West of the Shannon, peat bogs provide much of Ireland's fuel. East of the Shannon, the plains are rich grasslands, superb for cattle or horses. In fact, the Curragh, the finest stable and racetrack in the land, has 5,000 acres of grass uninterrupted by either a tree or a fence. But even in the center of Ireland, one is never far removed from the sea, for the whole island is only 150 miles wide and 275 miles long.

Ireland is a beautiful and gentle land. Tragically, its history has not always been so.

HISTORY

The Early Period

The earliest remains of humans in Ireland date from about 7000 BC. These hunters and food gatherers lived along the coasts and near the rivers. By 3000 BC Neolithic settlers had introduced agriculture and pottery. Their most spectacular accomplishments, elaborate Megalithic burial chambers, can still be seen today. At Newgrange one may enter the massive chamber by crawling through a tunnel 62 feet long. It is so constructed that only at the summer solstice does sunlight come down the tunnel and illuminate the interior chamber.

About 300 BC the Gaelic Celts used their knowledge of iron weapons to gain control of the island. Celtic Ireland was divided into some 150 local kingdoms under the loose control of the kings of the five provinces. Meath later became part of Leinster, but the four provinces of Ulster in the north, Leinster in the southeast, Munster in the southwest, and Connacht in the west have retained fairly similar boundaries to this day.

Saint Patrick

One of the high kings who ruled at the Hill of Tara from 380 to 405 AD was Niall, an ancestor of the O'Neills, an important family in Ulster until the 17th century. Niall's troops attacked both Britain and Normandy. On one raid, a young Briton named Patrick was brought back as a slave. After several years in Ireland, Patrick escaped to the Continent, where he entered a monastery. In 432, after being consecrated as a bishop, Patrick returned to Ireland. He spent Lent in prayer at the top of Croagh Patrick, a mountain overlooking the Atlantic in County Mayo. Bound by age-long tradition, even now, more than 50,000 people a year make the strenuous 2,700-foot climb to the top. And it is typical that some do it as an adventurous outing and some do it as a religious penance. In fact, thousands climb over the rough stones with bare, and therefore bleeding, feet. The story is told that two young men were climbing and one of them saw some attractive girls up ahead. He said, "Let's hurry and catch up with those girls." The other one replied, "Oh, I wouldn't dare. It's for too much foolin' with the girls that I'm havin' to make the climb."

Certainly Patrick was one of the most successful missionaries of all time. Within a few years after his death, the whole island was Christian. Celtic Christianity developed in unusual patterns. Instead of the bishop and his diocese being the chief authority, the abbot and the monastery were the center of ecclesiastical life. The emphasis on monastic life had three major effects on cultural developments.

First, monks often practiced extremes of asceticism. To this day, Irish Christianity has maintained an emphasis on self-denial and penance that affects the Irish

The ruins of Rocktown Castle, County Limerick

Ireland

character. Second, while the rest of Europe descended into darkness, Irish monasteries kept the light of western culture burning. Piety, painting, and learning were combined into one art form: the illuminated manuscript of the scriptures. Flights of imagination turned the letters of holy books into fantastic geometric shapes and celestial beings. The most famous illuminated manuscript, the Book of Kells, may be seen today in the library of Trinity College, Dublin.

Third, because monastic orders thought beyond the geographic boundaries of the diocese, Irish missionaries carried Celtic Christianity to Britain and the Continent. The Irish St. Colombo established a famous monastery at Iona off the coast of Scotland. But perhaps the most interesting missionary was St. Brendan—medieval manuscripts describe how he and a group of monks sailed in a leather boat from the coast of Kerry. They visited a land of sheep, then an island occupied by giant blacksmiths working at their forges, and later an area of great fog. Finally, they reached a new land of beauty and richness that was divided by a large river. Brendan returned to Ireland just before he died. The story has usually been dismissed as a fanciful legend. In 1977, however, a group of men built a leather boat and sailed from Brendan's creek in Kerry. They were blown to the outer Hebrides (where there are many sheep); wintered in Iceland (where volcanoes might be confused with giants' forges); were becalmed in the fog off the Grand Banks; and finally, in 1978, washed ashore in Canada. Perhaps Brendan, not Leif Ericson nor Christopher Columbus, was the first European to reach the New World.

Viking Raids and Norse Settlements

Unfortunately, the very success and more particularly the wealth of the monasteries brought trouble. Beginning in the 9th century, Viking raiders began to attack monastic and other settlements, plundering them for gold and valuables. Inevitably, the monks sought refuge in remote places.

The most spectacular of these is Skellig Michael, a tiny island off the coast of Kerry. Today, those who brave the four miles of rough seas in an open boat can climb the more than 600 steps cut into the stone face by monks over 1,000 years ago and visit the remains of the beehive huts perched 550 feet above the water. Tens of thousands of visitors come every year. But it remains shrouded in mystery. Its age is unknown, there are few references to it in written sources from the 8th century, and few artifacts have been found. UNESCO proclaimed it a World Heritage Site in 1996, and archaeologists are debating how best to preserve and study it.

Skellig Michael

By the 10th century, the Norsemen began to plan settlements. The Vikings established the first cities in Ireland near the mouth of important rivers. Dublin, Waterford, Cork, and Limerick all began that way.

At times the Celtic Irishmen intermarried with the Norse, and at times they tried to drive them into the sea. Brian Baru, after defeating the Norsemen in Munster, established himself as high king of all Ireland in 1002. Brian married the beautiful Gormflath, whose six feet of height was crowned with flaming red hair. Unfortunately, as so often happened in Irish history, treason destroyed a chance for national unity. Gormflath's half-Danish son by an earlier marriage plotted with his mother, his uncle, and other Danish chieftains to attack Brian. At the Battle of Clontarf in 1014, in which 20,000 men took part, Brian's forces were victorious and broke the Viking domination of Ireland. Tragically, at the end of the battle, a Danish soldier broke free and killed Brian in his own tent. It is even more tragic that neither Brian's brief unification of Ireland nor his freeing it of foreign domination proved lasting. No clear successor to him was able to establish control, and strife between local warlords continued as an Irish tradition. Because of these rivalries, new invaders arrived within 150 years.

The name Dermot MacMurrough has been a black one in Irish history for 800 years. It was he who invited British troops into Ireland. But it is easier to see the tragic consequences of his act in retrospect than it would have been in the 12th century. In fact, it was Adrian IV, the only Englishman ever to be pope, who set the stage. Wishing to bring the practices of Celtic

Christianity into conformity with the rest of Roman Christianity, Adrian issued the papal bull Laudabilitier in 1155 that granted Henry II of England permission to control Ireland. For 20 years, Henry did not make a move across the Irish Sea. However, when Dermot MacMurrough lost control of the kingdom of Leinster, he asked for help from the Normans, who had then been ruling England and Wales for 100 years.

Norman-Anglo-Saxon Invasion and Control

Strongbow, Earl of Pembroke, led a group of Normans into Ireland in 1170. He married MacMurrough's daughter, and for a while it appeared that an independent Norman kingdom might be established. A year later, however, Henry II himself brought a large force of British Normans into Ireland. With the murder of Thomas Becket less than 12 months behind him (see the United Kingdom chapter), Henry may have thought it was a good time for some foreign travel. He not only established Normans loyal to himself as local rulers, but he also did away with the Celtic form of worship and brought Irish Christianity under the control of the Roman Catholic Church.

Two legacies of the Normans are still plentifully evident in Ireland. Many of the great names of Ireland came with the Normans: Joyce, Fitzgerald, Barry, and Burke. These names can still be seen on many store and pub fronts. A person driving through Ireland also still sees the remains of castles, the prototypes of which were built by the Normans. These are usually rectangular stone towers three or four stories high. Most are in ruins, but a few,

Ireland

such as Bunratty, Blarney, Dungory, Cahair, and Knappogue, have been restored and are open for visitors or popular medieval banquets. Over 300 castles still stand in Ireland.

As the Anglo-Normans became settled in Ireland, they adopted more and more of the Irish ways. The old saying is that "They became more Irish than the Irish themselves." Eventually, of course, such assimilation began to threaten the rule of the British Crown. The attitude of the English was shown in the statutes of Kilkenny in 1366. These provided a punishment of the loss of lands for any Englishman who spoke Irish, married Irish people, or adopted Irish customs.

English authority was strongest in the area around Dublin, known as "the Pale." Outside this region, local rulers paid only nominal homage to the British Crown and British ways. Thus the expression "beyond the Pale" as a term of derision expresses things from the English point of view. While they had only small loyalty to Britain, the Irish rulers could hardly be described as ardent nationalists. Ireland was so fragmented politically that the idea of allegiance to Ireland itself was not an effective alternative. Rather, each local lord simply looked after his own interests.

Religious Intolerance after the Reformation

It is interesting but futile to speculate what would have happened to relationships between Britain and Ireland if the Reformation had not come to England. Perhaps Ireland would have gone the way of Scotland and Wales and become part of the United Kingdom. But the Reformation drove an irreconcilable wedge of hatred and mistrust between the English and the Irish.

England vacillated between Roman Catholicism and Protestantism through several monarchs, but with the crowning of Elizabeth I, the English were ready to try to export the Reformation. For the next 400 years, religion and nationalism would be intertwined in Ireland. In 1579, armed rebellion arose in the southwest of the island. As a reprisal against the rebels and as a reward to her soldiers, Elizabeth confiscated vast areas of land from the Irish, and gave it to Englishmen. On one such parcel of land, Walter Raleigh planted the first Irish potato. It was a crop well suited for growing by the Irish and they soon became dependent on it, much to their regret during the potato famine 275 years later, one of the greatest tragedies in Irish history.

By 1588 Elizabeth's rule was strong enough that, as the ships of the Spanish Armada wrecked against the rocky shores of Ireland, the Irish obeyed her orders and slaughtered the would-be invaders. Only

in Ulster in the north were the Spaniards spared. This was ironic; because Ulster held out against English rule, a sequence of events began that led in the 20th century to the north being the one area of Ireland loyal to the British Crown.

At the end of the 16th century, Hugh O'Neill led a rebellion in Ulster. He embarrassed Elizabeth's current favorite Essex but finally in 1601 was defeated at Kinsale by Mountjoy. In 1607 he and other Ulster chiefs fled to the Continent in "the flight of the earls." James I filled the vacuum by sending Scots Presbyterians to settle in Northern Ireland. These are the antecedents of today's Protestants in Northern Ireland loyal to the British. It is significant that the only Protestants in Ireland were imported.

Upheavals in the British monarchy brought violence to Ireland in the 17th century. Oliver Cromwell beheaded Charles I and in 1649 landed in Ireland. His purpose was to establish his brand of Puritanism in Ireland and end the possibility of rebellion. Tens of thousands of Irish were killed or driven into exile. Irish landlords in the fertile east were given the choice of death or migration to the rocky areas of the west. "Hell or Connacht" are still remembered as the only options open to them. By 1660, only one-quarter of the country was owned by Irish Catholics.

When James II, a Catholic, came to the throne of England, there was a chance of reconciliation. But there was an immediate rebellion of Protestants against James, who chose William of Orange, a

Netherlands Protestant, as king of England; the decisive battle was fought in Ireland in 1690. Protestants in Ulster still celebrate the anniversary of the Battle of Boyne, fought on Irish territory, where William defeated the forces of James. This greatly irritates their Catholic neighbors.

As retribution for support of James, the English confiscated more areas of Irish land and imposed the Penal Laws. These forbade Catholics to vote, to hold office, to send their children to anything but a Protestant school, or to have wealth above a set limit.

The Georgian Era

Much of Dublin and many beautiful country homes were built by the Protestant aristocracy during the Georgian era of the 18th century. The vast majority of the population, Catholic peasants, subsisted on potatoes grown on tiny plots of land. The success of the American and French Revolutions inspired hope among the downtrodden people. The ideals of equality and fraternity were imported from the Continent. Theobald Wolfe Tone founded the United Irishmen, a group that sought to include those of different religions in the establishing of a republic. In 1798 a French force, with Tone in attendance-landed in Mayo on the west coast. The British commander Cornwallis was more successful than he had been at Yorktown, and the French-Irish forces were soon defeated.

The English now tried to have Ireland conform to the pattern that Scotland and

The ancient mansion of Sir Walter Raleigh, Youghal

Ireland

Wales had followed years earlier. The Act of Union, passed in 1800, abolished the Irish parliament and gave the Irish representation in the British Parliament at Westminster. Robert Emmet tried an unsuccessful revolution in 1803; his statue stands today in Washington, DC, but his words were engraved on the heart of every Irish revolutionary who came after him: "When my country takes her place among the nations of the earth, then and not till then let my epitaph be written."

Further Attempts at Freedom and the Potato Famine

Two names dominate Irish attempts for freedom in the 19th century: Daniel O'Connell and Charles Stewart Parnell. But their periods of influence were separated by the most terrible tragedy Ireland ever knew. In the first half of the century, Daniel O'Connell worked to improve the position of Catholics. He won election to the House of Commons in 1828 even though, as a Catholic, he could no,t take his seat. A year later, the Penal Laws that accomplished this were replaced. In the 1840s O'Connell developed a large following that demanded the repeal of the Act of Union. However, when he obeyed an order by the British government to cancel a mass meeting in Clontarf, his political support soon failed.

By the 1840s more than half the people of Ireland were dependent on potatoes as their principal source of food. In the wet summer of 1845, blight attacked the crop, and it appeared again in 1846 and 1847. Famine and death spread across the stricken land. The relief efforts of the British government were too little and too late. In a population of 8.5 million, 1 million starved and another 1 million fled their country. English-speaking countries around the world, particularly the United States, received a transfusion of Celtic, Catholic blood that would, in turn, help shape their destinies. Even as the famine subsided, immigration continued, and for the next 40 years, 1% of the population left each year. Many found their way to America, where in the 2000 census, 10.8% identified themselves as of Irish descent, more than five times as many as inhabit the whole island of Ireland. One hundred years after the great famine, the population was only one-half what it had been before the blight struck.

As Irish immigrants prospered abroad, many did not forget the cause of Irish independence. Money and occasionally arms or leaders flowed back into Ireland and supported various movements. The Fenians, a secret society favoring armed revolution and also known as the Irish Republican Brotherhood, was founded in 1856 in Ireland and the United States.

In 1879, the Land League was founded by Michael Davitt and was supported by American money. It worked through parliament to achieve land reform. Charles Stewart Parnell became the leader of the Irish Parliamentary Party. He controlled enough seats in the British Parliament to tip the balance of power at various times. His Home Rule Bill passed the House of Commons but was defeated in the House of Lords. His next try for home rule might have been successful, but in 1890 a scandal broke when Parnell was the cause of a divorce between Kitty O'Shea and her husband. Although Parnell married Kitty, neither Victorian England nor Catholic Ireland would forgive him. How ironic it was that one man's illicit love of a woman delayed the possibility of home rule until it was too late to be effective.

In 1912, after severely limiting the power of the House of Lords, the House

The potato famine struck a severe blow to Ireland.

of Commons finally passed a Home Rule Bill, but by that time the Protestants in Ulster were afraid of being controlled by a Catholic majority. Sir Edward Casson organized the Ulster Volunteers, a military group armed with German guns, to oppose the move. The next year the Irish Republican Brotherhood and the Sinn Fein (pronounced "Shin Fane," meaning "Ourselves Alone") formed the Irish Volunteers to oppose the Ulster Volunteers.

But the outbreak of World War I caused Britain to postpone home rule for the duration of the war. With British attention focused on the Continent, the Irish Volunteers and the Irish Citizens Army staged an armed rebellion. On Easter Monday, 1916, rebels captured the center of Dublin. At the General Post Office, they proclaimed, "We declare the right of the people of Ireland to the ownership of Ireland and to the unfettered control of Irish destinies, to be sovereign and indefeasible. The long usurpation of that right by a foreign people and government has not extinguished the right, nor can it ever be extinguished except by the destruction of the Irish people. In every generation for centuries the Irish people had and have asserted their right to national freedom and sovereignty. Six times in the past 300 years they have asserted it in arms. Standing on that fundamental right and again asserting it in arms in the face of the world, we hereby proclaim the Irish Republic as a sovereign, independent state, and we pledge our lives and the lives of our comrades in arms to the cause of its freedom, of its welfare, and of its exultation among the nations."

Within a week the rebellion was crushed; because the British were at war, they reacted to the rebellion as treason and with great severity, executing most of the leaders. Eamon de Valera was spared because he had been born in the United States. Those executed instantly became heroes and martyrs to the Irish people, and hatred toward England became even deeper.

When World War I ended, the Sinn Fein again proclaimed an Irish Republic. De Valera was president, and Michael Collins led frequent terrorist raids on British installations. The British fought back with the Auxiliary Cadets (former officers) and the Black and Tans (former enlisted men). Both sides practiced atrocities, murders, burnings, and lootings. The Irish desire for freedom received worldwide publicity when Terrence McSwiney died in a British prison after a 74-day hunger strike. This strategy would later be used in the fight by India for its freedom from Britain and again in Ulster in the 1980s and 1990s.

The 32 Counties of Ireland

Strife and Freedom

The three years of fighting are still known by the Irish as "the Troubles," though many years in Irish history could qualify for that title. Parliament passed the Government of Ireland Act in 1920 that allowed for two types of home rule, one for the six counties in the north and another for the rest of Ireland. In early 1922 the republican government led by Arthur Griffith and Michael Collins accepted a treaty that made 26 counties a free state within the British Commonwealth and left the 6 northern counties a province of the United Kingdom. De Valera refused to accept the treaty and for a year and a half led a civil war against his former friends. Collins was killed in a battle, and Griffith died, but de Valera was forced to give up

his fight. William Cosgrave became head of the Irish free state; the boundary between the Free State and Northern Ireland was accepted in 1925.

Eamon de Valera returned to power in 1932 as head of the Fianna Fail ("Warriors of Destiny") Party that held a majority for 16 years. In 1937 a new constitution declared Ireland to be "a sovereign, independent, democratic state." Only formal ties with Britain remained.

Ireland was an important refueling stop for transatlantic military aircraft during World War II. It was officially neutral during the conflict, but tens of thousands of Irishmen served in the British armed forces. In 2013 the government pardoned 5,000 citizens who had fought on Britain's side. They had been branded as traitors

Ireland

By the sea in County Cork

after the war and barred from jobs in the civil service. Only about 100 were still alive.

In 1949, a coalition government led by John Costello took Ireland out of the Commonwealth and made it an independent republic. De Valera served as taoiseach, (pronounced "tea-such"), a prime minister, several times, but in 1959 he gave up leadership of the Fianna Fail and was elected president of the republic. During the 1950s, Ireland began a major push toward industrialization. Foreign capital was invited into the country and given tax incentives. By the mid-1960s, industrial output was growing at over 5% a year. Ireland joined the EC (now EU) in 1973, which gave a great boost to both its agricultural and industrial production. The improved economic situation brought about a rising standard of living. Automobiles and televisions became commonplace.

POLITICAL SYSTEM

A Written Constitution Derived from an Unwritten One

The Republic of Ireland (Eire) is Europe's newest independent state, having been founded in 1921 and having separated itself completely from Britain in 1949. It devotes much attention to strengthening a sense of Irish national identity, and the resentment resulting from recent British occupation is still very strong. Because of its long domination by Great Britain, it is hardly surprising that the Irish political system so closely resembles that of its former conqueror. Before Ireland gained its

independence, many Irishmen had served in the British House of Commons. Therefore, they had not only gained their parliamentary experience in Britain but had also contributed to the very development of the British political system.

In some important ways, however, Irish democracy differs from the "Westminster model" of Great Britain. The Republic of Ireland has a written constitution that it adopted in 1937. Article 2 of that document mandated the eventual reunification of Ireland: "The national territory consists of the whole island of Ireland, its islands and the territorial seas." This article was removed in 1998 as a contribution to a daring Northern Ireland settlement.

The Catholic Church

The constitution also pledges to support the teachings of the Roman Catholic Church, and until 2018 it banned blasphemy. Legislation in effect since January 1, 2010, bans the publication of material that grossly insults any religion, and it provides for fines to back up the ban. Except for the Vatican itself, Ireland has traditionally been the least secular state in all of Europe. The Catholic Church maintains considerable influence in social affairs. It controls all but 462 of the 3,940 primary and secondary schools. In 2011 school authorities in Dublin announced plans to remove hundreds of schools from the Catholic Church's control to reflect the increasingly diverse population. Foreign-born residents now constitute 17% of the population, up from 6% in 1991.

Until 2018 non-Christian and nonbaptized children experienced difficulties

securing a place in public schools; 85% of Irish favor ending all religious bias in the schools. Senator Donal Lydon once noted, "the Church has contacts at every level of society, in every corner. Its influence is everywhere. Any politician who ignores the views of the Church would need to be crazy." That is gradually changing as society is becoming increasingly secular.

In recent years, the church's political influence has declined significantly, as a younger generation is more reluctant to accept Catholic teachings, especially concerning sexual mores. This more liberal attitude was displayed in 2015 when it became the first country to legalize same-sex marriage by popular vote. Following a civil debate that lacked the emotional fights over divorce and abortion, three out of five voters approved. The Northern Irish assembly vetoed same-sex marriage. Three-fourths of respondents find the church's views on sex irrelevant. In the 21st century, 35% of the Catholics regularly attend Sunday mass, down from 87% in 1984 and 91% in 1974; in Dublin only 14% do so. Only 38% of Irish Catholics regularly take communion. Contraceptive devices have been legal since 1979. Ireland now has the world's largest percentage of married women under age 49 using them. Over 90% of girls age 18 to 24 use them. But that does not prevent 35% of all children from being born out of wedlock, up from 5% in the 1970s. The birth rate has fallen dramatically to two children on average, largely because more and more Irish women have entered the workforce: 54% in 2009, up from 7.5% in 1970. Nevertheless the birth rate is the highest in the OECD.

Following referenda in 1992 and 1995, Irish women were permitted to have abortions abroad; this was confirmed by a 2007 court ruling. By 2006 more than 4,000 women were going to Britain each year to have an abortion, up from 578 in 1971. This would be as if 500,000 American women had to go to Toronto each year to obtain an abortion. The abortion rate was over 10% by 2002. British abortion laws do not apply in the north, but a court ruled in 2015 that they should be available.

In December 2010 the European Court of Human Rights in Strasbourg ruled in favor of three Irish women plaintiffs that Ireland's laws and the constitutional protection for the "life of the unborn" violated their human rights. The court upheld Ireland's right to prohibit abortion in most cases. Only when there was a "real and substantial risk" to the mother's life could an abortion be performed.

In the face of furious opposition from the Catholic Church and antiabortion groups in 2013, parliament passed and the president signed a law allowing an

abortion when the mother's life is at risk or there is a possibility of suicide. This law amend the constitutional ban on abortion and codifies a 1992 Supreme Court ruling that permitted abortion in certain circumstances.

Public disgust and a bitter national debate over abortion and the influence of the church in Irish society were ignited in November 2012 when a practicing dentist from India, 17 weeks pregnant, died in a Galway hospital. The medical staff informed her that she was miscarrying. But despite her repeated pleas, they refused to perform an abortion as long as the baby's heart was still beating. She developed blood poisoning, which killed her. Her death emboldened the government to enact the legislation implementing the 1992 court decision. However, a strong anti-abortion lobby continued to exist.

In a May 2018 referendum, 66% of voters made abortion legal. In December this was ratified, 90 to 15, by parliament. Women can seek an abortion for any reason up to the 12th week of pregnancy and later in case of fatal fetal abnormality or risk to the mother's life or health. It remains illegal in Northern Ireland.

As a result of a close vote in 1995 (50.2%, with urban support outweighing rural opposition), couples are allowed to divorce after a four-year separation. The 60% yes vote in Dublin swung the result. All the parties and most of the media supported it. The campaign was bitterly fought: Opponents' posters read "Hello Divorce, Goodbye Daddy!" while proponents, irreverently referring to the spate of revelations about child-molesting and sexual transgressions by priests, waved signs reading "Let the bishops look after their own families!" These scandals involving clergy have shaken respect for ecclesiastical authority. The divorce rate has increased tenfold since 1996.

The government became involved in 2002 by ordering the police to set up a special team of detectives to investigate every case of sexual abuse involving priests ever reported. It also reached an agreement with 18 religious orders indemnifying them against abuse claims at state-financed schools they operated.

Critics charged that the government was slow to acknowledge the extent of the abuse and quick to exonerate the church. Taoiseach Bertie Ahern therefore ordered a retired judge to launch a new investigation. The report published in 2005 revealed one of the worst pedophile scandals ever in the southeastern diocese of Ferns. It identified 100 children who had complained of being sexually abused by priests. Some involved repeated rapes. It charged that the church and state had collaborated in covering up the abuse, and incriminated priests were transferred rather than punished. Compensation to victims could run into hundreds of millions of euros.

In 2014 the European Court of Human Rights overturned a series of Irish court decisions and ruled that an Irish woman was entitled to $157,000 in compensation because the government had not protected her from repeated sexual abuse in a publicly financed Catholic primary school in the 1970s. More claims are sure to follow.

A thorough inquiry nine years in the making was published in May 2009 that concluded that, over a half-century period from the 1930s through the 1970s, child and sexual abuse, as well as privation and a pervasive sense of fear and cruelty, was endemic in dozens of Catholic-operated institutions. It provided evidence that the government had colluded with the church to play down or cover up these transgressions. Many victims' groups were infuriated that no individual names were given for the hundreds of abusers, thereby preventing the explosive report from being used as the basic for prosecutions.

A second scathing 700-page report commissioned by the government and documenting the cover-ups and the widespread abuse in Catholic institutions appeared later in the year. It prompted the pope to act. He wrote an unprecedented pastoral letter on pedophilia in March 2010, apologizing to the victims and expressing his own "shame and remorse." This was seen as a vote of no confidence in the Irish bishops, and five resigned. Cardinal Sean Brady, the leader of the country's Catholics, apologized for not reporting abuses to the police. But he refused to step down after the deputy prime minister and three of the four parties in parliament called for his resignation.

In May 2010 the pope appointed a high-profile team of prelates, including the archbishops of New York and Boston, to investigate Irish dioceses and seminaries with a view to contribute "to the desired spiritual and moral renewal" of the church. Bishop Liam MacDaid, who took office in July 2010, presented a dark picture: "Society has forced us in the Irish church to look into the mirror, and what we saw was weakness and failure, victims and abuse."

Undying public controversy caused relations between the Irish government and the church to descend to an all-time low. The Vatican responded to the prime

Ireland

Former president Mary McAleese

minister's accusation that it had undermined the official inquiries into sexual abuses involving clerics by recalling its envoy to Dublin. Thereupon, the government closed Ireland's embassy to the Holy See.

Such unprecedented hostility affects young people's decisions to enter the priesthood. In 2009 more English youth were training for the priesthood (150) than Irish (99). In the 1980s over 150 new recruits entered Irish seminaries each year; in 2010 only 16 did so. In 2011 six men were ordained, making the average age of a priest 64 years. The situation is worse for nuns. Just two took final vows in 2009.

Former president Mary Robinson spoke of the country's "new pluralism," which "means the movement of a predominantly Catholic country, where the Catholic moral code and doctrines had a very significant place, to a society still influenced by the role of the Church but having other voices and having a sense of space between legislators and the Catholic Church." In the spirit of the times, the 30-year censorship ban on Playboy magazine was lifted in 1996.

Whereas Protestants in Northern Ireland outnumber Catholics by about 58% to 42%, in the republic they constitute only about 5% of the population. Since independence their numbers have declined by two-thirds. Many younger Protestants left; of the 115,000 who remain, most are elderly. Nevertheless, they have played and continue to play a role out of proportion to their size. They were important in creating modern Irish nationalism, from Wolfe Tone and his United Irishmen at the end of the 18th century to Charles Stewart Parnell and the home rule movement in the 19th. The republic's first president, Douglas Hyde, was one, as were great Irish writers like W. B. Yeats, Samuel Beckett, and Oscar Wilde. They were products of the Dublin Protestant middle class. Ireland's premier university, Trinity

in Dublin, was opened to Catholics only in recent years. Protestants created even such recognizable Irish products as Jameson whiskey and Guinness stout.

Two Languages

The constitution recognizes two official languages: English and Irish, the latter of which is a Celtic language, closely related to Scottish; Gaelic; and, more distantly, Welsh. It was spoken by a majority of Irishmen until the first half of the 19th century, when it rapidly lost ground to English. Irish is now "used frequently" by only about 5% of the people and is spoken as a native language by only about 2% (about 70,000 people) in seven small pockets along the western seaboard, an area known as the Gaeltacht. There are three dialects, and the speaker of one will not necessarily understand everything said in the other two.

Ireland is experiencing a resurgence of the Irish language. In 1996 polls, more than 1 million claimed "some proficiency" in it, and a half-million said they were "fluent" or intended to become so. Those numbers justified the creation of an Irish-language television station, called Teilifis na Gaeilge (literally "Irish TV"), which broadcasts homegrown soap operas and news and sports programs aimed primarily at educated and urbanized Irishmen. They also prompted the education ministry to create a dozen new all-Irish primary schools.

With state policy to promote the use of Irish, it is a required subject in the republic's schools. In Northern Ireland it is taught in Catholic schools, and 5,000 pupils attend Irish-language schools. Only recently did it become possible to receive a school-leaving certificate in the republic without passing an examination on the Irish language. Parliamentary documents are translated into it, and parliamentarians sometimes begin their speeches in the language. After a few sentences, though, they usually switch to English with the words "As I was saying . . ." Some persons wonder what good a sign does which reads "*Roinn na Plandeolaiochta. Aonad an Leicteron Mhiocrascóip*'," when the following words must be written underneath it to make it comprehensible: "Department of Plant Science. Electron Microscopy Unit."

Although Irish is still declining in the Gaeltacht areas, there is a trend among urban middle-class families to send their children to Irish-language schools. The state devotes €500 million ($685 million) to Irish instruction every year. When protesters confronted a government minister demanding that Irish be made an official EU language, he discovered when talking to them that they did not even speak the

language. Nevertheless, in 2007 the EU gave Irish the official status as the 23rd official language so that it could be spoken in the European Parliament. When it joined the EU in 1973, it had chosen English as its working language.

In 2005 a law came into force forbidding the use of English names in road signs, government documents, or survey maps. Another law mandates that, outside the Gaeltacht, signs bear the Irish version of the place names along with the English. A further change in road signs was made in 2005: Speed limits are now posted in kilometers per hour, not miles per hour.

The Supreme Court

As in most countries, a written constitution also calls for the Supreme Court to uphold that fundamental document. The republic has one consisting of a chief justice and five others. It is empowered to decide on the constitutionality of laws if the president of the republic asks for an opinion. This provision, known in the United States as "judicial review," is not present in Great Britain because there is no written constitution. However, English legal concepts and common law did replace the ancient Irish law (known as the Brehon law) by the 17th century. Thus Irish justice does bear an unmistakable British stamp. One British usage that was done away with in 2006 was that Supreme Court and high court judges are now addressed as "judge," not "my lord." The Supreme Court demonstrated its power in 1993 by declaring hundreds of EU directives unconstitutional because they had bypassed the Irish Senate.

The President

The most notable divergence from the "Westminster model" is that the Republic of Ireland does not have a monarch, and all links with the British Crown were severed in 1949. Instead of a monarch, the republic has a president, elected by the whole people for a seven-year term. This term can be renewed only once. The office is chiefly ceremonial, but unlike the British king or queen, Irish presidents have been leading political figures who continue to exercise considerable influence within the system, even if their powers are restricted.

The first woman president in Irish history, Mary Robinson, was elected in 1990. For years she had opposed Catholic positions on contraception, divorce, and same-sex couples. Her election signaled an important change from traditional social attitudes. She became one of the most popular presidents in Irish history, enjoying a 93% approval rating in 1996. Not inclined to shy away from controversy, she unofficially met Sinn Fein leader Gerry Adams in 1993 and shook his hand

Ireland

President Michael D. Higgins

in public in 1996, a political act that won her countrymen's praise. She became the first Irish chief of state to meet a British monarch. The fact that she is married to a Protestant manifests tolerance on this religiously torn island. In 1997 she became UN high commissioner for human rights.

Robinson's election as president in 1990 forced Ireland's leaders to take a fresh look at Irish society, which has proved to be more receptive to change than most had realized. She became Ireland's most respected politician and helped pave the way for many women to win seats in parliament.

Her successor was Mary McAleese, a Belfast lawyer and vice chancellor of Queen's University, who was the candidate of Fianna Fail. A resident of Northern Ireland, she was the first British subject to be elected president of Ireland. Under the Irish constitution, residents of the six "partitioned" counties of the north are considered citizens of the republic. She was a conservative Catholic who opposed the legalization of abortion and divorce, but she favored the ordination of women. She admited that she is an unabashed nationalist. She was not helped by the fact that she had a cousin serving a life prison term for an IRA murder. She disavowed any links with Sinn Fein and pledged to stand above politics, to "seek to heal the hurt of divided Ireland," and to "build bridges." In October 2004 she was reelected without opposition.

She was not able to run again in November 2011 because she had already served two terms. She was succeeded by Michael Higgins (known universally as "Michael D."), who captured 39.6% of the

votes, defeating entrepreneur Sean Gallagher (28.5%) and Sinn Fein candidate Martin McGuinness (13.7%). In 2018 he was reelected to a second term with 56% of the first-preference vote. On the same day, voters repealed the never-used constitutional ban on blasphemy. In his 70s, Higgins is a poet, writer, and political science and sociology professor, who did graduate work at Indiana University and who has a long record in politics. A former culture minister and head of the Labour Party, his political views are well to the left of the mainstream, and he harbors a dislike for free-rein capitalism.

The Parliament

Despite the differences described, the Irish political system developed by using Britain as a model. Irish government is parliamentary. This means that there are no checks and balances among three equal branches of government as in the United States. The lower house of parliament is supreme because unless the government can find a majority in it to carry forth its policies, that government must resign. Parliamentary government in the Republic of Ireland has usually been stable and durable. Conflict in the republic now takes place almost entirely within the parliamentary traditions and standards of conduct left by the British.

The Irish parliament (called the Oireachtas—pronounced "or-rock-tas") is bicameral. The upper house is the Senate (Seanad) composed of 60 members, 11 of whom are named by the prime minister and 6 by the universities. The remaining 43 are selected from 5 panels of nominees representing the national language and culture, agriculture and fisheries, organized and unorganized labor, industry and commerce, public administration, and social services. The Senate has the power to delay legislation for up to 90 days in order to try to amend bills. However, the lower house can always outvote it.

One might ask why such a weak body should even exist. Upper houses usually have the greatest importance in federal states where regional interests must be represented within the national government. However, the four traditional Irish provinces (Ulster in the north, Connacht in the west, Munster in the south and Leinster in the east) are not political units. Further, the 115 local authorities are supervised by the National Department of Environment. Local budgets are financed partly by grants from the national government, since local property taxes (known as "rates") cannot possibly provide enough revenue.

The Republic of Ireland is a unitary state, and political authority rests largely with the central government. This

centralized system exists even though local concerns are very important to Irish politicians. Thus, the Senate's purpose was never to represent provincial interests but instead to give some political power to certain groups, such as Protestants, which could not win it in free elections before the whole people.

Opposition to this weak Senate gained so much strength that the government decided to submit its abolition to a referendum in October 2013; the body survived by a close margin. One opponent, Peter Cunningham, described it as "the ultimate cosy club" that had "morphed into a salaried refuge for failed or retired politicians, party cronies and worthies whose activities have met with government approval." Many senators have other jobs and still receive a basic salary of €65,000 ($89,000) annually, plus up to €37,000 ($57,000) allowance for expenses.

Political power is centered in the lower house of parliament known as the Dáil (pronounced "Doyle"). This house is composed of 166 members known as Teachtái Dála, or TD for short, elected from 41 constituencies. Elections must be held at least every five years. The prime minister (called the Taoiseach—pronounced "teasuch") may choose to hold earlier elections if he desires to reestablish or widen his party's majority in the Dáil. The Taoiseach is by far the most important political figure in the republic. With his cabinet, which is composed of from 7 to 15 members, he establishes the country's policies and dominates his party in the Dáil in order to get his government's bills through parliament. He is also the best-paid head of government in the world. His salary is €310,000 ($450,000) per year, compared with the US president ($400,000) and the British prime minister ($387,700). In a gesture to share the pain with his fellow citizens, Taoiseach Enda Kenny reduced his pay in 2012 by €14,000 ($18,200).

Electoral System: Proportional Representation

In any democratic system, parties usually play a key role, presenting candidates and policy issues as alternatives from which to choose. They educate the voters; wage election campaigns; and, above all, rule or prepare to rule. Political parties are especially important in the Irish Republic because interest groups are far less tightly organized than in most other European countries. Thus, Irish parties are particularly important channels for interest groups expressing their concerns and wants at high policy levels.

Parties seek seats in the Dáil by means of a particularly complex electoral system—a form of proportional representation involving what is known as a single

Ireland

transferable vote in multimember constituencies. The voter marks his ballot by placing the numeral 1 opposite the name of the candidate of his first choice and may then place the numeral 2 opposite the name of his second choice, continuing on until he has numbered all the candidates. Thus the voter is able to say in effect, "I wish to vote for A, but if he does not need my vote or if he has no chance of being elected, transfer my vote to B. If B in turn does not need my vote, or he has no chance of election, transfer my vote to C," and so forth.

Thus, the system reflects more completely the voters' preferences for the three to five seats filled by each constituency. This makes it easier for smaller parties and independents to win parliamentary representation. At the same time, it is designed to prevent fringe politicians and a high number of small parties from winning seats in the Dáil and thereby adversely affecting the stability of the parliamentary system. It is therefore one of the better proportional representation systems in Europe. However, this complicated system enormously slows down the tabulation of the votes, and it often takes several days to determine the final results of an Irish election.

The republic's electoral system affects Irish politics in several important ways. By permitting voters to discriminate among candidates of the same party (as does the American primary system), it pits members of the same party against each other. Thus, the individual candidate's appeal must veer from the policy of the national party and be far more closely tailored to local concerns. Politicians compete with each other to perform a variety of services for local constituents, and this strengthens an important characteristic of Irish politics: Personality and personal ties become far more significant than national policy issues.

Moreover, the local political clubs, not the national parties (which have very small staffs), recruit candidates and wage campaigns. Although it is not required by law, Dáil members almost always come from the constituency in which they are elected. Also, most TDs continue to hold local political office at the same time. All of these factors represent a strong decentralized tendency in Irish politics: Politicians show strong loyalties to their local constituencies, but at the same time, the national party leadership needs to maintain strong party discipline as it seeks a majority in the Dáil. Without such discipline, no government could possibly survive.

Political Parties

Irish political parties are noticeably different from British parties, whose bases were traditionally rooted in different social classes. The Republic of Ireland is a more homogeneous country, and it has historically been economically underdeveloped. It has no major national, regional, religious, or racial differences that could become the basis for different parties. There are, of course, social cleavages, but these do not have the overriding significance that they do in many other European countries. It is more likely that the dividing line between the two major parties is determined by the position one's father or grandfather took on the signing of the Anglo-Irish Treaty in 1921, which divided the island and created the Irish Free State. In 1932, after a bloody civil war followed by intense domestic political rivalry, the party that had accepted the treaty (now the Fine Gael, pronounced Finna Gwail, meaning "Family of Irish") suffered an election defeat and relinquished power to the Fianna Fail (pronounced "Fee-anna Foil"), which had originally opposed the treaty. The 1932 elections firmly established democratic government, which stands or falls on the parties' willingness to alternate power peacefully, in response to the wishes of the voters.

The "pro" or "anti" distinction between the two major parties does not mean very much today. But the importance of family ties in Irish politics inclines Irishmen to vote as their fathers and grandfathers did, and it encourages political activists to become leaders in those same parties. It is hardly surprising that parties that are not formed along class or religious lines are not very ideological in their orientation.

North Americans who observe the two major Irish parties have the same difficulties distinguishing between them that Europeans express about American parties. Both parties in the republic are catchall parties that attract voters from all social groups. Both are rather conservative, antisecular, nationalistic and predominantly male. Both are what one would call Christian Democratic parties elsewhere in Europe.

The Irish party system had developed into two more or less stable blocs. In the past three decades, the government has alternated between the Fianna Fail and a coalition combining Fine Gael and the Labour Party. Traditionally Fianna Fail did not enter coalitions, but it must often rely on support from small parties, making its governments more fragile. Fine Gael. Labour coalitions were made easier by the fact that there is very little ideological distance between them.

Fianna Fail governed most of the time since 1932. It is moderate to conservative on economic matters; it still has a slightly anti-British attitude, although it has eliminated many of the more militant

Hon. Micheál Martin, Taoiseach of Ireland

elements in the aftermath of a party split in 1970 over the question of Irish unification. It attracts considerable support from businessmen and professional people, as well as parts of the urban working class. However, its greatest strength remains in the rural western regions. The native Irish speakers solidly support it because it has stamped itself as a party seeking restoration of the Irish language (at least nominally). It often sees itself as a grassroots party and demonstrates populist tendencies.

Fianna Fail was able to stay in power after 1989 only by forming a historic coalition with its most bitter political enemies, the Progressive Democrats. This was the first time ever that Fianna Fail shared power while ruling. In 1992 Charles Haughey (who was given a state funeral in June 2006) was finally forced out after it had been revealed that he had been aware of police bugging of two journalists' phones. He was replaced as Taoiseach by Albert Reynolds, a self-made pet-food tycoon.

As party leader Bertie Ahern led the party to victory in the 1997 elections. As usual, it took weeks of haggling and deal making before the new prime minister could go to the elegant Phoenix Park residence of the president and ask for permission to form a government. He is a populist Dubliner from a lower-class background who is separated from his wife and lived openly with his girlfriend. Ahern vowed to "cut taxes, cut crime and work for peace in Northern Ireland." Although reputed to be "green" or pro-Catholic on the volatile subject of Northern Ireland, he pushed hard for progress in the peace talks.

Riding on a tide of popular contentment with the economy in 2002, Ahern's Fianna Fail became the first government in more than 30 years to be reelected. He did it again in May 2007, when his party captured 78 seats, making him the first Taoiseach since Eamon de Valera to win three elections in a row. With 11 years in office, he became the longest-serving Taoiseach in modern Irish history.

His reputation as the "Teflon Taoiseach" failed him in April 2008. He decided to resign on May 6 before being pushed out of office because of a financial investigation against him. Half the electorate indicated in a poll that it no longer trusted him to run the country. He had become an electoral liability. In 2012 an investigative tribunal he had established found that he had lied about the source of large deposits (totaling €200,000 or $260,000) into his bank account while he was in office. He resigned from Fianna Fail rather than being expelled. Ex-Taoiseach Albert Reynolds, who died in 2014, was also accused of abusing his power.

Ahern had gained stature as a statesman in May 2007, when he helped facilitate a dramatic Northern Ireland agreement and became the first Irish leader to address both houses of the British Parliament. His last hurrah was a speech before a joint session of the US Congress just a week before leaving office on May 6, 2008. Bill Clinton and Tony Blair gave him glowing testimonials for his effectiveness in the Northern Irish negotiations. He also had presided over Ireland's most successful economic boom, which reversed the traditional emigration.

Ahern was replaced as Taoiseach in May 2008 by Brian Cowen, who had been in politics since age 24, when he succeeded to his father's parliamentary seat. In his long career, he had occupied most top cabinet posts, including the Foreign and Finance Ministries, and shown competence in each. When the Green Party withdrew its six members from the governing coalition, Fianna Fail lost its majority, and new elections had to be held in February 2011.

The result for Fianna Fail was a humiliation and a disaster. It sank to 15.1% of the votes. Going all the way back to 1932, it had never gotten less than 39%. It lost three-fourths of its seats, dropping from 78 to 20, and became only the third-largest party in parliament. This was its worst defeat in 8 decades. Voters flocked back in the February 2016 elections. Led by Micheál Martin, it captured 24% of the votes and 44 seats.

Fine Gael is a traditional establishment party that draws a disproportionate share of its votes from the upper and middle classes and from farmers with large holdings. Its leaders also tend to be drawn from somewhat higher social strata. Although it tends to be moderate to conservative on economic matters, the party has moved slightly to the left to accommodate

the Labour Party. Fine Gael is the most centralized and hierarchically organized in the republic.

In 1997 Irish voters continued a tradition maintained from 1969 to 2002: Never reelect a government, no matter how good its record. The parties were rudely reminded of an old saying in Irish politics: No good turn ever goes unpunished.

Its greatest triumph came in 2011, when it surged to 36.1% of the votes and 76 seats. Its leader, Enda Kenny, a former teacher and the longest-serving parliamentarian, became Taoiseach, presiding over a coalition with the Labour Party. Together they commanded two-thirds of the seats, the largest majority in Irish history. Both parties favor the abolition of the Senate, and Fine Gael seeks to reduce parliament by 20 seats. Fine Gael's coalition with Labour collapsed, and after an unprecedented six-week deadlock, Kenny won parliamentary backing to continue as prime minister heading a minority government.

Unlike in Britain, the Labour Party in Ireland has never articulated socialist or Marxist ideologies. In fact, by western standards, it is hardly a party of the left although it does have a left-wing minority. It had been virtually excluded from urban politics in the eastern part of the country, and most of the working class voted for one of the two major parties, especially the Fianna Fail. Its main electoral support is found among rural, agrarian workers. Its importance in Irish politics was greatly enhanced by the fact that until 1997 it had been an essential part of any ruling coalition led by either Fine Gael or Fianna Fail.

Labour experienced disaster in 2016. It collapsed to 6.6% of the votes and a mere 7 seats.

Minor Parties

Despite the proportional representation electoral system, which usually permits many parties to enter parliament, small parties had almost entirely disappeared from Irish parliamentary politics. Nineteen minor party representatives and independents did win seats in the 2011 elections. These included the environmentalist Greens, who had entered a governing coalition with Fianna Fail in 2007. This was the first time it had been in government. It was their departure from the government in January 2011 that prompted the election the following month.

The Progressive Democrats (PD) broke away from Fianna Fail in 1985 in protest against its hard-line Northern Ireland policy. It temporarily displaced Labour as third-largest party, a position that Labour had occupied since 1922. The PD appeared to break the mold of Irish party politics; it temporarily supplanted Labour as Fine Gael's favorite coalition partner, although

Fine Gael and PD compete for the same kinds of voters. It is approaching political irrelevance.

Polls long indicated that even though two-thirds of Eire's population believed ideally that Ireland should one day be a unified nation, the overwhelming majority abhorred the violent attempt to unify Ireland by bullets and bombs. It was precisely to overcome its isolation that the leader of Sinn Fein (formerly the political arm of the Irish Republican Army—IRA), Gerard (Gerry) Adams, ended the party's boycott of the Irish (though not of the British) parliament. As he stated, "We've lost touch with the people for the simple reason that we have not been able to represent them in the only political forum they know. To break out into the broad stream of people's consciousness, we have to approach them at their own level." To many traditionalists, this approach smacked of betrayal. As one die-hard remarked, "when you lie down with the dogs, you get up with the fleas."

Nevertheless, Sinn Fein is the only party with parliamentary seats in both parts of Ireland (and in London, although it refused to occupy its Westminster seats). Analysts concluded that the hard-left-leaning Sinn Fein's success was not primarily due to a rise of nationalist sentiment in the republic. Instead its young candidates exuded dynamism and concern in poorer areas on the island. It is Ireland's only truly leftist party. It appeals mainly to the urban poor, and has become the main opposition party.

In the February 2020 elections, Sinn Fein produced a shock win, capturing the most first-choice votes. Led by Mary Lou McDonald, it won 24.5% of the votes and became the most popular party. Despite being historic rivals, the two parties formed the first-ever coalition government, along with the Greens. Micheál Martin became prime minister, with Varadkar as deputy. After two years, they will swap positions.

Foreign and Defense Policies

A central reality in the republic of Ireland's foreign and defense policy is that the Irish live on a politically divided island and are a politically and religiously divided people. Few foreign policy issues can be treated entirely separately from these facts. Most Irish citizens and politicians in the republic want to see these divisions overcome, and no Irish republican government has ever recognized the division of the island as permanent. Most people in the republic do not use the term "Republic of Ireland," which implies permanent division, but instead refer to their state almost exclusively as "Ireland." But the unification issue is no longer as important in Irish politics as it once was.

Ireland

Younger leaders with no direct memories of the bloody struggle and with far greater interest in Ireland's economic development replaced the old revolutionary elite who fought for independence against Britain. A 2004 British Council poll of young Irish professionals revealed a dramatic transformation of Irish attitudes toward Britain: three-fourths have a broadly favorable view of Britain, and 81% described the relationship between the two countries as good to excellent. Irish unity remains important, but it is no longer as pressing as it once was. In fact, personal links with Britain are stronger than with Northern Ireland: Only half the respondents had ever visited the six northern counties, whereas 84% had been to London.

The Republic of Ireland lived for a long time in the shadow of Great Britain, although it has become a much more confidant nation and is no longer obsessed by its ancient hatred of the British. Because of Britain's part in Irish history and the continued presence of the British in Northern Ireland, the republic is inclined to remain neutral in conflicts where Britain is involved. It remained neutral in World War II. In fact, it even refused to observe blackouts in its cities at night. Thus German bombers were able to orient themselves by regrouping in the skies over Dublin and then flying in a direct line toward such British cities as Liverpool. In 1982, the republic also refused to go along with EU sanctions against Argentina when Britain, a fellow member, was engaged in an armed struggle for control of the Falkland Islands.

Ireland's policy of neutrality does not mean that the republic is ideologically neutral or politically indifferent. It shares the basic democratic, political, and economic values of other countries in Europe and North America. However, it is only one of four EU countries that have not joined NATO. This fact does cause disputes sometimes. For instance, when the Dáil debated the ratification of the EU's Single European Act (SEA), which calls for majority votes in the EU Council of Ministers and a completely free market, some members questioned how the republic could remain neutral and still take part in the security and foreign policy cooperation for which the act called.

The Supreme Court found that the SEA's political cooperation section was unconstitutional and therefore ruled that a referendum on amending the constitution was necessary. In the 1987 voting, 70% voted in favor of it, and 30%, against. This perennial question arose again in 2008, when the Irish debated whether the EU's Lisbon Treaty (a revision of the failed EU constitution) violated their treasured neutrality.

Ireland's long-established policy of military neutrality is increasingly irrelevant, since the country cooperates on European security matters, and Irish and British troops coordinate the fight against the IRA. In 1999 it decided to establish formal links with NATO through the Partnership for Peace (PfP). Following the September 11, 2001, terrorist attacks against the United States, Ireland offered its airspace and airfields to American military planes. In 2003 about 30,000 American soldiers passed through Shannon Airport during the military buildup around Iraq. However, Taoiseach Ahern declared, "Ireland cannot engage in support of military action because we work under the UN resolution."

It agreed in 2009 to accept two Uzbek detainees from Guantanamo Bay, Cuba, in order to help the US close the controversial prison. Ireland had served a two-year term on the UN Security council from 2001 to 2002. In 2010 it expelled an Israeli diplomat over the misuse of Irish passports by Mossad agents to assassinate a Hamas leader. The next year it expelled a Russian diplomat for using six stolen Irish identities to cover for spies operating in the US.

The republic is so enveloped by the military forces of the Atlantic alliance that it is able to keep its own defense forces very small. Internal security rests almost entirely with the unarmed police, the 10,000-strong Garda Siochana ("guardians of the peace"). External defense is the responsibility of the permanent defense forces that number 10,460, about 8,500 of whom are land forces. The navy has 1,110 personnel and 7 coastal and patrol vessels. The air force has 850 troops and is composed of fewer than 40 aircraft, including helicopters. Military service is voluntary, and there is also a reserve defense force of 14,875 that could be mobilized in time of crisis.

Ireland has contributed troops to UN peacekeeping units throughout the world, including in Kosovo (240 soldiers in 2010), Bosnia, Croatia, southern Lebanon, Cyprus, Western Sahara, Ethiopia/Eritrea, and East Timor. In 1991 the Irish government supported UN policy toward Iraq. Although Ireland played no direct role in the war, it did permit US military planes to refuel at Shannon Airport, thereby prompting many domestic critics to cry that its neutrality had been breached.

The European Union (EU)

Out of sheer economic necessity, Ireland joined the EU in 1973, at the same time that Britain entered. Ireland stood to benefit from EU regional aid and the Common Agricultural Program (CAP), which in 2002 accounted for 4% of its GDP, or $1.5 billion, and in no year exceeded 5% of its GDP. In three decades, such assistance has totaled over $32 billion. EU aid helps modernize Ireland's infrastructure. For a few years, CAP funds were a boon to Irish farmers, but their benefits were not lasting. Adjusting to CAP, western Ireland has been forced to change from its traditional dairy- and beef-farming economy to tourism and forestry. In 25 years its forestry industry is expected to be as important to the economy as its food industry is now. Its trade volume with Britain (to which 16% of its exports still go) remains important, especially since half its agricultural exports go to the UK. Brexit could devastate rural Ireland. The UK provides 39% of imports, but the EU provides 70.6% of imports and buys 57% of exports.

EU membership has served to shift Irish foreign trade and political attention away from Britain to a broader view of the rest of Europe. Brexit will adversely affect Ireland's foreign trade, direct investment, and the openness of its borders. Former president Robinson argued, "it lifts the burden of the relationship with our close neighbor. We are now partners with them in Europe. The history is still there, but it is less a tight connection and burden between us." For centuries Ireland had defined itself, in relation to Britain, as a victim. That is far less prominent now. Today it is more inclined to define itself in relation to Europe and the EU, in which it is recognized as an equal. It distinguishes itself from Britain and benefits from being the most pro-European anglophone country in the EU. This foreign policy reorientation has not altered the fact that hundreds of thousands of Irish still live and work in Britain, where they enjoy the same political, legal and social welfare rights as British citizens.

Some Irish worry that increasing integration with Europe may have negative effects on Irish culture. Arts Minister Sile de Valera, granddaughter of Eamon de Valera, said during a visit to Boston that EU regulations and directives "often seriously impinge on our identity, culture and traditions." Ahern's deputy prime minister, Mary Harney, also warned against a more centralized and bureaucratic Europe. She claimed that spiritually Ireland is "probably a lot closer to Boston than to Berlin."

In a June 8, 2001, referendum marked by massive abstention and indifference, a majority of Irish slapped the EU in the face by rejecting the Nice Treaty, which had laid out the process for enlarging the community. Many Irish were smarting from an earlier EU rebuke of the country's economic policy, were fearful of losing EU funding if a dozen poorer countries were admitted, and were uneasy that its neutrality was being threatened by Europe's acquisition of its own defense and security role.

A second referendum was held in October 2002, and this time the government spent 10 times more on the referendum campaign than it had the first time. Voters overwhelmingly endorsed the Treaty of Nice, 54% to 46%, with a turnout of 48.5%, giving the green light to EU institutional reform and enlargement and causing a sigh of relief throughout the community. Ireland is the only EU country whose constitution required that the new constitutional Lisbon Treaty be submitted to a referendum in June 2008. Voters rejected it. However, 60% of voters said yes in a referendum held in June 2012 to approve the EU fiscal treaty.

In 2002 Ireland gained more visibility in the EU when Pat Cox was elected president of the European Parliament. In the first half of 2004, Ireland assumed the EU presidency. It oversaw the entry of 10

new members and guided the discussions to salvage the new constitutional treaty on which the members could not agree. It assumed the rotating presidency again on January 1, 2013, celebrating 40 years of membership in the EU.

Leaders of the accession states were welcomed in a glittering ceremony in front of the presidential palace in Dublin on May 1, 2004. They looked to Ireland more than any other country as their model. Charles Grant of the Center for European Reform noted, "Ireland is a poor country dominated by a big neighbor, and all of the new countries except Poland are small countries dominated by big neighbors."

But it is poor no more, despite serious economic recession beginning in 2008. When it joined the EU in 1973, its per-capita income was a mere 62% of the EU average; by 2003 it had reached 136%. It slashed its top corporate tax rate from over 40% to 12.5% (6.25% of revenue from patents and intellectual property) and the state's share of GDP from 54% in the 1980s to only 33% in 2004. Foreign investment poured in. Unemployment fell from 17% in 1987 to 4.3% in 2006 and 5.3% in 2019. Cox stated the obvious: Membership "turned us from a stagnant, backward, failed part of the British regional economy into a modern and prosperous European country." This tiny land had become the third-richest country in the EU, and it is still one of Europe's richest nations. That was exactly what fascinates the new eastern partners and what they want for themselves. But this wealth had a significant consequence: Ireland became a net contributor to Brussels's coffers and therefore helped finance the assistance for the poorer new members.

There was nervousness throughout Europe over how unpredictable Irish voters

would decide in a June 2008 referendum over the EU's constitutional revision, known as the Lisbon Treaty. Ireland was the only member state whose constitution required such a plebiscite.

Polls indicated that voters would say yes, but on voting day, they shocked the rest of Europe, just as they had done in June 2001, when they rejected the Nice Treaty. This time, in a convincing vote of 53.4% against and only 46.6% in favor, voters said no to the reform that was intended to enable the enlarging EU to make quicker and more coherent decisions in vital areas. The results dramatized the inability of EU leaders to persuade citizens that they can benefit from reforms described in a long, dense, complex 277-page legal document.

At a time when economic growth was slowing and the real estate market was collapsing, it was easy for opponents of the treaty to exploit the fears of anxious Irishmen. Many worried about immigration and the possibility that Brussels could usurp their power to levy their own taxes, determine their own family law, and decide when and how to use their own armed forces.

The Irish government negotiated a compromise with the EU in an effort to salvage the Lisbon Treaty. It agreed to hold another referendum on October 2, 2009, after the EU offered assurances that Irish neutrality would be respected, that there would be no interference in Irish taxation or abortion laws, and that all member states would continue to have at least one commissioner in the European Commission.

Irish voters are notoriously unpredictable, but the severe economic downturn made it clear to many of them just how much Ireland needed the EU and the euro to stabilize its economy. The "yes"

Ireland

campaign also played on the fear of falling under British influence. The Irish know that one of the main benefits of EU membership is to boost their self-confidence in relation to Britain. Armed with much more knowledge about the treaty than they had shown in the first referendum, voters accepted it, 67% to 33%. The May 2012 referendum over the EU's policy of austerity was also a cliff-hanger, but it passed, 60% to 40%.

Reunification

The vast majority of the citizens of the Irish Republic and virtually all of its political leaders share the goal of reunifying all 32 Irish counties. But they eventually wish to see this accomplished peacefully and with the consent of the Northern Irish. In Northern Ireland, about 1 million Irish Protestants outnumber the half-million Catholics, so Irish unity must take a form palatable to the Protestants. Violence spilled over from Northern Ireland to the south. The Irish government outlawed the provisional IRA; government raids and arrests provide frequent reminders that the IRA can expect no tolerance within the republic. In 1982 a Dublin court convicted an Irishman for possessing explosives, even though the crime was committed in Britain. This was the first application of a 1976 law that was part of an ongoing Irish-British cooperation against terrorism in both countries.

In 1981 a US court convicted the Irish Northern Aid (NORAID) committee for failing to list the IRA as its principal foreign agent. The Irish government ordered its diplomatic representatives in the United States to boycott the 1983 annual St. Patrick's Day parade in New York City because the organizers of the parade had chosen an IRA supporter as grand marshal. In explaining its decision, the Irish government noted that the IRA's actions, which include collecting money from unsuspecting Irish Americans to finance violent operations in Northern Ireland, "have deepened the wounds of our troubled history and continue to postpone the day of Irish unity and reconciliation." Dublin frequently appealed to Americans not to support violence in Ireland. Funds from NORAID declined, and the IRA sought to fill its coffers by means of extortion and racketeering in Northern Ireland.

The Irish government realizes that unification can be accomplished only in cooperation with Britain and Northern Ireland. This has brought the Irish and British prime ministers together for periodic high-level meetings to discuss the developments in the area. This was dangerous, as was shown by the attempt on Prime Minister Thatcher's life in the grisly 1984 IRA bombing of the hotel in Brighton

Mr. David Trimble,
former leader, Ulster Unionist Party

where she was staying. She narrowly escaped death, and several Tory leaders were killed or wounded. The bombing inflamed anti-Irish sentiments to a height unequaled since the IRA murdered Lord Mountbatten in 1979, and it set back progress toward peace.

Nevertheless, consultation between representatives of Eire and the UK continues within the rubric of the 1985 Anglo-Irish Accord. For the first time, this permitted Dublin some say in Northern Ireland's affairs. The agreement enjoys majority support in the republic. In 1990 the pope appointed Bishop Cahal B. Daly, a fierce critic of IRA terrorism, as Ireland's primate. In 1993 optimism was ignited by a joint declaration by the British and Irish prime ministers offering Sinn Fein a seat at the bargaining table to discuss Northern Ireland's future if the IRA renounced violence. Prime Minister John Major promised that Britain would not stand in the way of a united Ireland if a majority of Northern Ireland residents supported such a step. Taoiseach Albert Reynolds pledged that there would be no change in the six counties' status without majority consent.

As a symbol of returning normalcy with Britain in 1995, Prince Charles became the first member of the royal family to make an official visit to the Irish Republic since 1922. Also in 1995, David Trimble, then leader of the Ulster Unionist Party, the main Protestant group, traveled to Dublin and met with Taoiseach Bruton. This was the first time since 1922 a unionist leader was received in Dublin. On November 26, 1998, Tony Blair became the first British prime minister since Ireland's independence to speak to the Irish parliament.

Talks involving eight Northern Ireland parties and the British and Irish

governments continued despite sporadic outbreaks of violence. In 1998 a majority in Eire backed the deletion from their constitution of the mandate to unify the island. As a result of the 1998 Good Friday Peace Agreement, followed by dramatic "yes" referenda votes for the accord in both the republic (94.4%) and Northern Ireland (71.1%), Ireland reached the doorstep of peace. Trimble and his Catholic counterpart, John Hume, received the 1998 Nobel Peace Prize for their role in reaching a historic peace agreement in Northern Ireland that year. Despite continuing setbacks, there is optimism that "the Troubles" will end.

In February 2005 the Dublin government named Sinn Fein leaders Gerry Adams, Martin McGuinness, and Martin Ferris as members of the IRA's ruling army council. Joined by the British government, it dropped the polite fiction that the leaders and organizations of Sinn Fein and IRA are separate. Ahern declared an end to "creative ambiguity." They are both to be regarded as one and the same. Justice Minister Michael McDowell called the IRA a "colossal criminal operation" and launched a major campaign against IRA racketeering. For decades the IRA has operated a range of criminal enterprises to finance IRA operations, including robbing banks and armored cars, counterfeiting currency and goods, smuggling fuel and cigarettes, and trafficking in drugs.

In February 2005 the Irish government ordered the police to move in on IRA money-laundering operations, believed to center on hotels and pubs. Three million pounds in cash were seized at the home of a businessman. Five young men were convicted in a Dublin court after their vehicles were found filled with fake police uniforms, stun guns, balaclavas, lump hammers, and lots of Sinn Fein election posters. The Irish and British governments agreed to share cross-border policing duties.

At Easter 2006 the Dublin government revived the tradition of commemorating the failed 1916 rebellion against the British by marching 2,500 soldiers and veterans down the main boulevard, O'Connell Street, where most of the fighting had taken place. To showcase the current friendly relationship, the British ambassador joined the leaders of the six main political parties in attendance. The republic is divided over whether the 1916 rebels were heroic patriots or trouble makers, and there was lively debate over whether the parade was an appropriate way to remember the event.

In an attempt a month earlier to demonstrate fairness and tolerance of a unionist alternative tradition, the government had permitted a march down O'Connell Street, past the post office, by 300 loyalists, most of them relatives of IRA victims. However, they were blocked by republican dissidents. The result was the largest riot Dublin had seen for a quarter-century. Gangs of young and drunken thugs wrecked cars and looted stores. The damages were set at €10 million ($15 million). Tanaiste (Deputy Prime Minister) Mary Harney admitted that the riots had brought "shame on the city, shame on the country."

On May 8, 2007, a power-sharing agreement in Northern Ireland was celebrated after three decades of violence and five years of rule from London. The last step in this process was taken in 2010, a year that saw major progress in the power-sharing and reconciliation process. In February, after almost two weeks of marathon negotiations, a landmark agreement was reached giving the Northern Irish government direct responsibility for policing and justice. This includes responsibility for police, prisons, and the prosecution service. This "devolution of policing" was the last missing piece of the Good Friday Agreement that established power sharing.

In March 2010 all the nationalist members and most of the unionists (except the UUP) voted for the historic measure in Stormont. In accepting it, Sinn Fein agreed for the first time to recognize and cooperate with the British state. Despite a series of bomb attacks by deadly splinter groups attempting to undermine the agreement, it took effect on April 12. The same day Northern Ireland's first justice minister in four decades was appointed, David Ford. Power sharing has provided considerable political harmony and has ended most paramilitary violence, even though it has not eliminated the last diehard bombers and gunmen. In May 2011 the Northern Irish governing coalition of the Democratic Unionists and Sinn Fein strengthened their control of the Stormont assembly by winning reelection in regional elections. This was a clear rebuff to militants on both sides who try to keep ancient animosities alive.

The Orange Order marches free of violence yet. Only three months after the handover of police powers, hundreds of rioters in Belfast battled the police with gasoline bombs, bricks, metal bars, planks, and concrete slabs, leaving 82 police officers injured. The violence, reminiscent of earlier times, erupted when the Protestant Orange Order rejected a new system for mediating the routes and timing the marches. Nevertheless, power sharing has enormously improved life in Northern Ireland.

The year 2010 also witnessed an electrifying apology by newly elected British prime minister David Cameron. On June 15 a 10-volume, 5,000-page final report

Irish village life

was issued on the events of January 30, 1972, a fateful day known as "Bloody Sunday." British paratroopers opened fire upon unarmed demonstrators during a civil rights march in the Bogside area of Londonderry, leaving 14 men dead and 13 injured. It was a deeply held nationalist grievance, and relatives' requests for an investigation went unanswered. In 1998 then–prime minister Blair ordered what became the longest and most expensive public inquiry in British history to be conducted.

After 12 years, more than 900 witnesses, and a cost of $288 million, Cameron stood up in the House of Commons to announce the conclusions: The soldiers had shown a "widespread loss of fire discipline. Some members of our armed forces acted wrongly." The demonstrators had not provoked the attacks. Even Martin McGuinness, who was present and probably armed with a submachine gun, did not "engage in any activity that provided any of the soldiers with any justification for opening fire. What happened should never, ever have happened." The shootings were "both unjustified and unjustifiable." And then the dramatic words: "On behalf of the government, I am deeply sorry." In Londonderry, thousands gathered at the site of the shooting and cheered as the prime minister's speech was broadcast live on giant screens.

London's Metropolitan Police released evidence in 2012 that agents working for the British army had worked with death squads in Northern Ireland. This included the 1989 murder of Belfast lawyer Patrick Finuncane, who had represented IRA terrorists. Two gunmen from the outlawed Ulster Defence Association broke into his home and shot him 14 times at point-blank range before the very eyes of his wife and three children. The report detailed how British intelligence was implicated in the murder. Then–prime minister Cameron

immediately went to Parliament. There he condemned the murder as "an appalling crime" and apologized to the family. (See United Kingdom chapter.)

The normalization of the Irish-British relationship was cemented in May 2011 by the first royal visit to Ireland since George V went in 1911. It was the capstone for the Northern Irish peace process. Loaded with symbolism, the visit would have been unimaginable without the dramatically improved bilateral relations since the Good Friday Agreement. Queen Elizabeth II laid a wreath in the Garden of Remembrance in Parnell Square, which commemorates the Irish who died in the struggle for independence. She also laid one in the National War Memorial Gardens, which honor the 50,000 Irish who died fighting in the British armed forces during the First World War. She then went to Croke Park Gaelic soccer stadium, where British auxiliary police had killed 14 Irish civilians in 1920 in retaliation for the deaths of British authorities. These ceremonies sent a powerful message to most Irish.

The monarch acknowledged a "troubled past," but she assured that the two countries are now "firm friends and equal partners." Deputy Taoiseach Eamon Gilmore said, "This is about closing the door and moving on from the past. . . . It's about normalizing the relationship." The ties are very strong: An estimated 6 million British have an Irish parent or grandparent, and Ireland is the UK's fifth-largest export market.

In 2012 she ended a visit to Northern Ireland by shaking hands with Martin McGuinness, who had belonged to the terrorist organization that murdered her cousin Lord Mountbatten in 1979. Elizabeth smiled but did not speak while McGuinness spoke to her in Irish, using words that translated to "goodbye and Godspeed." The brief meeting signified a new era. Prince Charles followed up in

Ireland

May 2015 by meeting with Gerry Adams in Galway.

In reciprocation, President Michael Higgins made the first state visit to Britain by an Irish president in April 2014. He and his wife, Sabina, stayed as guests of the queen in Windsor Castle. This was a rare privilege. Martin McGuinness, who died in March 2017, also took part in the visit. As a further sign of the two nations' improved ties, the British government announced that two years later it would be represented at the centenary commemorations of the 1916 Easter Rising against British rule.

When clashes in the assembly and Belfast streets broke out in July 2013, former American diplomat Richard Haass was asked to help find a compromise on three issues: how violent crimes committed during the Troubles should be investigated, whether and when the union flag could fly from public buildings, and what rules should govern parades. Months of negotiations, seven position papers, and visits by the British and Irish prime ministers failed to resolve the issues. But some progress was made in identifying areas of agreement and disagreement and on the issue of historical crimes. Until 2020, reunification seemed to be no more an unattainable fantasy. That is no longer true; it is becoming more likely. Sinn Fein's stunning electoral performance in 2020 shows how much attitudes have changes. The republic has become more welcoming and liberal. (See preceding United Kingdom chapter.)

ECONOMY

In the last half-century, Ireland has undergone an economic revolution. Despite the worst economic recession in memory (and the worst in the eurozone) that plagued the country in 2009 and beyond, fundamentals for the resumption of a strong economy in the future remain in place: a small, open, low-tax economy; an educated, English-speaking, adaptable, and young workforce; and strong European and Atlantic links with an Irish diaspora ready to led a hand. The influx of foreign investment as a result of generous incentives and the increase in trade have added significantly to the prosperity of Ireland. More than 1,100 foreign firms employ half of all Irish workers involved in manufacturing. Foreign companies are also responsible for 80% of the country's nonfood exports. It has also acquired an impressive high-tech industry. By 1986 it had already achieved the highest ratio of high technology to total exports of any EU country.

What made Ireland so rich so quickly? There is a combination of factors: It cut spending, taxes, and borrowing, and it adopted the euro. It established a social partnership between trade unions and management that keeps wages down and respects the opinions of the unions. Labor markets were liberalized, making businesses relatively free to fire and hire. Also employer social security payments are lower. The EU poured in transfers equivalent to almost 5% of Ireland's GDP. The European single market was a boon to trade.

Roughly a fourth of all American investments in Europe go to Ireland; this is more than America invests in China. The US is Ireland's largest source of foreign investment. It is the biggest trade partner for services, the second-largest for trade in goods, and the second-largest market for tourism. Educational standards, including in business administration, engineering, and the sciences, are kept high, and English is spoken.

Although Ireland's birth rate is falling, it still has a relatively young population. Finally, more people are working. More women are in the workforce (54%), and labor-force participation for both sexes has risen from 60% in the 1980s to 70% today.

Outmigration had temporarily ended, and immigrants poured into the country, one-third to one-half of whom had Irish roots. By one estimate, a quarter-million people immigrated between 1995 and 2000. The Irish government estimated that 14,000 Irish returned from the US after 2001, more than half of them from New York. The US Census Bureau reported that by 2005 the Irish population in the US had shrunk by 28,500 to 128,000; the number of illegal Irish had dwindled to 25,000 to 50,000. One million Irish with active passports live outside the country. Thirty-two million Americans have their roots in Ireland. This includes President Joe Biden. Prime Minister Micheál Martin called him a "stalwart supporter" of Ireland and the most Irish president since Kennedy. Biden proclaimed that "Ireland will be written on my soul."

The recession that began in 2008 and did continuing severe damage to the Irish economy reversed this inflow at least temporarily. The first to go were immigrants returning home to central Europe, but increasingly it was the Irish themselves, who left to look for greener pastures. In 2011–2012 they were leaving at the rate of 1,000 per week. Total emigration for those between 15 and 44 was 75,800 in 2012. Nearly 60% had university degrees. Almost half of Irish doctors were working abroad. One Irishman noted, "You don't go to parties any more. You go to going-away parties."

Like the UK, Ireland opened its doors to citizens of new EU member states after May 2004. There was an influx of 300,000 from those countries, mainly from Poland, who registered for work. This includes many students looking for temporary jobs while polishing up their English. Dublin's main afternoon newspaper, The Evening Herald, includes a Polish-language supplement, and there are other locally published newspapers and magazines available in Polish. Some Irish suspect uneasily that there are now more Polish speakers in the country than Gaelic speakers.

These newcomers were a key factor in the continued strong economic growth rate and for the construction boom. There is no evidence that they have displaced Irish workers, and they are still paid less than the Irish, although the gap is narrowing. But their presence sparked a debate over whether they are driving down wages. Trade unions pointed to Irish Ferries, which wanted to employ cheaper Latvian crews. Seven out of 10 newcomers are from Europe. There are tensions, but no anti-immigrant political movement has emerged.

Growth and prosperity in Ireland was dramatic. Less than 30% of all households are rented. The Irish entered the 1990s with a 50% gap between their living standards and those of the EU average. By 1998 income in Ireland had caught up with the European mean and surpassed Britain in per-capita GDP for the first time in history. Also, a variety of social welfare indicators in Ireland are as good or better than in Britain. Life expectancy for women is 83.5 years and for men 79.5. Ireland spends a higher percentage of its GDP on

A new generation of Irish youth, Kinsale

public education. Per capita consumption rose 10.5% from 1990 to 1996, twice the average rate of increase in the rest of Europe. Sustained economic growth, low inflation, a hard currency (the euro, to which some economists give credit that the recession was not even deeper), a healthy trade surplus, and relatively low unemployment (5.3% in 2019, a 10-year low) cohabited with a growing income gap between rich and poor.

It is an extremely productive, capital-intensive, and modern economy, only partly owned by foreigners, including companies like IBM, Intel, Fujitsu, Pfizer, Google, Facebook, and Motorola, as well as banks and financial institutions, like Citibank, Merrill Lynch, and Daiwa. Nine of the world's 10 top drug companies are there; one-third of all personal computers sold in Europe are manufactured in Ireland; it is the world's largest software exporter (ahead of the US). Dell's computer plant in Limerick was one of the company's most productive, but Dell shocked the country in 2009, when it left Ireland for a location in low-wage eastern Europe. HP Compaq is Galway's largest employer. The country is trying to invest more in research and development so that its own companies can grow to such status. Attracting foreign investment offers the island the best chance to recover economically and repay its debts. FDI pours in even after the recession, especially from America and particularly in the fields of pharmaceuticals, financial services, and information technology. By 2013 employment at foreign companies had returned to precrisis levels.

Agriculture has declined in importance in the last four decades—the percentage of the workforce employed in farming dropped from 43% to 4.7% in 2017; they produce only 2% of GDP. Industry's share in employment is 19%, producing 24% of GDP. Services account for 77% of employment and 74% of GDP. The agricultural life of Ireland benefited from EU membership, although income from the CAP helped fuel the rapid growth of welfare spending and thus contributed to the country's debt problem. Income in the farm sector has doubled in the past three decades, and today one-half of the value of agricultural production is exported. However, family farming remains relatively unsophisticated, and food processing has not developed as far as in some EU countries.

Two other sources of revenue are important to Ireland: tourists and pubs. By 2000 Ireland was the fastest-growing tourist destination in Europe, growing by 12% during the 1990s. Each year 5.5 million tourists (that is more than the number of Irishmen there are to receive them) visit the nation, despite the fact that Ireland is the only EU nation not directly linked to the Continent since the opening of the English Channel "Chunnel" in 1993. Americans account for 14% of the total, although they tend to spend more money than other visitors.

By 2019 the Irish drank in 8,400 pubs; the ratio of 1 pub for every 300 people was even more striking when one knows that half the population is under age 25, and thus the ratio of pubs to those old enough to drink was even higher. Annual alcoholic consumption per Irish adult jumped from 10.6 quarts of pure alcohol in 1985 to nearly 15.8 quarts in 2000, compared with the EU average of 9.5 quarts, despite high taxes on wine and spirits. This was the highest increase in the EU and brought with it more social problems, such as higher absenteeism on the job, auto accidents, and medical care costs.

With alcohol consumption up, both parts of Ireland moved to lower the legal driving blood alcohol content from .08% to .05%. This raised concern from an unexpected quarter—the Catholic Church. Since the number of priests is rapidly decreasing, more and more of them have to drive from church to church to say two or three masses per day. After each service, the priest must consume any communion wine left over since it is considered to be Christ's blood in the Eucharist; throwing it out would be blasphemous. The clergy must therefore sometimes drive impaired from parish to parish.

The air has been healthier since 2004, when smoking was banned throughout the republic in all pubs, restaurants, and workplaces (including company cars and trucks). Only prisons, police cells, psychiatric hospitals, and hotel rooms were exempted. In the decade since 2001, the smoking ban, changing drinking habits, and the economic recession reduced alcohol consumption by 21%. Such sobriety caused 833 pubs to close from 2007 to 2010.

The Irish economy is dependent on events outside of the country because of the important roles that trade and foreign sources of energy play in the life of the island. It is vulnerable to global recessions. It is a land that must import many essential raw materials. It does have a large quantity of zinc ore, as well as copper, sulphur, baryte, gypsum, and dolomite. Its only valuable energy source is peat, or turf bogs, which cover parts of the Central Plain and large areas along the south, west, and northwest coasts. It lacks sizable coal deposits, but it extracts natural gas near Kinsale Head.

Although recent discoveries on the ocean shelf may produce oil for Ireland, at this time the country has very little. Yet 70% of its energy needs are supplied by

Saucy Irish youth

oil. Thus, the Irish economy was drastically affected by changes in oil prices while remaining dependent upon unstable world trade for its strength. It generates no nuclear power. Peat provides 6% of energy.

Almost 90% of Ireland's GDP is generated by trade. Manufactured goods account for well over half the value of exports. Since 15% of these go to the United Kingdom (and the percentage is steadily declining) and over half to the continental EU members (a percentage which has steadily risen since 1973), Ireland is vulnerable to economic ups and downs in those industrialized countries. In 2002 it joined 10 other EU nations in adopting the euro. Ireland again presents an image of financial stability that foreign investors like.

In 2015, total public debt stood at 100% of GDP (down from 131% in 1987 but up from 25% in 2007). Its 2004 budget deficit was only .4% of GDP, well below the 3% limit required to meet the EU's convergence criterion for the European currency. These statistics changed dramatically after the 2008 recession. By 2021 its budget deficit was 5.3% of GDP, one of the largest in the EU. Taxes are kept low for foreign firms in order to attract them to

Ireland

FINANCIAL TIMES | Saturday June 14 / Sunday June 15 2008 | USA

USA $1.85 Canada C$2.50

LIFE & ARTS COVER STORY
The golden age of tennis
How Wimbledon sells a vision of a bygone era

COMMENT PAGE 7
Dick Fuld
Can the embattled chief executive put Lehman's house in order?

LIFE & ARTS PAGE 3
Diane von Furstenberg
The fashion designer has Lunch with the FT

Newspaper of the year

Inside

Jancis Robinson tastes Chilean wines
Life & Arts
Page 6

Irvine Welsh on Obama and the young Americans
Life & Arts
Page 2

Anish Kapoor: an artist with a magician's toolkit
Life & Arts
Page 16

Garden party Pope breaks with protocol for Bush visit to Vatican

Pope Benedict XVI yesterday broke with protocol by receiving George W. Bush in the Vatican Gardens, reviving a frenzy of speculation in Italian media that the US president might convert to Catholicism. 'Such an honour, such an honour,' Mr Bush said, as the pair entered the medieval St John's Tower for a private discussion **Report, Page 4** AP

Energy costs push up US inflation

By FT reporters

Fears of accelerating global inflation were further heightened yesterday when US consumer prices surged 0.6 per cent in May on the back of rising energy costs.

The jump in the US consumer price index was the largest since last November, as items such as air fares and petrol became much more expensive. However, core consumer prices – which strip out food and energy costs – were reasonably stable, rising only 0.2 per cent. The jump in US inflation came after it emerged that eurozone hourly labour costs rose 3.3 per cent – the fastest rate for five years. In Asia, India's inflation rate hit 8.75 per cent at the end of May – its highest level in seven years – prompting talk

---

invest in Ireland, making it the EU's biggest tax haven. New investors receive tax breaks, and overall corporate tax rates are 12.5%, far below the EU average of more than 30%. Personal taxes also began to be reduced sharply. Ireland still has Europe's highest VAT at 21%.

The economic growth that Ireland enjoyed since the mid-1950s was impressive. After averaging 6% from 1993 to 1998, it slowed down. It stood at around 4.6% from 2004 to 2007. In 2009, however, it was deep in negative territory (–7%), and by 2013 the economy had shrunk by a total of 20%. In 2015 it grew by 7%, by far the fastest in the eurozone, and it grew by almost 4.3% in 2021. Before the recession the economy had speeded ahead so rapidly that Ireland had not had time to revamp its infrastructure. Roads are often clogged, hospitals are overcrowded, and housing is tight and expensive.

Average Dublin real estate prices quadrupled in the decade 1994–2004. Average Irish homes in 2006 cost $450,000 ($600,000 in Dublin), nearly 10 times the average level of industrial wages. This affected a lot of people, since almost a third of the Irish population generating close to 40% of GDP live in or around Dublin. Elsewhere, housing prices rose by 14% in 2003 alone. However, the housing bubble

began bursting in 2007, falling almost 4% in that year alone and much more in the following years. In 2013 housing prices were nearly 50% below their peak in 2007; by 2019 they were 20% below. House prices in Dublin had risen by 10% in 2012 and continue to rise.

This severely hurt the economy, since a quarter of it was dependent on the property market, and construction accounted for 13% of economic output. With property values sliding, the banks, which held many bad mortgages, faced collapse, and bankrupt unfinished "ghost estates" became visible evidence of the disaster. The earlier Cowen government made the reckless decision in 2008 to guarantee the six largest banks' liabilities with public money, thereby devastating public finances and forcing Ireland to accept an €67.5 billion ($92.5 billion) bailout from the EU and IMF. Most of that money went to keep the banks afloat. It successfully exited its six-year bailout in December 2013.

Tax revenues plummeted, throwing the country's public finances into even further disarray and shooting the budget deficit upward. The government responded by charging public-sector workers a pension levy of 7.5% on average, which brought 100,000 of them into the streets of Dublin

to protest. Taxes were raised, and salaries were cut up to 20% for public workers. As unemployment grew, even more mortgage loans fell into default, and the banks found themselves in an increasingly desperate position without sufficient capital to cover their crippling losses.

Inflation might be higher were it not for a "social partnership" created by government, labor, and business to slow wage-rate increases and secure labor peace. Its 5.3% unemployment in 2019 was below the EU average of 7.9% in 2019 (25% for youth). The earlier low joblessness was partly due to the annual investment by offshore companies, creating directly or indirectly more than 300,000 jobs.

In order to deal with the deep economic recession, the Cowen government introduced the harshest budget in memory in 2009. Taxes were raised, a property tax was introduced, and public expenditures were cut by 6%, including drastic reductions in health care, education, and child and welfare benefits. A hiring freeze was declared. Public employees had their pay cut by an average of 15%, and Cowen cut his own salary by 20% in order to set a good example. Despite a mass public-sector strike over pay cuts in 2009, the largest strike in three decades, the Irish accepted the austerity measures as necessary. There was a sense that all were together in having to accept the bitter medicine.

As the country which had the EU's highest sustained growth in population (more than 8% in four years to 2006, the EU's fastest) and labor force, the republic must provide jobs for those Irishmen who continue to move back to Ireland and from the agricultural into the manufacturing and service sectors. But it must continue to provide work for the growing number of young persons and women who are entering the labor market. The economic boom was also attracting other nationalities, including the British. Immigration to this once-poor island exceeded emigration. Net immigration by 2005 was running about 30,000 per year, but that was reversed by 2011. By 2015 emigrants were returning in droves. Foreign direct investment was flowing in. The government's strategy to create jobs for the EU's youngest labor force was through rapid industrial development, backed by a corporate tax rate of 12.5%.

In the past high unemployment set in motion a disappointing wave of emigration. Almost a fourth of Ireland's adults have lived abroad at some point in their lives. The impressive economic growth reversed the population flight, and skilled workers were returning to Ireland. Labor became scarce in such sectors as electronics, computers, information technology, and building. American firms advertised in American newspapers to fill vacancies in their Irish businesses. The state training agency (FAS) conducted worldwide recruitment, known as Jobs Ireland, to fill vacancies.

The republic's population had soared to 4.7 million in 2012, the highest since 1871 and up 1 million in only a generation. Its population was growing by 2.5% annually and was projected to reach 5 million by 2019. This is true despite the fact that its fertility rate has plummeted and is slightly below the level usually required for a stable population. The country remains underpopulated when one considers that the Irish island had more than 8 million inhabitants in 1841. Both parts of Ireland have only 6 million today. The overall Catholic population has fallen from 91.6% in 1991 to 84% in 2013. The number of Muslims has quadrupled to 19,000 in the same period and is the fastest-growing segment of the population.

The Irish know that they need workers, given their declining birth rate. They have to offer work permits to foreigners in order to meet its labor supply requirements. But the Irish have conflicted feelings about the climate of fear and uncertainty that the resulting diversity has created. Their country has become multicultural, with 17% of the population foreign-born,

U2

Credit: Anton Corbijn

nearly as high a percentage as in the US. Such diversity has not provoked the kind of conflict found elsewhere in Europe. But there are undercurrents of racial unease, and regrettable racist incidents occur. This was made worse by an economic downturn. The government responded by denying automatic citizenship to immigrant children born in Ireland. This was overwhelmingly approved by almost 80% in a 2004 referendum.

Ireland grants to citizens of the eight former communist countries that entered the EU in May 2004 the right to enter the country to seek work. But like the UK, it sets a two-year waiting period for them to qualify for social benefits, although the attorney general indicated that such a waiting period might be illegal in the EU. No such limits apply to job seekers from Malta and Cyprus. Some returned home when the 2008–2009 recession struck.

The tradition of spirited trade-union activity has remained in Ireland. This is reflected in the 94 member unions of the Irish Congress of Trade Unions (ICTU), which have affiliates in Northern Ireland. About 60% of working Irishmen are members of unions, which were one among the strongest and most militant in the world. This is no longer true.

CULTURE

Ireland's culture, like its history, reflects the problem of a native people being dominated by a more powerful neighbor. For centuries the natives spoke Gaelic (usually called Irish); the Norman invaders spoke French; but as the English Anglicized them, they came to speak that language as it had evolved in the 14th century. As so many of the Irish-speaking people died or immigrated after the potato famine in the mid-19th century, English came to be the predominant language. Despite efforts

to require schoolchildren to learn Gaelic, only 2% of the population (located primarily in the rural areas of the west) speak Irish as a first language. The fact that road signs and official government publications are still in Gaelic is quaint but hardly necessary. In fact, it is so difficult to find someone who speaks it that fluent speakers can wear a lapel pin called a fainne to invite others to address them in Irish.

Because of the poverty in which they lived for many centuries, the Irish developed worldwide recognition in only one art form; it required no capital investment—the use of words. The Irish have always prided themselves in their ability to talk and write. Celtic history is rich in legend and folklore, and more recently, a number of authors, poets, and dramatists have achieved international prominence. Whenever one thinks of masters of the English language, the names of Irishmen come to mind. Jonathan Swift, Thomas More, James Joyce, Oliver Goldsmith, John Millington Synge, Sean O'Casey, and Brendan Beehan are influential in all of literature. And four Irishmen, William Butler Yeats, George Bernard Shaw, Samuel Becket, and in 1995 Seamus Heaney, won the Nobel Prize for literature. Born in Belfast the son of a potato farmer and cattle dealer, Heaney's poetry is stamped by the simplicity and nature images of his boyhood farm. With his characteristic modesty, he said that he is a mere "foothill of a mountain range" compared to Yeats and Becket. Beloved and popular on both sides of the Irish Sea, Heaney died in 2013, aged 74. Writers like Colm Toibin, Dermot Bolger, Mary O'Donnell, Evelyn Conlon, and Nuala Ni Dhomhnaill are widely read.

The Irish are indeed a musical people, but their music has most often taken the form of widespread participation rather than special expertise of outstanding composers or professional performers. The

Ireland

Celtic harp, along with the shamrock, is one of the most frequently used symbols of Ireland. Harp playing is heard wherever there are groups of expatriate Irish. Many American pioneer songs, bluegrass, and country music (but not western) have Irish roots. In rural Ireland, amateur nights where performers display a variety of talent are still popular. Even today, a visitor to a rural cottage may be told, "Now you mustn't leave until we have a little sing-song." Then all those present will sing together, usually unaccompanied by any musical instrument. The Cork jazz, Wexford opera, and Waterford light opera festivals attract thousands of visitors.

Among the famous Irish musicians is U2, a successful rock group and winner of two Grammy Awards in 1988. Although three out of four are Protestant, their unmistakable Irishness is revealed by the political content of some of their texts, which deal with fighting and dying on their island. The repertoire of the popular Irish American rock band Black 47 is also overtly political, as the title of its debut album, Fire of Freedom, indicates. Other musicians, such as Moving Hearts, Fleagh Cowboys, and Mary Coughlan, mix musical styles like rock and traditional and demonstrate that Ireland is still fertile ground for creative music. Ireland is also producing world-class films. A Dublin native, Glen Hansard, and his Czech partner, Marketa Irglova, won the 2008 Academy Award for best song, "Falling Slowly." It was the theme song for the Irish independent movie, Once, filmed in Dublin and funded by the Irish Film Board.

Celtic dancing (rhythmical patterns formed by four or eight dancers using rapid foot movements, with the arms usually held down at the sides) has spread around the world. Irish step dancing has burst out of the local parish hall and onto a world stage. The dance show-musicals Riverdance by Bill Whelan and Lord of the Dance starring Chicagoan Michael Flatley and Jean Butler are performing before packed audiences everywhere and are receiving global acclaim. After one performance, an observer claimed, "the speed and coordination took my breath away!" Another noted that Irish vernacular is being married to "American razzmatazz." These dance sensations were part of a larger cultural phenomenon in the 1990s. The Irish are becoming more urban, secular, experimental, self-confident, and less attached to nationalist certainties. Their once-rural-based arts are being transplanted to Dublin, where they find a new cosmopolitan expression and no longer serve a nationalist agenda.

Irish art in both Celtic and medieval times displayed a wild imagination with brightly colored swirls and fantastic figures best represented in the illustrated manuscripts. Until recently, Irish art has tended to copy work being done in England or on the Continent. But in the last quarter-century, there has been a revival of crafts that have used the old Gaelic and medieval symbols to create the beginnings of an indigenous modern art.

Until the 20th century, Ireland had only one university, Trinity College in Dublin, which was founded in 1591 by Queen Elizabeth I. Only recently was it opened to Catholics. In 1908 the National University of Ireland was founded. It has branches in Dublin, Cork, Galway, and Limerick. By 2015, two-thirds of 18-year-olds went on to higher education, compared with only 5% in 1960.

Education is free and compulsory for children through the age of 15. The system pays its teachers more in relation to average earnings than any other land in the OECD. It produces a well-educated workforce, especially at the upper end. This and the use of the English language are very appealing to foreign investors.

Both the postal and telephone services are operated by the government, which claims that 90% of all letters mailed reach their destination within one day. There are seven daily newspapers, five in Dublin and two in Cork. An autonomous public corporation operates radio and television broadcasting; licensing fees are charged, and advertisements also produce revenue.

Dublin, whose graceful Georgian buildings are now falling into the shadow of taller concrete and glass structures, continues to dominate the life of Ireland. A fifth of Eire's population lives within the city's boundaries, and over a quarter lives in greater Dublin. This reflects the fact that Ireland has become much more urban than it once was. It also means that some of Eire's poverty, which was largely confined to rural areas, is now more visible in the congested capital city. Dublin is the center of the nation's cultural, financial, and political life.

FUTURE

The Irish can be proud that Robert Emmet's vision has come true—his country has taken its place among the nations of the earth. They still aspire to unify with Ulster, and that appears to be plausible in the future. But election battles are now fought primarily on economic grounds and not over Northern Ireland. Ireland has reacquired the nickname "Celtic Tiger." Some prefer "Celtic Phoenix."

The economy has recovered, and a lot is going right. It has undeniable economic strengths, despite the deep recession that hit most industrialized countries. Economic recovery is steady and impressive. Unemployment is declining. Its exports are booming, but its reliance on foreign companies creates vulnerabilities to the ups and downs of the global economy. FDI is pouring in. Its flexible economy, with a 12.5% corporate tax rate, remains attractive to multinationals seeking a foothold in Europe. Its workforce is young, skilled, and adaptable, and the demographic outlook is favorable. Higher education has expanded dramatically. Almost a third of Irish students were the first in their family to attend university.

Its growing standard of living during the past half-century reached that of the EU, and for the first time in history, it overtook that of Britain. This wealth and success significantly increased the self-confidence and expectations of the Irish people and their demands on the government for continued prosperity.

The failure of any party or alliance to gain a majority in parliament and the frequent elections point to the difficulty any government will have in satisfying these aspirations. With typical Irish wit, two-time Taoiseach Garret FitzGerald, who passed away in 2011, said before the 1982 election, "Whoever wins the election should have first choice on going into opposition."

In June 2017 Kenny stepped down. He was replaced as Taoiseach by Ireland's first openly gay and youngest (38) government leader, Leo Varadkar. The son of a Hindu doctor in Dublin, he was trained as a physician.

By electing two female presidents in a row, including British subject from Northern Ireland Mary McAleese, and then the leftist Michael Higgins in 2011, voters signaled receptivity to reforms which enabled the country to enter the 21st century as a modern European nation. Sometimes the Irish say that their 1960s did not happen until the 1990s. In 1994 a bill was passed "without a ripple of controversy" legalizing same-sex relations. Public opinion loosened restrictions on abortion. Abortion and divorce are legal now. The diminished authority of the Catholic Church was visible in the May 2018 referendum to amend the constitution by giving women unrestricted access to abortions up to the 12th week of pregnancy. Two-thirds voted in favor. In May 2015 a majority of voters approved same-sex marriage in a constitutional referendum. A more liberal Ireland became the first country in the world to legalize same-sex marriage by popular vote. Being gay had been illegal until 1993. The traditional bastions of power and paternalism—state, church, and family business patriarchs—are under assault as never before.

Brexit, which was completed on January 1, 2021, threatens the open 500-kilometer border between the two parts. Dublin wants to maintain the open invisible border without customs checkpoints. Northern Irish politics have been unpredictable. Sinn Fein's withdrawal from power sharing in the north caused Stormont's dissolution for over a year, well into 2018. Mary Lou McDonald replaced the retiring Gerry Adams as party leader and seeks to soften the party's image.

Ireland is justified in being optimistic about its own future. It took vigorous steps to deal with its financial crisis. Its society is stable. It no longer suffers from a lack of confidence, and it is no longer as sensitive about its relations with Britain.

The government's chief challenges for the near future will be bringing the deadly coronavirus under control and adjusting to a Britain that is no longer an EU partner.

The queen's visits to Ireland in May 2011 and Northern Ireland in June 2012 turned a new page in the ties between the two countries, which she called "firm friends and equal partners." Nevertheless it commemorated the centenary of the Easter Rebellion in 2016.

At least one village watched the 2008 US presidential elections closely. Moneygall (population 300) in County Offaly unearthed records indicating that Barack Obama's great-great-great-grandfather, Fulmuth Kerney, grew up there before leaving for America at age 19. His line eventually produced Obama's mother, Ann Durham. A bemused Obama had to admit that "I've got pieces of everybody in me." His vice president, Joe Biden, is proud to trace his roots to Ireland.

When leaving for Paris in 1939, Irish dramatist Samuel Becket claimed that he preferred France at war to Ireland at peace. His country has changed dramatically. Frank McCourt, whose best-selling *Angela's Ashes* describes his youth in a poor and hide-bound Ireland before and during the Second World War, said about Ireland in the late 1990s, "When I go back I see it in a way the kids walk. The confidence. It's almost saucy. We have entered the age of Irish sauciness. God help us all."

France

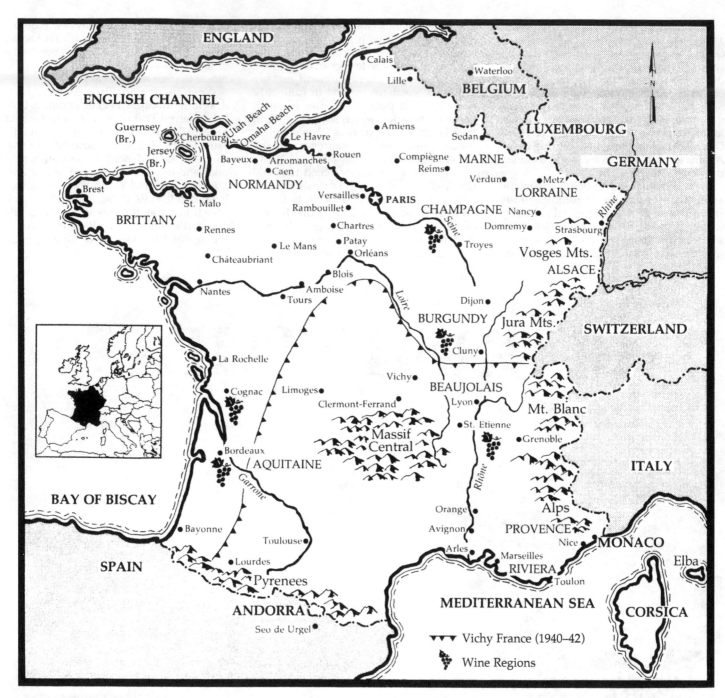

Area: 211,208 sq. mi. (547,026 km). This is the largest country in western Europe, four-fifths the size of Texas and four times the size of New York State.

Population: 65.4 million.

Capital City: Paris (pop. 2.4 million within city limits, 9.1 million within metropolitan Paris).

Climate: Pleasant, rather temperate, except in the south, where the weather resembles that of Florida.

Neighboring Countries: Belgium, Luxembourg, Germany (north and northeast); Switzerland (east); Italy and Monaco (southeast); Spain and Andorra (southwest).

Official Language: French.

Ethnic Background: Indo-European, of diverse origin.

Principal Religions: Roman Catholic (85%), Muslim (8.3%), Protestant (2%), Jewish (1%).

Main Exports and Imports: Capital equipment; consumer goods; automobiles and transport equipment, agricultural products, including wine and spirits; energy.

Major Trading Partners: EU (60.9% of exports and 67.3% of imports), Germany (16.8% of exports and 18.8% of imports), Italy (8.3% of exports and 7.6% of imports), Belgium (7.4% of exports and

11.1% of imports), Spain (7.5% of exports and 6.5% of imports), UK (6.7% of exports and 5.1% of imports), US (5.1% of exports), Netherlands (7.4% of imports), China (5% of imports).

Currency: Euro.

National Holiday: July 14, anniversary of the storming of the Bastille Prison in Paris in 1789, the spark that brought the French Revolution to an explosion.

Chief of State: Emmanuel Macron, President (since May 2017).

Head of Government: Jean Castex, Prime Minister (since July 2020). Unlike many nations where the presidency is merely ceremonial, France has a chief executive with broad powers. The prime minister concerns himself primarily with the daily workings of the government, and he also can wield great power if he is from a different party than that of the president.

National Flag: The tricolor—three broad vertical stripes, blue, white, red.

France is a land of visible contrasts. In many ways it appears divided. Within the past two and a quarter centuries, during which time the United States has had one continuous political system, France has experienced three monarchies, two empires, a half-dozen republics, and more than a dozen constitutions; its history is strewn with revolutions, counterrevolutions, and coups d'état, and its political party system is extremely fragmented. General de Gaulle, the founder of the present French Republic, once asked in exasperation how one could ever rule a land that has more than 300 different cheeses! Yet there is an underlying stability in contemporary France and a strong consensus concerning the importance of respecting individual rights and of maintaining a republican, democratic form of government. Indeed, France is one of a minority of stable democracies in the world and is therefore a haven for political refugees.

France also is highly centralized politically, economically, and culturally. The predominance of Paris is undeniable. No successful revolution ever began outside of Paris. King Henry IV's famous statement in 1593 justifying his conversion to Catholicism, that "Paris is worth a mass," was an early reminder that control over France must emanate from Paris and not from the provinces. The French capital often seems to be the place where French history is made and then merely presented to the provinces as the finished product. With a population as great as the entire continent of Australia (roughly one out of five Frenchmen lives in Paris or its suburbs), it is the residence of a fourth of France's civil servants and doctors, a third of its students and half of its university professors, two-thirds of its artisans and authors, a fifth of its factory workers and factories employing more than 25 persons, and two-thirds of its company and bank headquarters. Efforts since 1955 to decentralize the French economy have met with little success.

At the same time, France is a land of great diversity in terms of religion, landscape, language, customs, and styles of living. Such ethnic minorities as the Basques, the Alsatians, the Bretons, the West Indians, and the Corsicans preserve their own languages and cultures. Only in Corsica is there a serious movement for autonomy that enjoys any appreciable popular backing. There are other small and largely irrelevant movements in Brittany, the Basque region, and elsewhere. In general, ethnic diversity does not threaten the present French state to the degree that it does other European countries, such as Ireland, Belgium, and Spain.

France, it has often been said, is "weighed down by history." Frenchmen have a long memory for their own past, although they do not always agree about its high and low points. Yet, far from being a country exclusively living in the past, contemporary France is a highly dynamic and forward-looking nation. It is among the wealthiest, most technologically advanced, and most influential countries in the world. Clearly, France has a future, but Frenchmen would say that they have a *destiny*. From the time of the Crusades, the first of which was practically an entirely French affair, to the present day, Frenchmen have felt a sense of mission to civilize the world. In the 21st century, they still believe in "French exceptionalism," even as they grope for a clear French identity in the face of massive Arab and African immigration and de facto multiculturalism.

Perhaps no one expressed this mission better than the great realist de Gaulle, who opened his war memoirs with the following words: "All my life I have had a certain idea of France. This is inspired by sentiment as much as by reason. The emotional side of me tends to imagine France, like the princess in the fairy stories or the Madonna in the frescoes, as dedicated to an exalted and exceptional destiny. Instinctively I have the feeling that Providence has created her either for complete successes or for exemplary misfortunes.... But the positive side of my mind also assures me that France is not really herself unless in the front rank; that only vast enterprises are capable of counterbalancing the ferments of dispersal which are inherent in her people; that our country, as it is, surrounded by the others, as they are, must aim high and hold itself straight, on pain of mortal danger. In short, to my mind, France cannot be France without greatness."

The general, who once admitted that he preferred France to Frenchmen, disdained the petty squabbling of everyday politics. He denied that the essential France was to be found in the yawning provincial bureaucrat, the scandalous French president (Felix Faure) who died in the presidential palace while making love to his mistress, or the impetuous Parisian pamphleteer who plots to bring down the regime. He believed that one must inhale the heady air of the mountain peaks in order to see the true France: "Viewed from the heights, France is beautiful."

France is at the same time an Atlantic, continental, and Mediterranean country, and it is territorially the largest country in Europe west of Russia. The country is somewhat hexagonal in shape with rather regular contours. It stretches roughly 600 miles (960 km) from north to south and west to east. Through it flow five great rivers, the Seine, Loire, Garonne, Rhône, and Rhine, which originate in the central land mass (Massif Central) or in the mountains of the Alps and the Pyrenees. It faces three seas (the North Sea, the Atlantic Ocean and the Mediterranean) and has a coastline of more than 1,200 miles (1,930 km).

In the north, there are no natural barriers to separate France from northern Europe. Elsewhere, the Rhine River separates France from Germany, the Alps from

From atop Notre Dame Cathedral, a stone gargoyle stares vacantly over the Seine River and the rooftops of Paris to the distant Eiffel Tower.   Courtesy: Jon Markham Morrow

France

Switzerland and Italy, and the Pyrenees from Spain. The geographical relief of France begins from the coastline to the valleys, and then rises to plateaus, highlands, and finally to mountains, the highest being Mont Blanc in the Alps (15,777 feet; 4,807 meters) and Mont Vignemale in the Pyrenees (10,804 feet; 3,293 meters).

Although France is large, it has the lowest population density in the European Union (EU). Its total population and economic riches are very unevenly distributed geographically. If one were to draw a line on the map of France from the northern port of Le Havre to Grenoble and then on to Marseilles (which school children learn as the *diagonale du vide*—"diagonal of emptiness"), one could see two halves of a country as different from one another as northern Italy is from southern Italy. The western half of France contains 56% of the territory, but only 37% of its people, and is steadily losing population. It tends to be less industrialized, and its agriculture is based on small farms and is therefore less efficient. East of the line are 80% of France's industrial production and three-fourths of the industrial employees. Economic development is particularly rapid in the northeast of France and recently in the Rhône-Alps and Marseilles regions. Farming tends to be more intensive and efficient, and a far smaller percentage of inhabitants live agriculturally.

Geographic and demographic statistics can hardly convey the beauty that for centuries has been called *la belle France*. The visitor invariably finds himself charmed by the smell of rich vines heavy with grapes; by the rolling green countryside studded with more castles than one finds in any other country; by the towering cathedrals whose bells resound throughout the countryside; by the warm beaches along the Riviera; and by the majestic, snow-capped peaks. As one begins to realize how this beauty blends with the Frenchman's proverbial joie de vivre ("joy of living"), one sees why the Germans have always described the good life as "living like God in France."

HISTORY

The Early Period

Although France has played a prominent role in European history for at least 1,500 years, it did not become a national entity or even approximately achieve its present shape until the 16th century AD. The legend of French unity goes back to Vercingetorix, the chief of a Gallic tribe called the Arverni, who led a coalition in an uprising against the Roman occupiers in 52 BC. Although he placed his foot soldiers in a hopeless strategic position and squandered his cavalry before the critical phase of the battle had begun, resulting in his troops' and his own capture, he is seen as the first patriot and resistance hero of French history.

The French profess a close kinship to the Gauls. But the latter were a people who left no literature, no language, and no laws; who worshipped many gods and practiced human sacrifice; and who, according to the Roman arch at Orange, fought naked, their hair buttered and in a long looped knot, with drooping mustaches and long narrow shields. It is doubtful that such a race had a profound impact on the French people and their civilization. Frenchmen today are amused by the caricature of the early Gaulois in the popular *Asterix* comic books.

They no doubt owe far more to the Romans, who occupied for centuries much of what is now France. The Romans built towns, roads, aqueducts, and theaters. They provided examples of centralization, efficient bureaucracy, written law, and a periodic census. They brought education and culture to France and gave the French an appreciation of abstractions. They also left a tradition of grandeur, spotting France with statues and monuments. Finally, their language—vulgarized by common usage—later developed into French.

Even before the fall of the Roman Empire in the 5th century, France had become an invasion ground for tribes from all over the known world: Visigoths, Burgundians, Alemans, and Franks (Germans who eventually gave the country its name). In the 8th and 9th centuries, Charlemagne, the warrior king who established himself as "emperor of the west," absorbed what is now France into a huge political unit encompassing much of present Europe, from Saxony to the island of Elba, including Bavaria and most of Lombardy in Italy. This great empire, however, did not survive his death in 814 AD, and France again became fragmented.

The Capets Claim Paris

Not until a century and a half later did conditions begin to develop which were favorable to unity. In 987 the Capet family, who owned large tracts of land around the region now called the Île-de-France, raised a claim of dynastic leadership over France. The Capetians chose as their capital a small town nearby, which had been established in 100 BC on a five-acre island in the middle of the river Seine by a curly-headed Celtic tribe of fishermen and navigators called Parisii. The Romans had named this city Lutetia and had built it up to a town of from 6,000 to 10,000 inhabitants. The city had also served as capital for the Frankish king Clovis, who had defeated the last remnants of the retreating Romans in 486.

The Capetians adopted Francien, a Latin-based dialect spoken around Paris, as their official language. Hugues Capet, born in 938, was the first Frankish king who could speak no German, and as a result of the Capetian example, German and Latin soon disappeared from the early French court. French became the language of the elite, both at the court and abroad (for example, Marco Polo wrote about his travels to China in French), and the political and military successes of the French dynasty gradually led to the language's adoption by all the people. This language became a powerful agent in the formation and expansion of the French nation and civilization. For that reason, few peoples in the world try so hard to preserve and spread their language as do the French.

Crusades

The First Crusade in the 11th century, sponsored by the French pope Urban II and organized by the French cleric Peter the Hermit, was conducted almost exclusively by the French knights. While building castles in Lebanon and establishing a Kingdom of Jerusalem (which endured at least in name until the 15th century), they showed a zealous sense of mission in extending French civilization, which they tended to see as embodying Christian values. This became a major rationale for most French military and colonial enterprises in the centuries to follow.

A crucial by-product of the Crusades was the weakening of the feudal bonds which tied serfs to their lords. French noblemen were often left penniless by the military expenses they bore, and many times they obtained needed money by freeing serfs and selling charters to cities. By the 13th century, serfdom had almost disappeared in France, and cities had sprung up everywhere, partly because of the trade the Crusades had created. Spices and textiles from the Orient were highly desired by the Europeans, and cities became the crossroads for such trade. France prospered.

Another indirect example of French expansionism occurred when William the Conqueror invaded England in 1066, conquering the Anglo-Saxons by 1070. Although French largely displaced Anglo-Saxon initially, at least at the court, the latter soon revived, and the two languages were combined, enriching each other. Court decisions and proceedings by the 12th century were written in a curious combination of English, French, and Latin. But William retained his holdings in Normandy, Maine, Touraine, and Anjou within what is now France; this later became a source of friction between the French and the English. William's great-grandson, the incompetent King John of

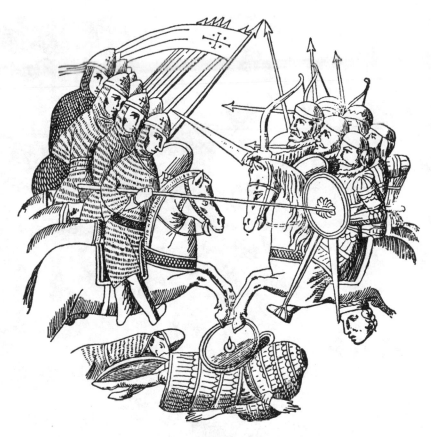

**Crusaders and Saracens in battle
(from a 12th-century stained-glass window)**

Charles VII crowned on July 17, 1429, in the way traditionally prescribed for French kings. Whenever she addressed the crowds as "Frenchmen," the response indicated that a new nationalism mingled with a divine mission was emerging.

Short-lived was the fortune of this girl. Dressed in men's clothing and violating the feudal law barring women from combat, she was distrusted by the clergy, the nobility, and even the newly crowned king. Mounted on a beautiful horse, she led her forces in a vain attempt to storm Paris and Compiègne, and though wounded by an arrow, she tried unsuccessfully to rally her troops. She was captured in May 1430 and delivered to the Duke of Burgundy, who was allied with the English and who sold her to them for a high fee. She was tried in Rouen by a French ecclesiastical court and, despite her own eloquent defense, was pronounced guilty of heresy. On May 30 she was burned at the stake in Rouen's marketplace, without the ungrateful king having made the slightest effort to save her.

Centuries later there is still no consensus in France concerning the legacy she had left. A monarchical France before 1789 had little use for saviors from the masses, and her mystical, religious aura made her out of place in an enlightened, revolutionary France. Nevertheless, Napoleon had a beautiful statue of her erected in Orléans in 1803, and the process to have her made a saint was initiated in 1869. Not until the humiliating defeat of France at the hands of the Prussians in 1870 was she embraced as a symbol of vengeance toward an outside power that had taken her native Lorraine. She was finally canonized in 1920.

Joan of Arc is to many Frenchmen the ideal symbol of patriotism: a pure lady warrior with a sense of mission who placed God solidly on the side of the French. She is undoubtedly the Madonna in de Gaulle's memoirs who incorporated France, since the great French leader also adopted the cross of Lorraine as his own symbol. His stubborn, righteous defense of France's destiny moved an exasperated Englishman, Sir Winston Churchill, to remark that "of all the crosses I have had to bear, the heaviest was the Cross of Lorraine."

Further Union Followed by Religious Wars

By 1453 the English had been driven from France, except for a tiny foothold in the northern port city of Calais. The Hundred Years' War had nevertheless been a cruel disaster for the French people. Within a century, the war and the plagues that had struck at roughly the same time had reduced the population by almost

England, lost many of the French territories in the early 13th century.

By the end of the 12th century, France, especially Paris (which by that time was the most populous city in Europe), was considered to be the world center of science and culture, having replaced Athens and Rome. In the 14th century, one-half of the people in the Christian world lived in what is now France.

Disorganization and Weak Monarchs

Despite the establishment of a unique language and a French dynasty, French history, until the 16th century, continued to be characterized most of the time by weak kings struggling against foreign rulers and by powerful, rebellious French noblemen, who often did not hesitate to ally with foreign powers against their king. Such division exposed France to the danger of absorption into a large kingdom dominated by England because of its control over much of France. But in the 13th and 14th centuries, three powerful French kings, Philippe Augustus, Louis IX (canonized in 1297 as Saint Louis), and Philippe IV (the Fair), succeeded in wresting control of some of the English domains in France. They began the slow process of patching France together, sometimes by legitimate feudal claims, often by intermarriage,

and very often by war. However, England maintained its huge foothold in Aquitaine, acquired in 1154 and encompassing most of southwestern France below the Loire River; England was also allied with the Burgundians north of the Loire. In the 14th and 15th centuries, the French kings waged a Hundred Years' War to finally drive the English out of France.

Joan of Arc

In the midst of this struggle, a female savior emerged from the small village of Domremy in Lorraine. At the age of 16, Joan of Arc, the daughter of a French shepherd, claimed to have heard the voices of the Saints Michel and Catherine commanding her to free the besieged city of Orléans and to have the French king crowned in Reims. Having persuaded a French captain to give her a horse and an armed guard and flying a white flag, she set off to find the king. She told a distrustful Charles VII that she would drive the English out of France and be "the lieutenant of the king of heaven who is king of France."

Dressed in a man's armor and displaying remarkable skill in improving offensive military operations, she liberated Orléans, defeated the enemy forces at Patay and Troyes, and amid enthusiastic crowds proceeded to Reims to have the 26-year-old

France

one-half. In the closing years of that century, Brittany, which had been independent, was integrated into France. Anne of Brittany, who in 1491 married the French king Charles VIII, sealed the union. She took her native Brittany as a dowry. Upon his death she married the next French king, Louis XII, in 1499 in order to preserve this union. Though France had made impressive strides toward territorial unity in the 15th century, the century to follow was not to be one of peace and unity.

In 1519 a minor German priest named Martin Luther courageously raised a challenge of faith to the powerful Catholic Church and began the Reformation that spread throughout the Christian world. A Frenchman, John Calvin, also developed a religious doctrine hostile to the church and was forced to flee to the Swiss city of Geneva, which he soon shaped into a Protestant "capital." He left behind a France seriously divided into two sects: the Huguenots (Protestant) and the Catholics. From 1559 until 1598, the Wars of Religion raged in France; this was a chaotic period dotted by eight distinct wars, assassinations, and massacres. These unfortunate events were related to the issue of the king's and other nobility's respective powers, as much as to theological matters.

The situation became particularly grave in 1572, when 4,000 Protestants gathered in Paris for the wedding of the 19-year-old King Henry of Navarre to Charles IX's sister. Henry, whose life was under threat, had announced his conversion to Catholicism, ostensibly to heal fanatical religious divisions in France. The Protestants were massacred on orders of the French king, and they promptly responded to this St. Bartholomew's Day Massacre by announcing that such a treacherous king was no longer to be obeyed. Henry quickly reassumed the Protestant faith, and the wars raged on. All involved finally realized in 1598 that the strife was without any redeeming value. Upon becoming king, Henry issued the Edict of Nantes, which promised Frenchmen religious freedom. Nevertheless, the religious issue continued to gnaw away at the unity of France for more than three centuries.

The French Century

The 17th century became "the French century" in all of continental Europe. This was a period when forceful French kings and brilliant royal advisers succeeded in reducing much of the French nobility's powers and in establishing the present borders of France. The glitter of the royal court soon dazzled Europe.

When in 1624 Louis XIII chose an ambitious cardinal to be his chief adviser, he gained at his side a tireless servant of the French Crown and the French state.

Joan of Arc triumphantly enters Reims.

Cardinal Richelieu was not a man given to courtly debauchery, theological hair-splitting, or listening for voices from God. "Reason must be the standard for everything," he said, and "the public interest ought to be the sole objective of the prince and his counselors." Raison d'état ("reason of state"), the interests of the community, became for him the overriding concerns.

Since Richelieu was convinced that only absolute monarchical authority could elevate his country to the highest rank in the world, he proceeded to neutralize any powers that could challenge the central authority of the king. He had torn down all castles not belonging to the king that could be used to resist royal authority. In a swashbuckling era presented so vividly in Alexander Dumas's *The Three Musketeers*, Richelieu dared to ban dueling, a favorite pastime of the nobility, on the grounds that weapons should be drawn only against enemies of the state. While not attacking religious principles, he whittled away at the privileges granted in 1598 to Protestants, believing that a free,

powerful Protestant party in France could easily undermine the centralized power of France.

At the same time, he sent money and troops to support the Protestants in the Thirty Years' War that ravaged Germany from 1618 to 1648. His reasons were simple: although Austria and Spain were fighting in the name of Catholicism, their victory in the struggle would have strengthened these great powers and thus presented a greater threat to France. Further, by sending French troops southward, eastward, and northward, France acquired territory along the way. France's borders thus moved outward. Clearly, the cardinal did not think religiously; he thought *French*. When he died in 1642 (followed in death a few months later by Louis XIII), he left behind an almost-unchallenged central authority, a powerful French army, a small but effective fleet, and a highly organized professional diplomatic service. He also established French as the new diplomatic language for the world, a position it enjoyed for more than 250 years. Above all, he left a tradition of total dedication to the power and glory of France.

Louis XIV, Cardinal Mazarin, and Anarchy

Louis XIV became king in 1643 at the age of five. This renowned monarch was able to build on the great works of Cardinal Richelieu and on the works of another cardinal who, though extremely unpopular, held France together against an angry and dangerous storm until the young king was ready to assume the reins of government. Cardinal Mazarin was a wealthy Italian, whose love of money did not prevent him from energetically serving the young king's mother and regent, Queen Anne, with whom he reportedly had more than just cordial relations.

Picking up where Richelieu had left off, Mazarin led France to victories over Austria. The Treaty of Westphalia in 1648 and subsequent victories over Spain left France the foremost power in Europe. Austria was seriously weakened, and Germany was fragmented, depopulated, and exhausted. French strength and German "weakness" through division remained a cornerstone of French politics until 1990. Indeed, many Frenchmen would have echoed the words spoken by the 1952 Nobel Prize for literature laureate and Gaullist political commentator François Mauriac after the Second World War: "I like Germany so much that I am glad there are two of them."

Having achieved a position of power in Europe, France became seriously weakened internally. From 1648 to 1653, it was rocked by a complicated series of civil disturbances which threatened the young king's hold on the throne and which in some ways anticipated the French Revolution that occurred a century and a half later. The parliament, the bourgeoisie (a class of persons who had risen socially above the level of peasants and manual laborers but who had no titles of nobility), and the Parisian mobs, all for their own reasons, created such an anarchical situation in Paris that the king and his mother were forced to flee to the palace of St. Germain, where they lived at Mazarin's personal expense.

Some French nobles invited the Spanish troops to reenter France, and Parisian mobs erected barricades and took law into their own hands. In the prolonged confusion, battles raged in the countryside and the streets of Paris, and finally Mazarin was forced to flee to Germany. However, after all order had disappeared, the key figures of this uprising, known as the *fronde* (named after the French word for "slingshot," used by rioters to smash windows in Paris), surprisingly lost their nerve, and this revolt against the centralized monarchy and the unpopular Mazarin gradually collapsed.

The 14-year-old Louis led his loyal troops in 1652 into a tired and shamed Paris. Louis never forgave the rebellious city and wasted little time in removing himself from the clutches of this beautiful but tempestuous and unfaithful mistress. The rupture between the king and Paris would later have disastrous consequences for the monarchy.

Louis Comes of Age

Immediately after Mazarin's death, the young king called a meeting of all the court's advisers and announced, "Now it is time that I rule!" No one questioned this. By then, the 23-year-old monarch's imposing physical dignity and his polished manners, combined with an unhesitating decisiveness, rapidly brought him respect within France, which sometimes bordered on worship. France was weary of chaos and was ready to kiss the hand that ruled with firm authority. His prodigious lovemaking at the court, which has certainly lost nothing in the telling, greatly irritated his mother. But it did not prevent him from being a hardworking and effective king. Almost no state affairs escaped his attention; in 1661 he commanded his ministers not to sign or seal any order without his permission.

The entire kingdom increasingly felt the impact of the royal government. When the affairs of state became too great for one man to handle, he developed a bureaucracy and efficient procedures to enable his government to absorb the workload. All aspects of French foreign affairs, defense, finance, commerce, religion, and the royal household were channeled through the king's court. He appointed officials to secure royal control over all activities in the various regions in France. He supervised all major appointments in his bureaucracy and the army. Although there is no evidence that he ever really said "I am the state," there was no question that he would have readily agreed with such an assertion. He actually worked very hard to live up to his rather arrogant motto: *Nec pluribus impar* ("None his equal").

As a symbol of his magnificence, the "Sun King" ordered that a royal palace be built in Versailles, which would not only be at a safe distance from Paris but also would be unsurpassed in all of Europe for its beauty and dignity. For 20 years he had this gigantic structure, with its surrounding gardens, fountains, and smaller palaces, built and rebuilt. His finance minister, Colbert, was exasperated by the project, which almost emptied the royal treasury and which could only be financed by selling many of the state's treasures. However, once finished, this palace became the assembly point for much of France's ambitious nobility. There Louis could keep an eye on them and busy them with ritual duties, such as buttoning his coat or escorting the servants who brought his food to the royal table. Louis's preeminence was such that nobles competed for the honor of performing even the most menial functions at his court. For instance, the princess of Ursins, who later became the queen of Spain, was considered one of the luckiest persons at the court of Versailles because she performed the task of handing the king his dagger and night pot each evening as he retired to his private bedroom.

Under the conscientious guidance of Louis XIV, France achieved an incomparable political, military, and cultural ascendancy. The arts bloomed, and France was the richest and most populous country in

Paris in the 17th century

France

Europe. It also acquired the most powerful army on the Continent, and Louis was more than willing to use it. He conducted almost continuously destructive wars. He thereby was able to establish France's present borders, but he ultimately converted almost every country in Europe into an enemy of France. He ordered that the Palatinate in the western part of Germany be burned, resulting in the destruction of Heidelberg, Mannheim, Speyer, Worms, and hundreds of smaller towns. His soldiers ripped the bones of earlier Holy Roman emperors out of their graves in Speyer, a sacrilege that was not soon forgotten in Germany. The Treaty of Utrecht finally established an uneasy peace in 1713, two years before the king's death.

Even if France gradually exhausted itself financially and physically through almost-continuous warfare, it was certainly well administered. Louis's powers were broad, and he used them with great energy. However, he could by no means be called a dictator in the modern sense. He had to deal with a limited national treasury, an absence of a national police force, ineffective and slow means of communication, and regions that still jealously guarded their remaining powers. All in all, he gave Frenchmen an era which they still proudly call "the grand century."

Stirrings of Discontent

The "Sun King" long outlived all of his children, and upon his death his five-year-old great-grandchild was crowned Louis XV. The new king ruled until 1774, when Louis XVI, a good man who never wanted to be king, succeeded to the throne. Both were rather weak and increasingly unpopular kings who were unable to guide their country's adjustment to the changes that occurred in French society during the 18th century. This was a formula for revolution. Greatly contributing to and benefiting from France's prosperity, the bourgeoisie resented its exclusion from political responsibility, which was almost entirely in the hands of the aristocracy. The rural peasantry, which comprised 80% of the population and owned 40% of the land, resented the aristocracy's rights to hunt on their land; its local police power; and its near-monopoly over rural mills, bake shops, and wine presses. The manorial lords appeared to live well without performing an obviously useful function.

The dissatisfaction with the aristocracy was fed by the enlightened ideas of the time. In the course of the 18th century, such thinkers as Montesquieu, Voltaire, and Diderot had brilliantly chipped away at the foundations of aristocratic society. An irreverent Frenchman named Jean-Jacques Rousseau had written in his bombshell

Louis XIV, the "Sun King." Probably painted at about age 55+, it indicates he had lost his teeth, was overweight, and had bunions from wearing high heels and a double chin.

book, *The Social Contract*, that "man was born free, but everywhere he is in chains," and he had proposed provocative ways of breaking these chains and creating a society of free and equal human beings. Rousseau was driven from France because of these ideas. He died in 1778.

Events in America that same year caused revolutionary ideas to pour in that brought the soup to a boil. A young revolutionary named Thomas Jefferson from Virginia had written, "all men are created equal and are endowed with unalienable rights." In rapid succession, the 13 colonies began to produce democratic constitutions, which were translated almost immediately into French and avidly read by intelligent persons grown weary of social hierarchy and inherited privilege. Benjamin Franklin, who was sent to France to persuade the government to help the American colonies in the struggle against the English, was lionized by France's high society. His rustic, egalitarian wisdom

The Mature Benjamin Franklin, 1777

was the talk of Paris. Most importantly, he persuaded France's leaders, who had lost their colonies in North America to the English in the Seven Years' War (1756–1763), to enter the struggle against the British. French assistance to the rebellious colonies was a very important contributing factor in the American victory; without the French army and navy, perhaps the ill-equipped and militarily untrained colonists would never have prevailed against their masters.

While the French government slapped its traditional enemy in the face, it had unknowingly allowed the bacillus of freedom to enter France through the back door. Some officers and many noncommissioned officers returned to France deeply moved by the events in America of which they had been a part, and they were very sympathetic and supportive of revolutionary movements in their own country. The world now had a concrete model of a large country ruling itself in a republican way.

Financial Woes Lead to Revolution

Another unforeseen consequence of France's aid to the Americans was that it brought France to the brink of bankruptcy; it doubled the national debt and consumed more than one-half of the crown's income. It was not an extravagant court that caused France's desperate financial situation; only 5% of the public expenditures were devoted to the entire royal establishment. The French Revolution did not spring from a naïve, spendthrift Queen Marie Antoinette (called by the people "Madame Deficit") who was reported (incorrectly) to have asked why the peasants did not eat cake if they had no bread.

One-fourth of France's budget was devoted to war costs, and a whopping one-half was needed to service France's debts. Other countries, such as England, had similar expenditures, but France's financial crisis could not be solved because of its archaic and unequal tax system. The aristocracy and the wealthy bourgeoisie either evaded or won exemptions from taxation. The church also refused to pay taxes, so the tax collectors could turn only to the poorest French citizens. Thus, although the country was generally prosperous, the public treasury was empty.

Louis XVI, who like his predecessor had often opposed the aristocracy and sought strength from the bourgeoisie, well understood the problem, but he was so weak and unpopular that he could do nothing about it. In desperation, he convened an Estates General in May 1789, the first such meeting in a century and a half. However, the class antagonism in France was such that the three classes assembled (clergy, aristocracy, and bourgeoisie) simply could not work out reform in cooperation.

On June 17, 1789, the bourgeois element (the "Third Estate") decided to declare itself the National Assembly. When the king panicked and closed the hall in which the Third Estate met, the latter moved to a nearby indoor tennis court and proclaimed in the Oath of the Tennis Court that it was the true representative of the people and that it would not disband until it had produced a constitution for France. This was a revolutionary step, unleashing explosive events that an irresolute king could not control. It was the first act in the French Revolution, which went through many stages and lasted 10 years. Whether or not these events represented "the end of history," as the Prussian philosopher Friedrich Hegel maintained, neither France nor the world would thereafter be the same.

Revolution

The events at the Versailles meetings stirred up crowds in Paris, who began to look for weapons in arsenals and public buildings. On July 14, 1789, a crowd went to the Bastille, which, like the Tower of London, was a stronghold built during the Middle Ages to overawe the city and to provide a place of detention for influential prisoners. When the official in charge of the stronghold refused to distribute any weapons, the crowd successfully stormed the fortress. The mob, infuriated that almost 100 persons had been killed, slaughtered the guards who had surrendered. They then beheaded the commanding official with knives and paraded around Paris with the heads of their victims on spikes. This bloody skirmish and macabre display was a harbinger of ferocious acts to come. Nevertheless, Frenchmen celebrate July 14 today as their major holiday.

The unrest and violence spread to the countryside as manorial lords saw their properties sacked and burned by bitter peasants. The more fortunate escaped with their lives, but royal power vanished quickly. The Marquis de Lafayette, a revolutionary-minded aristocrat who had been a favorite on George Washington's staff during the American War of Independence, was given command over the guard in Paris. He designed a flag for the new France to replace the blue and white fleur-de-lis ("lily flower"). He combined the colors of the city of Paris, red and blue, with the white of the House of Bourbon. Thus, the tricolor, which is France's flag today, represented a fusion of the new and old regimes.

The sudden acts of violence had frightened the ruling group into granting important concessions. On August 4, 1789, the nobles relinquished their feudal rights, and on August 27 the National Assembly promptly proclaimed the Declaration of the Rights of Man. The US ambassador to

Lafayette and Washington in Harlem, New York

France and author of the American Declaration of Independence, Thomas Jefferson, was asked to read and improve this French equivalent before its publication. He was also requested to sit in the National Assembly during the writing of the French constitution. He declined both requests for diplomatic reasons, although he was a passionate supporter in the young US of the French Revolution. This French declaration was one of history's most eloquent assertions of equality before the law; of the opening of public service to all classes; and

Thomas Jefferson
Courtesy of Special Collections, University of Virginia Library

France

Count de Mirabeau
Courtesy of Special Collections,
University of Virginia Library

LA MARSEILLAISE.

of freedom as an unalienable individual right, limited only by the freedom of others. An enlightened constitutional monarchy was established. The king was forced to return to the Tuileries Palace in Paris. There he would be under the watchful eye of France's new, moderate regime, guided by Count de Mirabeau, who, like many aristocrats, had concluded that the future lay with the Third Estate.

Revolution Out of Control

It is always a great misfortune when moderate and democratic revolutionaries cannot control the beast of revolution once it has been uncaged. As in Russia a century and a quarter later, a more radical "second revolution" often overtakes the first one, wiping away many of the democratic gains in the process. This misfortune befell the French Revolution.

The first signal for such a change came on the night of June 21, 1791, when the king and his family attempted to escape to Germany. Caught at Varennes, close to the border, two days later, they were brought back to the Tuileries without glory and locked up in their palace. After this clumsy move, the king's commitment to the new order was no longer credible, and the people's loyalty to the king, which had already been eroded, disappeared entirely.

This new situation greatly angered the other monarchies of Europe, especially those of Prussia and Austria. The moderate Girondists, members of a revolutionary club whose name derived from the department (state) of Gironde and who had gained a majority in the National Assembly in 1792, responded to what they saw as a clear external threat to the revolution. They declared war on Austria. It went badly for France, but it quickly added a new element to the revolution. Seeing the "fatherland in danger,"

the citizens took up arms, and patriotism rose to fever pitch.

Nationalism and revolution joined hands as the French national anthem, the "Marseillaise," indicates. First sung in April 1792, the words and music had been written by an army officer, Claude Joseph Rouget de Lisle, who was stationed in Strasbourg. It got its name from the fact that a battalion from Marseille was the first to sing it in Paris. It was banned under Napoleon and for much of the 19th century. Not until 1879 was it permanently adopted. Because the bloody text is often deemed inappropriate for modern Europe, there are frequent calls to change the words.

The newly unleashed popular tide became extremely difficult to control. The Tuileries Palace was stormed by a mob who forced a humiliated king to wear a red hat of the revolution and to drink with them from a common bottle. The constitutional monarchy was overthrown, and in September 1792 suspected royalists were hunted down and massacred in prisons, monasteries, and elsewhere. In December the king was tried and convicted of conspiring with the enemy (a charge which was no doubt true), and he was beheaded one month later. Scarcely had the king's head fallen into the basket of the guillotine

before France found itself at war with all the major monarchies of Europe.

Faced with a frenzied, imperiled nation, the moderates were pushed aside by the radical Jacobins, a revolutionary club who had met regularly since 1789 in the Jacobin Convent in the Rue Saint-Honoré and who was led by the fanatical Robespierre. A Committee of Public Safety was formed to cope with enemies abroad and at home. On October 10, 1793, the new revolutionary leadership declared that the government of France must remain "revolutionary until the peace." In clear text, this meant a "reign of terror," and political "trials" were begun at once.

On October 16 Queen Marie Antoinette was guillotined, followed by all the Girondists who could be arrested. For the next nine months, the guillotine would never cease from doing its grisly work. Until Robespierre and his followers' own execution in July 1794, France was subjected to a dictatorship in the hands of fanatically self-righteous people who asserted, "terror is nothing else than swift, severe, indomitable justice; it then flows from virtue."

Enlightened democrats make no claims to know absolute truth and therefore tolerate other men's views and weaknesses. By contrast, the ideologues who controlled

France in those bloody days had such an abstract conception of liberty that they lost sight of man. Out of love for humanity and the truth, they would have eradicated the human race.

The noted French author George Sand wrote that "during the terror, the men who spilled the most blood were those who had the strongest desire to lead their fellow men to the dreamed-of golden age, and who had the greatest sympathy for human misery. . . . the greater their thirst for universal happiness, the more relentless they became." Charles Dickens was no doubt correct when, in the opening sentence of his *A Tale of Two Cities*, he referred to the French Revolution, "It was the best of times, it was the worst of times, it was the age of wisdom, it was the age of foolishness." Perhaps at no other time could one see so clearly the worst and best in man.

Although Frenchmen today tend to remember mostly the noblest aspects of the revolution, the terror made it difficult then and now for persons outside of France to have a unified opinion of this first great European revolution. No doubt, many of the 17,000 victims of the terror were in fact enemies of the new republic. Only

15% of the executions took place in Paris, and more than half took place in western France, where the resistance to the new order was the greatest. Only 15% of the victims were aristocrats or clergymen. To some extent, then, the terror was a defensive measure. However, the number of innocent persons who were caught in the grinder was so great that the new republic disgusted highly respected friends abroad. Also, although France's foreign enemies were ultimately defeated, the French Revolution was knocked off its democratic path, and it was almost a century before France was able to return to relatively stable, republican government.

The French Revolution in Retrospect

The year 1989 marked the 200th anniversary of the French Revolution, and 5,000 events around the country commemorated this great convulsion. It created the opportunity for Frenchmen to look both back into their past and forward into their future. Not all Frenchmen cherish the spirit of 1789, as was shown by Catholic counterdemonstrations to remember martyrs in the Place de la Concorde on August 15, 1989, the production of a movie called

Vent de Galerne that depicts the savage repression of peasant rebels in the Vendée; the tracing of descendants of the 3,000 persons executed in Lyons by the Jacobins; and the widespread apathy in many parts of the country.

There has been a fundamental rethinking of the causes and meaning of the revolution, and many simplistic explanations have been replaced by a much more complex picture. Some myths were corrected: Only seven prisoners were freed at the Bastille; execution by guillotine often took several "chops," and only 10% of those beheaded were nobles; most of the revolution's victims were shot, burned, or drowned rather than beheaded; and the statement attributed to Marie Antoinette, "Let them eat cake!" appeared in Rousseau's Confessions at least two years before Marie arrived in France in 1770.

Frenchmen have even become more ambiguous about their heroes and villains. Polls indicated that the era's most revered character is the Marquis de Lafayette, who broke with the Jacobins and fled France. He became a favorite on the staff of General George Washington at age 19, living in his house and riding at his side in parades and into battle. Biographer Douglas Southall Freeman wrote, "Never during the Revolution was there so speedy and complete a conquest of the heart of Washington." A televised reenactment of Louis XVI's trial with the ending left open so that viewers could decide his guilt or innocence also produced astounding conclusions: Only 27% of viewers favored beheading him versus 55% who voted to acquit him.

It is therefore not surprising that the government decided to focus as little as possible on the bloody elements of the past and almost exclusively on the idealistic achievements of the revolution that have undeniable relevance for France's future, such as the Declaration of the Rights of Man and the Citizen. This focus on human rights and the question of what it means to be a citizen in a free and modern republic relates directly to France's future as a multiracial, multicultural society. Some citizens are also beginning to ask whether France needs to have such a brutal national anthem, which calls on them to "drench our fields" with the enemy's "tainted blood." According to a July 14, 1992, poll, 40% of the French find the lyrics too bloodthirsty, but 75% are staunchly opposed to altering the hallowed verses.

Napoleon

Robespierre was overthrown and beheaded on July 27, 1794. That date fell within the month of Thermador in the revolutionary calendar, which had been introduced on August 18, 1792, the date

The palace at Versailles

France

Napoleon returns from Elba (Karl Stenben).

the constitutional monarchy began. The notables who assumed power moved rapidly to restrict suffrage and eliminate the masses from political influence in a tired, internally paralyzed France. In 1795 they created a directory, led by five directors, but this new form of government could not create order in France.

In the midst of such instability, a brilliant young general saw his great opportunity. Born into an Italian family from Corsica in 1769, Napoleon Bonaparte had been educated in French military schools and had gained notoriety by suppressing an uprising against the directory shortly after its founding. An ingenious innovator of lightning military tactics combined with effective use of field artillery, he understood how to win the unswerving devotion of his soldiers. He achieved great victories in Italy, and in 1799, while his troops were conducting a major campaign in Egypt, he returned to Paris and seized power at bayonet point.

For the next 15 years, France followed this man, who, though slight of stature (barely five feet tall), was a great leader in many ways. He clearly preferred order to liberty, and he quickly moved to establish order in France. Despite his authoritarian style of rule, he was an immensely popular leader who quickly showed that he was, at least to some extent, a child of the revolution. He introduced financial reforms and tightened the centralized administration of France. He promulgated a new constitution and a civil code which reflected the major accomplishments of the revolution: popular sovereignty, underscored by Napoleon's practice of submitting every constitutional change to a plebiscite; trial by jury and equality before the law; a citizens' army; office holding based on competence; abolition of feudal privileges; freedom of religion; and freedom of speech and press (at least in theory). Though they had often been ignored in practice during the 10 years since 1789, liberty and equality had within a decade become so embraced in principle that they have remained permanent elements of French public life.

Napoleon may appear today as a greater friend of monarchy than of the revolution. He signed a concordat with the Catholic Church in 1801, reintroduced slavery in French colonies in 1802, and allowed émigrés to return to France and reclaim their unsold properties. In 1804 he crowned himself emperor of the French, and during his reign he divorced his wife, Josephine, in order to marry an Austrian princess. He also placed his brothers, son,

and marshals upon thrones throughout Europe as he proceeded from conquest to conquest. Nevertheless, in his own day, the other peoples of Europe saw him as a very embodiment of the revolution who carried its ideals to every part of Europe. These principles were always among his most effective weapons.

Napoleon remained a great military leader who sought both to secure France's "natural borders" and to pacify Europe under French leadership. This was essentially accomplished by 1802. However, his ambition was to be more than a peacemaker, and his lack of moderation not only sapped his own country's vigor, but it also ultimately doomed him to defeat. In May 1803 he began an endless series of wars aiming far beyond the mere protection of France's frontiers. Due to stunning victories, French domination by 1806 extended from Holland and the German North Sea coast to the Illyrian provinces along the east coast of the Adriatic Sea. Italy was completely under French control, and some territories (including Rome itself) were annexed to France. But his very successes helped to bring about his downfall.

His invasions stimulated nationalism outside France, and the other governments of Europe felt compelled to imitate France by making popular reforms and raising citizens' armies. Soon Napoleon discovered that he faced opposition, not just from hostile governments and ruling groups, but also from entire nations in Europe. He fought an unsuccessful guerrilla war in Spain, and in 1812 his Grand Army suffered a disastrous wintertime defeat in frigid Russia. The following year he was defeated at the Battle of the Nations in Leipzig that pitted France and its allies, chiefly the Rhineland Germans, against Prussia, Austria, Russia, Sweden, and England. His enemies pursued his disintegrating army into

Napoleon's tomb in Les Invalides

France

At the court of Napoleon I

the heart of France, capturing Paris itself on March 31, 1814.

Napoleon was forced to flee to the island of Elba, where the victors erected a small kingdom for him, but in less than a year, he returned to France in order to regain his empire. Though exhausted from long, sustained warfare, the French succumbed once more to Napoleon's magic. In 100 days he prepared a new army, but his dreams were crushed by a united Europe on the Belgian battlefield of Waterloo on June 18, 1815. His wars had claimed the lives of almost 2 million soldiers. This time he was held as prisoner on the small British island of Saint-Helena in the South Atlantic, while the victorious European powers gathered at the Congress of Vienna to reconstitute Europe.

Napoleon died in lonely exile in 1821, but the "little corporal," as he was often called, still casts a giant shadow in the memories of Frenchmen. He brought France pride, and he rests in magnificent glory in the Invalides, a military hospital in Paris, where the mutilated from his Grand Army were cared for. To this day, the elite professional officers of the French army descend at midnight to their knees at the foot of Napoleon's giant illuminated statue to receive their commissions at St. Cyr, the military academy he had created.

The Monarchy Returns

In 1815, with 150,000 occupation troops on French soil, the Bourbons were again placed on the throne. Although one spoke of a restoration and although 70,000

returned from exile abroad, few believed that the clock was to be turned back before 1789. The royal family was compelled to live in Paris under the eyes of a population that had never made the kings' lives comfortable. The new king, Louis XVIII, the brother of the ill-fated Louis XVI, wanted no part of the revolutionary flag, the tricolor. He did accept a constitutional order which left things more or less as they were before 1815; feudal customs and special privileges of the nobility were not reintroduced, and France's law code, formalized under Napoleon; the tax system; personal freedoms; centralized administration, and the principle of equality before the law remained.

Louis's other brother, who was crowned Charles X in 1824, showed that he had learned little about France since 1789. He believed in the divine right of kings to rule, and he tried to restore the earlier authority of the Catholic Church. His men sought revenge against former Jacobins and Bonapartists, and the ultraroyalists demanded restitution of their properties. In 1830 he made his final mistake by suspending liberty of the press, dissolving the French legislature, and so restricting the electorate that practically only noblemen could vote. While the oblivious king was hunting in Rambouillet, dissidents publicly waved the tricolor and erected barricades in the streets of Paris, some of which reached a height of up to 80 feet. One nobleman, sensing danger, noted to his friend, "Things look bad. They are singing La Marseillaise!"

Three days of bitter street fighting (known as the *trois glorieuses*) convinced Charles that he could not master the situation, so he set sail immediately for Scotland. No Bourbon ever ruled France again; their last king had failed to notice that although the French population had grown tired of revolution and war, it nevertheless continued to take equality and liberty seriously. However, unlike the Americans, the French did not experience one successful 18th-century revolution which established a new democratic political order once and for all. The French Revolution had to be refought at intervals, and each revolution left France divided. It remained a country with a seed of civil war.

Another monarchy was established in 1830. The new king was the 57-year-old Duke of Orléans, Louis-Philippe, the son of the renowned Philippe Egalité ("equality"), who had voted for the beheading of Louis XVI and who soon thereafter was also beheaded in the name of the revolution. Louis-Philippe had fought for the revolution at Valmy and Jemmapes and then had gone into exile, visiting the United States at one time. Despite his romantic past, the new king was an uninspiring man. He was intelligent enough to disavow the divine right of kings and to proclaim himself the "citizen's king." He restored the revolutionary tricolor as the nation's flag, lifted censorship, and doubled the suffrage (although only about 200,000 in a nation of 32 million had the right to vote).

He was a moderate, business-oriented king who brought France more prosperity at home and peace abroad. But the fact that he was the target of more than 80 assassination attempts indicated that his rule was not universally acceptable to Frenchmen. He did not pursue glory, a fact the poet Lamartine lamented, "France is a bored nation." Although an admirer of the king, even Victor Hugo wrote in that great work of fiction about post-Napoleonic France, *Les Misérables*, that "his great fault was that he was modest in the name of France. . . . His monarchy displayed excessive timidity which is offensive to a nation that has July 14 in its civil traditions and Austerlitz in its military annals."

An economic crisis in 1846 made the voteless urban workers in Paris nervous, and the middle classes wanted an end to the narrow elite composed of a few thousand noblemen and upper bourgeoisie. The influence of the extremely unpopular premier, François Guizot, who was reputed (incorrectly) to have advised those in power to "enrich yourselves," helped fan the republican and democratic revival which was gaining momentum. On January 27, 1848, Alexis de Tocqueville, who had gained a great reputation for his

109

France

perceptive study *Democracy in America*, told the French parliament, "I believe that at this moment we are sleeping on a volcano." The volcano erupted in Paris only a few days later. Wanting no bloodbath on his conscience, Louis-Philippe abdicated and departed for England.

The Second Republic, More Anarchy, and Another Napoleon

The Second Republic was declared, and a highly idealistic government under Lamartine's leadership proceeded to introduce universal male suffrage, to abolish slavery in the colonies again, and to guarantee every citizen a job by establishing national workshops at the state's expense. To the new leaders' surprise, their government suffered a crushing defeat in the first parliamentary elections in the spring of 1848. A new legislative majority eliminated the costly socialist experiments, most notably the national workshops. This action provoked desperate workers and idealists again to erect barricades in the streets of Paris and to resist the reaction that always follows each radically democratic experiment in France. In four bloody "June Days" of street fighting in Paris, General Cavaignac crushed the rebels, killing 1,500 and arresting 12,000 in the process; 3,000 persons were hunted down and executed later.

The frightful events in Paris set off rebellions in capitals all over Europe. French workers were left bitter and smoldering. Class hatred was hardened, feelings which remained a part of French life for the rest of the century and which, to a limited extent, continue to exist in France today.

After the June convulsion, there was a widespread desire for a return to order. A new constitution was written, calling for presidential elections by universal male suffrage. In elections held late in 1848, the winner by a landslide was a man who in the past had not displayed any political talent. He was not a dashing figure. He was short and rather paunchy, and his appearance was once described as that of a "depressed parrot." However, he enjoyed two immense advantages: His name was Louis Napoleon Bonaparte, and he was the nephew of the former emperor.

He had been raised in Germany and always spoke French with a slight German accent. He had served as a captain in the Swiss army and had participated in revolutionary events in Italy. In 1836 and 1840, he had made two almost-comic attempts to overthrow the dull regime of Louis-Philippe. In his trial in 1840, he had cried, "I represent before you a principle, a cause, a defeat. The principle is the sovereignty of the people; the cause is that of the Empire; the defeat is Waterloo!" Though he did not persuade the court,

The Café Concert by Edward Manet

he managed to associate his name in the minds of many Frenchmen with the Napoleonic legend, which had been experiencing a rise in popularity at the time. Streets in Paris had been named after Napoleonic victories, the Arch of Triumph that Napoleon I had ordered had been finally completed, and the "little corporal's" remains had been brought back to France and solemnly transported through the city before the wet eyes of thousands of nostalgic Frenchmen.

For his revolutionary activities in France, Louis Napoleon had been imprisoned for life in the fortress of Ham, where he spent his time in luxurious confinement, writing tracts on such topics as "The Extinction of Poverty." One morning early in 1846, Louis Napoleon slipped into workman's clothes and, with a pipe in his mouth and a board over his shoulder, walked out the front gate of the fortress. He was in England the next day, where he awaited his opportunity. In May 1848 his chance came, and he returned to France; by the end of the year, he had been elected France's president.

Louis Napoleon invoked the revolutionary principle of popular sovereignty, but he left little doubt that his would be an authoritarian regime. He once remarked, "I do not mind being baptized in the water of universal suffrage, but I do not intend to live with my feet in it." With his four-year term of office approaching its end, and with a hostile parliament that refused to change the constitution so he could succeed himself, he sent his troops to occupy Paris the night of December 1–2, 1851, and to arrest most of his opponents. When Parisians awoke the next morning, they learned that a coup d'état had just effectively put an end to the Second Republic.

In characteristic post-1789 style, Louis Napoleon asserted the sovereignty of the people as the first law of the land and promised a referendum on all constitutional changes. Also, in characteristic fashion, the Parisian population refused to accept this change without a fight. The barricades went up again; at one across the Boulevard de Montmartre near the Saint-Denis Gate, a military column panicked under the insults of the mob and opened indiscriminate fire on the fleeing citizens. Two hundred persons lay dead as a result of this unfortunate carnage. Although a terrified Parisian populace did not rise up again for 20 years, in 1871, Louis Napoleon's hope for a bloodless takeover was dashed; the December massacre was never forgotten or forgiven. Years later his wife, Eugénie, confided to a friend, "A coup d'état is like a convict's ball and chain. You drag it along and eventually it paralyzes your leg."

Observing the usual practice, Louis Napoleon proceeded rapidly to rewrite the constitution. He created a weak legislature and a strong president who could appeal directly to the people by means of plebiscites. After a year, he could no longer resist one last temptation: On the first anniversary of his coup d'état, he submitted a referendum to the people asking whether they favored "restoration of imperial dignity." Almost 8 million votes indicated yes against only a quarter-million who said no. On December 2, 1852 he was proclaimed Napoleon III, emperor of the French.

For all his talk of restoring France's glory, Napoleon III desired above all to establish order and to make it a prosperous, industrially advanced country. He expanded credit and stimulated new investment. Everywhere new industry and railroads sprang up. He liberalized trade, which boosted French commerce. Overall, French industrial production doubled under his rule; signs of dynamism were everywhere.

Perhaps the most lasting of his public works can be seen in the large cities, such as Marsailles and Paris. Napoleon III appointed Baron Haussmann to administer the department of the Seine, in which Paris is located. Haussmann completely transformed the city. He built the Paris Opera. He destroyed the narrow, medieval streets and laid wide boulevards and broad squares (such as the Place Étoile) with radiating avenues. It was noticed immediately that such wide boulevards would make barricade building, a periodic Parisian pastime, almost impossible and would facilitate military mobility inside the city. Nevertheless, these changes were badly needed to accommodate the capital's rapid growth and to make it a more modern, livable, and beautiful city. During the Second Empire, Paris was a prosperous, carefree, and culturally active

France

1900 Paris World Fair: Petit Palais

city that attracted admirers from all over the world.

In the first decade of his rule, Napoleon III restricted political parties and freedom of the press. He was a very popular ruler in France, however, and seeing that he had nothing to fear, he introduced greater political freedoms in the 1860s. He even took what at the time seemed to be a very radical step: He legalized trade unions and granted workers the right to strike. His regime certainly did not come to an end due to domestic resistance. Instead, he shared the fate of his uncle, falling victim to foreign policy entanglements. He conducted a very active colonial policy in Africa, the Near East, China, and Indochina, bringing the latter under French control in the 1860s.

In 1861 he decided to take advantage of the United States' preoccupation with its own Civil War by trying to establish a monarchy in Mexico dominated by France and ruled by Archduke Maximilian of Austria. In 1863 French troops entered Mexico City and placed the archduke on the newly created throne. But he never developed popular backing, and as soon as the American strife ended in 1865, the US invoked the Monroe Doctrine and demanded that France get out of Mexico. Napoleon III complied, and when by 1867 no French troops were left in Mexico, the naïve Maximilian, who had decided to remain with "his people," was executed by a firing squad. The Mexican adventure was a blunder that greatly diminished Napoleon III's prestige at home.

The fatal blow to the Second Empire was delivered in 1870, when the emperor tried to enforce France's long-standing policy of keeping Germany permanently divided. Provoked by the Prussian chancellor Otto von Bismarck, who sought to create a unified Germany under Prussian domination, the French government declared war against Prussia. Napoleon calculated that the southern German-speaking states would not support Bismarck and might even side with France, but he had made a grave miscalculation; southern Germans were swept up in the conflict.

War and Defeat

France entered the war extremely unprepared. Prussia had a far superior general staff, supply system, and strategy. Also, because of their faster mobilization, the German soldiers outnumbered the French, two to one. Smashing through Lorraine, the Prussian army cut Paris off from the two main French armies and delivered a devastating blow to the French at Sedan on the Belgian border. Napoleon III and more than 100,000 French soldiers were captured there, and the empire came crashing down. In Paris, a republic was declared, and the Parisians prepared for a long siege. The new government's 32-year-old leader, Léon Gambetta, escaped from the surrounded city of Paris by balloon and tried to raise a new army in the Loire area. However, the capture of the last trained French army in Metz in October 1870 demoralized the remaining untrained troops in France. In early 1871, after every last scrap of food in the capital had been consumed, including the rats in the sewers and the animals in the zoo, and after the trees in the Bois de Boulogne and the Champs Elysées had been chopped down for fuel, Paris and the troops in the provinces surrendered.

A humiliated France looked on as the German Empire was proclaimed in the Hall of Mirrors at the Versailles Palace. Germany then proceeded to set a very bad precedent by imposing a harsh peace on a prostrate France: Alsace and most of Lorraine, with their rich iron deposits and industry, were annexed by Germany. Further, France was required to pay the victor a very large reparations sum and to allow German occupation troops to remain in France until the sum was paid. For the next half-century, French policy would revolve around undoing these terrible losses. Referring to the lost provinces, Gambetta told his countrymen, "Never talk about them, always think about them."

France Drifts

While a new government under Adolphe Thiers saw no alternative to accepting this bitter peace, hundreds of thousands of Parisians saw the matter differently. They had suffered the most during the war and had been humiliated both by the Prussians' triumphant entry into Paris and by the transfer of the French capital to Versailles. Further, this traditional hotbed of republicanism resented the monarchist sentiment that dominated both the provinces and the newly elected National Assembly. Finally, Parisians greatly resented the new government's termination of the wartime moratorium on rents and debts and of all payments to the National Guardsmen, who had defended Paris and who, because of France's financial collapse, were now out of work and without subsistence. Again, Paris became a powder keg.

On March 18, 1871, the government sent cavalry troops commanded by two French generals to remove the guns from the promontory of Montmartre that overlooks the city. An angry mob attacked the cavalry and lynched the generals. Violence spread throughout the city, prompting the government's troops to withdraw hastily. Recalling the radical days of 1793, a new Commune of Paris, composed of radical republicans, socialists, and National Guardsmen, was formed. However, this strange mixture of idealists and rowdies spent more time debating socialist and political experiments than in preparing for their own defense. The government immediately besieged the city and, reinforced by French prisoners of war whom the Germans had released for just that purpose, prepared to storm the city.

The troops struck on May 21, and for one bloody week, the street battle raged. In the closing days of the struggle, the Communards, as the dissidents were called, shot their hostages, including the

111

France

archbishop of Paris, and set fire to many public buildings, including the Tuileries Palace and the Palais Royal. Finally the remaining Communards were trapped in Père-Lachaise Cemetery, where they were executed against the Mur des Fédéré (now highly revered shrines for socialists and communists all over the world).

The government's vengeance was severe: Any person caught wearing a National Guard uniform or army boots was shot immediately without trial. In all, about 10,000 Communards, who were out numbered, more than eight to one, were killed in battle or executed without trial. Thousands more were imprisoned or driven into exile. Both sides, fired by hatred, had fought like animals. It had lasted 72 days.

Reflecting on the events, the French novelist Flaubert wrote, "What an immoral beast the mob is, and how discouraging it is to be a human being." Karl Marx, in his widely read pamphlet *The Civil War in France*, made a legend of the Commune, and these violent events widened the gap created in 1848 between the workers and the political left on the one hand and the rest of France on the other. A constant reminder of this gulf is the beautiful white Sacre Coeur (Sacred Heart) Church that overlooks Paris from the top of Montmartre. Built to commemorate the suppression of the Commune, it remains for the French left a prominent and hated symbol of a reactionary France.

For a while a monarchist majority in the National Assembly pressed for the restoration of the monarchy, and Bourbon, Orléanist, and Bonapartist pretenders waited for the call. There were very good prospects for the aging Bourbon pretender, the Count de Chambord, who would rule as Henry V. But the count quickly showed how little he had learned about his own country. He insisted that the king have absolute authority, unrestrained by any constitution. He also insisted that the old fleur-de-lis flag of the former monarchy replace the revolutionary tricolor. Even the most die-hard royalists could see the folly of such demands.

Meanwhile the French people, who in the past 100 years had experienced about every conceivable regime and who were growing tired of provisional governments, pressed for a decision. In 1875 important constitutional laws were adopted calling for the establishment of a two-house parliament and a weak president. The wheel that always alternates in France between a strong parliament and a strong executive had again come full circle. The Third Republic lasted until 1940, longer than any French scheme of government since the revolution.

The capital was moved back to Paris from Versailles in 1880; July 14 was

Renoir's *The Luncheon of the Boating Party* (1881)

established as the national holiday, and "La Marseillaise" was made the national anthem. Paris began to bustle with artistic creativity. By the time the Eiffel Tower was unveiled at the World Exposition in 1889, Paris had assumed the place, in many foreigners' minds, as the intellectual and artistic capital of the world, of which it was often said, Every person in the world has two capitals—his own and Paris. Gertrude Stein put it this way: "America is my country, but Paris is my home." One can scarcely imagine contemporary culture without the creative contributions of artists, writers, and scholars in Third Republic France: impressionism in music and art (e.g., Renoir, Monet, Degas, Debussy) and the reaction to it (e.g., Bracque, Picasso, cubism, or fauvism); the positivism of Auguste Comte, the élan vital of Henri Bergson, and the discoveries of Louis Pasteur in medicine or Pierre and Marie Curie in physics.

Stung by its territorial losses in 1870, France, with Bismarck's encouragement, sought to reestablish a world empire such as the one it had lost a century earlier. It created French equatorial Africa and protectorates in Tunisia and Indochina (presently Vietnam, Cambodia, and Laos). Thus, by 1914 the tricolor flew in most of north, west, and equatorial Africa; in Madagascar, in several West Indian and South Pacific islands; and in small holdings elsewhere. Such a policy was not universally popular in France, but a colonial empire offered France the opportunity to resume expansion of its culture overseas. It also offered some economic benefits to France,

which was experiencing a slower rate of population growth and economic progress than Germany and Britain.

Many French industries remained small, family-owned, and cautious, a situation which persisted in France until after World War II. At the same time, there was considerable worker unrest and violent strikes during the Third Republic. Legalized trade unions tended to remain dedicated to direct, sometimes-violent action rather than to pursue gains through the parliamentary political process. Such "syndicalist" tendencies (to which French trade unions are still attracted) reveal that the deep wounds of the Paris Commune never healed entirely.

At the beginning of the Third Republic, more than half of the population lived in rural areas, and that number had declined to only about one-third by 1940. While the visitor to France has always been struck by the amount of acreage that is cultivated, many farms remained small and relatively inefficient. In the 1870s plant lice threatened the wine industry with extinction. Only by importing American plant grafts was this precious jewel saved. Thus, in a certain sense, French wine is actually American wine.

Third Republic Politics

The Third Republic was seriously rocked by religious disputes, parliamentary instability, scandals, a world war, and economic depression. The new republic moved in traditional French revolutionary fashion to reduce the influence of the Catholic Church. Its anticlerical policies included

France

the permission to divorce and the loosening of the church's grip on the school system. The result was a total separation of church and state in most of France by 1905.

The absence of party discipline and the distrust of any president who tried to play a guiding role in French politics (Third Republic presidents were said to be merely "old men who wore evening clothes in the afternoon!") produced a constant rotation of weak parliamentary coalitions. The resulting "parliamentary game" inclined French citizens to view politics with increasing cynicism and decreasing trust. Representatives rarely hesitated to vote themselves frequent and large salary increases. At the occasion of one such increase in 1905, a socialist member of parliament was heard to say "my indignation is matched only by my satisfaction."

Scandals further shook the confidence in France's political institutions. In the 1880s a dashing general named Boulanger was reputed to have wanted to put an end to the republic after gaining power legally. When he was summoned to the Senate in 1889 to answer to charges of conspiracy against the state, he lost his nerve and fled to Belgium, where he committed suicide two years later. Scarcely a year after his death, another scandal came to light. Since the 1870s a private French company had been attempting to build a canal across the isthmus of Panama. Unwise engineering and yellow fever bankrupted the company in 1889, but its directors bribed politicians and press in order to secure public subsidies for the project. The revelation of such bribery in 1892 helped convince many Frenchmen that all politicians were corrupt, an attitude which has by no means disappeared from France today. The French still tend to be far less shocked by political scandals than is the case in the United States.

A further scandal convinced many Frenchmen that it was not only politicians who could not be trusted but military leaders, as well. In 1894 Captain Alfred Dreyfus, the first Jewish officer to be assigned to the French general staff, was convicted of selling military secrets to the Germans and was sent to the infamous Devil's Island off the northern coast of South America. Later, probing journalists, aided by a skeptical army officer, discovered that the documents presented by the military had been forged and that Dreyfus had been framed. The army, seeing its honor at stake, refused to reopen the case, and many French conservatives and clergymen openly supported the army.

Dreyfus was later pardoned. He fought in the First World War and was promoted to lieutenant-colonel. He was awarded the Legion of Honor and died in 1935. But for more than a generation, this sordid affair,

Courtesy of Edwin L. Dooley Jr.

with its implications for anti-Semitism, the army, the church, and democracy in France, weakened the republic. Not until 101 years later, in 1995, did the French military formally and publicly acknowledge that the army had been wrong. On January 13, 1998, the 100th anniversary of Emile Zola's sensational headline article "J'accuse" ("I Accuse") in L'Aurore newspaper, Prime Minister Lionel Jospin laid a wreath on Zola's tomb in the Pantheon and called the Dreyfus affair "one of the founding events in the history of our country." In 2006 the French president and prime minister publicly honored Dreyfus on the 100th anniversary of his rehabilitation. Seven years later the entire secret military file used to convict Dreyfus was posted free online.

Until the 1890s Germany's chancellor, Bismarck managed to keep France diplomatically isolated in Europe. However, after the chancellor's fall from power in 1890, France was able to improve its relations with Italy and in 1894 to forge a military alliance with Russia. France's intense colonial activity led it into frequent conflicts with the greatest colonial power of the time, Britain. Nevertheless, after the turn of the century, France gradually settled its differences with England, and military and political cooperation between the two countries became much closer. The outlines of the Triple Entente alliance against Germany and Austria-Hungary before and during the First World War thereby emerged. Eventually, crises in Morocco and then in the Balkans brought about the devastating explosion which Bismarck had predicted shortly before his death in 1897: "One day the great European war will come out of some damned foolish thing in the Balkans." It did.

World War I

The outbreak of World War I in August 1914 unleashed an outburst of patriotic sentiment in all major countries of Europe. Even workers rallied to the French cause, and trainloads of enthusiastic troops left their hometowns in railroad cars with words "à Berlin" written on the sides. Although not openly avowed, many French undoubtedly viewed the affair as an opportunity for revenge of the dismal defeat of 1870 and recovery of the "lost provinces." Never since that time did France experience such unity of purpose.

The British and French armies were able to stop the German advance within heavy artillery range of Paris. Thereafter, the armies faced each other during four weary and bloody years of trench warfare. This unimaginative method of fighting made it exceptionally difficult for either side to win. The enthusiasm faded quickly, as 300,000 French soldiers lost their lives in the first five months. Colonel de Grandmaison's axiom that "there is no such thing as an excessive offensive" produced untold carnage on such battlefields as Verdun, where a half-million soldiers were slaughtered in the spring of 1916. A young captain named Charles de Gaulle, who was wounded three times and sent to a German prisoner-of-war camp for the last 30 months, noted, "It appeared in the wink of an eye that all the virtue in the world could not prevail against superior firepower."

The defeatism and demoralization which such mindless frontal assaults produced led to large-scale mutinies on the French front from April to October 1917. Miraculously, the Germans never heard about them at the time. They also produced a frame of mind which the novelist

France

German troops enter Paris, 1940.

Jules Romains described in his book *Verdun*, which first appeared at an unfortunate time—1938: "Men in the mass are seen to be like a school of fish or cloud of locusts swarming to destruction. The individual man is less than nothing—certainly not worth worrying about. . . . My most haunting horror is not that I see men now willing to suffer and act as they do, but that having so seen them, I shall never again be able to believe in their good intentions."

Ultimately 1 million fresh American troops in France tipped the balance, and on November 11, 1918, the exhausted and starving Germans saw no alternative to capitulation. France had technically been victorious, but it was left breathless and demoralized; 1.3 million Frenchmen had been killed, and more than 1 million, crippled. Northeastern France, the country's most prosperous industrial and agricultural sector, was largely devastated. France's enormous human and material losses inclined French leaders to demand a heavy price from Germany in the Treaty of Versailles.

Germany and its allies were branded as solely responsible for the war, and Germany was therefore required to pay exorbitant reparations. France regained Alsace and Lorraine, established temporary control over the German Saar, stationed its troops in Germany west of the Rhine, and obtained mandates in the former German colonies of Togo and Cameroons and in Syria and Lebanon, as well. While France's demands were somewhat understandable, they played into the hands of a future German rabble-rouser named Adolf Hitler, who promised to undo the hated treaty. The settlement is a glaring example of the fact that policies that may be righteous are not always wise.

The Post–World War I Era

The French expected to rebuild their land with the reparations from Germany, but when it became apparent that an impoverished Germany could never pay the sums demanded, the French set about to do the work themselves. Displaying remarkable resilience, the French had, by the mid-1920s, cleared away the rubble; rebuilt homes, factories, and railroads; and achieved a measure of prosperity which exceeded even that of Britain. Unfortunately, many of the economic gains were wiped away by the Great Depression that spread to France by 1932. The last European country to be affected by Black Friday on Wall Street, France was so jolted that, when democracies all over Europe toppled, France tottered also.

The Nazi seizure of power in Germany in 1933 further destabilized France by pumping new life into right-wing and, in some cases, openly fascist groups in France. The best-known was the Action Française, which had emerged from the Dreyfus controversy and whose leader, Charles Maurras, powerfully and eloquently railed against Jews, Protestants, foreigners, and the French Republic generally. Offshoots and competitors of Action Française such as the Camelots du Roi or the Francistes, bullied people in the streets, dressed like Hitler's storm troopers, and ceaselessly pointed to the difference between the vigor and effectiveness of the dictatorships in Italy and Germany and the tired, ineffective parliamentary system in France. Royalist and fascist groups, supported by thousands of students and some communists, gathered on February 6, 1934, at the Place de la Concorde and stormed the National Assembly, located just across the Pont de la Concorde. The police stopped the assault, but 21 persons lay dead, and more than 1,600 were injured in this violent action against the feeble republic.

Storm Clouds and Paralysis

As storm clouds gathered over Europe, France had only short-lived, stop-gap governments that could not begin to cope with the mounting crises. In desperate economic straits, no French government could propose military increases to counter the dictators. Also, the memories of the First World War were so horrifying in the minds of many Frenchmen that they could not tolerate the thought of participating in another war, for whatever cause. *Surtout pas la guerre* ("Above all, no war!") was the slogan of Action Française. It was uttered with all the energy of "Hell no, I won't go!" in the America of the 1960s and 1970s.

Pacifism was widespread and was manifest in the writings of many of France's literary figures. In a letter to a friend, novelist Roger Martin du Gard wrote, "I am hard as steel for neutrality. My principle: anything, rather than war! Anything, anything! Even fascism in Spain . . . even fascism in France! . . . Anything: Hitler rather than war!" The highly respected writer, Jean Giono, dared to write, "I prefer to be a live German than a dead Frenchman!" even the minister of public works, Anatole de Monzie, said publicly, "I prefer to receive a kick in the behind than a bullet in the head." French patriotism after World War I had become tinged with the fear that the costs of war were simply too great.

A state of mind took shape that prepared France for defeat in the next war. As noble as it may seem sometimes, pacifism usually plays into the hands of the world's bullies, as France was soon to see.

With the fascist leagues active in the streets of France, the parties of the left began to speak of unified action for the first time. In 1935 the Socialists and Radicals

General Charles de Gaulle, London

formed a Popular Front that won a great victory in 1936 parliamentary elections. Under Léon Blum, the first Jew and first Socialist to serve as prime minister of France, the Popular Front, with the parliamentary support of the Communists, proposed a 40-hour workweek, paid vacations, collective bargaining, and the partial nationalization of the Bank of France. However, Blum was unable to find a solution to the problem of lagging production, and in 1938 his government fell.

France was the helpless observer of an aggressive German government, which in the mid- and late 1930s reoccupied the Rhineland, sent troops and squadrons to Spain to fight for Franco in its civil war, absorbed Austria, and occupied part of Czechoslovakia. After World War I, France had not only constructed the Maginot Line, but it also sought to protect itself by surrounding Germany with enemy powers. It forged military alliances with Belgium, Poland, Czechoslovakia, Romania, and Yugoslavia. Hitler merely pointed to this encirclement to justify his own aggressive policies.

In 1930, before Hitler came to power, just 12 years after the end of World War I, the French parliament voted funds to build an allegedly impregnable defensive line against invasion from Germany. The Maginot Line consisted of an elaborate system of underground bunkers, fortifications, and antitank devices and extended all the way along France's border with Germany. It was based on a conclusion drawn from the previous war that all advantages lie with the defense. Colonel Charles de Gaulle disagreed. He warned at the time in his controversial book *France and Its Army* that modern warfare requires great mobility with tanks and aircraft. Regrettably the book was read only by the German commanders, who reportedly carried it with them when they invaded France in 1940. Unfortunately the designers of the line neglected one of the basic principles of fortress building: Protect all sides. It was thought that the line could stop at the Belgian border since that state was supposed to remain neutral.

This shield mentality naturally meshed with the pacifist feelings in the French population and political circles. Léon Blum, who apparently believed in the power of a strong world conscience that hated war, opposed the extension of military service from one to two years and continued to speak of the need for France to take unilateral steps toward disarmament, as if such a French policy could incline Hitler to be more peaceful. As his government fell, France was frozen with fear. Political parties and alliances were such that the country was ungovernable.

French resistance leader Jean Moulin

Complicating the scene was journalism at its lowest. Most political parties and groups printed their own newspapers that propagated untruths daily about opposing parties, groups, and people. There were 39 regularly published in Paris alone.

World War II

Thus, when Germany invaded Poland on September 1, 1939, and when France reluctantly and finally felt compelled to

Allied invasion of Normandy, June 6, 1944

France

General de Gaulle inspecting Free French troops, London

declare war three days later, it entered a disastrous conflict militarily and emotionally unprepared and half-consciously aspiring more to an armistice than to a victory. Germany and the Soviet Union quickly partitioned Poland, but Hitler delayed military action against France for three-quarters of a year. In France, one spoke of a "phony war," or a sitzkrieg, and precious little was done to prepare for a future onslaught. The German tank commander Heinz Guderian later wrote, "The relatively passive attitude of the French during the winter of 1939–40 incited us to conclude that the adversary had little inclination for war."

On May 10, 1940, Hitler unleashed his armies against France. Invading the Netherlands and Belgium (both neutral countries, thereby avoiding the face of the Maginot Line, which was unprotected from the rear), German forces used lightning warfare (blitzkrieg) tactics against a French army that was poorly and lethargically led and in some respects technologically outdated. French leaders refused to withdraw troops from the Maginot Line to confront actual German advances to the north, and their administrative confusion prevented badly needed French aircraft and artillery from being transferred to the actual front. This produced such disastrous reversals that the French government was forced to abandon Paris within one month. British prime minister Winston S. Churchill testified that French soldiers fought valiantly, but their political and military leaders were so quickly seized by defeatism that the French cabinet could not muster the tenacity or eagerness to persist after the shock of initial defeats.

Britain pleaded urgently that France both honor its earlier agreement not to seek a separate peace and even consider a political union of the two countries. The latter proposal was understandably unwelcome to a country that had spent centuries ridding itself of English domination and influence. A demoralized French cabinet, under the influence of the aging First World War hero, Marshal Pétain, chose instead to surrender on June 22, 1940, barely 40 days after the German attack.

The terms were very harsh. The northern half of France, including Paris, and the whole of the Atlantic coast to the Spanish border, were to be occupied by German troops at French expense. Alsace and the Moselle Department were annexed by Germany. The rest of France was to be ruled by a French government friendly to Germany. This government was to supply its conquerors with food and raw materials needed for the German war effort. The French army was to be disbanded and its navy placed in ports under the control of the Germans and the Italians.

The fate of the French navy especially distressed the British. They were unaware that the French naval commander-in-chief, Admiral Darlan, had secretly ordered his fleet commanders to scuttle his ships if the Germans or Italians tried to seize them. When the British tried to take control of the French squadron in Mersel-Kebir in Algeria, the French commander resisted. The British destroyed the squadron, an action that caused a wave of anti-British feeling in France. This sentiment played into the hands of the cunning Premier Pierre Laval and the 80-year-old Pétain, who had long opposed the Third Republic as a decadent, inefficient regime.

They quickly abolished the Third Republic and established a repressive Vichy Republic (named after the spa in France where the new government established its seat of power). Without prompting by the Germans, they denied Jews and Freemasons the protection of the law. In the July 1942 "Vélodrome d'hiver" roundup, 13,000 Paris Jews were arrested over two days and detained at that Paris sports stadium. A former police barracks outside Paris, called Drancy, served as a transit camp.

In all, 76,000 (including 11,000 children) of the 330,000 Jews in France at the beginning of the war were, with the help of the French police, deported during Vichy. Only 2,500 returned. In June 2006 a French court ruled that hundreds of Jewish families or their relatives are entitled to compensation paid by the French railway SNCF for its role in deporting them. In February 2009 France's highest court, the Council of State, formally recognized the nation's role in these deportations, but they effectively ruled out added reparations. In January

General Leclerc and his troops preparing to capture Paris

116

2011 SNCF buckled to pressure from the United States, which had threatened to stymie its bids for contracts to build high-speed rail lines from San Francisco to Los Angeles and from Orlando to Tampa. It offered its first formal public apology to Holocaust victims for transporting thousands of Jews to the German border, from where German trains took them to death camps. Restitution payments began in 2015. In 2019 payments of $402,000 were made to 49 Holocaust survivors and up to $100,500 to 32 spouses. Most lived in the United States. At the same time, some historians reminded the world that 1,647 French train drivers had been executed or deported and never came back.

Foreigners who had come to France to escape Hitler's persecution were penned up in French concentration camps and, unless they were able to escape, were later returned to Germany where an uncertain, usually fatal future awaited them. In fact, most Jews deported to Germany had been new arrivals in France who had fled Nazi persecution elsewhere. By the time Paris was liberated in 1944, about 60,000 Jews were left in the city, half of whom in hiding.

Some noted non-Jewish artists and intellectuals, such as Mondrian, Dali, and Chagall, fled to New York, while others, such as Sartre and Georges Pompidou, remained and coexisted with the occupiers. The Nazis decided that they would face fewer occupation problems if they permitted the French, especially Parisians, to be entertained. Despite censorship most French artists did just that. Singer Edith Piaf confessed, "My real job is to sing, to sing no matter what happened." Jean Cocteau expressed his astonishing opinion: "At no price should one let oneself be distracted from serious matters by the dramatic frivolity of war."

Many Frenchmen were relieved to have achieved a peace at any price; nevertheless, they felt a numbing feeling of humiliation and the awareness that this was a tragic debacle which had befallen the French nation. What followed was as much a French civil war as a war against the Germans. For the next four years, there were two Frances, one fighting against the Germans and one trying to ignore the conflict and to minimize damage to the French population. Any single Frenchman could find sound patriotic reasons for supporting either, and it was up to the individual to decide which France was his.

France still has not fully recovered psychologically from the terrible tension of the Vichy years. A poll in 1992 showed that 82% of Frenchmen considered the Vichy government to be guilty of "crimes against humanity," and 90% thought that their country should admit it. In a July 2004 ceremony to commemorate the "Vélodrome d'hiver" roundup, France's top public figures acknowledged the evils of anti-Semitism during the Vichy regime.

This lamentable event was portrayed in vivid accuracy in the 2010 film *La Rafle*, a box-office success in France. Until Jacques Chirac assumed the presidency in 1995, the opinion of every president was that the Vichy state was not France. This is despite the fact that Vichy put some soldiers on trial for the defeat and executed Gestapo spies.

In 1994 the trial of Paul Touvier captivated France. Convicted of murdering Jewish hostages in 1944, he became the first Frenchman charged and convicted of a crime against humanity. This was also the first time a French court blamed Vichy for its role in the Nazis' Final Solution. In 1995 Jacques Chirac became the first president to accept the responsibility of the French state for the arrest and deportation of Jews during Vichy. In 1997 the bishop of St. Denis admitted for the first time the French Catholic Church's guilt in "acquiescing by its silence" in the persecution of the Jews: "We beg God's pardon and we ask the Jewish people to hear our words of repentance."

Maurice Papon was a police supervisor in Bordeaux from 1942 to 1944, who, according to documents first revealed by the satirical *Le Canard Enchainé*, was instrumental in the arrest and deportation of 1,690 Jews; very few returned. Still defiantly maintaining that he had only done what the Germans had made him do and that he had been a loyal member of the resistance, he became de Gaulle's postwar

De Gaulle leaves Notre Dame Cathedral after the liberation of Paris. Courtesy: Central Audiovisual Library, European Commission

France

police chief in Paris, member of the National Assembly, Gaullist Party treasurer, and budget minister under President Giscard d'Estaing. He was found guilty in 1998 and sentenced to 10 years in prison, becoming the highest-ranking Frenchman ever convicted of complicity in crimes against humanity.

His trial had been the longest and most expensive in modern French history, and it forced the country to confront a part of its past that many still try to forget. After executing the Vichy leaders for treason, the policy was to keep France united, to avoid recriminations, and to draw a veil over the past. Vowing that he would "go into exile" rather than spend his last years behind bars, Papon fled to Switzerland. He was quickly apprehended. In 2000 President Chirac rejected his plea for release. Nevertheless, in September 2002, less than three years into his sentence, Papon was discharged under a law allowing early release for the ill and aging. He sparked anger when he walked unassisted from jail after the doctors had determined he was lacking in mobility. Controversy still surrounded him after his death in February 2007 at the age of 96. Many were shocked to learn that he had asked to be buried wearing his Legion of Honor medal he had received from de Gaulle's very hand.

During the war, France was the country from which the most art was looted; over a third of all privately owned art was stolen. Many of the most valuable treasures from state museums were rescued: *Winged Victory of Samothrace* was wheeled down a steep staircase, and the *Mona Lisa* was carried out of the Louvre on a stretcher and joined thousands of artworks hidden in southern France. The occupiers left what remained in the national museums untouched. It was a different story for Jewish collections. Thousands of treasures were seized and sent to the Jeu de Paume, which the Germans had set up as a kind of warehouse for stolen art. Hermann Goering visited it at least 20 times to help himself.

France has a respectable record in returning assets seized from Jews. A study in 2000 found that about the equivalent of $1.3 billion had been taken: 80,000 frozen bank accounts; 6,000 safe deposit boxes; 38,000 confiscated apartments; 50,000 "aryanization" cases to seize businesses and homes; and 100,000 works of art. About 90% of these were compensated in some form within a decade of war's end. Some were never reclaimed. France still has about $3 billion in unclaimed funds, earmarked for a National Foundation for Memory to keep alive the awareness of the Holocaust. In 2003 the government-appointed Commission for the Compensation of Victims of Spoliation recommended

One of hundreds of plaques honoring the fighters in the Battle for Paris

that the government and French banks pay Jews an additional $84 million.

While working together with the Germans, the Vichy government introduced what it called a "National Revolution." Although this was, in some cases, fascist in inspiration, it sought among other things to strengthen the role of France's regions; to introduce economic planning at the highest political level; to concentrate small agricultural holdings into larger, more efficient farms; and to stimulate population growth through family allowances for children. Postwar France actually built on some of these Vichy innovations.

The Vichy government's powers were drastically reduced at the end of 1942, when the Germans, in response to Anglo-American military landings in North Africa, occupied all of France. Vichy's prestige declined rapidly, and when Frenchmen were sent to Germany involuntarily in order to work in German war industries, the ranks of the resistance began to grow. Nevertheless, more Frenchmen fought on the Axis (German) side than with the Allies. In fact, the last SS unit that defended Hitler in his final days in the Berlin bunker was French. There was also much "horizontal collaboration," and about 20,000 women had their heads shaved in shame. French women bore an estimated 200,000 children sired by German soldiers. Known as "*enfants de Boches*," they suffered discrimination in France for a couple generations, and many were given to orphanages or put up for adoption. Ex–foreign minister Bernard Kouchner paid tribute to them in 2009, recognizing their misery.

By 1943 command over the entire French resistance movement had been gathered into the hands of General de Gaulle, who had fled to Britain in 1940 and who had organized there the Free French Movement. He reminded his countrymen by radio in a 3-minute, 400-word BBC address, "France has lost a battle, but not the war." Few French heard it since it was broadcast without prior announcement at 10 p.m. But by the time his 6'5" (1.96 meters) frame had stood up, he had appointed himself as the embodiment of all that is noble about France. Nevertheless, it would be a couple years before more Frenchmen would believe that he, rather than Pétain, had steered the right course for their country.

His claims to be the legal French government-in-exile and the sole spokesman for France greatly irritated Churchill and Roosevelt, who for a time found it politically wise to maintain diplomatic recognition of the Vichy government. Speaking of Churchill, de Gaulle said, "we are angry at each other most of the time." Further, when Admiral Darlan was assassinated three weeks after he scuttled the French navy, Britain and the United States recognized another French general as "chief of state" in French North Africa. Roosevelt greeted him warmly in Washington, which infuriated de Gaulle. His wartime experiences with the British and Americans did not leave him with a strong admiration for the two countries, and his resentment was to disturb these two nations' relations with France even after 1958, when he became France's leader.

The French resistance fighters helped protect unfortunate Allied pilots and often provided useful military intelligence and other support to the Allies. There is no doubt that resistance against the Germans was very dangerous business. De Gaulle later estimated that 20,000 French resistance fighters had been executed and more than 50,000 deported from France before the Allied landings in Normandy. But German documents reveal that this movement had not constituted an effective military threat to the Germans, as had the resistance movements in the Soviet Union and Yugoslavia. Still, when the Allies landed on the Normandy beaches (which today are sobering and moving sites for visiting and reflecting), the French resistance played an important part in destroying bridges, assembling paratroops for action, and providing Allied units with useful information. Also, French military units that had been organized in London under de Gaulle's overall command fought side by side with the Americans, British, and Canadians.

Local resistance forces and delegates from de Gaulle's headquarters in London assumed political control in liberated France, arresting or executing Vichy officials. On August 19, 1944, resistance fighters rose up in Paris against the German occupiers. Six days later, Free French units commanded by General Philippe Leclerc took control of the city, which a disobedient German commander had saved from senseless destruction by refusing to burn and destroy as ordered by Hitler. De Gaulle arrived with the French troops, and the following day he led a triumphant march down the broad Champs-Elysées.

The Vichy government fled to Germany, and for the next year and a half, de Gaulle's provisional government exercised unchallenged authority in liberated France. The resistance movement had brought together persons from all backgrounds and political convictions, and de Gaulle hoped that this predominantly young, patriotic, idealistic, but at the same time practical

core of Frenchmen would provide the spark for national revival and change. He announced during the war, "while the French people are uniting for victory they are assembling for a revolution."

His movement also encompassed French communists, although he was always suspicious that his desired revolution was not the same as theirs. Communists displayed undeniable courage and commitment after Germany had attacked the Soviet Union in 1941 "but never, as an army of revolution, losing sight of the objective, which was to establish their dictatorship by making use of the tragic situation of France. . . . I was quite as decided not to let them ever gain the upper hand or bypass me, or take the lead." He successfully blocked their efforts to gain a ministry controlling foreign affairs, defense, or the police. French Socialists and other groups also learned then and later what a mixed blessing cooperation with communists can be.

The End of Conflict and the Beginning of Bickering

De Gaulle engaged in feverish diplomacy in order to reestablish France's position in world affairs: He traveled to Moscow in November 1944, helped create the United Nations, fought successfully for a permanent French seat on the Security Council, and secured a French occupation zone in Germany as a victorious power. He also initiated a program of nationalizing the nation's coal mines, electrical production, natural gas, some banks, and other basic industries, such as the Renault auto company. Since many French business leaders had collaborated with the enemy during the Vichy years and since a national effort to rebuild the French economy was so obviously necessary, few people opposed such a policy.

Jean Monnet   Courtesy: Central Audiovisual Library, European Commission

Frenchmen shared an almost-universal desire for the creation of a Fourth Republic, but they split on the perennial French dispute concerning the kind of republic that was appropriate for France. De Gaulle stood aloof from these controversies, although it was widely known that he preferred a strong executive and a weak parliament. "Deliberation is the work of many men. Action, of one alone!" Sensing that the old bickering party and parliamentary activity was about to reemerge, that his coalition was collapsing, and that his views on the future republic were not gaining support, he announced in January 1946 his resignation as temporary president. He apparently expected a wave of popular support to swell in his favor, allowing him to strengthen his hand in shaping the new republic, but such a movement failed to materialize. For seven years he tried to return to power, but in 1953 he withdrew completely from direct involvement and lived for the next five years in the political desert, awaiting a crisis that would direct his countrymen's eyes again on de Gaulle, the savior.

In 1946 that kind of political regime was created which de Gaulle had most feared: a parliamentary system with a weak president—practically a restoration of the Third Republic which, in his eyes, had so thoroughly discredited itself and France in 1940. In the plebiscite of late 1946, a bare majority voted in favor of the new constitution, an ominous sign for the new Fourth Republic. There was no clear majority, either in the parliament or the nation, so subsequent political instability was hardly surprising. There were 10 governments in the first 5 years, and by 1958 Frenchmen had witnessed no fewer than 25 governments. A coherent policy was

Captain (later General) C. E. Vidal shaking hands with his French troops in Koblenz, Germany, 1945   Courtesy: The late general C. E. Vidal

France

very difficult to achieve, and the "parliamentary game" appeared more and more to be divorced from the pressing needs of the public.

The governments of the Fourth Republic were faced with many crises in economic, foreign, and colonial policy, some of which they mastered and most of which weakened or destroyed them. Nevertheless, it is a great mistake to view France from 1946 until de Gaulle's return to power in 1958 as a hopelessly paralyzed country. France had a resilient population, a rather competent and dedicated bureaucracy, and a few leaders with sound judgment.

Economic Growth and European Cooperation

France set about very quickly to repair the destruction from the long war and to reestablish economic strength. The results, with massive assistance of the United States' Marshall Plan, were impressive. Between 1949 and 1957, its GNP increased by 40%, and from 1952 forward, its growth rate was more than 10% a year, consistently among the highest in Europe. Frenchmen poured into the urban areas from the countryside, thereby dramatically changing the face of French society. Fortunately, French industry was able to absorb them. At the same time, agricultural production increased by 24% from 1949 to 1957. Government financial subsidies for families with children, coupled with the people's increasingly optimistic view of the future, helped bring about one of Europe's highest birth rates, a welcome development for a country which for more than a century had experienced relatively low population growth.

France's rapid economic growth was greatly aided by economic planning, which, in contrast to planning in communist countries, was entirely noncompulsory. These periodic plans set targets and suggested investments to French industry, with a view to making the economy as efficient and modern as possible. Perhaps most important, such planning helped Frenchmen believe strongly in the possibility of progress. The Marshall Plan assistance which the United States gave to France and other western European countries encouraged such planning. It even had a further long-term benefit for Europe: A condition for aid was that European countries discuss and agree among themselves how such help should be used. These discussions opened possibilities of European cooperation that laid the foundations for the creation of NATO and the EU.

The fruits of this were not long in coming. In 1950, France's brilliant foreign minister Robert Schuman proposed an imaginative European Coal and Steel Community, which within two years provided a common market for these two critical commodities among West Germany, France, the BENELUX countries, and Italy, a step unthinkable five years earlier. Seven years later, Schuman and his countryman Jean Monnet, de Gaulle's wartime representative for economic negotiations with Washington and London and from 1946 to 1952 chief of France's General Planning Commission, were key figures in the creation of the EU by the same six powers. The French were not inclined to transfer any French sovereignty to the EU; indeed, de Gaulle later reiterated that this was to be a "Europe of Fatherlands," that is, of entirely sovereign nation-states. Yet they have clearly recognized that French interests are best served in a cooperative, democratic Europe, and they have strongly supported such a Europe.

At one time France sought to extend European cooperation into the military sphere, as well. When the Korean War began in 1950, there was fear in Europe that the Soviet Union might be considering an aggressive assault against western Europe. When the United States suggested that West Germany be permitted to rearm, the French became uneasy. Therefore, the government proposed a European Defense Community (EDC) that would integrate German soldiers into an overall European command. There would be no German general staff. However, Britain refused to join, and French public opinion also gradually turned against it. In 1954 the parliament, not wanting French troops to be under supranational control, rejected the proposal. After the vote the Gaullist and communist deputies stood up and sang the "Marseillaise." France, however, remained a member of NATO, which had been formed in 1949 and which West Germany also joined in 1955.

The Empire Crumbles

While France's economic recovery and contribution to a unified Europe, which included former enemy powers, were glittering successes of the French Fourth Republic, the government was brought to its knees by the painfully traumatic disintegration of the colonial empire. The two world wars had stimulated a desire in colonies all over the world for independence, but many Frenchmen believed it was impossible to restore French power, prestige, and prosperity without aid from the colonies.

The first disaster occurred in Indochina, which the Japanese had occupied during the war. When the French attempted to reestablish control after liberation, a powerful native communist resistance movement called the Viet Minh and led by Ho Chi Minh opposed them. Fighting broke out in December 1946, and all French political parties, including the communists, initially supported the war effort. However, eight inglorious years of fighting without victory created powerful domestic opposition to continuation of the conflict. The United States refused in principle to help the French in a colonial war, although it did provide about $1 billion in financial assistance. When in 1954 France sought relief for its embattled stronghold Dien Bien Phu and a quick solution to the war by asking that the US use atomic bombs against the Viet Minh, the request was turned down. After the Viet Minh captured that garrison in the same year, the French agreed to a temporary division of Vietnam and to a permanent withdrawal

120

after free elections. For complicated reasons, such elections were never held.

Having had no time to recover from the shock of loss of Indochina, the French had to turn their attention immediately to a rebellion in Algeria that erupted in November 1954. Algeria was a much more complicated problem. Legally it was not a colony but an integral part of France, as Hawaii is part of the US. Located directly south of France, it (unlike Indochina) had an immediate strategic importance for the country. Further, there were more than 1 million French settlers living there, some of whose families had been in Algeria for more than three generations. Many were farmers, producing semitropical foodstuffs for France.

The Algerian rebellion shook France to the core. It unleashed conspiracies against the government, assassinations, and ill-fated military coups d'état. A half million troops were sent to Algeria to suppress it. It was a struggle that prompted the French military, which was left more or less to its own devices, to conduct unconventional warfare and atrocities against an enemy that often used terrorist methods and melted into the general population.

In response, French methods were sometimes unsavory. In 2001 a former French general in the secret service, Paul Aussaresses, wrote a book entitled *Special Services in Algeria 1955–1957*, in which he described in a matter-of-fact way how he and other French military routinely tortured and executed suspects, noting that as many as 3,000 suspects had simply "disappeared." He admitted having executed 24 suspected guerrillas himself and claimed to have only "followed orders." The book was a sensation in that he showed no remorse, and it reflected a "cold tone, lacking any hindsight and any humanity," in the words of the judge who fined him for "complicity in justifying war crimes." France has never officially apologized for its conduct during the war, which claimed the lives of 30,000 French men and women and at least a half-million Algerians.

The process by which Morocco and Tunisia gained their independence went much more smoothly. One of the most important and influential politicians to steer France through its crises in the 1950s was Pierre Mendes-France. Serving as premier from 1954 to 1955, he extricated France from Indochina, helped facilitate Tunisian independence in 1956, and began talks with Moroccan nationalists that would lead to France's withdrawal from the country. An ardent opponent of colonialism, he also favored concessions to Algerian nationalists.

The war brought an aging man out of retirement from the eastern village of Colombey-les-Deux-Églises: Charles de Gaulle. When the French military seized power in Algeria's capital city, Algiers, in May 1958 and soon thereafter on the island of Corsica, Napoleon's birthplace, many, especially French generals, believed that only de Gaulle could save Algeria or protect the country from civil war.

De Gaulle haughtily said that he would respond to the call of his fellow citizens only on his own terms: that he be granted unrestricted authority to cope with the crisis. In mid-1958, he was appointed prime minister, and he quickly went to Algeria and gave an enthusiastic French throng the highly ambiguous assurance "I have understood you!" He undoubtedly knew the situation was hopeless. In late 1958 an electoral college of notables elected him president of the republic. Parliament also approved his new constitution. This spelled the death knell of the Fourth Republic and the birth of the present Fifth Republic.

The de Gaulle Years in Power

Always a realist under his mantle of magnificence, de Gaulle was convinced that Algeria could no longer be held by force, but he proceeded very cautiously in seeking a settlement of the crisis. He did not want to provoke a military coup d'état in France itself. He shrewdly allowed all groups to think that he shared all of their own objectives. Sensing that the right time had come, he announced a referendum for early 1961 to decide whether Algeria should be granted self-determination. Fifteen million said yes; only 5 million said no. He thus had received a free hand to pursue negotiations with the Algerian National Liberation Front (FLN), and he directed Prime Minister Georges Pompidou to lead the negotiations.

This was an extremely unstable time in both France and Algeria, and de Gaulle felt compelled to assume sweeping emergency powers to master the situation. The cloud of a military takeover loomed over the country. Indeed, some French officers regarded the president's policy as "treachery" and formed the Secret Army Organization (OAS) with the aim of keeping Algeria French by any means possible, including terror, bombings, and assassinations. De Gaulle himself barely escaped three assassination attempts in 1962.

A breakthrough occurred in March 1962: France granted Algeria full sovereignty in return for the Algerian promise to respect the French settlers' lives and property, as well as French oil interests in the Sahara and military interests in a port city. Ninety percent of the people approved this settlement in a referendum. Three-quarters of a million French settlers from Algeria

"... the whole room might tilt everyone into the garden."

France

(known in France as *pieds noirs*—"black feet") and some Algerians who had fought for France (known as *harkis*) left for mainland France. The promise regarding oil interests was not fully kept by the Algerians.

De Gaulle had already offered all the other French colonies the option of becoming independent while retaining cultural ties with France. By 1960 all had accepted this option, with the exception of Guinea, which rejected all ties with the French community that was to be established. Thus by 1962 the French Empire had practically ceased to exist.

It now possesses five overseas departments (Guadeloupe and Martinique in the Caribbean, French Guiana in South America, Réunion, and since March 2009 Mayotte in the Indian Ocean); five overseas territories (New Caledonia, French Polynesia, Wallis, and Futuna in the South Pacific and French Southern and Antarctic Territories, a smattering of islands in the southern part of the earth); and one special-status territory (Saint-Pierre and Miquelon in the Atlantic near Newfoundland). The inhabitants are French citizens with a right to vote and economic subsidies that enable them to enjoy a standard of living comparable to that of metropolitan France. Far from weakening France, the shedding of the colonial burden freed its hand for a more assertive foreign policy in Europe, the Middle East, and elsewhere, and it eliminated the searing domestic division that stemmed from unpopular colonial wars. In the years that followed, de Gaulle was able to show his countrymen that it was possible to have a measure of grandeur without a colonial empire.

Prosperity and Social Benefits

While de Gaulle provided France with a constitution that could maintain a greater measure of political stability, he also sought to eliminate the bases of social conflict by introducing needed social reforms. The often enigmatic but always pragmatic general was a point of intersection between two seemingly contradictory forces. He was an agent of French modernization and also the guardian of the idea of French mission and grandeur. His task was to change France without discarding her glorious tradition. Among his followers were traditionalists, technocrats, social reformers, French nationalists, dreamers, and realists.

He continued work begun before 1958 to expand education opportunities, thus facilitating greater mobility, especially for workers and other formerly underprivileged groups. He stabilized France's currency and helped bring about a rise in real wages. He expanded the social security net that protects Frenchmen against ill health, unemployment, and old age. He

Subway entrance, Paris. The Louvre is on the left. Photo by Susan L. Thompson

also proposed that large firms distribute a portion of their shares to employees and include workers in the firms' decision-making practices, which some companies such as Renault, actually adopted.

In general, he furthered efforts to provide his countrymen with prosperity and higher common consumption standards shared by all. He could write with pride, "once upon a time there was an old country hemmed in by habits and circumspection. . . . Now this country, France, is back on her feet again."

Foreign Affairs—Estrangement from US Hegemony

With social peace and economic prosperity at home, de Gaulle could turn full attention to that which was undoubtedly his major interest: foreign affairs. He had been greatly displeased with France's position in the world when he came to power. Colonial wars had sapped almost all of France's attention and military strength. What was worse, the fate of Europe had been determined by the Soviet Union, the US, and Britain, and after the advent of the Cold War in 1946–1947, French security had fallen almost exclusively into the hands of NATO, with an American general in command. That is, France's security was basically in the hands of the US, a friendly but foreign country, which in his words,

"brings to great affairs elementary feelings and a complicated policy."

De Gaulle and all his successors knew that the Soviet Union posed a threat to western Europe, which ultimately needed American protection. He also knew that the United States' tolerance level toward its European allies was high. He therefore decided that France needed and could achieve foreign policy independence. He unquestionably also had bitter memories of what he considered a personal snub by Churchill and Roosevelt during the struggles of World War II.

His first step was to develop French atomic weapons. When he was informed in 1960 of the successful French explosion in the Sahara, he exclaimed, "Hurray for France!" This nuclear capability, known in France as the *force de frappe*, has come to be supported by most of the French political parties, including the Communist Party.

Seeking to strengthen the center of western Europe, he signed a Treaty on German-French Cooperation in 1963. It basically called for regular consultation and semiannual state visits between the leaders of these two European powerhouses. A disappointed de Gaulle later referred to this treaty as a "faded rose" because it had failed to persuade the West Germans to loosen their own ties with the US, as he had hoped. Nevertheless, it was an important and imaginative policy observed by all his successors. For example, the first meeting President Mitterrand had with a foreign political leader after his election was with the West German chancellor. Further, Helmut Kohl's first foreign visit after becoming German chancellor in 1982 was to Paris. De Gaulle had provided an enormous boost for a development which few Europeans would have considered possible in 1945: For the first time in European history, the idea of a war between France and Germany had become unthinkable.

In 1967 he announced an "opening to the east" which amounted to direct French contact with the Soviet Union and actual participation in the era of détente. In 1967, when war broke out between Israel and its Arab neighbors, de Gaulle, unfettered by a colonial policy in North Africa, chose to adopt an openly pro-Arab position. Although many Frenchmen were displeased by his anti-Israel (and occasionally unconcealed anti-Jewish) remarks, this policy was not reversed by his next two successors, who were only too well aware of France's dependence upon Arab oil. Mitterrand promised a more evenhanded policy toward Israel and the Arabs.

The US reluctantly honored de Gaulle's demand that American troops (whom he called "good-natured but bad mannered") be withdrawn from French soil, a move that greatly increased NATO's logistical problems. This was a logical step to follow his announcement a year earlier that France would withdraw from NATO's integrated command (although not from NATO itself). He did not oppose the presence of American troops elsewhere in Europe because he did not want to remove France from the NATO shield. It was always assumed that France would support NATO in the event of a Warsaw Pact attack against western Europe. This assumption was underscored by the fact that France continued to maintain 70,000 troops in West Germany and participates in many joint military exercises. De Gaulle was convinced that, in case of a ground war in Europe, Frenchmen would be more willing to make sacrifices to defend Europe because they would see this as primarily a French defense effort, not an American one. Thus, in his opinion, the western alliance would be strengthened, not weakened.

American leaders in 1967, bogged down in a hopeless Vietnam War, had little understanding for such logic. Many Americans remembered the many American soldiers buried in France as a result of World War II. However, after 1968, the White House had far more admiration for de Gaulle's character and policy. Kissinger noted in his memoirs that de Gaulle's policies, "so contrary to American postwar preconceptions, were those of an ancient country grown skeptical through many enthusiasms shattered and conscious that to be meaningful to others, France had first of all to mean something to herself."

The changes were by no means universally supported in France at the time, but by the early 1970s, they had been embraced by all political parties, including the communists. The basic Gaullist goal to create an independent Europe under French leadership and thereby to diminish US influence in Europe has not been accomplished. Nevertheless, his design to create an independent French foreign policy has been followed by his presidential successors, despite some changes in emphasis and style.

He gave France a role of which it could be proud, and he ultimately won the world's respect for his country. Kissinger recalled that the general "exuded authority" and told of de Gaulle's attendance at a reception given by former president Nixon on the occasion of General Eisenhower's funeral in Washington: "His presence . . . was so overwhelming that he was the center of attention wherever he stood. Other heads of government and many senators who usually proclaimed their antipathy to authoritarian generals crowded around him and treated him like some strange species. One had the sense that if he moved to a window, the center of gravity might shift and the whole room might tilt everyone into the garden."

The "Events of May" and de Gaulle's Exit

Under de Gaulle, France had not become a land of complete satisfaction and harmony. Many Frenchmen grew weary of his paternalism. His preoccupation with foreign affairs gradually slowed down the reformist impulse. While most Frenchmen shared in the increasing prosperity, income differences had actually widened during the Fifth Republic. Further, despite the educational reforms, only 1% of the children from the working-class families entered the universities. Class stratification was not breaking down as much as some would have liked. At the same time, some Frenchmen, especially the young and the educated, were becoming afraid that the new consumption-oriented society was not good for France; it became apparent that France's traditional schizophrenia about change and modernism had not been entirely erased.

Before departing for a state visit to Romania in May 1968, de Gaulle announced that France was an "island of calm" in a very troubled world. Scarcely had he arrived in Budapest when a furious storm erupted in France that brought the Fifth Republic to the brink of extinction. Student unrest at the new University of Nanterre, a slogan-besmeared concrete complex located at the edge of Paris, spilled over to the Sorbonne and to other universities in the country. Many small groups of anarchists and Trotskyite and Maoist students believed that the university was the ideal place to launch a revolution against the capitalist society. Trying to reestablish order, the police violated an old taboo by entering the university grounds. This tradition stemmed from the time when the universities actually exercised the privilege of ruling themselves, a privilege long since revoked by a highly centralized French regime.

With vivid pictures of the Paris Commune in their heads, students erected barricades in Paris, and night after night they battled police with bricks from the cobblestone streets for control of the Latin Quarter. For this reason, Parisian authorities later paved over all of the city's cobblestone streets, thereby eliminating this arsenal of projectiles. Miraculously, the chaos claimed only two dead.

De Gaulle's number 2 man, Prime Minister Georges Pompidou, was very conciliatory toward the students, but before he could restore order, French workers were on strike, and the French economy practically came to a standstill. The Paris Stock Exchange was burned, and the threat of civil war was in the air.

De Gaulle developed a bold plan of action. He quietly flew by helicopter to Baden Baden, the headquarters of the French forces in Germany, in order to assure himself that the French military no longer bore grudges against him and would help him in the crisis. Returning to Paris, he announced new parliamentary elections in a radio speech that reversed the entire situation.

The campaign that followed was one of the shortest (19 days) and crudest in France since 1945. De Gaulle presented the basic issue as a choice between himself or anarchy. He successfully raised the specter of a communist danger to France. He also freed the remaining OAS prisoners in order to placate the army and right-wing elements. Opposition collapsed when the communists decided that it was not yet time for a revolution in France and advocated a return to order. The elections held in June 1968 were a virtual landslide for the Gaullists. The left lost half its seats and found itself in utter shambles.

The "events of May" had so shaken de Gaulle's grip on power he decided that he needed to restore his authority. He announced a referendum for April 1969 and, as usual, warned that, if his recommendations were not accepted, he would resign. He combined a rather unpopular reform (a change in the election of senators) with a more popular measure designed

France

Honorable Valéry Giscard d'Estaing

to strengthen the French regions. It was clear, however, that the chief issue was de Gaulle's popularity and his continued presidency, and on election day 53% voted against him. The general was thus handed the first referendum defeat in French history—a stinging rebuke.

Never tempted by dictatorship over his country, he resigned immediately and returned for the last time to his estate in Colombey-les-Deux-Églises in eastern France. Many Frenchmen asked whether this would be the end of the Fifth Republic, but they soon saw that he had not left a political void. He had left a sturdy constitution, in many ways well tailored to French needs. He had left a successor who easily won the presidential elections and whose greatest contribution to France was that he showed how the Fifth Republic could survive its creator.

In a 2005 television poll, de Gaulle was elected as the greatest Frenchman of all time. This was not merely a matter of popularity. The general remains as a kind of moral guarantor of today's French state, as well as of the Gaullist Party. He provides comfort and inspiration in the midst of uncertainty, decline, political stagnation, and a never-ending search for French identity. In 2008 a multimedia museum was dedicated to him at Les Invalides in Paris, and another opened in his home village of Colombey-les-Deux-Églises.

Georges Pompidou and Valéry Giscard d'Estaing

The new president, Georges Pompidou, had been educated at one of France's elite Grandes écoles and had quietly taught French literature in a Paris lycée during World War II. He was characteristic of many successful French political leaders, including Mitterrand: highly literate and intelligent, with a humanistic education and a sharp, practical sense for the realities of modern and political economic life.

In foreign policy, Pompidou was only slightly less Gaullist than de Gaulle himself, although he was always more modest and less abrasive than the general had been. He did break with his predecessor's policy by allowing Britain to enter the EU. He stressed continued industrial growth and the protection of French economic interests in the world. He also sought to modernize Paris by constructing urban freeways and skyscrapers in the city. However, Frenchmen, who are always sensitive to any alterations of their capital, widely condemned this "Manhattanization" of Paris, and his successor therefore abandoned this face-lifting operation.

Pompidou died in 1974 and was succeeded by Valéry Giscard d'Estaing, who won a razor-thin victory over Socialist leader François Mitterrand. A product of the super-elite École Nationale d'Administration (ENA) and a former finance minister, Giscard, who possessed distinguished aristocratic looks and a logical and photographic mind, had emerged as leader of a cluster of parties in the center and moderate right of the French political spectrum which came to be known as the Union for French Democracy (UDF).

Giscard entered the presidency determined to establish a more relaxed style in the Elysées Palace. Calling himself a "conservative who loves change," he wore a business suit instead of formal wear to his inauguration and after the ceremony walked instead of motored down the Champs-Elysées. He allowed himself to be photographed in a V-neck sweater and took a ride on the Paris Metro. For a while, he even ate monthly dinners in the homes of ordinary Frenchmen, and once he invited a group of Parisian garbage men to breakfast in the presidential palace. But he, like US president Jimmy Carter, discovered that his people did not necessarily respect folksiness in their highest leaders. Soon he withdrew to the dignity of his office and eventually assumed such an aloof and aristocratic air that his political opponents were always able to score points with voters by attacking his "monarchical" style.

The only president to be elected under age 50, Giscard was a reform-minded leader. He brought question time to the National Assembly and gave the opposition the chance to challenge legislation in the constitutional court. He also introduced some social changes. During his term the minimum voting age was lowered from 21 to 18; divorce laws were liberalized; abortion was legalized; a minimum wage was made available to agricultural workers; and most of the emigrants housed in embarrassing shanty towns, known as

Honorable Jacques Chirac, ex-president of the French Republic

"Bidonvilles," on the periphery of France's metropolitan areas, were resettled in newly built public housing. He also made the decision to permit immigrant families to rejoin their relatives in France, a policy that later became highly controversial.

In foreign affairs he observed the basic Gaullist principles of French independence and active presence on the international scene. He modernized the force de frappe, sent warships to the Persian Gulf to underscore French interests in the area, and took an active hand in Zaire (Congo) and the former French West Africa. About 6,000 French troops, including Foreign Legionnaires, are stationed in Africa, where about 300,000 mainland French still live. The largest units are in Djibouti, Senegal, Ivory Coast, and Gabon.

He sent French troops in 1977–1978 to Shaba (formerly Katanga) Province in Zaire to halt an invasion of Angolan and rebel forces. While France continued to sell arms to Libya, Giscard approved French military operations against Libyan moves in Mauritania (1977 and 1979) and Tunisia (1980). He joined anti-Libyan efforts in Chad. He also approved the use of French soldiers in 1979 to help depose the butcherous leader of the Central African Republic, Jean Bédel-Bokassa, a man who figured in one of Giscard's most embarrassing and damaging scandals: While finance minister under Pompidou, he had accepted gifts of diamonds from Bokassa.

Giscard prided himself on his support of European cooperation. He increased France's role in NATO planning and exercises, although he never hinted at any willingness to lead France back into full participation. Sometimes, though, he chose to act alone, reaping condemnation not only from France's western allies but from many French, as well.

Giscard's main objectives were to reorder in a systematic and long-term way French industrial priorities. Industries such as textiles or steel, that could no longer compete in international markets were denied government subsidies and were therefore often forced to cut back on their operations. Future-oriented sectors, such as telecommunications, microelectronics, nuclear and aerospace technology, and seabed research, which could compete successfully, were granted support. To reduce French energy dependence on oil from over one-half of energy needs to less than a third, Giscard supported an atomic energy policy that made France Europe's largest producer of nuclear power.

On the whole, France was more prosperous and economically prepared for the future than when Giscard entered office. But his effort to strengthen the economy by making firms more competitive put many Frenchmen out of work. Combined with growing revulsion for Giscard's aloof and aristocratic manner and a scandal involving his acceptance of diamonds from an African dictator, a majority of the French voters in 1981 were convinced that it was time for change. Power passed to the Socialists under the leadership of François Mitterrand. Giscard died in 2020 at the age of 94.

GOVERNMENT IN THE FIFTH REPUBLIC

In his famous Bayeux Manifesto of 1946, de Gaulle repeated the rhetorical question posed by the ancient Greek thinker Solon: "What is the best constitution?" He answered, "Tell me first for what people and during which period." De Gaulle suggested to his countrymen, "Let us take ourselves as we are." He asserted that French political parties, as indeed most individual Frenchmen, traditionally obscured the highest interests of the country and thereby created confusion in the state. He admitted that a parliament is necessary, but it could not be entrusted with the destiny of the French nation. Due to its very nature, France requires a powerful, popularly elected president who stands above the parties, focuses on the "national purpose," and wields the supreme power of the state.

The constitution of the Fifth Republic, adopted in 1958 and still in force, reflects these convictions. It contains a workable compromise between the need for national unity and the legitimate expression of many political ideas, social classes, and interests; between the need for a strong executive and a representative parliament; between lofty politics and common, day-to-day politics. It also incorporated the Napoleonic practice of involving the citizens directly in the political process.

Beginning in 1962, they directly elected the president for a seven-year renewable term, lowered to five years in 2000; a reform in 2008 limits a president to two five-year terms. Through referenda, they are called upon occasionally to give opinions on major national policy issues.

The Presidency

The French president's constitutional powers are immense, and the character of the presidents since 1958 expanded these powers far beyond the letter of the constitution. Unless his party lacks a parliamentary majority (a situation called "cohabitation" that did not exist before 1986), he appoints the prime minister and cabinet, chairs all cabinet meetings, and actively directs the work of the cabinet ministers. Within any one-year period, he may dismiss the National Assembly (lower house of the parliament) for whatever reason he chooses and call new elections. He may question the constitutionality of any law and require parliament to reexamine any piece of legislation. He may submit any issue to a referendum, including constitutional amendments.

These infrequently held referendums almost always demonstrated confidence in the president and therefore invariably strengthened him with respect to the parliament. He is commander-in-chief of the nation's military forces, and he negotiates and ratifies all treaties. He may not issue decrees. But if, in his opinion, the republic is in danger, he can assume emergency powers that enable him to wield full executive, legislative, and military authority. He is formally obliged to seek the advice of the Constitutional Council and is not permitted to dismiss parliament during this time. There is no provision for terminating such emergency powers. In effect, the French president determines domestic and foreign policy and has veto power over every imaginable aspect of policy, including constitutional amendments. Unlike his American counterpart, though, he cannot veto an act of parliament. He can be removed from office if he is convicted in a special tribunal (not by the parliament) of high treason. In 2007 parliament approved a constitutional amendment creating an American-style impeachment procedure to check the president's powers.

Nicolas Sarkozy won approval in 2008 for further reforms that affect presidential powers: He cannot issue collective pardons, and his right to pronounce decrees was limited. In a kind of war-powers act, he must inform parliament within three days of any military operation abroad and seek its approval if it lasts more than four months. He can address parliament in a "state of the union" speech, abolished since 1875. When confronting the need to

Cafe life in Sarlat

France

Former prime minister François Fillon and former president Nicolas Sarkozy

ratify new membership to the EU, parliament, by a three-fifths vote, can authorize the president to seek such ratification either through a referendum or a parliamentary vote. Lacking such authorization, a referendum is required.

De Gaulle in 1964 described the presidency which he had created in breathtaking terms: "It must of course be understood that the indivisible authority of the State is confided in its entirety to the President by the people who have elected him, that no other authority exists, neither ministerial nor civil nor military nor judicial, which is not conferred and maintained by him."

Clearly this is hardly a presidency of the American type. The US president must deal with 50 powerful states and what has become the most powerful and assertive legislature in the world. One foreign minister complained that, in matters involving the United States, he had to deal with 535 secretaries of state. The French president traditionally appoints the prefects (governors) in the 101 departments (states, five of which are overseas) and until 1986 faced neither serious regional resistance nor a powerful legislature. In the 21st century, the power of prefects has been diminished by the requirement that they share responsibility with the departmental presidents and the 13 elected regional councils. Whereas the American president must deal with such nonconstitutional checks as an influential, independent, and often fiercely investigative press and electronic news media, the French president faced a

meeker press for a long time. Until 1984, radio and television networks were controlled by the government and were hesitant to attack the president openly.

In contrast, the American president must operate in an environment in which the Freedom of Information Act and various "sunshine" laws have made more visible the working of government. The French traditional cult of secrecy and more impenetrable bureaucracy are a haven for the chief executive. The public appears to be more used to viewing the state as something that is walled off.

Some prefer to describe French presidentialism as elected monarchy, in which the incumbent's whims and favors are crucially important. The French satirical magazine Le Canard Enchaîné (The Chained Duck) once put it, "There's the President, and under him there's a vast void. And afterwards there is a nothing. And below that, nothing. But finally one stumbles over the government." Edouard Balladur asked with a degree of exaggeration, "In which other democracy is the president in charge of the executive and the legislature and the judiciary; in charge of the order of business in parliament, where by intimidation, force or a reverential majority he gets the votes he wants; in charge of the promotion of magistrates and of the public prosecution that sends them cases; in charge of a government that moves only at his whim?" Only de Gaulle could live up to the impossibly high expectations the French have for their president: monarchical in stature but

able to connect with the people; extraordinary but "normal" at the same time; dignified at all times.

The powers of the presidency grew so much that President Mitterrand pledged to reduce them and to pass back to parliament some of the powers it had lost. He had always been a vocal critic of the Fifth Republic's constitution, as the title of his 1964 book indicated: The Permanent Coup d'Etat. In office, he did nothing to diminish presidential powers. Like all presidents, he succumbed to what political writer Denis Tillinac called the "Versailles syndrome."

Changes in the imperial presidency are underway. Growing public cynicism toward the political establishment emboldened journalists to break hallowed taboos against reporting on politicians' private lives. In 1994 the weekly Paris Match published a cover photo of Mitterrand in public with his daughter born from an extramarital affair two decades earlier. Mistress and daughter had been housed in government guesthouses and had traveled at taxpayers' expense. Although the magazine was sold out within hours, there was an outcry among public figures that it had crossed the line. Unlike in the US, this harmed neither Mitterrand, who made no attempt to conceal his daughter's paternity, nor his party. At his funeral in January 1996, his wife, Danielle, stood for the first time with his daughter out of wedlock, Mazarine Pingeot, and her mother, Anne Pingeot. In 2014, a young Swedish man announced that he is Mitterrand's son, the product of an affair the president had with a Swedish journalist.

Mitterrand died of prostate cancer. He had been informed of this condition several months after his election in 1981, but he ordered that it be kept secret. In 2005 a feature film on Mitterrand, Le Promeneur du Champ de Mars (The Stroller in the Champ de Mars, by Robert Guediguian), portrayed a cancer-weakened president in his final months in office with all his human frailties and missteps outside the view of the public.

In order to reduce the risk of seeing the same person occupy the presidency for 14 years, 73.5% of the voters in a 2000 referendum opted to reduce the term of office to 5 years, with no limit on the number of times to be reelected; parliament voted in 2008 to restrict the number of terms to two. All the major parties supported this reform. Even though only about one out of three eligible voters bothered to go to the polls to record their opinion, this change could alter the balance of power in the political system. Referring to such a significant shift by means of a referendum, political analyst Dominique Moïsi said this "ends Gaullism in a very Gaullist way."

The unusually long tenure of seven years had been designed to create a powerful chief of state who could provide France with the kind of stability that had been lacking in earlier republics. By the end of the century, France had achieved that stability, so an imperial presidency is no longer needed. The special aura of the magisterial presidential office declined. The reform reduced the periods of power sharing with parliament, known as "cohabitation." By making presidential and parliamentary elections coincide more frequently, France gains more coherent governments. However, critics argue that parliamentary elections only a month after presidential ones mean that the National Assembly has only a weak democratic mandate of its own, since it is filled with members who rode the president's coattails. The president still has the power to dissolve parliament once within a year's time.

The Prime Minister and Cabinet

The prime minister and the cabinet ministers (the "government") have usually been drawn from all the parties in the president's majority coalition, although some have belonged to no political party. They are forbidden from having seats in the National Assembly. Ministers, including prime ministers, must give up their seats to substitutes, and if they later leave the government, they can reclaim their seats only by persuading the substitutes to stand down and by winning a by-election. If the prime minister and president are from the same party, the former is responsible for explaining and gaining support for the president's policies and for ensuring that the president's overall directives are carried out in practice.

The prime minister executes the laws. He supervises the drafting of the budget, which is submitted to the parliament for overall approval but which parliament rarely alters. Finally, he determines the agenda of parliament; government legislation always takes priority. He is the president's lightening rod and is dependent on him; from 1958 to 1991, only one prime minister resigned voluntarily. None survived a full five-year legislative term until Socialist Lionel Jospin managed to do that from 1997 to 2002. Thereafter only one president—Nicolas Sarkozy—governed with the same prime minister for his entire term.

The Economist wrote that the prime minister must not upstage the president and must "let the president take the credit when things go well and to deal with the trouble when it all goes wrong." Of the 22 politicians who occupied the job from 1958 to 2018, only 2 (Pompidou and Chirac) went on to become president.

If the president's party does not have a parliamentary majority, then the president must select a prime minister whose party or coalition can get a majority of votes in the National Assembly. In this case, the prime minister is a very powerful political figure who establishes the main lines of French domestic and economic policy and shares with the president responsibility for foreign and defense policy. He appoints and instructs the top officials in the foreign ministry.

Parliament

The parliament has two houses: the Senate and the 576-seat National Assembly. Deputies to the National Assembly are elected for five years by universal suffrage. The president can call new elections before the end of the five-year term. The Senate has 330 members elected since 2003 for nine-year terms. One-third of them are renewed every three years by members of the National Assembly and elected officials at all levels down to municipal counselors.

Both houses of parliament have essentially the same powers with two exceptions: The National Assembly has the privilege of examining the government's budget first. Further, only the National Assembly can force the government to resign by assembling a majority against an important piece of government legislation. However, the Fifth Republic's constitution places severe limits on this latter practice, which in past republics had been abused and which therefore brought a merry-go-round of governments with extremely short life spans. Such a vote may be submitted only once during any legislative session, and all abstentions or blank ballots count automatically for the government. Also, if such a vote succeeds, the National Assembly is dissolved immediately, and new elections are called. This latter provision takes the fun out of the former "parliamentary game" of shooting down the government for the most trivial reasons and makes such a vote of censure a much more serious step for the parties and the individual deputies.

An additional limitation of the parliament's powers is that much of what is considered "legislation" in other democratic countries is defined in the French constitution as "rule making." The president signs decrees issued by the prime minister, thereby circumventing the parliament altogether for a limited period of time (ca. 18 months). There is a debate whether the president can refuse to sign a decree. Decrees authorized by parliament are called ordinances; an example was privatizations

France

while Jacques Chirac was prime minister from 1986 to 1988.

Approaching the 50th anniversary of the Fifth Republic in 2008, which has provided a degree of political stability unknown in France's past, President Nicolas Sarkozy commissioned his former mentor, ex–prime minister Edouard Balladur, to review the constitution. The latter submitted 77 reform proposals, some of them strengthening the presidency, such as allowing the president to address parliament (forbidden until 2008). Some would strengthen parliament's role: It would share the right to determine the daily agenda, which is now the government's prerogative; the government's right to pass laws by decree would be limited; parliament would get new powers over presidential nominations. Any changes in the constitution would have to be approved by a congress of both houses. One reform that must have pleased the president has already been enacted: his salary jumped from €101,000 to €240,000 ($310,000). This compares with the American president's salary of €343,000 ($450,000).

The number of parliamentary committees (which enable a parliament to develop the expertise to challenge the executive) is limited to six, and even these few committees are not permitted to amend a government bill before it comes to the floor. A party must have at least 15 deputies in order to form a parliamentary group. This brings committee assignments, subsidies, and other privileges. An increasingly weak parliament has been called "a device to provide majorities." There is little public interest in its debates, and people turn to their mayors rather than to their local deputies to pursue causes and grievances.

A final striking innovation in the constitution is the Constitutional Council, composed of nine members appointed by the president of the republic and of the presidents of the two houses of parliament for nine-year terms. Its purpose is to guard the constitution. De Gaulle did not originally design this body to protect individual rights but rather to protect executive power against parliament. It is ironic that today it emphasizes the protection of parliamentary and individual rights. In 1971 the Declaration of the Rights of Man became a reference used by the Constitutional Council.

Upon request of the three above-mentioned presidents or the prime minister or, since 1992, 60 members of either house of parliament, it can review the constitutionality of laws, treaties, elections, and referendums. The council cannot be compared to the far more prestigious United States Supreme Court, which possesses the power of unlimited judicial review. But in France a piece of legislation can be challenged in the Constitutional Council before it goes into effect; in the US, this can happen only after the law is in effect. For example, in 2012 the council ruled that the government's proposed 75% tax on incomes over €1 million ($1.3 million) was unconstitutional. Opponents of same-sex marriage also submitted the issue to the council in 2013 as soon as it was overwhelmingly passed in parliament.

From 1986 to 1988, when for the first time since 1958 the prime minister came from a different party than the president, the Constitutional Council was called upon to determine which powers and responsibilities belong to each office. It became the ultimate referee in the political system. A Council of State also exists to deal with administrative and public law. It provides recourse to individual citizens who have claims against the administration.

Decentralization

Since at least the 17th century, French national leaders consistently strengthened the powers of the central government at the expense of the regions and communes. In 1792 France was divided into 96 departments (plus 5 overseas departments by 2009), each headed by a prefect, a powerful and uniformed official appointed by and answerable to the national government. The prefect oversaw the work of locally elected mayors and councils in the 37,500 municipalities. For economic and administrative purposes, 22 regions, whose borders roughly approximate those of France's ancient provinces, each headed by a regional prefect, were created. They were later reduced to 13. The essential fact is that all important initiatives had either to originate or be approved in Paris. For example, the designs for school cafeterias, soccer fields, swimming pools, and other public facilities had to clear numerous bureaucratic and political hurdles in Paris.

This not only required personal connections and caused serious delays, but many Frenchmen feared that it also was creating excessive visual uniformity in a land admired for its rich diversity. Many observers also believed that centralization stifled individual civic action and stimulated suspicion toward the French state. Mitterrand took seriously his pledge to reduce the power the central government and the prefects had over subnational political units and to allow popularly elected regional and local assemblies and executives to handle their own affairs.

In the early 1980s, 10 devolution laws and 50 decrees designed to decentralize France were announced. Perhaps the most significant change was that the prefects, renamed "Commissioners of the Republic," were stripped of many of their administrative, financial, judicial, and technical powers. They must share responsibility with the elected presidents of the departments and the 13 regional councils, which were strengthened. Nevertheless, few French know or care much about their regional governments. Regional elections are mainly referenda on how popular the nation's governing party is. At the time of the 2010 regional elections, in which the Socialists won 21 out of 22 regions, voters were asked in a poll to name their regional president. Only 29% could do so.

During the 1980s local governments were granted more autonomy in spending, taxation, and borrowing. The result was more local activity to build new airports, wider streets, pedestrian zones, museums, concert halls, and stadiums. However, the shift of power from civil servants to local politicians also brought a higher level of local indebtedness and corruption.

Political Parties

It has always been difficult to rule France from the center, long referred to as the "swamp." Since the founding of the Fifth Republic, there has been a steady reduction in the number of parties with any hope for electoral success.

The Republicans

After numerous name changes, including the Rally for the Republic (RPR) and the Union for a Popular Movement (UMP), the Gaullist Party renamed itself the Republicans. It is a federation of parties that grew out of Jacques Chirac's successful electoral alliance in 2002, then called the Union for the Presidential Majority, with the same acronym. It merged several conservative and centrist groups.

Founded in 1976, the RPR and its successor seek to preserve the fundamental Gaullist values: foreign policy independence, caution toward a more united Europe, maintaining the institutions of the Fifth Republic, and economic and social expansion and progress. Even a third of a century after his death, de Gaulle basks in widespread approval. His predictions seem to have come true in the 1990s: the collapse of communism and the USSR; upheaval in eastern Europe; the unification of Germany, which Frenchmen accepted with only a little uneasiness; and the emergence of a Europe more independent of the superpowers. "Europe from the Atlantic to the Urals" was his concept before Mikhail Gorbachev picked up on it. In 1990, to celebrate his famous call for resistance on June 18, 1940, the obelisk at the Place de la Concorde was draped with a 35-meter-high radio model blaring popular songs of the time and coded messages from London to the Free French.

In May 1995 Jacques Chirac was elected president. But he was reduced almost to the status of a figurehead after the 1997 parliamentary elections, when the RPR crashed from being France's largest party, with 258 seats, to a minority, with only 134 seats. In 2000 the party picked the first female leader of a major French party, Michele Alliot-Marie, a law lecturer and later defense, interior, justice and foreign minister. The RPR struggled to unify itself and to find a new identity more compatible with the rise of a global economy and the EU and the reduced French role in the world.

Chirac and his party faced the 2002 presidential elections in serious trouble. They were mired in scandals that came perilously close to Chirac himself. During the 18 years Chirac was mayor of Paris (1977–1995), fictitious jobs were created at the taxpayers' expense, and grateful public-works contractors made contributions to parties, especially the RPR.

Chirac won a massive reelection as president in 2002, thanks to voters' revulsion for his chief opponent, Jean Marie Le Pen. He organized a conservative grouping broader than his RPR to win the June 2002 parliamentary elections—the UMP. It decimated the left.

Until his defeat in May 2012, the party's leader was Nicolas Sarkozy. In 2004 he won the party presidency with 85% of the votes at an American-style party convention complete with French flags, music, and a giant video screen. A first-generation immigrant son of a Hungarian nobleman (real name: Sarkozy de Nagy-Bocsa) and of a French mother with Jewish roots, he had made it known to his school classmates that he would be president one day. Unlike most of the elite, however, he studied law instead of attending the National School of Administration (ENA).

He entered politics at age 20 and became a mayor at age 28. Chirac heard him speak at a rally and told him, "You are made for politics." Sarkozy was a gifted orator. He was catapulted into national fame in 1993, when, as mayor of Neuilly-sur-Seine, he personally negotiated with a hostage-taker who had stormed a local kindergarten, while the police sneaked into the school and shot the man dead.

France needed a new generation of leaders, and Sarkozy most represented that new France. He brought to the presidency fresh ideas. He spoke of the erosion of the work culture and the importance of self-reliance, achievement, and social mobility. As interior minister, he pursued a law-and-order policy to crack crime and drug rings in immigrant neighborhoods.

He had an uncomplicated approach to America and advocated closer relations. Sarkozy came to the presidency without the usual French anti-Americanism. He offered a fresh start for Franco-American relations. He urged French youngsters to embrace as a role model Martin Luther King Jr., and he said his favorite author was Ernest Hemingway. During a highly publicized (and, in France, criticized) visit to the US in September 2006, he argued that "friendship is respect, understanding, affection, but not submission. . . . I ask our American friends to let us be free, free to be their friends."

In the first paragraph of the English translation of his best-selling campaign book *Testimony: France in the Twenty-First Century*, he called America "the greatest democracy in the world." Later in the book, he wrote, "I don't see why my country doesn't take inspiration from its great ally," and, "I love the value Americans place on work and the desire for excellence that you find everywhere." On election night he assured America that France would "always be at its side when it needs her." However, the realities of French politics require that he be cautious to leave some light between his foreign policy views and those of Washington. He acquired the tag of "*Sarko l'Americain*," and one of his Socialist opponents in the election called him "an American neocon with a French passport."

Sarkozy was a convinced Atlanticist, and in his first summer in office, "I came to visit the United States on holiday, like 900,000 French do every year. It's a great country." He paid an informal visit with both Presidents Bush at Kennebunkport, Maine, and was served his choice of hamburgers or hot dogs. Like the younger Bush, Sarkozy does not drink alcohol. He was granted the privilege in November 2007 of speaking to a joint session of Congress and was received with warmth and enthusiasm. Former undersecretary of state Nicholas Burns spoke for many Americans when he said, "we admire the way he has opened up to our country."

Confidential cables published by Wikileaks from American diplomats in Paris revealed a mixed view of the French president. On the one hand, he was "the most pro-American French president since World War II" and a "force multiplier" for American foreign policy interests. "Very much unlike nearly all other French political figures, Sarkozy is viscerally pro-American." He "identifies with America; he sees his own rise in the world as reflecting an American-like saga." He was especially fond of American movies and personally pinned the Legion of Honor on Clint Eastwood. During his tenure after 2007, the two countries had few foreign policy differences, and he changed the way many Americans view France. But he was high-maintenance and erratic. He had authoritarian tendencies and a tendency to decide policy on the fly. He was reported to be too impatient to consult with important allies before enacting his initiatives.

His willingness to reintegrate with NATO's command structure (on the condition that European defense capability is improved) is appreciated. His first foreign minister, Bernard Kouchner, made clear that France cannot pursue its interests through "permanent anti-Americanism." Both Frenchmen also have the hard-headed calculation that, if France's ties with the US are not strong, its weight in the world is diminished.

He persuaded the party to select its presidential candidate by means of primary elections involving all party members. He reached the presidency in May 2007, becoming the first French president born after World War II, the first Gaullist president never to have served under de Gaulle himself, the first Gaullist president since Georges Pompidou not to have graduated from ENA, and the first president whose father was not French. In the June 2007 parliamentary elections, his UMP became the first ruling party to be reelected since 1978.

Sarkozy and his party faced an uphill struggle to win again in 2012. His approval rating fell to only 22%, a record low for a president. In the first round of the 2012 presidential election, he placed second, with 27.2% of the votes, right behind François Hollande (with 28.6%) and ahead of Marine Le Pen (17.9%). He lost in the second round with 48.4% of the votes. He immediately announced he was leaving politics. The UMP was in a state of disarray.

Together, everything becomes possible.

France

The vacuum in the party, combined with his successor's disastrously low approval ratings, had prompted Sarkozy to announce that he would return to politics "out of duty and only because it is for France." Any plans were complicated by his need to face formal charges of "abuse of frailty" for allegedly playing on the weakness of 90-year-old L'Oréal heiress Liliane Bettencourt to secure a donation to his presidential campaign fund in 2007. That charge was dropped, but charges of corruption and influence peddling remained. Sarkozy's comeback failed. The party's primary was won by his former prime minister, François Fillon, whose campaign was paralyzed by a scandal. He had paid his wife almost €1 million of public money for work she did not perform. Winning only 20% in the first round of the 2017 presidential election, he was eliminated.

The Union for French Democracy (UDF)

Former president Giscard d'Estaing had founded his own Independent Republican Party in 1966, renamed the Republican Party (PR) and then Liberal Democracy (DL), which joined the UMP in 2002. In order to enlarge his electoral and parliamentary base, he forged in 1978 a larger, loosely knit group of parties called the Union for French Democracy (UDF), which was more pro-Europe and free-market-oriented than the UMP.

In addition to diverse centrist political groups, the UDF included the Democratic Force (FD), formerly the Center of Social Democrats (CDS). Centrist, devolutionist, and strongly pro-European, this was the last remnant of the postwar reformist Popular Republican Movement (MRP), which had played such an important political role in the Fourth Republic. It also included the Radical Party, a pro-Europe social democratic product of 19th-century liberal tradition and one of France's oldest parties. During the Third Republic, it almost dominated French politics and led a particularly determined campaign against the power of the Catholic Church in politics and society. This always undisciplined party shrank in importance after World War II.

The UDF was never a sufficiently powerful political base for Giscard, although it was constructed around him. Conservatives were always plagued by divisions and bickering. In 1996 the former president retired from politics. To make it look fresher, the party's name was officially changed in 2000 to Nouvelle UDF (New UDF). But it was a difficult task to make this loose collection of disparate parties into a credible political force. It allies with the Rebublicans in national elections.

National Rally

The phenomenal rise of the right-wing National Front (FN), led until 2010 by the tough-talking former paratrooper Jean Marie Le Pen, was the 1986 election's biggest surprise. Foaming against France's 4.2 million immigrants, whom he accused of being responsible for high unemployment and crime, the party won 9.7% of the votes. It did particularly well along the Mediterranean coast, where there is much hostility to North African immigrants.

The timely abolition of proportional representation in 1988 practically eliminated the party from parliament. But its 14% showing in the 1988 presidential balloting and 15% in 1995 indicated that racist fears and resentments on which the party feeds are strong in French society. Its high vote (e.g., 28% in Marseilles) in regions, towns, and suburbs with large concentrations of immigrants, unemployed, and crime, as well as in some rural areas, was a warning to the government to eliminate the seeds of discontent that keep the National Front alive.

The other conservative parties refuse to deal with this overtly racist, xenophobic party, which opposes greater European unity and the euro. A populist, Jean-Marie Le Pen presented himself as a supporter of the "little guy" against a corrupt establishment. The party's supporters are predominantly young, urban, poor, and unemployed.

In the 2007 presidential elections, his support was undercut by Sarkozy, who also talked about law and order, restrictions on immigration, and the need to address the underlying issues which had fueled Le Pen's strength in the past: uncertainty and insecurity, unease over immigration and crime, disillusionment with the political class, and a faltering economy. After a Paris court acquitted him of racism in December 2010, Jean Marie Le Pen announced his retirement from politics.

Le Pen's youngest daughter, Marine, became his political heir. A twice-divorced, young (age 47 in 2016), working mother of three, she was elected party president in 2011 with more than two-thirds of the votes. Toning down her father's notoriously aggressive rhetoric, she seeks to soften and decontaminate the party's image and broaden its electoral base. She calls the Holocaust the "summit of human barbarism." She is media-friendly, responding to aggressive questions with easy grace. She appears on TV talk shows and is poised and courteous. She displays common sense. She avoids her father's provocative and xenophobic statements and once quit the party in exasperation after one of his outbursts. She has gotten rid of the phalanx of skinheads, who used to accompany her father at rallies. Her change of style appeals especially to women.

However, she shares many of her father's objectives: withdrawal from the euro and NATO (thereby avoiding "submission to America"); support for Russia, reintroducing the death penalty; rejecting bailouts and globalization, limiting immigration; reerecting border controls; overcoming the alienation of a depraved globalized elite and the common Frenchman; and "French first" in housing, welfare, and employment. She claims not to be against Islam but for France's traditional secularism (laïcité). Above all, she insists that the National Front is no longer merely a party of protest on the political sidelines but a

"Le Pen: The people," National Front campaign poster

cannot win without a coalition of center-right allies.

The Communists

The main reason the left had difficulty assuming power in France is that it has always been fragmented, with two parties particularly prominent: the French Communist Party (PCF) and the Socialist Party (PS). The PCF was founded in 1920 when delegates to the Socialist Party congress walked out to join the Comintern, the external arm of the Soviet's party. It converted the Socialist newspaper *L'Humanité* into an organ through which the new party consistently advocated a hard-line, class-conscious revolutionary policy, closely attuned to the aims of the Soviets. In 1936 the PCF refused to join the Popular Front because Socialists dominated the coalition, and it loyally supported Stalin's nonaggression pact with Hitler, which was the prelude to the devastating German attack on France in 1940. Once the Soviet Union was invaded by Germany, though, the PCF joined the resistance to Hitler's Germany and fought valiantly, thereby winning the admiration of such diverse persons as de Gaulle and Mitterrand.

When the Cold War poisoned relations between the west and the Soviet Union, the PCF did not hesitate to orient itself toward the latter. The Soviet suppression of uprisings in eastern Europe in 1953, 1956, and 1968 all ultimately won the PCF's approval. In the 1970s a thaw in the party began to occur. It officially disavowed the Marxist-Leninist concept of "dictatorship of the proletariat" and accepted in 1972 Mitterrand's offer of a common program of the left, including both Socialists and Communists. The course was an entirely new concept for western European socialists, who had seen clearly what happened in eastern Europe after socialist and communist parties had agreed to cooperate.

The PCF showed itself to be a difficult partner. Mitterrand's PS could count on only about 5% of the vote in 1972, whereas the PCF consistently received over a fifth of the vote in any election (and a third of all workers' votes). Therefore the PCF believed that it would soon be able to control its "junior" member. It was badly mistaken. The PS grew very rapidly in voter appeal and eventually overtook the PCF.

The PCF had second thoughts about its Eurocommunist course. It openly supported the Soviet invasion of Afghanistan and was returning to its pro-Soviet position. This was disastrous. To halt its stunning erosion, the PCF saw no alternative in 1981 to joining forces with the Socialist Party, but this alliance collapsed within three years. The PCF suffered a steady decline in votes and membership, especially among the young and intellectuals. The

Street musicians in southern France

potential governing party: "I am here to build the National Front's accession to power." Her father was an ideologue, while she is a politician who wants to win.

She compelled other candidates on the right to adopt her themes. A frightened Sarkozy tightened immigration and citizenship laws, banned the burka in public places, condemned multiculturalism, and closed Roma camps on the outskirts of many cities. President Hollande continued the latter policy on the grounds that such settlements are unsanitary and dangerous. In addition to the up to 20,000 Roma in France, thousands have been deported or paid €300 ($370) to return home.

Marine's attempt to woo her voters legitimized the FN Party. In the 2012 presidential contest, she placed third in the first round, with an impressive 17.9% of the votes. While her father was strong in the south, she was effective in the north. A fourth of young voters, facing rising youth unemployment of 22.4%, voted for her. She picked up the discontented vote that used to go to the Communists. She refused to endorse either Sarkozy or Hollande in the second round, and Sarkozy won an estimated 58% of her voters. She failed to win a seat in the June 2012 parliamentary

elections, but her niece Marion Maréchal-Le Pen, a 22-year-old law student, captured one of the party's two seats. She is the youngest legislator ever elected in the Fifth Republic. These are the party's first seats since 1997.

Le Pen is the most dynamic force in France. FN rattled the political elite by coming out first in the May 2014 European Parliament elections, winning a quarter of the votes, and second in the March 2015 departmental elections, ahead of the Socialists and at the top of the first round of the December 2015 regional elections. She placed second in the first round of the 2017 presidential elections, with 21.3% of the votes, before the other parties ganged up on her and her party in the second round. She won 34% of the votes, twice as many as her father had gotten in the 2002 election. Her anti-immigration rhetoric will continue to resonate. The former domination by two main parties has given way to a four-party system. To distance itself from its early history as a radical fringe group, the party renamed itself National Rally in 2018.

To enhance the party's electoral prospects, Marion, who runs a school for the far right in Lyon, argues that the party

France

Socialists overtook the Communists in the traditional "red bastions" in the north. The PCF declined to where it stood a half-century ago.

The PCF shed such dogmas as the pledges to "abolish capitalism" and "nationalize the means of production." It entered the Socialist Party's governing coalition in 1997 and had four ministerial posts. It was staunchly opposed to the European constitution and helped defeat it in the May 29, 2005, referendum. One of its leaflets opened with the words "For years, one has been constructing Europe on the backs of the workers and against them."

The party is struggling to avoid disappearing completely and is trying to reinvent itself. If it modernizes its policies to adjust to a market-oriented new world not understood by Marx and participates in governments, it loses many of its core voters. If it does not do this, it becomes irrelevant and seals itself off from new voters. It got only a half-percent of the votes in the 2015 department elections. The PCF is fading from the electoral scene.

It loses many of its votes to other leftist groupings. They include such parties as the Workers' Struggle (Trotskyite, winning .6% of the presidency votes in 2012); the Revolutionary Communist Party; the Workers' Party (Trotskyite); and the Radical Party of the Left, led by Christiane Taubira, Guiana-born member of the European Parliament, the only candidate who was both black and female.

Although they are electorally insignificant, these far-left groups are still a strong political and social force in contemporary France. For example, the street demonstrations of 2008–2009 produced the New Anti-Capitalist Party, led by the telegenic Trotskyite Olivier Besancenot; it captured 1.2% of the votes for the presidency in 2012. A much more successful coalition of Communists and other far-left groups, the Front de Gauche (Left Front), led by firebrand Jean-Luc Mélenchon, attracted large, enthusiastic crowds during the presidential campaign and ended up with a surprising 19.6% of the first-round votes in the 2017 presidential election.

The Greens

The French public now focuses greater attention on environmental protection because of such highly publicized problems as the Chernobyl nuclear accident in the Ukraine, chemical factory accidents which polluted the Rhine and Loire Rivers, depletion of the ozone layer, global warming, and deforestation. They are also untainted by scandals, which have shaken other parties. French Greens (Les Verts) are on the left of the political spectrum, although they advocate protecting the high material standard of living rather than radically changing the structure of French society. They call for restraints on foreign capital in France and the preservation of small neighborhood stores, which are increasingly threatened by supermarkets.

Because of France's electoral system and because it lacks a tradition of pacifism, nuclear protest, or respect for the environment, the Greens do not have the political clout that their German counterparts do. Their standard-bearer is a German citizen, Daniel Cohn-Bendit. Known earlier as "Dany le rouge" (Dany the Red), he had been expelled from France for playing a leading role in the 1968 student rebellion. Known for his pugnacity, charisma, and rhetorical skills, he is an outspoken Europhile who already represented the German Greens in the European Parliament. He is the first foreigner to head an electoral campaign in France.

Led by Eva Joly, the "Europe Ecology, the Greens" captured a disappointing 2.3% of the votes in the 2012 presidential elections. They won 17 parliamentary seats in June, up from 4.

The Socialists

The ruling party since May 2012 is the Socialist Party (PS). It had become terribly divided over whether to support the EU constitution in the May 29, 2005, referendum. Although 59% of its members had voted to back it, deputy party leader and former prime minister Laurent Fabius defied the party line and opposed it. In June he and a dozen of his supporters who sided with the left and campaigned against it were ousted from their party positions.

The party entered the 2007 presidential elections with many ambitious contenders but one clear front-runner: Ségolène Royal. She is the daughter of an army colonel and graduate of the prestigious ENA, where she met her ex-common-law partner and father of her four children, then–Socialist chairman François Hollande. She was fresh, attractive, intelligent, and extremely media-savvy, with political experience as former minister for the environment and for family and education.

She experimented with a new style of participatory politics by engaging voters on her interactive website and posting her positions on a blog. Her entries were gathered into a book, since by tradition it is essential that serious French presidential candidates publish a book during their campaign. Because she lacked deep roots in the PS, she successfully attempted to shape public opinion before the 219,000 registered party members had a chance to elect the party's candidate in an open primary in November 2006. She won a landslide 60%, with 80% of party members participating.

Party leaders, including her then-partner, expressed outrage over her outspoken ideas, her populist methods, and her candidature in general. Former prime minister Laurent Fabius sneered, "Who will look after the children?" This remark would be a guaranteed vote-loser in many other democracies, also in France. At the end of a hard-fought election, she garnered a respectable 46.94% of the votes, and she led her party to a better-than-expected result in the parliamentary elections a month later, winning 205 seats, up from 140.

She had her eye on her party's leadership. That meant that her former partner, François Hollande, who had expected to be the party's candidate, had to step

Autumn in Paris . . . Susan and Wayne Thompson

Honorable François Mitterrand

aside in more that one respect. In her book published six weeks after the presidential election, *Behind the Scenes of a Defeat*, she admitted that she had asked Hollande to leave her home after cheating on her. This was very unusual for French politicians to be so open about their private lives. But the French press has become more intrusive, and she preferred that "things be clarified for everyone."

There was a bitter struggle for control of a divided Socialist Party, which, by the time of its leadership election in November 2008, had not won a presidential election in 20 years, although it held a majority of city hall and local posts. The bitter race left the party in full disarray and division.

The competition began to determine which Socialist would challenge Sarkozy in the 2012 presidential elections. Tops in the polls was Dominique Strauss-Kahn, a former professor and finance minister, who was managing director of the IMF, a job that gave him weight and credibility. He had already been tarnished by persistent rumors of serial womanizing and a 2008 sexual-harassment scandal. But by tradition the extramarital affairs of French politicians are tolerated and not reported in the press.

One of France's most popular politicians, he committed one of the most serious indiscretions in modern French political history. While staying in the exclusive French-owned Sofitel hotel in New York City, he is alleged to have forced a resisting chambermaid, who had entered his room unaware that he was naked in the bathroom, to perform a sexual act. She reported him, and police officers pulled him off an Air France plane within minutes of takeoff. He was charged with seven counts of attempted sexual assault and attempted rape and was kept in jail. After being granted bail, he was confined

to house arrest in a $50,000-per-month luxury townhouse awaiting trial.

The criminal charges were later dropped, but the alleged victim also charged him in civil court in New York. That suit was settled, reportedly by a $6 million deal with the maid. Back in France, legal proceedings were initiated against him for alleged "aggravated procurement in an organized gang," legal language for "pimping." He was part of a group that is said to have procured prostitutes for sex parties in Lille, London, and Washington. That is a crime in France, while prostitution is not. His wife had enough and ordered him out of the house. To add further humiliation, a play about the scandal in New York, *Suite 2806*, made its debut at the Théatre Daunou in Paris. Critics called it "a modern-day Marquis de Sade." In June 2015 all charges against him were dropped.

He resigned his post at the IMF. He was replaced by France's finance minister Christine Laguarde, who learned her perfect English in America on an exchange scholarship and worked her way to the top of a leading American law firm, Baker & McKenzie.

François Hollande would have had no chance to win the nomination through an online party primary and ultimately to capture the presidency without Strauss-Kahn's stunning indiscretions.

With a turnout of over 80%, Hollande won the first round of the 2012 presidential elections with 28.6% of the votes, and the second, with 51.6%. He was inaugurated May 15, the first Socialist to become president since François Mitterrand in 1981. His party swept the June parliamentary elections, capturing an absolute majority, with 314 seats, up from 202. Turnout dropped to a record low of 57%. The 2017 presidential election was a disaster for the

Prime Minister Jean Castex

Ex-president François Hollande

party. Hollande's popularity was so low (13%) that he did not seek reelection. The winner of the primary was Benoît Hamon, who captured only 6.4% of the first-round votes. Former prime minister Manuel Valls pronounced the party "dead."

Socialist Past

The PS was created in 1971 from the staunchly anticommunist French Section of the Workers' International (SFIO), François Mitterrand's own Convention of Republican Institutions, and various other socialist elements. Its rapid growth was partly due to the decline in some social groups which traditionally supported parties of the right: farmers, small shopkeepers, wealthy bourgeois families, and nonworking women. But the Socialist Party's success can be attributed mainly to the work of a man who was both farsighted and persistent but who, like de Gaulle, was also mysterious, elusive, and unknowable: François Mitterrand.

He was born into a piously Catholic bourgeois family in the Cognac region of France in 1916. His father was a railway stationmaster who inherited a thriving vinegar business. Brought up on Balzac's panoramic novels, Lamartine's romantic poetry, and Barrès's patriotic fiction, he acquired a love for literature, which remained his primary passion. He authored 10 books himself and certainly ranks with Léon Blum and de Gaulle as one of the most literary figures in French politics. His career did not always follow a consistently left-wing course. At age 18 he joined the youth group of the far-right Croix-de-Feu (Cross of Fire) and wrote for right-wing journals.

He studied law and political science at the Sorbonne in Paris. A sergeant in the

France

1988

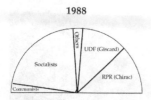

1993

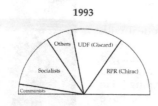

1997

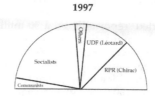

army, he was wounded in the chest at Verdun in 1940 and was sent to a POW camp after his capture. After two unsuccessful attempts to flee, he finally succeeded. Asked many years later why he thought he could win the presidency after two unsuccessful attempts in 1965 and 1974, he noted that in 1941 he had succeeded in returning to France only on his third try. He became a civil servant and admirer of Marshal Pétain. He was awarded the highest honor given by the Vichy state, the Francisque in 1943, and from 1986 to 1992, he laid a wreath on Pétain's tomb every Armistice Day. He also maintained personal contact with a number of collaborators, such as René Bousquet, who had overseen the deportation of French Jews.

Mitterrand joined the resistance movement under the cover names of "Morland" and "Monier" in mid-1943. He changed his address at least weekly and narrowly escaped arrest and almost-certain execution by the Gestapo a few days before being flown to England on November 16. There he was interrogated by British intelligence and transported to de Gaulle's Free French headquarters in Algiers before returning to France in early 1944. During this time he gained respect for French Communists and a strong distaste for de Gaulle, who had demanded that he subordinate his activity to the general's leadership.

Mitterrand was hardly a new face in Fifth Republic politics, having occupied many ministerial seats during the Fourth Republic under diverse governments. His political views continued to be very changeable, leading to charges that he was a political opportunist. In the Fifth Republic, though, he was a consistent and ferocious opponent of Gaullism, in part because he wanted power himself. He was a man determined to unify the left in order to take control of France's destiny.

His first task was to establish a program acceptable to his own heterogeneous party. He set a clear leftist course for the 1981 elections. However, he never mentioned the word "Marxist" in the campaign, even though the party's program did contain some Marxist references and principles. In the campaign, Mitterrand hammered away at the many inequalities in French society and Giscard's unpopular style. He presented himself as the "tranquil force" which France needed. His countrymen listened.

Mitterrand's 1981 Election

Mitterrand's triumph was the first time that an entire generation of Frenchmen had experienced a transfer of presidential power from right to left. One of his first acts in office was to dissolve the National Assembly and to call new elections. This reveals a fundamental characteristic of the French political system. Despite the powerful office of the presidency, no incumbent had been able to rule long in the face of a determined, reasonably cohesive opposing majority in the National Assembly because of its budgetary and legislative approval powers. For the first time in the history of the Fifth Republic, a president faced a hostile parliamentary majority. The elections in June produced a landslide victory for the PS, which won an absolute majority with 288 out of 491 seats in the assembly.

The new government wasted little time in seeking legislation for the most far-reaching of its proposed reforms: the nationalization of certain industries and the decentralization of the French political system. The Socialists promised France in 1981 fundamental changes. After it was clear by 1983 that his socialist revolution had failed, the Mitterrand government pursued a more austere economic course and stressed modernization rather than socialization of France.

As an intellectual force, Marxism became far less popular than it once had been. Partly because of Mitterrand's maneuverings, the

134

Communist Party became practically impotent and became locked in a steady decline. The trade unions, a traditional pillar of the PCF, became weaker than ever before in modern France.

Cohabitation—1986 to 1988

The 1986 electoral results created something entirely new since the beginning of the Fifth Republic in 1958: a president whose party was a minority in the National Assembly. The traditional conservative parties won a whisker-thin majority. Therefore, Mitterrand was compelled to appoint a conservative prime minister, Jacques Chirac.

Chirac had studied international relations at Harvard, paying his way by working as a waiter at Howard Johnson's. During the Algerian War, he served in the French Foreign Legion, after which he entered the prestigious Ecole Nationale d'Administration (ENA). His subsequent political rise was meteoric, working, as always, so energetically that Pompidou gave him the nickname "the Bulldozer." From 1974 to 1976, he had served as prime minister under Giscard. However, believing that he was given too little leeway to pursue his own policies, he became the only prime minister in the Fifth Republic to quit due to disagreements with the president.

Observers coined the word "cohabitation" to describe the relationship between a strong president and an equally strong prime minister who is not willing merely to execute the will of the president. This relationship changed the basic rules of the French political game from 1986 to 1988. It also showed that the institutions of the Fifth Republic are more adaptable and resilient in democratic politics than even de Gaulle had ever imagined.

The president's actual powers diminished somewhat, but they nevertheless remained formidable. "Cohabitation" was not a return to the parliamentary politics and "games" of the Third and Fourth Republics because the powers the president lost fell to a powerful prime minister, not to parliament. Nevertheless, it was a difficult relationship with which the French had almost no experience. Both the president and the prime minister had an interest in making this power sharing succeed. French politics has traditionally been characterized by polarization between the left and the right; the new experiment of cohabitation proved they could find common ground and cooperate with each other in the interest of the French nation. In fact, by election time in 1988, it had helped diminish the ideological gulf separating the major parties. Therefore, it actually strengthened French democracy. "Cohabitation" proved to be a workable alternative, and 70% of the French found it to be good.

Mitterrand could not stop a single policy the prime minister wanted to pursue. He was the first Fifth Republic president to have his wings clipped while still in office. He watched most of his power drain away from the Elysée to the Matignon Palace. However, by knowing how and when to assert his residual authority, he succeeded in halting the trend.

Having preserved his authority, President Mitterrand's popularity soared. By standing above the political fray and focusing on the nation's interests, he let Chirac, who was in the trenches doing day-to-day combat, acquire some serious political bruises. Mitterrand thereby enhanced his own prospects of reelection in 1988 and diminished Chirac's chances to win the presidency.

The End of the Mitterrand Era

The strength of de Gaulle's constitution had been demonstrated by the two-year "cohabitation" experiment, which coupled a Socialist president with a conservative prime minister. The 1988 elections led the country into yet another untested experiment: a minority government.

In presidential elections Chirac garnered only 46% of the votes to Mitterrand's 54%. In the subsequent parliamentary elections in June, the PS fell 14 votes short of a majority. Mitterrand appointed a popular and capable rival within his party, Michel Rocard, as prime minister with a cabinet containing some non-Socialists.

The minority government had to work with other parties to make the system work. But this is nothing unusual in Europe, where most major democracies have coalition or minority governments. The constitution had been designed in 1958 to enable a country with a fractious parliament to enjoy stable rule. No new elections can be called for 12 months, and governments cannot be brought down unless a majority unites against it. In other words, it is the opposition, not the government, which needs a majority. Rocard went far in introducing non-Socialist ideas on how an advanced economy should be run. He deserves much of the credit for transforming the PS from a party of doctrine to one of government.

In many ways Mitterrand had done more to transform French society and politics than de Gaulle. No one would have expected that he would be so able to convert the French to an acceptance of a market economy and the need for stable and rigorous economic management. In foreign policy he swept away some of the most important cornerstones of Gaullist foreign policy by nurturing a more trusting relationship with the United States

"The more just, the stronger France will be."

and by championing greater European integration, including in the field of defense. In a 1992 referendum to accept the Maastricht Treaty, only a hair-thin 51% voted *oui*. The narrowness of that margin in one of the EU's founding nations was a stinging blow to France's political elite. It was in the context of greater European integration and closer Franco-German relations that Mitterrand sought to contain an enlarged, unified, and dynamic Germany within a Europe whose map is being redrawn.

He oversaw the most ambitious building program in Paris since Haussmann remade the capital more than a century earlier. I. M. Pei's glass pyramid in the court of the Louvre had shocked Parisians at first, but it gave new life to one of the world's finest museums. The Grand Arch at the heart of the suburb of La Défense, completed for the bicentennial in 1989, is a majestic, modern, 360-foot steel-and-glass version of Napoleon's Arc de Triomphe. The Bastille Opéra, opened in 1989, has been less successful in winning public admiration, but numerous other *Grands Travaux*, such as a new National Library, leave Mitterrand's stamp on Paris. In 2003 a street in central Paris was named after him: Quai François Mitterrand runs beside the Louvre along the Seine.

Mitterrand's party, which had been in power too long and had run short on vision, ideas, and energy, was swept from power in the most devastating defeat in modern French electoral history. It was a hard verdict, but it was not an ideological one, since the Socialist Party had already shed most of its socialist ideology. Before

France

stepping down in May 1995, Mitterrand admitted that, with all the formal powers a French president has, he had "underestimated the ponderous nature of society, the slowness of its wheels, the weight of its traditions. You don't change society by an act of legislation."

Both of his families mourned at his funeral in 1996. During his 14-year presidency he lived officially with his wife, Danielle, but he spent most of his nights with his longtime mistress, Anne Pingeot, in a secret apartment. She and their daughter, Mazarine Pingeot, were sheltered in a variety of other houses paid for by the state.

The Chirac Era

Jacques Chirac's victory in the 1995 presidential election left the right in control of the presidency; with 80% of the seats in the National Assembly and two-thirds in the Senate, 20 of 22 regional councils, and four-fifths of the departmental councils; and in control of most of the big cities. Never in the history of the Fifth Republic had there been such a concentration of power.

Chirac promised a less monarchical presidency than that of his predecessor. He ordered that the fleet of military jets and helicopters at the disposal of the president and cabinet be disbanded and that ostentatious signs of power, such as motorcades with screaming sirens and motorcycles racing through the streets, be banned.

During his campaign, Chirac promised "profound change." As it became obvious that Chirac could not fulfill his campaign promises of lower taxes and bountiful jobs, his approval rating plummeted, and the worst strikes since 1968 broke out, involving millions of citizens, from civil servants and truck drivers to students, actors, and doctors. Demonstrators in 1968 had risen up against materialism and an allegedly soulless affluent society. Many French now revolted, not just because they refused to relinquish treasured welfare benefits and special privileges, but also because they had a feeling that life was getting worse and worse and that affluence and security might be slipping away from them. This is why strikers enjoy strong public support and why the government caves in to them so often.

President Chirac dissolved parliament and called new elections. In the June 1997 final round of elections, control of the National Assembly changed hands for the fifth straight parliamentary election in 16 years. Tired of Chirac's broken promises made only two years earlier, voters turned back to the Socialists, led by Lionel Jospin, a former diplomat, economics professor, and education minister.

Running in both 1997 and 2002 under a loose umbrella called the "pluralist left"

(*la gauche plurielle*), the Socialists captured 253 seats (including 12 Radical Socialists) in the 576-seat assembly. Since that was short of an absolute majority, the government Jospin formed had to rule with the support of the Communist Party, which won 38 seats, and the Greens, which got 7. President Chirac, who had disastrously misread the mood of the French public, was obligated to accept cohabitation for the third time in 11 years. Jospin became the first prime minister in the Fifth Republic to serve a full five-year term.

2002 Elections

The 2002 presidential elections left France reeling. In the first round, Chirac won just under 20% of the votes, the lowest ever for an incumbent president. Socialist challenger Prime Minister Lionel Jospin fell to a disgraceful third place, with about 16% of the votes, behind Le Pen, who won almost 17%.

Le Pen and his National Front benefited from the sense of insecurity that gripped the country, especially in the aftermath of the September 11, 2001, terrorist strikes against the US, which fueled fears of Arab terrorists moving within France's large immigrant minority. This feeling of insecurity was exacerbated by the physical attacks by Arab immigrants on French Jews and synagogues. Le Pen said, "I want to reestablish security throughout the territory."

Le Pen was thus a symptom of a wider political malaise, including the fear of globalization, ugly xenophobia, and gloomy feeling of decline. He spoke of France as a country "in regression": in its economy, its public safety, and its morality. The endless series of corruption scandals surrounding the political class, including Chirac, sickened many French, especially the "little people" to whom Le Pen appealed.

The shock to the nation caused by Le Pen's success in the first round brought millions of Frenchmen of diverse political persuasions into the streets demanding a massive show of opposition to Le Pen in the second round two weeks later. These were anti–Le Pen rallies, not pro-Chirac ones. The most common slogan for the demonstrations was "Vote for the crook, not the fascist." The usually neutral French media broke with tradition and endorsed Chirac. *Le Figero* carried a banner headline, "For France."

This worked. In the second round, Chirac captured an unprecedented 82% of the votes with a turnout of 80%. He faced the anomaly of having been elected by the largest margin in French history, outdoing even his hero, Charles de Gaulle, but having very weak support from the public. A Harris poll revealed a day after the tally that only 13% of voters supported him

because of his program; 75% gave as their main reason to shut out Le Pen.

Chirac's newly formed conservative Union for the Presidential Majority (UMP) dominated the parliamentary elections that followed on the heels of his presidential landslide. The right captured 399 of 577 seats, leaving only 140 for the humiliated Socialists. This victory not only left the right in control of the Senate and local government, but it also ended cohabitation of a conservative president and a Socialist government.

2007 Elections and the Chirac Legacy

An era came to an end in 2007: Jacques Chirac, the only remaining politician who served every Fifth Republic president since de Gaulle, left power after 12 years as president. He departed as the most unpopular president in the history of the Fifth Republic. He came into office in 1995 promising to "mend the social fracture," get people back to work, ease tensions in the explosive suburbs, cut taxes, and ensure prosperity. He accomplished none of these goals. Instead, he left a France that was frightened by high unemployment, growing debt, and a strong feeling of political and economic stagnation.

During his tenure, the French social system, while performing well in certain

Typical World War I monument seen in every French village

sectors, such as health care and public transportation, was in financial trouble. Yet he never stopped arguing that "our French model" must never be dismantled. His loss of the May 2005 referendum on the ill-fated EU constitutional treaty was a stinging personal rejection. He consistently backed down from pushing through unpopular reforms.

Nevertheless, he occasionally took some courageous stands: He spoke out against racism and anti-Semitism, and he admitted France's official culpability in deporting Jews to their deaths in concentration camps during the Second World War. He took the unpopular stand of advocating Turkey's membership in the EU. Although subsequent research revealed that he and his government wavered about whether to join the war against Saddam Hussein's Iraq in 2003, his ultimate decision not to participate was appreciated by a large percentage of his people. He enjoyed brief popularity, although France's diplomatic influence steadily declined after 2003.

He had more qualities to conquer power than to exercise it. A half-year before he left office, France 2 television aired a four-hour documentary on his presidency. This was the first time a sitting president had been assessed on prime-time public TV. One after another, political leaders told stories about his hunger for power, his opportunism, his betrayals and his nastiness. His tendency to change policies earned him the nickname, "The Weathervane."

It is no wonder that the three most promising candidates to succeed him—Nicolas Sarkozy (UMP), Ségolène Royal (Socialist), and François Bayrou (UDF)—all campaigned on anti-Chirac platforms in May 2007. In their varying ways, all ran against the current French system. This was especially remarkable for the winner, Sarkozy, who had occupied several posts in Chirac governments. Yet he and Royal were considered outsiders in their parties and were willing to challenge their conventional wisdom.

Twelve persons (down from 16 in 2002) competed for the presidency, but only 3 of them had a realistic chance. Three of the others were Trotskyites, one was a Communist, and one was an alternative, antiglobalization, McDonald's-hating gadfly (José Bové). The high turnout in the presidential voting (84%, the highest since 1974) was not only a testament to the vibrancy of French democracy but also a signal of how important voters considered these elections to be for their future. They gave the three leaders three-fourths (76%) of their votes.

Sarkozy won 30.5% of the votes in the first round and 53.06% in the second round by sticking resolutely to his central message: France must change, the French must work more and be rewarded for their work, law and order must be restored, and immigration must be tightened. This was the highest result for a center-right candidate since 1974 and 10 points higher than Chirac ever got in the first round. Surprisingly since his chief opponent was an impressive woman, he captured 52% of the female vote, as well as a majority of voters aged 25 to 44 and over 60.

Royal, the Socialist candidate, captured an impressive 25.5% in the first round and 46.94% in the second. She failed to transform her leftist party into a modern social democratic one in the center of the political spectrum. When she tried to do this in the second round and called for an electoral alliance with Bayrou, who had presented himself as a bridge builder between left and right, she lost credibility. She won 11 of 20 Paris arrondissements, many ethnically mixed working-class suburbs, large parts of central and southwestern France, and voters under age 24. In polls asking voters which characteristics most apply to the two top candidates, the only category in which she beat Sarkozy was "friendliness" (57% to 29%).

Bayrou won 18.6% in the first round, but he failed to get into the top two. A collective sigh of relief was heard when Jean-Marie Le Pen, leader of the extreme right-wing National Front, received only 11% of the votes and a humiliating fourth-place finish. In the second round, 63% of his voters turned to Sarkozy and only 12% to Royal. Sarkozy had succeeded in absorbing Le Pen's voters and, it was hoped, defanging them.

Entering the parliamentary elections a month later, in June 2007, Sarkozy became the first president in two decades to intervene in his UMP's campaign. This marked a change in style from Chirac's aloof stance. But the new president had won a mandate to reform the country. He stated after his victory, "The French people have chosen change, and it is change that I will implement." For this he needed a strong parliamentary majority. The French gave him that but without the margin that he had hoped.

The UMP captured 39.5% of the votes in the first round and 47.79% in the second. This left them 324 of the 577 seats, plus 22 seats of its ally, the New Center. With 60% of the seats, Sarkozy had won a solid legislative base for his reforms. The Socialists did quite well, winning 28% in the first round and 45% in the second, securing an impressive 205 seats, up from 140 in 2002. Bayrou created a new Democratic Movement (MoDem) for these elections, but it captured only 7.6% in the first round, winning a mere four seats, including his own. The other big loser was Le Pen's National Front, which won only 4.3% of the votes

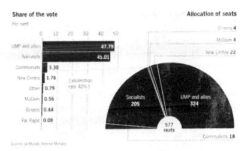

2007 parliamentary election
Source: *Financial Times*

and not a single seat. The Communists garnered 4.3% of the votes and 18 seats, while the Greens captured 3.3% of the votes and 4 seats.

Dubbed the "hyperpresident" in the press, the frenetic Sarkozy wasted no time in assembling the most diverse and inclusive cabinet in French history. He concentrated as much power in his Elysée Palace as possible, signaling his intention to be much more active in domestic politics than his predecessors. His prime minister was François Fillon, a lawyer and former education minister, who was a former enemy but later jogging buddy. His popularity ratings consistently remained above those of the president. This impertinence was usually grounds for a prime minister's dismissal in the Fifth Republic.

Sarkozy appointed a sleek 16-person cabinet, half the size of previous ones. It contained Socialists and centrists. Only one member (Higher Education Minister Valérie Pécresse) had attended the elite ENA. It included seven women. Nine were lawyers, including Christine Lagarde, a former top attorney of a large American law firm with a perfect command of English, who was tapped to be the country's and G-8's first female finance minister. *Forbes* listed her in 2008 as 1 of the 15 most powerful women in the world. In June 2011 she was chosen to be managing director of the IMF. To reach out to Socialists, he appointed longtime TV celebrity Frédéric Mitterrand, the late Socialist president's nephew, as culture minister.

Perhaps the most surprising appointment was Socialist Bernard Kouchner, who is consistently rated in the polls as France's most popular politician. His Socialist party called him a traitor and kicked him out for joining a conservative president's government. Cofounder of Doctors without Borders and former UN head in Kosovo, he is one of very few French who supported the US decision to go to war in Iraq, although he later criticized its management. As foreign minister, he visited Baghdad for three days, the first such trip since 1988, in a gesture aimed at healing the wounds caused by the war.

France

Kouchner was a longtime critic of French anti-Americanism (once calling it "the motor of French foreign policy"). He joined the president in toning down the rhetoric in Franco-American relations. He also gave the new government a strong human rights stamp. To assist both of them was a new American-style national security adviser, Jean-David Levitte, an ex-ambassador to Washington. Together, they attempted to conduct a foreign policy that was less "arrogant"; more sympathetic to America, Britain, and Israel; less friendly to Russia; and more transparent on Africa.

France faced the spectacle of legal proceedings against two of its disgraced political leaders. Former president Jacques Chirac was dogged by allegations of corruption from the time he was mayor of Paris, but he had immunity from prosecution as long as he was in office. With his immunity stripped from him in May 2007, he was called to court to testify on the charges stemming from his time as Paris mayor. He was charged with embezzlement of public funds relating to fake jobs. Putting an ex-president on trial is without precedent in modern French history; the last head of state to be tried was Philippe Pétain, who was convicted of treason. Chirac's lawyers argued that the constitution gave him immunity for acts done while president. Three-fourths (72%) of Frenchmen indicated that they favored treating Chirac as an ordinary citizen before the law, according to a 2007 poll.

Within a couple of years, they had lost their appetite to see him become the first former head of state to stand trial. In September 2010 the Paris City Hall dropped its charge against Chirac for embezzlement, and the UMP agreed to pay back €2.2 million ($3 million), the cost of the embezzled funds, interest, and legal fees.

He still faced charges for the 28 bogus jobs and misuse of public funds to further his own political career. He went on trial in December 2011. He did not attend due to "severe memory lapses." He was found guilty of breach of trust and misuse of public funds and given a two-year suspended sentence. Few political trials result in prison terms. His legal predicament did not diminish his standing in the eyes of his countrymen. In 2011 he was voted the most admired French politician. Sarkozy came in 32nd. In 2015 respondents rated him and his mentor, Charles de Gaulle, as the presidents who best embodied optimism.

In 2006 the Clearstream Affair helped paralyze the government, disgust the public, derail then–prime minister de Villepin's hopes to become president in 2007, and damage France's image in the world. It involved a baffling web of judicial and intelligence inquiries into secret investigations initiated by de Villepin alleging that Nicolas Sarkozy and other politicians had received kickbacks and bribes laundered through the Luxembourg clearinghouse Clearstream. French judges quickly determined that the accounts supposedly traced to Sarkozy were fabrications.

The scandal transcended the affair itself and revealed something about the power games played by the narrow political, industrial, and administrative elites. Even ENA's old-boy connections seemed to be at work in this scandal that was intended to undermine Sarkozy, who had not attended the powerful school.

On January 28, 2010, in the very courtroom in which Marie Antoinette was sentenced to the guillotine, the former prime minister was acquitted. Three of the other four persons on trial were found guilty.

2012 Elections

With a turnout of over 80%, Hollande won the first round of the 2012 presidential elections with 28.6% of the votes and the second with 51.6% to 48.4% for Sarkozy. Turnout was 81%. This was the first time since 1981 that a presidential incumbent had been defeated, and it ended 17 years of conservative rule. Hollande was inaugurated May 15, the first Socialist to become president since François Mitterrand in 1981. His party swept the June parliamentary elections, capturing an absolute majority with 314 seats, up from 202. Turnout dropped to a record low of 57%. Voters sent 108 women to the chamber, and 40% of all delegates were new. Seldom had a party been in such a commanding position. The Socialists already controlled the Senate, all but one of the regions, all

Socialists, not Sarkozy, "down in the dumps"

major cities, and most communes. Sarkozy left politics altogether, refusing to lead the right in legislative elections a month later. He left his party in disarray.

Unlike Sarkozy, the 57-year-old Hollande, the son of a doctor and a social worker, is a graduate of the prestigious National Administration School (ENA) and has deep political roots in rural France (Corrèze in the south-central part). At age 26, he was an adviser to former president François Mitterrand, and he later headed the Socialist Party for 11 years. In 30 years of politics, he had never been a governmental minister.

He is known and liked for his easy humor. He is affable and funny and has a preference for consensus politics and a dislike for confrontation. He is described as "calm, sure of himself, at ease everywhere, likeable and impenetrable." Because of his image as a soft-centered politician, his nickname is "Flanby," a reference to caramel pudding. Perhaps his biggest appeal to voters was his promise to have a "normal presidency," one of "dignity but simplicity," in his words. There would be no more talk of "President Bling-bling." Leading up to the election, he stopped tooling around Paris in his three-wheeled scooter.

He fathered four children with his previous unmarried partner and 2007 Socialist Party presidential candidate, Ségolène Royal. His next partner was twice married and twice divorced, Valérie Trierweiler, a journalist for *Paris Match*. They were the first unmarried couple to occupy the Élysée Palace together; some referred to her as the "First Girlfriend." This created some protocol concerns. For example, she was noticeably missing when the president met the queen at Windsor Castle.

The press, which has become more intrusive into politicians' lives, reported that Trierweiler had a poisonous relationship with Ségolène Royal. During the June 2012 parliamentary election campaign, Trierweiler posted a tweet supporting Royal's opponent. Royal lost her seat in La Rochelle. Hollande had wanted to appoint her as president of the National Assembly. In April 2014 Royal was named environment minister in a major cabinet reshuffle. Trierweiler was severely criticized by her deeply embarrassed partner and his party for this "Tweetweiler affair." She publically admitted that she had made a regrettable mistake. Such publicly discussed domestic problems with a former and present partner undermine the president's self-styled image as a "normal president."

He was everything but that. Just when he had enough troubles with a weak economy and the lowest approval ratings of any postwar president, a celebrity gossip magazine, *Closer*, photographed him secretly meeting in an apartment right across the street from the Elysée Palace with film actress Julie Gayet. He came and went on the back of a motor scooter driven by a security guard. The president was wearing a helmet with the visor down but was recognizable by his black shoes. *Closer* published a seven-page spread complete with photos of him and Gayet; the copies flew off the shelves, and the public and media were riveted to the story.

Trierweiler learned of the affair from the tabloid, and suffering an "emotional breakdown," she checked into the hospital "in shock" for a week before moving out of the palace. Polls in 2014 indicated sympathy for the president; 77% of French respondents considered this a purely private matter and believed that a president should not be judged on the basis of the women in his life. The French are tired of talk of "First Ladies." Nevertheless, Trierweiler's tell-all book, *Thanks for This Moment*, became an overnight best-seller in 2014.

Hollande made good on his pledge to have gender balance in the cabinet; 17 of 34 governmental posts went to women. He passed over left-leaning party leader Martine Aubry for the post of prime minister and appointed Jean-Marc Ayrault. Like the president, he had never been a government minister. After one year in office, his approval rating had dropped even lower than the president's. The party had been demolished in the May 2014 European Parliament elections and 2015 department elections. The only bright note was the election of Spanish-born Anne Hidalgo as the first female mayor of Paris. She defeated another woman, Nathalie Kosciusko-Morizet of the Republicans.

In keeping with tradition, the president fires the prime minister when things go wrong. In April 2014 Ayrault was replaced by the popular Barcelona-born Manuel Valls. As interior minister, he had cultivated a tough-guy, law-and-order image, cracking down on illegal immigration and crime. A centrist and reformist, he had once even proposed ridding the party of the name "Socialist." Laurent Fabius, a former prime minister, remained as minister of foreign affairs; he subsequently was appointed to the prestigious Constitutional Council. This and other choices reflected Hollande's instinct for compromise, since Fabius and the new president were old enemies.

The president had wasted no time in attempting to create a new image for his new government. He imposed a 30% salary cut for himself, the prime minister, and all ministers. They had to use trains for any trip less than three hours and respect red lights when traveling in their ministerial cars; these requirements were quickly dispensed with. They were told to turn over any official gift worth more than €150.

He had campaigned on a promise of an "exemplary republic" and made ministers sign an unprecedented ministerial code of ethics, which did not prevent scandals in his government, especially involving himself. For example, his budget minister, Jérôme Cahuzac, who was charged with combating tax evasion, was discovered to have hidden a large amount of money in a secret Swiss bank account. Polls taken after this shock found 77% judging all politicians corrupt, including 63% of those who voted for Hollande. To combat the stench of corruption, the president felt compelled to require a publication of all his 38 cabinet members' estate holdings. This was an unprecedented moment of transparency in France, and two-thirds of the French favored it.

In terms of policy, he reiterated his campaign promises of a fairer society. His proposed 75% top tax rate for those earning over €1 million ($1.37 million) was ruled unconstitutional by the Constitutional Council. It was dropped. His "soak-the-rich" policy caused some well-heeled French to leave the country. Its richest man, Bernard Arnault, took Belgian citizenship. Film icon Gérard Depardieu accepted Russian citizenship from President Vladimir Putin. The French star has long and deep connections with Russia, whose 13% flat income tax appears better than the French rates, which Depardieu claims took 85% of his earnings in 2012. He accused France of punishing "success, creation, talent."

He promised more than he could produce in a country slipping into recession. He expressed a strong antibusiness attitude and once said, "I hate the rich," and he declared war on the "world of finance." However, when the economy got worse, he had to make a U-turn in 2014:

Discarding the left's doctrine, he promised cuts in public spending and taxes in order to revive growth and create jobs. This pivot deepened a left-right rift in the Socialist Party. Valls exclaimed, "I love business!"

2017 Elections

These were the most unpredictable elections in Fifth Republic history. The winner's rise defied all the rules of the Fifth Republic. It was the first time an incumbent president was so unpopular that he did not seek reelection. It was the first time the candidates of the two established parties for over a half-century—Gaullist and Socialist—were both eliminated in the first round of presidential voting. For the first time, both had been selected by means of primaries. The victor, Emmanuel Macron, is the youngest president ever: 39 years. He is the first never before to have sought elective office. He had no party at the time he threw his hat into the ring. He quickly created a movement a year before the elections: En Marche, renamed Republique en Marsch! (Republic on the Move—LRM).

Born and raised in Amiens, he is the son of provincial doctors. A brilliant student of philosophy and an accomplished pianist, he studied at the prestigious École National d'Administration (ENA), during which time he had an internship in Nigeria. After graduation he earned a lot of money as an investment banker, then served as adviser to President Hollande and as minister of economy in his cabinet. He married his high school drama teacher, who is 24 years his senior. He speaks fluent English.

In his book *Revolution* and in his campaign, he argued for an open, tolerant, pro-European France. His platform called

France

for support of private enterprise, looser labor rules, a more competitive France globally, and deeper ties with the EU.

In the first round, Macron led with 24% of the votes to Marine Le Pen's 21.3%. This was the first time that two outsiders reached the final voting in the second round. As expected, many voters cast their ballots against Le Pen, not for Macron. Nevertheless, Macron won with 66.1% of the votes, while Le Pen got 33.9%, her party's best-ever result.

Macron faces difficulties. Reform is always difficult in France. Street demonstrations and union opposition can always be anticipated. Indeed, a mass protest movement was ignited in November 2018, called "Yellow Vest," which severely threatened public order and his increasingly unpopular government. Perhaps the greatest challenge is developing an effective relationship with parliament, whose support every president needs. Half of his 577 candidates for the National Assembly had never run for any office. Without a parliamentary majority, presidents must settle for a coalition or minority government. Working this issue most intensely is his prime minister, Jean Castex, a career civil servant and mayor of the village of Prades (population 6,000) in the Pyrenees.

FOREIGN AND DEFENSE POLICIES

German unification in 1990 led many French to fear that their country would be overshadowed by Germany and would be driven to the margins of international politics. That has not happened completely, although the euro crisis has made it obvious that Germany is the most influential country in Europe and that France has become the junior partner. France plays an important role as a medium-sized power willing to use its force abroad. Until April 2009 it preserved its independence by not rejoining NATO's integrated command structure, although it had progressively intensified its contacts with the alliance. For example, in 1994 it began attending NATO defense minister meetings again. In 1995 it rejoined NATO's military committee, which brings the service chiefs together, and its officers began working more closely with SHAPE. It did not join the Defense Planning Committee.

Sarkozy rethought his country's relationship with NATO. This was part of a wider shift of French foreign policy: a rapprochement with the US, warmer relations with Israel and the Middle East, and a reappraisal of France's interests in Africa. "Our strategic thinking can't remain frozen when the world around us has completely changed." He recognized NATO's permanence and importance in Europe and the world and said that France must

La France dit non à l'ultimatum

LES ÉTATS-UNIS, le Royaume-Uni et l'Espagne ont déposé vendredi 7 mars à l'ONU une nouvelle version d'un projet de résolution qui constitue un ultimatum à l'Irak. Dans ce texte, Bagdad est en effet sommé de désarmer, d'ici au lundi 17 mars, « une coopération entière, sans condition, immédiate et active » sur son désarmement, sous peine d'une action militaire. L'ambassadeur américain auprès des Nations unies, John Negroponte, a déclaré que la date du vote serait déterminée lors des consultations entre les membres du Conseil, lundi. En fait, ce vote pourrait avoir lieu dès mardi.

Face à cette accélération des événements, le ministre français des affaires étrangères, Dominique de Villepin, a affirmé à l'ONU que « résolution qui autoriserait le recours à la guerre », « La France, a-t-il ajouté, dit non à la logique de guerre (...). Nous ne pouvons pas accepter un ultimatum de trois jours les inspecteurs font état de progrès ». Le chef de la diplomatie française a proposé que les chefs

d'État et de gouvernement se réunissent la semaine prochaine au Conseil de sécurité, à New York, à l'occasion du vote sur la nouvelle résolution. Les États-Unis ont rejeté cette offre.

En matière de désarmement, le chef des inspecteurs de l'ONU, Hans Blix, a salué dans son rapport « une accélération des initiatives du côté irakien depuis la fin janvier ». « Vérifier le désarmement »,

a-t-il conclu, même avec la coopération active de l'Irak, ne prendra pas des semaines ou des années, mais des mois ». Colin Powell a qualifié ce rapport de « catalogue de non-coopération ».

▶ Nouveau projet de résolution : l'ONU sommée de constater avant le 17 mars que Bagdad n'a pas désarmé

▶ Le texte est déposé par Washington, Londres et Madrid

▶ Les inspecteurs font état de progrès et contestent les « preuves » américaines

▶ Villepin : « non à la logique de guerre »

Lire pages 2 à 4

SUPPLÉMENT
La mode de l'été 2003, énergique, sophistiquée, c'est de l'athlétisme pure soie

CORSE
Polémique sur la prison de Borgo   p. 8

SUPPLÉMENT
ARGENT
Placement immobilier

play "a full role." On a visit to Washington in November 2007, he indicated that he had already made his decision to rejoin the alliance's command structure on the condition that the US put aside its objections to expanding the EU's defense capabilities; Washington complied. In giving European defense a push, he stressed that this effort would not be in competition with the US and NATO but that it would complement them both. Nor would it be Europe's intention to duplicate the capabilities that NATO already has.

In March 2009 Sarkozy easily won a parliamentary vote of confidence, enabling France to rejoin the NATO integrated command structure. As a result, France was awarded one of NATO's top prizes: Allied Command Transformation in Norfolk, Virginia, which oversees changing NATO doctrine. It also took over NATO's regional command in Lisbon, the headquarters of the alliance's rapid reaction force, of

which France had been a founding member. In 2004 it had offered several thousand troops and two generals in key command slots to NATO's new rapid reaction force. French generals also commanded NATO forces in Kosovo and Afghanistan.

Beyond these two important commands, France's entry has limited military significance because it was already playing an active role in the alliance: It sat in 36 committees and joined 2 more. Its military had long favored reentering the command structure, had been participating in NATO planning, had taken part in all of NATO's wars, and had begun in 2004 assuming posts in the military command. Many persons in France's political and diplomatic elite did not like the idea, but an opinion poll at the time of entry revealed that 52% of French respondents supported the resumption of a full role in NATO.

Of its 10,000 soldiers deployed in missions abroad, one-third served under a NATO banner. In January 2007 it withdrew its 200 special forces troops working directly under US command in Afghanistan, but 50 remained to train Afghan commandos, and more returned. France also sent additional combat aircraft to Kandahar. By 2010 it had 3,750 soldiers in NATO's force in Afghanistan, including deployments in the dangerous southern part of the country. This was a risky move, considering polls at home showed that two-thirds opposed France's NATO commitment in Afghanistan. He turned down President Obama's request for more combat troops.

Chirac's meeting with British prime minister Tony Blair at St. Malo the end of 1998 agreed on a blueprint for such a new European defense. From 2003 on, British prime ministers met frequently with the French and German leaders to

ex-Prime Minister Édouard Philippe

give impetus to a kind of European military force that would complement NATO. Within the EU, France and the UK provide over two-thirds of military research funds and half the money for equipment. They spend the most on defense and are the only ones with nuclear weapons and permanent seats at the UN Security Council.

The creation of combined joint task forces (CJTF) allows some of NATO's European assets to be used in military operations where the US has no interest in participating. The concept is meant to work within NATO and not against it. Also, an agreement between the EU and NATO called Berlin-Plus makes available to the EU a variety of NATO planning capabilities and equipment for operations without NATO participation. After all, 21 of the 28 NATO members also belong to the EU. (The one exception since Brexit is Great Britain.) There is some disagreement on how Berlin-Plus should work. The French do not accept that the EU can act only when NATO chooses not to.

The wars in the Persian Gulf and the former Yugoslavia convinced France that it could not do much in military operations without NATO assets and American help. It put some of its ships and aircraft under American control in the Balkans. Its troops that enforced the Bosnian peace settlement served in a NATO force, which in December 2004 was converted into an EU-commanded force. France dispatched the largest foreign contingent—4,000 troops—to Bosnia to play the leading role in the UN Protection Force, led initially by a French general. Its combat pilots helped enforce the no-fly zone over war-torn Bosnia. When NATO created a rapid-reaction force in 1995 to protect UN peacekeepers in Bosnia, France contributed 1,500 elite troops and assumed overall command. France was a major participant in the Implementation Force (IFOR) in Bosnia, assuming responsibility for maintaining peace in the most complicated spot imaginable: Sarajevo. Its troops remained after IFOR ended.

Many of the country's leading intellectuals embraced the cause of direct military intervention in the Balkans, fearing that ethnic cleansing could spread across Europe. This mood reflected a sharp break with the pacifist traditions of French intellectuals. That support continued in 1999, when France contributed 61 combat aircraft and 5 ships to conduct an air war against Yugoslavia in a NATO attempt to stop ethnic cleansing in Kosovo.

Ex-president Sarkozy, former foreign minister Kouchner and President Emmanuel Macron had an Atlanticist view. Sarkozy stated that it is "unthinkable for Europe to forge its identity in opposition to the United States." After the US saw its influence and prestige in the world reduced by its Iraq policy and the presidency of Donald Trump, it no longer appeared as the "hyperpower" so many French had feared or distrusted. This made it easier for France to strengthen its ties with America.

The foreign policy of President Macron stands on two key principles: more solidarity among European countries and more assertion of European "sovereignty." They should do more for themselves.

Referendum on the EU Constitution

The strong Gaullist antipathy toward a more centralized Europe is gone. Nevertheless, France was the most nervous of all the 15 earlier EU members about the enlargement that came in May 2004: 55% opposed it, compared to 36% in the EU as a whole. Only 21% of French had ever traveled to any of the 10 new member states. The government fears its loss of leverage and leadership in an expanded EU, especially given the strong American influence in former communist countries.

Enlargement is painful for the French, who fear their voice is becoming diluted, their language threatened, and their jobs at risk. Europe once represented reassurance and comfort for them; now it seems to be a threat to their identity and prosperity. It used to be a means of spreading French values and influence outside France. Now the EU is seen as a way of imposing outside values and influences on France itself. Europe has been an instrument for preserving and multiplying French power. Now some perceive it as weakening France. France thought it could once dominate and control Europe; that is no longer possible with 27 members.

The country found itself in an unprecedented debate over Europe. This was manifested in the referendum on May 29, 2005, whether to ratify the EU constitution, drafted under the guidance of former president Giscard d'Estaing. Those who saw the wrong kind of Europe taking shape banded together to vote it down, 55% to 45%, with a turnout of 69%. What went wrong?

The entire French political establishment, elderly voters, the more affluent and better-educated, and two-thirds of voters in the 20 arrondissements of Paris supported the constitution. The unlikely coalition of opponents included renegade Socialists like former prime minister Laurent Fabius, the Communist Party, manual laborers (79% of whom voted no), Trotskyites, anti-globalization activists like José Bové, the anti-European right that advocates unfettered French sovereignty, the right-wing National Front, young voters, and baby boomers between ages 35 and 65.

The motives for rejecting it were multiple, but they mainly boiled down to one overriding concern: the specter of a bigger, more powerful Europe destroying the superior French social model and imposing upon the Continent the British economic model of reduced subsidies,

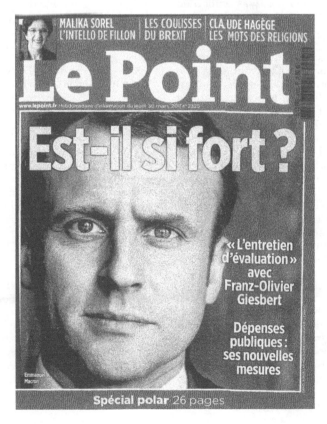

France

Vous faites quoi ces 3 prochaines années ?

L'Armée de Terre recrute dans plus de 400 métiers

ARMÉE DE TERRE
L'engagement par excellence
Ministère de la Défense

French recruitment poster

longer working hours, more flexible labor markets, and greater competition. The majority associated Brussels with free-market reforms that would endanger workers' protections and accelerate the "delocalization" (a favorite slogan in the campaign, meaning outsourcing) of their jobs to low-cost eastern Europe or China.

A deep anxiety over globalization came to the surface. This fear was embodied by a mythical Polish plumber, whose kind would flood France, undercutting its wages and stealing its jobs. "British liberalism," "competition," and "profit" were dirty words in the campaign. The French have an especially ambivalent attitude toward Britain, which has a lower unemployment rate and income per capita that overtook France's in 1995. Nicolas Sarkozy, who supported the constitution, asserted, "The best social model is the one that gives work to everybody. It is not, therefore, our own." Turkish entry into the EU symbolized borders that are too open. It unnerved voters, even though the constitution said nothing about Turkey, and the government promised a later referendum on Turkish accession. In general, the no vote was a protest against a Europe the French no longer recognized and a project they no longer dominated.

Perhaps the main source of opposition was a deep revolt against the political elite that does not seem to understand the concerns of normal citizens. It commits the people to ever-closer union in Europe without being able to explain to voters why this would be better for them. Related to this was a protest against an increasingly unpopular Chirac government. The 2007 presidential election was on the mind of every citizen who voted.

Chirac did what French presidents always do when they make mistakes and things go wrong: sack the prime minister and appoint another. This time it was his protégé, Dominique de Villepin, even though he epitomized the very mandarin class against which the majority appeared to have rebelled. He demonstrated more denial than understanding of the kind of new world in which France finds itself. "The French know it and tell it to us with force: globalization is not an ideal, it cannot be our destiny." He vowed to stay "deeply attached to the French model."

President Sarkozy recognized this unease. Although stating that he favors globalization and free markets, he used his first appearance at an EU summit meeting in June 2007 to eliminate the wording "free and undistorted competition" from the EU's objectives. He returned to France hailing this change as opening the door to greater protectionism, an industrial strategy, and "European champions." "A country that abandons its factories is a country that has lost its identity." The economic recession that began in 2008 strengthened this rhetoric.

Nevertheless, Sarkozy guided his country back into the EU's good graces. He strongly supported the new treaty that was adopted in Lisbon the end of 2007 to replace the more ambitious constitution his countrymen had rejected two and one-half years earlier. This time he decided to have the parliament, not the people, vote on the Lisbon Treaty. This succeeded in February 2008 after then–foreign minister Kouchner reminded the deputies, "All of Europe is waiting for this signal from France." Perhaps this caution was unnecessary. At the time the treaty was signed in Lisbon, polls indicated that fully 68% of French voters would have accepted it in a referendum. The Lisbon Treaty called for an EU external-action service, a kind of supranational foreign ministry. The first head of it was Pierre Vimont, France's former ambassador to the United States.

Franco-German Cooperation

Another important departure is a dramatic increase in France's military cooperation with Germany. The two neighbors created an experimental joint brigade, whose command alternates between French and German officers. In 1991 they agreed to expand that unit to a corps size—35,000 troops. Actually most of the units are stationed in their home countries, while Eurocorps headquarters in Strasbourg is only a staff. In 2009 the two countries went a step further by agreeing to the first permanent basing since World War II of a battalion of German troops in eastern France as part of a Franco-German brigade. The French eased some of America's and NATO's fears by conceding that this Eurocorps, which also includes troops from Spain, Belgium, and Luxembourg, could operate under NATO for international peacekeeping and in time of war. In Afghanistan it commanded NATO's peacekeeping forces.

France has close links with the FRG. Bilateral ties, EU integration, and NATO tether Germany securely to the west. German unity made Germany, not France, the leader of a strengthened Europe, and France seeks to act with Germany's support in the name of "European interests."

In January 2003 the two neighbors celebrated the 40th anniversary of the Treaty on German-French Cooperation in grand style. Former president Chirac and ex-chancellor Schröder met at the Elysée Palace, and 603 German parliamentarians joined 577 counterparts in the Palace of Versailles. The next day, the two leaders met in Berlin. In their Elysée Declaration, they agreed to increase the frequency of their special meetings to every six weeks; to appoint in each other's capital a "secretary-general for Franco-German cooperation" who would coordinate, prepare, and follow up their common European policies; to dispatch the relevant minister to the other country's cabinet meetings when discussing a subject of interest to the other (as did Finance Minister Christine Laguard in 2010); and to propose common Franco-German legislation to each other's parliaments. In 2004 three Germans joined the French civil service. In 2019 the two neighbors renewed their vows of friendship in the city of Aix-la-Chapelle (Aachen). De Gaulle's words still rang true: "Never forget that for France there can be no other alternative but friendship with Germany."

It is uncertain how durable this special Franco-German partnership is. From the beginning it was a reconciliation of opposites, and the two partners have always had worldviews that were not totally compatible. Although the two countries' interests converged in the early 21st century, including their publics' aversion to war in Iraq in 2003, they both continue to pursue their own national interests, which are not always the same.

A prevailing opinion in Berlin is that Franco-German agreement is a "necessary, but not a sufficient condition for moving the EU forward." Agreement between the two countries is still necessary for any serious EU initiative to get off the ground; if they can agree, a measure has a good chance of being accepted in Brussels. But they can no longer dictate policy. The French hand in EU leadership is diminished and more controversial in an enlarged EU. France's worst fear is that a Europe of 28 will be an unworkable, uncontrollable mess. In such an EU, the Franco-German partnership might end up dividing Europe more than unifying it.

They hope that such integration at the top, along with partner relationships between cities (numbering 2,500) and combined military units, will help warm their

citizens' hearts toward the other nation. A weakness in the relationship is that the two sides have to work so hard to maintain it. One French diplomat said, "It's the result of will and effort, not natural instinct." The reality is that the French and Germans are not particularly attracted to each other. One can see that in the choice of languages schoolchildren take. In 2006 only 800,583 French secondary-school pupils (15.7%) were learning German, and only 5% of German children were still learning French in their final year. But there is a reservoir of trust. A 2004 poll in *Liberation* revealed that 84% of French respondents said they trust the Germans, but only 51% trust the British. In 2006 educators in both countries completed a common history book to be used in their schools.

Both countries faced a change of leadership, with Angela Merkel the German chancellor after the September 18, 2005, elections and Nicolas Sarkozy the French president after May 2007. They did not find a comfortable and trusting rapport with each other. She was not amused by Sarkozy's self-promoting tendency to steal the limelight and to announce initiatives without informing her. Sarkozy could be unpredictable and abrasive. But both leaders agreed that the German-French "engine" remains important, even though it is insufficient to drive the enlarged EU.

The well-practiced institutional machinery remains in place and works as usual

with a new French president since May 2012. For all the talk of "Merkozy," Merkel and Sarkozy did not particularly like each other, but they learned to get along. Merkel's and Hollande's personalities are more alike, and they are both deliberative. There is a conviction in the Merkel government that the two nations are on different economic paths, with Germany far more positive toward the market economy, globalization, budgetary discipline, and penalties for those who do not obey the rules. France favors looser discipline, growth promotion, stimulus spending, and fiscal harmonization in the eurozone.

More serious is that the recession from 2008, and especially the euro crisis beginning in 2010, showed that the balance of power between the two countries had shifted in Germany's favor. The two partners are no longer equals; France appears to be the junior partner. Germany leads by default, not by choice. Thus, the euro crisis has changed the rules of European politics. The two still try to work out a common position ahead of important EU summits, so the shift in power is not obvious to everyone. However, until Germany's leaders agree on a measure, nothing happens, since Germany has become the European power that counts most.

Hollande announced during his campaign that "it is not for Germany to decide for the rest of Europe." That reveals major political change in Germany itself. It consults its own interests and no longer feels the need to please after the horrors of war. For example, Germany refused to follow France's lead and intervene militarily in Libya to enforce a UN no-fly zone in 2011.

A former French foreign minister lamented, "You can't call it the Franco-German couple any more because Germany has found its place as Europe's number one." France has difficulty adjusting to this new reality. The myth of an equal partnership is retained because it lends France an inflated diplomatic stature while it protects Germany from charges of unilateralism.

There is still a lot of symbolism in public view. On November 11, 2009, Merkel became the first German leader to commemorate on French soil Armistice Day ending World War I. She was invited to the Arc de Triomphe in Paris for a full military ceremony, where she publicly held hands with Sarkozy. She said in her speech, "When there is antagonism between us, everybody loses. When we are united, everybody wins." Hollande well understands that the special relationship between the two countries has traditionally multiplied French influence in Europe and the world. As has become traditional, Hollande's first foreign visit was to the German capital the day of his inauguration.

The Crisis. Why Obama is better.

France

Military Forces

The end of superpower confrontation meant that France had to reexamine the three pillars of its defense policy—its nuclear forces, its draft army, and its operational independence from permanent alliances. Without a Soviet threat, it had problems defining a clear purpose for its atomic force de frappe. It became difficult to maintain its expensive triad of forces, which in 1991 consumed a fifth of total defense spending.

Its underground nuclear test series in 1995–1996 unleashed a violent world out-cry, especially in Asia and the Pacific, where they took place. Taken aback by the worldwide protest, Chirac swore that these tests were needed to perfect computer simulation programs that would make further testing unnecessary. In 1991 the French had finally signed the nuclear Non-Proliferation Treaty (NPT) to emphasize the need to stop the spread of atomic weapons. They signed an international treaty banning nuclear testing in 1996. Not until 2009 did they admit that many of the illnesses suffered in French Polynesia were linked to the nuclear tests, and they agreed to pay compensation.

France continues to maintain the largest and most diversified military capability on the European continent outside of Russia, as well as a credible nuclear force. Despite the changed security environment in Europe following the end of the Cold War, a consensus remained to maintain as the ultimate security guarantee a minimal nuclear force posture for the purpose of "dissuasion," the French version of deterrence. There is little public debate over this. A significant change is that these nuclear weapons are to be linked to European security, not just the defense of French territory and interests. The French are aware that there is little current interest in Europe for such a link and that the establishment of a European defense identity would be a precondition.

French nuclear strategy also changed in 2001, with a move away from an "anti-cities," "all or nothing" strategy to a wider, more discriminate range of options. This is made possible by advances in the weapons' precision. In 2006 former president Chirac spoke openly of one new option for French nuclear weapons beyond the vague defense of France's "vital interests": retaliation against a terrorist strike against France backed by a sovereign state. He did not mention any specific countries, but he was probably thinking of Iran.

The consequence of France's decision to maintain only a minimal dissuasion policy is that major reductions in its nuclear force posture and infrastructure became possible. In the course of the 1990s, France reduced its nuclear spending by more than 50%. It started eliminating its 18 land-based nuclear missiles on Plateau d'Albion (completed by 2005), reduced to 4 its planned new ballistic missile submarines, and closed its plants at Pierrelatte and Marcoule that produce fissile material for atomic weapons. Of the five nuclear submarines in use at the end of the century, four are always operational, with two at sea. One sub has 16 M4 missiles, each carrying 6 warheads. Four new strategic subs carrying upgraded missiles entered the force: *Le Triomphant* in 1996, *Le Téméraire* in 1999, *Le Vigilant* in 2002, and finally *Le Terrible* in 2008. This submarine force represents four-fifths of the total French nuclear arsenal of 350 warheads.

An airborne component remains: Three squadrons of Mirage 2000 N planes are equipped with ASMP missiles, and two fleets of Super Etendards, equipped with ASMPs, are stationed on aircraft carriers. France keeps secret the scale of its nuclear capability. A study by the Federation of American Scientists suggested in 2009 that it had 348 warheads, of which 288 are on submarines, 50 on air-launched cruise missiles, and 10 on bombers.

The aircraft carrier *Clemenceau* was decommissioned in 1997, and the following year it was announced that the aged *Foch* would also be withdrawn from service. In 2000 after a four-year delay the *Charles de Gaulle* came on line. This is the first French carrier constructed to be interoperable with US Nimitz-class carriers. It has compatible catapults and color-coded systems, can receive US aircraft, and carries US-built Hawkeye planes flown by US-trained pilots who control the airspace around the carrier and guide planes to their targets. All French navy pilots train in America for a year, and 10 American officers serve as exchange officers on the ship under French command. Plagued by troubles, including the loss of a propeller during a shakedown cruise, the *Charles de Gaulle* must spend four months a year in port for maintenance. A second carrier, the *Jeanne d'Arc*, has been ordered to accompany it. In the summer of 2005, the *Charles de Gaulle* stole the show in a naval review of allied ships sponsored by the British to commemorate the Battle of Trafalger. In 2011 it saw action in enforcing the UN no-fly zone over Libya. It was the first non-American ship to command the Islamic State task force against IS positions in Iraq and Syria.

In 2010 France offered Russia the first significant purchase of NATO weaponry since the end of communism. It signed a deal in 2010 to sell to the Russian navy two technologically sophisticated Mistral amphibious assault ships, built at the troubled Saint-Nazaire shipyard. They are capable of carrying tanks, other vehicles, helicopters, landing barges, and more than 400 soldiers. In the aftermath of Russia's 2008 invasion of Georgia, Crimea, and southeast Ukraine, France's NATO partners were not pleased with this sale, and France postponed delivery indefinitely. President Hollande also joined the

French troops in Kosovo

Photo by Gerald Camier

France

German chancellor in negotiating a shaky cease-fire in Ukraine.

The 1991 Gulf War revealed that France's conventional forces were not equipped or structured to cope with faraway crises. Its draftees could not be sent out of France, and its equipment was found wanting. The war reinforced the case for a more professional army. Consequently, France began in 1996 to phase out its 10-month conscription and to create an all-volunteer army. By 2019 France had a total force of 209,000 troops, including 22,790 women. It also has 70,300 reservists. Over a five-year period, it disbanded 38 of its 180 regiments. This included 12 in Germany, where only 3,200 soldiers remained. In 2014 their last infantry regiment in Donaueschingen was disbanded, leaving no French soldiers permanently stationed in Germany. Army manpower was reduced from around 400,000 to 134,000, which includes 14,700 "marine infantry and artillery" and 13,490 women.

It also includes 7,700 members of the Foreign Legion. In the past, most senior noncommissioned officers and a few officers were German. The majority of legionnaires killed in the Indochina War were Germans. But that has changed. Recruits for the five-year stints now come from 136 countries; 80% say they join for economic reasons, not for adventure. Their service is a fast track to French citizenship, and they are eligible for French pensions after 15 years. Each must give up his name and choose an assumed one. Only 18% are French-born, and they must relinquish their passports and be issued one from another French-speaking country. East Europeans make up 40% of its new recruits, and Asians and Latin Americans are among the fast-growing cadres. Only about 1% are Americans. There are no women, and the command language is French. They serve with regular French military forces wherever the latter are deployed, especially in Africa.

The Foreign Legion deployed with US military forces in Somalia in 1992 and later in Afghanistan. They were part of peacekeeping forces in Kosovo, Rwanda, and Cambodia. Recruits must demonstrate computer and technology skills. They are now as likely to work side by side with French police and army fighting terrorism in metropolitan France. They also participate in humanitarian relief missions, such as in South Asia after the 2004 tsunami.

France has trained 2,300 special operations forces, and these elite troops have fought with the Americans and other allies in Afghanistan. The navy has 43,995 sailors, including 1,700 naval marines, 6,800 naval air, and 3,000 women. Its air force consists of 57,600 troops, including 6,300 women. There were cuts in the land-based nuclear-deterrence force, military bases, schools and hospitals, and civilian defense contractors; 16 warships are being decommissioned. The professional officer corps remains at about 38,000.

France no longer spends more than most European countries on defense: 1.7% of GDP in 2007. The government embarked in 2002 on a costly defense modernization plan and shifted France's strategy toward creating a force that can be projected anywhere in the world. It ordered a second aircraft carrier, new spy satellites, reconnaissance drones, 50 new Airbus A400M heavy-lift transport planes, 34 helicopters, and 57 Rafale combat aircraft. By 2008 total armed forces, including the paramilitary gendarmerie, rose to 446,000.

The goal was to catch up with Britain's armed forces in terms of professionalism, equipment, and global reach. The most dramatic step in this direction was the 50-year defense and security cooperation treaty signed in November 2010. It was driven by the need to restrain their defense budgets while maintaining their willingness and capability to project power globally. The two countries had explored such defense cooperation before, most notably in the 1998 St. Malo declaration following a meeting between Chirac and former prime minister Tony Blair. But the Iraq War in 2003 prevented progress. This was one of the few times the two midsized nuclear powers found themselves on opposite sides in a recent international conflict.

The main items in the treaty were a joint expeditionary force, combined training, and maintenance for the new A400M transport airplane and shared A300 aerial tankers. France offered Britain access to its jet pilot school, and both will cooperate in developing armed drones and ways of combatting roadside bombs. They will jointly operate aircraft-carrier strike groups with the aim of ensuring a permanent carrier presence at sea. Perhaps most dramatically, they will cooperate on nuclear weapons while retaining their independent deterrents and means: Britain depends on American equipment, while France develops its own.

France aims to improve its interoperability with allies but, at the same time, to protect its ability to act alone "should it be necessary" and to "assume the role of lead nation" in any coalition. Its independent stance had been challenged by the reality of emerging European defense identity, which the French government advocates. More than any western country, France was rocked by the breakup of the old world order. It can no longer pose as an independent force between two superpowers; such a state of affairs has ceased to exist. France no longer hopes to put itself in a position of leadership in Europe with the future possibility of heading a counterweight to American predominance in a more multipolar world. But it insists on its independence and the right to disagree with its allies.

Response to Terrorism and War in Iraq

When terrorists hijacked four commercial airliners and flew three of them into the World Trade Center and the Pentagon in 2001, killing 3,000 persons, including many French, France did not hesitate to help. It shed its usual hesitation toward collaboration with the US. President Chirac was the first foreign leader to visit Washington after the attacks. He told the American president that France stood in total solidarity" with the United States and "our forces will take part. We will assume our role in a spirit of solidarity and responsibility." Ex–prime minister Lionel Jospin also declared, "the struggle against terrorism calls for solidarity and cooperation. Our solidarity is first with America, the ally to which we owe victory over Nazism, the friend with whom we jointly affirm the ideal of democracy."

French public opinion backed these stands. A charmed Chirac escaped an assassination attempt when an assailant fired at him while he was passing in the annual Bastille Day parade. The July 14, 2002, event was dedicated to Franco-American friendship and featured marching West Point cadets and 75 relatives of victims of the September 11 attacks on the World Trade Center.

As military action against Afghanistan began, it had a refueling ship and an Exocet-rocket launching frigate patrolling the waters close to the war zone with the American and British navies. It quickly put intelligence agents on the ground to work with the Afghan opposition and dispatched special forces who fought under US command. It deployed 2,000 on 3 naval vessels, as well as combat and reconnaissance aircraft. It stationed some of its fighter-bombers in neighboring Tajikistan and ordered six of them back to the war in Afghanistan. It also sent some of its AWACS airborne control aircraft to the Balkans to relieve NATO AWACS planes for use in protecting the US East Coast. French leaders regarded America's turning to its friends as inevitable. One advisor was correct when he said, "America's power in the world may be unrivalled in military, political and economic areas, but in the era of globalization even a superpower cannot disregard the need for allies."

According to a book published in France in October 2004, *Chirac Contra Bush: L'Autre Guerre* (*Chirac vs. Bush: The Other War*), written by two journalists for *Le Parisien*, Cantaloube and Henri Vernet, France was prepared in the fall of 2002 to

France

provide from 10,000 to 15,000 troops for an invasion of Iraq. France agreed to Security Council resolution 1441 putting Saddam Hussein on notice to disarm. Chirac sent General Jean Patrick Gaviard to the Pentagon in December 2002 to discuss a French contribution. Reportedly they were especially interested because they believed that sitting the war out would have left French forces unprepared for future conflicts.

Another French author, Pierre Péan, in a best-selling book *L'Inconnu de L'Elysée* (*The Unknown of the Elysée*), wrote that France maneuvered for months while deliberating on whether to join an American-led invasion of Iraq. Research by former assistant secretary of state for public affairs under President Clinton James Rubin also showed France "scrambling to avoid a showdown with the United States." Rubin reported that the French government even advised at one point for "the Americans to bypass the Security Council altogether." French intelligence agreed in part with the analysis that Iraq wanted to acquire a nuclear weapon, but it could not prove it. After weapons inspectors seemed to be having success in Iraq and public opinion in France became so hostile, the French president changed his mind. Relations soured between the French and American governments. The Chirac government later refused to admit that there had been any hesitation on his part.

In the end, the French government opposed military action against Saddam's Iraq, with which France had long enjoyed lucrative commercial ties. Chirac and his ex–foreign minister (later prime minister) Dominique de Villepin argued that UN arms inspectors needed more time to complete their work and that such a conflict would breed even more terrorism and easily spill over into France itself, especially given its large Arab immigrant population, which solidly supported Chirac on this question.

Chirac, who enjoyed overwhelming backing within his own country and majority support in public opinion elsewhere on the Continent, believed that the crisis offered him an ideal opportunity to enact his version of the earlier Gaullist doctrine: that Europe must act as a counterweight to a much-too-powerful United States and that France, with German backing, must be the directing force in Europe. Whereas British policy aimed to promote unity with Washington rather than trying to rein it in, French policy sought the recreation of a multipolar world in which Europe, led by France, could stand up to the sole superpower. The UN Security Council would be the sole source of legitimacy for countries going to war. With its veto power, it could stop or limit the use of American military force whenever it chose to do so. In the

process, France's diplomatic weight and prestige would be greatly enhanced, and its interests, served.

This grand design ran into almost-immediate difficulties. Chirac's tactless remarks at an EU summit caused unexpected indignation throughout Europe that undermined any chances of placing France at the forefront of a united Europe. After 18 European governments, including most of those in central and eastern Europe, signed letters supporting US policy toward Iraq, he hinted in frustration that France might veto the application by former communist countries to join the EU. Chirac said that they "have not been very well behaved and have been rather reckless of the danger of aligning themselves too rapidly with the American position." Referring to Romania and Bulgaria, who were still waiting for an invitation to join, he stated, "if they wanted to diminish their chances of joining the EU, they could not have chosen a better way." The new partners in the east were furious.

Chirac's policy also poisoned France's relations with many of its other allies, including the US. When he declared on March 10 that he would veto "in all circumstances" any new resolution to bring about Iraqi disarmament, he unwittingly had called an end to all chances for a diplomatic settlement of the crisis. The US and Britain proceeded to defeat Saddam's regime in three weeks without France's support, even though the French government permitted coalition warplanes to use its airspace.

In France's own press and elsewhere, it began to sink in that France might have overreached its capacities. Chirac's condescending treatment of central European governments had split and weakened Europe rather than united it. The EU's nascent Common Foreign and Security Policy (CFSP) was left in shambles, thereby destroying any hope for a European pole dominated by France. France's dogged resistance to war had paralyzed the UN Security Council, thereby possibly weakening the only body in which France has equal standing with the US. France was temporarily left on the sidelines in a new post-Saddam Middle East, and it faced a difficult task in repairing its relations with the United States and Britain. Sarkozy, who almost never used words like "glory" and "grandeur" in his speeches, had also opposed the war in Iraq, but he saw a need to restore good relations with the US. He found a chastened America a more willing and cooperative partner.

In 2005 the US joined hands with France in a successful effort to order Syria to pull its troops and security forces out of Lebanon. The US and European allies asked France to take the lead in organizing

Guadeloupe

a peacekeeping force in Lebanon after the military conflict between Hezbollah and Israel was over. Paris ultimately dispatched 2,000 troops despite its nervousness about getting involved in a country as lethal as Lebanon and doing anything that could cost it goodwill with Arabs at home.

It also came to light in 2005 that the French and American intelligence services had created in 2002 a top-secret center in Paris, code-named Alliance Base, to analyze terrorist suspects' transnational movements and to develop operations to catch or spy on them. Funded largely by the CIA's Counterterrorist Center, it is directed by a French general assigned to France's equivalent of the CIA—the General Directorate for External Security (DGSE). It also brings together case officers from Britain, Germany, Canada and Australia. To play down the American role, the working language is French. Osama bin Laden declared France a terrorist target after it banned the burqk killed in Pakistan by American commandos. But the government redoubled its counterterror efforts.

Chirac phoned President Bush after the short war was over, expressing his pleasure that Saddam's government had been demolished and offering to be "pragmatic" about postwar reconstruction. France refrained from telling Washington, "I told you so," and it pledged to forgive some of Iraq's foreign debt. Chrac ordered its navy to cooperate with the US Navy in securing the sea lanes in the Indian Ocean; sent troops to Haiti under American command in 2004 to help create order after the Haiti's president was forced to flee; invited President Bush (as well as the German chancellor for the first time) to attend the 60th anniversary of the D-Day Invasion in June 2004, when 100 Americans were awarded the Légion d'Honneur; and publicly kissed the hand of Laura Bush when she visited Paris in 2003.

The French government seeks to reconcile its worst differences with the US. The United States remains France's largest trading partner outside the EU, with $50 billion in annual trade. Chirac dropped France's long-standing resistance to NATO's formal assumption of command over the international security force in Afghanistan. In 2005 France agreed to take part in NATO's effort to train 1,500 Iraqi security forces, albeit outside of Iraq.

After reelection in November 2004, President Bush made it one of his top priorities to restore good relations with Europe. In February 2005 he became the first American president to visit the European Union headquarters in Brussels, and he sent Secretary of State Condoleezza Rice to Paris a couple weeks later. The newspapers wrote of a "charm offensive." A former Stanford University professor, she gave a lecture to the political elite at Sciences Po and talked of a "new chapter" in Franco-American relations and of the need "to turn away from the disagreements of the past." This was desperately overdue. A German Marshall Fund poll in France had revealed at the time that 88% of French disapproved of Bush's foreign policy, and only 11% approved of his presidency. After Obama's election in 2009, that latter figure soared to 88% approval.

The French were receptive. Political analyst François Heisbourg concluded that it was not really rapprochement, but "we've both decided it's not in our interests to be at each other's throats." Americans appreciated this change: In May 2003 only 29% of them had a favorable opinion of France, but that figure rose to 62% by the end of 2009.

Americans shared the pain with the French on November 13, 2015, when France suffered the deadliest attacks on their soil since the battle of Paris in August 1944. Three teams of Islamic State terrorists killed 130 and injured 413. They made suicide attacks in a soccer stadium, shot 39 people in 3 restaurants, and gunned down 89 persons in Bataclan Theater during a rock concert. President Hollande declared that "France is at war" and announced a state of emergency that granted the police sweeping powers. His approval rating temporarily soared. The French were left with a sense of threat and shock.

Activism in Foreign Policy

France always tried to remain largely independent of other western industrialized

www.lemonde.fr

DIMANCHE 2 - LUNDI 3 MARS 2003

France-Algérie, les retrouvailles

▶ La première visite d'Etat d'un président français depuis 1962

▶ Une déclaration solennelle signée par Jacques Chirac et Abdelaziz Bouteflika

▶ Dans un discours devant le Parlement, M. Chirac devrait faire l'éloge de la démocratie

▶ ONG et familles de disparus s'inquiètent

Alger, la ville, le jour, la nuit

La guerre inéluctable de Washington

▶ Bagdad annonce la destruction de ses missiles

▶ Une « tromperie » selon les Américains

PATRIMOINE

Bartabas installe son Académie équestre dans les écuries du roi

nations in its dealing with the third world. No other country of comparable size maintains as big a military presence abroad. It had soldiers stationed in some three dozen countries and territories, including Germany (2,800), Kosovo (1,294), French Guiana on the northern coast of South America (1,435 army and an air unit), French West Indies (775 army, 450 navy and an air unit), and French Polynesia (640).

It maintains permanent military bases in three African ex-colonies: It has 1,690 army troops and an air unit on the east coast of Djibouti, 775 soldiers in Gabon, and 575 army troops and 230 sailors in Senegal. One thousand remained in Mali as part of a UN force. One of these bases will be closed in the future as France's relations with the continent are normalized. Like Sarkozy, President Hollande says that Françafrique, a pejorative term referring to those "networks of a bygone era," is over. It has been replaced by human rights and bilateral links free of postcolonial paternalism. France has troops in other African countries in order to protect French interests and citizens, who number about 130,000 in sub-Saharan Africa. In 2008 there were 2,600 French soldiers on a peacekeeping mission in the Ivory Coast, but 1,100 of them were brought home in 2009, and 1,000 more were withdrawn from the EU's Darfur peacekeeping mission.

When rebels tried to topple the government of Chad in February 2008, France had 1,500 troops on the ground to rescue 500 foreigners and the American and German

ambassadors. Although French troops did not enter the fighting, they were ready to evacuate President Idriss Déby, who had studied at the École Militaire in Paris, or prop up his corrupt government if necessary. Sarkozy declared "If France must do its duty, it will do so," despite earlier declarations that he intended to modernize France's Africa policy by refusing to defend dictators. It maintains 1,200 army troops and an aviation group in Chad. France keeps 5,100 soldiers in the Sahel (north Africa) as part of a counter-terrorism mission called Operation Barkhane.

France also sends two-thirds of its foreign aid to Africa, making it, the UK, and the US the continent's major patrons. Since 1990 it encourages the trend toward democracy in Africa by linking its aid to democratic reforms. It has lost to China its position as sub-Saharan Africa's top trading partner.

Although it convenes a Franco-African summit each year, it decided to trim its costs on that continent. Its military interventions have become rarer, although in 1992 it joined other allies to participate in the UN humanitarian relief operation in Somalia. It was the only European country to send troops to Rwanda in 1994. Its 2,500 soldiers managed to interrupt the first round of genocide and save thousands of lives.

Ex-president Chirac reiterated at a Franco-African summit in 1998, "The period of outside interference is over." That declaration had to be put aside in 2002, when French forces were rushed to the

France

French bread for euros
Courtesy: Central Audiovisual
Library, European Commission

Ivory Coast, a former French colony that was once a model of stability in West Africa. A bloody and confusing uprising got out of control, endangering 20,000 French nationals and prompting the rescue by French soldiers of 191 American schoolchildren trapped in the crossfire. Paris tried to mediate a peace pact.

By 2004 there were 4,600 French troops, including Foreign Legion and elite reconnaissance forces, trying to protect the government and enforce the oft-violated ceasefires. This was France's biggest foreign military commitment. France called on the UN to become more involved, and 6,000 UN peacekeepers, mainly from West African countries, were sent.

The Ivory Coast's government forces broke a longtime cease-fire in 2004 and bombed a French peacekeepers' camp, killing nine French troops and an American aid worker. France hit back immediately, destroying the entire Ivorian air force. Demonstrators then turned on Abidjan's sizeable French community, looting houses, burning businesses and schools, and forcing over 100 French nationals to flee in terror each day.

This festering crisis exposed the limits of France's new Africa policy of intervening less and resorting more to multilateral action. It maintains 1,000 soldiers in the Ivory Coast, but its base there had been downgraded to a temporary "overseas mission." It sent an additional 600 soldiers to the Ivory Coast in April 2011, when it answered a request of the UN to intervene militarily to save lives and to enable the winner of the presidential election, Alassane Ouattara, to assume the office that the loser, Laurent Gbagbo, refused to vacate. Although it supported the UN troops in the country, it retained its own command in Paris. The operation succeeded. The violence and killing were stopped, and the 12,000 French citizens were among the many who were protected.

In 2003 it attained EU and UN mandates to send its troops, accompanied by a small number of allied European soldiers including, for the first time, Swedes, to northeastern Congo to secure the airport around Bunia. This mission, called Artemis, was the first EU military deployment outside of Europe and was done with no coordination with NATO. President Sarkozy ordered more transparency in relations with Africa and downgraded a special presidential unit that once dealt with African heads of state.

France has long-standing interests in the Middle East. It sent a powerful 12,600-man air, naval, and ground contingent in 1991 to help drive Iraq out of Kuwait. This was a bold move, considering the large Arab population in France and the fact that Iraq had been France's best Middle Eastern customer and owed France $3 billion. In doing this it violated one of de Gaulle's most basic teachings: French troops should never be under US command. Former president Mitterrand answered critics, saying, "we are linked, we are allies, and we intend to do what we are committed to do." To renew French ties with Iraq, President Sarkozy visited Iraq in February 2009, thereby becoming the first leader of a European country that had opposed the 2003 US invasion to do so.

France demonstrated that it is ready to move outside its traditional area of operations and to match its military presence to its strategic interests rather than to its colonial links. In May 2009 France opened its first permanent base in the Persian Gulf: in Abu Dhabi in the United Arab Emirates (UAE). This is France's first permanent base outside of Africa, the first built outside of France since decolonization began in the 1960s, and the first in a country where it has no colonial ties. Its 500 naval, air, and ground troops there man a depot to support French maritime surveillance operations in the Gulf region. In March 2008 French forces took part in large-scale war games in the Gulf. In a separate deal, France also agreed to help the UAE build two nuclear energy reactors.

Other countries look to France to take the lead in deciding how to respond if Algeria, to which France annually provides $1 billion in aid, becomes a fundamentalist Islamic republic. France is torn between the desire to prevent Muslim extremists from coming to power and fear of making irreconcilable enemies out of potential rulers of Algeria. It supports the military junta in power, reinforced by its election, even though it has outlawed the popular Islamic Salvation Front (FIS). This policy creates problems within France itself.

France's nervousness is understandable. The threat of violence on French soil had become real. Out of a total of between 5 and 6 million Muslims in France in 2013, about 30%, or 1.5 million, are of Algerian

France welcomes the euro

origin. Authorities believe that fundamentalists wield influence over a small but growing minority of them.

In 2003 Chirac made the first-ever state visit to Algeria since independence four decades earlier, and he was welcomed with enthusiasm. The government in Algiers treated this high-profile visit as a momentous event in its postcolonial history. Its purpose was to redefine the tortured relationship with Algeria, gripped by a deadly civil war that had claimed at least 120,000 deaths. It was time for reconciliation.

Chirac, who had served there as a second lieutenant during the Algerian war, said that that conflict had been "a painful moment in our common history that we must not and cannot ignore, but it is time now to move forward." He signed a Declaration of Algiers, forerunner to a formal treaty underscoring a "special partnership" between the two nations. Everywhere he went, he was greeted with cries of "Visa, visa!" He promised to improve visa procedures, while his interior minister at home vowed to crack down on the large increase in visas issued.

In December 2012 President Hollande paid a delicate visit to Algeria. He acknowledged the "profoundly unjust and brutal" nature of France's colonial rule. However, he did not make an apology for France's conduct, although Algeria has long pressed for such. France's pro-Arab foreign policy, driven in part by domestic considerations, put the country in conflict with the US's basically pro-Israel leaning.

When revolutions in many Arab counters were sparked in early 2011, first in Tunisia and then in Egypt, France was caught off guard, and it was slow to support the demonstrators who were demanding democracy and to condemn the brutal government crackdowns. Then–foreign minister Michèle Alliot-Marie vacationed with her parents in Tunisia when the protests were gaining momentum, flying in a private jet owned by a tycoon close to President Ben Ali. She stepped forward to offer French security expertise to contain the street riots. She was sacked. Prime Minister François Fillon and his family also enjoyed similar perks during a holiday in Egypt; hotel bills, flights, and boat rides were paid by the Egyptian government. Sarkozy demanded that the cabinet members take their vacations in France.

The most embarrassing criticism came from an anonymous group of former and current French diplomats writing an opinion piece in *Le Monde*, accusing the government of "amateurism, impulsiveness and a short-term preoccupation with the image in the media. France's voice in the world has disappeared, and its foreign policy is dictated by improvisation. Europe is powerless, Africa escapes us, the Mediterranean won't talk to us, China has kept us down and Washington is ignoring us!" As a result, the 16,000-strong diplomatic service felt ignored, dispirited, and marginalized.

Realizing that he had made serious mistakes, the quick-footed Sarkozy pushed France's allies to intervene militarily in Libya after both the UN and the Arab League requested outside help to prevent a massacre. Intense meetings were held in NATO, which Sarkozy had initially wanted to sidestep. France angered the US and UK by making its first air strikes to enforce a no-fly zone without fully informing its allies. Sarkozy recognized the rebels' governing council without consulting with his allies or with his own foreign minister, Alain Juppé. He ordered that weapons be dropped to rebels on the ground. His actions were very popular at home, despite the fact that French soldiers were also fighting in Afghanistan and the Ivory Coast. *Libération* wrote that "France has pulled off a masterstroke." A poll indicated that 66% approved. Dominique Moisi claimed: "people are proud to be French again."

The same was true in January 2013, when President Hollande ordered fighter jets and attack helicopters stationed in Chad and France, along with 2,900 ground troops, to stop a jihadist offensive in Mali and to protect 6,000 French nationals in the region. France's EU and NATO allies, as well as the UN Security Council, supported the military action. The international legality of France's action was unquestioned.

Poster for the French census

The US supplied drones and intelligence assets, along with transport and refueling planes. The operation succeeded in pushing the attackers back, at the cost of five French soldiers dead. Hollande was showered with gratitude when he visited Mali: "*Merci* Papa Hollande!" Two-thirds (63%) of the French at home approved. This rare example of presidential decisiveness lent authority to a man with no foreign policy experience and a reputation for indecision. France leads the struggle against jihadism in the Sahel region. It has 5,100 soldiers in Mali and Chad, with headquarters in the latter's capital, N'Djamena, and bases in Niger, Ivory Coast, and Burkina Faso.

The end of 2013 into 2014 the French sent 2,000 soldiers as head of a UN peacemaking operation in the Central African Republic (CAR). The mandate was to break a cycle of Christian-Muslim sectarian violence described as "pregenocidal." The soldiers had no early success in stopping the violence, fanning French concerns that it could become a long and protracted fight.

President Hollande declared that "France wants to maintain its ability to react alone." It scrapped plans for a second aircraft carrier. The wars in Libya, Mali, and CAR pointed out deficiencies in intelligence gathering by drones, transport, and aerial refueling. These require help from its allies, especially the US and Britain. France joined the US-led air war in Iraq and Syria and became America's closest European ally in security policy.

Corsica

France also must deal with domestic terrorism from Corsica. Since the 1970s Corsicans suffered an average of 400 explosions a year by various and divided nationalist groups, who finance their operations by extorting "protection money" from local businesses. Supported by no more than 1 Corsican in 10, these groups do not agree among themselves about whether they are seeking independence or more autonomy. But in 1996 they took their struggle to the French mainland, bombing a courthouse in Aix-en-Provence and the Bordeaux office of the prime minister. The Corsican National Liberation Front (FNLC) claimed responsibility for the multiple explosions.

In 1998 the troubles escalated on "the impossible island." France's prefect, Claude Erignac, was murdered, and the assassins were never found. Bernard Bonnet replaced him and was given carte blanche to crack down on separatist terror, corruption, organized crime, and clan vendettas. He succeeded in reducing bomb attacks to 96 in 1998, armed robbery fell by two-thirds, and scores of separatist extremists were arrested. Dozens of local politicians and dignitaries were placed under investigation in some 80 corruption scandals.

In 2000 the French government sought to end the violence by recognizing the island's unique identity and history and by offering Corsica a limited form of self government. The 330,000 islanders have more authority over culture, education, economic development, and the environment. The teaching of the Corsican language (closer to Italian than to French) is required in all nursery schools. In December 2000, a large majority in the island's legislature approved this plan for greater autonomy. By 2018 the French state had granted greater autonomy to Corsica than to any other region.

The separatist Corsica National Liberation Front announced an unconditional suspension of its military actions in 2003. In 2014 it emphasized that it had given up its 40-year war against the French state. In 2017 nationalist parties won 56.5% of the votes in the territorial elections. Their demands were reasonable rather than emotional: fair recognition with France.

ECONOMY

After World War II, France experienced an economic miracle no less impressive than that of West Germany. The US Marshall Plan, economic planning, membership in the EU, and decolonization were important factors in this success. From the end of World War II until the Sarkozy presidency in 2007, the French state supervised economic planning through an official "planning commission," now disbanded. Managers, union representatives, and government officials drew up "Le Plan,"

France

and parliament debated and approved it. It usually extended for a five-year period and set economic targets; investment priorities; statistical analyses of past, present, and future economic performance, and needs. The aim was to sustain balanced economic growth.

Traditionally, there were no coercive measures associated with the plan, but the state always offered industries many incentives to participate: It provided useful statistics and analyses, granted tax relief and tariff concessions, awarded government contracts, or provided loans for investment funds. Even though the formal commission no longer exists, the spirit of planning is still alive.

France possesses enough raw materials to supply about half of its overall needs, and it has a diversified and modern industrial base and a highly skilled labor force, 22% of which is employed in industry (producing 20% of GDP) and 75% in services (producing 78% of GDP). Most of the job creation in recent years has come from the dynamic services sector. Women constitute 43% of the workforce, compared with 36% in 1968.

With its cultural riches and geographic beauty, France employs many people in its tourist industry. With 78 million visitors every year, it is the world's most visited country, ahead of the US, Spain, and Italy. In 2009 Chinese visitors to France were the biggest spenders. One sees this in department stores, which have introduced signs in Chinese. It is Americans' second-favorite destination after Britain. A film commission survey in 2005 concluded that 62% of tourists chose to visit France after seeing it in a film. But the French do not reciprocate. With more second homes than any other nation, 90% of them stay in France for their holidays. In 2016 it was the fifth-richest country in the world, despite the fact that it has only 1% of the world's population.

At 0.5% in 2021, its inflation was falling. The economic recession did not hit France as badly as most other European countries and the US. Salaries had not been rising fast enough to match price increases. Unemployment fell to 8.8% in 2021, and it's over 23.7% for the young under 26 years and non-EU foreigners, 22% for the unskilled workers, and up to half for Algerian and Moroccan immigrants in some suburbs. One major reason for the problem is the high cost of French labor. Employers must pay a high minimum wage, plus an added 50% in benefits. A French employer must pay twice as much in social charges as his German counterpart. It is politically impossible to create new jobs by cutting the pay and benefits of those working.

Half the households in France pay no income tax. To strengthen incentives to invest and to produce, the government lowered the tax rates in 2000. The top personal rates dropped from 54% to 52.5% and corporate rates to 33.3%; ex-President Hollande wanted to raise the top rate to 75%, but that was prevented by the Constitutional Council. Low-paid workers pay lower social security contributions, and the car license tax was abolished. Trumpeted by the government as the most dramatic tax cut in a half-century, the changes still leave the French with a higher tax bill than most of their competitors: 46% of GDP.

Government spending accounts for 57% of GDP, more than any other eurozone country and far above the OECD average of 38% and 37% in the US. In 2021 its budget deficit increased to 7.4% of GDP. Its public debt exceeds 90% of GDP and is rising fast. This was about seven times higher than in 1980 and exceeds EU guidelines for the euro.

The workweek was lowered to 35 hours for private companies and public workers. After fighting hard against the new law, employers discovered that, by averaging the hours over 52 weeks, they now had more flexibility to increase hours in busy periods and reduce them during slower times. They could respond better to seasonal demands. Thus workers found themselves doing shift work at awkward hours and six-day weeks. Also coffee breaks do not count in the 35 hours. Although wages were seldom cut, they were often being held down, and overtime was capped to the detriment of those wanting to earn more. The original law neither created new jobs nor boosted productivity. It is more difficult to judge whether a further aim of the reform—to balance work and life for the benefit of women—had succeeded.

The unintended results disappointed many employees, and some of them did what frustrated French workers always do: went on strike against the 35-hour week. More than 350,000 took to the streets in 2005 to defend it. While many private-sector employees concluded that the 35-hour week should be scuttled, the middle class in the public sector loved this latest entitlement, which permits French to work about 15%, or 300, fewer hours per year than Americans. A 2005 poll revealed that 77% of respondents liked their new lifestyles and did not want to work longer hours. However, it was blamed for 15,000 deaths in the 2003 summer heat wave, which depleted hospital and nursing home staffs.

In order to "increase the ability of workers to make their own choices," in the words of a government spokesman, legislation in 2005 scuttled the 35-hour workweek in all but name. It allowed employees to swap time off for money and to work as long as the 48 hours per week allowed by EU law. The state-imposed ceiling on overtime was progressively raised from 130 to 220 hours a year. Any time worked over 35 hours was made free of tax and social-insurance charges, and two-fifths of the companies employing more than 10 persons have taken advantage of this rule. In 2008 the 35-hour workweek was effectively ended by a new law that gave businesses the right to negotiate directly with employees to determine their working hours. The actual working hours in 2014 were 39.5.

The country has, in effect, a two-tier labor market: sheltered jobs for those lucky enough to have them and precariousness or joblessness for the rest, especially the young. It is a paradox, as the OECD confirmed in a 2005 study, that the French felt significantly less secure in their jobs than did Americans, Danes, Britons, or Canadians. That was a major reason for the "no" victory in the May 2005 referendum on the EU constitution. Without a more flexible labor market, unemployment will remain high.

The French labor code, which is longer than the Bible, has 30 pages detailing the procedures for dismissing an employee, beginning with warning letters and meetings with the person. Even after dismissal, an estimated 25% of cases end up in court, with the employee winning three out of four times. This nightmare makes employers reluctant to hire in the first place. The Hollande government and the unions agreed in 2013 to minor changes. Employers were given more flexibility to reduce working hours in times of economic difficulty, and the compensation courts can award to laid-off workers was lowered.

What unites the trade unions, civil servants, students, and the majority of the general public is a kind of conservatism: the wish to hang on to an idealized world of lifelong jobs and an economy insulated from the constraints of globalization, which has strongly negative connotations in France. Even free-market capitalism, which has made France the fifth-richest country in the world, is in disrepute: Only 31% agreed in 2012 that the free-market economy is the best system available. Leaders and media have convinced many French that they are victims of global markets. In his 2012 presidential campaign, ex-President Hollande proclaimed that his "main opponent is the world of finance," a damaging statement from which he later backed away.

That antipathy was hardened by the 2008–2009 recession. The crisis was not as severe as in other countries: No large bank had to be rescued, and there was no wave of mortgage repossessions. Therefore, domestic support for the "French model" of active governmental intervention in the economy increased. Three-quarters of young French

10 questions for discovering McDonald's from the farm to the restaurant

indicated in a 2006 poll that they would like to become civil servants, with ironclad job protection. Only a fourth of all jobs are in the public sector. "Jobs for life" are so protected and hard to get rid of that fewer and fewer employers produce them anymore. Two-thirds of young French who have a job a year after ending their schooling are on temporary contracts. By 2013, 8 out of 10 (82%) people hired were on temporary contracts, and half of those (four-fifths for the young) last less than a month. Without a permanent contract, one cannot rent an apartment or get a loan.

The government must avoid anything that smacks of what the French call "liberalism" (meaning a flexible labor market that responds to global challenges). Both unions and citizens fear the kind of global challenges that face all countries now, and they wish to build barriers against them.

It is a glaring contradiction that France, which is the world's seventh-largest exporter, has an economy that is, in fact, more and more open and globalized. France fully exploits the open world economy and benefits enormously from it. It had steady trade surpluses until 2007. For example, Jacques Rupnik, a specialist on eastern Europe, estimated that France lost 6,500 jobs to companies moving operations to eastern Europe. But these were dwarfed by the 150,000 jobs in France created by its trade surplus with these countries.

Its private sector boasts world-class producers of cars, cosmetics, and insurance.

A French company (Sodexho) feeds the US Army. In 2005 Cadarache in southern France was selected as the site for a €10 billion international nuclear-fusion reactor, the world's first.

At the same time, there is another French economy that coexists with the one that cowers before the threat of globalization. It is dynamic, highly trained, and comfortable in the private sector. French companies are brutally aggressive overseas. In the half-year to mid-2005, French companies bought $34 billion worth of foreign businesses, more than the $28 billion in all of 2004. French multinational corporations were the world's third-largest source of global cross-border takeovers. They are dynamically expansionist and are exploiting the globalized economy. Christine Lagarde, a former managing partner of a Chicago-based law firm and IMF boss as of 2011, rightly disagrees with many of her countrymen, asserting, "France has a lot to win out of globalization. We have incredible talents. We have great know-how. We have got a lot to offer."

France has usually had relatively peaceful labor relations. In part, this is because France's social security programs have taken much of the heat out of the issue of unequal income distribution. Only 8% of the workforce in the private sector belongs to labor unions (compared with 12% in the US and nearly 30% in Britain), and membership continues to decline. However, in the public sector, the share is about

one-fourth (compared with 37% in America). This gives France the least unionized workforce of any industrialized country.

Nevertheless, its unions are socially and politically strong in spite of their numerical weakness. The reason is that they have an ensconced place in positions of power. They conduct all national collective bargaining agreements, which apply to all employees within an industry, whether they belong to the union or not. By law since 1945, every company with over 50 employees must have a works council (*comité d'entreprise*), financed by the companies. This body, dominated by unions, must be consulted on many major decisions that go far beyond working conditions.

The unions and employers are joint managers of the health, retirement, and social security organizations. Unions belong to every labor tribunal. They also maintain a conflictual culture in industrial relations, where dialogue with the government is often piped through a megaphone by striking workers. The timing for strikes can seriously harm the national interest. This happened in March 2005, when strikes in Paris were called on the very day the International Olympics Committee was in the city to evaluate it for the 2012 games. Not surprisingly, it lost its bid to London.

Unions representing public-sector workers are a mighty force, and they insist at a minimum on preserving what their members already have. Unions were once the vanguard of the leftists, but they are now the country's most conservative force. With their secure employment, public-sector employees are sheltered from the globalized competition that demands change and adaptation.

The Communists once dominated the largest union, the General Confederation of Labor (CGT), but that link has been severed. By 2006 the CGT had lost two-thirds of its members since the 1970s, with only 700,000 remaining. The French Democratic Confederation of Labor (CFDT) displays moderation, as does the leftist but anticommunist Workers Force (FO). The powerful National Education Federation (FEN) and the white-collar Confederation of Supervisory Grades (CGC and CFE-CGC) organize teachers and engineers and skilled technical personnel. Some nonunionized French, especially in the public sector, belong to so-called coordinations, ad hoc bodies that serve as liaisons between competing unions or spring up in protest at the unions' inattention.

The Democratic Unitary Solidarity (SUD) union that emerged belongs to the anarchist-syndicalist tradition and preaches class warfare. A wave of "bossnapping" occurred at factories. Though not a new tactic in France, bosses were locked in their offices overnight and sometimes

France

roughed up in order to intimidate them and extract promises of job protection. While this would never be tolerated by the US public and politicians, the French government urged businesses not to press charges against the perpetrators out of fear that tensions would be heightened. In a 2009 poll, 45% of French respondents found such tactics acceptable, and two-thirds opposed any legal action against those who committed this form of coercion.

Although many signs of the old France remain, the economy is being modernized at an impressive rate. The Jospin Socialist government privatized far more of the country's industry than its center-right predecessors had done, leaving about 1,500 companies (compared with 3,500 in 1986) in which the state has a controlling share. It did all this without once using the word "privatize" in public.

One sign of the ascendancy of the "new economy" is the fact that half the graduates of the elite École Polytechnique now go into private business rather than into the civil service or large corporations. The result in the 21st century is an undeniable boom. Foreign investment plays a part in this. The US is France's largest source of foreign investment, and American companies employ 500,000 in France. Pfizer in France produces 80% of the Viagra consumed in America. Most of the shares in listed French companies are also owned by foreign investors, mainly American and British.

The Socialist government also quietly legalized practices that once raised ideological red flags: Stock options for young companies were legitimized in 1999, and private pension funds, heretofore illegal, appeared under the innocuous heading "workers' savings plans." Nevertheless, fewer than 13% of French own shares, compared to 23% of Britons.

Health care, costing 10% of GDP, remains among the best in the world, and the poor receive free treatment. In 2003 the government tackled an old health problem: cigarette smoking by a fifth of the adult population (50% of those aged 15 to 24). Taxes account for 80% of the cost of cigarettes, and three steep tax increases on tobacco raised the price of a package of cigarettes by 50% to €5.40 ($7), making France one of the most expensive places in Europe to smoke. For the first time, tobacconists responded by calling a nationwide strike, burning mountains of cigarettes in town squares. Although 90% joined in, the strike failed.

In 2006 lawmakers banned the sale of cigarettes to youth under 16 and cracked down on public smoking. Supported by an overwhelming majority of its population, France joined a European-wide movement by banning smoking in all public places. In 2008 this process was completed by including every commercial corner of "entertainment and conviviality," that is, bars, cafés, and restaurants. Some expressed amazement that this could happen in the country that gave the cigarette its name; has a Museum of Smoking in Paris; and even named a Parisian street after Jean Nicot, the 16th-century diplomat who took American tobacco to Catherine de Medici to treat her migraines and gave nicotine its name. The restriction on smoking contributes to the steady reduction of cafés in France from 200,000 in 1960 to 40,000 today.

A country where 82% of the women between the ages of 25 and 49 work, France is experiencing a rising birth rate of 2.1 children per woman, Europe's highest, even ahead of Ireland (1.99). This trend is encouraged by a number of government-funded programs, amounting to 5.1% of GDP, twice the EU average. They include free all-day nursery schooling at *écoles maternelles*. Mothers have four months of paid maternity leave and can chose not to work until the child is three and be guaranteed her full-time job when she returns. The state offers a monthly allowance of about $170 for two children, $400 for three, and $220 for every child thereafter. It is raised at age 11. Kids can go to subsidized summer camps. Families with three or more children are deemed *familles nombreuses* and are eligible for heavily subsidized rent and transportation, zero income tax, and state-funded parental leaves that can be extended for years.

Nevertheless, the French face a demographic time bomb: Whereas there are two workers today supporting one pensioner, by 2040 there might only be one. One thing the state cannot change is the expectation that women perform the lion's share of child care and domestic tasks at home: She spends an average of five hours per day on these, compared with only two hours for the man. She is also paid 26% less for her work than are men. In 2010 the World Economic Forum ranked France 46th in terms of gender equality, behind the US and most of Europe.

In accordance with its unsustainable traditional "pay-as-you-go" pension system, current workers are taxed to pay pensions of today's retired people. Public-sector workers could retire after 37.5 years with a full pension; the private-sector, after 40 years. This meant that many could retire at age 55 with a full pension. Railway, electricity, and gas workers and police could retire as young as 50 with full pensions, since the rules for such "special regimes" had been made in days past when such work was dangerous. Only 16% of French citizens aged 60 to 65 are still working. Given their high life expectancy, the average French man spends 24 years in retirement; a woman, 28. Ex–prime minister Raffarin noted, "Conceived more than 50 years ago, our retirement system no longer corresponds to the current and future demographic reality."

The government confronted the unions over this issue in 2003 and won. The reform brought public-sector workers in line with the private sector by 2008, requiring all persons to work 40 years (42 by 2020) in order to get a full pension. Government support for early retirement is being phased out, and the retirement age was to be raised from 60 to 62 in 2018. President Hollande pledged to lower it to 60 for those who began to work in their teens. Tax incentives are being introduced to persuade workers to invest in company-based savings programs like those in the US. Finally, a pension bonus is offered to those who work beyond 40 years. The public seems keenly aware of the growing pension deficit: Surveys in 2010 revealed that two-thirds believed the pension system was in

Trompe l'oeil: false painted storefront in Lyon. Which are the real pedestrians?

danger of collapse, and 64% thought the retirement age will have to rise. When strikes against the pension reform gripped France in October 2010, up to 3.5 million took to the streets.

But railway and metro strikes had lost much of their potency because a new law requires a minimum service in schools and on public transport. Also workers are no longer paid when they walk out. However that requirement does not apply to ports and refineries. A majority of respondents sympathized with the strikers, but at the same time, 70% agreed that the changes were "reasonable." The massive street demonstrations and strike action that greeted this reform failed to stop it.

Agriculture

Three percent of Frenchmen are now employed full time in agriculture (compared with more than a third in 1945); they produce a mere 2% of GDP. De Gaulle had once said, "A country that cannot feed itself is not a great country." France is self-sufficient in all foodstuffs, and it gets tropical produce from the Antilles and la Réunion. It is the major agricultural country in the EU, producing 21% of the community's total output (before enlargement to 28 members in 2013) and possessing about a third of all agricultural land within the EU. It is the world's fourth-largest producer of cereals and meat. Only the US exports more food and drink products.

France remains one of the world's leading producers of wine (which accounts for 17% of agricultural output), although by 2002 its wine industry was unable to sell all it produces. The country's largest wine-producing region, Bordeaux, supplies two-thirds of the French market and has avoided the worst of the slump. But wine-growers in Beaujolais, Burgundy, and elsewhere face ever-stiffer competition from aggressive wine-exporting countries like Australia, New Zealand, South Africa, and Chile. In 1996 it exported three times as much wine as these countries combined; a decade later it exported 15% less than they did. France's share of the American wine market fell from 26% to 16% in 2004 and from 37% to 23% in Britain.

The main reason for declining wine revenues comes from a dramatic reduction in wine consumption in France itself. Sipping wine throughout the day has gone out of fashion. The average Frenchman today drinks 56 liters of wine a year, compared with 120 in the mid-1960s. By 2005 only 23% of French drink wine each day. By 2009 Americans had caught up with the French in total wine consumption.

Desperate winegrowers even resorted in 2002 to suing the government unsuccessfully over its campaign against drunk driving, claiming that it is illegal

"Will they dare elect him?"   Courtesy: Sonia Fernandez

to discriminate between products, even those that make one intoxicated and those that do not. Speed cameras are everywhere now, and road accidents fell by 30% and traffic fatalities by 21% in the two years since 2002; during that same time wine consumption in restaurants declined by 20%. Regrettably more than twice as many people die in road accidents in France as in Britain.

As in other European countries, the farm lobby wields influence out of all proportion to its numbers. French farmers get around a sixth of the EU's farm subsidies through the Common Agricultural Policy (CAP), which consumes 40% of EU spending. This cornucopia means that Britain still pays two and a half times more into the EU budget than does France. EU subsidies account, on average, for 90% of a farmer's pretax income. Without it the average farmer would barely survive. But CAP funds are distributed very unevenly. A fifth of the largest and richest farmers, especially the grain growers, receive 80% of the funds. The largest 30 farmers, including Prince Albert of Monaco, annually get an average of over €390,000

($507,000). Some, such as wine producers, were traditionally able to compete well on the world market and therefore had no need for the assistance.

The importance of agriculture, not only for the French economy but also for the country's emotional rural roots in *la France profonde*, was demonstrated in the farmers' violent reaction to a compromise reached in 1992 between the EU and the US regarding GATT limits on agricultural subsidies. They took their tractors and manure to the streets of France, targeting not only the National Assembly and the European Parliament but also Coca-Cola plants and the 1,040 McDonald's restaurants, each of which serves 1,000 to 1,500 customers per day. France is the chain's second-most profitable national market after the US. All of them use only French farm products, and the head of McDonald's Europe, Denis Hennequin, is a Frenchman. McDonald's workforce of 50,000, many of them minority youth who can find employment nowhere else, make it France's largest private-sector employer. However, the facts that Coke had cornered half of the soft drink market by the mid-1990s and

France

McDonald's continued to grow steadily gave them symbolic value.

The emotion and fury of their clashes with the police underscored their intense concern about the effects a slash in subsidies would have on rural France. Ex-president Chirac was able to persuade the German government to postpone full-scale reform of CAP until 2013, and he refused even to consider an EU budget compromise that would reduce any of its free money from Brussels. By contrast, Sarkozy recognized the need for CAP to be overhauled after 2013. This was a dramatic change of approach, compared with his predecessor. Because more CAP subsidies flow eastward to the new EU members, France has become a net contributor to the fund.

Farming is part of France's culture. Since they are rooted in the land, farmers cannot be transferred from one location to another like factories. The main issue is protection of France's farm interests, not of its consumers. Food constitutes only 16% of an EU family's budget, compared with over 50% when CAP started in 1968.

Already barely surviving economically, many farmers would be forced off the land and into crowded cities, leaving depopulated regions behind them. From 1993 to 2004, the number of farms declined by a third to fewer than 700,000. Only half of these are run by full-time farmers; 40,000 farms go out of business each year. Without the CAP subsidies, an estimated third to two-thirds of the farms would go under, with as few as 150,000 remaining. Farms grew in size by 40% between 1995 and 2005, but they still are less than a fourth as big as the average American farm.

Energy

France is concerned about its future energy sources. Its energy consumption doubled during the 1970s. It is heavily dependent upon the importation of fossil fuels. It imports 96%. It obtains roughly half its needs from Persian Gulf countries, one-fourth from Mediterranean countries, and one-eighth from Black Africa. It imports 90% of its natural gas. Some is produced in the southwestern region of Aquitaine, but these wells are rapidly being depleted.

By 2011 the high tax levied on fuel (75% of the price) helped drive gasoline prices to above $8 per gallon. In the past, such costs sparked severe demonstrations in strike-prone France. Truckers, joined by farmers, ambulance and taxi drivers, and Paris tour-boat operators, stopped work and blockaded oil refineries and fuel storage depots. Paris and other cities were partially brought to a standstill. The government stated that it would not give in, but then it reduced diesel fuel taxes after all. This capitulation helped spark similar outbursts elsewhere in Europe. The events underscored that, while the "new economy" has contributed much to France's economic boom, the old economy remains very much alive.

Nevertheless, France produces about half the total energy it needs. The reason is that it launched a full-scale program to develop nuclear power, especially fast-breeder reactors. Now Europe's largest producer of nuclear power, producing half the EU's nuclear energy, it is the world's fourth-richest country in uranium, with 10% of all known reserves. Its Eurodif enrichment plant at Tricastin represents a third of the western world's capacity and feeds a third of the world's nuclear reactors. By 2012, 78% of its electricity (compared with 19% in the US, 19% in Britain, 28% in Japan, and 33% in Europe as a whole) was generated by 58 nuclear power plants employing 100,000 people. This is the highest percentage in the world. It gets another 12% from hydraulic generators and the rest from oil, coal, natural gas, solar panels, and windmills.

The last plant was completed in 1999. In 1994 it fired up the world's only working fast-breeder reactor, which creates plutonium while generating electricity. Nuclear power provides the country with the EU's cheapest electricity, except in Denmark. France even has an overcapacity in electrical generation that allows it to export about 13% of its production. Its nuclear industry has also given it an edge in developing nuclear technology. It is the world leader in reactor design and construction, supply of nuclear fuel, and treatment of waste. French engineers developed a new reprocessing technique that produces less nuclear waste than in competitor countries. This enabled it to win the contract to build in Finland the first of a new generation of pressurized-water reactors and to land in 2005 the world's first international nuclear-fusion reactor, a €10 billion project in Cadarache in southern France. Since 2007 France has signed nuclear cooperation agreements with Morocco, Algeria, Libya, the United Arab Emirates, and China. In 2004 it closed its last coal mine.

There were always critics who argued that France had become overly dependent upon a single energy source and that such heavy use was unsafe. The volume of this criticism grew much louder when a nuclear disaster struck Japan in February 2011. It unleashed a broad public debate. The government ordered a safety audit of all nuclear power plants and the review of a past decision to keep plants older than 30 years running. The nuclear safety authority concluded that billions of euros must be spent to make the 58 plants conform to new safety standards since the Fukushima disaster. In his 2012 campaign, President Hollande promised to shut 24 of the plants by 2025. A 2015 law will reduce nuclear's share of electricity generation from 78% to 50% by 2025.

France is unlikely to abolish nuclear power altogether. Its reactors are among the safest in the world. Its decision to build a single standard reactor design not only reduces construction costs but also enables technical personnel to be used interchangeably in all the sites rather than being trained to work only in one site. Nuclear waste is stored on-site at reprocessing plants. Because of violent local opposition, it has still not succeeded in finding a deep-storage site for nuclear waste. In the meantime, low-level waste is stored aboveground, while high-level waste is stored in vitrified form in both steel canisters and concrete pits at La Hague and Marcoule.

Lycée students take a break in Paris.

CULTURE

The French have long fought what some critics see as a futile battle to preserve the purity of the French language. This struggle is waged particularly against the powerful onslaught of the English language. One author even wrote a book with the provocative title *Parlezvous Frangluis?*, "franglais" being a combination of the words meaning "French" and "English."

The number of pupils learning English in school quadrupled in the 1980s, although a 2004 study found that French children speak English worse than all their neighbors. To combat this, the education ministry announced in 2008 that English instruction would be increased in the curriculum, with the goal that young French will be bilingual. "I've had enough of hearing that the French do not learn English. It's a big disadvantage for international competition," the minister said.

French scientists find it increasingly necessary to publish their works in English, and they often choose to deliver their lectures in English at international conferences held in France. English is the most frequently used language in the EU except at the European Court of Justice in Luxembourg. A 2007 survey of officials from the new EU member states revealed that 69% of them use English as their second language. To help them function in French, France offers them free crash courses at a castle near Avignon.

Jacques Chirac stormed out of an EU summit meeting in 2006, taking two ministers with him, when the French head of the EU's business organization, Ernest-Antoine Seillière, addressed the gathering in English. The former president (who speaks English) claimed to have been "profoundly shocked" that a French industrialist would speak English in an international meeting. Seillière explained later that he was speaking "the language of business."

Indeed he was. In many French companies, such as Danone and the oil giant Total, it is English that is spoken in the boardroom, in part because of the increased foreign presence there. Air France-KLM holds its meetings of "le strategy management committee" in English. Renault requires all of its management recruits to be fluent in that language. One French businessman recalled a meeting at the engineering group Alstom where English was spoken, even though every person in attendance was French. Business schools require much of their instruction and most of their readings to be in English. Commercial French is filled with anglicisms, including "le spin-off," "les road-shows," and "le cash-flow." At the same time, foreign companies must be careful. GE was fined €580,000 ($750,000) in 2006 for failing to translate English documents into French.

Sarkozy, who rejected the knee-jerk anti-Americanism that underpins much of the hostility toward English, no longer insisted that the French language be required at diplomatic events. However, in 2010 he appointed former prime minister Jean-Pierre Raffarin as his personal envoy to help French officials promote French in international institutions. The EU is becoming more and more an English-speaking organization.

Ordinary Frenchmen have adopted English words so quickly that in 1975 the parliament passed the Bas-Lauriol Law requiring that trade names, advertising material, product instructions, and receipts use only the French language. The text of the law even specified French replacements for such common expressions as "savoir-faire" (for "le know-how"), "boutique franche" (for "le duty-free shop"), "mini-marge" (for "le discount"), "aéroglisseur" (for "le hovercraft"), "credit-bail" (for "le leasing"), "matériel" (for "le hardware"), "gros porteur" (for "le jumbo jet"), "astronef" (for "le spacecraft"), "boteur" (for "le bulldozer"), "retrospectif" (for "le flashback"), "spectacle solo" (for "le one-man show"), "palmarès" (for "le hit parade"), "bala-deur" (for "le Walkman"), "mercatique" (for "le marketing"), and "zonage" (for "le zoning"). Some words escaped the sharp eyes of the language legislators: "le football," "le shopping," "le parking," "le living," and "le footing" (a word which is gradually being replaced in common usage by "le jogging").

Economic-Cultural Influences

Whether "le come-back" of pure French will succeed depends in part on "le marketing" of American investors in France. In 1983, the state's High Committee of the French Language stepped in to ban English words in the audiovisual field. Thus, "cameraman" and "close-up" became "cadreur" and "gros plan," and "drive-in theater" gave way to "ciné park." It also banned Anglo-Saxon terms in all government publications and speeches, legal contracts and schoolbooks. The counterattack has been generally successful in the computer field, such as "logiciel" ("software"), "la toile" ("the web"), "courrel" ("e-mail"), "arrosage" ("spam"), and "bogue" ("bug"), despite the persistence of a few terms, such as "un batch" of data or "un floppy disk."

In 1996 the High Committee sued the American sponsors of an English-only site on the World Wide Web because the material is not also available in French. It was thrown out of court in 1997 on a technicality. Former president Chirac argued, "the stakes are clear. If, in the new media, our language, our programs, our creations are not strongly present, the young generation of our country will be economically and culturally marginalized."

In 2005 he advocated setting up a French rival for Google's search engine, whose French-language version is used for 80% of Internet searches in France. Google was invented by two Stanford graduate students. In typical French fashion, this French version would be created by the government. In 2009 President Sarkozy promised $1.1 billion to scan French literary works, audiovisual archives, and historical documents. But when the prestigious National Library of France announced that it was negotiating with Google to digitize its collection, there was an outcry from the literary establishment that a company many regard with suspicion might be essential for the project.

The government has created a process to prevent English from dominating. Seven committees, including one in the Economy Ministry, suggest French replacements for English terms. These suggestions are sent to the Academie Française. If it and the Economy Ministry approve the changes, their use becomes mandatory for public bodies and law courts.

The French government wages a difficult battle. By 1995, 83% of high school pupils in EU countries were learning English (84% in France itself), compared with 32% learning French and 16% German. Only in Romania, whose Latin-based language is related to French, do more secondary-school pupils learn French than English. In an editorial, the *Washington Post* spoofed the apparent obsession with enforcing language purity by imagining a bureau in Washington sending a disk jockey a letter like this: "It has come to our attention that you have repeatedly used the word 'taco' to describe the comestible for which the officially sanctioned word is 'corn meal crispette.' Please be advised that . . ." A *Dictionary of Official Terms* contains 3,500 new French words for advertising, broadcasting, public notices, and official documents and those dealing with goods, services, and conditions of work. All international conferences held in France must allow participants to speak in French if they want and must provide French translations of foreign-language speeches and documents.

French is the mother tongue of about 90 million people in the world and the occasional language of another 60 million. As such, it ranks only ninth in the world, behind English, Spanish, and Portuguese. The French insist that it remain one of the two official languages in most international bodies, but only a tenth of the documents produced by the UN Secretariat are in French. Already, about 85%

France

of EU officials prefer to get information in English, which is their preferred second language. In an attempt to promote use of the language worldwide, France also foots the bulk of the bill for Francophonie, an assortment of 53 countries from Congo to Cambodia who enjoy "a shared use of the French language." Since French need not be the country's dominant or official language and since the membership includes such lands as Egypt and Moldova, it is doubtful that this organization is effective in achieving France's lingual goals.

France is the biggest domestic film market in Europe and the second-largest exporter of films after the US. It has the largest number of movie screens in the EU: more than 5,600. Fifty percent of the films French cinema fans went to see in 2002 were American, almost double the proportion a decade earlier but below the EU average of 70%. Of the tickets fans purchased in 2004, 47% were for American films, 38% for French, 4.9% for British, .8% for German, and a mere .2% for Italian. In 2011, French films accounted for 41% of all admissions in France. Four of the top five box-office films in 2004 were Hollywood blockbusters, as were two of the top three in 2006. The top film in 2005 was *Star Wars: Episode 3*, which did not quite reach the box-office champion of all time in France, *Titanic*. Steven Spielberg was invited to the presidential palace to receive the Legion of Honor award.

French cinema has made some impressive advances. In 2005, French films attracted larger audiences abroad than in France, increasing by 50% in only one year. Its films are appealing more and more to foreign general audiences rather than to the traditional art-house patrons; an example is Louis Leterrier's *Danny the Dog*. Three of its films were nominated for Oscars in 2005: *March of the Penguins*, *Joyeux Noël*, and *Darwin's Nightmare*. The first of these helped France have its best year ever in the US, where viewers tend not to like foreign-language films.

The French still make more films than do their European neighbors (200 features in 2005, compared with fewer than 40 in Britain). In the 21st century, the lead has been taken by a new wave of creative directors who are products of French film schools and criticism: Olivier Assayas, Catherine Breillat, Claire Denis, and Erick Zonca. The 2001 blockbusters *Le Fabuleux Destin d'Amélie Poulain* (*The Fabulous Destiny of Amelie Poulain*) and *Le Pacte des Loups* (*The Pact of the Wolves*) were smash hits in France and drew large crowds abroad. A decade later, *The Untouchables*, a feel-good French comedy, was the box-office smash. French films are making a comeback.

In 2008 a French performer, Marion Cotillard, won the Best Actress Oscar for her lead in *La Vie en Rose*, a depressing story of the life of singer Edith Piaf. A delightful animated story of a rat with a genius for smells who rescues a posh Parisian restaurant's kitchen walked away with several Oscars in 2008. Though an American film, *Ratatouille* was a hit in France and won praise from French chefs and the highbrow *Le Monde*, which called it "one of the greatest gastronomic films in the history of cinema." Not bad for a cute little rat with a golden nose! Jean Dujardin, who starred in the silent French film *The Artist*, became in 2012 the first French actor to win an Oscar as best actor. Although it was filmed entirely in Los Angeles, it received a subsidy from the French state.

Television has been influenced even more strongly by America. The most popular soap opera in 1992 was called *Santa Barbara*, and a French clone of the game show *Wheel of Fortune* topped the popularity charts. *Who Wants to Be a Millionaire* and *The Weakest Link* became the new hits. Reality TV made its debut in 2001 with *Loft Story*, which drew one of the largest TV audiences ever and divided France between millions of viewers who love such lowbrow entertainment and incensed critics who dismissed such trash television as the dumbing-down of French society. In 2004 the opening night of another reality-TV show, *La Ferme des Célébrités* (*Celebrities Farm*), attracted 46% of the TV audience. Viewers were fascinated by the celebrities' incompetence in dealing with farm life, something that has always had a special grip on the French imagination.

Ratings for American programs are as high as for French ones. About 70% of foreign TV shows purchased are from the US. Nevertheless, by law, 60% of TV programming had to be European (of which two-thirds French); 40% of songs on FM radio must be French, instead of less than 20% before the law was passed. Many of the teeth were extracted from this law in 1995, when the Constitutional Council ruled that it conflicted with freedom of expression. Nevertheless, in 2004 French music accounted for 63% of sales, up from 51% in 2000.

Anti-Americanism still exists on both the political left and right. De Gaulle's humiliation during World War II is no longer relevant, and thanks in part to the writings of Alexander Solzhenitsyn, Soviet communism fell from grace in French eyes. *Le Nouvel Observateur* even criticized anti-Americanism as "socialism for imbeciles." The dethroning of France as the world's cultural leader has hurt many Frenchmen. However, as ex-communist singer Yves Montand remarked, "if America has succeeded in invading us culturally, it is because we like it."

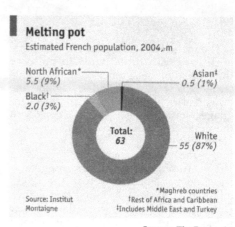

Melting pot
Estimated French population, 2004, m

North African* 5.5 (9%)

Asian‡ 0.5 (1%)

Black† 2.0 (3%)

Total: 63

White 55 (87%)

*Maghreb countries
†Rest of Africa and Caribbean
‡Includes Middle East and Turkey

Source: Institut Montaigne

Source: *The Economist*

In the 21st century, what antipathy existed between the two countries, which have never fought a war against each other, had been fueled by the 85% disapproval rating in France of President George W. Bush's foreign policy. However, the French did not seem to generalize this dislike: In 2004, 72% had a favorable view of Americans, and 68% agreed that what unites the two nations was more important than what separates them.

The inauguration of Barack Obama in 2009 was officially greeted by elegant events all over France, the grandest being held in the reception rooms of the 16th-century Paris City Hall. The new American president's triumphant trip to Europe to participate in three summit meetings in April electrified Europeans and filled the newspapers. He acknowledged in France that it was America's "oldest ally, our first ally," and he wowed an audience of schoolchildren in Strasbourg when he held a "town meeting." A swooning French commentator, Dominique Moïse, estimated that it would take a generation or two for France to produce a "French Obama." He called America a "source of hope" and concluded, "America, thanks to Mr. Obama, has returned to be the emotional center of gravity of the world." In 2009 the American president enjoyed an approval rating of 88% in France, compared with 57% in the US.

As France's economic and military influence declined, its independence from the US and its support from European allies seemed to be ways to enhance French power. Some French identify America with things they fear: globalization, capitalism, and the free market. The Socialist Party campaigned unsuccessfully for the new EU constitution under the banner "Strong in the face of the United States." Anti-Americanism is strongest at times of French uncertainty.

One earlier sign of America's acceptability was the hard-won contract negotiated by a Socialist government to build a $4 billion Disneyland 20 miles east of down-town Paris. It opened in 1992, promising to create 12,000 new jobs. The only saving grace for hard-line Americanophobes is that Disney himself is of French lineage; the family's name was not Disney at all, but D'Isigny.

In 1999–2000 the reaction against American popular culture was perhaps symbolized best by the antics of José Bové, a farmer who became something of a national hero for trashing one of McDonald's many new restaurants in the southern town of Millau. Using tractors, he literally brought down the roof. This act, along with protests at 40 other McDonald's establishments around France, was ostensibly in protest against the American decision to levy high tariffs on certain luxury foods imported from France, such as Roquefort cheese and *pâté foie gras*, in retaliation for the EU's and France's decision to ban American hormone-treated beef. By linking French culture with the protection of its food, Bové enormously widened his support within French society.

Chirac joined in by announcing that he "detests McDonald's food," and then prime minister Jospin also went on record that "I am personally not very pro-McDo," as the chain is called in France. How shocking it must have been when French nutritionists determined in 2004 that a Big Mac has a higher protein-to-fat ratio and is actually healthier than the French classic quiche lorraine. McDonald's cannot be blamed for the fact that 40% of French are considered overweight, according to a 2005 report by the French Senate.

The fact is that young French have always liked McDonald's since its first restaurant opened in the country in 1979. France is the chain's most profitable European country, the European manager is French, and the company is France's largest private-sector employer. KFC is expanding in its footsteps. A 2013 survey found that fast-food chains account for 54% of restaurant sales in France. In order not to turn Bové into a martyr, McDonald's decided not to take civil action against him. Instead it launched a publicity campaign stressing that its more than 1,040 franchises in 750 French cities are owned by French; employ thousands of French workers, especially minorities; and use French products almost exclusively (80%). Clearly more and more French love *malbouffe*, their word for "junk food." By 2009 the average French meal was wolfed down in 38 minutes, compared to 88 minutes a generation ago.

Bové's crusade tapped into far deeper issues gnawing at the French. They include fear of globalization and nostalgia for a bygone way of life, including long lunches. French voters on both the left and right instinctively mistrust globalization, which erodes French sovereignty and smacks of unrestrained free markets and American hegemony. The conventional wisdom is not that globalization should be prevented but that it should be regulated. President Hollande said in his 2012 campaign, "We're not just any country: we can change the situation."

The French government insists that the free-trade agreement that is being negotiated by the United States and European Union, which French businesses strongly favor, allow the right of "cultural exception." This permits the government to restrict foreign programs on TV and radio and to subsidize the French film industry. TV channels in France must ensure that 60% of their programing is European, including 40% French.

Academie Française

Since 1635 the Academie Française has striven, in the words of its first patron, Cardinal Richelieu, to "preserve the purity of the French language." The body itself selects individually 40 distinguished literary figures, known as "immortals." In 1932 they finally completed a French grammar book. They now meet every Thursday in order to compile a dictionary that is to serve as a criterion for good usage rather than as a list of all the words in the French language. After 60 years of work, the immortals reached the letter "R." Each word proposed for inclusion is first brought up before a special committee and then is voted on by the academy as a whole. In 1986 the academy added 912 new words; three-fourths of them were based on English or technical terms.

Such great French writers as Voltaire, Racine, and Victor Hugo were members, but no female writer, such as Madame de Staël or George Sand (pseudonym for Aurore Dupin, later Baroness Dudevant), ever managed to break the academy's all-male tradition. Finally, in 1980 it chose Belgian-born Marguerite Yourcenar, who at age 16 had begun to publish her string of poems, novels, and historical works, culminating in her monumental *Memoirs of Hadrian*. When World War II broke out, she decided to join the faculty of Sarah Lawrence College in New York, and she became an American citizen in 1947. After teaching 10 years, she moved to a wood-frame house on Mount Desert Island in Maine, where she could escape the literary circles and gossip of Paris and New York, which she detested. In 2015, the academy inducted its first non-French citizen: Dany Laferrière, a black writer from Quebec.

In December 2003 former president Valéry Giscard d'Estaing was elected into the academy with 19 out of 34 votes, despite vigorous criticism by some members, such as Maurice Druon, that "his works do not stand out in the history of French literature." His literary output consisted of four books on politics; two volumes of memoirs; and a steamy novel, *The Passage*, which *Le Monde* dismissed for its "total absence of originality." A year later he became the first former president to join. He was joined in 2010 by the sixth woman to become a member, Simone Veil. A Holocaust survivor who became a French minister, member of the Constitutional Council, and president of the European Parliament, she is one of France's most popular women.

All ambitious French politicians must write books as proof of seriousness, although campaign books seldom sell well. Excellent command of French is an essential prerequisite for the elite. Both top candidates for the presidency in 2007 came out with one or more during the campaign.

France

Dominique de Villepin has eight to his credit, including two collections of poetry. François Mitterrand wrote over 20. In 2012 François Hollande published *The French Dream*. Jacques Chirac seems to have been the least productive, with five to his name, including his student thesis, "The Development of the Port of New Orleans."

In 1989 the French Academy found itself in the midst of a storm over a proposal to simplify French spelling by, for example, eliminating the circumflex accent in such words as *être*, replacing the "x" on the end of such plurals as *bureaux* with a simple "s," writing "f" instead of "ph" (thus *filosofes*), and doing away with unexpected double consonants in words like *traditionnel* when the noun is *tradition*. A government survey had revealed that about 20% of the adult population is functionally illiterate, twice the percentage in Britain. One poll of teachers revealed that 90% favor making French easier to write in order to combat both such illiteracy and to enable French to hold its own as a world language.

Proponents of simplification point out that French has in the past been changed by decree and that another change is long overdue, since the last one came in 1832, when King Louis-Philippe ordered all public servants to conform strictly to the French Academy's dictionary. As expected, the opposition to change is strong and furious. One teacher warned his colleagues acidly to "keep your filthy hands off our language." Therefore, the academy ruled in 1991 that changes should not be enforced but should instead be subject to the "test of time." They have been blithely ignored.

The language watchdogs were stirred again in 1998, when the Académie Française, whose members wear green medieval costumes and carry swords when they meet, stoutly resisted female government ministers having themselves referred to as "Madame la Ministre" (the word being masculine). The "immortals" cringed when the Education Ministry declared that all women's job titles should be linguistically feminized: a female member of parliament should be a "députée"; a lawyer, an "advocate"; an inspector, an "inspectrice." In 2012 state administrators all over France received a memo banishing the word "mademoiselle" from official forms and registries, since it reveals a woman's "matrimonial situation," unlike "monsieur." Just how much the French admire their wordsmiths was revealed again on November 23, 1996, when André Malraux, a wartime hero, adventurer, and writer, was reinterred in the Panthéon. The ceremony was televised live on national TV, and his creative career was discussed exhaustively in the other media.

In 2013 American Supreme Court justice Stephen G. Breyer, who has worked hard to gain fluency in French, was inducted into a related prestigious French institution, the Academy of Moral and Political Sciences. This is one of five academies that belong to the Institute of France. It is limited to 50 French persons and 12 foreigners; Thomas Jefferson was a member.

Although all citizens of France can speak French, there are many tongues spoken by ethnic minorities, primarily on the periphery of the country. These languages include Provençal, Breton, Corsican, Italian, Catalan, Basque, and Alsacian. In 1993 the government faced protests because of its refusal to sign the European Charter on Minority Languages, adopted in 1988 by the European Parliament. In 1999 the Socialist government adopted only 39 of the charter's 98 clauses and again set off a wave of nationalist passion. The youngest member of the Académie Française, Jean-Marie Rouart, responded defensively, "At the very moment that our language is being bastardized by Anglo-Saxon expressions, it is to be undermined from within by having to compete with local dialects!"

Immigration and Ethnic Minorities

France's World Cup championship soccer team in 1998 demonstrated how multicultural France has become. Of 22 players, 8 were nonwhite (most of them born and bred in France), and another 4 of recent Armenian, Argentine, Kalmyk, or Spanish descent, not including the Bretons and Basques on the team. The same applied to its 2006 team, which came close to winning the World Cup, until the national emblem for minority accomplishment, Zinedine Zidane, intentionally head-butted an Italian player and was ejected from the game and from the sport in dishonor.

France has always been a magnet for foreigners, and today a third of all Frenchmen have at least one foreign grandparent. By 2010, 8% of residents were foreign-born. Six percent of the population had foreign passports in 1994. This was the same percentage as 25 years earlier, but then three-fourths were Europeans, compared with only 40% now; 39% of foreigners come from North Africa, and 6%, from sub-Saharan Africa. There is also a rapidly growing Chinese immigration.

Partly as a result of frightening unemployment, non-European immigrants face growing rejection and violence in communities where they live in large numbers. Except for music and sports, nonwhites are noticeably underrepresented in business, politics, media, and the professions. In parliament some nonwhites represent the 22 overseas French territories, but none has a seat from metropolitan France. In 2002, a black presidential candidate, Christiane Taubira, an economist from French Guiana, won 2.3% of the votes. A black journalist from Martinique, Harry Roselmack, was finally chosen in 2006 to anchor TF1's popular news program during the summer. Of the 555 deputies representing districts in continental France, none is of North African descent. Only 1 out of 36,560 mayors and none of the regional parliamentary members is nonwhite. Yet they are visible in the streets. Blacks officially number about 1.5 million, but the unofficial number is higher. Ex-President Sarkozy asked after a trip to the US in 2006, "Where is the French Condoleezza Rice or Colin Powell?" One would now add Barack Obama.

I.M. Pei's glass pyramid at the Louvre

Photo: Susan L. Thompson

Mosques spring up next to empty churches, and exotic North African commercial establishments are everywhere. Some Muslim girls wear scarves to school, igniting an emotional debate about whether such headgear should be permitted in secular schools. The French ideal envisions a secularized, uniform French identity as the most effective guarantee of national unity. Citizens in France are regarded as belonging to the whole republic, not to separate communities, and by tradition state schools are to be protected from all forms of religious proselytizing.

The issue came to a boil in 2004, when a law, unlike any other in Europe, was enacted prohibiting ostentatious religious symbols like head-scarves in public schools. It does not apply to private daycare centers. The law was directed against Muslim fundamentalists; in Chirac's words, "fanaticism is gaining ground." Many French, 69% of whom favored the law, are uneasy about culturally assertive Islam, and this fear is easily exploited by the far-right National Front. French feminists consider the headscarf a symbol of female oppression. To appear fairer, the law also banned the wearing of Jewish yarmulkes, Sikh turbans, and large Christian crosses.

Although 49% of North African immigrant women in France favored the ban (43% opposed it), thousands marched through the streets of Paris and other cities throughout the world to protest the action. Even the US State Department publicly questioned whether "it is really necessary to be outlawing their manifestation of their own faith" when people are "peacefully practicing their faith." In an attempt

to defuse the tension, the government appointed the first North African immigrant prefect, Aïssa Dermouche (in Jura), whose car was bombed within days of his assignment. The ban was widely accepted when schools opened in the fall of 2004. The Education Ministry reported in March 2005 that only 48 pupils had been sent home for wearing religious symbols, including 3 Sikh boys.

In 2011 the government banned a very prominent symbol of Muslim faith: the niqab, or head-to-toe burka, ruling that its wear was "incompatible" with French values and nationality. Only an estimated 2,000 women wear such a garment in France. Most French Muslims come from North Africa, where women only cover their hair, not their faces. Nevertheless, the National Assembly voted in favor of banning the full-face veil in public. A single vote was cast against the law, although the Council of State said there was no legal basis for the ban.

There is a fine of about $215 for wearing it, or the offender can be forced to take an official course on citizenship. A fine of up to €30,000 ($43,000) and a year in jail can be levied against anyone forcing a woman to wear it. If the victim is a minor, that fine can be doubled. Polls indicate that voters overwhelmingly support the ban by 80%, but its enactment sparked protests in Paris. The majority accepted Sarkozy's argument that the full-face veil "is not welcome in France" because it "hurts the dignity of women and is unacceptable in French society." Switzerland, the Netherlands, and Belgium have similar laws. Another target is polygamy. Despite being forbidden in 1993, there are an estimated 16,000 to 20,000 polygamous families in France.

In April 2011 the governing party sponsored a controversial three-hour public debate on the nature of secularism and the challenges of Islam. Sarkozy's desire was that a westernized version of Islam, one that fits within the behavioral and cultural norms of the France, take shape.

Called Beurs (Beurettes for females), a term that North Africans do not consider derogatory, French-born Arabs sometimes face resistance from their own families when they try to integrate into French society. The animosity toward them has helped far-right parties, such as the National Front, to make significant electoral gains in those areas. In their defense, an antidiscrimination lobby, SOS-Racisme has emerged.

France has the largest Muslim population in Europe: from 5 to 6 million, or 8.3% of the total population. Their numbers are growing by 3.4% per year; 30% are from Algeria; 20%, from Morocco; and 10%, from Turkey. More than half the prison

population is Muslim, and they are prime targets for proselytizing and terrorist recruitment. The percentage of population climbs in Marseilles to about 10% Arab and 17% Muslim. Half are French citizens. A third of French residents of North African descent live in about 750 suburban ghettos, where unemployment is three times higher than the nationwide rate.

Life is so desperate that, in one Paris park, Buttes Chaumont, radicals opened a training camp for Muslim boys in 2004 to prepare them for holy war in Iraq. Some were in their teens, and some spoke no Arabic. In 2014–2015, over 1,000 French Muslims were recruited to fight with jihadist forces in Iraq and Syria. The police, who pursue zero-tolerance policing, identified about 150 "no-go zones" in these dangerous suburbs (banlieues). Then–prime minister Valls called them "ghettos" for "apartheid."

In November 2005 they exploded with an intensity that stunned the entire country. Two boys in Paris were electrocuted in a high-voltage transformer. Rumors immediately raced through the city that they had sought refuge there from overzealous pursuing police. It turned out that there had been no pursuit, and the two officers present were later charged for failing to assist people in danger. But a wave of nightly clashes ensued. It spread to other cities throughout France. This was France's worst social turmoil since 1968. Mainly young Arabs clashed with police during three frightening weeks. More than 10,000 cars were burned; 255 schools, 233 public buildings, and 51 post offices were attacked or torched; 140 public-transport vehicles were stoned; and 4,770 people were arrested. One person died.

Using cell phone text messages, they coordinated their attacks and ambushed firefighters and police who arrived to restore order. The French government was shaken by its inability to contain the anger and violence. Finally it declared a controversial state of emergency based on a law not used since its enactment in 1955, during the Algerian War. This allowed local authorities to impose a curfew, restrict movement, and launch raids on residences 24 hours a day. The only sense of relief came from the gradual realization that there was no apparent Islamic inspiration to these riots.

In November 2007 even more ferocious violence erupted in another suburb (Villiers-le-Bel) north of Paris. As two years earlier, this was sparked by an incident in which two teenagers without helmets, riding a minimotorbike at 70 kilometers per hour, collided with a police car and were killed. For two bloody nights, scores of cars and buses were torched, and a police station, library, nursery school, local train

France

station, car dealer, shops, and a McDonald's were destroyed. Of 82 police injured, 6 were victims of serious gunshot wounds. The fact that rioters were prepared with shotguns signaled a worrisome escalation.

It is not as if the government had done nothing since the last round of violence. There have been large injections of public money (€6 billion annually) to renovate housing projects, demolish tower blocks, and improve lighting. But with youth unemployment doggedly remaining at 40% in the suburbs, the danger of explosion is always present. Since the uprising, violent attacks rose by 37%, and arson and car burning continued.

The prolonged violence was a crushing blow to the country's self-image as a model of social equality and tolerance. Its roots lie in the economic and social alienation of the mainly North African population, who face bad housing, poor schools, social exclusion, discrimination, and mass unemployment. A study in 2005 revealed that job applicants with French-sounding names were 50 times more likely to be granted a job interview than those with African- or Arab-sounding names. Ex-president Chirac admitted that France confronts "an identity crisis."

The second- and third-generation immigrants often do not feel part of French society, even if they are French citizens and say they are French. Because France's notion of supposedly color-blind equality does not acknowledge racial or religious minorities, there are no programs or concepts in place to help groups who face discrimination or social inequality. Minorities are forced to integrate with the strictly secular society, but they are victimized by discrimination. Like many other European countries, France is experiencing dangerous disenchantment.

It is this feeling that a radical comedian, Dieudonné, feeds on. He is well known for his provocative statements about the Holocaust and Jews, and he has had seven convictions for anti-Semitic hate speech and condoning terrorism. He popularized a gesture known as the *quenelle*, which many French interpret as a kind of Nazi salute. It is made with one outstretched arm straight down and the other hand held to the opposite shoulder. He insists that it is merely an expression of opposition to the established order. He has political ties with the National Front, and the government has attempted to prohibit his public performances.

Fears that France will one day have a fanatic Muslim majority are unfounded. North African women living in France have an average of 2.57 children, barely above the French rate. Only a tiny minority wants to establish a caliphate in Europe. One almost never hears the muezzin's call

to prayer. It is estimated that 15% to 20% of French Muslims do not practice Islam at all, and fewer than 5% attend mosque every Friday. About 70% fast during Ramadan.

France is vulnerable to a spillover of violence from the Middle East. This occurs when conditions of warfare and suicide bombings prevail in Israel and Palestine. Whereas incidents against Jews in the 1990s were mostly carried out by white supporters of Le Pen, most attacks are now committed by young North African men. This is a major reason ex-president Chirac was determined that France not become embroiled in the 2003 war in Iraq; French Arabs cheered the president for his decision to abstain.

France also has Europe's largest Jewish population (650,000, the fourth-largest after the US, Israel, and Russia). Like the vast majority of Muslims living in the country, two-thirds of Jews in France are

of North African origin. They share many cultural characteristics, including cooking. They become a soft target for Arab radicals in times of tension. Despite government pleas that passions that flare up in the Middle East not spill over into France, they do. A synagogue was gutted by fire in Marseille over Passover, and attacks on Jewish sites dramatically increased. In 2003 vandals torched a new two-story wing of an Orthodox Jewish school in Paris. The next year, a Jewish community center in the center of Paris was set on fire. On the walls of the ruins, the words "Death to Jews" were written. An appalling desecration in 2015 of 250 gravestones in eastern France had an obvious anti-Semitic motive.

Violent hate crimes quadrupled in 2002 to the highest level in a decade, and in 2004 they doubled again, reaching the highest level since France began keeping statistics on them. The number of attacks

against North Africans more than doubled in 2004. The majority was committed by supporters of the far right. However, two-thirds of attacks were aimed at Jews, mainly perpetrated by North Africans.

Parisian rabbis advise Jewish boys to wear baseball caps over their yarmulkes and girls to hide their Stars of David under their clothing to prevent attacks. The number of pupils in Jewish schools in greater Paris has doubled to 30,000 in a decade, with thousands more on the wait lists. The issue is the children's safety. More and more French Jews are also deciding to immigrate to Israel and the UK. The numbers climbed from 1,366 in 1999 to 8,000 in 2015.

Chirac declared that "an attack on a Jew is an attack against France," and Prime Minister Valls asserted in 2015 that "France without Jews is not France." The government ordered schools to show films like *Schindler's List*, *Sophie's Choice*, and *The Pianist* to combat the dramatic rise in racism. North African leaders in France condemn the violence but cannot stop it. Complicating the problem is that European public opinion is broadly critical of Israeli policy toward Palestinians. These attacks fed the existing fear of rising crime and a feeling of vulnerability to global terrorism since September 11, 2001.

With its large North African population and colonial history there, France is a kind of bellwether in Europe for dealing with a Muslim population. The center-right government elected in 2002 sought to create a model Muslim citizenry, which would be French speaking and law abiding, would honor the 1905 French law establishing separation between church and state, would incline females not to wear veils at work or school, and above all to consider themselves French first and Muslim second. The government adopted a two-prong strategy to achieve this: Give them a "place at the table" while at the same time regulating their activities through, for example, French intelligence monitoring of Friday sermons in mosques and prayer centers and deporting radical imams (clerics) who do not have citizenship.

To help integrate Muslims into French society, the government created in 2003 a French Council of the Muslim Faith (CFCM), with members elected by representatives of the country's mosques and prayer groups. It is a platform for discussions with local and national governments about such things as building more mosques and Muslim cemeteries and wearing veils in schools, an issue that seriously split the council. Catholics, Protestants, and Jews have had such councils for decades.

Participation was high, with 992 of 1,200 (1,600 by 2007, only 50 of which are deemed "extreme") eligible mosques voting. The authorities were not entirely pleased with the outcome of the elections, since fundamentalist Muslims in the Union of Islamic Organizations of France (UOIF) came in second and won a strong voice alongside moderate groups. This prompted the government to warn that it would deport immigrant Muslim leaders if they espoused violence or anti-Semitism. In new elections in June 2005, power was tilted away from the UOIF, the most radical grouping.

There is widespread uneasiness over the presence of millions of immigrants, the majority of whom are Arabs and blacks. A 1998 poll revealed that almost 60% of respondents thought there were too many Arabs in France (down from 71% five years earlier), over a quarter believed there were too many blacks (down from almost a half), and 15% said there were too many Jews. Four out of 10 admitted to being "racist" or "fairly racist," almost twice as many as in Germany, Britain, or Italy. Other polls revealed that half no longer feel "at home" in France and want a "large number" of immigrants to leave. Half expressed a belief in the "inequality of the races." Although 10% of respondents in a 2004 poll admitted disliking Jews, 23% expressed prejudice against North Africans. Thus the latter face much deeper discrimination than do Jews. Over half agreed in a 2008 poll that "western and Muslim ways of life are irreconcilable."

Earlier immigrant groups are often among the opponents of the new arrivals. Portuguese- and Spanish-born workers in the Marseilles area are among the National Front's most fervent supporters. But the polls show that racist feeling goes far beyond the 25% who vote for the National Front. About 28% of those who say they are "racist" or "fairly racist" vote for leftist parties. The elder Le Pen's ranting against "invading Muslim hordes" who allegedly threaten Frenchmen with the same fate as America's "Red Indians—annihilated by immigration," prove so seductive that the leaders of more respectable parties borrowed from his xenophobic vocabulary. Chirac once criticized their "odor" and "noise." Giscard d'Estaing warned of an "invasion" and called for nationality laws based on blood to replace the statutes that grant French citizenship automatically to anyone born on French soil.

There is positive news, though. A Pew poll in 2006 showed that only 46% of French Muslims considered themselves to be more Muslim than French, compared with 81% of British Muslims. A 2007 survey showed that the French are the most immigrant-friendly population in Europe: 52% thought that the number of immigrants in their country was "about right," compared with 43% in the US, 32% in Germany, and 20% in Britain. They were also more likely to invite a member of an ethnic minority into their home for dinner. Six in 10 white Frenchmen said in 1998 that they would not try to stop their child or sibling from marrying a Muslim. In fact, half of boys and a quarter of girls of Algerian origin in France have their first steady relationship with a white. Fremainville, a tiny farming hamlet just outside Paris, even adopted a black Marianne, the potent bare-breasted symbol of French republican liberty springing from the French Revolution.

The government responded by declaring that France "can no longer be a land of immigration." It introduced policies to stop the influx of foreign workers, refugees, and their families, as well as to tighten citizenship rules, while speeding the integration of foreigners already there. The number of other foreign immigrants was cut by a third. However, once they arrive, most illegal immigrants are unlikely ever to leave. For instance, close to 44,000 foreigners were ordered to leave in 2000, but only 9,230 were expelled. From 400,000 to 1 million illegal aliens remain underground, despite a dramatic increase in forced deportations.

France was largely avoided in the 2015–2016 flood of refugees to Europe. High unemployment and bad publicity about the National Front were important reasons, as was the difficult asylum process. Only 30% of applicants succeed.

In an attempt to get the problem under control, the government announced a tougher immigration policy in May 2006. Under the prevailing system, three-fourths of legal entrants were family-related. The new law aims to raise the proportion of skilled immigrants, who are lured by three-year "talent" work permits. Newcomers are required to take lessons in civic education and the French language. To crack down on sham marriages, those bringing in a family must demonstrate the financial means to support them. The National Assembly passed a law in September 2007 authorizing the use of DNA testing to see if foreigners who apply for visas are really related to the family members they want to join in France. The automatic right for illegals to remain after 10 years in France was ended. As in the past, the effort to deport those without proper papers is fiercely resisted, especially if it involves schoolchildren.

France's law-and-order ex-president, Nicolas Sarkozy, carefully explained, "France needs immigrants, but France cannot and should not welcome all immigrants." Determined to crack down on illegal migrants and people-smuggling networks, the center-right government that took power in 2002 made a decisive move. Under pressure by Britain, it closed

France

an overcrowded and uncontrollable refugee camp at Sangatte on the north coast set up by the Red Cross three years earlier. Located near the entrance to the "Chunnel," it had attracted thousands of immigrants who were trying to enter Britain illegally and who were willing to risk their lives to hop the fast-moving trains or follow the tracks through the darkness to the other end. After a new camp sprouted up in the dunes nearby, attracting 800 migrants, the government announced its closure by 2010. In 2014 a further camp was closed.

In 2010, as a part of its crackdown on crime and illegal immigration, the government closed 117 Roma squatter camps in central cities and deported 8,300 Roma back to their home countries, mainly to Romania and Bulgaria. They were given €300 ($420) and a one-way ticket home. Eight out of 10 voters applauded this, but it caused an outcry from the UN and the EU, which threatened an official reprimand. To try to stem the tide of immigrants pouring into France, the French and Italian governments agreed in April 2011 to restrict the Schengen rules for free movement across EU borders "in case of exceptional difficulties." France rounded up thousands of migrants, especially from Tunisia, near its borders and in trains and returned them to Italy. Any entrant who appeared to be a young North African is subject to questioning.

The French government cracked down on immigrants in other ways. It reduced the number of visas issued. It declared a zero-tolerance policy toward radical Muslims who incite violence, deporting imams (Muslim clergymen) who do. It used its newly merged (in 2008–2009) domestic intelligence service, the Direction Centrale du Renseignement Intérieur (Central Direction of Homeland Intelligence), to keep an eye on what goes on in mosques. Sarkozy wanted France to train imams; of the 1,200 or so in France, three-fourths are not French, and only a third speak French. The minimum age for girls to marry was raised from 15 to 18 in a bid to clamp down on forced marriages.

The judicial system pursues terrorists vigorously. For example, in May 2011 six men, some of them French citizens, were suspected of planning to go to Pakistan to train with Islamic militants and arrested. Since 2012 it is a crime to travel to militant training camps or fight in a jihadist war.

In March 2012 the police failed to prevent a 23-year-old Algerian French Muslim from Toulouse, Mohammed Merah, from killing seven persons in a shooting rampage. They could not explain how he had assembled a cache of firearms, including a Sten submachine gun. The gruesome crimes ignited a public discussion about the true identity of the young man: Was he

French or something else? Some blamed al Qaeda, but the left-wing newspaper *Libération* pointed to the all-too-frequent isolation in France of persons of North African heritage. "Merah is certainly a monster, but he was a French monster. . . . It was not Al Qaeda that created Mohammed Merah. It was France."

A satirical magazine, *Charlie Hebdo*, became the focus of a protest in 2012 for publishing a 65-page cartoon strip mocking militant Islamists and portraying the life of Muhammad. It rejected requests by the government to reconsider dealing with such an incendiary subject in that way. The paper again published cartoons of Muhammad in January 2015, with tragic results. Two gunmen burst into its offices and shot dead 10 of its editors in a staff meeting. They also killed two policemen before being captured and killed. A companion seized a Jewish grocery store and killed four shoppers. The culprits were French citizens, born in Paris of Algerian origin. This was the worst terrorist attack on French soil in over a half-century. Four million French, joined by a dozen European leaders, marched in the streets to show their solidarity with the victims. They carried signs proclaiming, "*Je suis Charlie*" ("I am Charlie").

Ten months later, on November 13, 2015, Paris suffered its bloodiest day since the Nazis were driven out, as Islamic State gunmen killed 130 and wounded 413.

On Bastille Day 2016, bloody tragedy struck in Nice, when a terrorist driving a rented truck veered into a packed crowd and killed 84 persons, including 10 children. It is no wonder that many French have a sense of siege and frustration. Polls show that most crave a stronger crackdown: 79% agreed that "Islamism is at war with France." In 2020, two women worshippers and a priest were beheaded in a church. A school teacher was also decapitated by a teen who objected to the instructor showing cartoons of the Prophet Muhammad in class.

Religion

Almost 9 out of 10 Frenchmen are baptized Roman Catholic, and two-thirds describe themselves as Catholic. The second-largest religion is Islam. Since 1905 churches in France have been separated from the state, except in Alsace, Lorraine, and the Moselle Department, which then belonged to Germany. In these areas, church-state relations are governed by the concordat, which Napoleon I signed with the Vatican in 1801. Protestants constitute barely 2% of the population, but their influence far outweighs their numbers in business, the civil service, and intelligentsia. Three former prime ministers, including Lionel Jospin, Michel Rocard,

and Couve de Murville, were Protestants. In the French public mind, Protestantism is almost synonymous with austerity and moral rigor.

Only 6% French still goes to mass weekly, according to a 2013 survey (down from 35% in 1961). The number of Catholic priests had fallen from 40,000 in 1940 to only 9,000 today. A 1997 poll by the Catholic newspaper *La Croix* indicated that two-thirds of the youth believe that the church has little influence on their lives. While 90% of Americans indicated in 2006 that they believe in God, only 50% of French respondents said that. Because of the principle of "secularity," whereby the state must be strictly separated from religion, the government's involvement in the pope's visit to France in 1996 sparked months of controversy and hostility. Also, many French resent any attempt by the Catholic Church to interfere in their private lives. Contraception is widely practiced, and abortion is common.

By 2007 the number of weddings had fallen by more than 30% in a generation. Only half of those weddings took place in church, compared with almost all of them only a quarter-century earlier. France has the lowest marriage rate in Europe, after Belgium and Slovenia; it was 40% below American figures. Marriage is in decline in most of northern Europe. In 1998, one in seven couples lived together outside marriage, a number seven times higher than a couple decades earlier and double the proportion a decade ago; only 7% of French respondents considered such an arrangement as "living in sin." After all, President Hollande and his partner cohabited in the Élysées palace Without being married to each other. French family structures have not disintegrated because society has accepted this.

The government decided in 1999 that it was time to offer some legal recognition to the new kinds of unions, although it refused to call them "marriages." It introduced "civil solidarity pacts" (PACS) allowing couples, of the same sex or not, to enter into a union and be entitled to the same rights as married couples in such areas as income tax, inheritance, housing, and social welfare, though it does not grant same sex couples the right to adopt children. Any two people sharing a home can sign a contract before a court clerk, and any partner can revoke it by giving the other person three-months advanced written notice.

Charging that this law further undermines the family, the Catholic Church, half the country's mayors, and 200,000 irate marchers in the streets of Paris vigorously protested it. A poll taken in 2000, one year after the PACs were introduced, revealed that 70% of respondents favored them.

The PACS had originally been intended primarily for same sex couples. By 2013, however, that situation had changed dramatically: The overwhelming majority of civil unions are between straight couples. More and more French are shunning traditional marriages, and PACS are almost twice as popular as marriages. They are easier to dissolve, but they confer fewer rights, especially regarding inheritance and pensions.

President Hollande and the Socialist government championed "marriage for all." In April 2013, after 136 hours of riotous parliamentary debate, same-sex marriage and adoption were made legal. The issue had been very divisive, prompting passionate, sometimes-violent homophobic street demonstrations. One attracted 1.4 million protesters. Catholic, Jewish, and Muslim clergy were unified in opposition, but 59% of French favored it, although only 40% supported adoption rights for married members of the LGBTQ community.

With the average French woman bearing only 1.8 children in the 1990s, there was fear that the country faced the prospect of a declining native population. But by 2011, the fertility rate had risen to 2.1%, the highest in Europe after Albania. More than 48% of all babies (59% of all first-born children) are now born out of wedlock, the highest rate in Europe outside the Nordic countries. This is mostly by choice, not by chance. Clearly illegitimacy no longer carries a stigma. Children born out of wedlock have the same inheritance rights as others, but unwed partners are not automatically entitled to inherit property after a companion's death. When then-president Chirac proudly announced in 1996 the birth of his first grandchild, no one seemed to care that his daughter Claude was not married to the child's father, an ex–judo champion turned television presenter.

Education

Control over the school system is concentrated in Paris. Education is free and compulsory between the ages of 6 and 16, and approximately 5 out of 6 children attend public schools. Mitterrand stirred up much controversy by promising to do away with private schools, which receive state subsidies, and to create a unified, secular school system. A half million persons protested in the streets against this policy, the largest public demonstration in French history. Such widespread protests prompted him to withdraw the contentious private school bill in 1984.

From ages 5 to 11, children attend elementary school, and then they spend 4 years in an intermediate school, called a college. After this, they proceed to a high school, called a lycée, which provides either vocational training or a baccalaureate degree leading to university study. It gives pupils a broad background that includes languages. In 1998, 75% were still in school pursuing the "bac," double the proportion only a decade earlier. In 2012, 90% passed it (compared with about 60% in the 1960s and 83% in 2007), a rate that diminishes its value, in the view of critics. Only 49% of immigrant boys and 58% of girls pass the bac. This gap contributes to their 40% unemployment rate. As the number receiving the bac grows, youth without it become sidelined in the job market. The examination for the baccalaureate is a traditional intellectual one.

France is one of the few countries that still include philosophy as one of its obligatory high school subjects. In a 30-page "letter to teachers," President Sarkozy complained about too much "theory and abstraction." That could be one reason 38% of pupils have to repeat a year by age 15. In 2008 the education minister revealed that his ministry was considering ending the preeminence of mathematics in the bac. In some lycées, history has been eliminated as a requirement for the bac.

Based on pupils' performance on the bac in 2005, all but 1 of the top 29 lycées in France are private. The exception is the famed Lycée Henri IV on Paris's left bank. This is why many parents choose private schools for their children: 14% of primary pupils and over 20% of lycée pupils go to private school, many of which are Catholic and some are Jewish. The state pays the teachers' salaries, and fees are normally under €3,000 ($4,100).

Any student with a bac is allowed to study at a university; universities are barred from rejecting students from entry. About 2.7 million students are enrolled in the 83 universities or special advanced schools, and about a third of these students are in the 17 universities in the Paris region. In 1968 a fourth of 18-year-olds and 4% of 20-year-olds were in a school or university; in 1990 the comparable figures stood at 55% and 22%. That latter percentage continues to grow. University fees are low.

The rapid growth of enrollment has brought severe overcrowding, and 40% drop out before completing their undergraduate degree. Universities are underfinanced, disorganized, and resistant to changes demanded by the outside world. Professor salaries are low by American standards. Graduates find that their degrees are now worth less and that there are too few jobs for them after graduation. The highest French university among the top 40 on Shanghai's Jiao Tong University's global ranking in 2011 was Université Paris-Sud, which placed 40th.

A group of eminent European scholars questions the methodology used in this ranking. Nevertheless, efforts are being made to improve French universities' world standing. For example, there is generous funding from a program called Idex to universities and grandes écoles that create clusters and pool their resources to compete with the world's top institutions. French business schools already enjoy better global visibility and are considered the best in Europe. Universities have world-class engineering, economics, and mathematics departments; they are ranked 14th in the world and 3rd in Europe, behind Oxford and Cambridge. An impressive new cluster is the University of Paris-Saclay. Launched in 2020, it merged twenty institutions specializing in science. Some call it a "MIT à la francaise."

The unemployment line never threatens graduates of the 220 elitist grandes écoles, of varying specialties who are selected by highly competitive nationwide examinations (*concours*) following two further years of intensive preparation in the lycée (called *prépa*) after the bac. At the top of the pyramid is a handful of ultraprestigious schools. Because they are so hard to get into, families celebrate acceptance at these institutions more than graduation itself. Many students at the universities still suffer from a sort of second-class status, as they watch the best jobs being filled by graduates from the grandes écoles. These extremely selective institutions are prestigious and produce an elite in teaching, industry, government, and the armed forces. They educate only 6% of French students but absorb 30% of the state's budget for higher education. They are well organized, well equipped, and overwhelmingly white and upper middle class. They account for 30% of the master's degrees and a third of the PhDs awarded in France. Half of the top 200 business bosses had attended a grande école.

Following the military debacle of 1870, the École des sciences politiques (called "Sciences-Po"), which offers advanced training in political science and economics, was created to improve the quality of senior civil servants. President Hollande, his three predecessors in the presidency, and at least a dozen prime ministers studied there. Half of its budget is financed by the state. It led France in offering a three-year undergraduate degree, followed by "*un master*." In 2003–2004 the Education Ministry advocated such degrees for all universities. All Sciences-Po students spend a year abroad, learn two foreign languages, and take at least a third of their classes in a language other than French. Some take all their courses in English. Over 40% are foreigners, including many Americans. It has established exchanges with American universities. It accepts 3,500 students yearly, for a total student body of 12,000.

France

Tuition is about $13,000 for undergraduates, and professors' pay is competitive. New subjects, including journalism, have been introduced.

Along with the elite School of Higher Commercial Studies, Sciences-Po has been a pioneer in offering classes in English. In 2013 the education minister proposed a bill that would allow other French universities to teach more courses in English, despite a 1994 law requiring that classes be taught in French. The goal is to attract more foreign students, who already account for 13% of all university students. The proposal was greeted by rage and protests.

In 2001 Sciences-Po caused a stir by introducing a kind of affirmative action plan, later temporarily ruled unlawful by a Paris court, to create a special admission track for secondary school students in seven poor neighborhoods whose population contains large concentrations of Arab and African immigrants. Such pupils are exempt from the stiff competitive entrance exams other applicants must pass, but there is no fixed quota. By 2012, the school's working-class intake had risen from 3% to 12%.

No one disputes that the grandes écoles have always recruited almost exclusively from a limited sociological pool of white, well-connected, and wealthy families. There is a growing minority of students from farm and working-class families. But these schools reject affirmative action on the grounds that it would dilute their standards. It would seem to violate the meritocracy through education, which is blind to race, religion, and ethnicity and which is the cornerstone of the republican ideal.

The École nationale d'administration (ENA, whose graduates are called Énarques) accepts 120 students (a fourth to a third female) by examination from the other grandes écoles each year for the 27-month program. It was set up after the defeat in 1940 and the shame of Vichy to train elite administrators who would put the interests of the state above their own. It was in Paris until 1992, when ENA was moved to Strasbourg. Study at ENA is particularly important to those persons aspiring to top civil-service positions.

Currently about two-thirds of such offices are held by Énarques, who form a highly useful informal network of contacts for each other. Only about 6,000 of its graduates are alive today. Among them were all the major contenders for the presidency in 1995—Jacques Chirac, Lionel Jospin, and Edouard Balladur—as well as former president Valery Giscard d'Estaing. The 2007 election pitted Nicolas Sarkozy, who was not an ENA graduate, against Ségolène Royal, who was. It is perhaps not surprising that Sarkozy included only one Énarque in his cabinet but nine lawyers. Dominique de Villepin and six out of his nine preceding prime ministers were Énarques, as was President François Hollande.

The mayor of Montpellier spoke bitterly of the influential Énarques: "France is still run by civil servants. There is no difference between a socialist Énarque and a neo-Gaullist Énarque. They are intelligent, incorrupt and absolutely convinced they are right. The country is run by thousands of little Robespierres." One conservative politician, Alain Madelin, even said in 1997, "Ireland has the IRA, Spain has ETA, Italy the mafia, but France has ENA." One contemporary reason for the disdain toward the highly selected Énarques is that ENA produces technocrats wholly imbued with a theoretical, state-oriented way of thinking that is not well adapted to a world of global capitalism.

The glory of ENA is fading somewhat. Between 1995 and 1999, applications for its notoriously difficult entrance exams declined by 30%. Sciences-Po, which supplies 90% of the external exam's successful candidates, has a special program to prepare students for the entrance test, but aspirants enrolling in that program have dwindled from 1,000 per year a decade ago to 200. A major reason is that, in France's changed economic environment, it is the private sector, not the civil service, which beckons ambitious young people.

In addition, there are three Écoles normales supérieures, one in Paris—ENS Ulm (in the Rue d'Ulm), which concentrates on the sciences and humanities—and two in Lyon, one of which focuses on the sciences and the other on the humanities. Both institutions in Lyon want to merge and become identical to their counterpart in Paris. These elite schools train the top lycée and university professors, who must pass a rigorous final examination called the agrégation.

Finally, there are the Hautes Études Commerciales (HEC) and other business-oriented schools. They do well in international comparison: In 2006 the British *Financial Times* picked 7 French business schools as among Europe's top 10. There are also the École des mines and similarly specialized schools, such as the military academy at Saint-Cyr. In 1794 the military École polytechnique was established as a military school. Now it trains top public officials. Cadets begin with one year in the military to undergo officer training and then spend two years doing top-level engineering and scientific study.

In protest against underfunding, overcrowding, decrepit buildings, insufficient security at inner-city schools, and bleak employment prospects, especially in nontechnical fields, lycée and university students often take to the streets. Teachers sympathize because half their classes have over 30 pupils, and some have over 40. One result is that one in four teachers requests a transfer or job change every year.

There were renewed strikes in 2003–2004 by university students protesting American-style reform plans to make the universities more autonomous and to offer a three-year degree followed by a two-year master's degree. The education minister backed off in 2005 and agreed not to modify the baccalauréat exam. Scientists also took to the streets or resigned to demand more state support for research to stem the brain drain abroad and to protest plans to cut funding and 550 permanent scientific posts. The frightened government pledged to restore 120 of the jobs and invest €3 billion more in research by 2007.

Sarkozy had to backtrack on some of his plans for university reform out of fear that the renewed student protests in 2009, led by the far left, would turn violent. However, he shook up the centrally run universities. As of 2011, 51 out of 83 universities had accepted his offer of autonomy. They can recruit their own faculty, establish their salaries, and seek funds from the

Azay-le-Rideau in the Loire Valley

private sector. They cannot select their undergraduates nor charge tuition.

The American film *Dead Poets Society*, which portrayed a rebellion against a hidebound educational system, had a profound effect on debates in France concerning reform of the school system. The government proposed reforms to humanize the grueling bac, which on average requires 45 hours of work per week, including homework, and leaves time for only one of five secondary pupils to participate in school team sports. A major stumbling block for change has been the resistance of powerful teaching unions. In the meantime, many French ask why their once-excellent educational system is soaking up more and more resources and producing students with less knowledge and fewer job prospects.

The Press

Financial difficulties have steadily reduced the number of daily newspapers to fewer than 100. The most widely read is *Ouest France*, published in Rennes, a regional paper with a circulation of 762,450, twice as many copies as any of the national papers. The best-selling national newspaper is the lively daily tabloid *Le Parisien-Aujourd'hui*, with a circulation of about 400,000. The largest and most influential of the national papers is the moderately leftist and intellectual *Le Monde*, with a declining circulation of 399,000 and a readership of 2.1 million. To compare, in 2011 the eight main French national dailies together sold 1.2 million copies a day (down 10% from the previous year), the same number as the *Daily Mirror* in Britain sells every day at newsstands.

The conservative *Le Figaro* (with receding circulation of 320,000) was purchased in 2004 by Serge Dassault of the airplane company of the same name. The left intellectual *Libération*, cofounded by Jean-Paul Sartre, also faces declining circulation, with 142,000. All three—*Le Monde, Le Figaro*, and *Libération*—have seen a large industrialist or banker take control or a significant share (Edouard de Rothschild in the case of *Libération*). All are from Paris. One of the few dailies with climbing sales is *L'Equipe*, an all-sports newspaper. As elsewhere, dailies face the challenge of the web.

In order to halt the growing concentration of the French press, the Socialist government approved in 1984 a law prohibiting publishers from owning both Parisian and regional newspapers and from controlling more than 15% of either Parisian or regional circulation. Many educated French read certain political and economic weeklies, such as *L'Express, Le Nouvel Observateur, Le Point*, and *L'Evenement du Jeudi*, which offer in-depth analysis and criticism.

The stock and trade of *Le Canard Enchaîné* is satire, a weekly that is thriving, with sales of 450,000 to 500,000. It was founded in 1915 by two left-wing journalists to circumvent army censorship during the First World War. It is owned by its staff of about 40 journalists and cartoonists and is so fiercely independent that it carries no advertising. Its investigative reporting can drive cabinet ministers out of office, but it has a strict ban on writing about the private lives of public figures.

As elsewhere in the world, many French have turned increasingly to television, radio, and the Internet for news. Fewer than 5% of French between the ages of 15 and 25 believe newspapers will be their first source of information in 5 years. The trends that face French newspapers are familiar in other nations: aging readers, plus competition from free newspapers, TV, and the Internet. Most face the prospect of being bought by investors to stay alive. Newspaper readership has dropped over 3 million since 1970.

Even *Le Monde*, founded in 1944 at the instigation of General de Gaulle to replace the collaborationist *Le Temps* and to provide journalism untainted by Vichy, is losing money and circulation. It was owned and operated entirely by its employees In the 1980s it temporarily improved its sales and financial condition by making its format more attractive and by selling and leasing back its headquarters building near the Opera.

In 2008 it faced another crisis. With losses and debts mounting, there was a drastic need for refinancing. But the staff associations resisted moves to improve efficiency and any solution that would eliminate their 60% controlling stake. Almost out of cash by July 2010, it was purchased by three businessmen for $139 million. They promised the staff full editorial independence and gave the journalists a blocking minority stake. But they attacked the unions head on, whose powers and featherbedding make it 40% more expensive to print newspapers in France than anywhere else in Europe. The papers must then charge higher cover prices, which drives down circulation even farther.

Renowned as rigorously intellectual and overwhelmingly serious, *Le Monde* received a black eye in 2003, when two journalists published a best-seller, *The Hidden Face of* Le Monde, accusing it of bias, conflicts of interest, hypocrisy, and business mismanagement. They argued that *Le Monde* twisted facts to cover up scandals, influenced French politics without declaring its interests, and hid the newspaper's financial weakness. The paper rejected the charges as an amalgam of "errors, lies, libels and calumnies." In 2003 it promptly fired Daniel Schneidermann, author of

a follow-up book, *The Media Nightmare*, which attacks the French press generally and *Le Monde's* reaction to *The Hidden Face* in particular.

Until 1984 the state had a monopoly on television and radio. Radio programs are produced by Radio-France, and French government holding companies partially own three independent radio stations (Radio Luxembourg, Europe No. 1, and Radio Monte Carlo), which broadcast from outside of France. Radio-France and the state-owned television companies were financed by annual license fees paid by those persons owning sets.

Critics charge that these companies, although nominally independent and responsible for their own programming, have been manipulated from the Elysées Palace. Mitterrand proposed reducing government influence over them by placing control into the hands of an independent board of directors that would include government officials, media specialists, and private citizens. In fact, little has changed in the management of the state-owned media.

The big changes in 1984 came with the legalization of private radio and television stations. So many private radio stations had cropped up that they could no longer be controlled. By legalizing them, the state broadcasting monopoly had been so irreparably punctured that it was only a matter of time until private television was permitted. More than 800 private radio stations exist already, providing a voice for all kinds of minority interests. Many local TV stations exist around the country. In 1987 the government took another momentous step by selling the largest of the old state networks (TF1) to the private sector. This was the first sell-off by any government of a state-owned TV network. The state kept two of the six channels.

To strengthen Franco-German familiarity with each other, the two countries started a joint satellite TV channel called Arte. However, its total audience had by 2003 stagnated to about 13 million viewers, 9 million of them in France. Many judge Arte as too highbrow and tend to associate it with Paris elites.

In 2006 France 24, the long-planned French rival to CNN and BBC World, went on the air with international news around the clock. It broadcasted in both French and English and was supposed to add an Arabic channel later. But the Sarkozy government produced a plan to strip it of its independence and to combine it with Radio France Internationale and TV5Monde to form France Monde. Broadcasting in English and Arabic was dropped.

The Arts

France continues to be a land rich and creative, and performing arts, although

France

no longer occupying the indisputably primary position in the world, are top-notch. Its artists have also declined from their pinnacle, but their past greatness is preserved for the world to admire in such great French museums as the Louvre, the Musée d'Orsay, the Beaubourg, and the beautifully renovated Picasso Museum. Such concentration of priceless art presents many tempting targets for thieves, as one saw in 2010. In January a pastel by Edgar Degas was lifted from the Cantini Museum in Marseilles. A week later works by Pablo Picasso and Henri Rousseau were stolen from a private villa. Then in May a single burglar broke into the Paris Museum of Modern Art and stole five paintings by Picasso, Matisse, George Braque, Modigliani and Fernand Léger worth a minimum of $114 million.

Traditions date back hundreds of years in literature, art, music, and the theater. The writings of Voltaire and Rousseau are landmarks in rich French enlightenment. The music of father and son François Couperin were classic; that of Frederic Chopin, Jules Massenet, Camille Saint-Saens, and Claude Debussy, richly postromantic. During the Third Republic before World War I, Paris was enriched by impressionism in art (e.g., Renoir, Monet, Degas) and the reaction to it (Braque, Picasso, cubism, or fauvism). During the same period, there was the positivism of Auguste Comte, the

élan vital of Henry Bergson, in medicine the discoveries of Louis Pasteur, and in physics the discoveries of Pierre and Marie Curie.

In 1988 Maurice Allais became the first Frenchman to win the Nobel Prize for economics, for his study of markets and efficient utilization of resources. This feat was repeated in 2014, when the same prize was won by Jean Tirole of the Toulouse School of Economics. France also won its 15th Nobel Prize in literature in 2014, when Patrick Modiano was honored for his 29 books, plus screenplays, that focus primarily on collaboration and the German occupation of Paris.

The job of French minister of culture is one of great influence and patronage. Today, the arts in France, as almost everything else, receive state subsidies amounting to 1.5% of the national budget. They are highly concentrated in Paris. To try to spread French cultural activity into the provinces, de Gaulle's minister of culture, André Malraux, created cultural centers in 10 provincial cities, financed and operated jointly by the central government and the municipalities. He was a leading French writer and art critic who incurred the wrath of Parisian traditionalists by ordering that all public buildings in Paris be sandblasted to eliminate centuries of soot which had accumulated on them.

These centers are designed to promote artistic creativity and to bring the performing arts into the provinces. In May 2010 the first regional branch of the Pompidou Museum opened in Metz. It can select from among the 65,000 artworks, the largest contemporary collection in Europe, which the Paris Museum has in storage. The centers also serve as places for discussions on contemporary problems. Despite such attempts, many still speak with some justification of "Paris and the desert."

FUTURE

France is undergoing introspection over its place in an enlarged Europe and a world seemingly dominated by American and Anglo-Saxon culture and economic practice. By 2017 it had slid to 25th place in the global ranking of GDP per capita. It has been overtaken by the Netherlands in terms of total exports. The euro crisis beginning in 2010 demonstrated that Germany has become the leader in Europe

and that France is now the junior partner in that important bilateral relationship.

President Macron's Republic on the Move (LRM) Party won a commanding victory in the June 2017 parliamentary elections. With a disappointing turnout of only 49%, it captured far more seats (62%) than the required 289 to win an absolute majority. The Republicans came in a distant second, and the Socialists placed last among the established parties. At first the nation rallied behind the new president, and there was a palpable sense that something dynamic was happening. That has changed. His approval rating has plummeted to under 40%.

Macron faces serious challenges in enacting the reforms which he advocated. As expected, his attempt to loosen the rigid labor laws triggered strikes by rail, airline, energy, and refuse workers. To calm a nervous public fearful of terrorism, the president pledged to tighten rules on immigration and asylum.

In November 2018 a lengthy, sometimes-violent protest exploded. It was set off by a rise in fuel prices and grew to include protest of income insufficiency and inequality, high taxes, and Macron's perceived arrogance and elitism. Calling themselves "Yellow Vests," they tagged him as a "president of the rich." A majority of the French agree with parts of their criticism. In response, Macron launched a "great national debate" and promised to listen to the grievances. Macron is struggling in the pools and striving to reboot his presidency. He changed his prime ministers, naming Jean Castex, a small-town mayor from the south. The party was hammered in the 2020 local elections. It failed to win a single big city; Paris remained in Socialist hands, and the Greens cleaned up.

France has been battered by the coronavirus: in Paris, one person became infected every 30 seconds, including Macron. The government's top priority in the future is to restore Macron's public image and recover from the economic slump brought on by the pandemic.

Long stretches of the banks of the Seine in Paris and rivers in other French cities, such as Bordeaux, are being returned to pedestrian and bicycle traffic. The roads are giving way to parks and gardens or, in the words of the mayor of Paris, "places of life, beauty and culture." No people do that better than the French.

The Principality of Monaco

Aerial view of Monaco showing the Port of Monaco

Area: .575 sq. mi. (1.95 sq. km).

Population: 35,427 (2013).

Capital City: Monaco-Ville.

Climate: Mild Mediterranean.

Neighboring Country: France.

Official Language: French.

Other Principal Tongues: Italian and Monégasque (a mixture of French and Italian) are also spoken.

Ethnic Background: French (50%), Italian (15%), native Monégasques (about 7,100), and diverse other European peoples.

Principal Religion: Roman Catholicism is the state religion.

Main Industries: Banking; tourism; postage stamps; gambling; small industries, such as cosmetics, chemicals, food processing, precision instrument manufacture, glassmaking, and printing.

Major Trading Partners: France, Italy.

Currency: Euro.

Date of Independence: 1338.

National Holiday: November 19.

Chief of State: His Serene Highness Prince Albert II, Sovereign Prince of Monaco, Marquis of Baux (b. 1958), performed duties since July 13, 2005, enthroned November 19, 2005.

Heir Apparent: Prince Jacques Honoré Rainier.

Head of Government: Minister of State (in effect, prime minister) Michel Roger (since March 2010), appointed by the prince. There is also a government counselor for foreign affairs, in 2010 Jean Pastorelli.

National Flag: Red and white horizontal stripes.

The Principality of Monaco is one of the smallest sovereign countries in the world,

smaller even than New York's Central Park. A densely populated, hilly city overlooking the Mediterranean Sea, Monaco is surrounded on three sides by the French Department of Alpes-Maritimes. The French city of Nice is nine miles (15 km) to the west of Monaco, and the Italian border is five miles (8 km) to the east. Three picturesque settlements are now unified into one city. Its older section, situated on top of a steep rock, has maintained its medieval flavor despite some characterless high-rise blocks on the skyline.

Overlooking crowded Riviera beaches and some of the most luxurious tourist resorts in the world is the 13th-century Genoese Palace, which was remodeled in the 16th century in Renaissance style. Here resides the prince of the House of Grimaldi, whose family has ruled Monaco, with periodic interruptions, since 1297. On January 8, 1997, the late Prince Rainier launched a year-long, $270 million celebration of his family's 700-year reign, the longest of any European dynasty.

Evidence of Stone Age settlements has been found within the present borders of Monaco. Founded much later by the Phoenicians, the city was known to the ancient Greeks and Carthaginians. Under the domination of the Romans (who called the city Herculis Moenaci Portus), Monaco was quite prosperous, and it was from Monaco that Julius Caesar set sail for his campaign against Pompeii. Its wealth was destroyed by the invading barbarians, who brought the once-mighty Roman Empire to its knees. In the 7th century, Monaco became a part of the Lombard Kingdom. Later it was absorbed into the Kingdom of Arles and was also subjected

to a period of Muhammadan control. In 1191 the Genoese took control of Monaco, but they ceded domination in 1297 to the reining Grimaldi family.

As a minuscule land in a restless world, the independent principality of Monaco always needed the protection of a stronger power in order to survive. It allied itself first with France. In 1524 it accepted Spain's protection instead, but it returned to French safety in 1641. In 1793 the radicalized French National Convention dispossessed the wealthy and aristocratic Grimaldi rulers and annexed the entire Monacan domain to France. After Napoleon's fall from power, the Congress of Vienna awarded Monaco to the Kingdom of Sardinia as a protectorate in 1814. France repossessed the principality in 1848 and, after greatly reducing its territory, granted independence to the present tiny remainder in 1861.

France today continues to assume responsibility for Monaco's defense, and a 1918 treaty stipulates that Monaco's policies must conform to French political, military, naval, and economic interests. A further treaty of 1919 stipulates that Monaco would be incorporated into France if the reigning prince dies without an heir. This means that the city's self-rule depends entirely on the royal family. A former adviser to the prince explained, "The independence is given to the prince, not to the people and not to the country, and this is why the prince is so important." With the birth of twins to the royal family in December 2014, the succession is clear: although Princess Gabriella Thérèse Marie was born first, her brother, Jacques Honoré Rainier, will be the future ruler.

The Principality of Monaco

His Serene Highness Prince Albert II and the late Prince Rainier III

Prince Rainier III died April 6, 2005. He had been Europe's longest-reigning monarch. Rainier had been educated in Britain, Switzerland, and France and had volunteered for service in the French army in 1944. He married the late American actress Grace Kelly in 1956. She epitomized American affluence and Hollywood glamour and attracted the world's attention to the ruling Grimaldi family. She met an untimely death in an automobile accident on the hilly roads of Monaco in 1982. Their offspring ensure survival of the principality. Grace's magic is still alive, as shown by the popular 2014 film *Grace of Monaco*, starring Nicole Kidman.

Since 1865, an economic union with France governs customs, postal services, telecommunications, and banking. The principality even used the French franc until it adopted the euro when France did in 2002. Although it is not in the EU, it was permitted to mint its own euro coins with its own motif on the back.

Monaco refuses to tax its own citizens, who number only about 20% of the principality's residents. Most of the rest are French. These 7,600 Monégasques also receive preferential employment and housing subsidies. The latter are needed since land, at €24,900 per meter (compared with €14,522 in central London and €6,667 in Paris), is the most expensive in Europe. Housing costs are also the world's highest; in 2010 an apartment was sold for €240 million ($350 million), a world record. They are guaranteed government service jobs, and all companies must make their first job offers to them. Their only penalty was that they were banned from setting foot in the casinos until 2011. There are 35,427 residents (including about 25,000 rich foreigners), but 43,000 commute daily into the principality to work.

Most Monégasques have second homes in nearby Italy or France in order to escape the tourist crush. They also go to France for higher education, but thanks to the principality's healthy economy, they return.

More than half the residents are French, many of whom choose to reside and to locate their businesses in Monaco in order to avoid French taxation. French protests of this situation in 1962 unleashed a serious dispute. Nevertheless, a compromise was worked out in 1963; all French companies that do more than 25% of their business outside of the principality were brought under French financial control. French living in Monaco must pay French taxes. Other nationalities do not. In 2000 verbal warfare broke out again when France threatened to punish the principality unless it took effective measures against money laundering, tax evasion, and drug barons. It demanded that Monaco impose a wealth tax on French residents and disclose details of bank accounts. Compliance would make the principality less attractive.

In 2008 trouble erupted again in the wake of a tax-haven scandal involving tiny Liechtenstein. Attention focused on the other two blacklisted ministates which the OECD declared "uncooperative states" in terms of taxes: Monaco and Andorra. The principality faced the dilemma of how to maintain its banking secrecy while not being misused for tax evasion.

Prince Rainier was not pleased, calling the French attitude "incongruous" and demanding a renegotiation of its treaties with France "to give Monaco back to the Monégasques." The principality likes to portray itself as a secure haven for the well-behaved rich. In response to EU pressure, Monaco agreed in 2003 to collect taxes on foreign accounts and to return 75% of the levy to the country of residence without revealing account holders' names. In 2009 it signaled its readiness to be more transparent and to fight tax fraud in order to stay off the OECD's blacklist of secretive states. It signed 24 tax agreements that got it off the OECD list.

Monaco has undergone a remarkable economic transformation in recent decades. At the end of the 19th century,

gambling and the belle époque casino accounted for 95% of the state's revenues. When Prince Rainier took the throne in 1949 at age 26, his realm was seen, in the words of Somerset Maugham, as "a sunny place for shady people." It was a glitzy but sleazy gambling center. The prince sought to upgrade its image in order to attract wealthy, respectable visitors, depositors, and residents and to provide long-term employment opportunities for native Monégasques. The principality derives half of its income from its 19.6% VAT, with another 13% coming from property sales. There are no income or inheritance taxes. Unemployment is official zero.

His main achievement was to stimulate the local economy by creating thriving banking and tourist industries. Benefiting from tax advantages, banks have doubled in number since the early 1980s to nearly 40. It is estimated that there is 1 cashier for every 400 residents. Tough laws permitting the seizure of profits from drug operations were introduced in 1993 in an effort to keep the banks' money clean. The principality now attracts over 7 million visitors each year. Many are day-trippers from Italy and France. More and more cruise passengers from giant liners are arriving every morning. The annual Grand Prix auto race attracts 150,000 alone. Tourist spending accounts for 25% of GDP. Monaco also has experienced a blooming of commerce and light industry.

In 1967 Prince Rainier won a long struggle with the Greek shipping magnate Aristotle Onassis over control of the famed casino of Monte-Carlo. Monaco's native citizens are not permitted to gamble in the casino, which is now owned by the Société

Monaco mourns the death of Prince Rainier III.

The Principality of Monaco

des Bains de Mer. Contrary to popular belief, less than 5% of the principality's revenues are now derived from its gambling royalties. Still, the social life of Monaco centers around the Place du Casino, with its lovely gardens. The Monte Carlo Philharmonic is one of the world's most recorded orchestras. The principality also boasts first-rate opera and ballet companies, as well as 55 galleries and 50 open-air sculptures.

The deceased prince also oversaw a major building program that changed both the look and the size of the city and won him the nickname "the Builder Prince." Few capitalist countries have such close ties between government and business. Since the town is hemmed in by its land borders, it could only expand outward into the sea. That is what happened. By filling land, he was able to expand Monaco's size by 23% at the expense of the Mediterranean. To win more space, a tunnel was built for the railway that used to dissect the principality. The old harbor was extended by constructing a pier to accommodate the largest cruise ships. Prince Albert II founded an ecology foundation and aims to make the environment his highest priority when developing the city.

Monaco's present constitution, which was promulgated December 17, 1962, reduced the prince's powers somewhat and increased parliamentary powers. Executive power is vested in the hereditary prince, who rules through his appointed minister of state. The latter official must be a French citizen and must be selected from a slate of three candidates put to the principality by the French president. Three state counselors (one of whom must be French) and palace personnel who are appointed by the prince assist the minister of state. France supplies senior civil servants, judges, policemen and firemen. The French judicial system applies in Monaco, and two Parisian judges form the Court of Appeal. Prisoners must serve their sentences outside the principality, usually in France, since its only jail can accommodate suspects awaiting trial but not convicted criminals. With 1 policeman for every 62 residents, this is one of the world's safest places.

Legislative power rests with an 18-member National Council elected by universal suffrage of native Monegasques for five-year terms. The prince shares the legislative powers in that he retains the right to initiate legislation. Although four political parties are now active in Monaco, one party, the National and Democratic Union (UND), dominated for four decades and controlled all 18 National Council seats. That ended with the 2003 elections, when the Union for Monaco coalition won an overwhelming majority.

The funeral of Prince Rainier III, attended by kings, queens and presidents, was held in the very cathedral where he had married Grace. On July 12, 2005, Prince Albert II, whose photo is displayed in every shop, assumed the duties of the throne to become the 31st descendant of Otto Canella, who had founded the house of Grimaldi. He was formally enthroned on November 19, 2005, with only one head of state (the Icelandic president) in attendance. He had graduated from Amherst College in Massachusetts and worked for a while on Wall Street and Moët and Chandon to learn finance and business.

He began early preparing for the transition to rule. He attended government meetings and assumed his father's duties during his frequent illnesses in the last years of his life. Albert was a member of Monaco's bobsled team in the 2002 Winter Olympics in Salt Lake City. He is also a passionate supporter of the AS Monaco soccer team. Non-French foreigners on the team do not have to pay income taxes. This enables the underfunded club to attract good players.

No sooner was his father laid to rest than a former Air France flight attendant from Togo announced that she had had an affair with Albert lasting several years and that her two-year-old son, Alexandre, had been fathered by him. She had been living in the prince's Paris apartment and had access to a villa on the French Riviera. After successfully suing the French weekly magazine *Paris Match* for €50,000 (about $65,000) for invading his privacy by publishing photos of him holding the child, Albert publicly recognized his paternity of the boy.

All Europe chatters about Albert's wife, Charlene, and his children.

The prince admitted in 2006 that he had also sired a daughter, Jazmin Grace, by a then-married California waitress on holiday along the Riviera, Tamara Jean Rotolo. Jazmin was born in 1992 and was a schoolgirl in Palm Desert, California. In 2011 he faced DNA testing for his third paternity. Given the fact that his sister Stephanie has three children out of wedlock and Caroline has two, this news did not shock the principality as one might have expected. Each child whose paternity he recognizes will have a share of his inheritance, estimated at over $1 billion. This will have no effect on the principality's dynastic succession, since only children born in wedlock are eligible.

On July 2, 2011, the 53-year-old monarch married Charlene Wittstock, a 33-year-old Zimbabwean-born South African national swimming champion, whom he met at a swim meet in Monaco in 2000. She is Monaco's first princess consort since Grace died in 1982, and her main duty is to have an heir. To qualify, she converted to Catholicism, the official religion, and took intensive French lessons. They live with their twins in the family's historic palace. To raise money for a needed renovation, the royal family sold 1,000 objects of Napoleon's memorabilia, including hats and stockings, raising €10 million.

France controls Monaco's foreign relations, and the principality is included in the EU through its customs union with France. Since 1993 it is a full member of the United Nations, and it serves on several UN specialized agencies. It also maintains 4 embassies (in Paris, Brussels, Bern, and Rome) and 110 consuls of its own, including ones in Washington and New York. In 1994 it signed a cultural convention under Council of Europe auspices. But because it is not considered to be either completely democratic or independent, it has never formally asked nor been invited to join the Council of Europe.

Monaco has no newspapers of its own, but there is a private radio station (Radio-Monte-Carlo) with programming in French, Italian, and Arabic. Also, Trans-World Radio has a seat in Monte-Carlo and broadcasts in four languages. One private television station (Tele Monte-Carlo) transmits programs in French and Italian.

FUTURE

Before his death in 2005, Prince Rainier III could look back on a half-century of successful rule in his ministate. With Prince Albert II and his 20-year-younger wife, Charlene; a succession to the throne; and an active program of home-based economic diversification, this minuscule 700-year-old principality can expect not only to exist but also to prosper in the coming years.

The BENELUX Nations

NORTH SEA

NETHERLANDS

GERMANY

BELGIUM

FRANCE

LUXEMBOURG

Belgium, the Netherlands, and Luxembourg are located at the crossroads of western Europe. Although they are collectively called BENELUX, a word derived from the first letters of each country's name, these small countries have developed differing traditions, national characters, and problems. Still, they have many things in common, and it is no accident that they cooperate with each other more closely than any other nations of the world. In fact, their example of international cooperation and their steady encouragement of tighter European integration have made them the core and motor for greater unity. The vast majority of the EU's institutions are located in Belgium and Luxembourg.

All three countries are very small and have no natural frontiers that could serve as barriers to unwanted intruders. They have therefore suffered recurrent invasions by all the great European powers. For a century and a half, they tried to keep themselves out of the grips of the major powers by declaring a policy of neutrality. But two disastrous world wars in the 20th century, which spared only the Netherlands from 1914 to 1918, left such a policy and the three countries in shambles. No one can easily forget the lines which the poet John McCrae wrote after visiting the Flemish battlefields: "In Flanders fields the poppies blow between the crosses, row by row."

Having paid a heavy price for their neutrality, all three countries became founding members of NATO in 1949. Its political headquarters are now located on the outskirts of Brussels, and its military headquarters, the Supreme Headquarters of the Allied Powers in Europe (SHAPE), are located outside of Mons, Belgium.

The Netherlands and Belgium have the highest population density of all Europe. All three have great numbers of foreign workers who bring both needed labor and social problems with them. These countries are not particularly rich in raw materials, but they have productive economies that have provided standards of living and social welfare systems for their populations that are almost unmatched in the world. Their central location and access to the sea made them prosperous trading nations, and the ports of Rotterdam and Antwerp are the largest and most active in Europe. With relatively small populations and high prosperity, these countries are heavily dependent upon trade and, therefore, upon economic and political conditions beyond their borders. Roughly half of these countries' GDP results from foreign trade. This heavy volume is an economic blessing, as well as a possible liability for the future.

To help secure their trade, they were pioneers in economic unions. In 1922 Belgium and Luxembourg formed the Belgium-Luxembourg Economic Union (BLEU), which made the two countries a unit for importing and exporting purposes. It also established a unified railway, customs area, and currency for the two countries. Luxembourg coined and printed money below 100 francs for local circulation, but Belgian currency remained dominant until the euro in 2002. The three countries' governments-in-exile in London in 1944 formed a customs union called BENELUX, which was later extended to include even noncustoms matters. Because of the striking difference in postwar recovery, BENELUX did not come into effect until January 1948.

In 1952 they were founding members with France, West Germany, and Italy of the European Coal and Steel Community (ECSC), with headquarters located in Luxembourg. Not only was it a farsighted idea to share these commodities, so crucial for heavy industry, rather than to risk fighting over them, but also the ECSC gave these nations the practice in economic cooperation needed to convince the six that a bold move to create a united Europe could succeed. The six signed the Treaty of Rome in 1957, and in 1958 the European Economic Community (Common Market) came into existence. Later the community grew, and its name was changed first to the European Community (EC) and then in 1993 to the European Union (EU) in order to emphasize that the union was someday to become a political one, as well as an economic one. None tried harder than the BENELUX countries to keep the idea of a united Europe alive in the 1960s, when the six were seriously split over the question of British entry.

All three countries are constitutional, parliamentary monarchies, whose monarchs are relatively popular, though not powerful. As modern constitutional monarchs, they "reign but do not rule." In contrast to the monarchy in Great Britain, which can be traced back more than 1,000 years, the BENELUX monarchies are young. The oldest, in the Netherlands, dates back to 1813. Throughout the centuries these small countries have been tossed back and forth among the great powers of Europe and have sometimes been forced together and sometimes split apart. A quick glance at their history shows why they have so much in common and are nevertheless different from each other.

Early History

The early history of these three countries is so intertwined that it is best considered by grouping them together.

About a half-century before Christ, after a long and destructive campaign, the Roman legions conquered the tenacious Celtic tribes, including the Belgeai and Treveri. In his commentary *The Gallic Wars*, Julius Caeser used the name "Belgium" to refer to all the territory we now call the BENELUX countries. This area, especially what is today Belgium and Luxembourg, was dominated for more than 300 years by the Romans, who built roads and villas and introduced agriculture, especially vineyards and fruit orchards. They also brought Christianity to the area, but it did not begin to flourish until the 6th and 7th centuries.

When Attila the Hun invaded what is now Germany, Germanic tribes were thrown into the Low Countries (the Netherlands) in about 300. Two centuries later another Germanic tribe, the Franks, invaded the area and established a linguistic frontier that exists today in the middle of what is now Belgium. North of the line, the Germanic tongues evolved into the Dutch language and into Flemish, a Dutch dialect spoken in northern Belgium. South of the line, vulgarized Latin, which developed into French, was spoken. Thus in Belgium the Latin and Germanic worlds met face to face and presented Belgium with a problem which, many centuries later, threatened to tear the country apart.

In the 8th and 9th centuries the entire territory that had been fragmented into many duchies, principalities, and other political units became a part of Charlemagne's empire. This was the time when the political center of gravity in Europe shifted from the Mediterranean to the northwestern regions. His great empire fell apart soon after his death, and for several centuries the BENELUX people saw their land converted into a constant battlefield between French and German contenders for control. During this time the Crusades opened up trade with the Orient, and especially Belgium experienced a flowering of trade and urban development. The beautiful canal city of Bruges became a wealthy city of trade and the arts. In the 15th century, the Dukes of Burgundy, who were among the most powerful in Europe, began to acquire control over what is now Belgium and Luxembourg by means of conquest, marriage, or land purchase.

Only the Netherlands was able to resist the Burgundian encroachment. As a country whose development had been retarded by its preoccupation with fighting back the sea, the Netherlands was not a very tempting target for Burgundian expansion anyway. At the end of the 15th century, the last descendent, Mary of Burgundy, married Maximilian of Austria, and the Burgundian holdings in the area passed into the Hapsburg family. Their son, Philip the Handsome, married the Spanish princess Juana of Castile; Spain and Spanish America also came under Hapsburg control.

A son born of this union in 1500 in the Flemish city of Ghent was destined to become one of Europe's greatest rulers. He became king of Spain in 1516 and the Holy Roman emperor in 1519. He was Charles V, and by 1543 he had unified all of what is now the BENELUX area, except the county of Liège, which led a separate existence until the 18th century. Charles ruled his far-flung empire from Brussels, a city established in 979 on the islands of the Senne River, which was then called "Bruocsella." His reign was a time of great economic prosperity and artistic and intellectual bloom for the "Seventeen Provinces," as the Luxembourg area was then called. This was the time of the great humanist Erasmus of Rotterdam; of Mercator, the

The Holy Roman emperor, Charles V

171

The BENELUX Nations

most widely known cartographer in the world; and of the painters van Eyck and Pieter Breugal.

The unity of the Seventeen Provinces might have survived if the Reformation which Martin Luther unleashed in 1519 had not divided Europe and with it the Low Countries. Charles V abdicated in 1555 in favor of his son Philip II, who had been raised in Spain; he decided to rule the empire from Madrid, leaving the administration of the Seventeen Provinces to governors. He was, however, determined to defend the Catholic faith, and he was cruel and inflexible in attempting to suppress the Protestant movement, which, in its Calvinist form, was particularly strong in the Netherlands. William of Orange-Nassau led Protestant resistance in the northern provinces. Because Spain was so severely weakened by its continuous struggles against England and France during the second half of the 16th century, the Netherlands was able to secure its independence in 1581.

Until Napoleon's conquests in the 1790s, the Dutch took control of their own destiny, while the Belgians and Luxembourgers continued to be dominated by other powers. In order to give the latter a sense of autonomy, Philip gave the southern provinces to his daughter, the Archduchess Isabella, and her husband, the Archduke Albert of Austria. It was a relatively happy time when the painter Peter Paul Rubens reached the height of his creativity. When Albert and Isabella died childless, the provinces reverted to Spain in 1621, and until 1713 the Hapsburgs fought over control of the area.

In one campaign in 1695, the French Marshal Villeroy, under orders of Louis XIV, bombarded the beautiful Grand Place in Brussels, with its majestic town hall, built around 1400; it survived only with its tower and its thickest walls. This disaster merely stiffened the courage and determination of the Brussels population, which began the very next day restoring the structure. The best artistic and architectural talent in the city joined in recreating one of man's greatest architectural treasures. Jan Van Ruysbroeck, the city's master mason, rebuilt the town hall. Wishing to retain the foundation and porch of the old bell tower while extending the new walls as far as possible, he placed the main portal of the town hall off-center with the central axis of the tower. Legend wrongly has it that he threw himself to his death when he discovered the error, but the "error" was in fact intentional. The Grand Place remains the vibrant heart of the city and has always been a favorite subject for painters and poets. It is a place for open-air markets, public meetings, political assemblies, royal receptions, and coronations. Earlier

it was the favorite place for launching revolutions and for public executions. Each year, on a summer evening, the Grand Place is transformed into its medieval setting for a historical procession called the "Ommegang."

Both Luxembourg and Belgium passed into the hands of the Austrians, who renamed Belgium the "Austrian Netherlands" and who ruled over these provinces until 1794–1795, when French troops snatched them away. The Austrians had exercised a benevolent dictatorship, but some Luxembourgers, Flemings, and Walloons were infected by the fever of revolution emanating from France and welcomed the changes that came with the French republican troops. Belgium fell to the French in 1794, and the following year French revolutionary forces conquered Luxembourg and the Netherlands, which had been greatly weakened by its series of wars against England.

The French occupation brought fundamental changes to the Netherlands, which had been ruled by an enlightened oligarchy, with a high official called a Stadhouder (not a monarch) at the top. Although it was not a modern democracy, in that leaders who were exercising power had been elected by universal suffrage, the Dutch republic had nevertheless been one of the most democratic countries in Europe, with the possible exception of Switzerland. The old republic had been highly decentralized, with each province stressing its independent powers. The new regime that the French created and called The Batavian Republic, named after one of the tribes who had populated the

country in the Roman period and who had revolted against Roman domination, was highly centralized in conformity with the French constitution.

The Napoleonic Code of laws and the selection of members of parliament on the basis of limited but free elections were also introduced. The Dutch grew restive under French control, especially after the Batavian Republic was abolished and Louis Napoleon, the brother of the French emperor, was made king of Holland in 1806. Quarrels with his brother forced Louis to abdicate in 1810, but only after he had tried unsuccessfully to have his son, who later became Napoleon III of France, crowned in his place. The Netherlands was annexed directly into the French Empire in 1810. Again, Napoleon's reversals gave the Dutch the chance to reassert their independence. In 1813, after Napoleon's defeat in the Battle of Leipzig, the son of the last Dutch Stadhouder, who had fled to England, landed at Scheveningen, not far from The Hague, and was proclaimed William I of the House of Orange-Nassau, king of the Netherlands. For the first time, the Netherlands became a monarchy with a Dutch monarch on the throne. Dutch troops took an active part in the final defeat of Napoleon.

In late 1794 French troops besieged the fortress of Luxembourg, which did not fall until mid-1795. It was annexed to France in the fall; French rule was very unpopular at first, but Napoleon was gradually able to smooth out many problems. When the French left the duchy in 1814, they left behind many positive and lasting gifts: the idea of equality, centralized and efficient administration, and the Napoleonic Code.

Gustav Wappers Episone of September Days 1830

172

The French were at first widely greeted in Belgium as liberators, and the introduction of the Napoleonic Code and an efficient, centralized administration was generally seen as an improvement over the old regime. Almost no one seemed to have realized at the time that decentralization would have helped Belgium's language groups to live together more harmoniously in a unified Belgian state. But the seemingly endless Napoleonic Wars soon sapped the Belgians' enthusiasm. After Napoleon began suffering disastrous reversals, especially in Russia in 1812, the Belgians joined the enemies of France. It was outside Brussels near a small town named Waterloo that the little dictator was defeated for the last time.

When the great powers of Europe met at the Congress of Vienna in 1814–1815, they combined the Netherlands, Belgium, and Luxembourg to form the Kingdom of the United Netherlands, with the monarch William I as king. European leaders, who suspected that they had supported the French too enthusiastically, distrusted the Belgians. They believed that the Belgians, therefore, needed to be controlled by the Dutch king. Further, the east Belgian cantons of Eupen, Malmedy, and Saint Vith were ceded to Prussia, whose borders had been moved as far west as possible in order to prevent any future eastward French expansion.

The union of the three countries did not last long. In 1830 the sparks of revolution flying from Paris landed in Brussels. The overwhelmingly Catholic Flemings and Walloons (Belgians who speak French) sensed religious discrimination by the predominantly Protestant Calvinist Dutch, despite the tradition of religious tolerance in the Netherlands.

Although it was the only thing that drew Flemings and Walloons together, Catholicism was enough to unify them against the Dutch. Such religious unity was later to prove the weakest of glue to hold the state of Belgium together. The use of Dutch in the south and in Brussels had been resented by the economically and culturally more influential French-speaking Walloons. The determination to elevate the French language above Dutch also was later to create extremely serious problems for this bilingual country. The eruption occurred in 1830, after an opera performance with a liberation theme. After a brief skirmish in Brussels, Dutch troops withdrew, and a provisional government proclaimed independence within three months. Seeing the utility of a buffer state on the European continent, the British announced that they would thenceforth guarantee Belgium's neutrality.

A liberal constitution, which is still in force, was proclaimed placing sovereignty in the people and providing for a constitutional monarchy. A German prince, Leopold I of Saxe-Coburg, who happened also to be a British citizen, became king in 1831. Since sovereignty was placed in the hands of the people, there was no doubt that the parliament, as the representative of the Belgian people, would be superior to the monarch. French was also declared to be the new country's official language.

The Dutch reacted to these events by attempting to invade Belgium, but the French and British announced their determination not to allow the Dutch to reassert their control. At a London Conference of 1831, a border between the Netherlands and Belgium was drawn, but this settlement pleased neither the Belgians, who claimed about half of Luxembourg, nor the Dutch, whose king wanted no settlement at all which would reduce the size of his kingdom. Finally, the Treaty of Twenty-Four Articles, signed in London in 1839, granted the Dutch a slice of northern Belgium. Belgium, in turn, was compensated through a grant of about half of Luxembourg's territory. Further, the great European powers guaranteed the neutrality of Belgium and Luxembourg. This settlement finally satisfied all but the Luxembourgers, who saw their already-tiny state reduced to about one-fourth of its pre-1815 size.

The Congress of Vienna had made Luxembourg (which means "Little Castle") an autonomous duchy, with the Dutch king as the grand duke, but Luxembourg lost all its territory east of the Moselle, Sure, and Our Rivers. The congress also made Luxembourg a member of the German Confederation and granted the Prussians the right to man the fortress in the capital city in order to be able to keep a closer eye on the recently defeated French. This arrangement meant that Luxembourg was wide open to Dutch royal ideas, Prussian military demands, and Belgium's liberal cravings.

At first the Dutch king ruled in a rather authoritarian way, and when the Belgians rebelled against Dutch rule in 1830, most Luxembourgers outside the capital city also arose. Although they were unable to establish their independence, Luxembourgers were gradually able to create separate institutions and administrations. Political autonomy was granted in 1839, and in 1848 the country received a liberal constitution similar to that of Belgium. The Dutch became more benevolent rulers and cooperated in Luxembourg's movement toward democracy and independence. Finally, in 1867 the Treaty of London, drawn up in an attempt to reconcile differences between Bismarck of Germany and Napoleon III of France, proclaimed Luxembourg an independent and neutral country. Only a year later, Luxembourg adopted a constitution that in revised form remains in force. Upon the insistence of Napoleon III, the Prussians withdrew from the duchy, and the fortress was razed.

The only disappointment for the Luxembourgers was that the Dutch king remained the grand duke. However, when in 1890 there were no male heirs to the Dutch throne, Adolf of Nassau, whose family was related to the Dutch ruling family, became the grand duke of Luxembourg and chose to reside in Luxembourg City. Nevertheless, the close historical ties with the Netherlands continue to be symbolized by the fact that the two countries have almost exactly the same flag.

From 1890 on, all three BENELUX countries have been fully independent and sovereign states. Proximity, economic interests, and political values continue to bind these three democracies very closely together.

The Monnaie Theater, Brussels, where the torch of liberation was lit

The Kingdom of the Netherlands

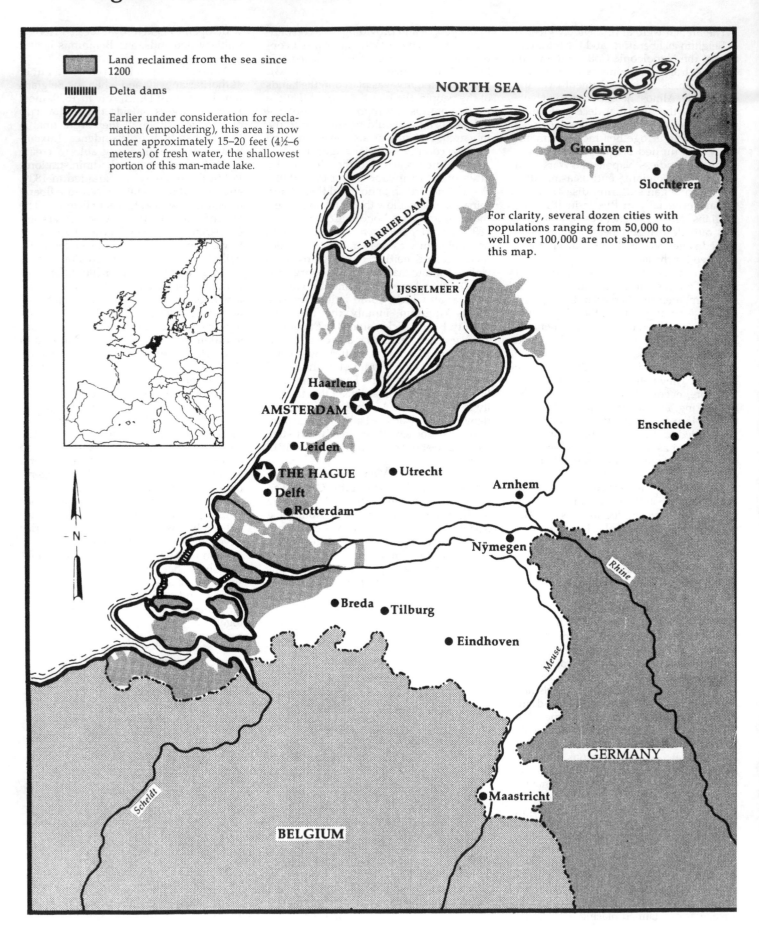

Land reclaimed from the sea since 1200

Delta dams

Earlier under consideration for reclamation (empoldering), this area is now under approximately 15–20 feet (4½–6 meters) of fresh water, the shallowest portion of this man-made lake.

NORTH SEA

Groningen

Slochteren

BARRIER DAM

IJSSELMEER

For clarity, several dozen cities with populations ranging from 50,000 to well over 100,000 are not shown on this map.

Haarlem

AMSTERDAM

Enschede

Leiden

THE HAGUE

Utrecht

Delft

Arnhem

Rotterdam

Nÿmegen

Rhine

N

Breda

Tilburg

Eindhoven

Meuse

GERMANY

Scheldt

Maastricht

BELGIUM

The Netherlands

Area: 16,163 sq. mi. (41,863 sq. km, twice the size of New Jersey and one-half the size of Virginia).

Population: 17.4 million

Capital City: Amsterdam (pop. 740,000). The city has more bicycles than people. The seat of government is The Hague (pop. 530,000, est.).

Climate: Temperate, with mild winters, cool summers.

Neighboring Countries: Germany (east); Belgium (south); England (west, 90 miles across the North Sea).

Official Languages: Dutch; Frisian in Friesland in the north.

Other Principal Tongues: English, German.

Ethnic Background: Frisian in the north, Saxon in the east and central part of the nation, Frankish south of the rivers.

Principal Religions: Roman Catholic (about one-third); Dutch Reformed Lutheran (about one-fifth); Muslim (5.5%, growing by 3.9% per year); Hindu (about .5%); about 40% profess belief in no religion.

Main Exports: Machinery and transport equipment; chemicals and plastics; agricultural products, largely dairy; processed foods; fish and fish products; petroleum products and natural gas.

Main Imports: Machinery and transport equipment, chemicals, foodstuffs, fuels, clothing and cotton, base metals and ores, pulp, pulpwood, lumber, feed grains, edible oils.

Major Trading Partners: EU (77% of exports and 46.3% of imports), Germany (29.9% of exports and 17% of imports), Belgium (16.1% of exports and 10.1% of imports), France (10.6% of exports), UK (8.7% of exports and 7.1% of imports), China (13.8% of imports), US (7.9% of imports).

Currency: Euro.

National Holiday: April 30, official birthday of former Queen Juliana. Liberation day, May 5, is celebrated every five years.

Chief of State: His Majesty King Willem-Alexander (b. 1967), since April 30, 2013. Married Maxima Zorreguieta of Argentina, 2002.

Heir Apparent: Her Royal Highness Crown Princess Catharina-Amalia Beatrix Carmen Victoria, Princess of Orange (b. 2003).

Head of Government: Mark Rutte, Prime Minister (since October 2010).

National Flag: Three horizontal stripes of red, white, and blue, almost identical to the flag of Luxembourg, which has a pale blue stripe.

Benjamin Franklin once said, "In love of liberty and in the defense of it, Holland has been our example." Indeed, when the Dutch declared their independence from Spain in 1581, they justified their act in words which in some ways are very reminiscent of those which Thomas Jefferson wrote in the American Declaration of Independence almost 200 years later: "As it is apparent to all that a prince is constituted by God to be the ruler of the people . . . and whereas God did not create the people slaves to their prince, to obey his commands, whether right or wrong, but rather the prince for the sake of the subjects. . . . And when he does not behave thus, but on the contrary oppresses them . . . they may not only disallow his authority, but legally proceed to the choice of another prince for their defense." Although their independence was not recognized internationally until 1648, the Dutch had already taken command of their own destiny and established a republic based on the ideas that government should be limited and directed exclusively toward the well-being of the people.

A 1,000-year struggle against the sea helped to shape a people who are hardworking, persistent, efficient, and imaginative. It is a fact of history that nations have expanded their borders at the expense of other nations. Even the Dutch call the Netherlands "Holland," though North and South Holland were traditionally merely the richest two provinces in the country. By official government decree, however, as of January 1, 2021, all communications will use "the Netherlands" as the country's name. It is one of the few nations whose expansion has been at the expense of the sea, not of other peoples. According to an old Dutch saying, "the Lord made heaven and earth, but the Dutch made Holland!" For centuries the Dutch built and strengthened dunes and dikes to hold back the sea.

Since the 15th century, they constructed windmills everywhere to convert the sea winds into energy to pump water back into the sea. Now they are being built or refurbished to kill two birds with one stone: to generate electricity and to save the roughly 1,040 remaining structures that are gradually falling into disrepair. Like tulips and Gouda cheese, windmills reflect that nature and tradition of the country. At a time when immigration is changing the face of cities, many Dutch want to look around them and see symbols of their roots. The government has built an enormous farm of mills far off the coast, and there are plans for a second wind farm.

Today, 40% of the country is below sea level, and if the Dutch were not constantly vigilant, about 60% of the country would become unusable for any purpose or disappear underwater from the North Sea or the Rhine, Meuse, and Scheldt Rivers and their tributaries. It is precisely in that portion that more than 60% of the Dutch live and work and that most of Holland's

HOLDING BACK THE SEA: DUNES, DIKES, DAMS

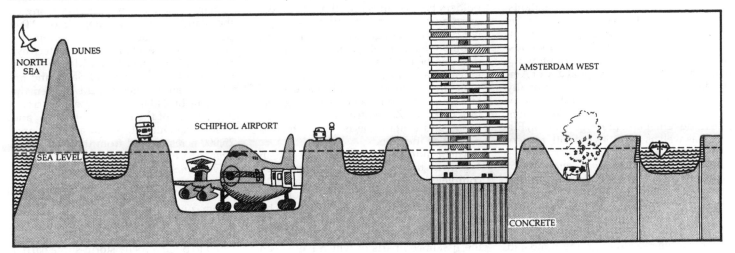

The Netherlands

The Barrier under construction . . .

. . . and completed in 1932

industry is located. Amsterdam is built entirely on piles and has so much water that it has 1,281 bridges. The visitor flying into Holland can scarcely imagine that Schiphol Airport, near Amsterdam, where he would probably land, is 4.5 meters below sea level. It is the only airport in the world that was once (in 1573) the scene of a naval battle.

Despite the almost-miraculous land reclamation the Dutch have achieved, there is still too little land. The Netherlands is the most densely populated country in Europe, with an average of almost 1,000 people per square mile (480 per sq. km). If the United States were as densely populated, it would have about 3 billion inhabitants. Of course, density is even greater in the horseshoe-shaped megalopolis surrounding a "green heart" of lakes and woods, called the Randstad (literally "rim-town"), which encompasses the capital city of Amsterdam (where merchants traditionally lived), The Hague (the seat of the government and the royal residence), Rotterdam (the trade center and the largest port in Europe), as well as the cities of Delft, Leiden, and Utrecht.

Its population density is twice that of Japan. Almost half the country's population lives in this area, which covers only about one-fifth of the total land area. Such concentration has made urban difficulties and pollution the most pressing of all Dutch problems, although the Randstad

provides a model for meeting the needs of its 7 million inhabitants.

The Netherlands is located on the North Sea at the mouth of three large rivers—the Rhine, the Meuse, and the Scheldt—and with the large port in Amsterdam as well, it truly deserves the name "Gateway to the heart of Europe." It has a predominantly low-lying, flat landscape; the highest elevation is only 323 meters. It is crisscrossed by lakes and waterways, which cover a total of 10% of the country's land area, about half of which consists of polders—land surrounded by dikes and drained artificially. There are many hundreds of such polders because in earlier times the areas were pumped by windmills, which were not powerful enough to drain them. Now, with modern technology, much larger polders can be created. Dutch hydraulic engineers have been among the most ingenious in the world and have successfully tackled projects one can only call gigantic in scope. The Zuiderzee (renamed Ijsselmeer) and Delta Projects have attracted particular attention.

The Zuiderzee Project was begun in 1920, with the expectation that it would be completed within 40 years. The idea was to seal off the Zuiderzee Bay in the northern part of the country from the North Sea by means of a 20-mile dam called the Barrier Dam. This created a large, freshwater lake, the Ijsselmeer, parts of which have been

pumped dry and converted into farmland and recreation areas. If needed, residential areas for Amsterdam also could be created. The Barrier Dam was completed in 1932, and four out of five of the planned polders were created. Extremely high costs, environmental worries, and disagreements concerning how the reclaimed land should best be used prevented the fifth from being completed.

In the 1950s a much larger project dramatically claimed a higher priority in the minds of the Dutch. On February 1, 1953, floodwaters from the North Sea surged into the Delta area in the southwestern corner of the country, covering many of the islands there and killing almost 2,000 persons. An audacious plan was promptly adopted to close off most of the waterways of the Rhine, Scheldt, and Meuse Rivers from the sea by a chain of dams and artificial islands. They would shorten the coastline by 440 miles, reverse the increasing salinity of the inland waterways and enable the Dutch to claim an additional 25,000 acres of land from the sea, if they ever choose to do so.

Only one dam across the Eastern Scheldt was left to be completed when a violent verbal storm erupted over the effect such a dam could have on the plant and animal life in the estuary. The environmentalists' influence was so great that parliament decided to build a costly storm-surge barrier instead of the planned solid dam. This change, which would better protect the ecological system, added more than $1 billion to the costs, delayed completion until 1986, required entire new technology, and could result in a barrier that might not last more than 50 years.

Queen Beatrix officially opened the Oosterscheldedam, assuring her subjects that "nature is under control but not disturbed." Indeed, this two-mile dam is "the ultimate insurance policy." This barrier, costing $5 billion, is the most expensive maritime project in the nine centuries since the Dutch have been building dikes to hold back the sea. It is a movable barrier, anchored by 65 concrete piers as large as grain elevators, which lowers 62 gigantic steel gates at the touch of a button to block off the rampaging North Sea whenever a serious storm threatens. Unless they are lowered, the tides continue to flow into the Rhine estuary as usual. This "compromise barrier" was a victory for the vocal Dutch environmental lobby. Large, manmade changes in the Netherlands' geography on the scale of the past are more difficult. But in 1997 the Dutch completed a storm-surge barrier to protect Rotterdam.

Experts calculated that the gates will need to be closed only once every five years or so. When another storm like that in 1953 raged again in 1995, a quarter of a million Dutch were forced to evacuate their homes. Such a dam could mean the difference between survival and total disaster for the inhabitants of Zeeland.

In 1995 the Dutch were caught looking the wrong way. Having focused on the North Sea, they were struck this time by man-made perils along the Rhine and Meuse Rivers. Marshes and floodplains once acted as sponges, soaking up surges of water. But in order to create residential and industrial property, people all the way along the river have dried out, asphalted, cemented, and buttressed with embankments the earlier waterlogged land. Changes in farming practices have also reduced the land's capacity to absorb rainwater. Worst of all, stretches of the Rhine have been straightened, reducing the meander to the sea and doubling the water's speed from Basel. This lessens the river system's ability to accommodate floodwaters. Holland's dikes held in 1995, but they were weakened by what many called "the flood of the century."

Alarm bells were rung, alerting the Dutch, 40% of whom live below sea level, that they must again mobilize for a renewed campaign to salvage their lands and themselves. This is especially urgent given the prospect of global warming. Children must learn to swim with their clothes on by age 6, and the government provides universal flood insurance to homeowners.

New parks, squares, and parking garages in Rotterdam double as a drainage system. In east Amsterdam new floating communities are beginning to be constructed. Houses, which start at about $600,000, are on floating platforms of reinforced concrete and rise with the floodwaters.

The Netherlands is still a country where the old can be seen alongside the new. Windmills are plentiful, although only about 1,000 serve their original purpose. For centuries the flowerbed of Europe, Holland in April almost seems like a gigantic bouquet of tulips, daffodils, narcissuses, and hyacinths. In a few isolated villages, one can find men in baggy pants and wooden shoes and women in floppy hats and bustling skirts. Yet the Netherlands is an extremely prosperous and heavily industrialized country, with a people whose dress is now more casual and modern. The Dutch stand out as among the tallest people in the world, with the average Dutchman six feet and woman five feet seven, three inches taller than their American-born counterparts. It is a dynamic country whose modern look prevails over the traditional.

HISTORY

The Emergence of the Netherlands

Protestant leaders in the northernmost provinces of the Spanish Empire signed, in 1579, the Declaration of Utrecht, swearing to defend liberty and religious freedom. Predictably the Catholic Spanish king was unwilling to accept such freedom in the area he controlled, so in 1581 the northern provinces declared their complete independence of Spain. William, Prince of Orange-Nassau, also known as William the Silent, became the first head (stadholder or *Stadhouder* in Dutch) of the newly born Dutch Republic. He was assassinated by order of Spanish King Philip II, but the young republic was able to resist Spanish efforts to reassert control. Aided initially by the English and by a fortuitous storm which decimated a mighty Spanish naval armada in 1588, the Dutch conducted a brilliant land campaign, led by Prince Maurice, son of William the Silent, and forced the Spanish to vacate the Netherlands in 1595. Although more wars with the Spanish followed, the Peace of Westphalia internationally recognized Dutch independence in 1648.

The 17th century was one in which the Dutch were involved in almost-constant war, but it was for them also one of commercial success, naval supremacy, and cultural bloom. It was the Netherlands' "Golden Age," and Dutch confidence and prosperity were vividly recorded in the paintings of the Dutch masters. It was the century in which Amsterdam quadrupled its population to 200,000 inhabitants and became a major point of departure for the entire world. It was also a city that even at that time was constantly *moving inland* as more and more land was reclaimed from the sea. In 1609 the Bank of Amsterdam was established, 85 years before the Bank

On top of the Zeeland storm-surge barrier

The Netherlands

Manhattan Island about 1627 . . . and today

of England, and Dutch financiers were among the most influential in the world. It was also a time of philosophical and scientific discovery.

Trade and Colonization

By the middle of the 17th century, the Dutch had 16,289 seagoing vessels and 160,000 seamen. Their traders could be found in every corner of the globe, most often representing such huge private companies as the Dutch East and West India Companies, which had been chartered by parliament, called the States General. They traded virtually all over Europe, and their activities extended to central Asia, where they had obtained the first tulip bulbs in the 16th century; India; Ceylon (now Sri Lanka); Japan; Formosa; and Indonesia, where they established a colony which they controlled until 1949. In 1652 they established a colony at a good stopping-off place on the southern tip of Africa.

This Cape colony was snatched by the British in 1806, but the Dutch descendants packed their belongings in 1836–1838 and moved in a "Great Trek" into the interior of what is now the Republic of South Africa and established the Afrikaner colony of Transvaal in 1852 and the Orange Free State in 1854. Ultimately these Dutch (together with French Huguenot descendants), who speak a dialect of Dutch called Afrikaans, became the predominant white group in the Republic of South Africa that was created from a union of Dutch-settled areas and British colonies. Until well into the 20th century, the Dutch retained great sympathy for their Afrikaner relatives, who had created an economically prosperous state in an inhospitable land and who had successfully resisted cultural assimilation by the British who previously had political control of the area as a colony. However, the Dutch gradually turned against the Afrikaners because of the latter's policy of racial segregation known as apartheid, an Afrikaans word meaning "separate." Until majority rule was introduced in 1994, the Dutch were among South Africa's most determined foes.

In 1609 a navigational failure brought the Dutch to North America. In that year Henry Hudson, an English sea captain in the service of the Dutch East India Company, sailed westward in search of a passage to the East Indies and China. He failed in his mission, but his ship, the *Half Moon*, bumped into what is now New York and cruised up a hitherto unknown river that now bears his name. It was the fate of America in its earliest days to be visited by seamen who actually wanted to get somewhere else. Hudson's contact with America resulted in the establishment of the Dutch West India Company and in subsequent settlement of the New World.

In 1614, six years before the Pilgrim fathers landed, the Dutch established Fort Nassau on an island just below the present-day city of Albany, New York, a city which the Dutch incorporated in 1652 as the town of Beverwych. In 1625 an even more important fort and town had been founded on Manhattan Island, and five family farms were established to supply the soldiers and merchants. The name of the town was Nieuw (New) Amsterdam, and it was soon to become the most important city in the Dutch North American colony, called New Netherland. Only a year later, the Dutch governor made the famous deal with the local Indians, buying the whole of Manhattan Island for 30 guilders' worth of merchandise, which by today's exchange rates is worth only about $12 but which was worth considerably more in 1625. It was nevertheless an extraordinarily favorable exchange for the Dutch.

In the next two decades, New Netherland continued to grow but at a much slower rate than the British colonies in New England and Virginia, whose populations outnumbered the Dutch settlers by at least four to one. New Amsterdam had a population that did not exceed 700 by 1647. Its boundaries, if one looks at a present-day map of New York City, extended to Pearl Street and to the northern wall, called *de wal*, which gave the name to what is now perhaps the richest street in the world, Wall Street. Under the last Dutch governor, Pieter Stuyvesant, the city grew to 1,500 (1664) and boasted two windmills and one church.

It was a very cosmopolitan city in which reportedly 18 languages were spoken. In strict accordance with Dutch West India policy, religious or other discrimination was forbidden. It was therefore much more tolerant than the Massachusetts Bay colony to the north. It was also much more fun to live in New Netherland. There were many inns for drinking and dancing, and sports were a favorite activity. One such sport imported from Holland was called *kolf*, which developed into modern golf.

The Dutch continued to found cities in their colony. Among them were what are now the Bronx, Staten Island, Breukelen (Brooklyn), Haarlem (Harlem), Bergen (now Jersey City), Hackensack, and Ridgewood. But the growth of New Netherland was halted abruptly by one of the three wars Holland fought against England in the 17th century. When British ships of war sailed into the harbor of New Amsterdam in 1664, Governor Stuyvesant saw no alternative to surrendering the colony to the English.

Although the Dutch won the colony back for a year in 1673–1674, their foothold on North America was lost. They also lost their settlements in Brazil, although they managed to hold on to Dutch Guiana (since 1975 the independent nation of Suriname) on the northern coast of South America and to a handful of Caribbean islands known as the Netherlands Antilles. It was partially dissolved in 2007, although the islands retain differing legal ties to the Netherlands. In October 2010 most of the remaining islands were made free, albeit remaining under the Dutch Crown and subject to Dutch foreign and defense policy. But Dutch influence did not totally disappear from North America. Governor Stuyvesant returned to his beloved city, renamed New York, to live on his farm on Manhattan Island. His *bouwerij*, the Dutch word for "farm," gave the name for a famous run-down area now undergoing gentrification in New York City known by its Americanized name—the Bowery.

In 2009 New York celebrated the 400th anniversary of Henry Hudson's arrival. The Dutch organized the events and paid $10 million of the costs. Thousands of Dutch came over to participate, including Crown Prince Willem-Alexander, who declared New York to be the greatest city in the world.

Holland and the United States

In 1775 the Netherlands was the first foreign nation to fire a salute to the newly designed American flag, and in 1782 it was the third country formally to recognize the independence of the US, after Morocco and France. It was America's major source for loans, although it must be said that Dutch lenders at the same time provided loans to the British.

The Netherlands also left influences in the New World that became a part of American history and culture. Many famous Americans, including James Madison, Martin van Buren, Zachary Taylor, Ulysses S. Grant, Jefferson Davis, Theodore Roosevelt, and Franklin D. Roosevelt, descended from Dutch settlers. Also, some words, such as "skate" (from *schaats*), "cookie" (*koekje*), "cole slaw" (*kool sla*), "cruller" (*krullen*), "halibut," and "pickle," as well as such seafaring expressions as "skipper," "marline," "hoist," and "yacht" entered English through the Dutch language. Perhaps the most famous, however, was the corruption of the popular Dutch name in the 17th century, Jan-Kees, which came to be applied to all persons from the United States: Yankees. Kids and boxers can be grateful to the Dutch for bringing rope-skipping to America. The first serving American president to visit the Netherlands was George H. W. Bush, who in July 1989 paid tribute to the contributions made by the Dutch in America, especially their strong spirit of freedom.

Decline and Political Change

In the numerous wars during the 17th century, particularly against the English, the Dutch did not always fare badly. One time, during the reign of Charles II of England, as Samuel Pepys described in his diary, the Dutch admiral de Ruyter sailed up the Thames, burning British warships at Chatham right outside of London Harbor

Golf and skating on ice, 17th century (van der Neer)

The Netherlands

and putting the city into a panic. This event was a high point in Dutch history and is still commemorated in Holland. The Dutch were also able to frustrate the plans of Louis XIV to conquer the Netherlands.

Nevertheless, Holland was exhausted by almost-continuous war, and it became clear by the end of the 17th century that the Netherlands had assumed a position in the world that was out of proportion to its resources and size. It was propped up to some extent in the 18th century by a close tie with England. When James II of England decided to remain a Catholic, parliament offered the throne in 1688 to the Protestant Dutch stadholder, Prince William III of Orange-Nassau, who had fought the English only ten years earlier. William reigned with his wife, Mary, the daughter of the deposed James II. The childless couple ruled until 1702, and it was after them that the College of William and Mary in Williamsburg, Virginia, was named, as well as Nassau Hall at Prince-ton University. The 18th century was for Holland one of political and cultural decline. When the French came again in 1795, the Dutch were unable to offer serious resistance.

The Netherlands for the first time in 1813 created a monarchy of its own. In 1848 the revolutionary tide in France, Belgium, and elsewhere in Europe reportedly converted King William I into a "liberal overnight," and he accepted a constitutional revision which made the government responsible to parliament rather than to the king. Thereafter, the Dutch monarch reigned but no longer ruled and became merely the first citizen of the kingdom. This was in effect the same position the Princes of Orange had earlier occupied as stadholders of the Dutch Republic and remains essentially true today.

After 1848 the Netherlands was confronted with tensions arising from industrialization. Though it came later than in Belgium or England, it nevertheless spawned a trade union and socialist movement. Holland also was confronted with struggles between the churches and the state, particularly over the creation of religiously affiliated schools that would be financed by the state. Not until 1920 was the present system of full state subsidies for parochial schools established. In all of these disputes, the Dutch displayed their characteristic willingness to abide by established rule of the democratic game and to find harmonious solutions to conflicts and differences.

The World Wars

During World War I, the Netherlands remained neutral and unoccupied. Sniffing the winds of change this mighty conflagration released, the Dutch did introduce universal suffrage for men in 1917 and for women in 1919. Because it had not joined Germany's enemies, the last German kaiser fled to Holland after his abdication, living there until his death in 1941. The war radically disrupted the trade on which Holland has always been so dependent, and after the war its prewar prosperity did not return. The economic depression of the 1930s created greater unemployment, which stimulated radical movements on the left and right.

FREE HOLLAND WELCOMES THE SOLDIERS OF THE ALLIES

WELKOM IN HET VRIJE NEDERLAND!

When the German army was hurled westward again in May 1940, the Dutch were unable to remove themselves from the melee. The Dutch army was facing east. The Germans flew around to the western part of Holland and attacked them from the rear. In the first large-scale aerial bombardment of a densely populated city, German dive-bombers destroyed 90% of Rotterdam's city center within 40 minutes. The German attempt to capture Queen Wilhelmina and the Dutch government by dropping crack paratroop units over The Hague failed, and the queen, Crown Princess Juliana, and the cabinet managed to escape to London; they worked during the entire war to bring about a German defeat.

Holland fell within five days, and a Nazi-appointed Dutch reich commissioner, an Austrian named Seyss-Inquart, ruled the country for the remainder of the war. This was an especially hard time for the Dutch, especially for Jews. The *Diary of Anne Frank*, whose setting is Amsterdam during the Nazi occupation, remains a moving testimony to the suffering inflicted upon the chief victims of Nazi racial theories and policies. Tragically the Frank family was not among the two-thirds of Jews who survived the war after going into hiding. In 2010 Miep Gies died. She had supplied the Frank family with food, books, and news, and she gathered up the scattered pages of Anne's diary on August 4, 1944, stowed them safely, and gave them to the family's only survivor, Anne's father, Otto. More than 100,000 Dutch Jews—three-quarters of the community—were deported and perished in concentration camps.

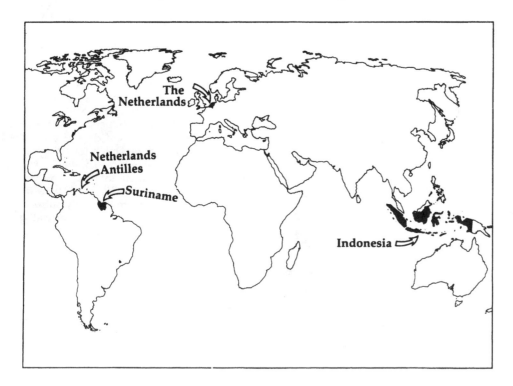

Unfortunately, some Dutch people were among the persecutors. As late as 1980, an art collector, Pieter Menten, was imprisoned and fined for his role in the murder of 20 to 30 Jews in Poland in 1941. In 2000, compensation payments totaling $240 million were offered to about 35,000 Jews for damages they or their relatives suffered in the Netherlands. In 2005, six decades after the war ended, the national rail company formally apologized for its role in deporting Jews.

Thousands of Dutch were active in the resistance movement against the occupation forces. Actress Audrey Hepburn grew up near the "bridge-too-far" at Arnhem. As a teenager she delivered messages from the resistance to soldiers in hiding. She suffered numerous illnesses due to her severe malnutrition; she subsisted on turnips, tulip bulbs, and nettles. Many did collaborate with the German occupation forces. Despite the successful Allied landing in Normandy in June 1944, because of strong German resistance north of the Rhine and Allied policy to drive toward Berlin, that part of Holland north of the Rhine was not liberated until May 1945; the area south of the Rhine was freed in September 1944. When the horror was over, the Netherlands was left with 280,000 civilian dead, vast expanses of flooded areas, wrecked harbors and industries, and an economy close to total collapse. Dutch memories and emotions remain strong.

Recovery

The very popular Queen Wilhelmina returned to Holland in 1945 amid enthusiastic cheers of her people, and the Dutch set about to mend their physically broken country, a task they were able to complete surprisingly quickly. In 1948, Wilhelmina abdicated in favor of her daughter, Juliana, and all would have gone well if the Netherlands had not been forced to face the same searing problem which was plaguing several other European powers at the time: decolonization.

The jewel of the colonial empire was Indonesia. In 1619 the Dutch East India Company had created a city it called Batavia (now Jakarta) on the island of Java. From this base the Dutch extended their control over most of the 3,000 or so islands of the Indonesian archipelago; for more than 300 years, they retained firm control over the colony, but their policy of drawing a rather distinct line between themselves and the native population was a major factor which fanned the flames of an independence movement in the 20th century. The islands were an attractive target for Japanese expansion after 1940. The Dutch government, which was trying to maintain a policy of neutrality in the Pacific war, could not organize a credible defense. Indonesia was captured in February 1942.

Decolonization

When the Dutch returned at the end of the war in order to reclaim what they believed was theirs, they found that they were not wanted by a native population whose leaders had declared the islands' independence in August 1945 immediately after the Japanese surrender. There followed four years of tension, military conflict, and American pressure. Finally a settlement was reached that recognized an independent Indonesia within a kind of union the Dutch equated with the British Commonwealth of Nations. In 2011 a Dutch court ruled that the state had been responsible for a massacre by Dutch soldiers of 430 Indonesian villagers in December 1947. The government apologized for the killing six decades later in December 2011.

This agreement by no means settled all the difficulties. The Dutch had insisted on retaining full control of their economic investments, which at the time accounted for almost 15% of their national income. Indonesia's flamboyant and unpredictable President Sukarno solved the problem single-handedly by simply nationalizing all Dutch properties in 1957. Relations between the two countries also remained sour because of the Dutch retention of West Irian, part of the island of New Guinea, which the Indonesians claimed. Finally, in 1962, an American mediator proposed the face-saving procedure of turning West Irian over to the UN, which seven months later transferred sovereignty to Indonesia.

After a painfully drawn-out severance from Indonesia, the Netherlands was more than cooperative in aiding its other colonies to gain their own independence. In 1975, Suriname was freed in the midst of widespread fears among the Surinamese that such independence would lead to violent racial measures against the whites and East Indian Hindustani. More than a quarter of the population fled to Holland in the final days before independence. In order to help Suriname adjust to its new status, the Netherlands promised it aid amounting to $100 million for each of the following 10 years. This was certainly one of the most generous foreign aid programs on a per-capita basis in history. However, because of the Surinamese government's flagrant human rights violations, the Netherlands suspended its assistance programs in 1983.

The Netherlands notified the six islands in the Netherlands Antilles that they must prepare for their independence. They organized themselves into four self-governing communities: Aruba, Bonaire, Curaçao, and the Leeward Islands (southern portion of Sint Maarten, Sint Eustatius, and Saba). The island of Aruba became an independent state in 1986 within the Kingdom of the Netherlands. It did not make its own foreign and security policy, and its highest court was still in the Netherlands.

In 2000 voters on the island of Sint Maarten opted to break away from the Dutch Antilles federation and become a separate country within the Kingdom of the Netherlands. Amsterdam feared that the islands would not be able to find a long-term alternative to economic dependence on Holland. Therefore, Dutch officials opposed Sint Maarten's independence, believing that it would be a bad precedent for the other islands.

On November 28, 2005, the Dutch government and the islands' other governments signed a new status agreement that went into effect July 2007. The Netherlands Antilles was partly dissolved. Curaçao and Sint Maarten became new associated states within the Kingdom of the Netherlands. Bonaire, Saba, and Sint Eustatius were directly part of the Netherlands as kingdom islands.

On October 10, 2010, the Netherlands Antilles was further dismantled. Curaçao, Sint Maarten, Bonaire, Saba, and Sint Eustatius became largely independent, with the first two islands becoming self-governing territories like Aruba. The last three became overseas municipalities with a status similar to Dutch cities. All remain under the Dutch Crown and are subject to Dutch foreign and defense policy. There is a vocal minority who demands full independence. The home country paid off 70% of the federation's $3.3 billion debt and temporarily oversaw Curaçao's debt.

The Dutch retain a military base in the area and send 60 Royal Marines to nearby Suriname twice a year for jungle-warfare training. Some Surinamese distrust the motives of the former colonial master, but Dutch leaders assure them that they are not creating an illegal base that could threaten the country's 1975 independence. Since 2000 the US Air Force maintains an airbase in Curaçao, and it also has planes in Aruba.

POLITICS AND GOVERNMENT

The Monarch

The Netherlands is a constitutional monarchy whose character is prominently visible during the investiture ceremony when a new king or queen begins to reign. The monarch takes an oath of allegiance to the constitution. Also, the royal crown is not placed on the head of the new ruler (for which reason the ceremony is called an investiture, not a coronation), but it and the other symbols of royal authority—the orb and the scepter—are arranged on a table around the constitution.

The Netherlands

Former Queen Beatrix with her children and grandchildren. King Willem-Alexander, top center.

The royal family is the House of Orange-Nassau, whose descendants are inseparably tied to the Netherlands' entire history as an independent state. This is one reason there is very little opposition to the monarchy in Holland and why most Dutch remain firmly attached to their monarchs. It was therefore a shock to many Dutch to witness the violent disturbances in Amsterdam, Rotterdam, and Utrecht on April 30, 1980, when the popular 71-year-old Queen Juliana, who died March 20, 2004, abdicated after 31 years as queen in favor of her daughter Beatrix. While orange flags and streamers were displayed everywhere and while the mood around the royal palace in Amsterdam was royally festive, elsewhere several thousand protesters waged such violent battles with the police that more than 50 policemen and 100 demonstrators were injured. The slogan of the protesters was "No apartment, no coronation," which referred to the serious housing shortage in the capital city. No doubt some of the protesters wished also to show disapproval of the monarchy and of a family who is among the richest in the world (worth an estimated $200 million). The family draws about €46 million ($55 million) a year from the state treasury for salaries and for maintaining a royal household with 250 servants and other assistants. However, the family's private fortune is secret. The area in which the ceremony was held had to be sealed off by the police. Few call for the abolition of the monarchy today.

Queen Beatrix was well prepared for her position, having studied law, politics, and history at the University of Leiden. She had a pleasantly dimpled smile and was extremely knowledgeable and interested in politics. But she tended to be a strong-willed and impatient person whose manner was often stiff and aristocratic. For a while her manner appealed less to her people than did that of her unpretentious mother, Juliana, who rode her bicycle in public, shopped in supermarkets, poured her own tea, and abolished the curtsy. But the nation's respect for Beatrix grew considerably after she became queen.

Beatrix's marriage in 1966 to a German diplomat, Claus, had created quite an uproar at the time. As a teenager he had joined the Hitler Youth. But the marriage became accepted, and Claus proved himself to be an effective promoter of good Dutch relations with developing countries. He acted as an adviser to the minister of development. Suffering from Parkinson's disease, he died in October 2002 at age 76.

At age 75 and after a reign of 33 years, one of Europe's longest, Beatrix abdicated on April 30, 2013, in favor of her eldest son, Crown Prince Willem-Alexander, age 45. He was crowned as the Netherlands' first king since the death of Willem II in 1890. He had served as a lieutenant on a guided-missile frigate. He is trained as a pilot. One of his favorite amusements is to fly twice a month as copilot for KLM's Cityhopper subsidiary that flies among European cities. He holds the rank of lieutenant-colonel. But he is not a career soldier. He studied history, but he is a specialist in water management and served on the International Olympic Committee. In 2002 he married Maxima Zorreguieta from Argentina. Since her father had been a cabinet member during the time of Argentina's military dictatorship, he was not permitted to attend the wedding.

On December 7, 2003, they had their first child, Catharina-Amalia Beatrix Carmen Victoria (called Amalia for short), who is crown princess and second in line for the throne, after her father. On June 26, 2005, they had their second daughter, Alexia Juliana Marcela Lourentien, and a third, Arianna, followed.

The king's younger brother, Johan Friso, suffered massive brain damage in February 2012, when he was buried in an avalanche while skiing in Austria. He lies indefinitely in a coma. A third brother, Constantijn, remains a part of the royal house and is in line for the throne.

Queen Beatrix was extremely hardworking and spent hours preparing for her speeches and meetings and reading proposed legislation. She was very frank in her inaugural speech about the unromantic side of being queen: "It is a task no one would ever seek. The glitter is visible, but not the burden and perpetual self-denial." Willem-Alexander has long been groomed to be king and is prepared for the challenges. In most matters the monarch is prevented from making any mistakes by the requirement that the appropriate

Princess of the Netherlands Maxima and King Willem-Alexander

cabinet member also sign all his acts and decrees. However, he is technically a part of the government, defined as the "king and his ministers." The monarch once played an important role in forming a government. In March 2012 six parties in parliament with a majority of seats largely eliminated that royal responsibility. Only when there is a deadlock in parliament can the king assume a minor role in this process. The royals are still popular, polling a 60% approval in 2021. But two royal vacations in Greece while the public was in lockdown because of Covid-19 were widely resented.

Forming a Government

The one public act the monarch was traditionally charged to accomplish independently was to coordinate the long coalition talks that are necessary to form a government after a parliamentary election. He largely lost that role. Because the Netherlands uses the proportional representation electoral system, many parties are able to win seats in the lower house, and no single party can even come close to winning a majority on its own.

The formation of a government out of almost a dozen parties that win parliamentary seats is therefore a very delicate task. According to the new rules in 2012, parliament selects within one week after an election one or more politicians to consult numerous party, parliamentary, and other political leaders in order to become intimately acquainted with the political climate. Then, acting independently, they name an informateur, who is usually a leading politician, whose task is to advise

parliament of the most promising formula for constructing a government. Next they appoint a formateur, a person who must seek to form a government in which he himself would probably be the prime minister. He is usually the leader of the party that has won the most seats in the election. His task includes the establishment of a program acceptable to several different parties. Such a broad program is necessarily moderate; no radical program would be acceptable to several parties. The entire process takes a very long time, usually two to four months. Fortunately the work is done carefully and normally results in a government that can survive for at least three years.

In the carefully constructed cabinet, ministerial seats are usually distributed according to the proportion of seats the various governing parties have in the lower house, the most important positions being that of prime minister and minister of finance. Cabinet members, including prime ministers, need not be members of parliament, and some ministers are specialists who had never even run for elective office in their lives.

Compared with other parliamentary systems in which a prime minister is the most important political figure, the Dutch system is almost unique in that it calls for a separation between the executive (cabinet) and the parliament. All cabinet members must resign their seats in parliament, and the new government need not seek the formal approval of the lower house. Nor is there such a thing as a vote of confidence, in which a majority in parliament can vote against the government, causing it to fall.

The government is, however, always free voluntarily to pose a "question of confidence" to the lower house if it chooses. It is acutely interested in maintaining a majority, without which it could not gain approval for important legislation, which is almost always written and submitted by the government, not by members of parliament.

The Parliament

The Dutch parliament, called the States General, remains powerful in comparison to many other parliaments in Europe. One reason is that the lower house has permanent committees that correspond to each ministry. Therefore, parliament members can develop the necessary expertise to question and control the work of the ministries. Further, parties in parliament do not require absolute discipline from their members, who according to the constitution represent the entire nation, not a regional or party constituency. Therefore, the government can never be absolutely sure that its measures will pass in both houses. It must design its legislation in such a way that it would be acceptable to more than a slim majority, and it must work very hard to persuade parliaments to support its programs. Parliament is by no means dominated or overshadowed by the cabinet.

The States General was first established in 1464 by the Burgundian kings as an advisory body. After independence in 1581, it considered itself the keeper of Dutch sovereignty and granted a hereditary official, the stadholder, the right to exercise executive power. The States General is bicameral, and both the First and Second Chambers meet in the Binnenhof (Inner Court) in The Hague. The First Chamber, or upper house, is composed of 75 members elected by the 12 provincial parliaments for six-year terms, with one-half of its membership being elected every three years. Since the provincial chambers are elected directly, the upper house usually has roughly the same party composition as the Second Chamber. This First Chamber cannot introduce or amend bills, but it is far more than a mere advisory or delaying chamber as is the British House of Lords. It has the right to approve or reject all legislation.

The Second Chamber is composed of 150 members elected at least every four years by all citizens 18 years or older. In contrast to most other European countries, elections are not held on Sundays. Nevertheless, voter turnout is high (78% in 2006), in contrast to US presidential elections, which are also held on Tuesdays and which now rarely attract more than 60% of the voters. One reason for the high participation is that Dutch law permits a

The Netherlands

family member or other designated individual to cast a person's ballot upon presenting a valid, signed voter card. The Second Chamber generally meets three days a week, Tuesday through Thursday, and its members are expected neither to reside in The Hague nor to give up their normal employment while they serve. About a third of its members are women.

Both chambers are regarded as the chief interpreters of the constitution, and together they are empowered to initiate the process to amend the constitution. If a majority in both houses finds a constitutional amendment necessary, then both houses are dissolved, new elections are held, and the amendment can then be accepted by a two-thirds vote in both chambers. No court in Holland has the right to declare a legislative act unconstitutional. The highest court of the land, the Court of Cassation, can only nullify a statute that is in variance with an international agreement. Its chief tasks are to ensure the uniform administration of justice and to serve as the court of high appeal for decisions made in lower courts. Presiding over those lower courts are independent judges who apply Dutch law. There are no juries; the Dutch want a professional administration of justice by judges who serve for life and who are as free as possible from popular influences.

Dutch law has its origins in Roman law. However, the Dutch copied and codified the French civil code in the 18th century. After a significant recent reform of its Citizens' Law Book (*Burgerlijk Wetboek*), based on a major comparative study in 1992, the Dutch private legal system now functions as a guideline for democratizing countries, such as Estonia.

Assisting the king and government as the highest advisory body is the Council of State, which is composed of a crown prince or princess over the age of 18 and no more than 24 persons appointed for life, although they normally step down at the age of 70. They are expected to have political, commercial, trade union, diplomatic, or military experience. The king officially presides over the council, although it is actually guided by a vice president who is selected from among the members. The cabinet can seek expert advice from the council and is always responsive to any constructive advice it might give.

Political Parties

At all levels of government, Dutch political parties play a key role in informing voters about the most important political issues, conducting election campaigns, and then forming coalitions to rule. Dutch political parties have always tended to represent particular subcultures in society, such as Catholicism, various shades

Ex–prime minister Peter Jan Balkenende with a picture of Harry Potter

of Protestantism, socialism, or liberalism. At the same time, they must adjust their aims to those of other parties in order to be able to participate in government. Therefore, compromise and mutual adjustment have been their basic rules. In a small country with such a highly homogeneous population, the range of political interests and opinions is somewhat narrower than in a large, multiracial, multilingual, and multinational country. Thus, a consensus regarding the political system and rules of the game has always been relatively easy to maintain in Holland, and this has made it less difficult for such a multiparty state to have such a high degree of parliamentary stability.

It has, however, become increasingly difficult to form coalition governments in Holland. This results partly from a change that is occurring in party politics. In the past, no Dutch government could ever be formed without the participation of confessional (religious) parties, particularly the Catholic Party. Therefore, the secular parties always had to moderate their programs in order to be able to coalesce with them. But as the importance of religion declines in Dutch society, fewer and fewer Dutch vote for a party exclusively for religious reasons. Therefore, the strength of the confessional parties has declined in recent years. Seeing this, the major secular parties have sharpened their own programs and have moved more clearly to the right or left in order to draw the formerly religiously oriented voters away from the politically heterogeneous religious parties. In other words, the major secular parties often have intentionally tried to polarize Dutch politics in order to attract more votes. They have even publicly stated that they are not interested in entering into any coalition with each other.

A couple dozen parties usually compete for seats. In 2017, 28 parties ran, and 13 won seats. Some of them, such as 50 Plus (pensioners), the Party for the Liquidation of the Netherlands, the God Is with Us, the Live or Die Together, the hard-line Communist Party of the Netherlands (CPN), and the Pedophile Party (which advocates lowering the age of consent and legalizing child pornography, bestiality, and hard drugs), could not seriously hope to win seats. But profiting from proportional representation, which grants a parliamentary seat for roughly 55,000 votes, several parties manage to win seats.

The Green Left, led by the youthful Jesse Klaver, which rallies radicals, socialists, pacifists, and communists, shot up to 9% and 14 seats in the March 2017 elections. Dutch voters are very sensitive to environmental issues. The crowded population, flatness, and the fact that half of it is below sea level make it a first victim to any rise in water levels due to the greenhouse effect. In fact, in 1989 a Dutch government became the first in Europe to fall in a crisis over the environment.

The leftist Socialist Party (SP), led by Emile Roemer, promotes an antiglobalization, anti-European platform. It blends leftist populism with nationalism and isolationism. It was prominent in the campaign against the new EU constitution in 2005. In 2017, the party won 14 seats. It received considerable support from the kinds of Dutch who had earlier voted for Pim Fortuyn and Labor.

The more conservative of the main secular parties is the People's Party for Freedom and Democracy (VVD, called "the Liberals"), led by Mark Rutte. He is a former human resources manage at Unilever. The VVD did very well in the 2010 elections. This was the first time in more than a century the party had won a national election. Rutte became the first Liberal prime minister since 1918. VVD did well in 2017, capturing 21% and 33 seats to be the largest party and the leading partner in a governing coalition. Rutte was one of the few European politicians to win reelection as prime minister during the euro crisis.

It is usually referred to as the Liberal Party because of its century-long struggle to reduce the influence of the churches in Dutch public life, especially in the schools. Individual freedom is its chief tenet, and it favors lower taxes, an even lower government deficit, a shrinking of the increasingly costly welfare state, higher criminal sentences, a strengthening of the police in order to curb crime and severe restrictions on immigration. It supports a free-market economy, but it also favors profit sharing with workers. It draws voters particularly from the upper and middle classes.

The VVD had been weakened by Geert Wilders's defection from the party in 2004. He is a hard-driving anti-Islam and anti-immigration campaigner. His Party for Freedom (PvdV) came out of nowhere in 2006 to capture 9 seats. He remains one of the country's most popular politicians. He is a skilled parliamentarian, and his outbursts introduced an adversarial style to debates, in contrast to the consensus politics to which the Dutch have been accustomed. He was put on trial in 2011 on charges of inciting hatred against Muslims. The Amsterdam court agreed that his comments were insulting but that they were protected in the interest of freedom of political speech. Because of his views on immigrants, he requires around-the-clock protection.

The PvdV had a disappointing result in the 2017 elections, winning 13% and 20 seats. Remembered for comparing the Quran to Hitler's *Mein Kampf* and calling Islam "Netherlands' biggest problem." He promised, "More safety, less crime, less immigration and less Islam is what the Netherlands has chosen." He did broaden his party's appeal by promising to cut red tape for small businesses; reduce taxes; increase care for the elderly; oppose further EU enlargement, especially to include Turkey; and withdraw Dutch troops from Afghanistan. He advocates LGBTQ and women's rights, opposes anti-Semitism, and is a strong supporter of Israel. He claims that the enemy is Islam, not Muslims. He called Islam a "backward" religion and demanded a ban on the Quran.

No party will coalesce with it. He is a Euroskeptic who lashed out against plans for financial bailouts to EU countries like Ireland and Greece. "Brussels is an undemocratic monster, a vampire that will suck us empty until we become an insignificant province of Greater Europe." Like 60% of Dutch, he thinks it was a mistake to get rid of the guilder, and he advocates a referendum on abandoning the euro. He demands that burkas and face-covering Islamic veils be banned, along with headscarves for police and employees in judicial institutions. He was widely ridiculed in 2012, when he criticized the queen for wearing a veil over her black hat while visiting a mosque in Oman. She tartly replied, "you adjust out of respect for religion." Nonwestern immigration and immigration through marriage should be reduced considerably. State subsidies for Dutch-language courses should be converted to loans, and failure to pass the tests could be grounds for refusing residence permits.

Wilders held talks with right-wing parties in other countries aiming to dismantle Europe and form an anti-EU bloc in the European Parliament. He met with Marine Le Pen of France's National Front. The two disagree on LGBTQ rights. In the Netherlands both the left and right support such rights. He also benefited greatly from the Dutch austerity fatigue. Like many Europeans, the Dutch are asking why jobs are hard to find, why they cannot sell their houses, and why things cost so much. Wilders has a simple answer: the EU.

Another major secular party is the Labor Party (PvdA). It is a moderate socialist reform party, which traditionally favors what it calls *Nivellering*, or the elimination of differences in citizens' power, knowledge, and income. It supports an increased workers' share of profits and decision making in the factories. To shake its aloof image, the party selects its new leader in a primary election open to all members, thereby breaking from its former practice of having the party elite decide behind closed doors.

The party made a spectacular comeback in the September 2012 elections, led by Diederik Samsom, a 39-year-old nuclear physicist and former Greenpeace campaigner. Labor was the big loser in 2017, losing three-fourths of its seats and holding onto only nine.

The rising star of the Labor Party was Jeroen Dijsselbloem. After only two months in office, he was elected as the new head of the Eurogroup of finance ministers. The term lasts two and a half years. His selection reflects the faith Europeans have in Dutch pragmatism and euro orthodoxy. With its triple-A credit rating, tough budget discipline, and close ties with Germany, it seemed natural to have a Dutch chairman as chair of this prestigious body.

The moderately left-wing party called Democrats 66 was founded in that year (1966) in order to present voters with a clear alternative to the established parties, especially the PvdA, whose strong, paternalistic leadership was widely resented at the time. It opposes the ideological approach to politics and sees itself as a practical, problem-solving party. It advocates reforms in the society and the constitution, such as the direct election of the prime minister. It is pro-Europe.

Once a trendy, intellectual party that appealed mainly to young voters from the upper and middle classes, it broadened its base temporarily. Led by Alexander Pechtold, it won the left's largest share of votes and 19 seats.

Fighting for its political life between the secular parties of the left and right was the Christian Democratic Appeal (CDA). Faced with the gloomy prospect of watching their voters run to the increasingly polarized secular parties, the three major religious political parties, which had long since severed their direct ties with the churches, decided in 1973 to join forces for electoral purposes. In a nostalgic ceremony of prayers and hymn singing in 1980, they went a giant step further by disbanding themselves entirely and becoming full members of the larger CDA.

The merger in 1980 brought birds of many different colors together, which are difficult to control. They all agree basically that Christian principles must be applied in politics and that both a free-enterprise economy and the present social welfare system should be defended. The fact that the CDA encompasses a broad political spectrum gives it the advantage that the party can easily form a coalition with almost every other party. Therefore, the CDA survived the secularization and polarization of Dutch politics.

In the 2002 elections the CDA emerged as the strongest party. Peter Jan Balkenende,

Prime Minister Mark Rutte

The Netherlands

a former professor of Christianity and head of the Christian broadcasting network, became prime minister.

Taking political responsibility for the drubbing in 2010, Balkenende resigned and announced that he was leaving politics. Its downslide continued in 2017, when it captured 19 seats.

Small parties captured 14 seats. The Christian Union (CU), led by André Rouvoet, retained its five seats. A new part arose in the 2017 election: Denk ("Think"). Three Dutch Turks won seats. Denk caters to Dutch Muslims and is the only ethnic party in parliament.

The 2012 elections revealed some important changes in Dutch politics. Voters' loyalty to parties has weakened, and parties are less able to count on their electoral support. Protest and radical parties have lost much of their appeal. At the same time, fragmentation continues. The combined support for the three main parties (Liberals, Labor, and Christian Democrats) has fallen from 80% of the votes in the late 1990s to a bare majority. Finally for the first time in Dutch history, the swearing-in ceremony for the new government was in public, transmitted live on television and the Internet.

The 2002 election campaign had witnessed the emergence of one of the Netherlands' most colorful and controversial politicians, who was assassinated a week before the elections. Pim Fortuyn was the antithesis to Dutch consensus politics. An openly gay sociology professor and ex-Marxist who became a prominent talk-show guest and columnist for the weekly magazine *Elsevier*, Fortuyn was an effective antiestablishment populist. He dared to express in public his reservations about the effects of burgeoning immigration on Dutch culture and society, something that Dutch political correctness had hitherto forbidden. Even many who did not agree with his views found his directness a breath of fresh air in a stuffy political environment. He formed his List Pim Fortuyn (LPF), which immediately captured a stunning 35% of the votes in Rotterdam's municipal elections. He expressed contempt for green politics.

On May 6, 2002, he was shot dead by an environmental activist, Volkert van der Graaf, who in April 2003 was given a shockingly lenient sentence of 18 years in prison, read amid the boos, curses, and sobs of Fortuyn supporters in the courtroom. This shocked his countrymen, who had never imagined that such violence could happen in their well-ordered country. He was the first Dutch politician killed since a mob lynched the De Witt brothers in 1672.

The follow-on party, List Pim Fortuyn, tried to capitalize on his notoriety, but it lacked the necessary discipline and leadership. It tried to attract votes by nominating political novices, such as a former Miss Netherlands beauty queen, but it continued to lose votes. It failed miserably as a governing party in Prime Minister Balkenende's ruling coalition, with four novice politicians in ministerial posts. The party's continuous internal feuding and power struggles blew the three-party government apart after only 87 days in office. Returning to the voters again in 2003, the Pim Fortuyn List was issued a rude rebuke for their irresponsibility. However, it could take some consolation in the fact that all the established parties adopted much of the Fortuyn platform, calling for tighter immigration policies and the need for more integration. In 2006 the party imploded. Picking up the pieces is Geert Wilders's anti-immigrant Freedom Party and the Socialists.

Unitary System, Regions, Municipalities

The Netherlands is a unitary, not a federal, state. There are elected provincial and municipal governments which deal with matters of regional or local concern, but about 90% of their income is channeled to them by the central government. In each of the 12 provinces, voters elect by means of proportional representation a provincial council. This assembly appoints from among its own members a provincial executive who is responsible for the day-to-day administration; retaining a French practice, the central government appoints a Queen's Commissioner, who presides over the provincial council and executive and seeks to insure that nationwide interests will not be overlooked. The provincial councils elect the members of the First Chamber in The Hague, a provision that helps ensure that provincial interests in turn will not be passed over by the central government.

Considerably more important in Dutch government are the municipal councils, which are also elected by proportional representation in the cities and towns. Each municipal council appoints aldermen from their own members who serve as the executive. Presiding over both the executive and the council is the Burgemeester (mayor), who is appointed by the central government for a six-year term. Although he usually does not come from the city in which he serves, he very often becomes the locality's most effective spokesman in The Hague. Increasingly, several municipalities are joining to form regional authorities to tackle such matters as the location of industry, housing, transport, and environment. The need for action on a larger scale than the municipality has led to a proposal to increase the number of provinces and to allow the new provincial governments to perform such tasks.

Other very important local bodies in the Netherlands and among the oldest form of democratic administration in Europe are the water control boards. Property owners within a board's jurisdiction elect a general council, which in turn elects an executive committee. The central government chooses the executive committee for the most important water control boards. These are responsible for what might be considered the most important task in Holland: defending the land against water.

Housing Shortages

The Dutch government must grapple with some very difficult problems. One of the thorniest is the desperate housing shortage in the Randstad. People disagree on how such a shortage arose and how it should be eliminated. The shortage is due in part to changed demands for housing. As young people leave home earlier, as the divorce rate climbs, and as an increasingly prosperous people demand larger and better-quality housing, the demand for existing housing increases. Like other European countries, the Netherlands is experiencing a dramatic increase in homeless persons. In a controversial effort to help them, Rotterdam began in 1993 distributing tent-shaped waterproof cardboard boxes to the estimated 3,500 homeless in that city.

About half of the Dutch housing stock is owner-occupied. Rotterdam is an exception, where nearly all the land is owned by the city, and 80% of its housing is rented. Private investors are discouraged from building more new apartments because the government forbids the returns on housing investments to exceed the returns paid on state bonds. No government has been able to find a way out of this trap. With low rents, many landlords refuse to pay for the kinds of renewal which much housing needs. According to the Amsterdam municipal council, as much as 60% of the city's housing is in need of renewal. In some districts, three-fourths of the houses have no bathrooms. Thus, rather primitive accommodations are hidden behind many of the stately facades that foreign tourists admire in the capital city.

On top of all this, the Netherlands experienced an end to its housing boom from 2003 on and an undeniable burst of the housing bubble from 2008. House prices fell by 6% in 2012 and 21% from their peak. Nevertheless it was hard to sell a house. The Netherlands is the only remaining country in Europe where mortgage interest is fully tax deductible. This has contributed to its huge mortgage debt levels, the highest in the eurozone. In 2013, 30% of homeowners owed more than their house was worth.

Social Welfare Problems

The government was confronted with the problem of how to finance its generous social welfare system. Unlike many western European countries, where welfare states were created after 1945 as a compromise between capitalism and socialism, and as an essential ingredient for social peace and political stability, Holland's welfare system (called the *verzorgingsstaat*) was built more on a Christian imperative rather than on a political necessity. It reached the limits of the welfare state and must realistically revise downward its earlier version of a new society. Both the Christian Democrats and the Labor Party cut back the welfare system.

It is understandable that the Dutch want to cling to the social welfare system. Parents receive special allowances for children, and widows and orphans receive special benefits, although widows who can work must do so. Health insurance has been privatized, is universal, and includes dental care. It covers treatment and nursing in institutions for the physically and mentally handicapped, nursing homes, hospitals, sanitariums and similar establishments.

Workers who are declared to be fully or partially disabled are entitled to benefits in amounts up to 70% of their wages. Since 1968, when these disability benefits were expanded, the nation's health has seemingly declined rapidly. In that year 5.5% of the workforce was considered to be at least partly disabled. In the 1990s this disability scheme (called WAO) was reformed slightly. The qualification criteria were tightened and benefit levels cut to 70% of previous salary. Nevertheless the number of claimants continued to rise, especially after psychological problems and stress were added. By 2002 nearly 1 million persons qualified for WAO out of a workforce of 7 million on the basis of complaints ranging from claustrophobia to chronic backache. Many had been added to the rolls because it was easier for employers to get unwanted employees on this list than to fire them. The government decided to do something about this outrage in 2003, when it tightened eligibility rules, reexamined all existing cases, limited levels of payments, and required those on welfare who can work to seek work.

All in all, only one out of two adults worked by the 1990s (compared with 63% in the US), which is one reason economic growth lagged behind most industrialized countries for years. All Dutch who cannot support themselves, including artists, are entitled to state aid. Employers and employees contribute 50–50 to the unemployment and health insurance, but the employers and, in some cases, the state treasury pay for all the other benefits.

Generous retirement benefits await all employees who contributed to special pension plans, but the government introduced tough measures in 2003 to end the practice of early retirement at only 57 years.

The luxurious social welfare system grew out of the unpleasant memories of the Depression of the 1930s and of the war. At first it was paid for by rising productivity and prosperity, and after large natural gas reserves were discovered in the late 1950s, budget deficits resulting from the social welfare bill were simply paid for by large government revenues derived from the export of natural gas. But the government, wishing to conserve the country's precious supply of natural gas, announced that all export contracts were to be terminated in the 1990s.

Public-sector spending is half of GDP. How should the welfare system be financed? The Dutch government believes that the welfare state can be maintained only if it is operated more strictly and efficiently. Therefore, in 1994 it privatized sickness insurance and shifted responsibility for social security from the government to companies. It hopes to improve greatly the ratio of active to inactive persons in a land where almost half the population lives on benefits.

In 2003 the government produced an ambitious reform package that sent the message that the days of cradle-to-grave government care are over and that the new society can expect more from its citizens in the way of individual responsibility. After four years the prime minister had cut spending, trimmed the welfare state by reducing benefits, scrapped incentives for early retirement, and introduced more competition in health care. When King Willem gave his first throne speech to parliament in September 2013, a speech written entirely by the government, he announced the end of the generous Dutch welfare state.

European and Third-World Relations

The Netherlands is a founding member of the EU and has long been one of the chief proponents of a more unified Europe. The Hague is the site of several supranational institutions, including especially the International Court of Justice, which is the supreme UN legal body in theory. This International Court meets in the stately Peace Palace built by money donated by the American steel magnate Andrew Carnegie. The Hague has, in a way, become the center of a world system of justice. The Balkan war-crimes tribunal, which tried the now-deceased Serbian ex-president Slobodan Milosevic for war crimes, is there, as is the International Criminal Court. The world appears to trust the Dutch sense of justice and fair play.

Holland has especially distinguished itself in development aid. In 2015 it gave 6.7% of its GDP, making it the eighth-highest per-capita donor. It is the fourth-largest financial backer of the UN refugee agency the UNHCR. One Dutch official commented, "development aid is a breed of sacred cow with us. We carry it out with the zeal formerly reserved for our country's Christian missionaries."

Peace Palace in the Hague

The Netherlands

By 2002 the Netherlands had also become the second-biggest net contributor to the EU budget (after Germany); in per-capita terms, it pays more into the EU coffers than any other member. Ex–prime minister Balkenende admitted, "For me it is difficult to explain why an ordinary Dutchman is paying six times more than a Frenchman."

Dutch voters shocked Europe on June 1, 2005, when they rejected a new EU constitution by two to one (62% to 38%, with a turnout of 63%) in their first ever national referendum. This was only three days after French voters did the same, although only 4% of Dutch said their decision had been influenced by the French "no" vote. When two founding members of the EU put their feet down on such an important issue, all of Europe pays attention.

An ever-larger Europe is in danger of losing its truest believers. It is all the more worrisome since they are two founding members on opposite sides of the ideological divide: France is in the "federalist" intervention camp, while the Netherlands is among the "Atlanticists," who favor a looser, less regulated Europe. All the main Dutch parties, representing 85% of the MPs, as well as the trade unions and almost all the main newspapers, supported the "yes" campaign. But by the time the "yes" campaign got going, the "no" voters had already set the agenda and were fighting on a broad front.

Opponents' reasons were many. The main one was fear that the Netherlands would lose influence in a Europe dominated by big countries. Close behind were concerns that their leaders had failed to consult the people; it was a kind of confrontation between the political elite and the Dutch people. The unpopularity of the then-government and its policies of austerity and immigration at a time of economic slowdown hurt. More than a fourth of the "no" voters opposed Turkey's entry into the EU, and many also feared they could lose control of immigration policy. The latter is especially important in a country that was still reeling from a Muslim extremist's terrorist act a half-year earlier. Almost a fourth feared a European superstate.

A third of "no" voters cited opposition to the euro, which is widely blamed for inflation; in 2005 only 39% of Dutch thought the euro has been a success. After the Dutch government fought hard for a strict interpretation of the rules on budget deficits in the eurozone, France and Germany simply overruled it and did what they wanted. Liberal Dutch voters feared that a more conservative EU might interfere with policies on soft drugs, same-sex marriage, and euthanasia. The vote was a slap in the face for the government, which vowed to slow the pace of European integration, reduce the relatively large Dutch contribution to the EU budget, and lay greater emphasis on the member states' sovereignty.

In 2007 the Dutch government voted in favor of the slimmed-down Lisbon Treaty that replaced the failed constitution. After much passionate debate, the cabinet and the main parties decided not to hold a new referendum but to allow parliament to decide whether to ratify the treaty.

The Dutch commitment to the EU has become shaky: One year after the referendum, three-fourths (74%) said membership was a good thing. Surveys in 2011 indicated that they were more likely than the Germans or French to see the EU's benefits. Few would give up the euro. Their country was the strongest advocate for compelling members to accept reforms or give up financial aid. A majority wanted Greece ejected from the EU, and 60% thought loans to other eurozone countries should stop. By 2013 a Gallup survey found voters split evenly, 39% each, on whether to leave the EU entirely. In 2014 a majority of voters were in favor of exiting the EU if that would lead to more jobs and economic growth.

Defense Policy

Its defense policy is based on its membership in NATO. Dutch troops are well trained and equipped and are considered to be among the best-prepared forces in NATO. One unique feature of the Dutch military is that it officially recognizes almost a dozen official personnel associations that function very much like labor unions, except that they have no right to strike.

Another unique feature is that the Dutch military was the first in the world to assign to combat units any woman who volunteers and who can satisfy the physical requirements. They also are permitted to serve on all naval vessels and to fly combat aircraft. The Dutch invested several million dollars on such things as developing backpack straps which do not irritate women's breasts, constructing separate quarters, and conducting studies to determine how valid the Israeli experience is that military units are more quickly demoralized when women are wounded than when men are hit. In 2001 there were 1,920 women in the Dutch forces, 7.6% of the total. They serve in all branches.

Other armies, including that of the US, watched the Dutch experiment closely, as

they did Holland's policy since 1974 to allow the LGBTQ community in the military. The LGBTQ community have their own Foundation for Homosexuality in the Armed Forces (FHAF), which represents gay interests in the services. For example, when Dutch troops serving in the Balkans in 1993 were sent complimentary copies of *Playboy*, gay soldiers were sent issues of a corresponding gay publication. Self-declared gay men and lesbians are officially welcome in the volunteer army.

The Dutch have abandoned conscription and created a flexible volunteer army designed to be used in rapid-deployment actions and UN peacekeeping operations. The force has been cut 37% from 101,000 to 41,000: 21,825 in the army, 9,420 in the navy (including 2,654 marines), and 9,559 in the air force. They are backed by 3,339 reservists, plus 6,078 Royal Military Constabulary. Stricter discipline and grooming standards have been introduced. Earrings and ponytails have been curtailed, and the use of cannabis was banned. The nonsaluting policy was not changed.

Some army bases were closed, and 2,300 of the army troops and 300 air-force personnel are assigned to a joint German-Dutch corps headquartered across the border in Münster. The command for this joint corps rotates between a German and a Dutch general, and English is the unit's official language.

The air force, which since 1977 has used the American F-16 fighter, has the task of protecting Dutch airspace and of contributing to the tactical air forces of the alliance. In 2013 it decided to buy 37 F-35 fighter jets produced by Lockheed Martin to replace is aging fleet of F-16s by 2023. The navy plays a part in defending the Atlantic, the English Channel, and the North Sea. Its most important assignment is to keep the Dutch coast clear of mines and to defend the Dutch ports, which are critical for NATO supply lines. To utilize their assets more rationally, the Dutch and Belgian navies and air forces coordinate some of their operations close to home. Several Dutch naval vessels were sent in 1991 to the Persian Gulf, and missile batteries were deployed to Turkey and Israel.

The US had reduced its troop level in the Netherlands from 2,200 to 525 in 2010. The UK has 120 soldiers in the country. In 2001 the Dutch entered a treaty with the US allowing American aircraft to use Dutch bases on the Caribbean islands of Aruba and Curaçao as staging areas to fight drug trafficking. Germany hosts 300 Dutch troops.

In the Balkans Dutch soldiers serve on the ground, in the air, and at sea. Their humanitarian image was badly tarnished by allegations in 1995 that they had stood aside after Srebrenica fell to Bosnian Serbs,

while 8,000 Muslim men and boys were butchered and while the women and girls were raped and expelled. The troops had been sent into the area under an ill-defined UN mandate, with none of the weaponry necessary to withstand the onslaught of thousands of Serb troops. The Dutch commander on the ground had separately sought air strikes but failed to get any support from allies, including the US.

The Dutch government absolved them in 1995 of any wrongdoing in that complicated and tragic situation. However, it commissioned an inquiry, which issued its report in April 2002 that Dutch troops had been sent on an "ill-conceived and virtually impossible mission." Nevertheless a Dutch court ruled in a 2011 civil suit that the Netherlands is liable for the deaths of three Bosnian Muslim men at Srebrenica and must pay compensation to the families. The Dutch Supreme Court upheld this decision in 2013, ruling that the three men were wrongfully ordered to leave the UN compound and faced certain death.

In 2014 a Dutch court ruled that the Netherlands (but not its peacekeepers) bears responsibility for turning over thousands of males, knowing that the Serbs would probably kill them. A further ruling in 2017 agreed that the Dutch peacekeepers could and should have done more to protect the men. It limited the Dutch government's liability to 30% of the damages. Even though the fault lay with the UN and some allies, the incident still haunts the Dutch conscience. Most Dutch feel ashamed, even though their soldiers had been put in an impossible situation. It prompted former prime minister Wim Kok to resign.

Determined to toughen the Dutch military for such difficult missions abroad, the government sent troops to Iraq and Afghanistan, as well as to Ethiopia, Liberia, Chad, and the Central African Republic.

In 1999 it deployed 1 ship, 16 combat aircraft, and 738 troops in the NATO air war against Yugoslavia to stop ethnic cleansing in Kosovo. A tenth of its peacekeeping forces there were female. Its maintenance of peacekeepers in the Balkans, Cyprus, and the Middle East underscores its changed emphasis from home defense to peacekeeping. In 2011 it heeded NATO's call to help enforce a no-fly zone over Libya.

Following the September 11, 2001, terrorist attacks against the United States, the Netherlands sent troops to Afghanistan, both to serve as peacekeepers and to fight alongside American and other allies to root out and destroy the remnants of Taliban and al Qaeda fighting forces. In February 2003 it joined hands with Germany to command all peacekeeping forces in Afghanistan for a half-year. After months

Hand-painting Delft porcelain

of debate in parliament and pressure from the US and NATO, the government decided in 2006 to deploy 1,700 troops in Afghanistan as a part of a NATO-led reconstruction mission. That number was raised to 2,160. What was important about the Netherlands' participation was that about 1,500 of its soldiers had the main NATO responsibility in the dangerous southern Afghan province of Oruzgan. By 2010, 21 of soldiers had been killed.

Fearing that the troops would be drawn into combat with Taliban fighters, D66 opposed the mission, but Labor decided to support it until at least 2010. The force included up to 1,400 troops dedicated to public-works efforts, with the remainder fighting with allied soldiers or flying and maintaining Apache helicopters and F-16 fighter jets. It has primary responsibility for Oruzgan Province. Its "population-based" technique of engaging local people and assisting them with development has been successful. For example, they seek to gain the locals' confidence by patrolling on bicycles. There are fewer Dutch fatalities. Since the arrival of Dutch forces, the number of kids in Uruzgan schools has leaped from 12,000 to 50,000, and 100 health centers have been created with 31 doctors (up from just 2 before). All this helps suppress the ghost of Srebrenica.

All of Europe, including the Netherlands, suffers from war fatigue. The government fell in 2010 because the Labor Party refused to extend their country's commitment to Afghanistan by another

The Netherlands

A residential area in Amsterdam

year. An exasperated Prime Minister Balkenende said, "People don't understand what we're doing." Dutch troops were withdrawn by the end of 2011.

During the 2003 American-British war against the regime of Saddam Hussein in Iraq, which most Dutch opposed, the government permitted the American and British allies to move troops, tanks, and other military supplies through the Netherlands to the Persian Gulf. This included airspace and airports, rail lines, and Rotterdam Harbor. Defense Minister Henk Kamp stated, "the Americans are our friends. They are here in Europe to help and protect us." The government also stood by NATO and shipped 3 of its 4 Patriot air-defense batteries and 370 soldiers to operate them to Turkey after France, Germany, and Belgium had blocked Turkey's request for NATO protection against Iraq. Kamp justified this action by explaining, "we are an independent country. We have certain obligations in NATO and no one can prevent us from honoring them."

During the crisis over Iraq in the early months of 2003, the Dutch government supported the American position politically while not alienating its European allies. In order not to inflame contradictions among Europeans, it declined to sign the letter of eight European NATO countries criticizing French and German opposition to the war. But after the rapid victory in April 2003, it agreed to provide 1,500 troops to help police postwar Iraq and to enable an equal number of US Marines to rotate home.

Its peacekeepers applied their preferred soft touch: eschewing armored vehicles,

helmets, and mirror sunglasses; encouraging interaction with the people; and generally making their soldiers accessible and vulnerable to their surroundings. In March 2005 it withdrew its remaining 1,400 troops. In 2010 an independent Dutch commission decided that the Iraq War lacked an international legal mandate and that the government had not fully informed parliament about its support for the US-led invasion.

The Netherlands was determined not to permit transatlantic ties to deteriorate any further. Referring to the countries that opposed the war, the then–foreign minister Jaap de Hoop Scheffer explained, "Belgium and France will not guarantee our security. Germany will not guarantee the security of the Netherlands. I cannot imagine a world order built against the United States." Ex–prime minister Balkenende put it this way: "The Netherlands has become a builder of bridges, both within Europe and across the Atlantic." Having proven himself as a master compromiser, Hoop Scheffer served from 2004 to 2009 as NATO secretary-general, the third Dutchman to occupy that post. Four out of five Dutch supported stringent sanctions against Russia for its aggression in Ukraine in 2014–2015. This stiffened when pro-Russian rebels shot down a Malaysian airliner with 193 Dutch citizens onboard. This was a greater share of its population than America's loss on 9/11. An investigation in 2016 concluded that the missile was fired from Russian territory and that the system was returned to Russia afterward. The investigators decided that any suspects should be prosecuted in Dutch courts.

In 2016 the Netherlands and Belgium settled a festering border problem. They swapped 35 acres of Belgian land by the Meuse River for 7 acres of Dutch territory. There are other anomalies. In the village of Baarle, the line zigzags through the middle of town and right through ships, living rooms, bars, and gardens.

ECONOMY

The Dutch economy is the sixteenth-largest in the world. It is almost entirely in private hands, and the government restrains itself from subsidizing or assuming a direct or indirect ownership of Dutch companies. Nor does it engage in compulsory economic planning. The state nonetheless is active in the economy. For example, it is a major participant in the Netherlands Gas Company. The state employs 12% of the nation's workforce, and including all social security programs, it spends half of the country's GDP.

The government is also closely tied in with the highly structured Dutch system for dealing with conflicts of economic interests. The labor unions (which have unionized about 40% of employees) send representatives to the Joint Industrial Labor Council, established in 1945; employers, primarily the Federation of Netherlands Industry and the Netherlands Federation of Christian Employers, send an equal number of representatives. The council not only engages in collective bargaining but also serves as an official advisory body to the government.

Another important body is the Social and Economic Council (SER), which is composed of 45 representatives: 15 each from the labor unions and the employers' organizations, 13 academics, and the heads of the central bank and planning agency. The government is required to ask its opinion on all proposed economic and social legislation, and the council is free to give unsolicited advice. The cabinet is not required to follow the advice, but if the council's recommendations are supported by a large majority of its members, it is very difficult for the government to disregard them.

The Netherlands has long since shed its traditional character as an agricultural country. Nevertheless, Dutch agriculture is important. It is very intensive, and farms in Holland, which are predominantly small, family operations, are the most productive in all of western Europe. There is a down side to such intensive farming: a poor environmental record. It lags behind it most other EU countries in air, soil, and surface-water quality, and it has extraordinarily high carbon emissions. A major reason is that it has the highest number of livestock per capita in Europe. Their

On the family tulip farm in northern Holland

manure is not recyclable. It has a swine population of 14 million and is Europe's leading pork producer and exporter. To keep up, the pig farms must expand, and that scares neighbors.

The Netherlands is the world's third-largest agricultural exporter after the US and France. The percentage of Dutch engaged in agriculture or fishing has dropped by two-thirds in the last three decades to only 2.5% of the total population, who produce 2% of GDP. Since three-quarters of them are unionized and their representatives sit in all economic advisory organs and political parties, they still can wield considerable political clout.

Two-thirds of the land is used for agricultural purposes, of which 62% is used for grassland, 32.5% for cultivation, and 5.5% for horticulture. A consequence of so much farmland is that the bulk of the population and industry is squeezed into the remaining third. Pollution is inevitable with so many people and so little land. The visitor notices much cultivation under glass.

Of course, no one can overlook the most beautiful crop of all: flowers. The Dutch have grown and exported all over the world a wide variety of plants ever since the first tulip bulbs arrived from central Asia in the 16th century. Their most splendid showpiece is Keukenhof and its environs, which in the months of April and May must surely be the largest and most colorful garden in the world.

The country is heavily industrialized. Its highly diversified industry employs 18.9% of the workforce and accounts for 24% of GDP. For such a small country, it has an exceptionally large number of big-name international corporations. Some of the most prominent industrial names in the world

are based in Holland: Phillips, Unilever, and Royal Dutch Shell. In 1993 the giant music company PolyGram NV purchased the legendary symbol of African-American music, Motown Records. Services provide employment for 78.9% of the Dutch and produce 76% of GDP.

Almost 70% of the industrial turnover is in chemicals and petroleum, metals, biotechnology products, food, drink, and tobacco. Chemical and petroleum industries, which include the processing of natural gas and the refining of oil, alone account for one-half of all exports. The Netherlands does have some lame industries, such as shipbuilding. It is, however, trying to gear up for future trade competition by exporting such sophisticated products as microcomputers and precision optical equipment. The government is strongly supporting the search for new Dutch markets abroad and does offer export subsidies to Dutch companies.

For centuries this has been a trading country, and today it is the world's eighth-largest trading nation. Over half of its GDP is derived from the export not only of its goods but also its services. It always has invested heavily abroad, ranking second behind the UK in total foreign investment in the US. It has always been a particularly important transit country because of its ports and inland waterways.

Of all goods loaded or unloaded in the EU destined for or arriving from overseas, 30% pass through Rotterdam, Europe's biggest port. It is the largest destination in the world for Russian exports and the biggest importer of Russian gas. The port moves almost half of all cargo entering or leaving ports between Le Havre in France and Hamburg in Germany. In 1996

the Dutch state and city of Rotterdam launched an investment program valued at $6.1 billion to boost the harbor's capacity. It includes building eight new state-of-the-art terminals capable of serving jumbo container ships. Because a deep channel was dug in the bed of the North Sea, the port can accommodate heavy tankers. Over half the cargo tonnage handled by the port now consists of crude or refined oils, and it is the world's chief oil port and "spot market," on which oil is bought and sold on a supply and demand basis. Pipelines have been constructed which can move petroleum to Germany and Belgium. Rotterdam alone provides more than 10% of the country's GDP.

Because of its inland waterways, which include western Europe's most important rivers, the Dutch ports of Rotterdam and Amsterdam have the capacity to transport goods by water to markets that serve over 200 million persons. Dutch companies are responsible for 40% of the EU's inland waterway transport. About 70% of the transport between the ports and the European hinterlands moves on water, but Holland also has an excellent road and rail net that is connected with those of neighboring countries. Finally, the national airlines, KLM (now linked to Air France), ties Schiphol Airport near Amsterdam to cities all over the world. Schiphol is Europe's second-biggest airport for goods transport.

The Netherlands' chief customer by far is Germany, whose unity was a powerful stimulus for Dutch goods and which accounts for 29.4% of exports and 16.1% of imports. Belgium buys 15% of its exports and provides 9.8% of its imports. In all, the EU accounts for 75.8% of its exports and 46.2% of its imports. US trade makes up 10.1% of its imports. But the US is Holland's largest source of private foreign investment; a fifth of American (and a third of British) investment in the EU goes to the Netherlands. In fact, the US invests 10 times as much in the Netherlands as in China and twice as much as in Mexico. The amount of American dollars per capita invested in the Netherlands is larger than in any other European country. The US has 1,100 companies there, including 42 of the top 50 American Fortune 500.

Energy

The Netherlands must, with a few exceptions, import almost all the raw materials its industries need. It has large salt deposits in the eastern part of the country, and it also is able to produce about 5% of the oil it needs. The principal exception is natural gas. Huge gas reserves were discovered in 1959 in Slochteren in Groningen Province. This became the largest-producing gas field in the world and contained about a third of all natural gas reserves in

The Netherlands

western Europe. Its gas reserves were the world's fifth-largest. The Slochteren fields produced 84% of the country's gas, and the remaining 16% came from Holland's continental shelf offshore. It exported about one-half of its gas, which was the country's most valuable source of foreign exchange. As its reserves dipped, it had to be more sparing with this dwindling treasure. Due to frequent minor earthquakes, production has been lowered by 20%.

The proceeds from these exports have not only kept its balance of payments in surplus since 1982, but the government, which claims a 90% share of all gas export income, also derived about 10% of its revenues from this source. In 1980 Holland renegotiated its 10-year gas sales agreements with its western European customers in order to bring the prices more in line with world energy prices.

When the Dutch first discovered their large gas reserves, they decided to exploit them very quickly because they saw that a rapid worldwide conversion to oil was in process. They foresaw the prospect of atomic plants supplying a high percentage of the industrialized world's needs in the future. Therefore, they rapidly converted 90% of Dutch homes and other buildings to gas heat. They also sought to sell their gas quickly while there was still a market for it. Almost all Dutch now regard this decision to have been a very serious mistake.

In the 21st century, natural gas accounts for about half of the nation's energy supplies, while oil accounts for 37%, coal 12.6%, and nuclear less than 1%; its one nuclear plant produces 4% of its electricity. In order to stretch out their gas supplies, the Dutch decided to terminate all gas export contracts in the early 1990s; to limit most of their own gas use to high-priority needs, such as home heating; and to mandate home insulation and the conversion of industry from gas to coal and oil. They also began buying gas from abroad, especially from Russia. The government negotiated contracts with Moscow, whereby Dutch gas companies would provide assistance in helping it extract gas, which would then be sent to western Europe. It also granted Gazprom use of a gas-storage facility in a depleted gas field north of Amsterdam. It is Europe's largest gas-storage facility. It is a part of the drive to make the Netherlands a gas hub for northwestern Europe and to increase its energy security.

Oil had to take up the energy slack, a fact which not only damaged Holland's balance of payments but also made it far more vulnerable to an oil boycott such as the nation faced in 1973–1974, when the Arab-dominated OPEC nations singled out Holland for its support of Israel. New discoveries in the North Sea enable the Netherlands to supply 20% of its own oil.

The future reliance on oil can be relieved also by increased use of coal and nuclear power. The Netherlands wanted to raise coal's share of electricity generation from the present 5% to 40% by the end of the century. This is made difficult by the fact that, since Holland has already shut down its coal mines, most of the coal will have to be imported. Also, coal has a frightening effect on global warming, a pernicious development that threatens the Dutch almost more than any other nation. Holland has two nuclear power plants, but there is strong opposition to nuclear power generation. The Labor Party even advocated the shutdown of the existing plants. With razor-thin majorities and with the 1986 Chernobyl nuclear accident in the Ukraine still in people's minds, shaky coalitions can seldom afford to touch such hot potatoes.

Holland's energy problems will not be alleviated by nuclear power nor that stereotype of the country: wind, which is used for only 5.2% of its electricity. Overall, renewable energy sources make up only 4.2% of the energy mix.

One healthy energy saver is bicycling. There are 1.3 bikes per person. More and more of them can be parked in underground bicycle parks, and at least nine commercial bike-sharing schemes exist.

Current Economic Situation

Dutch industry faced several problems even before the worst economic downturn in decades hit in 2008. The workweek has fallen to 36 hours. Wage costs are very high, and if one adds employer contributions to social security, wages are on a par with Belgium. Employers must also pay employees a holiday bonus of 8% of their annual pay. Normal wages are not indexed, but pensions and certain benefits are. The trade unions are still moderate, but they are often tempted to seek wage increases that could heat inflation (1.1% in 2021), and they resist reductions in social welfare benefits.

Despite high wage levels and the maintenance of extensive job protections and cooperation with the unions, unemployment was 3.8% in 2021, well below the EU average of 8.3%. Part of the success has been the willingness to create incentives to work by lowering unemployment benefits and to make the labor market less rigid by reducing job security and increasing temporary employment. Of all jobs, 15% are temporary (compared with 13% in the US and 30% in Spain).

By deregulating work hours and allowing previously unthinkable part-time work contracts, part-time employment now constitutes 40% of all jobs, the highest proportion in all Europe. Workers with such contracts continue to get benefits like vacation and health insurance, and

after six months they begin to accumulate pension rights. Thus the Dutch labor market combines flexibility with protection: Workers now accept more uncertainty in return for the reassurance of welfare assistance if all goes wrong.

It is women, 66% of whom work, who are most involved in this kind of work: 60% of working women in 2011 worked only part-time. Only 4% of them said they would like to increase their hours. This helps explain the pay gap between the sexes of 19% to 24%, one of the highest in the EU, and the underrepresentation of women in top government and business positions. But compared with other western countries, they consistently rank near the top in terms of well-being and happiness.

Unlike most European countries, the Netherlands actually created jobs in the late 1990s and early years of the 21st century, and this is a particular boon to younger Dutch. Success is due in part to the Dutch tradition of consultation and cooperation. It is also a small enough country that all the key political, labor, and employer figures know each other and can work together. There is hidden unemployment, such as early retirement and disability payments.

Its economy is growing (4.1% in 2021), and its budget surplus of 2.1% of GDP in 2021 is manageable. The resulting austerity put wind in the sails of extremist parties. Four out of five Dutch thought in 2013 that austerity was doing more harm than good. Its spending and taxes are sinking. In order to attract foreign investment and improve competitiveness, the government lowered corporate taxes from 34.5% to 30% by 2007, close to the EU average. Income taxes are high, but there is no capital gains tax. Its national debt, at 51% of GDP in 2004, is stable. Its welfare program has become less generous. Wealth is distributed unequally: the top 10% of households own 61% of net wealth (versus 75% in the United States). As an exceptionally open economy, which exports 70% of what it produces, it is a powerful voice against protectionism.

CULTURE

No longer a homogeneous country, the Netherlands has a growing nonwhite racial minority. However, except for about 400,000 in the province of Friesland northeast of Amsterdam who speak a German-Dutch language called Frisian and can use it to communicate with the government there, all whites speak Dutch as their mother tongue. Thus, the country avoids the terrible language problems found in neighboring Belgium. At the same time, the Dutch are very open to the world, and most schoolchildren learn English, German, and to a lesser extent French

The Netherlands

the Caribbean. But the national team was the only one in Europe invited to play in the 2008 Olympic Games. Five Dutch nationals played in the US Major Leagues in 2007. Nevertheless, soccer remains the favorite sport. Said one baseball coach, "Give a Dutch boy a ball, and he will usually drop it and try to kick it."

Religion

In the Netherlands religion has always been an important force shaping the national character. The Reformation took seed in Holland, and it was the attempt of the Spanish king to re-Catholicize Holland that sparked the Dutch rebellion in the 16th century. It remains a tradition for the Dutch royal family to belong to the Protestant Dutch Reformed Church. When the queen's younger sister Irene left the Netherlands in 1963 to marry Prince Carlos Hugo de Borbon y Parma, a Catholic pretender to the throne of Spain, the very enemy her forefathers fought for almost 100 years, she threw her family and her country into a rage. But in fact, the Netherlands was never thoroughly converted to the Protestant sect of Calvinism. Even today a third of the population is Catholic, 21% Protestant, 6% Muslim (rising by almost 4% every year), .5% Hindu, and 40% who profess no belief in religion at all. Still, those observers are to some extent correct when they say that every Dutchman is somewhat a Calvinist.

The Dutch take a moral approach to most human affairs. One sees this in the tone and content of Dutch politics. Moral arguments are invariably made to support many political issues, including social welfare, human rights, nuclear disarmament, environmental protection, and aid to developing countries. Some political parties are organized around religious principles. Although Dutch voters are less likely than they once were to vote primarily out of religious considerations, political parties often cannot resist the temptation to sprinkle their appeal with biblical messages, even if practical political considerations far outweigh religious ones. Most radio and television organizations and some newspapers have religious affiliations. Further, despite the fact that church and state are officially separated, the school system offers both religious and secular schools, with the state picking up the bill for both; 70% of these schools are privately owned, often nominally religion-based.

Despite their religious and moral approach to many human affairs and despite the religious strife that one still finds in the country, the Dutch have never practiced the kind of intolerance Calvinists practiced in, for example, the Massachusetts Bay Colony. Most of its people continue to practice some of the tolerance toward

and Spanish. Visitors who seek information from or contact with the Dutch are relieved that most Dutch have learned these languages rather well: Three-fourths speak at least one foreign language, 44% speak two, and 12% speak three or more.

Holland is a very pluralistic country in which diversity is institutionalized in a way that the Dutch used to call *Verzuiling*, or "columnization." This means the coexistence in political and social life of separate religious organizations which operate parallel to one another but which aspire to the same goals. Such columnization is no longer relevant, but diversity still is found in education, the mass media, sports and social clubs. Dutch schoolchildren are free to attend either state or private (mainly religious) schools. All are financed by the government, although religious schools receive some funding from religious communities.

Primary schooling lasts six years, and 70% of primary schoolchildren attend private schools. Secondary school pupils can choose either to go straight into vocational education, which would lead to careers in the trades, services, or sales, or into a general secondary education, which paves the way to the university. Approximately 60% of the secondary school pupils attend private schools. Parents can choose their

children's public school if they wish, and Dutch schools are permitted to select their pupils.

There are 14 universities, 4 of which are private. Only 3% of Dutch students of university age attend private universities, compared with approximately 50% in the US. Over 70% of university students attend state institutions. Many Dutch attend religious schools from the beginning through the university. Aside from some supervision to ensure minimum standards, the government does not attempt to influence the private schools.

When the elder generation was in school, the canals froze almost every year, but now it happens only once in a dozen years. In 2009 and 2012, temperatures plunged, and hundreds of thousands of Dutch skaters took to the ice. In an era when the country is struggling to maintain its identity in the face of a massive influx of immigrants, this was a way for the Dutch to reconnect with their past. Scenes like Pieter Bruegel's paintings of village festivals on ice are rare.

On the other hand, an American might scratch his head to see so many baseball (called *honkbal* in Dutch) teams and a membership of 30,000 in the Dutch baseball federation. Granted, many of the best players come from Dutch islands in

The Netherlands

other ideas and ways of living for which the Dutch were once famous and without which no democracy can function properly.

Some Dutch are increasingly inclined to cast off their tolerance and to attack violently those views they do not accept. For instance, when the pope visited the Netherlands in 1985, he was greeted by bottles, cans, bombs, and such obscene chants as "Kill, kill, kill the pope!" A majority of Dutch Catholics oppose the Vatican's teachings on contraception, abortion, celibacy, and the ordination of women, and John Paul had gone to Holland in the first place to heal these divisions. About 2,000 Dutch filed complaints of sexual or physical abuse against the church after it commissioned an inquiry; the actual number of victims could be 10 times that. Most offenses occurred decades ago. As many as 10 young men were surgically castrated in the 1950s. The church offered "sincere apologies" to all the victims of sexual mistreatment.

While religion plays a role in many facets of public life, church attendance is actually falling. The importance of religion in everyday affairs is no longer as great as it once was. Polls in 1987 indicated that 27% of Dutch adults attend church regularly (vs. 14% in the UK and 12% in France). The fact that both religions draw believers from all occupations prevents them from being linked closely with any particular social class, as is the case in Northern Ireland. There are fewer interfaith marriages than in most European countries.

The Dutch remain a family-oriented people, who tend to treasure family life and prefer private to public amusement. There is little outright class discrimination. Nevertheless, there is still a large income gap among citizens, and people of different social classes tend not to mix as frequently and as easily as in the US.

Diminishing Tolerance for Minorities

Holland was always a land of refuge. It absorbed religious refugees from England, Belgium, and France and Jews from Spain and Portugal. In fact, because of the tolerant and relatively enlightened and prosperous conditions inside the Netherlands, the Dutch never poured out of their country and colonized foreign lands in great numbers. Presently almost 20% of the population is visibly different ethnically from the native Dutch. The percentage in Rotterdam is one-half, and in Amsterdam, The Hague, and certain other large cities, it is one-third.

When Indonesia won its independence from the Netherlands, many people of Indonesian ancestry came to Holland and assimilated rather well. Exceptions were the 15,000 South Moluccans, Christians who had fought with the Dutch army. They had been promised autonomy, but the Indonesian ruler, Sukarno, forbade this. They could not get along with the new regime and were permitted to resettle in Holland. Their community has since more than doubled to 40,000.

When Suriname became independent in 1975, more than 140,000 Surinamese, who were Dutch citizens, left their newly freed country to go to Holland. The Dutch did almost nothing to stop or discourage them until the 1980s. Referring to these Surinamese, who now number 180,000, one Dutch clergyman spoke for many of his countrymen when he said, "they are here because we were there." The Netherlands continued to provide $1.5 billion of aid to Suriname annually. Surinamese and immigrants from the Netherlands Antilles continue to enter Holland.

In the 1960s, when the labor-starved Dutch economy was in desperate need of more workers, thousands of guest workers poured in from the Mediterranean area, primarily from Turkey, Morocco, Spain, and Italy. They concentrated in the cities of Rotterdam, Amsterdam, and The Hague, and today Dutch talk openly about "black schools" and "black zones," referring to schools and neighborhoods where non-whites are in the majority. The majority of the children under age 14 in the three largest cities are of "nonwestern background," mostly Muslim. Half the prison population is comprised of ethnic minorities.

These facts put wind in the sails of politicians like the late Pim Fortuyn, who helped break down the traditional political correctness about tolerance and the multiculturalism among all the mainstream parties except the Green-Left. Their insistence that newcomers integrate into Dutch society, learn the Dutch language, and realize that they cannot recreate their old lives at government expense in the midst of one of the world's richest nations has become official government policy.

Immigrant minorities are not on an economic or social par with the Dutch. The percentage of low-income households is three times higher among immigrants than native Dutch. Unemployment is also two to three times higher among these groups. Crime rates among young Moroccan males are three times higher than those of young white Dutch. In the 21st century, the gulf between immigrants and native Dutch is widening. A 2012 report concluded that immigrants felt less accepted in Dutch society in 2011 than in 2002. One politician talked in 2013 of a "tsunami of east Europeans," and rising unemployment made the Dutch more resentful of immigration. Only 28% of ethnic Turks and 37% of ethnic Moroccans identify themselves strongly as Dutch. The door remains open, with over 50,000 asylum seekers showing up in 2015 alone. Immigrants have a higher economic standard of living in the Netherlands than in many other European countries. There is no immigrant underclass and no real ghettos, and some enter the middle class.

The Dutch government bends over backward to serve them if they stay. More than 40% of immigrants receive some form of government assistance. This is a source of resentment among Dutch taxpayers. Mobile caravan schools have been organized for gypsy children, and all minorities are entitled to the same social welfare benefits as are the native Dutch. The Dutch Broadcasting Foundation beams television shows in five languages with subtitles. Since 1986 "outlanders" (as the resident foreigners are called) are permitted to vote or run for office in municipal elections. A 1998 survey on racism in Europe revealed that about a third of Dutch admit to being "racist" or "fairly racist." This regrettable statistic was nevertheless far below that in Belgium (55%) and France (48%).

The earlier Labor government claimed in 2002 that its tightening of the rules, especially on asylum, had cut the numbers of new arrivals by 25%. The center-right Balkenende government created a ministry of immigration and integration and tightened restrictions even further. They included admitting fewer immigrants and making it more difficult for ethnic minorities to bring a partner from their home country. Between 1997 and 2001, half the immigrants who entered the country had arranged for a spouse or family to follow. "Marriage migration" is a concern, since 60% to 70% of second-generation Moroccans and Turks marry somebody from outside the Netherlands; this impedes integration. The Freedom Party calls for restrictions on immigration via marriage.

Those seeking permanent residency have to pay in advance for a compulsory course on integration, and the sum is reimbursed only upon completion of the course. Newcomers must take about 600 hours of "culture classes." To receive a passport, immigrants must demonstrate competency in the Dutch language. Illegal immigrants' home countries were put on notice that they would not be eligible for Dutch development aid if they refuse to take back subjects whom the Netherlands had refused asylum. Those whose applications were rejected face criminal charges if they remain in the country.

Further steps were taken in 2006. An entrance examination tests whether applicants can speak some Dutch and are aware of the country's liberal values, even if they do not agree with all of them. Citizens of EU countries and of certain democratic states, such as the US, are not required to take it. The exam costs €350 and the preparation kit for it an additional €60. The government produced a two-hour movie, *To the Netherlands*, showing, among other things, women bathing nude and two men kissing. Its purpose is to cause applicants to ponder whether they really would fit into one of the world's most permissive countries. In response to fierce criticism, a blander film was released, with bare breasts and kissing deleted.

Many Dutch have never come to terms with the reality that the Netherlands has become an immigrant and multicultural country. A social worker in Utrecht admitted that, "as much as we are called a multicultural city, we are living next to each other, and not with each other." Holland's 20% visible ethnic minorities are a higher percentage than in France or Britain. About half the nonwestern population was born in the Netherlands.

Approximately 6% (over 1 million and rising) of the total population is Muslim; the figure rises to 24% in Amsterdam, 13% in Rotterdam, and over 10% in The Hague. About 400,000 are Turkish immigrants. In 2009 Rotterdam swore in the country's first immigrant mayor, Ahmed Aboutaleb. Born 47 years earlier in Morocco and since age 14 a Dutch resident, he had been a journalist and the central government's deputy social affairs minister. Judged too provocative, calls to prayer are banned in Rotterdam for the time being.

It was estimated that by 2020 ethnic minorities will constitute the majority in the four largest cities: Amsterdam, The Hague, Rotterdam, and Utrecht. Their birth rate is double that of native Dutch. Most come from the poorer parts of Turkey and Morocco, and the majority has citizenship. Two-thirds said in a 2005 poll that they would not want their daughters to marry a non-Muslim. Most take spouses from their home country, thereby delaying integration by a generation or more. Islam is a religion that now outnumbers Calvinism in the Netherlands. Polls in Amsterdam in 2007 revealed that more residents identify with Islam (12%) than with Catholicism and Protestantism combined. A minority of Muslim children attend 37 Islamic schools, financed by the state in the Dutch tradition.

The secret service recognizes that al-Qaeda is succeeding in recruiting young Muslims in mosques, cafés, and prisons in the Netherlands for a "holy war" against the US and its allies. In 2002 two men were accused in a Rotterdam trial of plotting to attack the American embassy in Paris. A year later Dutch authorities arrested an accomplice in a plot to send militants to Iraq for suicide attacks against US forces. Nervous Dutch authorities requested the US in 2003 to move its embassy from the middle of The Hague for security reasons.

In 2004 the nation was given a horrible shock by a second political murder in only two years. Theo van Gogh, a provocative film director and distant relative of the famous 19th-century Dutch painter, was murdered in Amsterdam in broad daylight while riding his bicycle to work. A 26-year-old Dutch Moroccan, Mohammed Bouyeri, emptied a magazine of bullets into Van Gogh's body, then slit his throat, and left a note with verses from the Quran and threats to other Dutch stuck to his lifeless body with a knife. The murderer was wounded in the leg and apprehended after a shoot-out with the police. This crime has been called the "Dutch September 11."

In 2005 Bouyeri was given a life sentence without parole, the first person to be convicted of terrorism in the Netherlands since its antiterror laws were toughened in 2004. Claiming to be waging a holy war against the "enemies of Islam," he said he dreamed of replacing the Dutch government with an Islamic theocracy and that he was supported by a network of like-minded fanatics. He rejected the validity of the Dutch legal system, admitted guilt, showed no remorse, and swore he would do the same again if he were ever freed. The most frightening thing about Bouyeri was that he had not been a victim of social exclusion. He had been a good student, spoke good Dutch, and was active in community affairs before falling in with extremist elements.

This grisly act of intolerance by a religious fanatic who had Dutch citizenship has convinced many Dutch that building a multicultural society has failed. This comes on top of a longer-term Dutch backlash that had fueled the spectacular rise of Pim Fortuyn, who was also gunned down in the street. Nine other Islamic radicals were tried and convicted in 2006.

Twelve more suspects from a radical Islamist cell, the Hofstad group, which had compiled a death list of Dutch politicians, were arrested a day after the van Gogh murder. Hundreds of police had conducted a 14-hour standoff. Two were jailed for 15 and 13 years for throwing a hand grenade at police officers, wounding five. The 30-man cell was mostly composed of second- or third-generation Dutch Muslims of Moroccan origin, but 2 were Dutch American converts. Police uncovered plans for blowing up Schiphol Airport, the Dutch parliament, the headquarters of the General Intelligence and Security Service, and one of the country's nuclear reactors. A number of the arrested had trained in Pakistan to carry out armed attacks. In the days after the van Gogh murder, there were attacks on Muslim sites. An Islamic elementary school in Eindhoven was bombed and two mosques burned. Former prime minister

Rembrandt, self-portrait

Balkenende visited a Turkish mosque in a show of solidarity.

Van Gogh, an outspoken critic of Islam, especially its treatment of women, had directed a film, *Submission*, for Dutch TV. It featured a Muslim woman in a see-through burka (head-to-toe robe) telling a story of abuse within her marriage. Text from the Quran condoning family violence was written on her naked body.

The script for the film had been written by an outspoken Somali refugee, Ayaan Hirsi Ali. She was a member of parliament who had to live for a while within the protected confines of a naval base to avoid murder. When she could finally live in a normal apartment, a court ordered her to move out after neighbors complained that her presence brought them into danger. She said she had entered parliament in order to highlight the oppression of immigrant women and to make politicians aware that key aspects of Islamic doctrine, as practiced today, are incompatible with an open society. Among her parliamentary goals was to outlaw honor crimes. She became a symbol for resistance to Muslim fundamentalism.

In May 2006 her life in the Netherlands faced a crisis. A TV documentary about her highlighted some embarrassing facts that she had already long since admitted publicly, including when she was vetted for parliament. Coached by groups helping immigrants, she had lied in her 1992 asylum application about the route she had taken, her real name, and her true date of birth. She insisted that she had come under duress, to flee an arranged marriage to a cousin from Canada.

Her political ally, friend, and party colleague Rita ("Iron Rita") Verdonk, the tough former immigration minister, decided she had to be even-handed. She

The Netherlands

withdrew Ali's citizenship and ordered her to leave the country. Ali abruptly resigned from parliament and a day later announced that she would accept a position in Washington at the conservative think tank American Enterprise Institute (AEI).

The expulsion order set off a political storm. Parliamentarians of all parties were enraged and held an all-night session to demand Verdonk to back off. After a further grilling from parliament, reprimands by cabinet members, and an order from the prime minister that her citizenship be restored, Verdonk relented. Ali's citizenship was returned to her, but the entire trauma caused the breakup of the governing coalition. The Hirsi Ali affair especially embarrassed the Dutch because it made them look both cowardly and anti-immigrant.

Another parliamentarian, Geert Wilders, had to go into hiding and required 24-hour police protection. He has six bodyguards and often sleeps in a protected prison cell with no windows. He noted, "The people who threaten us are walking around free and we are the captives." This kind of security is something entirely new for Dutch politicians. A soaring number of politicians, academics, and public figures have been compelled to go into hiding or accept 24-hour protection after receiving assassination threats. Elsewhere in Europe, Muslim terrorists unsettle the societies through indiscriminate attacks. In the Netherlands they single out individuals for assassination.

In the opinion of Amsterdam's former left-wing mayor Job Cohen, firebrands like Wilders are reaping what they have sown and are largely responsible for the situation that fear and suspicion among ethnic groups in the country are at a postwar peak. Wilders is an outspoken critic of radical Islam and immigrants, and radical Arab Internet sites call for his beheading.

He made everybody nervous when he announced in 2007 that he was producing a film that compares the Quran to Hitler's book *Mein Kampf*. He said the 15-minute film, entitled *Fitna* (meaning "civic strife" in Arabic), shows how the Quran inspires people "to do the worst things." The Dutch government tried but failed to persuade him not to broadcast it; warnings had come from all over the Muslim world. Since no television station would air the film, he temporarily put it on the Internet until the servers bowed to threats and took it off. It portrays Islam as a ticking time bomb aimed at the west, and it shows beheadings, violence against women, anti-Semitic tirades by imams, and the aftermath of the New York and Madrid terrorist bombings, including charred remains of victims. The clips are alternated with images of Quranic verses purporting to show from where the inspiration for such acts comes. It opens and closes with the same image of Muhammad with bombs in his turban published by a Danish cartoonist in 2005.

Wilders has radical suggestions: stopping all Muslim immigration, banning the Quran and the construction of mosques, and giving the 1 million Muslims in the Netherlands the choice of "going to their own countries" or renouncing their religion. He also proposed a general ban on wearing burkas, but the government decided that this would violate the freedom of religion guaranteed by the constitution. However, it did prohibit the wearing of burkas and full-face veils at schools and government workplaces. Wilders publicly questioned the loyalty of two cabinet members with dual citizenship (Turkish and Moroccan, in addition to Dutch).

After he had been invited in February 2009 to the House of Lords to screen his controversial film, the British government banned him from entering the country, saying his presence would threaten community harmony and public safety. A miffed Wilders commented, "This is something you'd expect from Saudi Arabia, not Britain." He appealed the ban, and it was lifted. The debate surrounding the Dutch parliamentarian did not diminish his voter appeal. In the June 2010 elections, his party shot up and placed third; it provides crucial votes for the center-right government.

The goal now is integration, meaning that the time has come for the growing Muslim minority (40% of whom come from Turkey and 34% from Morocco) to adjust to where they live and adopt Dutch values. The price for living in this open, law-governed society is to acknowledge the right of others to think differently. This conviction has entered the political mainstream.

More and more Dutch citizens feel threatened by the immigrant presence and the terrorist threat, and politicians have taken note of this. Laws were introduced permitting authorities to close mosques, confiscate Dutch passports from dual citizens, and deport radical imams (clergymen). Many demand that, in the near future, all imams be Dutch-educated. Universities are given subsidies to create theology departments that train Muslim prayer leaders. The Education Ministry now requires that any school (meaning Muslim school) that is opened must prove that it intends to transmit the values of Dutch society. In 2011 most parties in parliament, supported by two-thirds of the public, voted to ban the nonanaesthetized slaughter of animals used by Muslims and Jews to produce halal and kosher meat. This presented a rare sight of imams and rabbis marching together to protest the measure.

This comes at a time when Dutch are worrying about a general weakening of their social cohesion, symbolized in many minds by the omnipresence of immigrants. How far should liberal societies tolerate the intolerant? It is perhaps not surprising that half of Dutch respondents in a 2006 poll had a dislike of Islam, and 43% thought Islam is not a peaceful religion. But some political figures are calling on Muslim groups to accept the liberal Dutch society they live in or be forced to do so.

Political correctness has found its place. Some Dutch are offended by the black face of Zwarte Piet, who accompanies St. Nicholas on his Christmas rounds. They call it racism.

Sexual Tolerance

The hallmark of modern Netherlands has become to acknowledge common practices and to decriminalize them. An example is prostitution, which has long been legalized. However, brothels were not. In 2000 parliament passed a law making the 2,000 brothels legal and subjecting them to government regulation and regular inspections. A job category for the 30,000 registered prostitutes was created: "freelance workers." They have employment rights and the right to establish a trade union, a process that began in 2001. Not all "sex workers" like their new legal status because they have to pay taxes.

In 2007 the Amsterdam city government strong-armed Charlie Geerts, the property magnate known as the "Emperor of Sex," to sell his third of the city's famed red-light district windows and to convert the buildings into public housing. The mayor explained that prostitution, which remains legal, attracts money laundering and other criminal activity; he wants to gentrify the area. Indeed, more than 100 brothels and a dozen coffee shops were closed. City councilwoman Karina Schaapman, herself a former prostitute, calls the popular tourist district "a cesspit. There's a lot of exploiting of women and a lot of social distress. That's nothing to be proud of." In 2021, the council adopted a plan to shutter the district and relocate it to an "erotic center" in a different neighborhood.

Gay people and lesbians in the Netherlands have wider civil rights than anywhere in Europe. Since 1999 they could register their partnerships in a civil ceremony and receive almost the same rights and obligations as heterosexual couples. In 2000 the Netherlands became the first country in the world to allow same-sex couples to marry on the same terms as heterosexuals. They can take each other's surname, inherit their property, receive alimony, enjoy the same tax status, and opt for prenuptial agreements. The restriction that a same-sex couple may adopt only a Dutch child, not one from abroad, was lifted in 2005. As many as 8% of all marriages are of the same sex. In 2006 the Dutch ambassador to Estonia was transferred to Montreal when he complained that his black Cuban male partner suffered racist and homophobic abuse on the streets of Tallinn. In 2017 a pack of hoodlums brutally attacked two gay men holding hands. To show solidarity with the victims, the next day, hundreds of police, soldiers, athletes, actors, political party chieftains, and others held hands in public.

The Netherlands is also the first country to experience gay divorces, which must be obtained in court and which sometimes result in alimony payments. Polls indicate that most Dutch support these reforms, and it has ceased being a contentious issue. In the words of one of the bill's sponsors, Boris Dittrich, "A person's sex is not important for marriage."

Euthanasia

Another case of legalizing what has been long-standing practice is euthanasia. Passive euthanasia (halting life support systems to allow natural death) was long permitted, and doctors in the 1990s were virtually never prosecuted for assisting in thousands of suicides of terminally ill patients. In 1995, for the first time, a physician was found guilty of murder for ending the life of a deformed newborn who was unable to ask explicitly that a doctor do so. But as a sign of how torn even judges were over this issue, the court ruled that the doctor's actions were justifiable under the Netherlands' tolerant euthanasia laws and refused to punish him.

The Netherlands moved toward permitting voluntary euthanasia ("mercy killing" through fatal injections to hopelessly ill patients); 80% involve cancer patients. Only 4% of deaths (ca. 5,000 per year) are mercy killings, a number that is stabilizing. Polls have long indicated that three out of four Dutch support this, although the practice remains ethically troubling and controversial. A 2016 report revealed that patients had often declined treatment that would have helped or cited loneliness as a reason for wanting to die. Dutch courts stopped prosecuting and jailing doctors who, according to a 1993 law (the first of its kind in an industrialized nation), followed a detailed 28-point checklist: The patient had to be terminally ill and in a clear state of mind, and he or she, not family or friends, had to have asked repeatedly to die. A second opinion had to be obtained. A 2005 study showed that, of all the requests for euthanasia, nearly half are carried out; in a fourth the patient died before it could be done; 13% changed their mind; and physicians refused in 12% of the cases.

In 2000 euthanasia and assisted suicide were decriminalized under certain circumstances: A patient need not be actually dying. People over age 16 who suffer acute and unremitting pain may ask to die (parents may decide for sufferers under age 16). Doctors are not allowed to recommend suicide as an option and must inform the patient of all other alternatives known. They must get a second medical opinion and be sure that the patient's request is well considered and that he has acted voluntarily. In 2001, the Netherlands became the first country in the world to legalize mercy killing for terminally ill persons with "lasting and unbearable suffering" with no hope of improvement, as long as the volunteer's doctor and an independent consultant approve. An ethical storm broke out in 2016 over a proposal to allow healthy elderly persons who feel they have lived a full life to seek assisted suicide.

Drug Policies

In the early 1970s, the Dutch had another opportunity to show their toleration when Amsterdam became the favorite destination for long-haired, guitar-toting, young people who were called at the time "hippies," as well as other younger people with different lifestyles. While these young people horrified the established citizens almost everywhere they went, the Dutch accepted them with good humor and tried hard to find them temporary shelter and areas where they could meet freely. They also tried to look the other way when the visitors chose to use "soft" drugs or violate the sexual standards of Dutch society.

By the mid-1980s, though, Dutch patience with hard-drug trafficking and crime in Amsterdam had visibly begun to wear thin, and neighborhood vigilante groups were organized to protect against lawbreakers. On the whole, the crime rate

A coffee shop, not to be confused with a café (a bar) or coffee house (for coffee and tea).
Photo by Juliet Bunch

de Volkskrant

MAANDAG 4 FEBRUARI 2002 • 26 PAGINA'S

Kroonprins: Máxima brengt enorm offer

Van onze verslaggevers
AMSTERDAM

Prinses Máxima pinkt zaterdagmiddag in de Nieuwe Kerk een traantje weg bij de tango Adiós Nonino.

Emotionele inzegening in Nieuwe Kerk

Het weer

Opklarend

(above refers to ad images)

Rookbom past in Oranjefeest

Van onze verslaggever
Sander van Walsum
AMSTERDAM

Superster

Het Huwelijk
De kus, een offer voor hongerige wolven 10
De kleding was ingetogen, de make-up tranenproof 10
Iedereen steekt Máxima een hart onder de riem 11
Langoustinetaartjes en tartelette van knolselderij 11
De sabel en de bruidstaart: het huwelijk in beeld 12, 13
Huwelijksreis voert stel naar de camping 14

PRINS BERNHARD
'Wat een mooie bruid!'

Prins Bernhard (90), grootvader van de bruidegom:

Pieter Broertjes

Pagina 7: Commentaar
www.volkskrant.nl: Verslagen, persspiegel, fotogalerij, integrale tekst toespraken burgemeester Cohen en ds. Ter Linden

WILLEM-ALEXANDER & MÁXIMA
NU VERKRIJGBAAR OP COMPACT DISC!

NRC HANDELSBLAD

www.nrc.nl WOENSDAG 30 JANUARI 2002 Prijs € 1.15

Later zon

Amsterdam wordt gescreend en 'gebomcheckt'
• Binnenland: pagina 2

Gortdroge wetenschappers als oorlogshelden
• Film & Video: pagina 8

Ontslagen KPN-managers ontdekken nut van collectief optreden
• Loopbaan: pagina 14

Hermans haalt bakzeil over collegegeld

Premier Albanië afgetreden

Rel Japan: ontslag van minister

VVD wil enquête bouwfraudeleiden

President Bush in State of the Union:
Bestrijding terreur maar net begonnen

Door onze correspondent

WASHINGTON, 30 JAN. De oorlog tegen het terrorisme is nog maar net begonnen.

De Amerikaanse president George W. Bush waarschuwde gisteravond in zijn State of the Union-toespraak in het Congres, dat er nog zelfmoordcommando's in Afghanistan getrainde terroristen op vrije voeten zijn, 'als tikkende tijdbommen'. (Foto Reuters)

Brussel tikt

KLM zoekt

E-Plus helemaal

---

remains low compared with the US and many other European countries. But street crime increased dramatically. Dutch jails are known throughout Europe to be the hardest to enter and the easiest to leave. Even hardened criminals in prisons are permitted to vote and to have overnight visits with their families, girlfriends, or same-sex partners in special rooms with complete privacy. Two-thirds of all prisoners are hard-drug addicts, which points to a further problem.

Polls in 2008 showed that only 35% of Dutch had used cannabis by age 21, compared with 54% of Americans. It is still illegal to sell it without state supervision, but possession has been decriminalized. The state taxes the profits from the sale of cannabis, and police put the lowest priority on preventing its sale and use in small amounts. Marijuana is so tolerated that 700 coffee shops (down from 1,400 in 1995) put it on their menus and serve it to customers. It is a paradox that such establishments are permitted to sell cannabis products, but they may not grow cannabis. They have to resort to the black market. It is illegal to grow more than five plants for recreational use. In 2003 the Netherlands became the first country to make cannabis available as a prescription drug if it is approved by doctors to alleviate acute pain after conventional treatments had been exhausted or if other drugs had negative side effects.

There are some legal problems. Dutch law prohibits substances that have been "processed." Authorities are well practiced at turning a blind eye. When ecstasy tablets became popular in the 1980s, they were declared illegal. But the police were told to ignore consumption and to try to curb manufacturing.

Uncomfortable with its reputation as being soft on drug users, Dutch authorities cracked down on the larger-scale commercialization of soft drugs. Neighboring countries put pressure on the Dutch government to enforce stricter laws on drugs. The German government once blamed it for the vast amount of drugs crossing the German border. The Netherlands was sensitive to those concerns. Two cities near the Belgian border blamed the cannabis trade for a rise in crime and closed all its coffee shops by 2009. Owners were put on notice not to call attention to their wares, deal in carryout quantities, sell more than a sixth of an ounce at a time, or sell cocaine and heroin under the counter. Coffee shops caught selling cannabis to children under age 18 are shut down. As of January 2013, new government rules require that coffee shops become members-only clubs limited to 2,000 Dutch clients each and forbidden to serve foreigners. The European Court of Justice ruled that coffee shops have a right to refuse service to drug tourists.

The government pledged in 2002 to enforce the criteria governing the coffee shops more strictly and not to allow them to be located close to schools or the national borders. One earlier justice ministry spokeswoman had commented, "We want just enough to cater to our own citizens, not to the drug tourists." In 2006 a pilot program to regulate marijuana farming on the model of tobacco was introduced in Maastricht. It is estimated that the value of Dutch exports of cannabis is greater than the country's annual flower exports, which are worth $6.6 billion. After a top-level "weed summit" in 2008, Amsterdam ordered nearly one-fifth of its coffee shops to close by 2011 in an effort to protect children from drugs. All were located within 350 meters of schools. This was a part of a rethinking of the country's permissive drug policies. However, in a 2008 poll, 80% of Dutch citizens opposed shutting down the coffee shops altogether.

Police are cracking down on drug dealing at highway rest stops and parking areas. They have especially gone after the traffic in hard drugs, even though users are not arrested unless they commit other crimes. Such tolerance had been extended to ecstasy use. Although the country produces an estimated 80% of the world's supply, its trafficking and manufacturing are illegal. The government in 2002 pledged a crackdown on ecstasy, summarizing its tougher approach toward drugs: "The production of and trade in drugs in the Netherlands has reached unacceptable levels and must be tackled more firmly." Authorities believed that their tolerating soft drugs was responsible for the decline in the percentage of young people using hard drugs from 14% in the 1980s to only 1.6% in 1997, compared with 3% in Italy, 2.8% in France, and 1.5% in Germany.

Addicts are steered into treatment and are provided with clean new needles to prevent AIDS. In 2000 only 10% of AIDS victims in the Netherlands were intravenous drug users, compared with nearly 40% across Europe. The publicly visible use of drugs has caused some Dutch to wonder if their country has indeed become too permissive. Ed van Thijn, former mayor of Amsterdam, confessed that "in the past 15 years tolerance became synonymous with permissiveness and softness on law-and-order." In 1990, the Washington-based Drugs Policy Foundation awarded the Dutch government a prize for "its effective and humanitarian drug policies." Said one senior Amsterdam policeman, "We do not say that our way is right for them [Americans], but we are sure it is right for us." Nevertheless, in the 21st century, more and more European countries are inclined to follow the Dutch

Johannes Vermeer, *Girl with a Pearl Earring*   Mauritshuis, The Hague

lead in this matter and to turn away from America's more militant "war" on drugs.

The Dutch, as a people, are inclined to cling to tradition and to be conservative. At the same time, they are open to new ideas and are relatively tolerant toward all forms of individualism. This is why criticism and protest can be so firmly entrenched in the Dutch tradition but why the Dutch are at the same time not inclined to be revolutionary. Compromise is a highly developed art in the Netherlands, and protest groups have often been smothered by tolerance. It saps one's strength to beat one's head against a richly padded, sympathetic wall.

Media and Arts

"Columnization" is also found in the press and electronic media. Newspapers and magazines reflect the opinions of many diverse groups in society, and the average reader expects to find his own opinions expressed in the news he reads. Financial problems have resulted in the concentration of most newspapers in the hands of a few large companies, although 60% of the dailies still manage to take an independent editorial line. To help preserve their independence, the government provides financial support to newspapers and magazines that are undergoing reorganization to become profitable again. The major dailies, in order of circulation, are *De Telegraaf* (conservative, now with a Sunday edition), *Algemeen Dagblad* (neutral), *De Volkskrant* (progressive), *Het Parool* (center-left), and *Trouw* (Protestant). Top people tend to prefer the *NRCHandelsblad* (liked by intellectuals) and the *Financieele*

The Netherlands

Dagblad. The top magazines are *Elseviers Magazine* and *Elseviers Weekblad,* followed by *Vrij Nederland.* In a 2002 study by the professional group Reporters without Borders, the Netherlands ranked third in the world, after Finland and Iceland, in terms of press freedom. The US placed 17th.

There are three public television channels, which have difficulties competing with commercial channels. There is a public educational and cultural channel (Nederland 3), and five public radio stations. Also on the air are 400 local radio stations, including a handful that broadcast legally from abroad, especially Luxembourg. Commercial TV channels have operated since 1992. Programming is in the hands of both the state and a variety of private broadcasting organizations that largely operate free of government control. Some of these organizations represent the basic pillars of society. For instance, KRO is Catholic, NCRV is Protestant, VPRO is liberal Protestant, and VARA is socialist. Unlike many newspapers, however, the broadcasting companies attempt to broaden their appeals to include all social groups. They are, therefore, actually able to overcome some of the cleavages in Dutch society.

These four private organizations operate within the framework established by the government-related Netherlands Broadcasting Association (NOS). The NOS, a quasi-governmental broadcasting foundation, is charged with producing programs "in the general interest," such as news bulletins. The Ministry of Welfare, Health, and Culture is the authority that oversees its operations. The postal service, privatized in 1989, no longer collects fees to finance broadcasting; it is paid out of taxes. The NOS also controls the amount of advertising that may be broadcast.

When one thinks of Dutch culture, perhaps the first words that come to mind are the names of painters: Hieronymous Bosch, with his powerful and sometimes-terrifying scenes, brought to European art in the 16th century a form of symbolism which reflected the mind of a great visionary. In the 17th century, Rembrandt, Franz Hals, and Jan Vermeer established an artistic tradition through their vivid depiction of early Dutch life. In the 19th century, J. B. Jongkind became a precursor of impressionism, and Vincent van Gogh, in a short but wild life, helped create the romantic picture that many people have of artists. He sketched the drab and dreary life of persons living in working-class and rural areas in the late 19th century, going later to Paris and southern France, where he established his personal style of short brushstrokes in brilliant colors, which pointed the way to a new, expressive style.

Rembrandt's house in Amsterdam

The Netherlands has almost 1,000 museums, with 42 in Amsterdam alone. In 2013 the Rijksmuseum, now called the Museum of the Netherlands, reopened in Amsterdam after 10 years of restoration. Rembrandt's *The Night Watch,* probably the most famous Dutch painting, has top billing and location. It has 1.1 million objects in its collection and is busy renaming paintings with politically incorrect titles, such as *Negro, Indian,* or *Dwarf.*

There was less joy in the Kunsthal in Rotterdam. In October 2012 seven paintings by Picasso, Matisse, and Lucian Freud were stolen despite the state-of-the-art security. Investigators tracked the culprits to a Romanian gang, which sought a deal but burned at least three of the paintings.

In the Dutch artistic tradition of accurately recording the landscape around them, Hendrick Willem Mesdag painted in 1880 the world's largest panoramic painting, portraying Scheveningen, a fishing village on the outskirts of The Hague. Displayed in a museum in The Hague, called the *Panorama Mesdag,* the painting completely surrounds the viewer and gives him the most vivid possible impression of Holland in Mesdag's time.

Piet Mondrian, the greatest and most consistent renovator of modern Dutch art of the 20th century, began with experimental nature paintings, but gradually he departed from nature and sought harmonious and universal images. His paintings of lines and colors are among the world's most treasured modern artworks. M. C. Escher and Willem de Kooning also enjoy worldwide fame. The latter was born in Rotterdam in 1904 and came to New York City at age 22 as a stowaway aboard a British freighter. He became the undisputed leader of abstract expressionism and one of the most imitated artists in America.

The Dutch considered art to be so important for the society that they maintained, at public expense, some 3,000 artists who were unable to make a living. Although they had to demonstrate that they were full-time and professionally trained artists with talent, once they were selected, they merely had to deliver a modest number of paintings each year to the state in return for their pay.

Most of the paintings went into storage and were never seen again. Some critics argued that this subsidy lowered the quality of painting and was merely an example of the welfare state run wild. The government also helped to finance experimental theater, orchestra, ballet and film companies. Over 4% of the central government's budget was at one time devoted to supporting the arts. These subsidies have been heavily cut by 22% in 2012–2013; of 120 cultural arts organizations, a third became ineligible for government grants. Dutch businesses finance a variety of artistic groups from jazz to chamber music artists in order to improve their image with customers.

Historically, Holland is rich with philosophical and intellectual leaders. Hugo Grotius founded the study of international law. René Descartes, a Frenchman who was living in the Netherlands, developed a new starting point for philosophy when he asserted, "I think, therefore I am." Baruch Spinoza wrote treatises on the relationships between the human intellect, the state, and religious belief. Anton van Leeuwenhoek invented the microscope that thereby revolutionized the study of biology. Christian Huygens invented the pendulum clock, and the Dutch have been a very punctual people ever since.

There are more than 22 million people inside and outside the Netherlands who speak native Dutch, and as many as 35 million can read Dutch literature in the original. The Foundation for Promoting the Translation of Dutch Literature seeks to introduce the nation's writings abroad. Before the 16th century, literature was primarily composed of plays, religious literature, folktales, and stories of chivalry. In the 17th century, Joost van den Vondel's writings were read all over Europe.

The most noted author of the 19th century was Multatuli (pseudonym for Douwes Dekker), who worked in the colonies and observed the mistreatment of the native populations. His 1860 novel *Max Havelaar* attacked colonialism. The works of novelist Louis Couperus evoke the atmosphere of the turn of the century. After 1945, Holland rapidly lost its rural character. The postwar literature of such writers as Jan Wolkers, W. F. Hermans, and G. K. van't Reve often deals with the problems arising from life in a highly urban and industrial society. Harry Mulisch, whose book *The Discovery of Heaven* was voted in a 2007 newspaper poll "the best Dutch-language book ever," died in 2010. Prime Minister Mark Rutte said of his passing, "We all grew up with him. Mulisch presided over Dutch literature. This is the end of an era."

FUTURE

The legendary Dutch tolerance and consensus orientation have become frayed. The "polder model," the popular name for the practice of policy making by consensus between government, employers, and trade unions, was out of fashion for a while. Political correctness has weakened. The Dutch are willing to support politicians who openly defy the old rules and speak publicly of problems on many voters' minds, such as crime, immigration, and terrorism.

The March 2017 elections were widely seen as a bellwether for crucial elections in France and Germany; turnout was an admirable 82%. Geert Wilders' Freedom Party, which no other party wants to have as a partner, was second, with 20 seats. Growing anti-European and anti-immigrant feelings have their roots in the weak economy and in the influx of 50,000 asylum seekers in 2015. Prime Minister Mark Rutte's Liberal Party emerged as the largest party, with 33 seats. Green Left jumped from 4 to 14 seats. He turned to the Christian Democratic Appeal Party and Democrats 66 Party, each with 19 seats, as well as the Green Left to form a government. Seven months of haggling were necessary.

In the end Prime Minister Rutte cobbled together a diverse coalition government with a one-vote majority. Little binds the parts together, but all reject Wilders's opposition to the EU. Some things are going well. In 2009 their country was ranked highest of all OECD countries in terms of overall well-being, and in 2012 the UN's human-development index named it as the third-best country to live, after Norway and Australia. The Dutch looked nervously at Brexit. Except for Ireland, no country will suffer more; it could lose 3% of its GDP by 2030.

In January 2021, Ritte resigned over a child benefits scandal. However, he is a consummate political survivor and was favored to lead his fourth government in eleven years after the March 2021 elections. The main future task of any Dutch government is to bring the deadly coronavirus under control. This is no easy task. All over the country, rioters objected to the 9 p.m. curfew, the first since the Nazi occupation. The violence lasted three nights, and hundreds were arrested. It was the worst in forty years. Rutte apologized for allowing the royal family to take an

The Netherlands

autumn vacation in Greece. They cut it short.

The Netherlands faces the future with its first king since 1890, Willem-Alexander. He is Europe's youngest monarch. April 30, 2013, was a glorious day in Amsterdam, a mixture of pageantry, boisterous street parties, and church bells ringing out across the city. There was no religious blessing or coronation, since the Dutch monarch never wears a crown. He was "inaugurated." Polls show that support for maintaining the monarchy runs as high as 85%. Outgoing Queen Beatrix was beloved; the new king is regarded as a decent fellow; his wife, Maxima, who was an Argentine investment banker until they married in 2002, is wildly popular.

The Kingdom of Belgium

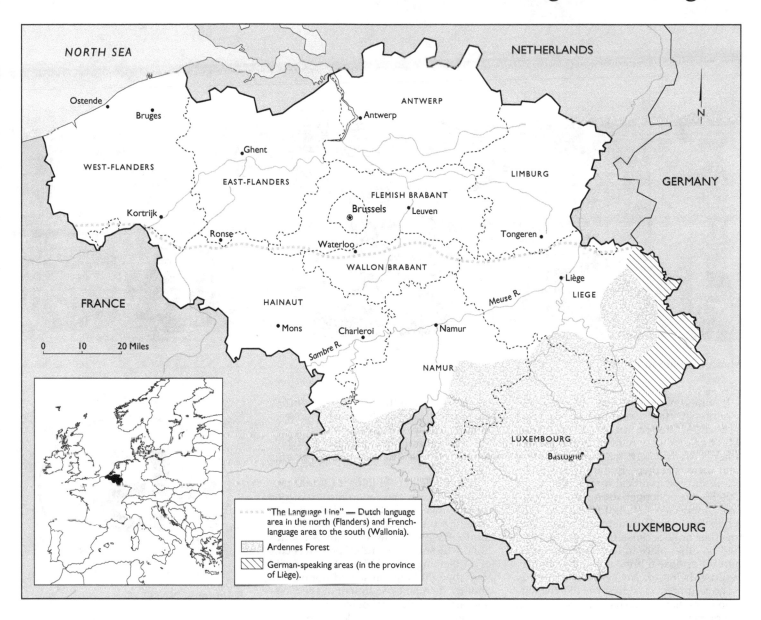

"The Language Line" — Dutch language area in the north (Flanders) and French-language area to the south (Wallonia).

Ardennes Forest

German-speaking areas (in the province of Liège).

Area: 18,991 sq. mi. (30,562 sq. km, somewhat larger than Maryland and about 200 miles, or 320 km wide, taken from its northwest to southeast points).

Population: 11.6 million (6.3 million in Flanders, 3.6 million in Wallonia, .95 million in Brussels, 2007).

Capital City: Brussels (pop. 178,552; Brussels capital region, 1.2 million, 2017).

Climate: Temperate, with rather mild winters and comfortable summers.

Neighboring Countries: Germany (east); the Netherlands (north); France (south); Luxembourg (southeast); England is about 54 miles (87 km) away across the English Channel.

Official Languages: Dutch (59%), French (40%). Both languages are spoken by about 10%, principally those living in and around Brussels, 80% of whose citizens are native French speakers. German is the native tongue for 1%.

Principal Religion: Roman Catholic (95%).

Main Exports: Chemicals, transport equipment, machinery, food and animal products, 70% of the world's cobalt, 60% of the world's diamond dealing, and 40% of cutting.

Main Imports: Chemicals, machinery, transport equipment, food, and animals.

Major Trading Partners: EU (72% of exports and 67.9% of imports), Germany (18.2% of exports and 14.6% of imports), France (16.4% of exports and 10.5% of imports), Netherlands (12.2% of exports and 19.6% of imports), UK (7% of exports and 5.9% of imports).

Currency: Euro.

National Holiday: July 21.

Chief of State: His Majesty King Philippe (b. 1960; since National Day, July 21, 2013).

Heir Apparent: Her Royal Highness Princess Elisabeth, Duchess of Brabant.

Head of Government: Prime Minister Alexander De Croo (since October 2020).

National Flag: Vertical stripes of red, yellow, and black, with the black stripe at the pole.

In some ways Belgium is a very unnatural country. It has no natural frontiers, such as a mountain chain or wide river, to set it off from its neighbors. It has therefore always been very vulnerable to foreign invasion. Belgians have no common language and are extremely sensitive about being forced to speak the one not used in their half of the country. Their tradition as a unified country is only a century and three-quarters old and is too weak to give its citizens a strong common identity. Unlike the Swiss, many Belgians never really developed the habit of thinking in terms of a single nation.

Belgium

Market Square in Bruges

It sometimes seems that there are just 6 million Dutch-speaking Flemings and 4 million French-speaking Walloons, who must try very hard to live with each other. Unfortunately, the forces that once held them together—Roman Catholicism, economic and political opposition to the Dutch—are no longer strong. Belgium appears almost like a shotgun wedding—like a hopelessly broken marriage which held together only because the partners could find no other place to live. Walloons, who bitterly oppose a breakup of the country because their economy depends so heavily on government subsidies, feel like the wife who fears that her husband is about to run out on her.

Economic performance and stable government, as well as language issues, are important in Belgians' minds. This is baffling to political scientists. Belgium may be the only dysfunctional state in the world that is both stable and prosperous and in which government services are efficient. Belgians have many trumps in their hands as they face the future. They are rather cautious, conservative people, a fact that causes some critics to call Belgium a private, family-centered country.

It also means that, while their conflicts are often verbally bitter and serious and sometimes erupt in street brawls between the rare hotheads, Belgians are very unlikely to resort to outright violence and terror to accomplish their goals. They have always shown a genius for compromise by very small steps. Thus, no one expects the community problems, as the language issue is called, to explode into a bloody and

tragic Northern Ireland–style conflict. However, they can still cause a government to collapse and can prevent a new government from being formed 18 whole months after elections are held, as was the case in 2010–2011.

The divide is beginning to sound permanent. Given this ongoing crisis, one can no longer be certain that Belgium will remain a unified country. The country's motto, "Strength through unity," sounds hollow these days. In a 2007 poll, over 60% of all Flemings and 40% of Walloons said they thought Belgium would not exist in another decade; close to half of the Flemings already favor that outcome.

It still has many valuable economic resources. It has a very skilled workforce with a proven willingness to work. Its economy remains highly productive; this has usually kept inflation low and has maintained for Belgians one of the highest standards of living in the world. Its central location in Europe remains a very significant trading advantage for the country. It is an important partner in a unified Europe and in the Atlantic alliance, and its capital city, Brussels, is in many ways the "capital of Europe," housing the headquarters for both NATO and the EU.

One in three residents of Brussels is now non-Belgian. One in four is Muslim, of which 70% are Moroccan and 20% Turkish. There are an estimated 30,000 foreign EU bureaucrats (dubbed "Eurocrats"), diplomats, journalists, lobbyists, and their families in Brussels and perhaps another 15,000 Europeans whose jobs are linked to the EU. Such massive presence and the

Belgium in NATO

decision to hold all European summits in Brussels starting in 2002 have prompted the European Commission to consider declaring the city the "capital of Europe." Some countries, including the United States, even send three ambassadors to this city: one to the king of the Belgians (i.e., to the government), one to NATO, and one to the EU.

Belgium is a picturesque country with scenery varying from Gothic medieval university cities to countless towns and villages located along winding rivers with steep bluffs. The country is mainly flat, but it rises toward the south, away from the North Sea coast and toward the Ardennes Forest. The country can be divided roughly into three geographic parts. In the north is the Flemish Plain, which extends westward from a 41-mile (60 km) North Sea coastline, with its sandy beaches and luxurious and expensive resorts. Flanders presents a pastoral landscape with small farms and most of Belgium's agricultural production. With 60% of the Belgian population in a little less than half the total land area, it is the most densely populated part of the country that itself is the second-most densely populated land in all of Europe, behind the Netherlands. Here are the Flemish cities of Bruges (with its many bridges which gave the city its name), Ghent, and Antwerp, all three filled with cathedrals and other medieval structures. Most of Belgium's newer industries are located in Flanders, which is the country's most economically dynamic section, a fact that greatly riles the Walloons today.

At the center of Belgium are rolling fields of grain and many villages with houses grouped around the parish church. In the middle is Brussels, and below it are heavy industrial centers, clustered around the formerly rich Walloon coalfields, which are now largely exhausted and closed. This was the area of the country's Industrial Revolution in the 19th century, which occurred in Belgium earlier than almost anywhere else in Europe. It is where such industrial cities as Mons, Charleroi, and the ancient and dignified city of Liège are located. South of the Sambre and Meuse Rivers is the third area, with no large cities or industries. It is a region of fields and pastures with woods thickening as one travels southward into the Ardennes Forest.

Running west to east, just south of Kortrijk, Ronse, Brussels, Leuven (Louvain), and Tongeren, is an invisible line established 1,500 years ago and now of far greater significance for contemporary Belgium than the geographic areas mentioned above. This is the language line that separates the Flemings from the Walloons. Along the German border is also the German-speaking minority numbering about 76,000 people. Because most Belgians live on "their" side of the language line, they have fewer language problems, now that Flemish (a language which differs from Dutch about as much as American from British English), French, or German is used exclusively in all affairs, including education, law, government, and business, within each respective region.

The people in the various sections do not look or act very differently, although some observers claim to notice differences in the people's characters—the Flemings being severe and serious and the Walloons being more outgoing, volatile, and fun-loving. In fact, the visitor would scarcely notice any difference at all if it were not for the fact that he hears different languages spoken on the streets and sees different languages on street signs and billboards. The language separation is greatly complicated by the capital city of Brussels, which has 20% of the country's GDP and 11% (1 million) of the country's population, 80% of whom speak French as a mother tongue. This city is situated uncomfortably north of the language line and is surrounded by Flemish speakers. It is over the hurdle of Brussels that all proponents of regional language reform have tripped. If Belgium ultimately holds together, it may very well be because Brussels is simply too entangled to unravel.

One would not expect language difficulties to trouble this small, cosmopolitan country that is located at the very crossroads of Europe and which has been one of the most persistent and constructive proponents of European integration. But it is exactly this problem that has caused many people to wonder how many more birthdays this country will be able to celebrate.

HISTORY

Shaky Independence

Belgium proclaimed its independence from the Netherlands in 1830, and its new king took the name of Leopold I. Because the Dutch king refused to recognize Belgian independence until 1839, Leopold's most immediate goal was to win recognition for his new state, a goal that was greatly boosted by his marriage to the daughter of Louis-Philippe, king of France from 1830 to 1848. Having adopted a modern liberal constitution in 1830, Belgium was scarcely affected by the storm of revolution that blew across Europe in 1848 and could turn its attention to economic development.

Following Britain's example, Belgium adopted a policy of free trade and plunged headlong into industrialization, using its large and easily extracted coal resources. This effort was aided by an agreement with the Dutch in 1863 ending tolls for the use of the Scheldt River, which passes through Dutch territory before emptying into the North Sea. For three centuries the Dutch had shut off the river to isolate Antwerp. This agreement enabled the Belgians to develop fully the port of Antwerp that now plays such a key role in their trade.

The rapid industrial growth also gave birth to an urbanized working class and ultimately to socialism, which along with liberalism and Catholicism became one of the three main political "families," or social cleavages, in Belgian society. Divisions still exist, although groups are now less hostile to each other than they once were. The liberal and Catholic "families" squabbled throughout the 19th and early 20th centuries over the relations between church and state, especially insofar as the schools were concerned. Their struggle roughly ended in a draw, and state financial support continues to flow to secular, denominational, and free schools.

King Leopold II actively engaged in colonial activity in order "to secure for ourselves a slice of this magnificent African cake." Henry Stanley, the famous Welshman who fought on both sides of the US Civil War after emigrating to America, proceeded on an arduous journey to Africa in search of the Scottish missionary Dr. Livingstone. He initially wanted Britain to take the Congo, but it already had too much on its plate and was not interested. Leopold summoned him to Belgium and engaged him to explore the Congo area of Africa (not on behalf of Belgium but on behalf of the king). Stanley accepted, left for Africa, and negotiated many favorable treaties with local chiefs that resulted in the establishment of the Congo Free State.

Conditions were harsh, since Leopold reportedly condoned labor and torture as instruments to produce wealth. Some say that about ten million Africans lost their lives during 23 years of Leopold's exploitation. Novelist Joseph Conrad, who was no anti-imperialist, described what he had seen in the Congo as "the vilest scramble for loot that ever disfigured the history of the human conscience."

Bowing to strong international pressures after a commission reported that administration of the colony was scandalous, parliament passed an act in 1908 annexing the Congo state of Belgium. But Leopold had already enriched his treasury with the immense copper deposits in Katanga Province (now Shaba) and with rubber from the Congo during his years of possession. While king, he did much to beautify and modernize Brussels.

King Leopold II of Belgium

Belgium

The smallest street in Bruges

In 2019, the Belgian government apologized for the first time for separating up to 20,000 Congolese children from their parents and placing them into largely Catholic orphanages and schools. A year later, King Philippe expressed "deepest regrets" over his nation's brutal colonial past. Statues of Leopold II all over Belgium were vandalized because he has been revealed to have been "a colonizer and genocider."

Another problem began to bubble in the 19th century: the conflict between languages. French so dominated the overly centralized bureaucracy, the court system, schools, and businesses in the entire country that ambitious Flemings felt obligated to observe the rule "French in the parlor, Flemish in the kitchen." In the long run, such suppression of the Flemings' language, and with it their identity as a people, could not last. In 1898 Belgium officially became a bilingual state, although it was not until 1932 that Dutch could be used in the national administration and not until the 1960s that Dutch became fully equal to French. Flemish is a dialect of Dutch, and it is the word "Dutch" that is used in the constitution and laws. An organization, Nederlanse Taalunie, exists to promote the correct usage of Dutch.

Failure of Neutrality and World War I

Since independence, Belgium tried to preserve its neutrality, which had been guaranteed by the great powers in Europe. However, when this was put to a test in 1914, the result was disastrous. Imperial Germany had set its gunsights toward France and demanded the right of free passage through Belgium for its troops. The Belgians refused, and the British announced that they would stand by the treaty of 1839 and support the Belgians to the end. Winston S. Churchill, the first lord of the admiralty, wrote later that the British cabinet had been "overwhelmingly pacific" at the beginning of August 1914, but "the direct appeal from the king of the Belgians for French and British aid raised an issue which united an overwhelming majority of ministers."

In a meeting with the British ambassador to Berlin, the German chancellor, who thought he was speaking off the record, expressed amazement that the British would go to war over a mere "scrap of paper." Of course, the treaty rested on more than paper. It was anchored to the British national interest of preventing the North Sea coasts from being dominated by a hostile power and of preventing any European power from dominating the Continent, as would have been the case if the Germans conquered France. The Germans conquered the Belgians in a few weeks, but their bravery against truly insurmountable odds was one of the most important factors in preventing a German victory in World War I.

The German violation of Belgian neutrality conformed with the German "Schliefen Plan," designed to meet the danger of a two-front war in the east and west through a strike at the heart of France on the well-fortified Franco-German frontier, which extended 150 miles (240 km) from Switzerland to Verdun. German forces were to be concentrated on the right flank, which would sweep through Luxembourg and Belgium into northern France. Paris would be enveloped, and the French troops would be pushed back toward the Moselle, where they would be met by the German left flank.

By late August 1914, this plan appeared to have succeeded. German troops, who had bypassed Antwerp and the Belgian coast, were dangerously close to Paris, with only a retreating French and British army before them. However, the German commanders grew increasingly nervous about the Belgian army, which was in a position to strike at the Germans' right flank and perhaps even to sever their lengthening lines of communication and supply in Belgium. Therefore, some German troops were detached from the main invasion force in order to contain the Belgian army in Antwerp. Seeing a chance to increase the Germans' nervousness, the British sent a brigade of marines (about 3,000 men) to Antwerp and leaked rumors of much more massive British landings and of totally fictitious British-aided Russian landings involving more than 80,000 troops.

This partly contrived danger to the German right flank, along with the Belgian army's refusal to surrender, influenced the German decision to avoid Paris and to slow down their advance. This interruption of momentum proved to be crucial during the four-day Battle of the Marne in September and turned the tide of the war. The Belgian military effort was an example of how seemingly hopeless defensive operations, when seen in a larger strategic context, can be crucial for overall victory.

The Germans occupied most of Belgium for the remainder of the war, although the king and the remains of the Belgian army held out in Ypres on a few square miles of unoccupied Belgian soil on the western tip of the country. This small salient was pulverized by four years of constant bombardment, and by the time the armistice was signed, it resembled a crater-filled lunar landscape. The three Ypres battles claimed an estimated 850,000 Allied and German casualties. So ferocious and frightening was the warfare that 700 French, 320 British, and 50 German soldiers were shot by their own side for refusing to continue the fight. Almost 85 years later, in 2008, a monument located in a quiet courtyard in the village of Poperinge, five miles from Ypres, was erected honoring these men.

Initially the Germans found some favor among some Flemings, who saw the possibility of liberation from Walloon control. Such sympathy, which was again manifested in World War II, created great distrust in Wallonia toward the Flemings and has still not been entirely forgotten by Walloons. However, the Germans also found some support in Wallonia. The REX Party, led by Léon de Grelle, was pro-German, and the Walloon Legion fought with the German military.

Further complicating the picture was a feeling on the part of some Walloons that the French had "defaulted" in both World War I and World War II and that Belgians had to pay a high price in helping pull French irons out of the fire. This strengthened the realization that union with France was unthinkable. Thus, although "estranged," the couple (Walloons and Flemings) had no choice but to remain in the same house.

German plunder of Belgian industry led to high unemployment and the mass deportation of Belgian workers to Germany, creating downright hatred. Even the German military commander in Belgium had to protest the policies he was asked to enforce. He remarked sarcastically that "a squeezed-out lemon has no value and a slaughtered cow gives no milk!"

The Interwar Period and World War II

After World War I, Belgium entered the League of Nations and was given the

Belgian soldiers mounted on bicycles, 1940

German-speaking area of Eupen, Malmedy, and Saint Vith, as well as a League of Nations mandate over two former German colonies in Africa, now called Rwanda and Burundi. It also abandoned its earlier policy of neutrality and negotiated a military agreement with France and Great Britain. As the clouds of war became more ominous in the 1930s, however, Belgium again proclaimed a policy of neutrality on October 28, 1936. It was thus without allies when, on May 10, 1940, German troops again invaded Belgium. After 18 days of bitter fighting, the Belgian army was forced to capitulate. The government escaped to London, but the king of the Belgians became a prisoner of the Germans.

Although Belgium was liberated after the Normandy invasion in the summer of 1944, war returned when Hitler threw his last tanks into the Ardennes Forest in order to recapture Antwerp and break the Allied advance. The decisive action took place at the southern Belgian town of Bastogne, where the surrounded US forces under General Anthony McAuliffe refused to surrender. When called upon to recognize the hopelessness of his situation and to give up, he answered defiantly, "nuts!" Fortunately, foggy weather broke and enabled the necessary air support to preserve the general's position. After the war, Bastogne's main square was renamed Place McAuliffe. In 2014 the Bastogne Military Museum opened. One out of four visitors is American. The Bastogne Historical Center was already opened to commemorate one of the most important battles of the war. Every December a "Nuts Festival" is held.

Postwar Reconstruction and "the Royal Question"

Belgium's postwar reconstruction was accomplished very rapidly. Partly because it had been liberated so quickly, the country had not been as heavily bombed and shelled as the Netherlands, and Antwerp was virtually undamaged. It adopted a financial policy to strengthen the Belgian franc, which soon became one of the most stable currencies in Europe. It also blocked all bank accounts and levied a high tax on fortunes acquired as a result of collaboration with the Germans.

From 1945 until 1950 Belgium was rocked by the so-called royal question. Unlike his Dutch and Luxembourg counterparts, King Leopold III refused to leave Belgium when the government fled. He argued that, as commander-in-chief of the armed forces, he was compelled to stay where he could help his people more than by leaving. He did deal with the German occupiers, and some of his countrymen claimed he had actually *collaborated* with them. Shortly before liberation, the Germans moved him to Austria, where he remained until 1950.

During the war he had angered many Belgians by courting and marrying his second wife, Liliane Baels, a Flemish commoner and daughter of an activist in the Flemish National Party. His first queen, Astrid of Sweden, had been beloved. In 1935 she died in an auto accident in Switzerland with Leopold at the wheel.

Until his wartime role could be determined, his brother Charles served as regent. A parliamentary commission appointed in 1947 returned a favorable verdict as far as the king's wartime actions were concerned, but the socialists and communists continued to oppose his return. In an attempt to settle the question once and for all, a referendum was held in 1950 in which 57.7% of all voters approved of the king's return. Significantly, 58% of the Walloons and 52% in Brussels were opposed, while only 28% in Flanders were against his rule. When he reentered Belgium in 1950, the resulting disorders were so intense that Leopold III felt obligated to abdicate in favor of his eldest son, Prince Baudouin, on July 16, 1951.

Ever since the "royal question" divided the country, the Belgian king has never been able to exercise the considerable influence on Belgian affairs that he formerly had. None of his acts is effective unless the responsible ministers countersign his orders. The king is the commander-in-chief of the country's armed forces, but a royal military staff in the palace has to coordinate any action with the defense minister. The king can make no independent decisions on the deployment of troops. Baudouin was a popular monarch who restored dignity to the Belgian throne while stripping it of much of its earlier pomposity. The monarch is now expected to be a symbol of the nation, but to perform this role, he often has to bend over backward to please the Walloons, whose hatred of his father, Leopold III, still smolders. Of course, overt efforts to satisfy the Walloons inevitably stimulate Flemish criticism.

The king is not a member of the government, but he can play a role in facilitating

Belgium

Former King Albert II and Queen Paola

the formation of cabinets. Since more than 30 have been formed since 1945, this is no small task. It is after parliament has been dissolved and a new cabinet is being sought that the king's influence is greatest. After elections he names an Informateur to advise him on who should form the next government. Then he names a formateur to do it. This person is almost always the leader of the party that got the most votes.

In the event of deadlock, the king must keep negotiations going, and he can ultimately influence the solution. In 2007–2008, when it took 10 months to form a permanent government after elections, the king played an indispensable role in keeping the parties talking to each other until a settlement was reached. The same occurred after the government fell in April 2010; 18 months passed before there was a government in place; this set a European record. He pleaded for a solution and kept appointing formateurs to keep negotiations going. He also ordered the caretaker government to make budget cuts.

This is the kind of practical political influence the monarch has. The fact that the king is a limited, if useful, monarch and knows what his boundaries are helps explain why there is no republican movement in Belgium. He is kept informed about political business through weekly meetings with the prime minister.

One of Belgium's most serious and prolonged postwar crises was the painful decolonization of the Belgian Congo, 76 times the size of Belgium, with a vastly larger population. Over 100,000 Belgians had settled in the Congo, and Belgium had certainly developed economic interests there, although it sought to avoid mutual economic dependence between the colony and mother country. Belgium opened up the colony to foreign investment and trade. In the 1950s winds of African independence began to reach gale proportions,

especially after French president Charles de Gaulle offered the French colonies in Africa their independence in 1958. A Congolese leader, Patrice Lumumba, emerged as a highly visible proponent of a free Africa. On January 4, 1959, riots broke out in the Congo; 42 persons died in events that deeply shocked the Belgians.

The Congolese had not been prepared for independence. Belgium quickly granted it on June 30, 1960. Unfortunately, a series of bloodbaths ensued, sparked by greed for power and wealth, as well as by tribalism. It was not until seven years later that the Congo became orderly, in part because of vigorous efforts of the Belgians and of UN troops.

In 2002 a parliamentary commission concluded that Belgium shared moral responsibility for the assassination in Katanga Province of Patrice Lumumba on January 17, 1961, seven months after being elected to lead Congo. It concluded that the Belgian government and king had known of plans for the police to kill him, but they did nothing to stop the assassination, which occurred in the presence of Belgian police and officials. Belgium's ex–foreign minister Louis Michel apologized to the Democratic Republic of the Congo on behalf of the government.

The copper, cobalt, and uranium mines in the southern Shaba Province are still of great interest to Belgium. When this province was invaded from Angola in mid-1978, Belgium and France sent paratroopers to evacuate white families and to secure the area. In 1979 the Belgian government again sent paratroopers to join its soldiers in training exercises near Kinshasa, the capital city. Thus, Belgium retains a great interest in its former African colonies, and the great bulk of its relatively large development aid (.48% of its GDP in 2015) has gone to the Congo, as well as to Rwanda and Burundi, which had been

granted their independence in 1962. The Congo is not always a grateful recipient of such aid, and by the end of the 1980s, Belgium's importance as a source of trade and aid had declined.

In 1989 Belgium halted all development plans there in response to President Mobutu's suspension of payments on Belgian loans. In 1990 it used its diplomatic influence to try to sort out civil unrest in Rwanda, and in 1991 it sent 750 commandos to help evacuate Belgian citizens from the riot-torn country. Its troops were under a UN mandate, and 10 Belgian soldiers were killed in 1994. The follow-up Rwanda Commission was Belgian, and ex–prime minister Guy Verhofstadt offered a gracious apology for any shortcomings his country might have shown.

In July 2010 King Albert II made the first royal visit to Congo in 25 years. The occasion was the country's independence day. The trip was criticized at home for seeming to bestow legitimacy on President Joseph Kabila's authoritarian regime. Once there, the king had to walk a diplomatic tightrope because of bad memories many Congolese have of former Belgian rule. He gave no speech, no Belgian soldiers were in view, and there was no public discussion of human rights. One senior diplomat remarked, "The truth is that Congo is the only foreign policy dossier where Belgium carries any weight, so of course a royal visit from the king is a talking point in Brussels."

The prime minister criticized in parliament the king's second son, Prince Laurent, for disregarding his government's written request that he not meet with Kabila without diplomatic guidance. It was hinted that his $400,000 stipend from the state might be at risk. Laurent's fast driving, expensive tastes, and blunt speech had often raised eyebrows. The king also faced criticism when it was learned that he had paid no sales tax on his new luxury yacht because it was said to be a "military vessel."

GOVERNMENT AND POLITICS

Overcoming the Language Barrier

Any discussion of Belgian politics always has to begin with the ever-present language problem. No major issue could be divorced from it, and it exhausted, paralyzed, and fractured coalition governments to such an extent that the country was scarcely able to tackle the extremely important economic problems which it increasingly faced. Belgium was seriously distracted.

Flemings have fought hard and successfully for the complete equality of their language and culture. The principle of equality is essential for both sides. Now cabinet

"The Flemish separatist temptation"

posts are distributed exactly equally between the French and Flemish speakers. This protects francophones, and the same principle applies in the Brussels regional government. The office of the prime minister technically remains outside of all language quotas or restrictions. However, given the permanent Flemish majority in the country, every prime minister since the 1970s came from Flanders until Elio Di Rupo occupied that post the end of 2011. Most francophone politicians do not master Dutch and therefore are not representative of the entire country. All discussions in cabinet meetings are conducted through simultaneous interpreters. Most major political parties are formally split along language lines, as are most military units and most labor unions.

Even the prestigious medieval Catholic University of Louvain, which had become a bilingual university, had to be split in 1968 because it was located in the Flemish area a few miles north of the language line. The French-speaking part was moved just below the language line and was renamed Louvain-la-Neuve ("The New Louvain"). When it came to deciding how to divide the holdings in the famous university library, one of the oldest in Europe, the only solution which was acceptable was that all books with an even file number would remain in Louvain (now called by its Flemish name of Leuven), and all books with an odd file number would be moved to the new campus.

The tension between Flemings and Walloons has been exacerbated by the economic disparities that have developed between them. In the words of ex-premier Leo Tindemans, whose government foundered on the rocks of language

regionalization in 1978, "the basic problem is not linguistic. It is the unequal economic development of two regions which speak different languages, have a different mentality and different dynamics, with the jealousy between them that often results and that can be easily exploited by politicians."

The economic inequality was becoming more apparent. Wallonia had once been one of the richest regions on the Continent, while Flanders was a poor, rural area. Some of the bourgeois elite in Flanders began to speak French at home, and to this day there is a sizable French-speaking minority of Flemings in Gent, Antwerp, Bruges, and Leuven. Then the tables turned with a vengeance. Wallonia's coal industry disappeared, and its antiquated steel plants are in desperate need of streamlining and restructuring. Other traditional industries, such as textiles, lost out to competition from third-world countries, where labor costs are very low. Thus, unemployment and labor unrest were higher in Wallonia. The EU declared Wallonia a "development area." Unfortunately, because of the psychological shock caused by crossing the linguistic border, unemployed Walloons are not inclined to move to Flanders to find work. Thus, there is little labor mobility.

While Wallonia faced an uncertain economic future, Flanders experienced an economic boom, based on research and development, high-tech manufacturing and such future-oriented industries as chemicals. Output per capita is higher in Flanders than in Wallonia. Because of Antwerp and the other thriving ports of Zeebrugge and Ghent, foreign investments poured into the area. Earlier, most foreign investment had gone to Wallonia, but by 1979 it received only 10% of the total. Brussels received the same amount and Flanders a gigantic 80%. By 2004 almost 80% of Belgium's exports originated from Flanders. Distrust made both decisive governmental action and the establishment of some kind of national consensus, so strong in the Netherlands and Luxembourg, almost impossible in Belgium.

Since the mid-1980s, Wallonia has experienced an economic turnaround, capitalizing on its location between Europe's two largest markets: France and Germany. In 2015 it still accounted for only a quarter of GDP (60% for Flanders, population 6.3 million). Investment, including high technology, has flowed in; industrial output has risen; and the economy has shifted from one in which 53% of the gross regional product is derived from industry and 42% from services to one in which 36% comes from industry (including chemicals, food processing, and light engineering) and 60% from services. Unfortunately services cannot provide sufficient employment for

its 3.3 million inhabitants; in 2015 Wallonia's jobless rate of 11.9% was still over two times as high as in Flanders. Wallonia receives significant structural funds from the EU. A major €4.5 billion investment program to modernize Wallonia's economy was dubbed by ex–prime minister Elio Di Rupo as the "Marshall Plan." This evokes the vast aid the US gave to a ravaged Europe after the Second World War. This plan has had some success, attracting €5 billion ($6.85 billion) in investments, including creative industries, between 2006 and 2014.

There was general agreement in Belgium that Wallonia and Flanders had to be given more powers to control their own affairs, but there was much haggling on the details. As early as 1963, the two respective languages were given supremacy in the two main regions, and Brussels was declared to be a bilingual city. In 1971 the constitution was revised to permit the establishment of two cultural councils within parliament with authority over certain cultural and linguistic matters. The revision also established the necessity for special majorities (mostly two-thirds) for legislation touching these matters. Such special majorities were demanded by Walloons, whom the Flemish outnumber, 60 to 40, and who have a lower birth rate, as well. The amendment called for the establishment of a federal state composed of two lingual communities and three precisely defined regions, each empowered to legislate within carefully drawn limits.

Eight years and a string of cabinet crises later, two-thirds of both houses of parliament approved an autonomy plan establishing regional assemblies and executives with authority over cultural and family affairs, public health, roads, urban projects, energy, environment, hunting and fishing, water resources, land use, housing, employment, and many other matters. In 2000 they gained control over agriculture and in 2002 over much of foreign trade. As a condition for creating a new government in 2011 and in a bid to cut financial transfers from richer Flanders and poorer Wallonia, significant amounts of power and 4% of national income were transferred from the federal to the regional governments. The latter received authority to raise their own taxes (within limits) and take charge of some dossiers, such as child-care payments.

Each has its own foreign trade department, and to raise its international profile, Flanders maintains "embassies" abroad called Flanders Houses. Brussels and Wallonia also have "delegations" normally located within embassies but sometimes with separate facilities. The regions receive a total of 10% of the national budget to finance these tasks. However, the

Belgium

central government retains control over national finances, social security, foreign and defense policy, justice, and police. Belgium thereby ceased being a unitary state and became more decentralized.

The new arrangement is messy. Borders differ for "regions," which deal with political, administrative, and economic matters within territorial areas, and for "communities," whose competencies relate to language, culture, radio-TV, and sports. These issues are linked to persons, not areas. Flemings choose to have one government for both, with its capital in Brussels, but Walloons and German speakers keep them separate. Also, some of the ministries at the federal and regional levels share the same responsibilities. There are one central government and five regional and community governments and parliaments—one Flemish, one in Brussels, two in Wallonia (with its regional capital in Namur), and one in the German-speaking area. There are a total of 58 ministers and junior ministers. In a country with one of Europe's highest tax rates, this seems wasteful and inefficient.

This act of parliament was an important step, and the establishment in 1981 of regional and community institutions has sparked enthusiasm and energies to improve life in the language regions. Nevertheless, there are still many problems in the two larger regions that must be solved. There are small language enclaves on the wrong side of "the line." In 1987 the Belgian government collapsed over such an issue. Because of its location, the small, predominantly Walloon town of Fourons (or Voeren, depending on where one stands on this dispute) had been transferred in 1963 to the Flemish province of Limburg. Although most of the inhabitants of the town actually speak a dialect of German among themselves, two-thirds consider themselves French speakers.

They elected as mayor a militant French-language campaigner, José Happart, who refused to speak Flemish or take a Dutch-language test. The Belgian Supreme Court ruled that Happart's appointment was therefore illegal. This village incident mechanically set off reactions which would be possible only in Belgium: Flemish ministers in Prime Minister Martens's cabinet threatened to resign if Happart was not sacked, and their French-speaking colleagues said they would leave if he was. Evicted from the mayor's office, Happart won a seat in the European Parliament and remained one of Wallonia's most popular politicians. An exasperated Martens had to resign over the issue, which he and many others considered absurd. He was understandably furious that such a parochial dispute could prevent

"Don't touch democracy!" Bilingualism in Brussels

his government from solving the critical economic challenges facing the country. In 1992 power sharing was introduced to such mixed communities. But Belgians remain acutely aware of the underlying message of the dispute: Never underestimate the importance of language factors in Belgian politics.

Belgium's high unemployment rate has created an interesting situation: In the past, the only Belgians who were bilingual were Flemings, since the francophones traditionally refused to learn Flemish. Brussels's bilingual status has placed a premium in the job market on the ability to speak both official languages, and that means that the Flemings there have a leg up on their Walloon competitors. This economic fact has bolstered a significant trend since the 1980s: Many Walloon parents, especially those living close to the language border, are sending their children to Dutch-language schools in order to improve their employment prospects. In more and more schools in French-speaking communities, some or all subjects are taught in Flemish so that pupils can become bilingual. This is occurring while fewer Flemish children are learning French.

The two regional governments, along with three additional separate governments of the country's francophone "communities" in both Wallonia and Brussels and of the tiny German-speaking "community" in the east, work alongside the traditional provincial and communal governments in Belgium. The country had always been divided for administrative purposes into nine provinces, each with a provincial council of 50 to 90 members and a governor chosen by the cabinet and officially appointed by the king. Four of the provinces are French-speaking—Hainaut, Namur, Liège, and Luxembourg (a large chunk of the Grand Duchy of Luxembourg which was transferred to Belgium in the settlement of 1839). Four are Flemish-speaking—East and West Flanders, Limburg, and Antwerp. In the 1990s Brabant, which had been bilingual, split into Flemish Brabant and Walloon Brabant, making 10 provinces today. Brussels is not a part of any province but is a region in itself.

In 1989 parliament passed legislation to devolve further power to the regions, and a special court was created to solve problems stemming from devolution. In 1992 an elected regional government for Brussels was approved, and the following year Belgium became even more federalized. The regional governments were granted all powers but those of the treasury, defense, and foreign policy. In 1995 their parliaments, as well as local parliamentary bodies, were directly elected for the first time.

There are potential problems in foreign affairs because the three regions have the right to sign treaties with other nations. Flanders signed one on water with the Netherlands and set up a network of 70 economic representatives in five continents; it also has its own diplomats in

King Philippe and Queen Mathilde with Crown Princess Elisabeth

Vienna, The Hague, Washington, Tokyo, and Brussels. Such separate foreign ties could diminish the standing of the federal government.

Local governments in Belgium have a long tradition stemming from the Middle Ages and have had much autonomy. Each has an elected council of aldermen, who serve six-year terms. As a holdover of Napoleon's reforms, the mayor (called Burge meester) is nominated by the city council, approved by the cabinet, and officially appointed by the king. Direct elections were scheduled to be introduced in 2006. He presides over the city council and is expected to ensure that national interests are considered. They very often become skilled defenders of local interests in opposition to the central government.

Since the early 1990s, Brussels is officially a bilingual Brussels Capital Region with enhanced competencies. The city is broken down into 19 bilingual and 6 Flemish communes. The latter are ruled by a separate Flemish regional council. There is sufficient language tension in the capital city and its suburbs that the Council of Europe formally rebuked Belgium in 2002 for violating minority rights. The facts that Dutch is an official language and that Brussels itself was once predominantly Flemish but is now about 85% francophone make Flemings all the more determined that only Dutch will be used in the suburbs regardless of the fact that 120,000 Walloons live there.

All local council proceedings and all official mailings must be in Flemish. Anyone showing up at a council meeting who cannot speak Flemish must bring interpreters. Belgium signed the Council of Europe's convention on protecting minorities.

However, all seven regional and national parliaments would have to ratify it, and few expect the Flemish parliament ever to agree.

It was the issue of the Brussels suburbs that was most bitterly fought over in the painstaking and seemingly endless 10-month negotiations to create a government after the June 2007 elections. More and more French speakers are moving into the tidy and prosperous Dutch-speaking suburbs on the Flemish side of the line. In some small towns and villages, they already constitute a majority, and there are francophone mayors and parties.

In November 2007 politicians from the Flemish majority called a vote in a parliamentary committee abolishing the bilingual rights of some of the 150,000 French speakers in the suburbs. An electoral district known as Brussels-Halle-Vilvoorde (BHV for short), which straddles the Brussels border, is to be split up in a way that francophones in the "Halle-Vilvoorde" part of it would lose their right to vote for francophone politicians from Brussels. They would also lose the right to have court cases heard by French-speaking judges. Nine out of 10 Flemings favor this move. However, the way this was done violated a long-standing taboo in the "Belgian pact." This forbade the two language groups from confronting each other directly by holding a straight sectarian vote. Walloon deputies stormed out as soon as the motion was proposed. This BHV matter is highly symbolic and explosive, and it blew the coalition government apart in April 2010. The issue was settled as part of the compromise leading to the creation

after 18 months of a new government in December 2011.

In general, government at the provincial and communal levels works rather efficiently and has been able to keep an important part of the governmental machinery running smoothly at times when the central government has been paralyzed. Also, city officials have much influence on the central government; more than three-fourths of the members of the Belgian parliament are at the same time local government officials, and this fact strengthens the ties between the national and local governments.

The Monarchy

Like a fourth of EU countries, Belgium is a constitutional monarchy in which the king exercises largely ceremonial powers. The established tradition is that he signs all legislation passed by democratic methods. That is why there was dismay in 1990, when former King Baudouin announced that he could not sign a bill liberalizing abortion within the first 12 weeks of pregnancy. The childless, devoutly Catholic monarch asked, "Would it be normal that I be the only citizen in Belgium to be forced to act against his conscience? Is freedom of conscience a privilege for all except the king?" The pragmatic Belgians found a way out of this dilemma: Invoking article 79 of the constitution on April 3, the government declared the king "temporarily incapable of ruling," and it hurriedly promulgated the abortion law in his absence from the throne. Then, on April 5, a joint session of parliament, invoking article 82, offered him his job back. This bizarre

Canal in Ghent

211

Belgium

episode prompted some Belgians to question again whether their country really needs a monarch after all.

After reigning for 42 years, King Baudouin died suddenly of a heart attack in Spain on July 31, 1993. Though his official powers were limited, he was popular among both Flemings and Walloons, and many credited him for helping preserve Belgian unity. Childless, he was succeeded by his brother Albert, while Baudouin's wife, Queen Fabiola, kept her title. Thus until Fabiola's death in 2014, Belgium had three queens because Albert's wife, Paola, retains her title of queen, as does the wife of current King Philippe, Mathilde.

King Albert II had never expected to become king and was a relative newcomer to the political world. He was familiar with the leaders of all three regions and was experienced in business. He had stated that he would step aside and allow his son Philippe to assume the throne. However, since the king's influence is considered essential to a smooth transition to greater federalism, he was persuaded to become king himself "in the interests of continuity."

He performed well, and his role in keeping the delicate and exhausting negotiations going over an 18-month period after the June 2010 elections was indispensable. Yves Leterme's government fell after only nine months. Albert held long talks with the five ruling coalition parties in an effort to fill the political vacuum. He also broke with tradition by ordering the caretaker government to reduce its budget. His down-to-earth genuine nature and his lack of arrogance appealed to Belgians, who forgave him for siring a daughter out of wedlock.

In 2018 his illegitimate daughter, Delphine Boel, demanded that Albert submit DNA evidence. He complied, and the DNA test confirmed her claim. Three out of four Belgians support her lawsuit. She will not enter the royal line of succession, but she will be in line to inherit a part of the former king's private fortune.

His popularity is confirmed by opinion polls: 70% of Belgians wanted to maintain the monarchy, with an equal percentage of Flemings and Walloons in favor of it. This remains true despite the expense.

King Philippe studied at Oxford and Stanford and qualified as a fighter pilot. In 1999 he married a glamorous speech therapist, Mathilde d'Udekem d'Acoz, who in 2013 became the kingdom's first Belgian-born queen. In 2002 they had a daughter, Elisabeth, now heir apparent, and the next year a son named Gabriel was born; a third child followed. Royals now learn Flemish and do a part of their schooling in Flanders. When officials at the Catholic University of Leuven decided in 2002

Children during Carnival at Binche, Hainaut Province

to award Philippe an honorary doctorate for his service to Belgian unity, 200 scholars signed a petition protesting the degree because of Philippe's earlier poor performance as an engineering student.

In July 2013 the 79-year-old King Albert II abdicated the throne to Philippe, who became the seventh king of the Belgians. The royal family's main contribution to Belgium is to be one of the few remaining symbols of unity. Albert's final words as king urged Belgians to be an "inspiration" for Europe, and the new King Philippe spoke of turning "our diversity into a strength."

Belgian parliamentarians used the handover as an opportunity to revive debate about limiting the few powers the king wields. They also went after the state tax-free funding for the royals. Albert's $16 million annual stipend as king, which included the expenses for representation and the court, was slashed to $1.3 million as an ex-monarch. The heir's salary was reduced from $1.2 million to $240,000, plus staff and expenses. The late Queen Fabiola especially infuriated the lawmakers by attempting to avoid steep inheritance taxes

by setting up a trust to shield her estate. She later dissolved this trust. Her allowance was cut from $1.7 million to $600,000. All royals except the king now have to pay taxes. The government ruled out any increased expenditures.

The National Government

Real power is exercised by coalitions of parties that can maintain a majority in the Chamber of Representatives, the lower house of parliament. This is never easy because the proportional representation electoral system enables almost 10 parties to win parliamentary seats. Governments are fragile and seldom last the entire four years for which a parliament is elected.

It is striking that few cabinets are overturned by votes in parliament. Members of parliament are firmly bound to the party leaders through party discipline, so it is the powerful party leaders who make or unmake governments. Even when cabinets fall, the new governments are usually formed after minor reshuffling of cabinet posts. For example, after 1978 Wilfried Martens was prime minister in six governments, and they came to be known as

Belgium

Martens I through VI. Thus, there is usually more governmental stability in Belgium than meets the eye.

This is particularly so because of the nature of Belgian political parties. Although they are very different ideologically and linguistically, they are normally willing to compromise in order to form a government. This stems in part from the tradition of elite cooperation in Belgium that has always helped to bridge some of the differences in the heterogeneous Belgian society. Nevertheless, the delicate compromises necessary to form and preserve a government make it very difficult to attack the country's pressing problems head-on. The process of forming a coalition is so complex that it took the daily *Le Soir* 20 installments to explain it to readers in the lead-up to the 2007 elections.

The Parliament

The Belgium parliament is bicameral, and both houses constitutionally have the same powers. However, tradition has made the lower house, the Chamber of Representatives, the more important. Its 150 members (reduced from 212 in 1995) are elected at least every four years by all citizens 18 years or older, who are required to vote; 34.7% of deputies are women. Nevertheless, in the 2003 federal elections, 10% of voters abstained in certain areas. Since 2003, parties are required to win at least 5% of the total votes to get any seats at all; this is intended to reduce the number of parties in parliament and make governments more stable. The great majority of its members continue to perform their normal jobs and commute to Brussels for parliamentary sessions. Most legislation is discussed first with the major Belgian interest groups and is introduced into the Chamber of Representatives before being passed on to the upper house.

The Senate accepts about 90% of the laws without change. The 181 senators are elected for four-year terms in three different ways. Fifty are elected by the provincial councils, 25 by the Senate itself, and the rest directly by Belgian voters. The heir apparent to the throne, presently Prince Philippe, is always a member, and the Senate almost always has roughly the same party composition as the lower house.

Both houses are empowered to amend the constitution by simple majority in both houses. However, such changes must first be announced in parliament and then voted on only after the next elections. A two-thirds majority is now necessary for certain language and cultural legislation. The highest court in the land, the Court of Cassation, whose chief justice is chosen by the government and formally appointed by the king, cannot declare acts of parliament unconstitutional. In

Honorable Herman Van Rompuy, ex-president of the European Council

the Belgian legal system, which is modeled on the French, there is no provision for judicial review, but the Court of Cassation can rule administrative acts unconstitutional. A separate body, the Council of State, is permitted to give advisory opinions on the legal suitability and constitutionality of major legislation. An arbitration court was created in the 1980s to act like a constitutional court to deal with federal competencies.

Political parties in Belgium follow the cleavages of society. There are specific language parties whose main objective is to preserve or extend the language rights of their particular groups. The three "traditional" parties spring from the three great movements in Belgium during the 19th century: Catholicism, liberalism, and socialism. Coalitions always require the participation of at least two of these, and one usually leads the opposition. None of the traditional parties is highly ideologically oriented, and all are rather flexible.

These parties have been challenged by three language parties whose demands in behalf of Walloons, Flemings, and residents of Brussels have been so appealing that these three language parties have increased their electoral strength enormously in the past two decades. This challenge was so great that all three traditional parties have split into separate French-speaking and Flemish-speaking parties that limit their appeal strictly to their own region. However, they are inclined to cooperate with their former party comrades when it comes to constructing a national governing coalition. There are no major national parties in Belgium today. One can scarcely imagine governing a nation with only regional parties. Energy is expended on the pettiest of issues.

The Christian Parties

Until 1999 the largest twin party was the Christian Democrats and Flemish (CD&V) Party, as it is known in Flanders, and the Humanist Democratic Center (CDH) Party in Wallonia. Participation of the CD&V and CDH was crucial in all coalition governments from 1958 to 1999. Recent prime ministers Leo Tindemans, Mark Eyskens (son of earlier Prime Minister Gaston Eyskens, who played a key role in the development of a satisfactory regionalization plan), Jean-Luc Dehaene, and Wilfried Martens were all from the CD&V. Martens was a particularly important integration figure for the party. He started his political career as an ultranationalist Flemish radical who painted over signs at the 1958 World's Fair because they were not written in both Flemish and French. He later became a convinced federalist and a model of adaptability. He was one of the few Belgian politicians trusted by both language groups.

Formerly a single Catholic party, it severed all its formal ties with the Catholic Church in 1945 in order to become the two mass parties they are today. Nevertheless, the two parties are still the only ones many Belgian Catholics find acceptable. Their program endorses a policy guided by Christian principles (liberally interpreted), and they have always been staunch proponents of state support for parochial schools. They favor a free-market economy and the protection of private property. At the same time, they advocate equality of opportunity, an active state role in the economy, and state assistance for those persons who cannot compete successfully in the capitalist economic order. These positions enable them to work sometimes with the socialist parties.

The CD&V is relatively stronger in Flanders than the CDH is in Wallonia, where the Christian socialists have always taken a backseat to the Socialist parties. Both find the bulk of their voters among the middle class, farmers, and Catholic labor movement, particularly within the Christian Trade Union Federation (CSC), Belgium's largest trade union. They also attract upper-class voters, such as prosperous merchants and high-ranking military officers.

The CD&V was confident as it entered the 2007 parliamentary elections. The Flemish party, led by the premier of that Dutch-speaking region, Yves Leterme, captured 30 seats based on about 30% of the votes there. He became prime minister at the end of Belgium's notoriously long postelection negotiations.

Leterme is the son of Dutch- and French-speaking parents, so he speaks both languages as a native. He was anything but a unifying figure, and his ascendance greatly heated up language tensions. He called the

Belgium

176-year-old Belgian state an "accident of history" that was so worn down that it amounted to no more than a king, a national soccer team, and well-known beer brands. He criticized King Albert II for not speaking Dutch well enough, and he once joked that Belgium's French speakers are too stupid to learn Dutch.

Leterme was replaced by a reluctant Herman Van Rompuy, a former budget minister and multilingual president of the lower house of parliament. His selection continued the three-decade tradition of having only Flemish-speaking prime ministers. Respected by both French and Dutch speakers, he led a relatively stable five-party ruling coalition for 11 months. By avoiding the big questions about language and Belgium's future, his short rule is remembered as a time of domestic peace. But his skill at compromise became so famous that the EU's European Council elected him as its first president, effective from 2010 to 2014. This was an international plus for Belgium, but it threw the country back into political turmoil.

Leterme was again appointed prime minister, but his five-party coalition collapsed in April 2010 over the seemingly insoluble issue of language rights in the Brussels suburbs. He remained as caretaker prime minister, and not until 588 days had passed without a government was a six-party governing coalition agreed upon in December 2011. This was a world record. This lamentable lack of a stable government not only was a European record. It also came at a terrible time for Belgium, since the country needed to adopt stringent medicine to overcome the consequences of the 2008–2010 recession. It had its credit rating downgraded and faced EU fines of hundreds of millions of euros if it did not agree on a government. It also assumed the EU's rotating presidency July 1, 2010, a high-profile challenge that usually requires a strong home government to be effective. In fact, Belgium's performance of its presidential duties was quite good. Laterme accepted a position with the OECD in Paris.

The Socialist Parties

The Socialist Parties (Socialist Party Alternative—Sp.a—in Flanders and PS in Wallonia) are a strong twin party nationwide. The Socialist Party is one of the oldest parties in Europe. It was never an extreme left-wing party and always sought to work within the constitutional system. Winning elections always took priority over doctrine. The best-known Belgian Socialist, Paul-Henri Spaak, former prime minister, foreign minister, first president of the UN General Assembly, and NATO general secretary, expressed the character of his party this way: "There are two kinds of Socialists—Socialists and real Socialists. Me? I am a Socialist."

Its program presents a parliamentary-reformist path to a socialist society. The party congress of 1974 defined the party's aim as democratic socialism, which gives each individual the possibility for full social, economic, and cultural realization. They once found their voters chiefly among lower-level employees and workers, especially those without strong ties to the Catholic Church and those who belong to the second-largest trade union, the Federation of Belgian Labor (FGTB). Today they are parties less for workers and more for intellectuals.

The Flemish party is generally less friendly to far-reaching reform than the Walloon party, which must stay left in order to compete in the more socialist Wallonia. The Socialists are considered to be especially useful coalition partners because of their ability to help control the powerful Belgian labor movement. Belgian Socialists allow their parliamentary candidates to be chosen by means of party primaries, with all party members entitled to vote.

In December 2011 Elio Di Rupo became prime minister, the first francophone since 1974. He represented other firsts: The son of Italian parents, he was the first prime minister of immigrant stock. He was also Europe's first openly gay male leader. He was criticized for his poor Dutch, but he vowed to improve his command of the language. According to an editorial in *Le Soir*, "Elio Di Rupo speaks Dutch poorly and will never speak it better. He is—everyone knows—feeble at languages."

His six-party coalition excluded the largest Flemish separatist party and lacked a majority among Flemish voters.

The Liberals

The third traditional party group is the Party for Freedom and Progress, renamed in Flanders the Flemish Liberals and Democrats (VLD) and calling itself "Open VLD." It is called the Mouvement Reformateurs (Movement of Reformers—MR) in Wallonia and Brussels. It absorbed the Democratic Front of French-Speaking Brusselers (FDF), which advocated a redrawing of the boundaries separating Flemish from French speakers.

Both parties are generally referred to as the Liberals. They pursue traditional European liberal policies, such as the limitation of the power of the state in society and the greatest possible freedom for private initiative. They generally want to prevent the socialization of the economy, to reduce taxes, and to cut state expenditures. They do, however, accept same-sex marriage and legalized marijuana. Perhaps the only expressly conservative parties in Belgium, they appeal mainly to middle-class voters, especially small businessmen and professionals.

Also divided by regions, the Liberals were the big winners in the 1999 elections and became the country's largest party after being in third place for more than 80 years. This electoral triumph represented the most dramatic turnover in Belgian political history. It repeated its victory in Flanders in 2003 and remained the senior member of the governing coalition.

"1 Walloon + 1 Fleming = 2 Belgians. Long Live Belgium!"

Charles Michel, president of the European Council

The Flemish Liberal leader was Guy Verhofstadt, who in 1981 at age 28 became the youngest major party leader in Belgian history. At age 32 he was already a vice premier and budget minister. Over the years he changed his conservative views and moved closer to the political center, especially since he had to lead a center-left governing coalition with the Socialists from 1999. He cast his earlier heroine Margaret Thatcher overboard and embraced Tony Blair's "third way."

As prime minister in league with the Socialists, he changed his priorities by showing sympathy with the antiglobalization movement; legalizing marijuana and same-sex marriage (including the equal right to adoption); becoming the second country, along with the Netherlands, to end the ban on euthanasia; and joining with neighboring France, Germany; and Luxembourg to oppose US policy toward Iraq.

The Liberals lost badly in the 2007 parliamentary elections, tumbling from first to third place in Flanders. This cost Verhofstadt his job as prime minister. Voters had become tired of him after eight years in power, and he was seen as not having backed Flemish interests strongly enough. It was the Flemish Liberals' departure from the government in April 2010 that prompted new elections in June. The party continued its losing ways.

Thirteen parties won parliamentary seats in May 2014. A relatively new party is the Greens, which are divided into Flemish and Walloon parties. They do meet together but make decisions separately. As in other European countries, they find voters among those who are concerned about environmental protection and nuclear dangers. They are convenient parties for expressing discontent and protest. They are the only partner parties whose French and Flemish factions cooperate easily in parliament. Charles Michel, leader of the French-speaking Liberals and 38-year-old son of former foreign minister Louis Michel, became prime minister after five arduous months of coalition talks. He formed a four-party government of both Liberals, the Flemish Christian Democrats, and the N-VA.

Flemish Independence Parties

The surprise winner of the 2014 elections was a relatively new party calling itself the New Flemish Alliance (N-VA). Its leader, Bart De Wever, is a portly young political writer and populist speaker, whose ultimate goal is Flemish independence. He had scorned Walloons as "dependents" who are addicted to transfers from the thrifty Flemish. He announced, "Belgium is a failed nation." However, he argues that Belgium is not ready for separation immediately, and he supports a gradual evolutionary process. "We do not want a revolution."

He accepted the king's request in 2010 that he act as informateur to create a new government. But in order not to frighten francophones any more than he already had, he announced that he would not seek the post of prime minister, preferring to concentrate on the right formulae for reforming the state and its finances in a radical way. He pledged to reach out to French speakers. His greatest success was to make the independence cause respectable and mainstream in Flanders. Not all the Flemings who voted for him truly desire an independent Flanders, but they want their fundamental problems solved. Almost half of all Flemings voted for parties that advocate independence.

The long period without a government, which seems to have become the norm, did not seem to bother De Wever and his N-VA Party. They did benefit from the prolonged stalemate, as the party's popularity climbed. Negotiations on constitutional reform have already produced many of the results the N-VA wants. Belgium is demonstrating without a sturdy central government that the country nevertheless functions quite well, and the people maintain a high standard of living. Most services are already provided by the regions anyway. De Wever makes no secret that he wants to see Belgium "evaporate" within the larger EU context. Even a Flemish army would not be needed as Europe develops its own military forces. It made sweeping gains in local elections in 2012, winning 38% of the votes in Antwerp and 30% across Flanders. De Wever became mayor of Antwerp.

Long familiar to Belgians is the hardline, anti-immigrant, law-and-order Flemish Bloc (Vlaams Blok), which changed its name in 2004 to Flemish Interest (Vlaams Belang—VB) and reformed itself as a new party with a new flag and program. Belgium's appeals court had banned it in 2004 for racism, advocating the forcible repatriation of immigrants, and saying such things as Islam and democracy cannot go together. Marching under the banner "Our people first!" it is the largest party in Antwerp, where it wins a third of the votes. Because of the scare of Islamic terror,

The Grande Place, Brussels

Belgium

many persons in Antwerp's sizable Jewish community support it. From 4,000 to 5,000 Flemish residents leave Antwerp every year, while 5,000 to 6,000 non-European immigrants arrive annually. It also does well in Brussels, where half the newborns are from Arab parents.

It continued its winning ways in the 2007 elections by overtaking the Liberals to become the second-largest party in Flanders. In the 2010 elections, it saw its support shrink as the New Flemish Alliance entered the scene with a more appealing and gradual approach to independence. Vlaams Belang lost 5 of its seats, winning only 12, and its share of the votes fell to 7.8% (a loss of 4.2%). The other parties continue to refuse to allow it into the governing coalition.

Its performance was helped by former beauty queen Anke Vandermeersch, who ran for a Senate seat and helped soften the bloc's edge. However, while beautifying the package, the message she delivered was the same: "We still are very much against the multicultural society. We need people who emigrate here to adapt. If they don't adapt to our systems, to our laws, to our values, they should go back to where they came from."

Filip Dewinter from Antwerp is one of the party leaders. The titles of his three books succinctly express his point of view: *Our People First*, *We Stand Alone*, and *Masters in Our House*. He opposes letting in more non-Europeans and insists that those already in Belgium "assimilate" or leave. Because of its views, no other Belgian party will team up with it, and this keeps it out of office, even in Antwerp. However, by closing ranks against the Vlaams Belang, forming what is known as the cordon sanitaire, the other parties

provided it with a monopoly on the protest vote until the New Flemish Alliance burst onto the political stage.

The party benefits from its ability to mix anti-immigration rhetoric with a call for Flemish autonomy or independence. Its insistence that taxes from Flanders should not be channeled toward poorer Wallonia attracts votes from the richest Flemish neighborhoods. The party is further strengthened by the fact that it is less reliant on a single, charismatic leader than are other European right-wing parties, although Dewinter is still its most visible leader.

It is changing its image from a radical to a conservative party without overt racial overtones. It does not mention immigration as much as earlier and states in public that its earlier program is no longer applicable. For example, when a Muslim woman felt compelled in 2005 to resign from her job following a series of death threats against her employer for allowing her to wear a head-scarf at work, both Dewinter and the king condemned the threats. The party is moving toward the political center while trying to hold on to its traditional voters. This frightens the other parties.

Foreign and Defense Policy

As a small country, Belgium's foreign policy is anchored in international organizations that seek to maintain peace and prosperity in the world, especially in Europe. The EU continues to give an important boost to this small trading nation, one-half of whose national income is derived from foreign trade. The first president of the EU until 2014 was a respected former Belgian prime minister Herman

Bilingual recruiting poster

Belgium

Women in the armed forces

Van Rompuy. He has received good marks as a behind-the-scenes mediator.

Belgium is also a founding member of NATO, but in recent years it has been among the alliance's least enthusiastic members, due in great part to its severe financial difficulties and to its preoccupation with its internal problems. Some of its equipment is outdated. It has a total active force of 28,500, including about 2,570 women; its reserves number 2,040. Its air force of 7,200 troops, including 800 women, modernized its force by purchasing American F-16 combat aircraft. In order to cut costs, Belgium is coordinating some of its air operations with the Dutch. The US maintains 1,274 military personnel in Belgium.

In December 2007 police detained 14 Islamic extremists on suspicion of planning to free from prison an al Qaeda supporter, former professional soccer player from Tunisia Nizar Trabelsi. In his trial he had been convicted of organizing an attack on a Belgian air base, Kleine Brogel, where about 100 American troops were stationed.

The navy, with bases in Ostend and Zeebrugge, has 1,605 personnel, including women, and is mainly a coastal defense force, composed of two frigates and a half-dozen minesweepers. The Belgian and Dutch navies are combined in a joint operational command based in Den Helder, Netherlands. In 1987–1988 it sent three of those minesweepers to the Persian Gulf to help in the allied effort to keep that important waterway open to world shipping. In 1991 it again sent four warships, including two minesweepers, to the Gulf, and in 1992 its troops were dispatched to the Congo, where violence threatened the lives of Europeans, and Somalia. In Somalia its soldiers were regarded as tough, unforgiving, disciplined (despite several incidents of racism and violence toward the local population), and skilled, traits acquired in previous interventions in Africa.

Belgium has an army of 14,013 soldiers, including 1,500 female troops. Troops are divided as much as possible into separate language units and generally into two armies. Most soldiers are stationed in Belgium. In 2010 it had 530 peacekeeping forces in Afghanistan. In 2011 it supported its NATO allies by helping to enforce a no-fly zone over Libya. By 2019 it had 1,000 troops abroad, including in Afghanistan and Mali. It takes turns with Dutch warplanes to patrol the airspace over Iraq and Syria and to conduct bombing raids against ISIS targets.

Critics, including high military officers, fear that the drastic cuts (.91% of GDP) deprive Belgium of the bare minimum needed to defend the country. In 1993 the government decided to participate in the Franco-German Eurocorps, the embryonic European army. This decision provoked criticism in Flanders because Dutch would not be one of the languages used. The memory is still alive that Flemish troops sometimes died during the First World War because they could not understand the orders of their overwhelmingly francophone officers.

In the leadup to the unpopular 2003 war in Iraq, the Belgian government took an aggressively critical stance, which boosted Prime Minister Verhofstadt's and Foreign Minister Louis Michel's popularity before the May 2003 elections. Teaming up with France, which Belgium usually supports unswervingly in NATO, it helped veto a request from Turkey for NATO protection, a decision that was popular with voters but was decried by many Belgian political veterans and business leaders. An editorial in *De Standaard* read, "Belgium is grandiosely overplaying its hand." A couple weeks later, the government relented, and it assisted its NATO ally Turkey.

Following the war, which Belgium vehemently opposed, it joined with France, Germany, and Luxembourg to create on paper a joint rapid-reaction unit built on the existing French-German brigade. Belgium offered to contribute commandos. In addition, the four said they would set up a multinational headquarters and a separate military center in the Brussels suburb of Tervuren to command and plan EU military operations when NATO is not involved. Belgium had even recommended that a "hard core" of EU countries form a defense organization entirely distinct from NATO, but that went too far even for its French partners.

The four invited other European nations to join their effort, but sensing that its real purpose was to weaken the transatlantic alliance, none did. Neither Belgium nor the other three pledged to raise their defense spending to cover the costs of these innovations, and the idea of a separate command in Tervuren was temporarily dropped.

Such a bold foreign policy places Belgium above its usual weight class in world politics. It did not shrink from publicly castigating the United States and such traditional partners as Britain. Perhaps the best example of a small country overstepping good sense and its own influence while seeking a special moral role in the world was a 1993 law granting Belgium "universal jurisdiction" to try the perpetrators of war crimes, crimes against humanity, and genocide even if there was no Belgian connection with the alleged crimes, victims, or perpetrators. Ten years later about 30 political leaders, including Palestinian leader Yasser Arafat, Israeli prime minister Ariel Sharon, and Cuban president Fidel Castro, had been charged under the law.

The sweeping law became untenable in March 2003, when Iraqis charged former president George H. W. Bush, Vice President Richard Cheney, Secretary of State Colin Powell, and Generals Norman Schwarzkopf and Tommy Franks in Belgium for alleged war crimes in Iraq. Powell issued a stern warning that Belgium's status as an international hub could be jeopardized by such legislation. At the June 2003 NATO summit, US defense secretary Donald Rumsfeld questioned whether the alliance could continue to hold meetings in Brussels and whether the US would withhold financing for the new NATO headquarters to be built across the street from the present building if the law remained in place. Under such pressure, Belgium all but scrapped the law, especially after ex-foreign minister Louis Michel himself was charged for authorizing the sale of machine guns to Nepal. He responded indignantly, calling the suit "mad, pernicious, irrational and malign" that would make Belgium a "laughingstock."

Realizing that it had overstepped its capacity as a moral force in the world, the Belgian parliament and government amended the law in 2003 by deleting the phrase "universal jurisdiction," limiting applicability to complaints in which either the victim or defendant is a Belgian citizen or resident for at least three years and granting automatic immunity to any official of a NATO or EU country or to citizens of a democratic country where they could be tried in their own courts.

ECONOMY

Belgium was one of the first countries in the world to become heavily industrialized; this was possible because of large deposits of coal and to a lesser extent of iron ore. The industrialized areas became

Belgium

Belgian cuisine: mussels and french fries   Photo: Juliet Bunch

heavily urbanized, and a well-trained and powerfully organized workforce emerged. Today, two-thirds of Belgium's workers are unionized, the highest percentage in western Europe. They are divided almost evenly among socialist, liberal, and Christian unions.

As in every other Belgian institution, language separations weaken the unity of the unions. The country experienced its first general strike in 58 years in 1993; it was aimed at the austerity program of a shaky government, which beat a tactical retreat. The government can weather many such labor disturbances because the mainly French-speaking socialist unions and the dominant Christian unions in Flanders cannot pull together sufficiently to bring the government down.

Over the years, a highly elaborate system of formal discussions between labor unions, employers, and the government has developed. These discussions facilitate the exchange of conflicting views and aim at establishing the framework for agreements in economic matters that would

protect the well-being and future of the entire country.

Sometimes this cooperation breaks down, but as a rule, the unions take a constructive, pragmatic approach to economic matters. They have much to show for their high productivity and cooperative policies: wages which, though declining in real terms, remain among the world's highest; one of the world's shortest workweeks (less than 38 hours); pensions; and social security benefits which until the 1980s were fully protected from inflation by means of indexing, which means that they were automatically raised to keep step with rises in retail prices. Such indexing took some of the heat out of labor relations, but it invariably contributed to inflation and to government spending deficits.

Like many European countries that were left in a condition of devastation and destitution at war's end in 1945, Belgium passed sweeping social welfare legislation within a few months which could give the people some economic hope for the future. Benefits were continually expanded. For

instance, generous unemployment benefits take much of the sting out of losing one's job. The state medical insurance reimburses three-fourths of all medical and pharmaceutical expenses and pays persons with long-term illnesses 60% of their salaries for the first two years and 40% for the next two years. Belgium's social welfare net has attracted many admirers, but such a net became extremely expensive. Its nominal costs multiplied twelvefold from 1960 to 1980, and the government exhausted domestic sources of credit to pay for them.

After 1978 the government had to borrow heavily abroad, not merely to finance foreign trade, but also to meet the budgetary demands created by what many consider to be an overly generous social welfare program. With its high standard of living and small domestic market, Belgium is extremely dependent upon foreign trade; over 80% of its GDP derives from it. It has many foreign trade advantages. Its location in the middle of major European economic centers and its membership in the EU are very significant.

Belgium lies within a 300-mile radius of a market containing 350 million consumers. About three-fourths of its exports go to the EU, and half flows to its three neighbors—Germany, France, and the Netherlands. In 2000 the Brussels, Paris, and Amsterdam stock exchanges merged to create Euronext, joined later by the Portuguese exchange and the London International Financial Futures and Options Exchange. Brussels is home to Euroclear, the world's largest clearance and settlement system for internationally traded securities, employing 1,800.

Also, it has the second-largest port in Europe and one of the most modern, best-equipped, efficiently operated, and busiest in the world—Antwerp. This port, which is owned by the city, is located within 250 miles of Frankfurt, Düsseldorf, Lille, Paris, Amsterdam, and London. Situated 45 miles (72 km) inland along the Scheldt River, its access to the open sea was always a problem because the Scheldt passes through Dutch territory before emptying into the North Sea. For centuries the Dutch, wishing to minimize competition for their own port of Rotterdam, limited or prevented traffic heading to Antwerp from passing though their territory. Excellent relations with the Netherlands finally enabled the two countries to sign a treaty eliminating such hindrance, and Antwerp now thrives.

The port has the largest underwater warehouse facilities in the world and is especially noted for its lightning-fast turnaround. More than 75,000 are employed by the port or by companies that in some way service the port. The port complex, which

Schoolchildren parading before the king.   Jan Verhas, 1878

covers 27,000 acres, contains entire industrial plants, including factories owned by such multinational companies as General Motors and Bayer.

Antwerp is the world's leading diamond trading center, accounting for 80% of the world's rough diamond trade and 50% of trade in polished gems. The value of this industry was demonstrated in 2013, when gangsters seized diamonds worth $50 million at Brussels Airport. The gems had been loaded into a private plane departing for Switzerland. A few months later, after trying to sell the diamonds in Geneva, 32 suspects were arrested in France, Belgium, and Switzerland, and about a third of the gems were recovered.

About half of the traffic entering and leaving the port is moved by Belgium's 930-mile (1,500 km) canal system, which links it to all major Belgian cities and rivers, which are easily navigable because of their slow current. The inland waterways also connect the inland ports of Brussels, Ghent, and Liège and plug into the Rhine River. Antwerp can call itself the gateway to Europe. The North Sea port at Zeebrugge is an important container terminal, and the one at Ostend is being restructured after losing much of its passenger trade following the opening of the Chunnel to the UK.

Backing up this inland waterway is a very well-developed internal transport system. Zaventem, outside Brussels, is Europe's fifth-most important airport. In 2002 the SN Brussels Airlines, formed from Delta Air Transport, a regional subsidiary of bankrupt SABENA, commenced operations. The first railway in Europe formally opened in Brussels in 1835. With its 2,536 miles (over 4,000 km), the Belgian railway net is now the densest in the world. The Eurostar line speeds passengers from Brussels through the Chunnel to central London in a little over two hours, and Thalys trains race to Paris in an hour and a half and provide links to the Netherlands and Germany. Its toll-free international motorways are plentiful and fully lighted at night.

Many of the factors that once made Belgium an economic powerhouse have now disappeared. Easily extractable coal, traditionally Belgium's only significant raw material, has been almost completely exhausted in the south, where most of the mines are closed. Belgium's steel industry, which grew up around the coalfields, had become inefficient and obsolete; EU policies to reduce European steel production have cost thousands of jobs in Belgium. Steel towns, such as Liège, Charleroi and Mons, are now economic and political trouble areas. The Belgian government felt compelled to subsidize many lame industries, particularly in the steel and textile

sectors. This aid almost always flowed to Wallonia and enabled labor unions to achieve higher wages in some of the lame industries, especially steel, than those paid in the more productive mills in Flanders. Indeed, the strike record in Wallonia is three times the rate per capita than in Flanders. This only increases resentment toward Wallonia, which many Flemings believe is in essence being subsidized by Flanders.

The world economic downturns since the oil shocks of 1973–1974 struck a hard blow at Belgium's trading position. A half-century ago, Belgium's own coal supplied 90% of the country's energy needs, but that figure has now sunk to about 20%. About 40% of its present energy needs are covered by oil; almost all of it must be imported, and most comes from the Middle East. The oil company Petrofina, now merged with Total, provides a small portion of the country's oil through its concession in the US, Canada, the Congo, and the North Sea. Natural gas provides for 17% of its energy consumption. It hopes to be able to develop on-site gasification of coal, which could have the effect of reviving the lagging coal-mining industry. About half of its energy is produced by seven nuclear power plants. In 2003 the parliament approved a law that would shut all of them down between 2015 and 2025 when each had reached the age of 40 years.

An unpleasant development for Belgium was the slowdown in foreign investment caused, in large part, by the country's high wage costs and drop in profitability of Belgian firms. The World Economic Forum

ranked Belgium 31st in its 2006 Global Competitiveness Report, behind Portugal but one notch above France. American investors, who in the 1960s accounted for 65% of all foreign investment in Belgium, had reduced their share to less than a third by the 1980s, and some of the most visible US firms, such as RCA, General Electric, and Holiday Inn, withdrew altogether.

This is a serious problem because multinational companies control an estimated one-third of all manufacturing jobs and almost one-half of all industrial assets in Belgium. Thus, their confidence in the Belgian economy is crucial. In 2010 General Motors announced the closure of its Opel Plant in Antwerp after consulting with the unions and exploring alternatives to a shutdown, as Belgian law requires. The last months of such negotiations often leave companies at a standstill. In 2013 other multinationals announced plant closures in Belgium: Caterpillar, Dow Chemical, AarcelorMittal, and Ford. After a bitter struggle, Ford had to pay each of the 4,000 blue-collar workers in Genk $190,000 plus additional payments to the white-collar staff. The government is trying to lure foreign investment by providing subsidies and giving capital bonuses and tax breaks, but the results are mixed. Companies are leaving largely because of costly regulation, high taxes, and high labor costs: For every euro paid to an employee, the employer must spend €2.52, considerably above the EU average of €1.86.

In 2008 the Belgian beer brewer InBev, the world's largest, purchased American icon Anheuser-Busch, which controls

Belgium

half the American market, for a stunning $52 billion. This created a new beer giant, Anheuser-Busch InBev, based nominally in Leuven but run out of New York. Worldwide, it sells a quarter of all beers and generate half the industry's global profits. The behemoth also produces Stella Artois, Leffe, and Hoegaarden. Its dominance grew even more with its $104 billion purchase of SAB Miller. Anheuser-Busch is one of several dozen "corporate champions" under fire from the EU for paying below the 34% corporate tax rate. Belgium has about 100 commercial beer makers (down from 3,400 in 1907), producing the largest range of beers in the world: about 1,131, including 6 Trappist ales and other abbey beers. The need to sell abroad has been enhanced by a 20% reduction of beer consumption in Belgium in the first decade of the 21st century. In 2010 Belgium exported 57% of its brew. Belgian brewers are showing increased interest in American craft beers, such as the Boulevard Brewing Company in Kansas City, which Duvel Moortgat purchased in 2013.

More than 10% of residents in Belgium are foreign. Foreign workers were once concentrated primarily in the Wallonian industrial areas and Brussels, but now they are spread throughout the country. The capital city has a particularly visible foreign presence. The thousands of EU bureaucrats, international businessmen, and especially foreign laborers now comprise a third of the city's population. There are an estimated 160,000 Muslim residents (25% of the total) in the Brussels region. The most common name given to sons born in Brussels is Mohammed.

Terrorists struck in March 2016. Two blasts ripped through the Brussels airport. Minutes later, at the peak of morning rush

hour, a bomb went off at the Maelbeek subway station. The attacks left 32 dead and more than 320 injured.

Foreign workers are a convenient target for extreme-right-wing groups, and they face discrimination in the larger society. The extent of the problem of integrating the predominantly African and Mediterranean workers was revealed by the passage of a law in 1981 directed against racism and hatred toward foreigners. It is now forbidden by law to put up signs such as "Foreigners unwanted" or "No entry for North Africans," as one once saw in Belgium. Public services may no longer be denied to foreigners.

Like many other rich western European countries, Belgium has become a magnet for persons from the third world seeking asylum. With the situation worsening, the government became a firm advocate of strict border controls. The government tightened controls on illegal refugees in 1993 and speeded up the application processing and deportation of such foreigners.

Belgian agriculture is still relatively efficient by European standards and provides 80% of the country's food needs. There are problems, however. Farm incomes have stagnated for years, but farmers have managed to stay afloat because of subsidies from the EU's Common Agriculture Program (CAP). Most Belgian farms are mixed, producing grains and raising livestock, and except for Italy, Belgium has the smallest farms in the EU. Therefore, there is a great need for amalgamation and modernization. But with a high unemployment rate in Belgium, the 1.2% of the population working in agriculture (producing 1% of GDP) must be kept on the land until some can be absorbed by industry, which employs 21.8% of the workforce and produces 22% of GDP, or services, which provide work for 77.1% and create 77% of GDP.

Despite some improvement, Belgium faces economic problems. Over a quarter of the budget is devoted to paying interest on the national debt. At about 100% of GDP and growing, this debt is one of the highest in the industrialized world. The government's stiff austerity program since the 1980s was partly successful. The government's borrowing, spending, and deficit had all been reduced until the global recession hit Belgium in autumn 2008. It had six budget surpluses in a row but showed a 5.1% deficit in 2021. Unemployment in 2021 was 6.1%. One out of three active adults works for the state. Inflation was 1.9% in 2021. In November 2011 Standard and Poor's lowered Belgium's long-term rating to AA, prompting politicians finally to form a governing coalition. The economy was growing in 2021 by 5.4% on an annual basis.

There are undeniable strengths. Tax rates continue to be reduced. The corporate income tax rate for large corporations has fallen from 40.17% to 33.99% (ultimately to 30%) and from 28.24% to 24.98% for small and medium-sized businesses. Belgium has maintained a current-account surplus for over a quarter-century. It has a close trading relationship with neighboring Germany, a healthy private sector, a high savings rate, and a visibly wealthy population.

After seven years of haggling, the EU and Canada reached a free-trade agreement in 2016. However, the Wallonia regional parliament voted to block it until its concerns could be met. It was finally amended.

CULTURE

Belgium has more than one culture, and to understand the cultural dimension of the country, one must unravel the strands of Roman, Frankish, Spanish, French, Austrian, German, and Dutch influences. With no common culture, there is very little feeling of Belgian national identity, especially among the Flemish. Unlike in Wallonia, there is a vocal separatist movement in Flanders. It is mainly when they are outside of Belgium that many Flemish and Walloons begin to feel like Belgians.

Today, Belgium is secularized, and few Belgians vote primarily along religious sect lines. Also, there is a trend away from doctrinaire religious positions on social and political matters, even among the Roman Catholics. Catholicism is still a significant social force, especially in Flanders. Catholics organize trade unions, youth movements, hospitals, sports clubs, political parties, and schools, and these organizations are thriving.

But 2010 saw the dramatic rise of tension between the Catholic Church and the state. There were about 500 accusations that priests had abused children. Belgium's longest-serving prelate, the bishop of Bruges Roger Vangheluwe, retired after admitting that he had molested "a boy in my close entourage" who was his own nephew. In April 2011 he ignited almost-universal condemnation by admitting that he had abused two of his nephews. He demonstrated no contrition and declared that he had no intention of abandoning the priesthood, although the Vatican ordered him to stop working until his punishment could be determined. Because of the statute of limitations, he faces no criminal charges.

While the church was investigating the charges, police raided the home of a cardinal, the offices of three bishops, and the offices of a commission created by the church to investigate such complaints.

Belgium

The Adoration of the Lamb by Jan and Hubert Van Eyck. **This has been stolen more frequently than any other artwork.**

Sint-Baafskathedraal, Ghent

They seized records, National Archive documents, and a computer. The pope was furious and called the actions "deplorable." The raids were signals that the church will no longer receive special treatment in criminal matters in this increasingly secular country.

The best example of the vitality of Catholicism is the separation of the school system into state schools, which accommodate approximately 43% of the pupils, and "free" (chiefly Catholic) schools, which are largely financed by the state and accommodate 57%. The long and emotional dispute over state support for Catholic schools was finally settled in 1958. The compromise that was reached probably put to rest the last religious dispute that would significantly affect Belgian politics. Such Catholic schools are open to all children and continue to be state-financed. They are reputed to be slightly better academically than other schools. There are state-financed Jewish schools in Antwerp, and there will probably be Muslim state schools in the future.

In 2003 same-sex marriages were legalized. This was followed the next year by legislation permitting same-sex couples to adopt children.

Far less permissive was the almost-unanimous parliamentary vote in April 2011 to ban the wearing of a burka, the head-to-toe garment that only a few dozen Muslim women wear in Belgium. Police can stop people masking their faces in public. The vote encouraged other countries, such as France and the Netherlands,

to follow suit. Schools are allowed to make their own rules on the wearing of head-scarves.

Belgium has become a launchpad for jihadis. It is the easiest place to buy smuggled weapons. The epicenter is the run-down former factory area in western Brussels Molenbeek. Half the perpetrators of the terrorist attacks in Paris in November 2015, in which 130 died, came from Molenbeek. Fearing a similar attack, Belgian officials ordered a four-day lockdown of the town. Over 500 Belgian citizens traveled to Syria or Iraq to fight for the Islamic State. This is by far the highest number per capita of any western state. It is difficult to coordinate counterterrorism efforts since Brussels is divided among 19 municipalities and 6 separate police forces.

Belgium attempts to control migration into the country and to assimilate refugees and immigrants who are already living there. Like other European countries, it confronts a frightening terrorist presence. Authorities have unearthed sleeper cells for future acts and face the difficulty in sorting out suspicious behavior from imminent danger. One Belgian woman, who converted to Islam during her two marriages with Arab men, became the first Belgian woman to die in a suicide attack in Iraq. Another French-speaking Belgian female, Malika El Aroud, was a fiery Internet jihadist who bullied Muslim men to fight and demanded that women join them. Calling herself a female warrior for al Qaeda, she accompanied her husband to Afghanistan in 2001 to train in an al Qaeda

camp. In May 2010 both were sentenced to eight years in prison for leading a cell that recruited fighters for training camps on the Afghanistan-Pakistan border.

In 2013 police arrested six men from a group called Sharia4Belgium implicated in a jihadist-recruitment drive for the insurgency in Syria. In 2015 many raids and arrests were made. The leader of Sharia4Belgium and 45 others were sent to prison. Some came from well-integrated families. Belgium had more jihadist fighters per capita going to Syria and Iraq than any European nation. Some returned home to continue the struggle, as was the case when four were shot dead at the Jewish museum in Brussels.

Parliament passed a controversial bill in 2005 giving police additional powers to fight terrorism. Belgium is aggressive in arresting al Qaeda suspects and in backing tough EU measures to combat terrorism in Europe. In 2008 they rounded up 14 suspected al Qaeda members on the eve an EU summit in Brussels. Anti-Islamic groups were not held responsible for an arson attack against a Shiite mosque in the Brussels suburb of Anderlecht in March 2012; it was attributed to Sunni-Shiite tensions.

It was a relief to see on June 7, 2009, that terrorist Muslims are the exception, not the rule: Mahinur Özdemir, a 26-year-old Turkish graduate in political science who wears a head-scarf, was elected to the Brussels regional parliament on a centrist ticket.

In Wallonia children are permitted to choose English as their first foreign language; 49.2% did that in 2007, in contrast to 42.3% who chose Flemish. In Flanders children start with French and begin English at about age 13. There has been an increasing tendency to use English as the common language between Flemings and Walloons, including in corporate boardrooms. Even José Happart admitted after a fierce TV debate, "after all, everybody will speak English in 20 years." There is, at the same time, an encouraging trend for ambitious francophones to buckle down and learn Flemish. Most educated Flemings continue to speak fluent French, although the percentage who can do so is declining. There are many variants of Walloon French, which is closer to the old rather than to the modern Parisian form. There is diversity at the university level. There are many universities, including four Dutch-speaking ones and four French-speaking. Some are Catholic, such as Leuven and Louvain-la-Neuve, and some are not, such as the University of Brussels, Ghent, and Liège.

The news media use both languages. The Radio Television Belge de la Communauté Culturelle Française (RTBF) and the

---

221

Belgium

A little piece of Belgium puts the country at the brink of implosion.

Vlaamse Radio en Televisie (VRT) are separate public utilities with state financing but without direct state intervention in their management. Both are run by 10-member administrative councils, of which 8 are representatives of political parties and are appointed by the parliament. Belgians were pioneers in radio broadcasting and now have numerous German, French, and Dutch channels. There are French- and Dutch-language television channels and many private channels.

There are newspapers in all three languages. The leading French papers are *La Libre Belgique* (Catholic) and *Le Soir* (independent). Flemish dailies include *Het Laatste Nieuws* (Liberal) and *De Standaard* (Catholic). One daily, *Grenz Echo*, appears in the German language. Most Belgian dailies have a political affiliation and are owned by one of four large chains, although each newspaper has a great measure of autonomy within each group.

Simply by driving through Belgium, one realizes that the country is filled with art treasures. One can see splendid medieval cities, such as Bruges, Ghent, Antwerp, Liège, Brussels, Leuven (Louvain), Tongeren, Namur, and Tournai, which are filled with castles, abbeys, and venerable public buildings. But it is in art museums throughout the world that one can best see the impact of Belgian artists.

Painting was the medium in which artists came to be known best of all, and by the 16th century, Flemish painting, with its bold personal expression and vitality, marked the high point of the northern Renaissance. Jan Van Eyck was the first Flemish master to arouse the admiration of Italian painters, and his brother Hubert Van Eyck also produced masterpieces of lasting value. Pieter Bruegel the Elder combined religious, moral, or satirical subjects with vivid descriptions of the Flemish rural environment. He broadened the art of landscape painting through a masterful, sweeping concept of nature.

Peter Paul Reubens became the most famous exponent of Baroque painting; he also was a noted diplomat and worked for Marie de Medici, Philip IV of Spain, and Charles I of England. His collaborator, Anthony Van Dyck, became the court painter of the English royal family. David Teniers was a master at painting highly realistic popular scenes. Flemish artists were pioneers in giving depth to painting instead of rendering a flat appearance. They paid very close attention to detail and to common people. Thus, they give us the most vivid picture imaginable of their surroundings and have kept their own time alive in the mind of the modern viewer.

Since ancient times, Belgian literature was bilingual. Until the 19th century, its painters overshadowed its writers, but after Belgium gained its independence, literature began to bloom. Hendrik Conscience attracted attention to his homeland through his novel *The Lion of Flanders*. Reminiscent of Sir Walter Scott's romantic novels, Conscience rekindled Flemings' pride and interest in their past. He also wrote other delightful novels depicting life in the Flemish countryside and towns that sparked a literary revival. Another great 19th-century Flemish figure was the poet Guido Gezelle, whose poems present religious sentiment with great eloquence. Karel van Woestijne was also a brilliant poet who wrote about the eternal conflict between body and soul.

Perhaps the greatest 20th-century authors are Hugo Claus and the late Baron Marnix Gijsen.

Walloon literature was revived under the leadership of Max Weller, whose literary review *La Jeune Belgique* encouraged experimentation and cosmopolitanism in the late 19th century. Charles de Coster wrote *Uilenspiegel* in 1867, a ribald tale so filled with the spirit of liberty that it became a symbol of Belgian resistance in both world wars. Perhaps the greatest French-speaking Belgian writers were Maurice Maeterlinck, who won a Nobel Prize in 1911; Emile Verhaeren; and Michel de Ghelderode. Paradoxically, all three were Flemish. Walloon writer Georges Remi (alias Hergé) invented a character in the 20th century, Tintin, whose adventures fascinated readers in both parts of Belgium. Steven Spielberg made a digital 3-D film of this likeable boy in 2011, and a museum was opened in Louvain-la-Neuve to honor him. With such a composer as Cesar Franck and ballet artist as Maurice Béjart, Belgium has also gained world acclaim in music and dance.

In general, Walloon literature is strongly oriented toward France, while Flemish literature is concerned chiefly with maintaining and broadening Flemish cultural identity. The state has established "houses of culture" all over the country. These houses enrich the quality of life of the communities in which they are located, but it is doubtful that they contribute much to welding together two so-distinct cultures. The Flemish community government and Dutch national government cosponsor similar "houses of culture" abroad and offer common literature prizes.

FUTURE

The German newspaper *Die Tageszeitung* called Belgium "the most successful failed state of all time." Despite serious economic difficulties and a dysfunctional central government, Belgium is still wealthy, even by the high European standards. It keeps muddling on, but every crisis seems to bring the fractured country a little closer to the precipice, without it falling off. Indeed, *Le Soir* described it as "a country on the edge of the abyss." Its greatest problem in the future will be to manage the perpetual and exhausting strife sparked by the existence of differing language communities who find it difficult to coexist with each other.

Language tensions got worse after the 2010 elections, in which almost half of Flemish voters supported parties that advocate separation into two sovereign countries. This has become mainstream thinking in the north. Such problems even seeped into the crowning ceremony of the

Belgium

2007 Miss Belgium pageant in Antwerp. When the shapely Alizee Poulicek, who is trilingual in Czech, English, and French, was asked a question in Dutch and had to admit she could not understand, she was booed. Caretaker Prime Minister Leterme had called the 176-year-old Belgian state an "accident of history" that was so worn down that it amounted to no more than a king, a national soccer team and well-known beer brands (which includes Anheuser-Busch).

The 2010 elections sent 12 parties to parliament and left the usual political mess. In 2007 it had taken 9 tense months (282 days) to form a multiparty coalition government. After the June 2010 elections, it took 18 months to agree to a government, even though the caretaker coalition under Yves Leterme had a majority in parliament. This was a new European record. The May 2014 elections sent 13 parties to parliament and required 5 months to produce a governing coalition. The May 2019 elections required 494 days to straighten out and produced a wobbly seven-party coalition government led by Prime Minister Alexander De Croo. He regretted that "we no longer have the certainty that we will ever return to normal."

The long period without a government did not seem to bother either Flemish separatist Bart De Wever or his N-VA Party. They benefited from the prolonged stalemate, as the party's popularity climbed. Negotiations on constitutional reform had already produced many of the results the N-VA wants.

Even without a sturdy central government, Belgium demonstrated that the country functions quite well. The people maintain a high standard of living. Most day-to-day services are already provided by the regions. De Wever makes no secret that he wants to see Belgium "evaporate" within the larger EU context. Even a Flemish army would not be needed as Europe develops its own military forces. King Philippe vowed to preserve unity and "to turn our diversity into a strength." The knowledge that Islamic terrorists are hatching their bloody plans in their midst focuses the attention of all Belgians.

Debate revolves around language and separation. One cannot imagine an amicable separation, such as the 1993 "velvet divorce" in Czechoslovakia, because any plan would have to find a solution for Brussels, which the Flemish claim as their capital. Political science professor Lieven de Winter said that "Belgians are at a crossroads where they are making a choice on whether they want to live together or not."

These tensions are not new. But in the opinion of former prime minister Wilfried Martens, who passed away in 2013, the current problems are made worse by the fact that politicians from the two regions do not share similar goals and lack the informal contacts they once had. "We are the center of the European Union. How could we give such a bad example to all the member states if we were to split?" The minister in charge of foreign affairs for the Flemish government, Geert Bourgeois, agrees: "We are two democracies with different parties and totally different needs. We speak different languages. We don't watch the same television. We don't read what is written in the south, and the Walloons don't read what our opinion-makers write." Only 1% of Belgians marry outside their own language group. The country is close to the point where the central government would be irrelevant. Power has been either devolved to the regions or passed up to the EU. What is left?

Many Belgians cling to their country. It is remarkable that, thanks to their efficient bureaucracy, Belgians' daily lives are barely disturbed by the prolonged crisis: Social security benefits and salaries are paid regularly, and the trains run on time. But the fragility of the decentralized Belgian state had been starkly displayed by the reaction to a fabricated TV "news" report on the French-language RTBF, December 13, 2006, the day before an EU summit. With a straight face, a well-known francophone news presenter interrupted the normal programming and announced that Belgium had just split apart after Flanders declared its independence. He cut to familiar reporters "on the spot" and showed film clips of the royal family departing from the Melsbroek Military Airport and of the number 44 streetcar being stopped

St.-Boniface Bridge in Bruges

Belgium

as it tried to cross from Brussels into the Flemish-speaking suburb of Tervuren.

The portrayal was so believable and realistic that diplomats called the foreign ministry to confirm whether it was true. Many Walloons panicked briefly. But all they would have had to do to verify that the report was a spoof was to flip on the Dutch-language channels. Few thought to do this. The incident was a scare for some Belgians, a hilarity for others, and a bad joke for the government. Coming in the midst of increasing talk about further decentralization, perhaps even separation, it demonstrated that the debate about Belgium's future is no longer restricted to political circles.

With its picturesque, cobblestoned, medieval towns, Flanders dominates tourism. The 200th commemoration of the 1815 Battle of Waterloo was an exciting event. An underground visitor center was constructed, and the monuments and roads at the site were refurbished. Perhaps this revealed more division: Dutch-speaking Belgians fought under the Duke of Wellington, while French speakers fought with Napoleon. The past is always present in Belgium.

The government's most urgent future challenge will be to defeat the deadly coronavirus, which hit Belgium particularly hard. It had one of Europe's worst infection rates.

The Grand Duchy of Luxembourg

Luxembourg City

Area: 999 sq. mi. (2,586 sq. km, somewhat smaller than Rhode Island).

Population: 560,000, of which over a third are foreigners.

Capital City: Luxembourg (pop. 80,000, estimated, fewer than half of whom are citizens).

Climate: Temperate, with mild winters and summers.

Neighboring Countries: Belgium (west); Germany (east); France (south).

Official Languages: Luxembourgish (a Moselle Franconian-German dialect with numerous additions of French words), French, and German.

Ethnic Background: Indo-European, Germanic.

Principal Religion: Roman Catholic (94%).

Main Exports: Iron and steel products, chemicals. International banking activities are extremely important.

Main Imports: Minerals, metals, foodstuffs, machinery.

Currency: Euro.

Major Trading Partners: EU (84.6% of exports and 90.1% of imports), Germany (25.4% of exports and 34.2% of imports), France (19.7% of exports and 26.5% of imports), Belgium (12.1% of exports and 15.3% of imports), US (3.2% of exports and 4.3% of imports).

National Holiday: June 23.

Chief of State: His Royal Highness the Grand Duke Henri (b. 1955), married

in 1981 to Grand Duchess Maria Teresa. He succeeded his father upon his abdication in 2000.

Heir Apparent: His Royal Highness Prince Guillaume, who married Stéphanie de Lannoy in November 2012.

Head of Government: Xavier Bettel, Prime Minister (since November 2013).

National Flag: Three horizontal stripes of equal width, red, white, and blue (the flag closely resembles that of the Netherlands).

Since the Roman legions came to what is now Luxembourg in 57 BC, the Luxembourgers have tenaciously clung to their separate existence. Caesar wrote that the Treveri tribesmen who resisted his troops "never submitted to commands except under the compulsion of an army." In the two millennia that followed, the Franks, Burgundians, Dutch, and Germans controlled this tiny land. But, unlike most small nations, the Luxembourgers never allowed themselves to be absorbed entirely by another power. They well deserve their national motto: *Mir wolle bleive wat mir sin!* ("We want to remain what we are!").

Luxembourg, which means "Little Castle," is the second-smallest independent state in the EU, after Malta, encompassing only 999 square miles, less than the state of Rhode Island. It has a growing population of 560,000, less than one-third that of Brussels and one-twentieth that of Paris. More than a third of inhabitants are not citizens. Nevertheless, it is one of the most prosperous countries in the world, with an industrial productivity and international significance far out of proportion to its size.

The northern half of the country, called Oesling, is a rugged territory of low mountains and Forests. It is a continuation of the Ardennes forest area of Belgium. The southern half is within the Lorraine Plain and is a rolling, wooded countryside. Because of its lush pastureland and fertile soil, this area is called the Gutland or Bon Pays (Good Land). It also contains most of Luxembourg's industrial centers and its capital city.

With its many international organizations and multilingual citizens, the capital is a very cosmopolitan city. Having only about 80,000 inhabitants, fewer than half of whom are citizens, it is no metropolis, but it is a charming, almost fairytale city built in the late 16th century in Spanish Renaissance style and remodeled at the end of the 19th century. Two rivers, the Alzette and Petrusse, flow through the city, which is located on a plateau, and through the centuries they have cut deep, narrow valleys with very steep sides dropping 200 feet. The old section of the city is perched on the highest part of the plateau. Located on one

Luxembourg

of the many narrow, twisting streets of the old city is the Grand Ducal Palace, built in 1573, with colorful guards always standing or marching in front of it.

HISTORY

The Early Period

Luxembourg's independence was established in 963 AD. Siegfried, the Count of Ardennes, hewed powerful battlements in the cliffs where Luxembourg's capital city is now located. Until it was demolished by international agreement in 1867, this almost-impregnable fortress was called the "Gibraltar of the north." In fact, the word "Luxembourg" meant "little fortress." The visitor can still climb on the ruins of this stronghold and wander in the maze of passages underneath it.

Independent Luxembourg was linked to the Holy Roman Empire, and in the beginning of the 14th century, Luxembourg's duke, Henry VII, was crowned Holy Roman emperor. Luxembourg ultimately provided four emperors during this heyday of the duchy's power. Henry's son John, a man very fond of travel, women, horses, and dice, became the king of Bohemia. After losing one eye in battle and the other to disease, he became known as John the Blind. His bravery became legendary in the Battle of Crecy in 1346 against the English. Unable to see, John galloped to the head of his troops by having his steed tied to those of several loyal aides and then ordering them to advance. Not surprisingly, he did not survive the battle.

John's grandson Charles IV was also a Holy Roman emperor and built the beautiful city of Prague, now the capital of the Czech Republic. The Luxembourgers' golden age of power gradually declined, and in 1443 the duchy was conquered by the Duke of Burgundy; for more than four centuries, foreign powers gave the orders in Luxembourg.

Neutrality and War

Luxembourg evolved into a neutral country in the 19th century, but this lasted less than a half-century. It was violated by German troops in August 1914. The Grand Duchess Marie-Adelheid remained in the country during the entire four-year occupation, and in the opinion of many Luxembourgers, she collaborated with the Germans. Whether this was true or not, she felt obliged to abdicate in early 1919, and her popular sister Charlotte ascended the throne. A referendum in 1919 confirmed the constitutional monarchy but proclaimed the people to be sovereign and introduced universal suffrage for men and women. This referendum established a fully democratic parliamentary form of government in the grand duchy.

As small countries often do, Luxembourg felt the need to seek a union with a larger power, so in a referendum in 1921, Luxembourgers voted three to one to enter an economic union with France. The latter country, however, advised Luxembourg to enter a close economic relationship with Belgium; both smaller countries agreed to this in 1922.

In 1940 Luxembourg was given another reminder that a policy of neutrality alone cannot guarantee the security of a country. German troops again occupied the tiny state in 1940 and within a few weeks virtually annexed it. In August 1942 Luxembourg was officially incorporated into Hitler's reich. When the population responded with a strike, about 30,000 Luxembourgers, or about 10% of the population and most of the country's young men, were deported. Many were forced to serve in the German army, and until liberation the population continued to suffer greatly from a brutal occupation.

Having learned from her sister's mistake in 1914, Grand Duchess Charlotte fled in 1940 with her entire government, first to London and then to Montreal. She worked tirelessly to ensure that Luxembourg would be recognized as an independent country at the war's end. Her son Crown Prince Jean served as an officer in the British army and landed with his unit, the Irish Guards, on the beaches of Normandy on June 11, 1944, five days after the first Allied troops had landed. On September 3 his unit entered Brussels, and on September 10 it crossed the Luxembourg border between Rodange and Pétange, exactly at the spot where his parents had left the country in 1940. The same afternoon he reached the capital city—his arrival was hailed by thousands of his countrymen. His father, Felix, had reached the

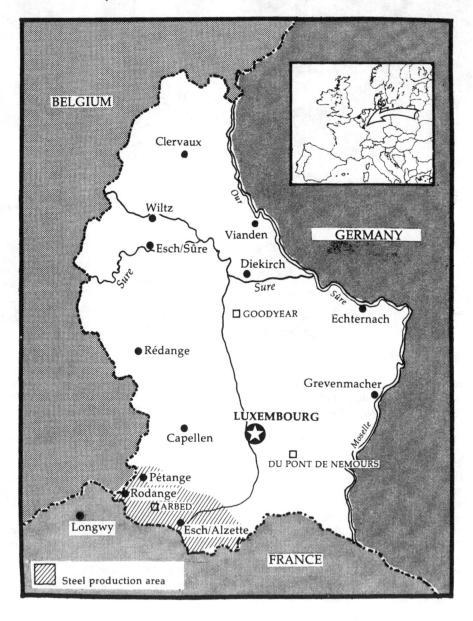

Luxembourg

city that morning with an American tank division.

Unfortunately, the war was not yet over for Luxembourg. Hitler's forces made a last offensive at the end of 1944 in order to stop the Allied advance toward Germany. During this Ardennes offensive, known as the Battle of the Bulge, the American commander General Omar Bradley made Luxembourg City his headquarters, but a large portion of the duchy was nevertheless recaptured by German troops. In the fiercely fought Battle of the Bulge, such destruction was visited upon the land that it took until 1952 to repair all the material damage. American losses were also very great, as one can see at the American military cemetery in Hamm, located about 1 mile from Luxembourg Airport. There rest 5,000 American soldiers, including General George Patton, who was killed in a jeep accident in December 1945. Most cities in Luxembourg have a street or square named after Patton, who is hailed as the country's liberator. Ettelbruck in the Ardennes unofficially calls itself Patton Town.

GOVERNMENT AND POLITICS

The Grand Duke

Luxembourg is a constitutional monarchy, whose constitution of 1868 was amended in 1919 to invest sovereignty in the people rather than in the Crown. Executive power is formally vested in the Grand Duke Henri, who assumed his father's legislative powers in 1998 and ascended to the throne in 2000, when his father, Jean, abdicated in his favor. He is the world's last grand duke and possesses no actual crown to wear. He is the sixth grand duke since 1890. Jean's decision to step down at age 79 followed a precedent set by his mother, Charlotte, who abdicated in 1964. Jean also ordered that Luxembourg's quota of euro coins, which went into circulation in 2002, bear Henri's head on them.

The grand duke, who underwent officer's training at Sandhurst in Britain, has been a popular monarch, and the Luxembourgers' enthusiastic response to his marriage in 1981 demonstrated this sentiment. Henri met a beautiful and intelligent Cuban exile, Maria Teresa Mestre, while both were studying in Geneva. Although she was not of noble birth, he chose to marry her, and their wedding in the Luxembourg Cathedral drew a large assemblage of European nobility. They have five children. In 2012 the oldest and heir to the throne, Guillaume, married Countess Stéphanie de Lannoy from one of the oldest noble families in Belgium. Henri is a very wealthy person with manorial residences scattered throughout the principality.

Grand Duke Henri, who takes his duties seriously, has considerable influence in

Prime Minister Xavier Bettel

the political process. As all constitutional monarchs, he "reigns but does not rule." To be effective, one or several members of the government, who alone assume political responsibility, must countersign his orders. Nevertheless, he could be an especially important figure in times of national crisis when either the parties are unable to form a government or the nation desperately needs a symbol of national unity. In normal times his actual powers are limited.

There is a serious ongoing discussion about reducing the grand duke's power, especially after he refused to sign a bill in 2008 permitting euthanasia. The constitution was quickly changed, making his signature unnecessary, but the calls became louder to bring his role more in line with that of other European monarchs. One scholar described it as an effort "to rid the

Constitution of the remains of absolute rule." If the reform succeeds, Henri would lose many of his executive powers, including that of commander-in-chief of the 900-soldier army.

Executive Power

Executive power is actually exercised by the president of the government (the prime minister) and his Council of Government (cabinet). The latter body is composed of 11 or 12 persons, each usually holding several ministerial posts. During the five years between elections, the cabinets are occasionally reshuffled, but the resulting "new" governments are seldom significantly different from the ones they replace. In order to try to create some separation between the parliament and the executive, as mandated by the constitution, all cabinet members are required to resign their parliamentary seats when they assume a cabinet post.

The cabinet drafts and submits legislation, which is debated in parliament. The most important professional organizations, especially the six official groups representing agriculture, handcrafts, commerce, civil servants, private employees, and labor, are consulted on legislation affecting their interests. The smallness of the country enables this process to work smoothly. Passage after two rounds of debate is usually a foregone conclusion, since the governing parties' approval had already been reached in advance. Particularly important legislation can be submitted directly to the voters in a referendum if the cabinet and parliament approve, but such referendums very seldom occur.

Legislative Structure and Powers

The grand duke must formally sign all legislation and appointments. The president

Former Royal Highnesses the Grand Duke Jean and Grand Duchess

Luxembourg

and Council of Government are not responsible to the monarch but to the lower house of parliament, the Chamber of Deputies. Its 60 members (lowered from 64 in 1989 to reflect the declining population) are elected every five years by a system of proportional representation tailored to a small or medium-size country, in which voters live close to the candidates and may even know them personally. Almost a fourth of deputies are women. Luxembourg is divided into four electoral districts, and seats are distributed to each depending upon population. The largest receives 23 seats, and the smallest, 7. Each voter is permitted to cast as many votes as there are candidates to be elected and may even cast two votes for the same candidate if he wishes. The seats are then distributed to the candidates who receive the most votes.

Summaries of parliamentary debates and election information are sent to all citizens of voting age, who are required to vote. As in all parliamentary democracies, if the president and Council of Government lose their majority in the Chamber of Deputies, then the grand duke can call new elections, although such early elections are seldom necessary.

Although the parliament is technically a one-chamber assembly, the 21-member Council of State traditionally functions as an upper house. It is appointed by the grand duke, acting upon the advice of the cabinet, Chamber of Deputies, and the Council of State itself. Mainly an advisory body, the Council of State must be consulted on all legislation and can actually postpone its enactment. Ultimately, however, the Chamber of Deputies can always override it. Eleven of the council's members function as the nation's highest administrative court. On the whole, the council plays an important role in the governing process.

Political Parties
Since 1925 no political party has ever been able to win a majority of seats in the Chamber of Deputies, so all governments are coalitions of two or more parties. Luxembourg's three main parties have led Luxembourg for about 50 years and have helped create a democracy based on party cooperation. Although each major party represents a distinct political subculture, they all seek a solution to problems in a way agreeable to all three, no matter which is in government at the moment. All three are willing to form coalitions with each other. Neither ideologies nor historical resentments prevent them from sharing responsibility for their nation's future.

The largest is the Christian-Social People's Party (CSV), which represents the bourgeois values of a predominantly Catholic population. Its votes are drawn primarily from practicing Catholics, although the gradual disappearance of church-state issues has greatly reduced the religious component of its program. It does draw votes from the nation's farmers and workers. The party's program calls for support of a social market economy and special attention to the needs of citizens who earn below the national average. It is a middle-of-the-road party which supports the extension of the country's already-generous social welfare system. With a loosening of religious bonds and a decrease of the number of farmers, the CSV gets fewer votes than it once did.

The CSV was for decades the key coalition party, and no ruling coalition since World War II has been formed without first trying to win its direct participation. In fact, only twice since the Second World War has another party produced the prime minister. Elections normally determine which junior partner CVS will choose. In 1994 Jean-Claude Juncker replaced as prime minister Jacques Santer, who left office to be EU president from 1995 to 1999. One of seven children of a steelworker and trade union militant, Juncker went to school in Belgium and studied law in Strasbourg. He came from the left of the CSV and joined the cabinet in 1984 at age 29. He quickly gained a reputation as an intelligent, well-connected man in the EU with integrity, a broad mind, and a knack for grasping both practical detail and conceptual problems. A chain-smoker, he has an unruly air and a common touch. By 2009 he was the EU's longest-serving leader with a reputation as a wily, multilingual political operator and negotiator, a blend of casualness and working energy.

Royal Highnesses the Grand Duke Henri and Grand Duchess Maria Teresa

He accepted the EU role as spokesman for the euro. After 19 years in office, Juncker resigned over a wiretapping scandal on the part of the country's intelligence service, the SREL. He was criticized for exercising insufficient oversight over the agency and not keeping parliament informed. In the elections called for October 2013, the CSV emerged as the largest party, winning 23 of 60 seats (down 3) and 33.66% of the votes (down from 38%). But it could not form a majority. Opponents accused him of spending too much time in Brussels on EU business. He became president of the European Commission.

The second-largest party is the Luxembourg Socialist Workers Party (LSAP), known generally as the Socialists. It was founded at the turn of the century to protect workers from the seamy consequences of industrialization. Because it views itself as the party of the working class, it is strongest in the highly industrialized south. The LSAP retained its 15 seats in the 2013 elections, winning 20.28% of the votes (down from 21.5%).

The third-largest party is the Democratic Party (DP), usually referred to as the Liberals. Its support is found primarily in the middle class, professions, and skilled working groups. It strongly supports a free-market economy and opposes excessive government control over the economy. In 2013, it garnered 13 seats (up from 9) and 18.27% of the votes (up from 15%). Its leader, 40-year-old Xavier Bettel, became prime minister. The mayor of Luxembourg City for two years, he had no EU political experience. He leads a three-party center-left majority, ending 50 years of center-right dominance.

The third party in what is called "the Gambia coalition" (because of its flag's colors) is the Greens (Déi Gréng). They hung on to six of their seven seats in 2013 (based on 10.13% of the votes). It profits from the unpopularity of the Cattenom nuclear reactor three kilometers (two miles) across the French border. Its slogan: "You decide! Your vote blows nuclear power away." It is in the government. The Greens entered the government following the November 2018 elections.

Small parties capture some votes. The Alternative Democratic Reform Party got 6.64% of the votes and three seats (down one). The Left, captured 4.94% of the votes and gained a seat, for a total of two.

The only party that never participates in governing coalitions is the Communist Party of Luxembourg (KPL). It finds its electoral support primarily in the industrialized south. Its electoral support has continuously declined. A major reason is that it never fully embraced the more moderate form of communism known as Eurocommunism, which seeks to respect

Luxembourg

Former EC president Jean-Claude Juncker

the democratic process and pursue policies oriented toward the particular needs of their own countries. The KPL's ideological rigidity has kept it in the political cold following the collapse of communism in Eastern Europe. It got 1.64% of the votes and no seats in 2013.

Local Government

For administrative purposes, Luxembourg is divided into 3 districts: Luxembourg, Diekirch, and Grevenmacher, which are further broken down into 12 cantons and 118 communes. Each commune has authority over local affairs and elects a communal council every six years. To maintain some measure of national control, the central government appoints a burgomaster (mayor) to every commune who presides over the communal council. All appointments must, however, enjoy the confidence and support of a majority among the locally elected members of the communal councils; no mayor is ever imposed on a commune. In order to make the system of local government more efficient, the central government has proposed that all the present communes be fused into a total of 30, with none having a population under 3,000. Local resistance so far has prevented the realization of this plan.

Defense and Foreign Policy

Two world wars in the 20th century convinced Luxembourgers that neutrality offered their country no protection whatsoever. Their government-in-exile supported the Allied cause, and in 1949 the country joined NATO. With such a small population, it cannot contribute many troops to the alliance. In 1967, it abolished its conscript army, created in 1945, but it maintains a voluntary army of battalion size (800 light infantry troops), including a 60-man band. There are 612 paramilitary

(gendarmerie). In 2010 it deployed 8 soldiers to Afghanistan and 23 to KFOR in Kosovo. More importantly, it provides storage sites for NATO equipment. In 2006 the US Army announced that it would close its facility in Bettembourg, where it stored equipment and material used to supply its troops on military deployments. Luxembourg pledged in 2002 that it would purchase an Airbus military transport plane to help provide lift to NATO or EU military units. Its air force consists of 20 planes.

In the aftermath of the 2003 Iraq War, which Luxembourg opposed, it joined with France, Germany, and Belgium to create a joint rapid-reaction unit built on the existing French-German brigade. Luxembourg would contribute a reconnaissance team. In addition, the four said they would set up a multinational headquarters and a separate military center in Belgium to command and plan EU military operations when NATO is not involved. The four invited other European nations to join their effort, but sensing that the real purpose of this effort was to weaken the transatlantic alliance, none did. The plan was therefore dropped a few months later. Neither Luxembourg nor the other three pledged to raise their defense spending to cover the costs of these innovations.

Luxembourg was a founding member of the EU, a fact that has greatly enhanced its prestige. It amended its constitution in 1956 to permit the transfer of certain of its sovereign powers to the EU. At first, the EU's founding fathers suggested that tiny Luxembourg, which is the geographic center of the six nations, become a kind of Washington, DC, for the new United

States of Europe. This never happened. EU officials travel back and forth from Brussels, Strasbourg, and Luxembourg, a necessity that many officials and observers find wasteful and irritating. It is now the home of many EU offices and institutions, a large part of which are located on the Kirchberg Plateau in the Europa Center, a cluster of EU institutions containing several of Luxembourg's few skyscrapers. In 2005 it was a vast construction site as Luxembourg expands and improves the EU officials' working environment in the wake of the May 2004 enlargement to 25 members. In all, about 9,300 EU employees and even more foreign business executives live in Luxembourg.

Among the EU offices located in the grand duchy is the secretariat for the European Parliament, which is the largest contingent, employing over 2,500 persons. There are also Euratom, the European Court of Justice, the European Audit Court, the European Investment Bank, and the European Currency Union. In 1988 Luxembourg won an important victory in its bid to become the center of the EU's legal operations. A new Court of First Instance was created there to assume some of the growing workload of the European Court of Justice.

The European Parliament used to meet there sometimes, and a new European Parliament building was constructed for these meetings. But in 1979 the parliament decided to hold all sessions in Strasbourg. This decision infuriated Luxembourg, which turned in vain to the European Court of Justice for help. A massive office complex was constructed in Brussels that includes an assembly chamber large enough

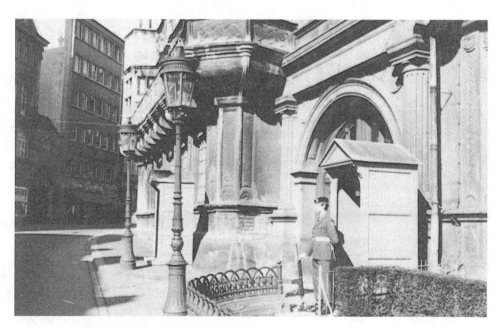

Entrance to the Grand Ducal Palace in Luxembourg

Luxembourg

for the European Parliament. Luxembourg tenaciously guards against Brussels its retention of the parliament's secretariat, a body of about 2,500 European officials who make the parliament work. Most of the parliament's committee work already takes place in Brussels, and all the major political groups within the parliament have established their headquarters there.

It has been estimated unofficially that 10% of all retail spending in the city of Luxembourg comes from EU employees and their families. Thus, their disappearance could severely affect retail businesses and property values. Thanks to the presence of these European institutions, Luxembourg is not only the richest member of the EU but also its biggest net recipient per head of EU funds. Luxembourgers converted their European Parliament building to other purposes, such as an international conference center.

Luxembourg's chief foreign policy goals are to be a significant partner in the building of a politically and economically integrated Europe. After French and Dutch voters turned down the ill-fated EU constitution in May and June 2005 referenda, Luxembourgers voted in favor of it (57% to 43%) on July 10, 2005. No one doubted that its parliament would approve the revived treaty signed in Lisbon in December 2007.

ECONOMY

Luxembourg is a highly industrialized and prosperous country. In 2014 it had the world's highest per-capita GDP. Since 1945, it has known a high degree of political and social peace. Its economy has always been based so heavily on iron and steel that it is often said, "Luxembourg is as much a gift of iron as Egypt is a gift of the Nile." This has been especially true since 1877, when the Englishmen Sidney, Thomas, and P. Carlyle Gilchrist discovered the Gilchrist-Thomas process for removing the phosphorus from Luxembourg's iron ore. Its largest steel company, Arcelor (formerly ARBED), was partly foreign-owned, but the Luxembourg state became its major stockholder. Only a fifth of its turnover was in Luxembourg; its operations were worldwide, and it had major plants in France, Spain, Germany, Belgium, Holland, and South Korea. ARBED, Usinor from France, and Aceralia from Spain merged to form Arcelor, the world's biggest steel producer with roughly 5% of global output.

The competition among the world's steel producers had become so strong that production outstripped demand. In response, Luxembourg reduced its production. In 1970 the steel industry produced nearly a third of the country's GDP; by 2006 that figure was down to less than 3%.

The Château de Berg, grand ducal country residence, an hour's drive from the capital

This forced the Luxembourg steel industry to restructure itself and ultimately to merge with two other foreign companies in 2002. This was also required by the EU, which now seeks to save the European steel industry by requiring it to modernize in member countries.

In June 2006 Arcelor agreed to a hostile merger with the Indian giant Mittal Steel to form the world's largest steelmaker in terms of market value, revenue, and output. The chief executive, backed by France, had vigorously resisted this move for over five months. But the selling price (€25.6 billion, or $33.3 billion) carried the day. Mittal contented itself with a 43.6% stake in the company and only three of the seven seats on the management board, but Lakshmi Mittal took over as chief executive.

There has been a gradual reduction of the steel industry's workforce in Luxembourg from 25,000 in 1974 to 6,500 by 2006. These reductions resulted in a rise in productivity per employee. Arcelor remains the country's biggest employer after the state. In order not to disrupt social peace, they were accomplished by retirement of workers as early as age 57 rather than by massive layoffs. It is this kind of practice that has enabled Luxembourg to have an unemployment rate among the lowest in the world and the best in the EU.

It has a labor shortage, and over 80% of new jobs are filled by cross-border workers, called Frontaliers—approximately 80,000 enter daily to work in Luxembourg, chiefly in the financial-services sector. Together with resident aliens, they constituted over 53% of the workforce in 2003; in the financial-services sector, that figure is two-thirds. Since Luxembourgers grew up speaking French and German, the foreign commuters face no language barriers. To ease the commuter traffic, the newly elected government in 2018 offered free public transport for all. The duchy still has the highest number of cars per capita (662 per 1,000 people; the United States has 800 per 1,000) in the European Union.

The country's political and economic leaders saw the problem of excessive dependence upon steel and banking well in advance, and since 1950, they have made a steady effort to diversify the economy. The Goodyear Tire and Rubber Company began building plants in the grand duchy in 1951 and is now its second-largest employer. The program got a particular boost from the industrial diversification law of 1962; this has been renewed regularly and provides state financial assistance for industrial development that contributes to the construction, conversion, and rationalization of industries, crafts, and commercial operations. The program has greatly stimulated the service industries, which now employ about three-fourths of the workforce, and has attracted over 60 new companies to Luxembourg, which have created employment for more than 11,000 persons. The most important newcomers have been American, such as DuPont.

The program has also helped to attract foreign banks to the country; the number of banks increased from 13 in 1955 to 230 in 1998 and then declined to 185 by 2002. Luxembourg has become one of the financial centers in Europe. Its financial-services institutions have assets of 20 times the country's economic output. When the Eurodollar market (in which Luxembourg had specialized) declined and London deregulated the British financial industry, Luxembourg shifted deftly to other retail banking services and maintains its place in the world market. This has greatly benefited the country. Banks employed 24,000 and generated a quarter of the GDP and a third of government revenue in 2004. Its diversified banking sector is generally considered to be healthy. One can almost speak of an economic revolution in the grand duchy.

In the 1980s, one job in banking was being created for every job that was disappearing in the steel industry. By 1988 the number of Luxembourgers employed in banking overtook those working in the steel industry, and that gap has continued to widen greatly. In 2006 financial services, such as banking, investment funds, corporate finance, and clearinghouses, accounted for 30% of GDP. Sometimes its easy business environment creates problems. This was the case in 2006, when a clearinghouse, Clearstream, landed in the middle of a French political scandal for allegedly laundering dirty money for high-level politicians. Although the indicated accounts turned out to be fabrications, the affair raised questions about what kind of money flows through the grand duchy. In response, it promised to scrap a law that gives tax exemptions to certain holding companies.

To attract funds to Luxembourg banks, the country had doggedly pursued its right to guarantee bank secrecy, despite pressure from the EU and US to cooperate more closely in cases involving crime, money laundering, and tax fraud. In 2013 the grand duchy announced that it would share information on individual depositors. Germany suffered most from the capital flight to Luxembourg. Along with other powerful neighbors, it pressured the duchy to harmonize its low tax regime (30.3% corporate tax) with its EU partners and abandon its zero withholding tax on foreigners.

Because the financial-services sector now accounts for almost a third of its GDP and employs 1 in 10 persons in the workforce, it remains the motor for the country's economic growth. Luxembourg resisted its partners' efforts as best it could. However,

it paid attention to proposals to reform EU banking policies. In 2008 it agreed, along with Belgium, to levy withholding taxes of 20% on foreign accounts and pass them on to other EU governments while keeping the bank secrecy rules in place. It eased its bank secrecy laws through a 2007 treaty with the US, and it indicated its willingness in 2009 to participate in talks on financial transparency. In 2013 it bowed to pressure and began forwarding information about foreign clients' accounts to their home governments.

Because of its low sales tax (VAT 15%) and its granting of negligible tax status to major corporation, the country has become a center for e-commerce, including iTunes, Skype, eBay, AOL, Amazon, Microsoft, and other large Internet companies, and such multinational corporations as McDonald's, Fiat, and Disney. This is part of its effort to diversify its economy from an excessive reliance on banking. It levies no taxes on up to 80% of net income generated from intellectual property. The result is a hub for technological innovation in Belval, 10 miles outside of Luxembourg City. It resisted EU efforts to get rid of its tax advantages and to go after it as a "tax haven."

Former prime minister Juncker admitted, "We have not made ourselves extremely popular in Europe." While he was prime minister and finance minister, Luxembourg attracted hundreds of multinational companies by offering them channels for funneling money through the duchy and reducing their tax burden to as low as 1%. He often personally lobbied the companies and was unapologetic for his role.

The financial-services sector has emerged as the economy's largest taxpayer. To keep the economy growing, the government introduced in 1986 the most sweeping tax reform in the nation's history. Taxes were cut, and loopholes were closed. Just over half the cuts are enjoyed by the business sector, prompting some critics of the reform to charge that it is a device primarily to improve the financial environment for bankers.

In 1991 further tax cuts went into effect. Luxembourg was the first EU country in 1997 to meet all the Maastricht Treaty convergence criteria for economic and monetary union (EMU). The banks had mixed feelings about the new euro; they shuddered at the cost of introducing it, estimated to be 4% of their total revenues. They also feared that the euro could bring with it an EU-wide harmonization of withholding tax, which could be a severe blow to Luxembourg's competitiveness as an offshore financial center. The country's government debt was a mere 20.5% of GDP in 2013. The global recession that began in 2008 harmed its economy, and

several of its local banks required government bailouts to remain solvent.

As a tiny but mighty economic dynamo and financial center in the heart of Europe, Luxembourg's influence over the regions it now borders has grown dramatically. It has adapted more successfully to new economic realities than have the German, French, and Belgian areas along its borders. Germany's Saarland and Rhineland-Palatinate, France's Lorraine, and Belgium's Wallonia have experienced retarded economic development and have in some ways become economic satellites of Luxembourg. This has been facilitated by the EU's "single market," which promotes the free movement of capital and labor. Employment opportunities in the duchy help relieve the high rates of unemployment in those neighboring areas. In such a Grande Région, as it has been called, the economic, social, and cultural ties will continue to deepen, and the borders between them will fade.

With a very small population and a high standard of living, Luxembourg is absolutely dependent upon foreign trade. Exports and imports account for 85% of its GDP, compared with 50% for Belgium, 20% for France, and 10% for the US. Such dependence indicates why Luxembourg's membership in the EU has been a matter of economic life or death. It sends 85% of its exports to its EU partners and gets 88% of its imports from them. At 4% of its total, Luxembourg's trade with the US remains relatively insignificant. Primary imports are iron ore, coke, and all energy sources except hydroelectricity.

Its steel companies own some coal mines in Germany, but its dependence upon imported oil, gas, and coal is a major problem. With the highest per-capita number of automobiles in Europe, oil is a particularly sensitive import, but by 1991 oil accounted for only 10% of Luxembourg's imports, down from 17% in 1973. To increase its energy supplies, an atomic plant along the Moselle River was planned, which would have supplied most of the power needs until 2000. However, the nuclear accident at Harrisburg, Pennsylvania, created political problems that caused the plans for this plant to be dropped.

Luxembourg also declined to join with France in developing a nuclear power plant at Cattenom, located only two miles (three kilometers) from the grand duchy. After the 1986 nuclear accident at Chernobyl in the Soviet Union, the Luxembourg government and, according to polls, 80% of the citizens began to worry more about the safety of the Cattenom plant. Winds blow west from Cattenom through Luxembourg. However, demonstrations and diplomatic protests have had no influence on the French in this matter.

Luxembourg

Museum of Modern Art on Kirchberg, Luxembourg City

An important factor in maintaining industrial production in such a small country has been the importation of foreign workers, especially from Portugal, Italy, and Spain. Together with their families, they now account for almost half of the population (43% of the total population) and come from 100 other countries. This is the highest percentage of foreign workers in the EU. If trends continue, the proportion will be one-half within the lifetimes of most living inhabitants. Over half of Luxembourg City's population is already foreign.

Nonnationals, especially immigrants from Portugal and Italy, hold about half of all jobs in the country. Foreigners provide 52% of the workers in all of Luxembourg's industries, although the percentages differ in the various economic sectors. They account for 85% of the construction workers, 66% of the craftsmen, and 35% of the laborers in the iron and steel industry. Of the overall population, 43% have foreign citizenship.

Foreign workers and their families are not permitted to participate in the national political life, although they can vote in European parliamentary elections. But even if there is little integration with the native population, they are generally well treated. Unlike in many European countries, there is no seriously destabilizing antiforeigner sentiment. This is partly explained by the fact that most immigrants share the same Catholic religion with 94% of the native Luxembourgers. In 2000 Luxembourg had the largest percentage of asylum seekers per capita in the EU. There was a public protest when 40 of them were deported in 1999.

The dependence upon foreign workers seems irreversible, given Luxembourg's alarmingly low birth rate. Unlike the case in most European countries after 1945, there was no baby boom in Luxembourg, and since 1960 the birth rate has steadily declined to one of the lowest in the world—since 1968 the native population has declined by about 1,000 each year. This is not only a serious problem for the very survival of a small nation, but it also creates an increasingly aging population who must be supported by fewer and fewer persons of working age. A fifth is already over 60 years of age, the largest percentage in the EU. Life expectance is rising: 74.9 years for men and 81.5 years for women. This will put increasing pressure on the country's generous pension system.

It is hoped that this unpleasant development can be rendered less serious by automating and modernizing industry. This would establish a productive industrial base that could create a high degree of wealth with fewer workers. The government provides a multitude of inducements to raise the birth rate: increasing family allowances, extending maternity leaves, and helping single or divorced women raise children. Few people are optimistic that these measures will reverse the demographic downturn. One parliamentarian worried, "Our country is like an aging couple. We live well, but we don't know what tomorrow brings. We have no grandchildren."

Maintaining economic stability and prosperity will remain a major task for the future. This will require maintaining not only a high level of productivity but also the labor peace that has prevailed since the end of World War II. There has been scarcely a strike since 1945. This enviable record is due to the well-organized process of consultation among employers, employees, and the government and to the great care taken not to allow the rate of unemployment to increase. In part, this has been successfully accomplished by introducing extensive public works and part-time work schedules, with the state paying for the hours not worked.

This daring policy is one that most observers agree will become too costly in the long run. Labor peace was also preserved by indexing incomes and pensions to adjust automatically to inflation, although such indexing fans the flames of inflation and damages trade competitiveness. In addition, this desire to maintain purchasing power clashes with the desire to increase social benefits, which already cover virtually the entire population.

Slightly more than half of Luxembourg's land is used for agriculture, of which 54% is used for grazing. A third of the country is planted with forests. Meat and dairy production dominate, accounting for more than 80% of the farm income. Wine production is also important.

Currently fewer than 6% of the population is engaged in agriculture, and this number is steadily declining. Yet even nonfarming Luxembourgers are not very far from the natural environment of their rural compatriots. A population density below the EU average, the absence of large cities, and the nearness of wooded areas, together with a relatively unspoiled countryside available for many kinds of relaxation, all contribute to making Luxembourg a pleasant place to live.

Luxembourg

CULTURE

Tiny Luxembourg has always been heavily influenced by its neighbors, and nothing shows this quite so clearly as the polyglot of languages that every Luxembourger masters. The everyday language of the people is Luxembourgish, an old Moselle-Frankish dialect of German, which has taken on many altered French expressions, such as *d'fotell* (*le fauteuil*, armchair). The language has become the country's one real symbol of national identity. Even modern Germans have difficulty understanding it.

This native language is spoken at home, in parliament, and sometimes in the courts, although documents and formal proceedings are in French. It also has a written form. Despite an official spelling, most Luxembourgers write it phonetically. There are no textbooks clarifying the grammatical rules. Some literature exists in the language, and local publishing houses are producing scores of books in it, spurred by such successful authors as Jhemp Hoscheit, who writes wildly popular children's books in Luxembourgish. Local radio thrives on it. There is a daily one-hour TV news broadcast in it since 1992. The 1990s witnessed a renaissance in interest in written Luxembourgish. A movement has risen to promote the language because many fear it will die in the face of massive migration to the duchy. The government declared it to be the official language and requires applicants for citizenship to study it. More and more foreign residents are learning to speak and write it as employees are increasingly required to use it in the workplace. It is the only native language of an EU member state that has not been made official in that organization.

The German language is primarily used in most primary schools, criminal court proceedings, churches, and the press, although it is not uncommon to see articles written in all three national languages on the same page of a newspaper—*Letzebuerger Journal, Luxemburger Wort, Tageblatt*. Finally, French is the language that is used most in administration, civil courts, parliament, the royal court, and secondary education. Since most immigrants living in Luxembourg come from countries (particularly Portugal, Italy, France, and Belgium) where Romance languages or French are spoken, French is an easily learned unifying language that binds the newcomers with native Luxembourgers. Two German invasions in the 20th century caused the elite to align itself more toward France and francophone culture. Until 2006 the country lacked a university, but a new one opened its doors in that year.

All Luxembourgers are completely trilingual, a fact that spares the country the terrible language conflicts that plague neighboring Belgium. In Luxembourg, culture, including theater, film, and literature, is very dependent upon the surrounding French and German worlds, and citizens have realistically accepted this without resentment. Luxembourgers' national identity is so strong and seems so natural that no language issue seems capable of altering it.

Luxembourg introduced Europe's first commercial radio station in 1934. In 1988 it seized the lead in the satellite broadcasting of commercial television when an Ariane rocket placed its Astra satellite into orbit. Luxembourg now has Europe's largest satellite operator, Societé Europeenne des Satellites (SES). It has 16 channels that can beam to Britain, France, Germany, and the BENELUX and Scandinavian countries.

Radio-Télé-Luxembourg (RTL) broadcasts to 500 million viewers across international borders. It purchased a second satellite, doubling capacity to 32 channels. It is the first European country to have an entire satellite system for TV. Some EU members, such as the UK and the Netherlands, oppose such open broadcasting, but Luxembourg is determined that the EU's principle of a "single market" should apply to TV viewing. This single market can also have other effects: Ufa, the TV and film subsidiary of the German media giant Bertelsmann, merged in 1996 with the Compagnie Luxembourgeoise Radiodiffusion (CLR/now CLT), one of the pioneers of the European media industry. One of Luxembourg's largest businesses, RTL is now a majority-owned subsidiary of Bertelsmann and remains Europe's leading broadcasting company with interests in 24 TV channels and 17 radio stations. It boasts 26 channels in 9 countries.

In 2006 the Grand-Duc Jean Museum of Modern Art opened on Kirchberg Plateau, overlooking the capital. Dramatically designed with much glass by the Chinese American architect Ieoh Ming Pei, it is the centerpiece of a vast cultural investment program aimed at transforming Luxembourg into a center for the arts. Lacking a world-class permanent collection, its first special exhibition featured the Luxembourg-born artist Michael Majerus. The grand duchy also inaugurated a new philharmonic concert hall (Christian de Portzamparc's Philharmonie) next door and a national library within walking distance from the new museum. A TGV fast-train line from France opened in 2007 to speed visitors to these sites.

THE FUTURE

Luxembourg's economic task will be to maintain the productivity, prosperity, and social welfare net it has achieved. It is already Europe's richest country in per-capita terms ($114,232 in 2011, compared with $48,112 in the US). Wages are 40% higher than in France. It receives more than one-tenth of the world's foreign direct investment. As an exporting nation, it worries about its increasingly uncompetitive cost structure.

The duchy's goal of becoming Europe's capital will remain unfulfilled, although its role in Europe is important. Jean-Claude Juncker was replaced as prime minister by Xavier Bettel, who leads a sturdy coalition after the November 2018 elections. In 2012 Luxembourgers enjoyed a royal wedding of Guillaume, heir to the throne, to Countess Stéphanie de Lannoy, who hails from one of Belgium's oldest noble families.

The Swiss Confederation (Confoederatio Helvetica)

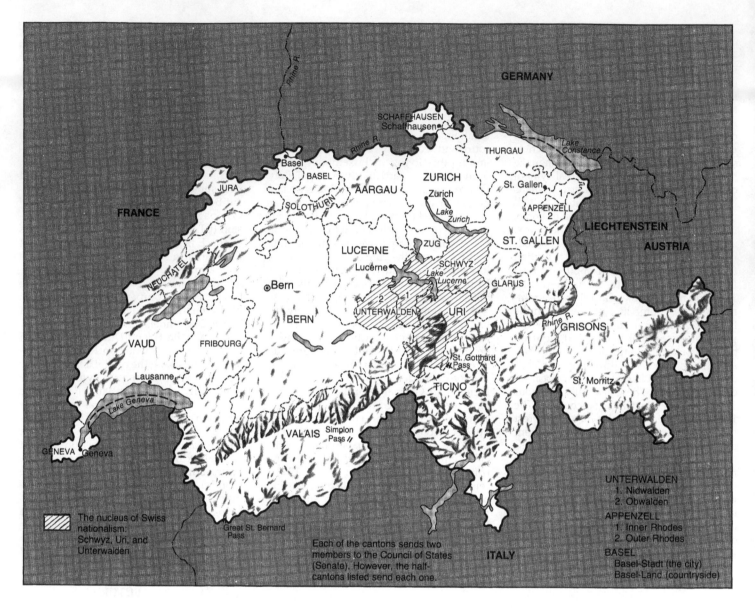

The nucleus of Swiss nationalism: Schwyz, Uri, and Unterwalden

Each of the cantons sends two members to the Council of States (Senate). However, the half-cantons listed send each one.

UNTERWALDEN
1. Nidwalden
2. Obwalden

APPENZELL
1. Inner Rhodes
2. Outer Rhodes

BASEL
Basel-Stadt (the city)
Basel-Land (countryside)

Area: 15,943 sq. mi. (41,292 sq. km). Roughly the size of Vermont and New Hampshire together.

Population: 8.7 million. Average annual growth rate is .1%. One-fourth of residents are foreigners.

Capital City: Bern (pop. 122,560).

Climate: Owing to great variations in altitude, rapid changes in weather are typical.

Neighboring Countries: France (west); Germany (north); Austria and Liechtenstein (east); Italy (south).

Languages: Swiss nationals—German (64%); French (20%); Italian (6%); Romansch (.5%), Other (9.5%). Total population: German (64%); French (19%); Italian (8%); Romansch (.6%); other (8.4%).

Ethnic Background: Swiss nationals—German (74%); French (20%); Italian (4%); Romansch (1%); other (1%). Total population: German (69%); French (19%); Italian (10%); Romansch (1%); other (1%).

Principal Religions: Swiss nationals—Protestant (55%); Roman Catholic (43%); Jewish (.2%); other (1.8%). Total population: Protestant (47%); Roman Catholic (49%); Muslim (4%); Jewish (.3%).

Main Exports: Chemicals, machinery, watches and jewelry, metals and manufactures, precision instruments.

Main Imports: Chemicals, machinery, motor vehicles, textiles, precision instruments.

Major Trading Partners: EU (56.9% of exports and 78.1% of imports), Germany (21.2% of exports and 34.1% of imports), US (10.8% of exports and 5.2% of imports), Italy (8.1% of exports and 11% of imports), France (7.5% of exports and 9.1% of imports), UK (5% of exports and 3.6% imports), China (4.5% of exports), Netherlands (4.6% of imports), Austria (4.6% of imports).

Currency: Swiss franc.

Date of Independence: August 1291.

National Holiday: August 1.

Chief of State: A seven-person collegiate Federal Council; ceremonial functions are performed by the federal president, a member of the Federal Council chosen by parliament for a one-year term. As of September 2010, a majority of four are women.

Head of Government: The federal president's position is merely "first among equals" in the Federal Council.

National Flag: Square with a white cross on a red field. The flag of the International Red Cross is exactly the same, except that the colors are reversed.

Few visitors ever leave Switzerland without feeling that they have been in one of the most extraordinary countries in the world. With its stark Jura Mountains; jagged snowcapped Alps with tidy, rustic villages dotting their valleys; and clean, mountain-fed lakes with such cosmopolitan, manicured cities as Geneva, Lausanne, Lucerne, Zurich, and Basel on their shores, Switzerland seems to be the epitome of natural beauty, cleanliness, prosperity, and stability. Its people speak a polyglot of languages, but such diversity does not threaten the country as it often does elsewhere.

In general, the Swiss are disciplined, thrifty, realistic, cautious, prudent about change, and ingenious about using the resources they have at their disposal. They are not an exceptionally outgoing people, but they are renowned for their tolerance. Therefore, Switzerland is a dreamed-of refuge for the political and economic disadvantaged and advantaged from all over the entire world.

A small, landlocked, mountainous country, Switzerland is located in the heart of western Europe. New Hampshire and Vermont could easily fit into the entire country, and 41 of 50 American states are larger than it. The Jura Mountain Chain covers approximately 10% of the country in the west and northwest and separates the city of Basel from the rest of the nation. Of the country's entire land area, 60% is located in the Alpine Mountain chain, which runs roughly west to east through the southern part of the country.

The country's many glaciers are melting as a result of global warming. This affects Switzerland's borders with both Italy and Austria. For instance, the border with Italy runs through the Alpine Monte Rosa Massif and in several places is established at the watershed. Because of diminishing glaciers, that watershed has shifted by as much as 10 meters (11 yards), taking the border with it. Switzerland also reached an agreement with Austria recognizing that this movement requires periodic alteration of the border.

Often called "the mother of rivers," Switzerland, or more precisely, the Gotthard Massif, is the watershed for some of western Europe's most important rivers: the Rhône flows through the canton of Valais, Lake Geneva, and France to the Mediterranean Sea. The Rhine forms the border with Liechtenstein, Austria, and Germany; it flows through Basel, where, because of its large harbor, one has the impression of being closer to the sea than to the Alps. It forms part of the border between Germany and France, and after flowing through the Netherlands, it empties into the distant North Sea. The Ticino River flows into Italy and into the River Po, which ultimately empties into the Adriatic Sea. Finally, the Inn River, rising in the Swiss Engadine Valley, flows through Austrian Tirol, and the city of Innsbruck and empties into the Danube, which is destined for the Black Sea.

The remaining 30% of Switzerland's land area is composed of the rolling lowlands of the Central Plateau, extending from the northern shore of Lake Geneva (Lac Leman) and northeast, past Lake Lucerne and Lake Zurich to Lake Constance (Bodensee). This part of Switzerland is one of the most densely populated and heavily industrialized areas in Europe. Here are located three quarters of the country's population, the bulk of its industry and agricultural crops, and most of its large cities, which by comparison with many other European cities, are relatively small. The largest is Zurich, with only about 720,000 inhabitants, including suburban residents.

Switzerland's central location has made the country a transportation hub for at least 2,000 years. Through it run important arteries connecting Paris with the Balkans, Munich with southeastern France, and northern Europe with Italy. This central location has, throughout the centuries, brought both prosperity and war to the fiercely independent Swiss people. It has presented them with their greatest opportunities and their greatest problems.

HISTORY

The Early Period

Since about 4000 BC, Celtic tribes settled the fertile plain between the Jura and Alpine Mountain Ranges. One such tribe, which had moved from the banks of the Rhine, called themselves Helvetians. Scribes at that time described the

An Alpine village, Château d'Oex, in the canton of Vaud

Switzerland

Helvetians as "wealthy with gold" and as "outdoing all others in martial valor." They also knew how to write, applying the Greek script to their own spoken tongue. These ambitious warriors had been seriously bitten by the restless spirit of the migrations and set their eyes on the lands of the richest empire in the known world: Rome. When they tried to move into what is now southeastern France in 58 BC, they clashed head-on with the legions of Julius Caesar, who decimated the Helvetian army. For the next four and one-half centuries, Switzerland was a Roman outpost, an important buffer between the Germanic tribes in the north and the Roman Empire.

The Helvetians prospered under Roman domination. The new masters built cities in which trade, arts, and crafts flourished. They secured the mountain passes and opened the Great Saint Bernard Pass for wagon trains in 47 AD. Thus, military and trade routes between the two halves of Europe separated by the formidable Alpine mountains were created, which proved to be of lasting importance for the future development of Europe. The Roman legions also brought Christianity to Switzerland in the 4th century AD.

As a Roman rampart and thoroughfare leading to the heart of the Roman Empire, the Helvetians were among the first to face the attacks by northern "barbarian" tribes who were bent on moving south against Rome. By the beginning of the 5th century, the Romans were compelled to withdraw, and the entire area lay open to invading Germanic tribes.

Two Germanic tribes moved to fill the rich vacuum left by the Romans. Christianized Burgundians settled in the western part of the country and gradually adopted Latin as their language. Ultimately their Latin idiom was the source of the French language. Shortly afterward, the hardy and uncivilized Alemans from north of the Rhine River moved into the central plains and the Alpine area. They refused to give up their Germanic tongue and eventually displaced the Latin language and the Roman culture wherever they settled. Only the Rhaetians, who were firmly settled in the southeastern part of Switzerland (now the canton of Grisons), and the inhabitants of the valleys on the southern slopes of the Alps (now the canton of Ticino) escaped Burgundian or Aleman mastery. They were able to continue speaking Latin, which gradually became vulgarized into Romansch and Italian, respectively. By the 6th century, the division of Switzerland into four separate language zones was established—three of Latin origin and the last, spoken by the majority, German.

From the 6th century on, another Germanic tribe, the Franks, established their control over large parts of Europe north of the Alps. During the reign of Charlemagne, who crowned himself emperor in 800 AD, the future Switzerland was absorbed into an empire that scarcely survived his death. Switzerland was partitioned in the 9th and 10th centuries between the Kingdom of Upper Burgundy and the Dukedom of Swabia, both parts of the Holy Roman Empire. Switzerland's history from then on was closely linked to Germany, particularly to the House of Habsburg in Austria.

Although the new masters tried very hard to impose feudal ties on the Swiss, these attempts were never completely successful. The Helvetians and Alemans both had firm traditions of local autonomy and of personal freedom, traditions clearly visible in Switzerland today. By the 13th century, when Europe's feudal orders had been severely weakened by the Crusades, important developments began to take place that ultimately resulted in an independent Switzerland.

In 1230 the St. Gotthard Pass was opened. Earlier, only two major, direct roads for crossing the Alps had been open, one in the west and one in the east of Switzerland. The opening of the Gotthard Pass now brought traffic to and from Italy through the heretofore relatively isolated central portion of the land. The great powers of Europe now eyed with much greater interest this valuable piece of territory astride a crucially important trade route.

At the foot of the northern slope of the Gotthard Massif, at opposite ends of Lake Lucerne, are located two small areas: Schwyz (from which Switzerland later got its name) and Uri. Far in advance of their time, these rugged mountain people met in assemblies to elect their leaders and to decide on the administration of common lands. In the 13th century, they rebelled against the local dynasties and achieved a semi-independent status linked with the Holy Roman Empire. Schwyz had adopted

The Oath of the Three Swiss (18th century)

its own banner, a white cross on a red field, the present Swiss flag.

The Beginning of Independence and Allegiance

The Habsburg ruler Rudolf I died in 1291, and two weeks later, representatives of Schwyz and Uri, joined by those of a third Swiss area, Unterwalden, which is located on another arm of Lake Lucerne, met on the meadow of Rütli. There they signed a peace alliance in the beginning of August 1291, declaring their right to choose their own judges from among men of their own valleys and pledging reciprocal aid if one of them were wronged by an outside power. Indeed this alliance proved effective in 1315, when 1,000 Swiss mountain men trapped and slaughtered 2,000–3,000 knights sent to reestablish full Habsburg control. Although this alliance does not seem very revolutionary today, it was a momentous step at the time and established the cornerstone for modern Switzerland. These voluntary agreements formed the basis for the Swiss *"Willensnation"*—a

Huge mural in parliament—Lake Uri, where Switzerland was founded

nation created not by blood ties but by the acts of diverse people's free will.

What it created was a loose confederation without central authority, army, police, court, or executive. Ultimate power remained with the individual states (called cantons after 1803). Decisions were made in regular meetings among the cantons' leaders and were made not by majority vote but by consensus. In other words, solutions had to be found to which all parties could agree. These principles of reaching agreement for all decisions, known in Switzerland today as "amicable agreement," and of working out problems in a confederal, not centralized, way have become deeply rooted in Swiss democracy.

The legendary William Tell of Uri, immortalized in Friedrich Schiller's drama, remains a symbol for the liberty these three "forest cantons" on the shores of Lake Lucerne pledged to defend. Forced by the tyrannical bailiff Gessler to shoot an apple from the head of his own child, Tell took revenge by shooting a fatal arrow at Gessler himself.

Present-day Switzerland gradually took shape in the following centuries as other cantons or cities joined this original alliance. The major motive for the cantons' joining or remaining in the alliance was usually to defend themselves against the Habsburgs' repeated attempts to regain or tighten control over them. The cities and territories of Lucerne, Zurich, Bern, Glarus, and Zug joined in the 14th century. At about the same time, Uri conquered the Italian speaking Leventina, a valley along the Ticino River on the southern slope of the Alps. This was the first time that a non-Germanic-speaking area became a part of the confederation. In 1477 Bern snatched stretches of land in the Vaud from the Duke of Savoy. Again, people who did not speak German were incorporated into the confederation. Later in joining were Fribourg and Solothurn in 1481, Basel and Schaffhausen in 1501, and Appenzell in 1513. The land between these cantons was gradually purchased or conquered, so that, by the early 16th century, Switzerland was a more or less contiguous territory.

Initial Alliance Organization

The terms for each entry were often different, and most maintained their own alliances with outside powers. Thus, Switzerland was at this time a "system of alliances," a patchwork of independent countries with different political systems. What they agreed to do was to assist each other militarily, to consult one another, and to hold conventions (diets) at fixed times and places. Only unanimous decisions were binding. There were certainly powerful disagreements among the members, which sometimes led to wars among themselves. This system of alliances was the first in Europe to combine cities with rural states, and there were persistent disputes stemming from the different interests of town dwellers and peasants. Also, some cantons wanted the confederation to expand in a westerly direction toward France, while others wanted it to expand in a southerly direction toward Italy.

The Swiss temptation to become a great power through territorial expansion was rapidly extinguished in 1515, when the French decisively defeated the Swiss forces at Marignano. The bravery of highland infantrymen was no match for modern cavalry and artillery in the plain. This disastrous battle, in which only about one-half the cantons chose to participate, made the Swiss realize two things: First, the headless confederation, with its web of alliances and no overall executive, did not permit ambitious Swiss projects beyond their territory. It decided thenceforth to make key decisions by majority vote, but it was no longer a match for the surrounding monarchies. Second, having eliminated the last vestiges of Habsburg influence from Switzerland in 1499, the Swiss decided to pursue a policy of maximum independence from the alliances and political intrigues of all other European countries. A treaty signed in 1521 with France became the only alliance signed by all the cantons of the confederation with a foreign power.

Arms, Mercenaries, and an Independent Tradition

In return for French protection and the right to trade freely with France, the Swiss obligated themselves to provide soldiers for the French king's infantry. At the same time, the Swiss were permitted to provide military units to other European states. This practice meant that, on occasion, Swiss troops faced each other on the battlefield. It was, nevertheless, often economically important for Swiss communities which accepted contracts for the troops. The hiring of mercenaries did not end until 1859, with the one exception of the colorful Swiss guards who still staff the Vatican today.

Due to the outstanding reputation of Swiss troops throughout Europe, these soldiers were very much sought after. Louis XI of France paid Swiss troops premium wages for their services, and when word got around that the Swiss were being paid so well, men from all over the French-speaking world attempted to enlist under the guise of being Swiss. Thereupon, Louis decided that a Swiss was only a person coming from a German-speaking canton, and anyone else who claimed to be Swiss was hanged promptly for "fake advertising."

The excellent Swiss military reputation stemmed from several things. First, Swiss troops served their own cantons' interests, fought under their own cantons' banners, obeyed their own officers, and were governed by their own codes. This made them far braver than other mercenaries, who were well known for the speed with which they left the battlefield at crucial times. Swiss troops, with their capacity to stick together and to offer themselves wholly to a collective, were prepared to fight to the last man.

The Swiss soldiers also had certain capabilities that were highly valued. They could march with great rapidity and they could operate very effectively in mountainous areas. Because they could scale cliffs so easily, they could capture fortresses better than any others. Therefore, before heavy artillery was perfected, the best weapon against a fortress was a unit of Swiss troops.

The Swiss infantry units also were the first to use a weapon that was terrifying to knights in armor—the halberd. This hand-wielded weapon, now frequently carried by the Swiss guards at the Vatican, basically stood in the same relationship to a knight's armor as a can-opener now stands to a can. Johannes von Winterthur recorded in his chronicle of a ghastly picture of row after row of dead knights lying on the battlefield, their helmets split wide open.

The Swiss were, and still are, a people in arms. This fact has been a key to Switzerland's survival as an independent country in the heart of Europe. It has also been a key to its establishment very early of an exceptionally high degree of personal freedom for more and more of its own people. Among the first things which European feudal lords did, in order to ensure their mastery over serfs, was to disarm them. Thus, in the rest of Europe, fewer persons were armed than in Switzerland. This meant not only that their rulers treated peasants and other citizens of Swiss cantons with greater respect. It also underscored the principle that gradually became accepted in Switzerland: that the people were sovereign and that no ruler could rule legitimately without their consent.

Although many Swiss did not achieve equality until the 19th century, the ruling nobility in other European countries were well aware after 1291 that a different kind of society existed in some parts of Switzerland, especially in Schwyz, Uri, and Unterwalden. They harbored fears that the Swiss example might destabilize the nobility and lead to the liberation of peasants all over Europe. For example the Burgundian king Charles the Bold once ordered that all captured Swiss soldiers be exchanged immediately so that they could not infect

Switzerland

peasants from elsewhere in Europe with their independent ideas.

While noblemen throughout Europe regarded Swiss progress toward democracy and respect for personal freedom as an ominous development, the Swiss themselves were never crusaders for their own ideas. They satisfied their yearning for freedom neither by trying to spread an abstract idea of justice throughout Europe, as the French did after their revolution, nor by trying to establish a *Pax Helvetia* in the entire known world as the Romans had done. Swiss democracy was always linked to moderation and the willingness to compromise. The Swiss almost always showed common sense by recognizing their own limitations.

The Reformation

Switzerland in the 16th and 17th centuries was shaken and divided by a development that changed the soul of Europe: the Reformation. From Swiss soil the great humanist Erasmus had long criticized the all-too-worldly popes and the many petty clerical abuses and had advocated a return to the simplicity of the earlier church. Only two years after Martin Luther had tacked his revolutionary 95 Theses on a cathedral door in Wittenberg, Germany, in 1519, Ulrich Zwingli, a priest, army chaplain, and humanist known as the "Reformer of Zurich," denounced on his own the abuses of the Catholic Church and began to preach sermons no less inflammatory than Luther's. Several Swiss cities followed his call, but the more rural cantons around Lake Lucerne resisted Zwingli by force. Ultimately he was killed in the violent atmosphere he helped to create. In the Peace of Kappel (1531), the cantons accepted a confessional division of the country into Protestant and Catholic cantons. Thereafter, all citizens in the same canton had to subscribe to the same form of Christianity. Where this was difficult, cantons split into half-cantons, as Appenzell did in 1597.

In Geneva, another city linked by alliance to the Swiss Confederation, a Frenchman named Jean Calvin (whose 500th birthday was celebrated in 2009) successfully established in 1541 a strict, Protestant religious government. His pious religious ideas spread quickly to central Europe and across the Netherlands to England and Scotland. Geneva itself became a strict city, where frolicking and frills of all kinds were frowned upon. For example, it was forbidden to wear chains, bracelets, necklaces, and gold objects. It became known as the "Protestant Rome." Interestingly, Calvinism as a faith had almost no impact on the rest of Switzerland; its theological radiation was felt chiefly outside the country. It did attract thousands upon thousands of

Statue of Zwingli, Zurich

skilled, ingenious, but brutally persecuted French Huguenots into Switzerland during the 17th century. These French Protestants were the first of many waves of immigrants seeking political or religious asylum in Switzerland. The Huguenots also brought skills in banking, trading, and manufacturing (especially watchmaking), which were of enormous economic benefit to Switzerland.

To its great fortune, Switzerland was able to remain almost completely uninvolved in the confused, bloody conflict known as the Thirty Years' War, which ravished parts of Europe from 1618 to 1648. The religious split a century earlier did slow the development of central institutions in the confederation. Yet, Switzerland was always fortunate to have its internal divisions overlap one another. The many differences among language and religious groups, as well as between urban and rural areas, had and now have the effect of pulling the Swiss back together. For example, two residents of the city of Zurich may belong to different religions, but the fact that they are German-speaking city dwellers means that they have important things in common. A French-speaking and a German-speaking Swiss may both live in a rural environment and belong to the same religion. These overlapping divisions and the traditions of tolerance, moderation, and readiness to compromise are important reasons a multilingual, multinational, multireligious Swiss state is still able to manage the searing problems of division so well.

Industrialization

Swiss ingenuity and the economic shot in the arm the Huguenots provided were especially crucial in the 17th and 18th centuries because the discovery of America gradually led to a shift in the center of world trade toward the Atlantic coast. One could almost say that Christopher Columbus had placed severe strains on the economic progress of Switzerland and of many other central European lands. In order to overcome the resultant economic stagnation, the Swiss had to raise capital to develop the country's manufacturing facilities, to expand Swiss banking operations, and to build a global trading network. These efforts later put Switzerland in a position to be one of the first countries on the continent of Europe to undergo an Industrial Revolution, a fact which has enabled the country to achieve a level of prosperity which is still envied throughout the world.

Democratic Ideals

Switzerland in the 18th century became a cauldron bubbling with explosive democratic political ideas that were to have a dramatic impact all over Europe. One reason was that a trend had gathered momentum in Switzerland since the 17th century which saw a narrowing ruling class, rich and often highly cultured, gaining hold over almost all the coveted public offices, monopolies, or privileges. Zurich became known as "the little Athens of the north," and after the 1760s Geneva became a magnet for such brilliant minds as Gibbon, Voltaire, and Rousseau. Jean-Jacques Rousseau, a citizen of Geneva whose politics made him unwelcome in France, challenged the very legitimacy of all contemporary regimes and societies. His opening to the famous *Social Contract* became a starting point for many revolutionaries, including Karl Marx: "Man was born free, but everywhere he is in chains." In Geneva, which had become known as the "political laboratory of Europe," such ideas helped ignite an unsuccessful revolution in 1782. This was the first in Europe since the American Revolution and seven years before the outbreak of the French Revolution.

As Germany's greatest poet, Goethe, said at that time, "With Rousseau a new world begins." The momentous events in France after 1789 unleashed aftershocks that ultimately shattered Switzerland's fragile confederal structure. In 1792 Geneva exploded, and the revolutionary fever spread throughout the confederation. Republican France intervened openly in Swiss affairs, and in 1798 French troops invaded Switzerland, partly in order to secure the Alpine passes. This was the first time since the Thirty Years' War

(1618–1648) that the confederation had been occupied by foreign troops. Further, in 1799 Austrian and Russian troops also entered Swiss territory, but the French drove them out. The ease with which the well-commanded armies conquered Switzerland was another reminder of its inherent weakness. Such an excessively decentralized Switzerland was completely unable to withstand a determined attack. By the end of 1799, war had ravaged large parts of Switzerland, and the French held the cantons firmly under their control.

The conquerors created a "Helvetic Republic," which was a highly centralized state modeled after France. This new republic was almost the complete opposite of the traditional Swiss Confederation and therefore sparked severe disorders within the country. It was replaced in 1803 by a new constitution drafted by Napoleon and called the Act of Mediation. This document permitted more decentralization, and it drew considerable inspiration from the newly developed US Constitution in that it combined federalism, separation of powers, popular sovereignty, individual rights, and the central government's authority over foreign and military policy. It reestablished the cantons, and to the older ones it added six new ones: French-speaking Vaud; Italian-speaking Ticino; partly Romansch-speaking Grisons; and the three German-speaking, St. Gallen, Aargau, and Thurgau. Thus, under French influence, Switzerland, which had hitherto been a predominantly German-speaking country, was converted into a truly multilingual state.

For the next 10 years, Switzerland remained a scarcely disguised French protectorate. Much to the disgust of many Swiss, it was compelled to supply a contingent of 16,000 men to the French army. In 1812 Napoleon's dominance of Europe received its fatal blow in the snows of Russia, and in 1813 Napoleon's enemies marched through Switzerland on their way to conquer France. When Napoleon escaped from Elba the following year and attempted to pick up his tattered imperial flag, Switzerland joined France's enemies in burying the Napoleonic Empire once and for all.

It received its reward at the Congress of Vienna, which put Europe back together in 1815. The European powers added three cantons: two French-speaking ones (Neuchâtel and Geneva) and the bilingual Valais, thereby completing the boundaries of present-day Switzerland. The congress also proclaimed the neutrality and inviolability of Switzerland. From that date on, Swiss neutrality has been an established principle of international law.

Although the French Revolution had been crushed, its ideals retained their force and popularity in many countries, including Switzerland. Pressure mounted in the cantons to achieve more democracy. Such efforts received a powerful boost at the time of the Paris uprisings in 1830, which prompted some cantons to regenerate themselves by establishing fully elective governments. They were also furthered by the Industrial Revolution, which created a confident middle class and a growing urban working group. Both demanded greater influence in the political affairs of their cantons. The democratic movement rapidly gained steam, and between 1830 and 1848, conservatives throughout Europe viewed Switzerland as a carrier of dangerous democratic germs that could infect the rest of Europe.

By 1847 proponents of an even more democratic national constitution had won the majority in more than a dozen cantons. As in the US, a civil war had to be fought between those insisting upon states' rights and those advocating a stronger federal government. The conflict lasted little more than a month and claimed only about 100 lives. But the federal victory was necessary for the pact among cantons to be converted into a truly federal constitution with institutions under which Switzerland still lives. A Swiss federal state with a democratic constitution inspired by the American Constitution and the 1803 Act of Mediation was created. This actually occurred before many revolutions had erupted throughout Europe in 1848, all of which ultimately failed. The only consequence of these outbreaks as far as Switzerland was concerned was that the European powers were far too busy with their own domestic problems to interfere in Swiss affairs at this crucial time. From 1848 on, Switzerland has been a democracy in the modern sense of the word. The Industrial Revolution, with a Swiss emphasis on watchmaking and fine machine tools and equipment, continued steadily during the balance of the century and the 20th century. Brilliant engineering enabled construction of a comprehensive rail system through the rugged terrain.

Rumblings and Difficulties during World War I

During World War I, tension between the German- and French-speaking populations erupted over a scandal involving a high-ranking Swiss military officer who had passed intelligence information to the Germans. Also, thousands of refugees poured into the country; many continued political activity involving other countries from Swiss soil, a practice that threatened the country's neutrality. Perhaps the best known of these was Vladimir Ilyich Lenin. He was living in Zurich in 1917 when the Russian Revolution erupted, and he reportedly screamed in exasperation that he would gladly sell his soul to the devil for the chance to return to his country to take

The church in Meiringen (Bern canton) has frescoes from the 11th and 12th centuries.

Switzerland

Scenic valleys in the canton of Bern

control of the upheaval. German leaders, desperately wishing to eliminate Russia as a battlefield foe, decided to support the Russian revolutionaries, who promised peace to their war-weary countrymen. Of course, the Swiss authorities were delighted to be rid of him and many other Russian radicals. The Germans provided him passage in a train closed to German officials of all kinds. As Winston Churchill later wrote, Lenin was sent "like a plague bacillus from Switzerland to Russia."

European wars always threaten the markets and raw materials that trade-dependent Switzerland needs in order to survive. Price controls and rationing had to be introduced during World War I, and the Swiss economy suffered greatly. In November 1918 the social discontent created by such setbacks exploded into a general strike with Marxist revolutionary overtones. Timely concessions, such as the introduction of a proportional representation electoral system, enabled the government to end the strike quickly and thereby to avert the danger of further domestic tensions.

Switzerland made three significant foreign policy decisions in 1920–1921. It turned down a request by the Austrians living in the Alpine area of Vorarlberg to become a part of Switzerland. It agreed to form a customs union with its small

eastern neighbor, Liechtenstein. Third, it decided to become a member of the League of Nations, whose headquarters had been established in Geneva. Thus, it decided that membership in international organizations did not violate Swiss neutrality so long as (1) the organization publicly recognized Swiss neutrality, (2) Switzerland be permitted to abstain from sanctions against other countries, and (3) Switzerland be permitted to maintain its universal economic relations with all countries of the world, a principle which it considers essential for its prosperity.

The Depression and World War II

The Great Depression of the 1930s inevitably affected Switzerland because of its dependence upon foreign trade. The social unrest the economic shocks helped to create spawned some radical political movements, such as the youthful Front groups that demanded a fascist order. Nevertheless, Switzerland managed to preserve its democratic order at a time when most of the democracies in Europe collapsed.

It also managed to remain neutral during World War II, which followed on the heels of the Depression. Such neutrality was not entirely a gift of the neighboring fascist dictators. Switzerland mobilized 430,000 soldiers and threatened to destroy all major tunnels and bridges. It declared

its determination to fight to the last man if it were invaded, although it was revealed after the war that only the heartland, including the St. Gotthard Pass and the Simplon tunnels, were to be defended to the end. This threat, backed by the Swiss military reputation and determination, helped to dissuade Hitler and Mussolini from attacking the country, which the former scornfully called "the anus of Europe."

But Switzerland did not remain free as a result of military deterrence alone. Faced with the prospect that it could share the fate of other occupied countries, it made compromises with Nazi Germany in the name of "neutrality" that now make it seem to many Swiss and non-Swiss that the country may have bought its freedom at a very high moral price. It continued to trade with Germany and Italy, and some of the products it sold were obviously used for armaments. Further, thousands of Jews and political refugees were denied entry into Switzerland and therefore ended up in prisons or extermination camps. An agreement with Germany in 1938 required Jews to obtain visas and have a special stamp in their passports. Elie Wiesel argues that the idea of stamping German passports with a "J" for "Jewish" came from the Swiss. Police officials who allowed Jews to enter the country illegally were punished.

Recently declassified Allied intelligence documents reveal the extent to which the Swiss also reaped handsome profits by serving as bankers both for the Nazis and their Jewish victims. Prominent Nazis were steady customers of Swiss banks: Hitler reportedly deposited royalties from *Mein Kampf*, and Hermann Goering made regular trips to Zurich to deposit art masterpieces stolen from museums in occupied countries. The banks purchased from the Nazis hundreds of millions of dollars of looted gold, and other looted funds were invested in Swiss enterprises. Bank secrecy was introduced in 1934 to accommodate Jews who wanted to deposit their assets quietly outside of Germany, and then those same secrecy laws were used to prevent the heirs from claiming those assets after the war. Jewish groups estimated in 1996 that the banks hold about $7 billion, including interest, that belonged to Jews who perished in the Holocaust, in addition to gold and other valuables looted from Jews. After years of denial, the government admitted that the Swiss secretly used some of these funds to compensate their own citizens for property confiscated by the communists in Poland, Hungary, and the former Czechoslovakia.

The Swiss refusal to discuss or deal with these problems cracked in 1996 under intense pressure from Jewish organizations, the American Senate Banking Committee, and other foreign governments.

Attempting to contain this gigantic public relations disaster, it formed one commission, chaired by former US Federal Reserve chairman Paul A. Volcker, to oversee the search for dormant accounts left by Jews. A second international historical panel was appointed to investigate the extent and fate of Jewish wealth and Nazi loot sent to neutral Switzerland during the war.

A further panel was set up under foreign pressure in 1996, composed of nine international historians with economists, legal experts, and researchers to assist them in examining the country's culpability. In 2002 it issued its massive final report that concluded that Switzerland's politicians and businessmen had failed the country on three counts: They contributed to the Holocaust by turning back 20,000 refugees, at times discriminating against Jews, even though they knew what fate awaited them in Germany. They helped the Nazi war machine by going further than necessary in trade and financial support. After the war, banks and art galleries were negligent about restoring property. At the end of 2002, the Swiss government supported a proposal to overturn the wartime convictions of people who broke the law by sheltering Jews and others fleeing Nazi Germany. The first pardon came in 2004, when a 79-year-old Jewish lady, who had served 15 days in jail for guiding other Jews across the border from France, was cleared. No compensation is allowed.

In 1997 Switzerland agreed for the first time to use the funds in Holocaust victims' unclaimed bank accounts to help survivors. It also set up a separate fund of about $200 million contributed by private banks to distribute to individuals who survived the Holocaust. In 1998 the two largest Swiss banks reached a $1.25 billion settlement of a lawsuit by Holocaust survivors and their descendants; $800 million is to go to bank depositors or their heirs and the rest to settle other claims, such as the looting of private property. Two major European insurers also reached an accord on life insurance claims for victims. In return, US cities and states canceled an economic boycott against all Swiss banks, institutions, and companies, and a $20 billion class-action suit brought against the banks was dropped. Ursula Koch, president of the Socialist Party, said, "we have to come to grips with our history." Nevertheless, a judge in Brooklyn claimed in 2004 that Swiss banks were still denying wrongdoing and were stonewalling the settlement of some cases. That seemed to have ended in January 2005, when a list of 3,100 newly released names of Nazi-era depositors was published.

While few Swiss are proud today of such past policies, Swiss national survival seemed to require them at the time. On the positive side, Switzerland was a base during the war for Allied spies, such as Allen Dulles, as well as for international Jewish agencies operating in Europe. It also offered protection to 300,000 refugees who would otherwise have joined the many victims of fascism. Switzerland did not entirely escape the destruction meted out in other parts of Europe. In April 1944 US squadrons mistakenly bombed the Swiss city of Schaffhausen, the only major Swiss city located entirely north of the Rhine River. Allied bombers also attacked other localities, such as Basel and Geneva.

In 1999 the Swiss government disbanded a special crisis task force looking into the country's role in the war. But it will take much longer for the bruised feelings to heal. The myth of wartime Swiss neutrality was exposed. Yet nothing in recent years unified this highly decentralized country as thoroughly as the world's condemnation of its actions during the war. The crisis opened Swiss eyes to their contemporary isolation. Many Swiss believe that their European neighbors and the US had abandoned them by bearing down on them so forcefully over Nazi gold.

POLITICAL SYSTEM

In many countries of the world today, ethnic, lingual, and regional diversity often create almost-insolvable problems of political and social instability. This has not been the case in Switzerland. Thanks to its tradition of tolerance and compromise, its economic prosperity, and its decentralized democratic order tailored to its particular needs, Switzerland enjoys a level of political stability envied in much of the world. But it is an undeniably complicated land. Napoleon Bonaparte confessed to a Swiss delegation in 1802, "The more I think about your country, the more convinced I become that the disparity between its constituent parts makes it impossible to impose a common pattern on it: everything points to federalism."

The constitution, adopted in 1848, was considerably revised in 1874 to establish national responsibility for defense, trade, and many legal matters. On the whole, it has served Switzerland well. Some Swiss now consider the much-amended constitution to be unwieldy and outdated, and since the 1960s the government studied the possibility of rewriting the document. In April 1999 voters, backed by all the major parties, approved a new constitution that abolished the gold standard for the franc and enshrined new rights in law, including the right to strike and the principle of equal opportunities for the handicapped.

The central elements of Swiss democracy remain unchanged: a federal form of government composed of powerful and confident cantons, jealously protective of their own powers; the participation of all major parties in the national, cantonal, and communal governments; a collegial executive elected by but not responsible to the parliament rather than a one-man executive elected directly or responsible to the parliament; a method of decision making known as "amicable agreement" involving consensus and respect for minority opinions rather than the majoritarian approach; and, finally, a system of semi-direct democracy at the national, cantonal, and communal levels.

Canton Customs and Government

A Swiss person tends to consider himself a citizen first of his commune or canton and second of Switzerland. Only the 2,800 communes can grant citizenship, but communal approval is normally a mere formality when the person meets all federal requirements. A quarter of the

The government procession at Nidwalden

Switzerland

country's residents are foreign-born, and about 12,000 foreigners become naturalized citizens each year. Federalism, reinforced by strong regional pride, is very much alive in Switzerland, and as a result, the 26 Swiss cantons have been considerably more successful in resisting the trend toward government centralization than most other countries, including the US. As is nominally true in the US, Swiss cantons in reality exercise all powers not explicitly granted to the federal government. In general, they have their own taxing authority, and the Swiss pay most of their income taxes to their cantons. The mix of spending among the federal, cantonal, and communal governments is approximately 30:40:30. The cantons have the right to manage their own affairs and the responsibility to enforce the law within their own boundaries.

A proposal in 1978 to create a federal police force was rejected in a national referendum. In 1982, 74% of the voters rejected the creation of a federal anti-terrorist unit. Cantons also have the authority to decide who has the right to vote in their elections.

Because 60% of all voters in a 1981 referendum agreed to amend the constitution in order to give women and men equal rights, it was inevitable that women would ultimately get to vote at every level. In 1990 the Federal Tribunal ruled that article 4 granting equal rights overrides article 74 giving cantons the power to decide their own voting rules. Thus, in 1991 the last holdout, Appenzell–Inner Rhodes, counted women's votes in its open-air assembly. The trend toward full equality for women was continued in a 1985 referendum that granted them equal marriage rights. The husband was no longer the legal head of the household who could decide where to live, to what schools the children should go, or whether the wife

could open a bank account or take a job. Since 1971 all women have been allowed to vote in national elections. Cantons also have the right to decide what kind of governments they will have, so long as they are democratic and conform to the federal constitution. All have chosen to have a collegial executive with a unicameral legislature.

On the last Sunday in April and the first Sunday of May, the citizens of the five mostly rural Swiss cantons of Obwalden, Nidwalden, Glarus, and the two Appenzell half-cantons of Inner Rhodes and Outer Rhodes gather in annual open-air assemblies to elect their leaders and judges, vote on important laws, approve the budget, and change their constitutions. In the early days, attendance at such assemblies, which date back to 1231, was required for all male citizens old enough to fight, which was usually 14 years. Participants came to the assemblies armed. Male citizens in Appenzell must still appear with side arms in order to vote; women were granted an exception to this rule. A large, ornate sword, which is the symbol of cantonal authority, is carried into the assembly area (called the "ring") with great pomp. In Glarus, the presiding official (called the Landammann) even wraps his arm around the sword during the entire session. In the past, the people dismissed the Landammann by the simple act of taking the sword away from him.

The assemblies begin, proceed, and end with ceremony and colorful folklore. They give vivid glimpses into Switzerland's past. Honored participants and guests are led into the ring by full-bearded attendants in long robes; baggy striped pants; fur or pointed hats and/or plumed helmets. They carry the cantonal insignias, seals, banners, keys, and other relics with them. The leaders stand on a wooden stage surrounded by attendants, while

the citizens stand or sit on long wooden benches. In Nidwalden, the assembly is opened by the blowing of a large, curled horn; a word from a priest; the introduction of honored guests; and an oath of the leaders to respect the constitution.

The visitor is usually so fascinated by the ceremonial aspects of the assembly that he forgets that the citizens have gathered in order to make policy, not to view a parade. There is a serious air, and participants in modern business suits and dresses far outnumber those wearing ornate traditional jackets and bonnets. All voters receive detailed information in advance on the issues that are to be discussed. Except in Appenzell, where there is no discussion at the assembly, each citizen has a right to speak. Speeches are well prepared and short, and normal voting is done by raising hands, with officials in red robes judging the results from an elevated platform.

A 1982 vote showed how uncertain the outcomes can be. In Obwalden the president of the federal senate Jost Dillier, one of Switzerland's leading national politicians, was voted out of office, even though he had no opposing candidate. Newspapers the next day wrote of "an absolute sensation," a "bomb which exploded." The Swiss emphasize continuity and stability so strongly that elected officials have no formal limits on the time they may serve. However, most retire when their terms expire. Dillier had violated two fundamental rules of Swiss politics. He had assumed too many offices in politics and business and thus had too much power in his own hands. Also, he paid more attention to politics in Bern than in his canton. Many said that he personified the "arrogance of power," and in Switzerland there is almost nothing which is more distrusted than obvious political ambition or heavy-handedness.

At the end of the four- to six-hour assemblies, ceremony again glosses over the differences that arose in the debates. The attendants lead the procession out of the ring and to the church or city hall, where the newly elected leaders are greeted before attending a banquet. The other citizens spend the rest of the day in a holiday manner.

In order to accomplish anything in such annual meetings, the canton must be rather small in size. It must also have a small and homogeneous population. Granting women the right to take part has created a particular problem by doubling the number of participants. Serious divisions between Catholics and Protestants or city and country dwellers have wrecked such annual assemblies. There are many tales of brawls at meetings, even though such disturbances of the peace traditionally carried a higher sentence than

The vote is taken in Glarus

at other times. To reduce the likelihood of these outbreaks, the consumption of alcoholic beverages at such meetings has long been strictly forbidden. Success requires concentrating on a few important issues, as well as discipline on the part of the individual citizens. Long-winded speeches would seriously try the patience of the participants, and filibusters would be a catastrophe.

One can call this form of direct democracy antiquated or mere ballast tradition. Yet every form of democracy has its advantages and disadvantages. This kind of colorful but serious gathering brings together several thousand citizens for public debate on political issues immediately affecting their lives. There have been practical reasons some such assemblies have had to be abolished. But none has ever been cancelled because of lack of public spirit or citizen interest.

Trends toward Centralization

There is an undeniable trend toward greater governmental centralization because of the many knotty problems of modern life. Such issues as environmental protection; nuclear energy; and especially economic matters including unemployment, inflation, foreign trade, currency controls, and planning, are increasingly seen to be problems with which single cantons cannot easily cope effectively. A rule of thumb is that, whenever the Swiss economy is in a slump, there is a stronger demand for shifting more powers to the central government. When the economic picture is rosier, then the resistance to such transfer stiffens.

Over the years the principle has developed that "federal law is superior to cantonal law." The cantons are, nevertheless, far from helpless in the face of this powerful pull toward the federal capital city of Bern. Any constitutional change requires a "double majority" in a national referendum—a majority of all Swiss voters and a majority in more than half the cantons. For instance, in 1973 a majority of Swiss voters supported a proposal to give the national government authority to unify the country's schools, traditionally a cantonal power. However, a majority of the cantons rejected the proposal, so each still maintains its own preferred school system.

The Bicameral Legislature

Both houses of the national parliament, including the Council of States, must approve all national legislation. This upper house, modeled after the US Senate, is composed of 2 representatives from each canton, regardless of size—and the cantons vary in population from 15,000 in rural Appenzell Inner Rhodes to 1.2 million in Zurich. The cantons are free to decide how representatives are chosen; in fact,

The Swiss Parliament, Bern

the 46 members are elected directly by the people in all but 4. This Council of States tends to be far more conservative than the lower house of the national parliament, especially insofar as cantonal prerogatives are concerned. As is true of other Swiss political offices, the title of parliamentarian carries neither great influence nor prestige. Parliament meets for approximately 16 weeks a year, divided into 4 sessions. Deputies are given only a part-time wage for their service and are even freed two days per week during the sessions to perform their regular jobs.

As the United States' leaders saw in the 1780s and as Belgium's leaders realized in the 1970s, federalism is a very important means of enabling a heterogeneous population to live together in harmony; it certainly has been a key ingredient in Switzerland's success as a multinational, multilingual state. Switzerland has had the

flexibility to adjust its federal order when a serious problem developed, such as that which emerged in the bilingual canton of Bern. The French-speaking inhabitants in the Jura Mountains that border France sensed discrimination by the canton's German-speaking majority and desired to live in an autonomous canton of Jura. Mass demonstrations were organized, and a few extremists even planted bombs in prominent public places to underscore this separatist demand. In a national referendum held in 1978, 82% of all voting Swiss and a majority in virtually all cantons approved the creation of a new Jura canton, the first new canton to be created in 130 years. Thus, instead of suffering a festering problem with a separatist minority, Switzerland now has an additional canton exercising all the powers enjoyed by all the other cantons. Again, federalism was able to act as a tranquilizer.

Switzerland

Below the cantons are some 2,800 communes of greatly differing size. They choose their own system of local government (with approval of the cantons). Some elect their own parliament, but most have a traditional community assembly that normally meets indoors where all citizens over 18 can show up and express their opinions. They elect their own officials and assume general responsibility for granting citizenship; administering public lands, such as the forests; and supplying citizens with water, gas, electricity, bridges, city administrative offices, schools, swimming pools, sanitation facilities, fire services, and police protection. They have to submit to some supervision by cantonal governments, but their right to self-rule is guaranteed by the federal constitution, and they can appeal to the Federal Supreme Court if their autonomy is excessively infringed upon.

Political Parties

At all levels of government in Switzerland, political parties play a key role. In contrast to most other European parties, Swiss parties did not grow out of parliamentary groupings or honorary societies but were mass parties from the very beginning. This was because Switzerland had introduced universal manhood suffrage as early as 1830. As in the US, Swiss parties were, and still are, organized primarily at the communal and cantonal levels, and the national parties are little more than umbrella organizations for local parties, some of which even have different names than the larger national parties. As decentralized bodies, the national parties are all able to perform an important integrative function by cutting across most subgroups in Switzerland. The major Swiss parties encompass all language, regional, religious, and occupational groups. Decentralization also permits maximum flexibility for local and regional solutions to problems.

Swiss parties have a few other important characteristics. First, organized interest groups are represented formally in the parties to an extent unknown in most other countries. Second, the parties demand almost no "party discipline." Members are left more or less free to vote as they please, and it is therefore often difficult to pin a particular policy to a particular party. Third, conflicts within the parties are settled by the principle of "amicable agreement." The majority tries to find solutions acceptable to the minority rather than merely voting it down. This is widely accepted as the best means of finding a common denominator for all the diverging language, religious, and economic interests. At the same time, it makes parties and governments very cautious and deliberate and therefore helps give Swiss

government and all major parties their rather conservative hue.

The principal parties' voting strength has remained stable since the end of World War I. In 1919 the four major parties received 88% of the vote; in 2007 they received just under 80%. All four support the existing political order, and until December 2007 none presented itself explicitly as an opposition party. For this reason, no major party and no government traditionally had a firm party or governmental program against which one could easily evaluate its performance. That began to change in 2003. Because of the proportional representation electoral system, votes for the 200-seat National Council (lower house) seldom produce dramatic shifts in political power. Until 2007 elections normally renewed the governing coalition.

The most traditional and oldest party is the Free Democrats/Radical Democratic Party (FDP/PLR), led by Philippe Müller. In the October 2015 federal elections, it obtained 33 seats, based on its 16.4% of the votes. Founded in the 19th century as a radical (which in the traditional European sense means anticlerical) and liberal (meaning traditionally that it favored an expansion of individual rights and a reduction of governmental power) party, it now defends the economic and social status quo and is friendly to business. It has very close connections with private economic groups and influential molders of opinion in the mass media, schools, and universities. It is no longer the most influential party.

The Christian Democratic People's Party (CVP/PDC), led by Christophe Darbellay, won 27 seats in 2015, winning 11.6% of the votes. It received only one seat on the Federal Council. The bulk of its voters are practicing Catholics. It does recruit members and voters from all language and occupational groups, but although it has attempted to leap beyond the confessional barrier by attracting Protestants, it has not been very successful in doing so. The party sees itself as a "dynamic center" party.

From 1935 to 2003, the Social Democratic Party (SPS/PSS), led by Christian Levrat, received more votes than any other party, but now it has slipped into second place, obtaining 18.7% of the votes and winning 43 seats in 2015. Founded in 1904, it was originally a working-class party dedicated to the class struggle. But the fascist threat and the economic crises in the 1930s convinced Social Democrats that support of reform policies in the existing Swiss state was its best course. It officially changed its program in 1959 and is now a moderate party that wants to reform the capitalist economic system by expanding the social

Christoph Blocher

security net, reforming the tax structure, and evening out incomes. Its voters were once found only in the working class, but many intellectuals now support it. It helps to form every government in Switzerland, but it always tried to project an image of the "opposition within the government," a role it must now share.

The Swiss People's Party (SVP), led by Toni Brunner, climbed in 2015 to 29.4% and 65 seats. It conducted a determined anti-immigration and law-and-order campaign. It plays on fears of "asylum chaos." It remains the largest party since 1919. Its votes came mainly from the smaller rightist parties and increasingly from the FDP. The SVP traditionally tried to represent the interests of farmers, small businessmen, and craftsmen, and it gets most of its votes in small towns and rural areas. It is more conservative than the FDP in the sense that it has been openly skeptical of any sign of a welfare state and European integration. The SVP captured the most votes in the 2020 election and is still the largest party, with 26%. It declined in that election, however, while the Green and Liberal parties garnered 20%. The SVP is losing momentum.

The SVP is not an extreme right-wing party. It is deeply conservative, nationalist, and populist. It exploits extremist ideas and plays on deep-seated fears of cultural dilution and being overwhelmed by larger neighbors. But it is committed to democracy and the constitution, and it vigorously defends popular rights and direct democracy. It does not advocate sending all immigrants home, only those who have committed a crime. It is a modern party that is well funded, dynamic, and professionally organized. It normally did well only in the rural German-speaking east, but it now wins seats in French-speaking areas. Its phenomenal electoral

"Stop; yes to ban on minarets"

"Mass immigration? Twice no!"

success not only upset governing traditions, but it also threw the entire political landscape into chaos.

Founded by outspoken and charismatic billionaire industrialist Christoph Blocher, one of the world's richest 300 people, the party appealed to voters worried about high taxes; closer ties with Europe; Swiss participation in peacekeeping operations and NATO's Partnership for Peace; a flood of illegal immigrants and asylum seekers, whom he blames for a rise in crime; and easier citizenship laws. He touches a nerve by implying that the EU would swallow their nation and jeopardize its direct democracy by accumulating powers in Brussels.

Some of his party's campaign posters were so racist that the UN high commissioner for refugees sternly rejected them. One showed a black face and the slogan "The Swiss are becoming Negroes." It was withdrawn after an outcry of protests, but others displayed mug shots of criminals and the text "Our Dear Foreigners." In the defeated referendum in 2004 to ease citizenship rules for second- and third-generation foreigners, Osama bin Laden was portrayed on a Swiss ID card, and black and brown hands were depicted taking Swiss passports out of a box.

A 2007 poster depicted three white sheep kicking a lone black sheep off the Swiss flag; it bore the caption "For Greater Security." One of its posters demanded, "Stop massive immigration!" Such provocations ignited a clash in Bern during the 2007 campaign, when hundreds of leftist demonstrators tried to disrupt a march of about 5,000 SVP supporters.

The demonstrators threw bottles and rocks, and the police responded with tear gas. Such violence at election time was unknown in such a placid land. It is significant that, in the 2007 elections, a black man, Ricardo Lumengo, was elected to parliament for the first time.

The SVP success also reflects a continuing reaction to limits on bank secrecy and embarrassing disclosures about the country's role as the Nazis' banker during the Second World War. Blocher proclaimed, "As far as Switzerland is concerned, the threat to boycott Swiss banks in America is pure extortion." Many Swiss voters agree. Blocher's electoral fortunes have risen as some of the country's defining myths have weakened. The bankruptcy of Swissair, rising unemployment (hitherto unknown), increasing numbers of visible minorities, the international assault on bank secrecy, and the discovery of al Qaeda terrorist cells have shaken Swiss pride in their unique land and stimulated a mood of self-doubt. Blocher offers a vision of Switzerland's return to its old values of prosperity and robust independence.

He made his mark in a September 2006 referendum, when 68% of voters endorsed a tightening of asylum and immigration laws. Asylum seekers face faster expatriation or loss of welfare benefits if they cannot present a valid identity document within 48 hours; three-fourths cannot. Voters also approved a law requiring foreigners to integrate into Swiss society. In 2010 the SVP again won majority support (52.9%) for a referendum calling for the automatic expulsion of foreigners convicted of crimes, including murder, rape, drug dealing, and social security fraud. Since foreigners compose 23.3% of the population but commit 60% of the murders and 57% of burglaries, this measure made sense to voters. The SVP again succeeded in 2012 to gather more than 135,000 signatures supporting a future referendum to stop "massive immigration" of those seeking asylum and work and to examine the financial resources of those wanting to move in.

In February 2014 the SVP achieved its greatest success by engineering a narrow 50.3% referendum victory requiring a constitutional amendment setting quotas for immigration, including from EU countries. This violates treaty commitments with the EU, Switzerland's largest trading partner by far. The government, businesses, unions, churches, and most media and civil society organizations opposed the measure. But the SVP argued it was necessary if Switzerland were to retain its identity in the face of immigration. The deep anxiety was not primarily directed toward poor immigrants but against rich neighbors who allegedly clog

the trains and interstate highways, overcrowd schools, and drive housing costs so high that many Swiss can no longer afford to live in cities like Zurich and Geneva. The results revealed significant divisions: French-speaking cantons voted against it, but German and Italian cantons were for it. The cities were opposed, while rural areas were in favor. Nine months later, voters again defeated overwhelmingly a proposal to curb the influx of foreigners. In 2020, voters defeated an SVP initiative to end free movement across borders for EU and Swiss citizens, and the SVP could not block a favorable vote (63.1%) to give anti-discrimination protection to gay and bisexual people.

The 2007, 2011, and 2015 electoral outcomes called into question the "magic formula" for distributing seats among the four main parties. As the smallest of the four parties, the SVP always had to be content with only one seat in the Federal Council, the Swiss governing body, while the other three each got two. As the largest party now, the SVP demanded and received two. Blocher became justice minister.

The SVP's leading role in the government after 2003 represented the first political alignment to the right in more than four decades. It signaled a more confrontational style of government, which strains the consensual system. Blocher told the *Neue Zürcher Zeitung*, "Our success is a clear sign that people want another type of politics." Traditionally ministers are expected to come to unanimous decisions behind closed doors, whereby the outside

Switzerland

world hardly ever learns how individual members argued. One of the least popular ministers in the Federal Council, according to polls, he often publicly alluded to disagreements with his fellow cabinet colleagues, a practice that is discouraged.

Blocher showed little respect for the traditional team spirit of collective responsibility. He combined a place in the government with an outsider's role, disapproving of legislation at odds with his party's policies. The consequence was almost-constant tension and an end to the tradition that ministers drop their party loyalties to serve the state. Consensual politics came to an end after a half-century.

He paid the price in December 2007, when parliament, in a surprising vote, rejected Blocher and elected two other SVP members (Samuel Schmid and Eveline Widmer-Schlumpf) to the cabinet. As he had warned, he disowned the two who had accepted the cabinet positions, yanked his party out of the government, and announced that the SVP would be an opposition party. He rudely gave Widmer-Schlumpf, who became president in 2012, a 100-day ultimatum to resign from office and the SVP, but she resolutely refused. She was publicly insulted and even received anonymous death threats. Many viewed such warnings as a serious challenge to democracy in a country where ministers ride the streetcar and move around without bodyguards. These are uncharted waters for Switzerland. Since it is the largest party, the SVP can paralyze the government and threaten to call for a referendum for any legislation it does not like.

Any citizen over age 18 can found a political party by gathering only 100 to 400 signatures, depending on the size of the canton. That explains why so many parties run at election time. In 2011 they included the Anti-PowerPoint Party, the Animals' Party ("to give animals a political voice"), Subitas (demanding equal rights for men), the Swiss Fool's Party (seeking to restrict top management salaries at public companies), the Party-Free Switzerland (for those who are sick of parties), and the Swiss Pirate Party (against all restrictions in the Internet).

The Federal Government

The federal government, with its seat in Bern, is composed of a bicameral parliament, similar in some ways to the US Congress, and of a powerful seven-man executive elected by parliament. The National Council, elected every four years by male and, since 1971, female voters over 18 years of age, represents the interests of all Swiss. Because elections almost never produce significant changes in the parties' strength in parliament, Swiss elections are never the heated, highly publicized affairs

Former president (1982) Fritz Honegger with the author's two daughters, Katie and Juliet Thompson, April 1982

they are in the US and many other European countries.

Both houses have equal powers. Although all bills are now drafted by the government and presented to parliament, both houses must examine them. Once both have passed a piece of legislation, the executive may not veto it, and the Supreme Court may not declare it unconstitutional. In drafting legislation, the government, by tradition, consults all interested groups inside and outside parliament. This is a clumsy, time-consuming process, but it helps to ensure better results: Potential objections to the legislation are ironed out in advance. It also reduces the possible danger of a law being overturned in a referendum.

Both houses meet to elect the seven federal councillors (Bundesräte, singular: Bundesrat). They have steadily become more powerful in the Swiss political system. The parties carefully select on the basis of party membership and political experience at the federal or cantonal levels. Highly charismatic figures are very seldom chosen because of the traditional Swiss aversion to a personality cult of any kind. The recommended candidates are almost always elected. Their terms are four years, during which time they cannot be removed by parliament for any reason. They are traditionally reelected until they voluntarily choose to retire. The stability-conscious Swiss like little turnover of their top leaders. Thus, strictly speaking, Switzerland does not have a parliamentary system as in most European democracies. The federal councillors are addressed as such, and each heads what is called a "department" (such as finance or justice), not a "ministry."

Since 1959 they have been selected according to a so-called magic formula: two councillors are chosen from each of the three largest parties in the National

Council and one from the fourth-largest. At least two councillors must be from the French- or Italian-speaking sections, and it is usual that one comes from each of the country's three largest cantons—Zurich, Bern, and Vaud. Finally, no two councillors may come from the same canton. One can imagine the compromises necessary to satisfy such a "magic formula."

Each directs one of seven ministries, called departments. Together the seven form the government, and they play the predominant role in drafting legislation, executing laws and dealing with the outside world. Until 2007 they made decisions collectively according to the principle of "amicable agreement." They are nominated by the major parties, but they are expected to cease being "party men" once they are in office. Therefore, they have no coherent government program.

There was no formal opposition either within the government or the parliament before the SVP stormed out of the government in December 2007. This did not mean that a party could not oppose a particular issue; what it meant was that none of the major parties consistently opposed the government with a view to replacing it. In other countries such an "all-parties government," also known as a "grand coalition," is formed only in times of national emergency. Switzerland always had them. Due to Christoph Blocher's decision to take the country's largest party, the SVP, into opposition, a more adversarial system has replaced the earlier consensual practice. It is uncertain whether this change is permanent.

The year 1984 had seen a break in the tradition of parliament's more or less automatic acceptance of the parties' nominations to the Federal Council. Polls indicated that 64% of citizens thought it was time to have a woman federal councillor, so the Social Democrats nominated Lilian

Young woman gathers signatures opposing centralization of power

Uchtenhagen, a respected economist. Reportedly grumbling that she was "too emotional," "too elegant," "not enough of a mother figure," and "unable to stand the strain of high office," a majority in the Federal Assembly in a joint meeting of the two chambers rejected her.

The widespread bad feelings caused by Uchtenhagen's rejection no doubt helped Elisabeth Kopp, a lawyer and leading member of the Radical Democratic Party, to win a seat on the Federal Council in 1984. Unfortunately Kopp became implicated in Switzerland's biggest scandal in years. In 1989 she resigned because of accusations that, as justice minister, she had used her influence to protect her lawyer husband against charges of complicity in a major drug-money-laundering operation by leaking confidential information to him about the inquiry. She was later acquitted of violating the official secrecy laws.

In 1993 it was time for another woman to be named to the Federal Council. She had to be a Social Democrat from a French-speaking canton, and parliamentarian Christiane Brunner fit that bill. However, an overwhelmingly male parliament rejected her, some say for sexist reasons: She was a thrice-married blonde who liked flashy clothes, opposed the military, and was said to have had an illegal abortion and posed in the nude. She denied the latter charge.

Switzerland had never experienced what followed: Thousands of women gathered in front of parliament, spattering paint and eggs, and chanting, "We have lost the first battle, but only the first!" They were right. Ex–trade unionist Ruth Dreifuss of the SPS was promptly elected

as interior minister. A close friend of Brunner, she concluded, "I reassure people because I look a little plain." In 1999 she became the country's first female and first Jewish president. When Simonetta Sommaruga of the Social Democratic Party was elected in September 2010, women claimed the majority of four out of seven seats. This was quite an achievement for one of western Europe's last countries to allow women to vote.

Every year the parliament elects from among the seven a president and a vice president for one-year terms. They are not permitted to succeed themselves immediately, and by tradition, the vice president is elected president the next year. The president of the confederation is only a "first among equals," representing the government in ceremonial functions. In times of emergencies, he or she may assume greater powers than the other councillors. Under no circumstances can he be recalled or impeached. Serving as president in 2012 was Finance Minister Eveline Widmer-Schlumpf.

Swiss presidents are so inconspicuous in comparison to French or American counterparts that most Swiss, when asked, are unable to name their own president in any given year. In a country in which the most glamorous figure is the head of the central bank, the president needs neither bodyguards nor staff cars, and he or she lives in her own house during the term of office. He or she goes unguarded to movies or restaurants. When Kurt Furgler (1981) traveled to work or around the country, he either drove his own car or went by rail. Only when his schedule was particularly tight was he transported by helicopter.

Once, when he was being flown to an appointment, his helicopter developed engine trouble and was forced to make an emergency landing. Undaunted, he merely walked to the nearest road and hitch-hiked the rest of the way.

The Courts

Since the Federal Supreme Court has no power to judge on the constitutionality of federal laws, it does not have the same prestige or importance as does the US Supreme Court. It is chiefly the highest court of appeals for civil and criminal cases. Its judges are selected by both houses of parliament, meet together for six-year terms, and must be chosen from all language and regional groups that the entire population is represented. Its seat is not in Bern but in Lausanne. The administration of justice remains primarily a cantonal affair, but the supreme civil and criminal laws of the land are the federal code of civil law, in force since 1912, and the federal code of penal law, enacted in 1942.

Direct Democracy

Many European democracies permit citizens to vote directly on some particularly important political issues rather than to leave virtually all such decisions to the parliament. This is called "direct democracy" because the will of the people is not filtered exclusively through parliament. In most countries this instrument is used very sparingly, particularly because it has often been a favorite tool for dictators to legitimize their power over a frightened people. The Swiss have never needed to fear such abuse in modern times, and direct democracy is a very important part of the political process at all levels of government.

If at least 100,000 voters sign a petition demanding a constitutional change, then such an "initiative" must be submitted to a direct vote of all Swiss. Initiatives have a 1-in-2 chance of succeeding if they are put forward by parliament, whereas the success rate is only 1 in 10 if voters launch them. If at least 50,000 demand a petition that an act of parliament or an international treaty be approved by all the voters, then a "facultative referendum" is held. Parliament can declare an act to be too urgent to allow time for a referendum, but one is mandatory if parliament adopts any constitutional changes or approves of an international treaty of supranational or security character which affects the country's sovereignty.

Most Swiss now cast their votes for initiatives and referendums by mail. They are held on an extremely wide range of subjects: abortion, conscientious objection to military service, modernizing the armed services, restructuring civil defense, mandatory wearing of safety belts, increasing

Switzerland

federal powers to tax and to control unemployment and inflation, mandatory retirement ages, executive pay, a $24.65 minimum wage and a state-provided basic income (both rejected), tax breaks for wealthy foreigners, minimum gold holdings for the central bank, gun control, bans on automobile driving and on leaded gasoline, daylight savings time, nuclear power, rent controls, euthanasia, worker participation in management, expelling foreign criminals, and many more topics. In 2004 voters backed proposals for some of Europe's harshest laws on violent criminals and pedophiles. "Extremely violent and dangerous criminals" can be incarcerated for life unless "scientific findings" show they are cured or no longer dangerous. In 2005 Switzerland held Europe's first referendum granting more rights to same-sex couples. If registered, they have had from 2007 the same tax and pension status as married couples except that they can neither adopt children nor undergo fertility treatment.

By threatening to organize an initiative or referendum, interest groups in Switzerland can almost always secure a serious hearing for their concerns within the government or parliament. This ensures that they will not be overlooked in the decision-making process and that the government will try to establish a consensus for all its acts. Still, the problems associated with direct democracy have increasingly become the subject of discussion. The first problem is that the number of referenda and initiatives at all levels has sharply increased. Between 1914 and 1934, there was an average of 8.5 referenda per year. At present, the average has climbed to more than 30, and this includes neither the many referenda at the communal and cantonal levels, nor

the up to 4 national initiatives per year. Constitutional changes since 1871 have been made an average of once every 13 months, and the frequency has risen in recent years. Further, the issues on which the people are asked to decide have become more and more complex, and fewer and fewer citizens are able to form a firm opinion about them. From 1971 to 1997, only 5 of 68 national initiatives passed.

The cost of gathering signatures by convincing enough people of an issue's importance has become very expensive, and the Swiss government must now spend more than 4 million Swiss francs (about $3 million) to conduct a referendum. The increasing dissatisfaction with this form of democracy is demonstrated by the rapidly decreasing voter participation. Few referenda, initiatives, or national parliamentary elections attract more than 50% of the voters, and no one is surprised if only one-third of the eligible voters choose to vote on an issue; the average was 40% by 2004. In fact, Switzerland is the only democracy in the world where voter participation (45% in federal elections) in major elections is lower than in the US. Nevertheless, Switzerland, with only 4.7 million voters, accounts for an estimated half of referendum ballots worldwide.

The people also express their will on emotional social issues through referenda. The Swiss try hard to find acceptable compromises with the youth because they fear that failure could damage or destroy a very delicate but essential ingredient of Swiss democracy: the inclination and ability to solve serious problems by means of consensus. Without its traditional "rules of the game," which include tolerance and compromise, Swiss democracy would lose much of its uniqueness.

Foreign Policy

Swiss foreign policy is based on five main pillars: (1) armed neutrality; (2) universality of diplomatic and economic relations with all countries of the world regardless of regime or foreign policy; (3) the readiness to provide its "good offices" to other countries (for instance, Switzerland represented the US in Cuba and still in Iran, where no US diplomats are allowed; it also represents Cuba in the US, Iran in Egypt, and Israel in Ghana); (4) providing its own territory for international organizations and conferences; and (5) solidarity with other peoples of the world, especially when it comes to humanitarian actions.

There are many international organizations with headquarters in Geneva, including many UN specialized agencies, such as WHO, ILO, ITU, and WTO. Numerous nongovernmental organizations have their headquarters in Geneva, such as the World Council of Churches, the International Committee of the Red Cross (for war emergencies), and the International Federation of Red Cross Societies (for natural disasters and peacetime emergencies). The latter organization was founded in 1864 by the Swiss businessman Henri Dunant, who had been shocked by the carnage he had witnessed on Italian battlefields during the campaigns of Napoleon III. Switzerland's close links to the Red Cross are still symbolized by the latter's use of the Swiss flag with reversed colors. The Red Cross is an important vehicle for international humanitarian actions involving prisoners and refugees.

Switzerland is often criticized for its mediocre record for foreign aid. In 2015 it devoted .48% of its GDP to helping developing countries, compared with 1% for Sweden. The US spent only .19%, but that does not include private giving. Yet, the quality of its assistance is very high, and there is scarcely a nation in the world that is more generous in time of crisis.

Switzerland is not a member of NATO, and its and Austria's neutrality separates NATO's northern and southern halves. However, it joined the Partnership for Peace within NATO in order to strengthen its cooperation with that alliance. Its citizens also voted in 2001 to allow their soldiers to train with NATO forces. Earlier, its political leaders never publicly commented on foreign political events, such as elections or coups d'état, or on foreign military actions, such as the Soviet Union's invasions of Czechoslovakia in 1968 and of Afghanistan in 1979. This changed in August 1990, when for the first time Switzerland applied the UN sanctions against Iraq, which had invaded Kuwait. However, it staunchly opposed the military action taken by the US and Britain against Iraq in 2003 and closed its

Montag, 4. März 2002 · Nr. 52

Der Zürcher Zeitung 223. Jahrgang

Neue Zürcher Zeitung

INTERNATIONALE AUSGABE

Blutiges Wochenende im Nahen Osten
Über 20 Tote in Israel – Rund 30 palästinensische Opfer

Ja zum Uno-Beitritt der Schweiz
Knappes Ständemehr – deutlicheres Ja des Volkes

248

airspace to military planes on their way to the front.

Until 2002 the Swiss conception of neutrality had prevented the country from joining the UN. It joined many of the specialized UN organizations, and it pays more than a half-billion Swiss francs ($500 million, more than 72 Swiss francs per inhabitant). Geneva is the seat of the UN's European headquarters. It has held that the UN's provision for sanctions against member states is incompatible with Swiss neutrality. The Swiss Federal Council and parliament gradually reached the conclusion that Switzerland could no longer remain outside the UN, which they believed would officially take note of Swiss neutrality. They were supported by most university-educated Swiss and by the country's most prestigious newspapers.

The Swiss government has steadily nudged the country in the direction of greater international involvement. In a 2002 referendum, a majority (54%) of Swiss finally voted to join the United Nations. They concluded that their country, which sits in the middle of Europe, could no longer remain on the sidelines in an era of global politics and interwoven economics. Support for the move came from the government, most political parties, business, and trade unions. Foreign Minister Joseph Deiss noted, "Switzerland needs the world and the world needs our country." The September 11, 2001, terrorist attacks against the US boosted the vote because it shattered the Swiss sense that their country could remain outside of and immune from world events. In September 2002 it became the 190th member of the United Nations. President Kaspar Villiger said, "The people realized that they are no longer an island. We can be neutral—and be a good member of the UN."

Switzerland participates in international peacekeeping missions and helps finance UN peacekeeping operations. In 1989 it took the bold step of actually sending unarmed but uniformed medical personnel, administrators, and observers to Namibia and later to Western Sahara. Since the Swiss constitution forbade sending troops abroad, this was not an ordinary military unit: All were volunteers, and a third were women, only a few of whom are members of the country's tiny women's military services (known best for their former work with carrier pigeons that has been abandoned with Army 95). Nevertheless, this marked the first deployment of Swiss troops abroad since the Battle of Marignano in 1515. Switzerland also sends officers and aircraft to assist the UN in the Middle East.

Following an unusually bitter campaign preceding a 2001 referendum, a narrow majority (51%) approved of arming Swiss soldiers participating in peacekeeping missions. Heretofore, they had been unarmed in accordance with the policy of neutrality. The government wanted to avoid such situations as in Kosovo, where its peacekeepers had to rely on German and Austrian troops for protection. Opponents had displayed posters showing the battered corpse of an American soldier in Somalia, with the words "Die for foreign powers?" The country's neutrality continues to prevent its soldiers from performing peace-enforcing operations, as opposed to peacekeeping ones. In 2005 it had 220 soldiers deployed in Kosovo and a smaller contingent with three helicopters under EU command in Bosnia. It participates in UN missions on the Golan Heights, in Afghanistan, and since 1953 along the DMZ between the two Koreas.

In 1996 it broke with its tradition by allowing NATO troops to pass through its territory and skies on their way to implement the peace in Bosnia. By giving sanctuary to 400,000 refugees from former Yugoslavia, it also turned its back on its refugee policy before and during the Second World War. In 2010 it agreed to provide refuge to two Uighurs confined at the Guantanamo Bay detention center. It was feared that the two Chinese Muslims would be killed if they were sent home. The growing internationalism is strongest in the French- and Italian-speaking parts of the country.

Military Service

The Swiss have traditionally been armed to the teeth in order to demonstrate their determination to defend their neutrality and in order to dissuade any belligerent in a European war from viewing Swiss territory as a military vacuum and thereby inviting invasion. There is no general staff in peacetime, and parliament creates the rank of general only in wartime. There is only a skeleton standing army—about 1,500 career officers and NCOs. Defense spending has fallen to 9% of the confederation's budget and less than 2% of the nation's GDP.

The Swiss buy some of the most sophisticated military hardware available, including US fighter aircraft. They also produce a wide range of military equipment that they sell—subject to certain restrictions—to countries as diverse as Australia, Turkey, Egypt, Saudi Arabia, Burma, Guatemala, and Angola. Switzerland has built a network of bomb shelters that would protect 90% of the population in the event of nuclear attack.

Every Swiss male must serve in the national militia from age 20 to age 42 (age 52 for officers and 62 at the latest for generals). It has been aptly noted that Switzerland "has been in a state of war every weekend since 1945" and that "Switzerland does not have an army, it is an army!" Although there is a civilian service for those citizens who are morally or religiously opposed to all forms of military service, this service lasts 1.5 times longer than the minimum requirement for ordinary military duty. Avoiding the draft has become easier than before. Many young Swiss succeed in claiming to be mentally or physically unfit. Those who for any legitimate reason cannot perform military service must pay a fee to the Swiss state. If they want to do so, women can also serve in the armed forces, except in combat missions. After 18–21 weeks of basic training, soldiers are assigned to militia units and are required

Swiss soldiers

Switzerland

to perform three weeks of duty every other year. Special units, such as militia pilots and tank formations, serve two weeks each year. Thus, the country could mobilize 351,000 soldiers within 48 hours.

The Swiss soldier is permitted to take his equipment, including his assault rifle, home with him. Many keep it all after leaving the military, but the police must approve of such purchase. Civilian buyers must also obtain a police permit. Only 24% of Swiss own guns. They used to be permitted to keep five sealed magazines of live ammunition, but since 2007 ammunition must be kept at secure army depots. He is required to practice his sharp-shooting regularly in rifle associations. Former reservists are permitted to buy a weapon for private use.

This policy of having so many weapons in the society came under close scrutiny after a grisly massacre that occurred in 2001. Using a semiautomatic weapon, a man burst into the cantonal parliament in Zug and shot dead 14 people and wounded as many more before killing himself. This was the first time in more than 100 years that any Swiss politician had been murdered and was the biggest mass murder in the country in living memory. The man had never been in the military. Guns are easily available, and he had probably purchased his weapon in a shop that sells semiautomatic weapons legally or from another person, also legally. In 2013 it happened again when a drunken man armed with an assault rifle killed three women in the village of Daillon.

Although gun laws vary depending upon the canton, any citizen without a criminal record can buy one after an identity check and official approval. One may keep it locked up at home. There are an estimated 2–3 million guns in circulation, 1 for every 3 inhabitants. The total number of gun deaths, including accidents, was 6.2 per 100,000, second to the US rate of 9.42 and more than double the rate elsewhere in Europe.

This practice of keeping guns at home is being widely criticized. A 2007 poll had found that two-thirds (65%) were opposed to storing military guns at home, and three-fourths (76%) said it was not "necessary for the army's mission." Some worry about occasional shooting attacks and suicides using a few of the estimated 2 million guns at home, half of which were issued by the army or police. But such traditions die hard, especially since the "porcupine" military doctrine has existed for generations: All the guns in closets or basements throughout the small but mountainous country are believed to act as millions of quills to deter invaders. In 2011 the emotional question was submitted to a referendum, and 56% of voters and a majority of cantons opposed a ban on army firearms in homes.

The Swiss ability to shoot straight is widely respected. As the Swiss often remind listeners, "William Tell was a man of courage and integrity—and he was a good shot!" The last German kaiser, Wilhelm II, was also given a friendly reminder of this. Once, after inspecting a Swiss army unit, he turned to one of the Swiss soldiers and asked what his comrades would do if the German army were to invade Switzerland with twice as many soldiers. The answer: "In that case, each of us would have to fire twice!"

In 1989 the government decided to add some American firepower by acquiring several thousand shoulder-fired Stinger antiaircraft missiles and 34 F/A-18 fighter airplanes. In 2005 parliament made the unusual move of rejecting Defense Minister Samuel Schmid's defense budget because it contained funds to purchase two Spanish military transport aircraft. He wanted them in order to make Switzerland less dependent on others to move its troops. The military has only helicopters to move soldiers, or it must charter planes. There is some question about the readiness of Swiss military aircraft. When in 2014 the copilot of an Ethiopian airliner hijacked his plane and steered it toward Geneva in the hope of getting refugee status, the Swiss air force was unable to scramble fighter jets because, as a spokesman explained, the hijacking occurred outside business hours. "Air bases are closed at night and on the weekend" for budget and staffing reasons.

In 1989 the revered armed forces, which in a country with so many ethnic divisions is one of the few truly national institutions, was seriously buffeted by the winds of détente. The end of the Cold War greatly diminished the likelihood that Switzerland would ever face a serious external threat. For that reason, work began in 2015 to remove the explosives that had been installed in 2,000 structures, such as bridges and tunnels. They would have been detonated in case of attack.

Swiss feel less need to be as well armed as before, and they are reexamining their policy of armed neutrality. In a 1989 referendum, in which 68.6% of the eligible voters participated (the largest turnout in 15 years), 35.6% voted to abolish the military. Although the president at this time, Jean-Pascal Delamuraz, had called the initiative "an idiocy as big as the Matterhorn" (one of the highest and best-known mountains in Switzerland), the results severely shook the armed forces. A coalition called Switzerland without an Army was able to resubmit the question of disbanding the armed forces to the voters in 2001. It was again overwhelmingly rejected; only 21.9% voted in favor of the initiative. Arguing that "young men have better things

to do," pacifists and leftists again had the question of conscription put to a referendum vote in 2013. Three-fourths (73%) chose to maintain it. Even though it had survived three times in a quarter-century, the votes pointed to resentment against the army's influence in society, which has in any case diminished. The networking advantages have declined.

The army embarked on reform and rehabilitation. Former general Heinz Häsler admitted that "everything must be done to restore the people's confidence that military defense is needed." In 1994 voters were asked to decide on the questions "Does Switzerland really need an army?" and "Does Switzerland need 34 new fighter airplanes?" Both votes passed by a small majority.

By 2010 the armed forces had been reduced to 22,059 active soldiers (including 18,000 conscripts), in part by shortening the service time and declaring many draftees as unfit. The air force numbers 27,151. Switzerland could mobilize 155,000 soldiers in an emergency. Civil Defense numbers 80,000, but they are not part of the armed services.

Switzerland converted from a "static force" to a "dynamic force." The professional support comprises about 1,500 instructors, pilots, and professional soldiers (to protect the underground installations). As a result of the most extensive armed forces reform since 1907, called Army 95, the minimum total service time (after basic training) is 295 days for soldiers, 900 days for officers up to the rank of captain, and 1,200 days for colonels.

In 2003, three-fourths of the voters agreed in a referendum to plans for reducing and professionalizing the military, ignoring arguments that such a reform could undermine the country's traditional neutrality. Quaint remnants of the past, such as bicycle units, were disbanded, going the way of carrier pigeons, whose use had ended only in 1994. The number of men in active and reserve service was drastically reduced. With the reforms completed, the army had shrunk to about half its size, and the remaining soldiers are more mobile, more flexible, better trained, and better equipped. Military service was shortened. For most soldiers it is over by the time they are 26.

At the same time, civil defenses were refocused from war to national catastrophes and terrorist attacks, and it will be possible for recruits to opt for civil defense duty instead of the armed forces. The Cold War requirement that all residences and businesses have their own nuclear fallout shelters was also relaxed. The government claims that Switzerland already has sufficient bunker places for almost the entire population.

Switzerland is home to about 400,000 Muslims, or 5.5% of the population. For years the Swiss assumed that their country would be one of the last for Islamic terrorists to attack or to use for planning attacks. That has changed. In 2006 police arrested a dozen suspects who allegedly conspired to shoot down an Israeli airliner flying out of Geneva. A North African man was also seized and charged with preparing to blow up the Spanish Supreme Court. An intelligence report in May concluded that the country has become "a jihadi field of operation" and predicted a rise in terrorist actions. The chairman of the Parliamentary Intelligence Oversight Committee noted realistically, "Switzerland is no longer able to exclude itself from the rest of the world in the face of a globalized threat."

Christoph Blocher, of the populist SVP, turned his attention to Switzerland's Muslims, fighting such things as minarets and veils. Most are from the Balkans (especially Bosnia and Kosovo) and Turkey and are not particularly zealous. Very few women wear head-scarves, and almost none wear burkas. However, there is deep-rooted fear that "creeping Islamization" and immigration would erode Swiss values.

Blocher demanded a referendum over construction of mosques with minarets in Swiss cities, even though Islam has never been very visible. Also, there has been next to no Muslim terrorism in the country. Muslims are sometimes the victims. In 2016 a gunman entered an Islamic center in Zurich and severely wounded three worshipers. There were only 4 minarets in the entire country and no more than 150 mosques. The call to prayer is never heard.

The referendum took place in November 2009. Although the central government and most parties opposed the ban, 57% of all Swiss and majorities in 22 of 26 cantons voted to forbid mosques with new minarets. This was the most dramatic move any European country had made to keep Islam out of sight. The SVP's referendum poster portrayed a Swiss flag with dark shapes resembling both minarets and missiles rising out of it.

Foreign Workers

The Swiss Democrats, formerly called the National Action for People and Homeland (NA), aims its arrows toward what it sees as a threatening perversion of the Swiss character caused by foreign workers, rapid urbanization, and growing concentration of power in Switzerland. This openly patriotic and nationalist party reached its zenith in 1970, when a majority of Swiss voters was almost persuaded in a referendum to limit the numbers of foreign workers. In the 1990s the less democratic, neo-Nazi Patriotic Front entered the anti-immigrant scene.

In their opposition to foreign workers, the REP and NA unquestionably touch a very sensitive nerve in Switzerland. The country has traditionally been very hospitable to political exiles; for example, it took in 16,000 Hungarians after 1956 and 14,000 Czechoslovaks after 1968. Swiss industry learned very early that high levels of production could be achieved only by attracting foreign workers. No one doubts that the hotel and restaurant industries would never be able to survive without foreign workers. About half of these workers are Italians, followed by Germans and Spaniards.

In 2008 foreign workers accounted for a quarter of the labor force. About 60% come from EU countries and another fourth from former Yugoslavia. All western European citizens are now free to work in Switzerland. An additional 150,000 people cross the Swiss border every day to go to work. In all, there are about 850,000 "guest workers" in Switzerland.

As classrooms in Swiss schools sometimes swell with foreign children and as run-down areas with predominantly foreign residents begin to appear in some cities, cultural clashes are inevitable. That was the case when Muslim parents objected to mixed swimming classes and the traditional morning handshakes pupils give their teachers. In fact, this same problem is seriously testing the tolerance of many European countries. In a 1994 referendum, a majority of voters accepted a government ban on all forms of racism, including a belittling of the Holocaust. However, an incident with American billionaire Oprah Winfrey in 2013 suggested that racism is alive. When the African American media owner and philanthropist visited an upscale Zurich boutique and asked to see a handbag, she was refused on the grounds that the item was "too expensive." Amid the furor over this slight, 43% of Swiss respondents in a poll said they thought their countrymen were racist.

In five referenda since 1970, Swiss voters, not wishing to tarnish Switzerland's image as a land of refuge or to harm its economy, rejected proposed laws to limit the percentage of foreigners. A proposal in 2000 to limit it to 18% was defeated by 64% of voters in a referendum. For a while, the Swiss government responded to the discontentment by quietly reducing the percentage of foreigners in Switzerland to 17% of the total population. It could do this because, although foreign workers enjoy many rights and social benefits while in the country, many must renew their work permits every year. However, the country's dependence upon such labor is so great that by 2004 the percentage of foreign residents had grown to 20% and continues to rise. In 2002 voters rejected

by the closest referendum margin since 1891 (50.1%) another proposal to curb the number of asylum seekers; none of the French- or Italian-speaking cantons approved of the proposition. In the previous year, only 12% of asylum applications had been accepted.

Those with permanent work permits and the same employment rights as Swiss nationals slightly outnumber those with limited rights. Foreign workers must live in the country four years before they are permitted to bring their families. In one French-speaking canton, Neuchâtel, long-term foreign residents are permitted to vote in local elections.

In 1997, the Swiss Statistical Office calculated that, with declining birth rates, the working population would be reduced by almost a third by 2050 if the level of immigration were kept stable. This meant that the foreign population would have to expand to a total of 23% by 2017 for the country's workforce to be kept stable. By 2014 it had reached this percentage.

ECONOMY

The overall Swiss economy is one of the most efficient and prosperous on Earth. In 2012 the World Economic Forum named it the world's most competitive; the US was seventh. But there are at least two economies, not one. There is the efficient export sector, dominated by such large world-class companies as Nestlé, Novartis, Roche and Swatch and such banks as UBS and Credit Suisse. Then there is the inefficient domestic sector that only survives by being protected. Its per-capita GDP and income were at one time among the highest in the industrialized world. Now Luxembourg, Norway, and the US are richer as measured by GDP per head at purchasing-power parity. Even tiny neighboring Liechtenstein with its postage stamps and tremendous number of banks does better. In 1950 income per head was 80% above the European average; now it is only 14% above. The Swiss work longer than any nationality in the OECD (44.5 hours average per week). In 2002 they turned down a referendum proposal to mandate a 36-hour workweek. The economy is firmly based on the principle of free enterprise. In 2013, two-thirds of voters rejected severe limits on executive pay.

The public sector accounts for a lower percentage of GDP than in most other European countries, and some public companies, such as telecommunications, are being privatized. There has traditionally been little protection for their industries, so Swiss companies have always been stimulated by international competition to adapt in order to survive. However, as in all modern states, the Swiss state

Switzerland

Cheese making

intervenes more and more in the economy. It offers export risk guarantees to exporters who doubt the viability of their customers. But it scorns central planning and other attempts to limit the flexibility of private firms.

The Swiss economy is influenced heavily by several basic factors. First, Switzerland is a very small country with almost no exploitable raw materials. This includes, most importantly, oil. Switzerland meets more than three-fourths of its energy needs with oil, and almost every drop must be imported from as many diverse sources as possible. It must also import natural gas—which constitutes about 4% of its energy consumption—and nuclear fuel for its five nuclear plants, which produce almost 40% of its electricity. In 2003 voters rejected proposals to impose a 10-year moratorium on new atomic plants, to require existing ones to be closed after 40 years of service, or to close nuclear power plants after 30 years. But in the wake of the 2011 nuclear disaster in Fukushima, Japan, the government called for a phasing out of the five nuclear reactors at the end of their design lives.

One of its few natural resources is mountainous terrain for waterpower, which provides the country with about 56% of its electricity. In 2008 this fact helped put Switzerland in 1st place among 149 countries in an international ranking of environmental performance. The US was in 39th place. The only other natural resource

is wood, available because forests cover one-fourth of the country.

Second, Switzerland has insufficient farmable land to feed its population. Since it has pasturelands, much of which is in or at the foot of mountains, it has a productive dairy industry. Milk has always been plentiful, and long ago the Swiss discovered that, by converting it to cheese, it could export its milk to the world. This discovery made it famous for cheese. Its sunny hillsides also enable every single canton to produce excellent, mostly light-dry white wine, which supplies well over one-half the Swiss market. Unfortunately, there is very little left over for export. Only 6.3% of Switzerland is suitable for grain crops, and this is the chief reason for its excessive dependency upon food imports. In 2005 voters approved a five-year ban on growing genetically modified organisms (GMOs). In terms of calorie intake, Swiss agriculture produces only 60% of the national requirements, or 45% if one takes into consideration the imported feed component of milk and meat production.

Switzerland is willing to pay a high price to keep farms operating in remote areas of the country in order to reduce the wartime vulnerability of its food supplies and to look after the countryside. Farmers comprise 3.5% of the labor force, compared to 22% prior to World War II. They produce only 1% of the GDP, but they earn an average of 50% more than other European farmers. This has been due largely

to the fact that Switzerland subsidizes agriculture and forestry more generously than does the EU's CAP. However, Swiss subsidies have been reduced in the 21st century. Tariffs on agricultural imports average 50%. This makes farming the least market-oriented sector of the Swiss economy. It also raises food prices, which are 40% higher than the OECD average, compared with 10% for France and Germany. In addition, heavy mechanization and the government-sponsored effort to combine more than half the arable land into larger farms more suited to efficient agriculture help keep farming alive.

Third, the lack of raw materials and sufficient homegrown food has forced the Swiss to make the most of their human resources. This means that they have had to industrialize and, above all, to become a trading nation. Almost no European country with such a high standard of living has reached such a high degree of dependence on the world economy. Almost two-thirds of its GDP is derived from foreign trade in goods and services. Exports account for a third of GDP. This high volume of foreign trade is also made necessary both by Switzerland's small domestic market stemming from a small population and by its high level of prosperity.

Germany is its most important trading partner. The lion's share of Swiss trade is with European countries, particularly with the members of the EU: 54.9% of its exports and 72.9% of its imports. Of course, it benefits from being strategically located at the junction of Europe's main trade routes and from having an excellent road and rail network that plugs into the transportation nets of its neighbors. However, it has faced severe problems with terrible fires in key tunnels that are essential to through-traffic.

Switzerland has an almost-unique problem for a European trading nation: It is landlocked. It does have one important port on the Rhine-Basel. It maintains 29 merchant ships on the high seas and is in 50th place among 111 nations that maintain a merchant fleet. However, its lines to its overseas trading partners are very vulnerable.

This was one reason it maintained its important air link through Swissair, a semi-public corporation that went bankrupt on October 1, 2001, a day the prestigious *Neue Zürcher Zeitung* called "the blackest day in Switzerland's economic history." It was the first collapse of a European flag carrier, and its demise was a huge blow to Switzerland's image as a solid business and financial center. Already terribly indebted before the September 11 terrorist attacks, it could not secure the funds to continue. It also caused the collapse of Belgium's Sabena, which was partly owned

Switzerland

by Swissair. In 2002 the defunct Swissair was combined with Crossair, which flew routes within Europe, to form Swiss International Air Lines, known as "Swiss." It added international flights and used two-thirds of Swissair's planes. It was bought by Germany's Lufthansa in 2005. The airports at Zurich and Geneva remain among the busiest in the world.

Ground transportation was made faster by the completion of the Gotthard train tunnel. At 35 miles, it is the world's longest, 4 miles longer than the Channel Tunnel.

Industrial Sector

Swiss industry, which was fortunate to survive World War II almost unscathed, produces a wide variety of quality, precision goods. It has some heavyweight multinational corporations, 12 of which are on the Fortune 500 list, led by Nestlé (which ranked number 12). Four out of Europe's top 10 multinationals in terms of market capitalization are Swiss: Novartis, Nestlé, Roche, and UBS. Thanks to its lowered corporate tax of only 8.5%, plus cantonal taxes, as well as its central location, good transport links, well-trained multilingual workforce, and high quality of life, it has become the European headquarters of choice for many foreign multinationals, such as Colgate-Palmolive, DuPont, Catepillar, General Motors, Proctor & Gamble, Polo Ralph Lauren, Estée Lauder, Hewlett-Packard, Phillip Morris, and Oracle. American and French companies prefer Geneva, while German multinationals like the German-speaking cantons. However, most of its factories are by world standards relatively small and widely dispersed throughout the country.

About a fifth (20.3%) of all employed persons work in industry and 72.5% in services. Over a fourth (26%) of the GDP is derived from industry, compared with almost three-fourths (73%) from the growing service sector.

Approximately one-sixth of all employees work in the machine and equipment sector. It provides one-third of Switzerland's exports. It specializes particularly in equipment that does not lend itself to mass production, such as generators and turbines. It produces over 15% of the world's textile machines and roughly 13% of the precision instruments. The country provides about 1% of the world's arms exports. In 1997 three-fourths of voters approved continuing arms sales despite reports that Switzerland had delivered about a fifth of the equipment for Iraq's atomic program. It is also a leading chemical exporter. Three Basel firms alone produce roughly 10% of the world's need for medicines, and Swiss chemical plants provide 13% of the world's production of paint materials.

The chemical industries in the Basel area created great concern and international consternation in 1986. Accidents at the chemical plants of Sandoz and Ciba-Geigy spilled masses of toxic waste into the Rhine, undoing much of the hard work in the preceding 15 years to revive a river that had been declared ecologically dead. Countries all along the Rhine protested the Swiss handling of the disasters and the fact that information about them was withheld for many hours by Swiss authorities. These incidents were also a rude awakening for the Swiss, who had comfortably contended that nothing like that could happen in their country because their technology was too good and they were so careful.

Two of Switzerland's traditionally most important industries, watchmaking and textiles, have faced serious challenges. The textile industry is a victim of high labor costs and the rising value of the Swiss franc, which has priced many textile products out of the market; they cannot compete with cheaper Asian products.

In 1970, Swiss watchmakers had a third of the world's sales. By 1984 that share had fallen to 10%. Benefiting from the technological spin-offs of space exploration, the US watch industry moved rapidly into the field of digital, electronic, and quartz watches regulated by computer chips, and Japan was close behind. Swiss watchmakers responded by restructuring and investing effectively, diversifying into such products as heart pacemakers, and shifting some of the production facilities to foreign countries with low labor costs. To the horror of traditionalists, many "Swiss" watches bear the stamp "Made in Hong Kong under Swiss supervision." Two Swiss firms (SSIH and Asuag) have also merged to form the world's second-largest watch producer—Industrie Horlogère Suisse—and have met the challenge of the electronics revolution by introducing robots to produce such big, midprice sellers as the "Swatch."

As a result, the restructured watchmaking industry has recovered steadily since 1982. It now employs 40,000, compared with 90,000 in 1970. It is also making advances in microchips for watches. Switzerland now has a 60% share of the world market, and watches account for 8% of exports. Top-quality timepieces, such as Rolex, are among the most coveted in the world. Exports sank by a tenth in 2016–2017, as smartphones are also status items.

The undisputed leader is Swatch, the world's largest watch producer. It is best known for its low-cost but stylish plastic timepieces. They make a lifestyle statement and get much of the credit for making Swiss watchmaking healthy again. But Swatch also owns upmarket brands, such as Omega, Longines, and Breguet. As the country's dominant supplier of mechanical watch movements, it sent tremors through the entire Swiss industry in 2005, when it announced that it would no longer supply them to other watchmakers. That means that the latter must either make their own movements or no longer advertise their watches as "Swiss-made," since the law requires that the movements, not just the assembled watch, be produced in the country.

Strikes in key sectors of the economy were almost unknown since 1937, despite the fact that nominal wage increases are traditionally the lowest of all industrialized countries. This fact is crucial for Switzerland's ability to maintain its international competitiveness. Consensus and conservative continuity are the foundation of the country's stability and steady economic progress. Wage negotiations are conducted at the local level, and the government stays out of them. Nevertheless, 2002 saw the first nationwide strike in Switzerland in 55 years. Construction workers protested their employers' refusal to sign a contract to allow early retirement at age 60.

A chronic problem had been a shortage of labor. That helped ensure that Switzerland did not have the unemployment other European nations face. In 2021 it was only 3.4% overall and 5% for young Swiss. The labor shortage compelled Switzerland to attract foreign workers, who comprise a fourth of the labor force and are essential to Swiss prosperity. In earlier years the country could cope with the threat of unemployment by simply sending some guest workers home. However, criticism of this policy shamed the government into granting more permanent visas.

Tourism

An essential aspect of the economy is tourism, which accounts for about 8% of the overall national income. It is the fourth-largest foreign-exchange earner. Swiss tourists spend about one-half of that income outside Switzerland. This industry is threatened by the high value of the franc. Nevertheless, it was ranked in 2007 as having the most competitive travel industry in the developed world. No one who has seen pictures of Switzerland's majestic mountains, its sparkling spring-fed lakes and streams, or its beautiful meadows and valleys should have any difficulty understanding why the tourism industry is so successful.

It has also been the salvation for rural areas that would have become almost completely depopulated due to the economic and cultural attractions of the cities. Since the tourism trade is concentrated largely in otherwise economically disadvantaged

Switzerland

areas, rural Switzerland has been kept alive and prosperous. Of course, some veteran travelers miss much of the color and folklore of the earlier rustic Switzerland, but they sometimes forget that such folklore often masked great poverty.

Banking

Since the 16th century, Switzerland has been among the world's major banking nations. Geneva became an extremely successful banking city, which aroused admiration and exasperation throughout Europe. Voltaire once advised that, if one sees a Genevese banker jump out the window, one should jump after him because there is bound to be gold on the pavement. The French novelist Stendhal called them "the foremost money men of the Continent. In this métier, they have the foremost of virtues, that of eating less each day than they earn!" The US also profited from this talent when the scion of a wealthy Geneva family, Albert Gallatin, was appointed secretary of the treasury in 1801. Later, as the US ambassador to France and Britain, Gallatin adroitly negotiated commercial relations between the US and Europe.

Switzerland has more banks than it has dentists—1 per 1,400 residents. The number of banks has declined from 495 in 1990 to 356 in 2002. The biggest banks are in Zurich, but Geneva still has 140 private banks that provide a fifth of the jobs in the city of 180,000 inhabitants. Half of all banking business comes from outside the country. The traditional strength is in private banking, which is personalized service for the rich. They had a reputation for secrecy, security, and efficiency. Financial services by banks account for 11% of GDP, twice that in Zurich and Geneva, and 200,000 jobs. If one includes insurance and pension funds, the figure rises to 16%, ahead of commerce and tourism at 15% and engineering at 9%. However, they have begun to lose ground to the three big world banking centers of New York, Tokyo, and London. A third of its smaller banks have merged or closed. The banks' dealings with the Nazis tarnished their reputation.

Swiss banks have profited from Switzerland's political stability and hard currency, which is the most highly treasured in the world. By attracting funds to Switzerland, the "gnomes of Zurich," as the Swiss bankers have been called, in turn help to drive up the value of the franc. Combined with the Swiss National Bank's successful policy of restricting the domestic money supply, the high value of the franc has kept Switzerland's inflation rate (.3% in 2021) under control. This is because, with its valuable franc, it can buy raw materials abroad more cheaply than it could if its currency were worth less. Of course, the rise in the franc's value can increase the price

of Switzerland's exports, thereby hurting Swiss industry. However, the extremely low inflation rate helps keep down the price of Swiss exports and thereby keeps the export industries competitive.

A very important ace which Swiss bankers held in their hands is the country's bank secrecy laws, which sometimes make their banking system look like the Ali Baba caves. Their banks hold an estimated one-third of the world's total offshore assets and about a third of the world's clandestine personal wealth. These laws were introduced initially in 1934 to protect Jewish victims of Nazi persecution. They differed from bank secrecy laws in other countries in that bank information was also withheld from revenue authorities, and any breach of banking secrecy was a criminal offense. Yet since 1991 absolute secrecy is no longer possible. Swiss courts can order banks to divulge information or to freeze accounts, as they did when the US Congress began investigating insider trading. In October 2018 the ban on whistleblowing was eased, and swaps of account information with other countries were permitted.

A 1973 treaty with the US permits the divulging of bank information in cases where US authorities could prove that a criminal offense is under investigation. This does not include US tax evasion, which does not violate Swiss laws. After 1983 Swiss authorities were willing to extend legal assistance to other foreign governments seeking evidence to convict persons accused of tax fraud or other penal cases. The code was tightened in 1989, when the laundering of money obtained through illegal activities was made a criminal offense. This law was in part a result of American pressure, as was a 1985 measure dealing with insider stock trading.

The Swiss froze assets of deposed dictators Nicolae Ceausescu (Romania) and Manuel Noriega (Panama) and of the Medellin drug cartel. They agreed to cooperate with investigations on unclaimed Jewish assets from the Second World War. In 1997, for the first time, they took action against a ruler still in office, Zairian president Mobutu, who by the time of his death was said to hold $4 billion in Swiss bank accounts. In 1998, Switzerland's highest court ordered $500 million in assets belonging to the late Philippine ruler Ferdinand Marcos to be returned to the Philippine central bank. In 2001 Switzerland cooperated with the United States' antiterrorist campaign by freezing 24 bank accounts linked with al Qaeda.

A year later it returned to Nigeria more than $1 billion the late dictator Sani Abacha and his family had embezzled and placed into Swiss accounts. A $500 million more were returned in 2005, when the court determined that the remaining

funds from Abacha "were clearly of criminal origin." In 2011 the assets of North African dictators Ben Ali (Tunisia), Gaddafi (Libya), and Hosni Mubarak and his two sons (Egypt) were frozen, as were those of Laurent Gbagbo (Ivory Coast), who refused to relinquish the presidency after losing an election.

In 2004 the accounts of Russia's formerly richest man, Mikhail Khodorkovsky, and 20 other Russian citizens were frozen. The sum linked to the Yukos oil group alone amounted to $5 billion. In August 2007, while Khodorkovsky sat in a Russian prison, the Swiss Supreme Court ordered authorities not to turn over bank documents that Russia was seeking on the grounds that the Russian investigation of Yukos was politically motivated. This was the first time the court rejected an international request for this reason.

The Trade Union Federation and the Swiss Socialist Party have long demanded that banking operations be opened even more to public scrutiny, and American law gave strength to these demands. Many other Swiss grew uncomfortable with the notion that their prosperity might partly be based on the huge deposits of dictators and drug kings, especially as drug consumption was a problem in Switzerland itself. Finally, in 1991, Switzerland abolished its "Form B" accounts, which allowed clients to conduct bank transactions through intermediaries without revealing their own identities. Banks must know who is behind each account.

Desiring to ward off dirty money in the first place, Swiss authorities tightened their "know your customer" rules in 1997 and introduced one of the world's strictest money-laundering laws. Bankers must report suspicious deposits or transfers to a special police office, and they must relinquish account details requested in criminal investigations. Legal procedures were streamlined to make it easier for foreign police or prosecutors to get assistance. In 1999–2000, authorities froze more than $1 billion in bank accounts. However, they need cooperation from foreign governments, which must be willing to prosecute.

In 2003 Switzerland grudgingly agreed with the European Union that it would discourage citizens from EU countries from using Swiss accounts. The EU is aggressively cracking down on tax evaders, and the trail all too often leads to the Alpine banking center. The drain on Swiss banking assets seems relentless, a very serious problem for a country whose banks manage about a third of the world's private savings (ca. $3 trillion). It reached an agreement with the EU to collect withholding taxes of 35% for bank account interest and to return 75% of it to the country

Jean Tinguely's *Chaos I* in Columbus, Indiana

Photo by Claude and Victor Thompson

of residence without providing account holders' names.

By 2005 the flood of foreign money pouring into Switzerland had become a trickle for several reasons. It is no longer so attractive because of its new savings tax and laws on money laundering. Declining tax rates elsewhere in Europe reduced the fiscal incentives. Some countries have offered amnesties to entice wealthy foreigners to repatriate their funds. Nevertheless, in 2012 Switzerland still sheltered around $2.1 trillion, or 27% of offshore wealth.

Finally, its banks have been subjected to aggressive litigation, especially from the United States. The largest Swiss bank and world's biggest wealth manager, UBS, admitted in 2009 to having violated US law. Some of its bankers had referred clients to accountants and lawyers who set up secret offshore entities to conceal assets from the IRS. They encouraged Americans to destroy records and use Swiss credit cards to prevent authorities from tracking their purchases.

UBS agreed to divulge some of the 46,000 secret accounts (estimated worth $18 billion) of wealthy Americans whom the IRS suspects of using offshore accounts to avoid taxes. It agreed to pay the US $780 million to settle the investigation into its activities. It announced that it is closing American clients' offshore accounts. In 2014 the country signed a multilateral convention to fight tax evasion.

The IRS uses the treaty as a springboard to force about a dozen other Swiss banks, such as Credit Suisse and Wegelin, the country's oldest bank, to turn over names

and financial information on American depositors, while continuing to probe former UBS and other bankers. This deal was backed by parliament, which decided in June 2010 not to submit the question to a referendum. This deal encourages Switzerland's neighbors to follow the American lead, and it is a watershed for Swiss banking. Both the US and France praised Swiss efforts. There is a near-consensus among Swiss bankers that, while they should preserve their country's prized banking secrecy, their traditional methods of managing undeclared wealth, which attracted a third of all wealth kept offshore, cannot be sustained in a world of increased financial transparency.

Some Swiss have grown uneasy about the scores of wealthy foreigners who come to their country. Several cantons have gotten rid of their special tax regimes for wealthy outsiders. In a 2013 referendum, over two-thirds (68%) voted in favor of curbs on corporate wages. Shareholders are given a binding say on executives' overall pay packages. "Golden hellos and goodbyes" are banned.

The European Union

Switzerland is a member of several economic international organizations. In addition to the OECD, IEA, and WTO, it has belonged since 1960 to EFTA, which is now largely irrelevant. Although Switzerland signed an agreement with the EU that removed all tariffs on industrial products in 1972, it could not become a full member for three reasons: First, it would have had to relinquish a portion of its sovereignty

to the EU; second, its neutrality could be affected; third are economic reasons. For example, it gives much higher subsidies to its farmers than the EU allows.

The EU's push toward greater unity stimulated Swiss fears of isolation. In 1992 the Federal Council formally applied for membership. In that year the Swiss voted to join the IMF and the World Bank. But in December they rejected, by a whisker-thin 50.3%, their country's entry into the European Economic Area (EEA), a link between the EU and EFTA. German speakers in the large cities said yes, but they were outvoted by rural and small-town German speakers, whose traditional fear of being absorbed by a larger Germany was revived by the EU. By contrast, French-speaking Swiss, who have no fear of France, said yes. In a step to align their fiscal policies to the EU, voters in a 1993 referendum approved the introduction of a value-added tax (VAT).

The rejection of the EEA put the application to the EU, for which there is no parliamentary or popular majority, temporarily on ice. In a 2001 referendum, 77% of the voters in an unusually large turnout again rejected a proposal to enter negotiations to join the EU. French-speaking cantons were most inclined to favor entry. This blocked the government's hopes that talks with the EU could get underway during the 2003–2007 legislative session. Thus EU membership is unlikely before 2015 or later, especially after the SVP's electoral success in 2003. Its laws have already been made "Eurocompatible" in most sectors. It has negotiated a series of sector-by-sector bilateral deals with the EU that give it access to most EU markets without loss of sovereignty. It can opt out of whatever EU legislation it or its citizens dislike. By 2005 its citizens were free to live and work anywhere in the EU.

In a June 2005 referendum, 55% of voters chose to join the 13 EU countries in the Schengen passport-free travel zone. It would retain customs checks on shoppers and trade. The government reacted angrily when the EU commissioner for external affairs Benita Ferrero-Waldner said immediately after the vote that Switzerland would not be allowed to join Schengen unless its voters also voted yes on a more controversial question in a September 2005 referendum. The Swiss government denied that there was a legal link. Fortunately, backed by business groups and opposed by nationalists, a solid 56% of voters voted in that referendum to endorse the plan to open up the country's job market to workers from the EU's 10 new member states and to pay them an equal wage. In a February 2009 referendum, 59.6% of voters extended that right and included workers from the newest EU members, Romania and Bulgaria.

Swiss voters share many of the same fears that motivated French and Dutch voters to vote down the ill-fated EU constitution in May and June 2005: that eastern Europeans will swamp them and take their jobs from them. The country had already been criticized by the UN in March 2005 for introducing some of the toughest asylum and immigration controls in Europe. They would require refugees to produce a passport or identity papers to apply for asylum. Welfare payments would be cut off if those ordered to leave the country tried to remain.

Therefore, Switzerland has not suffered economically by not joining. However, this bilateral approach is both cumbersome and complicated as the EU constantly evolves. The Swiss worry about the fact that, if it were ever to enter, their country would be the second-biggest financial contributor after Germany. But its small population means that it would be one of the smaller and therefore less influential members. Most of all Swiss fear the effect EU membership would have on their unique political system.

In May 2004 the government and the EU accepted a series of treaties to clear the way for a new savings tax regime, for the country's entry into the EU's Schengen passport-free area in 2006–2007, and for enhanced cooperation in areas like fraud. Whether and when they would be ratified remained an open question. It feels its close ties with the EU. Swiss voters approved a law in 2006 to give the 10 newest EU members $800 million in economic aid. It also had to accept EU criticism that its tax rate in some cantons, where profits foreign companies make in EU countries are not taxed, are a form of state subsidies.

The chances that Switzerland would soon join the EU are slim. If it did, its manner of governance would create a constant dilemma. How would the EU deal with a member that could call a referendum on every major EU decision? Even the most pro-European Swiss treasure their country's unique system of democracy. Most voters, as well as the government and business, seem to prefer the web of about 120 bilateral agreements and treaties rather than formal membership.

Refusal to join the EU hurts some industries, such as chocolate. To retain their market shares in other European countries, chocolate makers shifted their production outside of Switzerland, thereby dulling the magic ring of "Swiss chocolate." At least they retain a huge market at home: The average Swiss consumes more than 22 pounds of chocolate per year, more than do Americans (10 pounds) or any nationality.

CULTURE

Switzerland is a multilingual country. The most widely used official language is German, spoken by 64% of the citizens. Actually, most German-speaking Swiss speak one of many different dialects of Aleman German, which differs from valley to valley and which is spoken very differently from that which is heard in Berlin. The other official languages are French, spoken in pure form by 18% of the Swiss, and Italian, spoken by about 8%.

A fourth "national language" is Romansch, a collection of five not always mutually intelligible Latin-based dialects spoken mostly in the more isolated valleys of Grisons. Some linguists argue that it is the closest living language to the late Roman Empire vernacular. In the 19th century, local monks developed a written language, and its first daily newspaper, *La Quotidiana*, appeared in 1997. It is spoken by about 40,000 (.6%) of the Swiss, all of whom also speak Swiss German. That number has been declining as tourism has helped encourage slightly more than half the residents in Grisons to speak German at home and at work.

To fight against this trend, linguists are busy standardizing the idioms and spelling and translating many texts, including income tax forms, into Romansch. TV and radio airtime is also being increased and broadened to include comedians and local pop groups. In 1996 the Swiss voted in

a referendum to elevate Romansch to the status of a "semiofficial" language, meaning that speakers may use it in dealings with the federal government. The government spends about $4 million each year to promote this quaint language.

Although only a minority of Swiss is fully multilingual, as are Luxembourgers, the fact that the language groups are separated and largely concentrated in single-language, autonomous cantons prevents the language diversity from being a major problem as in Belgium. It is true, though, that French- and Italian-speaking Swiss somewhat resent the dominance of German in the federal institutions in Bern.

In 1998 a new language problem emerged: The most populous canton, Zurich, decided that English, not French, should begin at an early age, perhaps in the first grade. Its officials argued that in the contemporary world pupils need more than the 1 or 2 years of English they used to get before age 16, when they can leave school. Education officials in 11 of 19 other German-speaking cantons want to follow Zurich's lead. This produced an uproar, especially in the French-speaking cantons. Many fear such a change could erode Swiss identity. But with no national ministry of education, it is difficult to establish and maintain one common policy in the cultural field. Federal interior minister Ruth Dreifuss argued in 2000 that English "should not be like a steamroller" crushing the country's languages. But she recommended that all Swiss children have a fair command of three languages, including two of Switzerland's official ones. As in the EU, English already serves as a lingua franca in Swiss business.

Zurich also took the lead in reintroducing High German in the classroom after the promotion of dialect had been successful in the 1970s. A 2005 study showed that teaching in the local dialect may hold pupils back both academically and in terms of employment.

Switzerland is also multireligious. While Protestants outnumbered Catholics by nearly three to two in 1900, Catholics, who now comprise 49.4% of the population, presently outnumber the Protestants, who comprise 47.8%. Each canton is free to decide whether to have complete separation between church and state, as in Geneva. The federal government does exercise some control over the churches by reserving the right to approve bishoprics and by banning members of the clergy from the National Council. Not until the 1970s did the government permit the Jesuits to resume activities in the country. However, one cannot say that serious tensions exist among religions or between the churches and the state. Religion also plays an insignificant role in Swiss politics

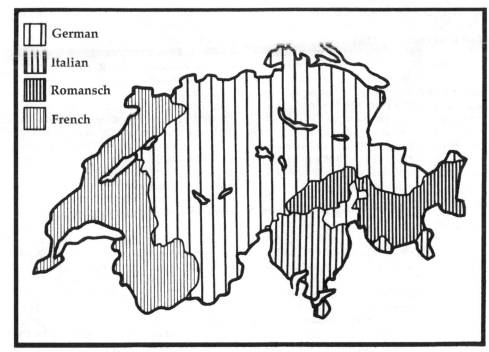

| German |
| Italian |
| Romansch |
| French |

Language Areas

today, except when such issues as abortion are the subjects of referenda. Nevertheless, 58% of Swiss voted in 2005 to grant more rights to same-sex couples.

The cantons organize their own school systems, and this enables the schools to reflect their religious, lingual, and cultural uniqueness. All children enter primary school at age six or seven. After four or five years of primary school, the children enter one of three different kinds of "upper school": An extended primary school makes the lowest academic demands; a second type, called a *Realschule*, prepares pupils for a commercial or technical career; and a *Gymnasium* prepares pupils for the universities. After the mandatory eight or nine years of schooling, pupils can enter an apprenticeship, and roughly 80% do this, or they can continue their general education, aiming toward specialized training or the university. There are seven cantonal universities, one business and social science university in St. Gallen, and two federally operated technical universities in Zurich and Lausanne.

The level of Swiss scientific achievement was demonstrated in March 2010, when its Large Hadron Collider, a 16-year $10 billion international project involving a 17-mile underground magnetic track outside Geneva, began to make subatomic particles collide. It seeks answers to the Big Bang theory of how moving bodies fragmented in the universe. It overtook America's Tevatron as the world's most powerful particle accelerator. The following year an experiment at Cern, the world's largest physics laboratory, showed particles

traveling faster than light. This upset a fundamental tenet of science and has scientists still scratching their heads.

Radio and TV operate under government license and are administered by a mixed state and privately owned body, the Swiss Broadcasting and Television Corporation (SRG). The SRG broadcasts in four languages from six radio studios and in German, French, and Italian from three television stations. Broadcasts from neighboring countries and private companies are also received.

With about 231 newspapers, the country also has the greatest number per capita in Europe, although it has declined by 40% since 1939. Zurich has one of the most highly respected newspapers in Europe, the *Neue Zürcher Zeitung*, which celebrated its 225th birthday in 2005. Known affectionately as "*Die alte Tante*" ("the old aunt"), it has changed very little since the 1930s. It is invariably highbrow and studiously avoids gossip. Perhaps that is why the average age of its readers has climbed to 50 and its circulation has fallen to 160,000.

Switzerland has a wealth of folk art and music and a rich cultural tradition of its own. The Swiss foundation, Pro Helvetia, seeks to both preserve and stimulate Swiss cultural activities. Yet the cultural and intellectual life of Switzerland has always been enriched by foreigners who were drawn to it or who sought refuge there. Such towering figures as Hans Holbein the Younger, Germaine de Staël, Franz Liszt, Richard Wagner, Friedrich Nietzsche, Thomas Mann, Jules Verne, Albert

Switzerland

Einstein, Karl Barth, Karl Jaspers, and Hermann Hesse chose to live and work part of their lives in Switzerland.

The proximity of great cultures that surround the country both stimulates Swiss writers and thinkers and draws their minds away. Any Swiss writer who does not feel himself a German, French, or Italian or who does not share in the intellectual life of the neighboring country where his native language is spoken risks becoming narrow and provincial. But if he takes a much wider view, his work risks losing its Swiss character. Indeed, many Swiss writers have been frustrated and bored with the narrow confines of the small, bourgeois, and neutral Switzerland. The Swiss psychoanalyst C. G. Jung once described Switzerland as a country "beneath the battle," and two of the 20th century's greatest playwrights, Max Frisch and Friedrich Dürrenmatt, both Swiss, have expressed in their works gruesomeness and disillusionment and have generally debunked the lives of those around them.

Still, many Swiss artists have found great international recognition. Paul Klee, who was brought up in Bern and who later fled Nazi Germany, brought Swiss painting to the world stage. His modern art is represented in the great galleries around the world. The art theoretician and one of the greatest architects in history Charles-Edouard Jeanneret (better known as Le Corbusier) designed buildings throughout the world, although he built very little in his native Switzerland. The modernist sculptor Jean Tinguely, with his "free and joyous machines," ranks as one of the world's most inventive contrivers.

An ingenious example of his work can be found in Columbus, Indiana. Using pieces he had found in the Columbus junkyard, he created his indescribable *Chaos* with such intriguing moving parts that the viewer can neither wholly understand nor forget it.

In February 2008 Switzerland was stunned by two spectacular art thefts. The first took place in the town of Pfäffikon, where thieves stole two Picassos worth an estimated $4.4 million. A week later, in nearby Zurich, three men wearing ski masks walked into a low-security private museum in broad daylight and stole the first four paintings they saw, valued at $163 million. A van Gogh and a Monet were found a week later in an unlocked car in the parking lot of a mental hospital a few hundred yards away in perfect condition. But the most valuable painting, Cézanne's *Boy in a Red Vest*, valued at $91 million, and a Degas remained missing. The Kunstmuseum Bern inherited 1,600 priceless paintings collected during the Nazi time by the father of Cornelius Gurlitt, who hid them until his death in 2014. Works suspected of being looted were returned to the heirs of their owners or kept in Germany. The rest can be admired in Bern.

One of the most important influences on the Swiss culture has been and always will be nature. Perhaps the incomparable Swiss landscape is the focus of the greatest pages in its literature and of its greatest art. They evoke those magic moments when a person surrenders himself completely to the beauty of the world around him, when a person feels himself included for a moment in a great harmony.

Foreign writers could scarcely escape this magic effect of the Alps. Friedrich Nietzsche conceived his *Zarathustra*, which expressed his bold, heroic, overproportional philosophy in the Alpine Engadine, and Thomas Mann set his *Magic Mountain*, one of the 20th century's greatest novels, in the crisp, sanitary Alpine air above Davos. Perhaps Hermann Hesse, who had been drawn permanently to Switzerland, expressed it best: "Everything merges into one, distance vanishes and time is done away with."

FUTURE

The Swiss are ruminating about their role in the modern world. Such problems as an aging population, hostility toward Muslims and immigrants, political scandals, and laundering of dirty money have prompted the country, in the words of a Swiss official, "to redefine Switzerland by examining our internal problems and by looking at our future role in Europe and in the 21st century." The government decided to be cooperative with the US in revealing untaxed offshore accounts held by wealthy Americans, thereby weakening its traditional bank secrecy.

It will continue to enjoy a high degree of domestic stability and comfortable life. According to Mercer's 2008 Quality of Living Survey, Zurich and Geneva were ranked first and second (along with Vienna) in terms of quality of life, and Bern and Zurich were tied for second in terms of personal safety. The economy successfully reinvented itself in the face of globalization and is running well. In 2012 the World Economic Forum ranked Switzerland as the most competitive country on Earth. It will remain a prosperous country with economic growth in 2021 of 3.5%, unemployment at an astonishingly low 3.4% (5% for youth), inflation at .3%, a budget deficit of 1.2% of GDP, and its franc at record highs after it ended its cap against the euro in 2015. Exporters and the tourism industry were hurt by this. There is no housing bubble: Prices rose 77% in the past decade, fueled by immigration.

As a member of the UN since 2002, its foreign policy has a much more international orientation, and its policy of neutrality continues to undergo change. Christoph Blocher's Swiss People's Party continues to transform the basic rules of Swiss government. Consensus politics and amicable agreement are weaker, and adversarial politics has become the rule.

The country's major challenge in the future will be to eradicate the deadly coronavirus.

"Distance vanishes, and time is done away with."

Liechtenstein

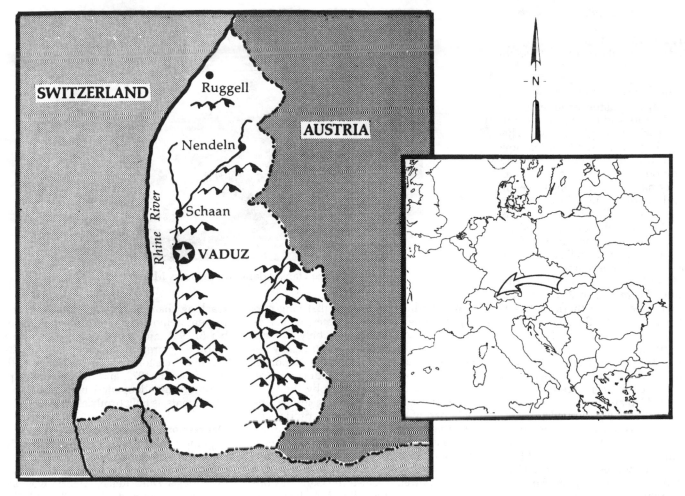

Area: 62 sq. mi. (160.475 sq. km)

Population: 35,000, est.

Capital City: Vaduz (pop. 5,000, est.).

Climate: Alpine, with cool summers and cold winters.

Neighboring Countries: Switzerland (northwest and south); Austria (northeast).

Official Language: German (Aleman dialect).

Ethnic Background: Alemannic German. More than one-third of the residents are foreigners, chiefly Swiss, German, Austrian, and Italian.

Official Religion: Roman Catholic (80%).

National Holiday: August 15 (birthday of Prince Franz Josef II, father of current reigning Prince Hans Adam II).

Main Industries: High technology; metal industry, especially production of small machines; textiles; ceramics; chemicals and pharmaceuticals; timber; hydroelectric power; building equipment; processed foods; tourism postage stamps.

Main Trading Partners: EU (45%), EFTA (19%), Switzerland (27.3%).

Currency: Swiss franc.

Date of Independence: January 23, 1719.

Government: Hereditary constitutional monarchy.

Head of State: His Serene Highness Prince Hans Adam II (b. 1945). Since August 2004 Crown Prince Alois conducts the day-to-day affairs.

Head of Government: Adrien Hasler (since February 2013).

National Flag: Two horizontal bands, blue over red, with a gold crown in the blue field. (The colors of the House of Liechtenstein are gold and red.)

Liechtenstein is an almost-unknown Alpine country with a territorial size slightly smaller than the District of Columbia and one-twentieth of that of Rhode Island and a population of only about 35,000. In fact, about the only thing big about this pint-sized state was the name of its late ruler, who died in 1989: Prince Franz Josef II Maria Aloys Alfred Karl Johannes Heinrich Michael Georg Ignatius Benediktus Gerhardus Majella von und zu Liechtenstein, Duke of Troppau and Jägerndorf, Count of Rietberg. It is the last existing intact remnant of the Holy Roman Empire and is the world's only remaining German-speaking monarchy. Its people, who have a strong feeling of independence and tradition, maintain their country's sovereignty without soldiers.

Separated from Switzerland by the Rhine River, a torrent rushing straight down from the mountains, which at times threatens the country's fertile valley, Liechtenstein is squeezed between the Swiss cantons of Grisons and St. Gallen to the west and the Austrian province of Vorarlberg to the east. One-third of the country, which is approximately 15 miles (25 kilometers) long and an average of 4 miles (6 kilometers) wide, is a rolling, green, and fertile area located in the Rhine Valley. Most of the country's population, industry, and agriculture are located in this area. The remaining two-thirds is composed of the rugged foothills of the Raetian Massif, with peaks ranging from 5,900 feet (1,735 meters) to 8,600 feet (2,599 meters), that form part of the central Alpine chain which runs east and west through the southern half of Switzerland. Surveyors recharted and remeasured the borders in 2006 and concluded that they were one mile (or 2%) longer than previously assumed. Thus the tiny principality grew by a half of a square kilometer, or roughly 50 football fields. This forward-looking relic of the past is a land of almost-unsurpassed natural beauty, colorful tradition, and economic prosperity.

Liechtenstein

HISTORY

The Early Period

Situated on one of the oldest north-south transit routes in Europe, Liechtenstein was a logical area for continuous settlement since the Stone Age. In 15 BC the Romans under Caesar Augustus conquered the Celtic inhabitants and established an important highway through the area. This road helped open the land that is now Germany to Roman conquest, trade, and administration. Later, it provided good access for German tribes or troops seeking wealth and power in Italy. Liechtenstein also lies astride the Basel–Vienna route, a thoroughfare that also brought soldiers and traders to the area. The remains of Roman villas and the castle in Schaan testify to the former Roman presence.

Parts of the Alemannic (Germanic) tribe moved into the region in 264 AD. Like many other tribes of northern and eastern Europe at the time, the Alemans had pulled up stakes and sought richer territories in western and southern Europe. They drove the Romans out of the area very quickly and have remained ever since. Today's citizens are descendants of these ancient Alemans and still speak their melodic dialect of German, which is also spoken in sections of eastern Switzerland and southern Germany.

The land was subsequently ruled by a variety of noble houses until Prince Hans Adam von Liechtenstein, an Austrian nobleman with a family residence near Vienna, purchased the Lordships of Shellenberg in 1699 and Vaduz in 1712. The calculation of the prince, who had tried for years to buy territory anywhere between Italy and the Elbe River, was that, by purchasing these two independent lordships which were fiefs of the Holy Roman Empire, he could persuade Austria's Kaiser Karl VI to upgrade the united lordships to the status of the Imperial Principality of Liechtenstein. Karl did just this on January 23, 1719, and the House of Liechtenstein, which gave its name to the new principality, thereby gained a coveted seat in the Imperial Diet of the Holy Roman Empire. Karl's declaration made Liechtenstein the 343rd state in the empire and gave the principality its present form. The new ruling family remained in Vienna, caring very little for the small land that had brought it privilege and honor. For 187 years, Liechtenstein was ruled from a distance by an absolute monarch.

Napoleon

In 1806 Napoleon drove out the Austrian troops who had occupied the principality since 1794 and made the country a member of the Confederation of the Rhine. Its ties with the Holy Roman Empire

Prince Hans-Adam and Princess Marie

ended with the demise of that long-paralyzed conglomerate of states, which, as was often said, was neither holy, Roman, nor an empire. Liechtenstein officially became a free and sovereign state. Napoleon respected Liechtenstein's independence, which was confirmed later by the Congress of Vienna in 1815. It is, in fact, the only part of the Napoleonic territorial system that survived unchanged to this day.

It is almost inconceivable that a country as small as Liechtenstein could exist without some form of economic union with a greater power. It joined the German Confederation after the fall of Napoleon, and in 1852 it joined a customs union with the Austro-Hungarian Empire. From 1876 until 1918, the principality was a part of an even tighter customs and tax arrangement with the Austrian province of Vorarlberg. Its close ties with Austria made it unavoidable that it lent its support in Austria's feud with Prussia over the future shape of a unified Germany. Nevertheless, Liechtenstein maintained a rather free hand. It resisted all efforts to draw it into the First World War as an ally of Germany-Austria.

After World War I

The links between Liechtenstein and its eastern neighbor were severed in 1918 with the collapse of Austria-Hungary. World War I brought about the collapse of centuries-old dynasties all over Europe in the face of revolution, famine, misery, and the widespread evaporation of former ideals. Liechtenstein's partner, Austria-Hungary, had been whittled down to its German core, a mere splinter of the earlier multinational empire. Such a ruined and chaotic country could no longer offer a promising future to Liechtenstein. In fact, Austria's collapse and dizzying postwar inflation wiped out Liechtenstein's entire savings. Therefore it saw the need for far-reaching changes. It both proclaimed the present democratic constitution on October 5, 1921, and reoriented itself toward its other, more fortunate neighbor: Switzerland. A customs treaty was signed with that nation in 1923, and this relationship, updated and deepened by subsequent agreements, is now firmly established.

Depression and World War II

In the 1930s Liechtenstein was severely shaken by the economic depression and narrowly escaped being swallowed up by Hitler's Third Reich. Austria was absorbed by Germany in 1938, and the shadow of the swastika was cast over Liechtenstein's border. The 85-year-old monarch Franz I was without heirs, and he feared that his death would be the signal for a Nazi takeover of the principality. He therefore appointed as regent one of his grand-nephews, the present monarch's father, Franz Josef II. On July 26, 1938, Franz Josef II ascended the throne. A small minority of Liechtensteiners had actually been attracted to Nazism, and in March 1939 local Nazis attempted unsuccessfully to overthrow the government. This determined minority remained undaunted and continued to publish a semiweekly Nazi newspaper. A few of them even joined the armed sections of the Nazi SS.

Not included in the Swiss defense system during World War II, Liechtenstein miraculously managed to maintain its neutrality throughout the conflict. German troops could have captured the country within a half-hour, especially since the 50-man auxiliary police corps was under orders to offer no actual or symbolic resistance whatsoever. This corps occupied itself chiefly with trying to control the great number of foreign deserters, conscientious objectors, and refugees who streamed into the country.

After Germany's collapse, the border posts were strengthened, and a barbed-wire barricade was strung along the entire border with Austria. However, in the night of May 2, 1945, the barricade was trampled and crossed by armed soldiers of the First Russian Army of Liberation, who were fleeing from Red Army units that had been ordered to send them back to the Soviet Union. They were disarmed and interned with thousands of other refugees in camps near Ruggell and Schaan. Despite attempts by a Soviet investigating team that came to Vaduz to demand possession of all Russians, these refugees remained until 1948, when they were permitted to emigrate to Argentina.

POLITICAL SYSTEM

Liechtenstein is a constitutional monarchy in which sovereignty is theoretically shared by the hereditary monarch from the House of Liechtenstein and the people. The prince's constitutional powers were dramatically increased as a result of a referendum in 2003, in which 64.3% of voters supported his proposals to strengthen his political prerogatives. Only 35.7% opposed them, with a voter turnout of 87.7%. The reforms made the ruling prince the most powerful monarch in Europe within his realm.

This was confirmed in another referendum held on July 1, 2012. Voters were asked to decide whether to strip the prince of his right to veto referendum results. He threatened to resign if the measure passed. It failed: 76.4% of voters rejected it. Few dare speak out against him. It cannot be said that this royal "reigns but does not rule."

His acquisition of sweeping powers caused concern in the Council of Europe. It set up a commission that concluded that the constitutional revisions are "a serious step backward" and could "lead to the isolation of Liechtenstein within the European community of states." Former prime minister Mario Frick agreed, "We have made ourselves an international laughingstock." However, both the prince and two-thirds of Liechtensteiners waved off these worries. In the prince's words, "the princely house and the people of Liechtenstein can walk hand in hand into the future."

The country has a 25-member unicameral parliament elected by proportional representation for four-year terms. The voter turnout at elections is quite high, ranging from 76% to 95% (84.6% in 2009), and citizens 18 years of age or older are permitted to vote. Not until 1984 were women granted the right to vote and to hold public office. Earlier, an antiquated law stripping all locally born women of

their citizenship if they married foreigners was repealed. Liechtenstein has ceased being politically a "man's world."

As in Switzerland, the highest executive authority is a collegial board. All five members of the cabinet serve four-year terms. The majority in parliament selects the leading member (called the head of government). The deputy chief is chosen in the same manner, and by tradition is from an opposition party. Parliament also chooses the remaining members (called government councillors). The prince formally appoints all of them. Since 2003 he can unilaterally dismiss the government, which is responsible to both parliament and to the prince.

The prince must formally approve all legislation, although he has not vetoed a law since the 1960s, when he disapproved of the legislature's proposed change in hunting rights. Since 2003 he can kill legislation passed by parliament by not acting on it for six months. He has the right to introduce legislative proposals in the parliament. In time of emergency, he can, with the permission of the head of government, decree laws without seeking approval from parliament.

In 1993 he flexed his constitutional muscles by dissolving parliament and calling new elections after the ruling party revolted against its leader, Markus Büchel, whom it accused of incompetence. Such a rejection of a parliamentary no-confidence vote is inconceivable in any other European monarchy. The prince noted, "There is no majority for a figurehead," and the 2003 referendum confirmed this.

In the past the prince made no attempt to dominate the political process. However, in 1997 he demanded and later received the right to approve the appointment of judges. He had said he would pack up his family and move to Vienna if this power were denied him. Even one of his critics in parliament, Peter Wolff, admitted that losing the prince would be a terrible setback: "The monarchy gives us our national identity." The speaker of parliament agreed, asserting, "Without the prince, we are nothing." The referendum gave him the power to approve all judges and to be removed from the jurisdiction of the constitutional court.

The prince found solid support among the political parties and the people. Citizens were divided on his proposed constitutional changes, which some saw as an excessive strengthening of the monarchist element. Some local politicians resent his semifeudal powers, although they want to retain a constitutional monarchy. The constitutional struggle culminated in the 2003 reform, which for the first time grants citizens the right to call a referendum to express any displeasure in the prince's performance. If that were to happen, various males in his extended family could decide whether to replace him. According to custom, the prince receives no pay from his subjects. He accepts a token expense allowance of 250,000 Swiss francs, and he pays no taxes. His popularity helps give stability to the country's politics.

The prince is married to Prague-born Countess Marie Aglae Kinsky, and they have four children. When Crown Prince Alois, who graduated from Britain's famed Sandhurst military academy and Salzburg University law school, was married to Duchess Sophie of Bavaria in 1993, the entire Liechtenstein population was invited to join the festivities in a garden

The prince and princess of Liechtenstein with their children—(on the stairs) HSH Princess Tatjana and HSH Prince Maximilian and (left and right) HSH Prince Constantin and HSH Hereditary Prince Alois

Liechtenstein

The castle at Vaduz, residence of the reigning prince of Liechtenstein

party. Having won the referendum after a decade of bickering and criticism, Prince Hans Adam II, who remains head of state, handed over day-to-day responsibility to Alois on August 15, 2004.

Liechtensteiners generally know how to reconcile their love for the royal dynasty with their right to self-rule. Thus, their traditionally firm attachment to the monarchy was rather surprising to the outsider, considering the facts that the first time their ruler even visited the tiny country was in 1842 and that the rulers declined to live permanently in the land until 1938. Until then, princes always preferred the splendid family palace, Burg Mödling, near Vienna. But when he ascended the throne in 1938, the quiet and unassuming Prince Franz Josef II, who had been born in 1906 and educated in agriculture and forestry in Vienna, chose to reside in the 100-room medieval castle perched on a high cliff crowning Vaduz.

The royal family possesses an art collection whose estimated value is at least $500 million. In the closing days of the Second World War, two subjects drove a postal bus and a truck, both with trailers, through Austria, picking up the art that had been stashed in many hiding places. They evaded scattering soldiers and unpredictable control posts on the highways to bring the works to Vaduz. Only small parts are displayed in the Vienna and Vaduz palaces, and most works are in storage.

In 1989 Franz Josef II died, less than one month after the death of his wife, Princess Gina; he collapsed at his wife's bedside and never recovered. His successor, Hans-Adam, is an economist who has long administered the family's wealth, estimated at €5 billion ($6.5 billion). This makes it Europe's richest monarchy, 10 times wealthier than the British royal family. This includes the principality's largest

bank (LGT) with subsidiaries in London and New York, electronics and "software" investments in the US, and land holdings in Austria twice the size of Liechtenstein. It also owns jointly with the International Paper Company a 75,000-acre farming operation in Texas. Its rice business, RiceTec, supplies 20,000 US grocery stores.

In one of Europe's most complicated and high-profile cases, the prince is demanding that the Czech Republic return lands confiscated after World War I, 10 times the size of the principality. It began in 1991, when he discovered a painting in a museum in Cologne and on loan from Czechoslovakia that had been stolen from his family collection. A decade later he took Germany to court to recoup over €1 billion worth of property that it claims Germany had illegally expropriated to pay its postwar debts to Czechoslovakia. Prague keeps the properties on the grounds that Liechtenstein's royals are German speaking and therefore German in nationality; that gave Prague the right to confiscate the property. The prince argues that postwar Allied-sponsored legislation exempted neutral Liechtenstein, which was the only country to refuse to recognize the infamous 1938 Munich Agreement that ceded the Sudetenland to Germany, from paying Germany's reparations. Prague refuses even to recognize Liechtenstein officially, let alone discuss the case.

Political Parties

The two main political parties have programs that are difficult to distinguish from each other. They appeal to electors who, not surprisingly in such a small country, are often inclined to vote for the man rather than the party.

The February 2013 elections to the 25-seat parliament were the first in which four parties won seats. The centrist Fatherland Union (VU) was the big loser, capturing 33.5% of the votes (down from 47.6%) and 8 seats (a loss of 5). Coming out on top was the conservative Progressive Citizens' Party (FBP), which won 40% of the votes (down from 43.5%) and 10 seats (a loss of 1). FBP leader Adrian Hasler became prime minister. A left-wing environmentalist group, the Free List (FL), which advocates a more representative monarchy and an end of bank secrecy, captured 11.1% of the votes (up from 8.9%). It cleared the minimum 8% hurdle necessary for winning any seats, receiving 3 (up from 1). New to parliament are the Independents, who benefited from citizens' unhappiness over the government's austerity policy. They garnered 15.3% of the votes and 4 seats.

Liechtenstein has an independent judiciary and a legal system based on Swiss, Austrian, and its own law. Numerous Austrians and Swiss citizens occupy judi-

cial posts in Liechtenstein. Nevertheless, the principality can stand up to its powerful neighbors, as it did in 2012, when it refused to hand over to Austria documents seized in the office of a former finance minister's attorney. For administrative purposes, the country is divided into 11 communes, which are governed by mayors and city councils elected locally every three years. A civil service staff of approximately 600 officials administers the government's political decisions.

This is a sovereign state that, because of its extremely small size, has chosen to align itself politically and economically very closely to Switzerland. This places severe limits on its powers, but as a sovereign state, Liechtenstein is free to take back its full powers at any time. It does differ with Switzerland on some diplomatic issues. In 1980 Liechtenstein broke with the Swiss policy and supported the US-led boycott of the Moscow Olympics to protest Soviet intervention in Afghanistan.

He also announced Liechtenstein's entry into the UN rather than to wait for the Swiss to make up their minds. In 1992 it announced that it would not enter the EU, even if Switzerland decided to do so. The voters accepted the referendum on the European Economic Area (EEA) Treaty in 1992 under the condition that the customs union with Switzerland be maintained. Unlike Switzerland, it joined the EEA in 1995. In 2007 it joined the EU's greenhouse gas trading system. The royal family cashes in over €900,000 ($1.17 million) of EU agricultural subsidies each year from its farming and wine-growing estate in Wilfersdorf, Austria.

EEA membership gives it most of the advantages of EU membership and few of the burdens. Prince Hans-Adam called it "the best of all possible worlds for Liechtenstein. We have our cake and eat it too." The greatest beneficiary is its manufacturing sector, which accounts for almost half of the country's 20,000 jobs and which is almost totally dependent upon exporting.

Liechtenstein belongs to several special organizations associated with the UN, such as the International Court of Justice, the International Atomic Energy Agency, and the UN Conference on Trade and Development. It belongs to EFTA (to which a substantial amount of its exports go), the OSCE, and the Council of Europe in Strasbourg, at which it has taken its turn as chair.

At one time, Liechtenstein maintained embassies only in Bern, Switzerland (which in turn represents its tiny partner throughout the world), and in Vienna, Austria. It now has eight foreign missions, including in such international centers as Brussels, Berlin, New York, and Washington. Relatives of the royal family oc-

Prime Minister Adrian Hasler

cupy plum ambassadorships in Germany, Austria, and Brussels. It has agreed not to conclude trade or customs treaties with other states but is bound by most treaties into which Switzerland enters. In general, it avoids any international dealings that would displease Switzerland. It has renounced its right to coin its own money, with the exception of gold coins that have no legal value as currency; Swiss currency has been used since 1921. Swiss officials have full responsibility for all customs questions arising out of the 1924 customs union.

Beautiful postage stamps are printed in Liechtenstein, which it sells profitably throughout the world. In fact, such sales provide 10% of the government's revenues. Switzerland once shared responsibility for the postal, telephone, and telegraph systems, although Liechtenstein owned the equipment. In 2000 the principality assumed full control of its postal and telecommunications systems.

Swiss border guards also control Liechtenstein's boundaries. Officially, all able-bodied males to age 60 are required to be ready for military service. However, there has in fact been no army since 1868. It maintains merely a 55-man police force.

Liechtenstein was most recently invaded on March 1, 2007, a dark and rainy night, when 170 confused Swiss infantry soldiers mistakenly crossed the unmarked border into Liechtenstein during a routine training exercise. After two kilometers of marching, they realized they had made a mistake, so they turned around and sneaked back home undetected. After a few hours sleep, they called the Liechten-stein authorities and apologized for the embarrassing border violation.

ECONOMY

The visitor to Liechtenstein most often remembers the romantic side of this Alpine retreat, which seems to have slumbered almost unnoticed into the modern age. What he often overlooks is the fact that this principality is the second-richest, second-most industrially productive country in the world when measured in per-capita income terms. Only Brunei, with its tremendous oil deposits, earns more per person each year. This economic prosperity tends to change the traditional overall picture of this nation. Though traditional in so many ways, it has shown itself to be extremely open to progress in research, technology, and production. Before World War II, more than a third of the population worked on the land, and there were only four factories.

Now only 1.7% of the population is engaged in agriculture, and there are 45 factories. This leap into the modern industrial age is a result not only of extraordinarily stable political conditions but also of minimum investment requirements, a very liberal tax policy, and strict bank secrecy. The tax laws encouraged about 75,000 foreign businesses, often called "letter box companies," to maintain nominal headquarters in Liechtenstein. It also allows the establishment of anonymous foundations, of which there are about 50,000, more than there are inhabitants. About 30% of GDP and a third of Liechtenstein's total fiscal revenues are derived from such companies and foundations. The government prefers to call this "wealth management," and it traditionally refused to assist foreign tax evasion investigations. It is untrue that no individual or company pays taxes there. Income taxes range from 8% to 10% for individuals and 6% to 18% for companies. Property is also taxed.

It grew tired of its reputation as a country that caters to persons and groups who want to hide "dirty" money. French and German reports had linked it to Russian and American organized crime and South American drug dealing. Such criticism prompted Prince Hans-Adam, whose family owns Liechtenstein's largest bank (LGT, managed by second son, Prince Max), and the elected government to appoint a financial investigator from Austria to look into corruption.

A police raid in 2000 led to the arrest of a handful of leading citizens, including the brothers of the economics minister and the chief judge. The embarrassed principality amended its laws to facilitate the search for dirty money, dubious depositors, and other shady individuals who maintain mailbox corporations. It reached an agreement with the EU in 2003 to collect taxes for bank account interest and return 75% of it to the country of residence without providing account holders' names. In 2005 it returned to Germany about 2.6 million Swiss francs, which East German embezzlers had deposited in the closing days of their sinking state.

In February 2008 disaster struck when Germany revealed that it had a disc purchased from an anonymous former LGT employee for nearly €5 million containing the names of thousands of investors who were hiding money in the principality. British tax authorities also paid the same informant. After Germany announced that it would share the information on accounts with any government that wanted it, Liechtenstein was faced with its greatest financial crisis ever. Berlin accused it of "encouraging lawbreaking" and threatened to oppose its entry into the EU's Schengen Area to end border controls. The usually quiet and reflective Crown Prince Alois shot back against this "attack" on his country and accused Germany of "trafficking in stolen goods." He canceled an exhibition of the royal family's paintings in Munich.

Although his spirited defense won him adulation at home, he faced charges from many European countries, which successfully pressured Liechtenstein to adopt OECD rules on secret accounts and to loosen its bank secrecy laws. They demand the same kind of transparency standards as the United States negotiated with Vaduz, committing the principality to provide financial information on US citizens who invest there and who are being investigated or prosecuted in the US for tax evasion. The agreement went into effect for two years from 2010. In 2013 the Liechtensteinische Landesbank agreed to pay a fine of $23.8 million to US authorities and agreed to press ahead with automatic exchange of tax information. Liechtenstein had also reached an accord with British tax authorities in 2009 requiring that the tiny country's banks ask their British clients if their tax records are in order. In April of that year, the G20 had declared a clampdown on tax havens.

Determined to change its shady image in order to attract tourists and legitimate investments, the principality set up the Image Liechtenstein Foundation in 2002 and hired a global branding specialist, Wolff Olins, to polish up its image. When day-to-day power was transferred to the crown prince on August 15, 2004, a new national logo was unveiled. Called a "democratic crown," it is red and blue, the royal colors, on an aubergine-colored background. It is used on official documents and on materials in the private sector.

Liechtenstein

Liechtenstein's industry is very diverse. High technology and the metal industry, which specializes in small machines, are the leading ones, followed by the ceramic, chemical, and pharmaceutical industries. The country produces a wide range of goods, including ultrahigh-vacuum technology; miniature calculators; boilers; textiles; furniture; varnishes; fountains; canned foods; prefabricated houses; and protective coatings for spaceship windows and artificial teeth, for which it is one of the world's biggest producers. One of its companies even produced a component for a solar wind experiment that went to the moon with the Apollo astronauts.

Because it has practically no natural resources, Liechtenstein has no heavy industry. The relatively small size of factories and the fact that the firms have been consciously dispersed throughout the country away from urban areas has had the favorable effect of both preventing large industrial plants from dominating the landscape and of preserving the country's environment from the kind of damage that has often accompanied rapid industrialization in other countries. This fortunate situation greatly benefits not only the inhabitants but also the country's tourism industry, which is the nation's fourth-most important source of income. With tourism down in 2003, an innovative "rent-a-state" program was introduced. It offers the whole principality except the Vaduz Castle as a destination for conventions and corporate retreats. For a daily fee of about $320 to $530 per person for groups up to 1,200 people, an organization could reserve entire hotels, restaurants, meeting places, and sports facilities and even temporarily put their own logos on buildings.

The thriving economy has enabled the residents to enjoy a high standard of living and a generous social welfare system. It has also brought certain economic and social problems to the country. First, since there is almost no domestic market for its high technology products, Liechtenstein is overwhelmingly dependent upon exporting. It is extremely vulnerable to international developments that might adversely affect world trade. Second, with only 1.7% of its population working in agriculture, it must import 70% of the food needed to nourish its well-fed population. Third, the small size of the domestic workforce has necessitated the importation of foreign workers. Approximately 12,000 such workers, who come chiefly from Switzerland, Austria, Germany, and Italy and who are often accompanied by their families, now constitute a third (33.3%) of the country's population. Adding 6,500 commuters who come daily to work, about 60% of the workforce is foreign.

This large percentage of foreigners has placed strains on the tolerant and hospitable Liechtensteiners. They can seldom be absorbed into the political life of the country; an ancient practice permits foreigners to become citizens only if the popular assemblies in 1 of the 11 communes approve them individually. Few of the foreigners ever gain the right to vote. In 2000 a new law was passed to make it easier for foreigners who have been living in the principality for 30 years to become citizens.

Many native Liechtensteiners became concerned about the possibly negative social effects that the presence of so many foreigners might have on the country. Therefore, since 1962 the government has placed severe limits on the influx of foreign workers. This policy has produced undeniable economic difficulties. Without an available pool of labor, Liechtenstein's domestic industry cannot grow. Because of this limitation, almost all of the country's major industries, which need to expand because of the high volume of orders, have begun to transfer substantial portions of their production activities to foreign countries.

Liechtenstein has a good network of roads but has no airport and no rail service to the capital city. The railway facilities in the north of the country linking Switzerland and Austria are owned and operated by the Austrian Federal Railways.

CULTURE

As a small country with very few citizens, Liechtenstein is heavily dependent culturally on its German-speaking neighbors. Two German-language newspapers appear in the capital city of Vaduz: the *Liechtensteiner Vaterland*, published six times weekly by the Fatherland Union, and the *Liechtensteiner Volksblatt*, published six times weekly by the Progressive Citizens Party. Except for a Liechtenstein station called Radio L, all radio and television programming comes from Switzerland, and the Liechtenstein postal ministry pays fees for this service.

Cultural efforts receive generous subsidies from the government. Permanent art collections are maintained in two museums. In the second half of the 1980s, a new art museum was supposed to be built in Vaduz to display the bulk of the prince's collection of paintings, sculptures, old weapons, and furniture. However, bickering and red tape held up the construction. Most of these treasures are stored in the royal castle in a five-story depot as large as a medium-sized department store. A few can be seen in a new museum that replaced the old Engländerbau in 2000. An impatient Prince Hans-Adam reportedly thought about establishing his own art museum by blasting a huge cavern into the cliff under his castle in Vaduz. The high cost of constructing the new museum was such a political hot potato that it prompted new parliamentary elections in 1989 to try to sort it out. Theater am Kirchplatz in the town of Schaan attracts leading performers from throughout the world.

Liechtenstein's people are 80% Roman Catholic, and in 1999 it finally got its first archbishop. His limited political influence was displayed in 2005, when an initiative he had supported to prevent abortion, birth control, assisted suicide, and living wills was favored by fewer than one in five voters. Nearly 80% ratified a government counterproposal that brought the principality's birth control and abortion laws in line with European standards.

The school system offers kindergarten, elementary, and secondary educations and is modeled largely after the Swiss school system. There is one elite *Gymnasium* (high school) in Vaduz for those pupils who wish to pursue university studies. Students must enter universities outside the country, since none exists locally. The literacy rate among the country's citizens is 100%.

FUTURE

Liechtenstein's close association with Switzerland and its highly advanced and diversified economy will continue to be crucial for its existence as a sovereign microstate in the modern world. It can be expected to remain politically stable, despite the fact that one-third of its residents are foreigners. After constitutional reform in 2003, the principality has Europe's most powerful monarchy, with everyday powers being wielded by Crown Prince Alois. This was confirmed in a July 2012 referendum. Liechtenstein will remain somewhat vulnerable economically because of its dependence upon exports, a static domestic labor pool, and dubious financial services. It suffered its greatest economic crisis in 2008, when the names of thousands of tax evaders fell into the hands of European tax authorities. This led to a loosening of its bank secrecy and greater transparency in its financial-service sector, which accounts for 30% of the principality's GDP.

The government's chief problem to be solved in the immediate future is to bring the deadly coronavirus under control.

Greece

Area: 50,961 sq. mi. (131,900 sq. km, somewhat larger than Louisiana).

Population: 10.4 million.

Capital City: Athens (pop. 3.2 million). The number in the Greater Athens area, including Athens, Piraeus (its port), and surrounding municipalities is estimated to be 5 million.

Climate: Generally mild, with the summer hot and dry, tempered in the vicinity of the coast, where sea breezes blow in every afternoon.

Neighboring Countries: Turkey (east, across the Aegean Sea, with many scattered Greek islands lying close to the Turkish coast, bordered on the northeast by European Turkey); Albania, Bulgaria, Macedonia (north).

Official Language: Greek.

Other Principal Tongues: There is a small Turkish-speaking minority (about 1.5% of the population) in Thrace.

Principal Religion: Greek Orthodox (98%).

Main Exports: Food and beverages, machinery, transport equipment, petroleum products, chemicals, nonferrous metals, textiles.

Main Imports: Machinery and transport equipment, chemicals and plastics, foodstuffs, automobiles, petroleum and fuels, iron and steel.

Major Trading Partners: EU (49.9% of exports and 51.9% of imports), Germany (8% of exports and 10.7% of imports), Italy (9.6% of exports and 9.3% of im-

Greece

ports), Turkey (7.9% of exports), Cyprus (6.9% of exports), Bulgaria (5.6% of exports), Cyprus (6.2% of exports), Russia (9.2% of imports), China (5.7% of imports), Netherlands (5.5% of imports).

Currency: Euro.

National Holiday: March 25 (Independence Day).

Chief of State: Katerina Sakellapropoulou, President (since January 2020).

Head of Government: Kyriakos Mitsotakis, Prime Minister (since 2019).

National Flag: Four white and five blue alternating stripes, with a white cross on the upper left-hand corner.

Greece is a land with many islands that, at times in the past, has been the geographic, military, economic, cultural, or philosophical heart of the western world. Its mainland portion is for the most part mountainous and hilly. Its geographical position at the intersection between east and west and between the Balkans and the Mediterranean has made it a springboard to the Orient and a thoroughfare for invasion by Muslim peoples heading west. For ancient Romans, Christian crusaders, and European merchants, Greece was the doorway to the east. For Arabs, Turks, Serbs, and Bulgarians, it was an important gateway to western culture. Throughout the centuries, Greece's position at the bridgehead of three continents inevitably drew it into most conflicts between the peoples of Europe, the Near East, and North Africa.

This central position of Greece remains largely unchanged in the 21st century.

Even today Greece retains its key geostrategic position. With its many islands, it is the heart of the Aegean Sea and the eastern Mediterranean. But contemporary Greece is much more than that. It is a society that is experiencing a shift from traditional values and economic ways to those more compatible with Greece's new role as a full partner with the prosperous and advanced states of western Europe. It is a land that is open to the major influences of the modern world. All changes in Greece are always viewed from outside the country with a mixture of hope and anxiety.

HISTORY

Greece is both a very old and a very new country. Not until 1829 were Greeks able to end four centuries of Turkish domination and to create an independent nation-state. However, the Greek state which was proclaimed in that year and the country's contemporary society and culture bear little resemblance to the ancient Greece which so many people have admired throughout the centuries. The large body of Greek classical literature and the many magnificent ruins reflect the grandeur of the ancient past. But the modern Greek's approach to life and his understanding of himself have been shaped far more significantly by the Byzantine past (324 AD to 1453), the Orthodox Church, and four centuries of Turkish domination than by the Greece of antiquity. At the very most, today's Greek shares with his ancient forefathers an ardent passion for political

discussion, a talent for daring economic activity, and a proverbial hospitality.

The Early Periods

Nevertheless, a presentation of Greece without the classical period would be unthinkable, for ancient Greece was the cradle of western culture and civilization. Most western philosophical, political, scholarly, and artistic achievements have their roots in Greek antiquity. Ancient Greece has served in many respects as a model worthy of imitation or, at the very least, as an almost-inexhaustible, examinable reservoir of human experience and thought. It is rightly referred to as the founder of western thought and culture. That torch still to a degree burns today.

It is often the case in history that the new and the extraordinary emerge at the point of contact between various cultures and peoples. From roughly 1600 to 1200 BC, Greece attracted a flood of Indo-Germanic tribes from the north, who came into contact with older cultures from Crete, Egypt, and other areas of the Middle East. These highly intelligent and agile newcomers borrowed the Phoenician letters and numbers and developed a written Greek language; they took the religiously oriented astronomy of the Middle East and developed it into mathematics. They also freed the ancient Egyptians' great but static art of sculpture from its immobility and produced an art capable of portraying the idealized likeness of man.

When the first Greek immigrants arrived on the coast of the Aegean Sea, they

The Parthenon in Athens (temple of Athena, goddess of wisdom) dominates the Acropolis, that flat-topped natural stronghold of early times which was the heart of the city.

Photo by Susan L. Thompson

came upon a highly developed culture, whose mysterious ruins on the island of Crete provide evidence of the Minoan culture, named after the legendary king of the island, Minos. It began to rise around 3000 BC and had developed brilliantly by about 2000 BC. The unearthed palaces, ceramics, and frescoes give exciting glimpses into a highly developed and cultivated civilization. The Minoans apparently maintained a very powerful fleet because excavations provide no evidence of fortifications. The origins of this culture, its social structure, and its decline remain a mystery to the present day.

The Greeks began to burn and sack the Minoan strongholds around 1400 BC, and a new culture emerged—the Mycenaean, named after the town of Mycenae in the Peloponnesus—the peninsula forming part of the mainland of Greece. The remains of this culture can be seen around the Peloponnesian coasts and up the eastern seaboard of Greece all the way to Thessaly (Thessaloniki), as well as in the southern islands of the Aegean Sea, the islands of Rhodes and Cyprus, and the west coast of Asia Minor. Through the decoding of many clay reliefs from this period (roughly 1600 to 1150 BC), we know that the civilization was organized in small, Greek-speaking governmental structures. Even the names of Greek myths appear as historical realities in these carvings, so this society unquestionably provided material for these myths and system of religion.

It was around 1200 BC that the legendary siege and destruction of Troy (a city whose ruins can be seen on the northwestern coast of Turkey) is said to have taken place. This exciting tale, which may even contain a tiny bit of truth, came from the alleged kidnapping of Helen, the beautiful wife of the Spartan King Menelaüs, by Paris, a prince of Troy. King Agamemnon of Mycenae, Menelaüs's brother, led a 10-year Greek expedition to Troy to recapture the queen. Finally the Greeks pretended to give up the fight, leaving behind a large wooden horse as a supposed gift of congratulations to the "victors." During the night the gullible Trojans broke a hole in their walls to bring the fatal trophy into the city, and Greek soldiers sprang out of the "Trojan horse" and captured the city from within.

A System of Religion

Sometime between 900 and 700 BC, the Greek poet Homer described the siege in the *Iliad* and the *Odyssey* and the Greek warriors' adventures on their way home. The same author may not have written these long poems. Nevertheless, they are the beginning and, in some experts' view, the best of Greek literature. They quickly became the standard texts that were memorized by Greek pupils and influenced western literature as have few other works. They also reflected, and may even have influenced, the Greeks' view of the gods, who, they thought, took a direct part in their daily lives. Homer poetically presented a host of particular gods, with well-defined characteristics, names, and places of residence.

Zeus, ruler of the heavens, was of primary importance. Hera, his wife and sister, was queen of the heavens. Poseidon ruled the sea and unleashed earthquakes, and Hades lorded over the underworld. Athena was the goddess of wisdom and skills, including those of the household; Aphrodite, of love and beauty; Eros, her son, god of love (thus the word "erotic"); and Apollo, of youthful manly beauty, light, healing, and young men's arts, such as archery, music, prophecy, and poetic inspiration. Artemis, sister of Apollo, was goddess of the moon, wild animals, and hunting; Demeter, of grain; Hephaestus, god of fire and metalworking; Hermes, messenger of the gods and god of the roads; Ares, of war; and Dionysus, of wine (and thus, drunkenness).

All Greeks ascribed to the gods at least some influence over their lives and cities, but it would be a mistake to think that Greek life was dominated by fear of the deities, as was the case in some primitive societies. Religious dogma, clergy, or temples never profoundly shaped Greek political, economic, and intellectual life. They sought human achievement and pleasures, and their endeavors were, on the whole, secular rather than religious. In this respect, the Greeks distinguished themselves from most other ancient civilizations. Nevertheless, the authority of the gods continued to be invoked in order to bolster political authority within the cities. Therefore, as the philosopher Socrates experienced in 399 BC, a person could lose his life for defaming the gods in public, especially within earshot of impressionable young people.

City-States

The onset of a second migratory wave into Greece, from 1200 to 900 BC, led many Greeks to flee across the Aegean Sea to the Near East, on whose coasts they founded such cities as Ephesus and Miletus. Athens was located on the peninsula of Attica, an inverted triangle about 20 miles (30 km) wide at the base and 35 miles (56 km) from top to bottom. Attica, which had allegedly been united by the legendary King Theseus, was able to remain an undisturbed enclave during this second migration.

As was often the case, geographic factors left their stamp on Greek history. The mountainous terrain, with small river valleys and almost no large plains except in the north, favored from the beginning the formation of a kind of small political organization known as a polis (from this the words "politics" and metropolis" are derived). The polis was a city-state, which in some cases included a number of small towns. Its limited size later made possible the unprecedented development of democracy in some Greek cities, especially Athens, and it helped stimulate the development of political awareness and interest among the citizens of the cities.

The Greeks' passion for politics was one reason the philosopher Aristotle defined humans as "political beings." However, the intense interest in politics and the small scale of Greek political units were also factors which helped perpetuate the never-ending and exhausting conflicts among the various city-states. These conflicts helped prevent the integration of the

Detail from a piece of Minoan pottery

Greece

Greek settlements into a larger political order, such as a nation-state, as we know it today. Citizens in the city-states viewed the world strictly on the basis of their narrow local patriotism and never developed a sense of Greek national identity. For the Greeks, including the Athenians, there was hardly a period of more than two years that was free of conflict with other cities. In general, the history of ancient Greece is one of almost-constant war.

Had it not been for the temporary predominance during the 8th to the 6th centuries BC of the cities' aristocracies (often called "oligarchies") who gradually dislodged the cities' kings from power and who maintained some close ties among the various city-states, Greece would probably have suffocated very early in the stifling spirit of provincial narrow-mindedness. It is because of this aristocratic class that the poetry of Homer, with its portrayal of the Olympian world of the gods, became standard references for all Greeks. The aristocracy was also responsible for developing the Greek education of man in the arts, as well as in athletic competition.

The periodic gathering of Greeks for the Olympic Games, first organized in 776 BC at the city of Olympia in the western Peloponnesus and thereafter held every four years, reflected the spirit of competition which became a precedent for the knightly tournaments in the European Middle Ages. Those with Olympic prowess and the virtues espoused by the noble class greatly overshadowed those persons who merely showed the simpler virtues, such as trading skills and industriousness, and sometimes they even overshadowed sculptors and architects who adorned the cities in which the Greeks lived. There can be no doubt that the Olympic Games brought Greeks together and showed them some common ideals. But these games never succeeded in creating peace or political unity in the Hellenic world, any more than have the modern Olympic Games eliminated wars or divisions among the peoples of the world today.

The governing cliques of aristocrats did begin to establish the political principles that the privilege of ruling should be passed around periodically and that rulers should not be above an established body of rules of law. Such laws were independent of the will of the temporary ruler and could be invoked if the rulers appeared to be abusing their powers. Thus, a notion of "limited government" by consent of the governed existed in most Greek cites from the 8th century on. This was a principle that was scarcely known in any other civilization of the era.

Politically, the aristocracy's domination over the masses was already being challenged from the 8th century. Rapid

Greek legend tells of Hero, a priestess of Aphrodite, whose lover, Leander, swam to her each night across the strait between Europe and Asia. On one stormy night, he drowned, his lifeless body washing to the shore. In grief, she cast herself into the raging waters.

population growth, increasing tensions among the social classes, and changes in warfare (which made citizen armies militarily superior to ones based primarily on noblemen) became important factors in further Greek developments. Increasing conflicts between the aristocracies and the common citizens created the right kind of conditions by about 600 BC for dictators to seize power in most of the cities. The threatened or dispossessed noblemen called them *tyrannis*, or "tyrants," a word which had formerly been applied to absolute rulers and one which still retains its negative connotation.

It is true that most tyrants disregarded many previously established laws and conventions. But most came to power by promising to break the power of the aristocracy, and the common citizens usually favored them. They frequently launched conspicuous building programs to create public works which would both provide people with jobs and improve the economic base; living conditions; beauty; and, therefore, the prestige of the city. They also proclaimed laws that would benefit small tradesmen, artisans, and farmers, and sometimes they gave subsidies to these groups. To pay for these policies, they often expropriated the property of the noblemen (and of their own opponents). Such property could thus be dispersed to some persons who had possessed none. They often abused the power they wielded, but because they did tend to have an ear attuned to the wishes of the lower classes of citizens, they, too, made a contribution toward the development of democracy in Greece.

Those Greek cities that had only small agricultural hinterlands close by could relieve the pressures created by rapidly growing populations only by founding colonies overseas to which their excess people could emigrate. Between 750 and 550 BC, such Greek colonies were created along the coasts and on the islands of the entire Mediterranean and Black Sea, including one at Byzantium (later Constantinople, now Istanbul, Turkey). Greek colonies sprang up from the eastern coast of Spain to the mouth of the Dnieper River in what is now the Soviet Union and from what is presently the French Riviera and Sicily (where Syracuse was built) to the toe of Italy, which, along with Sicily, became known as "Greater Greece."

By means of these colonies, the Greek language, culture, and influence were extended over much of the known world. Almost all of these colonies quickly broke the umbilical cords that tied them to their mother cities and became politically independent. There was no all-powerful overlord to subordinate the cities through taxes or military means as was the case in the Middle and Near Eastern Empires. They continued to share similar viewpoints on ruling, culture, and religion, and they almost always maintained sentimental ties. They also traded with the older Greek cities, and such trade was the foundation for an enormous growth of wealth in the entire Greek world. This wealth provided some Greeks with leisure, which was essential for their being able to produce beautiful poetry, usually about various forms of love. Leisure was also the starting point for rational, systematic speculation about nature. Thus, the Greeks began to free philosophy from mythology, which had characterized speculation in other ancient cultures.

The philosopher Plato coined the expression that the Greeks sat around the Mediterranean like frogs around a pond. In a short period of time, the Greeks showed themselves to be daring seafarers, traveling as far as Britain. It was the Greeks who gave meaning to the saying that "oceans are bridges," and they established the foundations of a Greek maritime predominance that indirectly continues to exist today.

Athens and Sparta

As could be expected, these cities often became bitter rivals. In the motherland political developments came to be dominated by the rivalry between the land power, Sparta, and the sea power, Athens. By the late 8th century BC, Sparta had

Frieze of a Greek athlete

acquired the entire southern part of Peloponnesus. Its expansion had always been of a military rather than of an economic nature, and it did very little colonizing. The political organization of Sparta consisted of the exclusive domination by a warrior caste over the subjugated masses, who practically were kept in a condition of slavery and who were responsible for the economic maintenance of their masters.

According to law, all members of the warrior caste were equal and were not allowed to possess private property. The elite, whose reputation of being unconquerable lasted until the 5th century BC, was shaped from early youth by strict breeding and upbringing in a collective (thus the expression "Spartan discipline"). They performed permanent military service until age 60 and had a very restricted private life. The Spartans' thoughts centered almost exclusively on the triangular fortress, the mess hall, and the battlefield. Most standard forms of pleasure and luxury were abolished in order to make military life more attractive. This kind of life would appeal to few people today, but a form of it was presented as an ideal state in one of the greatest books ever written, *The Republic* by Plato.

The Spartan political system blended elements of monarchy, aristocracy, and democracy. Two kings had limited power and had supreme authority only in time of

war. A Council of Elders, whose members were elected by an assembly of soldiers, made the really important political decisions. The brand of Spartan perfection, whose purpose was permanent military preparedness, tolerated no change and therefore soon became frozen in conservative rigidity.

Athens, a late bloomer among the Greek city-states, assumed a unique position from its onset because it encompassed the entire Attican Peninsula and became master of the sea. Perhaps most important, it developed a new kind of political order. As we have seen, the domestic political conflicts between the nobility and other classes of citizens had gradually led to the rise of tyrants in most cities. In the course of the 6th century BC, a few of these cities experienced the emergence of a more democratic political order, in which the principles of equality before the law and the right to vote were extended to that part of the inhabitants who were citizens. Foremost among these was Athens.

Athenian law was codified and made public by 621 BC. This enabled anyone who could read or who was informed to compare the behavior of the city's rulers with the established laws. In 593 the highly respected public figure Solon introduced a complete legal reform that provided the lower classes with financial relief, legal protection, and a powerful voice in the

Greece

city's government. The reform abolished property requirements for participation in the Assembly, which elected the city's leaders and which served as the final court of law for important cases, including those for public officials accused of abusing their power. For such cases, the judges were selected by lot from the entire citizen body.

The reform also transferred from the upper class to the other classes the right to determine the Assembly's agenda. Thus, the lower classes gained an important influence, perhaps even control, over the election of the city's officials, over legislation, and over the Athenian judiciary. These reforms cannot be said to have secured democracy in Athens, but they laid the foundation for the Athenian democratic tradition. It was not until the reform of the statesman Cleisthenes in the years 508–507 BC that the power of the aristocracy was completely broken and all the important political decisions began to be made by democratic institutions.

The most important organ in the Athenian political system, and that which wielded legislative authority, was the Assembly, in which all citizens could attend and vote. This form of parliament did have some important drawbacks. One was that citizenship in Athens, as well as other Greek cities, was denied to women, foreign residents, and slaves. Slave ownership was widespread. Small farmers and shopkeepers usually had two or three, and the rich could own thousands. In general, slaves were at least as numerous as were citizens. In any case, never did anything close to a majority of adult residents have the right to vote in the Assembly, so Athenian democracy, as advanced as it was for its time, was still ruled by a minority.

A second drawback stemmed from the fact that the Assembly met on a regular basis every 9 or 10 days. Since such meetings were too frequent even for most of the passionately political Athenians, few citizens attended most sessions, and the wealthier ones, who had more leisure to pursue their political interests, were often able to dominate the proceedings. Not until the 5th century BC were citizens paid to attend the sessions so that they could receive financial compensation for being away from their work.

The government's supreme executive functions were performed by the Council, composed of 500 representatives drawn by lot from the 10 districts of the city. For the sake of convenience, the Council was divided into 10 committees, each of which served a tenth of a year, during which time the chairmanship changed daily. The Council and the committees always remained subordinate to the Assembly, though. The sovereignty of the people was, in principle, exercised through the Assembly, but those who really had the decisive influence were the ones who could have their point of view accepted by the often-fickle and easily changeable majority in the Assembly. This fact put a high premium on the ability to speak eloquently and persuasively in public. Thus, these skills formed the basis of Athenian education. It also gave rise to a whole new profession: sophistry, so named because the sophists claimed to make men wise (*sophos*). Sophists made good money by teaching people how to win arguments in the Assembly and courts of law.

The volatility and changeability of the majority within the Assembly meant that policy could switch suddenly, and yesterday's powerful and honored leaders could be disgraced and dismissed the very next day. This led to great political instability and to a form of permanently latent revolution in Athenian political life. It is not surprising that many a leader was sent into exile, not because he had disregarded Athenian law or interests, but because his political opponents had successfully seized the chance to get rid of him. It is clear that such a political order was an ideal setting for golden-tongued demagogues and intriguers. This is one reason such profound political thinkers as Socrates, Plato, and Aristotle condemned democracy as an inferior type of political organization.

Only the most competent politicians who could persuade the masses at any moment could conduct a coherent and consistent policy under these circumstances. These leadership qualities were best reflected by Athens's greatest political figure, Pericles, who from 461 to 428 BC was able to guide the city to the summit of its power, glory, prosperity, and architectural achievements. Of course, there were courts of law in which all citizens' rights were to be protected. But Plato's description in the apology of Socrates's trial in 399 BC indicates that court proceedings could be uproarious and outrageous affairs, in which political or personal interests often weighed heavier than the evidence, to say nothing of justice.

With all its shortcomings, though, Athens extended wealth, luxury, leisure, and political power more broadly among its citizens than did any other city. Also, democracy was an essential step in the direction of placing ultimate political power in the hands of the ruled instead of those of arbitrary rulers. In Athens, the citizens exercised final control over all aspects of government. This first great example of

Simplified map of Sparta and Athens with certain major cities of the area

democracy in action influenced western political thought from then on and helped to inspire the democratic revolutions of the 18th, 19th, and 20th centuries AD in America, western Europe, and modern Greece itself.

Athens existed under conditions of almost-permanent mobilization and imperialism, maintained by sea power and the exploitation of allies. It was able to survive a grave external threat to itself and to the rest of Greece in the first decades of the 5th century BC, namely that of the mighty Persian Empire to the east. The power of this great empire already extended into India and, by the middle of the 6th century, to the Greek cities along what is today the western coast of Turkey. When these cities, especially Miletus, revolted in 500 BC, they were brutally crushed by the Persians within a few years.

The easterners, under the great King Darius, decided to eliminate the sources of support for the Greek cities under their control and especially to punish Athens for its aid to the rebels. Darius threw his military forces against the Greek mainland in 492 BC and conquered Macedonia and Thrace. However, during a violent storm, his navy was wrecked off Mount Athos. But he resumed the operation two years later, landing an expeditionary force of 20,000 troops on the Attican coast.

A far smaller force of heavily armored and battle-hardened Athenian citizen soldiers boldly attacked the Persians on the Plain of Marathon. They easily smashed their foes, who suffered 6,400 dead,

An Athenian lady

compared with only 192 Athenians dead. A messenger ran as fast as he could for 26 miles (42 km) in order to bring the news of victory to Athens, where he reportedly died upon arrival. The modern marathon runs, in which both Olympians and many thousands of avid joggers now participate, commemorate the feats of both the Athenian soldiers and their prodigious messenger. Athens's victory secured for it enormous importance and prestige in all of Greece, and it ushered in the Golden Age of Athens, the 5th century BC, when its power and cultural achievements were at their peak. When the great dramatist Aeschylus later composed his own epitaph, he did not praise his artistic achievements but rather the fact that he had stood and fought at Marathon.

After Darius's death his crown prince, Xerxes, laid careful plans for a final blow to Greece. It certainly is wrong to assume that the Greeks displayed solidarity and fraternity with each other in the face of the Persian threat. Such concepts, as well as nationalism, were still unknown in the ancient world, as many Greeks showed in this great struggle. Xerxes was able to persuade the Greek trading power in the western Mediterranean, Carthage (located near the present-day city of Tunis in Tunisia), to tie down the western Greek forces by means of an attack against Sicily. All of northern Greece offered Persia indispensable support. Greek architects and engineers built the pontoon bridge over the Dardanelles and dug a canal in order to spare the Persian fleet from having to sail around the perilous Mount Athos. Most of the sailors in the Persian fleet were Greeks, and Athenians who had been driven out of their city served the Persians as highly paid military advisers. Basically, only a large part of those cities in central Greece and the Peloponnesus, including Corinth, Thebes, and a couple dozen smaller city-states, fought under the leadership of Sparta and Athens.

In the summer of 480 BC, the numerically vastly superior Persian units, with an estimated 100,000 foot soldiers and 1,000 ships, descended upon central Greece. They confronted the Greeks' first line of defense at Thermopoly, where, in a legendary effort, a Greek force of 7,000 courageous soldiers, under the command of Spartan King Leonidas, held back the entire Persian army for a week before withdrawing. The enemy was then able to march almost unopposed into Attica and to occupy and completely destroy Athens, which had been evacuated just in the nick of time.

The Athenians were by no means defeated. In the narrow straits between the Attican coast and the island of Salamis, the Athenian admiral Themistocles lured

the Persian fleet into a trap and destroyed it. Also, the land battle at Plataea in 479 BC demonstrated the superiority of well trained and motivated citizen soldiers over a huge immobile army, which was largely composed of a colorful mixture of diverse peoples who had been involuntarily drafted into service and who had been left on the Greek mainland without logistical support. At the very same time, the news arrived that the Sicilian Greeks had stopped the Carthaginian invasion and that the remainder of the Persian fleet in Asia Minor had been cornered and destroyed at Mount Mycale, located immediately north of Miletus. After these sobering dual victories, the Persian threat was ended, and many of the Greek cities on the Aegean coasts rebelled anew against Persian domination. For the next 280 years, the Greek world was spared from any serious external threat until the Roman Empire absorbed all of it in 190 BC.

The Delian League and the Golden Age

Athens, which had carried the main burden of the Persian War, took quick advantage of its undisputed mastery at sea in order to construct a widely spun web of alliances, which extended throughout the entire Aegean area and which Athens dominated. After Sparta had relinquished its leadership in the Greek alliance against Persia, Athens organized in 478–477 BC the Delian League, which maintained a common treasury on the island of Delos, where the league's representatives occasionally met. As the largest contributor, Athens was assured political and military predominance within the league. Soon, its allies discovered that they were veritable subjects of Athens, especially after 454 BC, when the treasury was transferred to Athens and when meetings of the Council were terminated.

Athens experienced an almost-unbelievable economic upswing, and it had a democratic order that inspired both loyalty on the part of its own citizens and some admiration and support on the part of the lower classes in the other Greek cities (to the chagrin of their nondemocratic leaders). Conditions were favorable to a cultural flowering that still testifies to Athens's Golden Age. Out of the rubble of Athens emerged the classical Athens, with its grandiose structures on the Acropolis (literally "high city," which in most Greek cities was first a place of refuge from enemies and later the place for temples). Under the leadership of Pericles, the living conditions of the poor were improved. After a few unfortunate military adventures, Pericles again launched Athens's deliberate, major policy of colonization, sending settlers to Thrace, Euboea, and Naxos in

Greece

An artist's concept of ancient Athens at its height

447 and then on to other Aegean Islands, Macedonia, southern Italy, and the Black Sea. These settlements provided land for Athens's allies and poorer citizens, as well as markets for its trade.

Art, science, and philosophy flourished. Sculpture achieved its eternal classical form under such artists as Phidias and Plyclet. The dramatists Aeschylus (525–456), Sophocles (496–406), and Euripides (485–408) produced timeless tragedies. It is characteristically Greek that the victory over the Persians did not produce feelings of superiority among the Greeks. In his famous tragedies, Aeschylus portrayed the Persians with sympathy and sorrow. In bitingly critical comedies, Aristophanes took hilarious but deadly shots at the politics of the day. He is the only 5th-century author of comedies whose complete works survived. On the southern slope of the Acropolis, these dramatists presented plays in festivals, at which winners were chosen. A special tax on the rich enabled those from all classes to enjoy the performances.

In the writing of history, Thucydides approached his subjects far more systematically and analytically than had Herodotus in his narrations. Thucydides presented a concept of history as a structure of interlocking effects, which themselves become causes in human affairs. He sought to delve into the motives and interests of conflicting parties in historical events, and his historical method is still important today. In medicine, Hippocrates demanded that the body be studied as a whole. Hippodamus of Miletus redesigned Piraeus (which was and is, in effect, the port of Athens) and introduced gridiron planning for cities instead of building towns with wildly winding streets.

A Second Round with Sparta

The enormous growth of Athens's power and its imperialist foreign policy again led almost unavoidably to a collision with Sparta, the second greatest power in Greece. When Athens turned on its major trade competitors, Corinth and Megara, which had been joined by Thebes, Corinth appealed to Sparta for help. The tension boiled over in the Peloponnesian War, which lasted almost three decades, from 431 to 404, and which ended in Athens's defeat and ruin. This war was conducted with a brutality that had been almost unknown up to that time. Because of the alliance systems which Sparta and Athens had built up, almost every city in Greece was ultimately drawn into the conflict.

Based on what he witnessed in this war, Thucydides, the former Athenian general who had been exiled from Athens during the first part of the war for failing to save Amphipolis from the Spartans, developed his pessimistic view that man's insatiable striving for power was the sole motor of history. In his fascinating classic book *History of the Peloponnesian War*, he described very impressively the restless and unlimited political passion that was a basic characteristic of the Greeks, along with the yearning for perfection and order in art and philosophy. On the one hand, Greeks were politically volatile and unreliable; on the other, they left timeless works.

As a sobering example, Thucydides described the political mistreatment of a small state by a more powerful one. When the island of Melos refused to join the Athenian naval league, the Athenians stormed the capital city, killed all the men, and sold the women and children into slavery. And that was done by a democratic Athens. Thucydides's observations on foreign relations remain largely valid today. Military power and the willingness to use it are significant factors in international politics. Modern countries, large and small, must still adjust to this reality or suffer the consequences. The challenge to men remains to create a system of international law and widely respected codes of international conduct that would greatly diminish the significance of military force in human affairs.

At the onset of the war, Sparta marched into Attica and drove much of the rural population into the city of Athens, where close quarters and insufficient sanitary conditions created ideal conditions for a deadly plague, which broke out in 430 and which reduced the population by a third. It so frightened the rest of the people that, as Thucydides described so vividly, all respect for morality, social ties, and law broke down for a time, since all individuals expected to be dead by the next day. The great leader Pericles died in 429. Fortunately for Athens, the Spartans were unable to launch any decisive attacks, so an armistice was arranged in 423 and a peace treaty in 421.

This first phase of the war accomplished nothing. Athens was interested only in having a temporary breather, and in 415 it sent an expedition under the leadership of the wealthy, brilliant, and handsome

The Lions of Delos, guardians of Apollo's sacred island   Courtesy: Dorothy L. Lewis

young general Alcibiades to Syracuse (a former colony of Corinth) on the island of Sicily. As happened so often in Athens, he no sooner left the city with his large army and navy than his political enemies at home turned on him and demanded that he return home to stand trial. Knowing that he would be returning to sure death, Alcibiades fled instead to the Spartans, whom he persuaded to recommence hostilities against Athens in 414. The next year, the Syracusans proceeded to decimate the Athenian force.

By 412 both Syracuse and Persia had entered the war on Sparta's side, and Athens's allies along the Ionian coast had revolted. These setbacks so discredited the democratic order that an oligarchy was temporarily established, but the people in Athens could not accept this for long. Therefore, Alcibiades was called back to Athens as the city's supreme commander, and democracy was restored. However, Athens was so ridden by party squabbles and demagoguery that it could not possibly conduct a successful war against its enemies. After a stinging naval defeat, Alcibiades was again driven into exile, and the Persians ultimately executed him. Demagogues in Athens persuaded the volatile majority to execute most of the successful commanders, and after its last fleet was destroyed in 405, the Athenians were exhausted. In 404 they surrendered to the Spartans, and Athenian greatness came to an end. In fact, none of the Greek cities ever fully recovered from the wounds they suffered in this terrible war.

The Athenian Empire had existed for a shorter period of time than had any of the famous empires of antiquity; it had risen and fallen in three-quarters of a century. It

was also the smallest of the great empires, comprising only a corner of Greece; most of the Aegean Islands; and colonies along the western coast of Greece, in Asia Minor around the Black Sea, and in southern Italy. It probably never had a citizen population of more than about 60,000, and the population of Attica was certainly never more than a half-million; in all likelihood it was a lot less.

The Postwar Period; Socrates, Plato, and Aristotle

The Peloponnesian War accelerated the breakdown of morality, restraint, and harmony among citizens in Athens and elsewhere in Greece. Greek politics was in a state of chaos. The probing, analytical minds of Greek thinkers had revealed that the gods in which Greeks had believed did not really sanction the moral order or back up the laws of the various cities as the people had thought. These insights created problems for the rulers, who now had greater difficulty persuading their people to obey them. If the gods did not determine what was just and what was not, then who did? What was justice? That was the fundamental question that a stone carver and former private in the Athenian infantry liked to discuss at the Athenian marketplace (agora) with anyone who wanted to talk about it.

His name was Socrates, and he particularly attracted a following of young, rich, and ambitious Athenians who were itching to become rulers themselves. He impressed and entertained them by skillfully cross-examining influential and supposedly wise men in public on subjects dealing with justice and morality. In reality, he was teaching by questioning. He was

invariably able to reveal that they did not really know much about these subjects. He claimed not to know anything about these difficult concepts, but because of his skepticism and willingness to examine any question at its very roots, the oracle of Delphi (a pronouncement by a religious group with political clout) declared him to be the wisest of all men.

The rulers of Athens did not agree. Aristophanes revealed in his hilarious play *The Clouds* that most of the people regarded him as a mere gadfly who taught young people how to lie, to avoid paying their debts, and to turn against their parents with a good conscience. He was perceived to be undermining the already-corroded authority of the city, and he was therefore put on trial in 399 BC for allegedly defaming the gods and corrupting the youth. He was condemned to death. But this questioning stone carver, who never wrote a word (he was described by others, such as Plato or Xenophon), influenced western civilization as almost no other human being.

After the fall of Athens in 404, the greatest power in Greece was Sparta, which established oligarchies in most cities. Even Athens experienced a "reign of terror" under the "30 tyrants," led by a former pupil of Socrates and cousin of Plato—Critias—whose bloody deeds did much to ensure his teacher's execution. The heavy Spartan hand provoked revolutions everywhere, and Greece experienced a long period of power struggles with Persia, Sparta, Athens, and Thebes as the main contenders. By about 370 BC, Spartan predominance in Greece ended once and for all.

Greece entered the 4th century BC in pitiful condition. The constant war had devastated much of the countryside, impoverished or destroyed many of the cities, and disrupted the patterns of travel and trade. It was a time of growing piracy and of economic depression. However, it was also a time of continued intellectual achievement. The most influential sculptor of antiquity, Praxiteles, was creating individual statues which could stand alone in their perfection rather than having to blend into an architectural setting.

The philosopher Plato, a rich Athenian from a very influential family, focused on the legacy of one man who, in his opinion, stood out in the madness of Athens: Socrates. His poetic and literary style, filled with brilliant argumentation, common sense, and moral concern, as well as with beautiful myths and metaphors, greatly enhanced his prestige in his own day and his scholarly reputation right up to the present time. He founded a school in the Athenian suburb of Academia (from which the words "academy" and

Greece

"academic" are derived), which survived until the Christian emperor Justinian closed it in 529 AD.

Out of this school came his most famous pupil, Aristotle, who classified the various branches of knowledge, created much scientific terminology, advocated close scientific examination and experimentation, and established standards of definition and proof. He, too, created a school, called the Lyceum (after which the French high school, "lycée," is named). In 1997 this school was accidentally unearthed on a construction site for a Museum of Modern Art, 600 meters from Athens's central Constitution Square. The large ancient complex that was rediscovered includes a central courtyard and palaestra (wrestling area). Although he had very little impact on his own contemporaries, his writings, which were preserved by Arab scholars and rediscovered in medieval Europe, became the basis of scholarship and university teaching in Europe and the US until the 19th century.

Philip of Macedon and His Son Alexander

The mainland of Greece had fallen into such political chaos that it was left to the mercy of Philip II of Macedon, a kingdom of a Greek-speaking population in the north (now the independent state calling itself Macedonia). Macedon was culturally attracted to Greece, and Philip brought to his court outstanding Greek artists, writers, and scholars, including Aristotle, who tutored the monarch's son Alexander.

Macedon was a different kind of political entity than the city-states of Greece. It was a large kingdom, not a city.

Philip was able to extend his rule into Byzantium in what is now Turkey. He could take advantage of the web of rivalries among the Greek cities to the south so that he brought one city after the other under his influence. The warnings of one of antiquity's most famous speakers, Demosthenes, fell on deaf ears in Athens, and by the time he could organize a coalition of the most important Greek cities against the Macedonian king, it was too late. Philip's victory in 338 BC, followed up by finishing operations in the Peloponnesus, signaled the end of the cities' freedom. The king proclaimed a general peace and organized the Greek cities in a league under his control.

Philip had already begun preparations for war against Persia when he was assassinated in 336. His son Alexander, later known as "the Great" (356–323), who had just turned 20 when he became king, turned a new page in the book of world history. In a breathtaking campaign, the young commander in only nine years conquered the Persian Empire that had reached its greatest expanse, and he also won parts of south Asia as far as the Indus Valley. By the time he arrived in Susa with his army, which had completed a 12,000-mile (20,000 km) march, Alexander ruled over an empire which stretched from Greece over Asia Minor, the Phoenician coast, Egypt, Mesopotamia, Babylon, Persia, and beyond.

It is true that the Persian Empire had been weakened by palace intrigues and rebellions, but nothing fell into his lap without his having to earn it. On the contrary, bitter struggles demanded the entire strategic genius of the young commander, and his army had to engage in constant and exhausting individual combat with wild mountain men; to face inconceivable perils in the extensive deserts and dry highlands; and to master difficult technical challenges, such as the siege of the sea fortress at Tyre in Palestine.

He also had the political sense to assume the right titles in order to win the loyalty of his newly conquered subjects. He became the "Great King" in Persia and the "Divine Pharaoh" and "Son of the God Amon" in Egypt. The Greek cities bent to his demand that he be proclaimed no less than a Greek god. Genius, energy, ambition, and charismatic leadership so united in the person of Alexander the Great that he could inspire thousands to perform the most incredible feats, and he was honored as a demigod during his own lifetime.

The fascination for this great and unfathomable personality remains alive today, especially since his campaigns of conquest were not like the marauding of Mongols, who left nothing but devastation and terror in their wake. He placed the stamp of Greek civilization on the entire Near and Middle East, not by simply forcing the Greek culture on conquered peoples, but by attempting to foster an ingenious synthesis of the Greek and oriental cultures. The most visible expression

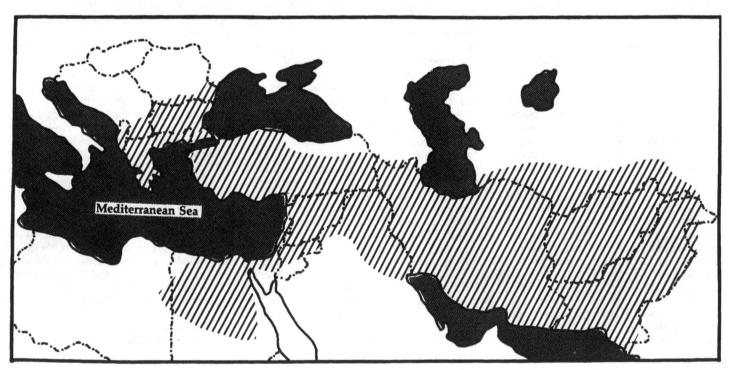

Alexander the Great's empire at its height

Greece

Alexander

of this attempt was the mass marriage in Susa (today in western Iran) of 10,000 Greek Macedonians with Persian women in the year 324 BC.

A by-product of Alexander's success was the release of the Jewish people from Babylonian captivity. They gradually returned to Palestine, but many, referred to in the Bible as Samaritans, adopted some Greek customs, much to the consternation of those who had struggled to preserve their faith intact.

When Alexander died on June 13, 323 BC, at the age of only 33, the gigantic empire which he had created fell into three large parts, which had been divided among his three main generals and which ultimately developed into a relatively consolidated system of states: the kingdoms of Egypt, Macedonia, and Seleucid (the latter encompassing the bulk of the former Persian Empire). There were also minor states that developed, such as Pergamum, Rhodes, and Syracuse. The thread of Hellenistic culture ran through all of these states. The century following Alexander's death witnessed constant border wars caused by the conflicting interests of the three major kingdoms. Also, a new rising power in the west, Rome, conquered all the Greek cities in Italy by 270 BC. These conquests not only increased Rome's power but also enhanced the influence of Greek culture on Rome itself. Much of the Roman Empire retained Greek culture and usages, including the grisly custom of execution by crucifixion.

The creative genius of the old Greece had not entirely dried up after the death of Alexander. This was a time when the Greek heritage was preserved in great libraries in Alexandria (a Greek city and the capital of Egypt) and Pergamum (now in Turkey), where scholars carefully collected, classified, evaluated, and edited classical texts and theories. Thinkers, such as Euclid (in mathematics), Archimedes (in physics), and Theophrastus (in botany) absorbed what had previously been done in their fields. Their works later became the point of departure for the Renaissance in the 15th and 16th centuries AD. Eratosthenes calculated rather accurately the circumference of the earth in 295 BC. The astronomer Aristarchus even proposed the revolutionary theory that the earth revolves around the sun. Another thinker, Hipparchus, refuted his theory incorrectly in the 2nd century BC. Ptolemy's explanation of the astronomical constellation was accepted for many centuries before it was disproved by the discoveries of Kepler and Galileo.

The classical Greek language gradually gave way to dialects and became a learned language of scholarship. The more simplified Greek that emerged facilitated communication among many different peoples. Greek remained the international language of administration, diplomacy, business, teaching, and theology. It is no surprise that simplified Greek was the language of the first written New Testament known to exist. Greek knowledge, customs, and administrative talents migrated to Rome as Greeks were taken as slaves by the Romans, who used them according to their knowledge and talent, often as civil servants.

The Roman and Byzantine Eras

The road from classical to modern Greece passed through the gates of the Roman and Byzantine Empires. Byzantium, along with later Turkish domination, shaped modern Greece far more than did the Greece of Homer, Pericles, and Socrates. Rome had conquered the entire Greek world by 190 BC, and in 394–395 AD, the Roman Empire was divided into a western and an eastern half. The latter, initially Rome but later ruled from Byzantium (later Constantinople and now Istanbul), was the offspring of the union of classical Greece and Christianity. With Christian faith, Roman administration, and Greek thought and language, Byzantium remained the preserver of classical philosophy and culture. This remains the empire's greatest legacy to the west, providing the foundation for the later Renaissance (see "Italy").

In a swift tide of events, the Romans expelled the Jews from Palestine (Israel) in 70 AD; they had already widely become dispersed throughout the Mediterranean area prior to that date but became more so after the Diaspora (dispersal). Many settled on Greek islands, and a substantial number, together with Jews in Rome itself, were converted to Christianity in the first centuries AD in spite of oppression.

Until the 11th century AD the Byzantine Empire, of which Greece was only a small part, was the leading country of its time in terms of military power; area and population; differentiated administrative organization; education level of its people; and splendid mosaics and buildings, the most impressive example of which is the Hagia Sofia Church (now a mosque) in Istanbul, Turkey. From Byzantium the Slavic Balkans and Russians were Christianized, not by means of fire and sword, but by means of an alphabet. The monks Cyril and Methodius developed the Cyrillic script, which was molded to display graphically the Slavic languages and which Russians and other Slavic peoples, such as the Bulgarians and Serbs, now use. At its peak, the empire under Emperor Justinian (527–565) extended to all of Italy; parts of Spain; North Africa; and the Middle East, including Syria and Palestine.

This colorful mixture of peoples was ruled by a theocratic (religiously oriented) monarchy. The state and Orthodox

Greece

Church were united in the person of the emperor, whose rule was absolute. Tsarist Russia later adopted this term, and the word "tsar" was derived from the Latin word "caesar" (emperor). For a long time, Byzantium served as a rampart against the onslaught of Islam. However, rivalry with the Roman Catholic west, whose Fourth Crusade resulted in the plundering of Constantinople by Catholic knights in 1204, brought about a change. For a while, Frankish knights and Italian merchants dominated Greece, and Slavs who were moving southward threatened the empire. The constant battle against the Muslim pirates and later against the Turks weakened the empire and reduced it in size to Greece and the capital city. In 1453 the remainder of the empire fell into the hands of the Turkish Sultan Mohammed II, without the Christian west lifting a finger to help.

Islamic Rule: Church Preservation of Greek Culture

Greece lived under the sign of the Islamic half-moon for almost 400 years, until it won its independence in 1829. But it was Byzantine tradition, embodied and preserved by the Orthodox (which literally means "worshipping correctly") Church, which provided the strength of survival and the sense of cultural independence. The church kept Greek identity alive; operated underground schools; guarded Greek literature and culture; fought any attempt to diminish the use of the Greek language; and, with the approval of the Turkish masters, took full responsibility for such acts as baptism, marriage, and burial, which until the early 1980s remained the exclusive privilege of the church.

The Turks also granted the Orthodox Church tax exemption and the right to conduct court cases in civil matters. Thus, the church was responsible not only for religious matters but also for most legal and civil administration over Orthodox Christians. This was because of the Turkish masters' desire largely to avoid contact with "infidels." In contrast to some other Islamic peoples, the Turks placed no importance on the religious conversion of their subjects. Such intense Orthodox political involvement in, and even control over, political, social, and religious affairs created in Greece a kind of close union between church and nation that was almost unique in the world. This union only now is breaking down as the Greeks are becoming increasingly secular and as the church's political and social influence is being strongly challenged. Nevertheless, much of the prestige which the church still enjoys today stems from the Greeks' awareness that in the past the Orthodox Church kept the Hellenic flame burning during four centuries of Turkish domination and that, as the chief patron for Greek nationalism, the church was at the forefront of the struggle for Greek independence in the 1820s.

The Turks left their traces in Greece, even though the war of independence almost totally removed any visible traces of Turkish rule. Remains of medieval cities or of mosques can hardly be found in the country today. One does notice elements in the Greeks' everyday life, though: the warm hospitality and generosity, the food and the manner in which coffee is prepared and drunk, the men's habit of sitting around cafés in midday while the women are at home working, the music, the distinctly Balkan folklore, the peasant dress, and the reels of red tape and almost-impenetrable bureaucracy all reflect heavy Middle Eastern influences.

On the other hand, the unpleasant memory of long Turkish subjugation; the bloody and emotional struggle with the Turks to regain Greek independence in the 1820s; and the effort, which continues to this day, to extend Greece's borders to include all Greek-speaking peoples have combined to create a deep-seated antipathy that always plays a prominent role in Greek politics.

Revolt

Exasperated by Turkish maladministration and inspired by the ideals of liberty ignited in Europe by the French Revolution, the Greeks revolted against the Turks in 1821. This struggle immediately stimulated sympathy in all of western Europe, where the love for Greek antiquity was great and where, only a few years earlier, the young British poet Lord Byron had written of Greece lamentingly in *Childe Harold's Pilgrimage*, "Trembling beneath the scourge of Turkish hand, From birth to death enslaved; in work, in deed, unmann'd." Byron even went to Greece to fight for its independence, and his death as a result of fever at Missolonghi on April 19, 1824, lent the struggle an almost-divine consecration in the eyes of many western Europeans.

Frieze of a water bearer

Greek history kept alive under Turkish occupation

As so often in 19th- and 20th-century Greek history, foreigners' admiration for Greek antiquity helped focus attention on modern Greece's problems. The Russian poet Pushkin found this fact disgusting. He wrote acidly, "This enthusiasm of all cultured nations for Greece is unforgivable childishness. The Jesuits have told us all that twaddle about Themistocles and Pericles, and so we imagine that the shabby nation of robbers and traders are their legitimate successors." Pushkin was certainly too hard on the Greeks, but it is true that foreign observers were all too apt to show disgust at Turkish atrocities in this brutal struggle and to overlook such behavior when the Greeks committed them. For instance, there was hardly a reaction to the Greeks' hanging, impaling, and roasting alive 12,000 Turkish prisoners who had surrendered at Tripolitsa, but the outcry was deafening when the Turkish governor later systematically executed 30,000 Greek survivors at Chios and sold another 46,000 into slavery. The atrocities both sides were committing did not hinder the French, British, and Russians from joining the struggle against the Turks in 1827, and by 1829 Turkey had to sue for peace.

A Wobbly Monarchy

In an ambassadorial conference in London, the major powers and Greece finally defined the boundaries of the new Greek state, which was much smaller than present-day Greece. The first border extended only as far north as the line extending from the Gulf of Volos on the east to the Gulf of Arta on the west. This excluded such islands as Crete and Corfu. At the same conference, Prince Otto of Bavaria was named king of Greece and was placed on a royal throne that wobbled and shook almost continuously until it was finally abolished once and for all in 1974. The new king made one mistake after another. This foreigner refused to convert from Roman Catholicism to Orthodox Christianity in a land where the Orthodox Church was inextricably linked with the very idea of the Greek nation. Then he tried to impose tightly centralized government upon a people who had just fought for their independence. The first governor established himself on the island of Aegina in 1828. For idealistic reasons, Athens, a dusty village of 5,000 inhabitants at the time, was declared capital with the constitution of 1834.

It is not surprising that the Greeks could never settle down under such rule and that the two unfortunate elements in subsequent Greek politics developed like malignant cysts in the very heart of Greek politics. First, an unbridgeable gap between monarchists and republicans was created. Second, the Greek military began meddling in Greek politics. Such activity was partly the consequence of and partly the cause of the political instability that afflicted the country for the next century and a half.

This chronic instability and absence of even a minimal consensus ultimately left the Greek political landscape littered with the wreckage of two dynasties. Absence of political stability ultimately resulted in 5 removals of kings from power (1862, 1917, 1922, 1941, and 1967), 7 changes of constitution, 3 republics, 7 military dictatorships, 15 revolutions and coups (of which 10 succeeded), 155 governments (43 since 1945), 12 wars, and a bitter five-year civil war. Thus, in certain ways, modern Greek politics until 1973 was like a pendulum swinging constantly between the extreme democracy of Athens and the iron military sentiments of Sparta.

About the only thing the Greeks could agree on was that their borders had to be extended until all Greeks were citizens of the Greek state (a goal referred to as the "Great Idea"). Thus, where domestic politics divided them, intense nationalism, which can bubble to the surface of any Greek almost instantly, united them. The settlement of 1832 had not created a natural and mutually acceptable frontier between Greece and Turkey, and every Greek government pursued an ingathering policy of some kind to rectify this. This meant constant friction

Greece

and occasional war with Turkey, which greatly nourished the hatred Greeks seem almost always to bear toward their neighbor to the east.

It took time, but the Greeks have, with the notable exception of Cyprus and small pockets of Greeks in southern Albania, accomplished their "Great Idea." In 1864 the British turned over to them the Ionian Islands, including especially Corfu. In 1881 Greece received a third of Epirus and the bulk of Thessaly, but when it conducted naval actions against the Turks in Crete and the rest of Thessaly a few years later, the Turks declared war on Greece in 1897. They routed the Greek army and even threatened to take Athens—a humiliating defeat for Greece.

The emergence before World War I of one of Greece's greatest 20th-century political leaders, Eleutherios Venizelos, brought Greece many benefits. He introduced important reforms to establish a modern state. An admirer of western European democracy, he created the foundations of a state of law in Greece, expanded the school system, initiated a land reform program, legalized trade unions, and created agricultural cooperatives. He was also able to utilize his international prestige and diplomatic skill to win for his country a handsome chunk of the spoils of distribution to the Balkan nations resulting from the Balkan wars against Turkey in 1912 and 1913. Greece received a part of Macedonia, the island of Crete, and the Aegean Islands. These additions enlarged the Greek land area by 75% and its population by 70%.

World War I and Another Greek-Turkish Round

When World War I broke out, King Constantine I tried to remain neutral, but British and French pressure, which included the landing of French troops on Greek soil, caused the king to abdicate. Prime Minister Venizelos was able to have his country declare war on Germany and its allies. Its reward from its new allies was western Thrace, which it received in 1918, and a British promise of a part of Turkey around Smyrna (now Izmir).

On May 15, 1919, British ships transported Greek troops to Smyrna in order to collect its booty, but this adventure ended in a catastrophe. American president Woodrow Wilson opposed any carving up of Turkey in spite of its support of Germany in the war. Further, the greatest political leader in Turkish history, General Kemal Atatürk, who created the modern Turkish state, revived his exhausted and humiliated countrymen, who had been decimated during the war, and organized a heroic defense of Smyrna.

After the British stopped supporting the Greek expeditionary force, the Turks delivered a devastating and fatal blow to the Greeks. In bloody revenge, the Turkish sword swung freely, and practically the entire Greek population was either killed or driven out of the area around the coast of Asia Minor, where Greeks had lived for 3,000 years. The French and British declared themselves to be neutral in the face of this massacre and refused to take Greek refugees onboard their ships, although it had been the British who had made promises to the Greeks that had unleashed this tragic adventure in the first place. In the end, 600,000 Greeks perished, and almost 1.5 million were forced out of Turkey. In return, Turkey agreed to the repatriation of about 400,000 Muslims living in Greece.

Continued Political Conflict

The one positive thing this unfortunate conflict did produce was clearly defined borders between Greeks and Turks (except in Cyprus), with only negligible minorities on the wrong side of the lines. But the disaster sent Greek politics into a tailspin again. Venizelos and the king were forced into exile. The first Greek Republic was established in 1923, followed by military coups in 1925, 1926, 1933, and 1935 and a restoration of the monarchy in 1935 but one in which real power was held by General Joannes Metaxas. The latter suppressed most political groups and led a right-wing dictatorship until he was subsequently removed from power by the German conquerors in 1941.

World War II

Greece entered World War II on the side of Britain and France. On October 28, 1940, the Greek government said *ochi* ("no") to a host of unacceptable demands made by the impetuous Italian dictator Benito Mussolini, who boasted of a "promenade to Athens." Italian troops entered Greece from Albania. Although the British hurriedly sent a limited number of troops to Greece from North Africa, the Greeks themselves were able to drive Mussolini's poor-quality forces back into Albania, where they could have destroyed the entire Italian army if Metaxas had not feared German retaliation.

Since Hitler had already decided that Greece, the "Achilles heel of Europe" should not be allowed to fall into enemy hands, it mattered little what the Greek general feared. Hitler sent his storm troopers into Greece; their numerical superiority broke the Greek resistance on April 6, 1941. The last British bastion in Greece, the island of Crete, was taken within two months after the attackers launched the largest airborne operation against the island that the world had ever seen. The Germans then divided Greece into occupation zones, awarding the lion's share to the defeated Italy, which perhaps could at least tend to a conquered country.

The suffering and humiliation of occupation created a resistance movement in Greece. Metaxas had destroyed all political parties and thereby had created a political vacuum. Therefore, the Greek communists, who had built up an underground apparatus, were able to form an effective resistance organization, the Greek Liberation Front (EAM), which had a fighting force, the Greek People's Liberation Army (ELAS). Not until 1943 was an anticommunist competitor created, the Greek Republic Liberation League (EDES).

The British supported both partisan groups in order to disrupt the Germans' supply links with their troops in North Africa. When the Italian fascist regime collapsed in 1943, its occupation forces left Greece after selling a large part of their weapons to the Greek partisans. The Germans responded to the resistance activity in Greece by shooting hostages and devastating entire villages. These measures merely drove countless young peasants into the arms of the communists.

Civil War

Even during its struggle against the Germans, ELAS began preparing a civil war against its Greek opponents. At first, Soviet leader Stalin honored the agreement he made with British prime minister Churchill at the Tehran conference from November 28 to December 1, 1943, to divide the Balkans into spheres of influence, with Greece falling at a ratio of 90% into the British sphere and 10% into the Soviet. Romania would be the reverse, while British and Soviet interests in Yugoslavia would be 50–50.

However, from March 1944 on, the Soviets began supporting their Greek comrades. Therefore, when the Germans pulled out of Greece in October, the communists were in a very good position. They controlled about 90% of the country when the exile government arrived at Athens from Egypt accompanied by about 15,000 British troops. Fearing defeat in a democratic election, ELAS resisted by force, and it took a full month of bitter house-to-house combat for the British and the Greek government troops to drive the communists out of Athens. Fighting again broke out in December 1944, but the communists suffered such losses they decided to lay down their arms temporarily.

The first elections, which were held on March 31, 1946, under the supervision of 1,200 American, British, and French troops, produced a resounding victory

Greece

for the conservative royalists. Also, in a referendum held on September 1, 1946, to determine the future form of government, 68% of those voting supported the restoration of the monarchy. Along with the stern anticommunist measures of the right-wing extremist Colonel George Grivas, this referendum made reconciliation with the communists impossible. They also made it difficult for noncommunist liberals and republicans to give the new regime their enthusiastic support.

With the aid of the Soviet Union, Yugoslavia, and Bulgaria, the Greek communists resumed their armed struggle, which lasted three more years. Key factors in the ultimate noncommunist victory were American economic and military assistance to Greece (as a consequence of the Truman doctrine, which promised aid against communist threats to Greece and Turkey) and Yugoslavia's break with the Soviet Union in 1948. After the latter event, Yugoslav leader Marshal Tito closed the Yugoslav-Greek border, thereby preventing needed supplies from being shipped to the Greek communist rebels.

In 1949 the communists finally gave up the struggle, which had cost them about 80,000 casualties and the government forces about 50,000. This tragic conflict polarized Greek politics for years, sapped Greece's economic resources, and caused considerable destruction in the country. The civil war complicated the problem of reconstruction, despite generous infusions of Marshall Plan assistance from the US. Thus, while World War I lasted in reality 10—not 4—years in Greece, World War II had also, in effect, lasted a decade in the battered country. The only tangible benefit from the settlement after the second conflict was that Greece was awarded the Dodecanese Islands in 1947.

Restoration and Recovery; the Status of Cyprus

The government turned to the task of restoring and improving the country's economy. It led Greece into NATO in February 1952 and into a Balkan Pact in August 1954, which was supposed to forge a military link among Greece, Turkey, and Yugoslavia. This pact has, for all practical purposes, remained a dead letter because of Greece's chronic tensions with Turkey. Such tensions were again rekindled in 1954 as a result of events on the island of Cyprus, which had been a British base since 1878 and a Crown colony since 1925 and more than 80% of whose residents are Greek. Cyprus had long aroused the emotions of Greek nationalists, and the goal (called enosis) of bringing the island's residents under Greek authority had long existed. Enosis was supported on the island

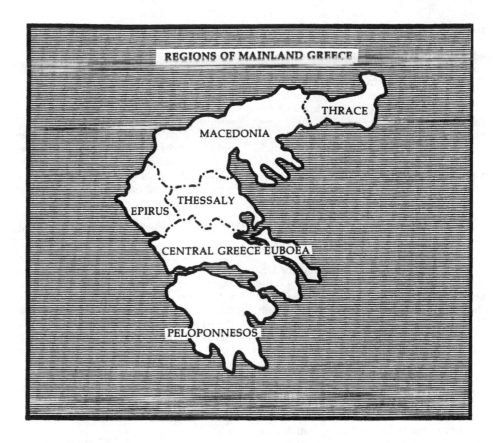

by the Orthodox Church and by a large number of educated Greeks.

When some of them launched an indiscriminate terrorist campaign in 1954 in order to try to stimulate international sympathy for their cause, the Turkish minority on the island fought back. Although Cyprus was ultimately granted independence, the problems of how the two groups should administer the island and what kind of relations Cyprus should maintain with Greece and Turkey have been and are a continuing, chronic irritant in the relations between the two NATO allies and with the European Union.

POSTWAR POLITICS

During the postwar period, Greece was a parliamentary democracy. King Paul succeeded his brother King George II in 1947. But there also was a strong military involvement in politics. Present party alignments emerged. There was almost-continuous political instability after the communists were defeated, and cabinets sometimes lasted only a few months.

From 1954 to 1963, the key figure in Greek politics was Constantine Karamanlis, who later became president and who tried to steer Greece more closely toward western Europe by establishing economic links with the EC. Almost two decades later, as prime minister and president, he finished his work by overseeing Greece's

entry into the EC as a full member in 1981. He and many of his countrymen hoped that entry into the EC would help secure democracy in Greece.

The years from 1963 to 1965 were characterized by the sweeping social reform efforts of Georgios Papandreou and by a situation in which neither the supporters of the monarch nor of parliamentary democracy could prevail. The political temperature in Athens rose extremely quickly in 1965. Young King Constantine II, who had ascended to the throne at the age of 23 when King Paul died in 1964, almost immediately locked horns with Papandreou over a number of constitutional issues, especially that involving control of the army. The king accused the prime minister of trying to infiltrate the military by means of a left-wing organization called Aspida, headed by Papandreou's son Andreas (who became prime minister in 1981 and again in 1993). Papandreou saw the matter differently—he wanted to fire his defense minister because the latter balked at dismissing right-wing plotters within the army. In any case, King Constantine dismissed Papandreou in mid-1965, an act which set off two more confusing years of stopgap governments, trials, riots, strikes, and political polarization, which cleared the way for the military to act.

On the eve of the May 1967 parliamentary elections, in which Papandreou's Center Union Party was favored to win,

279

Greece

perhaps with the electoral help of communist groups, a group of military officers seized power, pointing to the alleged communist danger and claiming to have the support of the king. It turned out that he had not even been informed about the plan. When they began arresting and exiling parliamentary leaders, including both Papandreous, King Constantine attempted a clumsy coup of his own, which failed miserably and which forced him to flee the country. Not until 1993 did a stable and democratic Greek republic inform Constantine, who had just announced his hopes of reclaiming the throne some day, that he could leave his London exile and return to Greece as a private citizen any time he wanted.

Some Greeks are convinced that the US, through the CIA, had a hand in this military coup, even though it is admitted that there is no absolute proof and even though President Lyndon Johnson publicly denounced the coup. Reference is made to a so-called Prometheus Plan worked out by the king and the army for a military coup in the event that the elections produced a government with communist participation. It is alleged that NATO approved this plan. Further, Andreas Papandreou frequently reminded his listeners that, during the Nixon administration, Vice President Spiro Agnew, himself of Greek descent, traveled to Greece, thereby allegedly giving the dictatorship "full support."

It is, of course, true that the US maintained its military presence in Greece and made arms sales to the new military rulers. Whether the rumors of US complicity or foreknowledge of the coup are true or not, these allegations did help to create in Greece an anti-American feeling that remains strong. President Bill Clinton's state visit to Greece in November 1999 unleashed pent-up rage. Leftist groups organized daily protests, mobilizing more than 10,000 before the American embassy. They forced the Greek government to close off the Athens city center and Clinton to pare down the visit to only 24 hours. Every November 17, the anniversary of a 1973 student uprising that helped topple the country's military rulers, demonstrators march on the American embassy in Athens because of alleged US backing for the junta that seized power in 1967.

The bombing in Kosovo, which 90% of Greeks opposed, ignited the renewed anti-American fervor. But Clinton addressed the deeper cause, offering a near-apology for the American stance during the seven years of repressive military dictatorship: "When the junta took over in 1967 here, the United States allowed its interests in prosecuting the Cold War to prevail over its interests—I should say its obligation—to support democracy, which was, after all, the cause for which we fought the Cold War. It is important that we acknowledge that." The audience erupted in applause.

Military Dictatorship

The seven-year military dictatorship, first under the leadership of Georgios Papadoupoulos and, after November 1973, under the chief of the secret service Colonel Demetrios Ioannides, is remembered as a long and brutal period. The "colonels" converted Greece into a military camp, in which political opponents were persecuted by all the means of state terror.

The regime put itself on the wrack when in 1974 Ioannides decided to overthrow the government of Cyprus's mercurial Archbishop Makarios and to try to install a government on the island subject to command from Athens. This heavy-handed action merely provoked the Turks to invade Cyprus and ultimately to partition the island. Since the Turks used American weapons in this invasion (referred to as Attila), many Greeks place partial responsibility on the Americans' shoulders. This is a deliberate distortion, however, since the Turks were using weapons received as a member of NATO and there was no authorization by the US to use them for an invasion of Cyprus. The use of such weaponry violated American law, and even when the US thereafter cut off all arms sales to Turkey for several years, this event, which was clearly out of American control, created even more resentment in Greece against the US. In effect, the Americans were criticized both because they allegedly supported the "colonels" and because they allegedly did not.

Fortunately the crisis created a situation the "colonels" could not handle. Greece had been brought to the brink of war with Turkey, so important senior officers withdrew their support from the discredited Ioannides and called for Constantine Karamanlis to return from his Paris exile and to reassume the reins of power as the leader of a government of national unity. Thus, as in Portugal the same year, a foreign policy crisis cleared the way for the establishment of a democratic political order.

After years of intense political instability and harsh military rule, Greeks adjusted very well to democracy after 1974.

October 1944: Prime Minister Georgios Papandreou on the Acropolis as Greek women carry the national flag to be raised over liberated Athens

When Andreas Papandreou called for *allaghi* ("change") in the 1981 parliamentary election, a near-majority of his countrymen responded. Greeks knew well that, for the first time in decades, change meant a transfer of power from one democratic party to another, not a change of regime involving the destruction of democratic rule.

Despite many political and economic problems, Greece is experiencing unprecedented stability. The traditional Greek cycle of volatile democracy–military dictatorship, often punctuated by coups, has come to an end. Now the two largest parties, which received 85.9% of the votes in 2004, firmly accept the parliamentary system. Also, the soldiers have returned to their barracks once and for all, and Greek politicians no longer have to calculate the military's possible response to any decision. Despite the invariably inflated election rhetoric, the Greek body politic is no longer divided into hostile, enemy camps.

In some European countries, monarchs symbolize national unity, but in Greece they almost always tended to divide, not unite, the nation. Therefore, 69% of those who went to the polls voted in a referendum held on December 8, 1974, to abolish the monarchy and to establish a republic.

In 1981 the Greek leadership nervously allowed Constantine II to return briefly to Athens to attend the funeral of his mother, ex-queen Frederika, at the Tatoi Palace on the outskirts of Athens. They feared that his presence in Greece, after 14 years of absence (first in Rome, later in London, where he was in the sales and public relations business), might destabilize the new regime. They permitted him to land at a military airbase near the palace and remain in Greece a few hours to attend. The leaders' risk paid off because only 2,000 chanting admirers appeared to greet the king.

It became clear that what little support the monarchy had enjoyed earlier had largely evaporated. This realization bolstered the confidence and long-term stability of the republic. When the king and his family unexpectedly returned for a two-week holiday in August 1993, scuffles broke out between royalists and leftist protesters, prompting the government publicly to disapprove of the visit. An irritated President Karamanlis noted, "such affairs do not threaten democracy or our system of government but hold the country up to ridicule." In 1994 parliament stripped the king of his citizenship and remaining property in Greece.

At the European Court of Human Rights in Strasbourg in late 2002, Constantine received an award of about €20 million as a settlement of the royal claims, a sum lower than that accepted by the Greek government. In February 2003 he also got two palaces in Athens and Corfu, some compensation, but no pay. Since he refuses to adopt a surname, allow his name to be entered into the record of citizens, and carry an identification card, he cannot get a Greek passport.

PRESENT GOVERNMENT STRUCTURE

The Presidency

On June 7, 1974, a new constitution went into effect that described Greece as a "presidential parliamentary republic." Considering the Greeks' experiences during seven years of military dictatorship, it is not surprising that the new constitution contains extensive guarantees of individual rights and civil liberties. The head of state is a president without executive powers, who is elected for a five-year term by the parliament, which meets for this purpose as an electoral college. The constitution requires consensus in electing the president. A successful candidate must win a two-thirds majority on one of the first two ballots or 60% on a third one. If the third ballot fails, parliament is dissolved, new elections are held, and a simple majority of deputies in the new house elects the president. This form of indirect election means that no president can claim to have a direct mandate from the people and thereby challenge the political direction taken by the majority in parliament. The presidential powers are largely ceremonial, and a responsible minister, that is, the government, must countersign most of his acts.

The parliament voted in 1986 to reduce the president's powers even further. He can no longer appoint the prime minister. He can dissolve parliament only if two governments fall in rapid succession. He can no longer call a referendum on what he regards as a major issue, address the people directly when his opinions differ from those of the government, or proclaim a state of siege.

The president's powers and actual influence in Greek politics depend upon the respect he enjoys in the eyes of the citizens or of the leading politicians. The president until 1985 was Constantine Karamanlis, one of the most highly respected leaders in Greece and widely regarded as one of the major architects and protectors of the democratic regime. No prime minister could overlook his views on important issues. He was succeeded by Christos Sartzetakis, a respected supreme court justice who became famous for cracking the notorious Lambrakis murder case in 1963 and who was immortalized as the incorruptible judge in the movie Z, which portrayed Greek politics during the last years of the monarchy. In 1990 Karamanlis was again elected to a five-year term.

He was followed in 1995 by lawyer Constantinos Stephanopoulos, who had sought exile in Paris during the military dictatorship and who had never been implicated in a scandal. In 2005 the New Democracy government nominated an ex–foreign minister and a founding member of PASOK, Karolos Papoulias, for the presidency. He won by a record majority in parliament, receiving 279 of the 296 votes cast. He was succeeded in March 2015 by Prokopis Pavlopoulos. In January 2020, the first woman was elected as Greek president: Katerina Sakellaropoulou.

Parliament and Prime Minister

The most powerful political office in Greece is that of the prime minister, who must be able to find a majority for his policies in the 300-seat unicameral parliament (Vouli). All Greek citizens 18 years or older can vote. Voting is mandatory, although not all eligible voters go to the polls. For example, in September 2015, the turnout was 56%. Greek media are prohibited from publishing opinion polls in the final two weeks of an election campaign.

The members of parliament are elected by a modified form of proportional representation that favors the larger parties. Members of parliament (MP) are elected for a four-year term in 56 constituencies and in 1 multimember nationwide constituency for 12 MPs. A bonus of 50 seats is allocated directly to the party or coalition that gets the most votes. The remaining seats are distributed proportionally. This system is designed to increase the chances that one party will have a parliamentary majority even when none wins a majority of the votes cast. For instance, in the September 2015 elections, Syriza received 36.5% of the votes, but it won an absolute majority of the seats (145 of 300). Having gotten the most votes, it received the 50 bonus seats.

In the two dozen general elections following 1951, the government has changed the electoral system nine times within six months of the polling in order to maximize its seats. In 1989 the system was brought closer to a strict proportional representation system, which improves the chances of small parties and thereby makes it more difficult to form a majority. This was further tweaked in 2007 to help little parties. A party must win at least 3% of the total votes in an election to qualify for any parliamentary seats. This eliminates minuscule parties. For example, in September 2015, eight parties cleared this threshold and got seats, but the Ecologists-Greens won only 2.53% of the votes and received none. In May 2012, 32 parties entered the election.

Greece

Because instability had long been a curse in Greek politics, it is logical that the framers of the present constitution would seek ways to ensure stability within a democratic framework. Parliament is elected for four years, but the prime minister can arrange for early elections for any reason, especially in the event he cannot maintain a parliamentary majority. This happened in 2009.

Since 2003 a deputy is prohibited from holding other jobs. His influence depends largely on whether his particular party permits him to disregard the party's recommendations or policy when votes are taken. For instance, under Andreas Papandreou PASOK forbade its deputies to vote against the party leadership and would refuse a maverick deputy the chance to seek reelection under the PASOK label. A traditional source of influence for the deputy was *rousfeti* ("influence peddling"), by which he used the bureaucracy to get special favors, including jobs, for his constituents. This was a way for him to win and to maintain votes, but the massive migration from rural areas into the cities reduced its effectiveness. In the cities people are no longer so inclined to turn to their local political bosses and deputies for help or favors.

The traditional need for some practice like *rousfeti* reflected the difficulty Greek citizens have in attracting the attention of an overgrown and often lethargic, indifferent, or corrupt bureaucracy in order to find solutions for individual or collective problems. At the same time, *rousfeti* helped to bloat or paralyze the bureaucracy because jobs were often filled or created for friends or constituents of influential politicians. Appointments and subsequent promotions were too often based more upon friendship and connections that upon merit.

In Greek political ideology, it is better to have a friend or relative hired or advanced rather than having a merit system. Added to the problem are job security for even the most incompetent workers; exaggerated respect for tradition, which leaves little room for new ideas; lack of management skills; and excessive fear of being blamed for mistakes: If you don't do *anything*, you can't be blamed for doing *something*. Even simple transactions required as many as a dozen signatures. A bureaucrat's typical response is understandably *avrio, avrio* ("tomorrow, tomorrow"). Every prime minister vows to limit patronage and corruption, but seldom is noticeable progress made.

Greece's high unemployment rate in the 21st century is in part due to the collapse of public-sector patronage as a way to win the voters' favor. Politicians do not have the opportunities they once had

to divvy out jobs to their friends. There are also more jobs in the private sector than there used to be. However, patronage is still deeply entrenched, and party heavyweights control most public-sector appointments, from hospital directors to university professors and local government officials. Corruption is still rife in state enterprises and in hospitals, where envelopes with cash are given to well-paid doctors in the hope of greater attention to the patient's needs.

PASOK tried to make good its promise to decentralize power in a highly centralized country. The central government traditionally sent 55 nomarchs (governors) into the provinces to exercise nearly total power over local decisions. Local government received all their revenues from Athens and did not even have the right to levy taxes. The government doubled the financial grants to local governments and set up committees, composed of city councilmen, farmers, workers, and employers, to advise the nomarchs, whose control over the city councils was reduced. In 2010 the government passed legislation to reduce the number of states from 76 to 13 and the number of counties from 1,034 to 370.

Evzone (a Greek regiment) presidential guard in the traditional white foustanela
Courtesy: Jon Markham Morrow

POLITICS AND PARTIES

One of the most encouraging developments in Greek politics since 1974 is that the military no longer threatens to intervene in politics as it once did. Although soldiers were apparently still hatching plots in 1975, they concentrate now on purely military duties. Nevertheless, no Greek politician, especially no leftist prime minister, would dare overlook the remote possibility that the officers might return to their earlier self-appointed political role of "straightening up the mess" of democratic politics.

In order to help pacify the military, Andreas Papandreou increased their housing allowances and pay sharply. Also, his stridently nationalistic rhetoric was well received in the mess halls. As irritating and exaggerated as his nationalism may have been to foreigners, it did serve an important domestic political purpose of reconciling, if not totally integrating, ultraconservative and military circles with the democratic regime.

Parties are, in traditional Greek style, personalized in that they are built around and largely dominated by respected figures. They are run from the top. Central headquarters selects electoral candidates and controls patronage. In Greece, politics revolves more around persons than policies.

PASOK

PASOK sprang from the Panhellenic Liberation Movement (PaK), an underground guerrilla group established to fight against the colonels' junta from 1967 to 1974. It grew extremely rapidly since its founding as a political party in 1974. It climbed from 14% of the vote in 1974 to 25% in 1977 and to 48% in 1981, to become the first nonconservative government since 1974. PASOK's rise to power would have been unthinkable without the inspiration and leadership of one man, Andreas Papandreou.

Young Andreas got a PhD in economics from Harvard University and became an American citizen in 1944. After serving in the US Navy, he taught economics at such American universities as Minnesota (where he met and married his first wife, Margarete), Northwestern, and Berkeley.

When in 1963 his father asked him and all other Greeks living abroad who could contribute to the nation's development to return to Greece, Andreas agreed. When the "colonels" seized power in 1967, he and his father were imprisoned. During the coup soldiers had come to the Papandreou home looking for them. Finding they were not there, they put a gun at the head of young George Papandreou, who became prime minister in 2009, and

**Former prime minister
Andreas Papandreou**

Ex-President Prokopis Pavlopoulos

It saw itself as a left-wing party, as European socialist and social democratic parties go. For years it refused to join the Socialist International because Andreas Papandreou claimed that it was dominated by the social democratic parties in northern Europe, especially the German SPD, which he had branded as the European representative of "monopoly capitalism." Nevertheless, PASOK is extremely flexible (some say "opportunist") and can present itself in almost any democratic way, depending on the political climate and realities of the time.

As a governing party, it faced the typical problems of a radical party that finds itself in power and responsible for confronting concrete problems. The party was aware that the change for which many Greeks voted in 1981 was not socialism but something less, and the party acted accordingly. This caused tension within the party.

Before the 1989 elections, Papandreou's popularity plummeted because of a serious financial scandal and his public love affair with Dimitra Liani ("Mimi"), a divorced airline stewardess half his age. She began serving as his official consort. Some feared that she influenced his political decisions. Pictures of her in the nude published in Greek newspapers shocked many Greeks.

To minimize electoral damage in socially conservative Greece, Papandreou divorced his wife a few days before the election. But he had already sacrificed the respect of many citizens. Many Greeks cringed in 1993, when he named Liani as his chief of staff, a powerful post managing his work schedule as prime minister and controlling access to him.

Many thought that he was determined to make the unpopular Mimi his successor. They were irritated by the way she interfered in government, screened access to the prime minister, and summoned ministers for meetings. She deepened the divisions within the party and strengthened fears that it would be punished severely at the next elections. In 1999 she was charged with fraud, embezzlement of public funds, and tax evasion.

In 1996 Andreas Papandreou was replaced as prime minister by Costas Simitis, a mild-mannered, statistics-quoting technocrat and reformer. He narrowly won the 1996 and 2000 elections. For the first time in Greece's postwar history, the Socialists won three electoral victories in a row.

Rapport with America was enhanced by the appointment in 1999 of the soft-edged George Papandreou as foreign minister. Born in the US of an American mother and speaking perfect American English and Swedish, he grew up in the US, Canada, and Sweden and studied at Amherst, Harvard, and the London School of Economics.

He greatly benefited from his family's name and connections. But whereas his father was confrontational, the son is more inclined to build bridges and emphasize the positive. He is highly sensitive to the political realities of the outside world. He worked hard to improve Greece's relationship with Turkey, whose entry into the EU he favored. Few Greek foreign ministers were as respected by their NATO and EU opposite numbers.

Seeing that it was heading for defeat in the 2004 elections, PASOK chose George Papandreou, the country's most popular politician at the time, to succeed Simitis as party leader. In his eight years as prime minister, Simitis had achieved good relations with its neighbors, especially Turkey. But he had largely failed to reform the state and to rid the country of much of its corruption. Greeks were tired of PASOK in power; after all, they had ruled in all but 3 of the preceding 22 years. They liked Papandreou's style, his soft-spoken talk of social inclusiveness, his folksy Internet diary on the web, and his willingness to use his personal authority to break foreign policy molds. He was respected in part because of his name recognition. After all, politics in Greece is a family affair.

He served as prime minister and his own foreign minister, a post he had held from 1999 to 2004. However, as the financial crisis worsened, Papandreou's own approval rating plummeted to only 22%. He clumsily announced that he would call a referendum on the austerity measures his government had agreed upon. He was forced to back down in the face of an outcry from creditors, the EU, and Germany, which demanded an assault on tax evasion, the end to rampant public-sector patronage, privatization of state entities, and an improvement of competitiveness. No prime minister could have achieved this in so short a time.

demanded that he tell where they were. He coolly answered, "I don't know." Andreas was kept in solitary confinement for eight months before he was released, thanks in large part to the efforts of his American wife and the US embassy. He again went into exile, first to Sweden and then to Canada, before returning in 1974.

Papandreou was a brilliant speaker with a knack for accurately reading the pulse of his audience. However, his eloquence often lapsed into demagoguery. He is very intolerant of criticism or diverging views. He ran PASOK and the Greek government with an iron hand.

PASOK's voter appeal was not limited to one class or group. Young voters were especially attracted to PASOK. It established a network of local organizations all over Greece and had a populist strain, and it was very nationalistic, directing its venom toward the US, Turkey, NATO, and the EU. Nationalist appeals always brought in the votes in Greek elections, and they combined with the populist appeals to help PASOK win votes from a wide spectrum of groups, including farmers, workers, employees, and midlevel civil servants.

At first PASOK presented itself as a somewhat-Marxist movement for national and social liberation, and even shortly before the 1981 election, Papandreou announced, "we plan to change the system, not to embellish it." Experience indicates that too much Marxism is bad politics in most democratic countries. The party quickly backed away from it.

Greece

**Former prime minister
George Papandreou**

In 2011, after only two years, he stepped down. This was a humiliating end for Papandreou, who became the first Greek prime minister in a half-century to be forced out of office by his own cabinet.

It confronted disaster in the September 2015 elections. PASOK experienced its worst result ever, slipping to fourth place, with only 17 seats.

Communists

Greek communists are divided into two main parties. The Greek Communist Party (KKE) is a rigid Marxist-Leninist party. It greeted the August 1991 coup against democracy in the USSR as a "welcome return to order." It is the only party in Greece today that had existed before 1974. The KKE has a well-organized and highly disciplined cadre and base. It controls much real estate around Athens, including a shipping company. Its domestic and foreign policy is predictable: state control over the economy and withdrawal from NATO and the EU.

In the 1989 elections, the KKE forged an "Alliance of the Left and Progress" with the Greek Communist Party of the Interior (KKES) and other small groups. KKES is so named because its leaders had remained in Greece after the civil war instead of fleeing to eastern Europe. It advocates a softer, Eurocommunist line, more in tune with the Greek democratic political order. Most of them went to the KKE. Another moderate communist party is Sinaspismos, which never wins seats.

The communists' success in playing "kingmaker" after 1989 enhanced their political legitimacy. It helped Greeks to bury the hatchet that had been bloodied during the civil war. The term "civil war"

officially replaced the previous term for the struggle: "bandits' war." The 40th anniversary of the last battle in the mountains of Epirus was redesignated a celebration of "national reconciliation." Some 16 million files the security police had kept on politically suspicious persons were burned, and full pension rights and social benefits were extended to anybody who had fought on the losing side. KKE captured only 15 seats in September 2015.

Syriza

Benefiting most from deep dissatisfaction with the economic situation and PASOK was the populist Radical Left Coalition (Syriza, or SYN), a leftist coalition of a dozen far-left factions popular with young voters and led by the young and charismatic Alexis Tsipras. He had joined the pro-Soviet communist party while in high school. His appeal was simple and impossible: reject the "barbarous" loan agreement with the EU without abandoning the euro and the EU itself. Place the banks under state control. The EU is bluffing and would be hurt more than Greece if the country had to abandon the euro. He also called for free meals for students and pensions as high as final salaries. He refused to join any government that supported the austerity plan.

The January 25, 2015, elections were a charm for Syriza. Voters had had enough of austerity and sacrifice and rewarded it with 36% of the votes and 149 seats. To form a majority ruling coalition, Tsipras allied with the 13 MPs of the right-wing, antiausterity Independent Greeks (ANEL), whose leader, Panos Kammenos, became defense minister. As an atheist, Tsipras did not hold a Bible during his swearing-in or accept the usual blessing from Orthodox priests. However, they conducted a swearing-in for MPs in parliament. Presiding over parliament was a woman, Zoe Konstantopoulou. When creditors rejected the government's antiausterity policy, prompting 40 hard-left Syriza MPs to bolt, Tsipras called snap elections in September 2015. His party won again, capturing 35.5% of the votes and 145 seats. Coalescing again with ANEL, the government enjoys a narrow majority of 153 seats. The new center-left To Potami (The River) won 11 seats.

The New Democracy Party

New Democracy (ND) sprang up quickly around Constantine Karamanlis. He later became a cabinet member before the colonels overthrew the government in 1967. He was jailed briefly and later escaped to exile abroad. Returning to Greece in 1974, he served as minister of foreign affairs until 1981.

It is a party of the center and the reformed right, which is committed to

democracy and social reform. It defines itself as a modern, pluralistic party. It is liberal in the European sense in that it favors a limitation of the state's role in the society and economy. It advocates a free-market economy but one that does not overlook the economic needs of any groups, including those citizens with low incomes. New Democracy's foreign policy is strongly oriented toward the west, and it was Karamanlis who guided Greece into the EU and back into the NATO command structure. Although it introduced many needed changes, it became tinged with accusations of corruption and favoritism, whose roots are deeply embedded in Greek politics and society.

In 1997 it picked a new leader, Costas Karamanlis, nephew of the party's founder. It got a boost from the first woman to be elected mayor of Athens, Dora Bakoyanni. This was a major accomplishment in a country with so few women in elective office. For example, after the 2004 parliamentary elections, there were two women in the cabinet and 40 women in parliament, including the first-ever female speaker, Anna Psarouda-Benaki. Like Karamanlis himself, Bakoyanni is the product of a famous political family, being the daughter of former prime minister Mitsotakis. This is very important in Greece, where voters feel loyalty for familiar family names. She inherited her family's huge network of personal connections on Crete. In 2006 she became the country's first female foreign minister.

Karamanlis steered his party toward the center on domestic policy and toward his predecessor's sensible policy of conciliation toward Turkey and healing the division of Cyprus. While still in opposition, he had built a personal relationship with Turkish leader Recep Tayyip Erdogan, who invited him to address his party's congress in 2003. Ex–foreign minister Petros Molyviatis remembered the occasion, "Watching 7,000 Turks giving a standing ovation to a Greek leader was unprecedented." In 2008 he made the first prime-ministerial visit to Turkey since his uncle Constantine Karamanlis had done so 49 years earlier.

Greeks grew tired of the many corruption scandals attributed to the ND government. In May 2012 ND was buried in an avalanche of disgust over the government's austerity program. Although it remained the largest party, it plunged to 20%. Whereas ND and PASOK had dominated Greek politics since 1974, they now had fallen to only a third of the votes, down from 77% in 2009. The political center had lost much of its legitimacy. In the September 2015 elections, New Democracy was soundly defeated by Syriza, capturing only 28.3% and 75 seats.

Syriza has led the government since 2019 under a new leader, Kyriakos Mitsotakis. Son of a former prime minister and with degrees from Harvard and Stanford, he offers a steady reformist hand for his floundering party.

Golden Dawn

The most threatening party to Greek democracy has been Golden Dawn, a far-right party that makes no pretense of being nonviolent. Its cult of violence is unique among European far-right groups. It was founded in the early 1980s by sympathizers of the military dictatorship from 1967 to 1974. It ran unsuccessfully in national elections since 1994, but it won 7.1% and 18 seats in the malaise election of September 2015. Since it opposed Greece's agreement with the EU and other lenders, it lured much of the protest vote.

Led by Nikos Michaloliakos, it is unapologetically fascist, as its Nazi salutes and swastika-like symbol indicate. It denies that the Holocaust had happened and organizes torch-lit parades led by young men in black T-shirts. Its structure is modeled on Hitler's leadership principle. It has tried to mute its neo-Nazi image and focus on unwanted immigrants. It calls for a "clean Greece, only for Greeks, a safe Greece." Its vigilante squads are known for their violent treatment of nonwestern immigrants. It taps into rising Greek nationalism, which is increasingly anti-German because of Germany's hard-line approach to Greece's debt problem. One newspaper published a fake photo showing Chancellor Angela Merkel in a Nazi uniform. An opinion poll in May 2012 found that 78% of respondents have an unfavorable view of Germany.

Most tolerance ran out when one of its supporters stabbed a popular rap singer, Pavlos Fyssas, to death in front of dozens of bystanders following an argument over a soccer game. This act sparked a national and international outcry, and mass rallies were organized to express widespread disgust. One unwelcome reaction was the gangland-style drive-by shooting of two party members outside a party office. A previously unknown leftist guerrilla group claimed responsibility for the killings. A party cannot be banned, so the government had to make a case that the party is a criminal organization. The party's leader Michaloliakos, most of its members of parliament, and other supporters were arrested and jailed in a crackdown, and $1.2 million in state funding to the party was stopped.

In the 2019 elections, Golden Dawn lost all its MPs and failed to reach the 3% threshold for entering Parliament. In October 2020, a court found the party leaders guilty of running a criminal organization.

They face prison terms of up to 15 years. The party itself was not banned.

To circumvent the government's crackdown in the lead up to the May 2014 European Parliament elections, its leaders announced the formation of a new party called National Dawn. Like its parent party, its appeal is largely explained by promises to restore jobs and order. This call resonates in a country where unemployment reached 23.5% in 2017; youth joblessness approached 60%.

FOREIGN RELATIONS AND DEFENSE POLICY

Any government in Athens formulating Greece's foreign policy finds a complicated web of problems that confound most people who examine it. The ingredients include an American military base in Crete; Greek membership in NATO, along with Turkey, the traditional enemy to the east that is competing for Cyprus; air-traffic lanes; offshore oil; mineral rights; and the delineation of international and territorial waters and the continental shelf. None of these problems can be sorted out and dealt with separately, and each problem with Turkey is overladen with heated emotion, the roots of which run more deeply than anyone can imagine.

Greece occupies a very important strategic location in the Mediterranean, which is a major lifeline for Europe. Much of Europe's oil moves through the Mediterranean, and this southern flank of NATO is a vital staging area for any possible European or American military operation in the Middle East. In order to bolster NATO muscle in this region, the US has naval air facility in Suda Bay, Crete, with an airfield nearby. The US Sixth Fleet is trained and equipped to operate without bases in Greece in case their use would be denied.

Greece still buys most of its weapons from the US, as well as from Germany, France, and Britain. The Greek and Turkish air and naval forces are roughly equal in numbers. However, with 542,000 troops, the Turkish army outnumbers and outguns the Greek forces. The term of service for conscripts is 14 months, 16 months for navy and air force, depending on the branch. In 2004 the government expressed its intention to reduce military service gradually to six months and to use border-area residents as reserve forces. A professional army is still far off. In 2010, of 156,600 total troops, including 5,520 female volunteers, 93,500 were in the army (including 35,530 conscripts); 20,000, navy (including 4,000 conscripts); and 31,500, air force (including 11,000 conscripts). In 2010, 145 of its soldiers were deployed in Afghanistan, and 588, in Kosovo. In Cyprus, 950 soldiers and 200 officers and

NCOs are seconded to the Greek-Cypriot National Guard.

Among NATO and EU countries, Greece spends the highest percentage of its GDP for defense: almost 5%, over three times the percentage spent by most other NATO nations. In 1997 Greece launched a $16 billion weapons modernization program, completed in 2007. It included purchase of an AWACS early-warning aircraft; 60 new warplanes; and other aircraft, including training and transport planes and helicopters. In 2005 Greece decided to purchase from the US 40 F-16 (block 52) fighter airplanes to be delivered by 2009. This was a bitter disappointment for the European allies that produce the Euro-fighter. There will also be new tanks, antiaircraft systems, and warships, including submarines and nine surface ships. It upgraded its antiaircraft capability by procuring 6 long-range American-made Patriot missile systems, 21 short-range Russian-made Tor missiles for the army, and 11 French-built Crotale missiles for the air force and navy.

It is unlikely that Greece will again leave the NATO command structure after having reentered it in 1980. It had left that command structure in protest against the Turkish invasion of Cyprus. However, when Greece sought reentry, it ran up against a Turkish wall. Any NATO member can veto entry into the alliance or its command structure, and Turkey wanted to use its veto to force Greece to make concessions in the Aegean and in Cyprus. On its part, Greece became so anxious to rejoin that it even wanted to make its reentry a precondition for the renewal of the US base agreements, thereby giving the Americans a powerful motive to help it. It was primarily American diplomatic efforts that smoothed Greece's path back into NATO.

The basic traditional problem remains but in significantly diminished form: that Greek eyes are cast eastward toward Turkey. Confrontation with Turkey is no longer a permanent operating factor in Greek foreign and defense policy. Greece contributed to its allies' war effort against Iraq in 1991 by sending one frigate. But Turkey's participation was much more visible.

In the 1990s both acquired huge quantities of modern offensive weaponry free of charge, as the US and Germany transferred to them hundreds of helicopters, tanks, and artillery under the terms of the 1990 CFE Treaty. The purpose of this conventional forces agreement was to diminish the threat of surprise attack in central Europe. But it was an arms bonanza for Turkey and Greece and, in the opinion of some observers, created less, not more, stability in the Balkans. In 1998 the US stopped all military aid, in the form of

Greece

credits for purchasing American weaponry, to both Greece and Turkey.

The government supports reconciliation with Turkey, its accession to the EU and a unified Cyprus in the EU. It favors "a really European Turkey" and publicly supported the Annan Plan for creating an all-Cyprus federation, which failed in April 2004 after Greek Cypriots voted against it. (See following chapter on Cyprus.)

The Balkans

While Turkey remains Greece's top concern, the dramatic changes in the Balkans and the breakup of the former Yugoslavia are very worrisome to Greeks. They feared that Macedonia to the north could make irredentist claims on their province with the same name. This prompted Athens in 1992 to oppose Macedonia's right to use that ancient Hellenic name when it declared its independence from Yugoslavia. In 1993 a compromise was reached to allow Macedonia to enter the UN under the clumsy temporary name of "Former Yugoslav Republic of Macedonia (FYROM)." Greeks called the country either FYROM or the capital's name, Skopje; they referred to the people as "Skopjans." No flag was hoisted because of Greece's objection to its 16-point star. Greece was at odds with all its neighbors.

Through American mediation in 1995, Greece and North Macedonia agreed to take steps to end their quarrel. Greece agreed to (1) recognize North Macedonia as a sovereign and independent state; (2) lift its trade blockade imposed against North Macedonia, which was hurting both countries financially; (3) stop vetoing EU aid to North Macedonia; and (4) endorse its membership in the OSCE.

In return, North Macedonia agreed to redesign its flag and change two articles in its constitution eliminating any hint of a claim on the Greek province of Macedonia. Liaison offices were established in each other's capitals, and both countries enjoy mutual "unimpeded movement of people and goods." Trade is thriving. In 1999 the Greeks flew supplies to North Macedonia to help that country cope with the flood of refugees from Kosovo. The policy of friendly support continued as a part of Athens's policy to promote stability in the Balkans. In 2001 Greece deployed 411 troops to North Macedonia as part of a NATO force to disarm Albanian rebels, and it is North Macedonia's largest investor.

Their relations with each other have been greatly improved as commerce has gained precedence over historical arguments. Greece supports North Macedonia's application for EU and NATO membership. They opened a pipeline from Thessaloniki to Skopj. The refined oil is shipped north to Kosovo in a second pipeline. Greeks own North Macedonia's biggest bank, a leading supermarket chain, and a mobile-phone operation. Both countries are worried about armed Albanian militants, who often maintain close ties with organized crime. Greece's policy in the Balkans is to maintain cordial relations and discreet communication with all groups, including Muslim ones.

Washington gave an assurance that it would recognize any name that is eventually agreed on between the two countries. Greeks objected to North Macedonia's decision to name its main airport after Alexander the Great and to erect on Skopje's main square in 2011 a gigantic 92-foot 30-ton bronze statue that resembles ancient depictions of Alexander the Great.

In 2008 the Greeks delayed North Macedonia's admission to NATO, even though North Macedonia had accepted "Republic of Macedonia (Skopje)." They pointed out that they would accept the name "Macedonia" with an "Upper" or "New" before it.

In January 2019 an agreement was finally reached. In 2018 the two governments agreed on the name "North Macedonia" and on North Macedonia's entry into NATO and the EU. North Macedonia agreed to "claim no relation to the ancient Greek civilization of Macedonia." It held a referendum in September to adopt the deal, but only 37% participated. A two-thirds parliamentary majority accepted it in the face of violent street protests. The deal barely squeaked through the Greek parliament in January 2019. Despite the fact that 70% of Greeks opposed it, the agreement went into effect.

Greeks made a great effort to establish good relations with the new regimes in Bulgaria and Romania. Since entering the EU in 2007, Bulgaria forms Greece's first border with the EU. This is good for trade. Greeks are already among the three largest investors in Bulgaria, Romania, and Serbia, and overall Greek investment in the Balkans is increasing. By 2003, an estimated 3,500 Greek enterprises were active in the broad Balkan area, with investments

Zeus, from Artemision, ca. 450 BC

286

amounting to €4 billion. Greece is now the top foreign investor in Bulgaria, Albania, and North Macedonia. Its banking sector represents 16% of banking activities in the region, and Greek banks open a new branch in a Balkan country almost weekly.

Even in Istanbul there are 50 to 60 Greek companies, up from 3 or 4 only a decade ago. Companies in Greece are increasingly transferring manufacturing operations to the lower-wage Balkan countries. Average per-capita income in the Balkans is less than one-fifth the level in Greece. The Greek vision is an integrated and open Balkan market of 65 million people, with its own economy in the lead. Its trade with southeastern European countries more than doubled between 1996 and 2005. In short, it is the region's business center.

Greece is strengthening its relations with the Black Sea countries and Russia. In 2007 it signed a long-delayed agreement with Russia and Bulgaria to construct an oil pipeline by 2011 to convey Russian crude oil from Burgas on Bulgaria's Black Sea coast 175 miles (280 km) to Alexandroupolis in northern Greece. Russia holds 51% of the shares, with Greece and Bulgaria each holding 24.5%. Since this deal excluded Turkey, Ankara was not pleased.

In July 2005 the Greek and Turkish prime ministers had launched a landmark cooperative project to build a natural gas pipeline connecting the two countries. Inaugurated in November 2007, it carries natural gas from Azerbaijan 170 miles (295 km) through Anatolia in Turkey to Thrace in Greece beneath the Marmara Sea and eventually underneath the Adriatic Sea to Italy. This project highlights the American role in encouraging Greece and Turkey to reduce dependence on Russian energy supplies by tapping Caspian Sea resources. Their electric grids were linked by 2007. Construction of the continuing undersea gas pipeline between Greece and Italy began in 2008. In the same year, Greece formally agreed to host a section of Russia's South Stream gas pipeline, thereby furthering Greece's goal to be a regional transport hub for oil and gas shipments to Europe.

Athens utilized its traditionally close ties with Serbia to try to mediate a settlement to the bloody war in Bosnia. This effort led to friction with Turkey, against which Greece and Serbia share a historical antipathy. Greece forbade Turkish planes from flying over its airspace on their way to helping NATO enforce a no-fly zone over Bosnia. It refused in 1994 to endorse NATO ultimatums against Bosnian Serbs or to participate in any military action in Bosnia. In 1995 Turkey used its veto to prevent the establishment of a NATO rapid-deployment headquarters in Thessaloniki and a land and air headquarters in Larissa.

Greece welcomed the Bosnian peace agreement in 1995 and the lifting of UN trade sanctions against Serbia and Montenegro, which had hurt the Greek economy. It agreed to send a contingent of 1,000 troops to join NATO's multinational peacekeeping force in Bosnia, and it donated $7 million in reconstruction funds. In 1997 it put pressure on the Serb president to recognize opposition victories in local elections.

Albania presents a special problem. In 1987 Greece had officially ended the state of war with Albania and had sent the first cabinet-level delegation since 1940. In 1991 Mitsotakis became the first Greek prime minister to visit Tirana. Since 1994 Greece has been the largest investor in Albania. The partial opening of its borders resulted in thousands of ethnic Greeks from a part of Albania called North Epirus and other parts of Albania fleeing to Greece. After decrying their plight for decades, Greece could hardly shut them out.

In 1993, after some 300,000 Albanians had poured into Greece, the breaking point was reached. With illegal immigrants being blamed for rising crime and lowering wage rates, anti-Albanian sentiment prompted the government to try to detain and expel the estimated half-million Albanians who entered Greece illegally in the three previous years. Deportations of Albanians began in 1993, and there was some frighteningly loose talk in Greece about autonomy for the Greek minority in North Epirus. Albania retaliated by cutting the number of Greek-language schools. Rarely had Greece's relations with Albania been worse.

A tentative rapprochement was reached in 1995, when Greek police arrested members of the Greek terrorist North Epirus Liberation Front, and the foreign minister visited Tirana. But when Albania later rejected Greece's request for the establishment of three Greek schools in southern Albania, Athens suspended the planned signing of an agreement on employment opportunities for the estimated 150,000 illegal Albanians residing in Greece. In 1997 Greece sent a sizable peacekeeping contingent to Albania as a part of a multinational force to restore public order. To demonstrate impartiality, its troops were not deployed in the south, where the Greek ethnic minority is concentrated. Athens also opened new border crossings and increased its economic assistance to the small, destabilized neighbor. In 2009 the two countries signed an agreement delineating the continental shelf and maritime borders in the Ionian Sea.

Today 10% of Greece's population are immigrants, most of them legal. About 130,000 immigrant children are enrolled in Greek schools. Greece announced in 2006

that it would open its doors to workers from all the new EU member states.

In 2001 Greece conducted a vast drive to register hundreds of thousands of illegal immigrants, nearly all from Albania, so that they could acquire the proper papers and live and work without fear of deportation. Most have residence permits, which they can lose if they lose their employment. There are about 1.5 million immigrant workers in Greece, over half of them (58%) Albanian. The approximately 800,000 Albanian immigrants mostly work on farms and construction sites and in services. Until the economic crisis from 2008, they sent an estimated €1 billion back home in the form of remittances; by 2012 that had fallen by half. Even though they have integrated rather well, with most of their children speaking better Greek than Albanian, they find it difficult to gain acceptance.

The hardships they face were described in a best-selling book written by an Albanian immigrant and journalist, Gazmend Kapllani, *A Small Diary of Borders*. He regrets that only a handful of Albanians, those considered to be of Greek origin, are granted Greek citizenship. The children of immigrants born in Greece are not entitled to citizenship.

Russia is home to about a half-million Pontians, who are of Greek origin, having once lived along the southern coast of the Black Sea, which the ancient Greeks called "Pontos." Few of them speak modern Greek. By 1991 about 25,000 of them had found their way to Greece. They are a resourceful people who had already become masters of survival in the Soviet Union. Nevertheless, there were some protests against their being resettled in Thrace, one of Greece's poorest areas.

Other immigrant waves came from Bulgaria, Romania, Ukraine, Georgia, Pakistan, Russia, Moldova, Turkish Kurdistan, and Poland. By 2009 Greeks' hospitality was wearing thin, as unwanted immigrants from countries like Pakistan, Afghanistan, Iraq, Sudan, and Somalia washed ashore via Turkey. In 2008 more than 146,000 illegal immigrants arrived, up from 100,000 the year before and with no sign of abating in the years that followed.

Uncontrolled immigration overwhelms Greece at a time of extreme economic distress. Reception facilities are too small, too few, and understaffed, and they became overrun. In 2011 the European Court of Human Rights ruled them so squalid that they violated the prohibition on "torture or inhuman or degrading treatment." An estimated 300,000 illegals were already in Greece, and they kept coming. There was a backlog of over 60,000 asylum applicants. Only 1% were accepted (although 11% gained that status upon appeal).

Mount Lycabettus, Athens

Greece had become the gateway of choice for the overwhelming majority (80%) of migrants trying to reach the EU. In 2016–2017 more than 1 million migrants passed through, and 62,000 were trapped in Greece, which is stretched to the limit to cope with them. The numbers were reduced by an EU-Turkish agreement to curb human smuggling. Most entered from Turkey, which removed visa restrictions for North Africans. Making the problem even more complicated is the rule that illegal immigrants found anywhere in the EU must be returned to the country of entry, usually Greece. The EU agreed to send a team of armed guards to help Greece patrol its border.

When it announced it was going to build a fence along part of its border with Turkey, there was an outcry by immigrant rights groups. Most mines were removed from the border area because some immigrants had stepped on them. But in 2012 the government approved the fence with fixed night-vision cameras. It would cover a 6-mile (10.5 kilometers) dry-land break in the Evros River, where most immigrants cross the border. While most want to proceed to other richer EU countries via Hungary, many end up in Athens, often sleeping rough. Few can find jobs, and some turn to crime. They stir strong anti-immigrant feelings, and right-wing extremists, such as Golden Dawn, sometimes attack them. The EU has paid Greece to house migrants while their asylum claims are processed.

In 1999 Greece found itself in a difficult situation when NATO launched an air war against Serbia in an effort to stop ethnic cleansing in predominantly Muslim Kosovo. Greek leaders had been friendly to Serb strongman Slobodan Milosevic in the past. Most Greeks are fiercely pro-Serb, as are most of the country's newspapers and TV stations. Both nations are Orthodox Christian, and Greek churchmen are not shy about stirring up emotions against Muslims, although the church as a whole is not anti-Muslim. But the government decided that Greece's wider interests—closer ties with western Europe and joining the euro—required that it support NATO.

As the alliance's sole Balkan country at the time, Athens said it could not join an attack against a neighbor. However, its airbases provided logistical help for AWACS surveillance flights over Yugoslavia, and it permitted supplies to pass through its port of Thessaloniki. Also, its good relations with Belgrade enabled Greece to be the only NATO country that could actively support such non-governmental organizations as the Red Cross inside Kosovo. Simitis distanced his country from Serbia's leaders while improving relations with the

In traditional costumes of their region, young men from Crete perform a line dance.

rest of the Balkan countries. Greece sent 1,000 peacekeeping troops to Kosovo.

Following Milosevic's fall from power in October 2000, Foreign Minister George Papandreou was the first EU minister to meet Yugoslavia's new president, Vojislav Kostunica, and stressed that Europe must seize the opportunity to transform the Balkans from a crisis region to one of stability and democracy. To put its money where its mouth is, Greece pledged $455 million over five years for Balkan reconstruction. Speaking in the European Parliament, Kostunica asserted that Greece was Yugoslavia's "window to the outside world." Greece now views the Balkans more from a commercial standpoint than from a strategic one. Their hope is that the oil flows and shopping trips and cross-border business deals will help prevent a renewal of armed conflict.

Greek-Turkish Hostility in the Aegean

Greece insists that its airspace extends 10 miles around each island rather than 6 miles, which Turkey recognized. Also, now that there are proven oil reserves in the Aegean, Greece is determined to maximize its economic rights on the continental shelf. Each country claims that the Aegean is a part of its continental shelf, and Turkey questions Greece's possession of the eastern Aegean Sea. Actually, both have shown noteworthy restraint in the past, accepting a 6-mile offshore limit in the Aegean, compared with the internationally accepted 12 miles. An exception occurred in August 2020 when Greek and Turkish frigates collided in disputed waters after a clumsy maneuver.

When Turkey occupied northern Cyprus in 1974, many Greeks asked, "What

good is NATO to us if it cannot prevent the Turks from invading Cyprus or from threatening Greek interests in the Aegean?" Cyprus remains an issue, although both Turkey and Greece supported a UN effort in 2004 to overcome the island's division. Pending a future settlement that satisfies a majority of both Turkish and Greek-Cypriots, 35,000 Turkish troops will still occupy 37% of the island, although the Turkish minority comprises only 18% of the population.

In 2005 Greece supported France's objection to the opening of accession talks between Turkey and the EU until Turkey formally recognizes Greek Cyprus and opens its ports to Cypriot-flagged shipping, something that Ankara resists. Prime Minister Karamanlis increased the pressure by postponing his planned visit to Turkey. Accession talks began anyway. While continuing their demands on Turkey, most Greeks desire to see it pursuing peace and respectability through the EU. Ever since Turkey became a candidate for the EU, both Greece and Cyprus have sharply reduced their defense spending.

Greece focused on extracting NATO guarantees against possible Turkish incursions in the area. This was a guarantee that NATO was understandably unprepared to make against a fellow member. Greece also turned to the Americans to secure a more precise formulation of a vaguely worded guarantee that former secretary of state Henry Kissinger had given in 1976 that the US would not stand idly by if either Greece or Turkey attempted to resolve their disputes by force. This was a delicate request for the US The Americans hinted that they might be prepared to give Greece a firmer

guarantee if it would first try to mend its fences with Turkey.

At NATO's 1997 summit, the American secretary of state got the Greek prime minister and Turkish president to endorse a broad declaration of good neighborly relations in a nonaggression pact. But they rejected Washington's requests to cancel military maneuvers in sensitive areas. Instead they engaged in dogfight challenges over the Aegean, violated a moratorium on military overflights of Cyprus, and steered so closely to each other that two naval vessels nearly collided close to the Turkish coast. Nevertheless, in 1997 Mesut Yilmaz became the first Turkish prime minister to visit Greek territory since 1988. The occasion was the first summit of Balkan leaders since the breakup of Yugoslavia. The meeting was hosted by the Greeks on the island of Crete and ended with a pledge to work together to ease tensions. The Greek and Turkish prime ministers took the opportunity to hold private talks.

In the months before the dawning of the 21st century, an almost-miraculous change in popular attitudes occurred in both Greece and Turkey. After the Turkish prime minister asked Greece to endorse a bilateral agreement on combating terrorism, the PASOK government decided to drop long-standing objections to engaging in direct negotiations with Ankara.

Then a mutual disaster occurred. An earthquake struck Turkey on August 17, 1999, killing at least 15,000 people. Greek nongovernmental organizations rushed blankets, clothing, and medical supplies to the stricken region, while Greek families on Greek islands off the Turkish coast offered to host children made homeless by the quake. Three weeks later a terrible earthquake struck Athens, killing 140. The Turks instantly sent rescue teams. The television images of Turks searching for Greeks trapped in the rubble stirred deep emotions that laid the foundation for undreamed-of rapprochement and optimism that the two nations could cooperate with each other.

The fruits were quick to come. In December Greece supported Turkey's candidacy for the EU, and Ankara subsequently announced that it backed Greece's efforts to recover the Parthenon (Elgin) Marbles from Britain. George Papandreou became the first Greek foreign minister to visit Turkey in almost four decades, and in 2000 Prime Minister Simitis accepted an invitation to become the first Greek head of government to visit Turkey since the late 1950s. The two countries tackled numerous "soft issues," reaching agreements on such matters as tourism, commerce, the environment, combating organized crime and terrorism, and preventing illegal immigration. They set up a joint

Greece

Greek-Turkish team to handle disaster relief. After their newly acquired habits of cooperation had been strengthened, they confronted the truly divisive problem of Cyprus in 2004, and they are doing so also in the Aegean.

A positive signal had been given in 2000, when, for the first time in more than 20 years, Turkish marines were permitted to land in Greece during NATO exercises in the Aegean. Defense ministers from both countries met in Greece for the first time to discuss how to cut military spending. At the beginning of a 17-day NATO exercise in 2000 designed to showcase the new era of friendship between Greece and Turkey, Greek military planes landed in Turkey for the first time in 28 years. Greek frigates also called on a Turkish port. By 2006 both sides were busy implementing confidence-building measures, including a telephone hotline between both countries' military forces, avoidance of military exercises in the Aegean during the tourist season, and cooperating on air-sea rescue training.

But then an old controversy broke out that seriously set back the two nations' year-long attempt to improve their relations. Turkey objected to Greek flights over the Greek islands of Lemnos and Ikaria in the Aegean. Turkey considers the islands to be demilitarized zones, whereas Greece denies that there are any such international agreements. Greece maintains a large military presence on Lemnos, and Turkey has always claimed that Greece has no right to do so. Greece immediately withdrew from the maneuvers. To make matters worse, Russian-made antiaircraft missiles locked on to Turkish planes that flew close to the Greek-controlled part of Cyprus. Although Greeks did see in the crisis a danger of war, NATO's former supreme commander General Joseph W. Ralston was called in to help broker a truce, and the other allies were relieved that the dispute had not led to war.

The rapprochement at the highest level continues, pushed especially by two ex–foreign ministers, George Papandreou and Ismail Cem. In 2001 they strolled together down the streets of Kusadasi, Turkey, and planted an olive tree near the ruins of an ancient temple; they agreed to clear land mines from their common borders; they decided to bid jointly to host the European soccer championships in 2008. Papandreou made an unprecedented overture during a visit to Ankara in 2001 to discuss with Turkish leaders the possibility of mutually agreed defense cuts. In 2002 they traveled together to Israel and the West Bank to offer their joint help in the search for peace and to show that traditional foes can choose a "different path."

They signed an agreement to build a pipeline to transport central Asian and Iranian natural gas through Turkey to a Greek port and then on to western Europe. Christo Doulakis became the first Greek finance minister to visit Turkey, and Greece no longer blocks Turkey's EU application. This consensus among Greeks and their government in supporting the warming of ties with Turkey and a just and lasting settlement of the Cyprus problem prompted ex–foreign minister Molyviatis in 2005 to call the present "the golden age of Greek diplomacy." In January 2008 Costas Karamanlis became the first Greek prime minister to make an official visit to Turkey since his uncle did it 49 years earlier.

The improvement of the diplomatic climate is not irreversible. There are many festering disputes, including Cyprus, seabed exploration rights, territorial waters, and airspace rights. In May 2006 two of their F-16 fighters collided in midair as they shadowed each other in disputed Aegean airspace near the island of Karpathos. The Greek pilot was killed. Dogfights over the Aegean continue. Trade and investment have remained limited, even though cross-border trade doubled from 2002 to 2006, and an increasing number of foreign tourists pass from the Greek islands to the Turkish coast.

But the policy of reconciliation continued under ex–prime minister Karamanlis and his successor, George Papandreou. The latter's first visits abroad as prime minister were to Istanbul and Cyprus. He said; "We must free Cyprus of the walls that have no place in the EU." He told Turkish prime minister Recep Erdogan; "We have proved we want good relations with Turkey, and we support her European course." But, he continued, Turkey "must also take the steps required by the EU so that the accession course can move forward." Erdogan made a return visit to Athens in May 2010, and the two countries signed 21 agreements. Due to Greece's severe financial crisis, it is cutting its defense operational expenses by 25%, and this appears less threatening to Turkey. There are good grounds for confidence that their differences will be settled peacefully.

Terrorism

The November 17 Movement, Greece's deadliest terrorist group, claimed responsibility for a spate of attacks against US targets, including the murder of four American officials, an antitank rocket blast at a Citibank branch in 1998, and bombings of tourist sites in 1999 in protest of the NATO bombing of Yugoslavia. Since 1975 it killed 23 persons, starting with CIA Athens station chief Richard Welch

and continuing in 2000 with the daylight murder of the British defense attaché at a spot along a busy Athens street where US Navy captain George Tsantes and his driver had been murdered in 1983. Most of its victims are Greeks, usually political conservatives.

American intelligence and law enforcement experts widely suspected that the Socialist government tolerated November 17 because the group's overtly leftist and nationalist standpoints and strident anti-Americanism resonate with many Greeks. Its ideology had evolved from hard-core Marxism to nationalism and antiglobalization. Until 2002 not a single November 17 member had ever been arrested. When suspects were picked up, they were treated leniently. In 1999, for example, a woman was caught attempting to firebomb the US consulate in Thessaloniki. After a few days' detention and a small fine, she was released.

In 2002 Greek police made a rapid-fire series of raids arresting leading members of the November 17 terrorist group, named after the date in 1973 when soldiers and tanks crushed student-led protests in Athens. Known for its fanatical secrecy and ruthless precision, the organization had completely outwitted authorities during a 27-year spate of murders, robberies, and bombings. The break came after a botched bombing attempt on June 29, 2002, left an injured terrorist on the scene who revealed information to the police that led to the sudden raids throughout Greece.

The captured operatives included an unassuming shopkeeper (Nikos Papanastasiou); a hospital telephone operator (Pavlos Serifis), who was accused of being the group's second in command; and a translator of French texts, Alexandros Giotopoulos, whom Serifs fingered as the gunman who killed the CIA Athens station chief Richard Welch in 1975. That was the assassination that initially attracted attention to the terrorist organization. Also arrested were a bus driver, a religious icon painter, and an elementary school teacher. Since the Welch murder, the group claimed responsibility for 22 more victims (including three Americans), the latest being the British defense attaché Brigadier Stephen Saunders in June 2000.

In September 2002 Greece's most wanted man, Dimitris Koufodinas, walked into an Athens police station and announced that November 17 was "finished." A series of revelations led to weapons stashes in Athens apartments. In March 2003 what the Greek press called the "trial of trials" began in a specially protected maximum-security courtroom in the country's largest prison, where the leaders of the 1967–1974 junta had been tried. The court rejected the suspects' charges that their crimes were political, not criminal, and it forbade TV coverage of the lengthy trial.

Even for prisoners condemned to multiple life sentences, Greek law permits a maximum sentence for murder of only 25 years, with the right to apply for conditional release after only 20. In the trial that lasted until November 2003, the suspects faced 2,000 charges. Guilty verdicts were rendered against 15 of the 19 members of the November 17 terrorist group. Four were acquitted for lack of evidence. The leader, Alexandros Yiotopoulos, got 21 life terms, the heaviest penalty in Greek legal history, and Dimitris Koufodinas got 13 life terms. The remaining 13 received sentences ranging from eight years to life. Many were disappointed that the trials did not shed more light on the group itself and why it was able to act with impunity for 27 years.

The US must spend more on diplomatic security in Greece than almost anywhere else in the world. The State Department's annual report in 2000, *Patterns of Global Terrorism*, placed Greece second only to Colombia in the number of terrorist attacks. In 2007 the far-left Revolutionary Struggle fired an antitank grenade into the heavily fortified American embassy. When claiming responsibility, the group blamed US policy in Iraq and the Middle East. There were no injuries and little damage, but the attack underscored continued anti-American sentiment and the potential for more homegrown terror.

The US was spared by an elaborate letter-bomb plot in November 2010 that targeted foreign embassies in Athens, as well as the French president and German chancellor in their capitals. It was the work of a domestic terrorism group known as the Conspiracy of Cells of Fire, which seeks to inspire an uprising against the Greek capitalist state.

There were serious concerns about terrorist violence during the 2004 summer Olympics in Athens. They embarrassed the government of former prime minister Simitis, which strove to convince the other EU countries that Greece is a well-run, law-abiding country. He agreed to a reorganization of the antiterrorism police and to new antiterrorist cooperation with the US, UK and EU. The government also hoped that the trial would reassure the world that it could deal effectively with any kinds of terrorists who might threaten the 2004 summer Olympic Games, in which a record 202 nations participated. They were the first to take place since the September 11 terrorist attacks in the US and a particular worry following the March 11, 2004, Islamic militant attack in Madrid that killed 192 persons.

The government allotted $1.2 billion for security during the games, more than three times the amount spent four years earlier in Sydney, Australia. Security was coordinated by Greek authorities and by a seven-member intelligence advisory group that included the US, UK, France and Israel. The FBI and CIA were directly involved in the planning, and the US Department of Energy supplied millions of dollars' worth of radiation detectors to deal with "dirty bombs."

Greece asked NATO for help and received pledges of 24-hour air surveillance by AWACS aircraft. US battleships patrolled offshore. The Czechs kept a bio-logical warfare detection battalion on standby for the games. No NATO forces served on Greek soil. For that the Greeks themselves assigned more than 50,000 police, army, and other security personnel. To get ready, 1,500 Greek police officers and soldiers, joined by 400 American special-forces troops and soldiers from other allied nations, held a two-week exercise in March 2004 to train for "catastrophic scenarios." A June 2006 bomb attack on Greece's culture minister by the left-wing Revolutionary Struggle demonstrated that foreigners are not the only targets. No one was hurt.

When terrorists killed 3,000 persons in New York and Washington on September 11, 2001, the Greek government did not waver in its support of America's response to this mortal terrorist threat. It put sympathy ads into six major US newspapers, reading "Greece, the birthplace of democracy, mourns with America at this difficult hour. We have joined with the United States in the fight against terrorism. Our common values of freedom, democracy and humanism will prevail. Together we stand."

Greece provided to the US and its other allies the use of its airspace, air bases, and naval facilities on Crete. It shared intelligence and investigated suspect bank accounts. It offered to replace American peacekeepers in Bosnia and Kosovo (where Greece already had peacekeeping troops) if the US soldiers would have to be withdrawn for service in Afghanistan or elsewhere. It dispatched a naval frigate to patrol the Arabian Sea. Its aircrews were among those of the NATO allies who manned five AWACS reconnaissance aircraft dispatched to the US to help patrol the East Coast; this was the first time since the Revolutionary War that the US needed foreign troops to protect its own territory.

Finally, Greece sent two C-130 transport planes and 128 soldiers (mostly engineers and medical personnel) to Afghanistan to support the war against the Taliban and al Qaeda. In 2005 it deployed a 45-man mobile medical unit, and at the end of the year,

it dispatched 44 air force officers to assume the administration of the Kabul Airport for four months. In late 2008 the Greeks sent a warship to join the inter-national naval effort to defeat piracy off the Somali coast. Nevertheless, Greeks are the only western Europeans who are not granted visa-free travel to the United States.

About 90% of Greeks opposed the US-British war effort in Iraq, but Greece's role as EU president muted the government's criticism of the war. It did permit allied military aircraft to fly over Greek airspace on their way to bomb Baghdad. In 2005 it contributed €300,000 ($390,000) for training Iraqi security forces and military doctors in Greek hospitals. In the aftermath of the August 2006 Lebanese War, it helped more than 13,000 Americans who had to flee the country, and it contributed two naval ships and a Navy Seals unit to the international peacekeeping efforts.

Entry into the EU

Greece joined the EU in a hurry, primarily in order to strengthen democracy but also to benefit the economy. The EU, in contrast to NATO, was popular in Greece, and it is quite lucrative as well. Greece receives handsome annual subsidies from the EU coffers. In the 21st century EU structural aid amounted to more than 1.5% of GDP annually. Greece still lacks the necessary administrative capacity to administer all these funds. In 2005 it had to repay almost €500 million ($650,000) in aid it had misspent; this was the first such instance in EU history.

In 2006 Greece succeeded in securing over €20 billion ($26 billion) through 2013. But these EU funds decreased thereafter because needier new member states have a more urgent claim on them. Greece also receives stern economic warnings and advice from Brussels. This is bitter but needed medicine; aid does not flow to Greece unconditionally.

Greece did not make the most of its first decade in the EU. In 1981 its per-capita GDP was 58% of the EU average, but by 2006 it had risen to 77.3% of the EU average (90% of the eurozone average in 2009). Its citizens were asked to make sacrifices in order to get ready for the European single currency. With a government deficit at 4.2% of GDP in 2017 and a total national debt at 180% by 2017, it did not qualify for the euro on the first round. But it appeared to meet the convergence criteria by 2000, and it was invited to join the eurozone in 2001.

The Greek government had provided false budget deficit figures between 1997 and 2003 that disguised Greece's repeated breaches of the EU budget ceiling. When the European Commission discovered this

Greece

in 2004, it ordered Eurostat, its statistical service, to begin supervising Greece's finances very closely. It admonished the country for widening the budget deficits, recognizing that at least half the overruns in 2004 were due to unexpected cost overruns to finance the Olympic Games.

Brussels showed renewed skepticism in 2006, when Greece changed its method of measuring its economy by including parts of its large black economy, such as prostitution and money laundering. This increased the GDP figure by about 25% and both lowered the budget deficit and the public debt figure. In any case, possessing the euro gave Greece a stronger sense of security and confidence. It also made it easier to borrow money, which it did with abandon. That led Greece into deep financial crisis.

Rescue by the European Union

During the first decade of the 21st century, Greeks had enjoyed a steady increase in their living standards. Wages were rising, pensions were generous, consumers could buy more and more things, and lots of money was in circulation. Thanks to its joining the eurozone, the government could borrow money on the same low terms as economic giant Germany, and it did so freely. Both main parties competed with each other by seeing who could outbid the other in terms of distributing borrowed money to voters in the form of benefits and jobs for life. Tax collection was poor, corruption was rampant, the underground economy was huge, and a

construction bubble was developing. But as long as the good times were rolling, who cared?

As the debts began to come due, people started to take notice. Six weeks after his PASOK Party's election victory on October 4, 2009, George Papandreou went to the EU in Brussels with a woeful admission: Greece's budget deficit was twice as high as it had reported and three times larger (12.7%) than it had promised the European Commission it would be. More than a third of government borrowing was from the European Central Bank via emergency lending. The public debt was rapidly heading toward 160% of GDP. Public finances were a mess.

Papandreou's revelations caused Greece's credit rating to be downgraded to junk status, the first to happen to a eurozone member. The interest rate it had to pay for its international borrowing shot up, while markets in Europe and America were rattled. Greece's economy constitutes only 2.3% of the eurozone's total GDP. But what if Greece defaulted? Nobody knows.

The Greek leader turned to the EU partners for help, and the newly elected president of the European Council Herman Van Rompuy said, "The eurozone will never let Greece fail." Not all partners wanted to join in at first. Germans asked why they should give billions to people who live beyond their means, do not pay their taxes, and retire a decade earlier than Germans do. But all feared "contagion" from the Greek meltdown. Finally, at the end of April 2010, a deal was struck to provide

the Greeks with €110 billion ($145 billion) in loans, €30 billion ($39 billion) of which coming from the IMF. The idea was to give Greece a breathing space of a few years to change their economy and economic culture fundamentally.

In return, the Greek government committed its people to a harsh fiscal retrenchment. Some Greeks fear it will spell the end of the cradle-to-grave state compact. The measures included pension freezes and reform; raised taxes on fuel, alcohol, and cigarettes; a jump of the VAT from 19% to 23%; and a reduction by 30% in employees' bonuses for Easter, summer, and Christmas. Government spending was slashed, including for defense, social security, and government operating expenditures. Only one person would be hired for every five civil servants who retire; one out of four workers is now employed by the state. Bonuses for private bank managers would be taxed at a rate of 90%. Tax exemptions would be abolished, tax collection performed more energetically, and the gigantic underground economy (comprising from 12% to a fourth of GDP) forced into the open. Labor reform would make it easier to fire workers. The goal was to bring the budget deficit down to 3%. Parliament accepted these changes.

The IMF demanded that Greece do something about Hellenic Railways, which loses €3 million ($3.9 million) a day, more than $1 billion each year. Conductors earn up to $130,000 per year, often driving empty trains. Its total debt is $13 billion, or 5% of GDP. Greece must now see that this debt, along with the off-balance-sheet obligations of other state-owned enterprises, be included in the country's official debt.

Greece must also increase its economy's competitiveness and dynamism. An important step would be to open up the approximately 70 professions that are protected from competition. They include pharmacists, lawyers, engineers, architects, taxi and truck drivers, welders, notaries, street market venders, and newsstand operators. They all require expensive limited licenses, and they charge fixed prices. One Greek economist said, "Greece is the last Soviet-style economy in Europe." The country must reduce the powers of unions and eliminate patronage, for which the two main parties became dispensing machines.

The average retirement age is 61.5 years (eurozone average: 61.2), but about 14% fall into an early retirement category of age 50 for women and 55 for men. Among the 560 job categories qualifying for early retirement, there are some dangerous jobs, such as coal mining and bomb disposal. But they also include hair dressers (who have to deal with dangerous chemicals) TV and radio presenters (whose microphones

Altar boys in Serres

may have bacteria on them), and musicians playing wind instruments (who can get gastric reflux when they blow).

Many Greeks believe that the EU's and IMF's intervention into Greek affairs was tantamount to "a partial surrender of sovereignty." They staged strikes and went into the streets to protest the long-term austerity to which their country had been committed. On one hot day, three bank workers were killed when a gasoline bomb burned down their building. Despite the obvious unpopularity of the austerity measures, 64% of respondents considered the measures "necessary." However, 57% thought they would probably be insufficient to overcome the crisis. They were right.

Some economists fear that the economic medicine could plunge Greece into a depression and kill the patient. Some doubt that the reform is sustainable and suspect that Greeks lack the political will to do what is needed. What makes this crisis different from earlier ones is that the stakes have never been higher. Public support for the austerity became increasingly hostile in July 2011 as parliament considered and finally narrowly adopted budget cuts, new taxes, privatization, and reforms. They were necessary to qualify for the next vital round of European Commission/IMF/European Central Bank (troika) bailout funds to avoid defaulting on Greece's unsustainable debt, which climbed to 180% of GDP in 2017.

Hundreds of protestors camped out in Syntagma Square to keep up the pressure on the government; a general strike and violent protests indicated that some Greeks think the old days of living well on borrowed money can return if only they shout loudly enough. Many blame Germany for the austerity they must now practice. Chancellor Angela Markel's six-hour visit in October 2012 was the first by a major European leader since the debt crisis began in 2009. She was greeted by 40,000 protestors carrying banners reading "Out with the Fourth Reich" and "Angela, You Are Not Welcome!" A squad of made-up Nazis atop a jeep waved the swastika and gave her the Hitler salute. A spokesman for the right-wing party Independent Greeks asserted, "We have scores to settle with Ms. Merkel. Her policies are destroying Greece." Protesters surrounded a German diplomat in Salonika in the north and poured coffee and bottles of water on him.

Many are protesting against the entire political class that has gotten their country into this mess. But disaster would befall Greece if nothing were done: Public- and private-sector wages would plummet even farther, its banks would crash, and it would be kept out of the world debt markets for years. In the midst of all this,

Greece assumed the EU's rotating presidency in the first half of 2014.

Greece has had unstable government ever since. Syriza sailed to election victory in January 2015. However, it ran into a brick wall afterward in trying to persuade the troika and German government to renegotiate the terms of the bailout and write down at least half of Greece's debt. Europe is left with agonizing questions: Can Greece avoid austerity? How? Will it leave the euro (which four out of five Greeks want to keep)? If so, how and when would that happen? Would other Mediterranean countries follow? How would the EU be affected? Can it survive? Nobody knows. While wrestling with these problems, Greece faced one of the most serious crises in EU history: an overwhelming flood of refugees from the Middle East.

ECONOMY

Herodotus wrote almost 2,500 years ago, "Greece always has poverty for a mate." After Portugal, it is the poorest country in western Europe; more than 15% of Greeks live below the poverty level defined by the EU. It is always tempting to use western European standards when analyzing the Greek economy. In one sense, this is appropriate because many Greeks do, in fact, want to share western life and values. But it must be remembered that Greece is geographically isolated from the rest of western Europe and is Mediterranean and Balkan in character, as well as western European.

Greece has undeniably changed greatly since the 1940s, when foreign occupation and a destructive civil war stood in the way of economic improvement. In the 1950s it began to experience an economic boom, and from 1964 to 1975, it had an annual growth rate of over 10%. Between 2000 and 2006, that rate was over 4%, fueled by Olympic construction projects. From 2007 to 2012, in the midst of the global recession, its economy shrank by a fifth. By 2021 it was growing at an annual rate of 3.5%. Personal consumption rose almost as spectacularly, and improvements in living standards were visible. Half of the Greek families living in the cities own their own homes, and the figure is even higher in the countryside.

This is one of those countries in which real earnings and the actual standard of living are higher than official statistics would indicate. The secret lies partly in the flexibility and resilience of the Greeks and in the tightly knit family, which is marked by hard work, saving for the future, and the drive to get ahead.

It also lies partly in the extensive "underground" economy. It has almost become

the norm for Greeks to hold down second and even third jobs, for which persons are paid in a way that goes unnoticed by the tax collectors and statisticians. It has been estimated that the underground economy may constitute 12% to 25% of Greece's GDP. Greece is a cash-based society, with much work done without invoices and receipts. This thriving underground economy is one reason more and more foreign refugees and mostly illegal migrant workers were immigrating to Greece, especially from Poland and the Philippines.

Shipping

Ever since Jason and the Argonauts sailed away to find the Golden Fleece, Greece has been the world's leader in shipping. Today it has the largest merchant fleet in the world owned by one group of nationals—16.5% of the world's merchant fleet is Greek-owned. About three-fourths of the ships fly the Liberian, Cypriot, Maltese, or Panamanian flags for reasons of legal convenience. Most owners are based in Athens, and they invested so much in new ships that 612 of a total of 3,700 Greek ships were new in 2007. For the first time, the average age of its ships fell below the world average of 14.4 years. Greeks own two-thirds of the EU's total merchant fleet and half of its tonnage. Greece was therefore given the chairmanship of the EU shipping committee.

Shipping is a vital part of the economy, providing about 114,000 jobs. It is estimated that 1 family out of 11 is directly or indirectly dependent upon shipping for its livelihood. After tourism, it is the country's top foreign exchange earner and has helped to alleviate Greece's chronic balance of payments deficits. Names like Onassis, Niarchos, Goulandris, and John Spiros Latsis are inextricably identified with this entire industry. The tax-free

Greece

status of shipping magnates is enshrined in the constitution.

Until the global recession in 2009, Greek shipping reaped handsome profits from delivering China's growing raw material imports. Greek ferries transport more than 10 million passengers a year. Recruiting can be a problem. Greek law requires that all captains be Greek nationals, and most personnel must be Greek or EU citizens. The rise in living standards on the mainland and islands have made the seaman's life of loneliness, long absences from families (the average time away is seven months), and the danger from storms less attractive. Greece's 10 training academies produce too few officers to man the ships. Therefore, shipowners are compelled both to pay extremely high wages and benefits, at EU levels. But they may hire more than 25% of their crews from outside of Greece, especially from Asia, and pay them less.

Tourism, Immigration, and Industry

Its ancient ruins, beautiful beaches, and almost-perpetual sunshine, combined with the people's well-deserved reputation for hospitality and friendliness, have long made Greece a favorite tourist land. It welcomed 16.4 million tourists in 2011, more than the total Greek population. One-third come from Germany and the UK. An increasing number of Russians

(1 million annually) are coming. Crete is the most popular destination, with more than 2.2 million visitors each year. It ranks among the top 15 tourist destinations in the world. Tourists leave large amounts of their currencies behind by the time they depart, 18% of GDP. Tourism is Greece's largest source of foreign currency and its biggest industry, employing a tenth of the population, or a fifth of the workforce.

But there are problems with tourism. It is seasonal, so many facilities are not used in the off-season. It is vulnerable to a recession, such as the global downturn beginning in late 2008. It fell by 10% in 2009, and bookings continued to fall sharply in 2012. Many tourists are scared off by protests, strikes, and street violence caused by the recession. Further, it tends to be concentrated in Athens and the islands, which become terribly overcrowded in the high season. Efforts to encourage tourists to visit less-frequented places, particularly northern Greece, have not been successful. Since the arrival of the euro, Greece has lost its price-competitiveness compared with its Mediterranean rivals. Turkey, with beautiful beaches, friendly people, low prices, and almost as many ancient Greek ruins as Greece itself, is luring precisely the kinds of middle-class tourists as is Greece. Only 2% of tourists are Americans.

Finally, Greece lies close to the Arab world. This has scared some tourists away. As the 1991 Gulf War showed, Greece is very sensitive to travel advisories issued by the US government. Not until 2006 did the government decide to allow foreign investors to build large new resorts with world-class accommodations and golf and other sports facilities.

An increasingly prosperous Greece has a growing number of immigrants, who number about 1.5 million working in the country. Including their families, at least 1 million residents in Greece were born elsewhere. Most live around Athens, and many of them perform many jobs Greeks no longer want to do, such as hard farm labor. Thus the economy could hardly function without them. That is why changes in the law resulted by 2006 in more than 400,000 immigrants acquiring work and residence permits and joining the social security system.

Their presence in such large numbers is a considerable challenge to what is called "Greekness," everything that has to do with Greek culture, language, and history. The number of immigrant children in Greek schools had risen by 2006 to over 130,000. In 2006 Greece opened its doors to workers from all the new EU member states. However, citizenship remains severely restricted. Law requires that illegal migrants arrested by the police be released within three months. Those denied asylum are released with a deportation order, and most of those go underground or move elsewhere in the EU.

Traditionally Greece has been relatively tolerant of foreigners. But in the early 1990s, the country lost control of its borders, and hundreds of thousands of people poured over its frontiers. Some of them brought with them unwelcome problems, such as organized crime and illegal trafficking in women and children for the sex industry. The same applies to Cyprus, which is located less than 40 miles from the shores of Turkey, Syria, and Lebanon. The furious debate ignited by proposals to build a mosque in Athens in time for the 2004 Olympic Games showed just how sensitive the issue of accommodating outsiders is. There are at least 100,000 Muslims in or around Athens. Their presence taps into lingering resentments against Turks, with whom many associate Islam. Parliament had authorized a mosque for Athens in 2001, but not until 2006 were actual plans for constructing such a place of worship announced.

As measured by its employment structure, the Greek economy has become more modern: 70% of its workforce is engaged in the services sector, producing 82% of GDP, and 16.7% is employed in industry, creating 14% of GDP. Manufacturing is

A Greek newspaper reports on the London bombing of the Queen's Horse Guards

concentrated primarily in small, artisan industries. The average number of workers is 45, but about 95% have fewer than 10 workers, and about 80%, fewer than 4. Only companies producing basic metals, tobacco, paper, textiles, chemicals, and petrochemicals are in the medium to large-scale category. The 100 largest Greek companies combined do not approach the size of General Motors.

By EU standards Greek production methods are often antiquated, and the management style is more appropriate to small, artisan, family businesses than to modern, aggressive ones. These are all too often one-man shows, in which the family head runs almost everything and is very hesitant to delegate authority. One result is lower productivity than elsewhere in the EU. For example, manufacturing exports per capita are only about 4% that of the EU average.

Another problem with Greek industry is that it tends to be heavily concentrated in the Athens-Piraeus and Thessaloniki areas. About 30% of the Greek population, 40% of all enterprises, and 50% of the total labor force producing half of the country's GDP are located in and around Athens, a sprawling megalopolis of 3.2 million. The capital is growing by 100,000 each year, despite the problems of smog (primarily from 1 million motor vehicles), high rents, poor sanitation, and traffic chaos. There was a consensus that the best way of solving the city's traffic and pollution problems was to expand the subway system. Prodded by the Olympic deadline of 2004, much was done to accomplish this. By extending the metro, improving the suburban rail line, and creating a streetcar from the center of Athens to the beaches, traffic has been reduced, and so has pollution.

Although Greece is not highly developed as a whole, it has pollution problems similar to those of many highly industrialized countries, thanks to the fact that its industry is greatly concentrated. For several years the government has tried to do something about this problem. Athens is formally closed to new industry, and permits for modernization or expansion of existing plants are issued only under the condition that there be no further pollution. Also, large investments have been steered to northern Greece, and this area is now the fastest-growing region in terms of population.

The two main trade unions are the General Confederation of Greek Workers (GSEE) and the Civil Servants' Union. Together they represent more than 2.5 million workers and had traditionally been under the thumb of the government, which gave unions their money and usually managed to get their men installed in union leadership. Therefore Greek union leaders were almost always conservative.

Former prime minister Andreas Papandreou allowed the unions to finance themselves through members' dues and thereby gave them more independence from the state. Also, strikes became easier by eliminating such restrictions as cooling-off periods and by making it more difficult for employers to use the "lockout" response to a strike. The result is that Greece loses the most workdays to strikes among the OECD rich countries: 580 per 1,000 employees per year, compared with 197 for Spain, 113 for Italy, 16 for France, 5.3 for Germany, and 2.4 for Austria.

Both their ability to disrupt daily life and the limits to their influence on the government were shown from 2008 to 2010, when they repeatedly created labor unrest to protest the government's plans to reform the fragmented pay-as-you-go pension system and the EU-mandated austerity and reform program. It is one of the most generous in the EU and also so underfunded in a country with the EU's fastest-aging population that it would go bankrupt if unreformed.

Agriculture

Greek agriculture has always been limited by the facts that the land is 80% mountainous, the soil is rocky, and the climate is dry. Only 28% of the land is arable. Greece has the lowest proportion of forest cover of any EU country. That is diminishing rapidly because of fire destruction, which by the beginning of the 1990s had already claimed 1.5 million acres (or 4.8% of Greece's total surface area). Despite the massive exodus to the cities during the past three and a half decades, the farm population is still 13% of the total, producing 4% of GDP.

Living standards of Greek farmers have risen. Their frame of mind has also changed considerably in the last quarter-century. They are now outspoken and ready to underscore their protests against low crop prices by blocking roads with their tractors, as they did in January 2009. More than 9,000 tractors blockaded the main roads leading to Athens and to Greece's northern neighbors. The government halted it only by granting €600 million ($780 million) in subsidies the farmers had demanded. They are also far better organized. The government devoted an increasing share of its budget to modernizing agriculture, but Greek farms are still too small and fragmented to be competitive. That is a major reason agriculture produces only 3.8% of GDP. About 12% of the workforce claim to be farmers, but this includes many who have second jobs in the cities or in tourism.

The European Court of Justice gave cheese farmers a boost in 2005 by declaring that only Greece could call the salty, crumbly white cheese sold all over the world "feta."

A further source of foreign exchange has been the remittances sent back to Greece by the close to 1 million Greeks living elsewhere in Europe. The country's fishing industry lands over half of the Mediterranean's total fish catch and employs 10,000 persons in places where there are few alternative job opportunities.

Resources

Greece is not rich in raw materials, but it does mine nickel, bauxite, chrome, zinc, asbestos, and lignite (brown coal). It also has deposits of uranium, gold, and silver. Heretofore it has had very little domestic oil and rapidly became very dependent upon import sources. Fortunately, the Greeks' energy consumption is the lowest per capita in western Europe, mainly because there is little need for heating in the warm climate.

The dry climate prevents a dramatic expansion of hydroelectric power, and the hundreds of scattered islands complicate energy delivery to the far reaches of the country. Greece is nevertheless determined to increase its domestic energy production. With so much sun and coastline, solar and tidal power is a possibility in the distant future. Greeks have been nervous about pressing ahead with plans to construct a nuclear plant that could supply a fifth of the nation's power. The major

Greek student in Warsaw

Greece

reason for their hesitation is that the country is very prone to earthquakes, which could dangerously damage a power plant. With its sizable lignite deposits, it still uses this brown coal for 60% of its electricity generation, despite the negative environmental consequences. Renewable energy (primarily hydroelectricity) accounts for only 12% of its power. It can import harder and cleaner-burning coals to replace the lignite. The goal is to reduce the oil component of electricity from 40% to only 2%.

The greatest hope is that offshore oil extraction can increase. In 1981 Greece began extracting its first barrels of low-quality Aegean crude oil from Prinos, near the holiday resort island of Thasos in northern Greece. Its production is expected to supply from 8% to 10% of oil needs. Promising oil deposits have also been found off the Ionian Islands between Paxoi and Zakinthos, facing Italy. However, the extent to which Greece can use Aegean oil depends upon its ability to settle its differences with Turkey, which also raises conflicting claims in this disputed area. Dependency on imported oil will continue.

Most of Greece's trade is with the EU, the Middle East, and North Africa. While Lebanon was in flames, Athens grew fast as a regional trade center for the Middle East, with many international businesses maintaining regional offices in Athens. However, Greece has not been a Mecca for foreign direct investments. The 2006 World Competitiveness Report ranked Greece 42nd (up from 50th) out of the 60 countries it surveyed. It pointed to several obstacles for investors, including an inefficient bureaucracy, high income and corporate tax rates (cut to 25% in 2007), ill-defined land use, and popular resistance to the idea of foreigners benefiting from the development of Greek assets. The processing of investment applications is slow, and the issuance of licenses and permits, even slower. Many investors lack the patience to wait two years to complete the paperwork.

The Current State of the Economy

The budget deficit has been brought down to a respectable 3.2% in 2021, if one excludes interest payments. Public-sector debt stood at 185% of GDP in 2019. This is the highest in the EU and triple the EU average of 64.2%; it is hard to imagine that it can ever be repaid. Inflation was .2% in 2021, and unemployment declined slightly to 16.7% in 2021. The figure for youth under age 29 is 60%. No wonder many want to emigrate, as 400,000 have done to Germany. Economic growth was 3.5% in 2021.

The economy is in need of radical restructuring, and Greece still has a long way to go to get out of its deep hole of debt and to catch up with the rest of western Europe. Per-capita income was 90% of the eurozone average in 2011, but it is declining as austerity bites. The "new economy" has yet to arrive. Greeks own fewer computers per capita than any other nation in the EU.

There is plenty of bad news for an economy that has shrunk by a quarter since 2008, where a fourth of the workforce is without a job, where incomes have been reduced by a third, where corruption and tax evasion are still rampant, and where 15,000 civil-service jobs have been eliminated. The days are over when civil servants worked less and got higher pay and pensions than the private sector. But there is also positive news. Having received €240 billion ($257 billion) in bailouts since 2010, there is less talk of "Grexit" and default.

Greece received a temporary stimulus by pushing to be ready for the 2004 Olympics. A new metro line and airport in Athens were completed. A new highway around greater Athens was begun, as was a major project to link the Peloponnese to mainland Greece by a bridge. A new highway from the Adriatic to the Turkish border will speed up east–west travel and help tie the two cautious neighbors more closely together. All these projects contributed to the highly successful Olympic Games in 2004. Now Greeks face the difficult decisions of what to do with all their new specialized sports facilities; 21 of the 22 Olympic venues are shuttered, empty, and locked while taxpayers shell out millions in maintenance fees. Some were used temporarily to house tens of thousands of asylum seekers stranded in Greece.

CULTURE

Before the Byzantine Empire fell under the Turkish onslaught, the Greek culture had largely fallen into a state of religiously induced rigidity. Under Turkish domination, cultural life oriented itself more around the simple roots of peasant and shepherd life. That is the reason for the fact that modern Greek culture, with its exotic charm, is strongly shaped by and fused with folklore.

Gazing down from the Acropolis . . . and looking back on the glory of ancient Greece

Greece

Priests and soldiers commemorate the patron saint of Serres.

Literature and Arts

In modern Greek literature, one finds a strong orientation toward folk themes and styles. In the works of its most famous novelist, Nikos Kazantzakis (1883–1957), who was nominated for the Nobel Prize several times, one gains a deep insight into the suffering and the liberation of the Greek people. His novel *Alexis Zorbas*, which was filmed in the 1960s, became an enormous success. Greek music long kept its distance from the western cultural tradition, and this film, as well as *Never on Sunday*, helped introduce to western ears the oriental sound of the bouzouki through the artistry of composers Mikis Theodorakis and Manos Hadjidakis. Greece has produced some leading classical musicians, such as singer Maria Callas and composer Dimitri Mitropoulos. Classical music is rapidly gaining in popularity, and Athens has a new concert hall, the Megaro Mousikis, for presentations of all musical styles.

The lyricist Georgios Seferis (1900–1971) received the Nobel Prize in 1963 for his attempt to synthesize Greek folklore with the western cultural tradition. Odysseus Elytis was also awarded the Nobel Prize for his surrealist poetry. The hope and the suffering of the Greek left during the turmoil and civil wars of the 1930s and 1940s are chronicled by the astoundingly prolific Yannis Ritsos, one of Greece's most popular poets, especially among those who are young and on the political left. A staunch supporter of the Greek communists, he published 86 books of his works in 48 languages, and he reportedly has 40 more ready for publication. Like many contemporary Greek artists, he has had much experience with arrests and exile because of his political activities and writings. This also applied to Mikis Theodorakis, who was an active communist, and to Melina Mercouri, who became the PASOK minister of culture and science. After dying of lung cancer in a New York hospital in 1994, she lay in state at the Athens Cathedral. She effectively shut down the city by attracting 300,000 admirers to line her funeral procession.

Language

Modern Greeks cannot understand the classical Greek language, although the modern dialects do retain some features of that earlier, far more complicated language. Despite the changes over time, the Greeks are the world's only people (except the Chinese) who can look at a 2,500-year-old inscription and recognize it in their own language. A proposal by the education minister in 1987 to restore classical Greek to the higher-education curriculum revived a century-old dispute. Opponents say that teaching two Greek languages would slow down educational reforms, and communists and leftists branded the proposal as reactionary. But classicists responded that even Marx, Engels, and Lenin learned ancient Greek. In 1992, after a 16-year hiatus, ancient Greek was reintroduced in junior high schools.

At present there is one modern Greek language, since Katharevousa is no longer in use. The latter was devised in the 19th century to purify the language as much as feasible and return it to a form at least approximating classical Greek. It was used in the church and for a long time in the administration, courts, elevated literature, and universities. The less formal and simpler Demotiki ("people's language") is exclusively used by 90% of the people. Those who only read it felt like quasi-illiterates whenever they entered those circles where Katharevousa was used. Since the restoration of democracy in 1974, the formal version has lost its privileged position. It was eliminated from the schools as part of a series of educational reforms introduced in 1976. The language used in church liturgy is a mixture of some modern Greek and even more ancient Greek as reformed

Greek students at the College of Europe, Bruges

Greece

A monastery on the Mount Athos Peninsula

during the Hellenistic Age. It is the language in which the Old and New Testaments were written.

Educational System

The school and university systems need improvement. Reform has focused on unblocking the bottleneck leading to the Greek universities. The government traditionally limits the number of openings to anticipated numbers of jobs for graduates. The country must face the problem of ill-equipped schools and universities staffed by poorly paid teachers, who refuse to submit to any form of peer review or commit themselves to higher teaching standards. The universities are safe havens for violent demonstrators, since the police and military are banned from entering the campuses after tanks rammed the gates in Athens in 1973, killing 22. The anniversary is marked every gear by marches that sometimes turn violent.

There are pockets of excellence within the university system, but the state universities tend to be chaotic, highly politicized, ill-adapted to the requirements of the 21st century, and often unprofessional in hiring staff. Surveys show that only 30% of students at the 23 universities attend courses regularly, and the average graduate takes 7.6 years to complete the first degree. Graduation rates are among the EU's lowest. One result is that about 5,000 Greek scientists and professors have gone abroad, mainly to America, to work.

With government hiring frozen and businesses scaling back, young university graduates are seeking better jobs abroad. There is a general sense that they face a blocked society at home. A 2010 poll indicated that 7 out of 10 graduates wanted to work abroad, and 4 out of 10 were actively seeking such employment. Greece sends more students per capita to foreign universities (about 10%) than most other countries, despite free tuition. Britain is the favorite choice, followed by America and Germany.

Some private universities sprang up to fill gaps. But a government effort in 2007 to change the constitution to end the state monopoly on higher education by encouraging private, not-for-profit universities failed. The very idea, along with tightening state funding, making academic standards stricter, and imposing a time limit on completing degrees, sparked prolonged strikes and disturbing street violence in Athens in 2007. Unrest broke out again in 2013, when Athens's two main universities were subject to strikes after their funding had been cut. Exams and classes were cancelled, professors were not allowed to work in their offices or meet their students, and left-wing radicals patrolled the campuses to enforce compliance. Polls showed that 99% of respondents objected to the aggressiveness and vandalism of these riots. Students and teachers seem always to favor the status quo. The government introduced another reform in 2011

that took away from students the right to have a say in electing university administrators and imposed a four-year deadline for completing their first degrees. It also permitted private sponsors to fund scientific research and business and technology programs.

No doubt drawing on his experience in the US, Papandreou proposed that a system of junior colleges be established for those applicants not accepted to the universities. Such reforms inevitably run into opposition by educational bureaucrats and the highly revered professors. Nevertheless, a 1982 Higher Education Law replaced the earlier university system built around a few almighty professors with broader American-style departments. It also created about 2,000 new teaching positions and permits undergraduate representatives to participate in university decision making.

In 1987 two new institutions, the University of the Aegean and Ionian University, opened their doors to all Greek students on many Aegean and Ionian islands. These branch campuses strive both to provide practical education and to revive Greek literary and artistic traditions. The professors are encouraged to live at the university sites. This avoids the problems at mainland provincial universities, where professors often appear only briefly during the week before returning to Athens. Greek student life remains highly politicized, and lecture halls and laboratories are still overcrowded in the metropolitan universities.

Cultural Heritage

**His All Holiness
Ecumenical Patriarch Bartholomew**

Many Greeks are aware that the country's rapid economic growth and modernization have sometimes done violence to Greece's cultural inheritance. This is very much the case with Athens. When it was declared to be the capital of the newly independent Greek nation in 1833, it was "nothing but a pile of filthy ruins," in the words of Austrian historian von Prokesch-Osten, who visited the village at that time. When the German archaeologist Ludwig Ross saw the settlement, which had only 5,000 largely poor inhabitants, he was astonished. "One has difficulty believing that one is in Athens!" The new king, Otto I of Bavaria, brought in noted German architects, such as Leo von Klentze, Ernst Ziller, and Friedrich von Schinkel, who designed and built glittering neoclassical buildings for the city.

Unfortunately most of these buildings fell victim to the construction boom after World War II, a period when there was little interest in conserving the monuments of the past. "Growth" was the consuming reality, and no major city in Europe grew as fast as Athens. At the turn of the last century, it had 120,000 inhabitants. In 1920 it had already 300,000, and by 1950 it had reached 1 million. At the beginning of the 1960s, the number had passed the 2 million mark, and by now greater Athens has almost 5 million inhabitants.

Almost miraculously, there are no slums in Athens, and the crime rate is lower than in any other major European city. But one must live amid countless blocks of unembellished apartment buildings, traffic jams, and noxious clouds of smog, called *nefos* by the Greeks; it is a mixture of smoke, dust, sulphur dioxide, carbon monoxide, and nitrogen oxides produced by industrial discharges and car exhaust gases. Surrounded by mountains, Athens is as vulnerable to air pollution as is Los Angeles and Denver. When it rains, the

sulphur dioxide in the air turns into sulphuric acid that dissolves stone, especially the marble of the city's few remaining monuments.

The previous government tried to make a start at controlling this by limiting the use of high-sulphur oil, but this measure had little effect. It also halted the movement of new industries into the area. Cars with alternating license numbers were banned from the center city, but public transportation was greatly improved in preparation for the 2004 Olympic Games. More trees were planted in order to beautify the dusty cityscape. The pollution problem has been somewhat alleviated since the Olympics. The Parthenon, which dominates Athens's horizon, was linked with the city's other antiquities in a new four-kilometer-long archaeological park to display the capital's magic during the 2004 spectacle.

The remaining classical structures in Athens can almost be counted on the fingers of both hands. The previous and present governments have mounted an all-out effort to save the most precious jewel of classical Greece: the Acropolis in Athens. This monument to man's sense of beauty and proportion has led a tortured existence. It has been battered by wars, earthquakes, and plunder from such varied groups as barbarian invaders and British diplomats. During the Turkish occupation, the temples were converted into mosques and at one point were even used to house the harem of the Turkish commander.

Many of the marble statues and friezes can be seen in the British Museum in London, and the Greek government has formally demanded their return. In 2004 former British foreign minister Robin Cook, supported by 50 MPs, launched "Marbles Reunited," an initiative of British citizens who believe that the Parthenon Marbles should be returned to Athens. British opinion polls in 2003–2004 showed that up to 80% of respondents are in favor of restitution. The Greeks hoped in vain to have them back in time for the 2004 Olympics. On a much smaller scale, the Getty Museum in Los Angeles agreed to return a few ancient Greek artifacts taken illegally out of Greece. Italy returned on permanent loan a chunk of the marbles that Lord Elgin had given to a friend in Sicily on his way back to London.

The four major buildings remaining atop the 512-foot (158 meter) hill now face their most serious challenge: tourists and air pollution. Three million tourists visit the Acropolis each year. They not only marvel and walk upon the stones but also, in a few cases, scratch, pound, or etch their names in the stones. Acid rain is an even more formidable enemy, eating away at the marble. Earlier suggestions to cover the entire Acropolis with a plastic dome

Greece

were rejected as unfeasible. But many original statues are being placed into museums and are replaced on the site by copies. Also, next to the Parthenon, the huge Doric temple that once housed the gigantic statues of the goddess Passas Athena was closed to tourists. Work is now being done on all the temples to strengthen them. By the time the restoration is completed, the 230 restorers will have worked twice as long as the original builders and sculptors in the 5th century BC. One stonemason on the project marveled at his ancient counterparts, "The attention to detail, the huge amount they knew about working marble—it makes you feel you're a beginner."

At one time one could wander and climb unimpeded within this magnificent structure, but now one may view it only from the outside. In anticipation of the eventual return of the Parthenon Marbles, a new state-of-the-art museum opened in June 2009 at the foot of the Acropolis that houses all the sculptures from the temples. It includes a huge, empty space exactly the size of the Parthenon so that the 54 meters of frieze remaining in Athens could be reunited with the other 75 meters in London. This would allow the original sculptures to be seen in relation to each other as they once were. Other sculptures are displayed on the top floor, surrounded by glass walls and roof so that the visitor can look back and forth at the Parthenon while admiring the artworks. The Greeks hope that this spectacular $200 million structure will invalidate the persistent British argument that Athens had no adequate place to display the Parthenon Marbles. They also hope that it will lure visitors back to their museums and archeological sites, whose numbers had declined in the few years before 2009.

Another segment of its heritage it fought hard to bring back to Greece is the Olympic Games, although no one contemplated trying to hold them in the ancient location. The first modern Olympics had been held in Athens in 1896. Greece's hopes to stage the centennial games in 1996 were dashed when Atlanta was picked over Athens. A stunned Melina Mercouri exclaimed, "Coca-Cola has prevailed over the Parthenon!" But jubilant Athenians won their bid to host the 2004 games.

Preparations for the 2004 games were long plagued by slow progress, infighting, sobering cost overruns, and worries about security. One special problem Greeks faced in rushing to finish all the needed construction projects was that builders had to be on the lookout for delicate remnants of the ancient past. When workmen turned up artifacts, work stopped immediately until archaeologists could be dispatched to the site; the artifacts were unearthed, photographed, and documented;

the information was passed on to the Hellenic Ministry of Culture; the Central Archaeological Council determined how to handle the findings; and archaeological excavation was completed. The costs for any such delays were borne by the builders. The Greeks hoped the games would provide an economic and development stimulus. They calculated an annual .5% boost in GDP until 2004, 30,000 to 40,000 new jobs per year, 14 new hospitals, 38 major new road works, and athletic and tourist facilities.

Foreign interest in the treasures of classical Greece remains strong. It is in part maintained by such institutions as the American School of Classical Studies located in Athens. This is an academy for rigorous classical scholarship and archaeological excavation founded 100 years ago by a group of scholars from Harvard, Yale, Brown, Johns Hopkins, and Cornell Universities. It now has about 100 students and faculty from the US and Canada and an endowment of $8 million.

At the same time, Greeks maintain strong ties abroad, primarily with the US. There have been two waves of immigration to the US in the 20th century, and now over 3 million people of Greek descent live permanently in the US. The third-biggest Greek city in the world is Chicago, and Greeks in America have, on the whole, been very successful. They include not only such well-known entertainers as Maria Callas and Telly Savalas (Kojak) but also former presidential candidate Michael Dukakis; ex–vice president Spiro Agnew; and Admiral James G. Stavridis, who assumed NATO's top command as SACEUR in 2009.

Greek Americans form a potent lobby in the US Congress. Sometimes they can even put pressure on Greece. For instance, in 1963 they erected a statue of President Harry Truman honoring his providing Greece with arms and money to defeat the communists in the Greek civil war. However, some Greeks saw this as a symbol of American tutelage. In 1986 left-wing extremists blew it off its pedestal. The former Socialist-Communist majority in the Athens City Council voted to get rid of it altogether. At first Papandreou refused to intervene, but Greek American delegations persuaded him to reconsider.

As elsewhere in the past, the Greek Orthodox Church holds the Greek communities in the US and Canada together by organizing schools, cultural events and activities, social welfare, and even camping holidays. As delighted audiences all over the world saw in the film *My Big Fat Greek Wedding*, this event is a rite and celebration that is unforgettable. Marriage remains strong in the homeland. Greeks marry more and divorce less than other

EU citizens, and they have fewer children out of wedlock: 4% of births, compared with Sweden's 55%.

Some progress has been made in the field of social reform, especially in matters involving women's rights. The 1974 constitution includes a provision that all laws that foster inequality between the sexes had to be wiped off the books. Such things are easier written than done in a country with such a powerful state church and in one which the man, as head of the household, always had the right to decide all family matters literally by decree.

The PASOK government was able to break the church's monopoly on marriage and to permit civil marriages. By the 1990s only 3 out of 20 couples in the cities married outside the church. But atheists can now marry in Greece. Further, there are no more criminal prosecutions for adultery. The government also prepared legislation to permit abortion on demand, although it in fact was already widely available. In the 21st century, it has an exceptionally high incidence of abortion. Along with rising prosperity, this contributes to a dramatic plunge in the fertility rate. Combined with prodigious longevity, especially among women, this is having a frightening demographic effect. By 2015 the number of Greeks between ages 15 and 24 will have fallen by almost a quarter, and the number of octogenarians will have increased by 70%.

Parliament enacted in 1983 a series of important laws to protect women; it permitted divorce on mutually declared grounds of incompatibility and made it possible to name a child without baptism and to register the name with the civil authorities rather than with the church. It made it legal for a Greek woman to keep her own name after marriage, to have custody of small children, and to choose which schools they attend. It guaranteed to Greek women equal pay for equal work and forbade employers both to discriminate in hiring and to fire women for being pregnant. Greece has one of Europe's lowest percentages of women in the workforce. The government also proposed family planning centers and social benefits to unmarried mothers.

Orthodox Church

The Greek Orthodox Church remains influential in Greece, although many Greeks no longer care about religion. Except for the Turkish-speaking minority concentrated in Thrace and constituting only about 1.5% of the total Greek population, 90% of Greek citizens are baptized and belong to the established church, whose position and powers are fixed in the constitution. At least 5 million adherents live abroad. Greece is the only country in the world today in which Orthodox Christianity is the official religion. Although only 4% of Greeks say they attend church regularly, religion remains a part of their daily lives.

The ecumenical patriarch of the Orthodox Church (currently Bartholomew) is the spiritual head of world Orthodoxy, but he has no jurisdiction over the Church of Greece. Since the great split with the Roman Catholic Church, he has always resided in Istanbul (formerly Byzantium), Turkey. Life in Islamic Turkey has not been easy for the patriarch, who must be a Turkish citizen and travel with a Turkish passport. His flock within Turkey has shrunk to only 3,000. During crises between Turkey and Greece, he must worry about being expelled from Istanbul, thereby surrendering his primacy over the other Orthodox patriarchs, especially the Russian Orthodox leader, as heir to the Byzantine tradition.

His place as head of world Orthodoxy is tenuous. Relations with the resurgent Russian Orthodox Church are not good. By tradition he is considered the first among equals of over 135 million adherents of Orthodox Christianity, including 1.5 million in the US. He was permitted to restore the shabby buildings of his patriarchate, in part because of an appeal made to Turkey by former president Carter.

The church has, in the past, been able to use its influence to delay social reforms. In causing these delays, it sacrificed much of its prestige in a society that is increasingly secular. The government had widespread approval for its plans to cut off state financial aid to the church and to amend the constitution in order to make all religions equal in the eyes of the law.

It also continued the efforts begun by New Democracy aimed at expropriating the landed wealth of the church, which, after the state, is Greece's largest property and enterprise owner. It owned forest and agricultural land, office and apartment buildings, bank shares, islands, and businesses, in addition to churches and monasteries filled with treasures. Much of its land had been abandoned by Turkish landowners, and the state has often challenged the church's claim to it. Much of the land is not used at all, in part because it is too hilly or mountainous.

In 1987 parliament approved a bill expropriating the church's huge, 350,000 acres of landholdings and distributing them to farm cooperatives. The bill also called for putting laymen in charge of church administration. In an expropriating mood, the government also announced plans to take over most of former King Constantine's property in Greece, estimated to be worth about $40 million. Not surprisingly, the church announced at first

that it would not comply with the new law. An amicable face-saving compromise was found, though. In his first journey to Greece in a quarter-century, the patriarch agreed to a church-state committee to administer monastic lands and to leave the rest of the property under the control of the Holy Synod.

The leader of the Orthodox Church inside Greece from 1998 until his death in 2008 was His Beatitude Archbishop Christodoulos of Athens and all Greece. Although he succeeded the late Seraphim, who had been put in power by the right-wing colonels who ruled Greece from 1967 to 1974, he found himself at loggerheads with the government. He was a tireless meddler in

politics. His message was stridently nationalist, and he expounded the tired conspiracy theory that "the world's big powers are working against the interests of Hellenism." He railed especially against the "eastern barbarians" (the Turks) and called upon Greeks to "liberate Constantinople." Since Orthodoxy is the country's established religion, such populist pronouncements were especially embarrassing to Greece's diplomats. His popularity rating of 75% was far higher than any politician, and he was able to raise church attendance. He worked to heal the centuries-old grievances with the Roman Catholic Church, and in 2006 he met the pope in Rome. But he avoided the sensitive subject of dogma.

Hermes (or Youth), **4th century BC, Athens National Museum**

Greece

Elected by a conclave of 74 bishops in the main cathedral in Athens to take his place was Metropolitan Ieronymos of Thebes, a 70-year-old bishop, who has not courted conflict. The process lasted only four hours, when bells pealed and the light of an ancient lantern outside flashed on to signal his election. Minutes later, dressed in traditional black robes, he appeared on a balcony to acknowledge the cheers of thousands of faithful. He was enthroned February 16, 2008.

In general the church's influence is declining, although it will remain for a long time a political, social, and economic force to be reckoned with. In the rural, mountainous areas, attendance at the breathtaking, ritualistic services is very high. A curious custom exists in some of these areas—a shortage of land means a shortage of cemetery land. A person is buried for a certain number of years; the women of the parish then dig up the bones, clean them and place them in the cellar reliquary of the church with those of thousands already there. A new burial plot is thus created. In 2008 Greece's highest court, the Council of State, approved a government petition to legalize cremation, which the church had opposed.

One place where the religious flame also burns brightly is Mount Athos, or the Holy Mountain, as many Greeks call it. It dates back to the 7th century, when a group of hermits fled there and founded their "Garden of God," and it is one of the world's oldest Christian communities. Covering 225 square miles in an isolated forested and mountainous peninsula in northern Greece and overlooking treacherous waters in which many a seaman drowned, Mount Athos contained 180 monasteries sheltering more than 10,000 monks in the 11th century. Now it has shriveled to about 20 monasteries and only 1,400 monks (up from 1,146 in 1972).

Mount Athos is beset with numerous problems. One is that female tourists who sail within sight of the monasteries and sometimes even land illegally have challenged its long-standing total ban on women (and even on female animals). It can no longer maintain the 20 monasteries and 1,700 auxiliary buildings, 300,000 feet of frescoes, 20,000 icons, 13,500 Greek manuscripts, and a vast collection of relics and treasures which are irresistible objects for thieves.

The Greek state gives Mount Athos about $300,000 annually, but neither this nor the income it derives from subsistence farming, rent from outside properties, and timber trading enable the monks to make ends meet. The entire area is an autonomous republic within the Greek state, and it rules itself entirely through an annually elected governing body of 20 abbots. All the monks categorically refuse to unite or reconcile their differences with the western churches, which they regard as heretical and corrupt. They all criticize the Greek state's decision to open diplomatic relations with the Vatican, as well as the Orthodox Church's ecumenical steps toward the Catholic Church in Rome.

One group of 117 Esfigmenou monks, which regards the dialogue with the Vatican as betrayal, was branded by the patriarch as "schismatic" and was ordered off the sacred ground in 2003. They refused to budge and stocked enough food to last for a two-year siege. Their dispute was taken up by Greece's highest administrative court. One young member of the group drove a tractor accidentally off a cliff while trying to dodge the police during a standoff.

In all, a minority of about 300 zealots within the compound accuses the other monks of religious impurity. This fanatic minority struggles with them over control of the monasteries. On several occasions, the Greek police have been called in to deal with violent skirmishes between zealots and moderates. Still, all the monks agree that Mount Athos is a gateway to higher spiritual levels and ultimately to heaven. One abbot explained with confidence that "for the rest of the world, we are a lighthouse, battered by the waves, but still lighting the way, as we have done for centuries."

Media

Since 1974 Greece has been a country that enjoys freedom of speech, and Greek newspapers make full use of this liberty. Although the newspaper readership is low by western European standards (about 80 per 1,000), about 85 papers appear daily. Athens alone has 14 morning dailies. Few could survive without the tax-free newsprint and guaranteed loans provided by the state. Greece's large public banks also give aid. Although only two papers are official party organs, *Rizospastis* (Communist) and *Avgi* (radical right), most other papers have a clearly recognizable political line.

Most foreign observers remark that the journalistic standards of the Greek press are rather low, with sensationalism and extreme politicization taking priority over objective reporting. News columns tend to be as politicized as the editorial pages, but this seems to be what most Greek readers expect of their favorite newspapers. Only such Athens morning papers as the independent *Kathimerini* and the prosocialist *To Vima* even make a stab at objective news reporting. In 1991 the editors of seven newspapers went to jail rather than comply with a new law which, precipitated by the 1989 assassination of Mitsotakis's son-in-law by the November 17 group, prohibited them from publishing statements from terrorists. This measure reminded too many Greeks of the censorship practices during the military dictatorship from 1967 to 1974.

There are three state-owned television channels: two in Athens (ET1 and NET) and one in Thessaloniki (ERT3). They are financed by the state and by advertising fees. Since 1989 there are also many private channels, which are financed by advertising fees: 10 major ones in Athens and 13 smaller ones in other large cities. Countless local community channels broadcast throughout Greece. The programming consists of American films (70%); Greek films (20%–22%); other European programs; and the normal fare of news, sports, documentaries, interviews, and entertainment. There is also a mix of state-owned and private radio stations.

After exhaustive consultation among political parties and other interests, a bill for regulating privately owned press and media was introduced in parliament. The aim is to restrict the excessive concentration of media ownership and the development of communications monopolies. It

Goodbye to the world's oldest currency!

would prohibit companies that accept contracts with the state to have ownership in a mass media company. Also, no individual would be permitted to own more than a 25% stake in a television station. Finally, it would prohibit simultaneous participation in more than two media categories, such as television and publishing.

FUTURE

Greece is a country that is trying to absorb a half-century of rapid economic and social change. A predominantly rural way of life and a traditional system of values have been largely swept away. Greek democracy has become sufficiently robust to absorb a good deal of passionate debate and unrest. Repeated riots and strikes have been fueled by unemployment, bad administration, endemic corruption, and a string of financial scandals.

The last several governments had pledged to root out corruption, but it is deeply entrenched in Greek society. None has succeeded. Transparency International's 2012 corruption perceptions index ranked Greece 80th out of 183 countries. Politicians are widely denounced as "thieves and traitors," reflecting a widespread opinion that the corruption of those in government is responsible for causing the financial collapse. Despite a poll revealing that two-thirds of respondents thought the government was failing to go after tax evaders, the crackdown on tax cheats prompted hundreds of arrests.

One reform has stuck: a renewed ban on smoking in many public places. Fines of up to $700 await violators.

Four out of five Greeks want to keep the euro, but only a minority was willing to rescue it by continued belt tightening, restoring healthy public finances, and increasing international competitiveness. Nobody knows what the consequences would be if Greece were forced to abandon the euro, but no one wants to test it.

One can see the consequences of the draconian measures to reduce government spending. Wages and pensions have been cut by a quarter, and property taxes have tripled. Since thousands have defaulted on their mortgages or can no longer pay their rents, the number of homeless has skyrocketed in Athens. Combined with reductions in welfare services, this creates a new class of urban poor: One out of five now lives under the poverty line. One-third of children do. Hard times mean more childless and one-child women. The result is one of Europe's lowest birth rates: 1.3.

A feeling of insecurity is strengthened by nonstop antiausterity protests, rising crime, looting, and violence against immigrants and property. Fortunately things are not yet as bad as one unemployed

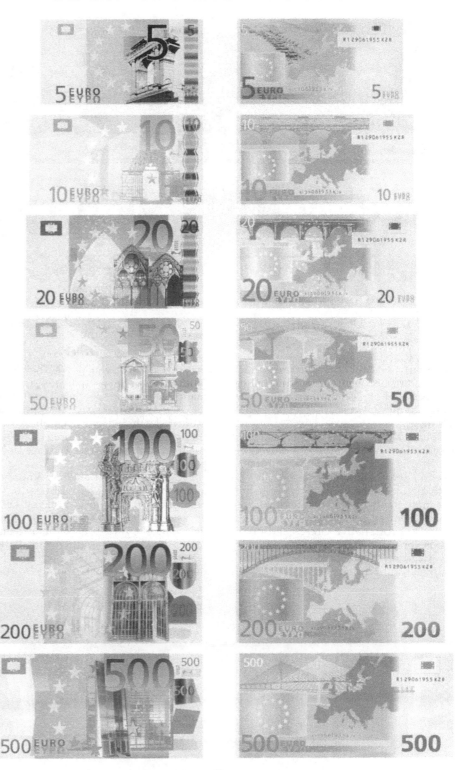

THE EURO BANKNOTE DESIGNS
LES MAQUETTES DES BILLETS EN EURO
DIE ENTWÜRFE DER EURO-BANKNOTEN

EUROPEAN MONETARY INSTITUTE

Greek letters on euro notes

FINANCIAL TI

MONDAY 26 JANUARY 2015   WORLD BUSINESS NEWSPAPER

$300bn woman
The Calpers boss on fighting
fund fees — BUSINESS LIFE, PAGE 10

Falling foul of Beijing
Chinese economist who defended
Qualcomm breaks silence — PAGE 7

Greek leftists' victory throws down challenge to euro establishment

● Syriza claims momentous poll win ● Inspiration for similar parties across continent

Athenian construction worker thinks: "We are finished as a nation. The country has been sold off. We have no say in anything anymore. Greece is owned by the Germans."

Golden Dawn exploited this feeling of desperation and introduced a dangerous new form of racist nationalism unthinkable in Greece a few years earlier. It violently pounced upon the country's 1.5 million immigrants and demanded that they all be deported immediately. To drive a wedge between native Greeks and immigrants, it handed out food to those hurt by the crisis only if they could show a Greek ID. Black-shirted party members roamed

the streets in menacing packs. Their leader, Nikos Michaloliakos, delivered melodramatic, fist-shaking speeches. They claimed they were not neo-Nazis, but appearances indicated otherwise. Michaloliakos and some of its MPs and supporters have been jailed on criminal charges and face 15-year prison sentences.

Relations with Turkey have improved, and the government continues to seek better ties with this former enemy. Differences over the long-standing division of the island of Cyprus will continue to make this difficult. Cooperation with Balkan neighbors is tense as they close their borders to migrants from Greece.

Greece stopped punishing North Macedonia for not changing its name. In January 2019 Greece accepted the name "North Macedonia," thereby opening the door to North Macedonia's entry into NATO and the European Union. In 2018 and 2019, tens of thousands gathered in the streets to protest as the two countries held successful talks to resolve the long-standing dispute.

The major future challenge facing the center-right Mitsotakis government is to eradicate the deadly coronavirus and to recover from the economic damage it has caused.

The Republic of Cyprus

Marketwoman in Nicosia: "Try these luscious grapes!"

Photo by George Tsappas

Area: 3,572 sq. miles (9,251 sq. km), the third-largest island in the Mediterranean. Cypriot Republic 59%, Turkish Republic 36%.

Population: 891,000 Greek Cypriots; 274,440 Turkish Cypriots, including an estimated 80,000 Turkish settlers and about 40,000 Turkish troops in the north.

Capital City: Lefkosia (Nicosia; pop. 307,000). Capital for both parts, the world's only divided capital.

Climate: Rainfall is usually moderate, but periodic droughts may be severe. Summers are usually hot, humid on the coasts, dry inland; winters are mild, except in the mountains.

Neighboring Countries: Turkey (40 miles north across the Mediterranean); Lebanon and Syria (65 east across the Mediterranean); Israel, West Bank, and Gaza Strip (southeast across the Mediterranean); Egypt (south across the Mediterranean).

Official Languages: Greek and Turkish. English is widely used.

Ethnic Background: The people are divided by language and tradition into Greeks (about 78%); Turks (about 18%); Armenian, Maronites, and Latins (about 1%); foreigners (3%).

Principal Religions: Most Greek Cypriots profess Greek Orthodox Christianity; most Turkish Cypriots profess Sunni Islam, but tiny religious minorities also are found.

Major Exports: Grapes, citrus fruits, potatoes, and grain. Light manufactures include textiles, food products, and pharmaceuticals.

Major Trading Partners: Greece (22% of exports and 17% of imports), UK (14% of exports and 9% of imports), Germany (7% of exports and 9% of imports), Italy (11% of imports), Romania (3% of exports), France (3% of exports), Lebanon (3.4% of exports).

Currency: Euro in the south since 2008. Turkish lira in the north.

Former Dependent Status: British colony (1925–1960).

Independence Date: August 16, 1960.

National Holiday: October 1; November 15 (Turkish Republic).

Chiefs of State: Nicos Anastasiades, president of the Republic of Cyprus since March 2013. Ersin Tatar, president of the Turkish Republic of Northern Cyprus since October 2020.

National Flag: The Greek Cypriot flag has a white field with an outline map of the island in rich gold above two sprigs of green leaves. The Turkish Cypriot flag has two horizontal red bars and between them a red crescent on a white field.

Cyprus is a pleasant, often dry island barely larger than Delaware. It is in the northeast part of the Mediterranean Sea, located 65 kilometers (40 miles) off Turkey's coast. Along the entire scenic sweep of the northern coast are the Kyrenia Mountains, often snowcapped in the winter. The higher Troödos range in the west-central region, covered with forests and vineyards, is crowned by a peak reaching 6,401 feet above sea level. This lofty mountain is called Chionistra by Greek-speaking Cypriots, but in English it is often known as Mount Olympus in imitation of the more famous mountain in northern Greece. Between the two mountain ranges lies the central plain of Mesaoria, a rich agricultural region surrounding the capital, Lefkosia (renamed in English from Nicosia in 1995). Thanks to the normally adequate rainfall that favors it, more than half the island's total area is cultivated.

HISTORY

As early as 6000 BC, this island was inhabited by people who built curious

Cyprus

round houses, herded sheep and goats, raised a few crops, and wove textiles. The first mention of the island in written records occurred in the Nile Valley, whose ancient inhabitants traded with it, as did the Phoenicians and Greeks at a later time. Christianity began to spread on the island in the 1st century AD, when it was part of the Roman Empire. By the 5th century, a Cypriot Church with its own archbishop was recognized.

Cyprus remained part of the Byzantine Empire until 1191, when Richard the Lionheart of England conquered the island on his way to the Holy Land as part of the Crusades. The following year King Richard sold Cyprus to Guy de Lusignan, a former Crusader king of Jerusalem. From the Lusignan period, which lasted until 1489, come numerous examples of Gothic architecture in the form of castles and fortifications.

The merchant states of Genoa and Venice in turn sought control of Cyprus as a link in their trade with the Orient. Genoa held the port of Famagusta from 1373 to 1464, but it was Venice which finally wrested control from the Lusignan rulers. Fearing competitors and the growing Ottoman Turkish Empire, the Venetians built massive fortifications at the main ports. They taxed the Cypriots heavily; required free labor from them; and attempted to impose Latin Christianity on them, as the Lusignan rulers before them had also done.

Because of the unpopularity of the European rulers, the Cypriots were not unhappy to see the Ottomans drive them out in 1570–1571. As Ottoman subjects until 1878, the Cypriots—most of whom Christian—were permitted civil autonomy within their religious community. The reestablished office of archbishop for the Cypriot Orthodox Church became their link with the Ottoman government. The important role of the religious community and its head has persisted up to the present in varying forms. Poor administration and heavy taxation later in the Ottoman period led to much dissatisfaction.

The Ottoman government agreed at the Congress of Berlin in 1878 to let Britain take over the administration of Cyprus but not sovereignty. The Ottomans were to receive part of the revenues and, in case of need, British aid in warding off Russian encroachment on Turkey's northern borders. Following Turkey's entry into World War I on the side of Germany, Britain annexed Cyprus in 1914 and in 1925 gave it the status of a Crown colony. Britain continued to regard it mainly as a military base to defend the Suez Canal. It therefore did not pay much attention to the internal affairs until they became difficult after World War II.

The grievances of the Greek Cypriots, aggravated by an economic depression after World War II, found political form in the idea of enosis (union) with Greece. Some Greek Cypriots had long felt themselves part of the Greek nationalist movement. Enosis basically rejected Cypriot independence in favor of becoming part of Greece. As the idea gained support among Greek Cypriots, opposition to it grew among the Turkish Cypriot minority.

When the determined and energetic Makarios was elected archbishop and ethnarch of the Cypriot Orthodox Church in 1950, the enosis movement gained more political impact. British concessions came too late, and rioting came to characterize life on Cyprus. Murder and intimidation accompanied the breaches of the peace after the formation in 1955 of the EOKA, an underground terrorist military force fighting for enosis.

Pressed by worsening conditions, negotiators from Britain, Greece, and Turkey met with representatives of both Cypriot communities and finally reached an agreement in Zurich in 1959. The Zurich Agreement rejected both union with Greece and partition of the island. Instead, it granted Cyprus independence under a constitution containing collective safeguards for the Turkish minority. Britain, Turkey, and

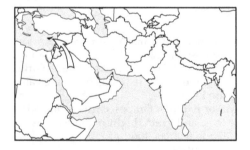

Archbishop Makarios

Greece received the right to intervene, either jointly or singly, to uphold the constitution. Britain also retained sovereignty over about 99 square miles of territory for two military bases.

As specified in the constitution, Cyprus became independent, with a Greek Cypriot president, Archbishop Makarios, and a Turkish Cypriot vice president, Dr. Fazil Küchük. However, independence did not dispel the old attitudes and suspicions. Turkish leaders used their constitutional veto to block laws and development programs allegedly favorable to the Greeks. Soon major government functions came to a halt, and in 1963 fighting broke out between the two communities. The constitution had failed to solve the conflict between the Greek Cypriot goal of majority

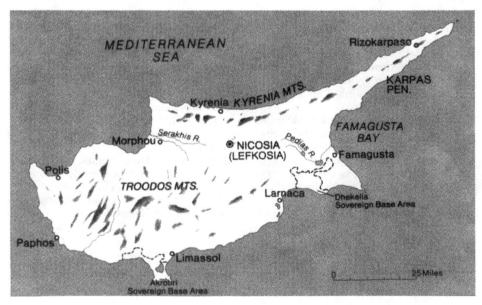

rule throughout the island and the Turkish Cypriot goal of its partition.

To halt the violence, the United Nations voted to send peacekeepers (UNFICYP), who arranged cease-fire agreements between the two sides. They patrolled areas of possible renewed fighting. Established in 1964 for six months, this international force became the longest-serving group of UN peacekeepers.

For the next decade, general peace prevailed, but there was little cooperation between the two communities. The House of Representatives met with only the 35 Greek members present; the 15 Turkish members met separately and denounced the measures taken by the Greeks. Though representatives of the two factions met occasionally, they found no formula to resolve the constitutional issues. The Greek majority could not impose its will by force because of the constant threat of invasion by Turkey on behalf of the minority's interests.

The year 1974 proved critical. In January EOKA's leader died, and sentiment for enosis began to fade more rapidly. In sharp contrast to the multiparty democracy enjoyed by Greek Cypriots, Greece suffered a military dictatorship linked to NATO. Determined supporters of enosis saw the chances for union with Greece slipping away and, in a desperate effort, engineered a coup by the national guard. Archbishop Makarios himself barely escaped into exile.

The Turkish government seized the coup and the following disorders as an opportunity to invade Cyprus. Its forces attacked in July, rapidly seizing Greek inhabited villages and towns in the north, as well as Turkish ones. Successful in military terms, and arguably legal by the Zurich Agreement, the assault captured 37% of the island, ostensibly to protect the rights of 18% of the population.

The invasion displaced from 150,000 to 200,000 Greeks from their homes, farms, and businesses; an estimated 40,000 Turkish Cypriots fled in the opposite direction. The resort towns of Famagusta and Kyrenia lost practically their entire populations, and some small villages fell vacant. Other serious human rights violations included the disappearance and apparent execution of prisoners. Unique works of art and other antiquities were stolen from churches in the Turkish-occupied zone, a crime rendered easier by alleged neglect or even the connivance of officials and the military.

The invasion had an enormous political and economic effect on the Greek Cypriot community. It discredited the coup leaders, and Glafcos Clerides, speaker of the house, became acting president until Makarios returned. An expanded UNFICYP monitored an uneasy peace between the Turkish army and the Greek Cypriots along the Attila Line dividing the two zones.

When Makarios died in 1977, Spyros Kyprianou succeeded him. He then won his own term. A hard-liner, he demanded that the territorial division should be proportionate to the population of the two zones. In addition, he demanded a strong (and inevitably Greek) federal government.

Equally uncompromising, the Turkish Cypriots continued to demand most of the territory north of the Attila Line (keeping 37% of the island for their 18% of the population) and virtual independence for their Turkish region. The two communities periodically bowed to international pressure and held talks on a settlement, but neither proved willing to compromise.

In 1981 Turkish Cypriot leaders finally approved an investigation of over 1,600 Greeks who had disappeared during the invasion, to little avail. In 1996, besides noting that hundreds of Turks were missing, as well, Denktash finally publicly admitted the obvious: Prisoners turned over to the Turkish Cypriot militia had been executed.

In some technical cases, the communities worked together. Water from the Turkish-held town of Morphou, purified by a Greek processing plant, was restored. The Greek sector supplies electric generating capacity for Turkish Lefkosa, while the sewage passes from the Greek to the Turkish side for treatment. Nevertheless, the Lefkosia (Nicosia) Airport was closed, and the Varosha resort near Famagusta was shuttered.

POLITICAL SYSTEMS

Political System in the South

The Republic of Cyprus has a presidential form of government. Under the 1960 constitution, the president is elected by universal suffrage to a five-year renewable term of office. If a candidate in a multiparty election does not succeed in winning an absolute majority in the first round of voting, there must be a runoff election between the two top vote-getters. The one who gets a simple majority wins.

The president is vested with executive power. He appoints and chairs the cabinet, called the Council of Ministers, which has 11 ministries. They are responsible for initiating legislation, coordinating and supervising the public services and finances, and processing bills and the budget before they are presented to parliament. Members may be chosen from outside parliament, but they may not sit in the House of Representatives after joining the Council of Ministers.

The unicameral parliament—House of Representatives—was enlarged in 1985 to 56 seats, each elected by direct universal suffrage for five-year terms. The proportional representation electoral method is used, and parliamentary and presidential elections are not scheduled at the same times. Three seats elected in a separate vote are reserved for special representatives of the Maronite and Armenian minorities. Voting is compulsory, and heavy fines are levied for nonvoting.

A Turkish soldier guards Greek Cypriot prisoners, July 1974.

Cyprus

ΙΔΡΥΤΗΣ: ΝΙΚΟΣ ΧΡ. ΠΑΤΤΙΧΗΣ

Ὁ ΦΙΛΕΛΕΥΘΕΡΟΣ

20 ΣΕΛΙΔΕΣ
ΤΡΙΤΗ
3 Ἀπριλίου 1990

ΗΜΕΡΗΣΙΑ ΕΦΗΜΕΡΙΣ ΕΙΣ ΤΗΝ ΥΠΗΡΕΣΙΑΝ ΤΟΥ ΚΥΠΡΙΑΚΟΥ ΛΑΟΥ

ΛΕΥΚΩΣΙΑ ΕΝΩ ΕΤΟΙΜΑΖΟΝΤΑΙ ΟΙ ΕΝΑΛΛΑΚΤΙΚΕΣ ΕΙΣΗΓΗΣΕΙΣ

ΠΡΟΣ ΠΑΓΚΟΜΜΑΤΙΚΗ ΤΩΡΑ ΣΤΗΝ ΑΘΗΝΑ

Ἀμέσως μετὰ τὶς ἐκλογές

ΔΙΑΦΩΝΕΙ Ο Γ.Γ. ΤΟΥ ΑΚΕΛ

Λένε ὅτι ὁ Νικολάου πλήρωσε τὸ «πρόστιμο» στὸ Λονδίνο

ΛΕΜΕΣΟΣ Τάφηκαν χωρὶς νεκρώσιμη ἀκολουθία τὰ τέσσερα «θύματα μαγείας»

ΣΤΙΣ 14 ΑΠΡΙΛΙΟΥ Θάτσερ καὶ Μπους συζητοῦ τὸ Κυπριακὸ καὶ ἀντιδρ ἔντονα ἡ Ἀγκυρα

Lefkosia's *O Phileleftheros* headlines the third interparliamentary union congress held in Cyprus in April 1990.

Parties range across the political spectrum. Those winning seats in the May 2011 parliamentary elections were the right-of-center Democratic Rally (DISY), who came out on top, receiving 34.27% of the votes (up from 30.3%) and 20 seats. The communist Progressive Party of the Working People (AKEL) climbed to 32.67% (up from 31.1%) and 19 seats. The moderate nationalist Democratic Party (DIKO) slipped from 17.9% to 15.77% and 9 seats. The Movement for Social Democracy (EDEK) maintained its position with 8.9% and 5 seats. The relatively new right-wing European Party (EVROKO) fell to 3.88% (from 5.8%) and 2 seats. The Greens rose to 2.21% and 1 seat.

In the February 2008 presidential elections, the victor was Demetris Christofias of the communist AKEL Party. He had studied political science in Moscow and spoke fluent Russian. He was the first communist to run for the presidency and was the first communist ever to rule in an EU country. Despite the fact that AKEL has not formally renounced Marxism-Leninism, he was no red firebrand. He abandoned AKEL's former Euroskeptic position, and his party is friendly toward business. In fact, it controls a wide range of businesses, including an investment company.

Replacing him after the February 2013 presidential elections was Nicos Anastasiades, leader of the conservative Democratic Rally (DYSY) Party. He won 57.5% of the votes and defeated the AKEL candidate, Stavros Malas, who garnered 42.5%. Turnout was 81.6%, relatively low

for Cyprus. Anastasiades was the most prominent politician to support the Annan Plan to unify the island. It took him years to make his political comeback.

The independent judiciary is modeled on the British system. A Supreme Court stands above lower Assize and District Courts. Most statutes and regulations relevant to business are in English.

The south has a national guard of 10,050, including 9,100 conscripts who serve two years. There are 50,000 reservists, composed in large part of former conscripts, who remain reservists until age 50 (60 for officers). Greece sends 950 soldiers and 200 officers and NCOs to the Greek Cypriot national guard. There are 750 paramilitary forces. They face 35,000 Turkish troops north of the line.

Political System in the North

The 1985 constitution for the Turkish Republic of Northern Cyprus provides for a strong president, a prime minister, and an elected legislature of 50 seats. Although the constitution allows for an independent judiciary, individual freedoms are more limited than in the south. Military forces from mainland Turkey control the local police, and journalists questioning such links have been arrested on dubious charges.

In December 2003 a landmark parliamentary election ended in a draw. The Republican Turkish Party, which supported the Annan Plan for reunifying the island, won more votes than Rauf Denktash's National Unity Party, which opposed it. But

both received 25 seats apiece. In effect, the election was a referendum on Denktash's rejection of the UN plan. The two parties had no alternative to forming a coalition government in 2004.

The outcome of the April 2009 parliamentary elections eliminated much of the optimism for progress in the negotiations. The winner was the National Unity Party, led by 72-year-old Dervish Eroglu. It captured 44% of the votes and 26 out of 50 seats, while Talat's ruling Republican Turkish Party fell to only 29%. Eroglu became prime minister. His victory was a consequence of widespread disappointment that negotiations between the two parts were going nowhere.

As in the south, the political system is characterized by a strong presidency

President of Cyprus, Nicos Anastasiades

308

elected for a renewable five-year term. In April 2005 Talat easily won the presidential election with 56% of the votes on a platform of reuniting the divided island and joining the EU. He was defeated in the April 2010 presidential elections by then–prime minister Dervish Eroglu, who captured 50.4% of the votes, compared with Talat's 42.8%, and became president.

Although widespread disappointment in Talat's failure to bring about a settlement worked against him, there was also a demographic factor at work. In general, Turkish Cypriots tend to vote for the Republican Turkish Party, whereas mainland Turks tend to vote for Eroglu and his National Unity Party. This has become relevant in elections, since settlers from Turkey now outnumber indigenous Cypriots in the north. There are an estimated 140,000 Turkish Cypriots. There are 50,000 citizens from Turkey, plus 35,000 soldiers and about 100,000 transients of Turkish nationality. This not only effects voting, but also some Turkish Cypriots believe their unique identity is under threat. Settlers from Turkey are more socially and religiously conservative, and they look different because many wear their traditional village clothing. One northern politician noted that the Greek and Turkish Cypriot communities "have more in common with each other than with these people from Anatolia."

After the 1974 invasion, the Turkish community organized itself north of the Attila Line (Green Line) across the island that the Turkish troops had established. In the absence of an agreement, the Turkish Cypriot Legislative Assembly proclaimed the independent Turkish Republic of Northern Cyprus in 1983. Only Turkey recognized this new state, while the Security Council of the UN asked that the independence move be withdrawn. Rauf Denktash, nicknamed "Mr. No" and former vice president of the entire island, became president. In April 2015, the longtime mayor of northern Nicosia, the world's only divided capital, was elected president in the Turkish north: Mustafa Akinci. He is respected for advocating reconciliation. He met dozens of times with his Greek counterpart, crossing the Green Line together and joining Anastasiades to issue New Year's greetings on TV. He was beaten in the October 2020 elections by Ersin Tatar, a hardline supporter of the two-state model.

Despite surviving for a generation, the Turkish sector technically remains an international illegality. It is recognized only by Turkey, although the EU offered in 2004 to provide it with financial and trade benefits. Travelers can fly to northern Cyprus only from Turkey, greatly hindering business and tourism. Its products lack convenient access to foreign markets.

Ex-President Mustafa Akinci, Turkish Republic of Cyprus

International copyright laws are often not honored, thus permitting local bargains in counterfeit sports clothing and videos.

Per-capita incomes now average only about one-half the Greek level. Even this meager existence depends on subsidies from mainland Turkey, which funds most major public works and is the main employer. However, this requires use of the Turkish lira, one of the least-valued currencies in Europe. The Turkish Cypriot state is starved of capital, faces a trade boycott, attracts few foreign investors, and lures less than a tenth of the tourists who are vacationing in the south.

THE SEARCH FOR CYPRIOT UNITY

Initial attempts to bring peace to the island during the 1970s and 1980s failed even in the humanitarian task of discovering the fate of the 1,600 Greeks and 800 Turks listed as missing persons. Greece suffered a shocking setback in 1983, when Turkish Cypriots declared an independent Republic of Northern Cyprus, thereby undercutting UN efforts to find a solution to that conflict. Currently 1,200 UN peacekeepers patrol the line that divides the two communities, and the capital city of Lefkosia (Nicosia) is the world's last divided capital.

The Greeks long suspected that the Turks might try to seize other Greek islands lying close to the Turkish coast. Although such fears may seem farfetched, the Turks maintain a 125,000-man Army of the Aegean equipped with 110 landing craft on their southwestern coast. Turkish politicians have sometimes refused to recognize that the Aegean Islands are Greek, and they actually demonstrated in Cyprus that they

were willing to use military means to back up their aspirations in the area. In 1996 US diplomatic intervention was required to defuse a crisis over Turkish occupation of an uninhabited Greek island, Imia. Greeks conveniently forget that the Greek majority in Cyprus, particularly under Archbishop Makarios, had sometimes abused the Turkish minority Cypriots.

In 1992, the UN secretary-general proposed a "bizonal and bicommunal" settlement that required concessions from each side. "Bizonal" implied that the Greeks would have to abandon demands for one strong government for the whole island. Instead, a weak central administration would have been limited mostly to customs, the post office, the central bank, and the diplomatic corps. The two ethnic zones would have remained and administered themselves with great autonomy. This would have required the Turkish community to accept the withdrawal of most Turkish military forces and a reduction in the size of the zone from 37% to 28%. This would have allowed one-third of the 1974 refugees to return to their homes, while the other Greek and Turkish refugees would receive compensation. This proposal was unacceptable to both sides.

Greece's long-standing position until 2004 was that the Greek Cypriot side is the only legitimate government and the Turkish part was a breakaway entity that must rejoin the national government. Further, Turkish troops and settlers had to be withdrawn, and effective guarantees had to be given to a Cypriot Republic. The Turkish position until 2004 was that all talks must presuppose equal legitimacy of the two sides and that any solution must be based on a federation of two separate Cypriot states.

Former Greek Cypriot president Glafcos Clerides spurned earlier UN talks on Cyprus. To strengthen his hand, he won Russian agreement to sell 300 sophisticated surface-to-air missiles. The Turks said they would destroy them the moment they arrive. Also, a 1993 defense pact with Greece permitted construction of a military air base at Paphos that could accommodate Greek F-16s deployed there in time of crisis. One American official noted that "these are acid concerns for Turkey-Greek jets and Russian missiles on Cyprus." To prevent military conflict, an American diplomatic mission in 1997 got Clerides to postpone receipt of Greek F-16s. He also announced that the Russian missiles would not be deployed on Cyprus. Instead they were removed in 1999 to the Greek island of Crete, placing Turkey well outside of the missiles' 90-mile range.

In 1997 the EU decided to consider Cyprus's application for membership, but it rejected Turkey's three-decade-old

Cyprus

Anguish: Clutching large photographs of missing loved ones, mothers and wives plead for information about men who have not been heard from since the Turkish invasion of July 1974, a full generation ago.
Courtesy: Embassy of Cyprus

One clear impetus behind the negotiations was "accession," the planned expansion in 2004 of the European Union to include Cyprus and nine other nations. Partly because it met the economic criteria for membership and partly because Greece had threatened to veto all other new members if Cyprus was not admitted, the EU governments pledged to admit Greek Cyprus, even without a settlement over the Turkish zone. This decision has proven unfortunate. Cyprus has played a destructive role in the EU, undermining EU attempts to help Turkish Cypriots, preventing closer ties between the EU and NATO, and creating serious obstacles to Turkey's membership negotiations.

Despite months of negotiations with Clerides and even urgings by the Turkish prime minister, in early 2003 Denktash rejected a new UN plan accepted by the EU. Ironically, his rejection diminished the pressure for a Greek acceptance of the UN plan. It featured strongly in the presidential elections of early 2003, when President Clerides promised that, if elected, he would serve only until Cyprus joined the union. However, Tassos Papadopoulos, his leading rival and strong critic of the UN plan, managed to unite both right-wing and left-wing sides against Clerides. He defeated him, ending Clerides's 40 years at the helm of the island's politics. As the Greek Cypriot leader during the final negotiations, Papadopoulos demanded better terms for Greek refugees from areas that would remain Turkish.

Things moved very quickly in 2003 in the wake of the EU's "big bang" enlargement. Voters went to the polls in the north and strongly backed prosettlement politicians in local elections. In February a third of the population in the north gathered in a

application. Greece refused to allow a linkage between Greek Cypriot EU entry and a final settlement of the island's division. It threatened to veto further EU expansion if such a linkage were made. The EU ultimately accepted Greece's position in 1999. Turkey objected in vain to an arrangement whereby a Greek Cypriot government would be admitted to the EU, while Turkish Cyprus and Turkey itself were left out. That could end Turkey's chances of ever joining because accession decisions are made by unanimous consent.

To the north of the dividing line, resentment among Turkish Cypriots grew toward the presence and role of the 35,000 Turkish troops, in addition to the approximately 150,000 Turkish settlers who came since 1974. Turkish Cypriots, who number about 140,000, find themselves in a minority vis-à-vis these settlers and soldiers. They were almost completely dependent on Turkish government handouts. For these reasons, public opinion in the north swung heavily in favor of a settlement that would have permitted unification and EU membership for the entire island in 2004.

After two decades of discussing the bizonal, bicommunity proposal, Denktash broke off negotiations in 2000. He demanded a new framework: a confederation of two independent states. While the practical difference may be nil between a federation of autonomous regions and a confederation of independent states,

Greek Cypriots feared that the Turkish terms amounted to creeping recognition for the northern republic.

Hopes rose on both sides of the buffer zone after the Cypriot president, Glafcos Clerides, met with Denktash several times in late 2001 and early 2002, even crossing into the Turkish zone. Taking a humanitarian approach to the missing persons, they sought to find mass graves and identify the dead rather than concentrate on details of their capture.

Ancient theater at Curium (Limassol)

huge demonstration and marched through the streets shouting anti-Denktash slogans and carrying signs reading "Yes to peace, yes to the EU." On February 28 UN secretary-general Kofi Annan met in The Hague with the leaders of both parts of the island to ask them if they accepted his compromise plan to have a referendum on unification a month later. The Greek Cypriot president said yes, but Denktash said no, thereby having to bear the stigma of sabotaging the UN plan. In April the south turned down his offer of a six-point confidence-building plan just two weeks before Greek Cypriot leaders signed the EU accession document at the union's summit in Greece on April 16. In July parliament approved entry unanimously.

In an attempt to prevent isolation and to keep the pot from boiling over, Denktash stunned everybody at the end of April 2003 by throwing open the three-decade-old dividing line between the two parts and allowing citizens from both areas to cross into the other side for one-day stays. Within a week, 160,000 Cypriots had flooded both ways over the border to visit their old homes, to observe how the other people live, and to see for themselves just how much each community had grown apart from each other. Most found the mingling experience exhilarating. Cyprus's most famous refugee is Titina Loizidou. In December 2003 the European Court of Human Rights ordered Turkey to pay her €1.2 million ($1.56 million) for denying her the "peaceful enjoyment of her property" in Kyrenia. Similar cases are likely to follow.

Other long-awaited steps quickly followed, including reopening telephone lines, clearing minefields, removing trade barriers on Turkish goods, granting work permits and health benefits to Turkish Cypriots, and making it possible for Orthodox Christian Greek Cypriots to marry Muslim Turkish Cypriots. By the end of 2003, there had been 2.2 million border crossings; around 6,000 Turkish Cypriots cross into the more prosperous south each day in order to work or seek medical care. The government in the south was ambivalent and tried to put moral pressure on its citizens not to go north and spend money, particularly in hotels, which it described as "stolen property." Nevertheless, the mutual fear that sustained the Cyprus problem for so long has largely disappeared. Some southerners visit the 20 casinos in the north, since the Orthodox Church opposes such establishments in the south.

The Annan Plan, 2004

In 2004 a UN plan devised and personally negotiated by Secretary-General Kofi Annan and strongly supported by the EU and the United States, brought the two

Rauf Denktash,
ex-leader of the Turkish Cypriots

sides as close to accepting an agreement as they had ever been. The formation in January of a new Turkish Cypriot coalition government that included the Republican Turkish Party, which supports a settlement to end the division, set the stage for a new round of unification talks.

On February 13 the leaders of Greece and Turkey accepted the UN road map for reunification before Cyprus joined the European Union on May 1. Turkish prime minister Recep Tayyip Erdogan decided to put his weight behind an agreement because he knew that a settlement of the Cypriot issue is a precondition for Turkey's opening of negotiations to join the EU. It has been an official candidate for membership since 1999. He persuaded the Turkish generals that his way, not the obstructionist tactics of Turkish Cypriot president Denktash, was best for Turkey's future. Erdogan acted courageously in reversing decades of Turkish policy.

For several years the leaders of the Greek and Turkish governments had worked to lower the tensions between the two former archenemies. In October 2003 they had decided to cancel their annual naval exercises in the eastern Mediterranean and not to participate in planned naval war games with their rival communities on Cyprus.

Six weeks of intensive UN-sponsored talks followed in New York, Cyprus, and Switzerland. In the end, the two Cypriot presidents were unable to agree. But under the February 13 accord, they were obligated to help the UN organize separate referenda on Annan's plan, scheduled for April 24, 2004.

The UN plan called for a federation of two politically equal states under a weak central government. A "United Cyprus Republic" would handle relations with the EU. It would be governed by a

nine-member presidential council of six Greek Cypriots and three Turkish Cypriots. Three members would have no voting rights, thereby ensuring that the Greek majority could not simply outvote the Turkish minority. The presidency would be by rotation.

The area under Turkish control would have been reduced from 37% to 29% of the land area, allowing 120,000 Greek Cypriots to return to their homes and live under Greek Cypriot administration. The port city of Famagusta would be returned to the Greek Cypriots. Approximately 50,000 Turkish Cypriots would have been uprooted. There would be limitations on the settlement of one ethnic group in the area controlled by the other for 19 years or until Turkey had entered the EU, whichever came first. Finally, Turkey and Greece would gradually reduce their military presence on the island from the present 35,000 Turkish and 6,000 Greek soldiers to no more than a total of 1,600 by 2018.

In the lead-up to the referendum on both sides of the line, the presidents of both parts of Cyprus opposed the plan. Most Greek Cypriots largely objected to limits on the right of all Greek Cypriot refugees to return to the homes they had fled in 1974, while permitting tens of thousands of Turkish settlers who arrived after the 1974 invasion to stay. In other words, not all Greeks could reclaim their lost property. Most Turkish Cypriots favored the plan because it was their ticket to greater prosperity and membership in the EU. The Greek Cypriots were aware that they would enter the EU on May 1 no matter what the outcome of the referendum in their part of the island. They would then have a veto over the future EU entry of both Turkish Cyprus and Turkey itself. Turkish Cypriots knew that they would enter the EU only if voters in both parts of Cyprus accepted the plan.

The outcome of the referenda on April 24, which was the first time Cypriots had ever had a chance to vote on any peace plan since 1974, was disappointing but not surprising. With a turnout of 88% in the south and 87% in the north, the results were predictable: 76% of Greek Cypriots rejected the plan, while 65% of Turkish Cypriots voted in favor of it. Opinion polls showed that three-quarters of Greek Cypriots opposed the UN blueprint because they distrusted Turkey. They believed that the Annan Plan offered too little restitution for the more than 160,000 people who were forced to flee to the south during the 1974 invasion. It would have left too many Turkish soldiers on the island (6,000) pending a withdrawal plan whose execution was not guaranteed. Turkish Cypriots sensed that they were on the brink of a historic change, and many supporters

Cyprus

demonstrated outside the home of Rauf Denktash, urging him to resign.

Denktash, who passed away in 2012, remained rejectionist to the end, promising to step down if the plan had been accepted. In practice, however, he had seen his power diminished as a growing number of moderate Turkish Cypriots showed that they want to coexist with like-minded Greeks. They won a moral victory by casting off their previous image as the main obstacle to a unified federal republic, which both sides claim to want. Cyprus became the only European country with UN peacekeeping forces (1,200) patrolling its interior.

Current Situation

On May 1, 2004, the Greek Cypriot Republic entered the EU under a cloud of resentment for having turned down a compromise that many outside observers considered fair. The EU moved immediately to share the benefits of EU membership with both parts of the island and to send a positive signal to those in the north who had voted "yes." It agreed to end the economic isolation of northern Cyprus by allowing Cypriot goods to pass freely over the partition line without the need to prove that they are of purely local origin. These goods would enter the EU tariff-free. This would be a long step toward ending the international trade embargo against the north imposed in 1974.

To reward the north further, the EU decided to redirect to its use €259 million ($337 million) originally earmarked to back a political settlement. It made another offer of €139 million ($181 million) in 2006. Through maneuvering in Brussels, the Greek Cypriot government prevented all these steps from being taken. The north also added its own complication, refusing to accept the aid until its ports and airports are opened to EU traffic.

In the face of withering international criticism, former Greek Cypriot president Tassos Papadopoulos insisted that UN efforts to reunite the island would continue despite his own energetic opposition to them. He also pledged not to use his island's EU membership to block Turkey's effort to join. Few believed that. He added a proviso: Turkey must behave "like a European country" and adhere to European law and principles. Papadopoulos's true stance was intransigence rather than to work with the Talat government in the north. The UN-backed plan to reunify Cyprus as a bizonal federal state was on extended hold. Polls showed that three-quarters of Greek Cypriots continued to oppose the UN plan, and 48% in 2006 favored living separately from Turkish Cypriots, while only 42% wanted to coexist.

The south has a hammer hold on Turkey, whose start of accession talks in October 2005 complicated matters. Ankara agreed to sign a protocol to its customs union with the EU in 2005. But it emphasized that this did not mean it recognized the Greek Cypriot administration. Nor would it open its ports and airports to all EU members until the embargo against northern Cyprus and its ports is lifted. It was unacceptable to some EU countries for a country to want to join an organization without recognizing one of its members. Progress stalled.

Cypriots on both sides of the line are entitled to European citizenship, and Turkish Cypriots have the right to request Cypriot passports. Many apply for a Greek Cypriot passport so that they can work within the EU. "We're fed up with being isolated," said one businessman. "We want to join Europe." About 40,000 Turkish Cypriots had received Greek Cypriot passports by 2006, and others were in line to get them. These enable them to work outside their northern enclave and to vote or run for office in Greek Cypriot elections. More than 30,000 immigrant workers are employed in the south, and 6,000 Turkish Cypriots cross the Green Line every day to work in the south, mainly in the booming construction industry.

By investing in Cypriot bonds, real estate, banks, and companies, foreigners could acquire permanent residence and citizenship. The EU strongly opposed such "golden passports" and forced the Greek Cypriots to end the practice in November 2020.

In January 2007 Turkish Cypriot authorities sent a positive signal by ordering the

Greek Cypriot student at the College of Europe, Bruges

demolition of a foot bridge that had been an obstacle to opening up Ledra Street, the main thoroughfare that runs through the heart of Nicosia's tourist area. The south responded two months later by tearing down a heavy wall that had separated the two parts of the capital for four decades and replacing it with less daunting sheets of aluminum. However, it made clear that civilians could not cross it freely until Turkey removed its troops stationed in the area. This particularly ugly part of the Green Line had stretched along Ledra Street.

The February 2008 presidential victory of Demetris Christofias, who had been a rejectionist in the previous election but now pledged to "build bridges," showed that Cypriots on both sides want an end to division. Both the candidate he defeated, Yiannakis Kassoulides, and ex–northern Turkish president Mehmet Ali Talat, who stems from the same leftist camp as Christofias, promised to support his efforts. This signaled an end to a four-year stalemate in bringing the two parts of Cyprus together.

The two presidents met and decided to restart formal peace talks. They promptly opened the Nicosia city center's Ledra Street crossing. Although the Turkish Cypriots had opened five other checkpoints in the preceding years, this one is especially symbolic because it is in the heart of Nicosia. Mines had to be removed, and Turkish soldiers stationed there had to be moved out of sight. This dramatic step will eventually help revitalize the center of the divided capital, parts of which had practically become a ghost town. Another successful confidence-building measure is the launching of investigations, funded by the EU and bilateral donors, to locate the sites of mass graves of victims of the 1974 war, exhume the remains, and identify as many as possible for the families.

The EU was relieved to see former president Tassos Papadopoulos defeated. He had irritated them to no end by exploiting the south's EU membership to force Turkey to accept concessions over Cyprus and to stymie EU-funded projects in the north. In December 2008 he died of lung cancer. In a bizarre series of events, his body was secretly exhumed and stolen from a Nicosia cemetery in 2009 by a man who wanted to trade the body for his brother's freedom from a life prison sentence for murder. The culprits were caught, and the body was reburied.

Former northern president Talat was also burdened by having to follow Turkey's guidance on major issues. However, with prosettlement leaders—Christofias and Talat—on both sides, the chances of a successful outcome seemed to be greater. For the first time since the island was divided in 1974, the leaders of both communities wished to negotiate a settlement.

Weekly substantive talks began in September 2008 with the backing of the Turkish government in Ankara, which knows that it will never be permitted to enter the EU as long as Cyprus is divided. In October Christofias cancelled an annual military exercise to improve the atmosphere for the negotiations. The UN dispatched Australia's foreign minister, Alexander Downer, to moderate the talks. UN secretary-general Ban Ki-moon visited for three days in February 2010 to try to lend a hand. However, when he met with the then-president Talat in the latter's office on the Turkish side, critics protested that his visit could be interpreted as recognition of the northern regime. In fact, many Greek Cypriots avoid any form of cross-border relationships out of fear that they would imply recognition.

Over 100 fruitless meetings were held in the 30 months after September 2008. Greek Cypriots spout platitudes about wanting reunification, but they do not make the hard political decisions to bring it about. In April 2009 northern Turkish voters threw out the party that most favored negotiation. Northern Turkish ex-president Dervish Eroglu had long favored a two-state solution and was uninterested in federation. Many Greek Cypriots shy away from a federal state, knowing that they would have to finance it in the early years.

The UN is deeply frustrated, but it continues to call on the parties to put in more work to reach a settlement. After months of quiet diplomacy by the US, the two Cypriot presidents met again in February 2014 on the UN's Green Line to relaunch the search for unity based on federalism. This effort was dubbed in Nicosia the Obama Plan. Because of disagreements over offshore gas reserves and the Greek insistence that all Turkish soldiers be withdrawn, the negotiations easily were stalled. Optimism was rekindled in 2015, when Presidents Anastasiades and Akinci met dozens of times. Talks in Geneva in January 2017 again failed.

The EU is sick and tired of the constant Greek Cypriot disruption of EU business because of the Cyprus dispute. For example, in 2020 it held up the EU's intent to levy sanctions against Belarus because such sanctions were not applied to Turkey. Cyprus assumed the six-month rotating presidency in July 2012. Talks cannot continue forever. Young Cypriots already have no memory of a united Cyprus, and the Green Line is starting to look like a permanent border. Although it is easy to cross the north–south checkpoints, half of Greek Cypriot students have never visited the north, and 43% do only rarely. The two peoples lead separate lives.

A Greek Orthodox priest at his easel   Courtesy: Embassy of Cyprus

ECONOMY

Greek Cypriots are 70% urban and 30% rural. The agricultural contribution to the economy varies, owing to occasional severe droughts. Water from the small rivers is used for irrigation, but this is insufficient during an extended period of below-average rainfall. So great has been the shortage of water that running water was not always available in homes. However, several desalination plants in Greek areas now provide water for households, industry, and some irrigation there. Tankers can transport water from Turkey to the northern zone. Tankers from Eleusis in Greece sail to Limassol laden with water that can be pumped into the island's Southern Conveyor pipeline for delivery to households.

The largest share of arable land is sown in cereal crops, but there is not enough grain produced to meet domestic needs. Production of olives, an important part of the diet, likewise falls short of domestic requirements. The agricultural exports are mainly citrus fruits, potatoes, raisins, carob beans, and wine. The Orthodox Church is the largest landowner, a fact that lends it secular influence in the countryside.

Although copper was previously the chief Cypriot export—indeed, the island's name comes from the mineral—mining currently plays only a minor role in the economy. Light industry expanded substantially in recent years, and the British bases provide both jobs and foreign exchange. Nevertheless, the island still imports a far greater value of goods than it exports. The island's only globalized industry is shipping. By 2005 the Cypriot-flagged fleet totaled 1,084 vessels, down from 1,475 in 2000. This makes it the

world's eighth-largest fleet, down from fourth a few years earlier.

There is possible good news on the horizon: the prospect that abundant offshore oil and natural gas could be tapped by a US-based company. Exploratory drilling was ordered to begin. Turkey strenuously objected, arguing that such these resources belong to both parts of the island and that their exploitation must await settlement of the island's political status. It threatened to send gunships.

The island was shaken by a massive explosion at a naval base in July 2011 that destroyed the nearby Vasilikos power station, killing 13. This took out half of the country's electricity supply, caused repeated blackouts, and sparked angry protests by thousands. The powerful blast was triggered by 98 containers of seized Iranian munitions stored carelessly in the open at the base for two and a half years. A public inquiry found that former president Christofias was responsible, and criminal charges were filed against the defense minister and top military chief for negligence and manslaughter.

The 1974 Turkish invasion necessitated a drastic reorganization of the economy. For instance, all of the tobacco farms and more than half of the citrus groves and grain lands fell under Turkish occupation, although they were mostly owned by Greek Cypriots exiled to the south. Though not as experienced in this work, Turkish Cypriots took over these agricultural resources. Citrus fruit now comprises half of the exports from the Turkish zone.

Although more than half of the tourist facilities are in the 37% of the island occupied by Turkey, few tourists go there aside from a half-million Turks each year. All tourists to the north must fly over Turkey

Cyprus

since there are no direct flights into northern Cyprus from elsewhere. The opening of the border for Cypriots does not apply to foreign visitors. The south bans tourist visits from the north.

By contrast, Greek Cypriots who were cut off from the hotels and restaurants they owned at Famagusta, Kyrenia, and elsewhere have built new tourist centers in the south, mainly along the southern coast. So well managed is their tourism business that the number of visitors both from Europe and Arab countries has grown by leaps and bounds. Britain alone accounts for 55% of the tourists. With more than 2 million tourists each year, the number of tourists entering the country triples the size of the south's population. Their need for hotels and apartments boosts the construction industry.

Tourism is the main industry in the Cypriot economy, accounting for 12% of GDP in 2007 (down from more than 20% in 2002) and about 45% of foreign earnings. A problem is that it is rated a more expensive destination than its rivals Greece, Turkey, and Croatia. In 2009 it reported a 10% reduction of visitors and a 15% loss of tourist revenue. Less fortunate visitors are those trapped in the sex industry. The US State Department lists the island as having Europe's worst record for trafficking of women.

Both sides experienced a property boom, especially in second-home sales, triggered by entry into the EU in 2004. This opened up the property market to non-Cypriot citizens. In the three years following membership, more than 120,000 such homes were purchased by foreigners. In the south most families own their own homes, and many have villas or apartments by the sea. The economy suffered a lingering housing bust during the 2008–2010 recession.

In the north, construction on land formerly belonging to Greek Cypriots is a source of division and tension. As much as 80% of the property there belongs to Greek Cypriots who fled south in the 1970s. The Turkish Cypriot government transferred deeds to Turkish Cypriots from the south, settlers from the Turkish mainland, and the Turkish military. However, the EU's European Court of Justice ruled in 2009 that Greek Cypriots who had fled after 1974 can reclaim their land even if the northern government had sold it to others. It ordered courts throughout the EU to enforce this judgment. This was done in 2010, when a court in the UK ruled that a British couple must demolish their home in northern Cyprus. There will be more demands for demolition of holiday homes and hotels built on Greek Cypriot lands. The Greek Cypriots' policy on seized property in the north is clear: The original owners can decide if they want to return, sell their property, or accept compensation for it. The 2008–2010 recession ended a boom in holiday-home and other construction on both sides of the line.

Services now employ twice the labor force as agriculture in the Greek sector. Three-fourths of the south's GDP comes from the services sector. Until the 2013 financial crisis, its GDP per capita was 80% of that in the EU15 and the highest among the 10 new states that entered the EU on May 1, 2004. The good times are temporarily over. One middle-class Cypriot said, "We woke up and suddenly everyone was poor in Cyprus."

The country does have some strengths to fall back on. Its infrastructure is good, the British-based legal system is transparent, it has a strong middle class, and its educational system is sound. Young Cypriots, who face 30% unemployment, twice the national average, are mobile and multilingual. They enjoy the sixth-highest rate of university education in the EU and are in second place in terms of students abroad.

Violence and difficulties elsewhere in the Middle East helped Cyprus become a center for banking, insurance, and shipping activities. In 2007, financial services accounted for about 7% of GDP, and the number of foreign companies registered increases by 20% annually. In 2011, its outsized banking sector had assets of more than seven times GDP. Simple regulations, 12.5% corporate taxes, a skilled population, and lots of lawyers and accountants encourage companies to locate regional headquarters on the island. Cyprus is a particular hub for Russian businesses; Russians were the source of a third of bank deposits. Unable to raise money after 2010 on international capital markets, it borrowed €2.5 billion ($3.28 billion) from Russia at below-market interest rates. This favorable loan reflected Moscow's interest in protecting wealthy Russian depositors with billions parked in the island's banks. The Cypriot finance minister returned to Moscow in 2013 to ask for a further €5 billion loan, but he left empty-handed.

The Greek Cypriot Republic's bank secrecy attracted funds in need of laundering and avoidance of taxation. It became a tax haven. Foreign currency deposits held by nonresidents constituted about half of total bank deposits. Because of the common language and physical proximity, Greece was a logical place for Cypriot banks to expand their operations and to buy Greek sovereign bonds. Cyprus is also considered to be a more business-friendly country than Greece, which is burdened by bureaucracy and corruption. But this made Cypriot banks vulnerable to contagion by the serious problems facing the Greek state and banks. If Greece had to default or restructure its crushing debts, Cyprus would inevitably be thrown into a severe bank crisis of its own, especially since the assets in Cypriot banks were eight times higher than GDP. It was a disaster waiting to happen, and it did happen.

The largest expatriate community is Russian, with an estimated 60,000 residents around the port of Limassol; 25,000 are eligible to vote. In 2000 Cyprus agreed

The Annan Plan, 2004

Land to be handed back from Turks to Greeks under UN scheme

British sovereign territory

Source: *The Economist*

to cooperate with international efforts to curb abusive and criminal tax-avoidance schemes. It received US approval in its efforts to fight money laundering and the drug trade. Credit-rating agencies upgraded its credit worthiness.

Until the global recession that began in 2008, the Greek Cypriot economy was booming, with GDP growing annually by just under 4% from 2004 to 2007, but down to −7% in 2014. Inflation stood at 3.5% in 2009, and unemployment had risen from 3.9% to 16% by 2015, twice that for young people. To attract foreign investment, the government reduced corporate taxes to 12.5%, the lowest in the EU. The south achieved its first budget surplus in 2007 and qualified to adopt the euro in 2008; by 2011 its budget was in deficit by 7%. Reducing this would be very difficult under any circumstances. Its total foreign debt was 61.7% of GDP in 2011, close to the 60% desired by the EU. However, if its banks' liabilities were included, its debt in 2013 would be 145%. More than half of the outstanding bank loans in 2015 were nonperforming, including those of 13 of 56 members of parliament. Many shops are shuttered. It initiated deep spending cuts, including in defense. The retirement age was lifted from 60 to 63.

But then the bottom dropped out of the economy and the banking system. By March 2013 Cyprus desperately needed a €10-billion ($13 billion) bailout from the EU, IMF, and ECB (called the troika). The latter offered to help but insisted that €5.8 billion be raised from the offending government and the bank depositors themselves. There would be no more "casino economies," little countries with banking sectors many times larger than GDP that violated the rules and made other partners vulnerable. They must pay a price for their mistakes. The richer EU countries also disliked Russian involvement in Cyprus and had no desire to bail out Russian money launderers.

At first, the government agreed to making all depositors pay, including insured depositors with less than €100,000 in the bank. But this drove protesters into the streets, and parliament angrily rejected it. A second agreement was accepted, sparing the small insured investors, but large depositors were hit hard. The country's second-largest bank, Laiki, was shut down, and its large depositors lost almost all their money. Those with over €100,000 in the largest, the Bank of Cyprus, suffered losses of up to 60%. It was restructured. Banks were closed for a week, and currency controls were imposed for the first time in the eurozone. In the end the banking system was drastically overhauled and reduced by half. The reforms made the economy and banks stronger.

Not surprisingly, Cypriots were angry and insulted. Many felt they had been victimized and bullied into accepting the draconian solution, with the threat of being tossed out of the euro if they refused. President Anastasiades accused EU leaders of "blackmail" to get him to agree.

CULTURE

Cypriots, whether Greek or Turkish, Christian or Muslim, share a number of basic cultural traits. In both groups the rural population is generally poorer than the city dwellers. Women of both groups traditionally led rather restricted lives and with very few exceptions did not participate in public life nor enter the professions. That is slowly changing. Greek Cypriot women increasingly enter the professions and exercise rights similar to those in the rest of Europe. The two communities were already socially separate before the geographical separation of 1974. This social avoidance resulted from reciprocal suspicions and hostility rooted more in tradition and emotion than in culture.

It has not been the similarities but the differences that have been emphasized by the two communities. This is reflected by the remark "There are no Cypriots living on Cyprus, only Greeks and Turks." In the cities, members of the two communities often cannot be distinguished by appearance, but in the countryside the style of clothing worn is frequently distinctive. They celebrate different holidays. The Greeks celebrate Easter in the spring, while the Turks celebrate their Islamic Bairam (at the time of pilgrimage to Mecca) at different times in each year according to a lunar calendar. Then the national holidays of Greece are observed by one community, and those of Turkey, by the other.

The Church of Cyprus is one of the largest and most influential investors in Cyprus. It has extensive holdings in banks, real estate, and other interests. An Eastern Orthodox church, its archbishop is Chrysostomos II. In the midst of the 2013 financial crisis, he went on TV and offered the church's properties as collateral so that the government could issue more bonds to raise money.

Greek Cypriots traditionally dominated trade and industry, and this gave Turks the feeling that they were economically oppressed, although relative to their numbers, Turks traditionally owned more farmland. Education in the respective communities has tended to follow the systems used in Greece and Turkey and was largely separate even before 1974. Those countries are also the sources of most of the books and periodicals read by the two communities.

For decades, Cypriot students wishing to study most disciplines at the university level were forced to go abroad, and a high proportion did so. However, the University of Cyprus opened in 1992, incorporating the existing teacher-training institute. There are now 10 universities on the island, after 3 colleges in the south were upgraded to university status in 2007. The six Turkish universities in the north have 32,500 students, most from mainland Turkey. The four southern universities educate 5,500 students. Three of them are private: European University Cyprus, Frederick's University, and Nicosia University.

The Greek Cypriot government refuses to recognize any institution of higher learning in the north. This means that degrees from Turkish Cypriot universities are not recognized in western Europe. Fewer than 100 Turkish Cypriot students cross the border to study in the south. Scholars in the south are prohibited from collaborating with their counterparts in the north. They are even discouraged from traveling there, especially with students.

A Nicosia University dean lamented, "Students from both communities show a marked lack of curiosity about their compatriots." In attempt to eliminate the stereotypes each has of the other, history teachers from both communities are engaging in joint discussions to find ways to contribute to reconciliation. The Turkish Cypriot government adopted a new set of history textbooks that take a constructive approach to intercommunal relations and cooperation.

FUTURE

A mood of optimism has arisen on the island of Cyprus. The prospects are encouraging for a breakthrough in unity talks, even though they broke down again in 2017 over the issue of Turkish troops. Negotiations resumed between the two presidents. The key is for Cypriots on both sides of the Green Line to be persuaded that a deal is not a zero-sum game and that both sides would benefit. Reconciliation appears to be less elusive. However, the election of Ersin Tatar as the northern president may set back efforts to unite Cyprus under a power-sharing model.

The economy will remain in trouble. It will be a challenge to attract businesses. The World Bank placed it 36th in its "Doing Business" rankings, and the World Economic Forum ranked it 58th on its competitiveness table. Foreign, particularly Russian, money may go somewhere else. Unemployment surged to 17.5% in 2014 (40% for youth). EU help will be hard to get. Presidential elections in February 2018 and October 2020 did not change this reality.

The Italian Republic (Italy)

A rainy morning in Rome

Area: 187,176 sq. mi. (301,225 sq. km, about twice the size of California; about 750 miles—1,200 km—from north to south and from 95 to 155 miles—152 to 248 km wide).

Population: 60.4 million.

Capital City: Rome (Roma in Italian; pop. 2.5 million, est.).

Climate: From late spring to early winter, the days are generally sunny and warm. Midsummer is quite hot in all but the north, where in the winter (the rainy season throughout the country) temperatures can sink to below freezing; the south is consistently warm.

Neighboring Countries: France (west); Switzerland and Austria (north); Slovenia (northeast), with Croatia, Bosnia-Herzegovina, Montenegro, and Albania paralleling its eastern coastline across the Adriatic Sea, 50 to 100 miles (80 to 160 km) away.

Official Language: Italian.

Principal Minorities: Predominantly German-speaking people with Austrian culture in South Tirol (Alto Adige); Albanian-speaking people in Calabria and Sicily; Greek-speaking people in Grecia-Salentin (Puglia) and some places in Calabria; French-speaking minority in Aosta-Valley; Slovene-speaking minority in the Trieste-Gorizia area; Catalan-

speaking minority in northeast Sardinia (Alghero).

Principal Religion: Roman Catholic.

Main Exports: Engineering products, transport equipment, chemicals, textiles and clothing, foodstuffs.

Main Imports: Engineering products, energy products, chemicals, transport equipment, foodstuffs, textiles and clothing.

Major Trading Partners: EU (56% of exports and 53.7% of imports), Germany (13.1% of exports and 15.6% of imports), France (11.6% of exports and 8.3% of imports), US (6.1% of exports), UK (4.7% of exports and 2.7% of imports), Netherlands (5.2% of imports).

Currency: Euro.

National Holiday: June 2 (1946), anniversary of the republic.

Chief of State: Sergio Mattarella, President (since February 2015).

Head of Government: Mario Dragui, Prime Minister (since February 2021).

National Flag: From the pole, three equal vertical stripes of green, white, and red.

Italy is easily recognized on every map by its boot shape. This narrow peninsula with the Apennine Mountain Range as its backbone extends from the Alps almost to the North African coast. It is flanked by the

largest islands of the Mediterranean: Sicily (15,500 sq. mi.; 25,000 sq. km) and Sardinia (14,300 sq. mi.; 23,000 sq. km) in the western basin of the Mediterranean. With its own coastline extending almost 5,000 miles (8,000 km) and its mild climate, Italy has lured people for thousands of years. However, most of its settlers did not come as polite guests but rather as plunderers or conquerors who used force to overrun the land.

In the long course of Italian history, almost all the peoples of Europe have at one time or another either occupied or settled the country. From the ancient Greeks to the Spaniards, from the ancient Germanic tribes and Arab Saracens to the Holy Roman and Austrian emperors, peoples of the world have left their traces in Italy. This almost-uninterrupted chain of foreign domination dating back to the classical period has decisively affected the traditions, behavior, and mentality of the Italian. At the same time, it has provided a basic impulse for Europe. Roman rule, which extended from the Mediterranean area through present-day Germany and France, as well as all the way to Hadrian's Wall in Britain, and the Renaissance (meaning "rebirth") in the 14th and 15th centuries decisively shaped western civilization.

Italy

In northern Italy the visitor witnesses a modern industrial and urban life. But in the south one finds the many typical characteristics of a developing nation, with illiteracy, high unemployment, and unproductive agriculture. Whoever takes the so-called sunny freeway to a village in the region of Abruzzi in central Italy finds himself in two different worlds: on the one hand, modern construction and, on the other hand, a medieval mountain village that has had electricity for little over a half-century. Old women clothed in black sit in front of their houses and look distrustfully at the stranger.

Even by western European standards, Italy is a prosperous nation. At the same time, one is astonished by the social differences between the rich and poor. It has the sobering task of defending a 5,000-mile coastline. Given the strong centrifugal forces of highly diverse regions and countless competing political groups, it is no wonder that Guilio Andreotti wrote in his memoirs that Italy is almost ungovernable.

HISTORY

One of the major contradictions of Italian history is that the heroic epoch that was invoked and emulated by Mussolini, Italy's fascist dictator from 1922 to 1943, is actually not Italian history but rather the history of a single city, Rome. This city rose to become the ruler of the entire Mediterranean world and, much more, of Europe. At one time, a person could truly say, "all roads lead to Rome." Italians themselves interpret differently the significance of Rome's earlier power and influence. If one were to ask inhabitants of southern Italy,

particularly someone from Calabria or Sicily, whether they consider themselves descendants of the Romans, one would immediately receive a vigorously negative response. Even in the north, the people, with their Celtic roots, do not consider themselves descendants of the Romans. Southern Italians view Roman history as the beginning of perpetual foreign or outside control. The present form of this control is the economic predominance of the north over the south.

In a strict sense, Roman history cannot be called Italian national history because the concept of "the nation" was completely unknown in the ancient world. Yet, one cannot understand modern Italy without first viewing some of the principal features of Rome's development. This still-vibrant past has had tremendous impact not only upon Italy itself but also upon western Europe as a whole. The most evident examples of Roman heritage are found in the Romance languages, which include modern Italian, Spanish, Portuguese, Romanian, and French. Without its Latin components, English would never have developed as it did and certainly would be incomprehensible to people today. The grammatical structure and vocabulary of all modern Germanic languages was strongly influenced by Latin (including the old rule that the verb comes last, which gives non-Germans so much trouble). In law, civil administration, literature, art, and engineering, ancient Roman civilization established the standards for many centuries.

The Early Period

The history of ancient Rome is long and exceedingly complicated and is

punctuated with magnificent victories and achievements, as well as ignoble failures, corruption, and civil war. That history can be divided roughly into three periods: it was ruled by kings from roughly 753 BC (according to Roman legend) until 509 BC, when a revolt led to the establishment of a republic, governed by elected consuls. The Roman Republic lasted until 45 BC when Julius Caesar established an empire subsequently ruled by emperors. In 185 AD this mighty empire began to fragment. It was divided under Emperor Theodosis in 395 AD into a western empire, led from Rome, Milan, and Trier in present-day Germany, and an eastern empire, ruled from Constantinople (now Istanbul) in Turkey. The former empire finally collapsed in 476 AD, whereas the eastern one continued to exist for another 1,000 years.

According to their own legend, the Romans were descendants of a group of Greeks who had accompanied Aeneas, one of the sons of the Trojan King Priam. Aeneas, who many historians would say was not Greek, had escaped from the burning city of Troy and had sailed across the Mediterranean Sea before being blown ashore at the mouth of the Tiber River. There he allegedly founded a city called Lavinium. In fact, Italy was settled around 1200 BC by Indo-European tribes which moved into the area from the west, and since the Trojans were Indo-Europeans themselves, there might have been some truth in the Roman belief that they were descended from the Greeks.

The settlers in the Italian Peninsula broke up into various warlike tribes: The Etruscans settled around the present city of Viterbo, located about 66 miles (110 km) north of Rome. The Umbrians also settled north of Rome around the present city of Perugia. The Samnites built up their civilization south of Rome, while the Latins were based around the Tiber River. At the bottom of the peninsula and on the island of Sicily, the Greeks and Phoenicians established colonies, which thrived on trade and shipping.

Roman legends tell us that the city of Rome was founded in 753 BC by a Latin chief named Romulus, one of the infants allegedly reared by a she-wolf. The new city was situated on a hilly site about 20 miles (32 km) inland from the former city of Lavinium in order to be out of reach of Phoenician and Greek raiders. Romans believed that Romulus made himself king of Rome and ruled until 716 BC. He was succeeded by Numa Pomilius, who came from the Sabine tribe and who is said to have introduced Rome's first religious institutions, which were largely copied from those of the Etruscans and Greeks. Many Greek gods were worshipped, although the Romans gave them different names.

Florence: Medieval parade

An Etruscan soldier

For instance, Zeus became Jupiter, Hera became Juno, Hermes became Mercury, and Athena became Minerva.

Under the rule of the Roman kings, the city's influence and control began to expand beyond the original seven hills, named the Palatine, the Capitoline, the Esquiline, the Aventine, the Caelian, the Quirinal, and the Viminal. The most powerful foes were the Etruscans, a fierce but civilized people who had perfected the use of iron. The Etruscan leader Tarquin reportedly defeated the Romans and became king. Although it still became the leading city of the Latin League, a loose association of cities bound together for purposes of defense, Rome's subsequent kings were of Etruscan descent and were known as "the Tarquins"; they were elected by a small group of noblemen.

Under the Tarquin kings, Rome's class system became more firmly shaped. On top was the patrician class, consisting of free Romans who had the right to attend the assembly of aristocrats who advised the king. Eventually this assembly became open to all Romans who owned property.

The plebeian class was composed of freed slaves who had immigrated to the city. The third class was composed of slaves, who had some rights but who were not citizens. Only patricians and plebeians were allowed to serve in the army. Soldiers were at first required to provide their own uniforms, weapons, and supplies, and they were paid by being able to share in the booty gained in victorious campaigns.

The last king was also named Tarquin, but his people called him Superbus because of his arrogance. He ruled very badly, involving Rome in expensive wars, arresting and murdering Roman citizens without trial, and generally subjecting the city to a reign of terror. Finally, in 509 BC two patricians staged a successful revolt and drove out the last of the kings, although it was not until 496 BC that the final attempt by the Etruscans and Sabines to restore the monarchy in Rome was suppressed.

The Republic

Because the kings had made themselves so hated, the Roman Republic was declared, which was ruled by two consuls elected by the People's Assembly each year for a one-year term. The first two consuls were the leaders of the revolt, Brutus and Collatinus, who were the most important founders of the republic. Later, officials below the level of consuls were elected in pairs, and the normal career path to the post of consul was through a series of lower offices.

The republican constitution was not wholly democratic in the modern sense because it granted considerably more power to the patricians than to the plebeians and because most slaves were entirely excluded from politics. Only the election of the civil servants, consuls, and judges by the People's Assembly can be regarded as democratic. There can be no doubt that a few influential Roman families wielded a disproportionate amount of power and authority. In general, the nobility and large landowners ensured that all political functions were carried out honorably. Yet it was possible for common people with talent to acquire great political prominence and to influence Roman politics. For example, the well-known politician Cicero, who did not come from one of the few influential families in Rome, was the most famous orator of his time. Despite his great influence and fame, he suffered his entire life from an inferiority complex about his humble background.

The Roman constitution succeeded in solving many social crises and enabled Rome to establish and maintain a citizen's army. Realizing that victories were their own, these citizen soldiers were eminently more motivated than the disorderly mercenary armies of oriental dynasties. For the ancient world, the Roman civic virtues, such as discipline, obedience, and bravery, were of great importance. They made their control over other peoples legitimate. Three essential pillars for the Roman state's strength were the exclusively Roman understanding of the commonwealth as res publica ("affairs of the people"), from which the word "republic" is derived; the right of political participation, which was the highest goal of every distinguished Roman; and the disdain for all purely private matters.

In the Roman Republic, important steps toward limited government were made: The very existence of a constitution, as long as it is observed, places limits on rulers' power. The Roman republican constitution, which was unwritten, especially embodied many principles essential for the development of modern democracy and did limit the state's control over citizens in several important ways. It was based on the separation of power between the executive and the legislature. Two consuls, who were elected by the People's Assembly composed of all citizens, provided the executive leadership. However, the electoral system gave more votes to those citizens who paid more taxes. Therefore, upper classes always had a majority of votes. The highest executive authority alternated each day from one consul to the other, although the consul not having the highest authority could veto decisions made by the other except in times of war. The yearly election and the mutual control over each other prevented the concentration of power in one person's hands.

The fact that the civilian rulers had command over the military, even in times of crisis, prevented the development of a "state within a state" and the use of war as an end in itself instead of as a political means. The daily alternation of supreme command over the military, however, caused many defeats, the most famous occurring in Cannae in 216 BC. But these changes helped to prevent a military dictatorship. In time of extreme emergency, the People's Assembly could appoint a dictator to exercise full political powers until the grave dangers to the city had passed. The only exception to such a dictatorship limited in time was Julius Caesar, who, at the end of the Roman Republic, was appointed dictator for life.

The Senate wielded limited legislative power and had authority over foreign policy, including the declaration of war and ratification of treaties. In domestic policy it had only advisory power. In contrast to the consuls and other civil servants, Senators, who numbered up to 300 at any one time, were not elected; rather they consisted of retired high government officials, including all former consuls.

Italy

To protect themselves in courts of law, the plebeians forced the establishment of Tribunes for the People, elected by the People's Assembly and to whom any plebeian could turn for help whenever he believed that he was being treated unjustly. These People's Tribunes could even veto decisions made by the Senate, and they could eventually veto any law. It was considered to be a very serious crime to attack the tribunes during their term of office. Plebeians won the right for themselves (and for slaves) to stand for election to all city offices and thereby ultimately to gain seats in the Senate. Plebeians also won the right to marry patricians, thus making class lines less rigid.

Very significantly, the plebeians were able to have a written legal code adopted in 454 BC. These laws were published on 12 bronze tablets, known as the Twelve Tablets of Law, and were kept in the heart of the city, known as the Forum. Every Roman schoolchild was expected to know them by heart, and they ultimately became the foundation of Roman law and of the legal systems of many modern European nations. Roman laws embodied all the important rules pertaining to contracts, the protection of private property, marriage and divorce, and inheritance. Because private property was at the core of Roman legal thought, offenses were most frequently punished by requiring payment of property. The victims of petty theft and robbery and the families of murder victims were compensated by means of fines and confiscated property. The Romans had no clear-cut criminal law, with the exception of a political penal code for corruption, abuse of public office, and high treason.

Two important preconditions for the rise of Rome were the still unexplained decline of Etruscan rule over northern and central Italy in the 5th and 4th centuries BC, as well as the Roman domination of the various tribes in Italy and the Greek cities in the south. Rome had been constantly threatened by various tribes within Italy and by Gauls who poured into the peninsula from the north. Once it was even captured and burned. The city was saved several times by such heroes as Cincinnatus and Camillus.

One Greek city in southern Italy, Tarentum, even sent for the help of Pyrrhus, king of Epirus in northern Greece, who arrived in 280 BC with a huge fleet carrying a herd of elephants and 25,000 troops. This army clashed with the Romans outside of Heraclea in 280 BC; the Romans fought extremely well, but when Pyrrhus sent his elephants roaring and screaming against the enemy troops, who had never seen such beasts before, the soldiers panicked and retreated. Though he won the battle, Pyrrhus had lost far more soldiers than the Romans had, and his weakened troops therefore were eventually beaten at Benventum. Today, the words "Pyrrhic victory" refer to any success achieved at too high a price.

Punic Wars

The victory over Pyrrhus, along with other swift and successful campaigns, established Roman domination over the Italian Peninsula in the first part of the 3rd century and permitted them to cast their sights farther for the first time. It is no surprise that Italy hurled a serious challenge against the major naval power in the western Mediterranean at the time: the Phoenician metropolis of Carthage (located a few miles outside the present city of Tunis in North Africa). Carthage had numerous colonies extending all along the coasts of North Africa and Spain, and it dominated Sardinia and the western part of Sicily.

In the first Carthaginian (Punic) War (264–241 BC) between the land power Rome and the sea power Carthage, Rome demonstrated its unusual adaptability by skillfully utilizing its allies in order to acquire sea power itself and by gaining the three large islands, Sicily, Sardinia, and Corsica. From 218 to 202, after the Romans had finally expelled the Gauls from the

Built by the first Tarquin king, the Circus Maximus, seating 300,000 Romans, saw the first chariot races.

Italy

The Roman Senate

mainland peninsula, Carthage, which had been provoked by Roman meddling in Spain, sought revenge in a second round of battles known as the Second Punic War.

The Carthaginians, led by a brilliant young general named Hannibal, threatened the very heart of Rome's Italian domain. In 218 BC he moved an army of 100,000 foot soldiers, 1,300 cavalry, and 40 elephants from Spain over the Pyrenees and Alps right into Italy. But the climate was too cold in the mountains, and he lost all his elephants and many of his troops during this journey. Nevertheless, he was able to assemble an army on its soil in 218 BC. Although the Romans tried to avoid open battle, except at Cannae, Hannibal's forces succeeded in destroying several Roman armies through skillful maneuvering, but they were never able to take Rome; he remained until 203 BC, when he received word of an end run that the Romans were planning on Carthage itself. He departed hastily to his city's rescue but to no avail. In the third Punic War, Roman troops captured the city and destroyed it, salting the soil in the hope that nothing would ever grow again. From this harshness came the expression "a Carthaginian peace." At last, Rome was unchallenged master of the western Mediterranean. A treaty between Rome and Carthage, now outside Tunis,

ending the Punic Wars was finally signed in 1987 AD.

Roman Imperialism

Rome could now direct its sights eastward toward Greece. Between 198 and 190 BC, Rome won victories in Greece, which not only again opened the Roman door wide to Greek cultural influence but it also gave the Romans a firm foothold in Asia Minor. This was the beginning of Roman imperialism. Hitherto, diplomatic balancing and management of conquered peoples were the primary factors in Roman foreign policy; in the new phase, it adopted different methods of power politics. Punitive expeditions against disloyal allies and the destruction of cities like Carthage and Corinth in 115 BC revealed the foreign political pattern for the conquest of the eastern Mediterranean area. By 63 BC nearly all the countries in the Mediterranean region were paying tribute to Rome.

The burden of constant war and of administering the enormous empire overextended the resources of a small state that had started on the banks of the Tiber River at the foot of the Palatine Hill. It had transformed itself into a large and powerful metropolis.

The Romans' encounter with Greece during the conquest of the eastern

Mediterranean area influenced Roman life and thought in such a way that the Roman poet Horace could write that the "conquered Greeks conquered their victors." Greek slaves taught the children of the wealthy in the Roman Empire. The Greek language assumed a role during the republic that in some ways corresponded to that of the French language in the 17th and 18th centuries. However, the Romans clung to their traditional political and cultural norms and deeply mistrusted foreign influences. They were willing to adopt those technical and institutional achievements of other peoples that the Romans considered worthy of copying. For instance, many weapons systems were patterned after those of the conquered peoples. The critical examination and adoption of whatever was considered better, combined with the steadfastness of a self-reliant identity, gave Roman policies their dynamism and flexibility.

After many years the republican constitution became increasingly incapable of solving the many social problems of such a large realm. The defense of the vast empire, with its many administrative requirements, called for an effective central bureaucracy, but the old republic did not have such an institution and was therefore unable to perform many essential

Italy

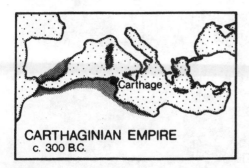

CARTHAGINIAN EMPIRE
c. 300 B.C.

functions. Numerous military campaigns claimed thousands of casualties and therefore left large tracts of land either to fall fallow or into the hands of the large landowners. Further, following the campaigns, many unemployed soldiers drifted into Rome, thereby adding to the city's mounting problems.

In earlier times no one was permitted to enter the city of Rome with weapons. Standing armies with nothing to do and former peasants who had lost their land to large landowners broke down the old customs that had integrated the army with the society and the state. At this point, the earlier observation of the Greek philosopher Aristotle applied to Rome: Masters of weapons are also masters of the state.

The political order in the Roman Republic began slowly to disintegrate, and widespread dissatisfaction, lawlessness, and corruption ran riot throughout the realm. The citizens' rights were gradually whittled away; the parties particularly established themselves in the social circles of the later republic from 133 to 45 BC. The Senate Party represented the interests of the nobility and the large landowners, while the Popular Party was supported by the masses.

The Republic Falls; the Empire Arises

Early in the 1st century BC, civil war between these two groups broke out which lasted on and off for most of the remainder of the century. The leading figure in this struggle was Gaius Julius Caesar, the best-known leader within the Popular Party. Born into a patrician's family but always possessing strong plebeian sentiments, his extraordinary bravery and endurance endeared him with his troops. He was a talented general, politician, orator, poet, historian, mathematician, and architect. William Shakespeare called this unique man "the noblest man that ever lived in the tide of times." In 60 BC he was elected consul and set about to accomplish his two chief objectives of establishing order in Rome and the empire and reconciling the conflicting classes. He spent nine years in Gaul (presently France) and Britain. This enabled him not only to win victories for Rome but also to write an eight-volume

history entitled the *Gallic War*. This remains one of the most important books of ancient history.

When he wanted to return to Rome in 49 BC, the Senate informed him that he was to disband his army and to return to Rome alone. Sensing that he was about to be arrested, he decided to cross the Rubicon River and to march his army against Rome itself. For four years he confronted his enemies, including his former friend and son-in-law Pompey, in battles in Greece, Egypt, North Africa, and Spain, before returning in 45 BC as master of the entire Roman world.

Julius was acclaimed dictator in 45 BC. He proceeded to try to restore order and to introduce such measures as founding colonies inside and outside of Italy to provide new lives for Rome's unemployed, providing grain for the hungry, enabling non-Romans to become members of the Senate, and making all residents of Italy Roman citizens. He also made no secret of his conviction that Rome could survive only if it had one ruler with absolute power that included the right to name his successor.

Fearing the restoration of kings, a group of senators let by Brutus and Cassius murdered Caesar in 44 BC in the theater of Pompeius, which was being used temporarily as the Senate. This act, vividly dramatized by Shakespeare, again thrust Rome into a civil war that touched every part of the realm. Not until Octavian, Caesar's grandnephew, established order in 31 BC did the bloody civil war come to an end. He became the first emperor of Rome, under the name of Augustus (meaning "the revered"), and his successors bore the title of "Caesar" in honor of Julius. The Roman Republic was dead, and the Roman Empire had commenced. The Caesars served for life and were selected in many different ways. Most of them were not from the city of Rome. Some even came from Spain (Trajan), Africa (Lucius Septimius Severus), or what is now Yugoslavia (Diocletian).

Peace and Prosperity

Augustus restored order and revived trade, and his people again experienced the rare combination of peace and prosperity. He launched a building program in the empire and its capital that enabled him to say toward the end of his life in 14 BC, "I found Rome a city of brick and am leaving it a city of marble." Despite a string of less capable emperors, his life's work lasted almost two centuries.

There are many preconceived ideas about Roman emperors. They are often portrayed as degenerate beasts who practiced tyranny with Caesarean insanity, only to fall victims to palace revolts

or poisonous death. This is only an anecdotal and superficial understanding. It is true that they sometimes directed political cruelty against other members of the noble class who might have presented a threat to them, but the Roman Empire and its citizens drew many benefits from the emperors' efforts.

It was precisely the centralized bureaucracy, which the emperors created, which made the Roman Empire the blooming civilization as we know it today. Some were wise and learned men, such as Marcus Aurelius, whose published volume *Meditations* is still a highly valued philosophical work. Impressive ruins bear eloquent witness to prosperous Roman cities from Germany to the desert sands of the Sahara. The empire reached its greatest expansion under Emperor Trajan from 98 to 117 AD. From Iraq to Scotland, from Cologne to Libya, one spoke Latin and lived according to Roman law and customs.

A dark shadow over the cultural splendor of the Roman classical period was the fact that much of the economic prosperity was achieved by means of slave labor. Modern estimations are that, at any one time, between 300,000 and 500,000 slaves provided a luxurious life for many citizens of Rome, which by the 2nd century AD had grown to a city of over 1 million inhabitants, including slaves. Our present view of humanity inclines us to judge harshly the treatment of the ancient slaves, who, without rights or status, could be sold or even killed by their masters. Under Roman law they were considered to be nothing more than "animated tools." However, slaves were actually valuable property, especially an educated Greek.

The degree of suppression endured by a slave depended upon his type of work. Naturally, those slaves who served in public office, including the highest administrative positions, or who as scholars instructed the children of wealthy Romans were much better off than those who worked on the large plantations. The exploitation of the latter led to two slave revolts. In 136 BC the slaves in Sicily rose up under their leader Syrer Eunus and established a short-lived slave republic in the city of Enna. From 73 to 71, Rome trembled before the legendary slave leader Spartacus, who led 90,000 rebellious slaves in southern Italy.

Very early the conscience of many persons was stirred by the injustice of slavery. In Plautus's comedies the slaves always played the intelligent and superior roles. Stoic philosophy rejected such servitude entirely. In making a judgment against human bondage in the Roman world, one must remember that slavery existed in modern times, as well. In addition, the history of human suppression

Statue of the emperor Trajan in Rome

and exploitation is a very long one. To say that a worker during the period of early capitalism in Manchester or a mercenary Hessian soldier bought by the English to fight against Washington's army during the American Revolution was better off than an ancient slave would be deceptive.

The Decline and Fall of the Empire

The emperors considered their main task to be the security of the empire's extensive borders. However, as the threat of invasion became greater and greater, the ancient Roman world was unable after the beginning of the 3rd century AD to withstand the mounted attacks of Germans, Slavs, Huns, Persians, Turks, Mongolians, Berbers, and later, Arabs.

In 284 AD Diocletian, the son of a freed slave from Illyria (along the eastern Adriatic coast) became emperor. He realized that the Roman Empire had grown too large to be governed by one man, so in 285 AD he divided it into an eastern and a western part. He assumed rule over the eastern portion, with its seat in Nicomedia in Asia Minor. The subsequent western emperors held court at Milan and Trier. Emperor Constantine, who became sole emperor of Rome in 324 AD, continued the reorganization of the empire initiated by Diocletian. He built a new city on the site of the former Byzantium, a strategically important crossroads between Asia and Europe, and named it after himself:

Constantinople. From then on, the Roman Empire was administered from that city, and Rome lost much of its significance. There, Roman civilization mingled with that of Greece and Asia.

Disciples of and converts to Christianity had been circulating amid most parts of the empire since the 1st century AD, converting many who held the ancient Greek and Roman beliefs in the classical gods to their belief in a single, almighty God. These beliefs and moral teachings were those of a mortal who claimed to be his son. A gradual Christian penetration of the Roman society and the emergence of Christianity to that of a state religion were not as commonly supposed. They were only persecuted when they directly challenged the traditional classical understanding of a state religion as a form of political loyalty. It would not have been possible for Christian beliefs to spread unless there had otherwise been an attitude of relative religious tolerance. In spite of some use of torture and martyrdom, this faith continued inexorably to grow, eventually becoming the most powerful and dominating concept of the western and Middle Eastern worlds. It was supplanted by Islam to a large degree in the Middle East after the life of the prophet Muhammad.

Constantine decided to accept Christianity and to make it the empire's official religion. After his death in 337 AD, there was less and less cooperation and coordination between the eastern and western parts of the empire. While Constantinople was a safe distance from the marauding tribes of Europe, the western part became the object of sustained attacks by Goths, Visigoths, and Vandals. Rome was temporarily captured and sacked in 410 AD, and in 476 the East Gothic chief Odoacer marched his troops into the city and deposed the last western Roman emperor, Romulus Augustulus. Thereafter, sheep grazed on the overgrown ruins of the Forum, once the scene of the power behind the heart of the empire.

Rome Destroyed

The destruction of Rome was without precedent. But many aspects of this great empire have been salvaged for posterity, including its literature, which was protected in the Christian cloisters, and its law. Further testimonies to the splendor of the Roman past are the unique accomplishments in architecture, such as domes, columns, and basilicas, and in engineering, such as bridges, aqueducts, and highways. Most of the important European roads today follow the same routes established by the Romans. Therefore, Italy's past is significant not only to Italians but also to all persons touched by Western civilization.

The Middle Ages

During and after the Middle Ages, Italy was so fragmented into feuding and ever-shifting states, papal holdings, kingdoms, and foreign dominions that even well-educated Italians have difficulty comprehending their own history during that time. In the Middle Ages, as well as in modern times, Italy was characterized by foreign domination, inner strife, and parochialism of the Catholic Church. Over a span of 1,000 years, Byzantines, Germanic tribes, Arabs, Germans, Normans (Scandinavians), Frenchmen, Spaniards, and Austrians marched across the land and levied taxes or subjugated the dependent minor princes in the peninsula to servitude.

Ideals, such as freedom, unity, and independence, first became political realities in 1861 with the "Resurgence," or unification movement. With Italy's past in mind, it should be no surprise that Italians' identification with their state developed very slowly. The political culture was stamped with a combined feeling of powerlessness and distrust toward the state.

After the fall of the Roman Empire, centuries of gloom and of alternating domination, particularly by the Germans and Lombards, afflicted the peninsula until the Frankish King Pippin, father of Charlemagne, introduced in the 8th century AD a territorial order in Italy. It was divided into a Lombard-Frankish area in the north and a Byzantine area in the south, ruled ultimately from Constantinople. The results of this fateful division continue to be evident in the economic and cultural contrasts between the north and the south right up to the present day.

Along with the division of Italy, the so-called Pippin Deed had another extremely far-reaching consequence for the political development of Italy. The deed assured the pope an ecclesiastical state in the middle of Italy. Centuries later this was the last political entity in the nation that resisted unification with the national Italian state.

Meanwhile, during the later Middle Ages, as the north was involved in and profiting from the constant conflict between the German emperors and the popes, the south was undergoing an entirely different development. The Byzantines, who were also occupying Sicily, could no longer fend off the attacks of the Muslim Saracens from North Africa.

The Byzantines, who had become Eastern Orthodox Christians, could not count on the Roman Catholic Church for assistance in upholding their occupation. Around 900 Sicily blossomed into a rich and fertile garden under the new Muslim rule. The Saracens, reputed to be bloodthirsty pirates along the coast of Italy, exercised a clever and tolerant reign in which an enormous cultural flowering unfolded.

Italy

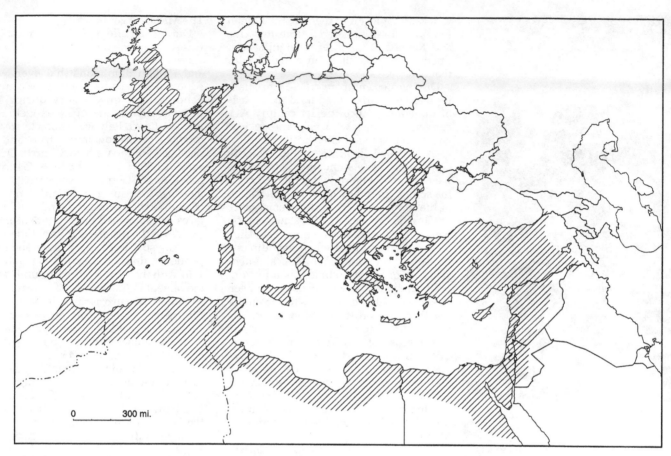

The Roman Empire at its height

They introduced lemons, oranges, cotton, and pistachio nuts, the last being the island's most important agricultural export today. Only an entirely new actor who entered the world scene could put an end to such a rule.

The Power of the Holy "Roman" Empire

In 1080, through a shrewd marriage policy, southern Italy under the Normans (Vikings) became joined with the Holy Roman (actually German) Empire under Friedrich II of the Staufen dynasty. Known to his contemporaries as "the wonder of the world," Friedrich was an enlightened emperor who was as at home in the world of politics as in the world of scholarship. His reign was the last golden age in Italy before a long period of conservative-clerical foreign domination. Despite their different lifestyles, Friedrich succeeded in uniting the original inhabitants of southern Italy, the Byzantine Greeks, and the Muslim Saracens in a life of harmonious coexistence. Under his rule a cultural and economic high point was achieved which was unparalleled in Europe at the time.

The new spirit of tolerance, as well as the encirclement of the ecclesiastical state by Friedrich's territories, did not please the pope. The long-standing dispute between the German emperors and the pope reached a climax with the appeal for a crusade against Friedrich. Many had hoped that a divided Italy would develop into a model state under the reign of the House of Staufen. These dreams were shattered, however, when the Frenchman Charles of Anjou, protégé of the pope, overthrew Staufen rule in Italy. Southern Italy suffered terribly under the domination of the Anjou family until 1282, when the mounting hate against the uninhibited French arrogance erupted. The absolute monarchy of the French in southern Italy was consumed with uninterrupted wars and could not withstand the attacks by the Aragonians from Spain, who through intrigues were able to undermine every French military unit.

Disunification

As a result of the disputes between the pope and the German emperor, the small and fragmented states and cities in northern Italy were able to achieve a certain degree of political independence. Loyalty to one side or the other varied, depending upon the political advantage at the time of a given battle.

The cities knew well how to exploit to their own economic advantage the disputes of the popes and the German emperors and the Crusades, which began at the end of the 11th century. The latter were medieval efforts directed at reclaiming Jerusalem from the Arabs. Of all cities, Venice profited most from these efforts. The Venetians did not in any way share the religious fervor or self-sacrifice of the German, French, and English knights. The knights and pilgrims en route to the Crusades and Jerusalem poured into rival Venice and Genoa in droves.

One of the most notable Crusades was the fourth, which took place from 1198 to 1204. The aged, composed, and politically gifted doge (leader) Dandolo of Venice was able to redirect the course toward Constantinople and agreed to transport the crusaders to their destination on the condition that they stop along the way and plunder Constantinople for Venice. Thus, instead of becoming conquerors of holy cities held by Muslims, the crusaders attacked and plundered a Christian capital city. The *Quadriga*, a large statue of four horses from the Hippodrome in Constantinople and now above St. Mark's Cathedral in Venice, bears witness to this strange event. In this way, a troublesome trade rival was seriously weakened. Venice was so powerful that it was not even perturbed

Ideal of virility: Tiziano Vecellio, *Portrait of a Man* **(***The Englishman***)**

Ideal of feminine beauty: Tiziano Vecellio, *Portrait of a Young Woman* **(***La Bella***)**

by the resulting excommunication of the Venetian leaders by the pope.

Despite the continuing conflict, no other country in Europe achieved at this time the degree of economic development that took place in Italy. One of the most well-known and powerful families of bankers, the Medici, had gained far-reaching political influence in their home city of Florence, as well as in France, where marriage joined Catherine de Medici with King Henry II. In the economically developed cities of northern and central Italy, the transition had been made from a less productive barter economy to a money economy. The bases of this affluence were the development of industry and trade, especially with the Middle and Far East.

The Reawakening (Renaissance)

In 1492 the Italian Christopher Columbus discovered the "new world." Some would say that this ended the strategic importance of the Mediterranean Sea and the Italian Peninsula. But in the 14th and 15th centuries, northern Italy was the cradle of an intellectual and cultural rebirth known as the Renaissance. This reawakening was indirectly stimulated by Venice's refusal to support Constantinople when that city was subjected to a determined Turkish attack. When that last remnant of the Roman Empire finally fell in 1453, many highly cultured Greeks emigrated to Italy from Constantinople and gave the Renaissance movement a significant boost. They

helped to reawaken Italian interest in the Greek classical authors. Had it not been for the efforts of the Italian scholars, who laboriously collected and preserved many ancient Greek works, the originals we possess today would have been lost forever.

In the depths of the foaming cauldron of bickering city-states, a fundamentally new approach to life was born. Man was no longer the *viator mundi* (pilgrim seeking heavenly salvation) of the Middle Ages, concerned with the universal principle of salvation. He became the *faber mundi* (the creator and master of the world), who shaped his own destiny. Self-assured individualism and rational thought were reflected in the Renaissance conception of the state. Autonomous states were directed by paid public officials according to the guidelines of "reason of state," and carefully calculated business considerations determined politics and administration. Wars were conducted by mercenary enterprises (known as condottieri) that dared to do battle in the same way as one dares to make capital investment, that is, only if a profit is certain. The Florentine Niccolò Machiavelli developed the theory of politics that in no way was based upon religious principles.

Correspondingly, scholars who had until that time been considered as *ancillas theologiae* ("slaves of theology") divested themselves of that status and began working independently of theology. Above all,

rediscovery of the classical authors advanced this secular conception to that of a rational principle. Spurred on by their Latin predecessors Dante, Petrarca, and Boccaccio, they created new literature in Italian (sometimes intermingled with Latin) but later a total variant of the historic language of Rome.

The universal man with his comprehensive wealth of knowledge represented the new ideal of the Renaissance man. The universal genius Leonardo da Vinci was a painter, artist, engineer, doctor, architect, and politician and is a particularly prominent example of vast numbers of creative persons who contributed enormously to his culturally rich times. Inspired by the classical model of rounded arches that tied together the central construction, architects developed a totally new concept of space through emphasis on the vertical, with clear, well-formed proportions. Donatello and Michelangelo surpassed their classical predecessors in expression and monumentality. In painting, the central perspective was developed which strove for ideal anatomical proportions that were at the same time more realistic. Masaccio, Botticelli, Raphael, and da Vinci, the best-known painters of their time, were the leading lights of an art movement that influenced the entire field of European painting.

Secular-Religious Relations

The popes themselves were responsible for directing the focus of the Renaissance from the religious realm to the secular princes and scholars. For instance, Pope Julius was Michelangelo's patron. As learned patrons of the arts, the popes accelerated the inner disintegration of the church—the reconstruction of St. Peter's Cathedral, sponsored by member of the Medici family Pope Leo X, could only be financed by his system of indulgences (paying for forgiveness of sin). This way of raising revenue unleashed the Reformation in the early 16th century. When the popes became staunch supporters of the Counter-Reformation, Italy ceased being the center of the Renaissance, which thereafter found a more congenial setting in France.

In the conflict between the Habsburgs and the French, which was the central problem for the western European states until the 18th century, the autonomous Italian city-states lost much of their independence. The plunder and devastation caused by the rival French and Habsburg armies, as well as pillaging and destruction by pirates from North African Barbary states, came to dominate life in Italy. The south gradually faded under Spanish domination and became unhinged from developments in the rest of Europe.

Italy

Da Vinci design and backward handwriting

The War of the Spanish Succession (1701–1713), which endangered the European balance of power between the Habsburgs and France, brought northern Italy under the domination of the Austrians and southern Italy under the control of the Spanish Bourbons. The popes retained their political hold over much of central Italy. Due to uncontrolled cuttings, the rich forests of Puglia, where Friedrich II had so happily hunted, were reduced to withering grasslands.

It is hardly surprising that the shock waves of the French Revolution of 1789 soon were felt in Italy, where feudal institutions and conditions were still present. French republican forces invaded Savoy and Nice in the fall of 1792, and in March 1796 a concentrated French campaign began in Italy. This resulted not only in temporary French domination of most of northern and central Italy but also in brilliant victories for a young French general who soon became the leader of France, Napoleon Bonaparte.

In early 1798 French forces invaded the Papal States. The pope fled, and a Roman Republic was established. Although the French were temporarily driven out of Italy in the latter part of 1799, Napoleon, who had seized power in late 1799, renewed his Italian conquests and soon secured much of Italy under his control. When Napoleon made himself emperor of France, he also placed an Italian crown on his head, thereby becoming king of Italy, with all of northern and central Italy under his authority. In the spring of 1806, French forces occupied the rest of Italy, and on March 30, 1806, Napoleon's brother Joseph was proclaimed the king of the Two Sicilies. When Joseph became king of Spain in 1808, French general Joachim Murat was crowned king of Naples.

Exit Napoleon

Although Napoleon's hold on Italy was finally broken in 1815, his legacy remained. He had decreed important reforms in the country. These included the Napoleonic Code, which, together with Roman law, remains the foundation of

Dante in Florence

Italian law today. He confiscated much of the Catholic Church's property, ended feudal privileges and immunities, and improved roads and education. He thereby gave Italians a crucial impetus for political, social, legal, and economic reform.

The restoration of the old regime after the Congress of Vienna reestablished Austrian domination in northern and central Italy. The pope was granted the Vatican's pre-Napoleonic holdings again, and the Bourbon king Ferdinand I of the Two Sicilies again became ruler of southern Italy. But the spark of the enlightenment, Italian nationalism, and the right of Italians to establish a democratic state continued to ferment within a few secret societies of bourgeois intellectuals.

Fragmented Italy

Prince Metternich of Austria stated correctly in 1815 that Italy was not a nation but rather a "geographic concept." The only state within Italy that played an active role in Europe was Piedmont-Savoy, where the unification movement originated. The remainder of Italy was either under foreign control or ruled by small splinter states. A contemporary example is tiny Campione d'Italia within Switzerland, population 2,000. The parochialism that had its roots in Italian history also resisted the liberal ideas of the French Revolution and those of the few "middle and upper-class romantics" who dreamed of Italian national unification. Numerous

uprisings, usually started by the secret societies against the established rulers, from 1820 to 1831 were all crushed.

The revolutionary movement was not strong enough to overcome Austrian domination without outside help. The major European powers had concluded that the balance of power in Europe was more important than Italian unity. Further, the most important secret resistance movement, the Carboneria (literally "Charcoal Burners") had been so loosely organized, so heterogeneous, and so unable to define its aims clearly that it was incapable of uniting in crucial moments.

It was these kinds of problems that certain subsequent Italian nationalists tried to avoid. The traveler to Italy notices that in every town, streets and plazas bear the names of Mazzini, Cavour, and Garibaldi. They made up the triple constellation of the "Resurgence," the name they gave to Italian political unification in 1861.

Gradual Unification

In 1831 a young Genoan political thinker, Giuseppe Mazzini, founded the Young Italy movement. He had remained the intellectual head and prophet of the unification drive for a free, independent, and republican Italy, although he was unable to lead that movement to success. He died in 1872, bitterly disappointed about the kind of Italian state that had been created.

In 1848 uprisings again occurred throughout Italy, and the pope was even temporarily driven out of Rome. But with the aid of French troops, the rebellion was quelled. With its failure, nationalists' eyes turned increasingly toward the Kingdom of Piedmont-Sardinia, whose capital was Turin and which was ruled by one of the oldest ruling families in Europe, the House of Savoy. It had been the only regime in Italy that had fought hard for freedom from Austria.

The new Piedmont King Victor Emmanuel, who was to become the first king of a united Italy, was a man of rough manners and visible virility. He became a popular focus of attention for those who wanted change. But that he was also a politically shrewd man was revealed by his appointment as Piedmontese prime minister of a man whom he personally detested: Count Camillo di Cavour. He was not brilliant, but he was a pragmatic man who was well aware that Italy could never become independent as a result of spontaneous mass uprisings of idealists. The political hold of Austria had to be broken, and he knew that Italians would need the help of a foreign power to do this. Therefore, he turned to the new French emperor Napoleon III.

The French leader agreed to support Piedmont in any war against Austria

Scene typical of the Renaissance: Dante in Florence

under the condition that, in the event of victory, France be rewarded with Nice and Savoy. The deal was sealed by the marriage of Victor Emmanuel's 15-year-old daughter Clotilde with Napoleon's lecherous cousin Jerome. With such a commitment tucked away in his breast pocket, Cavour sought a way to bring about war with Austria. Two blunders by the latter country played directly into Cavour's hands. One was Austria's decision to impose military conscription on its dominions of Lombardy and Venetia, a move which drove many draft-dodgers into Piedmont. The tension which arose as a result of Piedmont's refusal to turn these young men over to the Austrian authorities gave Cavour the excuse he needed to begin military preparations.

The second blunder was committed just when the French emperor was beginning to have second thoughts about the promises he had made earlier to Piedmont. In the spring of 1859, Austria issued an ultimatum to Piedmont, demanding that it either disarm itself or go to war. Cavour, of course, chose the latter and with Napoleon's assistance faced the powerful but indecisive Austrian army and defeated it at Magenta on June 4 and at Solferino on June 24 and conquered all Lombardy and Milan.

After these important victories, Napoleon grew weary of the war and concluded an armistice with the Austrians at Villafranca on July 11. Cavour was understandably furious at the French, but the movement toward Italian unity had gained such momentum that it could no longer be stopped. Revolutionary assemblies in Tuscany, Modena, Parma, and Romagna voted in August 1859 to unite with Piedmont; France and Britain spoke out against any foreign (i.e., Austrian) intervention to foil these popular decisions. In March 1860, plebiscites in the four areas confirmed the steps taken by the assemblies. True to his earlier promise, Cavour delivered Savoy and Nice to the French.

Southern Unification

With most of northern and central Italy now unified, the cauldron of unification began to bubble in the south. In the spring of 1860, revolts broke out in Sicily that gave a chance to reenter the center stage in Italy to a highly talented military adventurer, Giuseppe Garibaldi. A former member of Mazzini's Young Italy movement, he had spent 13 years as a soldier of fortune in Latin America, where he became a master in the leadership of irregular forces and guerrilla warfare. He had raced back to Italy in 1848, when he heard of the revolutionary activity there.

He formed military forces first in Lombardy, then in Venice, and finally in Rome, where he served under Mazzini to defend the Roman Republic which had just been created. From April to the end of June 1849, Garibaldi's legion, clad in red shirts and Calabrian hats, had defended the "Eternal City" valiantly against French troops who protected the pope. Prolonged resistance had proved to be impossible, so Garibaldi fled with his troops to the tiny independent republic of San Marino, where he disbanded his army and went into exile.

Revolts in Sicily in 1860 again drew him into southern Italy, and in May he packed his 1,000 irregulars, mostly students, poets, and soldiers of fortune, into rickety steamers and set a course directly to Sicily. When he arrived at Marsala, he declared himself dictator of Sicily and proceeded to defeat piecemeal the confused and divided Neapolitan troops who were supposed to defend the island. By mid-July he poised for his strike against the Bourbon Kingdom of the Two Sicilies with its capital in Naples.

Riding a tide of popular enthusiasm, Garibaldi's army, which had swollen to 10,000 men, crossed the Strait of Messina in mid-1860, and his units produced panic among the Neapolitan troops whenever they appeared. On September 7, a jubilant Garibaldi entered the city of Naples far in advance of his troops. In less than five months, he had conquered the Kingdom

A foreign-dominated, politically fragmented peninsula

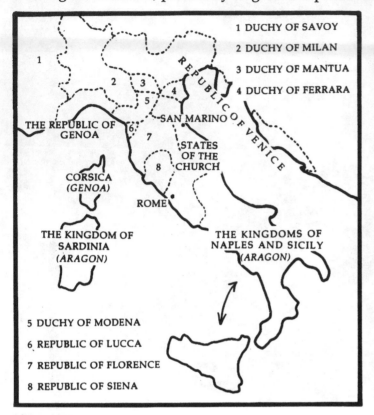

1 DUCHY OF SAVOY
2 DUCHY OF MILAN
3 DUCHY OF MANTUA
4 DUCHY OF FERRARA

THE REPUBLIC OF GENOA

CORSICA (GENOA)

THE KINGDOM OF SARDINIA (ARAGON)

SAN MARINO

STATES OF THE CHURCH

ROME

THE KINGDOMS OF NAPLES AND SICILY (ARAGON)

5 DUCHY OF MODENA
6 REPUBLIC OF LUCCA
7 REPUBLIC OF FLORENCE
8 REPUBLIC OF SIENA

About 1450

SAVOY
MILAN
PIEDMONT
REPUBLIC OF GENOA
GRAND DUCHY OF TUSCANY
SAN MARINO
REPUBLIC OF VENICE
STATES OF THE CHURCH
CORSICA (GENOA)
ROME
KINGDOM OF SARDINIA
KINGDOM OF NAPLES (AUSTRIA)
KINGDOM OF SICILY (AUSTRIA)

1 MANTUA
2 PARMA AND MODENA

About 1722

FRANCE

NAPOLEON'S "KINGDOM OF ITALY" (1804–1813)

SAN MARINO

OCCUPIED BY FRANCE

CORSICA (FRANCE)

ROME

KINGDOM OF SARDINIA

KINGDOM OF NAPLES (France, 1806–1813)

KINGDOM OF SICILY

Under Napoleon, 1804–1813

LOMBARDY (FROM AUSTRIA)
VENETIA
PIEDMONT
SAN MARINO
GRAND DUCHY OF TUSCANY
STATES OF THE CHURCH
CORSICA (FRANCE)
ROME
KINGDOM OF SARDINIA
NAPLES
KINGDOM OF THE TWO SICILIES (RULED BY SPANISH BOURBONS)
SICILY

1 PARMA
2 MODENA
3 LUCCA

The Unification of Italy, 1849–1870

of the Two Sicilies, a country of 11 million inhabitants.

He immediately set his sights again on Rome, which was still defended by French troops. Not wishing to lose entirely the initiative for unifying Italy, Cavour ordered his own troops to march southward into the Papal States. On September 18 they crushed the pope's forces at Castelfidardo and then defeated a remaining Neapolitan army at Capua. These successes prompted the Piedmontese parliament to annex southern Italy. In October plebiscites in Naples, Sicily, the Marches, and Umbria revealed overwhelming popular support for union with Piedmont.

On October 26, 1860, Garibaldi met Victor Emmanuel II at Teano. The warrior greeted Victor as king of Italy and shook his hand. When the monarch asked him not to start a war against the Vatican, Garibaldi reportedly replied, "*Obbedisco*!" (I obey!) and resigned his command the next day. He retired on the rocky island of Caprera, refusing to accept any reward for his services. He was subsequently called the "hero of the two worlds" as a tribute to his military adventures in South America and Europe.

In February 1861 Victor Emmanuel II was proclaimed king of Italy. A new Italian parliament representing the entire peninsula except Rome and the province of Venetia assembled. Shortly thereafter Florence became Italy's new capital until 1870.

Differences within the Union

The historical differences between northern and southern Italy were not overcome through the unification and establishment of a monarchy. Despite the initial enthusiasm in southern Italy for joining the newly unified state, the northern rulers considered the southern half of the autonomous Italian national state more as a conquered province of the north. They displayed little respect for traditional practices in the south, regarding the people as backward and rural, and merely included it in a highly centralized governmental administration that was imposed on all of Italy. Therefore, the Italian king's popularity in the south disappeared almost overnight, and southerners again began to look northward with distrust and resentment that has yet to disappear.

The new national leaders next turned to the province of Venetia, which was still in the clutches of the Austrian Empire. When the latter entered a war in 1866 against Prussia, however, Italy immediately sided with the victorious Prussians, who granted their allies the prize Italians had wanted. Only Rome remained outside the new Italy.

The End of the Church State

The ecclesiastical state under the pope remained a drop of melancholy in the

Giuseppe Garibaldi

Courtesy of Special Collections, University of Virginia Library

wine of the unification. The Vatican resented the reduction of its secular power in the unification of Italy. As the new Italian state was officially declared in 1861, it was taboo even to speak of Piedmont and that part of Italy ruled by it. But when France became locked in war against Prussia in 1870, French troops could no longer defend Rome against the rest of Italy. Hence, in September royal Italian troops marched into Rome unchallenged, and the national capital was transferred to the city without delay.

The ecclesiastical state came to an end, and the popes withdrew in bitterness behind the Vatican walls with utter contempt for the Italian kingdom. This papal rejection of the Italian state nipped in the bud all attempts to integrate Catholic elements in politics, and the Catholic prohibition against political participation

gained strength especially in the more independent-minded south. It hardened many Italians' distrust toward their state, a problem that remains today. Leading liberals asserted their strong anticlerical position despite the church's opposition. Only in the second decade of the 20th century did the church support an Italian Popular Party (the Popolari), founded in 1919 and a forerunner of the now-defunct Christian Democratic (DC) Party. Those historians are certainly correct who argue that an earlier integration of moderate Catholic forces would have helped stabilize Italy's political system and would have helped to prevent the later rise of fascism.

Continued Instability

The first years of unification were overshadowed by political instability, social opposition, and an ever-growing gap

Italy

Monument in Rome commemorating the unification of Italy

between north and south. The inhabitants of the South continued to be looked down upon as backward, illiterate semi–North Africans. The people were also disadvantaged by the new liberal leaders' dropping of trade barriers, which clearly favored the industrially powerful north.

The one-crop agrarian society of the south bore the full economic weight of foreign grain imports. Malnutrition, health problems, and child labor abuse set in motion an enormous emigration wave from the south. From 1886 to 1890, over 200,000 people left their homeland every year, most of whom sought refuge in the United States. Today, 25 million Americans are of Italian and/or Sicilian descent. The fact that most of their ancestors came from southern Italy helps explain why Americans often have a one-sided view of Italy, namely that of the impoverished south rather than the more opulent north.

Parliamentary proceedings degenerated quickly as deputies became so concerned about clinging to their seats that they avoided taking clear-cut stands on the pressing issues of the day. By means of a method which came to be known as *Trasformismo* ("Transformism"), prime ministers and cabinets disregarded party affiliation and made delicate bargains with any interested deputies from the left, right, or center in order to patch together a short-lived parliamentary majority. In the process, all political groups became highly fractured, and cabinets changed so constantly that no coherent and consistent governmental policy was possible. Major questions were avoided or postponed, and when domestic pressure for change became too great, governments tended to divert attention from them by taking refuge

in such emotional campaigns as anticlericalism or colonialism.

Colonial Ambitions

In order to cope with the problem of a surplus of workers and to divert attention from the domestic political paralysis and tensions, Italy embarked on a colonial policy which was not only unprofitable but also robbed it of its strength. After a casualty-ridden expedition into the East African coast of Eritrea (formerly in Ethiopia), Italy temporarily conquered this area in 1889–1890. A subsequent campaign in Ethiopia ended in catastrophe soon thereafter, costing the lives of 15,000 poorly equipped soldiers when the Ethiopians drove them out. Italy took Libya and the southeastern Greek Islands (Dodecanese) from Turkey, which was in the process of disintegration.

All of these foreign adventures could not distract from the domestic social tensions and conflicts. Rebellions, violent protests, assassinations, and bloody reactions against the forces of order became so commonplace by the turn of the 20th century that many observers believed that the young kingdom could not survive.

The most outstanding politician in the early 20th century was Giovanni Giolitti, who tried to fuse the liberal bourgeoisie and socialists who supported the state from 1903 to 1915. He was able to guide some progressive legislation through a highly undisciplined parliament. Factory laws were passed, insurance companies and railways were nationalized, trade unions were legalized, agricultural cooperatives were subsidized, and collective bargaining was encouraged. However, he could not overcome the widespread impression among the people that Italy

was not only standing still but was also decaying.

Sick and tired of these internal conflicts, a movement of bourgeois intellectuals under the leadership of the poet Gabriele D'Annunzio and the political thinkers Gaetano Mosca and Vilfredo Pareto gained respect and practically declared war on the parliamentary system. D'Annunzio called on young Italians to seek fulfillment in violent action that would put an end to parliamentary maneuvering, general mediocrity, and dullness that characterized public life. Mosca and Pareto called for a new political elite who understood how to use power and to put an end to materialist values.

A jingoist National Party was created in 1910 under the leadership of Enrico Corradini, who never tired of painting an attractive picture of martial heroism, of total sacrifice of individualism and equality to one's nation, of the need for reestablishing discipline and obedience, of the grandeur and power of ancient Rome, and of the personal gratification which comes with living dangerously. Many Italians needed only the travails of a long and disappointing war to make a dangerous leap toward fascism. They heard its extremist appeals with enthusiasm.

World War I

Although Italy had allied itself with Germany and Austria-Hungary in 1882, it declared its neutrality at the outbreak of World War I in 1914 on the grounds that its allies were waging an aggressive war. For more than 10 years, it had pursued, under Giolitti's leadership, a policy of peaceful reconciliation in Europe. Italy did, in fact, enter World War I against Austria and Germany in 1915. In Hemingway's *A Farewell to Arms*, one sees that the Italian war against Austria was neither easily won nor advantageous for Italy. It lost 600,000 men in battle, and the Italian economy was wrecked by the war. The public debt swelled, inflation ran out of control, and many of the demobilized soldiers left one kind of army for another: that of the unemployed.

To make things worse, the aftermath of the Paris peace settlement following the war never fulfilled Italy's high expectations. Trentino and the city of Trieste became part of the country, as did the Istrian Peninsula and the German-speaking part of South Tirol, which even today remains a bone of contention between Austria and Italy.

Postwar Chaos

Italy had entered the post–World War I era as a society badly off balance. Without relief, lawlessness in the countryside and towns, strikes in the cities, and sharp and

Benito Mussolini

Benito Mussolini: Il Duce

often-violent domestic differences of opinion polarized the political scene. The war had brought revolution in Russia and with that revolution a breaking away in Italy and elsewhere of radically revolutionary communists from the more moderate socialist parties. The establishment of the Communist Party of Italy (PCI) scared many anti-Marxist Italians, who became sympathetic to the idea of a strong leader who could protect Italy from the communist revolution. This included many wealthy landowners and industrialists.

The war had also frustrated the dreams of many Italian nationalists, who had believed that Italy should become a major Mediterranean and Balkan power. Millions of returning veterans were bitter about the fact that their country seemed to show no appreciation for the suffering and sacrifice they had endured. Even appearing on the streets in uniform was bound to evoke abuse. Finally, the traditional Italian parties and elites were almost wholly incapable of coping with the domestic political situation. Therefore, a vacuum and a constituency were created for a charismatic opportunist with extremely flexible principles and an emotionally appealing but intellectually fraudulent political theory: Benito Mussolini.

Mussolini and the Fascists

Born the son of a blacksmith and a schoolteacher in 1883, Mussolini had been educated in a seminary but had been expelled because he reportedly stabbed another student. After teaching school for a few years, he fled to Switzerland in order to avoid military service. He grew tired of exile after a couple of years and returned to Italy to serve in the army, rising like Hitler to the rank of corporal. He then became a prolific journalist, an activity he performed quite effectively and which helped launch a meteoric career in socialist politics. He left behind 44 volumes of his collected writings. In 1911 he was jailed briefly for his inflammatory articles against Italy's colonial policy in North Africa, and in 1912 he was named editor-in-chief of the major Socialist Party newspaper *Avanti!* (*Forward!*) of Milan. His writings and speeches sometimes took excursions into anarchism, and they were always radical. At the Socialist Party congress at Reggio in mid-1912, he was among those party members who vehemently rejected a moderate course for the party and insisted that socialism must destroy the "bourgeois experiment" of democracy.

He never veered from his bitter opposition to liberal democracy, but after the outbreak of World War I, he revealed how fluid his political convictions really were. Unlike his former socialist comrades, he strongly supported Italy's involvement in the war. He maintained that it was one of the country's finest hours and that the conniving, greedy politicians at home had betrayed the young heroes. He had coined the slogan "war or revolution," which clearly presented the only alternatives as he saw them. The moving and persuasive eloquence with which he used the Italian language, his undeniable charisma and showmanship, and his appearance of raw manliness (although he was in reality often a timid man in times of crisis when daring moves needed to be taken) greatly appealed to the lost, the frightened, and the bored.

They flocked to the many loosely knit fasci (groups) that sprang into existence in imitation of the Fascio di combattimento (fighting group), which Mussolini had founded in Milan in 1919. Mussolini wanted to weld a coalition with the non-communist left, but he found little support for such a union. It took a couple of years for him to gain full control of the fascist movement, named after the Latin word *fasces*, which means a "bundle of sticks around an ax," an ancient Roman symbol of state authority. Not until 1921 was the Fascist Party formally created. Mussolini quickly saw that the government's inability or unwillingness to step in and bring the rural and industrial violence under control offered a welcome opportunity for the Fascists to present themselves as the protectors of life, property, law, and order.

His Squadristi (black-shirted bully squads) roamed the streets unimpeded and intimidated voters and opponents. When the Socialists proclaimed a general strike in August 1922, the Italian public became exasperated with this newest in a series of crippling strikes. It did nothing as the Fascists sacked or smashed trade union or Socialist Party headquarters and presses all over Italy, including those of *Avanti!*, the paper which Mussolini once edited. They also seized control of the city councils in Cremona, Ferrara, Livorno, Parma, and Ravenna. These brazen but unopposed acts were merely the prelude to a Fascist coup d'état that had been long-planned.

After delicate negotiations with royalist and church circles to assure their acquiescence, Mussolini mobilized his Black Shirts for a "March on Rome" on October 22, 1922. Mussolini demonstrated that he was not entirely confident such a seizure of power would succeed by remaining close to the Swiss border in order to be able to escape into exile just in case the march failed. The prime minister tried to persuade King Victor Emmanuel III to sign a declaration of martial law in order to deal with the crisis, but the latter refused. Informed that there would be no resistance whatsoever, Mussolini took a night train to Rome, where the king appointed him prime minister. After so much violence and lawlessness, Rome fell to the Fascists without a shot being fired. This outrageous act of political adventurers would have been foiled if the forces of order had only shown the smallest bit of courage.

Step by step, Mussolini (who named himself Il Duce, "the leader") transformed Italy into the first European dictatorship outside of Russia. He combined workers, employers, and other groups into organizations called corporations. This corporate structure was intended to convey the mistaken impression that class and other social conflicts had been or were being eliminated. It therefore was used to justify the abolition of trade unions and strikes, which were allegedly no longer necessary to protect workers.

Italy

Mussolini and his "Black Shirts"

His power was ensured through the introduction of censorship, a strict administration, a youth movement led by the state, a sham one-party electoral system, the incarceration of all political opponents, and the creation of a feared secret police (OVRA). The slogan "*credere, obbedire, combattere*" ("believe, obey, fight") reflected the new ideal. Although the king remained on the throne and the bicameral parliament was permitted to go through the motions as if it were functioning, all power by 1925 rested with Mussolini and his Fascist Party, whose organization reached from 10,000 fasci (local) party groups all the way up to a Fascist Grand Council of about 20 men. All other parties were outlawed.

Fascist "Theory" and Administration

In the Fascist ideology Mussolini had helped to concoct, freedom had allegedly been created through authoritarianism, and nobility and heroism had been established through discipline and sacrifice. The state was glorified, and liberalism, democracy, and socialism were condemned. On top of that allegedly well-ordered state stood the leader, Mussolini, a man with a knack for sensationalism, self-dramatization, effective oratory, and heavy-handedness toward those who were weaker than he.

The subsequent persecution of all opposition forces was restrained in comparison to the terror in Nazi Germany. He hesitated before acceding to German demands to round up Jews. In the end, 8,600 Italian Jews perished. In 2009 the diaries of Clara Petacci, his mistress who was executed with him in 1945, were published in book form (*Mussolini segreto*) after 50 years in the archives. They reveal that Il Duce was anti-Semitic and racist: "I've been a racist since '21." She wrote that he said, "These disgusting Jews, I must destroy them all," and "I shall carry out a massacre, like the Turks did."

The dead-end policies to establish an autarkical (internationally independent) economy corrupted the initial economic successes resulting from protective tariffs and grandiose state-sponsored projects. The antiquated relationships of the property owners toward the peasants in the agrarian south remained unaffected, and the power of the Mafia was temporarily broken. Of far-reaching importance, however, were the Lateran Treaties (February 11, 1929) with the Vatican. Mussolini settled the long-standing dispute with the church over its role in Italian politics by granting it extensive opportunities to influence political and social affairs within Italy (see Vatican City State).

World War II

Italy was ill-prepared for the wars it fought, at first on a small scale against Ethiopia in 1935 and then later against Germany's enemies in World War II. After Mussolini's attempts to conquer Albania and Greece in 1941 had failed, Italy and Il Duce became more dependent upon Hitler than the Italians had intended. Their initial enthusiasm about the adventure of war soon turned to resignation and disappointment. Although Italy was supposedly a "partner" in the Axis, Hitler and the Germans in some ways considered it as much a problem as an asset insofar as the war effort was concerned. Although Mussolini was arrogant and boastful in public, he was rather timid in reality.

Things got worse when the Americans, British, and Canadians began to launch successful attacks against the Italian homeland. In mid-1943 British and Canadian forces landed on the east coast of Sicily and took Syracuse, while General George S. Patton's troops landed in the south of the island and took Marsala and Palermo. They then joined the British forces to expel the Germans who were in control of Sicily. The Allies next turned toward the Italian mainland and began bombing Rome on July 19.

The sober reality of war right in the city of Rome brought the downfall of

Mussolini. The Fascist Grand Council, formerly a malleable tool in Mussolini's hands, which had not met since 1939, demanded his resignation, which the king ordered the next day. The former Duce was arrested as he left the royal palace, but German paratroopers rescued him later in a daring, precision operation. Totally at the mercy of Germans, Mussolini eked out a temporary existence as head of a puppet fascist state in German-occupied northern Italy until April 28, 1945, when communist partisans murdered him and publicly hanged him and his mistress upside down. A few days later, his protector, Hitler, shot himself and had his body burned in Berlin to escape such ignoble public treatment.

Unfortunately, long, drawn-out negotiations in the summer of 1943 between the Anglo-American Allies and the new Italian government under Marshal Pietro Badoglio enabled the Germans to improve their defenses in Italy. Therefore, when an armistice could finally be signed and an amphibious assault could be launched the very same day against the mainland on September 3, 1943, the Germans were well-prepared. The British Eighth Army under General Montgomery landed with little difficulty on the coast of Calabria. By contrast, the American landing at Salerno thereafter was resisted fiercely and almost ended in disaster.

The rugged and hilly Italian terrain, combined with the dogged German resistance under Marshal Kesselring, rendered every mile of northward advance in the peninsula painful and costly. The Germans had dug in their heels along the so-called Gustav Line, in the center of which was located the almost-impregnable 1,700 foot (510 meters) Monte Cassino, which guarded the road through the Liri Valley toward Rome. In order to try to circumvent these formidable defenses, the Americans made another amphibious landing at Anzio, located only 33 miles (53 km) south of Rome. But the American troops were pinned to the slopes overlooking the beach under murderous fire for four months until they could finally break free. In April 1944 Monte Cassino finally fell at the cost of thousands of American lives and after the Allies had made the much-criticized decision to bomb the Benedictine Abbey there, which the Germans were effectively using for observation purposes.

In June 1944 Allied troops entered Rome. When seven Allied divisions were withdrawn shortly thereafter in order to take part in an amphibious landing in southern France, the possibility of driving the German armies entirely out of Italy quickly disappeared. Italy therefore remained partially occupied by the Germans until the end of the war. On the plus side, the Italian invasion diverted German troops who

Uniformed police: carabinieri

Courtesy: Jon Markham Morrow

otherwise would have been available elsewhere. The expertise gained—in complex amphibious operations at beaches like Anzio and Salerno; in fighting as a large, multinational coalition; in occupying a big, fractious, defeated country; and in reorganizing civil society and infrastructure from the ground up—were very useful in the subsequent invasions of France and Germany. Tactically, it was a costly mistake, since Italy presented no threat, and the terrain made it a defender's battlefield, not an invader's. This is reflected in the tremendous number of Allied casualties. Three-quarters of 1 million American GIs served in Italy, and 23,501 of them were killed in action.

The Italian resistance to the Axis powers was militarily significant in the course of the war. After the war the resistance became a symbol of solidarity, and it should have helped the Italians to put aside some of their many regional, political, and social differences. Unfortunately, the adhesive effect of the resistance proved to be weaker and more transitory than many had hoped.

After the war, Italy found itself again in the strange position of being both the conqueror and the conquered. Regular troops and partisan units had fought against the Germans ever since the fall of Mussolini in mid-1943. However, the fact that this same Italy had been an ally of Nazi Germany and had led attacks against Albania, Yugoslavia, and Greece had not been forgotten. Historian R. J. B. Bosworth calculates that, through his wars, Mussolini was responsible for the deaths of 1 million people. In contrast to Germany, Italy was able to preserve its national unity, but this

was due chiefly to the crucial assistance of the influential Italians living in the United States.

The peace treaty that took effect September 15, 1947, required Italy to renounce all claims on Ethiopia and Greece and to cede the Dodecanese Islands back to Greece and five small Alpine areas to France. In addition, the Istrian Peninsula (including Fiume and Pola) was awarded to Yugoslavia. Trieste was made a free city until 1954, when it and a 90-square-mile (135 sq. km) zone were transferred to Italy. The remainder went to Yugoslavia. In addition, Italy was required to pay reparations to the Soviet Union and Albania.

GOVERNMENT

A majority of Italian voters in a national referendum held in June 1946 chose to abolish the monarchy and to establish a democratic republic. Not until 56 years later, in 2002, did parliament agree that the ban against Italy's male royalty from entering the country would be lifted. Victor Emmanuel, who left Italy at age nine, pledged allegiance to the Italian Republic. He and his son Emmanuel Filiberto live in Switzerland, where Victor was jailed in 2006 on charges of racketeering, gambling, and prostitution.

With the unpleasant memories of a dictator and a rigid one-party state fresh in their minds, the framers of the postwar constitution made two important decisions which have made it difficult for the country's political institutions to cope with some of Italy's festering economic and social problems. First, they greatly curtailed the powers of the head of government in

Italy

order to make the reemergence of a dictator almost impossible. Second, they adopted the proportional representation system of voting that gave parliamentary seats to as many parties as possible.

Italy is a centralized, unitary state. As in France, the prefect in each of the 106 provinces is appointed by and accountable to the central government. The 20 regions each elect regional parliaments and wield limited political power, but they still are chiefly administrative units for the central government. Five of these regions have had special statutes for a long time: Sicily, Sardinia, Valle d'Aosta, Friuli-Venezia Giulia, and Trentino-Alto Adige. This broadening of regional government led to an actual decentralization of political power in Italy.

Within Trentino-Alto Adige, known in Austria as South Tyrol, are two partly German-speaking special provinces, Trento and Bolzano, which enjoy autonomy. They retain 90% of the taxes they collect. They benefit from a separate German-language school system and legally mandated bilingualism. The German-speaking South Tyrolean People's Party (SVP) has swept every election since 1848. Italian speakers make up a quarter of South Tyrol's population and dominate the provincial capital, Bolzano. When 113 of the 116 municipalities in Alto Adige signed a petition in 2006 asking Austrian authorities to help protect their language rights, they touched a raw nerve in Italy.

The other 15 regions were created in 1970. In 2001 a further devolution of power in the regions was approved in a referendum. The reform made the 20 regions responsible for everything, including raising taxes, not constitutionally granted to the central government in Rome. In September 2004 parliament accepted measures to grant the regions new powers over health, education, and law and order.

In a June 2006 referendum, voters rejected by a wide margin of 61% to 39% a proposal to change more than 50 of 139 articles in the constitution. Turnout was 52%; 50% is required for any referendum to pass. Originally conceived by the Northern League, the reform would have transformed Italy into a quasi-federal state by devolving more powers to the regions. It would also have reduced the size of the legislature and strengthened the power of the prime minister by allowing him to disband parliament (which only the president can do) and appoint and fire cabinet members (of which the president must now approve).

The Constitutional Court judges the constitutionality of laws, decisions made by state or regional councils, and accusations against the president. It is made up of 15 judges, 5 of whom are nominated by the president, 5 by parliament in joint session, and 5 by the magistrates' Supreme Council. In 1985 the Italian government revised the 55-year-old concordat with the Vatican ending the status of Roman Catholicism as the state religion; Italy became a secular state. The church accepted the civil court's right to decide on marital annulments, previously the exclusive right of the church, and it agreed that religious instruction in public schools would be optional.

Post–Cold War Renovation

A political earthquake occurred in Italy that has brought about profound changes in the country's parliamentary system and party politics. Italians have always known that there was corruption in high places, but what they have now learned is taking their breaths away. It began in 1991 with the arrest of a Socialist Party official in Milan (Mario Chiesa) who was caught taking bribes on a cleaning contract in a home for the elderly. But it developed into an explosion that affected the nation's entire political order.

Investigations (called Operation Clean Hands) into embezzlement, illicit bribes, and kickbacks to political parties and politicians in return for public-works contracts have produced the greatest public corruption scandal in modern European history. The estimated $11 billion in annual rip-offs was equivalent to the government's annual deficit. The investigations uncovered evidence that the Mafia and top government leaders might have cooperated for years. None of the traditional parties escaped unharmed; all were discredited.

Until the collapse of communism in Europe, Italians had grudgingly tolerated misgovernment by leaders mainly preoccupied with party intrigue and devious fund-raising because it seemed like the alternative would have been rule by the Communist Party of Italy, which had discomforting links with the Soviet Union. With that danger gone, most Italians saw no reason not to confront head-on the rot in the political establishment. By mid-1993, more than 2,600 persons in the political and business elite, including top corporate executives, party chairmen, and three former prime ministers, had either been arrested or were under investigation. Entire regional and local governments had been jailed or forced to resign.

Voters' disgust came to a head in a historic referendum in April 1993. Voting on eight separate questions, over 90% voted to abolish state financing of political parties, and 83% chose to scrap the system of proportional representation in the Senate. Designed in the postfascist era to prevent another single party, such as Mussolini's, from gaining power, this system created government by weak coalitions of quarrelsome partners and by an oligarchy of often-corrupt party leaders.

The 1993 referendum was a stunning rebuke to politicians and their machinery of power. Operation Clean Hands officially came to an end in 2003. However, in the preceding decade, all of the institutions and parties discussed below were changed or influenced by the rage and determination that had been expressed.

The pressure was kept on by a best-selling book published in 2007 by two journalists—Sergio Rizzo and Gian Antonio Stella—entitled *La Casta* (*The Caste*). They describe the many privileges and perks of the deeply entrenched political class. They estimate that from 600,000 to 700,000 live off the political machine. There will always be plenty of Italians clamoring to win parliamentary seats. Few benefit from high-paying jobs more than members of parliament (MPs). They have the highest salaries for parliamentarians in all of Europe: €16,000 ($22,000) a month, including funds for staff members, whether they have any or not. After only 30 months, they are eligible for a lifelong pension beginning as early as age 60. With such frequent elections, there are three times more retired parliamentarians than active ones. The turnover continued in the 2008 elections, when 40% of the elected MPs were new. It is little wonder that the annual cost of Italy's parliament is the highest in Europe. The number of sitting MPs "in trouble with the law" remains high, although the number had fallen from 91 to 70 after the 2008 elections. One of them was former prime minister Silvio Berlusconi.

Parliament

Italy is a parliamentary democracy with a bicameral legislature. The Chamber of Deputies is composed of 630 members elected until 1994 and then again from 2006 by proportional representation in 32 electoral districts at least every five years. The 2005 electoral reform aimed to add more stability to governments by strengthening party leaders, reducing the number of parties in the chamber, and giving a reward to the electoral coalition that wins the most votes. Deputies are dependent for reelection entirely on their party leaders, who decide where to place them on the party's electoral lists. This makes rebellions within the party almost impossible. A party linked to a coalition needs to win at least 2% of the votes to win a seat. A party running independently must get at least 4%, and a coalition of parties needs to capture at least 10%.

The winning coalition is guaranteed a minimum of 340 seats, however narrow the margin of its victory. The intent is to increase the chances of a stable governing coalition composed of as few parties as possible. For example, in 2008 the center-right coalition led by Silvio Berlusconi's People of Freedom Party got 344 lower-house seats based on 46.81% of the votes. The center-left coalition around the Democratic Party got only 246 seats, although it won 37.54% of the votes. The 9% advantage gave Berlusconi a 98-seat majority, more than enough to move into the prime minister's magnificent residence in central Rome, the Palazzo Chigi. This huge majority, combined with the fact that only 6 parties (plus 3 minuscule parties that took only 4 seats) won seats (compared with 23 parties in the previous parliament), created a stable government that could serve out its full five-year term. In 2015, parliament passed a new electoral law that guarantees a majority of seats to the party (no longer the alliance) that wins the most votes. The 2008 elections produced the first Italian parliament with more than 20% women.

The Senate is composed of 315 elected members. Every five years members representing the 20 regions (the exceptions being the Valley of Aosta, which sends a senator, and the province of Molise, which sends two) are elected. Beginning in 2006, members are elected by proportional representation. As in the lower house, the new system aims to reduce the number of parties with seats. A party linked to an electoral coalition needs at least 3% to win a seat. One running alone must get 8%. A coalition of parties must win at least 20%. Seats are distributed on a regional basis. The winner in each region receives at least 55% of the region's seats. It is possible for an electoral coalition to win the most votes but receive fewer seats. For example, in 2006, Berlusconi's center-right won 50.2% of the votes but got only 156 seats. Prodi's

Former president Scalfaro addresses the Chamber of Deputies.

center-left garnered 48.9% of the votes but received 158 seats.

In contrast to the Chamber of Deputies, the Senate contains some nonelected members. Every ex-president of the republic is a senator for life, and the president appoints five other senators for life based on their outstanding achievements in social, scientific, or artistic and literary fields. The oldest senator elected was 99-year-old Nobel Prize winner Rita Levi Montalcini.

The 3.4 million Italians living abroad elect 12 deputies and 6 senators to represent them; these are added to the 630 and 315 members. The constituencies for these seats are huge: Europe (including Russia and Turkey), South America, North and Central America, and Africa-Asia-Oceania-Antarctica. The speaker of the Senate is a powerful political figure and is the equivalent to the vice president of the republic. He takes over if the president is unable to perform his duties.

Both houses have identical powers. Both function and make decisions independently, and both must pass a bill before it is forwarded to the president of the republic for signature. The government must have the confidence of both chambers. The legislative system is slow and cumbersome, making passage of laws difficult. Because of the electoral system, almost the same constellation of parties is represented in both chambers with the same proportion of parties in the standing committees. The Senate has 11 such committees, and the Chamber of Deputies, 14. In both houses party politics determines all aspects of the legislative process. In 2015, parliament approved a reform of the Senate that, if

it had been accepted by a referendum, would have weakened the upper chamber and taken away its veto power. The Senate would have 100 regional and municipal representatives. The referendum was defeated in December 2016. A reform in September 2020, approved by the referendum, cut the number of seats in Parliament by around a third.

Since 1988 party discipline is easier to maintain because of the elimination of secret voting, which had permitted dissidents to vote anonymously against their own parties and bring down their own governments; the result was perennially weak government. Secret balloting had been one stumbling block to efficient rule under a constitution that had been designed four decades ago primarily to prevent another Mussolini from coming to power. Until 2006 no Italian legislature had lived its full five-year life. Italy's 952 lawmakers have the highest parliamentary salaries in Europe: €20,000 ($26,000) per month, including per-diem living expenses and personal staff. At a time of austerity, when the average Italian takes home less than €2,000 ($2,600), such opulent salaries cause widespread disgust.

Presidency

The president is elected by the members of both houses of parliament and by three delegates from each regional council for a seven-year term. Any citizen over the age of 50 is eligible. In order to maximize the possibility that the president be a national unifying figure and impartial, a two-thirds majority is required. But if such a special majority cannot be reached after three

President Sergio Mattarella

Italy

ballots, then a simple majority is enough. This was the case in May 2006, April 2013, and February 2015.

The president is an influential player in the political system. He can veto a law, but a simple majority in both houses can override his veto. All acts of the president require the countersignature of the appropriate cabinet minister, who assumes political responsibility for these acts. He formally declares a state of war, calls elections, and appoints the prime minister. He can also dissolve parliament and call new elections, except in his last six months in office.

The presidency is gaining in influence. In 1991 Francesco Cossiga grew tired of his figurehead role and proclaimed his intention "to shake a few pebbles out of my shoes." He startled the nation by becoming more involved in everyday politics. His moves caused a storm of controversy. In 1992 he decided to give "a shock to the political classes" by resigning two months before his term ended. He charged that Italy's traditional politicians had ignored the electorate's reform message in the parliamentary elections. He died in August 2010.

His successor, Oscar Luigi Scalfaro, broke long-standing practices in 1993 by not consulting the ruling parties before selecting the first prime minister not to belong to a political party: Carlo Azeglio Ciampi, a respected civil servant and head of the independent Bank of Italy. Scalfaro charged him with enacting sweeping political reform, trimming the budget, and then bowing out after early elections. In the past, party leaders dictated the political direction to the president. But in 1993 it was President Scalfaro who delivered the marching orders to the party chiefs.

In May 1999 Ciampi became president. He demonstrated that the president is no mere figurehead. In 2003 he refused to sign into law a controversial reform of the media sector that Berlusconi's government had pushed through parliament. A year later he blocked changes to the judicial system that seemed to curb the independence of judges and prosecutors.

On May 10, 2006, Giorgio Napolitano was elected. A moderate communist leader until 1989, whom Henry Kissinger called his "favorite communist," and president of the lower house, he represented the integration of former communists into the current political system. At 80 he was the oldest man ever to be elected to the office. No less a luminary than Cicero would approve. He once said, "Old age, especially an honored old age, has such great authority that it is of more value than all the pleasures of youth." In February 2015, Sergio Mattarella was elected president. A Constitutional Court judge from Sicily whose brother had been gunned down by Mafia henchmen, he is known as a determined foe of organized crime.

Normally the most delicate political act in which the president is fully involved is the formation of a cabinet. A prospective candidate for the prime-ministerial post is charged by the president to form a government. The candidate suggests the composition of the new government after extensive consultations with the possible coalition partners. Whether the prime minister can win and maintain a majority for his cabinet in both chambers is always the decisive question.

The president has no executive power, but he can be a quiet power broker. Napolitano worked for months laying the groundwork for transferring the prime-ministership from Silvio Berlusconi to Mario Monti in 2011. Monti's technocratic government was often referred to as "a government of the president." At 80%, Napolitano enjoyed the highest popularity rating by far of any politician. He was the first president in the history of the republic to be reelected.

Political Parties and Alliances

In 2018 Italy installed its 66th government since World War II. Until 2001 the average duration of each had been 7 months; by 2014 an average government's lifespan was 393 days. All governments are coalitions, with disagreement on a single point sometimes bringing down a prime minister. To understand why Italian governments are often so unstable, one must examine the past and current basic party structure.

The multiparty system has traditionally been highly fragmented. However, beginning with the 1996 elections, many of the numerous parties grouped themselves into two loose alliances. The *Washington Post* aptly described them at the time as "not coalitions but collages, fragments of political movements thrown together without a cogent denominator other than the aim of power. As such they are prone to instability."

On the center-right were the parties that formed Silvio Berlusconi's People of Freedom (formerly House of Liberties). They included his own People of Freedom (formerly called and then later renamed Forza Italia, "Go, Italy!"). He was considered to be politically dead, but by opposing austerity and an unpopular property tax, his party surged to second place in 2008. Berlusconi prompted new elections in 2013 by refusing to support the Monti government. He tried again but failed to bring the government down in 2013, causing a split in his party. Angelino Alfano led many followers to break away and establish the New Center-Right (NCD), which remained in the government.

The National Alliance (formerly the neofascist Italian Social Movement, MSI), led by Gianfranco Fini, who was appointed speaker of the Chamber of Deputies, was absorbed by People of Freedom. Coalition allies were the Northern League, led until April 2012 by Umberto Bossi, and its southern Italian equivalent, the Movement for Autonomy.

In March 2009 Berlusconi's electoral coalition People of Freedom (PDL) became a political party that absorbed the National Alliance and 11 smaller parties, including a rightist faction led by Alessandra Mussolini. The Northern League did not join the new party. Berlusconi was the uncontested political master of the country until he stepped down as prime minister after losing a vote of confidence in November 2011. After the 2013 elections, he had a veto on forming a government.

In the vanishing center was the Union of Center and Christian Democrats (UDC, led by Pier Ferdinando Casini), a breakaway minority from the former ruling Christian Democrats (DC). His dream of holding the balance between left and right remains just that—a dream.

On the center-left is the Democratic Party (PD). Its coalition partner was Italy of Values. PD consciously excluded far-left parties from its coalition. As a result, the Communists were routed in the 2008 elections and for the first time in the history of the republic were not represented in parliament.

Until February 2009 the PD leader was Walter Veltroni, popular former mayor of Rome, who had begun his career at age 21 as a Communist on the Rome City Council. He later edited the Communist daily newspaper *L'Unita* for five years. In October 2007 he won a huge primary majority to lead the new party, which he promised would be "a new force" with a "new language." He professed admiration for America's big-tent Democratic Party, especially John Kennedy, and he openly modeled himself and his new party on presidential candidate Barack Obama. An author of over a dozen books, including a novel, he wrote the preface for the Italian edition of Obama's book *The Audacity of Hope* and wrote, "Obama is innovative, unifying and post-ideological." He included Obama's image in his election videos and even adopted as its slogan, "*Si puo fare!*" ("It can be done!"). While Berlusconi flew everywhere during his campaign, Veltroni traveled throughout Italy on a green campaign bus called "Pullman."

After suffering a humiliating regional election defeat in Sardinia in 2009, Veltroni passed the leadership on to Pierluigi Bersani, who had arisen from the Communist Party. In traditional leftist fashion, PD experiences constant intraparty squabbling.

In the February 2013 national elections, it led all parties, capturing 29.5% of the votes and 340 seats in the Chamber of Deputies and 31.6% and 113 seats in the Senate. It could not form a government on its own because it fell short of a Senate majority. It looked in vain for a coalition partner. After nine weeks of stalemate and Bersani's resignation, his deputy, Enrico Letta, was able to put together a grand coalition with Silvio Berlusconi's People of Freedom Party and become prime minister in April 2013. Letta was unseated as party leader in December 2013 and as prime minister in February by his party colleague Matteo Renzi, mayor of Florence.

PD had replaced "The Union," a broad nine-party coalition led by outgoing prime minister Romano Prodi. The old "Union" had included the "Olive Tree" coalition, a patchwork of ex-Communists, liberals, greens, some former Christian Democrats, and a few independents. Created in 1996, they had together made history by becoming Italy's first leftist government, under Prodi. They broke a long-standing taboo by including nine former Communists in the ruling coalition, more than from any other single party.

In 2006 Olive Tree coalition took power for 20 months by combining the moderate ex-communist Democrats of the Left (DS, formerly the Communist Party of Italy, PCI) and Margherita (Daisy) Democracy Is Freedom. Prodi stepped in to organize the disparate groups for the April 2006 elections and moved the left closer to a unified party. He suggested an American-style primary election to select the left's leader (himself), who would thereby enjoy an unparalleled degree of legitimacy. That was done in October 2005, with the members of all the parties in the coalition having a vote; Prodi won 75%. To prevent the incessant warring on the left, he proposed a broad-based Democratic Party like its American namesake. The hard-line Refounded Communists, which broke off from DS in 1998, ran its own candidates. Groups on the left have their own daily newspapers wherein they passionately debate issues in which the average voters have little or no interest.

The shift to such a unified right and left had begun in 1993, when the entire political landscape began to change. Before that the political fronts in Italy were polarized and rigid. The problem was that parties cornering roughly a third of the vote—the PCI and the MSI—were unacceptable as coalition partners, leaving only two-thirds within which to find a majority. Neither of the two largest parties was capable of winning a majority. No governing coalition could be formed without the participation of the defunct Christian Democrats and the Socialists.

Together with the Social Democrats, the Liberals, and sometimes the Republicans, these two parties could paste together a wobbly temporary majority in parliament composed of five parties (called the *Pentapartito*), which were generally more interested in their own survival and in delivering maximum benefits to their own special constituencies than in providing stable government capable of dealing with Italy's pressing problems.

The DC and the Socialists were never natural partners for reasons of ideology and strategy. Any coalition between them was by nature unstable because the partners were fierce competitors. The DC could not win a majority by itself, and most Italians did not accept the Communists as ready for a place in the government. Thus, about a dozen small parties held the balance. This ensured incoherence and produced a string of short-lived governments with narrow attention spans.

Even elections could not always produce a government; they could create only the raw materials for one. They seldom settled questions; they merely deferred them. Following elections, an acceptable coalition, composed almost invariably of the same parties which were in the last one, was hammered together only after a drawn-out process of bargaining. It could take weeks or months until the many demands of powerful party and factional leaders had been satisfied and balanced. While there was a certain stability inherent in this process, the damage to the political system was clear. Widespread corruption and cynicism toward rulers flourished in a fragmented political scene in which politicians were well entrenched with little possibility of being displaced. Nobody expected major changes. One voter remarked before the 1992 polling, "we all know that when the vote is counted we will be right back where we started."

That is changing as Italy is moving toward a two-party system (or at least two opposing blocs) with fewer and fewer parties in parliament. In 2006, 39 parties won seats in parliament; in 2008 only 6 succeeded, all moderate. Even though the two main parties are still young and somewhat undefined, Berlusconi's People of Freedom victory in 2008 offered the reasonable hope that Italy's 62nd postwar government would be stable and durable, lasting five full years. After all, he was the only postwar prime minister to have survived a full term, from 2001 to 2005. The left-leaning *La Repubblica* wrote of "an electoral tsunami that redraws Italy's political landscape." Becoming prime minister for the third time in a clear and convincing win, Berlusconi announced confidently, "Now we'll govern like major western democracies, with one major party in power

Former prime minister Romano Prodi, ex-president, European Commission

and one major party in opposition." That lasted until November 2011.

THE RIGHT

People of Freedom (Again Forza Italia)

At the head of this party is one of Italy's richest men (the world's 51st richest, according to Forbes in 2008), Silvio Berlusconi, an entrepreneurial superstar whose business empire, Fininvest, includes three TV networks dominating commercial television, Italy's largest department store chain, the top-selling newsmagazine, and an array of other investments, including the AC Milan soccer club. His opponents charge that he misused his three TV networks, which control 45% of the Italian audience, to propagandize voters. Indeed, in 2009 the New York watchdog organization Freedom House downgraded Italy in its global media survey from "free" to "partly free," ranking it 73rd in the world. Critics also claim that a politician with such vast and varied investments cannot escape from conflicts of interest.

He is a man with telegenic good looks, enormous energy and determination, an excellent business brain, an uncanny ability to connect with ordinary people, and a shrewd understanding of the nature of power. He is a polarizing figure who has a knack for enraging critics with remarks construed as sexist, racist, or homophobic. For example, he advised women who seek future happiness and financial security to "look for a wealthy boyfriend." He complimented President Barack Obama for his suntan. He announced, "It's better to be passionate about beautiful women than gay."

Italy

He claimed to have been forced into politics "to keep my country from falling into the hands of the communists." Centrist reformers had failed to organize an effective bloc against the Communists' momentum. Its deputies tend to be young, ambitious professionals and businesspeople who helped change the character of the parliament by lowering the average age (40% under age 50 and 25% under 40), raising the percentage of university graduates to 75, and increasing the number of women representatives from 51 to 170 (of whom 70 are from the conservative ruling parties). People of Freedom had to coalesce with the autonomy-seeking Northern League, with its roots in the rich and industrialized Lombardy region around Milan (Berlusconi's hometown), and its southern equivalent—the Movement for Autonomy. People of Freedom absorbed the National Alliance before the 2008 elections; its voters are concentrated in the impoverished south, and it advocates a strong central government.

In its first attempt at governing, Berlusconi's heterogeneous coalition could not give Italy what has eluded it for more than four decades: stable government. In December 1994 it collapsed after only eight months when the Northern League walked out. Berlusconi had refused to separate himself from his business empire. When he was formally placed under investigation for his business dealings, including tax fraud and corruption, he could no longer survive as prime minister.

Berlusconi was convicted in 1997 for false accounting (though his 16-month sentence was commuted). In 1998 he was sentenced to two years and nine months in prison for bribery, but his parliamentary immunity and the appeals process kept

Berlusconi creates his new party in 2009.

Ex–prime minister Silvio Berlusconi

him out of jail. In 2003 he became the first sitting Italian prime minister to be called to give testimony as a criminal defendant in his own bribery trial. He has often been convicted, but he almost always manages to escape punishment because Italy's statute of limitations and interminable judicial delays make it almost impossible to convict someone of a white-collar crime. In 2013 Berlusconi was sentenced to a year in jail for publicizing a wiretapped phone call; he was also found guilty of tax evasion. Many Italians believe that he remains in politics primarily to protect himself from the justice system.

Berlusconi used his majority in parliament to pass laws that make prosecuting corruption cases more difficult. They included a retroactive measure to restrict the use of evidence gathered abroad, especially secret bank account records; the decriminalizing of false bookkeeping convictions; amnesty for illegal transfer of funds outside Italy; change of venue for trials away from judges who are "legitimately suspected" of bias; and immunity for the country's top five posts from facing trial while they hold office. In July 2008 his government passed a law giving him, as prime minister; the president; and the heads of the two parliamentary chambers immunity from prosecution during their terms.

The Constitutional Court partially lifted this grant of immunity in 2011, so he was ordered to trial on some of the most embarrassing charges yet: that he paid an underaged alleged prostitute from Morocco (stage name: Ruby Heartstealer, thus "Rubygate") for sex at orgies (called "bunga bunga" parties) at his Milan mansion and that he abused his position to hide the fact. When she had been picked up on charges of theft, he vouched for her character and sent an aide to collect

her, lying that she was a granddaughter of now-deposed Egyptian president Hosni Mubarak. Both deny having sex with each other, but tapped phone calls appear to indicate otherwise. She admitted receiving €7,000 ($9,500) from him the first time she attended one of his parties, and he admitted to have given her the equivalent of $87,000 to save her from a life of prostitution. While the age of consent is 14 and prostitution is legal, having sex with a prostitute under 18 is not. As if these charges and convictions were not enough, he was also convicted of tax fraud and bribing a lawyer to lie in court. The "Teflon tycoon" had his hands full; denied a seat in the Senate, he had to face these challenges without immunity. He was ordered in 2014 to serve one year doing work in the community. He worked one day a week in an Alzheimer clinic. He was banned from running for public office for two years. In 2015 the highest court dropped all sex charges, but his chances for a comeback are low. Approval for his party has halved to 13%.

He never enacted a law to deal with his conflicts of interest, and his family did not divest itself of the nation's three largest private TV channels. In any other democratic country, he would probably have been forced to resign but not in Italy. Berlusconi's approval rating sank to a mere 22% by the time he stepped down in November 2011. A poll published in *Corriere delle Sera* revealed that only a third of Italians trust the judicial system.

This impression was hardened by the case against American student Amanda Knox, who had been accused and convicted of murdering her British roommate in Perugia in 2007. Four years later an Italian court overturned the verdict, pointing to mishandled evidence, including DNA (none from Knox was found at the scene of the crime); bungling police and magistrates; and failure to go beyond circumstantial evidence and to establish a motive. She returned to the US a free woman. However, her nightmare was not ended. In March 2013 an Italian court overruled that acquittal and demanded that she return to Italy for a new trial in 2014. Because the American legal system protects defendants from being tried twice for the same crime and because the rule of "reasonable doubt" was ignored, she was not extradited, despite a new 28.5-year sentence (which was later overturned).

Berlusconi had been the dominant figure in Italian politics since 1994 and after 8.5 years had been the country's longest-serving prime minister since Mussolini. His ruling coalition had been Italy's longest-serving government since the return of democracy in 1945 and the only one to

**Future and Freedom for Italy
Gianfranco Fini**

serve out a full five-year parliamentary term. It provided unaccustomed continuity. His Forza Italia Party was weakened by a split in October 2013, when Angelino Alfano led a few dozen members of parliament, including all 5 of PdL's ministers, to create the New Center Right (NCD). The rebels had had enough of Berlusconi's autocratic style of leadership and rejected the boss's call for new elections as soon as possible. Berlusconi was the longest-serving postwar prime minister, but his political star has fallen. His attempted comeback in 2018 failed, as his party captured only 14% of the votes in the March national elections.

National Alliance

Until 1994 the neofascist Italian Social Movement–National Right (MSI–DN) could be found at the outer-right fringe of the party spectrum. It understood how to capitalize on the disadvantaged population of southern Italy. But protests against the establishment and disappointment over the center-left governments never took it over 7% of the votes. In terms of a political program, the MSI maintained entirely the tradition of Italian fascism.

But then came a new and intelligent young leader, Gianfranco Fini, who steered the party away from the corporatism and exaggerated nationalism of old fascism and gave it a new program (which he calls "postfascism") and a more respectable name: National Alliance. The MSI was dissolved in 1995. The fascist hard-liners who could not accept this change broke away and created their own Fiamma Tricolore, which languished in irrelevance.

Fini studiously avoided contacts with extreme-rightist groups elsewhere in Europe and condemned anti-Semitism, attacks against foreigners, and skinhead violence. Emphasizing clean government, law and order (including reintroduction of the death penalty), stricter immigration controls, family values, and the preservation of Italian unity, he transformed the party into a broad-based mainstream conservative political force, modeled on the French Gaullists, and a major player in Italian politics.

Having been excluded from government for a half-century, it could not be blamed for corruption and poor performance, as could Italy's traditional parties. Fini declared during the campaign, "Italy no longer divides itself between fascists and anti-fascists, but between thieves and those with clean hands!"

The reward came in the 1994 elections, when it more than doubled its previous electoral score. Capitalizing on the dramatic decline of the former Christian Democrats, who had long dominated the south, the National Alliance became the strongest political force in the southern half of Italy, including Rome. Fini later became a respected foreign minister.

Fini moved resolutely to disavow the party's fascist roots. He referred to the fascist past as "shameful pages of history" and denounced the racism of Mussolini's regime. He visited Israel and advocated that legal immigrants be permitted to vote in local elections. This was too much for Alessandra Mussolini, granddaughter of the fascist dictator and niece of actress Sophia Loren. She temporarily left the party but held on to her parliamentary seat as an independent. A strident feminist, she became a member of the European Parliament. She briefly created her own far-right Social Alternative Party, but she joined Berlusconi's People of Freedom in 2008. Some other National Alliance members are critical of Fini's turnaround.

Fini, who became leader of the Chamber of Deputies in 2008, was one of the most popular politicians on the center-right and is the man to watch. By joining forces with Berlusconi in the 2008 elections and agreeing to merge his party with the People of Freedom the following year, he was positioning himself to be Berlusconi's successor, even though the latter disliked him. He often clashed with Berlusconi, especially over tough immigration policies, attempts to reduce parliament's role in the name of greater efficiency, and the use of votes of confidence to rush through bills.

That the party was on a roll was demonstrated two weeks after the 2008 parliamentary elections, when Gianni Alemanno of the National Alliance won 54% of the votes and defeated former Rome mayor and national culture minister Francesco Rutelli to become Rome's mayor. It is the first time since Mussolini's time that a conservative has been elected to that prominent post. Alemanno was a former MSI youth leader who served 14 years in parliament and then as agriculture minister in Berlusconi's previous government. His election created some unease, especially after youthful supporters greeted him following his victory with straight-armed "Roman" salutes, chanted "Duce! Duce!" and screamed abuse against communists and foreign immigrants.

Fini quit the alliance in July 2010 and formed his own Future and Freedom for Italy (FLI) parliamentary party. He took with him 33 members of the lower house and 10 from the Senate, thereby depriving the government of its majority. To complicate matters, Fini and his followers formally remained in Berlusconi's People of Freedom Party, and some even stayed in the government. However, Berlusconi could no longer count on their votes in parliament. The National Alliance had become irrelevant by the 2018 national elections. Also a direct heir of the Fascist Party and Mussolini is the passionately nationalist Brothers of Italy (FDI). It is particularly strong in the south and by 2021 had the backing of 16% of Parliament.

Northern League (The League)

In the 1990s all of Italy's established parties anxiously witnessed the rise of leagues seeking regional autonomy in the north. The most successful was the *Lega Nord* (Northern League), led until April 2012 by Umberto Bossi. He was replaced by Matteo Salvini, whose enhanced approval rating, at 33%, is impressive.

The league traditionally stands for federalism and devolution of power to the regions. It capitalizes on local dissatisfaction against what is seen as misrule by Rome, which does not seem to act vigorously enough to stem the wave of immigrants and to reverse northern Italy's subsidizing of the south. It charges, with considerable justification, that too much of those funds end up in the pockets of Mafia contractors. A clean-government party, the Northern League benefited from the country's massive corruption scandals. Its spokesman Roberto Maroni announced, "our purpose of breaking up Italy is not linked to ethnic or religious identities, but to economic issues." Nevertheless, there is a whiff of racism in its appeals. The party's emphasis has shifted from separating to immigration and the euro.

Emboldened by its strong election showing in 1996, the league proclaimed northern Italy an "independent and sovereign" republic called "Padania" (for the River Po) and called on the United Nations to recognize its right of self-determination. Unlike the Basque country in Spain and France, Padania has never existed before.

Italy

Nevertheless, its supporters are playing government. They moved their 15 "ministers" into a Renaissance building in Venice and swore in a self-nominated "parliament" in their "capital city" of Mantua. In 1997 they held unofficial parliamentary elections and charged the assembly with writing a new constitution that would make Padania either independent or loosely confederated with Italy. Advocates waved their own flag, wore green shirts, and called themselves "citizens of the north." They called on northerners to refuse to pay their taxes to Rome.

By 2008 Bossi abandoned those calls for Padania secession. Despite such colorful trappings, opinion polls suggested that most northerners opposed secession, although many agreed with some of the league's criticisms. Bossi had not helped his cause in 1997 by referring to the pope as a "foreigner" and to Romans as "pigs." Urban voters tended to dislike his populism and vulgarity, such as saying that the Italian flag belongs in the toilet. This remark brought 1 million Italians into the streets in Milan and Venice to demonstrate for national unity. In 2005 the league began a campaign to scrap the euro and reintroduce the lira. It got mileage out of his anti-immigrant and anti-Islamic stance and its argument that spending money on the south is useless, since it ends up in the pockets of Mafiosi and corrupt politicians.

In April 2012 scandal caught up with the party. Prosecutors accused the party treasurer of channeling public funds to Bossi family members and close associates. More than 10% of the Lombardy regional assembly was under investigation for corruption. No wonder that only 10% of Italians said in 2012 that they had faith in the main parties.

The Northern League's strength stems from its strident anti-immigration, anti-crime, anti-EU, and antiglobalization rhetoric. Newcomers to Italy are branded as a social and cultural threat. It remains fiercely independent. It pressed for greater financial autonomy for the north as the price for its support. It is characteristic that the party's leaders refused to join in the March 2011 festivities celebrating the 150th year of Italy's unification.

By 2018 it abandoned its separatist longings, dropped "northern" from its name, and sought votes in all of Italy. It won 17% of the votes in 2018. Its combative populist leader is Matteo Salvini. Although he became interior minister with authority over the police, security forces, and immigration, he became the most powerful leader in an unstable populist coalition with the Five Star Movement. Polls showed that, within a few months, the league was supported by a third of the electorate.

Former prime minister Matteo Renzi

THE VANISHED CENTER

Union of Center and Christian Democrats

In the center only the Union of Center and Christian Democrats (UDC), led by Pier Ferdinando Casini, retains a parliamentary presence. It is a breakaway minority from the former ruling Christian Democrats (DC). With only 36 seats in the lower house and a mere 3 in the Senate, its hopes of holding the balance between left and right remains an empty dream.

What happened to the political center? Until 1994 the Christian Democrats had been the dominant party since 1945 and as such was hit the hardest by the political storm raging in Italy. It had placed in office all prime ministers until the Republican Giovanni Spadolini held the office from 1981 to 1982. The DC formed coalitions with all parties except the PDS (Communists) and MSI (neofascists). By 1983, 64% of all mayors, 57% of city councillors, 90% of the managers of state-operated businesses, 94% of all savings and loan presidents, and 58% of all bank presidents were members of the DC. In addition to the broad spectrum of closely related organizations in all sectors of the society in which the DC Party exercises influence, the party received special support from the Catholic Church. Two-thirds of the DC's 1,200 sections had been founded in 1946 at the insistence and under the influence of local clerics.

Ideologically, the DC built upon the two larger middle-class parties of the prefascist period. The Catholicism of the old Popular Party and the economic liberalism of the old Liberal Party were the pillars for the DC's political conception. In accordance with the Manifesto of Milan of 1943, the DC defined itself as a "Catholic

People's Party" encompassing all classes. It had no binding party program. Instead, it was the classical example of the "catch-all party."

The DC's adaptability and its openness to coalitions toward both the right and the left were why for so long it survived political and economic crises without suffering large electoral losses. However, it refused to agree to a "historical compromise" (*Compromesso storico*) with the Communists. Its heterogeneity helped it to stabilize Italian society and guarantee the proper functioning of the parliamentary system. But it was shaken by scandals that left few of its talented leaders untainted.

Staring electoral disaster in the face, DC renamed itself the Italian Popular Party (PPI) in order to try to improve its image and appeal. The new name was designed to signal a return to the Catholic values of Luigi Sturzo, the priest who had founded the Popular Party in 1919.

A minority refused to stay in the Popular Party, forming instead the Christian Democratic Center Party, which was largely irrelevant. To gain some name recognition, it recruited actress Gina Lollobrigida to be a candidate for the 1999 European Parliament elections. Also losing their political significance were the Italian Republican Party (PRI, the Republicans), the Social Democrats (PSDI), the Italian Liberal Party (PLI), and Italian Renewal. The only center party left standing in 2008 was the Union of Center and Christian Democrats. It rebuffed Berlusconi's request for support. Eleven of these small parties or groups joined Berlusconi's People of Freedom Party in 2009. All of them are in decline.

THE LEFT

Since the 2008 elections, the left is dominated by the new center-left Democratic Party (PD, formerly the Olive Tree Coalition), modeled in many ways after its American namesake. It absorbed the former Radicals and formed an electoral and parliamentary agreement with the much smaller Italy of Values Party, led by Antonio Di Pietro. No other leftist party survived. For the first time since the Second World War, the Communists—represented by The Left–The Rainbow (which included Greens)—were routed and are absent in parliament.

Walter Veltroni was unable to hold the reins. He was replaced in 2009 by Dario Franceschini, who was succeeded as leader within months by Pierluigi Bersani, who had served in five center-left governments. After the party came out on top in the February 2013 national elections, his deputy, Enrico Letta, was able to put together a grand coalition with Silvio

Berlusconi's People of Freedom Party and become prime minister in April 2013.

Letta did not survive a year in the top job. He was displaced as PD party leader in December 2013 and as prime minister in February 2014 by the youngest (age 39) prime minister in Italian history, Matteo Renzi, the brash, dynamic, and charismatic "can-do" mayor of Florence (nicknames: "demolisher" and the "scrapper"). Polls indicated he was the country's most popular politician, although only 29% approved the ruthless way he dispatched his predecessor and party colleague, Letta. He was the third unelected prime minister in a row (after Bersani and Letta). He is a confident and forceful outsider untainted by the country's old political class. He led a fragile left-right coalition government composed of the PD, Deputy Prime Minister Angelino Alfano's New Center Right, and Mario Monti's Civic Choice. It had a pact with Berlusconi's Forza Italia. His young 16-minister cabinet contained 8 women; one of them was Italy's first female defense minister, Roberta Pinotti.

Renzi promised sweeping radical reform in 100 days. A new and complex electoral law would strengthen governments to enact their policies. An unelected Senate would be turned into a weakened regional body, which would eliminate the need for a government to have a majority in both chambers. Public administration would be shaken up, and the tax system, reformed. "Our country is rusty, bogged down, immobilized by an asphyxiating bureaucracy, by rules, norms and codicils that paradoxically don't eliminate illegality."

Renzi's promises did not come true. The referendum on his reforms was defeated 60% to 40%. He resigned as prime minister and was replaced by former journalist and

Demonstration by the largest union, the CGIL

foreign minister Paolo Gentiloni. This was Italy's 66th government in 70 years. The PD Party was the biggest loser in the 2018 national elections. Its vote collapsed to a mere 19% and 118 seats in the lower house. Renzi was forced to resign as party leader. A breakaway group, Free and Equal (LEU), won only 14 seats. Renzi founded a new party, Italia Viva, in September 2019. Although tiny, commanding only 3% in Parliament, it was able in January 2021 to leave the governing coalition and bring the Conte government down.

The Communists

One of Italy's oldest parties, the Socialist Party, founded in 1892 and one-time political home to Mussolini, has all but disappeared. The various communist parties grew out of the now-defunct Communist Party of Italy (PCI), which had emerged in 1921 and disbanded in 1991. It split into the Party of Democratic Socialism (PDS) and the Refounded Communists (Rifondazione Comunista). In 1998 PDS joined several smaller parties and became the Democrats of the Left (DS), which became the largest party on the left with 1.5 million members. In the same year, the Italian Communist Party broke off from the Refounded Communists. The old PCI overcame its political and social isolation of the 1950s and 1960s because it was able to reach beyond its traditional base in the industrial working class and to gain new voters from the middle class. A traditionally atheistic party, it could exist in a country closely associated with the Catholic Church because it quietly dropped

atheism as a part of its platform. It also ceased being a Marxist-Leninist cadre party and instead became simply a leftist worker's party. It rejected the concept of its first postwar leader, Palmiro Togliatti, who had wanted to introduce socialism into Italy through revolution. History had proven that efforts to change Italian society through revolution simply helped to drive an uncertain middle class into the arms of the fascists.

In the 1960s the PCI was the first western European communist party publicly to reject the Leninist doctrine of a revolutionary seizure of power followed by a dictatorship of the proletariat. That is, it turned down the model of the Soviet Union and sought its own path to socialism.

This enabled the PCI to accept Italian membership in NATO and the EU. As western Europe's largest communist party, it could become the leader of so-called Eurocommunism, a movement that discarded Marxist-Leninist orthodoxy as the basis of its ideology. The movement recognized parliamentary democracy as a prerequisite for socialism, which, it believed, could be achieved through a wide consensus of reform-oriented forces. It also rejected the planned economies found in eastern Europe, although this rejection did not imply total acceptance of a free-market economy. It is no surprise that these policies led to tensions with the Soviet Union. The DS criticized Moscow over the Soviet occupation of Afghanistan in 1979 and the introduction of martial law in Poland in 1981. Other Italian parties cautiously welcomed such criticism.

Ex–prime minister Paolo Gentiloni, PD

Italy

In contrast to that of its voters, the social structure of the party members has not basically changed. The reservoir of the party is still industrial workers, who make up approximately three-fourths of its membership. An important lever for accomplishing party goals is the largest union in Italy, the CGIL, with 4.32 million members. It was led in 2012 by a woman, Susanna Camusso. One thing that weakened the party is that the number of industrial workers has declined in Italy's modernizing economy. Also, the growth of the service and white-collar sectors reduced the power of trade unions, and that has adversely affected the DS. The new groups in which the party was able to attract voters and members, such as the intellectual and technical elites, as well as the civil-service workers, remain under-represented in the overall party membership. However, just the opposite can be seen in the party's leadership organs. In the 36-member party directorate, a majority has full university credentials.

To hold on to the votes of young and well-educated people, the DS loosened the leaders' grip on the rank and file by making public criticism of the party no longer grounds for expulsion and by permitting elections to the party's central committee to be held in public. The formerly closed way of making party decisions was replaced by free and open votes in all party committees, from the national to the local levels. It formally embraced the market economy and did not oppose the privatization of nationalized industries. It accepted NATO and American bases in Italy, and it rejected unilateral nuclear disarmament.

In 1991, the DS cast off both its name and hammer-and-sickle symbol and sought membership in the Socialist International. The events in eastern Europe had left the party with no choice. One member admitted, "in terms of Italian politics, this is our Berlin Wall that has come crashing down." The new insignia was a spreading tree, with the hammer and sickle practically hidden in the roots. With the total collapse of Moscow-led communism in Europe, the other parties lost their rationale for excluding the DS from government. It is now willing to enter a governing coalition with any major party. It was the main pillar of the Olive Tree coalition.

In October 1998, DS leader Massimo D'Alema became the first ex-Communist to form an Italian government. A pensive former editor of Italy's largest leftist newspaper, *L'Unità*, which after a makeover still sells 50,000 copies a day (down from 300,000 in its heyday), and author of many books, one of which is aptly entitled *La Grande Occasione* (*The Big Chance*), D'Alema admires Tony Blair's style of reform and attacked irresponsible trade

Former prime minister Mario Monti

unionists. He broke a record by bringing nine parties into his government, sarcastically dubbed "the first center-left government of the center-right open to the radical left." It included Communists, ex-Communists, various Greens, and centrists. This government fell in April 2000.

In 2006 D'Alema became foreign minister. Another former prime minister from DS, Giuliano Amato, became interior minister. In April 2007 D'Alema proposed that DS merge with Democracy and Freedom (Margherita), a suggestion that appalled some of his fellow former Communist comrades. D'Alema called for primaries to choose the first leader for the newly united Democratic Party.

Hard-liners broke from the DS and formed a separate party, Refounded Communist Party, led by Fausto Bertinotti. It advocated Italy's withdrawal from NATO and opposition to further European integration. The party refused to join the Olive Tree coalition, which, in Bertinotti's opinion, was too "heavily weighted on the side of centrists and moderates." But it joined the Prodi government in 2006. Bertinotti was elected president (speaker) of the Chamber of Deputies. However, in 2008 he resigned his party leadership after his electoral coalition, The Left–The Rainbow, which included Greens, was decimated at the polls, winning only slightly more than 3% of the votes. The Communists had become politically irrelevant by the 2018 election.

Monti's Nonparty Government

In November 2011 Silvio Berlusconi's center-right government lost its majority in the lower house of parliament and lost a crucial vote of confidence. Berlusconi

announced that he was stepping aside from frontline politics and had no intention of being prime minister again. But he still leads his People of Liberty Party. Berlusconi faced trial on charges of abuse of power and paying for sex with an underaged prostitute. Although the charges were dropped, it was this kind of behavior that brought about his divorce from Veronica Lario, whom the court awarded nearly €100,000 per day, or €35 million annually, in maintenance.

Given the danger that neighboring Greece's serious economic problems could spill over to Italy, the country's leaders decided that a government of experts, not of politicians, was needed until new elections were due in 2013. Nicknamed "Super Mario," Mario Monti is respected throughout Europe for his successful tenure as competition (antitrust) commissioner at the EU. He gained a reputation as a man of measured words and bold action. He elevated Italy's standing in the EU after many European officials had grown tired of Berlusconi's antics and Italian influence had diminished.

Monti appointed a small cabinet of 17, composed of well-regarded technocrats. There were bankers, seven professors like himself, ambassadors, and bureaucrats but no politicians. He assumed the portfolio of finance minister without pay. Critics noted a shortage of women. There were three, who occupy senior posts. Young people were also underrepresented in a cabinet whose average age is 64, the highest in the history of the Italian Republic.

This government acted with a rapidity unknown in Italian politics. In its first six weeks in power, it passed more economic measures than Italy had in a decade. It pulled Italy back from economic catastrophe. It introduced spending cuts and tax rises, as well as pension reform by raising the retirement age. It bore down on tax evasion. It put public finances on track to balance the budget and to start paying down the gigantic national debt of 133% of GDP. It sought to stimulate growth by opening up closed professions, such as notaries, lawyers, pharmacists, and taxi driving. It attempted to simplify bureaucracy and took on the daunting challenge of ending the two-tier labor market of overly protected older workers and younger ones and females, called "precarious workers" in Italy, who lead an uncertain existence from one temporary contract to the other, even if they are lucky enough to enter the job market. The unions opposed his objective to make it easier to hire and fire.

As expected, he ran up against a wall of vested interests, and strikes by pharmacists, taxi drivers, self-employed truck drivers, lawyers, and railway workers shook the country. His austerity and

Report of car-bombing

reform policy became increasingly unpopular, and the economy could not grow fast enough to show citizens the benefits of such prudent finances.

For a while his government maintained support from parties of the right and left and enjoyed an approval rating of 62% in spring 2012, far above the established parties. But the reforms undertaken would have taken a decade to complete. Monti stated repeatedly that he would step down after the spring 2013 elections. His prediction was not correct that "the parties will not dare go back to the acrimonious, superficial and tough confrontation that animated parliament. The image and style of the public debate has changed."

He decided to found and lead a Civic Choice Party in the February 2013 elections. But its performance was the biggest disappointment for Italy's eurozone partners. The Party placed a distant fourth, winning only 10.6% of the votes and 45 seats in the Chamber of Deputies and 9.1%

and 18 seats in the Senate. His thrashing indicated deep disillusion with his austerity measures. His embrace of German chancellor Angela Markel and her policies also played a major role in his undoing.

The Five Star Movement (M5S)

A new antiestablishment party led autocratically by an eccentric former stand-up comedian Beppe Grillo, provided much more than comic relief. In 2013 the Five Star Movement (M5S) captured 25.6% of the votes and 108 seats in the lower house and 23.8% and 54 seats in the Senate. It put an end to the drift toward a two-party system. By refusing every form of governing coalition, it brought Italian politics to a stalemate. It saw itself as a protest, antiestablishment, and opposition party. It espouses environmentalism and pacifism. Grillo himself has no parliamentary seat, and the party has no headquarters. After a few years of being perceived as clownish and eccentric, the party transformed itself into a more normal party. thirty-one-year-old leader Luigi Di Maio declared unmistakably, "We want to govern."

The party is fueled by the resentment toward the political establishment and the sacrifices forced on Italians by the euro crisis. It is staunchly anti-EU and anti-immigrant. It is especially strong in the south. Its chief aims are to replace political parties and parliamentary government with a web-based, semidirect democracy. Members of parliament would enact the will of the people as expressed in referenda on the web. It talks of a true participatory democracy. It would abolish labor unions but introduce a 20-hour workweek and an income for everybody. Legislation would eliminate corruption, and the environment would be protected. It is the first Populist Party with a serious chance to win power. In 2016 it won two key mayoral races, in Rome and Turin. It has the opportunity to prove its claim that amateurs are the best politicians.

Fourteen of its senators and five of its deputies quit in protest against Grillo's autocratic leadership and refusal to cooperate with other parties. The party's fortunes are rising. It was the big winner in the March 2018 national elections. It got 37% of the votes and 222 lower-house seats (up from 109) and 112 Senate seats (up from 54). The party and the league won half the votes, and after months of frustrating haggling, they formed a shaky populist government. They both agree the EU, its fiscal rules, the euro, and immigration are the problems.

SOCIETY

Civil Society and Terrorism

Italian society has often been characterized as an "uncivic culture." According to studies made by Almond and Verba in the late 1950s, two-thirds of the Italians refused to have anything to do with politics or to discuss the subject with anyone. Only 3% were proud of their state institutions, and only 10% approved of political participation.

An updated version of this study in 1980 revealed that Italians have become much more inclined to engage in direct political action, especially in the form of demonstrations, strikes, blocking of railroads or highways, or even political violence. Many Italians cling to the view that laws have been made to be evaded, that taxes are hostile acts of the state against the individual, and that one who does not successfully embezzle the government when one has the opportunity is considered a fool. Public institutions were long regarded with an unparalleled carefree air. The citizen's contempt and irritation toward his state was almost nihilistic, as is manifested in the widely used expression *"piove, governo ladro"* ("It's raining on this corrupt state"). The political revolution in the 1990s showed that toleration of corruption and indifference toward elected representatives have dramatically changed.

For centuries the state meant nothing more to Italians than suppression by foreigners of subordination to the Doge princes, who themselves were dependent upon others. It has been difficult for Italians to believe that the state is working for their interests. One Italian expressed in 1993, "We expect little of our politicians, and that's what we get."

The permanent crisis of the modern democratic state in Italy is scarcely suitable for developing a stronger sense of public spirit among its citizens. The work of many heterogeneous factions organized into many groups has made the establishment of a political consensus difficult. In Rome alone, over 25,000 politically active organizations have been counted. Some of these groups refuse to observe the democratic rules of the game and have become parts of the powerful terrorist movements that seek to achieve their political goals through violence. Terrorists on the extreme right have tried to upset the political system by means of countless indiscriminate bomb attacks. They have not been brought entirely under control.

The extreme leftists, the Red Brigades, posed a great problem for Italian domestic security through their precisely planned and executed attacks and kidnappings of high-ranking personalities. Their objective was to undermine the state and then to provoke a fascist reaction, which, they hoped, would be the prelude to a "proletarian" revolution, although the working class in Italy shows almost no sympathy for such aims.

Italy

They planned a spree of kidnappings and commando-style raids on jails to free arrested terrorists. As a final bloody crescendo, they imagined the massacre of the entire Christian Democratic leadership at a DC gathering in Rome. This campaign was foiled by the determination of the Italian government to put an end to left-wing terrorism. The government was greatly aided by the crack antiterrorist units, which had been created in order to achieve the same level of expertise as that of the astonishingly well-informed, well-armed, and well-trained terrorists. Very importantly, it did this without abandoning democracy or an observance of civil rights. But the causes of such violence remain: an immobile political system, a corruption-ridden bureaucracy, and the bleak economic outlook for many young Italians.

In 1999 there was a frightening reminder of Red Brigade terrorism when one of the government's top advisers, Massimo D'Antona, was gunned down as he walked to work. Prime Minister D'Alema vowed, "We are faced with a terrorist band that the state intends to find and to hit." In July 2005 three of the murderers received life sentences for this crime, and one got nine years.

In March 2002 Marco Biagi, a top economic adviser who was helping the government draft controversial changes to the labor laws, making it easier to lay off workers, was murdered in Bologna. Authorities had ignored Biagi's pleas for protection. Forensic tests indicated that the assassination was the work of the Red Brigades. A Red Brigade member arrested a year later admitted that the assassination had been part of the group's strategy to derail the government's plans to reform Italy's labor laws. One of the murderers, a turncoat, was sentenced in 2005 to 16 years in prison. In October 2003 six further suspects were apprehended in raids throughout the country.

In March 2004 a breakthrough occurred in the battle against the Red Brigades. A gunfight broke out on a train from Rome to Florence when police asked two Red Brigade suspects to show their identity cards. A police officer and one suspect were killed, but police found notebooks filled with information about the gang. The clues gained from them led to a series of raids and arrests across the country. One of the apprehended, Cinzia Banelli, became the first Red Brigade suspect to turn informant since the group returned to action, disclosing hiding places, secret codes, accomplices, and crimes committed. In February 2007 police arrested 15 people accused of belonging to the Politico-military Communist Party (PCPM), a descendent of the Red Brigades.

Italians' worries about violence in their midst were fueled again in 2001 by the radical Islamic terrorist strikes in New York and Washington on September 11. Police authorities determined that al Qaeda cells were operating in Italy and were planning violent attacks against such targets as the US embassy. Police made many arrests of suspected terrorists. For example, in September 2002 they followed a tip from US naval intelligence and seized a ship carrying 15 suspected terrorists. They also raided a farmhouse near Venice in January 2003 and arrested five Moroccans in possession of explosives and chemicals, plus maps of NATO bases in Italy and the London Underground. Police have shut down money-transfer operations suspected of financing terrorist groups and concluded that Italy was being used by international terrorist groups as a transit and logistics center.

Cooperation with the Americans has been close, perhaps too close to suit some Italians. Berlusconi is vocally pro-American. But American diplomatic cables published by Wikileaks in 2010 described him as "feckless, vain and ineffective as a modern European leader" and as a canny survivor and sometimes erratic partner on the international scene. He "seems determined to be best friends with Russia." Therefore he criticized the Americans' missile defense project, NATO's eastward enlargement, and Kosovo's independence in 2008. He was also the only European leader to defend Russia's military attack against Georgia in 2008.

In 2005 an Italian judge ordered the arrest of 13 CIA operatives (and 13 more in July 2006) on charges of kidnapping for carrying out an operation of "extraordinary rendition" on Italian soil. It occurred in February 2003, when a Muslim cleric, Abu Omar, who was suspected of belonging to a militant Islamic organization, was bundled into a van and transported back to his native Egypt, where he was jailed, tortured, and released. The CIA claims that its Rome station chief had informed his Italian counterpart at the time and had received implicit approval for the operation.

Evidence emerged in 2006 that Italy's military intelligence service, SISMI, had indeed been notified of the plans and had perhaps aided the CIA. In a letter the SISMI chief had told political leaders at the time of the CIA's operation. A judge ruled in February 2010 that Italy's secret services had indeed been informed. In February 2013 Italy's former head of intelligence was sentenced to 10 years in prison for his part in the rendition. A year later he and four other Italian intelligence leaders and agents were acquitted.

In 2007 an Italian judge indicted 26 CIA operatives for the kidnapping. The warrants never led to any arrests because the agents were no longer in Italy. They had used false papers. A State Department legal adviser confirmed that, if Italy were to request the extraditions, the US would not comply. Italy did not request.

In 2008 the long-delayed trial of the CIA operatives in absentia and former Italian intelligence officials began. The Americans pleaded not guilty. The trial was suspended and later resumed. In 2009 the judge convicted 23 of the Americans. He acquitted three because they had diplomatic immunity, but they were tried in absentia in March 2014 and given a guilty verdict. All but one of the agents had already left the CIA.

In December 2010 and again in September 2012, an appellate court in Milan upheld the convictions and raised the sentences from five to seven years. They were also ordered to pay $1.33 million in damages to the abducted Egyptian cleric. Probably none will serve jail time, and no money will be paid. But they are legally considered fugitives and are subject to an EU arrest warrant. One is a dual American-Portuguese citizen who was detained and extradited to Italy by Portuguese authorities in April 2017. She has asked for a pardon. This was the first time an allied country had placed CIA agents on trial.

Italians' fears were heightened after the July 2005 bombings in the London Underground stations and the flight of one of the suspects to Italy, where he was tracked down and arrested by Italian police. A poll in *Corriere della Sera* found that 82% saw a serious risk that they will face similar deadly attacks. Sensing the popular mood, the government gained approval for many new security measures. They include strengthening border checks, the right to hold terrorist suspects for 24 hours (up from 12) without turning them over to a magistrate, broader access to the records of Internet service providers (including Internet cafés) and telephone and cellular companies, permission to take DNA samples from suspects, jailing suspects who provide explosives training, placing limits on pilots' licenses, quick expulsions for foreigners considered to be a danger to national security or who assist in terrorist activities, criminalizing the recruitment and training of people for terrorist activities, sequestering assets of firms suspected of financing terror, and checking on mosques and Islamic centers.

The Mafia

Organized crime is the country's number 1 plague. The most famous is the Sicilian Cosa Nostra, whose power extends from Sicily to Rome and the industrialized area farther north. Its regional competitors include the Sacra Corona Unita in Puglia; Camorra, an umbrella term for dozens of

344

Neapolitan Mafia clans; and Ndrangheta from Calabria, the "toe" of Italy. Camorra smuggles uninspected Chinese goods into Europe, imports arms from eastern Europe and transfers them to Basque terrorists, launders money, and reportedly has its hand in the highly lucrative business of collecting and disposing of trash. It is widely believed that it dumps forbidden toxic wastes gathered from Camorra-affiliated companies all over Europe into public landfills around Naples.

Of all these groups, Ndrangheta is the most ruthless and prosperous, having cornered the market for cocaine smuggled into Europe. Its annual narcotics income was estimated in 2008 to be as much as €40 billion ($64 million). It has eclipsed Cosa Nostra and the other mobs in power, wealth, and international reach. It enjoys the advantage that there is little public protest in Calabria against it, while there is a growing outcry in Sicily against the outrages of Cosa Nostra.

Ndrangheta and other crime families have expanded their operations to the more prosperous north of Italy, where their influence is far greater than had been suspected. Dozens of mobsters and corrupt politicians have been arrested in Rome and Milan. They remind Italians that traditional mafias are pervasive.

The Mafia accumulated enormous wealth from lucrative bogus public-works contracts, "protection," and international drug traffic, of which Sicily became the European center following the severance of the "French Connection" in the 1970s. The Mafia has lost ground in the global drug trade, supplying only an estimated 5% of the American market in 1993. As a result of its being progressively pushed out of international drug smuggling, it has become more dependent on its traditional extortion business. A 1996 survey revealed that 23% of businesses paid racketeers an average of 10.7% of their annual sales.

A decade later Sicilian entrepreneurs pay an estimated €8 billion ($11.2 billion) in "*pizzo*" (protection payment) to the Cosa Nostra each year. A small but growing number of mainly young businessmen defy the mob by refusing to pay protection. A grassroots movement in Naples is determined to resist the Camorra mob by refusing to pay, and an international audience is taking note of that. This is progress, although nobody knows how many businesses still pay *pizzo*. The 2008 national budget contained tax breaks for those courageous entrepreneurs. Also this illicit means of collecting money actually makes Cosa Nostra members more vulnerable to the combined pressure of the government and businesspeople who refuse to pay.

Italian mobsters also face competition from ruthless imitators from Russia, Colombia, China, and other countries. Italy is not merely a transit point for drugs, which increasingly flow into the veins of Italians themselves. It gives the country the shameful distinction of having the largest number of addicts in Europe.

With its wealth the Mafia has shifted its emphasis to becoming an entrepreneur. The Mafia bought into countless businesses and penetrated a portion of the Italian banking system, which it needs to launder its "hot" money. Whereas the Mafia's main profits were once from the drug trade, they are now from government contracts and extortion. In 1996 the Italian trade association Confcommercio estimated that a fifth of all trade and construction enterprises in Italy were controlled by organized crime and that the authorities discover no more than 8% of illegal businesses.

When the 2008–2009 economic recession produced a severe credit crunch, cash-rich Mafia gangs profited by offering loans to an estimated 180,000 small businesses who could not get them from banks. They also used their huge cash reserves to buy property and companies at discount prices. Italy's economic advancement over the years has helped the five main Mafia organizations to become even richer. It is estimated that their activities are equal to about 7% of Italy's GDP, and their profit is an estimated $200 billion annually.

The competition among Mafia and Camorra families for larger shares of the drug trade unleashed ruthless gang wars that left the streets and countryside strewn with hundreds of bloody corpses. In 2005 a turf war over the drug trade erupted in Naples, claiming at least 135 lives. It also led the Mafia to aim its ugly pistol at the political process itself. In 1979 it began liquidating top Italian political officials in Sicily who stood in its way. The government responded to this deadly challenge by making membership in a Mafia clan a crime, by legalizing the confiscation of suspects' estates if they cannot demonstrate that their income was legally acquired, and by sending the new leader of the secret services to Sicily as that island's regional prefect. In 1987 courageous judges and prosecutors in Palermo, relying heavily on testimony from 14 Mafia members who broke the code of silence, convicted 338 Mafiosi of crimes ranging from murder to drug trafficking in the biggest Mafia trial in Italian history. For the first time, the leading mobster bosses received the stiffest sentences.

In the 1980s and 1990s, the Mafiosi maintained a steady wave of killings, not only among themselves, but also against the Italian state. In 1988 they murdered an

Prosperous shoppers in Florence

active judge for the first time. The government cooperated with US officials to crack a powerful transatlantic drug ring. Despite the scores of bosses arrested, all agree that only the tip of the iceberg had been shattered. Authorities are able to prosecute criminals more quickly because of a 1989 judicial reform aimed at streamlining the system. One headline read, "Perry Mason has finally entered Italy's old and decrepit courtrooms."

The criminal families not only expanded their operations into northern Italian cities but also began influencing municipal and regional elections by murdering or intimidating candidates. In 1991 five persons, including a member of a city council, were shot; one victim was even beheaded; his head was used for target practice. This horrified the Italian public and prompted the government to assume the authority to dissolve any city council or local authority infiltrated by the Mafia and to send judges, even against their will, to man understaffed courts in the three regions most plagued by gangs: Calabria, Sicily, and Campania. The government created in 1991 a special post, dubbed the Italian FBI, within the attorney general's office to coordinate the fight against organized crime.

Italy is fighting to prevent itself from falling under the control of unelected

Italy

international criminals. At stake is the freedom of Italians to be ruled by leaders they elect rather than by those who reap undreamed-of profits from feeding human vices. After the Mafia murdered two top anti-Mafia officials (Giovanni Falcone and Paolo Borsellino) in 1992, the government deployed 7,000 soldiers to Sicily in July to crack down on the mob. This was the most drastic step taken since 1945 against a domestic disorder and the first time troops were used in a large-scale crackdown on the Sicilian mobsters. Also in 1992 law-enforcement officials joined Spanish, British, and American police to arrest Italians working with the Cali (Colombia) cocaine cartel. The biggest organized crime sweep in almost 10 years put scores of Mafia suspects in jail, including several mayors and three members of parliament.

Armed with strengthened antiracketeering laws permitting wider use of phone taps, property searches, confiscation of property of convicted or suspected Mafia people, state reimbursement to businesses that suffer for defying the racketeers, and guarantees of protection for state witnesses, police maintained this momentum in 1993. A startling development occurred when the late Pope John Paul broke the church's long tradition of silence on Mafia matters and lashed out against organized crime. The Mafia's two top leaders, Salvatore ("Nitto") Riina and Benedetto Santapaola, as well as the only woman known to have headed an Italian crime syndicate (the Camorra around Naples), Rosario Cutolo, were captured. In 1996 one of the most powerful and ruthless bosses in the history of the Corleone clan, Giovanni Brusca (nicknamed "the Pig"), who had masterminded the murder of Falcone and Borsellino, was captured by 200 black-hooded special police troops.

The key has been a crumbling of the long-standing code of silence. By 1997 more than 1,200 arrested Mafiosi were collaborating with investigators. The growing number of *pentiti* ("penitents") has prompted Mafia organizations to retaliate brutally, departing from the older code of honor not to attack women, children, judges, government officials, and innocent bystanders. It has also been expensive for the taxpayer to take care of more than 6,000 people, including families, who need escorts, protection, money, shelter, special schools, and churches. But organized crime really does seem to be on the run.

The resulting confessions of these *pentiti* not only led to the dramatic arrests of Mafia leaders. They also opened perhaps the most explosive chapter in Italy's mega-corruption scandal: that top Christian Democratic leaders, especially seven-time prime minister Giulio Andreotti, may have cooperated with and protected the

Chatting at the market

Mafia. No Italian politician had as many revealing nicknames as he: "Machiavelli," "Mephistopheles," and "the Fox." Prosecutors claim that the Mafia had guaranteed his party votes and political control in Sicily in return for government contracts for Mafia-controlled companies and protection from police crackdowns. Andreotti denied the charges but agreed to have his senatorial immunity lifted in order to clear his name in court.

Commencing in 1995, this trial was a humiliating ordeal for Andreotti; two-thirds of respondents in a 1995 poll though he did indeed have a "relationship" with Mafia. The press called it "the trial of the century." In 1999 he was acquitted on charges that he had associated with the Mafia and had ordered it to kill an investigative journalist (Mauro De Navro) in 1979. The court decisions did not dispel all doubts about his activities, and in November 2002 this verdict was overturned in a court of appeals, and Andreotti was sentenced to 24 years in jail. He quickly appealed this reversal, as the country was aghast at this never-ending ordeal based on the testimony of a Mafia turncoat. A year later Italy's highest court overturned the conviction, and he was formally acquitted. In May 2003 he was absolved of another charge of having connections to the Mafia, and finally, in October 2004, the highest criminal court acquitted him of all charges that he had colluded with the Mafia. In 2006 he was an unsuccessful candidate for speaker of the Senate. He died in 2013.

Andreotti's seemingly interminable legal entanglement ignited attacks on the controversial use of over 1,100 *pentiti*, on whose testimony all his cases had been based. This questioning became a furious public debate in May 2003, when a mobster convicted of a grisly murder was released from prison after only seven years behind bars. Enzo Brusca had kidnapped an 11-year-old boy and held him captive, before strangling him and dissolving his body in acid. In 2001 parliament had already toughened the *pentiti* law by limiting the window for providing information and requiring them to serve at least 10 years of a life sentence.

Some Italians now believe that organized crime can finally be defeated. No longer able to act with impunity inside Italy, the Mafia and other organized crime groups are increasingly expanding their operations into other European countries. In 1998 one of the new generation's top bosses in Sicily, Vito Vitale, was arrested. Then in 2006 the "boss of bosses," Bernardo Provenzano ("Binnu the Tractor"), was captured at a lonely run-down farmhouse in Sicily. Sentenced in absentia to life in prison in 1963, he had been on the run 43 years, sleeping in caves, stables, and secluded cottages. He had been supported by a vast invisible web of protection that included businessmen and possibly prominent politicians. He is said to have steered the Mafia away from murder and into such rackets as drug dealing. He died in 2017 at age 83, after 10 years in prison.

The arrests continued. In 2007 Salvatore Lo Piccolo (nicknamed "the Baron"), the most senior Mafia "boss of bosses" still at large, was captured with his son and two other mobsters in a house near Palermo. He had been on the run for 24 years. An ecstatic chief anti-Mafia prosecutor declared that the mob had been "decapitated." Another gang leader, Pasquale Condello, was snatched in 2008 after 20 years on the run. At the same time, Italian and American police arrested over 100 Mafia suspects in New York and Sicily, striking a fatal blow to the second largest crime group in the US, the Bambino family. This operation was repeated in 2010, when 25 mobsters in Sicily, New York, North Carolina, and Florida were apprehended.

One of the largest raids in recent years was made in 2008, when 89 more arrests were made involving dog teams and helicopters and 1,200 Carabinieri. Operation Perseus was intended to stop an attempt by Cosa Nostra's senior mobsters to reconstitute its governing board and choose a new leader after previous waves of arrests.

The year 2010 saw some of the most dramatic roundups. In January 1,200 police officers arrested 100 Mafiosi in Palermo and Tuscany. That culminated a several-month effort in which 17 of the country's 30 most-wanted fugitives had been nabbed. In July 3,000 police and Carabinieri swooped upon Italy's richest, most aggressive, and most dangerous syndicate, the Ndrangheta (pronounced n-DRANG-gay-tah). Over 320 suspected members were arrested, including its top boss, 80-year-old Domenico Oppendisano. Police confiscated millions of euros in property, money, weapons, and drugs. The interior ministry claimed that, in the two years to July 2010, police had arrested 6,433 Mafia suspects across Italy and seized assets of €15 billion ($21 billion).

Italians remain fascinated by the Mafia. In January 2008 they were treated to a six-part TV miniseries called *Il Capo dei Capi* (*The Boss of Bosses*) about imprisoned chief

Salvatore (Toto) Riina, who reportedly watched it faithfully from his cell. Seven million viewers (28% of the total TV audience) were glued to the series. Ironically, the American gangster series *The Sopranos* was a flop in Italy.

Despite the fact that many bosses and their underlings are behind bars, the Mafia is far from destroyed. No part of Sicily is free of its influence, and extortion and protection rackets remain commonplace. In 2008 a magistrate in Calabria worried about the deeply rooted mob: "There is a virus, but no anti-virus." There is, however, some good news. About half of businesses pay protection, but in the 1990s four-fifths did. While at that time the levies amounted to a tenth of the businesses' turnover, they are now half that.

The Italian Family

Despite the complicated historical development and the division into numerous interest groups, the Italian family has traditionally been responsible for Italy's national identity and strength. It is the most important institution and focal point of Italian life. Its strength permits society to function when government fails. Its significance has changed due to the modernization that accompanies industrial life. Just half of women have jobs.

An OECD study in 2009 concluded that, within the Italian family, the husband has 80 minutes more leisure time than does the wife. This is the greatest gap among the 18 countries studied. A survey a year later concluded that women with jobs outside the home still spend 21 hours per week on housework; American women spend 4. In 2010 the World Economic Forum placed Italy 74th in the world in its Global Gender Gap rankings. Other European countries strive to narrow gender inequality, while the Berlusconi government led in the other direction. Only 7% of corporate management posts are held by women.

Perhaps it is not surprising that many women are unwilling to take on an added burden of raising children. Italy reached zero population growth in 1987. By 2017 the average mother was producing only 1.3 children (up from 1.25 a few years earlier), compared with 2.7 in 1964 and the European average of 1.6. The figure is especially low in the south (1.4), which is a region of emigration. Government programs, such as "fertility day," have failed. Italy spends 1.1% of its GDP on child care and other family incentives, less than half that spent in France. Only 10% of toddlers have access to preschool nurseries, and a fourth (27%) of women quit work after bearing a child.

Italy now has one of the world's oldest populations: One in five is in retirement. This is a ticking bomb for the nation.

Current projections foresee Italians over age 65 accounting for a third of the population in 2050, up from 15.3% in 1991. The entire population could decline to 47 million in 2050. However, thanks to immigration, the population could hold steady at 60 million.

Italians live long: 85.7 years for women and 80.3 for men. After becoming, in 2005, Europe's third nation (after Norway and Ireland) to ban smoking totally in public places, they may live even longer. The ban includes offices, bars, restaurants, and discotheques, unless they have separate smoking areas with ventilation. In most years now, deaths outnumber births, and only immigration somewhat stabilizes the population.

The influence of the Catholic Church remains important, and it takes an active and overt role in politics. A reminder was given in June 2005, when a referendum took place to decide whether to abrogate parts of a 2004 fertility law that banned research using stem cells from embryos. The law also imposed stringent requirements on test-tube pregnancies. In order to pass, a majority had to turn out to vote, and a majority had to vote yes. Pope Benedict XVI and the country's bishops and priests told the faithful to boycott the referendum. As a result, only 26% showed up to vote, and 90% of those voted yes. Italians once again showed the power of their church. This action convinced some students and academics that the pope was hostile to science; he had once argued in 1990 that the

SPECIAL REPORT: THE FUTURE OF THE CAR IS SMALL

Newsweek

ITALY'S MESS

HOW A LOVELY COUNTRY BECAME EUROPE'S ECONOMIC AND POLITICAL DISASTER ZONE

Italy

church's verdict against Galileo had been "rational and just."

In 2008 he had to cancel a speech at the prestigious Sapienza University in Rome because of protests by professors and students. In a 2010 poll almost two-thirds (62%) of Italians disapproved of how Benedict managed the church. The church supported the Berlusconi government because of its prochurch policies on family life and social issues. However, the prime minister's sex scandals strained those relations especially after a report surfaced that, at one of his parties, a prostitute had dressed as a nun and then performed a strip-tease act.

To cool down a dispute with the Vatican in May 2006, then–prime minister Prodi publicly reprimanded his health minister for supporting trials of the RU-486 abortion pill, even though polls show that Italians strongly favor the 1978 law legalizing abortion in the first trimester. Same-sex marriages are forbidden, but in 2016 civil unions were legalized, albeit without the right to adopt children. The Catholic Church opposed such unions. In 2007 the government supported the Roman municipal council officially designating two blocks of bars and restaurants leading up to the Colosseum as a recreation ground for the LGBTQ Community.

Young Italians must postpone marriage for economic reasons. They do not finish university until about age 27. Youth unemployment is over three times the national average (43%, higher in the south). Caught in an employment trap of one after another short-term contract, they cannot afford to leave home until they are around 30, to say nothing of having children inside marriage. In 2015, four out of five (79%) Italians under the age of 30 still lived with their parents. A "baby bounty" of €1,000 ($1,300) to couples for every child after their first has little effect on procreation. In contrast to most northern European nations, only 9.6% of Italian babies are born out of wedlock (EU average: 28%; 55% in Sweden). Divorce law was liberalized to permit Italians to end a marriage after only 12 months (6 if not contested) without going to court.

The worsening age distribution presents a ticking bomb for the pension system. In 2001 pensions claimed 60% of welfare spending, compared to an EU average of 45%. By 2013 the annual pension bill was 14% of GDP and rising to 17% by 2035 if future entitlements are not adjusted to rising life expectancy. It is estimated that by 2030 about 42% of Italians will be pensioners, the highest proportion in Europe.

The government introduced a pension reform in 2003 that brought hundreds of thousands of protesters into the streets. It had to water down the reform to get it

passed in 2004. Only Greece has a lower employment rate than Italy. Only 30% of Italians aged 55 to 64 have jobs. Starting in 2013 the retirement age was raised to 61 if contributions were made for 36 years. The country cannot afford its current pension system. That is why the European Commission prevailed on the cabinet to raise the female retirement age in the public sector by 4 years to 65 starting in 2012. This is the same age as for men.

The Bureaucracy

Many political decisions are made within the various interest groups rather than in the official political channels. Italians therefore have a good understanding for the term "under government" (sottogoverno). Italian bureaucracy, with 1.7 million civil servants, has been reproached for its general inefficiency, inflexibility, and corruption. Government employees have alarming absenteeism, and far too many who report for work either do nothing or use their time to do outside work in order to have a second income.

Government officials are, for the most part, recruited from the south, where an administrative position is for many the only opportunity for a job. The emphasis on authority, exaggerated bureaucracy, and official government patronage and nepotism which characterizes public offices can be traced back historically to the behavioral patterns of the precapitalistic feudal states of the south. It is a curious phenomenon that, in this land of contradictions, the north conquered the south during the "Resurgence" partly through its economic predominance; however, the south conquered the north through the Italian bureaucracy.

The South

The main domestic problem remains the structurally underdeveloped south (Mezzogiorno). It comprises 40% of Italy's land area and 35% of its population but only 24% of its GDP. GDP per person is more than 40% lower in the south than in the center and north. It receives only 1% of foreign direct investment (FDI) coming into Italy. The reason is organized crime, which is based in the south and which bleeds companies of the cash they might otherwise invest in R&D. When describing the Italian social and economic situation, one can speak of an industrialized state that has some characteristics of an underdeveloped country. Four-fifths of the industry is concentrated in the Turin-Milan-Genoa triangle. Although roughly one-third of the population is concentrated in the south, half of Italy's unemployed live there. In 2006 the jobless rate in the south was three to four times higher than in the north.

The problem is bound to get worse because illiteracy is higher and education is worse. In the Shanghai ranking, only 3 southern universities are among Italy's 20 best ones. Talented young and educated southerners too often join the brain drain out. The average income per capita in the south is 70% of the Italian average, and it is widening. The per-capita productivity is 40% to 60% under that of the north. In the 21st century, most of the gaps in the labor market in the dynamic north of Italy are being filled by workers from central and eastern Europe, no longer by immigrants from the south of Italy. There are, of course, significant differences between regions within the south. For instance, Calabria and Campania are very depressed, while such areas as Abruzzi and Molise are catching up with the north. Clearly prosperity is not being shared equally throughout Italy. The south faces even more intensely a problem that threatens manufacturers in all of Italy: Too many of its industries—textiles, shoes, machine tools—are vulnerable to global competition, especially low-cost China.

The traveler coming from the modern, industrialized north to Calabria or the Basilicata in the south has the feeling that he has left a highly developed country and has landed in an underdeveloped one. In order to compensate for this historical disadvantage, a governmental agency called the Cassa per il Mezzogiorno was established in 1950 to channel resources to the south and stimulate improvements. It accounted for a few worthwhile projects, including a turnpike from Milan to Palermo, which opened up the south to tourism. However, overall results were disappointing. Profit seekers in the north benefited excessively, and the Mafia and the Ndrangheta used fraud to amass fortunes from the money it provided. It was therefore abolished in 1992.

The culmination point for misery in the south is Naples, the "capital of poverty," as the Turin newspaper *La Stampa* described it. The city, with its 1.3 million inhabitants, among which over 100,000 are unemployed, is practically incomprehensible. Speculation on construction projects has been boundless. Also, the absence of a sewage system has transformed the once-renowned gulf into a cesspool that is five times more polluted than Italy's other coastal waters. Neapolitan newspapers read many days like a hair-raising chronicle of crime and catastrophe. The number of stolen vehicles is estimated at 40,000 annually. There are not enough orphans' homes to accommodate the deserted children of desperate parents living in a city known traditionally to be family-conscious. It is surprising that Naples has not collapsed under the pressure of such massive problems.

In 2007–2008 the extent to which the public sector fails its citizens was demonstrated by the fact that Naples went months without trash collection. This was merely the latest rubbish emergency the city had faced in the preceding decade and a half. Garbage collectors stopped their rounds on December 21 because the dumps in and around the city were full.

la Repubblica

Fondatore Eugenio Scalfari — Direttore Ezio Mauro

L'autodifesa di Milosevic "Ecco le stragi della Nato"

Ciampi: basta con le risse

Ma le nomine Rai tornano in alto mare. Ed è scontro sul Csm

Stop alla protesta delle stazioni oggi scioperano scuola e trasporti

Tony Blair il fascino di un hobbit moderno

A controversial modern incinerator was never built. The local organized-crime organization Camorra was also involved, since it reaps large profits from disposing often-toxic wastes from all over Europe in illegal dumps. Then–prime minister Prodi tried desperately to deal with the stinking problem, even sending in the army to clear the city's trash. The inability to solve this putrid problem was an important reason his center-left government was voted out in April 2008. The problem was so bad that in May 2008 the EU's European Commission filed suit against Italy in the European Court of Justice in Luxembourg, charging that the state had failed to meet its obligations to its people.

Foreign Relations and Defense

Italy joined the UN in 1955, but the two main pillars of its foreign policy are membership in the EU and NATO. It was a founding member of both. Conscription has been abolished, and in 2000 the first female volunteers entered the military. In 2019 it had a total of 181,000 soldiers. The army has 108,300 troops; the navy, 34,000 (and two aircraft carriers: the *Garibaldi* and the *Cavour*); the air force, 42,935; and the marines, 2,000. There are 41,867 reservists; 107,967 quasi-military Carbinieri; and 142,933 paramilitary forces of varying kinds. In 2010 these forces were deployed around the globe: 91 act as trainers in Iraq; 2,795 fight in Afghanistan; and 1,892 are peacekeepers in Kosovo and 300 in Bosnia.

Italy's forces are supplemented by 3,015 US ground troops; 4,076 air force personnel mainly in northern Italy; and 4,400 US naval personnel in the Sixth fleet based in Naples, including 55 marines. A spat over American plans to expand the size of its army base at Vicenza in northwestern Italy in order to unify all three elements of the 173rd Airborne Brigade, a rapid-reaction force of 4,500 soldiers, helped bring the Prodi government down temporarily in 2007. He favored the enlargement, but

Italy

Piazza San Marco, Venice

Photo by Vincent Campi

almost two-thirds of the city's residents and the most leftist groups in his nine-party coalition opposed it. He was quickly restored to power, and the construction plans proceeded, backed by a July 2008 ruling by the Council of State, Italy's highest court.

Although it occupies a strategically important position on NATO's southern flank, its defense spending accounts for less than 2% of its GDP. This has dire consequences for the Italian navy, which must leave the defense of Italy's extensive coastline to the army and the air force, which are concentrated in the north. The navy is capable of defending only merchant vessels in the Mediterranean.

NATO membership for a country that had the largest communist party in western Europe caused some tensions. However, as the PCI moved steadily away from Moscow and renamed itself the PDS (then DS), it increasingly accepted national defense within NATO. The dilemma still gives Italian foreign policy one of its major characteristics: It is normally conducted quietly and with the utmost discretion in order not to allow foreign policy to become part of the always-heated domestic cauldron.

Italy has long sought to play a more assertive role in the world, especially in Mediterranean affairs. It became the first European NATO ally to accept, without condition, US medium-range cruise missiles, which began to be deployed at Comiso, Sicily, in 1983. Italian willingness to contribute to strengthening NATO was again shown in 1988, when its government termed the eviction of American F-16 fighter aircraft from Spain as "disastrous" and agreed to their being based in southern Italy. The end of the Cold War made that relocation unnecessary.

In 1991 it sent 10 Tornado aircraft and 5 naval vessels to the Persian Gulf to support its allies' war effort against Iraq. In 1993 Italy was one of the first countries to send troops on the UN humanitarian mission to Somalia, part of which had been ruled by Italy until 1960. Links with Somalia remained strong. Most educated Somalis still speak Italian, and many studied in Italy. In late 2008 the Italians sent a destroyer to join the international naval effort to defeat piracy off the Somali coast.

When NATO launched an air war against Serbia in 1999 to try to stop ethnic cleansing in Kosovo, Italy stuck with the alliance. Although its own aircraft were not involved, it sent 2,000 troops to Albania to administer humanitarian aid, and it permitted NATO pilots to use 14 bases in Italy, including especially Aviano in the northeast. Although some parties, such as the Northern League and the United Communists, opposed the air strikes, then–prime minister D'Alema, a former Communist, declared, "we'll be loyal to the end."

The Italian government responded without hesitation when radical Middle Eastern terrorists attacked the World Trade Center in New York and the Pentagon in Washington on September 11, 2001. It offered the aircraft carrier *Garibaldi*, 2 frigates, Harrier jump jets and Tornado aircraft, a supply ship, and 2,700 troops including 150 paratroopers. It also organized a rally in Rome called "USA Day" on November 10. On the same day, leftists organized a peace rally. This reflected the ambivalence and division within Italian society over the issue of going to war in Afghanistan.

Opinion polls revealed only a slight majority favoring such participation.

When the US and Britain went to war in Iraq to unseat dictator Saddam Hussein in March 2003, most Italians opposed the conflict. But the Berlusconi government backed the American and British allies by offering Italian airspace, ports, highways, and bases, provided that they were not used for actually launching attacks against the enemy. After the three-week conflict was over, Italy joined several other European allies in agreeing to send 3,000 soldiers to help humanitarian efforts in Baghdad, while maintaining 650 troops in Afghanistan. They suffered casualties. Italy also endorsed the call to cancel some of the $1.73 billion debt Iraq owes it. Berlusconi had already announced the withdrawal of Italy's 2,600 troops from Iraq by the end of 2006. Subsequent prime minister Prodi, who called the war in Iraq a "grave error," completed this.

Italy under Berlusconi tried to help heal the wide transatlantic rift that had developed over the Iraq crisis. It asserted itself in world affairs more than its predecessors, and it was less deferential to France and Germany within the EU. "Italy makes the Euro-Atlantic relationship a priority." Fearful that Italy wields too little international influence, Prime Minister Renzi picked fights with the EU and Germany and boasted, "I'm the leader of a great country." In 2015 Italy's influence in the EU was enhanced by the appointment of Foreign Minister Federica Mogherini as its top foreign policy official.

Immigration and the Balkans

One of Italy's thorniest future foreign policy problems is immigration. According to Catholic charity Caritas, by 2011 immigrants living there legally constituted 4.5% of the total population. Adding those who are illegal, the number is over 3.7 million, or 7.9% of the total population. Half are from eastern Europe. They contribute about 10% of the country's GDP, often taking jobs Italians refuse to do. They keep the country's population up and are needed because a majority of Italian women do not work. They head mainly for the center-north, but many work in agriculture in the south. To raise awareness about their contributions to Italy's economy, immigrant workers stayed home and boycotted shopping for one day in March 2010.

More than 700,000 new immigrants arrived every year, but that number had ebbed from 1 million in 2015 to about 100,000 by 2018. Nevertheless, its blocking rescue ships from its ports incensed EU leaders. Of the illegals who have slipped in, 10% come by sea and 15% over land, and 75% overstay their visas. Many Italians fear that some of these illegals are involved in prostitution and drug rings in the major cities. Other European countries fear that Italy could be a gateway into the EU, since Italy is a member of the EU's Schengen group, which lifts border controls for those persons already inside an EU country. But it is increasingly a place where immigrants want to remain.

Especially unsettling are the large number of Romanians (especially Roma, or gypsies) who poured into Italy after their country entered the EU in January 2007. By the end of the year, it was estimated that 556,000 had arrived. Many sleep in illegal camps or shantytowns on the outskirts of major cities. Over a third of all

Lucca

The Spanish Steps, Rome

Composer Puccini in his hometown, Lucca

crimes are committed by foreigners, with Romanians topping the list. Sensational incidents in Rome have spread terror. A Romanian woman was caught on closed-circuit security cameras killing a subway passenger by stabbing her in the eye with an umbrella (for which the assailant was sentenced to 16 years in prison).

After another woman was raped and brutally murdered by a Romanian immigrant, the government issued a decree permitting local authorities to expel from the country any EU nationals considered to be a threat to public safety. Earlier loopholes in the law had made it difficult to deport immigrants. The dramatic electoral success of the anti-immigrant Northern League in 2008 and the subsequent election of the first right-wing mayor (Gianni Alemanno) of Rome since Mussolini's time underscored the rising concern over crime in Italians' minds. Alemanno pledged in his campaign to demolish 85 unlicensed Roma encampments, expel 20,000 allegedly criminal foreigners, and generally crack down on lawbreaking.

Until recently Italy was a land of emigration, but its long coastline facing North Africa has made it a natural bridge between the burgeoning populations of Africa and the Middle East and the rich nations of Europe. Not wishing to damage its good relations with its Arab neighbors on the other side of the Mediterranean and Adriatic Seas, Italy has not wanted to impose quotas. Its Muslim population has risen steeply to about 1.5 million, and the vast majority of them are immigrants who have little chance of ever getting citizenship. Only an estimated 4% regularly attend a mosque. Because of the discovery of numerous Muslim terrorist cells, Italians have mixed feelings about these new

Italy

arrivals. There are attempts to reach out to them. The chairman of Rome's city council Giuseppe Mannino said, "Rome is a city that is open to everybody." To encourage its growing number of illegal residents to register with the authorities, it offered its generous welfare benefits to non-EU citizens, but this merely stimulated even greater immigration.

In a country that thought it was above racism, daily headlines now report racial strife. Nowhere was that more visible than in Florence, where the presence of hundreds of North African street vendors sparked protest marches to decry the influx. Gangs of white rowdies set upon the newcomers with baseball bats and iron bars. Some of the worst riots involving immigrants that Italy had experienced in years broke out in January 2010 in Rosarno in Calabria. These pointed to rising racial tension, especially among the young.

To the east, the collapsed communist regimes in Albania and Yugoslavia have enhanced the specter of an immigration flood. Waves of Albanians, traveling across the Adriatic Sea in overcrowded boats, were washed ashore in 1991, only to be penned in coal docks and inside a local soccer stadium, which they proceeded to wreck out of anger toward their reception. One Caritas relief worker complained, "the police threw food at them like in a zoo."

In 1997, for the first time since the Second World War, Italy led a multinational force, including 6,000 of its own soldiers, to restore order in Albania, a country with which it has close historical and cultural ties. Violence and anarchy had broken out when thousands of people lost their savings in shady financial pyramid schemes. By the end of the year, order had been restored, and thousands of the Albanian refugees began to be deported. In 2010 it still had 1,892 peacekeepers in Kosovo and 300 in Bosnia. The Balkans are simply too close and too unstable not to warrant Italy's full attention. In the words of Lucio Caracciolo, editor of *Limes* magazine, they "have become our top foreign policy priority."

Stung by the criticism, the government adopted a new policy to prevent the exodus of impoverished Albanians. Italian naval vessels help Albania patrol its shores. It also established a large emergency aid program within Albania itself. Italian soldiers distribute food and advice on improving the infrastructure as a forerunner to a longer-term program to help stabilize the Balkan country's ailing economy.

By 2003 the main immigration route into Italy had changed. Instead of coming from the east into the southeastern region of Apulia, more immigrants now come north from Africa and land on the southern and southwestern shores. Italy also adopted a tougher law in 2002 making it harder for new immigrants to obtain residency permits. That made it easier for law enforcement authorities to expel those who do not have the right papers or consistent employment, to levy higher fines and criminal sentences, and to mete out stiffer penalties for employers and immigrants who violate the regulations. Non-EU immigrants must be fingerprinted upon arrival in Italy.

Until the outbreak of the Arab Spring revolutions in 2011, the number of illegal immigrants was reduced. But chaos and violence in Tunisia, Libya, Iraq, and Syria opened the floodgates again. Foreign Minister Franco Frattini warned of "an exodus of Biblical proportions" from North Africa and the Middle East. After hesitation and a persuasive phone call from President Barack Obama, Italy's government agreed to join the UN-NATO air offensive over Libya.

About half of immigrants arriving by sea enter Italy at its southernmost part, Lampedusa, an island 180 miles (310 km) north of Libya. Of those who make it to Italian soil, two-thirds are denied protection and should be repatriated. However, that is often impossible because they arrive without papers indicating their origin. Most join the mass of illegal residents. Since they cannot work legally, they are responsible for a disproportionate number of crimes.

ECONOMY

The motor that keeps the country operating, despite all of the crises, scandals, strikes, poverty, and natural catastrophes, is the Italians' ability to improvise and adapt to existing conditions. Such extraordinary resilience and resourcefulness have taken shape through centuries of foreign domination and of continuous threats along the coastline from pirates and conquerors. The everyday problems merely stimulate these qualities and enable one to understand why so many informed commentators on the state of Italian affairs are inclined to say with confidence that "the situation is desperate but not hopeless."

Italy has a private enterprise economy, although the government has a controlling interest in some large commercial and industrial firms. Electricity, transportation, telephone, and telegraph are largely owned by the state. Three TV channels are dominated by the state RAI network, although voters in a 1995 referendum chose to allow private shareholders to buy a stake in them. Silvio Berlusconi's Fininvest owns three other channels, with 65% of the advertising market, and voters in 1995 decided that he should not be forced to give up control of two of them.

The changes in wage indexation stabilized inflation (.8% in 2021), despite a VAT of 19%. Italy suffers from chronically low productivity growth, the worst being the public sector, one of Europe's most expensive and inefficient. This is partly explained by the abysmally poor educational scores in international comparisons and the low level of computer literacy at the workplace.

Even though inflation is low, criticism against the euro is audible because it has allegedly increased the cost of living. After the Northern League called for a return of the lira, Berlusconi also blamed the nation's economic problems on the way his nemesis Romano Prodi, while prime minister, had steered Italy into monetary union. "Prodi's euro conned us all." In 2011–2012 fears grew that Italy could be pulled into the sovereign debt crisis experienced by its Mediterranean neighbors and threatening the credibility of the euro.

In the first five years of the 21st century, its economic growth averaged only .7% per year, the slowest of all the G8 and large OECD countries. It was 5.8% in 2021. GDP has fallen in real terms by almost 10% since the inception of the great recession in 2008. It has barely grown at all since the euro's launch in 1999. Its lack of growth over two decades is Italy's most persistent economic failure.

In 2006 its per-capita GDP fell below that of Spain. In 2008 it dropped below the EU average for the first time. Productivity growth is static, and competitiveness has declined. In 2005 the World Economic Forum ranked Italy 47th in the world in competitiveness, just one notch above Botswana. Tourism dropped by a quarter after the September 11 terrorist attacks and the discovery of al Qaeda cells in Italy. In 1970 Italy was the world's top tourist destination; today it is in fifth place, after France, the US, Spain, and China. In 2010, 42 million tourists visited. But Italy does have a modern economy: 68% of the workforce is employed in services, who produce 74% of the GDP, while 28% is employed in industry, who produce 24% of GDP.

Italian firms have invested heavily in the latest technology and have some of the most productive factories in Europe. Italian companies are also actively investing outside the country. Northern Italy shows particular dynamism. Of Italy's 20 regions, the 3 northern ones—Lombardy, Veneto, and Piedmont—produce almost 40% of the GDP. Lombardy alone generates 30% of the country's exports. The country has a high level of entrepreneurship: A third of all Europe's small- and medium-size enterprises are based in Italy.

Prodded by its desire to join the EU's single currency (euro), Italy made some economic progress since 1992. By 2021

Italian students celebrating the end of a course at the College of Europe.

the budget deficit had grown to 5.2% of GDP. Its total national debt is 133% of its GDP, the second-largest in the eurozone after Greece. This limits the government's ability to introduce expensive stimulus measures. Servicing that debt consumes a tenth of its GDP and a fifth of government spending. This leaves very few funds for needed investment in productivity improvement and research and innovation.

At 1.1% of GDP, Italy's R&D is below the EU's average of almost 2%. Italy needs to be more internationally competitive. Fortunately, much of its debt is funded domestically by banks, insurance companies, and individuals, thereby helping slow the flight of capital from Italy. This is thanks largely to Italians' disposition for saving: They save 15% of their earnings, the highest rate in the EU. Much of it is in government securities. Thus, most of the interest payments are recycled into the economy. The low level of household debt (57% of disposable income) is much lower than the eurozone average of 93%.

Partly because of the shaky ruling coalitions that require expensive concessions to keep all partners satisfied, it has not been easy for any government to make big cuts in government spending and borrowing. Public spending accounted for 52.5% of GDP in 2010. The financial system both in banking and the stock market must be further modernized. Obstacles to business exist, such as rigid hiring and firing laws, high employers' social security contributions, widespread price controls and corruption, inefficiency, and organized crime, which scares away foreign investment. These fuel unemployment, which was 9% in 2021 (above the eurozone's 9.5% average) and one-third for young Italians. The Berlusconi government reformed the labor

market by making it easier for companies to hire temporary staff. Renzi's legislation to strengthen that drove 1 million protestors into the streets. Joblessness is much higher in the south than in the north. It is also higher for women, whose emancipation Italians say they want. Italy has the smallest proportion of participation in the workforce (57% and only 50% for women) in western Europe. Living standards are stagnant or declining.

Some argue that the south will get an economic boost from the construction of a bridge over the Strait of Messina linking Sicily with the mainland. The world's largest suspension bridge, it will stretch 2 miles (3.3 km), three times longer than the Golden Gate bridge, and have 12 lanes for cars, trucks, and trains. Its towers will soar 1,230 feet above sea level. The failure to build this long-discussed bridge had become a symbol of the country's inability to modernize its road and rail infrastructure.

Others argue that it would only benefit a few construction companies, the Mafia, and organized criminals who will be able to travel more quickly to the mainland. It would be in private hands and would charge more than boats now do. The project was scrapped in 2006 because the benefits could not justify the high costs. But it was resurrected by the subsequent Berlusconi government in 2008.

A further problem is Italy's lag in innovation. A 2003 survey revealed that it holds a mere 1.8% of the world's high-tech patents, compared with Germany's 15% and France's 7.3%. Its citizens' scientific knowledge, Internet use, and vocational training are low compared with many other European countries, and the resources it allots to research and higher education are inadequate. As many as 5% of its university graduates (60,000 annually) leave the country to work elsewhere, and 70% of those who leave are university graduates. It is one of the few rich European countries that is a net exporter of university graduates. That is why the Education Ministry announced plans in 2003 to improve schools; to have pupils begin school at an earlier age; to study computers and English from the start; and to stay in school for a minimum of 12 years, 2 years more than before. There is a demonstrated need for improvement. Italian children (especially in the south) did badly on the OECD's PISA cross-national comparisons. Although it has a few excellent private universities, such as Bocconi and Università Cattolica in Milan, none of its universities are in the world's top 100, according to the two chief international rankings of higher education.

Nevertheless, Italy remains a visibly prosperous country. A reflection of such prosperity is the fact that almost two-thirds

of Italians were homeowners by the end of the 1980s, and one Italian family in four has a second home. One explanation of such economic well-being, which defies the gloomy statistics, is the celebrated "submerged economy," a parallel unofficial economy, mainly behind the backs of government statisticians and tax collectors. The black labor market is estimated to constitute 16% of GDP, about 60% above the OECD average. It could be as high as 30% of GDP. Tax revenues equal about 45.6% of GDP, and it is conservatively estimated that tax evasion amounts to around 15% of GDP. This kind of economic activity is done at home, in the streets, or on the job while the boss is looking the other way.

Under- and noninvoicing to avoid the VAT are common practices, and declarations of income are often much too low. For example, in 2008 most dentists and lawyers declared less than €50,000 ($70,000), restaurant owners €20,000 ($28,000); and taxi drivers only €11,500 ($16,000). In an effort to improve public finances, the Prodi government made some progress in tax collection. Days before leaving office

Garibaldi

Italy

in May 2008, it posted on the Internet all 40 million tax returns so that journalists could report on the pitiful underpayment of taxes. The government vowed to crack down on tax evasion. This was not the first time an Italian government has promised that, and Mario Monti did the same.

If the production of goods and services from such a submerged economy were able to be included in the official economic figures, an estimated 10% to 30% would have to be added to the national wealth. This black economy makes the country's high unemployment figure less serious politically than in many other western European nations. Also, whereas unemployment prevails in large parts of the south and in some cities in the industrial north, there are other regions where the demand for jobs must be filled with such guest workers as Tunisians in Sicily and Yugoslavs in Trieste.

Italy's dependence upon oil and raw material imports is excessive: It must import 86% of its energy needs, twice the western European average. It has almost no domestic energy sources, except small amounts of natural gas (chiefly in the Po Valley) and very few other raw materials. Domestic oil production meets only 7% of needs, and its diminishing natural gas covers only 12% of consumption. It imports about 16% of its electricity. Its vulnerability to disruptions is demonstrated by periodic power outages. Hydro-electricity from dams mostly in the north was once the largest domestic source of energy, but it is of decreasing importance. Wind power generates 1.2% of electricity, and Italy is still Europe's leader in geothermal power, using steam produced by hot rocks.

Government plans to expand nuclear power production were dealt a severe blow in an emotional 1987 referendum vote which stopped the building of atomic power stations, even though the country possessed an advanced nuclear industry. Italy has no functioning nuclear plants. In the face of a global energy shortage, the government announced plans in 2008 to resume building them. But in a June 2011 referendum, 94% of voters rejected laws that would have restarted the nuclear program. It takes 20 years to construct nuclear plants, and the country's sluggish bureaucracy guarantees that nothing happens quickly.

Such extreme dependence on energy imports explains the heavy Italian investment in a trans-Mediterranean gas pipeline, which began in 1982 to bring Algerian gas to the economically depressed southern Italy. Another pipeline brings 28% of Libya's natural gas to Europe via Italy. Its large state-owned ENI jointly owns with Russia's Gazprom the giant South Stream pipeline that will deliver natural gas from Siberia via the Black Sea and the Balkans. Romano Prodi declined a proposal by the Russian president to head that project after leaving office in 2008. In a further effort to ensure its energy supply, Italy increased its reliance on coal from 14% to 33% by 2013.

The country's periodic trade deficit results mainly from the import of consumer goods and even agricultural products that Italy itself produces. It is only 80% self-sufficient in food. It does have impressive trade successes, though, in clothing, shoes, and mechanical goods; 90% of its total exports are manufactures. Almost 60% its trade is with its EU partners.

Agriculture

The percentage employed in agriculture has dropped over the years from 38% in 1951 to 3.7% in 2017. Italy's agricultural population generates only 2% of GDP. The rather unproductive Italian agriculture suffers from the small size of farms and the advanced age of farmers. Also, about a fourth of the farmland is underutilized, and about a tenth is not used at all.

A major agricultural obstacle is, of course, the problem of hill farming. More than 40% of Italy is classified as hilly, and such terrain merely intensifies the country's other agricultural problems of fragmentation and low productivity. Only about 23% of the land is classified as plain, most of it in the fertile Po Valley in the north, the Pontine Valley south of Rome, and parts of Puglia in the south, although the latter is strapped by severe irrigation problems. The Po Valley is Italy's breadbasket, producing cereals, dairy products, and sugar beets. In the south, Mediterranean produce predominates, such as citrus fruits, olive oil, wine, and tomatoes. But Italy is faced with a particular dilemma as far as this kind of farming is concerned. On the one hand, it is inefficient. Yet, if farming in the south were reorganized, many agricultural workers would lose jobs.

One vintage Italian product, wine, has fallen on hard times. Domestic wine consumption has halved, especially in the south, where thirst increasingly demands beer and whisky. Production is still relatively impressive, supplying 30% of Europe's wine (second only to France) and 18% of the world total. The EU buys 56% of its exports, and the US, 6%. With regard to the cheese to go with that wine, the European Court of Justice ruled in 2008 that the word "parmesan" can apply only to the product made near the Italian city of Parma, not the fake varieties produced elsewhere, such as Germany.

Government-Owned Enterprises

Italy's enormous budget deficits in the past can be partly explained by the huge losses by some of the businesses that are

wholly or partially owned by the state, the almost-uncontrollable system of social expenditures, and the hostile attitude of the citizens toward taxes. The state's hand in the economy is large. In contrast to many other European countries, where left-wing governments once nationalized many companies, such work was done in Italy by Mussolini. The three large state-owned industrial groups—IRI, ENI, and EFIM—account for about 10% of GDP. Some of the firms controlled by these huge holding companies are not profitable. These debt-ridden enterprises are an economic burden in a country in which most private concerns report a profit.

Therefore, the government decided to reduce the state's ownership in the economy. It is in no great hurry to privatize, and it has made no commitment to divest itself totally. The reason is political. Few of the country's leaders were convinced that privatization was a good way to improve the economy. During the 1990s the proportion of the banking system in state hands declined from 70% to 20%. The nation's flag air carrier, Alitalia, limped along to bankruptcy. Its union, as well as Prime Minister Berlusconi, rejected an initial bid by Air France–KLM to buy it in 2008. However, its future prospects were so dim that Air France–KLM was permitted in 2009 to buy a 25% stake in the relaunched slimmed-down airline, which had merged with Air One. It received a near-monopoly on the main domestic routes, and it flies to 50 foreign destinations.

Unions

In the view of many analysts, it is an encouraging sign that the Italian trade unions, which in 2013 organized 35% of Italy's workforce (down from 39.2% in 1990), have lost a considerable portion of their power and influence, especially among the youth. Renzi calls them an "outdated force." In the past the unions had made the Italian worker one of the most protected in Europe, and they had gained a practical veto power over the country's economic and social policies.

Marchionne divides his time equally between the two companies.

Italy enjoys better industrial relations than it once had: From 2002 to 2004, it annually lost 113.2 working days per 1,000 employees to strikes, compared with 580 for Greece, 197.4 for Spain, 34.7 for the UK, and 16 for France. Enhanced competitiveness enabled production and export of subway cars for the Washington, DC, Metro.

The heavy political involvement of the unions has caused them to lose touch with the rank-and-file members, who are more interested in bread-and-butter economic issues. In the midst of a recession, more and more Italians have also come to the conclusion that private enterprise and market-oriented management are necessary if the country's prosperity is to be maintained. Further, the unions were forced to budge on wage indexation, which had kept the motor of inflation well lubricated. The result is a generally favorable economic outlook. At the same time, despite the fact that things miraculously turn out to be less serious than they are usually predicted, the country continues to face some serious economic challenges.

Italy also has powerful professional guilds (*ordini*), which do not always get their way. For example, a state body, the Corte dei Conti, ruled in 2005 that all graduates of the recently revamped university system have the right to use the title "*dottore*" ("doctor"), even though it takes only three years, to graduate. With two additional years they can be called "*dottore magistrale*," while the title "*dottore di recerca*" adorns those who complete advanced research degrees equivalent to an American PhD. The guilds argued that this cheapens the title. But they fought a losing battle in a society that loves inflated titles. Graduates of professional schools are addressed by their occupation (e.g., Architect Verdi or Engineer Rossi). Even postelementary school teachers are called "*professore*" ("professor").

Italian universities are chronically short of funding. But the main reasons that not a single one is in the top 100 of the world university ranking are the overwhelming power of the tenured professors (often called *baroni*, "barons") and the predominance of a system of connections (*raccomandazioni*), which are more important than academic qualifications in hiring. The average age of a full professor is 63. The barons stifle innovation and treat their staff and departments as personal fiefs. Nepotism is also rife. The result is a 55% dropout rate, the highest in the developed world, and a meager 17% of Italians with postsecondary degrees, compared with an OECD average of 33%.

The reversal in trade unionists' fortunes came since the Communists lost votes in successive parliamentary elections and since a massive strike against the Fiat automotive company collapsed in 1980. The country's leading private-sector industrial group, Turin-based Fiat, had to keep its overseas prices competitive with those of other countries. Now only 30% of Fiat's workforce is unionized. Its cash position was so good by June 2009 that it could buy a controlling 20% share in Chrysler. Its chief executive Sergio Marchionne issued an ultimatum to the unions in 2010: Either modernize their labor practices, or risk a move by Fiat to another country. Two-thirds accepted the offer. Fiat merged the two companies, which made it a model of transatlantic cooperation in the auto industry. In 2014 Fiat announced that it would acquire the 41.5% of Chrysler it did not already own. A strong leader,

Italy

CULTURE

No other country has both profited from and been stifled by the wealth of its historical inheritance as has Italy. This inheritance has attracted educated tourists for over 200 years. Annually, 42 million tourists visit its incomparable art treasures and generate 8% of GDP. They seek to enjoy the usually mild climate. In addition, approximately 80 million individual pieces of art await restoration. The most dramatic reappearance in 1999 was Leonardo Da Vinci's *Last Supper*, which had undergone a meticulous 21-year restoration in Milan.

Italy possesses 30,000 churches; 20,000 castles; 3,000 archaeological sites that are of value to art historians; and shelters in its 712 museums countless important works of art. According to one UNESCO estimate, Italy possesses more than two-thirds of western civilization. With 39 (2 more than Spain), it has more sites on the UN's coveted UNESCO World Heritage List than any other country on earth. Its most recent additions were the Etruscan necropolises of Cerveteri and Tarquinia, as well as the picturesque hills and villages of Tuscany's Val d'Orcia.

Only one who understands the ambivalent attitude of the Italian toward his history and state can excuse the fact that the money used by the state to maintain the irreplaceable wealth of arts corresponds to the amount needed to construct 18 miles of freeway. Since 1909 the immeasurable cultural inheritance has been administered by a small group of 284 highly placed civil servants. However, Italy alone cannot be expected to bear the burden history has placed upon it; the entire civilized world is also, to some extent, responsible for the vast historical wealth.

UNESCO provided a considerable contribution in order to save Venice, which was threatened by uninhibited industrial exploitation of the hinterlands. In 2003 one of the largest public-works projects in a long time was launched to save Venice, which is threatened by rising sea levels and the sinking of the city itself, which had been built on a soggy foundation. It is flooded nine months a year. A series of 79 sea gates were being constructed to rise from the ocean floor if high tides in the Adriatic threaten to swell the lagoon in which Venice is located. This grand project was shelved by the Prodi government as too expensive, but the Berlusconi government in 2008 resurrected it.

Many European and American organizations provided aid to cover damages caused by the catastrophic flood in Florence in 1966. It continues to face flooding, with the low-lying parts of the city inundated about every three years. In 2008 it reached the fourth-highest level since 1872

and brought the transport system to a halt. Rainwater continues to run down some of the Uffizi's interior walls.

Florence was again shaken in 1993, when terrorists exploded a car bomb in front of the 16th-century Uffizi Gallery, which houses the world's most important collection of classic Italian art, including priceless paintings by Leonardo da Vinci, Michelangelo, Raphael, and Titian, and which is visited by more than 1 million persons each year. Six people died, 3 paintings and many medieval manuscripts in the library were destroyed, and 21 canvases and 3 statues were damaged.

The Uffizi's cash flow problem was dramatized in 2002, when the state electric company threatened to cut off its power if it did not pay its long-overdue €250,000 bill. This was symptomatic of a larger problem: The state spends much too little on maintaining the country's cultural treasures: only .2% of GDP (compared with 1% in France), which was reduced further by the Berlusconi and Monti governments. The culture budget was halved between 2006 and 2012. Since the idea of tax deductions for private donations is only beginning to take hold, the private sector lacks an incentive to step in and help. In 2008 three-fourths of corporate donations went to sports, mainly soccer.

Not until 1993 did state museums begin to allow private companies to operate services like ticketing, bookstores, and restaurants and cafés. The earlier Berlusconi government introduced an experiment to see if some of Italy's treasure trove could be privatized. A new state agency, Patrimonio dello Stato, was created to evaluate Italy's cultural patrimony and decide what could be sold or leased in order to generate income. The government promised not to sell off any treasures that are part of the country's national identity, such as the Colosseum, the Leaning Tower of Pisa, or the Uffizi. Nor would private owners ever possess a majority stake or hold leases longer than five years. In 2008 the former boss of McDonald's in Italy, Mario Resca, was put in charge of the 3,600 museums and archaeological sites in order to improve their management and to upgrade the sites. Sometimes the treasures are hidden. This was the case in 2016, when the Iranian president gave a speech in the renowned Capitoline Museum. All nude statues were encased in large white boxes.

Pompeii, which draws 2.6 million visitors each year, is so dilapidated that the government declared a state of emergency. There has not been a systemic maintenance of the site in the last half-century. In November 2010 two buildings collapsed: the frescoed House of Gladiators, followed several weeks later by a 12-meter wall protecting the House of the Moralist.

In Rome large chunks of stone and mortar are dropping from the Colosseum and the Trevi Fountain. The same is happening to Florence's Duomo.

The government announced in 2002 that it would return to Ethiopia the prized Obelisk of Axum, dating from the 3rd century AD and looted by Mussolini's soldiers in 1937. It is believed to be a grave marker for a king from the Axumite Empire. It was erected near Rome's Circus Maximus. Italy's past reluctance over its repatriation stemmed from a worry shared by many European countries: Once such repatriation of antiquities begins, where does it stop? The first part of the 160-ton monument was shipped in April 2005.

According to Italian law, any classical artifacts found on Italian soil belong to the state, even if they originated in Greece. The Ministry of Culture negotiated tenaciously with the Getty Museum in Los Angeles concerning the return of 46 antiquities from the American collection taken out of Italy under questionable circumstances or purchased from dishonest dealers. The Getty Museum offered 26 in 2006, which Italy's culture minister denounced as not meeting its demand for a comprehensive agreement, which was reached the following year. New York's Metropolitan Museum of Art agreed to return 21 disputed antiquities to Italy, and 3 other American museums also handed over artifacts. In all cases, such transfer was in exchange for long-term loans from Italy of artifacts of "equal beauty and historical and cultural significance." Such a quid pro quo was not possible for New York philanthropist Shelby White, who was persuaded to give up 10 classical antiquities. She became the first private collector to return art to Italy.

The unique Byzantine churches of Ravenna are threatened, the cathedral in Milan is unstable, and there is danger that the Palatine Hill in Rome will collapse. Unfortunately, the international contribution has never been used in full because of competition and disputes among the different bureaucracies. The burden of history has not only left its imprint on the political culture and on the problem of southern Italy (*Mezzogiorno*) but also literally threatens to slip out of the Italian state's control.

Italy's extraordinary significance for the development of western civilization from antiquity through the Middle Ages and the Renaissance in the areas of science, the arts, architecture, and finance is well known. The Italians have also accomplished much in more recent times. The recognition of Italian as the language of music indicates the influence it had on the developing years. During the Baroque period (17th–18th centuries), such composers as Domenico Scarlatti, Antonio

Vivaldi, and Luigi Boccherini, just to name the most important figures, were prominent (Bach was a great admirer of Vivaldi's works).

The 19th century also produced world-renowned composers, such as Gioacchino Rossini, Giuseppe Verdi, Gaetano Donizetti, and Giacomo Puccini. Even today, Italian composers, such as Luigi Dallapiccola, Bruno Maderna, and Luigi Mono, are conspicuous. No singer of opera is a star until he performs at the incomparable La Scala in Milan. In December 2004 it was reopened after a three-year overhaul, staging the same obscure opera by Salieri with which it first opened in 1778.

Without even taking into account the countless artists of the 15th, 16th, and 17th centuries, Italian artists include modern painters, such as Amadeo Modigliani and Giorgio de Chirico, and sculptor Marino Marini, who have maintained Italy's reputation in the international art world. In 1906 and 1936, respectively, Giosuè Carducci and Grazia Deledda received Nobel Prizes for literature. Significant writers, such as the novelist Giovanni Verga and the romantic poet Gabriele D'Annunzio, lead a long list of splendid literary figures. In lyric poetry, Giuseppe Ungaretti, Eugenio Montale, and Salvatore Quasimodo (who won a Nobel Prize in 1959) have made important contributions. Dramatist Luigi Pirandello and novelists Curzio Malaparte, Cesare Pavese, Tomasi di Lampedusa, Ignazio Silone, and Alberto Moravia dominated the Italian literary scene until after World War II. The critical realist Italo Calvino enjoys postwar popularity.

International film, opera, and theater festivals, as well as modern art exhibits, reflect the ever-vibrant cultural life of Italy. In terms of cinema, Rome is to Italy what Hollywood means to the US Italian directors have been and still are the leading film figures in Europe. Such names as Vittorio de Sica, Federico Fellini, Luchino Visconti, and Pier Paolo Pasolini have decisively affected European films. With his commercial Italian western (often referred to jokingly as "spaghetti western"), director Sergio Leone captivated masses of moviegoers all over the world. Italian cinema's stellar position was shown in 1999 by Roberto Benigni's *Life Is Beautiful*, which won two Oscars, including the best foreign-language film, and the Grand Jury Prize at the Cannes Film Festival. Italians continue to see many American feature films, and in 1999 two-thirds of its foreign TV programs were purchased from the United States.

In the natural sciences, the Italians have also distinguished themselves—Galileo Galilei, Luigi Galvani, and Alessandro Volta played a prominent role in the research of electricity. Guglielmo Marconi won a Nobel Prize in 1909 for his discovery of the wireless telegraph. One cannot overlook another Nobel Prize winner, Enrico Fermi, who investigated the peaceful use of the atom.

For the first time since Italy's creation, the press is no longer controlled by political power and parties but by the normal business groups in the Italian economy. Major dailies include Rome's *La Repubblica* and *Il Messaggero*, *Il Giornale*, and *Il Sole 24 Ore* (important financial newspaper), and Turin's *La Stampa*. Milan's *Corriere della Sera* sets the tone of national political debate. But when this venerable newspaper saw its revenues falling and the age of its readers rising in 2013, the wealthy Agnelli family doubled its stake in the paper to 20%. *Il Foglio* is a clever four-page daily. The Communist *L'Unità*, founded by Antonio Gramsci in 1924, is no longer widely read, but it still sells 50,000 copies a day (down from 300,000 in its heyday). Italians buy no more dailies than they did in the 1930s—6 million, compared with 22 million in the UK. In 2012 the Monti government confirmed its predecessor's cutting of public subsidies for as many as 100 smaller newspapers, including for *L'Unità*. The major newsweeklies include *L'Espresso* and *Panorama*.

As in France, the guardians of the language worry that English is encroaching on the Italian language. They deride the resulting mixture as "Italiese." The Academia della Crusca was founded in 1570 to promote the primacy of Florentine Italian, and the government maintains 89 Italian cultural institutes throughout the world to serve as disseminators of the Italian language. In 2005 the government jumped into action when the European Commission decided to drop Italian and Spanish and use only English, French, and German in some news conferences. The EC backed off. This reaction underscored the fact that, while many Europeans are willing to merge their currencies and cede some sovereignty to Brussels, they are not ready to give up their languages.

Despite its problems, Italy remains a prosperous, democratic country, in which civil rights are protected far better than in most countries of the world. It sometimes looks maddeningly chaotic. Even the

Italy

PANORAMA

Esclusivo: Expo e tangenti

COMPAGNI DI COOP E DI GOVERNO

Primo Greganti

Giuliano Poletti

Matteo Renzi

RIECCO PRIMO GREGANTI**: GARANTIVA COPERTURA POLITICA PER GLI APPALTI ALLE COOPERATIVE ROSSE. RAPPRESENTATE FINO A TRE MESI FA DA** GIULIANO POLETTI**, CHE** MATTEO RENZI **HA VOLUTO A TUTTI I COSTI MINISTRO DEL LAVORO.**

hottest film in Italy in 2008 was entitled *Caos Calmo* (*Quiet Chaos*). But the Italian brand of chaos has a refreshing sweetness to it, which is precisely why millions of non-Italians are fervent admirers, even lovers, of this country and its friendly people. Perhaps a touch of chaos is essential to the renowned Italian *dolce vita* ("sweet life").

FUTURE

That Italy will survive its multifaceted ordeals is due largely to the fact that the Italians have an unshakable ability to adapt to existing circumstances with imagination and practicality. Some tendencies toward integrating the otherwise-centrifugal political forces are evident in the widespread rejection and struggle against corruption, terrorism, and organized crime. Pressure for reform of the political system continues. However, in 2014 Transparency International ranked Italy 69th among 175 nations in terms of corruption. Pressure on the Mafia and the other organized crime families is being stepped up considerably, but it is doubtful that they will ever be stamped out completely.

The novelty of a nascent two-party political system did not last, as the March 2018 elections demonstrated. Three hostile blocs emerged, including an eccentric Five Star Movement. All three of the largest parties are still young, divided, poorly defined, and disinclined to compromise.

The 2018 national elections were a stinging rejection of traditional parties and the country's political establishment. They produced a badly hung parliament with none of the three main groupings close to a majority. The big winner was the Five Star Movement, which captured about a third of the votes. Populist parties won more than half. Five Star's Beppe Grillo had branded the 2013 postelection negotiations as "an orgy worthy of bunga bunga," and another commentator called them "the mother of all stalemates." Italians experienced the same in 2018.

It took several months for Five Star and the league to agree to a fragile governing coalition. It was Europe's first all-populist government, which is bad news for the European Union. Italy was long one of the European Union's most Europhile members; it has become one of its most Euroskeptic. Its message is stronger borders, drastically fewer migrants, taking back control from the elites, and "Italians first." For months it resisted the European Union's fiscal discipline regarding its 2010 budget before bowing to the union's demands. The controversy is a test of whether a populist government can defy the rules that hold Europe together.

Matteo Renzi raised expectations too high by promising radical reforms in his first 100 days in office. An unelected prime minister, his fragile left-right coalition did not survive. His constitutional referendum failed.

The economic recovery will remain a big story. Italy is the eurozone's third-largest economy. Renzi shared the frustration of his predecessors: "Ours is a rusty country, bogged down and chained by a suffocating bureaucracy." In January 2021, his tiny Stalia Viva party left the Conte government, which brought about its collapse. President Mattarella summoned former head of the European Central Bank, Mario Dragui, to form a new government.

The former governor of the Bank of Italy, Mario Draghi, who earned a doctorate in economics at the Massachusetts Institute of Technology, is ready to lead. There are many courageous anti-Mafia campaigners, who risk their lives to reduce and maybe one day eliminate that scourge on Italian society. One of these is the president, Sergio Mattarella. The country continues to be a magnet for tourists. There is always room for some optimism in Italy. It is peaceful, civilized, and rich.

On March 17, 2011, Italians celebrated the 150th anniversary of Italian unification. That was the day in 1861 that King Victor Emmanuel proclaimed the founding of the Kingdom of Italy. However, the party was muted because many Italians are ambivalent about unification. The governor of the formerly German-speaking province of Bolzano said he would not join the festivities because "we were taken away from Austria against our will." The leader (until April 2012) of the Northern League, Umberto Bossi, called the celebrations "useless" and ordered his party faithful to work on the 17th as if it were a day like any other. Italy is as fractured as ever—politically, economically, and geographically.

Former prime minister Giuliano Amato, the chairman of the anniversary committee, argued, "We need to stay together in order to keep arguing." Two polls in 2010 determined that only 11% of Italians believed unification was a mistake. Over half said Italians were not a "single people," and 15% would be happy if the north would break away. But 88% were proud of their country.

In the near future and with a new government, Italy will battle a recession while struggling to combat one of Europe's worst cases of coronavirus.

The Republic of San Marino

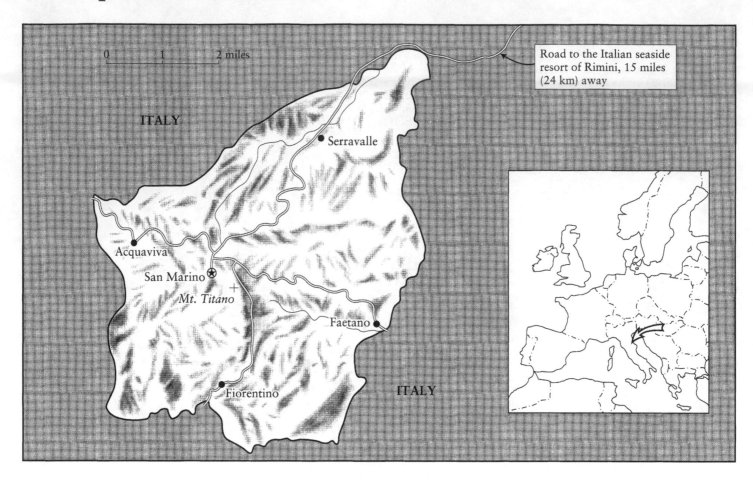

0   1   2 miles

ITALY

Road to the Italian seaside
resort of Rimini, 15 miles
(24 km) away

Serravalle

Acquaviva

San Marino ⊛

Mt. Titano

Faetano

ITALY

Fiorentino

ITALY

Area: 23.6 sq. mi. (61 sq. km).
Population: 31,716 (UN 2010).
Capital City: San Marino (pop. 4,500, est.).
Climate: Mild and temperate.
Neighboring Country: Italy
Official Language: Italian.
Ethnic Background: Italian.
Principal Religion: Roman Catholic.
Main Industries: Tourism, postage stamps, cotton textiles, bricks, tiles, cement, furniture, craft goods.
Main Trading Partner: Italy.
Currency: Euro.
Independence: 4th century AD.
Government: Republic.
Chiefs of State: Two captains regent, selected every six months. In 2012, Italo Righi and Maurizio Rattini.
Heads of Government: Secretary of state for foreign and political affairs (Fabio Berardi) and secretary of state for budget, financial, and internal affairs (Pierre Marino Mularoni).
National Flag: Two horizontal stripes, one white on the top and one blue on the bottom.
National Holidays: April 1, October 1.

Known today chiefly to collectors, who prize this tiny country's beautiful postage stamps, the most serene Republic of San Marino is a landlocked historical curiosity

situated on the slopes of Monte Titano in the eastern part of central Italy, to which it is linked by a customs union and a treaty of friendship. The last remaining relic of the self-governing Italian city-states, San Marino is the smallest republic in the world (except Nauru), and it always has wanted to stay that way. Its residents once refused Napoleon's offer of more territory on the grounds that the country's small size and poverty were the greatest guarantors of its independence. It has an irregular rectangular form with a maximum length of 8 miles (13 km). The country's setting is dominated by the 2,424-foot-high (739 meters) Monte Titano, whose three summits are crowned by ancient fortifications. The medieval-looking capital city with its red-roofed stone houses is located directly below one of these fortifications and is surrounded by triple walls. Of its 31,000 residents, roughly 3,000 are noncitizens, mainly Italians. An additional 20,000 of the people (known as San Marinese) reside abroad, principally in Italy.

San Marino traces its origin to 301 AD, when St. Marinus (from whom the country derives its name) and a small group of Christians fled to Monte Titano to escape religious persecution. In memory of their founder, the San Marinese do not date years according to Christ's life but instead

begin counting the years from 301 AD. For instance, the year 2021 in San Marino is 1720. By the 12th century, this tiny territory had become self-ruling. It has always managed to maintain its independence chiefly thanks to its geographic isolation, its mountain fortresses, and its skill in playing rival noble families against one another. By the 15th century, it was a republic ruled by a Grand Council composed of 60 men from San Marino's leading families.

During the Italian unification struggles in the 19th century, San Marino offered asylum to revolutionaries, including the hero Giuseppe Garibaldi. This assistance enabled it to gain a guarantee of independence from the Kingdom of Italy in 1862. Abraham Lincoln had been made an honorary citizen in 1861. San Marino remained neutral in World War II until September 1943. In November of that year, it was temporarily occupied by German troops. In June 1944 it was damaged by British bomber pilots who were attempting to dislodge the occupiers.

The Statutes of 1600, enlarged in 1926 and revised in 1939, serve as a constitution. They established a parliament, the Great and General Councils, with 60 members elected every five years by universal suffrage since 1960. This council in turn elects two captains regent, largely ceremonial figures who formally exercise executive power for a period of six months. During their semiannual investitures on April 1 and October 1, the Noble Guard and Great and General Councillors all dress in brightly colored uniforms and parade through the capital's streets. The captains regent cannot be elected for a second term until three years have elapsed. In 1981, for the first time in the country's history, a woman, Maria Lea Pedini Angelini, was chosen. The council also elects from among its members 10 persons who serve as secretaries of state in the Council of State, the principal organ of executive power. These secretaries of state each head a government administrative department.

The secretary of state for foreign and political affairs and the secretary of state for budget, financial, and internal affairs are in fact the highest and most powerful government executives of San Marino. Finally, the Great and General Councils elect a supreme appellate judicial body, the Council of Twelve, which hears appeals from the decisions of San Marino's two full-time judges, who need not be citizens. These judges decide on the basis of San Marino's own civil and criminal legal system, which has understandably been influenced greatly by Italian law.

The country has many political parties, which are heavily influenced by their much larger counterpart parties in Italy. They include the Christian Democratic Party (DCS), the Party of Socialists and Democrats (PSD), the Popular Alliance, the United Party, and the New Socialist Party. Like their Italian counterparts, these parties are not rigidly bound to doctrine. In the November 2008 elections, two electoral coalitions faced each other. The Pact for San Marino won 54.2% of the votes and 35 seats. Its largest partner was the Christian Democrats, continuing their dominance by winning 31.9% of the votes and 22 seats. The Reform and Liberty coalition

Monte Titano dominates San Marino.

captured 45.8% of the votes and 25 seats. Its largest party was the Party of Socialists and Democrats, which garnered 32% of the votes and 18 seats.

A unique election feature is that the state pays 75% of the return fare for any San Marinese living abroad to come home and vote in general elections. Over 5,400 did just that in 1988, returning from as far as Detroit, where many live.

This tiny mouse roars against the United States if it gets an urge to do so. In 1982 its parliament voted to "deplore" American policy in El Salvador and authorized a symbolic $4,500 contribution to the rebel forces there.

All parties in San Marino favor a broad social security system that, among other things, provides health care from state funds. Children up to the age of 12 receive a guaranteed summer holiday on the seaside and up to the age of 14 a free public education. Those wishing to study further are eligible for state scholarships to Italian high schools and universities. Finally, the state of San Marino finds work for all citizens who cannot obtain employment privately. If no work at all can be found, then the state provides unemployment benefits amounting to 60% of the person's normal salary. Citizens inform themselves by the state-run radio and TV—San Marino RTV—and two daily newspapers: *La Tribuna Sammarinese* and *San Marino Oggi*.

This country has no army because Italy provides for its defense. It does have a military corps that performs parade duty during national celebrations. It has a gendarmerie that maintains public order. In 1988 San Marino entered the Council of Europe, and in 1992 it joined the United Nations. It has sent athletes to the winter Olympics since 1976.

It is the smallest recognized soccer nation. With only three professionals on its national team (citizens only), it competes internationally in order "to demonstrate that we have dignity." That is about all it gets. Of 109 matches it played from 1990 to 2012, it won 1, tied 2 and lost 106, scoring 17 goals and surrendering 468. It was given a 5,000-to-1 odds of qualifying for the 2014 World Cup.

There are utterly no natural resources, so earnings must be made from farming (chiefly wheat and grapes), raising livestock, light manufacturing (chiefly cotton textiles, bricks and tiles, cement, and pottery), the sale of postage stamps, and tourism. Diplomatic relations between the EU and San Marino were opened in 1983. Its goods have free access to the EU. It not only adopted the euro in 2002, but it also was permitted to mint its own euro coins with its own motif on the back.

It began to attract capital by being a tax haven. However, in 2000 it agreed to

cooperate with international efforts to curb abusive and criminal tax-avoidance schemes. It reached an agreement with the EU in 2003 to collect taxes for bank account interest and return 75% of it to the country of residence without providing account holders' names. It aspires to be a financial center like Luxembourg, with light regulation and banking secrecy. Thanks to foreign investers, it is still one of the world's richest countries measured by per-capita GDP. It set up a central bank in 2005 and established eight banks since 2000, with insurance companies arriving thereafter.

Tourism accounts for over 50% of GDP. During the summer months, from 20,000 to 30,000 foreign tourists visit San Marino each day. Unfortunately, the San Marinese welcome these tourists with solid rows of souvenir shops on both sides of the principal streets. Without doubt, it has more tourist stands and shops per capita than does any other country in the world. This creates an excessively commercialized air in this naturally beautiful mountaintop republic. Several handsome hotels and restaurants relieve this monotony. There are no railroad or airport facilities.

FUTURE

Although legally independent, San Marino has always been very vulnerable to pressure from the Italian government, political parties, and trade unions. This situation will certainly continue. Its beautiful setting and the curiosity this tiny republic stimulates ensure that tourism will continue to be a lucrative source of income. However, a shortage of energy will continue to exist, and San Marino will have difficulty finding the necessary funds to finance badly needed expanded water and electric power systems.

The Vatican City State

Area: .15 sq. mi. (.40 sq. km).
Population: 1,000 (est.).
Climate: Temperate.
Neighboring Country: Italy.
Official Language: Latin. Italian is the working language at the Vatican.
Religion: Roman Catholic.
Currency: Vatican lira, interchangeable with the euro.
National Holiday: June 30.
Chief of State: His Holiness Pope Francis (formerly Cardinal Jorge Mario Bergoglio from Buenos Aires, Argentina), elected pope March 13, 2013.
Suffrage: Limited to cardinals less than 80 years of age, who elect a pope for life.
National Flag: Yellow and white stripes parallel to the staff, with the papal insignia on a white field.

St. Peter's Square

Vatican City is the world's second-smallest state. One can stroll leisurely around the full length of its borders in less than one hour. Located in the heart of Rome, near the west bank of the Tiber River, and surrounded by medieval walls and the Church of St. Peter, this tiny dot on the Rome city map is often said to wield more influence in the world than the entire nation of Italy. The reason is that this is the headquarters of the Roman Catholic Church, the largest body of Christians in the world. Building began in the 8th century to create a residence for the popes. By the Middle Ages, the Vatican had come to control a large part of Italy and was one of the most important and influential powers in European politics. In 1870 the government of the newly founded Italian state annexed the extensive Papal States throughout Italy. The pontiffs rejected all offers of financial compensation, choosing instead to withdraw behind the Vatican's walls in defiance.

In 1929 the pope chose to sign the Lateran Treaty with the then-fascist government of Italy. This treaty established the independence and sovereignty of the State of Vatican City, fixed the relationship between the Italian government and the Catholic Church, and set a cash payment for the earlier seizure of papal property. A revision of this treaty in 1984 ended the status of Roman Catholicism as Italy's state religion. Despite the loss of much of its property, the Vatican has very extensive investments throughout the world, especially in Italy.

The church's wealth is widely assumed to be massive. Financial operations are handled by the Institute for the Works of Religion (IOR), better known as the Vatican Bank, whose depositors are Catholic religious orders, Vatican employees, and clergymen. For 2,000 years until 1987, the Vatican kept its financial operations strictly secret. Popes Benedict and Francis

inherited a bank haunted by suspicion of corruption, money laundering, and even links to organized crime. In February 2013, two weeks before abdicating, Benedict appointed a German lawyer and financier, Ernst von Freyberg, as bank president, with a mandate to clean up its reputation and to get the bank on the "white list" of states that comply with international standards against money laundering and tax fraud. He was succeeded by French financier Jean-Baptiste de Franssu. Francis created a new secretariat of the economy to oversee the Vatican's financial affairs. The Vatican Bank closed the accounts of about 900 organizations and embassies and 3,350 clients. Francis made it more transparent and returned it to its original purpose: sending money to missionaries and church groups around the world.

Italy has no extradition treaty with the Vatican. According to article 22 of the Lateran Treaty, the Vatican is obligated to surrender to Italian custody anyone who enters its grounds in order to escape from Italian law. However, article 11 states, "central bodies of the Catholic Church are free from every interference on the part of the Italian state." During the Second World War, even the Mussolini government did not try to get possession of Jews and political refugees who had hidden within the Vatican's walls.

The Lateran Treaty established extraterritorial status but technically not papal sovereignty for 13 areas outside Vatican City. These are chiefly the major Catholic churches in Rome and the pope's summer residence of Castel Gandolfo. In an agreement of 1951, the Vatican's radio station (Stazione Radio Città del Vaticano) also was placed under Vatican jurisdiction.

This created tensions in 2001, when citizens charged that the electromagnetic emissions from the Vatican Radio's large towers on the outskirts of Rome cause cancer.

Insofar as the purely political functions of the Vatican are concerned, all executive, legislative, and judicial authority is vested in the pope. He appoints a governor and organs to administer the Vatican. The College of Cardinals serves as the chief papal advisers, and the Roman Curia carries on the central administration of the Roman Catholic Church's religious affairs.

The pope is treated like a king, but few outsiders see the infighting that goes on within the Vatican walls. It was rumored that a major reason Pope Benedict stepped down in 2013 was his inability to bring the power struggles among the different parts of the hierarchy under control. A high church official who had worked for a decade in the Vatican said this of a pope: "Whoever is appointed, they get absorbed by the structure. Instead of you transforming the structure, the structure transforms you." Francis, who combines toughness and compassion, is determined to change this.

In 2012 a stream of embarrassing leaks of Vatican documents fell into the hands of the Italian press. They provided the basis of a sensational book by Gianluigi Nuzzi, *Your Holiness: The Secret Papers of Benedict XVI*. One after another behind-the-scenes conflicts was publicized. Faced with these revelations, the pope appeared increasingly isolated and unable to bring his infighting underlings under control. Doubly disappointing was the fact that the source of these "Vatileaks" of the confidential papers was the pope's own butler,

Paolo Gabriele. He was convicted of stealing the documents, but the pope forgave him for his transgression. The same happened to Pope John Paul II's personal notes, which he had ordered to be burned. They were published in a book, I Am Very Much in God's Hands, by his secretary, the archbishop of Krakow.

Many in Rome are convinced that a plot within the Curia forced Benedict's resignation. Pope Francis has moved decisively to confront management problems and overhaul the Curia. There should be more transparency and collegiality and fewer "narcissists" in the Vatican. He appointed eight cardinals to oversee this reform.

Order within the small state is provided by a colorfully dressed regular army of Swiss guards. Recruitment is held in the cantons of Freiburg, St. Gallen, and Lucerne; the men must be between 20 and 30 years old. They carry old-fashioned halberds, but they always have machine guns hidden close by. Perhaps former Soviet foreign minister Andrei Gromyko was wrong in calling them "the world's least frightening army." Nevertheless, Francis changed the guards' commander to soften their military image.

Plainclothes Swiss guards and agents from the papal gendarmes always accompany the pope everywhere when he confronts audiences and crowds within the Vatican, just as Secret Service men accompany the president of the United States. One difference is that the agents never turn completely away from the pope in order to scan for potential troublemakers. Paul VI ruled that it was disrespectful for the guards to turn their backs on the pontiff. In 1998 a disgruntled guard fatally shot his commander and wife and then killed himself. This was the first time in 150 years that this had occurred, and it prompted

Author (left) with the papal nuncio to the United Nations

the Vatican to review its recruiting procedures and administer psychological exams for new guards.

Within the Vatican live fewer than 1,000 persons, all of whom have Vatican documents rather than other passports. They are chiefly permanent Vatican employees, the largest number being priests and nuns. Cardinals are considered to be Vatican residents whenever they are in Rome. When a citizen of the Vatican leaves the city limits of Rome, he automatically becomes a citizen of his original nationality (or of Italy if the original nationality does not permit dual citizenship).

Vatican City has within its borders its own telephone system, a post office (which uses the Vatican's own stamps), a radio station, a pharmacy, several stores, and a banking system with its own coins and the only cash machines in the world with instructions in Latin. It was also granted permission to mint its own euro coins with Pope John Paul's profile on the back.

In addition to the Church of St. Peter and the Vatican Apostolic Palace (which was expanded in the 15th and 16th centuries to become the largest palace in the world) with all its museums and library, the Vatican contains a score of administrative and ecclesiastical buildings, a "village" of apartments, and the beautiful Vatican gardens. There is a small railroad station at the perimeter of the Vatican that is connected by 300 meters of track to the Italian state railway station.

Almost 300 permanent diplomatic representatives (known as nuncios) in 176 capitals throughout the world conduct the Vatican's external dealings; 78 countries

maintain missions in Rome, including the United States since 1984. By tradition, papal nuncios are granted the first rank at any diplomatic ceremonies they attend. The Vatican also has permanent observer status at the United Nations (some of whose human-rights conventions it has signed) and at 15 other intergovernmental bodies, including the African Union and the Organization of American States. Since 2006 its guards attend meetings of the Organization for Security and Cooperation in Europe (OSCE), and in 2008 it joined the international police organization Interpol. The Vatican even considered joining the EU's antiterrorist body Eurojust.

Nuncios (all priests) are trained at the Pontifical Ecclesiastical Academy in Rome and are known to be very knowledgeable, highly cultured, and facile in languages. According to leaked American diplomatic cables in 2010, US diplomats often rely on the church's worldwide network of prelates for intelligence. Nuncios have a policy to be only lightly protected and never to pull out of dangerous situations. There are seldom more than two people in each mission, and their time is devoted chiefly to the life of the church, including the appointment of bishops. Their "headquarters" is the Section for Relations with States in Rome, which has only 18 diplomats and 29 other staff. A Pontifical Council for Justice and Peace serves as a kind of overseas-aid mission, while an independent Rome-based body, the Sant'Egidio Community, specializes in mediation work in crisis areas.

The Vatican possesses priceless cultural treasures, including the Vatican Museums;

His Holiness the late Pope John Paul II

Vatican City

Fresco in the Sistine Chapel

the frescoes by Michelangelo in the Sistine Chapel; frescoes by Pinturicchio in the Borgia Apartment; Raphael's Stanze; and the Church of St. Peter, where such art treasures as Michelangelo's La Pietà are displayed. In 1983 more than 200 of these irreplaceable artworks toured the United States, where they were viewed by millions of Americans in New York, Chicago, and San Francisco.

The Vatican Library contains a valuable collection of manuscripts from the pre-Christian era to the present. They include notes by Michelangelo and Galileo. All are being digitized. It also publishes an influential daily newspaper, L'Osservatore Romano.

The Vatican owns a press that publishes books and pamphlets in all languages of the world. In 2003 it published the latest edition of a two-volume Latin dictionary containing 15,000 modernized Latin words. The Vatican's Latin Foundation, set up in the 1970s to keep Latin alive in the church after it had been decreed that mass could be celebrated in local languages, is behind the project. Although Italian is the working language of the Vatican, Latin remains the church's official language.

Francis decided not to conduct the 2014 worldwide gathering of bishops in Latin, using Italian instead. An up-to-date dictionary is needed for encyclicals and other scientific documents. It is not easy to keep Latin alive after more than two millennia, and many of the dictionary's new words are compounds of existing Latin words. For example, "dishwasher" is "escariorum lavator," and "disco" is "orbium phonographicorum theca."

Sensitive to allegations that the Vatican had done little to condemn the Holocaust or help Jews during the Second World War, the Vatican intervened to support the relocation of a cloister located on the edge of the Auschwitz death camp in Poland. The Holy See's relations with Jews had been strained for 2,000 years. But in 1965 the Vatican repudiated the doctrine of collective Jewish guilt for the death of Jesus. This was documented in Nostra Aetate (In Our Time) published in 2002. The Vatican official in charge of Jewish relations, Cardinal Walter Kasper, stated in that year that Catholics and Jews may still disagree on some things, but they do so as brothers. In 1993 it signed an accord with Israel leading to full diplomatic relations the following year, and in 1994 it published a document acknowledging its past mistakes that had contributed to anti-Semitism.

In 1997 the pope condemned the actions of many Christians before and during the Holocaust, saying that they contributed to the rise of anti-Semitism and then failed to help as Jews were being eradicated. Jewish groups criticized the fact that this strong statement fell short of an apology, which they have been demanding. In 1998 the church, while defending the actions of Pope Pius XII as having been a quieter form of resistance against the Nazis, officially apologized for failing to take a more active role in stopping Nazi persecution of Jews. It also declared Edith Stein, an Orthodox Jew who had converted to Christianity and died at Auschwitz in 1942, to be a saint. One year after becoming pope, Benedict XVI was welcomed in Poland by 2 million faithful. He visited Auschwitz to signal reconciliation and called the Nazis "a ring of criminals." In July 2016 Francis also visited Auschwitz.

Until 1975 the foreign diplomatic representatives to the Vatican had to be men. When the West Germans sent a woman counselor to its mission, they were reminded of the Vatican's "tradition that forbids Vatican officials from having business contacts with ladies." Finally the former African dictator of Uganda Idi Amin forced the Vatican to accept a female mission chief. The church's ban on women priests is under increasing attack by Catholics. In 1987 it was revealed that a priest who had served in southern Italy for 25 years had undergone a sex change and became a woman. Church practice holds that an ordained priest remains one whatever his transgressions might be. Therefore, the church granted her early retirement with the usual pension. The church often acts slowly: In 1992 it formally rehabilitated Galileo Galilei, whom the Inquisition had condemned in 1633 for daring to prove that the Earth orbited the sun rather than the other way around. The Vatican announced in 2008 that a statue to Galileo would be erected and also that Martin Luther would be rehabilitated.

Italy assumes responsibility for defending the Vatican and for patrolling St. Peter's Square. When the Turkish gunman who shot the pope in May 1981 was captured, he was taken initially to the Commissariato Borgo, the Vatican police headquarters. He was then bundled very quickly into an armored car and driven to central police headquarters in downtown Rome. Not until March 2006 was there evidence "beyond any reasonable doubt," in the words of an Italian parliamentary commission, that the Soviet Union's military intelligence (not the KGB) was behind the assassination attempt. The motive was Moscow's fear of the pope's support of

Reprinted with special permission of King Features Syndicate

Vatican City

Solidarity in Poland. The pope requested clemency for Agca, and the Italian president pardoned him in 2000. He was extradited to Turkey to serve a sentence for a prior crime, and he was released in 2006.

By the end of the decade, though, Mikhail Gorbachev's glasnost had led to better relations between the Holy See and eastern Europe, and the pope launched a campaign for a "Europe without spiritual frontiers." The reconciliation between communism and Christianity was crowned by Gorbachev's historic audience with the pope (whom he addressed as "Your Holiness") in 1989. A Vatican diplomat said, "Catholicism and communism are ideologies that cannot be reconciled. But there is space for common endeavor in the social, cultural and humanitarian fields."

Gorbachev expressed interest in the pope's call for a third road between capitalism and socialism, a new social order that would combine social justice with economic efficiency and political pluralism. The USSR wanted to be a full partner in a common European civilization, and the pope holds one of the keys to that community. In 1991 he named spiritual leaders for Soviet Catholics, published a social doctrine for societies returning to capitalism, and convened an unprecedented synod of bishops from the two halves of Europe to meet in Rome.

In 1996 Pope John Paul II received one of the world's last communist leaders, Fidel Castro. In return, the Cuban dictator renewed his country's invitation of the pontiff; Cuba was the only Latin American nation the pope had not yet visited. The pope arrived in Cuba in 1998 to large and enthusiastic crowds. One million Cubans assembled to hear him read mass at Revolutionary Square. The political importance and influence of the pope were visible in the easing by Castro (who for the first time as president wore civilian clothes in his own country) of religious intolerance before the pontiff arrived and his public composure while the pope admonished the Cuban church to fight for "the recognition of human rights and social justice" and to take "courageous and prophetic stands in the face of the corruption of political and economic power." The pope also won the release of 299 prisoners. However, in 2003 he decried the harsh sentences against dissidents meted out by the Castro regime.

Fourteen years later, in March 2012, Pope Benedict XVI visited Cuba for 48 hours. As a sign of the pontiff's influence, Cuba's leader, Raúl Castro, released 2,900 inmates, some of them political prisoners, as a "humanitarian gesture." Benedict told Cubans to "strive to build a renewed and open society, a better society, one more worthy of humanity." He explicitly

criticized Marxist political systems and the US embargo on Cuba. His words were not reported in the Cuban news media. Cuba leaders were pleased that he refused to meet with dissidents, who had urged him to see them.

The Vatican looked forward to a grandiose diversion to celebrate the dawning of the third Christian millennium in 2000. More than 30 million visitors journeyed to Rome for the event. Fearing that this celebration would be marred, the Vatican suggested that it would have been a "matter of common sense" for Italian officials to ban a World Gay Pride parade in Rome in July. Many persons were offended by posters highlighting God's hand touching Adam's private parts in Michelangelo's masterpiece in the Vatican's Sistine Chapel. However, the Holy See took no formal steps to stop the parade, especially since the most recent concordat between the Vatican and the Italian state, signed in 1984, deprives Rome of the "holy status" Mussolini had granted it in 1929. The event drew 70,000 participants. The pope bitterly denounced it as an insult and an offense to Christian values, saying that same-sex sex acts are "contrary to natural law." That view had changed by 2020.

A Vatican glossary of sexual terms that appeared in 2003 asserts that gay people are not normal and that the increasingly large number of countries that allow same-sex marriages are inhabited by people with "profoundly disordered minds." Nevertheless, the pope argued that gays should be treated with "respect, compassion, and delicacy" because "homosexuality" is a "disorder." Believing that "homosexuality" might be partially responsible for the many sexual abuse scandals involving priests, the Vatican ordered seminaries in 2005 to bar candidates for the priesthood who "practice homosexuality," have "deeply rooted homosexual tendencies," or support "gay culture." It

did not call for the removal of gays who are already priests. In 2016 Francis said the church should seek forgiveness from gays for the ways it had treated them.

The church has sexual problems of its own, as its clergy are charged in many countries of sexually abusing believers. In 2019 an embarrassed Vatican confirmed clergy abuse of nuns, and the German Roman Catholic Church announced the abuse by at least 1,670 church workers of at least 3,677 children over seven decades. All American cardinals were called to Rome in 2002 to be lectured on the impermissibility of such behavior. However, when the United States Conference of Catholic Bishops approved a zero-tolerance policy on sexually abusive priests in 2002, the Vatican demanded major revisions.

According to American diplomatic cables released by WikiLeaks in 2010, the Vatican learned important lessons from the American sex abuse scandal of 2002. They include "to act quickly to express horror at allegations, to label the alleged acts both crimes and sins, and to call in the local leaders to discuss how to prevent recurrences." The church created a fast track for punishing American priests and bishops, including a zero-tolerance policy by which priests are suspended at the first accusation of abuse.

Far more than his predecessor, Benedict was open about the abuse and harm that sexual abuse has created: It reached a "degree we could not have imagined." Knowing that many people judge his papacy by his response to this crisis, he met many times with victims to express his personal sorrow, condemned priests and bishops for their actions, and made it clear that it is the welfare of children, not the church's reputation, that counts.

In April 2008 Benedict made his first visit to the US as pope and made the first papal visit to the White House in 30 years. The crowd in the Rose Garden sang "Happy Birthday" to celebrate his 81st birthday. He celebrated huge masses at Nationals Park stadium in Washington and in St. Patrick's Cathedral in New York. But his trip was dominated by the sexual abuse scandal involving 12,000 children and 5,000 priests and costing the church $2 billion in settlements. In Philadelphia the church suspended 21 priests from active ministry following accusations of improper conduct with juveniles. A half-dozen bankrupt dioceses were closed. In 2008 a federal appeals court allowed a lawsuit against the Vatican over alleged sexual abuse. This was the first time such a high court recognized that the Vatican could be liable for negligence in thousands of cases of sexual abuse in the US. In 2018 a Pennsylvania grand jury reported that 301 priests had abused more than 1,000

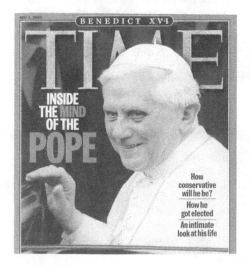

Vatican City

children in 70 years; all had been covered up. Such shocking revelations have cost the church popularity. Only 51% rate Francis favorably, and a mere 31% like his response to the scandal.

In 2001 John Paul II apologized to China for errors of the colonial past and pleaded for diplomatic relations, broken in 1951, in order to protect the 10 to 12 million Chinese Roman Catholics from continued persecution. This is made difficult because the Vatican maintains diplomatic relations with Taiwan. But in 2006 the Vatican hinted that it is willing to break with Taiwan and recognize Beijing in order to improve the lives of the practicing Catholics in China. In May 2008 the China Philharmonic Orchestra performed Mozart's Requiem with the Shanghai Opera House Chorus for Pope Benedict XVI in the Paul VI Audience Hall at the Vatican. This was an unprecedented event aimed at signaling a possible thaw in the chilly China-Vatican relationship. This came in 2018, when the pope recognized the legitimacy of seven bishops appointed by the Chinese government and lifted an order on excommunicating them.

The church also clashed with Russia's Orthodox Church in 2002 when it created four new dioceses in that country, which has an estimated 1.3 million Catholics. Orthodox leaders charged that Rome seeks to poach converts. On the Pope John Paul II's 100th foreign trip during his papacy in 2003, he reached out to leaders of the Orthodox Church to try to heal the rift that has divided the two faiths since the Great Schism of 1054. In 2004 he agreed to establish a joint committee to help improve relations with the Russian Orthodox Church. He also called on the Catholic majority in Croatia to seek reconciliation with Orthodox Serbs. In 2004 he returned the bones of two saints to Ecumenical Patriarch Bartholomew I to underscore his determination to reconcile with Orthodox Christianity and forge pan-Christian unity. He was canonized in April 2014.

The Papacy of Pope Benedict XVI (2005–2013)

John Paul II passed away a few days after Easter 2005. The able hand of Cardinal Joseph Ratzinger, the guardian of theological orthodoxy during most of John Paul II's reign, organized the pope's memorable funeral in St. Peter's Square. It was attended by 300,000, including 3 US presidents, the secretary of state, and dozens of other heads of state and government. This was the first time in history any American president had attended a papal funeral. Millions more watched on huge screens all over Rome. Not only did the world's 1.2 billion Catholics (17.4% of the world's population) mourn the loss of their spiritual leader, but also 2 billion people all over the globe, one-third of the world's population, turned on their televisions to witness the departure of an extraordinary man who had accomplished extraordinary things.

It was also Cardinal Ratzinger who organized the election of a new pontiff. Centuries of tradition govern the process. Nine days of official mourning (known as novemdiales) follow the burial. The conclave must be held no sooner than 15 days after the pope's death and no later than 20 days. All cardinals under the age of 80 can vote. Of the 117 electors who qualified, 58 came from Europe (20 from Italy, the largest national contingent), 21 from Latin America, 14 from North America, 11 from Africa, 11 from Asia, and 1 each from Australia and New Zealand.

During the process cardinals are not permitted to use phones, computers, radios, televisions, cameras, or recording devices. Phone lines are disconnected. All cardinals take an oath of secrecy and may only confer with each other. They may negotiate but not make deals. The winner must have a two-thirds majority. If after 12 days and 30 votes no candidate has achieved that, the cardinals can change the rules. They can either elect the pope by a simple majority or by holding a run-off vote between the two top candidates in the most recent ballot. After each vote, the ballots are burned with the addition of special chemicals, and the smoke exits from the Vatican palace roof. Black smoke indicates an inconclusive vote. White means the world has a new pope. In 2005, for the first time, the traditional white smoke for a winner was accompanied by the ringing of bells.

Emerging as the winner after only four votes in fewer than 24 hours was the 78-year-old Ratzinger himself, the first German pope in 482 years. He took the name Benedict XVI. The son of a police officer from rural Bavaria, he, like most young Germans, had joined the Hitler Youth and served briefly in an antiaircraft unit before deserting in 1944. Like his brother, he became a priest, and his sister became a nun. A religious scholar and powerful intellectual, he held professorships at the Universities of Tübingen and Regensburg and is a gifted linguist (10 languages, including heavily accented English, French, and Italian). After serving as archbishop of Munich for only four years, Pope John Paul II called him to Rome to head the Congregation for the Doctrine of Faith, the Vatican's ministry for maintaining orthodoxy. He was no doubt elected pope because of his deep knowledge of the Vatican bureaucracy, leadership qualities, intellectual prowess, and reputation for shoring up the fundamentals of the faith.

In the first months of his papacy, Benedict XVI waived the traditional five-year waiting period and ordered the launching of a fast-track process to make his predecessor a saint. In fact, this is the fastest in modern times, beginning 15 days sooner than Mother Teresa's record. She was made a saint on September 4, 2016. During his 27-year papacy, John Paul had produced more beatifications (1,338) and canonizations (482) than all previous 263 popes combined. He had also changed the sainthood process to make it faster, cheaper, and less adversarial. He eliminated the office of "devil's advocate" and dropped the required number of miracles. The objective is to show the secular world that sanctity is still alive. Francis continued the reform, making the process less murky and costly.

A special commission reviewed John Paul's life and work and looked for miracles. One is required for beatification and a second for canonization. On May 1, 2011, he was beatified in a celebratory mass and day-long prayers beside John Paul's coffin attended by more than 1 million believers in Rome and many more on television. On April 27, 2014, both he and an earlier pope, John XXIII, were declared saints: John Paul II for encouraging the fall of communism and John XXIII for the liberalizing Second Vatican Council from 1962–1965.

Benedict and his successor confronted enormous challenges, including how to stem the church's erosion in Europe. This traditional bastion is in decline, even in such predominantly Catholic countries as

"The pope is coming [to Austria]."

Italy, Ireland, and Spain, the country that changed more than any other.

Benedict committed gaffes that caused offense and embarrassed the Vatican. In 2007 he had to apologize to the Muslim world, which now claims a greater share of the world's population than Catholicism (19.2% to 17.4%, or 33% if all Christian groups are included), for a speech in which he seemed to equate Islam with violence by describing it as a "cruel and inhuman" religion. His support of Pope Pius XII (1939–1958) for sainthood caused an old argument to flare up whether Pius had done enough during the Second World War to save Jews from Nazi persecution. This constantly strains relations with Jews. The Vatican harms its case by refusing to open up critical diplomatic files in its archives.

However, Benedict had an innovative impact in other ways. He exonerated Jews from the charge of killing Christ; reached out to Muslims, Orthodox Christians, and disaffected Anglicans; did far more than his predecessor in atoning for the sins of child abusers in the church; and endorsed the use of condoms under certain circumstances to protect life in this HIV age. He created a new Vatican department to "re-evangelize" secular parts of the world. He became the first pope to grant a TV interview. One in six humans on earth were baptized Catholics, but many Europeans and North Americans describe themselves as "cultural Catholics" while blithely ignoring the pope's teaching when it does not suit them.

Its former political influence in Italy was greatly diminished by the collapse of the Christian Democracy Party. Nevertheless, Pope John Paul II gave a historic address to the Italian parliament in 2002, the first time this had ever happened. Appealing to Italians to meet the "crisis of the birth rate," he received a standing ovation. The appearance was a sign that the turbulent relationship between Italy and the church has become warmer.

Its political influence has not completely vanished in Italy. A reminder was given in 2005, when a referendum took place to decide whether to abrogate parts of a 2004 fertility law that banned research using stem cells from embryos. The law also imposed stringent requirements on test-tube pregnancies. In order to pass, a majority had to turn out to vote, and a majority had to vote yes. Pope Benedict XVI and the country's bishops and priests told the faithful to boycott the referendum. As a result, only 26% showed up to vote, and 90% of those voted yes. Italians once again showed the power of their church. It urges greater "morality" and "legality" in public life.

In Spain only 14% of young people described themselves as religious in 2005. The Spanish Socialist government aggressively pursued an agenda that contravened almost every tenet of Catholic doctrine. It legalized same-sex marriage in 2005 and allowed same-sex couples to adopt children. It introduced fast-track divorce and relaxed abortion rules. The archbishop of Madrid said his country had turned into Sodom and Gomorrah. Benedict XVI himself called "homosexuality" "intrinsic moral evil."

There was no dramatic doctrinal change under a pope who considered rock music a "vehicle of anti-religion" and who opposed women priests. He did, however, reach out to other faiths and order the church to rethink its ban on condoms, though not for the purpose of contraception. The church is experiencing its greatest growth in Africa and is alert to the impact that AIDS is having on that troubled continent. Benedict surprised many by being an activist leader.

The Papacy of Pope Francis (2013 to present)

On February 28, 2013, Benedict became the first pope in almost 600 years to retire from the papacy. He said his physical and mental health was giving out, but it was widely assumed that uncontrollable power struggles within the Vatican wore him out. The conclave of 115 cardinals (those under age 80) assembled in Rome. Many thought it was time to choose a pope from Africa, which has 186 million Catholics, or 18.3% of the total population, or Latin America, which accounts for 40% of the world's 1.2 billion Catholics. On March 13, 2013, the cardinals settled after only 28 hours on 76-year-old Jorge Mario Bergolglio of Argentina as the 266th pope. He had been the runner-up in 2005.

Known as an attractive mix of piety, humility, and shrewd administrative skills, he represents many firsts: the first non-European in 1,200 years (Syrian-born Gregory III was elected in the 8th century), the first Jesuit, the first pope from Latin America, the first southern pope. He chose the name Francis to honor St. Francis of Assisi and St. Francis Xavier, the first Jesuit missionary. He has a strong common touch and enjoys great popularity. He even has his own magazine, a 68-page weekly called Il Mio Papa (My Pope). Each issue has a pull-out centerfold of the pope accompanied by a quote.

He has focused his priesthood on the interests of the poor and is recognized for his simplicity. As archbishop in Buenos Aires, he rode the bus to work, lived in a normal apartment instead of the bishop's place, and cooked his own meals. He now lives in the more modest quarters within the Vatican. He is a conservative on doctrine, opposing abortion, euthanasia, same-sex marriage, and adoption by same-sex couples. He wants to show more understanding for these issues. In 2020, he voiced his support for same-sex unions. He said that "homosexuals have a right to be part of the family" and that "they are children of God and have a right to a family."

Two-thirds of American Catholics, who constitute 20.8% of the nation, and half the non-Catholics find him a change for the better. Their enthusiasm has not inspired more Americans to attend Sunday mass regularly (only 22%) or go to confession. However, over half (54%) said he was doing a good or excellent job on addressing the sex abuse scandals. His approval rating among US Catholics is 63%. Of the thirteen new cardinals Francis appointed in 2020, one was the first African American: Wilton Gregory, Archbishop of Washington, D.C. His most immediate problem is to tackle feuding and scandal in the Vatican, and he must deal with the ongoing problem of sexual abuse by priests. The pope showed his diplomatic finesse in 2014 by brokering a historic agreement by Cuba and the United States to normalize relations.

FUTURE

The fact that a third of mankind and the world's major political leaders observed John Paul II's funeral in April 2005 demonstrated that the influence and spiritual attraction of the Roman Catholic Church have not disappeared, even if they are weaker than they once were. It faces the future more confidently with a unique Pope Francis.

The Sovereign Military Order of Malta

The Roman Catholic Sovereign Military Hospitaler Order of St. John of Jerusalem, of Rhodes, and of Malta

Area: The Malta Palace (Palazzo di Malta) and the Villa Malta, about three acres.

Population: International membership in the order is about 9,600, all of whom retain their own nationality.

Neighboring Countries: Located in Rome, Italy.

Religion: Roman Catholicism.

Chief of State (Head of the Order): The Prince and Grand Master, His Most Eminent Highness Frà Matthew Festing (79th Grand Master).

Flag of State: A plain white cross on a red field (of the Grand Master), the white Maltese Cross on a red field.

Only with a magnifying glass can one see the world's smallest country on a Rome city map. Completely surrounded by a wall and with a territorial size equivalent to half a football field, the Sovereign Military Order of Malta (SMOM) is the only country in the world which has *no* citizens whatsoever and which is small enough to be assigned a street address: 68 Via Condotti, a very elegant street just a stone's throw from Rome's famous Span-ish Steps. By peeping through the key-hole of the main gate of Villa Malta on the Aventine Hill, a palace which is also part of SMOM, one can gain the kind of view normally available only to astronauts: One can see three sovereign countries, namely the SMOM, Italy, and the Vatican.

The prince and grand master is elected by the Council Complete of State and is duly confirmed by the pope. Today this an-cient entity maintains diplomatic relations with the Holy See, on which it depends as a religious order but not as a sovereign, and with 100 nations (but not with the United States). It has permanent observer status at the UN. It issues passports and postage stamps. It has delegations to the Council of Europe and UNESCO. It sent a delegate to the UN Millennium Sum-mit in New York in September 2000, who was imaginative in getting himself and his sovereign order noticed. Publication of the official photograph of world leaders was delayed because a man in the photo could not be identified. It turned out that he was Count Carlos Maruulo di Condojanni, grand chancellor of the Sovereign Military Order of Malta, who somehow slipped past security into history.

It enjoys the same status of extraterrito-riality that the Italian government grants to any embassy; that is, it is considered to be foreign soil. On January 28, 1961, the civil courts of Rome declared the order an "international sovereign society." Issuing its own passports and conducting its af-fairs without interference, this tiny state is truly an oddity in the contemporary world.

The hospital-infirmary dedicated to St. John the Baptist was founded in Jerusa-lem about the middle of the 11th century. Originally connected with the Benedic-tines but later independent, it was admin-istered by a monastic community dedi-cated to the care of those Christians who fell ill during their pilgrimages to the Holy Land.

In the same century, Pope Urban II urged the formation of a great crusade in order to sweep the Muslims from the cradle of Christianity and to expand the reach of the Roman Catholic Church. In 1096, a grow-ing army, led by French knights and joined

The Sovereign Military Order of Malta

by noblemen and simple folk from many nations, progressed on horseback and foot across Europe and toward the Holy Land. The crusader knights were young, ranging from 16 to 30 years, and they were brimming with enthusiasm, self-confidence, a strong taste for adventure, and (for many) visions of riches. They seized Jerusalem in 1099 and surrounding areas in a series of bloody battles. During the first years, the hospital's prior installed some of them into the Order of St. John of Jerusalem as defenders. To confirm their intense dedication at the time of their induction, they held out their swords, which were blessed under flickering torches.

In 1113 the community of the Hospital of St. John was recognized by the pope as a religious order of the church, free from all lay interference. This was the germ of the order's sovereignty. In the 1130s, because of the need to protect the sick, the pilgrims, and the Christian settlements in the Holy Land, the order acquired the ad-

**HMEH Frà Andrew Bertie,
the former prince and grand master**

ditional military character and became a monastic-chivalric order, in which monks were knights and knights took the monastic vows. The order's military edge was first felt in 1118, when its knights did more than protect; they openly attacked the Muslims. Stories of their bravery made them living legends, and new recruits continued to join their ranks every year.

In 1187 the overwhelming forces of Saladin, sultan of Egypt and Syria, drove the knights, who suffered terrible losses, from the Latin Kingdom of Jerusalem. All of them were at least wounded, and only a handful survived, including the grand master. Those who remained escaped. The kingdom and the order continued at Acre (Akka). In even greater numbers than before, knights came from all over Europe to join the struggle against the "infidels." There were eight Crusades until 1291, but each grew weaker. The crusaders were never permanently able to wrest Jerusalem from Muslim control. The Muslims wiped the kingdom out in 1291, and the order moved to Cyprus. But the Knights of St. John remained dedicated to their task of defending Christianity.

They used Cyprus as a base for the next 120 years, continuing to battle the Muslims on or around the Mediterranean Sea. The island was never considered ideal for their purposes because the coastline was too extensive to defend adequately. In 1310 the knights attacked and captured Rhodes, a beautiful island of meadowlands and forests lying some 25 miles (40 km) off the southwestern coast of Turkey. Establishing their headquarters there, they continued to expand their navy and constructed a

The Malta Palace, 68 Via Condotti

The Sovereign Military Order of Malta

watchtower on the nearby islet of Simi in order to foil any naval attack.

In the following years, their control extended over most of the islands off the western coast of Turkey, some little more than outcroppings of jagged rock. Their activity excited admiration throughout Europe because the knights could effectively challenge Turkish domination in the Mediterranean Sea. In recognition of this role, Pope Nicholas V recognized the grand master of the order as the sovereign prince of Rhodes in 1446.

The Turks overran Asia Minor and were moving into Europe—in 1453 they put an end to the Byzantine Empire and pro-

ceeded to launch attacks on Rhodes. Over and over the Turks made massive attacks against the island, but not until 1532 did they succeed in overwhelming the knights and forcing them to leave. During the following eight years, the knights were homeless, but in 1530 the Holy Roman Emperor Charles V gave the order the island of Malta, on which they built the finest hospital in Europe at that time. Included were the nearby islands, as well as the African mainland fortress-city Tripoli, a city which the knights soon abandoned.

During the next 268 years, they vigilantly patrolled the waters to protect trade routes for Christian merchants. They con-

tinued to raid Turkish ships and those of Barbary pirates (see the Republic of Malta).

The prince grand master of the order, who since 1630 has the rank equal to that of a cardinal, was the undisputed ruler of Malta and was a sovereign who entered into treaties with other nations and enjoyed the usual rights accorded to a chief of state. Of course, the order's very existence, powers, privileges, and immunities remained under the protective umbrella of the Roman Catholic Church, and these were therefore respected throughout Christendom. Splendid architectural monuments, churches, public buildings, and fortifications still bear witness to the order's sovereign rule in Malta.

It took periodic interest in acquiring territory in the New World. In 1653 Louis XIV of France gave the order four Caribbean islands—St. Kitts, St. Martin, St. Croix, and St. Barthélemy—but it later decided to sell them to the French West India Company.

In 1794 it approached James Monroe, the US ambassador to France, with an offer of ports, provisions, and protection for American sailors in the Mediterranean in return for lands in America. Monroe responded that the order was welcome to purchase land but that such property could not become a part of another sovereign government and would have to remain under the jurisdiction of the United States. Although the order was not interested in buying under these terms, its personal ties with the United States have remained strong—approximately 1,500 out of 9,600 of the order's knights are presently living in the US, and they include such prominent American Catholics as former treasury secretary William E. Simon; the late Clare Boothe Luce; William F. Buckley Jr.; and the late Terrence Cardinal Cooke; archbishop of New York. However, Americans can never ascend to the highest ranks of the order because only persons of long-standing nobility are admitted to high leadership positions.

Napoleon's forces, engaged in a campaign against Egypt, occupied the island of Malta in 1798 and drove out the order. The knights were overwhelmingly French and were reportedly somewhat sympathetic to the French general. But they again found themselves without a home. This was followed by what has been called the Russian coup d'état (1798–1803).

Tsar Paul I of Russia was a bitter opponent of the French Revolution and also had hopes of setting up a Russian naval base in the Mediterranean. He had shown himself as a friend of the order. He now had himself proclaimed grand master by a handful of knights who had gone to live in Russia instead of the grand master Frà

Interior courtyard of the Malta Palace

The Sovereign Military Order of Malta

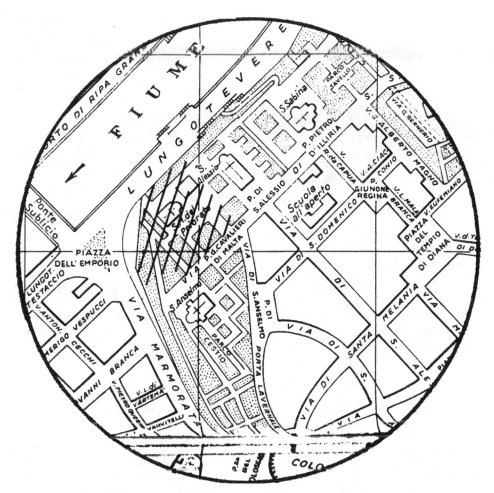

Location and grounds of the Villa Malta on the Aventine Hill

European powers once again to give the order a base. Various islands were considered, but no nation seemed interested in donating even a small one to what they considered to be a fading order of knighthood. The sovereign order's headquarters moved to Sicily and then to Ferrara. Finally, in 1834 the 16th-century Malta Palace in Rome, which had been the order's embassy to the Papal State since the early 1600s, became the order's headquarters and remains so to the present time.

Maintaining health institutions throughout the world, from small dispensaries and leper colonies to 10 hospitals, the order has returned to its original mission of caring for the sick. Yet those persons who dismiss the Sovereign Military Order of Malta as being neither sovereign nor military are only half-right. It no longer performs a military function, despite the shining swords that the knights still bear on festive occasions. It does perform an admirable humanitarian function in a world that, in many places, is still largely gripped by disease and misery. It is a sovereign entity by international recognition, even if it only has three acres in Rome to call its very own. It is legally seperate from the Holy See. But in January 2017, Pope Francis demanded the grand master's obedience and resignation.

Ferdinand von Hompesch, who had abandoned Malta to the French. This proclamation of a married non-Catholic as head of a Catholic religious order was wholly illegal and void; the Holy See never recognized it, which was a necessary condition for legitimacy. Accordingly, Paul I, who was nevertheless accepted by many knights and a number of governments, can only be regarded as a grand master de facto, never one de jure. This was only a brief interlude. Paul was murdered in 1801 and was succeeded by his 24-year-old son Alexander I. The new tsar helped the order to return to legitimate rule. In 1803 Frà Giovanni Battista Tommasi was elected grand master.

In the meantime, the British had seized the island of Malta from Napoleon in 1801. They specified in the 1802 Treaty of Amiens with France that Malta must be restored to the order. This never happened, though, and Britain continued to rule the island until it became independent in 1964. Surviving knights scattered throughout Europe attempted after 1802 to persuade

Peeping through the keyhole of Villa Malta

371

The Republic of Malta

Mdina, old capital of Malta

Courtesy: Alexandra Schaerer

Area: 122 sq. mi. (316 sq. km, one-tenth the size of Rhode Island, twice the size of Washington, DC). Smallest and most densely populated in the EU.

Population: 460,000 (UN, 2015).

Capital City: Valletta (pop. 21,000, est.).

Climate: Mild and sunny Mediterranean.

Neighboring Countries: Italy (north), Libya (south).

Official Languages: Maltese, English. Italian is also widely spoken.

Other Principal Tongues: Italian is understood.

Ethnic Background: Mixture of Phoenician, Carthaginian, Arab, Sicilian, Norman, Spanish, Italian, British.

Principal Religion: Roman Catholic (98%).

Main Exports: Tourism, machinery, transport equipment, ship repair, clothing, food manufacturing and processing, textiles.

Main Trading Partners: EU (42.3% of exports and 67.3% of imports), Italy (40%), Germany (15%), France (9%), UK (6%).

Currency: Maltese lira.

Former Colonial Status: British Crown colony.

Date of Independence: September 21, 1964, within the British Commonwealth of Nations; republic declared on December 13, 1974; parliamentary democracy.

Chief of State: George Vella, President (since April 2019).

Head of Government: Robert Abela, Prime Minister (since January 2020).

National Holiday: Republic Day, December 13.

National Flag: Two large vertical white and red stripes with a gray cross in the upper left-hand corner.

Malta is a small but historically and strategically important group of five islands (two of which are uninhabited) in the central Mediterranean Sea, 60 miles (96 km) south of Sicily and 180 miles (290 km) north of Libya. After Monaco, it has the greatest population density in Europe and the third-greatest in the world, with 1,196 persons per square kilometer, three times that of the Netherlands. For centuries Malta, with its well-sheltered anchorage and the largest natural harbor in the Mediterranean, has been squarely in the middle of the many struggles to control the Mediterranean Sea and, with that, the traffic between Europe, Africa, and the Middle East. Because of its strategic importance and small size, Malta has always been dependent upon exterior powers.

Malta's people and culture today clearly reflect the influence of the many conquerors who have dominated the islands. Ethnically, the Maltese people are predominantly of Carthaginian and Phoenician origin. The latter named the islands Maleth, meaning "hiding place," from which the country's present name is derived. The Maltese culture is a mixture of Italian and Arabic traditions. Maltese is a Semitic language arising from the mixture of Arabic and Sicilian Italian, with influences from English and French. It is the only Semitic language that is written in Latin script, and it is the only official language in the EU that is Semitic. To the stranger it sounds very much like Arabic.

Because of long British rule, many Maltese speak impeccable English. Today Britons constitute only 2.1% of the population, which is dominated by 95.7% Maltese. The official language since 1934, Maltese is the most widely used medium of communication. It is also the language of instruction in the schools, which are patterned on the British educational system, and is used by one television and nine radio networks. Scholars disagree whether the European or the Arabic component predominates in the Maltese character and nature, but they do agree that the Maltese have a distinct culture and identity of their own.

HISTORY

The Early Period

Archaeologists have uncovered evidence of Neolithic cave dwellers from approximately 3800 BC on Malta, and it is probable that the islands were a center of Mediterranean civilization before Crete was. Between the 9th and 6th centuries BC, the Phoenicians, Greeks, and Carthaginians established colonies in Malta, and the islands' inhabitants came into contact with Semitic cultures along the southern and eastern rim of the Mediterranean. In 218 BC the islands fell under Roman control.

Christian Beginnings

According to biblical legend, a Roman ship carrying St. Paul crashed on offshore rocks in 60 AD, and Paul saved himself by swimming shore. The Maltese still use the favorite saying when everything seems to go wrong, "Don't forget that even St. Paul was shipwrecked on Malta!" He wasted no time in converting the population, and the majority of Malta's population has been Christian ever since.

Arabs and Normans

When the Roman Empire approached total collapse in the 4th century AD, Malta fell under the domination of Constantinople. Until the 16th century, the islands were ruled successively by Arabs, who came in 870 AD and placed their indelible stamp on the Maltese; by Normans, who displaced the Arabs in 1000 AD and who improved Maltese political and legal structures; and later by other European nations.

Control by the Knights

In 1520 Malta came under the control of the Order of the Hospital of St. John of Jerusalem (otherwise known as the Knights Hospitalers, or the Maltese Knights), a Roman Catholic religious order. It had been founded in Jerusalem before the Crusades in order to protect Christian pilgrims. Later, it had established its headquarters on the Greek island of Rhodes, before being driven out by the Turks. The Holy Roman emperor of the time, Charles V, granted Malta to the knights, which they turned into a fortress against Islam.

Their military mission was to keep the Turks out of the western Mediterranean and to clear the southern Mediterranean of pirates. Their raids on the immense Ottoman Empire so enraged the Turkish sultan that he sent a huge army of 40,000 men and a navy of 200 ships against the heavily fortified islands. The four-month Turkish siege was one of the bloodiest in history, and of 9,000 Maltese knights and soldiers, fewer than 1,000 survived unwounded. But their valor, under Grand Master Jean de La Valette, a shrewd military tactician after whom Malta's present capital city was named, forced the Turks to withdraw. Never again did the Turks attempt to penetrate the western Mediterranean.

The victorious and prosperous knights began to build the capital city of Valleta on a rocky headland. They built innumerable splendid baroque palaces, churches, and public buildings, financed primarily by

The Republic of Malta

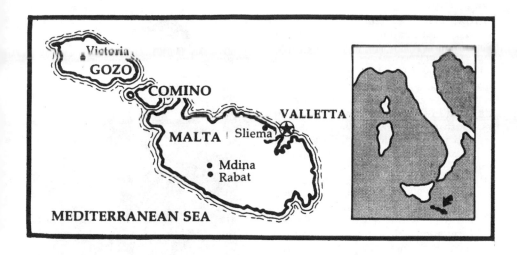

cise executive power, but who remain responsible to the House of Representatives. An indirectly elected, largely ceremonial president serves as the head of state for a five-year term. In 2004 former Prime Minister Eddie Fenech Adami was elected. He was succeeded in 2009 by George Abela, who was followed by Marie-Louise Coleiro Preca and then by George Vella.

The government of the country is highly centralized in the capital city, although Sliema is actually the country's largest city. There is little established local government. The major exception to this is the island of Gozo, which has a locally elected Civic Council which rules that small island in conjunction with a commissioner appointed by the central government in Valletta. Malta has an independent judicial system consisting of lower courts and a Constitutional Court, a Superior Court, and a Court of Appeal.

POLITICS

Only two political parties have a significant number of seats in the House of Representatives or play an important role in Maltese politics. The ruling Labour Party (LP) sees itself as a socialist party and depends upon the support of workers and the powerful trade unions. From 1961 until 1971, the LP was embroiled in such a bitter struggle with the Catholic Church that the church declared any vote or other active support for this party to be sufficient grounds for excommunication. The lifting of this ban in 1971 enabled the party to maintain its position.

For many years the character of the LP was shaped by the personality of its mercurial former leader Dom Mintoff, who stepped down as prime minister in 1984. His handpicked successor, Carmelo Mifsud-Bonnici, succeeded him. The LP favored an independent and neutral Malta playing the role of bridge between Europe and the Arab world and an anticolonialist foreign policy involving close ties with the Third World. To strengthen its European credentials, it joined the Council of Europe in 1965.

The LP advocates foreign investment and economic help to industrialize the islands. At the same time, it seeks the redistribution of property and income in order to create a more egalitarian society. In many ways, these last two objectives are in conflict with one another. Under Mintoff's premiership the government took over broadcasting, telecommunications, oil and gas, and a full or majority interest in all banks. It also established a national airline and shipping line, and it introduced a minimum wage, a 40-hour workweek, and mandatory wage increases to keep pace with inflation.

booty from their naval adventures against the Turks. Many of these structures still survive and testify to the great prosperity of that time. The famed Sacra Infermeria Hospital, whose construction began in 1571, was recently converted to a magnificent and modern Mediterranean conference center in an attempt to make Malta a major trade center.

Napoleon and British Rule

Napoleon Bonaparte seized the islands in 1798. Because of sympathetic French knights, his troops scarcely had to fire a shot. However, realizing that he would be unable to defend the islands against the British navy, he decided to return them to the knights soon thereafter. Not wishing this to happen, a sizable number of Maltese rebelled and demanded to be placed under British sovereignty. Always attentive to the strategic needs of its empire and navy and bracing itself for a bitter struggle against Napoleonic France, Britain gladly accepted in 1800. The Treaty of Paris confirmed British sovereignty over Malta in 1814. The Maltese knights never returned to the islands as rulers, but each June they return from all over the world in full regalia for the Feast of St. John at St. John's Cathedral.

Throughout the 19th century, a British governor ruled Malta, and its economy grew almost entirely dependent upon the proceeds from British military facilities on the islands, a dependence which Malta has never been able to overcome successfully. Immediately following World War I, the British granted internal autonomy to the Maltese, but the experiment failed, and in 1933 Malta reverted to its status of a Crown colony. During World War II, this "unsinkable aircraft carrier," as Winston S. Churchill called it, heroically resisted brutal German bombing (at the cost of 7,000 lives) and refused to surrender, even though the islands were frequently cut off from supplies for months at a time.

Cannon still sound every day at noon to commemorate the siege. Malta played an extremely significant role in the successful Allied efforts in North Africa, Sicily, and southern Europe. In 1947 the islands were again granted self-government, but a British-appointed governor maintained control over foreign affairs, defense, and currency.

In 1955 the Maltese Labor Party won a parliamentary majority and made a radical proposal for full integration of Malta into the United Kingdom. This proposal, which now appears highly surprising in view of the party's later stand on independence, received the support of three-fourths of the voters in a referendum in 1956. However, negotiations to work out such integration broke down two years later, and by 1960 the Maltese support for the tie had disappeared. Independence, not integration, became the new goal, and the Nationalist Party, which had won the 1964 parliamentary elections, achieved this the same year.

GOVERNMENT

The constitution of 1964, which had made Malta an independent parliamentary monarchy within the British Commonwealth, was revised in 1974 to create a republican parliamentary democracy. A 65-member unicameral parliament, called the House of Representatives, is elected by universal suffrage of all citizens over the age of 18 on the basis of proportional representation (PR) using the single-transferable-vote system at least every five years. Since 1987 any party that wins a majority of the popular vote is assured a majority of parliamentary seats, despite PR. In deference to the country's Catholic majority and past, all members of parliament take the constitutional oath of loyalty in the traditional manner, by kissing a cross held out to them. The majority party appoints the prime minister and cabinet, who exer-

The Republic of Malta

The LP clashed with the Catholic Church because of Mintoff's decision to nationalize hospitals and schools. He expelled all nuns and doctors who refused to comply with the state takeover of the hospitals. He refused all state assistance to the country's private (mainly Catholic) schools, which educate about a third of all Maltese children. The government's campaign against Catholic schools was stepped up in 1984, when it was announced that private schools could no longer charge tuition. This move was followed by widespread violence, including a raid on Catholic Church headquarters, reportedly led by Mifsud-Bonnici.

Hostility between the church and the LP had been intensified when the latter introduced a bill to authorize state seizure of about three-fourths of the church's property in Malta. Not surprisingly, Vatican spokesmen warned that such action would have "predictable repercussions on religious peace." But in 1985 Mifsud-Bonnici signed an agreement with the Vatican designed to end the controversy over government control of Catholic schools.

The church remains influential in Malta, where 98% are Catholic. Divorce was legalized in 2011, but abortion is illegal, regardless of circumstances. A 2005 poll revealed that 55% opposed divorce, while only 38% found it necessary. Opposition to abortion was even more pronounced: 95.7% opposed it in cases where a woman becomes pregnant outside marriage; 85.7%, in cases of incest. Even 76% opposed it in cases of rape.

When the pope visited the country in 1990, half the entire population gathered in a large square to see him. Benedict XVI returned in April 2010 to celebrate the 1,950th anniversary of St. Paul's shipwreck on the island. He also met with a small group of victims of sexual abuse by priests, expressing his "shame and

President George Vella

sorrow." Same-sex couples have equal marriage and adoption rights. Malta has become on of the most gay-friendly countries in the EU.

Under the leadership from 1992 to 2003 of Alfred Sant, a pragmatic Harvard PhD in business administration and former diplomat in Brussels, the party shook off its confrontational socialist image. He severed the party's formal links with the trade unions and admitted that economic liberalization had benefited Malta. Not all LP militants supported these changes. In the 2003 and 2008 elections, it lost again, receiving 48.8% of the votes. Led from 2003 to 2020 by Joseph Muscat, a 39-year-old former journalist and member of the European Parliament, the party won a majority of seats in parliament by capturing 54% of the votes in the March 2013 elections. Amid corruption allegations, Muscat called a snap election in June 2017 and won another five-year term. He was replaced as prime minister in 2020 by Robert Abela.

The opposition Nationalist Party (NP), led from 2004 to 2013 by Lawrence Gonzi, stands much closer to the Catholic Church and to the Maltese middle class. It wishes to safeguard Malta's Catholic Church and European traditions. The NP advocates Malta's following the example of other minute European states, such as Andorra, Monaco, and Liechtenstein, in lowering taxes so that foreign wealth and business enterprises are attracted to the islands. This reduces the island's dependence on financial handouts from other countries and brings prosperity to Malta. The NP advocates closer relations with Europe and the US.

The land is bitterly polarized in many ways: labor unions based in the dockyards versus the middle class, clans with generations of hostility, villages divided in their loyalty to competing saints, and townships torn by rivalry between clubs which parade on holy days. But the transition from violent confrontational politics succeeded. Party allegiance no longer dominates every issue, and the pervasive tension is gone.

A third party, the Democratic Alternative, is politically active, but it is irrelevant in the House of Representatives. It got only 2% of the votes and no seats in 2008 and 2013. It describes itself as "green-progressive" and focuses on corruption and social and environmental issues. It publishes a monthly newspaper, XPRESS.

Foreign and Defense Policy

Malta had difficulty solving its major long-standing economic and foreign policy problem: how to survive economically without the rental fees paid by Britain for use of Maltese defense facilities. In 1971 the strong-willed Mintoff abrogated the

Prime Minister Robert Abela

Mutual Defense and Assistance Agreement of 1964; after months of difficult negotiations, a new seven-year agreement was reached, tripling the rental fees Britain was required to pay. He again demanded an increase in 1973. Britain finally decided it could live without Malta's base facilities and withdrew from the island in 1979, after 179 years of military presence there. Mintoff hailed this as "the day of light, freedom day, the day of the new Malta."

The economic problems caused by the loss of more than $70 million in revenue were not solved by that freedom. No country was inclined to help Mintoff.

A modest amount of development assistance the People's Republic of China had given Malta since 1971 to construct a dry dock to handle tankers was much too small to solve Malta's problems. Therefore, Mintoff turned to that oil-rich state to the south, whose leader had shown himself willing to support practically any state or group whose policies are directed against the industrialized west: Libya. Mintoff announced in 1979, "Europe showed us the cold shoulder, but Libya heartily and spontaneously accepted our suggestions for collaboration." Libya's flamboyant and erratic leader, the late Colonel Muammar al Gaddafi, took a 500-man delegation to the ceremony in Malta marking the British withdrawal and promised the country unlimited aid.

Gaddafi delivered oil and gasoline to Malta almost without charge, and the Maltese government was able to derive even greater profit from this gift by imposing a stiff local consumption tax on the petroleum. Libya also invested approximately $150 million in the islands, entered a defense pact with Malta, and provided heli-

374

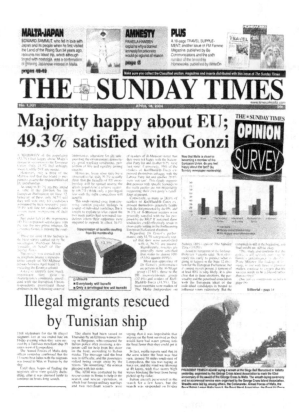

copters and coastal patrol boats. Gaddafi proudly proclaimed Malta as the "northern outpost of the Arabic world" and even aspired to introduce pure Arabic as Malta's official language (Arabic is no longer compulsory in secondary schools). Such pronouncements merely aggravated many Maltese, who from the beginning had misgivings toward this strange marriage of convenience. NP leaders called it an exchange of "one type of colonialism for another."

The marriage was scarcely a year old when a disagreement erupted. Both governments claimed oil rights in the waters between the two states. An angry Mintoff declared Libya "a danger to peace in the Mediterranean" and expelled as "security risks" 50 Libyan military personnel who had been sent to train Maltese helicopter pilots. By 1984 differences with Libya were settled. Both countries agreed to submit their dispute over oil rights in the sea to the International Court of Justice, which rendered a decision satisfactory to both parties. They signed a military cooperation treaty, under which Libya would help to train and supply the Maltese forces and help to protect Malta "in case of threats or acts of aggression." The treaty became meaningless after civil war broke out in Libya in February 2011.

In 1981 Malta had signed an agreement with the Soviet Union, which pledged to respect Malta's neutrality in return for the right to store up to 300,000 tons of oil on the islands. Mintoff claimed that Moscow

was not committed to defend the island if Maltese territory were violated.

Under Fenech Adami, Malta steered a more pro-western course. The NP has a tradition of strong sympathies with Italy. Under Labour rule, Malta had already secured assistance from its nearest northern neighbor. Arguing that Maltese neutrality was in Italy's and NATO's interests and

threatening to allow the Soviet navy to use the harbor of Valletta, it persuaded Italy to support Malta. The Italian government rather liked the idea of assuming greater responsibility in the Mediterranean area. In 1980 it promised Malta technical assistance and financial support. Until 1994 Italy covered a third of Malta's budget deficit.

The islands, which for five years had maintained a consultative arrangement with NATO, received in 1981 military guarantees from Italy, which stationed 47 air force personnel in Malta to operate two helicopters. In exchange, Malta formally declared neutrality and promised not to allow any foreign military bases. In 1987 the Maltese constitution was changed in order to entrench both nonalignment and neutrality and to forbid foreign military bases.

In 1986 the former LP prime minister admitted having tipped off Gaddafi minutes before the American bombing raid on Libya, thereby possibly saving the Libyan leader's life. The NP government did not show such "even-handedness." Malta maintained economic ties with Libya and renegotiated its friendship treaty with it. But Fenech Adami emphasized that he had widened the political distance with Gaddafi and that the military clauses, which had obligated Malta to warn Libya of American air strikes, had been removed. Fenech Adami's government severed air links with Libya and honored the UN embargo imposed after Libya's complicity in the bombing of a Pan Am plane over Lockerbie, Scotland, appeared obvious.

After the 1998 election, the new NP government renewed the country's EU appli-

The Republic of Malta

cation. In one of his first acts, Sant formally withdrew Malta from NATO's Partnership for Peace program "because it contradicts our constitutional neutrality." Malta allots about 3.5% ($29 million) of its budget to the maintenance of its small army, navy, and air force of 1,954 active troops and 167 reservists. There are also 47 Italian air force personnel stationed in Malta flying two AB-212 aircraft. However, it could never defend itself alone.

Malta's most pressing foreign policy problem by far is the influx of unwanted illegal immigrants from Africa. It looks south to a 2,000-mile (3,200 km) North African coastline, located less than 250 miles (400 km) away. The passage can be made in open fishing boats, which often capsize, or overloaded rubber dinghies, which can make the journey in 36 hours. In the four years to 2006, almost 6,000 migrants had washed ashore. In proportion to the resident population, this would be like the US being inundated by 3.5 million migrants. Many used it as a back door to the EU after it joined in 2004. Because of the high costs and diplomatic complications, Malta cannot return them to their homelands, and many feel trapped in their dingy barracks or tent cities where they are confined.

Malta pleads for help from the EU, but many of its partners are facing the same problem. The leader of a Maltese anti-immigrant party said, "We have never had minorities, and we don't want minorities." Foreigners constitute 4% of Malta's population. This threatened to shoot up when Gaddafi's brutal regime began to collapse in February 2011 and descended into chaos. Given its proximity to Libya, Malta became a stepping stone for many countries, including the US, to evacuate their nationals from Libya by air and sea. Even a British warship filled with Britons and two air force jets flown by Libyan defectors found their way to the tiny island.

But the Maltese worried about the newcomers who want to stay. The home affairs minister Carmelo Mifsud-Bonnici said, "This volcano that has been in hibernation for the last 40 years has erupted." How can up to 6,000 African refugees be accommodated or processed? He asked, "What can Malta do? In the time of the Knights of St. John there were 20,000 people here. Now there are 400,000. We are at our limits." Migrants found a safer path to Europe through Turkey and Greece and between Libya and Italy. The influx through Malta has largely stopped. It sometimes prevents refugee ships from landing.

Malta occupied the EU's six-month rotating presidency the first half of 2017. This brought to its handsome capital Valletta important EU meetings. Its focus was the EU burden sharing of immigration. In 2018 Valetta, Europe's smallest capital, was named Europe's cultural capital. Hundreds of events took place.

ECONOMY

Malta is a highly overcrowded ministate with four-tenths of 1 million people on only 122 square miles (316 sq. km). Only one-third the size of New York City, it has one vehicle for every two residents, making it Europe's most traffic-congested nation. It has no natural resources, except limestone, and its terrain is very unsuited to agriculture. It can supply only about 20% of its food needs, and only 6% of its population can find employment in agriculture. Its major agricultural products are potatoes, cauliflower, grapes, wheat, barley, tomatoes, citrus fruit, cut flowers, hogs, poultry, and eggs. Desalination plants provide half of Malta's freshwater.

Its major industry, thanks to its deep-water harbors, is ship repair. This provides 5% of total employment, although it has fallen on hard times. In an austerity move, the workforce at the docks was cut by 3,000. In the related area of aircraft maintenance, Lufthansa services its smaller planes at Malta's airport and plans to do the same for its wide-body fleet in the future. The government's efforts since independence to diversify the economy have had modest success, and Malta now has some light-manufacturing enterprises in the clothing, textile, building, and food- processing sectors. Foreign investments contributed significantly to this success, but they have meant that more than half of Malta's industrial production is in foreign hands. Maltese industry will be lucky if it can continue employing a fourth of the workforce. Not wanting to compete as a low-wage economy, it faces a particular obstacle in that it must import so many raw materials in order to export finished products at a profit.

An Achilles' heel was the fact that more than half of its exports are textile products. In the industrialized nations to which it exports, there are increasingly loud demands to erect barriers against textile imports in order to protect their own clothing industries. Diversification has reduced this problem. Malta must still import most consumer and industrial needs, including fuels and raw materials.

A fourth of its GDP is derived from tourism, its biggest revenue earner. The number of foreign tourists who visit Malta is three times as large as the country's population. The government believes that, with 1 million tourists every year (predominantly Britons), the three islands have reached the saturation point. Therefore, it aims to restructure the industry to attract more up-market tourists. This would bring more income from fewer visitors. They ar-

Advertising for tourists in Germany

rive at the country's two usable airfields and one major and two minor harbors.

In order to try to overcome Malta's economic stagnation, the former NP government liberalized the economy, which was overprotected and state-dominated. Through "tax holidays," it lured foreign investment from the west. Sometimes companies are granted a corporate tax rate of 5%. Some other countries and the OECD criticized its status as a tax haven. Therefore, in 2000 it joined five other small states in agreeing to cooperate with international efforts to curb abusive and criminal tax-avoidance schemes.

It has high hopes for its financial-services industry, which is attracting most of the incoming investment and which is supported by a small government-owned stock exchange located in a former military chapel. It lists only 13 stocks. There are about 250 hedge funds. Its financial-services sector is eight times as large as its GDP. It is considered to be healthy and run conservatively.

Malta largely completed its first priority of improving the infrastructure by overhauling the telecommunications network and building a new power station, desalination plants, and a second airport terminal. It attracted some higher-skill and technology industries, such as pharmaceuticals, to replace traditional ones, like textiles, which are threatened by low-cost competition from North Africa and Asia. The government has sold off a variety of state-owned businesses, including the telecoms provider Maltacom, bought in 2006 by Dubai Tecom.

With one or more cars per family, there is an air of prosperity in the country. Growing wealth has created the same phenomenon in Malta as in other developed European countries: a lowering of the fertility rate to only 1.5 (2.1 are needed to maintain the population level). Malta has the EU's lowest female-participation rate in its workforce. Life expectancy is 81 for women and 77 for men. The feeling that Malta is already performing rather well was an important reason many voters did not view EU entry as an urgent necessity.

Since 1971 Malta has had a special trade relationship with the EU, to which it sent 68% of its exports and from which it bought 78% of its imports in 1990, the year in which it applied for full membership. The government drafted all its legislation with eventual EU membership in mind. Prime Minister (later president) Fenech Adami had announced, "Malta is a European country. To us, this will be a homecoming." In 1999 the EU invited Malta back to formal talks leading to membership.

The talks went so well that Malta won more concessions than any of the other nine accession countries. Its workers are allowed unrestricted entry into EU countries, although it won the right to bar foreign labor for seven years. It also secured the right to block nonresidents indefinitely from buying second homes on the islands.

In 2003 the government was ready to put the emotional question of membership to the voters. Rallies for and against joining drew thousands of people. Many Maltese feared that Europe would take away the hard-earned independence they had finally won in 1964. As the least populous country in the EU, Malta risked being overshadowed by the large EU nations and might not have a voice that would be listened to. The Labour Party led the charge against EU membership. However, arguing that membership is vital for Malta's economy and international credibility, the government prevailed. In the March 9 referendum, 53.6% supported accession, while 46.4% said no.

Malta's constitution required that the referendum be confirmed by a general election. Interest was at such a high pitch that planeloads of Maltese returned to vote, benefiting from reduced fares by state-owned Air Malta. In an election whose central issue was the EU, the government won almost 52%. Four days later ex–prime minister Adami traveled to Athens to sign the EU accession treaty, with formal membership following on May 1, 2004. The accession of Malta and Cyprus strengthened the EU's Mediterranean dimension. Malta replaced Luxembourg as the smallest country in the EU. It is also the most socially conservative, given the fact that abortion is illegal. The pope praised this during his 2010 visit. It joined Schengen in 2007. The government created consternation in the EU in 2014, when it vowed to sell EU passports to wealthy investors for €650,000 ($890,000) plus the purchase of at least €350,000 ($480,000) of property and €150,000 ($205,000) in government bonds. Applications poured in, but the EU launched legal action against such "golden passports" on the grounds that they give shelter to criminals and the corrupt.

In the past two decades, Malta has experienced robust annual economic growth (7% in 2017). Its public-sector finances are solid, with an overall public debt of 73% of GDP in 2013. In 1993 employment in the service sector overtook private direct production for the first time, signaling that Malta has a modern economy. Malta's per-capita income, at €11,170 ($17,000), exceeds that of Portugal and Greece and is the highest of any of the 10 countries that entered the EU in May 2004. Real growth has remained strong in recent years, and unemployment (5.8% in 2014) and inflation have stayed low. A source of possible vulnerability is the fact that its banks' assets are eight times the size of its economy.

The large government budget debt (6% of GDP in 2004) was brought down to 1.6% in 2015 in order to qualify for the euro, which went into circulation on January 1, 2008. Malta is a good example of how countries are inspired to reform their economies in order to meet EU entry requirements. Many of the Maltese government's austerity measures, such as freezing public employment, would have been unimaginable without the lure of the euro. Three-fourths of its trade is with the EU. As central-bank governor Michael Bonello noted, "For a trading nation like ours, it is one headache less." Of course, problems remain in addition to the 2009–2010 global recession. Internal market rigidities weaken competition and deter productive investment. Malta must reform its pension system and deregulate and privatize its economy. These matters remain contentious in the domestic political context. The generally peaceful country was stunned in late 2017 by the brutal assassination of Daphne Galizia, a well-informed anticorruption blogger who routinely excoriated the elites for their incompetence and negligence. Her last blog states, "There are crooks everywhere you look now. The situation is desperate."

FUTURE

Malta looks into a future of prosperous alignment with Europe as a full member of the EU. It adopted the euro in 2008, and its financial sector is eight times the size of its GDP. This makes it vulnerable to economic contagion from nearby Greece, Italy, and Cyprus. The economy is thriving, with a steady 7% growth and record low unemployment. Prospects for the tiny island nation looked good. But 2017 shined an unwanted international spotlight on Malta: Star investigative journalist Daphne Caruana Galizia, whose writings described a "climate of fear" and a "web of corruption" reaching the government, was murdered. Suspected of protecting friends who might have been involved in the murder, Joseph Muscat was replaced as prime minister by Robert Abela of the Labour Party.

Source: BBC

Source: BBC

Maltese celebrating an EU referendum victory

Iberian Peninsula

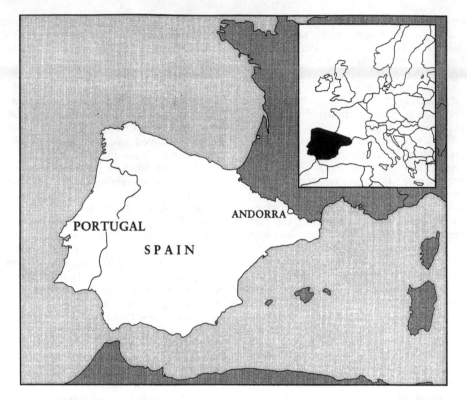

Contemporary Mutual Relations

The Iberian Peninsula is located at the southwest periphery of Europe, separated from the rest of the Continent by the high Pyrenees Mountains. Most of the population is settled around the coastal areas, with certain prominent exceptions, most notably Madrid, where a third of Spain's inland population is concentrated. The land area is distributed very unevenly among the three countries on the peninsula; Spain occupies about 85% of the space, and Portugal occupies most of the rest. Tiny Andorra has a very small chunk of mountainous land in the northeastern corner, and Britain still controls a strategically important toehold on the rock of Gibraltar at the southern tip of Spain.

Spain and Portugal do not have identical characteristics and problems. But they undeniably have very much in common. Perhaps most obviously, if one casts a quick glance at the globe, are their strategically significant locations. They are placed between the continents of Europe and Africa and face the Atlantic and, in the case of Spain, the Mediterranean Sea.

They possess islands in the Atlantic Ocean that are important links between the Western and Eastern Hemispheres: the Canary Islands are Spanish, and the Azores and Madeira are Portuguese. The Spanish also possess the Balearic Islands in the Mediterranean, the largest of which is the tourist mecca of Majorca. Spain also owns a few islands off the Moroccan coast and the cities of Ceuta and Melilla on the northern coast of Morocco. In 1987 the

Portuguese agreed to relinquish to China their small enclave of Macau on the southern coast of China. It was their highly valuable strategic positions which enabled Spain and Portugal to escape prolonged international isolation and to regain a status of relative respectability after 1945, despite the fact that until the mid-1970s they had authoritarian political systems that were repugnant to most persons in the democratic countries of the world.

These lands were formerly mighty colonial powers that spread their languages and cultures to colonies in Latin America and Africa, which were many times greater in size and population than the mother countries. Their empires have by now almost completely disappeared. The process of decolonization brought the fascist regime to its knees in Portugal in 1974 and was a consequence of the collapse of fascism in Spain in 1975.

Portuguese and Spaniards speak languages that are derived from Latin and that are very similar to each other. Although their words are spelled and pronounced somewhat differently, they understand the gist of what each other is saying. However, the Spaniard, except in Galicia, generally has more trouble understanding Portuguese than vice versa. Both countries are also predominantly Roman Catholic, and the Catholic Church has traditionally wielded considerable power and influence in them.

Both countries have similar political backgrounds, traditions, institutions, and problems. They had monarchies that

collapsed in the first third of the 20th century because of chronic political turmoil and violence. In neither country did experiments with republican and democratic forms of government go well, and in 1926 in Portugal and 1936 in Spain, the military seized power. Such seizure was quick and bloodless in Portugal but painful and bloody in Spain. The carnage that lasted for three years in Spain was portrayed with great force by Picasso's unforgettable painting *Guernica* and by Ernest Hemingway's moving novel *For Whom the Bell Tolls*.

Both countries lived under fascism for several decades. In the mid-1970s, they reemerged from fascism but experienced different transitions. Portugal dived headlong into revolutionary and democratic government and passed through two tense years of political experimentalism and uncertainty until it could gain its balance in the political center. By contrast, Spain experienced in 1975 a long and carefully planned entry into democracy and a restoration of the monarchy, which proved to be one of the major bulwarks of democracy.

During the last decade and a half of fascist rule, Spain underwent rapid and extensive industrialization. By contrast, Portugal did not, and it entered its new democratic era as the poorest country in western Europe. Although Spain was one of its poorest countries, its economic head-start over Portugal strengthened the inclination of Spaniards to regard the poorer, smaller Portugal in a condescending, patronizing way. In the 21st century, both experienced an economic boom until the worst recession in three decades hit in 2008.

In 1983 the Spanish prime minister traveled to Portugal for a summit designed to bury "historical ghosts." He called for "a new era in our relations." His Portuguese counterpart responded by announcing, "the mistrust and reservations which many Portuguese continue to feel toward Spain are no longer justified. Portugal has survived eight centuries of independence and national identity, and Spain, a great country, has respected and will continue to respect our independence." Clichés remain, though. Some Portuguese still see Spaniards as explosively talkative, opinionated, aggressive, arrogant, sociable, and dressed beyond their means, with a barely concealed contempt for Portugal, while the Portuguese are quieter, more reserved, and self-deprecating.

In 1986 they again pledged closer cooperation and agreed on frequent and regular meetings between the heads of their governments. As a symbol of closer ties, they agreed to build a bridge over the Guadiana River frontier. In 1989 they adapted their narrow-gauged railway systems to the one used in the rest of Europe so that rail cars will not need to be changed at Iberia's frontier with the rest of Europe. Portugal launched a major effort to streamline and modernize its rail system and highways toward Spain. Due to the recession, a planned high-speed rail line that would have linked Madrid and Lisbon in three hours rather than nine and therefore was seen as a milestone of modernization was canceled in 2012.

The results of their cooperation are clear: Between 1985 and 1989, trade trebled between them, and it doubled again in the 1990s. By 2015, 7.3% of Spain's export trade was with Portugal, and it is Portugal's largest supplier and its third-biggest market. In 2015 Portugal bought 31.5% of its imports from Spain, more than from any other country. Portugal sends 22.6% of its exports to its eastern neighbor. Spain trades more with it than with all of Latin America. After the US, Spain is the largest investor in Latin America, which provides 10% of Spain's direct foreign investment. Spain invests more heavily in Portugal than anywhere else in Europe. By 2003 there were over 2,500 Spanish firms in Portugal, compared with only 400 in 1989. Spanish banks control about one-sixth of Portugal's banking. Many multinational corporations deal with Portugal through their headquarters in Madrid. About two-thirds of foreigners visiting Portugal are Spanish. Portugal has about 300 companies operating in Spain. Its income per capita was half that of Spain in 1991. By 2012 its per-capita GDP had increased to $21,900, compared with $31,770 in Spain.

The relationship is asymmetrical, partly because of the different size and partly because of their past: Spain began encouraging competition and entrepreneurship during the Franco years, while Portugal did not. Spain was also largely free of the costly colonial wars, disruptive revolution, and political upheaval that set Portugal back. Some Portuguese worry about Spain's economic influence on them. In 2003, 40 Portuguese economists and business leaders published an open letter entitled "Patriots' Manifesto," warning against the steady move of their country's economic decision-making centers abroad.

Portugal and Spain have long traditions of military intervention in politics. Since the 19th century, soldiers in the peninsula have viewed themselves as the guarantors of their nations' sovereignty and integrity. Although soldiers in both lands symbolically show their loyalty to the state by kissing the respective national flags at ceremonial occasions, their commitment to democracy was not entirely certain, as the attempted coup d'état in 1981 by elements within the Spanish military revealed. In the constitution of Spain, the military as an institution is granted explicit political

powers. From the 1974 revolution until 1986, the highest political office in Portugal, the presidency, was occupied by high-ranking officers. The potential political activity of the military sets these nations off from the rest of western European nations, where the military is indisputably subordinate to the elected political leadership. Nevertheless, by the 1990s, democracy had set deep roots in both countries, and the danger of military intervention had diminished significantly. This adjustment to the western European norm was strengthened by Spain's entry into NATO in 1982 (Portugal was a founding member in 1949), as well as by both lands joining the EU in 1986.

The Early Period

Many things that Portugal and Spain have in common stem from 2,000 years of shared history. The most ancient human remains found on the peninsula, and so far in all of Europe, date from 800,000 BC. They were uncovered at the Atapuerca archaeological site in Burgos in northern Spain. It is likely that the first settlers began arriving on the Iberian Peninsula from 3000 to 2000 BC and were followed by waves of Celts, Phoenicians, Greeks, and Carthaginians from the rest of Europe and Africa. Most of the settlers were firmly unified under Roman rule by 19 BC, although individual tribes and cultures in the interior and northern parts of the peninsula continued to exist.

Tensions between the center and the periphery have continued to plague Spain and Portugal to the present day, although they are certainly less significant in contemporary Portugal than in Spain. The Romans brought the Latin language to the peninsula, from which both modern Spanish and Portuguese developed. They also brought Roman law and administrative practices. In the 4th century, they introduced Christianity to the area. From the important Roman cities in the south

Spain under Roman rule

and east of the peninsula came many of the Roman Empire's great leaders, such as Hadrian, Lucan, Marcus Aurelius, Seneca, and Trajan.

Visigoth and Muslim Rule

The collapse of Rome in the 5th century AD was followed by three centuries of rule in Spain by the Visigoths, who had stormed the peninsula by force. Taking advantage of divisions and quarrels among the Visigoth leaders, Moors from North Africa began crossing the Strait of Gibraltar in 711 AD. Within a very short time, Muslims controlled virtually all the Roman cities in the south and east of the peninsula. Iberian art and commerce bloomed under the new Muslim rule, which was, on the whole, tolerant toward Jews and Christians.

Christians ensconced in strongholds in northwestern Spain hammered away at the Muslim realm in Iberia. It was further weakened by quarrels and intrigues among the Muslim rulers themselves, whose grip on the peninsula began to loosen. The newly emerging kingdom of Castile, which combined with Leon and whose military prowess is symbolized by its hero El Cid, and the kingdom of Aragon, which in 1137 combined with Catalonia, slowly but steadily pushed back the Muslims. Their rule in most of the peninsula had been broken by the mid–13th century, although a small Muslim kingdom hung on in Granada until 1492.

Muslim Decline; Portugal and Spain Separate

While the reconquest of the peninsula from the Muslims was taking place, Portugal began to sever its ties with Leon and to establish itself as an independent country. In 1095 Count Henri of the House of Burgundy became the direct ruler over Portugal, and in 1140, after a nine-year rebellion against the king of Leon-Castille, Henri's son Alfonso Henriques declared himself to be the king of Portugal. The Burgundians ruled Portugal until 1383, during which time Portugal's borders were expanded from the original Oporto and Coimbra. Lisbon was snatched from the Muslims in 1147. Since the second half of the 13th century, Portugal's boundaries have been the same as today, with the exception of the district of Olivenza, which Spain took in 1801 and continues to hold.

Portuguese Exploration and Conquest

As a country facing the sea, Portuguese sights were always directed outward, and the bulk of the population was attracted to the coast because of this maritime and external commercial orientation. By 1337 their mariners had already landed on the Canary Islands. Overseas exploration was particularly encouraged by Prince Henry

Iberian Peninsula

The Iberian Peninsula about 1150

the Navigator (1394–1460), a farsighted and imaginative man who established a maritime school to assemble and extend his country's knowledge of the sea. Portuguese mariners explored the African coast, and in 1488 Bartolommeo Dias rounded the Cape of Good Hope and reached East Africa. In 1497 Vasco da Gama set sail for India. He not only reached it, but he also returned to describe the land to a receptive and curious Europe. Pedro Alvares Cabral landed in Brazil in 1500.

Such activity stimulated important advances in cartography and astronomy and also helped redirect the attention of Europe outward toward the larger world. It enabled Portugal to build up a massive empire which included Mozambique, Angola, and Guinea-Bissau in Africa; Brazil in South America; East Timor, Macau (which the Chinese gave to Portugal as a reward for its fight against pirates), and Portuguese India (with its capital of Goa) in south and southeastern Asia; and the Atlantic islands of the Azores and Madeira. Portuguese naval squadrons were stationed permanently in strongholds in or around the Atlantic and Indian Oceans. The Portuguese also began to send settlers to some of these imperial holdings, especially to the Azores, Madeira, and Brazil.

These colonial activities brought advantages to Portugal, as they did to Spain. They provided it with gold and other precious stones, silks, and spices, which were treasured in Europe at that time, and needed foodstuffs, especially wheat. They also provided an occupation for those portions of the feudal nobility who could no longer be supported by domestic agricultural production. Settlement in the colonies offered many Portuguese the hope for a better life. Finally, the desire to convert the peoples of the world to Roman Catholicism furnished the enterprise with a spirit of crusade and gave it a religious and spiritual justification.

Spanish Colonial Activities

Portugal's most avid competitor was its only neighbor—Spain. Spanish attention had remained largely focused on Iberia until 1492, which was a very significant date. In that year the Spanish captured Granada, the last Muslim foothold on Spanish soil. The triumphant entry into that city of Ferdinand and Isabella, whose marriage had sealed the unity of Aragon and Castile, signified the end of the seven-and-one-half-century reconquest of the Iberian Peninsula. Thus, Spain took shape as a unified kingdom over an ethnically diverse area three and a half centuries after Portugal. The year 1492 also saw one of Spain's darkest historical chapters: the expulsion of its Jewish community. It is estimated that 3.5 million Sephardic Jews are alive today, and about 800,000 live in

Israel. Approximately 100,000 still speak Ladino, a Spanish-based language. In 2013 the Spanish government decided to offer Spanish citizenship to those who can certify that they belong to this group without requiring them to renounce their present citizenship or to move to Spain. Portugal did the same in 2015.

The reconquest sparked a flourish of Spanish literature and artistic achievement that lasted at least two centuries. It also allowed Spaniards to concentrate their energy on overseas expansion and exploration. As every American schoolchild knows, the year 1492 was significant for another event: Christopher Columbus, a native of Genoa (Italy) working for the Spanish, sailed west in search of India but instead bumped into the island of Santo Domingo in the Caribbean. His discovery opened the eyes of Europeans to an entirely new part of their world and launched an era of Spanish colonialism that spread Hispanic culture and languages to dozens of modern-day countries.

In order to minimize a potentially dangerous rivalry between Spain and Portugal in the wake of Columbus's discovery, the sovereigns of the two countries agreed in the Treaty of Tordesillas (1494) to divide the world in such a way that Spain would receive the Philippines (named after the Spanish king) and most of the Western Hemisphere (including large chunks of the contemporary US, such as California, the Southwest, and Florida), with Portugal receiving what is now Brazil and parts of Africa and Asia. Both countries continued generally to observe this agreement, which had the pope's approval, but to their consternation, other interested powers, especially Britain, France, and the Netherlands, did not.

Like Portugal, Spain had several different motives for establishing and maintaining an empire. Dominican and Franciscan friars were always close on the heels of the conquistadores in order to convert and educate the native populations. Also, the conquistadores, the royal court, and the private companies that stood behind them clearly sought wealth, status, and power. The Spanish kings insisted that all trade with the colonies be conducted through Seville and be reserved for Castile, although most of the trade was actually organized by Genoese and southern German merchants.

The Spanish kings also claimed one-fifth of all precious metals imported from the New World. Such metals greatly enriched the Spanish treasury, but they also heated inflation within Spain and created serious economic distortions. This wealth was used to add glitter to the royal and noble courts, to finance massive Spanish imports, and also to finance Spanish armies and navies. These military forces were constantly embroiled abroad maintaining an empire which encompassed the present-day BENELUX countries; Italy; and, through the Hapsburg throne, all of the Austrian Empire. Throughout the 17th century, Spanish money and troops also supported the Catholic struggle against Protestantism. Since almost none of its wealth was invested in productive facilities within the home country itself, Spain remained poor despite its temporary wealth.

Temporary Unity

The 16th century had been Portugal's "Golden Age," but it was dealt a devastating blow in the aftermath of events in Morocco, where King Sabastião and much of the nobility were slain while trying to protect the kingdom's holdings there. Spain claimed the Portuguese throne on the grounds that the mother of King Philip II of Spain was descended from Portuguese nobility. Thus, in 1580 the two countries were united in a dual monarchy, which was supposed to leave the Portuguese with domestic autonomy. In fact, Spaniards were appointed to Portuguese offices.

Despite initial economic advantages that Portugal gained through a dropping of customs barriers between the two lands, it was compelled to enter and to help finance through heavy taxes a costly and protracted war against England. This cost Portugal not only most of its lucrative markets in the Orient but the bulk of its fleet, as well. Both consequences directly benefited England and the Netherlands. Disillusioned about Spanish rule and taking advantage of a revolt in Catalonia, the Portuguese also revolted. French support helped the rebellion succeed in 1640, when the House of Bragança was established as the Portuguese ruling family (which it remained until the monarchy fell in 1910). The Portuguese still mark the anniversary of this revolt that ended Spanish rule, and much of their subsequent history can be summarized as a struggle against absorption by its big neighbor. The Spanish did not accept Portuguese independence without a fight, though, and until 1668 they struggled unsuccessfully to win back the country. As late as the early 20th century, King Alfonso XIII, grandfather of currently reigning King Juan Carlos, was considering the annexation of Portugal.

In order to guarantee that it would never again fall under Spanish domination, Portugal entered an alliance with the sea power Britain, which always had a sharp strategic eye for coastal countries that could be useful allies. This alliance lasts into the 21st century. The struggle against Spain affirmed and strengthened Portuguese national identity, which still defines itself most clearly in terms of its distinctiveness from the Spanish nation. The loss of many of its colonies and markets in the Orient necessitated a shift of Portugal's colonial attention from the Indian Ocean to Brazil. The revenues from Brazilian sugar, coffee, diamonds, gold, and other minerals became extremely important to the Portuguese economy.

Separation

The separation of Portugal from Spain was, for the latter, merely one of a series of foreign political setbacks following the destruction of the Spanish Armada, a mighty fleet sent to subdue England in 1588. Spain squandered its wealth on endless wars on the European Continent, and its European holdings were gradually whittled away. The last blow was the War of the Spanish Succession that erupted after the death in 1700 of Charles II, the last of the Hapsburg rulers in Spain. This conflict ended in the establishment of a Bourbon dynasty in Spain. In practical terms, this meant French domination of Spain's foreign policy. Occasionally Spain seemed about to be ready to rear its proud head once again and to assert primacy in its own affairs. However, any chance of Spain's restoring its former imperial grandeur and power was undercut by that social and political convulsion which changed Europe irrevocably—the French Revolution and the accompanying French military conquest of most of Europe.

As an ally of England, Portugal intervened much earlier, in 1793, in the war against revolutionary France. In 1807 the French entered Portugal, prompting the royal court to flee to Brazil. French troops also invaded Spain, and in 1808 Napoleon placed his brother Joseph on the Spanish throne. Many Spaniards valiantly resisted this foreign invasion, as Goya's powerful paintings portray.

The Grand Army was nevertheless able to conquer most of the peninsula by 1809. Yet its hold on Spain was only temporary. The English Duke of Wellington, supported by Spanish guerrillas, advanced from Portugal and delivered a crushing defeat at Talavera in 1809. By 1811 the French had been driven out by British troops and by Portuguese soldiers who had been placed under the command of an English general, Lord Beresford. In the Portuguese king's absence, Beresford continued to dominate Portuguese politics long after Napoleon's troops had departed. Wellington defeated the French again at Vitoria in June 1813.

Both Spain and Portugal faced the post-Napoleonic era with restored monarchies but with the liberal ideas of the French Revolution in the heads of many of their citizens. These ideas would not permit a quiet return to the authoritarian government of earlier years. Also, these new notions, combined with the long rupture in reliable communication with their American colonies, spelled the end of their empires in the Western Hemisphere. The Spanish and Portuguese had fought heroically for their national independence. Now their American colonies decided to do the same.

Driving the Moors from Spain

381

Spain

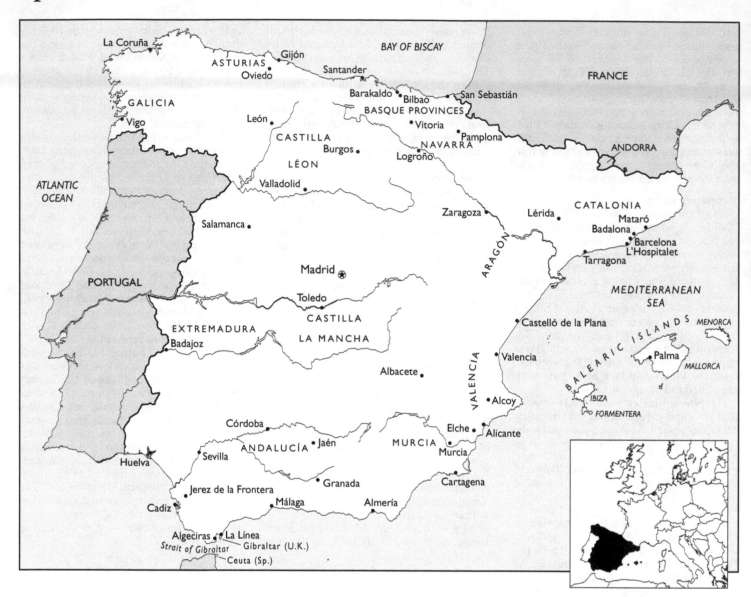

Area: 194,897 sq. mi. (504,750 sq. km), some 640 miles (1,034 km) from east to west, 530 miles (848 km) from north to south. Slightly more than twice the size of Oregon.

Population: 46.8 million.

Capital City: Madrid (pop. 3.2 million, almost 6 million in greater Madrid region).

Climate: Varying from Madrid's 2,000-foot (610 meters) elevation, making the area cold in winter and hot and dry in summer, to the Mediterranean coast that is hot in summer, mild in winter.

Neighboring Countries: France, Andorra (north); Portugal (west); Morocco lies only eight and a half miles across the Strait of Gibraltar.

Languages: Spanish (primarily the Castilian dialect), with Catalan, Basque, Galician, Valencian, and regional languages which are once again flourishing and comprise an important part of the tongues spoken every day.

Principal Religion: Roman Catholic.

Chief Commercial Exports: Machinery, iron and steel, fruits and vegetables, footwear, textiles, energy products.

Major Trading Partners: EU (66.6% of exports and 56.9% of imports), France (17.7% of exports and 11.4% of imports), Germany (10.1% of exports and 12.5% of imports), Portugal (7.9% of exports), Italy (7.8% of imports and 6.8% of imports), China (5.9% of imports).

Currency: Euro.

National Holiday: October 12 (1492), *Dia de la Hispanidad* (Columbus Day). This holiday was called *Dia de la Raza* until it was changed before the Franco era. A second national holiday is December 6 to commemorate the passage of the present constitution by referendum in 1978.

Chief of State: His Majesty King Felipe VI (b. 1968). Married Princess Letizia Ortíz, May 22, 2004. Proclaimed king of Spain, June 19, 2014.

Heir Apparent: Her Royal Highness Crown Princess Leonor of Asturias (b. 2005).

Head of Government: Pedro Sánchez, President of the Government (since June 2018).

National Flag: Three horizontal stripes of red, yellow, and red, with the center yellow stripe twice as wide as the red ones. The Spanish royal crest is set off-center on the left of the flag.

For as long as most people could remember, Spain was, by European standards, a poor, thinly populated country on the edge of the Continent and separated from the rest of Europe by more than the high peaks of the Pyrenees Mountains. Its people had produced a language and a high culture which had been spread to most countries in the New World, but in politics it appeared excessively passionate, polarized, and generally ungovernable by any other means than authoritarianism.

The Spanish kings had never thoroughly integrated this heterogeneous country, and at times it threatened to split apart, with the Basque and Catalan Provinces in the northeast leading the way. Unceasing political instability prevailed, punctuated by longer or shorter periods of authoritarian rule. The last such interlude lasted until the end of 1975 and was guided by a diminutive general named Francisco Franco, called El Caudillo ("the leader"). His fascist regime made Spain an embarrassment to and, for a long time, an outcast in western Europe.

After Franco's death Spain began to move in a different direction. Indeed, he would scarcely recognize the land he claimed to have "saved" in 1939. Wishing both to create a parliamentary democratic order and to avoid a bloody repeat of the turmoil and civil war of the 1930s, the major contenders for political power have displayed a remarkable willingness to cooperate with each other and to moderate their political demands.

Spain's regions have been offered autonomy statutes that reduce Madrid's hold on the country's politics. Communist and socialist-led trade unions operate freely and act with moderation and responsibility. Many political parties compete for seats in the national parliament, but Spanish voters have overwhelmingly supported the moderate democratic parties in the political center. A king, picked and trained by Franco, has shown unswerving determination to create and to preserve a democratic order and has therefore won the admiration of most of his countrymen. Spain also moved into western Europe by joining NATO and by entering the EU, which enjoys a broad consensus within the country.

It is true that every November the anniversary of Franco's death still brings some Spaniards out into the streets to wear and wave fascist paraphernalia and to hear inflammatory speeches against the new democratic order. There is also a small minority within the army that sometimes vents its dissatisfaction with the new Spain and makes democrats nervous. But democracy in Spain, as well as in Portugal, is working. The Pyrenees are no longer the edge of Europe.

CONTEMPORARY HISTORY

The Post-Napoleonic Period

The liberation of Spain from French occupation and the restoration of the Bourbon dynasty by no means brought the country peace and stability. Spain's isolation from its American colonies during the Napoleonic Wars had loosened its grip and had given Latin American leaders a taste of local rule they liked. They therefore revolted. Again, the Spanish treasury was drained by protracted war far from its own territory. After the disastrous Spanish defeat at the battle of Ayacucho in 1825, the vast and mighty Spanish Empire had been reduced to the islands of Cuba, Puerto Rico, the Philippines, and three Pacific archipelagos—the Carolinas, the Marianas (which included Guam), and Palaos. Spain kept these archipelagos for one year and then sold them to Germany in 1899.

Spanish domestic politics was marred by almost-continuous political, social, and economic crises. This turmoil began with the king's revocation in 1814 of the admirably liberal Cadiz Constitution, which had been approved in 1812. By 1820 the dim-witted Ferdinand VII had alienated many important groups, especially the liberals and the military, and in the midst of widespread demonstrations and riots throughout the country, the military revolted. In an unsuccessful attempt to salvage his throne, the king allowed the Cadiz Constitution to be proclaimed again, but it was exactly such democratic constitutions which most of the conservative monarchs of Europe could not tolerate. Therefore, in April 1823, French armies again invaded Spain on behalf of most other European powers (with the notable exception of England) and restored Ferdinand VII to absolute power.

The next decade and a half were filled with reaction and unrest, followed by another quarter-century of rule by generals and a scandal-ridden Queen Isabella II, who was finally deposed in 1868 by military officers. When they tried to appoint a Prussian Hohenzollern to the throne, they provided the spark for the war between France and Prussia in 1870, which resulted in German unification. A brief and unsuccessful republican experiment ended again in military intervention and the restoration in 1874 of the monarchy under Alfonso XII, the son of Isabella II. A parliament (Cortes), for which only property owners could vote, was also created. In order to achieve some measure of stability, the Conservative and Liberal Parties agreed to alternate power. However, this system of turno político had broken down by the end of the 19th century.

The Spanish-American War and Ensuing Turbulence

Spain was badly shaken in 1898 by its war against the United States. This conflict was sparked by an explosion of dubious origin on a US vessel, the Maine, which was anchored in Havana Harbor. American soldiers, including those led by Theodore Roosevelt's "Roughriders," entered the battlefield with the cry, "Remember the Maine!" The war left Spain with 200,000 dead in Cuba, a sorely humiliated officer corps, an empty treasury, and a denuded empire. The US took Cuba, Puerto Rico, Guam, and the Philippines, and Spain retained only a smattering of holdings in West Africa and Morocco.

Widespread domestic dissatisfaction increasingly began to manifest itself again, urban workers began to be attracted to Marxism and syndicalism (radically political trade unionism), and anarchism infected the downtrodden workers in Barcelona and the peasants in southern Spain. Corruption and inefficiency in Madrid, combined with bitter disappointment at losing the 1898 Spanish-American War (called "the Disaster") and many colonies, stimulated separatist sentiments in the Basque and Catalan regions. Political parties took shape. Political violence became commonplace, and Spanish politics was in a state of utter confusion. Between 1902 and 1923, the country averaged one government every 18 months.

Spain managed to remain neutral in World War I, but in 1921 it experienced such a stinging military reversal at the hands of the Moors at Annual in North Africa that public pressure forced the government to conduct an investigation of that institution which had never contented itself with mere military matters—the army. However, before the investigation could be completed, the military's rage at such "impudence" boiled over. The army seized power in 1923 and formed a government under General Miguel Primo de Rivera. Primo de Rivera's government banned all opposition parties, slapped severe controls on the press and the universities, and openly expressed great admiration for the kind of fascist political order that Mussolini was establishing in Italy.

The new Spanish leader did launch an extensive public-works program and, with the help of the French, ended the war in Morocco in 1926. But without the support of the masses or of the youth or intelligentsia, Primo de Rivera's authoritarian government could not survive the jolt which the worldwide depression gave to Spain and most other European countries at the end of the 1920s. He therefore resigned in January 1930. Demonstrations in favor of a republic and elections in which republican candidates won in all important cities became so worrisome that King Alfonso XIII was forced to flee the country April 13, 1931. The almost-immediate proclamation of the Second Republic (the first being in the early 1870s) unleashed such enthusiasm from its supporters that 200 churches were burned to the ground. Of course, such anticlericalism had been building up throughout the 19th century. This helps explain why the church supported Franco so strongly and why he protected it in turn.

Spain

Many Spaniards today look back very carefully to Spain's entry into democracy in 1931 in order to try to ensure that earlier mistakes which helped lead to the downfall of the democratic republic would not be repeated. The new constitution of December 1931 legalized all political parties and created a unicameral Cortes (parliament), to which the government was responsible. The new government under Manuel Azaña launched a full-scale attack on the old ruling pillars: the church, the army, and the wealthy. The Jesuit order was expelled, and fully state schools were established in order to eliminate religious influence over education. Large estates were confiscated, and the beginnings of a land reform were introduced. Railroads and the Bank of Spain were nationalized, the eight-hour workday was introduced, and the army officer corps was reduced by almost half.

It soon became clear that many of the new government's reforms were unrealistic. Both the delay in their implementation and the fear that they might actually be implemented brought peasants, workers, anarchists, fascists, and monarchists out into the streets. Spain was bubbling with conspiracies and intrigues. It experienced one government after another; in the five years of the republic, there were 18 different governments. This came to a head shortly after the beginning of 1936, when a Popular Front on the French model, composed of socialists, communists, anarcho-syndicalists, and Basque and Catalan nationalists, was formed and won an electoral victory. The assassination on July 13, 1936, of the former finance minister under Primo de Rivera, Calvo Sotelo, was the cue for the army to launch a long-planned coup against the republic.

Civil War

On July 18, 1936, a diminutive general, Francisco Franco, flew to Morocco from the Canary Islands and drew his sword against the republic. Within a few days, the revolt spread to garrisons within metropolitan Spain, and within 10 days troops were flown in German planes from Morocco to secure strategically important positions. Unlike early military rebellions, which usually succeeded very quickly, this one thrust Spain into a savage three-year civil war that not only destroyed democracy and liberty in Spain but also temporarily moved the country into the center of the world political conflict between the proponents and opponents of fascist dictatorship.

The revolt was successful in certain parts of Spain but not in such key cities as Madrid. Also, the provinces of Catalonia and Basque strongly supported the republic because the latter had guaranteed them a large measure of autonomy. Further, Franco did not have the support of the navy, the air force, and part of the army.

It is probable that the coup would have collapsed within a few months if Franco had not received crucial military assistance from fascist Germany and Italy. The Italians sent more than 1,000 planes, 4 infantry divisions, tanks, artillery, and other military equipment. The German contribution was smaller but highly effective. The Germans sent a tank battalion. The major contribution was the Condor Legion, composed of four fighter-bombers, four fighters, one reconnaissance, and two seaplane squadrons. The German aerial bombing of the city of Guernica on April 26, 1937, outraged world opinion and prompted an indignant Pablo Picasso to paint his famous Guernica. Sixty years later Germany agreed to donate almost $2 million to the city in symbolic compensation for the destruction.

The republic called for help, but France and Britain refused to respond to its calls and limited their reactions to verbal protests. It did have on its side some loyal army and naval units, as well as units hastily formed with trade unionists, students, and Catalan and Basque nationalists. In addition, 40,000 international volunteers came to fight for the republic. They were generally poorly equipped and insufficiently trained and were organized in such brigades as the Ernst Thälmann (German) and the Abraham Lincoln. The latter unit counted 2,800 Americans. In 2007 a new Spanish law allows former members of the International Brigades to apply for full Spanish citizenship without relinquishing their existing passports. Some elderly Americans have done that.

This conflict inspired to action many idealistic young people throughout Europe and the United States, who saw in Spain the only determined struggle against fascism. The Soviet Union also sent limited aid in the form of advisers, technicians, tanks, and aircraft. However, the Soviet Union itself was in the grips of a terrifying purge at home, which spilled over to communist units fighting in Spain. In such a state of paralysis, the Soviets withdrew their aid to the republic a year before the end of the war.

Ultimately the military balance tipped in favor of Franco's fascists. In the spring of 1939, armed resistance in Catalonia was broken, and soon thereafter Franco's forces entered the severely bombed and starving capital of Madrid. The human costs of this brutal civil war were extremely high: More than a half-million Spaniards were killed, and at least as many were forced to emigrate. The war left most Spaniards with an intense fear of another such armed conflict on their own territory.

Franco and Fascism

Despite Hitler's pressure and threats, Franco did maintain an official policy of neutrality during World War II, although

A victim of the civil war amid the ruins of her home

384

General Francisco Franco

he openly sympathized with Germany and Italy. He even sent a "Blue Division" of volunteers to fight on Germany's side against the Soviet Union from 1941 to 1943. But Franco was always sensitive to the direction political winds blew, and after disastrous German setbacks on the eastern front in 1943, he decided to maintain his official policy of neutrality more strictly.

Franco created an authoritarian, fascist regime, supported by the army and initially by the Catholic Church. This regime remained fundamentally unchanged until his death in November 1975. He always was skillful in playing different groups against each other, but he did not dare create any democratic institutions. The Cortes was restructured so that it could not effectively challenge Franco; in reality it was a cheerleader for the rulers. The news media were subjected to close censorship. Franco abolished all political parties except his own Movimiento Nacional (National Movement).

The right-wing Falangist Movement, which had elaborated fascist ideals for Franco in the early days, gradually declined in influence and ultimately became strictly an agency to administer the bureaucracy. The Catholic Church's support of the regime gradually waned as the years went on, but the Catholic lay organization Opus Dei did grow in influence, especially within the educational and economic spheres. The Opus Dei became more open to progressive ideas and was a force behind Spain's rapid industrialization and robust economic growth that began in the 1960s.

Although Franco was the undisputed dictator from the very beginning, in 1947 he officially made himself chief of state for life, with the right to appoint his own successor. He declared Spain to be a monarchy, but not until 1969 did he name Prince Juan Carlos of Bourbon, whom he had educated and groomed for years to prepare him for his new role, to be the new king upon his death.

Isolation and Economic Progress

Because of Franco's open sympathy with Germany and Italy during World War II, the victorious Allies initially isolated Spain in the international community and for years refused to allow it to enter the UN. But the Cold War brought many former enemies onto better terms with each other, and Spain was no exception. The emerging hostilities between the Soviet Union and the nations in the Atlantic alliance greatly enhanced the value of Spain's strategic location. Therefore, in 1953 the US reached an agreement with Franco providing for American financial assistance in return for the right to establish four air and naval bases in Spain. This agreement was of great military significance for the US, but Franco's many opponents never regarded it kindly. The former socialist prime minister Felipe González, for instance, admitted that his attitude toward the US had always been negative, in large part because the picture of President Dwight D. Eisenhower smilingly shaking hands with Franco had remained firmly etched in his memory.

All in all, the fascist movement failed to stimulate much mass enthusiasm in Spain. It rested on widespread apathy fed by most Spaniards' intense desire for order after the civil war. Franco had created a panoply of corporatist organizations that were designed to mobilize and control the diverse elements of society. But as years passed, dissatisfaction and unrest began to manifest themselves, since Spain's fundamental problems had by no means been solved. Labor and student unrest, high inflation, growing opposition with the church, increasing Basque extremism, and revolutionary events in neighboring Portugal beginning in 1974 continually chipped away at the foundations of the fascist state. Yet only one event could wipe away the trappings of fascism and set the process of democracy in motion: the death of Franco, which finally occurred in November 1975.

King Juan Carlos

The most visible sign for a new democratic spirit of reconciliation and national unity quickly became King Juan Carlos de Borbón y Borbón. Even former Communist Party chief Santiago Carrillo had to admit, "without Juan Carlos, Spaniards would probably be fighting each other again." Few persons had expected that the monarch would become a major linchpin for democracy in Spain.

Franco had chosen Juan Carlos (the grandson of former King Alfonso XIII) over the head of his father, Don Juan, who lived in Portuguese exile and who had always been an outspoken critic of Franco. From his father, Juan Carlos had learned several very important lessons: to install a democracy in Spain, to shun the everyday dealings of political parties, and never to play the army against the people.

Young Juan Carlos was an uninspiring pupil and rather introverted, especially after accidentally shooting his brother with an air gun at age 16. Remembering a suggestion the Italian fascist leader Benito Mussolini had once made to him, Franco brought the nine-year old Juan Carlos back to Spain in 1947 and had him educated under his watchful eye. The boy was sent to the army, navy, and air force academies in Zaragoza, Marín, and San Javier, respectively. He enjoyed his life at these academies, making contacts within the

Prince Juan Carlos as a schoolboy

Spain

military that later were to be important to him as king. He had plenty of time for his favorite hobbies of athletics, ham radios, and fast motorcycles. He also became a jet pilot, and he flew himself around Spain for official visits.

When Franco decided in 1964 that the young prince had had enough education, he entered a very trying phase in his life waiting for a task. He married Sophia, sister of the former Greek King Constantine, a public relations agent in London who was one of the king's few close friends. Not until 1969 was he officially proclaimed the crown prince after he had sworn allegiance to Franco's basic principles before the parliament and after he had had a serious argument with his own father over his decision to accept the Spanish Crown from Franco's own hand. He was therefore distrusted by Don Juan and by many Spanish democrats, who thought that the prince had become El Caudillo's stooge.

Many in Franco's coterie also distrusted him because he did not ingratiate himself to them. Their suspicions were fed by the fact that Juan Carlos began establishing contacts with political opponents of the Franco regime, including, through an intermediary, communist leaders in Paris. With Franco on his death bed in late 1975, Juan Carlos gave a revealing glimpse of his sentiments by flying to Spanish Sahara and telling the troops there that they would have to withdraw because Spanish colonialism had come to an end.

He was installed as king after Franco's death, but he proceeded cautiously.

Immediately after being sworn in, he rushed to visit Franco's body lying in state. In fact, the Spanish experiment of making a step-by-step transition from a dictatorship to a parliamentary democracy, while continuing to observe the existing laws of the land, was unique in European history. He temporarily retained Franco's last prime minister, Carlos Arias Navarro. Through wise appointments, he gained influence over the Council of the Realm, a small body whose only clear function was to ensure that the new regime would remain within the bounds of Francoism. By the summer of 1976, he was able to have Arias eased out of office and to have a man with reformist designs, Adolfo Suárez, appointed in his place. The king gave Suárez unmistakable instructions to proceed as rapidly as possible toward the goal which Juan Carlos shared with most of his countrymen: "to restore sovereignty to the Spanish people."

As king, Juan Carlos set about to demonstrate that the bitter controversies of the past could be ended. When he visited Mexico three years after becoming king, he requested that veteran republicans who had fled from Franco's rule be invited to the Spanish Embassy, where he received them with demonstrative cordiality. Also, in a public speech, he called the civil war a fratricidal tragedy; Franco had always referred to it as a "glorious crusade."

He chose to live in the relatively small Zarzuela Palace outside of Madrid rather than the stately palace his ancestors had built in the middle of the capital. He

prevented anything like a palace clique to congeal around him. He realized that most Spaniards, especially the young, are not ardent monarchists. After all, by 2013 kings had reigned for only half of the previous 90 years. Not since 1885 had a reigning Spanish king passed the Crown on to his offspring, as Juan Carlos did to Felipe VI in June 2014. Spanish royals lack the aura of timeless, inevitable continuity that is essential for monarchy. Many Spaniards had given their lives to establish or protect a republic. Juan Carlos kept protocol to a minimum and tried to lead a relatively austere private life. His patience, tact, shrewdness, and courage in guiding the nation won him respect even from some Spaniards who had always considered the very word "monarchist" an insult.

Seeds of Democracy

The National Movement (Movimiento Nacional), which Franco had formed out of various political movements, was withering on the vine. The best-known component of the National Movement was the fascist-oriented Falange, named after the infantry formations which Alexander the Great had called "phalanx." The trappings of fascist salutes; paramilitary youth organizations; and the calls to revitalize Spain through order, authority, and hierarchy remained, but membership in the National Movement had for most Spaniards become a mere formal prerequisite for a government job. In fact, many of Spain's foremost reformers after Franco's death, including Adolfo Suárez (who died

The ancient city of Toledo, capital of Spain under Roman rule and home of the illustrious artist El Greco

in 2014), under whose premiership Spain became a modern parliamentary democracy in the second half of the 1970s, had attained political prominence within the National Movement.

Spain felt its way slowly and nervously out of the authoritarian political order created and maintained by Franco. Many Spaniards looked back uneasily to the 1930s, and they saw certain parallels between that period and the 1970s. At both times political parties were legalized after dictatorships had ended, and the Communist Party supported the young democracy both times. At the beginning of the two democracies, the vast majority of Spaniards voted for the moderate parties of the center. Also, world economic crises set in at the inception of both Spanish democracies. Basque and Catalan nationalists demanded autonomy, and a fraction of their numbers resorted to grisly violence to provoke the military and press for their aims. Thus, in both eras, Spanish democratic leaders had to face a declining economy, a wave of strikes and demands for better wages, and extremist violence while creating a political order which would later be, in the words of King Juan Carlos, "a just order, equal for all," supported by "public activity as much as private activity, under legal safeguards."

Economic Progress

Despite the parallels between the 1930s and the 1970s, one must notice also the many significant differences between Spanish society in the heyday of Franco's rule and in the 1970s. One difference was

the evolution of the church in Spain, traditionally one of the most conservative in the entire Catholic world.

A further development that favored the post-Franco democratic experiment was economic progress. The recession of the 1970s was not nearly as deep as that of the 1930s and did not shake the democratic foundations of the European countries, as was the case earlier. Most important, Spain's economic structure has changed drastically since Franco seized power. El Caudillo sought to establish complete Spanish self-reliance, which amounted to sealing Spain off economically from the rest of the world. An international outcast after World War II, Spain was not permitted to receive Marshall Plan assistance. This greatly widened the gap between Spain and most of the rest of western Europe. But in 1950 the UN lifted the trade boycott against Spain, and capital and modern production and business ideas began to enter the country.

The result was a doubling of industrial production in the course of the 1950s. This upswing did bring a doubling of prices, which stimulated labor unrest, but it also gave Spanish technocrats the courage to draw up a Stabilization Plan in 1959. This significant plan devalued the peseta to a level that would favor Spanish exports, began to eliminate some unnecessary economic controls, buried the old economic isolation policy (known as autarky) in theory as well as practice, and headed Spain in a dynamic capitalist direction. This new direction was good not only for the living standards of the people but also for the

later stabilizing of democracy. In the last decade of Franco's rule, economic growth in Spain was an enviable 7% per year, one of the highest in western Europe.

Rapid economic growth not only increased the size of the middle class and gradually began to level out class differences, but it also changed the country's outlook and demography. As Spaniards' economic expectations grew, their eyes turned more toward western Europe, where democracy and prosperity were linked. Their contact with other Europeans was enormously increased by the lightning expansion of the Spanish tourism industry, which soon made Spain the number 1 tourist country in all of Europe. Although the bulk of Spain's tourists flock to the beaches, seldom venturing into the interior, they brought millions of Spanish into direct contact with western Europeans and their ideas and spending habits.

Many Spaniards themselves began to pull up stakes and seek a better economic life elsewhere. In the 1960s more than 3 million Spaniards moved from the poorer countryside into the country's major industrial areas, especially Madrid, Catalonia, and the Basque country. Well over 2 million Spaniards left the rural areas for industrialized countries north of the Pyrenees, especially to France, West Germany, and Switzerland, sending much-needed foreign currency remittances back to Spain. Entire villages were deserted.

The trend greatly reduced the number of Spaniards engaging in agriculture and left many pockets of rural poverty, especially in the south and in the province of

West of Madrid in the foothills of the bleak Sierra de Guadarrama stands El Escorial, the brooding, magnificent blue-gray slate and stone symbol of the unchangeable spirit of Spain. Combining a royal palace, basilica, monastery, and art gallery, it was built by Philip II, heir to the boundless riches of the New World, the most powerful monarch of the 16th century.

Spain

A younger royal family: (left to right) Princess Elena, now King Felipe, Queen Sophia, King Juan Carlos I, and Princess Cristina

Galicia. Such rapid industrial growth also left more polluted air, sea, rivers, and tap water in Spain. It transformed quiet, picturesque fishing villages into loud, overcrowded mass tourist places with tasteless and cheaply constructed hotels, an army of souvenir vendors and thieves, and much higher prices. Large parts of the beautiful coastline were scarred with factories, chemical and power plants, and blocks of apartments. Also, many of the suburbs around industrial cities shot up almost overnight and were often built without paved streets or medical, educational, and leisure facilities. Some became slums and centers for delinquency and crime. Spain paid a price for its rapid industrialization.

Yet Spain's social base had changed significantly. Workers increasingly began to own their own homes or apartments. They also began to buy cars and take vacations far from home. These so-called years of development in the final decade of Franco's rule (at least until the 1973 oil crisis) laid an important foundation for democracy after Franco died in 1975. As Germany had already demonstrated, young democracies thrive and grow stronger in an environment of economic prosperity.

Although Franco had tried to keep the people by and large politically apathetic, more and more Spaniards began under Franco to make public demands on the political system through strikes and demonstrations. Workers began to support the illegal trade union movement that grew out of the 1950s. Workers' committees (Comisiones Obreras) emerged in larger factories

to represent workers in negotiations with the management. By the 1970s they had successfully infiltrated the official unions, thereby weakening that prop of the Francoist system. In 1967 workers acquired the right to strike as long as such strikes were peaceful and strictly nonpolitical.

Franco's Legacy

The changes in the Catholic Church, the economy, and the social structure had already eaten away at the roots of Francoism long before El Caudillo had closed his eyes for the last time. But the main reason Spain's second attempt at democracy had a better chance to succeed was that Spaniards had a good memory. They remembered that four decades earlier half of Spain conquered the other after untold suffering and grief and that years of authoritarianism had followed. This time, Spaniards were ready for reconciliation with each other.

The willingness to ignore the things they once fought over has been referred to as a *pacto de olvido*, an agreement to forget. For example, even after more than two decades of socialist rule, many plazas still bore Franco's name, and almost all monuments and memorials one-sidedly honored Franco's rebels. This is no longer the case, even in his birthplace. In 2016 the Madrid city government published a list of 27 streets and squares it plans to rename. In 1977, two years after his death, an amnesty was granted to his collaborators, and unlike in several other European countries, there was no collective

declaration of guilt or rejection of the past, even though hundreds of thousands of Franco's opponents had been killed, sent to concentration camps, or forced into exile. There were no war-crimes trials or purges of the security apparatus. There was also a compromise on the new constitution: The left accepted a parliamentary monarchy instead of restoring the republic, while the right agreed to devolution for Catalonia, Galicia, and the Basque country, which it had fiercely opposed.

In 1980 the new democratic regime dared to sponsor the first balanced exhibition of the civil war. Videotapes, old news films, and tapes of the songs of both sides were played. Documents, flags, weapons, posters, and newspapers were shown. Rather than rekindling old passions, the exhibition seemed to strengthen a very powerful sentiment in contemporary Spain—never again civil war.

By 2014, half of all Spaniards either had not been born when Franco ruled or were too young to remember him. They form a new political class of Spaniards not involved in the old regime. Democracy has been firmly established and reinforced by NATO and EU membership, and it now seems less dangerous for the country's cohesion to glance backward into Spain's past. A flood of books on the Franco era has appeared, as well as a major exhibition (officially opened by the king) on the history of those forced into exile and a popular TV series, Cuéntame cómo pasó (Tell Me How It Happened), based on the day-to-day life of an ordinary Madrid family as Spain began to change in the 1960s. Many communal graves of republican fighters and sympathizers have been located for excavation and transformation into memorials. Groups of volunteers dig up mass graves and have returned thousands of remains to families for reburial. About 500 mass graves have been found in Andalusia alone. Perhaps the most famous victim whose remains are being sought is Federico García Lorca, widely considered the best 20th-century playwright and poet, executed at age 38 in 1936. Retrospection is no longer taboo in Spain, and the deal that led to the amnesty law is breaking down.

The generation of ex–president of the government José Luis Rodriguez Zapatero, elected in 2004, was too young to have taken part in the negotiated amnesia following Franco's death in 1975. One of his Socialist Party's campaign pledges was to change it. In 2007 his government passed a statute, known as the Law of Historical Memory, formally condemning Franco's rule for the first time. It mandated the removal of all fascist symbols, forbade all political acts at gravesites, dismissed the verdicts of the summary trials staged by Franco's nationalists during the civil war, and required local governments to fund the excavation of mass graves so that those republican victims who had been denied a decent burial could finally have one. The law honored not only the many war dead, including the hundreds of priests and nuns murdered by republican supporters, but also the countless victims of persecution by the later Franco regime. This was very personal for Zapatero: His grandfather, a captain in the republican army, was executed by Franco's forces in 1936. The law was opposed by the opposition Popular Party on the grounds that it is a mistake to revisit the past.

A further reminder of the country's undigested past was given in 2008, when an attempt to provide words to the national anthem, *La Marcha Real* ("The Royal March"), failed. The earlier text was dropped after Franco's death and never replaced. This left sports fans with nothing to sing when their anthem was played at contests. Therefore, the Spanish Olympic Committee launched a contest to seek proposals for the lyrics, and it received 7,000 entries. One was chosen, but then it had to be withdrawn a few days later amid criticism that it harked back to the fascist past. It opened with *Viva España* "Long live Spain"), the rallying cry of the Franco dictatorship. Anything smacking of fervent patriotism remains suspect. A further problem is the fact that this is one of Europe's most decentralized countries, with many groups within its borders that consider themselves "nations." One can hardly imagine a stirring anthem that would satisfy both left and right and not offend Basques, Catalans, or Galicians.

GOVERNMENT

Monarch as Head of State

Like his father, King Felipe VI works hard and is informed about the minutest details of his country's policies. However, unlike Franco, the monarch does not attend cabinet meetings, and he usually keeps himself aloof from day-to-day political affairs. He preserves his real political authority for critical issues and times. Some Spaniards were critical of Juan Carlos's outspoken support of joining NATO's integrated command structure and the EU's single currency. But communist leader Julio Anguita's demand in 1996 that the king resign unleashed a public furor. Polls in the same year revealed that the monarchy was Spain's most highly rated institution.

The king operates under strong constitutional constraints. However, he is able to influence the complexion of the government, and he is the supreme commander of the armed forces. He performs all the ceremonial duties of a chief-of-state.

Sometimes Juan Carlos could be very direct. In 2007 he participated in an Ibero-American summit of 19 Latin American countries plus Spain and Portugal in Santiago, Chile. When Venezuela's mercurial president, Hugo Chávez, kept interrupting the proceedings, repeatedly calling Spain's former ruler José María Aznar a "fascist," the infuriated king turned to Chávez and told him, "Why don't you just shut up?" Juan Carlos later stormed out of the meeting when Nicaragua's president, Daniel Ortega, supported Chávez and attacked Spanish businesses. His comment was a big hit back home. A ring tone featuring his words, "Por qué no te callas?" netted more than $2 million sales in a couple of weeks. Websites, T-shirts, and coffee mugs dedicated to the incident were on the market by Christmas.

The former king and Queen Sophia were at one time repeatedly voted as Spain's most respected public figures, but even she could step out of line. In 2008 she granted a series of candid interviews to a journalist that appeared in a book by Pilar Urbano, The Queen Up Close. Throwing her usual caution and neutrality to the wind, she attacked same-sex marriage, abortion, and President George W. Bush's "wars of vengeance and destruction in Iraq and Afghanistan." This enraged her husband and liberal Spaniards.

In the 21st century, the monarchy was probably respected more than it was at any time since 1800. Its popularity was strengthened in the aftermath of the March 11, 2004, terrorist bombings in Madrid, when then–crown prince Felipe led a march of millions through the streets of the capital to protest terrorism and to commemorate the victims of the attacks. This was the first time he had participated in a public rally.

In May 2004 Felipe married the commoner and divorced Letizia Ortíz, a beautiful and intelligent woman with a PhD from Mexico. She was a nationally known TV journalist. It helped her pass his parents' strict muster that she hails from Asturias along Spain's northern coast. This seemed particularly appropriate, since she was marrying the Prince of Asturias, the title given to a crown prince.

The wedding was a welcome diversion and catharsis for a shocked nation. Security concerns were so great that the Schengen Treaty permitting free movement across EU borders was suspended for a week, and Madrid's city center was blocked to traffic for almost 24 hours. There is a historical precedent for such caution, since his great-grandfather Alfonso XIII was almost killed at his wedding in 1906, when a Catalan anarchist threw at the newlyweds a bomb wrapped in a bouquet of flowers.

Felipe and Letizia have two daughters, Leonor (b. 2005) and Sofia (b. 2007), who are next in line for the throne after their father. All political parties are in agreement that the law of male primogeniture should be abolished in order to permit a woman to ascend the throne before her younger brothers. Such a constitutional change requires a referendum, and some fear that it could degenerate into a plebiscite between monarchists and republicans that could threaten the monarchy itself.

The years 2012–2014 were bad ones for Juan Carlos. His family was acutely embarrassed by a corruption scandal centered on his son-in-law Iñaki Urdangarin, Duke of Parma and husband of third daughter Cristina. A former Olympic handball player from a wealthy Basque family, he was investigated for tax evasion, money laundering, misuse of public funds, and siphoning €6 million ($8.2 million) from his nonprofit Nóos Foundation. The couple ran up company credit card and mortgage debt, and their mansion in Barcelona and three other properties were seized to pay them. Cristina was implicated and became the first close relative of a king in modern times to stand in a criminal trial. She faced the lesser charges of tax fraud, and she enjoys no immunities or privileges.

The ex-king himself blundered badly in taking part in an expensive elephant hunt in Botswana in the midst of Spain's deepest recession in decades and just weeks after claiming he could not sleep at nights because of youth unemployment. The only reason the public found out was

Spain

**Ex-president of the government
Mariano Rajoy**

that the increasingly frail monarch, who was honorary president in Spain of the WWF, a worldwide conservation group, had to return home early for emergency hip-replacement surgery. Since Spaniards were almost universally critical of him, he went on TV to apologize to the nation: "I'm very sorry. I made a mistake, and it won't happen again."

For the first time, the royal family's popularity sank below 50%. Only half the respondents in 2013 said they had a good or very good opinion of his reign, down from 72% a year earlier. Two-thirds (62%, up from 45%) told pollsters in 2014 they wanted Juan Carlos to abdicate in favor of the far more popular and untainted 46-year-old Felipe, who was self-assured, knowledgeable, and well-prepared for the job. (He did so shortly thereafter.) Fifty-five percent wanted the country to remain a constitutional monarchy; 36% favored abolishing the monarchy altogether. The decline in support is especially strong among the youth and political left.

One commentator noted, "The protective shield of the royal family has simply disappeared." The royal family is sometimes booed and ridiculed in public. Taboos concerning the king's private life have fallen away, and almost anything has become fair game. How did Juan Carlos acquire so much personal wealth when he started with almost nothing? How does the family spend its €7.78 million ($10.65 million) budget? The king agreed to publish details about this: He received a salary of €292,752 annually ($400,000), plus €152,233 ($208,500) for "cost of representation." Queen Sophia was paid €63,234 ($86,630), plus €68,505 ($93850)

for "representation." Princess Cristina gets nothing. Roughly half of the family's overall €7.78 million budget is spent on personnel.

Why did Juan Carlos give a former lover €65 million, paid out of illegal involvement in a Saudi rail contract? Spain's supreme court opened an investigation, which prompted the former king to go into voluntary exile. Juan Carlos is toxic, and Felipe will struggle to win back the respect he had won.

A handsome six-foot-five former Olympic yachtsman, Felipe VI is the first Spanish king to attend university: the School of Foreign Service at Georgetown. He speaks four languages, including French and Catalan, and attended all three Spanish military academies. Unlike his father, he is rigid and distant, rarely showing emotions. But he restored popular faith in the royal house. Monarchist sentiment has fallen sharply. Parliament had to approve of his accession. The event on June 19, 2014, was devoid of pomp and glamor. No foreign royals or statesmen were present, nor was his father. The crown was not put on his head, nor was the scepter put in his hand. He said his task is to represent a "renovated monarchy for a new age."

Parliament and Government

The king influences the selection of the president of the government and the cabinet, and he formally appoints both. The cabinet is technically not responsible to the Cortes. However, according to recent practice, a government is expected to have a majority in the Chamber of Deputies or at least to have the support on key votes of a majority of deputies. The leader and most important political figure is not called "prime minister," as in most European democracies, but "president of the government."

A national referendum in December 1976 established a bicameral parliament. In another referendum in December 1978, 87.8% of all voting Spaniards approved of a new constitution, which contained few traces of Francoism.

The upper house of the Cortes, the 259-seat Senate, is the less important chamber. Senators are elected in two ways: 208 are chosen by direct election in provincial constituencies in an electoral system that gives each voter four votes. Each provincial constituency selects four senators regardless of population. This is designed to protect the interests of the smaller provinces. There are variations for the Balearic and Canary Islands. The enclaves of Ceuta and Melilla choose two each. The remaining 51 are chosen through proportional representation in the autonomous communities (regions). Each region chooses one senator and an additional one for every 1 million

inhabitants. The senators are designated by the parliament of each region in a manner that differs from region to region. This complicated system is one indication of the extent to which Spain had become a federal state. The king is no longer permitted to appoint senators.

The 350 members of the lower house, the Chamber of Deputies, are elected by a modified form of proportional representation by which voters choose from a list established by each party. Independent candidates are forbidden to run for election unless they can combine to form a list. Seats are distributed to the various provinces according to population, with the smallest province receiving at least three seats.

The electoral system is designed to favor the large parties at the expense of the smaller ones. For example, in the 2008 parliamentary elections, the two largest parties won 84% of the votes and 323 of 350 seats; that percentage is steadily shrinking: 73.4% and 296 seats in 2011 and 50.7% and 213 seats in 2015. Parties have the power to expel maverick parliamentarians from the party but not to take their seats away. This possibility strengthens members' loyalty toward their parties. One can only marvel at the way the Spanish, who were not permitted to vote in free elections for more than 40 years, could in the early years of the democracy competently sort their way through more than 60 parties and groups, using two different electoral systems at the same time, and produce a similar result in both houses of the Cortes. In 2011, over a third were women.

Political Parties

In 1977 Spain's major parties signed the Moncloa Pact with each other, named after the small governmental palace in Madrid. By signing this pact, the parties agreed to drop their party dogma for the good of the country. The voters appreciated the major parties' moderation. In the first free elections since 1936, the Spanish showed their preference for the parties that are unmistakably in favor of the democratic order. The more radical parties of the left and right found themselves represented in parliament but without anything close to a majority.

Political parties entered the post-Franco era with well-founded nervousness. In Spain's past, parties were always plagued by division. Like Greece, Spain was one of the few European countries to experience a civil war in the 20th century. The political parties had been in the thick of that tragic struggle. From 1939 to 1975, they had been unable to operate freely, and most of them had been driven underground or into exile, where their members were often isolated from each other and where their leaders had great problems in establishing and maintaining unity. They also had difficulty following political developments within Spain

When Franco died, the parties had to organize themselves very quickly. Fortunately Spain had an intelligent and able king who could stabilize the transition while the democratic parties prepared themselves. Portugal had not been so fortunate and had to experience two years of chaos before the moderate democratic parties could gain their footing.

The Socialists

Only two of the major parties existed before 1975. The Spanish Socialist Labor Party (PSOE) which, together with the Catalan Socialist Party and the Basque Socialist Party, is generally referred to as the Socialists. Founded in 1879, it is the oldest Spanish party. Yet it acquired a young image after a thorough change of leadership in the early 1970s.

Its former leader Felipe González was an attractive and charismatic man who was a labor lawyer and who had engaged in anti-Francoist underground activity. He and the other leaders were able to lead the PSOE from a radical leftist Marxist stance during the Franco era to a pragmatic political course that sought to open the party toward the political center. He was a master of compromise, tactics, and organization.

A majority within the PSOE decided in 1976 to call itself Marxist, over the urgent protest of González. The latter argued that the party should return to the ethical and undogmatic socialism of the party's founders and consider Marxism merely as "an interesting intellectual exercise, but not the holy writ." He, himself, publicly declared that he was not a Marxist. González resigned in protest, and as a result the popularity of the party plummeted. Therefore a special party congress was called in 1979 to vote by 86% to reinstate him as head of a moderate party executive committee. The PSOE is still a party with a broad political spectrum, but González brought the left wing within the party largely under control. The PSOE calls for a classless, pluralistic, democratic, and decentralized Spain with a market economy. Its slogan is "Socialism is freedom!"

The party is strong in industrial centers, and many large cities have Socialist mayors. It is also strong in the agricultural region of Andalusia. It is the only socialist party in southern Europe that has strong support from a significant independent trade union, the UGT. It also has a well-developed local base, so it is the only Spanish party with solid roots in the factories, local neighborhoods, and national and regional parliaments.

González was sometimes accused of abandoning socialist principles by failing to redistribute wealth. The charge is not entirely fair. During his four terms, education spending rose, an the school leaving age was raised to 16 and the number of university students doubled. Health services and pension rights were extended to the entire population, and a nation-wide unemployment benefit scheme was created. His moderate, pragmatic party personified Spain's post-Franco modernization.

González stepped down as leader in 1997. At the end of his era, Spaniards reflected on the dramatic transformation their country had undergone during his rule: Spain is solidly democratic. Francoism has lost its force, even though old Francoists have suffered little persecution. The army no longer intervenes in politics. The country is more decentralized, with more power having passed to the regions. The nature of Spanish socialism has changed to the extent that most now refer to themselves as "social democrats," and the middle class is no longer hostile to Socialists. In foreign affairs, he led Spain into the EU and NATO, and he permitted the US to retain its military bases in the country.

The party got a new leader in 2000: José Luis Rodríguez Zapatero, a 39-year-old lawyer from northern Castile who had won his first Cortes seat at age 26. Polls had indicated that his party would lose the 2004 elections, but everything changed in Spain on March 11, three days before the elections, when terrorist bombs in commuter trains killed 191 persons and injured more than 1,400. The conservative government's initial insistence that the Basque terrorist group ETA had committed the bloody act came to be perceived by many voters as deceptive and self-serving. The quickly emerging realization that the perpetrators were Islamic terrorists led some voters to blame the Aznar government's policy of supporting the US war effort in Iraq, which had been very unpopular in Spain, for allegedly bringing their country into the gun sights of fanatic religious killers. Zapatero had pledged to withdraw the 1,300 Spanish troops from Iraq, a promise that three-fourths of Spaniards favored.

A traumatized people, which gathered in the streets by the millions to protest terrorism, decided in record time to vote against the conservative government, whose leader's authoritarian and divisive style was increasingly resented. Voter turnout increased dramatically from 69% in 2000 to 77% in 2004. In a poll, 86% of respondents expressed the belief that the terrorist attacks had influenced the results, and 20% said they had galvanized them to vote. The Socialists were reelected in March 2008. Turnout was 75%. They still fell short of an absolute majority and had to turn to regional parties to put them over the top.

In the midst of the economic recession that boosted unemployment above 20% and required very austere measures to combat, Zapatero's approval rating plummeted. Zapatero will be remembered for the social issues he passionately championed. Same-sex marriage and accelerated divorce were introduced, abortion was decriminalized, and equality of the sexes was embedded in law.

In the parliamentary elections on November 20, 2011, the party was led by Alfredo Pérez Rubalcaba. The Socialists chose the date November 20 for its symbolism and warning to the electorate not to vote for the right: It was the day of death for both Franco and the Falange movement's founder, José Antonio Primo de Rivera. The Socialists lost a third of their seats. This was its worst defeat in 35 years. It was even worse in December 2015 and again in June 2016 under a new leader, Pedro Sánchez. It fell to a historic low of 22% and only 85 seats. Sánchez was reborn as leader. In June 2018 he took advantage of a string of PP corruption scandals to call for a vote of no confidence. He won and became president of the government in a shaky coalition of Podemos and Catalan and Basque nationalists. The two-party system has become a four-party one. His 17-member cabinet contains 12 women.

A few regional parties won seats in the Cortes. They include Basque Nationalists (PNV/EAJ), Amaiur (radical Basque nationalists), and Convergence and Union (CiU, Catalan nationalists). The Republican Left of Catalonia, the center-right Canary Coalition (CC), and the left-wing Galicia Nationalist Bloc (BNG) also ran candidates. Finally, there was Union, Progress, and Democracy (UPyD). Imagine having to sort through these minuscule parties to form a majority. Emerging from a Catalan party called Ciudadanos (Citizens) was a new national centrist party led by Albert Rivera. In 2015, it shot up to 40 seats. It is fiercely opposed to Catalan independence.

Emerging rapidly since its creation in January 2014 is the far-left antiestablishment party Podemos (We Can). Led by charismatic 38-year-old political science professor Pablo Iglesias (known simply as "the one with the ponytail"), it challenged PSOE and PP. Calling conservatives "the enemy," Podemos rails against corruption, austerity, and economic control by the EU and Berlin. It proposes higher taxes for the rich, a restructuring of Spain's external debt and the 35-hour workweek, and changes in the laws that "allow the rich to keep stealing from us." It captued 69 seats in 2015 and 71 in 2016. This inability to overtake the Socialists was a huge disappointment. It was the big loser. In January

Spain

2020, it entered a minority government with the Socialists.

The Communists

The Spanish Communist Party (PCE) has deep historical roots. Founded in 1920, it was heavily involved in the Spanish civil war on the republican side. The Communists worked closely with the Soviet Union's participants in the civil war. This collaboration was too close and gave Spanish Communists a clear look at Marxist-Leninist practices. This fact helps to explain why the exiled party was the first communist party in Europe to reject the Soviet model of communism and the notion of the dictatorship of the proletariat. It condemned the Warsaw Pact invasion of Czechoslovakia in 1968, as well as similar actions against Afghanistan and Poland in 1979 and 1981. In 1977 former party chief Santiago Carrillo published a book, Eurocommunism and the State, in which he repeated his contention that the Soviet model had so discredited itself that it was beyond rescue. The party continues this moderate, independent course. After Franco died, King Juan Carlos had sought Carrillo's advice. When Carrillo died at age 97 in September 2012, the king was one of the first to pay his respects. He called Carrillo "a person fundamental for democracy."

The party's operations within Spain began again long before the death of Franco. It built up party cells in the factories, neighborhoods, youth groups, hospitals, and even government ministries. It is still the most disciplined and best organized mass party in Spain, despite factional splits. The working class provides 80% of its voters, who are predominantly male. Its strongest areas are in the industrialized zones of Madrid and Catalonia.

Despite its turn from Stalinism and despite its pragmatic approach and support for the democratic regime, it had little electoral success. In the 1979 national parliamentary elections, it received only about 10% of the votes, and it has declined steadily ever since. Combining forces with other elements of the old Marxist left under the banner United Left (IU), it wins a few seats. It is able to lure the votes of some dissatisfied socialists.

It has become almost irrelevant in Spanish politics. While its cells are well entrenched in numerous organizations in the country, it lacks popular support. Its membership had fallen to about 62,000 from its peak of 200,000 in 1978. Although it is supported by the Workers' Commissions, this most powerful trade union federation is losing ground to the socialist-dominated UGT.

Some Spanish are still aware of the remorseless and cunning tactics that the

EL PAIS

MIÉRCOLES 14 DE ABRIL DE 2004
Año XXIX. Número 9.813

DIARIO INDEPENDIENTE DE LA MAÑANA

EDICIÓN EUROPA
www.elpais.es

España y varios países europeos piden a sus ciudadanos que salgan de Irak

Un portavoz de EE UU afirma que hay 40 secuestrados de 12 países

La inseguridad de Irak y la oleada de secuestros de extranjeros en los últimos días —un portavoz de EE UU en Bagdad informó ayer de que hay 40 rehenes de 12 países— ha hecho saltar las alarmas en varias cancillerías acreditadas en la capital iraquí. España, Alemania, Francia, Portugal y la República Checa han pedido a sus ciudadanos que no viajen al país árabe y que salgan todos aquellos cuya presencia no sea imprescindible. "Hay que extremar las precauciones", afirmó ayer el encargado de negocios español, Marcos Vega.

El clérigo Hazem al Arayí, al ser detenido ayer en un hotel de Bagdad. / AP

El diplomático aconsejó ayer a los residentes y periodistas españoles que, mientras dure la actual situación, "lo prudente es que se reduzca el personal al mínimo imprescindible y que quienes tengan que estar en Irak eviten desplazamientos por carretera y restrinjan sus movimientos al máximo". Francia, Alemania y Portugal fueron más lejos y recomendaron a sus ciudadanos salir de Irak.

El Gobierno francés exhortó al centenar de compatriotas que se encuentran en Irak a que abandonen el país y pidió el aplazamiento de cualquier viaje previsto. "La situación evoluciona como lo temíamos desde el comienzo de la crisis", afirmó ayer el

RELEVO CON DOSSIERES. El presidente del Gobierno en funciones, José María Aznar, y el líder del PSOE, José Luis Rodríguez Zapatero, cerraron ayer en La Moncloa, durante un desayuno, el traspaso de poderes. En esta ocasión primó la cordialidad y se alcanzó un compromiso: los ministros entrantes, que previsiblemente jurarán sus cargos el domingo, recibirán informes sobre la situación en cada departamento. Página 17 / Editorial en la página 12

Zapatero depende de ERC para salir investido en primera votación

Former presidents of the government, Aznar and Zapatero

Communists used during the civil war to gain control over socialists and leftist republicans. Their heavy-handedness caused many Spanish to forget their more moderate actions during the popular front days before the outbreak of hostilities. Although the PCE now advocates a "peaceful road to socialism," there are several other ultraleft and violent groups in Spain that call themselves "communist." They help keep alive the inclination of many Spaniards to associate communism with unrest and violence.

The hardest nut for the splintered PCE to crack was the presence of an attractive Socialist Party for Spanish voters who want a moderate, democratic leftist-oriented party. In fact, the Communist Party faces a dilemma: It knows that no party in Spain has a chance without a democratic program and policy. But the more the PCE moderates itself and embraces democracy, the more it becomes indistinguishable from the PSOE and Podemos. Thus, there is little reason to vote for the PCE, which has become politically marginalized.

The Political Right

The existence of two parties on the political left that once could together capture about half of the votes presented a serious challenge to the more conservative political forces. The die-hard supporters of the Franco dictatorship had to learn through stinging electoral defeats that Francoism

could not survive in Spain without El Caudillo himself.

The two dominant parties in Spain—the PSOE and the People's Party (PP, until 1989 called the Popular Alliance, or AP)—support the democratic order; this makes the present political situation far different from the early 1930s.

The most conservative of the major parties, the People's Party, was refounded, renamed, and revamped in 1989. At first it thought it could win votes by hammering against crime and the alleged Marxist danger and thereby polarizing the society. Young thugs identifying themselves as AP adherents roamed the streets with sticks and bicycle chains attacking persons wearing Socialist badges. The result was a miserable showing in the 1977 elections.

In post-Franco Spain, the word "right" is still a red flag for many voters, who want to see any conservative policies advocated from the center-right. The party decided to move closer to the political center and to draw a clear line between itself and the antiregime parties on the right. It rejects violence, supports the monarchy, advocates reforms and a "social market economy," and opposes monopolies. It seeks a broad alliance of voters.

Its former leader was Manuel Fraga Iribarne, one of Spain's most colorful politicians. Like almost all earlier leaders of the party, he was a high functionary in the earlier regime. But he became a strong proponent of parliamentary democracy. He was such a skilled and hard-hitting speaker that he even scared some people in his own party. His party became Spain's second-largest political force, despite its lingering associations with the Franco era. Fraga left the national scene to become head of Galicia's regional government. This left the party free to construct a more modern alternative to the socialist government. In the 2005 regional elections, the defeat of Fraga and his PP cut the last political tie to the Franco era.

The party was led until 2004 by José María Aznar, who was able to do what other conservative leaders had failed to accomplish: unite former Francoists, Christian Democrats, and free-market liberals. A master of consensus politics, he insisted, "I am a centrist." He narrowly escaped an assassination attempt in 1995. The People's Party has the fewest members of any other major party and is well represented only in the upper civil service and the army. PP is particularly strong in small towns and predominantly rural areas. Its views are expressed by La Razón, a newspaper that few read. Most conservatives read El Mundo, which often supports the PP. The monarchist, conservative Madrid daily ABC is not important.

Approaching the 2004 elections, Aznar honored his promise to serve only two terms as president of the government. He turned over leadership of the party to his handpicked successor, Mariano Rajoy. But because of the tragic bombings on March 11, 2004, emotional and angry Spanish voters threw out the PP government, despite the economic accomplishments which had made it the favorite for reelection. It vehemently rejected allegations that the Aznar government had deliberately sought to conceal evidence of the Islamist threat and that it had withheld information from voters to deny any link between its unpopular occupation role in Iraq and the Madrid bombings.

Post-Franco Spain has undergone five peaceful transfers of power, from the center to the left, then from the left to the right, again back to the left in 2004, then to the right in 2011, and back to the left in 2018. This demonstrates that democracy has come of age. In another way, Aznar's government represented a Second Transition (the title of his 1994 book): It brought to power a new generation of leaders in their 30s and 40s who were students when Franco died in 1975. The PP's leadership allayed Spanish fears that the old Francoist right would dismantle the welfare state and that fascist intolerance might return to Spain. Aznar had a strong historical motive to operate by consensus. Most of his policies—privatization of industries, full integration with NATO, and fiscal

Colonel Tejero brandishes a pistol on the podium of the Cortes.

austerity to qualify for the euro—continued the Socialists' program.

Aznar benefited from a booming economy and from his brand of government that purged the authoritarian reputation that once haunted the country's conservatives. His governance did not provoke the trade unions or the students, and street violence was practically unknown on his watch. He gradually withdrew subsidies from ailing industries; privatized nearly every publicly owned enterprise, including the steel industry, which he made competitive; closed the shipyards in Cadiz; lowered top tax rates from 56% to 48% and public spending from 48% of GDP to 40%; reshaped the welfare state; loosened the rigid labor market; and balanced the budget. Under his rule, Spain was the fastest-growing large economy in Europe. His stewardship of the economy was his government's greatest gift. He strengthened the delicate consensus that has maintained stability in Spanish politics since Franco's death. Aznar directed the country's politics into the center.

Aznar challenged nationalists' hold in the regions, and his party did well in elections there. His policy was one of national unity. He and his successor stressed that the constitution mandates that Spain remain one country. He refused to grant the Basques a referendum on self-determination or to talk to ETA terrorists until they renounce violence. He also enacted a controversial ad hoc criminal law threatening the Basque regional president if he dared conduct a referendum. Following the defeat of his party in 2004, he accepted a visiting professorship at Georgetown University in Washington, DC.

The PP achieved its biggest election victory ever in the 2011 elections. It raised its share of the vote from 40.1% to 44.63% and its seats from 154 to 186, an absolute majority. This was the largest parliamentary majority of any party in three decades. The PP already controlled two-thirds of the regions and 40% of the town halls.

Mariano Rajoy, a model of persistence who had already lost two elections, emerged as president of the government. The PP lost a third of its seats in the 2015 elections, but it captured 137 in 2016. This was short of an absolute majority in parliament. Although it won the most votes, it could not form a government. For 10 months Rajoy was democratic Spain's first caretaker president. Finally, in October 2016, the Cortes elected him as head of a minority government, ending the deadlock.

By June 2018 voters had grown tired of him and of a string of scandals involving the PP. He lost a vote of confidence and was replaced as president and as party leader. The new PP leader was Pablo Casado.

The Military and Politics

While Spain's parties are doing much to pull Spain's democratic forces together, there are certain elements that place strains on the Spanish constitutional order: the military, regional separatists, and a governmental bureaucracy in need of reform.

After Franco's death the civilians carefully removed the 40,000-man National Police from military control and gave the Ministry of the Interior equal power with the military over the 75,000-man Civil Guard. The latter troops, highly efficient, proud, and dressed in dull-green uniforms and black patent-leather tricorn hats, have been used since 1844 as an internal security force by the central government and under Franco as an apparatus of repression. No country can ever make an absolutely clean break with its past, and an essential fact of Spain's past is the military's arrogation to itself of special political responsibility. Every officer takes an oath "to preserve the unity of Spain," and article 8 of the constitution names the military as ultimate arbiter of Spanish sovereignty and constitutional rights.

Most of Spain's officers are politically conservative and highly disciplined. Most will obey whomever is in power. After the inception of democracy, many officers openly grumbled about the new kind of politics, which, they say, gave free rein to criminals, terrorists, opponents of a unified Spain, bickering political parties, and assertive trade unions. They also resented what they saw as politically motivated military promotions and neglect of the military's needs. By the end of the 1980s,

Spain

only about 9% of the central government's budget was spent on defense.

Soldiers also criticized the civilian government's failure to cope with domestic terrorism. These groups include the Basque separatists (ETA), a leftist-sounding GRAPO (the Spanish initials for "Groups of Antifascist Resistance First of October," which scarcely exists anymore), the rightist Apostolic Alliance, and the Warriors of Christ the King. All aim to destroy confidence in the government, polarize society, and (except ETA) provoke the armed forces to take over power and establish a dictatorship. Their motives are, of course, different.

The ultrarightists want a dictatorship for its own sake, and the ultraleftists want one as a prelude to some kind of Marxist paradise. It cannot be denied that these terrorists know their country's history very well. Domestic violence has time and again destroyed the constitutional order and provoked the establishment of dictatorships to restore order. Fortunately none of these groups poses a serious threat today. The chief terrorist threat to Spain now comes from radical Islamic groups.

The 1981 Attempted Coup

One event especially showed that the essential political issues of parliamentary supremacy and civilian control over the military had not yet been entirely solved within the first decade after the restoration of democracy. On February 23, 1981 (known in Spain as 23-F), only three weeks after President of the Government Suárez had announced his resignation, thereby plunging Spain into a parliamentary crisis, a colonel in the Civil Guard, Antonio Tejero Molina, led 186 armed guardsmen into the ornate Chamber of Deputies and held the parliament and the cabinet hostage for 18 hours. The aim was to overthrow the fledgling democracy and replace it with a regime in which the army would play a guiding role. It was the most outrageous event in the Cortes since 1874, when General Manuel Pavia rode his horse up the steps of the parliament building and dismissed the horrified deputies.

The intruders roughed up Deputy President of the Government and Defense Minister Manuel Gutierrez Mellado, a liberal general in the army, and unleashed bursts of machine-gun fire toward the ceiling, forcing most deputies to take cover under their desks. The only captives who refused Tejero's order to lie on the floor were Suárez, Mellado, and Communist leader Santiago Carrillo. Since the plotters forgot that the session was being televised, Spaniards outside the Cortes were able to witness the shameful spectacle. Tejero had received a slap on the wrist only a year earlier for his part in a

harebrained plot to kidnap the cabinet, and he was not acting alone. Other officers were also involved. The regional commander in Valencia put his troops on alert and sent his tanks into the streets, and all but two of the nine regional commanders hesitated to do anything while waiting to see if the coup (called el golpe in Spain) would succeed.

It was at this critical juncture that Juan Carlos, who had fortunately canceled a long-planned trip to the US in order to be in Madrid during the political crisis, acted to save Spanish democracy. He ordered the creation of a "governmental commission" composed of ministerial undersecretaries to assume provisional civilian governmental power while the cabinet was in

EL PAIS

DIARIO INDEPENDIENTE DE LA MAÑANA

SÁBADO 13 DE MARZO DE 2004
Año XXIX. Número 9.782

EDICIÓN EURO
www.elpai

MILLONES DE CIUDADANOS CONTRA EL TERROR

España se echa a la calle

Millones de españoles tomaron ayer las calles para expresar su rechazo a la violencia terrorista tras el atentado perpetrado el pasado jueves contra cuatro trenes de cercanías de Madrid, en el que han muerto hasta ahora 199 personas. En muchos lugares, los manifestantes gritaron una pregunta: "¿Quién ha sido?". Por primera vez, el príncipe Felipe y las Infantas participaron en una manifestación. En Barcelona, el vicepresidente Rodrigo Rato y el ex ministro Josep Piqué fueron increpados por los manifestantes al grito de "asesinos".

En Madrid, hasta dos millones de personas marcharon bajo un aguacero intenso por el centro de la ciudad para probar su unidad contra el terrorismo. En la cabeza de la manifestación, junto al príncipe Felipe y las infantas Elena y Cristina, se situaron el presidente José María Aznar, los ex presidentes Leopoldo Calvo Sotelo y Felipe González, y los primeros ministros de Francia, Jean Pierre Raffarin; Italia, Silvio Berlusconi, y Portugal, José Manuel Durão Barroso. El presidente del Parlamento Europeo, Pat Cox, y el presidente de la Comisión Europea, Romano Prodi, se unieron

también a la manifestación. Barcelona reunió a un millón de personas contra la violencia en una manifestación encabezada por el presidente de la Generalitat, Pasqual Maragall. Abundaron las pancartas críticas con el PP, que relacionaban la matanza terrorista con la implicación de España en la guerra de Irak.

En Euskadi, las manifestaciones atrajeron a miles de ciudadanos, aunque los representantes de los partidos políticos eligieron marchas separadas. En las concentraciones se escucharon gritos de "Aznar, asesino" y "No a la guerra".

Aznar y Acebes insisten en apuntar a ETA y la banda lo desmiente

El presidente del Gobierno, José María Aznar, y su ministro del Interior, Ángel Acebes, mantuvieron ayer en sendas conferencias de prensa que la principal línea de investigación sobre el atentado contra los trenes de cercanías de Madrid apunta a ETA. Mientras tanto, un supuesto portavoz de la banda terrorista negó la participación de ETA en la masacre de Madrid a través de un comunicado remitido ayer por la tarde al diario *Gara*. Acebes contestó: "No nos lo creemos".

La investigación policial ha determinado que el explosivo y

los temporizadores utilizados en los atentados contra los cuatro trenes de cercanías es similar a los encontrados en la furgoneta que estaba aparcada junto a la estación ferroviaria de Alcalá de Henares. En esa furgoneta también halló la policía cintas con versos del Corán, lo que abrió nuevas sospechas sobre la participación en los hechos de grupos islámicos violentos.

IU y PSOE reclamaron transparencia al Gobierno al informar sobre los descubrimientos de la policía en relación con los atentados.

ATOCHA, ZONA CERO
La plaza de Atocha se convirtió ayer en la Zona Cero de Madrid, donde cientos de miles de ciudadanos expresaron su rechazo a la violencia terrorista que ha dejado 199 muertos en la capital.

Spaniards protest by the millions against terrorism.

captivity. He skillfully turned one of the highest-ranking plotters, his military tutor in the 1950s and chief military advisor after 1975, General Alfonso Armada Comyn, away from the venture by declaring that the plotters would "have to put two bullets in me before they take over" and then dispatching the general to help suppress the uprising.

The king then turned to his many contacts within the army to assure them that he opposed the coup and would die to defend Spain's democracy. Ironically, one can thank Franco for having sent the king to the military academies and thereby having provided Juan Carlos with so many friends within the armed forces. He persuaded the officers of the elite Brunete armored division on the outskirts of Madrid to keep their tanks in the camp and out of the streets of Madrid. If the capital city had become filled with tanks, it is likely that the coup would have acquired uncontrollable momentum. The king phoned all the captains-general in the nine military districts to coax or pressure them into supporting him.

Finally, at 1:15 a.m., he went on national television, wearing a general's uniform and sitting in front of the royal coat of arms, to announce that "the Crown, symbol of the permanence and unity of the nation, cannot tolerate, in any form, actions or attitudes attempting to interrupt the democratic process." This announcement was a tremendous comfort to a people who place great importance on symbols. The next morning Tejero saw that he was alone and gave up.

Spanish democracy had passed an important test. According to opinion polls, only 4% of Spaniards wanted the coup to succeed, while 76% were hostile to it. Most soldiers had supported their civilian rulers. Only hours after the abortive coup, the king met with political leaders and warned, "I invite all to reflect and reconsider postures that might lead to greater unity in Spain and more agreement among the Spanish people."

All democratic forces thereafter had to be more cautious and to strive much harder to adopt policies and wage settlements that rest on a consensus, which would include the military. Reforms were slowed down, and a conscientious effort was made to woo the military. For the first time, the army was given an actual role in a stepped-up campaign against Basque terrorism by being deployed along the French border. The Cortes passed a law defining states of alarm, siege, and emergency, during which times certain civil rights dealing with press freedom, search, and detention could be revoked.

Spain's political leaders were faced with a dilemma as to what to do with the plotters.

If they cracked down too hard, they might provoke an unfortunate military response. Spanish history clearly shows that nothing is more dangerous than a humiliated military. However, if the coup leaders were not given stiff sentences, then they might be encouraged to try again. After all, most of the key figures in the coup had been given the mildest suspended sentences for their part in earlier attempts to overthrow the government.

One year after the coup attempt, 32 officers and one civilian were brought to trial before 1 military tribunal. In the closing statements, no defendant showed the slightest regret or guilt for his actions, and instead all stressed their love for Spain, their honor as officers, and their wish to save the motherland. Tejero probably best expressed the standpoint of a person who learns nothing and understands even less: "I would like to express my utter contempt for those high-ranking officers who have betrayed their motherland." He and the other major conspirator, General Milan del Bosch, were sentenced to 30 years in jail.

The potential strength of the far right was also demonstrated at the time by the Fuerza Nueva ("New Force"), which had wanted to turn back the wheel of history. Although this and other ultraright groups never got many votes, they were visible and audible. The leader was Blas Piñar, a highly skilled demagogue who was at his best in rallies, complete with outstretched arms giving the fascist salute, fascist paraphernalia everywhere, and the sounds of Franco's hymn, "Cara al Sol" ("Face the Sun") blaring in the background. At one time this group could mobilize 300,000 Spaniards in the streets of Madrid every November to honor their dead idol, and their bullies roamed the streets menacingly. The Fuerza Nueva idolized the military, especially those soldiers who seized the Cortes in 1981, and it promised to help establish a "free Spain." Few Spaniards cared much for its notion of freedom. It disappeared because it had been ignored by those it had hoped to protect: the church, conservatives, and the military.

González bent over backward to quiet the soldiers' nerves. Shortly after assuming office, he visited the crack Brunete armored division, which had been deeply implicated in the 1981 plot. He picked up on the initiatives of his predecessor to modernize the army by streamlining and professionalizing it and by giving it better equipment. In 1983 the government moved to tighten control over the military by appointing a single chief of defense responsible to the defense minister. It moved the Brunete armored division to Extremadura on the Portuguese border.

It reduced the number and rank of Spain's most senior officers. In 1985 the

defense minister abolished the guarantee that every officer would be promoted at least to the rank of brigadier general before retirement. But he had to concede the right that all would be made colonels, a policy unheard of in any other western army. In 1989 Spain introduced promotions based on merit, and those who cannot perform satisfactorily are retired early. These were important steps toward greater professionalization.

Spain has come a long way since the 1981 plot, but the military's history of intervening in political disputes continues to cast a shadow. In January 2006 the supreme commander of the country's ground forces General José Mena Aguado expressed his concern about increasing Catalan autonomy. He cited article 8 of the constitution, which establishes that the armed forces are responsible for defending the country's "territorial integrity" and "the constitutional order." "It is our obligation to warn that there could be serious consequences for the armed forces as an institution." He hinted that other soldiers shared his views.

The government's reaction to these impermissible comments was swift and firm. He was placed under house arrest, relieved of his command, and retired early from the army. An army captain who published similar opinions in Melilla Hoy was disciplined by his superiors and admitted afterward that his chances for promotion were doomed.

Terrorism

Spain has known terrorist violence by radical Basque separatists for decades, and that form of violence has not disappeared. But the variety that poses the most danger to Spaniards today is Islamic radicalism, stemming particularly from Morocco, with which Spain has had troubled relations over the years. Al Qaeda inspiration but not direction is apparent. Al Qaeda has claimed many times that it seeks to reestablish "al-Andalus," the vast area of Spain the Moors ruled for 800 years until 1492.

On March 11, 2004 (referred to in Spain as 11-M), Spaniards suffered their most savage attack since the civil war from 1936 to 1939. About a dozen terrorists left 13 backpacks and gym bags in commuter trains as they pulled into three crowded stations, including the central Atocha Station, during the morning rush hour. Each contained about 25 pounds of high explosives. The detonators were wired to cell phones, and when they rang, 10 bombs went off almost simultaneously. The force of the blasts crumpled rail cars like aluminum cans and scattered burned and twisted bodies alongside the train tracks. The ghastly result was 191 dead (47 of

Spain

whom were foreigners) and over 1,400 injured, many seriously. Suddenly the Spanish had experienced the shock and the terrible confusion Americans had on 9/11. An estimated 11 million Spaniards took to the streets in cities all over Spain to show solidarity with the victims and with each other. In Madrid, 2.5 million shouted, "We were all in that train!"

Three of the bombs had failed to detonate, permitting the police to examine the cell phones and cell phone cards inside the bags and thereby trace the presumed perpetrators of the crime. Arrests were made quickly, and on April 3 seven of the Islamist terrorists, including the cell leader, suspected of carrying out the rail bombings blew themselves up after police cornered them in a suburban Madrid apartment. The same kind of explosives was found under tracks 40 miles south of Madrid used by the country's high-speed AVE trains a couple of weeks later. Fortunately the bomb had been poorly wired, and it failed to ignite.

The investigations focused on the Moroccan Islamic Combatant Group, which was linked to both al Qaeda and the 2003 suicide attacks against Spanish interests in Casablanca, Morocco. They revealed that the equipment and explosives used in the bombings had been financed by the sale of hashish and ecstasy. As in the US, there is now more cooperation among police and intelligence services, as well as with Spain's allies, to try to deal with this deadly problem.

Spanish authorities are aggressively pursuing suspected terrorists in the courts. In February 2007, a trial for 29 (7 of whom had already blown themselves up and 2 who had fled) began in connection with the March 11 attacks. This was the largest legal proceeding against terrorism to take place in Europe to date. Most were Moroccans, and all but one (the Spaniard who provided the explosives) were from North Africa or the Middle East. The trials were held in a high-security building constructed for that purpose on the outskirts of Madrid.

In November 2007 the court sentenced 21 persons. Seven were acquitted, and only three were found guilty of murder. The rest were convicted of belonging to an Islamist terrorist cell. Most were angry young North Africans who had settled in Spain. They had been inspired by al Qaeda, but they were not directed by it. The Madrid bombings had changed Spanish politics by opening up a rift between left and right over who ordered the attacks and how to counter terrorism in general.

Since the Madrid bombings, police are very aggressive in breaking up suspected Islamist plots. Police arrested 11 men on charges of belonging to a group that recruits people to carry out suicide attacks in Iraq. They arrested five men on suspicion of planning to bomb the country's High Court and Real Madrid's Bernabeu soccer stadium. They disrupted a plot by a cell of Islamic radicals to blow up the headquarters for the country's top anti-terrorism investigators and judges. They uncovered a Pakistani cell suspected of planning an attack in Barcelona. In January 2008 they apprehended 14 men (12 Pakistanis and 2 Indians) on suspicion of planning a suicide attack on Barcelona's public transportation system. In August 2017 the Islamic terrorist organization ISIS took responsibility for another bloody attack in Barcelona. A van driver deliberately plowed into strollers along a favorite tourist street, killing 15 and injuring 80 more. Laws in place to deal with Basque terror allow the state to imprison terrorist suspects for up to four years without trial.

The picture that emerged was a complicated and mixed one; the Madrid conspiracy was wider and more destructive than previously suspected. Most suspects were Moroccan, but some come from elsewhere, such as the local leader of the cell responsible for March 11. He was Tunisian and was a successful real estate agent before turning radical. A few were native Spaniards, such as the miner who provided the explosives for the March 11 bombings. Some were radicalized Muslims, while others were common criminals. Based on a two-year investigation, authorities concluded in 2006 that ETA played no role in the Madrid bombings and that, while the terrorist threat is homegrown, a major inspiration was the Iraq and Afghanistan Wars, even though the al Qaeda cells were well established in Spain long before the conflicts and took part in the planning of the September 11, 2001, attacks in New York and Washington. In 2004–2005 Spain began trying 22 Spain-based Muslims charged with providing logistical support to the September 11 killers. Authorities have arrested hundreds of Islamic terror suspects since the 2001 attacks in America. Spain agreed in 2010 to help America close the Guantanamo detention center by accepting five of its inmates. Police have cracked down on Islamic militants who recruit and dispatch young volunteers to fight in Syria, Iraq, Libya, and Mali.

Spain faces the problem of how to deal with attacks in the future. The dangers make their dealing with the country's 1.1 million Muslims (most of whom are legal Moroccan residents) more difficult. Even though a 2007 poll revealed that only 16% of them thought that suicide bombing was often or sometimes justified, the question remains, How would they affect Spain's immigrant population of 4.5 million (12.3% of the population—higher than in France, the UK, or Germany—and half of them undocumented) and the growing hostility toward foreigners within its borders? Polls in 2010 indicated that two-thirds of Spaniards thought immigrants were making it harder to find a job, and a third believed they received less pay as a result.

Many cities have toned down their traditional festivals that for three centuries celebrated the expulsion of the Muslim rulers by staging provocative mock battles between Christians and Moors and by destroying effigies of Muhammad. The Cortes rejected a motion in July 2010 to forbid the wearing of burkas. Also a Spanish Islamic Council of eight members was created in April 2011 to search for common ground with local Muslims.

The authorities consider organized crime to be as big a threat as terrorism and are particularly worried about its ability to corrupt local politicians, judges, and police officers. They are detaining Mafia bosses of diverse origin, including eastern Europe. Spain is determined to crack down on crime syndicates that have flocked to the Mediterranean coast to launder money through the booming construction and real estate businesses.

Regionalization and Decentralization

A second element that places a heavy strain on the democratic regime is the attempt to decentralize Spanish government and to grant a satisfactory measure of autonomy to the regions. For reasons related to the Muslim conquest, the prolonged expulsion of them, and the vast overextension of imperial power, Spain was never a fully integrated country. This is true of many other European countries. Madrid is in the middle and is therefore a logical site for the capital. It is surrounded like a bull's-eye by the harsh, sparsely populated, mainly Castilian Meseta. Around this tableland is the more densely populated and highly diverse periphery.

Tension between the center and the periphery has been a constant factor in politics. Even today, a fourth of all citizens speak another language in addition to Castilian Spanish. There are economic disparities. For example, Catalonia, the Basque area, and Madrid produce half of Spain's GDP, while almost half the population in Galicia and a third in Extremadura and Castile still work on the land, compared to only 6% in Catalonia and the Basque region. New industries and tourism have helped narrow the gap between these rich and poor regions.

Most Spaniards note regional idiosyncrasies, and many clichés are current: Cordobans are stoic, Galicians are stubborn and moody, Catalans and Valencians are artistic and entrepreneurial, Andalusians are a bit wild and Moorish, and Castilians

Spanish autonomous communities

monetary, customs, and strategic industrial policy, as well as full responsibility over the national police and criminal law. Health, welfare, local administration, local roads, and education were gradually transferred to the regions, but that transfer varies in degree and was still incomplete as Spain entered the new century. The central government negotiates with each of the 17 regions on the powers that should be granted to each. There is still staunch opposition to federalism. The system has to be renegotiated between the regions and Madrid every five years.

The Cortes vets all charters and usually waters them down. No charter gives a region the right of secession, and references to nations are carefully worded. For instance, Andalusia is a "nationality," not a "nation." The Catalans' charter states that they consider their region a nation, but the rest of Spain does not. In June 2010 the constitutional court nullified the Catalans' earlier referendum to approve its new charter by striking out parts of 14 of 223 articles and reinterpreting 27 more. Most important, it ruled that the Catalan language cannot be considered as superior to Castilian Spanish and that Catalans can call themselves a "nation," but it has no legal value. Therefore only Spain is a legal "nation," according to the constitution. More than 1 million Catalans demonstrated in the streets of Barcelona to protest this ruling.

Since the death of Franco, who had banned the public use of Euskera (Basque), Catalan, and Gallego (in Galicia), regional languages and history has been emphasized. Madrid was forced to back down in 1997, when a committee of experts drew up a list of 100 teaching points to be used in history classes all over Spain. Regional minorities, especially in Catalonia and the Basque area, considered the idea that Spain had a unified history to be reactionary and intolerable. However, the question was not put to rest. Government education officials in Madrid argued in 2000 that Castile should regain its place at the heart of Spanish history and as the source of the country's main language. The central government has the ultimate authority to inspect and supervise schools, although the regions have input. Regions establish a large part of the curriculum and approve textbooks before they are published. The result is that children learn widely varying things in different parts of the country.

Relations with the demanding regions are never easy for Madrid. Four regions—Catalonia, the Basque country, Galicia, and Andalusia—have more autonomy than the others. As a price for Catalan support for the Aznar minority government in 1996, the central government agreed to increase the proportion of locally raised

are austere and noble. Yet all benefit from being a part of the larger Spanish economy and are held together by such strong common interests that no region would vote for secession.

The regions particularly were suppressed under Franco, who in part justified his military coup and subsequent rule as the preservation of unity. Franco gained the lasting hatred of the Basques after ordering the devastating bombing of Guernica on April 26, 1937. This situation did not change immediately after Franco's death, and in the Basque country, there were some regrettable incidents involving the suppression of cultural events. But in modern Spanish history, transitions to greater freedom and democracy were always accompanied by demands for more home rule in the regions, and the post-Franco era was no exception. Fortunately the new leaders had pluralist political sentiments and were therefore willing to make many compromises.

Spain introduced in 1979 the most ambitious plan to decentralize political power since the foundation of the Federal Republic of Germany in 1949. It would have been much easier if the country had officially adopted federalism, which would have established clear lines of responsibility between the center and the regions. But Catalan and Basque nationalists would accept only a "confederation of several nations."

It has already become one of Europe's most decentralized states. Between 1994 and 2000, the central government shed 45,000 employees, and the regions gained 235,000 more.

There are 17 autonomous regions, plus the 2 enclaves of Ceuta and Melilla on the Moroccan coast. Each has its own government and parliament though with differing degrees of power. They have responsibility for health, schools and universities, social services (but not unemployment benefits), culture, and urban and rural development. Basques and Catalans have their own police forces and civil law. The Basque country and Navarra collect their own taxes and pay Madrid for the services they receive. Other regions live on funds and grants from Madrid. Regional governments and local governments dispense three-fourths of all public spending. About a third of the income tax collected in the regions returns to them. There is still constant controversy between the center and the regions over the funding of public services. Regional governments conduct their own foreign policy, and some have aid budgets; self-confident Catalonia even has shadow embassies and delegations in such capitals as Brussels and London.

Ultimately Spain is supposed to have a fully federal system, with the central government reserving for itself the exclusive right to conduct foreign, defense,

Spain

income taxes the Catalans may keep from 15% to 30% over five years. This percentage differs in each region, so Spain in effect has 17 different tax systems.

Basque Separatism

Basque nationalism was the Achilles' heel of Spanish democracy. There are 2.2 million Basques in Spain (just 5% of the country's population) and about 200,000 in France, which declared in 1981 that it would no longer permit its territory to be used as a base for illegal operations in Spain. The relative prosperity of the Basque area had long attracted immigrants from poorer Spanish regions. The result is that half of the residents are not Basque. Only a quarter of the people speak Euskera (Basque).

An ancient people of obscure origins and speaking a language which is unrelated to any language of Europe and which almost no outsiders speak, the Basques have always been sharply aware of their separate identity. This awareness was greatly enhanced by the suppression of things Basque during the Franco era. People were forced to adopt Spanish names, and local administration and police work was placed in the hands of non-Basques who had no comprehension or sympathy with the local language or culture.

Acting more like an army of occupation than a protector of public safety, the Civil Guard antagonized the local population to such an extent that the latter could not help sympathizing with a group of Basque nationalists and student activists that took shape in 1952 under the name of Euskadi ta Askatasuna ("Basque Country and Freedom," or ETA). In 1968 ETA began resorting to violence to accomplish its aims. This caused it to split into a militant, hypernationalist wing called ETA-Militar, staffed by predominantly young, well-educated Basques from middle- and working-class backgrounds, and a more moderate wing that now disavows violence. Since 1968 ETA was directly responsible for 812 deaths by 2003, when the organization temporarily stopped its frenzied killing. In the next four years, it killed "only" 4 persons, but by 2009 the death toll had reached 825.

ETA-Militar reportedly received training and material support from Libya, Cuba, Yemen, and Palestinian terrorist organizations. It was closely linked to the only Basque party that opposed regional autonomy in 1980, Herri Batasuna ("Popular Unity"), renamed Euskal Herritarok (EH) in 1998. Both organizations demand a revision of the Spanish constitution that would be a prelude for an independent Euskadi, based on the right of self-determination. Only a third of Basque voters had supported Spain's new constitution in 1978.

EL PAIS
DIARIO INDEPENDIENTE DE LA MAÑANA

JUEVES 23 DE MARZO DE 2006
Año XXXI. Número 10.516

EDICIÓN EUROPA
www.elpais.es

LA BANDA AFIRMA QUE "LA SUPERACIÓN DEL CONFLICTO, AQUÍ Y AHORA, ES POSIBLE"

ETA anuncia un "alto el fuego permanente"

Zapatero pide prudencia y serenidad para un proceso "largo y difícil" al que convoca a todos los partidos políticos

ETA declaró ayer un "alto el fuego permanente" que entrará en vigor mañana, según un escueto comunicado en el que la banda concluye: "La superación del conflicto, aquí y ahora, es posible". El presidente, José Luis Rodríguez Zapatero, pidió "responsabilidad, prudencia y serenidad" ante un proceso que se anuncia "largo y difícil", para el que convocó a todos los partidos. "Hasta ahora nos unía el espanto del horror; confío en que ahora nos una una esperanza", declaró Zapatero, quien hizo en el Congreso una apelación al PP y a su líder, Mariano Rajoy: "Nos han separado muchas cosas, pero sé que ustedes también desean la paz. Tenemos que recorrer juntos este camino". Rajoy lamentó que el alto el fuego anunciado sea sólo "una pausa" de ETA y no la "disolución" definitiva de la banda.

La banda terrorista, que ha cometido 817 asesinatos en los últimos 36 años, anunció el alto el fuego en un vídeo remitido a la televisión pública vasca. En él, una terrorista encapuchada, escoltada por otros dos miembros de ETA, lee un comunicado en el que explica las intenciones de la banda: "Impulsar un proceso democrático en Euskal Herria para construir un nuevo marco en el que sean reconocidos los derechos que como pueblo nos corresponden (...). La decisión que los ciudadanos vascos adoptemos sobre nuestro futuro deberá ser respetada". En el comunicado no hay ninguna referencia a la violencia callejera ni a la extorsión de los empresarios.

La tregua de ETA llega tras 1.028 días sin muertos de atentado. En los últimos meses, Zapatero ha reiterado su confianza en que se acercaba "el principio del fin" de la banda. En agosto de 2004, cuatro meses después de asumir el poder, el presidente recibió una carta en la que ETA le pedía establecer una comunicación con su Gobierno. Fue el arranque del actual proceso.

Zapatero anunció que se tomará tiempo para analizar si "se dan las condiciones para pedir el aval del Congreso ante un posible diálogo" con ETA. Rajoy le ofreció su apoyo siempre que no se pague un precio político y las fuerzas y cuerpos de Seguridad y los jueces sigan actuando contra los terroristas. **Páginas 15 a 31**

Rajoy minusvalora la tregua porque es sólo "una pausa" ● El presidente del Gobierno recibió la primera carta de la organización terrorista en agosto de 2004 ● La sociedad vasca acoge la noticia con esperanza y cautela ● París, Londres y Washington hablan de "paso decisivo" para la paz

Tres terroristas de ETA anuncian el "alto el fuego permanente" en un vídeo remitido a la televisión pública vasca. / AP

La UE busca una política energética común pese a sus divisiones internas

Los jefes de Estado y de Gobierno de la UE debaten desde hoy en Bruselas la puesta en marcha de una política europea de energía. Los Veinticinco están divididos sobre las ofertas de compra de firmas del sector y las medidas adoptadas por los Gobiernos para proteger su mercado nacional. INTERNACIONAL **Páginas 2 y 3**

CAROD descarta que ERC vote 'no' en el referéndum sobre el Estatuto de Cataluña. ESPAÑA **Página 32**

CUATRO AÑOS de cárcel para el dueño de un bar de Barcelona por exceso de ruido. SOCIEDAD **Página 35**

ARQUITECTOS DE ÉLITE debaten en Barcelona sobre la construcción del entorno. CULTURA **Página 40**

That document declares Spain's unity to be forever indivisible, and most parties outside of the Basque region consider that wording to preclude any form of referendum on self-determination. However, that is precisely what all Basque nationalists, including the majority who renounce violence, demand. Opponents retort that any tampering with that clause would lead quickly to the dissolution of Spain.

Short of amending the constitution, there is little else Madrid can offer Basques. They already have wide autonomy; a parliament; the power to raise taxes; and control over most aspects of education, health, transport, and local police (although antiterrorism is a federal matter). Nor are Basques the victims of discrimination. In fact, the reverse is more likely correct. They man the police force and otherwise have good jobs. Their language is spreading and is used in the schools.

The major political force in Euskadi is the more conservative Basque Nationalist Party (PNV), formerly led by Josu Jon Imaz. He spoke of creating a civic society for all Basques, not an ethnic one; condemned ETA; and ruled out pacts with Batasuna. By 2008 it had dominated Basque politics for three decades, and it won the September 2016 provincial elections. It is rural, conservative, and Catholic. A party calling itself Eusko Alkartasuna (EA) broke away from PNV, thereby dividing the moderate Basques.

The Basque subsidiary of the Socialist Party is the Partido Socialista de Euskadi (PSE), which regards itself as progressive, modern, and secular; it appeals mainly to nonnationalists. By 2012 it was the ruling party. The PSE is not to be confused with the Abertzale Sozialistak (AS), which the Spanish Supreme Court declared in May 2007 to be front group for the outlawed Batasuna. There is a Basque branch of the People's Party. More and more Basques are political moderates. They are no longer so afraid to speak out against ETA.

The central government has recognized their specific needs by granting Basques the right to raise their own taxes and pay none to the federal treasury, as well as to form an all-Basque police force of 6,000 to replace the Civil Guards and National Police. Schools, roads, courts, and police are all run by the Basques themselves. There are three types of schooling available: in Spanish, Basque, or a mixture of both languages. Fewer than 15% of the schools teach only in Spanish. The predominance of Basque (Euskerra) was shown in 2008, when regional education authorities turned down free copies of Al Gore's film An Inconvenient Truth, because it had not been translated into Basque. A 2000 poll determined that almost two-thirds of Basques feel both Basque and Spanish. A groundswell of opinion sees violence as futile and profoundly damaging to the Basque economy; opinion polls in 2009 suggested that only a third of Basques support full independence, and only a tenth support ETA's violent means. ETA and EH supporters came to realize that their extremism was so unpopular that it undermined their cause.

The autonomy measures cut into public support for the separatist alternative. Also, the antiterrorist campaign by the Spanish police increased French cooperation, and disillusionment among many Basques with the brutality shown by ETA reduced the number of terrorist attacks and paved the way to temporary cease-fires in 1998 and 2006. Spaniards were greatly relieved that ETA terrorists had not disrupted the Barcelona Olympics in 1992. Prior to the games, the Spanish and French authorities had launched a determined campaign against ETA.

In 1992 ETA's top leaders were arrested, but authorities found the organization to be more complex than had previously been imagined. Its fighters were equipped with advanced technology, weapons, lots of money, and a backup leadership ready to take over in case the top members were arrested, as was the case. ETA traditionally based its command and support structures in southwest France. There its armed units were equipped and trained and then sent across the border into Spain to make its bloody strikes.

As ETA became more isolated, it attacked higher-profile targets. In 1995 José María Aznar, who was president of the government from 1996 to 2004, barely escaped death when a car bomb went off near his home. ETA also failed in an attempt to assassinate King Juan Carlos in 1995. The mastermind for that attempt, Ibon Gogeascoechea, was arrested in 2010. A year later two more participants in this abortive plot were arrested: Julián Atxurra Egurola in France—whose three southwest

departments, together with the four northern Spanish regions the Basque terrorists claim for the independent Basque country they dream of—and Eneko Gogeaskoetxea in Cambridge. The house in which Egurola was captured was a true arsenal, containing explosives, timers, grenade launchers, antitank rockets, machine guns, pistols, and ammunition.

The September 11, 2001, terrorist attacks were a shock to Spaniards and created more backing for the president of the government's tough stand against ETA. The government reacted by arresting many al Qaeda suspects, sharing intelligence with the US and other allies, and cooperating with police authorities in France and elsewhere. The Americans responded by putting 21 ETA names on their "wanted" list. A series of ETA attacks in 2002 persuaded Aznar that it was time to outlaw its political arm, Batasuna, and the Cortes approved in June 2002. The Spanish Supreme Court agreed to this in March 2003 under a new law allowing political parties to be banned if they do not condemn terrorism and if they maintain even tenuous links with terrorist groups. In 2013 Batasuna dissolved itself in France.

Two months later the United States and EU acceded to Spain's request to add Batasuna to their list of terrorist organizations. The moment Batasuna became illegal, the PNV became more radical in its objectives. Batasuna was seriously weakened by the arrests of scores of members and many top leaders and by the squeeze on its financial assets abroad as a result of increased international cooperation. The arrests and convictions continued in October 2007, when the Batasuna leadership was apprehended at a secret meeting, and in December 2007, when 47 Basques were sentenced for links with ETA.

In 2003 the Spanish government closed down the only newspaper printed in the Basque language, Euskaldunon Egunkaria, for allegedly aiding ETA. This did not dissuade the more moderate PNV regional government under Juan José Ibarretxe from guiding through a divided regional assembly in October 2003 a plan for a referendum to determine whether the Basque region should become a "free state associated with Spain." A Euskobarómetro poll a month later revealed that 32% of Basques favor the status quo; 31%, a federal model of greater autonomy; and only 31%, independence. His plan would involve its own foreign policy, separate courts, and representation in the EU. Citizens would have dual Basque-Spanish citizenship, and they would perhaps share the monarchy. It would fall far short of ETA's claims to a greater Basque state that includes the province of Navarre and part of southwest France. Such a state was

rejected by a majority of Basque voters in their April 2005 regional elections.

Zapatero announced that, while his government would not amend the 1978 constitution to permit secession of any part of Spain, it would be more flexible and offer Basque nationalists an alternative that would not violate the constitution but address Basques' concerns. That alternative would not include independence. In May 2005 he got the Cortes to accept an explosive motion supporting "dialogue between the competent authority within the state and whoever decides to give up violence." The country was ready for this. The March 2004 train bombings in Madrid had eliminated most residual support for terrorist groups and reduced their political audience. The government had also come as close as is possible to defeating ETA terrorist operatives. With most of their senior commanders in jail, 600 other members incarcerated in Spain and 200 more in France, more than 700 arrests in Spain and France since 2000, and its support at home halved since the 1998 ceasefire, ETA had been greatly weakened and degraded to more an irritant than a serious security threat. This is especially true after the 2004 Madrid bombings, which strengthened public revulsion against terrorism in general.

On March 22, 2006, a woman wearing combat fatigues, a white face mask, and a black beret and flanked by two similarly clad guerrillas made a dramatic announcement in a video: ETA was prepared to shift from violence to "a democratic process in which our rights as people will be recognized." The organization declared a permanent cease-fire with the aim "to drive a democratic process in the Basque country." The Zapatero government responded cautiously but resolutely to ETA. Talks started in the summer of 2006. The opposition PP, which nearly defeated ETA while in government, accused the president of bowing to terrorism.

In December 2006 whatever peace had prevailed was shattered by an ETA bombing at Madrid's Barajas Airport, which flattened a five-story parking garage and killed two Ecuadorians sleeping in their cars. This act made a mockery of Zapatero's optimism about a peace process on which he had staked so much of his political credibility. He called off the peace talks. In March 2007 the opposition PP, which had fiercely resisted every socialist attempt to solve the Basque problem, organized a mass demonstration of several hundreds of thousands in Madrid to demand tougher government action against separatists. This coincided with the dedication of a towering monument located outside Atocha railroad station to those killed in the March 11, 2004, bombings.

Spain

Complaining that the government had not reciprocated, ETA called off its 14-month cease-fire in June 2007. There was a surge of ETA attacks in the months leading up to the March 2008 national elections. But a series of joint Spanish-French intelligence operations proved how close their working relationship is and how thoroughly they have infiltrated ETA by netting a whole bevy of top ETA leaders. In May 2008 López Pena, the top commander, was detained in Bordeaux. In November Garikoitz Aspeazu (Cherokee), ETA military chief, was nabbed in France. A US intelligence agency gave a helping hand by tracking his e-mails to his favorite Internet café. A month later his replacement, Aitzol Iriondo, was captured. In April 2009 the new leader and military chief Jurdan Martitegi Lizaso was grabbed in France, and nine more ETA operatives were arrested. Ibon Gogeaskoetxea was military leader only 10 months before being nabbed in February 2010. Two months later, his successor, Carrera Sarobe, was apprehended.

Each of these arrests forced ETA to reorganize, and that distracted it from killing. In an attempt to escape the pressure from the Spanish and French governments, ETA moved some of its operations deeper into France and Portugal. In 2010 ETA killed a French policeman in a shootout outside of Paris; this was the first time it has murdered a member of the French security forces.

The most dramatic political setback for ETA came in the March 1, 2009, regional elections. For the first time in 29 years, the nonnationalists defeated Juan José Ibarretxe's nonviolent PNV and took over the government. The new lehendakari (premier) was socialist Patxi López, who must cooperate with the regional PP to maintain a majority. López pledged to bridge the divide between nationalists and nonnationalists.

The Spanish Supreme Court helped by banning two small nationalist parties that were ETA front groups that supported PNV in parliament: Herri Batasuna and Batasuna. That decision was backed up by the European Court of Human Rights in 2009. To get around this ban, Batasuna launched a new party, Sortu (Create). Its statutes say it opposes violence and that ETA acts against the people's "fundamental rights and freedoms." Despite the thousands who marched in Bilbao in support of it, prosecutors claimed it, too, was a front group for Batasuna and barred it from fielding candidates in the May 2011 local and provincial elections.

In the October 2012 Basque elections, the Socialists were voted out of power, and the PNV came back on top, winning a third of the votes. Its leader, Inigo Urkullu, became president. Parties supporting continued ties with Spain won another third. Herria Bildu, a coalition of separatist groups, including the former political wing of ETA, took a fourth. Polls in 2012 indicated that a majority of Basques had "little or no" interest in independence.

ETA got weaker by the month. It is thoroughly penetrated, its leaders are apprehended as soon as they are appointed, it is steadily losing public support, and 300 ETA terrorists are in jail. Its morale and manpower are being sapped. Its recruiting and rate of killing declined dramatically. It can no longer pursue its goals by the double-edged sword of terrorism and political activity. It is split between military and political wings and is inoperative. It can no longer collect "revolutionary taxes."

Because of its weakness, it announced a permanent cease-fire in January 2011 that would be "verifiable by the international community." Having heard such promises before, the central government promptly rejected it. But on October 20, 2011, ETA again proclaimed a definitive end to its four decades of terror that claimed 829 lives.

A weakened ETA was in a bad negotiating position, but the government still had work to do. ETA had weapons and explosives caches in the Basque region and France that needed to be decommissioned. It put a small quantity of weapons, explosives, and munitions beyond use in March 2014 and offered to destroy more under the eyes of international monitors. However, the Spanish government insisted ETA must disband and disarm entirely, verified by Spanish police.

In April 2017 ETA apologized for decades of violence. It disbanded after providing French authorities with a list of arms caches. It created a new party—EH Bildu—that renounces violence.

In the meantime, the Basque economy is doing well. Its unemployment is half the rest of Spain, and its tourist industry and exports are growing fast. It has become a center for engineering products. No wonder half of all Basques oppose independence and regard ETA as a failure.

Catalonia

Viewed from Madrid, Catalonia appears almost as the model of civic responsibility, when compared with its Basque neighbors. It is much larger, with a population of 7.3 million; almost one-sixth of Spaniards live there. Catalans are Spain's richest and culturally most illustrious minority. The architect Antoni Gaudi, cellist Pablo Casals, and painters Joan Miró and Salvador Dalí were all from this region. Its capital, Barcelona, is one of Europe's most stylish and fun metropolises. International business surveys conducted by Cushman & Wakefield consistently rank it first in the world in terms of quality of life. It receives 20 million tourists each year. In the past its literature and language, spoken by about 4 million persons (some Catalans claim 10 million), was suppressed. Under Franco one could be put in jail for singing "El Cant dels Segadors," the Catalan national anthem.

Catalans are a pragmatic and patient people who are inclined to wait for more promising times rather than to revolt. As one Castilian observer noted, "the difference between the Basque and Catalan nationalists is that the Basques want to leave Spain and the Catalans want to run it." Some Catalan political parties want autonomy, not independence, with the same taxing power as the Basques now have and with their own court system. In 1992, the Olympic Games were held in Barcelona 500 years after Columbus's discovery of America. They were a source of great pride for Catalans. All events and results were announced first in the Catalan language and then in Spanish, English, and French.

Since 1979 Catalonia has had an autonomy statute similar to that of the Basque country. However, by the time it was able to manage many of its own affairs, an important change had taken place. The region's dynamic industry and commerce had attracted so many immigrants from the poorer Spanish regions that nearly half of the region's population was no longer of Catalan origin. A minority of the newcomers refused to learn the Catalan language or to adjust to the cultural traditions in the area. Some become enthusiastic Catalans.

Schoolkids are required to receive their education in Catalan. After years of teaching it, almost everybody now speaks it, and half speak it all the time. Catalonia had a struggle to define its own identity within the Spanish nation. But by the end of the last century, the Catalan language had revived remarkably. About 95% of the residents can use it. The regional government is strict in enforcing its use. In 2004 it fined the Spanish postal service €30,000 ($42,000) for not having all its labels and stamps in Catalan. The 2006 autonomy statute officially made Catalan the "preferential" language, but Spain's constitutional court struck that down in 2010. The statute says that it is the duty of all residents to learn it. Strangely, Barcelona is the center of Spain's publishing industry, and three-fourths of all books purchased in the region are in Spanish.

Barcelona's clout in Madrid was dramatically increased by the fact that both the Socialist and PP governments became dependent on the seats of the two-party alliance, Convergence and Union (CIU), to have a majority. The skillful former leader

Jordi Pujol had by 2000 won six regional elections by proclaiming both Catalan nationalism and loyalty to Spain. He knew how to use the CIU's leverage. With the Socialists, he negotiated a measure of fiscal autonomy for the Catalan government to keep 15% of the income tax raised in the region. In 1996 he forced the newly elected Aznar to raise that to 30% within five years. He also stepped up the campaign, supported by all parties, to make Catalan the language used in the schools.

When the blockbuster film Harry Potter premiered in 2001, he insisted that it be dubbed in Catalan, not in Castilian Spanish. In 2008 education authorities turned down free copies of Al Gore's film An Inconvenient Truth, for the schools because it was not in Catalan. A 2010 law requires that at least half the copies of every film from outside Europe be dubbed in Catalan. But in one 2010 study, fewer than 10% of moviegoers preferred films in Catalan rather than in Spanish when given the choice. Pujol kept his focus on his central ambition: a loosely federated Spain in which the king of Spain would become the "king of the Spains."

Pujol stepped down in 2003, although his party, the nationalist Convergence and Union (CIU), had come out on top in elections to the 135-seat regional assembly. The Catalan Republican Left (ERC), a leftist proindependence party, joined the Socialists and Greens to form a governing coalition under the leadership of Pasquall Maragall.

Maragall pressed ahead with plans for a new statute recognizing the region as a nation. He got a powerful boost after the 2004 Spanish elections, when Zapatero's new Socialist government became dependent on the votes of regional parties, including those in Catalonia, to support his

minority government. Zapatero owed his March 2008 reelection to the overwhelming vote he got in Catalonia. Everywhere else, the PP captured the most votes.

Zapatero agreed to respect Catalan aspirations and to support the elevation of the Catalan language to official status within the EU. However, Maragall and the ERC were furious when Spain's foreign minister asked the EU in 2004 to make Catalan, Valencian, Basque, and Galician official languages. Catalans consider Valencian to be a mere dialect of Catalan. An ERC spokesman accused the government in Madrid of "ignorance, lack of culture and bad political faith." In the end, only Catalan won EU recognition as an official regional language, along with Irish.

In June 2006 three-quarters (74%) of voters in the region approved the Catalan Statute of Autonomy, which had been approved by the Cortes earlier in the year. Many voters greeted the statute with a gaping yawn. In polls before the referendum, 70% admitted they knew nothing about the new charter, half said the result was of little or no concern to them, and few had read it. The low turnout of only 49% cast some doubt on its legitimacy. But the law passed nevertheless. Much of the campaign had revolved around symbolic issues, such as the right to call Catalonia a "nation," which its charter does. Article 2 of the Spanish constitution already recognizes that the country contains different "nationalities." But the constitutional court ruled in 2010 that, while Catalan can call itself a "nation," that is legally irrelevant.

Catalonia now has more taxing powers and pays less to Spain than it did before although it was not allowed to include a revenue-sharing formula in its new statute. It gained authority over immigration

and judicial matters, but its courts cannot override Spain's highest courts. Despite its limitations, the statute could be a model for other regions, including Andalusia, Galicia, Valencia, the Balearic Islands, and the Basque area. However, it was fiercely resisted by the PP and was unpopular elsewhere in Spain. In 2012 Catalonia put the Rajoy government on notice that pressure for "divorce" would grow if it attempted to impose strict controls on regional budgets. Regions now account for a little more than half of public spending and manage schools and hospitals. Catalonia insists on more financial autonomy and lower transfers to poorer regions.

Artur Mas hoped the November 2012 regional elections would give him an absolute majority, but that did not happen. His Convergence and Union (CIU) Party had its worst result since 1980, winning only 31% of the votes and 50 of 135 seats. Many voters went to the vehemently antiseparatist Citizens Party or to the Republican Left of Catalonia (ERC). To demonstrate the sharp increase in separatist sentiment in a dramatic way in 2013, hundreds of thousands of Catalans formed a human chain on their national day, September 11, from the French border 250 miles across Catalonia to the southern resorts on the Mediterranean Sea. This put them on a collision course with Madrid.

The two main separatist parties, CIU and ERC, announced that they would sponsor a consultative (nonbinding) referendum on November 9, 2014, on whether to secede. However, in March 2014 the highest court in Spain ruled that no region had a right to self-determination. In April 2014 the Spanish parliament overwhelmingly rejected such a referendum on the grounds that Catalonians alone could not decide something that affects all of Spain. Mas retorted, "We will find a way to sidestep every obstacle that appears in our path." In a November 2014 nonbinding referendum, 80% voted in favor, but turnout was only 37%. The Spanish government called it "useless and sterile." The fractious independence movement received another blow when it was revealed in 2014 that Jordi Pujol had hidden undeclared money in Switzerland for 35 years.

Catalan separatists won the September 2015 regional elections with only 48% of the votes. Any subsequent referendum would require over 50%. Nevertheless, a resolution was adopted that mandated a move toward independence. This was promptly rejected by Spain's highest court and national government. In January 2016, Artur Mas was replaced as Catalan leader by a more radical politician, Carles Puigdemont, who vowed to expel the "invaders" from Catalonia. Despite vehement objection from the constitutional court

The sign was written in both languages—Spanish and Catalan. The Spanish was crossed out, leaving only the Catalan with the added comment, "In Catalonia, in Catalan," meaning that, in Catalonia, it has to be written in Catalan.

Spain

and central government, Puigdemont promised a binding referendum on independence in 2017.

Events moved quickly after October 1, 2017, when separatists won a referendum on independence despite a constitutional court ruling that it was illegal. On October 27 the Catalan parliament declared independence. President Rajoy removed the leaders of the Catalan government from office and called for new elections on December 21. Separatist parties won again with 47.5% of the votes. Madrid declared direct rule in Catalonia, while Puigdemont and a few other leaders fled to Brussels to avoid persecution for rebellion. They faced 30 years in prison, but their arrest warrants were later dropped. Even King Filipe VI, who seldom comments on political matters, accused the separatists of "inadmissible disloyalty" and of creating "a situation of extreme gravity." Puigdemont was replaced as party leader by Quim Torra, a hard-line separatist who rules with a fragile coalition of separatist parties. The rhetoric remains confrontational.

Catalonia is booming economically, and its 7 million people generate 20% of Spain's GDP; its economy is the size of Portugal's. Pujol's favorite statistics were that Catalonia has 6% of Spain's territory, 13% of its population, 25% of its exports, and 38% of its industrial exports. Barcelona is still Spain's industrial heart. Foreign investment pours in. However, because of the political turmoil, 2,000 businesses have moved their headquarters out of Catalonia. Catalonia receives $50 million each year in EU grants and since 2006 is authorized to negotiate directly with the EU on matters affecting the region. It has its own seat in such international bodies as UNESCO.

Other Regions

The other Spanish regions are also making their way toward one form of autonomy or the other. About half the inhabitants of País Valencia (the provinces of Valencia, Castellón, and Alicante) speak Valencian, which is related to but not the same as Catalan. However, the majority is in favor of autonomy while remaining consciously within the Catalan cultural community, which also embraces the Balearic Islands, Andorra, and Roussillon in France.

Spain's largest region, Andalusia, approved its autonomous statute in 1981, and voters in a 2007 referendum approved a revised charter that calls their people a "nationality." It is one of Spain's poorest regions, with an illiteracy rate estimated at 30% but accounting for half of Spain's population growth. It needs all the financial assistance it can get from the wealthier regions and the EU.

Catalonian symbol

In order to stimulate the region's economy and build up its infrastructure, its capital, Seville, hosted "Expo 92," 500 years since Columbus set foot on Santo Domingo. Visitors saw the pavilions around the 15th-century Santa María de la Cuevas, where Columbus planned his last voyage to America and where he is buried. His voyages were retraced by reproductions of the Niña and Pinta and two of the Santa María, which sailed to San Salvador and New York, where three of the ships remain as part of the Metropolitan Museum's permanent collection. The second Santa María proceeded through the Panama Canal and on to Japan, where Columbus had hoped to arrive.

In Galicia, 28.4% of eligible voters went to the polls to approve overwhelmingly its autonomy statute. Aragón, Asturias, and other regions are also moving toward limited self-government. In the Canary Islands, the separatist Union of the Canary People demands self-determination for the islands and the removal of the Spanish army.

Bureaucracy Reform

A third major problem facing Spain was to reform the bureaucracy while maintaining a reasonable level of services. Large numbers of state employees had some trouble adjusting to the new democratic environment, where public servants are really expected to serve the public. Many functionaries long regarded their positions as practically their own property, and many old usages have persisted, such as the right of each department to collect fees for the services it performs. Also, financial inspectors expected to receive a percentage of the taxes they collected.

Each department still has a strong sense of self-interest and internal loyalty that often takes priority over serving the public. They are often inefficient and excruciatingly slow, especially when it comes to paying money they owe. They are also greatly overstaffed. This was made worse by such measures as the requirement that the government bureaucracy absorb 35,000 members of Franco's disbanded sindicatos, or state-controlled unions. Work had to be created for this vast unproductive

group, and there was understandably lots of sitting or standing around in many of the departments.

González moved quickly to create the kind of civil service appropriate to a democratic and modern Spanish state. His government began immediately to enforce the conflict-of-interest law passed by the Cortes in 1982. Civil servants, cabinet ministers, members of parliament, and top executives of state companies are allowed to have only one job and one salary. Civil servants, who had become accustomed to a 26- to 28-hour work week, are required to be at work at 8 a.m. and to work eight and one-half hours, with a half-hour lunch break. Also, the first Spanish ombudsman was appointed, with the task of looking into complaints of abuses and neglects inflicted on the people by ministers, administrative authorities, or public servants.

In 2006 the Zapatero government abolished the midafternoon two-hour lunch break for civil servants by limiting lunch to one hour beginning at noon. The aim is to stop the practice of pushing the workday into night and keeping parents away from their families. It is hoped that the private sector will follow suit. Already some large firms, like Coca-Cola and Ibérica, have decreed 45-minute lunch breaks and clock out at 6 p.m. But the private sector is slow to change the traditional siesta. Spain has the longest working hours in Europe.

FOREIGN AND DEFENSE POLICY

Franco's death enabled Spain to modify its course in foreign policy. In February 1976 Spain relinquished Spanish Sahara, with its rich phosphate deposits, to Morocco and Mauritania, with the hope that the inhabitants could determine their own future. Algeria greatly resented this solution, and a bloody struggle occurred over control of this colony. Morocco simply annexed the former colony.

The major change in Spain's foreign policy, however, was that it turned its primary attention toward Europe. Spain was the only country in western Europe that did not belong either to the EU, EFTA, or NATO. It had been permitted to join the UN in 1950 and eventually became a member of virtually all world bodies.

Latin America

Spain's entry into western Europe signaled certain other foreign policy changes. Franco established a special relationship with Latin America, where there were many authoritarian regimes similar to his own. The king left no doubt when he was awarded a prize in Germany for his work toward European unity that, although Spain is rooted in Europe, it is also a part of the Hispanic world. Spain's support for Argentina during the Falkland Islands conflict underscored this fact.

The earlier socialist government showed its special interest in helping to bring about peace talks in Central America, if Spain had been asked to do so. During a visit to Cuba in 1986, Cuban leader Fidel Castro referred to González as "dear friend Felipe" and pinned Cuba's highest distinction, the order of José Martí, on his lapel. In the mid-1990s, Spain became the leading investor and a key western economic and diplomatic intermediary for Cuba, which, unlike the Philippines, still exerts an emotional pull on Spaniards.

Relations cooled after Aznar and the PP came to power. But in 1999 King Juan Carlos became the first Spanish monarch to visit Cuba, joining the leaders of 14 Latin American countries and Portugal for an Ibero-American summit. In 2010 Foreign Minister Moratinos worked with the Catholic Church to broker a deal to take in 20 of the 52 Cuban dissidents imprisoned by Fidel Castro in 2003.

The Socialist government that came to power in March 2004 was determined to reinforce Spain's relations with Cuba. Madrid disagrees with the American embargo against Cuba, and in December 2004 it restored diplomatic relations with Cuba, followed a month later by most other major European countries. When Foreign Minister Moratinos visited Havana in 2007 without meeting with dissidents, US secretary of state Condoleezza Rice criticized him. But Moratinos insisted that the Americans

"should trust in a faithful, solid ally like Spain."

The Zapatero government tried to play an active role in Latin America. In March 2005 it announced plans to host a summit in Colombia of three South American leaders from Venezuela, Colombia, and Brazil to forge closer cooperation against terrorism and drug trafficking. Venezuela's leader Hugo Chávez greeted the opportunity to have Spain as a possible ally to offset a tense relationship with the US. In April 2005 Spain agreed to sell Venezuela $2.3 billion in military equipment, including a dozen unarmed transport and maritime surveillance aircraft and eight patrol boats to combat smuggling. This was Spain's largest-ever defense contract. Washington was not pleased and tried to block it by forbidding Spain to outfit the planes with American surveillance electronics. But Madrid announced it would get the electronics from other NATO allies and go ahead with the deal.

This sale fit Spain's earlier policy of deliberately courting left-wing and populist regimes in Latin America. However, by 2007 it had cooled toward the mercurial Chávez as he became increasingly autocratic. It also became less supportive of Chávez's admirer in Bolivia, Evo Morales, when the latter nationalized the gas sector, in which the Spanish energy giant Repsol had major stakes.

In February 2019 Spain led its European allies in recognizing opposition leader Juan Guaidó as Nicolás Maduro's

legitimate successor as president. As many as 208,300 Venezuelans have sought refuge in Spain.

Bolivia announced in 2012 the nationalization of Transportadora de Electricidad (TDE), which belonged to Spain, but it gave ample warning and promised to pay fair compensation. The same cannot be said for Argentina's announcement in the same year that it would renationalize 51% of its largest oil company, YPF, thereby depriving Repsol of its majority control purchased in 1999. Spain, which is Argentina's biggest foreign investor, was furious. To smooth feathers in 2014, the Argentine government gave $5 billion in compensation to Repsol. In return the latter withdrew a sweeping international lawsuit.

Despite the importance that Spain places on hispanidad, its growing European focus weakens its ties with Latin America, although the region is Spain's most important growth market. Its historical links with its colonies were severed much earlier than were those of Britain and France. The major trade partners are Venezuela and Mexico. Spain is the leading foreign investor in Latin America after the US. This is visible in Cuba, where Spanish hotels are everywhere. The Spanish could never really dominate Latin America; the size of Spain's economy is roughly the same as Brazil's and almost twice the size of Mexico's.

Since 1991 both Spain and Portugal maintain formal ties with Latin America and the Caribbean through annual summits, bringing together the leaders of 21 countries and 489 million people. This is merely a forum for discussion, and it serves mainly to twist arms for trade deals. In May 2010 Spain hosted the EU-Latin America summit in Madrid. The meeting made clear that the global balance of power is shifting to powerhouses like Brazil.

Latin Americans no longer need Spain to achieve their global goals. They do not see Spain as the place of opportunity it once was. In the decade to 2007, about 1.5 million Latin Americans moved to Spain. That direction has been reversed as many return home. Young and educated Spaniards follow them. This outward movement lifts a burden from the labor market, since most are unemployed. For the first time since records have been kept, Spain's overall population is falling. The foreign-born population was 6.6 million in 2014, down from over 7 million just two years earlier. President Rajoy noted in 2012 that more than 1 million Spaniards live in Latin America. Many more leave to seek work in wealthier European countries, such as Germany, Switzerland, or Britain.

In 1992, Spain had hoped to celebrate in grand style the 500th anniversary of Columbus's voyage. But it found at a meeting

Roman bridge in Orense, Galicia

Spain

in Madrid of 19 presidential guests from Latin America and Portugal that the New World has mixed feelings about that explorer who sailed under the Spanish flag.

North Africa and Spanish Enclaves

Franco had also established another special relationship with the Arab states. Until 1986 Spain did not recognize Israel, for instance. But since Franco's death, the Arab states have shown little gratitude for this long-standing policy. Morocco has refused to help implement self-determination for the almost totally nomadic residents of former Spanish Sahara.

With the backing of Arab states, Morocco periodically revives its claims to Ceuta (where 15,000 out of a total population of 85,000 are Muslims and which is located only 14 kilometers from the Spanish mainland) and Melilla (where 27,000 Moroccans and 45,000 Spaniards, including 15,000 soldiers, live). These are the remnants of a string of fortresses Spain built in North Africa after Andalusia was reconquered. These bases have lost most of their strategic importance, and the Spanish and Moroccan militaries exercise and interact with each other quite well, even though Morocco has never formally recognized Spain's footholds there. There is tension between Arab residents (many of whom are illegal) and Spaniards, who show no signs of wanting to be ruled by Morocco.

In 1997, Spain fenced off the enclaves to prevent illegal immigrants from using them to gain access to Europe. The reason is that Spain's per-capita GDP is 12 times higher than that of Morocco. However, these 20-foot-high barriers were not too difficult to overcome and did not prevent the enclaves from becoming centers for illegal immigration to southern Europe. The razor-wire barriers around Melilla were breached in 2005, when close to 700 Africans, some of whom trekked for two years to get there, scaled the fence in a predawn rush. Newer, higher, and more high-tech walls in three layers were built, but they continue to be swarmed by desperate Africans who are not deterred. In 2014 alone, the treacherous barriers were crossed by 2,000 Africans. Some attach hooks to their wrists and screw them to their shoes to grip better. Some try to swim around the barriers, and others use fake papers to blend into the 25,000–30,000 people who cross the border every day to work or buy goods.

In 2006 Zapatero defied decades of Moroccan warnings and made the first visit by a Spanish leader to the enclaves since 1980. The Moroccan newspaper Le Matin called it an unnecessary provocation for him to visit "the last vestiges of a colonial occupation." He wanted to reassure the two cities that Spain would defend them and their borders and be tough on immigration.

Morocco is aware of the steps the Spanish government has made to improve bilateral cooperation. Spain combats Islamic terrorist groups that also threaten Morocco and helps Moroccan officials establish closer ties with the EU. Spain also has a 1992 agreement obligating Morocco to take back sub-Saharan Africans who try to enter the enclaves by land. That caused an international outcry in 2005, when Morocco rounded up the migrants and abandoned them several hundred kilometers in the desert without food or water.

Although Ceuta is only a 90-minute boat-ride from mainland Spain, it is a dangerous trip. One Moroccan association in Spain claims that about 4,000 persons perished in this way from 1997 to 2003. Arabs in the enclaves have the same rights as Spanish citizens. Muslim leaders negotiated with local Spanish officials to improve their social and political conditions, but resistance to their demands remains strong within the Spanish majority.

In order to press its sovereignty claim over the enclaves, a group of Moroccan gendarmes occupied on July 11, 2002, the tiny, uninhabited island of Perejil (Parsley, but known in Arabic as Leila) located 200 meters off the North African coast and claimed by both Spain and Morocco. Moroccan marines quickly replaced them, and escalation followed rapidly. The Spanish government dispatched five warships, a submarine, and helicopters and other aircraft to the area and put the 7,000 troops of Spain's Foreign Legion, who defend the two enclaves, on alert. On July 17 Spanish commandos recaptured the island without firing a shot, and a Foreign Legion unit moved in to hold it.

President Zapatero meets Moroccan King Mohamed VI in Casablanca.

Moroccans accused Spain of hypocrisy for demanding that Britain hand over Gibraltar while refusing to talk to them about doing the same for the enclaves. US secretary of state Colin Powell was asked to mediate the crisis. After he made an estimated three dozen phone calls to both parties, a deal was reached to return the island to its previous demilitarized status. Spanish troops left, and both sides agreed not to send troops there again.

Following a post-Franco tradition, newly elected president of the government Zapatero made his first foreign visit to Morocco in April 2004. Relations improved markedly after he took office. To symbolize an improvement of relations in January 2005, King Juan Carlos made his first state visit to Morocco in more than a quarter-century.

Defense Policy and NATO

Spain's strategic location brought it into an indirect relationship with NATO through a series of bilateral defense agreements with the US beginning in 1953. According to the provisions of this agreement, the US would provide military assistance to the Spanish armed forces in return for the right to have air bases in Torrejon and Zaragoza, a naval base in Rota, and scattered communications installations throughout the country. About 10,000 US troops are stationed in Spain. The periodic renegotiation of these agreements has never been pleasant or easy.

In 1982 Spain became the first country to enter NATO since Germany did so in 1956. Although a majority within the Cortes approved membership, the PSOE and PCE opposed it, and public opinion polls indicated that more Spaniards were against NATO membership than for it. There is an undercurrent of neutralism in Spain. Nevertheless the earlier government pressed on without a referendum on the issue in order, in the words of the former defense minister, "to bring us back into European and democratic circles and to strengthen the democratic system in Spain."

Thus, not only would Spanish defense be boosted, but also its officers would be brought into closer contact with foreign officers who are committed to democracy and civilian rule. Army officers would have to learn foreign languages, travel to other NATO countries, and acquire modern military skills. They would have to accept a promotion system based not on mere seniority but on professional competence, as was already the case for young officers in the Spanish air force and navy.

Modernization is also desirable for strictly military reasons. The army is poorly equipped and has very few mobile units that are up to NATO standards. The air force is competent, but it is scarcely large enough to provide for Spain's own

Source: *The Economist*

air defense needs. Therefore, the government decided to purchase 72 American-made F18A fighter planes. It also acquired an aircraft carrier, called the Príncipe de Asturias, equipped with a dozen vertical take-off Sea Harrier jets and leading a task force that will include four new antisubmarine frigates. Still, Spanish studies concluded that Spain has half the necessary capability for defending its own airspace; the US provided the other half from its bases in Zaragoza and Torrejon (now vacated).

The armed forces had by 2019 been reduced to 121,000 active-duty forces (79,736 army; 17,950 navy, including 5,300 marines; and 21,600 air force), including 3,800 women. It has a total reserve strength of 309,000, and there are 80,210 paramilitary forces, of which 79,950 are Civil Guard. Soldiers are no longer required to perform nonmilitary duties, such as serving as chauffeurs of officers' wives, doing laundry, or making house repairs, with the commanders taking payment on the black market. Also, serving better food lifted morale. When possible, recruits serve near their homes, and they are never posted outside of Spain. The government announced plans in 1996 to phase out conscription in favor of a smaller, better-equipped professional army, and this was completed in 2002. It was to be paid for by raising defense spending, but that did not happen. It actually declined to only 1.4% by 2000.

One consequence of ending the draft was that the military gained a more positive image in the eyes of many Spaniards, who had associated it with fascist rule. Beginning in 2008 the forces were flooded with applications. At first there were five candidates for every vacancy, but the number of candidates shot up as the recession got worse. Almost a tenth of the soldiers—and as many as a third in combat units—are immigrants, mostly from Latin America, who have been permitted to join since 2002. They can only serve up to six years, unless they obtain Spanish citizenship through the normal channels. The defense

Spain

Spanish students at the College of Europe

ministry does not expedite the citizenship process.

NATO also derived important advantages from Spain's entry. It is well situated for resupply from the US. Spain also provides important bases and surveillance posts to protect Mediterranean and Atlantic shipping routes, and it can help deny the exit of enemy ships from the Mediterranean into the Atlantic.

In 1979 the Spanish required the US to withdraw its nuclear weapons from Rota. The African Union has issued a resolution supporting independence for these enclaves, as well as for the Canary Islands. Partly for that reason, the Spanish have declared the latter to be out of bounds for NATO facilities. Spain insists that Spanish officers command all units on Spanish territory. Until January 1, 1999, Spain remained outside NATO's integrated military command structure. It is now an active NATO member.

Despite his 1982 electoral rhetoric, González became more pragmatic about his party's opposition to NATO. He brought it to accept the view that Spain's democracy and political stability, as well as its commitment to Europe, would be best served if Spain remained inside of NATO. He considered it the "logical consequence" of Spain's entry into the EU, which took place on January 1, 1986.

Nevertheless, in March 1986, he fulfilled his earlier promise to allow Spaniards to express their opinion in a referendum. This was the first time that a member of either NATO or the Warsaw Pact permitted a popular vote on continued membership. Polls had indicated that a majority was against remaining in NATO. To sweeten the pill, González set terms: Spain would not join the integrated command structure, would not permit the entry or stockpiling of nuclear weapons on its territory, and would negotiate the progressive reduction of the US military presence in Spain.

The results stunned many anxious observers: 52.5% voted in favor of continued membership, while fewer than 40% voted for withdrawal. An earlier opponent, Socialist foreign minister Javier Solana, was named NATO secretary-general in 1995. The opposition parties were left shocked and divided, while González's moderate and pragmatic brand of socialism was reinforced. More important, Spain had finally and dramatically ended centuries of isolation. No longer would the French be able to joke that Africa begins at the Pyrenees.

In 1988 González carried through with his promise to reduce American military forces in the country. No reductions were sought at Rota, which plays a key role in supporting the US Sixth Fleet. But the 5,000 American servicemen and 72 F-16 fighters of the 401st Tactical Air Wing at Torrejon, which is located only 12 miles from Madrid and had become a convenient symbol for anti-US protesters, were ordered to leave by 1991. The bilateral defense agreement in effect since 1953 was renewed in 2001, allowing full use of the naval base in Rota and the nearby Morón Air Base near Seville. The two allies agreed that it would be a permanent US Marine base for rapid-action operations primarily in Africa. It can accommodate 3,000 marines. Torrejon could be used for fuel stops. There were 1,274 US troops left in the country by 2010.

Spain's government made a crucial decision during the 1991 Gulf War against Iraq to support its allies actively. Before the fighting began, it sent three warships to the Persian Gulf to help enforce the UN embargo against Iraq. When the air war commenced, Spain permitted the Americans to launch B-52 bombing raids escorted by Spanish fighter planes from Morón Air Base, a base jointly used by both air forces. It ferried bombs to the US planes and even supplied ordnance from its own stocks when the Americans ran low. At first, this was highly unnerving and unpopular in a country whose last war outside its borders was in 1898, when Cuba was lost to the Americans. However, public opinion swung around when reports of Iraqi atrocities in Kuwait began arriving.

It was an enormous political risk for González, but it paid off handsomely. He said, "That is what allies are for," and "for the first time in modern history, Spain has stood where it should be." It marked a defining moment in Spain's effort to end its long isolation and shoulder more international responsibility. It buoyed Spanish confidence and helped sweep away memories of neutrality in the First World War and fascist sympathies in the Second.

In 1992–1993 Spain again demonstrated its expanded role in international affairs and the increased professionalism of its military by deploying the Spanish Legion to war-torn Bosnia. This elite unit had been formed in 1920 as a colonial force for Africa and gained a fearsome reputation in the civil war on Franco's side.

Spanish troops participated in the international force sent to Bosnia in 1995 to implement the peace agreement. The contingent in Bosnia (numbering 1,200 in 2004) was the largest Spanish force to be deployed outside the country since the Blue Division fought in Russia on the side of Nazi Germany. In 1999 Spain sent four F-18 fighter aircraft to join NATO's air war against Serbia that aimed to stop ethnic cleansing in Kosovo, and it permitted American military aircraft to stopover at bases across Spain.

Public opinion was mixed concerning this action, especially after the Spanish ambassador's residence in Belgrade had been mistakenly damaged in a bombing raid. It sent peacekeeping forces to Bosnia and deployed 320 there in 2010. In 2004 it had 1,300 peacekeepers deployed in Kosovo. However, it was unable to bring itself to recognize Kosovo's independence from Serbia in February 2008 out of fear that Basques would see that as a precedent and push even harder for their own independence. It withdrew its soldiers from Kosovo in 2009, leaving 10 soldiers. In 2010 it had 1,045 peacekeepers in Lebanon (UNIFIL). It also offered in 2000 to provide 10% of its military personnel to a future EU rapid-reaction force. By 2004 it was already the largest contributor to the NATO

Response Force (NRF), with 2,200 troops, plus ships, aircraft, and helicopters. In 2004 Spain also dispatched military medical teams to the Asian countries devastated by the tsunamis.

Following the September 11, 2001, terrorist attacks against the United States, Spain offered unhesitating support to its ally and sent troops to Afghanistan to participate in the peacekeeping effort after the defeat of the Taliban. In May 2003 Spaniards mourned the death of 62 of their peacekeepers on their way home after a four-month tour in Afghanistan. The 15-year-old Ukrainian Yak-42 plane, chartered by a NATO agency, crashed into a mountain in bad weather while trying to land in Turkey. It was the worst accident in Spanish military history. Spain also lost 17 soldiers in a single helicopter crash in Afghanistan.

In 2010 it had over 1,500 troops deployed in Afghanistan. In 2005 NATO had agreed to expand its mission in the country after Spain committed its troops to western Afghanistan. It moved almost all of its troops out of the relatively secure capital city of Kabul. It set up a provincial reconstruction team (PRT) and protected four other PRTs operating in the area. Its soldiers left Afghanistan entirely by 2015.

Iraq

Spain served on the UN Security Council during the Iraq War in 2003. The Spanish government and president of the government worked hard to strengthen the strategic relationship between Europe and the US. He opposed any signs of resurging anti-Americanism: "We don't always have to agree on everything. But I don't see what's to be gained by beating the drums every time there is a divergence." President George W. Bush appreciated this consideration. In his maiden trip to Europe as president in 2001, he made his first stop in Spain, and his description of former president of the government Aznar was sincere: "José María is a man of principle and a man of courage."

Aznar had a dramatic opportunity to display this in the 2003 crisis in Iraq. While polls indicated that as many as 90% of his countrymen opposed war against Saddam Hussein's regime, he steadfastly supported the US and UK. Although he sent no combat troops to Iraq, he dispatched 200 soldiers to help defend Turkey within the NATO framework, a hospital ship with 900 personnel onboard, a frigate, an oiler, and mine-clearing and chemical weapons decontamination units. After the war he sent 1,300 troops to participate in the postwar stabilization force in Iraq, although he forbade them to engage in combat missions.

Until they were ordered home by the new Socialist government in April 2004,

a Spanish brigade served in a division with Ukrainian forces, led by Poland, and a Spanish officer was the deputy commander. Spain utilized its traditionally close ties with Arab nations to help mediate between the US and the Arab world. Aznar emphasized his conviction that "Europe and the United States have to act together. Any weakening of the Atlantic alliance is directly opposed to Europe's interests." When France and Germany moved to block US policy in Iraq, Aznar enlisted seven other like-minded European leaders to sign an open letter praising a strong US-European relationship.

However, Aznar's deeper motives were to put an end to Spain's peripheral position in Europe and within the EU and to move it into the center of continental foreign policy, heretofore dominated by France and Germany. He saw this as a second transition in Spain following the successful transition to parliamentary democracy after Franco's death in 1975. As one of his aides put it, he hoped to make Spain "one of the few and not one of the many." He himself said, "Spain can no longer be just a nice country. It has to assume its responsibilities." The country's newly established economic strength gave the government confidence that Spain could support a more activist foreign policy and form its own alliances.

By siding with the US and the UK, he furthered his twin goals of raising his country's international profile and gaining American support for his government's fight against Basque terrorists. This policy was fraught with domestic political dangers because not all Spaniards were convinced that a prominent international role is good for them. Since the civil war and Franco's military dictatorship, they are distrustful of military displays. Some were also convinced that Aznar had degraded himself to being a yes man for the American president. There was no doubt that

Spain's international stature and visibility had increased during Aznar's rule.

The Socialist victory in the March 2004 elections brought a dramatic change in Spain's foreign policy. The Socialist Party had always denounced the shift away from the large European continental powers Germany and France and toward the US and Britain. President of the Government Zapatero reoriented the main focus of Spanish foreign policy from being a global player back toward Europe and the EU. He pledged to "return to the heart of Europe" and restore previously "magnificent" relations with France and Germany. This included accepting those countries' views on the new EU constitutional treaty. In February 2005, Spaniards were the first to hold a referendum to ratify the constitution; 77% voted in favor, although only 42% turned out to cast their votes. By contrast, the French rejected it solidly in May. He emphasized that the chief goal is to forge a common EU foreign policy that can deal with the United States as an equal. "It is Europe that must have a great relationship with the United States before any individual country. That will make Europe strong."

He announced a two-track approach toward the United States. On the one hand, he tries to portray Spain as a reliable ally. Foreign Minister Moratinos said that the terror attacks in Madrid on March 11, 2004, proved that Spain "needs the United States more than ever." On the other hand, Zapatero rails against the US policy in Iraq, describing it as a disaster, "neocolonial," and a "huge mistake." He accused both British prime minister Tony Blair and President George W. Bush of having gone to war "on the basis of lies." He suggested publicly that American voters should follow the Spaniards' example and change their leadership by supporting John Kerry for president in 2004. He even offered to go to America and campaign for Kerry,

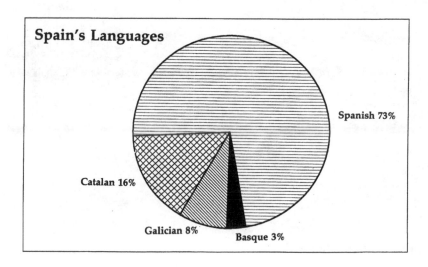

Spain's Languages

Spanish 73%

Catalan 16%

Galician 8%

Basque 3%

Spain

who found this unusual intrusion into the domestic politics of another country embarrassing and unwelcome. President Bush showed his displeasure by refusing to accept a congratulatory call from the Spanish leader after his reelection.

Within 24 hours of taking office, Zapatero announced the withdrawal of Spain's 1,300 troops from Iraq. He had spoken during the campaign about such a prospect only in the event that the United Nations did not assume a leading role in the transfer of sovereignty to Iraqis. Sensitive to charges of "appeasement," he insisted that the withdrawal had nothing to do with the March 11 terrorist attacks and that Spain would continue its help to rebuild Iraq by honoring its pledges made at the Iraq donor's conference. Spain provided €20 million ($28 million) to help finance Iraq's successful elections on January 30, 2005. It left several dozen troops in the country to help train Iraqi forces. Taking a swipe at Aznar, he pledged that Spanish troops would never again be sent on foreign missions "behind the backs of its citizens." In 2019 King Felipe celebrated his 51st birthday by visiting Spain's remaining soldiers in Gran Capitan Military Base in Baghdad.

Zapatero was one of the few European leaders who had never visited the White House. He was shocked that he had not been invited to a November 15, 2008, conference in Washington to discuss reforms to the international financial system. The parties were the G8 countries and 12 large developing countries that together form the G20, of which Spain is not a member. After waging an intense diplomatic battle

to get an invitation, it came, thanks to the intervention of the then–French president Nicolas Sarkozy. He got his handshake with President Bush in the White House and hoped this visit would burnish his image as a world leader.

This is not a role that came naturally to him. He had spent little time outside Spain and speaks no foreign language except a little French. His main initiative was a nebulous "Alliance of Civilizations," which few countries understood or signed on to. He was an admirer of Barack Obama, who paid the Spanish leader a welcome compliment by saying in public, "I am glad to call him a friend." However, he found it acutely embarrassing when Obama declined to attend the US-EU summit held in Madrid during Spain's six-month EU presidency the first six months of 2010.

Gibraltar

The Spanish government also hopes that NATO membership will prepare the way for Spanish sovereignty over Gibraltar, a piece of rock three and a half square miles (six sq. km) in size, where a Muslim army under Tarik ibn Zeyad (thus the Arab name for the rock, gib al-Tarik) landed an army from North Africa in 711 to begin the conquest of Spain. England snatched the rock during the War of the Spanish Succession in 1704 and has held it ever since.

The 34,000 Gibraltarians are not of Spanish descent, although they tend to speak more Spanish among themselves than English. Their habits are more English, though. They lunch at noon, not in mid-afternoon, and eat and drink more British fare. They read English newspapers, and

**Chief Minister of Gibraltar
Fabian Picardo**

their currency is sterling, albeit Gibraltar sterling. They are descendants of various Mediterranean immigrants brought to Gibraltar and include Genoese, Catalans, Jews, Portuguese, and Maltese. The Spanish maintain that the population is artificial and the mere remnant of a foreign naval base and is therefore not entitled to self-determination in the decolonization process. The UN has upheld this claim.

Britain, on the other hand, maintains that no change in the status of Gibraltar could be legitimate without the approval of the population. The preamble to Gibraltar's 1969 constitution reads that Britain "will never enter into arrangements under which the people of Gibraltar would pass under the sovereignty of another state against their freely and democratically expressed wishes." Gibraltarians remain ardently pro-British and profoundly suspicious of Spain. They have their own miniature Westminster-style democracy, and the attempted coup in Madrid in 1981 helped confirm their preference, expressed in a 1967 referendum, when 12,138 voted to remain British subjects; only 44 voted against it.

In 1969 Spain sealed the border between the mainland and the rock. In 1980 Britain agreed to negotiate a settlement. When Prince Charles and his bride decided to visit Gibraltar during their honeymoon cruise, Juan Carlos refused to attend the wedding in London. Also, the Falkland Islands conflict in the spring of 1982 caused further delays. Spain was the only western European land not to support the British in the crisis, and many Spanish see parallels between the Argentines' claim to the islands and the Spanish claim to Gibraltar. Nevertheless, both sides continue to profess the desire to settle their differences. During the Falklands War, Spain did prevent a number of Argentines from launching an attack on Gibraltar from Spanish territory.

View of the port of Gibraltar

Photo by Eugenia Elseth

Goya's epic painting *El 3 de mayo de 1808*, which hangs in the Prado Museum in Madrid, commemorates the resistance to the French invasion, which placed Napoleon's brother Joseph on the Spanish throne.

Spain made a goodwill gesture in 1982 by opening the border to pedestrians. In 1985 it was opened to vehicular traffic. Britain and Spain reached an agreement in 1988 to share Gibraltar's airport, although until 2006 Spain maintained restrictions on airlines approaching Gibraltar and denied them use of its airspace. Planes had to leave from Britain and perform dangerous approaches onto the Rock. The area is so small that its airstrip could not accommodate large aircraft. The road from the border closed every time a plane landed or took off because it crossed the runway; that was fixed when the new airport was finished. The airport is also built on an isthmus that Spain does not recognize as British territory.

In 1997 Spain proposed "shared sovereignty" of the Rock. Although the British rejected it, they noted that the Spanish no longer rule out the idea of Gibraltar's independence, only that "independence will never be granted against Spanish wishes." That is not the same as insisting that the Rock must one day be Spanish.

The concept of "shared sovereignty" was central to the talks that recommenced in 2002. It will be at the heart of any agreement, even though former chief minister Peter Caruana, who refused an invitation to attend the talks unless he were to be granted a veto, rejected the concept, as did 99% of the Rock's population (with 85% voting) in a 2002 referendum on the single question, "Do you approve of the principle that Britain and Spain should share sovereignty over Gibraltar?" London refused to recognize this polling, which was an effort of the Gibraltar government to thwart British plans for a compromise with Spain. It complicates the British government's effort to settle this lingering sore point with Spain once and for all.

The UK's interest in holding on to the colony has waned, and it would like to be rid of it. Gibraltar no longer has the enormous strategic value it once had. The British navy has mostly departed. Mines, long-range missiles, and nuclear weapons make it far easier to block the strait of Gibraltar than to keep it open. The Rock does contain 30 miles of underground tunnels, a hidden strategic command center, and berths for atomic submarines, all of which are important for NATO.

In 1991 Britain withdrew the last of its ground forces stationed there. That was an economic blow, since spending by British soldiers and their dependents amounted to 18% of Gibraltar's revenues and provided a fourth of the jobs. Tourists replace some of the losses. Their numbers leaped from 600,000 in 1984, the last full year of the Spanish siege, to more than 3 million annually in the 1990s. The Rock also lives well from offshore finance and Internet gambling, among other things.

Tensions remain. Spanish leaders are always wary of any moves by Gibraltar to represent itself on the international stage, insisting that it operate through the British foreign office. In 2013 a dispute arose over Gibraltar's constructing an artificial underwater reef made of concrete blocks and metal spikes. The purpose was to stop local Spaniards from overfishing in what the Rock regards as its own waters. Spain retaliated by deliberately slowing traffic across the border.

In 2000 Spain and the UK agreed to allow banking and insurance firms based in Gibraltar to sell products across the EU and to have identity cards issued in Gibraltar recognized throughout the EU. In the same year, the OECD named Gibraltar as an unfair tax haven. Gibraltar's priority is to transform itself from such a haven that is condemned by European governments and international organizations to

Spain

Philip II by Sánchez Coello 1531–1588

becoming a normal financial center with low taxes. The low-tax economy is booming. It grew 30% over four years from 2008, and it was 10.6% in 2015. Unemployment scarcely exists. Every day 10,000 workers commute to Gibraltar from nearby Spanish towns.

The vast majority of residents opposed Brexit and favored the European Union. The UK and Spain held talks after Brexit went into effect on January 1, 2021, to ensure that no border checks would be required for commuting workers.

After the sovereignty negotiations collapsed with the referendum in 2002, the UK and Spain agreed to set this paramount issue aside and to concentrate on cooperation. A trilateral "forum" was created in 2006 to tackle practical mutual problems without backing away from their differing views on sovereignty. It has eased tensions. In July 2009 Spain's foreign minister drove into Gibraltar, thereby becoming the first Spanish minister in 300 years to set foot in the disputed British territory. Spanish critics called him a "traitor," but his visit was part of the current dialogue and cooperation.

The airport got a new terminal that straddles the border so that passengers can exit directly either into Spain or Gibraltar. Its opening was delayed by several years. One can take direct flights from Spanish cities to the colony. Border controls are relaxed. A Spanish ferry service began operating from Algeciras across the bay to the Rock in 2009. Spain now recognizes Gibraltar's international dialing code, making direct dialing possible. The government-operated Cervantes Institute, which promotes Spanish culture around the world, opened a branch on the Rock. Residents can work on either side of the border, and some Gibraltarians even live on the Spanish side and commute to work on the Rock.

ECONOMY

At one time, Spain was a country with a layer of wealthy persons stretched thin over a large population who lived in varying degrees of poverty. Its industry was small, highly protected, unaggressive, and suffering from a general mental inertia. Its agriculture was unproductive, by comparison with other western European nations north of the Pyrenees. The chronically unstable political conditions in the 19th and 20th centuries always hampered economic development and delayed the Industrial Revolution. In the 1940s Spain's national income had fallen to the level of 1906–1907, and not until 1954 was the 1936 level reached.

All of that has changed now that the country has undergone an almost-miraculous economic transformation. The Spanish are now prosperous, and they have the 13th-largest economy in the world, the 5th-largest in Europe, and the 4th-largest in the eurozone. The economy accounts for 12% of the total GDP in the eurozone and 10% of the EU's GDP.

Before the real estate bubble burst, 83% of families owned their own homes, giving Spain one of Europe's highest home-ownership rates. However, since the typical Spaniard had 80% of his assets tied up in real estate, the bust brought massive impoverishment. In 2006 Spaniards had built more than France, Germany, and Italy combined. Housing prices more than doubled between 1995 and 2007, but by 2012 average residential property had dropped in value by a fourth since its peak. The construction boom drove the economy, accounting for 18% of GDP, twice the share in other European nations. But the economy became overheated, and in 2007–2012, the bubble burst, causing a painful slowdown in economic growth. One million new homes stood empty (down to 700,000 in 2014), which had an impact on diminishing property tax revenues, bad loans on banks' and savings and loans' (cajas) books, and growing unemployment: 1 million in the construction industry lost their jobs.

It cannot be denied that Spain had come a very long way since the 1950s. Its economy grew at an annual rate of 3.6% from 1994 to 2007, double the EU average. It slowed down to 1.8% in 2008, then rebounded to 2.8% in 2018. Per-capita GDP had climbed to 90% of the EU average in 2004, up from 68% in 1986, when it joined the EU. Its prosperity was boosted by moderate trade unions.

Prosperity is distributed geographically unequally. In Catalonia, the Basque country, and Madrid, incomes are 25% higher than the national average, and in most of Andalusia, Extremadura, Galicia, and Castilla-la-Mancha, incomes are 30% below the national average. In 2019 unemployment eased down to 14.7% (lower in the Madrid and Basque regions), double the 8.6% EU average. Youth joblessness under age 26 is stuck at 23%, the highest in the EU. Immigrants suffer almost one-third unemployment; many are returning to their home countries, including Latin Americans. Job insecurity is everywhere. With joblessness so high and home values so low, Spaniards are frightened, and everybody feels poorer. This caused a collapse in consumer spending. Young people are so desperate that the military recruiting stations are full, and there are 30 applicants for every opening with the police.

As in all Mediterranean countries, Spain has a sizable "submerged economy," which accounts for an estimated one-fifth to one-fourth of GDP in good times, higher in bad. Up to one-third of the unemployed has an income from unofficial work. Taking this into account, the real unemployment figure is lower. Joblessness is also unevenly distributed. It is much higher in Andalusia and Extremadura. It is a testimony to the resilience of the extended-family-based society that the Spanish can bear joblessness. Spaniards are reluctant to move too far from home, and that is an advantage in bad economic times, when their lifelines are their extended families. Also many young people reside with their parents, whether they want to or not. Almost two-thirds (62%) of Spanish women are in the workforce, but their unemployment is almost double that of men.

In an attempt to maintain Spanish firms' economic competitiveness, the Socialist government introduced the concept of "temporary contracts" in 1984, followed by other labor-market reforms in 1994, hoping to make it easier for companies to hire and fire. These measures antagonized labor unions and voters, who had grown accustomed since the Franco era to life-time job guarantees. But enough obstacles remain to make Spain's labor market one of the world's most rigid. Employers must pay 20 days' salary for each year of employment to workers "fairly" dismissed and 45 days' to those "unfairly" dismissed. The courts almost always rule that dismissal is "unfair." A hesitating Socialist cabinet agreed in 2010 to a very limited reform of the labor market. It makes it slightly cheaper to fire workers so that more permanent employees can be hired. It also restricts an excessive use of temporary workers. Rajoy's PP went a little further.

Not wishing to hire full-time employees who would receive this kind of protection, employers can, since 1984, hire them on

The horror of April 26, 1937, in Guernica . . .

. . . and Picasso's stark depiction—*Guernica*

411

Spain

Guggenheim Bilbao Museum

"temporary contracts," which provide no job security. Thus, a two-tier labor market has developed: one for older workers and civil servants, with such protection that they have little incentive to be productive or to restrain their pay demands, and one for younger ones, who stagger from one short-term contract to another without building real careers. By 2019 over a fourth (compared with 13% in the US and 12% in Germany, Italy, and France) of all workers and two-thirds of young people under age 25 had such contracts. Four-fifths of new jobs are short-term contracts. When a recession hits, as it did in 2008, it is primarily these temps and immigrants who swell the jobless ranks. On the positive side, these give Spanish companies a competitive edge over their French and German rivals. In 2006 the World Bank ranked Spain 30th out of 155 countries studied in terms of competitiveness.

Nationwide collective-bargaining agreements are negotiated for each industry. This makes it hard for individual firms to adjust their employment conditions to their own particular economic circumstances. The result is unemployment higher than it should be.

Economic growth stalled but then picked up to 6.8% in 2021, among the fastest in Europe. Spain once surpassed the United States as the largest foreign investor in Latin America, but that was reversed in 1999, when Spanish investments there declined rapidly. Latin America provides 10% of Spain's direct foreign investment. In 2021 the budget deficit was 7.4% of GDP. Controlling spending is difficult in decentralized Spain because 17 regional governments account for half of it. Unemployment in 2021 was 16.2%.

The total foreign debt stood at 53% of GDP in 2011; by 2019 it was 98%. The real danger is in the private sector, where indebtedness stands at 178% of GDP. Public spending fell from 48% of GDP in the mid-1990s to 40.8% a decade later. Government employment has been cut. Perhaps most significantly, the historical phenomenon in Spain of disinterest or lack of prestige accorded to business activity has disappeared.

There are serious problems. Spain has an aging population, with a birth rate among native Spaniards of 1.32, one of the world's lowest. However, immigrants are more than offsetting the shrinking native population. Inflation fell from 14% in 1981 to .9% in 2021. Productivity is low. Exports are weak, and the trade deficit, high. Corporate taxes and wages are significantly higher than those of its competitors, making it more difficult to compete. Perhaps the greatest problem is the failure to invest sufficiently in research, development, and technology. In 2010 it was investing only 1.35% of GDP in research and development, compared with an EU average of about 2% and 2.6% in the US. Although R&D tripled between 2000 and 2008, private spending on it was negligible. Its number of active patents is 300 per 100,000, compared with 5,800 in the US. It has a weak technology base, and high-tech manufactured exports account for only 5% of its total, compared with 32% in the US and 40% in Ireland.

It has caught up with many other western European countries in terms of social welfare benefits. Almost a third of its unemployed receive some form of assistance, and the social security system is able to provide free or cheap medical care, although its facilities are often overcrowded. It provides pensions, welfare and other social assistance. From 80% to 85% of its funds are provided by a payroll tax on employees. This tax increases labor costs, though, by about 35%.

Madrid was the biggest net beneficiary of EU funds by far, something that changed after 10 new and poorer members joined the EU in 2004 (and 2 more in 2007). It received annually about $7.5 billion in EU regional, social, and "cohesion" funds, plus $6.75 billion from the EU's Common Agriculture Policy (CAP). The total was more than €90 billion ($117 billion). After subtracting Spain's $6.4 billion in annual payments into the EU budget, it chalked up a net gain of almost €8 billion each year, or roughly 1% of GDP.

In recent years EU funds financed from 30% to 50% of infrastructure construction in Spain. In general, that money was used wisely, as one sees from its up-to-date infrastructure and general prosperity. Its roads and railroads are modern and well laid out, helping connect poorer regions to more developed ones. Its new interstate highways are first-rate, and most of them run north, connecting the country with Europe. The Spanish government accepted that it would receive fewer subsidies after 2007, although EU guidelines still permitted subsidies to four of the 17 Spanish regions. It phased in the cuts slowly. Starting in 2012 Spain became a net contributor to the EU budget.

It is no wonder that most Spaniards thought that membership in the EU was both beneficial and good. It brought prosperity, and per-capita income rose. But belonging to the EU was never primarily a matter of money for Spain. It was a symbol of European norms of social progress, democracy, and freedom. It is also a context within which Spain's strength and size can count. Few members were more positive toward the EU than Spain. This is why so many Spaniards were disappointed and hurt when the EU, backed by the IMF, demanded that Spain adopt one of the EU's harshest austerity policies to bring its budget deficit down to 3% of GDP. Enthusiasm for the EU declined. In 2008, only 4% of respondents thought the

EU was bad for Spain; in 2013, that had risen to 37%.

That inflation is under control is partially due to the largely responsible way in which the major labor unions, the communist-controlled Confederation of Workers' Commissions (CCOO), and the Socialist-dominated General Workers' Union (UGT), which work closely together, responded to the economic challenges facing the country. Only one worker in seven (15%) belongs to a union. Yet Spain has the EU's second-worst record for days lost in strikes per 1,000 employees (197.4), after Greece (580).

As in all European countries, the rapid rise in energy prices in the 1970s exacerbated the country's economic problems. Spain is dependent on imported oil for about 60% of its total energy needs. It is only able to produce domestically 2% of the oil it uses. It receives 60% of its natural gas from Algeria via a pipeline through Morocco.

In years of normal rainfall, Spain can provide 15% of its power generation through hydroelectricity. However, since 2004 it has experienced a series of droughts that are increasingly worrisome for the future. Scientists predict that, because of global warming, most of the country will be desert within a half century. Water is already so scarce that, during the summer

months, it must be brought by ship to Barcelona from Marseilles and from a desalination plant in Almería.

It has had modest success in relieving its excessive reliance on imported oil by increasing its use of hydro-, coal, and nuclear power. Local opposition to atomic power has caused Spain's nuclear ambitions to be revised downward. Nevertheless, in 2011 nine nuclear power plants were generating about a fifth of Spain's electricity.

Its greatest hope lies in renewable sources to provide for its future energy needs. They account for almost a third of electricity; of this, wind produces over 14%, and solar, 2%. Its natural conditions are favorable for them: It is Europe's second-most mountainous country, after Switzerland, and it is one of Europe's least populated. Combined with the increasing desertification, Spain has the right climate and geography for wind and solar power. It is already the world's second-largest producer of wind energy, after Germany and slightly ahead of the US. It is also in the front ranks in solar power and biofuels. Gas produces close to a third of its electricity, and coal, 13.5%. The renewable industry suffered from the recession, and investments dried up.

Spain has a modern economy, with 20.7% of the workforce employed in industry (producing 23% of GDP), and 74.9%, in

services (turning out 74% of GDP). Its industries are, as a rule, much smaller than in most EU countries. It has few multinational corporations. Of the FT-500 top European companies in 2008, only 14 were Spanish. Businesses tend not to be as high-tech as in some competitor countries. Half of Spain's biggest companies, including all the auto industry—Europe's third-biggest—and 9 out of 10 top exporters, are owned by foreign companies.

The conservative government had privatized most of the economy. However, a Spanish Society for Industrial Participation (SEPI, which replaced the earlier state holding company National Institute of Industry, INI, created during the Franco era) controls companies that still remain under state control. The state monopolies on telephones (through Telefónica), petroleum (though Campsa) and tobacco (through Altadis, earlier named Tabacalera) have ended, although the state retains some shares in those specific companies.

Foreign trade accounts for 38% of Spain's economy, and the emphasis is on Europe. About two-thirds of total Spanish merchandise exports go to the EU, up from half in 1985, and about 53% of its imports are from the EU, compared with 37% in 1985. Thanks in part to incentives for investment, Spain attracted needed foreign investments. This is no one-way street. Spanish companies also invest heavily in Europe and North and South America. Such activities make Spanish companies global leaders in some industries.

A major problem that cooled the enthusiasm of foreign investors and seriously burdens the economy in certain areas of Spain is the terrorist activity, especially in the Basque country, traditionally one of the most industrialized and economically dynamic regions in Spain. There the ETA forced "revolutionary taxes" on the companies and kidnapped and even killed some leading industrialists and engineers. These tactics prompted other businessmen to leave with their families. The al Qaeda–related bombings in Madrid on March 11, 2004, gave potential investors pause, but they had little economic effect. Nevertheless, Spain will not be wholly attractive for business activity and investments until terrorism has been brought under complete control.

The "primary sector" of agriculture, forestry, and fishing employs 4.4% of the Spanish, produces 3% of the GDP, and constitutes less than 20% of its exports. Its horticulture, poultry farming, wine, and fruit growing are highly productive, but its meat and cereal production is low. Despite the large size of its territory and agricultural population, Spain is not entirely self-sufficient in food. It remains one of Europe's major wine growers and is

Secluded, elegant entrances to several Andalusian homes

Spain

the fourth-largest exporter to the US, supplying 5% of the American market. However, Spain finds it increasingly difficult to compete with wines from countries like Australia, New Zealand, Chile, and South Africa.

It needs to reorganize its agricultural production. But the results of such improvement would be to increase rural unemployment and thus stimulate the flight into the cities and industrialized countries. Among the rural problems which must be solved in order to improve the country's agricultural output are insufficient water supplies, especially in the south; forest and brush fires; soil erosion; the preponderance of small, uneconomical farms in the north and the west; and the existence of large underutilized estates in the south.

A Spaniard eats an estimated three times more fish than the average western European. To supply this immense seafood appetite, the country has built up the largest fishing fleet in the EU and the third-largest in the world. This caused concern over Spain's entry into the EU, and members fight bitterly over fishing quotas. Spain accounts for a fifth of the EU's catch. In 1988 a French coast guard vessel fired on Basque fishing boats that were exceeding Spain's quota. Canada captured a Spanish vessel overfishing off its coast in 1994 and found onboard doctored records and illegal nets designed to catch undersized fish. Despite being caught red-handed, Spanish public opinion was enflamed by this "act of piracy." One of its diplomats proclaimed, "We may not be big in anything else, but in fish we are a superpower."

Two of Spain's major economic assets have been the sun and the sea, and since the 1960s Spain has been one of Europeans' favorite tourist countries. It is the world's fourth most popular tourist destination. With 57.7 million overnight foreign tourists in 2012, it is close behind France as Europe's leader in terms of tourist earnings. Tourism is an important source of income and employment. It is Spain's biggest earner of foreign exchange and generates 12% of GDP directly or indirectly and 13% of jobs. In the Balearics and Canaries, the figures rise to more than a third. It continued to thrive and grow during the economic crisis. It benefited from problems elsewhere, such as in Egypt and Turkey.

However, Spain became expensive for the mass tourism market. Also, the tourism industry is vulnerable to recession at home and in the rest of Europe and to international terrorism. It had only 1 million American tourists in 2002. Not only do Americans spend more money on vacation, but they also are more likely than Europeans to visit cultural sites in the interior of the country as opposed to sunning themselves on Spain's beaches. For a long time, Spain relied on its beaches and good weather to attract tourists, but as the euro hardened, prices rose, and many tourists looked elsewhere. This presented challenges to the industry.

In order to stimulate both tourism and its economy in general, Spain decided in 1988 to modernize its railroad, which was one of Europe's oldest, slowest, and financially troubled. It adapted its narrow-gauge railway system to the one used by the rest of Europe and introduced its first high-speed train (known as AVE, Alta Velocidad Espanola, or Spanish High Speed) between Madrid and Seville in 1992. Its AVE trains are punctual, clean, and highly profitable. The project to create a similar AVE line from Madrid to Barcelona was completed in 2008. That trip takes about 6 hours by car, but only 2 hours and 38 minutes by AVE. Now more Spaniards take the AVE to Barcelona than fly, despite the fact that the price is just as steep: $200 one-way. In 2009 the high-speed trains gained a third more passengers in only a year. In 2010 the king opened a new line from Madrid to Valencia, Spain's third-largest city. This boosted Spain over France as the European country operating the largest high-speed rail network.

The government is building 9,000 more kilometers (6,000 miles) of high-speed lines. The objective is to have a station within 50 kilometers (30 miles) of every inhabitant. There is a confused patchwork of old and new track and systems, and sometimes 21st-century AVEs have to run on 19th-century tracks. Although the AVEs are generally safe, there was a tragic derailment in July 2013 near Santiago de Compostela of a train traveling at more than double the speed limit, killing 79 and injuring 140. There was only one driver at the controls, a man who was talking on his mobile phone seconds before the crash. He had earlier boasted about speeding.

Lines were planned to connect with Lisbon, but they were postponed for financial reasons. Future links to France will require an eight-kilometer tunnel through the Pyrenees. In December 2010 a start was made when a new rail passage across the Pyrenees Mountains was opened between Figueres in Spain and Perpignan in France. Since 2010 Spaniards can fly with a larger airline group after British Airways and troubled Iberia merged.

CULTURE

Languages

Spain's culture and language have taken root far beyond its own borders. In fact, 450 million speak Spanish as a mother tongue in nearly two dozen countries. It

As only the Spanish can dance it—
El Flamenco

has more native speakers than any language other than Mandarin Chinese. It is the only real challenger to English as a world language. Spanish is by far the favorite foreign language in American high schools and universities, and as many as 35 million citizens and residents of the US speak Spanish as a mother tongue.

The official language in Spain is the Castilian dialect of Spanish. It differs in some respect from the many different dialects of Spanish spoken in South and Central America, to say nothing of the Basque, Galician, and Catalan languages. The most audible difference is that the "s" or soft "c" sound in Castilian Spanish sounds like the English "th" sound. Since 1713 the Royal Spanish Academy exists to preserve Spanish grammar and oversee the simplification of spelling. For instance, in 2010 it announced that "ch" and "ll" will be dropped.

There are, of course, many languages spoken within Spain itself, and three are especially important. In Galicia one speaks Gallego, which is more similar to Portuguese than are other Spanish languages. In Catalonia, Valencia, and the Balearic Islands, variations of a separate language called Catalan are spoken. It is a Romance language closely related to Provençal and Languedoc, spoken in France. It has a rich written literature and has always been a crucial cultural tool for preserving Catalan national identity. Catalans want the EU to recognize their tongue as an official language.

Basque, a language with neither Romance nor other Indo-European roots, is spoken mainly in the villages of the Basque country and is seldom heard in the

Días 15 y 16 agosto 1987 - 7 tarde

se celebrarán, si el tiempo no lo impide,

UNA GRAN NOVILLADA SIN PICADORES y
UNA SOBERBIA CORRIDA DE TOROS

SABADO 15 · NOVILLADA SIN PICADORES

SEIS soberbios novillos, SEIS, de
DON VICTOR LOPEZ CHAVES
de SALAMANCA, para los ESPADAS

JOSE JULIAN DENIS
MAREGIL - MARTINEZ - LORE

DOMINGO 16 GRAN CORRIDA DE TOROS

SEIS bravos toros, SEIS, de
«BRANCO NUNCIO» [BN]
de EVORA (Portugal), para los ESPADAS

Carlos Escolar FRASCUELO
FERNANDO GALINDO
SANCHEZ CUBERO

PLAZA DE TOROS **LAS VENTAS**

COMUNIDAD DE MADRID · TOROS MADRID, S. A.

---

two major Basque cities of Bilbao and San Sabastian. It remains, however, a very important vehicle for Basque identity. Some Spaniards are concerned about the number of English words that are slipping into their language, such as "football," "tweet," and "selfie."

Literature and Arts

Spain was always a crossroads between the European and Islamic Oriental cultures. Indeed, some of Europe's greatest writers wrote in Spanish. During the "Golden Age" of the 16th and 17th centuries, Cervantes wrote his classic, Don Quixote, a humorous story of chivalry and lofty, idealistic aspirations beyond all human capacity to achieve. Today, the word "quixotic" is used in English to refer to any naïve venture which, because of hopeless odds, is doomed to failure from the very start. Since Cervantes's death in 1616, the location of his grave was a mystery until 2015, when remains that may be his were found in the Convent of the Barefoot Trinitarians in Madrid. In the 20th century, Spain produced several internationally renowned poets, most notably Juan Ramón Jiménez, who won a Nobel Prize in 1956, and Federico García Lorca, who was murdered during the civil war.

Its novelists, such as Manuel Vázquez, José Heirro, Soledad Puertolas, Arturo Perez-Reverte, Antonio Muñoz Molina, Almudena Grandes, Miguel Delibes, and Manuel Rives, have international reputations. In 1989, Camilo José Cela was awarded the Nobel Prize for literature. Author of 60 disturbing and powerful books, Cela lived an exciting, risky, and iconoclastic life, disdaining authority in all forms. His regular newspaper columns and television appearances also helped make him a legend in Spain.

In art Spain has also distinguished itself. El Greco (words which mean "the Greek" and applied to Kyriakos Theotokopoulos, who lived and worked in Toledo) established his own characteristic style in the 16th century. Diego Rodríguez de Silva Velázquez painted revealing and astonishingly uncomplimentary portraits of the Spanish court during the 17th century, and Francisco José de Goya painted powerful portrayals of revolution and resistance in the 18th and 19th centuries.

In the 20th century, Salvador Dalí, Joan Miró, and Pablo Picasso inalterably influenced modern painting. Because of political disagreements, these artists lived a part of their working lives outside of Spain. Dalí's personalized quirky museum in the

former theater of his Catalan hometown of Figueres, just south of the French border, is unforgettable.

The most ringing protest against Franco and, of course, against war itself was Picasso's *Guernica*, which he painted for the Spanish pavilion of the Paris World Fair in 1937 in order to invoke the memory of the German bombing of the Basque city of Guernica. He then lent the painting to the Museum of Modern Art in New York and ordered that it not be returned to Spain until democracy had been restored in his homeland. In 1980, after a long legal wrangle with Picasso's heirs, the painting was finally returned to the magnificent Prado Museum in Madrid. In 1992 it was moved to the new modern art museum Centro de Arte Reina Sofia. Spanish viewers, who often exclaim in museums, are hushed when face to face with the shrieking victims portrayed in this stark mural. The Thyssen-Bornemisza Museum in Madrid opened in the 1990s to rave reviews.

A major addition to Spanish culture is the Guggenheim Museum in Bilbao, opened in 1997. Costing $171 million to build, this is the anchor project in an effort to preempt Basque violence by emphasizing national pride and culture in a positive way. Basque officials requested that Guernica, the work of art most symbolic of the region, be moved or lent to the museum, which is located only 12 miles from the town of Guernica. Citing the painting's deteriorating condition and concerns over its safety in the Basque area, the request was turned down. This decision sparked fierce controversy. Nevertheless, the experiment of stimulating the entire Basque region through this art magnet is a smashing success. In its first 18 months, tourism in the Basque country increased by 28%, most of it attributable to the museum. It has become a symbol of the area's economic and cultural resurgence that could be secured by the permanent end of separatist violence. In an effort to give a similar cultural boost to the south, a museum in Malaga to honor its most famous son, Pablo Picasso, draws large crowds.

Cinema

Over two-thirds of all films shown in Spain are American, and only 16% are Spanish. Spanish directors have created some very good ones, even in the Franco era. Luis Garcia Berlanga premiered his rebellious comedy Bienvenido Mr. Marshall (Welcome Mr. Marshall) in 1953. Luis Buñuel, who for decades lived in exile in France, Hollywood, and Mexico, was especially acclaimed for his playful and charming films. He aims his subtle but deadly arrows toward the Spanish bourgeoisie, from which he is descended.

Spain

In 2000, Spanish director Pedro Almodovar's film, All about My Mother, won the Academy Award for best foreign-language film, and his 2002 film, Talk to Her, won the Best Original Screenplay Oscar. He comes from a poor village in La Mancha to the south of Madrid, and his loyalty to his roots, despite past criticism of some aspects of Spain, endeared him to most of his compatriots. Two cabinet ministers accompanied him to Hollywood, and in accepting his statue, he dedicated the prize "to Spain and Spaniards." The entire country cheered, and King Juan Carlos and former president of the government José María Aznar sent him congratulatory telegrams.

Others are hard on his heels, such as the female film director and screenwriter Icíar Bollaín (Take My Eyes), Julio Medem (Sex and Lucía) and Alejandro Amenábar (The Others). Amenábar's Mar Adentro (The Sea Inside) took an Oscar in 2005. Javier Bardem, who acts in both English and Spanish, can almost single-handedly make a film succeed. Spain's film success has also helped Latin America: Over half of Spain's co-productions in 2002 involved at least one Latin American country.

The kinds of Spanish films that have won international acclaim are facing domestic competition from another kind of movie which has sprung alive after 1975—pornography. Barcelona has become one of Europe's centers for this. Spain has developed such a tolerant society that it seems unaffected by this type of license. Prostitution (though not pimping) is legal, and even conservative newspapers publish explicit ads for their services.

Two-thirds of the foreign TV films purchased are from the US. Only slightly more than 10% of Spaniards go to the theater, despite heavy state subsidies of theater tickets.

More follow bullfighting: 40% according to polls, although a 2008 survey revealed that 70% of Spaniards disapproved of the sport, especially the young, and only 1 in 10 Spaniards ever attend a bullfight. Bullfighting nets over $1 billion every year, but the number of bullfights is plummeting. It is an expensive spectacle. A normal event requires six bulls, which cost from $25,000 to $100,000 a head. The price for a matador can run from $25,000 to $120,000 for a single afternoon. No wonder ticket prices have shot through the roof. Catalonia banned it in 2012. The constitutional court overturned this ban in 2016, ruling that bullfighting is enshrined in the cultural patrimony of the Spanish state. President Rajoy fiercely defends the sport and is doing what he can to keep it alive. TV again airs fights, and parliament declared bullfighting a protected national cultural pastime, stoking tensions with Catalonia, where it was banned.

Media

The lifting of censorship in Spain brought a flowering daily and weekly press, even though newspaper readership remains low. Only about 8% of Spaniards buy a newspaper, which is half as many as in France and a fifth as many as in Britain. One in seven young adults claims to read any printed medium at all.

Three of the best papers in Europe now come from Spain: Cambio, a weekly modeled on Time; the conservative daily Vanguardia (circulation 198,000); and the liberal, broadly pro-Socialist daily El País, which is unloved by the police, army, and church. El País, which aims to be the global newspaper in Spanish, is the leading paid daily, with a circulation of 434,000 (and declining) copies; it often supports the Socialist Party, for which it is criticized. As a sign of its political influence, former Socialist president Felipe González banned its reading before cabinet meetings out of fear that members would be swayed by its opinion. Advertising revenues for all newspapers have fallen by two-thirds since 2007. The facts that El País is heavily indebted and was forced to lay off a third of its workforce in 2012 reflect the depth of Spain's recession.

A new nationalist daily, Público, hit the stands in 2007. To the left of El País, it is irreverent and aims to attract young people who had not bought newspapers before. El Mundo (312,000) is its livelier conservative rival. La Razón (149,000) is another voice on the right. Even the right-wing monarchist daily ABC (279,000) improved its standards and converted to democracy. Most papers are partisan in one way or the other. As of 2006, the largest general-circulation newspaper, with a total readership of 2.3 million, was the free sheet 20 Minutos, which surged past El País. With another free paper, Metro, nipping at its heels, about half of all newspapers in Spain are distributed free.

It is no longer an offense to question the honor of the royal family or the legitimacy of the monarchy or the unity of Spain. That changed in the wake of so many scandals. The press has become much freer to delve into the personal peccadilloes of the royals. The press is technically forbidden to challenge the honor of the armed forces. But this is changing. For the first time in Spanish history, people can generally speak and write about politics and religion without fear of being jailed.

Television is the real molder of society. Polls indicate that about two-thirds of adults form their political opinions from television, which 87% watch daily. The state remains a large owner and voice in the media. It appoints the heads of state TV and radio, as well as of the national news agency EFE. Critics say this limits the objectivity and selection of images and news. Others argue that the private sector provides an adequate balance. The autonomous governments also run regional channels. In 1991 private TV was established. There are two central and seven regional public-sector channels, four private channels, a subscription company called Canal Plus, and the state's two main TVE networks which also operate TVE Internacional and a rolling news channel,

Plaza de Colón, Madrid. The column has been moved to the street island.

24 Horas. The private channels, Antena 3 and Tele-5, have more viewers than TVE-1. Two of the private channels appeared: Cuatro in 2005 and La Sexta in 2006.

Catholic Church

The church had been one of Franco's chief supporters, and he repaid the favor by restoring its role in the schools and by granting it generous state subsidies. He effectively had the power to appoint bishops, a prerogative which Juan Carlos eliminated. On Spanish coins Franco was called "leader of Spain by God's grace."

In the 1960s, though, the church's support for El Caudillo began to change. Many Spanish priests adopted the ethic of social justice. They formed social action groups and spoke out in support of disadvantaged workers and peasants. Priests in the Basque country, Spain's most fervently Catholic area, sometimes publicly supported the Basque nationalists.

In the 1960s the Catholic lay organization Opus Dei (Latin for "God's Work"), which began its existence in 1928 as a highly conservative effort to become firmly rooted in the society's elite, changed its thinking. It became an important force for rationalizing the economy. From a force for reaction, Opus Dei became one of Spain's most important forces for industrial innovation. Although it had largely lost its influence on public policy by the end of the 1980s, its Spanish membership had by 2006 settled at 35,000 of the world total of 85,000. Pope John Paul II ordered in 1982 that Opus Dei become a "personal" bishopric, meaning that its members owe spiritual allegiance to its head, not to the local bishop. In 2003 he canonized its founder, José María Escriva de Balaguer, who died only in 1975.

By 1972 most of Spain's bishops were moderate. Franco's displeasure was demonstrated by his government's threat in 1974 to cancel the concordat (treaty) with the Vatican. Most Spaniards favored maintaining this concordat with Rome; it provides the state with a voice in appointing bishops, while the church receives a modest subsidy. The church had changed from a major foundation for the Franco regime to a skeptical semiopponent. However, in 2000 it decided not to plead forgiveness for siding with Franco after the civil war.

The church now claims to stay out of party politics, but critics accuse it of meddling in electoral politics. In 2008 the church urged voters not to support parties that talked with ETA; favored abortion and gay rights, including same-sex marriage; and advocated reducing the importance of religion in the school curriculum.

In the 1980s, the church accepted the Socialist Party's law permitting the sale of contraceptives. But it fought in vain to

prevent the full legalization of abortion and divorce, problems that could not be so easily hidden in the medicine cabinet. It is understandable why many Spanish supported the reform to depenalize abortion in 1985 in such cases as rape or where the mother's life is in danger. The government changed the law in order to permit abortions within the first 12 weeks of pregnancy for whatever reason. Illegal abortions have become rare, and 90% of terminations happen within this 12-week period. They can also take place within the first 22 weeks if there is a risk of fetal malformation and at any stage of pregnancy if the mother's mental or physical health is at risk.

According to a July 2010 law, a woman has a right to abortion and need not fear imprisonment. She is allowed to abort within the first 14 weeks of pregnancy with no restrictions. Parental permission for 16- and 17-year-olds is not required, although parents must be informed. The Rajoy government sought in 2014 to tighten restrictions on abortion, allowing it only if it were the result of rape or if having the baby would endanger the mother's health.

The church hierarchy and the conservative opposition expressed outrage and are helpless against Europe's steepest drop in the birth rate, from 19 births per 1,000 Spaniards in 1975 to 11 by 1989. By 2002 the average Spanish woman had become the least reproductive in the EU, with a birth rate of only 1.22 children, down from 2.8 in 1975 but up in 2006 to 1.35. Italy and Greece were close behind, with 1.25 and 1.3, respectively. This is well below the 2.1% needed to keep a population steady. The immigrant population helps bring this rate up. Despite the fact that Spaniards have the longest life expectancy in the EU (86 years for women and 79.5 for men), the overall population is expected to decline.

It is influenced by the fact that 62% of Spanish women are already in the workforce (compared with 75% in northern Europe), and 70% under age 30 have or are seeking employment. Although Spanish families are still cohesive and close, they continue to become less male-dominated than they once were. The government introduced tough penalties for wife beating and discrimination against women at the workplace.

Spain

The government announced some important social changes. Calling himself a "radical feminist" and promising to make sexual equality an "emblematic task," Zapatera appointed nine women to his cabinet in 2008 (up from eight in 2004), including Defense Minister Carme Chacón, who died unexpectedly in 2017 at age 46. He sponsored a law that requires that between 40% and 60% of the candidates in elections be women. By 2017, 139 members of parliament out of 350 were women. The mayors of Madrid and Barcelona were leftist females. He emphasized that women earn one-fifth less than men for the same work, that Spain has one of the highest female jobless rates in Europe, and that only 10% of business executives are female. His government introduced fast-track divorce. It also liberalized abortion laws, eliminated required religious instruction in public schools, legalized same-sex marriages, and granted same-sex couples the right to adopt children.

In 2007 a far-reaching new gender-equality act came into force. It mandates equal pay for equal work. It requires companies with more than 250 employees to implement "equality plans" and become more "family friendly." Since office hours still sometimes end at 8 p.m. or later, many women have to drop out of the workforce when they have children. Female unemployment is almost double the rate for men. In 2007, two-thirds of companies had no women on their boards, and fewer than 6% of directors were female. The law requires listed companies to balance men and women on corporate boards. They must be 40% to 50% female.

Families have become less heterosexual. Spain has a vibrant, flamboyant, and politically active gay community. Some form of civil unions short of marriage were already in place in most of the 17 autonomous regions by 2004. Same-sex marriage was favored by two-thirds of Spaniards in 2005. By a vote of 187 to 147, the Cortes legalized same-sex marriages in June 2005. This included the rights to adopt children and inherit each other's property. In the first half of 2006 alone, there were 4,500 same-sex marriages that included army officers and politicians of the conservative People's Party.

The changed environment in Spain is reflected by opinion polls, which indicated that fewer than 15% of Spaniards considered marriage to be indissoluble. Yet the roots of social conservatism in Spain were also revealed in the fact that it took six years after Franco's death to pass a liberal divorce law, which permitted civil divorce by mutual consent one year after the couple had been legally separated. The debate exasperated church leaders so much that they told Spanish

Catholics that the law does not apply to them.

The former Socialist government wasted no time in enacting an agenda that contravenes almost every tenet of Catholic doctrine, including fast-track divorce, relaxed rules on abortion, and legal stem-cell research. The archbishop of Madrid Cardinal Rauco Varela, despaired, "Madrid has turned into Sodom and Gomorrah." Spain has become the main battleground in the new Pope Benedict XVI's attack against the evil of "moral relativism" encroaching all of Europe.

The church's stand on these issues does not persuade many Spaniards, 82% of whom consider themselves to be "culturally Catholic" and are formally members of the church. In his May 2003 visit to Spain, Pope John Paul II pleaded with the people, "Do not break with your Christian roots!" He claimed, "the Christian and Catholic faith constitutes the identity of the Spanish people." His successor, Pope Benedict, made a one-day visit to Spain in July 2006 to carry the message that the family was "founded on indissoluble marriage between a man and a women." The king and queen saw him off at Valencia Airport.

Most Spaniards favor the strict separation between church and state, which was enshrined in the constitution in 1978. A 2006 poll revealed that, while 80% still call themselves Catholics, only 42% say they believe in God. In 2010, 38% professed devotion to a particular saint, image of Christ, or the Virgin Mary. In 1975, 61% had claimed to go to mass regularly; by 2011 that figure had fallen to 13% (even less in urban areas); 46% of those saying they are Catholic admit that they "almost never go." Further polls in 2010 revealed that only 28% call themselves practicing Catholics, while 46% describe themselves as nonpracticing.

In 2004 only 12% of young Spaniards between ages 13 and 24 said they go to mass every week; in 2005 only 14% described themselves as "religious." A year later, 80% of young Spaniards said they distrusted the church, to which they gave a lower approval rating than to NATO and multinational corporations.

Even the clergy is shrinking. In 1952 Spain had 77,800 priests and 7,050 seminarians studying for the priesthood; today the figures are 18,500 and 1,800. From 10% to 15% of parishes have no priest at all. In 2009, for the first time, weddings in the town hall outnumbered those in church. Clearly secularism is advancing. The church is still strong culturally and is rooted in one half of a divided society. It can mobilize supporters, for example in opposition to more liberal abortion laws. But it does not sway Spaniards' behavior.

Although Spain is officially a secular state, the government and church are closely intertwined. Since 1979, Spaniards can check a box on their income tax designating about a half-percent (.052%) of their taxes to the church. However, the number of taxpayers doing so has steadily declined to under 40%. The government makes up the shortfall of what the church needs with direct subsidies, which account for about 30% of the church's income.

Education

The role of the church in contemporary Spanish society is not a burning political issue. It has largely turned away from active intervention in politics. But it does raise its voice on certain issues, such as religious instruction and parochial schools. The church energetically defends its influence on parochial schools, which about a third of all Spanish schoolchildren attend (twice the figure even of the Franco years) and which have a higher social reputation. These Catholic schools are fully funded by the government. The church is willing to accept some standards and guidelines by the state, such as teacher training and financial accountability. But it wishes to avoid any state control over the content of education in its schools, which it insists must remain religious.

The first Socialist government before 1996 aroused the ire of the church by passing legislation guaranteeing the right to free secular education and thereby reducing the church's influence in the schools. The government also announced that, for the first time, books and teaching materials would be distributed free of charge to some 200,000 schoolchildren attending rural public and private schools. The school-leaving age was lifted to 16.

The second Socialist government refused in 2004 to allow a controversial law to go into effect that would have made religious instruction a required part of the curriculum in state schools. Instead the government allows optional religion courses while integrating religion as a cultural topic in other subjects. All regions permit religious instruction, but it is optional.

Spain must seek to improve education. In 2007 it spent only half the OECD average on schools. One-third of secondary pupils drop out before graduation, twice the EU average. Also, 70% of Madrid 14- and 15-year-olds fail their mathematics examinations. Spain ranked only 29th in the world (behind Morocco and South Africa) as an attractive research and development location. Although it has three world-class business schools—IESE, IE, and ESADE, all private—not a single one of its 83 universities was among the world's top 150 compiled by Shanghai's Jiao Tong University. Its public universities are snarled in a rigid, bureaucratic system that does not contribute to academic excellence. About a third of university students drop out before graduation, and only a third complete their studies on time.

Drugs and Immigration

Spain has replaced the Netherlands as the most important conduit into Europe for illegal drugs. European addicts receive 40% of their cocaine via Spain. In part this is explained by the more open borders to other EU partners, the congenial Spanish-speaking environment for Latin American drug runners, and the 1983 decriminalization of possession of small quantities of soft or hard drugs for personal use. Drug use by individuals in the privacy of their homes is tolerated. The government had made the country's drug laws among the most lax in Europe, and the rapid spread of drug abuse brought a reaction.

Spain has Europe's highest incidence of drug abuse and AIDS (along with Portugal). It is faced with an epidemic: It has an estimated 100,000 heroin addicts, and cocaine use has spread into the middle class. It is reckoned that 1.5 million smoke marijuana often. Most of Spain's heavy drug users are young. The earlier Socialist government had tried to fight back by increasing maximum prison sentences, fines, and indictments for drug traffickers, but critics called these measures too little, too late.

Racial violence was a shock for many Spaniards, despite polls that suggest that they are more tolerant of outsiders than are most other Europeans. By 2010 Spain had 5.6 million foreigners (4.4 million legal), or 12.3% of the total population (the highest in the EU), compared with only 1.6% in 1998.

This includes Europe's largest Romanian (mainly Roma—gypsy, called gitano in Spain) community outside of Romania, numbering 530,000 registered residents. If one includes illegal and unregistered, the number of gitanos climbs to about 800,000. Their number quadrupled between 2006 and 2011. Spain has spent more on social programs for them than any other EU country. Some success has been achieved. Nearly half own their own homes, and 92% live in standard apartments or houses. Only 4% live in shacks. Half are formally employed. All their children attend elementary school. Unfortunately the school dropout rate between ages 12 and 18 is a stunning 80%. Because of the country's high unemployment, severe restrictions were placed on Roma entering. Since 2011 they need a work contract before settling in Spain.

Until 2009 foreigners could bring in their families only one year after receiving a residency permit, but this now applies only to spouses and children under age 18, not to parents and parents-in-law. Moroccans have more trouble integrating than do other large immigrant groups, such as Latin Americans and eastern Europeans.

Spain overtook France as the favored European destination for immigrants behind Germany. That was a dramatic change from the 1950s and 1960s, when it was a net exporter of people. Spain remains open to many newcomers. They are good for a growing economy. But they are among the first to be fired when the economy suffers. About a third were without jobs in 2010. About 2 million paid into the social security system. This is important for a country trying to maintain its pay-as-you-go pensions while experiencing a declining birth rate. It decided in 2006 to lift restrictions on the movement of labor from the EU's new members. But most troubling, it is the closest thing in the EU to a frontier with Africa, with nautical distances of 9 miles (14 km) at the Strait of Gibraltar and land borders along the enclaves.

Most immigrants arrive by plane and, until the 2007–2009 recession, quickly got jobs on building sites or in households. Of those arriving by sea in 2006, the greatest flood was pouring over the shores of the Canary Islands, a 600-mile (1,000 km) week to 10-day journey on dangerously flimsy boats from countries as far south as Mauritania and Senegal. An estimated 1,000 have perished at sea. As an area that depends on 12 million annual tourists, the islanders feel a mortal economic threat. In 2005 alone, 4,700 illegal immigrants were registered in the Canaries, and that number was topped in the first six months of 2006.

Spanish law gives authorities only 40 days to determine the country of origin and deport an illegal alien. This is often impossible, since most migrants get rid of all their passports and identification documents before they set sail. Thus many are turned over to the Red Cross and are allowed to remain in Spain or migrate elsewhere in Europe. In desperation, Spain asked for EU help. Because of the backlash against out-of-control immigration in Europe, the organization agreed in May 2006 to deploy patrol boats, planes, and rapid-reaction aid teams from eight nations to the Canaries. Its European Refugee Fund can be used to pay the cost of sending illegal migrants back home.

Spain also enlisted the help of African countries, including especially Morocco, by offering equipment for patrolling shore lines and all kinds of economic aid. It offered Senegal cash to help repatriate immigrants who are returned to Dakar Airport but lack the money to get back to their villages.

In 2005 the government offered another three-month amnesty, under which 700,000 illegal immigrants were given work and residency permits if they could prove that they had resided in Spain since August 2001 and had a six month work contract. Ecuadorians made up a fifth of the applicants, followed by Romanians, Moroccans, and Colombians. Other EU countries were not happy with this amnesty, since legal residents can freely move within the union.

In 2000 the government created a department for integrating immigrants. Most immigrants live along the Mediterranean coast and in the main cities. Madrid and Catalonia are the favored destinations, with the former preferred by Latin Americans and the latter by North Africans. Demography experts calculate that Spain will need 12 million immigrants until 2030 in order to prevent the population from shrinking below its 2000 level. They help lift Spain's low fertility rate. One in seven children is born to an immigrant mother. A half-million immigrant children attend schools.

The March 11, 2004, terrorist bombings in Madrid focused the spotlight on Spain's ambivalent attitudes toward immigrants. Of the 191 who died in the attack, 47 were foreigners, and all of the suspects arrested were foreigners, most of them Islamic militants from Morocco. Opinion polls reveal that hostility and mistrust toward foreigners are growing, as well as the perceptions that immigrants burden the social welfare system, take jobs from Spaniards, and drive up the crime rate. Verbal abuse and derogatory graffiti are more noticeable, but there was no violent backlash against the Muslim community. They also worry about the effect of so many foreigners on their Spanish national identity. As the government responds by tightening up legal immigration, the illegal variety rises, despite the redoubled efforts to deport illegals and to prevent others from trying to enter the country illegally.

Defenders of immigration as a necessity for the country's demographic health point out that the low-paid newcomers do work that Spaniards do not wish to do, and they actually increase employment. For example, cheap nannies enable more Spanish women to work. The tourism and construction industries depend on foreigners. Immigrant workers are net contributors to the welfare system and generate more than twice the tax revenue they consume. Nevertheless, a majority of Spaniards believe there are too many foreigners in the country.

When its booming economy went into recession, the government introduced in 2008 a program that allows immigrants to take their unemployment benefits in a lump sum, amounting to about €20,000 ($28,000), if they go back to their native countries and promise not to return for three years. There

Spain

were few takers. But the decade-long immigration surge has stopped. By 2010, the number of working-age foreigners was falling as unemployment for immigrants reached 30%. Recession proved to be far more effective than policy in stemming and then reversing the flow.

FUTURE

Spain's future is promising. Spaniards have created one of the most tolerant and permissive societies in Europe. Spain has a democratic constitution. The royal family sacrificed much of their popularity through scandals, but the new king, Felipe VI, vowed to restore respect for the monarchy. Voters avoid extremist parties, trade unions show responsibility and moderation, and politicians are inclined to cooperate with each other. Time has dampened most of the passions over the civil war, fears of military coups, and emotions over NATO. The government decided in 2018 to remove the remains of Franco and José Antonio Primo de Rivera from the monumental Valley of the Fallen outside Madrid to a less prominent place. It shall be converted to a democratic memorial.

Its stability and democratic confidence allow it to reexamine its Franco past cautiously and to identify remains of executed victims during the civil war without tearing the nation apart.

Separatist terrorism in the Basque region has been dealt a series of serious blows by arrests of its top leaders and by elections. ETA promises a definitive end of its terrorist activities. In 2017 it apologized and revealed the locations of its weapons caches. After March 11, 2004, a greater threat facing the country is radical Islamic terrorism, stemming primarily from Morocco. The liberal, parliamentary order has sunk its roots deeply. It has already long outlived the earlier republic, during which 18 governments fell before Franco took full control. Nevertheless, in 2020 about two-thirds of Spaniards declared themselves dissatisfied with democracy in their country.

The economy was seriously troubled by its worst recession since the civil war. The five-year recession is over, but due to the coronavirus Spain still has not regained all the ground it lost. The EU is slowly loosening austerity. Economic growth of 6.8% is among the fastest in Europe. Its housing market is picking up. Unemployment (at 16.2%) is serious. The budget declined slightly to a 7.4% deficit in 2021. Its gaping current-accounts deficit has leveled out.

Voters blamed President Rajoy, the EU, and Germany for the austerity that was required. He sought to introduce real labor reform, snip away red tape that hurts businesses, shore up the hated banks, reduce the budget deficit, and lead his

King Felipe VI and family

countrymen out of the housing and unemployment crises.

Faith in politicians is at rock bottom. Parliamentary elections are contested by a left-wing Podemos (We Can) party that feeds on the frustration of many Spaniards. The centrist Citizens Party (Cs) has also grabbed seats. It is catching up with PP and could possibly displace it as the main party of the center-right. The votes produced two large parties that could not construct a majority coalition. The result was a hung parliament that was confused and fragmented. Months of haggling brought no resolution, so new elections were necessary. Pre-election polls predicted a dramatic resurgence of the far-left Unidas Podemos bloc, but that did not happen. The once-mighty Socialists also stumbled. The PP again emerged as the largest force in parliament, but its 137 seats offered no chance of achieving an absolute parliamental majority. In June 2018 Mariano Rajoy was replaced as president of the government by Socialist leader Pedro Sánchez. He leads a weak minority government with Podemos.

A major threat to Spain is the political turmoil stoked by the independence movement in Catalonia. That conflict represents one of the biggest crises Spain has faced since Franco's death in 1975.

Madrid staunchly opposes Catalonian separation, now supported by half of Catalans. The region remains volotile. Despite political passions, Spain is experiencing no surge in extremism or violence and no overt expression of antipathy toward immigrants.

As serious as the independence movements are, the coronavirus plague is far more deadly. Prime Minister Sanchez calls it "the most serious situation the country has faced since the civil war." Spain is suffering one of Europe's most severe outbreaks.

On December 6, 2018, Spain commemorated the 40th anniversary of its democratic constitution. The country has changed out of all recognition. It is more than twice as rich, is socially tolerant, has a vibrant democracy, and is fully integrated into Europe.

Portugal

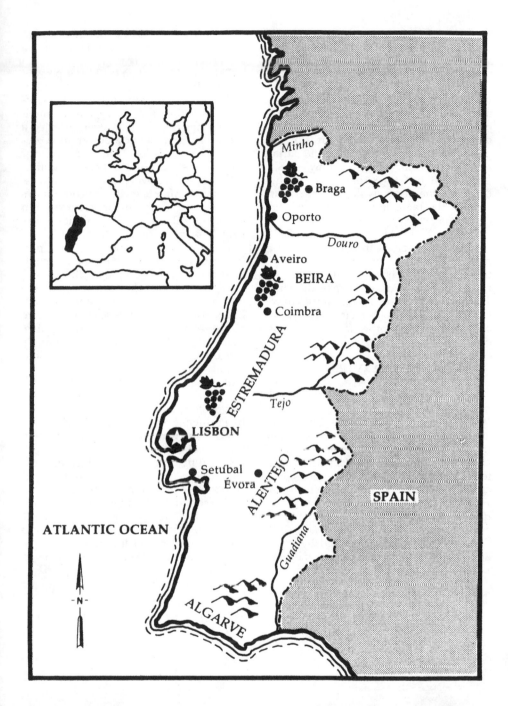

Currency: Euro.

National Holiday: June 10 (Luiz de Camões Day, and Day of the Portuguese Communities).

Chief of State: Marcelo Rebelo de Silva, President (since January 2016).

Head of Government: Antonio Costa, Prime Minister (since November 2015).

National Flag: From the hoist, green and red vertical fields, the green being somewhat less than half of the flag. The Portuguese coat of arms is imposed where the two fields meet.

Portugal entered the 1970s as a conservative, industrially underdeveloped country at the bottom of western Europe's economic barrel. It had an authoritarian political order that suppressed all signs of genuine opposition. It therefore was an embarrassment to its NATO allies, which sought to defend democracy on both sides of the Atlantic. It was embroiled in a multitude of hopeless colonial wars in an attempt to maintain control over an empire more than 20 times the size of the mother country.

Yet by the 1980s, Portugal offered an almost entirely different picture. It had undergone a revolution that, though claiming almost no lives, drastically altered many aspects of the country. It is now a thriving democracy in which persons of all persuasions can speak and act openly. Although it is one of western Europe's poorest nations, with the Continent's highest infant mortality and illiteracy rates, it was willing to accept the economic challenge of entering the EU. It is a country now entirely stripped of its colonial empire, but it is much healthier and stronger as a result. It is a democratically ruled member of NATO with an army radically reduced in size but with military facilities of great strategic importance for the alliance.

The Portuguese are tolerant, friendly, polite, and patient. They have an expression for that: *brandos costumes* (mild ways). It is a mixture of understanding tolerance and acquiescence. They form a relatively cohesive society. Without these qualities, the Portuguese would not have survived so well the radical changes that have occurred in the country since 1974. The population is largely homogeneous. But there are over 100,000 blacks from the former African colonies; 10% of Lisbon's population is black, some of whom have been the targets of racist attacks. There are also about 90,000 gypsies, who have not integrated as well in Portugal as they have in Spain.

Few European countries have such a large portion of its population living abroad as does Portugal. Since the 15th century, the Portuguese have emigrated in large numbers, first to Brazil and then,

Area: 35,553 sq. mi. (92,082 sq. km), not counting the Azores or Madeira; about the size and general shape of Indiana—380 miles north to south, and 140 miles at its widest point.

Population: 10.2 million (2021 est.).

Capital City: Lisbon (pop. 2 million). Lisboa in Portuguese, pronounced Leesh-boa.

Climate: Mild and rainy weather in late fall and early winter but cold and snowy in the mountains. From June to September, the days are hot, but the air is rather dry.

Neighboring Countries: Spain (north and East); Morocco (southeast, 140 miles across the ocean).

Language: Portuguese.

Principal Religion: Roman Catholic.

Chief Commercial Exports: Machinery, transport equipment, foodstuffs and tobacco (wine, canned fish, tomato paste, olive oil), chemicals, minerals, clothing and footwear, cork, wood and wood products.

Major Trading Partners: EU (74.4% of exports and 73.6% of imports), Spain (24.65% of exports and 30.7% of imports), Germany (13.3% of exports and 12% of imports), France (11.9% of exports and 6.7% of imports), Angola (5.4% of exports), UK (5.1% of exports), Italy (5.2% of imports), Netherlands (4.7% of imports).

Portugal

after Brazilian independence, to such destinations as North America, Venezuela, Angola, and Mozambique. However, after 1955 the greatest number of Portuguese emigrants, two-thirds of whom left agricultural areas in Portugal, went to industrialized western European countries, especially France and Germany, in order to find employment. From 1960 until 1972, 1.5 million Portuguese left the country. Emigration has slowed down considerably due to the dramatic economy and political improvements in Portugal after 1974.

The US is now the single country that accepts the greatest annual number of Portuguese emigrants. Indeed, more than 1 million Portuguese live there. Most of them are from the Azores. By 1987 the total number of Portuguese living abroad was more than 4 million—roughly 40% of the country's total population. They send back billions in remittances every year.

Portugal is a rectangular-shaped country, a little larger than the state of Maine but with 10 times as many inhabitants. It has a long Atlantic coastline, along which most of the country's inhabitants live, and it has only one neighbor: Spain. The country is separated into northern and southern halves by the Tagus River. The north is cooler and more mountainous, with small family farms and three-fourths of the entire population. The south is hotter and drier, with rolling plains and large farms, called latifundios.

Astride the line between the two halves is Lisbon, where the Tagus empties into the Atlantic Ocean. The capital city is located on seven hills and still reflects a physical character shaped by its Moorish past. It is

the heart of a highly centralized country and has all too often in the past looked down upon the rest of the country and has seemed to be uninterested in the fate and welfare of the regions. With all its suburbs, it counts almost 2.5 million inhabitants. It and greater Oporto, which is Portugal's only other major city and has 800,000 residents, have attracted three-fourths of the population that is active in the industrial and service sectors of the economy.

Portugal has three main rivers: the Douro in the north, which empties near Oporto; the Tagus in the middle; and the Guadiana, which forms part of the border with Spain and then empties into the Gulf of Cadiz. All originate in Spain, but almost none is navigable between the two countries. Indeed, the transportation links between Spain and Portugal remain difficult. This is a major reason both countries have stood for so long with their backs practically toward each other facing different directions.

CONTEMPORARY HISTORY

In 1834 Portugal became a constitutional monarchy in a setting of bitter power struggles and intrigues among rival claimants to the throne and between conservatives, who supported the Catholic Church and the nobility, and liberals, who wished to reduce the power of those groups. Except for a relatively brief respite between 1851 and 1910, the century preceding the military takeover of power in 1926 was an era of restlessness, discontent, and civil disturbances. It was peppered by wars and revolts which so shook the land that

conservatives and liberals finally agreed to avoid bloodshed by alternating power in a system called *rotativismo*.

This rotation system could not prevent the steady erosion of support for the monarchy, caused by financial and colonial difficulties and by the rising political ambitions of the middle class, which wanted a greater share in political power. In February 1908 King Carlos I, a man of absolutist inclinations and a lust for personal gratification, and the crown prince were both assassinated. After a spell of uncontrollable political turbulence, the monarchy fell in October 1910. As usual, the military was heavily involved in this overthrow.

The monarchy was replaced by a parliamentary republic, whose main accomplishments were to separate church and state, to end Catholicism's status as the official state religion, and to terminate religious instruction in state schools and state aid to religious schools. But the republic could not find solutions for the country's economic problems or the political factionalism, extremism, terrorism, anarchy, riots, strikes, and attempted coups d'état, which continued to be a part of daily political life. The republic was further weakened by Portugal's participation in World War I, which in no way unified the many leading groups behind a common objective.

Not only were many politicians corrupt and incompetent, but also the rapid turnover of governments prevented any policy continuity. Portugal had an average of three governments per year until 1926, when the military stepped in again and took political power into its own hands. The military takeover was not followed

Lisbon from the Tagus River

422

by a bloody civil war, as in Spain a decade later. The reasons are that the years of political havoc had not thoroughly polarized Portuguese society, as had been the case in Spain. Also Portugal has, in general, a more homogeneous, less fragmented society than its neighbor, Spain.

Military-Fascist Rule

In order to attack the financial problems, especially inflation, which the years of chaos had exacerbated, the generals in 1928 named an economics professor from the University of Coimbra, Dr. Antonio Oliveira Salazar, as finance minister. In 1932 he became leader of the only legal party and prime minister, the post that until 1974 remained the heart of political power in Portugal. He established a fascist state, called the Estado Novo (New State), which he guided until his incapacitation in 1968. In 1933 a constitution was promulgated that had a few trappings of parliamentary government, such as a unicameral National Assembly and a directly elected president.

The corporatist character of the new constitution was embodied in an advisory organ called the Corporative Chamber. This allegedly united all classes by bringing together representatives of diverse economic and professional groups in order to evaluate all legislation. Over the years other organizations were established to encompass workers, employers, craftsmen, landowners, rural laborers, fishermen, women, and youth in order to lock all citizens tightly into a bundle of groups, all directed from the top by Salazar. There was only one legal political party, the União Nacional (National Union), which never played a central role in Portugal, as did the Nazi or Fascist Parties in Germany and Italy.

The Portuguese political system was complicated in theory, but it was rather simple in practice. With the advice of trusted cronies from industry, the military, and the church, Salazar made all crucial political decisions. Freedom of press and assembly were curtailed, and all written and electronic communications were censored. Critical professors were dismissed, and strikes were outlawed. As every Portuguese knew, the secret police (PIDE) was ever present. It is estimated that 1 in 400 Portuguese were paid informants.

When the Spanish Civil War broke out in 1936, Salazar ordered the creation of a "Portuguese Legion" to fight on General Francisco Franco's side. About 6,000 Portuguese fought against the Spanish Republic. Portugal also tolerated the transport of munitions from France across its territory until mid-1937, when the British, Portugal's closest ally for three centuries, pressured Salazar into closing its borders to such war material. On March 17, 1939, Franco and Salazar signed a nonaggression and friendship pact, which was amended on July 29, 1940, to obligate both governments to discuss their mutual security interests with one another whenever the "independence or security" of one of the countries is endangered. That pact remains valid.

Portugal, like Spain, did not become linked militarily and diplomatically with Germany and Italy before and during World War II. Portugal even profited from its neutrality; the country became one of Europe's major centers for spies from all belligerent countries. However, Salazar's sympathies were revealed when he ordered a day of national mourning after Hitler had committed suicide.

Portugal's valuable strategic position and long-standing relationship with Britain enabled it to become a founding member of NATO, and in 1955 Portugal was admitted to the UN. However, Portugal remained in an economic, social, and political condition of stagnation and immobility, ruled and administered by an aging dictator and a tight clique of generals, admirals, and bureaucrats, who, through a swarm of spies, rendered the population submissive but increasingly dissatisfied and restless.

In 1968 a law professor, Dr. Marcelo Caetano, assumed leadership over this regime, which was in the process of rapid decay. He had high hopes of reforming and liberalizing the authoritarian system that his predecessor had created, but it had become far too late for such reform. Portugal had just about reached the exploding point, and all that was needed was a spark. That spark came in 1974 from the same institution that had stepped into the Portuguese political sphere many times before and that had established the half-century dictatorship in the first place in 1926—the military.

Colonial Problems

The last straw was the seemingly endless wars in Portugal's African colonies, which the Portuguese preferred to call ultramar (overseas territories). The Portuguese settlers had always mingled more easily with nonwhite native populations than did the British, French, and Belgian colonizers. One still sees the results of this in Brazil, where blacks and whites seem to live together relatively harmoniously (albeit under a predominantly white elite). Also, nothing resembling an official apartheid ("separateness") policy ever developed in the Portuguese colonies, such as in formerly British and Dutch South Africa.

A certain conviction that Portuguese rule was both good and tolerable for the subject peoples, combined with the economic importance for Portugal and with the fact that there were over 1 million Portuguese living in the colonies, led Portugal to hang on to its empire long after the other European nations had decided to relinquish theirs. Foreign Minister Franco

Salazar greeting Spain's Franco

Portugal

War in Angola: A troop carrier swerves to avoid a road trap.

Nogueira even wrote in 1967 that the Portuguese considered themselves "to be an African nation." The obvious point, however, was that the bulk of the native populations in the colonies did not consider themselves to be *Portuguese*.

In 1961 India simply invaded and annexed the miniterritories of Goa, Damão, and Diu. Since 1913 the Portuguese had had to quell occasional native uprisings in Africa. In 1961 these uprisings reerupted, first in Angola around such groups as the Popular Movement for the Liberation of Angola (MPLA), the Angolan National Liberation Front (FNLA), and the National Union for Total Angolan Independence, (UNITA), then in 1963 in Mozambique (led by the Front for the Liberation of Mozambique) and in Guinea-Bissau. The Portuguese government decided to hold on to the African colonies at all costs, fearing that their loss would spell the doom of the Portuguese state. In fact, it was this decision more than any other that led to the ultimate downfall of the Portuguese fascist regime.

Military Unrest

By 1974 there were 170,000 men in the Portuguese army, 135,000 of whom were stationed in Africa. The lion's share of these troops was four-year conscripts, who increasingly resented their role in quelling native rebellions against a regime that fewer and fewer Portuguese wished to preserve. The need to expand the size of the army to cope with the African wars brought many young men from the lower classes and the universities into the officers' corps. These groups had earlier been largely excluded from the officers' ranks and were more inclined to sympathize with the rebels' aims. These young officers gradually lost faith in the kinds of arguments that had long been used to justify the protracted colonial struggle. Many became inspired by the revolutionary ideas espoused by their African adversaries. They grew to dislike strongly their more traditional military superiors. These radicalized lower-ranking officers formed the illegal Movement of the Armed Forces (MFA), which became the core of opposition to the regime.

Their convictions and confidence were enormously strengthened by the appearance in February 1974 of a book that must be considered one of the most significant in modern Portuguese history: *Portugal and the Future*. It was written by the monacled General António de Spínola, the former commander in Guinea-Bissau whose legendary bravery in battle had won him the admiration of the lower ranks. Spínola advocated a political solution to the colonial question and the establishment of a sort of Portuguese commonwealth of nations, similar to that of the British. It is not surprising that Dr. Caetano reportedly could not sleep the night after he had read the book.

The "Carnation Revolution"

Plotters in the MFA went to work on a plan to overthrow the regime. The key discussions took place at a series of innocuous picnics, making this the only revolution in history to be hatched at picnic gatherings. In the night of April 25, 1974, troops numbering about 5,000 occupied Lisbon in a well-planned operation. Since most officers had become indifferent to the survival of the regime, there was no resistance to the surprise coup. Some nervous PIDE agents (which the underground press had called "Gestaportuguese"), who had fled to their headquarters in panic, had reportedly fired on a small crowd (reports differ, but the total casualties did not exceed four). Except for these, not a shot was fired to defend a fascist regime that had ruled Portugal for about a half-century. Rarely in history has such a fundamental political change occurred with so little loss of life.

The plotters formed a Junta of National Salvation, which abolished the PIDE and announced that the colonies would be granted the right of self-determination and that political exiles would be permitted to return to Portugal. Political enthusiasm burst into life, and public debates, rallies and street demonstrations seized a nation in which such things had been forbidden for 48 years.

For two years Portugal was rocked by a succession of provisional governments and confusing revolutionary turmoil. While this turmoil was fired by much emotion, it occurred in the traditional Portuguese style of little actual bloodshed. The new leaders were in such a hurry to cut their former colonies totally loose that they made little effort to try at least to introduce a stable transfer of power in the colonies to groups that might have been willing to legitimize their rule through democratic elections. The MFA's strong Marxist bias inclined it to hand over power in the colonies to like-minded revolutionaries.

Decolonization and Internal Turmoil

Most of Portugal's land area and its worldwide population were reduced by 65% overnight because of the rapid Portuguese withdrawal from the African territories and Timor in the Far East. This created a particularly great refugee problem for the home country. Between 1974 and 1976, at least a half-million refugees poured into Portugal, mainly from Angola. In March 1977 the new Marxist leader ordered the expulsion of all persons holding Portuguese passports, so a new wave of expellees began to pour in. The US helped pay for the airlift of the *retornados* (a term Portuguese dislike today because it implies the returnees were not welcome) and gave Portugal more than $1 billion over five years to help cope with the financial crisis.

The returnees arrived in a chaotic Portugal with few possessions and with currencies that were not accepted in Portugal. Many were convinced that their home government had sold out to revolutionary terrorists and were therefore deeply embittered and inclined toward active, anticommunist, and conservative politics. Their

Portugal

The military coup, April 25, 1974

bitterness was also stimulated by the facts that there were almost no jobs for them in Portugal and that the government could provide only meager financial assistance. Many only found shelter in shantytowns that cropped up everywhere. In some places, especially in Algarve, the government commandeered luxury hotels for the returnees, a logical and humanitarian action which, however, almost bankrupted the country and deprived one of Portugal's most important industries, tourism, of many needed facilities. Ultimately the returnees were dispersed more evenly throughout the country and slowly began to find work. But the initial problems for the shaken country were immense.

There were moderates within the ruling MFA, such as General Spínola, whom the MFA had appointed immediately as provisional president, who believed that the new leaders had moved too far to the left. As a result of unsuccessful countercoups against the leftist elements within the leadership in September 1974 and again in March 1975, the moderate elements within the government were purged and, in some cases such as Spínola himself, were driven into exile.

Those leaders who remained were highly critical of what they derided as "bourgeois democracy." The avowedly procommunist Colonel Vasco Gonçalves advocated the creation of Soviet-style "committees for the defense of the revolution," and the swaggering admirer of Fidel Castro, General Otelo Saraiva de Carvalho, championed the notion of "people's power" to replace the political parties. These leaders, along with a more pliant presidential replacement for Spínola, General Costa Gomes, allowed the communists and the far left to assume control of the trade unions, the news media, and local governments.

They ordered the soldiers not to intervene when left-wing mobs broke up socialist and conservative political gatherings. They nationalized major industries, insurance companies, and banks, and they looked on approvingly as workers seized factories and as peasants took over land in the central and southern provinces. Roughly a fourth of Portugal's forest and croplands were seized, and most of them were converted to forms of collectively owned farms. But these new farms, especially in the province of Alentejo, where farming had traditionally been done on large estates called latifundios, were so inefficient that, by the end of the 1970s, Alentejo produced about a third to half of the grain and livestock it had supplied before the revolution.

The MFA's revolutionary economic experiments were devastating for the country, and they aroused intense opposition. It almost seemed that Portugal was going to return to the political havoc that had stricken the country before 1926. But the politically naïve and inexperienced captains, who suddenly wore colonels' and generals' brass on their shoulders, lost sight of one important factor: the Portuguese voter.

They had announced that they intended to hold power for three years, but they did not prevent the holding of elections in April 1975 for an assembly that would produce a new constitution. They dismissed the elections casually as a mere opinion poll that could not possibly lessen their grip on political power. However, the results stunned them. In the first free election in a half-century, 92% of eligible voters turned out to give a massive vote of no confidence to the heavy-handed, revolutionary-authoritarian rulers. Over 70% of the voters supported the three moderate democratic parties, and only 17% supported the soldiers' only friends, the communists and their allies.

The officers in power made it clear that they had no intention of honoring the results of the election. Instead they moved to

Portugal

eliminate entirely the freedom of the press. The supporters of the democratic parties thereupon poured into the streets to show their disapproval. Beginning in July 1975, anticommunist riots erupted in the north in reaction to a communist bombing campaign there. This massive resistance jolted the majority of military officers out of their state of indifference. When far-left paratroopers supporting General Otelo tried to seize full power for themselves on November 25, 1975, Lieutenant Colonel Ramalho Eanes led a crack commando force to foil the uprising. Eanes, who had heretofore been almost unknown, took the revolution back to its democratic purpose. In the aftermath, all communists and extreme leftists were purged from the MFA and from all governing bodies, and the communists' hopes of taking command over a radical revolution were dashed.

A decade later, Otelo was put on trial for his continuing support for leftist revolution. The press dubbed it the "trial of the century," and it lasted 19 months. He was convicted in 1987 of belonging to a terrorist organization, Popular Forces of April 25 (FP-25), which was suspected of being responsible for at least 15 assassinations of businessmen and landowners and for attacks against the US embassy, NATO warships, and the residences of German airmen. Forty-seven codefendants were also convicted. In 2001 a Lisbon court acquitted Otelo of terrorism charges.

In the mid-1970s, foreign observers were left dizzy by all the fundamental shifts, from right to left and then back to center, where Portugal was to stay. Most Portuguese had wanted a revolution, but they had wanted a moderate democratic revolution, one that would bring them a stable and just political order, protection of individual rights, and ultimately economic prosperity. The last 50 years had brought them enough tyranny and extremist politics. Within a year and a half, the Portuguese revolution had been tamed.

In February 1976 the MFA signed a pact with the political parties that greatly restricted the political role of the military. In April 1976 the assembly that had been elected a year earlier to write a new constitution completed its job. Elections in the same month produced another victory for the moderate democratic parties. Eanes, who had been promoted to the rank of general, was elected president in June 1976, an office he occupied for a decade. One month later he swore in Portugal's first truly democratic government since 1926. Within a few months, the radically revolutionary military officers disappeared from the political stage. In 1996, Portugal's first contemporary history museum, charting the transition from dictatorship to democracy, was opened in

Leiria. It contains official archives of the 1974 armed forces revolt.

GOVERNMENT

The Arrival of Democracy

One of the most astonishing aspects of Portuguese events after April 25, 1974, often called the "Carnation Revolution" because of its bloodless character, was the speed with which the Marxist flirtation expired and the extent to which the revolution became tamed. Within two years, the swaggering officers who had seized power and set Portugal on the fast track toward a radical socialist state had disappeared almost completely. The rigidly orthodox Portuguese Communist Party (PCP) saw much of its electoral support evaporate.

Within two years the moderate democratic parties could claim the support of more than 80% of the voters. Also, a president was in office who had snatched the revolution from the clutches of the extreme left, even though he had moderate leftist sympathies and saw the revolution as something more than the mere establishment of a politically democratic system. He had left no doubt whatsoever that he would support democracy with all the vigor that his serious and ramrod frame could muster.

The salvation of democracy in Portugal was aided by other important factors. First, the extremists were effectively challenged by a democratically oriented Portuguese Socialist Party (PS), led by Mario Soares, a product of one of the country's most prominent families and one of the most respected Portuguese political figures. His popularity within Portugal helped him counter the communist grab for power by presenting a responsible, socialist, democratic alternative to the Stalinist, heavy-handed, Moscow-oriented PCP. Also, his prestige abroad helped bind Portugal's untried democracy to the west. The PS was also aided by the existence of attractive social democratic models in other western European countries, such as Germany.

A second factor was US financial assistance. In addition to helping finance the return of many refugees from Africa to metropolitan Portugal, the US granted $1.5 billion in economic assistance from 1975 to 1980. This was the largest contribution any single western country made to the $2.3 billion worth of aid given to Portugal during that period. The US also provided it with long-term, low-interest credit to purchase grain and animal feeds. This example of enlightened self-interest

Former president Ramalho Eanes

426

Lisbon: panoramic view of Ponte Vasco da Gama Bridge over the Tagus River

reflected the earlier insights of the Marshall Plan in the rest of Europe after World War II—the best policy against Marxist appeals is economic success. The US held itself aloof from Portugal's domestic battles and thus enabled the democratic forces to expose the blatant communist attempts to seize power, backed by money from the Soviet Union.

A final factor, and perhaps the most important, was the fact that the Portuguese were tired of 50 years of dictatorship and desperately wanted an effective economy to scrape the country out of the bottom of the western European economic barrel

and to set it on the path to stability and prosperity.

In spite of the success in grabbing the revolution out of the eager hands of the extremists, there were significant visible traces of revolutionary enthusiasm left in the constitution and the political and economic system, which could only gradually be erased. One was the far-reaching nationalization of much of the economy; article 10 of the constitution called for "the collectivization of the main means of production." Second, the constitution of 1976 ruled out the idea of a market economy and placed severe limitations on any nonsocialist government.

Article 1 called for "Portugal's . . . transformation into a society without classes." Article 2 obligated the nation's leaders to "assure the transition to socialism through the creation of conditions for the democratic exercise of power by the working classes." A third remnant was the appointment of the Revolutionary Council, the governing body of the old Armed Forces Movement, as a kind of watchdog of the revolution. Article 273 of the constitution gave the army the duty to "secure the continuation of the revolution." This body was composed of 14 military officers chosen among themselves, the heads of the three branches of the armed services, and the president of the republic, who was chairman of the council. It had the power to block or even to veto parliamentary legislation, a power it was not afraid to exercise.

A New Constitution

A fourth remnant is the strong presidency, elected every five years by direct,

universal suffrage. A president may be reelected only once. The president relinquished in 1981 the post of supreme commander, and he can no longer control promotions within the armed forces. According to the 1982 constitution, the government is responsible only to the parliament and not to the president. The latter can dismiss a government only after consulting the constitutional committee. But as the country saw in 2004 and 2005, the president indeed retains the power to appoint prime ministers, dissolve parliament, and call new elections; former president Jorge Sampaio called this crucial power his "atomic bomb." A president can veto or delay or block legislation by sending it

Prime Minister Antonio Costa

President Marcelo Rebelo de Sousa

Portugal

back to parliament or to the 13-judge constitutional court, most of whose members are elected by parliament. Although the president's formal powers may seem limited, his influence is considerable. The reason is that, with so many changes in governments (by 1987 there had been 17 in 13 years), the presidency has been the center of political continuity.

The former president General António Ramalho Eanes can undeniably take more credit than anyone else for establishing order and discipline among the country's highly politicized military officers and for purging the leftist extremists within the army. In February 1976 he signed a pact with the leaders of the major political parties that demoted the army to a less direct political role. He ruled as a quiet, shy, serious, and very hardworking man from a peasant background. Although he was seldom seen smiling, he was unquestionably the most popular man in Portuguese politics at the time. This is very important in Portugal, where, as in many young democracies, politics is highly personalized. Names tend to be more important than programs.

The winner of the 1986 presidential election was socialist Mario Soares, who jubilantly proclaimed that his election marked "the end of Portugal's transition to a genuine democracy." The event was a watershed in Portuguese politics, in that none of the candidates was a military man. It signaled the definite return of the soldiers from politics to the barracks.

Soares relinquished the presidency in 1996 to fellow socialist Jorge Sampaio, a lawyer and former Lisbon mayor who defeated Cavaco Silva 53.8% to 46.2%. This was the first time since 1974 that voters chose a president from the same ranks as the ruling party. Sampaio speaks excellent

"Force and Confidence. Advance Portugal." Jose Socrates in happier days

English, having spent part of his boyhood in Baltimore and London. He was comfortably reelected in January 2001.

He demonstrated how powerful the presidency can be when he decided in July 2004 that, for the sake of stability, no new elections would be held when José Manuel Barroso stepped down as prime minister to become president of the European Commission. After the new prime minister, Pedro Santana Lopes, seemed to have lost control after only five months, despite commanding a majority in parliament, it was Sampaio who ordered the parliament to be dissolved and new elections held in 2005, again for the sake of long-term stability. This was unprecedented, but it was within the president's authority.

In 2006, Anibal Cavaco Silva, who had served as prime minister from 1985 to 1995, won the presidency. An economist who studied at Britain's York University, he is a pragmatic Social Democratic politician. He was the first president since the overthrow of the dictatorship in 1974 who was not of the left. He crushed former president Mario Soares, who at age 81 won an embarrassingly low 14%. It was an inglorious end to Soares's noble political career. He died in 2017, age 92. In January 2016, charismatic TV commentator and center-right politician Marcelo Rebelo de Sousa won 52% of the votes to defeat nine opponents for the presidency.

Changes in Government Structure

There are some institutions, policies, and trends that have steadily reduced the revolutionary stamp on political life. One is the unicameral parliament, called the Assembly of the Republic, with 230 seats

elected for a maximum four-year term by proportional representation in 20 multimember constituencies. At the head of the majority within the assembly is a relatively strong prime minister. Since 1974 regional governors or parliaments have not been able to block either the prime minister's or the president's powers because Portugal is a highly centralized, unitary state. It has also developed a stable political system. From 1975 to 1985, the average life of a government was only 10 months. The average from 1975 to 2005 was two years. Since 1987, all but one government has served out its full four-year term.

For administrative purposes Portugal is divided into 18 districts, each with a governor appointed by the Ministry of Internal Administration upon the approval of the prime minister and his cabinet. A plan to devolve more power to the regions failed in 1998, when an overwhelming 64% of voters in a referendum rejected it; the majority feared that it would destroy national unity, undermine budgetary discipline, and create another wasteful layer of bureaucracy. A few months earlier, only a third of voters turned out to express their opinion on the country's strict abortion laws; since a majority did not vote, the results were invalid. This had been Portugal's first-ever referendum, a device whose introduction a year earlier had been hailed as the completion of a finely balanced constitution.

All institutionalized control by the military over the civilian government was eliminated, and military officers were banned from politics. This meant that a civilian Council of State and Constitutional Council, appointed jointly by the parliament, the

Ex–prime minister Pedro Passos Coelho

government, and the president, replaced the Revolutionary Council. There is a Constitutional Court of 13 justices, most of whom are elected by parliament. The adoption of the new constitution in 1982 marked the formal end of the "Carnation Revolution" and the coming of age of Portugal's parliamentary democracy.

A further move to strengthen the Portuguese incentive to remain on the road of democracy was the decision in 1976 to seek entry into the EC (now EU) and thereby to tighten the links that bind Portugal to the older democracies of western Europe. Perhaps the most important trend that has reduced the revolutionary stamp on public life in Portugal has been the string of electoral victories for the moderate democratic political parties. This is particularly significant for a country in which all earlier attempts at democratic rule collapsed partly because of a paralyzing multiparty system.

POLITICAL PARTIES

Social Democratic Party (PSD)

The Social Democratic Party (PSD) changed its name from the People's Democratic Party (PPD) in order to give itself a sharper programmatic definition. It is a moderate, progressive, and organizationally decentralized party without a rigid ideological position. It is an avowedly anti-Marxist party which supports basic democratic freedoms and the market economy. It draws its voters mainly from the middle class in small and medium-sized towns, from the independent professions, and from mid- and upper-level technical cadres. It is traditionally strongest in the Azores and Madeira Archipelagos and in northern and central Portugal.

Under former leader Aníbal Cavaco Silva, it became in 1987 the first party since 1974 to win a majority of either votes or seats. It was also the first time that the parties of the left did not win most of the votes. For the first time since the founding of the republic 81 years earlier, a democratically elected party won two consecutive absolute majorities. This was a stunning change for a country whose only previous periods of political stability were under fascist dictatorship.

After winning the March 2002 elections, José Manuel Barroso, a former foreign minister who had lived seven years in the US and taught at Georgetown University, became prime minister. In 2004 he stepped down to become EC president. Thanks to his fluent French acquired while working on an MA in political science in Geneva, he was acceptable to the French.

The 2009 defeat prompted a change of leadership to Pedro Passos Coelho, who had grown up in Angola, the son of a

country doctor, and who was married to a physiotherapist from Guinea-Bissau. He is strikingly handsome and uses his trained baritone voice to sing fado and opera. In the June 2011 early elections, he led his party to a decisive victory, capturing 38.66% of the votes and 108 seats. Turnout was 58%. It formed a comfortable coalition of 132 seats with the People's Party in the 230-seat national parliament. Conflict over the bitter economic austerity medicine nearly tore the governing coalition apart. Nevertheless, this was the first government to survive a full four-year term.

The unpopular austerity was the main reason Coelho's coalition lost the October 2015 elections. His Forward Portugal alliance won 38.4% of the votes but only 107 of 230 seats. He lost his majority and was forced into opposition.

The People's Party (PP)

The People's Party (PP, formerly called the Democratic and Social Center, CDS, or Christian Democrats) is the newest and most conservative of Portugal's four major parties. It has an anti-Marxist, Euroskeptic, Christian, and humanistic orientation and a politically moderate leadership. It is

the only major party that rejects socialism as a goal. It finds its members and voters chiefly among industrial management, the service industries, independent farmers, and the *retornados* from the former colonies. Women also vote disproportionately for it. The party is strongest in the north, where the influence of the Catholic Church has not sunk as rapidly after 1974 as in Lisbon and the south.

It is decentralized and organizationally weaker than the other major parties. It does have the backing of the major industrialists' association, the CIP. It was the junior member of the government led by the PSD, but this coalition was unable to construct a governing majority after the 2015 election.

Socialist Party (PS)

Along with some close associates, Mario Soares had founded the Socialist Party (PS) in Münstereifel, Germany, in 1973, with the helping hand of the then-ruling Social Democratic Party of Germany. When the Portuguese revolution erupted in 1974, Soares rushed back from his Paris exile, and the PS was thrust into the forefront of the turbulent events without having time

Portugal

Young communists call for action in Faro (Algarve).

to become well organized for its new role. The PS and Soares certainly share much of the credit for channeling the revolution into a democratic direction. But after being the country's most important political party for a few years, its extreme fragmentation and organizational difficulties, along with the widespread unsatisfied economic expectations of the Portuguese, caused it to suffer a string of election failures, which shook the party's confidence.

The party is organized in a decentralized way. Unlike all other Portuguese parties, its voting strength has traditionally been spread fairly evenly over the entire country and was found primarily in the working and lower-middle classes. It is backed by the moderate General Union of Workers (UGT), which since 1979 increasingly challenged communist domination of the organized labor movement. The party program was officially Marxist, but the existence of a rigid and stubborn Communist Party to its left, with which the PS refuses to form any coalition, pushed the party toward the political center. In the minds of most politically active Portuguese, the desire to overcome economic difficulties has replaced earlier aspirations of establishing socialism.

The Socialists ruled Portugal from 1995 to 2002 and again from 2005 to 2011. It got new life under the leadership of a dynamic and charismatic leader, José Sócrates.

In the 2005 elections, the Socialists achieved an overwhelming victory, winning an absolute majority in parliament for the first time in the party's history. The left parties together won nearly two-thirds of the seats. After four prime ministers in four years, the four uninterrupted years of Socialist rule provided the stability for sustained economic reforms that most

Portuguese regarded as essential. The party won the 2009 elections but lost its majority.

In March 2011 Sócrates was forced to resign as prime minister and call elections two years early in June 2011. The Socialists suffered their worst defeat in two decades, falling to 28% of the votes and only 74 seats. They moved into the opposition, and Sócrates gave up his party leadership and retired from frontline politics. He soon became caught up in an upsurge of legal action against top establishment persons. He was detained for investigation into alleged tax fraud, money laundering, and corruption. He was arrested and placed under house arrest.

Leading the Socialists into the October 2019 elections was Antonio Costa, former mayor of Lisbon. He is the first candidate chosen by a primary. To forge an anti-austerity minority, he entered an unprecedented, fragile leftist coalition with the radical Left Bloc (BE) and the hardline Communist Party (PCP). This kind of leftist minority coalition was copied in Spain.

Portuguese Communist Party (PCP)

The final major party is the Portuguese Communist Party (PCP), once led by Alvaro Cunhal, then Carlos Carvalhas, and Jerónimo de Sousa. The PCP is still fairly orthodox. During the fascist rule, many of its leading functionaries were either in prison or in exile in the Soviet Union. Cunhal himself was in prison eight years and was too bitter and frozen in his thinking to change. It is Portugal's oldest party and is the only one with roots in the first republic from 1910 to 1926. This is also the country's best-organized party. It was a tight, clandestine group during the fascist period, and when the revolution came in 1974, it was immediately prepared to jump

into the political fray and attempt to take all the reins of power in its own hands.

Its major base of power since the summer of 1975, when its patrons within the army lost most of their own power, was the landless farmers in the Alentejo region, where the party helped organize collectivized agricultural enterprises (UCP) and the trade unions, especially the powerful General Confederation of Portuguese Workers (CGTP-Intersindical), which organizes almost three-fourths of all trade union leaders. The PCP has also attracted some intellectuals.

Geographically the party's electoral fortresses were the agricultural area of Alentejo and the industrial zone around Lisbon. In the north, it faced almost complete rejection, except in the city of Oporto. The disillusioned, more educated party members defected in droves. Among the party's problems are a general deradicalization of the working class and the rise of a younger wing within the PCP that advocates less dogmatic policies.

In the 2015 elections, the PCP and the Bloco de Esquerda (Bloc of the Left, BE), an undogmatic communist electoral alliance founded a decade earlier, did well. The Left Bloc doubled its share of votes to 10.2% and 19 seats. The communists captured 8.3% of the votes and 17 seats. They support the Socialists in parliament. A dozen other parties have failed to win seats.

Foreign and Defense Policies

Because of its small size and limited economic prowess, Portugal is accustomed to playing a low-key role in international affairs. In 2004 José Manuel Barroso departed from this mold and stepped into the international spotlight to become the president of the European Commission. It was significant that he had grown up under fascism: He hates bullies and is a person who had stood up to a dictatorship's police when he was a young man.

Many regard the EC presidency as the most important international post ever held by a Portuguese citizen. Added to this top spot are the EU's ambassador to the United States Vale de Almeida, formerly a personal aide to Barroso, and Vítor Manuel Ribeiro Constancio, who moved from the post of governor of the Bank of Portugal to the vice presidency of the European Central Bank. Being a part of an integrated Europe is a major foundation stone for Portugal's foreign policy. In 2009 Barroso was elected to serve another five years. In October 2016, former socialist prime minister Antonio Guterres was unanimously chosen as secretary-general of the United Nations. For 10 years he had run the UN refugee agency. Named as theoretical physicist, he is considered intelligent, multilingual, pragmatic, and competent. In 2021, Portugal occupied the presidency of the EU for six months.

Its defense policy has long been based on its membership in NATO. Its Atlantic location is central to its approach to the world. It was access to this body of water that enabled it to expand its language and culture to far-flung lands. As a traditional ally of Great Britain since 1386, it was a founding member of the Atlantic alliance in 1949. In fact, its historical partnership with the UK is the longest-standing pact in Europe. Portugal's major contribution to the alliance has never been in the form of combat troops.

During the decade and a half preceding the 1974 revolution, Portugal's army was bogged down in colonial wars, but between September 1974 and November 1975, these millstones were cast off one by one: first Portuguese Guinea (now Guinea-Bissau), then Mozambique, Angola, the Cape Verde Islands, São Tomé, and Príncipe.

In 1996 Portugal and its six former colonies, including Brazil, fulfilled a long-held ambition by uniting their 230 million people (of whom 183 million are Brazilians) in the Community of Portuguese-Speaking Countries (CPLP). Its task is to protect their common language and promote cooperation. The post of secretary-general is rotated alphabetically every two years. The African Union has designated Portuguese as one of the organization's official languages, and China has observer status because of Macao. Portuguese is a global language, spoken on every continent, but it is not an international language used in business and diplomacy.

Ex–prime minister Sócrates reaffirmed the country's three-sided foreign policy in 2005: "Portugal's external policy is a strategic triangle that unites our commitment to being at the heart of Europe with our Atlantic ties and our commitment to the Lusophone community." The country was a partner in the attempt to stabilize Iraq after the March 2003 war, but many Portuguese, including the Socialist government's foreign minister Diogo Freitas do Amaral, were critical of Washington's Iraq policy. He was particularly blunt, calling the war "illegal" and even comparing President George W. Bush to Hitler. His appointment was controversial because Portugal's relationship with the US is a key element in its foreign policy.

Macau

The only actual colony that remained until the end of the century was Macau, a tiny (6 sq. mi.) outpost on the southern coast of the People's Republic of China, 40 miles (64 km) across the Canton River Estuary from Hong Kong. Only about 10,000 of the estimated 427,000 are Portuguese,

although 110,000 hold Portuguese passports and can therefore live and work anywhere in the EU if they choose. Few of the Chinese who live there speak Portuguese. In fact, English is used far more than Portuguese. After the 1974 revolution, Lisbon wanted to give up the colony, which is an important trade outlet and source of foreign capital for Beijing. In 1979 officials from both countries met secretly in Paris, where the Portuguese acknowledged Chinese sovereignty over the territory and agreed to administer it until China wanted it back. China assumed full control on December 19, 1999, after 442 years of Portuguese rule.

Although nominally under Portuguese administration, Portuguese officials made no pretense of being in charge. Indeed, all it would have taken for the Chinese to regain control of the colony earlier was a phone call from Beijing. There is little popular agitation for greater democracy, as in Hong Kong. The Chinese promised to respect Macau's western, capitalist society and economy until at least 2050 and leave it with considerable autonomy in local affairs. Macau has overtaken Las Vegas to become the world's largest gambling center.

The Portuguese were a bit nostalgic. Fernando Lima, a journalist and author of

several books on Macau, wrote, "At least Portuguese can look back with some pride. We created a special culture you don't find anywhere else in the world, a melting pot of people of mixed-European, Indian, and Asian descent."

East Timor (Timor-Leste)

Technically speaking, Portugal still had another colony until 2002, namely Portuguese Timor. Neither Portugal nor the UN ever officially recognized the annexation of this half of the Timor Island by Indonesia on July 17, 1976. A quarter of East Timor's population died as a result of Indonesia's invasion, and a native independence movement still resists Indonesian authority. The situation recaptured the world's attention in 1991, when Indonesian soldiers and police opened fire on peaceful demonstrators, killing dozens in front of western journalists' cameras. All over Portugal, flags were flown at half-mast, newspapers appeared with black bands, and ceremonies and church vigils were held. Portugal's talks with Indonesia on this issue in 1992 ended with no concrete results.

In 1996 the Nobel Peace Prize was awarded to José Ramos-Horta, a US-educated human rights activist whose

Portugal

leftist Portuguese father had been deported to East Timor (also known as Timor-Leste), and to Roman Catholic bishop Carlos Filipe Ximenes Belo, a native of Timor who had studied in missionary schools in Portugal and Rome. President Jorge Sampaio, whose country had provided refuge for many East Timorese dissidents and had conducted the UN-sponsored negotiations with Indonesia for 12 years, called the award "a wonderful surprise" that reflects the two men's "indefatigable work in the service of human rights and peace in the territory." Portugal was rewarded by being given a two-year seat on the UN Security Council in 1997. Ramos-Horta went on to become president of the new country, but he almost died of an assassination attempt in February 2008.

The situation changed dramatically in 1998, when the Indonesian government of longtime ruler Suharto was overthrown, and the new leaders offered the 800,000 Timorese the opportunity to choose autonomy or independence. In May 1999, following more than 15 years of UN-sponsored negotiations in which the Portuguese were more closely involved than any other nation, Portugal signed an agreement with Indonesia calling for a referendum on August 8. A majority voted for independence, but violence continued. Portugal dispatched 1,000 troops to help reestablish and keep the peace.

The UN decision to make Portuguese the official language of independent East Timor ignited an intense protest and debate about what it means to be East Timorese. Only 10%, most of them older people, speak it. Proponents, like resistance fighter Joao Carrascalo, argue, "we have a strong and long link with Portugal. They were benevolent colonialists. It makes sense for us to speak the language." Opponents, such as youth leader Nino Pereira, disagree: "If that [Portuguese] is

what they want to speak, how are we supposed to be involved in the new government? The old people have this nostalgia with Portugal, but they have to realize that we are moving forward. The colonial days are over." In 2001 voters elected a constituent assembly that produced a constitution. In 2002 East Timor became an independent state. In 2013 the mandate expired for the UN mission promoting stability. East Timor is Asia's youngest nation and one of its poorest.

The Azores

The Azores, nine mountainous and beautiful islands of volcanic origin which are located about 1,000 miles (1,600 km) west of Lisbon, are a vital stepping stone for NATO airborne forces moving toward the Mediterranean, Middle East, Persian Gulf, or Africa. Former president Eanes was certainly correct in calling them "a pillar of support in the defense of Europe." American air force general Larry Wright underscored this: "Whoever controls the Azores controls the Atlantic."

Of particular importance is the US air base at Lajes on the island of Terceiram, which the US leases from Portugal, renewable every five years. Lajes is a refueling station, and about 250 US aircraft touch down each month. It is also a base for P-3 Orion maritime surveillance planes that patrol 2.5 million square miles in the North Atlantic.

A serious financial dispute arose in 1988, when the US announced that it would provide less aid. The prime minister noted, "expectations are not being met." Many of his countrymen had the impression that Portugal was being taken for granted, now that democracy had been stabilized. Unlike the situation in Spain concerning Torrejon Air Base, where the issue was political, not financial, there is no public resentment over the American military presence at Lajes. In 1988 the Portuguese government announced that it did not want the F-16 fighter-bombers that were being evicted from Spain to be redeployed in Portugal. It called for a formal review of the base agreement, and a solution was found in 1989: The US supplied the Portuguese armed forces with 20 F-16s, as well as a battery of Hawk ground-to-air missiles, 57 antisubmarine, combat and utility helicopters, air defense radar, and a hydrographic vessel. US financial aid for 1989 was set at $150 million, down from $208 million in 1985. All this assistance enables Portugal to shift its military emphasis in NATO from leasing bases to a more active antisubmarine role in the mid-Atlantic.

In the 1990s the US pulled some of its military assets out of the Azores after Soviet activity in the Atlantic had ended. It announced in 2015 the withdrawal of an

additional 500 soldiers from Lajes, leaving only 165 soldiers. The civilian workforce was cut in half to 400. This was a blow to the local economy, where unemployment was already 15%. The US also has an underwater terminal on the island of Santa Maria to monitor submarine movements in the Atlantic and a network of underground supply areas throughout the islands whose contents can be airlifted to any trans-Atlantic area within hours. France also operates a missile-tracking station on the island of Flores. Because of its need for a rapid-deployment capability for the Middle East and elsewhere, the US maintains its military facilities here, aimed at providing a "viable support base" eastward and southward.

When in 1975 the leftist Portuguese government allowed Cuban planes carrying troops to Angola to use Santa Maria for refueling stops, a pro-American Azores separatist movement sprang up, but it withered again when more moderate leaders came to power in Lisbon. This movement indicated the basic strength of the ties between the 200,000 residents of the Azores and the US, where more than 600,000 Azoreans now live, mainly on the East and West Coasts. The issue of possible abuse of landing rights reemerged in 2007, when allegations were made that CIA-operated planes with suspected terrorists refueled on the islands; there was no evidence of that.

A dispute in 1986 over the elevation of the Azorean flag and anthem to equal status with those of the motherland served as a reminder of local pride. They had been waved and played in official ceremonies since 1980. Nevertheless, because of the symbolic importance, President Soares vetoed the islands' revised autonomy statute, which had been approved by the Portuguese parliament. This was the first use of the presidential veto under the 1976 constitution, and it indicated how a flag and anthem question can revive Lisbon's fears of possible Azorean separatism. Demonstrating the homeland's continued responsibility for the autonomous archipelago, when the Azores were unable to finance their debt in 2012, Portugal granted them a bailout of €135 million ($168 million).

The Madeira Archipelago

The Madeira Archipelago is not only the home of a desirable aperitif wine, which rivals sherry for popularity. It also guards the southern approaches to Europe and the Strait of Gibraltar and is the southernmost NATO territory. The island of Porto Santo has excellent airport and deepwater port facilities, which at times has been used for military purposes, such as in 1978, when it was used as a refueling stop for aircraft carrying Belgian troops to Zaire. NATO

Azores

Portugal

Stripping cork. Portugal provides half the world's supply.

military planners are very interested in Madeira because the Spanish made it clear that their Canary Islands, which lie only 300 miles (480 km) south of Madeira, would not be considered NATO territory once Spain entered the Atlantic alliance.

Portugal is wary about allowing Madeira to become a military bastion like the Azores. A major reason is that this could create a conflict with the African Union, in which voices have long been raised that the Madeira Archipelago is colonized African territory and should therefore be liberated. After all, Madeira lies only 350 miles (560 km) west of Morocco. Lisbon is trying to forge closer links with its former African colonies in order to regain some of their lucrative markets and to send them some of their excess workforce.

Mozambique and Angola

Both Mozambique and Angola, the two richest of the former colonies, have realized the benefits the more skilled Portuguese could bring to their countries and have asked the Portuguese to return under a new guise. This reconciliation with its former colonies has been made politically easier since Portugal supported the black African position toward South Africa. One-seventh of the white South Africans are of Portuguese origin.

In 1991 Portugal mediated the Estoril Accord, ending Angola's 16-year civil war. The key mediator in the talks was José Manuel Barroso, who went on to become Portuguese prime minister and then president of the European Commission. Portugal also participated, along with American, Russian, and Angolan observers, in the political-military commission to supervise the truce and prepare for elections. It sent peacekeeping forces to Mozambique

in the early 1990s. Portugal supported peaceful change in part because it wants to avoid the kind of refugee flood it experienced in the 1970s.

Emotional and language ties with Africa are still strong, but economic links became weaker. By the 1990s only about 1% of Portugal's foreign trade was with Angola and Mozambique. However, by 2013 oil- and diamond-rich Angola, whose economic growth in 2010 was 8.5% of GDP, had risen to Portugal's fifth biggest export market, with 5.4% of its total exports. As President Cavaco Silva's first visit to Angola signaled in 2010, Portugal increasingly places its economic recovery on Angola and hopes that the language and cultural links will give it an advantage against the Chinese. Angolans have become major investors and spenders in Portugal.

It faces stiff competition with the Brazilians, who are also active in Lusophone Africa. There are difficulties in doing business in Angola. It is one of the least business-friendly environments, mainly because of corruption. In the 2009 Transparency International's corruption index, Angola ranked 162 out of 180 nations, while Portugal was 35th. Nevertheless, over 100,000 Portuguese are living and working in Angola, an increase of almost 24,000 in 2009 alone. By 2011, thousands of Portuguese were arriving in Angola each week, including persons with professional qualifications. They are part of the largest wave of emigration in Portugal's history. In 2011 alone, 150,000 left, mainly to Brazil and Angola. They were going to work for Angolans. The same reverse brain drain is happening in Mozambique, where Portuguese dentists, doctors, lawyers, architects, and engineers are moving to seek better professional opportunities. An estimated

20,000 Portuguese were living in the capital of Maputo in 2012. This is a unique inversion between colony and mother country.

Defense

After the 1974 revolution had been tamed, Portugal could afford neither politically nor economically to continue maintaining a large land army. Therefore by 2010 the size of the armed forces had been cut from nearly a half-million to 43,330 politically obedient troops (26,700 army; 10,450 navy, including 1,430 marines; 7,100 air force), including 2,300 female volunteers and 9,100 conscripts. Compulsory service dropped to four months for all services. It is scheduled to disappear altogether as Portugal shifts to a professional army with modern rapid-reaction capability. There are 210,900 in the reserves (up to age 35) and 47,700 paramilitaries (including 26,100 National Republican Guard). The military's share in the budget fell from 50% in 1970 to less than 10% by 2000. What Portugal can contribute to NATO is the use of strategically important facilities on the mainland, where NATO has naval and air facilities, and in the Azores and Madeira island groups, which are autonomous parts of Portugal.

In 1991 it supported its allies' war to dislodge the Iraqi aggressors from Kuwait. It sent 900 troops to Bosnia to help NATO implement the 1995 Dayton Peace Accords. In 2010 it still maintained peacekeeping forces in Bosnia (52), Kosovo (300), and Lebanon (146). In 2009 it sent a warship with special forces to the waters off Somalia to help prevent pirate attacks on shipping. Its diplomatic support for the US is not due exclusively to the fact that the US provides Portugal economic and military aid and stations 727 troops on its soil. The two nations now share democratic values and common interests and therefore have a solid foundation for good relations. Portugal became the most outspoken advocate of helping President Barack Obama close Guantanamo Bay Detention Center by offering to accept up to three detainees. Foreign Minister Luís Amado said, "The time has come for the European Union to step forward."

Portugal is trying to improve its relations with the nations of the Middle East. Portugal was the first ally to heed President Carter's call in 1979 for sanctions against Iran when Iranian mobs had seized the US embassy. It also levied sanctions against the Soviet Union when it invaded Afghanistan, although President Soares's visit to Moscow in 1987 signaled a normalization of relations with Russia.

Portugal supported the US, UK, and Spain in the 2003 war in Iraq, although it supplied no troops or military aid. It hosted in the Azores a summit of the

Portugal

leaders of these three allies on March 16, 2003. It culminated in a final 24-hour notice to the UN Security Council to act, or a decision to take military action would be made without the UN. After the conflict, it dispatched 120 peacekeepers to Iraq (all of whom have been withdrawn). It maintains 145 troops in Afghanistan, but it reduced its force in East Timor from 655 to only 3 observers in 2010. It turned to Washington for help in rebuilding its neglected armed forces. At its 2003 summit, NATO decided in Portugal to locate a sea-based joint task force and a rapid-reaction force there. In 2009 a French officer took over the alliance's regional command in Lisbon.

ECONOMY

Under fascist rule, Portugal's economy was relatively isolated and sheltered from the rest of Europe. Its industry was primarily in the hands of rather inefficient family businesses, which were protected from stiff western European competition and which had a comfortable export and import monopoly with their country's African colonies. A third of the Portuguese worked in agriculture. After 1974 much of Portugal's economic situation changed for the better.

The 1974 revolution did, however, create additional economic problems beyond the temporary scaring away of tourists and their much-needed foreign currencies. Most of the earlier large private industrial and financial groups were broken down, and a wide range of economic activities that were not foreign owned was brought under state control. These included banks, insurance, airlines, railways, electricity, oil, gas, petrochemicals, cement, breweries, tobacco, wood pulp, steel, shipping and shipbuilding, urban transit, trucking, metallurgy, chemicals, food processing, and textiles. Many of these sectors were combined in a huge, publicly owned conglomerate called Quimigal.

In all, 60% of Portugal's industry was nationalized after 1974. These nationalized industries exacerbated Portugal's problems. In 2007 government expenditures still accounted for 42.4% of GDP (down from 47.7% in 2005). Although many firms escaped the sword of nationalization because of their small size, it is not surprising that an immediate result of this policy was that investment capital was scared away. Productivity dropped, and because wages were doubled after 1974, inflation soared. Such nationalizations merely added to the weight of Portugal's already-cumbersome bureaucracy.

The Cavaco Silva government vowed in 1985 to end state domination of the economy, which he blamed for keeping Portuguese living standards so far below the western European average. His reelection in 1987 boosted his program to begin gradually selling off most industries and financial institutions nationalized after 1974. Cavaco Silva noted, "the state should control only companies of particular importance to public service," such as power, water, and public-transport utilities. The government's extensive media holdings, including newspapers, were also earmarked for sale, save one television and radio channel. "The era of state paternalism is over."

Progress on this privatization program was slow. One problem was that there are too few large Portuguese groups with enough money to buy what is up for sale. Not wishing to sell most of these assets to foreigners, rigid but ineffective limits on how much foreigners can buy were established. Beginning in 1993 foreigners could buy control in state firms on a case-by-case basis; that included the national airlines, TAP-Air Portugal. The Coelho government announced in 2011 that water utilities (49%), the postal service, and the state-owned broadcasting media would be put on the auction block. In 2012 a 21% stake in the national electric company, EDP, was sold to China.

A welcome reform after the 1974 revolution was the lifting of the ban against strikes and independent trade unions. However, in the heady days after the revolution, the well-organized communists seized control of the major labor union, the CGTP-Intersindical. This union drives a hard bargain and became accustomed to getting what it demands. It is highly politicized and is able to threaten the government through potentially crippling strikes. In 2012 it called a general strike to protest the government's austerity policy.

The decolonization of Portugal's empire forced Portugal to compete with other nations for markets and brought close to 1 million bitter and penniless *retornados* to the motherland. What was worse, it cut off the country's most important sources of raw materials, especially energy. With no fossil fuel resources of its own, it must import about 80% of its primary energy needs. It can produce only about 20% of the energy it needs, and it brings in all of its oil and 83% of its coal. It generates 58% of its electricity from foreign oil, and it imports substantial amounts of electricity from Spain and France. Its bill for energy imports is about 10% of GDP, compared with only 1% in 1973. It does have the alternative of using its one untapped energy source, namely the 8,000 tons of proven uranium reserves, mostly located in the northern area of Urgerica, to produce nuclear energy.

It manages for several reasons. It has the lowest per-capita energy consumption in western Europe and also the lowest ownership of automobiles per inhabitant, although the number of cars doubled between 1985 and 1990, causing congestion in Lisbon. Of increasing importance is the fact that it is among the top three countries in Europe (after Sweden and Austria) in terms of renewable energy sources. Almost one-fifth of its total energy needs and about 45% of its total electricity production is met by alternative sources. That percentage is growing, as is energy demand in general, and it was hoped that they would constitute 60% of the country's electricity by 2020. In partnership with Renault and Nissan, Portugal is on the brink of creating a network of battery-recharging and -swap stations for electric vehicles.

Unlike most other European countries, which have already developed their own hydroelectricity to a maximum, Portugal's is only half-used, and it is building 18 hydropower projects. The Guadinana River

Wine-growing country around the Douro River Valley, home of port wine

434

Europe celebrates EU enlargement.

was dammed to create western Europe's largest reservoir, and a project is moving along to dam the Sabor River. Recurrent droughts and environmental protests plague hydroelectric plans and make this source less certain. Portugal is already one of the world's top 10 producers of wind power. One of the world's largest wind farms is being built in the northwest Alto Minho region. Outside the town of Moura, the world's biggest photovoltaic power plant is being constructed to take advantage of the country's abundant sunlight. General Electric's huge solar energy plant contains 52,000 solar panels capable of lighting and heating 8,000 homes. Portugal will start up the world's first commercial wave-driven power plant off the coast of Porto, and planners hope that 20% of electricity needs will one day be met by wave power.

Agriculture and Fishing

Portuguese agriculture is traditionally inefficient, and 10.5% of all Portuguese are engaged in agriculture (down from 44% in 1960). Farming contributes 2% of Portugal's GDP, 8.3% if one includes fishing and forestry. Portugal continues to have proportionately the western Europe's largest agricultural sector. The country must still import half of its food and animal feeds. Food makes up one-fifth of the nation's total imports. Portugal is dependent on the Americans for a large portion of foodstuffs, including 90% of its wheat.

It has the lowest per-capita productivity in western Europe. It is only about 40% of the EU average and two-thirds that of Spain and Greece. This is due to several factors, including the rocky, hilly soil; the low level of mechanization; the inefficient

collective farms in the south; the insufficient size of family farms in the north; and the farmers' general resistance to change. Portuguese farmers' inability to compete successfully within a single European market has left a majority of them living at subsistence levels on incomes a third as big as their Spanish counterparts.

The revolution of 1974 did not create Portugal's agricultural problems. However, the initial leaders' fervor created particular problems in the south, where the land conquered from the Moors in the 13th century was distributed in large tracts to Portuguese nobility. These large landowners often lived in Lisbon and had their large estates worked by low-paid agricultural laborers. These large estates were ripe for picking in revolutionary times.

The communists, supported by the ruling leftist military leaders, seized many of the estates and converted them into large collective farms. In other cases, they forced the owners to hire more workers than could be employed profitably. By the 1990s more than half the seized estates had been returned to their original owners, and all owners have received some compensation for their former holdings. Nevertheless, about one-fifth of Portugal's forest and cropland remains collectivized. But these collectively owned farms have on the whole been poorly managed. They therefore now produce only a third to a half of the grain and livestock that they supplied before the revolution. Because of legal tangles, the government did not move as fast to decollectivize farming in the south as it had hoped.

Portugal faces a problem of what to do about its inefficient farming and antiquated fishing fleet, which is already unable to withstand competition in its home waters. Also, it has few agricultural products that can compete in the EU. The ones that can are wines, tomato concentrate, and cork. The heart of its wine growing is in the Douro River Valley, from which port wine (named for the city of Oporto) comes.

Portugal's fishing fleet is the oldest and least productive in all of western Europe. Many of its vessels have no engines. It has world-class ship repair; its repair yards are among the world's biggest and handle more tonnage than their top four competitors together. In 1969 the Portuguese government granted Spain, which has a fishing fleet that is larger than that of all of the first 15 EU countries combined, unrestricted rights to fish in Portugal's waters. Most leaders in Lisbon now view that decision as a cardinal error and have been trying hard to undo it.

Portugal's chief export is cork, of which it provides half of the world's supply (most of the rest comes from Spain) and 68% of the wine corks. The industry creates 3%

of the country's GDP, but it is threatened by the rising popularity of synthetic corks and twist-off caps, which are capturing more and more of the world market. It has invested heavily in research to improve cork effectiveness as a stopper. This substance is the bark that is stripped off the cork oak trees every 11 years, a process which leaves the trees a bright red color. Cork production suffered a setback in the mid-1970s, when, following the seizure of large estates in Alentejo, thousands of cork trees were uprooted to make way for wheat, a crop unsuited for the region. The communist-inspired wheat drive at least temporarily destroyed cork growing there.

In order to irrigate more than 272,000 acres in the Alentejo region, the government closed the giant Alqueva Dam in 2002 in order to create the largest artificial lake in western Europe. Filled, it submerges the village of Luz, 1 million trees, and hundreds of Stone Age rock drawings. Environmentalists decry the damage this project does to nature. Droughts and resulting forest fires are a perpetual threat to the country.

Membership in EU

Portugal's political leaders, supported by a large majority of the population, chose a formidable challenge to prepare their country for a more prosperous future—entry into the EU. Before becoming a full member in 1986, it was a member of EFTA. In 1972 Portugal had entered into an agreement with the EU, providing free trade of industrial products. Its leaders, as well as those in the EU member countries, hoped that such entry would help solidify the democratic foundations in Portugal, as well as provide a mighty boost for the country's economy. In 2016, about three-fourths of its exports and imports were with EU countries, more

Former prime minister and EC president Manuel Durão Barroso

Portugal

than double the proportion a dozen years earlier. Exports constitute 30% of its GDP.

Portugal has developed a modern economy that employs 25.6% of its workforce in industry (producing 21% of GDP) and 63.8% in services (creating 77% of GDP). By 2008 the country had reached a tipping point, where it exports more technology than it imports, invests more in science and research than ever before, and earns more from its export of business services than from cheap textiles and footwear. It is clearly evolving from a low-cost manufacturing economy to a knowledge-based one. The introduction of greater incentives through a reform of personal taxation, which some observers described as the most punitive in all of western Europe, stimulated the economy. Corporate taxes fell to 20% in 2006 but were raised to 27.5% during the 2010 austerity year. Portuguese industry enjoys other advantages. Its smallness and fragmented nature lend it flexibility.

Its poor remain the poorest in western Europe, and the gap between the rich and poor within the country is widening and is the biggest in Europe. More than 2 million Portuguese (a fifth of the population) live on less than €350 ($490) per month; that is under the poverty line. The sluggish economic growth (an annual average of only .6% from 2001 to 2005 and 2% in 2017) offers little hope of rapid recovery. Since 1999 its economic growth has been among the

Fado star

slowest in the eurozone. Its basic strength was in the cheapness of labor, the lowest in western Europe, but that advantage is eroding. Its GDP per capita grew from 55% of the EU average in 1975 to 79% in 2010 and 75% in 2014. In terms of GDP per head, the Czech Republic, Malta, and Slovenia have all overtaken it. The OECD estimated in 2005 that it would take another 40 years to catch up with the EU average.

Its productivity was only 40% of the EU average in 2007. Part of the reason is that its research and development is up to only 1.55% of GDP, higher than Spain but still below the EU average of 1.9%. However, it is improving. Its 7% unemployment rate in 2021 was below the EU average of 11.2%. Joblessness is especially serious for young Portuguese. The rate is over 50% for those aged 15 to 24 and 28% for ages 25 to 34. It would have been higher if so many young Portuguese had not emigrated. No wonder many of them see the labor market as primarily protecting the jobs of older workers. Far too many of the jobs available to young people are internships or temporary contracts, which by 2011 were more common than permanent employment. Living standards had risen visibly, but failure to rein in wage increases created serious problems.

Entry into the EU brought needed social and regional funds to Portugal; from 3% to 4% of its GDP was derived from financial transfers from Brussels, a total of $30 billion between 1986 and 2003. Those funds began to decline in 2006, and new ones are going to new members in central Europe. However, these monies made a

real economic difference. One can see this in Portugal's infrastructure. In 1987 it had only 240 kilometers (144 miles) of freeways; by 1998, it had 840 kilometers (504 miles). This is more in terms of distance per inhabitant than in any other EU member state. Critics say these freeways do not link the poorer and richer regions as they should, nor do they tie in well with Spain's road network, leaving Portugal relatively isolated from Europe. Its railway system has not been modernized at the same pace as its roadways. A planned high-speed rail link from Lisbon to Madrid was canceled in 2012.

This country, which was so successful in establishing a democratic political order despite enormous problems and the absence of a democratic tradition, is meeting the economic challenges associated with becoming a full economic partner in Europe. It met the qualifications to adopt the euro. The euro was considered a "good thing" by half the people in 2014; only 38% thought it "bad."

In 2001 Portugal became the first country to exceed the 3% limit for a budget deficit and to face a penalty. The prior conservative government was compelled to impose painful budget cuts, freeze civil servants' pay, and raise the sales tax to 19%. It tried to make the overstaffed, underproductive, and expensive public-sector workers more efficient. As of 2004 automatic promotion and guaranteed top performance reports were scrapped, and promotion is now based on merit.

These measures sparked widespread strikes among civil servants. The budget

Vasco da Gama, Museum of Ancient Art, Lisbon

deficit was down to 2.6% of GDP in 2007 (the lowest since Portugal's return to democracy), but it shot up to 8.6% of GDP in 2010, before declining to 4.3% in 2020. Total public debt had been reduced to 63.6% of GDP by 2007, but it was 131% in 2016. It is expected to decline gradually to about 80%.

Portugal experienced neither a bursting housing bubble, as did Spain, nor a bank crisis, as Ireland. Nevertheless, these dire economic developments, made worse by the euro crisis stemming from Greece from 2010 on, forced the Socialist government to take unpopular austerity measures. These were practically forced on it by the EU partners, who feared that Greece's problems could happen in Portugal, a country that constitutes only 2% of the eurozone economy. Whereas being in the euro club had brought only benefits since 2001, now it involved pain as well as gain.

The austerity policy adopted by the Coelho government in 2011 was required as a condition for the €78 billion ($115 billion) bailout from the EU and IMF. The outgoing Socialist government had already responded to a decline in tax revenues by introducing a "crisis tax" on wages and large companies. The value-added tax (VAT) rose by 1% to 21%, and income tax rates were upped by 1.5%. Coelho raised them even farther to help meet the deficit-reduction targets. Public-sector employment was cut by 20% across the board and 30% in some cases. Some public works

The National Theater, Lisbon

were postponed, such as a new Lisbon airport. To these measures Coelho added such things as cuts in unemployment assistance and pensions over €1,500 per month and increases in copays for doctor visits and medicine. It overhauled labor laws and intensified the privatization program. These were the biggest cuts in government spending in a half-century.

Protest demonstrations and strikes against austerity continued to 2015 during the Coelho government. Critics called the required austerity "brutal," "a crime against the middle class," a "fiscal atomic bomb." The Constitutional Court struck down as discriminatory some of the planned cuts in public-sector pay, pensions and benefits, sick leave, jobless benefits, university tuition, and the 14th-month holiday bonus for civil servants and pensioners. One expert called the court "the biggest impediment to the country's clean exit from the bailout." Universal health care and education is widely viewed as fundamental to the 1974 revolution. Nevertheless, the government persisted in cutting the budget and benefits. The EU praised the government and granted it up to seven years to pay back the bailout loans. German chancellor Angela Merkel made a six-hour visit to the country to support its painful policies, but she was greeted by shouts of "Merkel out!"

Among the controversial measures the prior Socialist government had already taken was to raise the minimum retirement age for state employees in stages from age 60 to 65, the same as in the private sector. Incentives to work longer were introduced. They make up one-sixth of the workforce and under the constitution cannot be fired. People with fewer than two children are expected to contribute more toward their pensions. These steps are crucial if the country is to solve its pension crisis. Retirement benefits are among the world's most generous, with some people receiving more than they did while working. Since 2010, the population has shrunk by 3%. Given a birth rate that has fallen by 35% between 1975 and 2005 (from a 2.6 fertility rate to only 1.5), more than a third of the population will be over age 65 in 2050, compared with 17% in 2005.

Belem Tower, 16th century, Lisbon

Portugal

The state hired only one new state employee for every two who left. It lowered their sickness pay from 100% to 65% and reduced the maximum personal income tax to 42% (thereby limiting tax evasion). Despite demonstrations and strikes by judges, public prosecutors, doctors, nurses, teachers, police, soldiers, and other state workers against radical changes to their pension, health, and pay benefits, the government stuck to its guns. Courts were forced to stay open during the summer, except for a one-month holiday. To cut red tape and to stimulate the creation of new businesses, the time needed to set up a new company was lowered to less than an hour, the fastest in the EU.

Tourism continues to be an important component of the economy, accounting for approximately 15% of its GDP and providing employment for 1 in 10 workers. However, tourism officials would like to attract visitors year-round to areas beyond the beaches of the Algarve, which now produces about half of Portugal's tourism earnings. One form of tourism that is increasingly popular is "wine tourism," especially in the Douro Valley.

Foreign investment is coming in, two-thirds of it from the EU. With about half of its GDP derived from foreign trade and tourism, Portugal is one of the most open countries in Europe. It is therefore natural that it became a part of the world's largest economic market, and it is doing well. Its huge Autoeuropa car plant, owned by Volkswagen, accounts for 12% of exports. The US is one of the country's leading investors, and among the major American firms active in Portugal are Ford, Microsoft, Texas Instruments, Compaq, Johnson

& Johnson, Unisys, Citibank, and Chase Manhattan. General Motors sparked strikes in 2006, when it rejected its workers' cost cuts aimed at keeping its van factory in Portugal open. The US purchases almost 6% of Portugal's exports and provides over a quarter of its non-EU imports. An active American Chamber of Commerce in Portugal promotes this important bilateral trade.

Since the 1990s the state has been selling off its interests in oil, gasoline, natural gas, electricity, banks, and telecommunications companies. In 2000 it unloaded an additional 20% of the national power company, Electricidade de Portugal. It sold most of its remaining interest in Portugal Telecom (PT). In 2004 the state sold a stake in Portucel, the state-owned pulp and paper company. It announced the sale of a large part of Galp Energia, the country's dominant oil utility. However, the government maintains close ties with formerly state-owned firms. It keeps "golden shares" that allow it to veto mergers, even when it retains only a minority stake in a company. It also has a "golden visa" scheme that gives investors the right of residence.

The existence of a lively "submerged economy" makes it more difficult to get an exact picture of Portugal's economic condition. This kind of activity is done at home, in the streets, or on the job while the boss is looking the other way. It takes place behind the backs of government statisticians and tax collectors. If the production of goods and services from such an invisible economy were able to be included in the official economic figures, an estimated

Portuguese student

10% to 25% would have to be added to the GDP, and real unemployment would be below the official figures.

CULTURE

Portugal is a nation whose cultural influence extends far beyond its own borders. Today over 200 million people speak Portuguese. Its outward-looking orientation was beautifully reflected in its greatest literary figure, Luiz de Camões (1524–1580),

Robed freshmen students are initiated into the University, Lisbon

438

who wrote poetry and dramatic comedies. In 1572 he published perhaps the greatest piece of Portuguese literature, *Os Lusíadas* (*The Lusitanians*), a long epic poem celebrating Portuguese history and heroes. His story is linked with that of Vasco da Gama's voyage to India and is infused with much Greek mythology. In general, Portuguese today are nostalgic about their country's great past, and they have a term for this yearning: *saudade*.

Portuguese culture has also been enriched by experiences or influences from abroad. For instance, the novelist John Dos Passos and the undisputed king of march music, John Philip Sousa, were both sons of Portuguese emigrants and received their artistic inspiration in the US. No one who has heard fado (meaning "fate") music sung in Portugal can ever forget its deep feeling for love, nostalgia, and yearning. Used during the fascist era to promote nationalism (along with Fatima and football), it has become the country's most successful cultural export.

In 1998 a Portuguese writer won the Nobel Prize for literature for the first time. Jose Samarago, who died in July 2010, was born into a home with no books, grew up in poverty, never went to the university, and toiled as a metalworker until the fall of dictator Antonio Salazar enabled him, an active communist, to publish his first novel in 1974. The best known of his imaginative novels are *Baltasar and Blimunda* and *The Year of the Death of Ricardo Reis*. Some contain page-long sentences and no proper names. He expressed his hope on receiving the honor that "Portuguese will become more visible and more audible." Earlier in the century, Egas Moniz had won the Nobel Prize for medicine.

Portuguese journalist

Students at Coimbra University

Immigrants from Portugal's former colonies changed the face of Portuguese society and made it much more heterogeneous. Historically the Portuguese were an emigrant people, settling all corners of the globe. By the 21st century, the flow had reversed, and Portugal had become a net importer of labor. In 2005 there were roughly 256,000 legal immigrants in the country, almost half of them from Africa. An increasing number comes from central and eastern Europe. By 2011, 4.3% of residents were from other countries. The 2008 recession produced a reverse brain drain. From 2007 to 2012, about a half-million Portuguese emigrated to seek work. Unlike in some other European countries, this ethnic mixing has not been accompanied by serious racial tension. In 2005 newcomers were issued high-tech identity cards in an effort to fight illegal immigration.

Influence of Brazil

Perhaps the greatest foreign cultural influence comes from Brazil. Soap operas from there fill Portugal's airwaves with Brazilian slang, songs, accents, and dress. Many imports are aired on Portugal's two state-owned and -run channels, RTP 1 and 2; on its two newer private commercial channels, SIC and TV1; and on a multitude of cable and satellite channels.

Chiefly because of its small size and high degree of centralization, there are few different dialects spoken within Portugal, except in Miranda do Douro in the northeast. But of the 230 million persons in the world who speak Portuguese as a native language, only a little over 10 million live in the mother country; 195 million live in Brazil and speak what writer Eca de Queiroz calls "Portuguese with sugar." At newsstands one finds many Brazilian publications mixed with Portuguese ones:

Lisbon alone has five morning and four afternoon papers, the most popular being the tabloid *Correio da Manha*. In 1991 the last state-owned daily newspaper, *Diario de Noticias*, established in 1864, was sold into private hands; it is respected as a serious paper and has been given a modernized look. Other dailies are *Publico, Correio da Manha*, and the *Jornal de Noticias*. There are also hot-selling weeklies, such as *Expresso, O Jornal, Semanario*, and *Independente*. *The Portugal News* is available for English readers.

It is not surprising that the Portuguese spoken outside, especially in Brazil, is changing the language spoken in this small country. Oral expression is being strongly penetrated by Brazilian words and idiomatic phrases. The economic prowess of Brazil has meant that the Portuguese being learned by foreigners abroad is now primarily Brazilian. Most magazines on Portugal's newsstands are from Brazil.

A passionate debate began in 1986 over whether Portugal should simply recognize this fact and negotiate a linguistic agreement with Brazil and other former colonies. Proponents argue that a common structure of the language must be preserved and that the constant evolution of the language should be incorporated in the mother country. Critics decry the "crime against the patrimony of the Portuguese language" and "a disgusting resignation to Brazil's economic interests." It cannot be expected that, in the long run, any effort to erect a barrier against the flood of foreign cultural influences could succeed in a country like Portugal that is adapting itself so quickly to the changing world it faces. Millions of Portuguese really want no such barrier anyway. Nevertheless, the government established tough requirements that 40% of all TV shows have to be in Portuguese. Three-fourths must be produced in Portugal.

Education

Postrevolutionary Portugal inherited considerable educational problems. These included a shortage of schools and teachers, a clear and discriminatory separation of the elite lycée (high school) from the trade schools, a poor geographic distribution of educational facilities throughout the country, and especially the concentration of higher education along the coast. By the 1990s there were 12 state universities, 14 polytechnic schools, and a growing number of private universities, created to accommodate the swelling student population.

For a couple of years after the ancien régime was swept from power, the educational system became the wet clay in the hands of leftist and Marxist teachers and reformers. Many Marxist textbooks replaced the outdated books from the

Portugal

Salazar era, schools were taken over by management committees which excluded most parental influence in the schools, and pupils were examined on their "collective work" and even had a voice in the grades they received.

When the Socialist Party finally gained a firm grip on the reins of government in the second half of 1975, the textbooks were changed again to reflect the more moderate and pluralistic character of the new leadership. Parents were again given some say in the school system, the former strict grading system was reintroduced, and hundreds of leftists were removed from the schools and the Ministry of Education. With order restored in the schools, the education system was more or less back where it had been in 1974, but the ground had been laid for important changes.

In 1977 a system of preschool instruction was introduced. About 80% of children receive preschool education today, compared with only 1% in 1960. Secondary schooling was established at 11 years; a 12th year came in 2009. All pupils now receive six years of elementary education. To prepare for the high-tech world, each primary school pupil is issued a laptop computer, and almost every school is equipped with high-speed fiber-optic Internet connections and one PC for every five pupils. English as a second language is compulsory from age six. About 900 primary schools with fewer than 21 pupils each were closed.

Since a major reform in 2009, all children must remain in school for 12 years. In that year, 31% had dropped out before they had finished secondary school. This was more than double the 16% EU average. In 2005 a bold reform called Novas Oportunidades (New Opportunities) was introduced, permitting adult and young dropouts to complete their secondary education. This has been a runaway success, with about 1 million people registering for courses in the five years after 2005. Progress has been steady. The percentage of the population with a secondary education had increased to 63.2% in 2010. A further improvement is that 180,000 out of 351,000 secondary pupils were in courses that equip them with specific job market skills, while the rest were in college-preparatory courses in 2010. The percentage of young people who are university graduates has climbed to 35%. After the one-year transition class, qualified students can enter the university for a "short advanced education" of two to three years or for the "diverse superior courses" of four or five years. About 70% of the population age 18 to 24 attend higher education, compared to 9% in 1974.

The educational system remains a matter of concern. Portugal spends 5.7% of its national income on public schools and universities, a relatively high proportion by OECD standards. It also spends more per student in secondary education than most countries, in part because its teachers' salaries are relatively high, consuming 93% of spending on education, compared with the OECD average of 75%. Its average ratio of one teacher to nine students is one of the highest in the world. But the outcomes are nevertheless among the worst in Europe. Portugal is trying to overcome this at the highest level by entering into research partnership agreements with leading US universities, including MIT, Carnegie Mellon, the University of Texas, and Harvard Medical School.

All kinds of scholarly and cultural endeavors are generously supported in Portugal by the Gulbenkian Foundation, established and richly funded by a foreign oil magnate who made Portugal his home. Since the foundation is massively involved in supporting a wide range of cultural activities, is private, and has carefully steered clear of government control, it was able to support research with critical political implications, which the politicians in power viewed with some distrust. The Luso-American Foundation sponsors scholarships for American students of Portuguese descent and provides funding for hiring American professors at MBA programs at Portuguese universities.

Cultural activity also got a boost in 1986 with a new law (called the Maecenas Law) that concedes tax breaks to corporations that support cultural initiatives. Up to 60% of any "cultural financing" costs can be written off taxes. Since only about 1% of the national budget is allotted to culture and public support is very scarce, this new measure is most welcome.

Religion

Portuguese society has experienced major social transformation, but religion had not changed as quickly as in many other western European countries. Divorce was permitted after the revolution. The Catholic Church continued to oppose birth control, but Portuguese of childbearing age are inclined to ignore that.

Despite bitter protests by the Catholic Church, parliament voted in 1984 to permit abortions following rape or whenever medically advisable. Nevertheless, until 2007 it had the strictest abortion laws of any EU country, except Ireland. Legal abortion was rare, and illegal abortions continued. It was estimated in 2002 that as many as 40,000 women a year had them. One 23-year-old female journalist stated, "I would say 60% of the women I know have had abortions. If they're rich, they go to Spain, and if they're not, they go to midwives, often in really bad conditions."

The trial and conviction in 2002 of a female abortionist who performed illegal operations in a clean, modern clinic provoked outrage among prochoice groups. But in 2004 a judge in Aveiro dropped charges against seven women who had abortions deemed to be illegal. The dramatic lowering of Portugal's infant mortality rate from 85 to only 6 per 1,000 births reinforced the conviction of supporters that abortions should be conducted in modern hospitals, not in back rooms. In a February 2007 referendum, 59% of voters backed the legalization of abortion on demand within the first 10 weeks of pregnancy. Since fewer than 50% of eligible voters (31%) turned out to cast their ballots, the result was not binding on the government. But the Socialist-dominated parliament approved of the reform anyway.

Religious superstitions and symbols remain strong. One sees "Our Lady of . . ." various things everywhere. A popular pilgrimage site is the shrine of Our Lady of Fatima, where the Virgin reportedly appeared to three shepherd children in 1917. Hundreds of thousands of pilgrims attend candlelight masses at the rural shrine twice a year.

In a 2010 poll, 84.5% of Portuguese described themselves as Catholics. However, they are no longer conscientious churchgoers. Only 18.7% said they practice their religion, and a mere 10.3% confessed that they attend masses regularly. About 2 out of 3 choose to get married in a church, compared with 9 out of 10 in 1960. Portugal is one of the few countries that grant paternity leave. The divorce rate has shot up to approximately 14,000 a year, from only a few hundred before the 1974 revolution. A fifth of all babies are born out of wedlock, compared with 1 in 14 in 1970. Portugal has the second-highest rate of teenage pregnancy in Europe, after the UK.

Three children reportedly visited by the Virgin at Our Lady of Fatima

In 2008 parliament rejected same-sex marriage. However, despite polls indicating that only about 40% of Portuguese supported the idea of same-sex marriage, on January 1, 2010, it became the sixth European country to legalize it, in the face vigorous opposition by the Catholic Church. Couples cannot get fertility treatments or adopt children. Popular opposition to it was muted. To add insult to injury, two divorced mothers in their 30s became the first couple to take advantage of the new law and scheduled their wedding in May 2010 during the pope's four-day visit to Portugal.

Perhaps the greatest social change involves women. Before 1974, a woman had to get her husband's permission to go into higher education, take a job, or get a passport. She could not be a diplomat or a judge. In 1960, only about a fifth of women of working age had paying jobs. Now the proportion is 63%, at the top end of the EU range. Women account for about half the workforce and 60% of university students and graduates, up from a fourth in 1960. The majority of new judges are female. As a result of increased education and employment possibilities, fertility rates have plummeted from the highest in Europe to among the lowest. Portuguese are also living longer: 81.9 years for women and 75.4 years for men.

Reflecting a shifting attitude in Europe, Portugal adopted in 2002 a new approach to the problem of drug addiction by decriminalizing all personal drug use and possession of less than a 10-day supply for one person. This applies to all drugs, including heroin and cocaine. Users (now officially called "consumers") are no longer viewed as criminals but as victims of a drug culture that tough laws cannot control. This does not mean that use is legal. Anybody caught in possession has the drugs confiscated and is sent before a government commission that counsels and encourages the user on treatment. It can levy fines and community service.

The Cato Institute, an American think tank, studied the new approach and concluded that none of the "nightmare scenarios" opponents predicted have come true. Drug use in Portugal is among the lowest in the EU, and there is little evidence of "drug tourism." One worrisome fact was that Portugal once had the highest HIV infection rate in all of Europe. But the share of heroin users who inject the drug with needles has fallen from 45% before decriminalization to 17% by 2009. Drugs account for only 20% of HIV cases, down from 56% before. Since 2008 Portuguese lungs have benefited from a ban on smoking in all public places.

FUTURE

Portugal has undergone a dramatic transformation since joining the EU in 1986. The economy experienced an unprecedented boom and has been modernized and liberalized. Poverty still exists, and the income gap is among the largest in Europe. But standards of living have risen, and most Portuguese have benefited.

The Socialist Party, led by Antonio Costa, entered the campaign for the October 2015 elections as foes of austerity, which, it claims, had brought only poverty. It won the elections. He formed a stable parliamentary minority supported by two hard-left parties. This unique coalition is thriving. It restored state pensions, wages, and working hours to prebailout levels and has complied with the eurozone fiscal rules. Tourism and startups are booming. Costa, whose government emerged victorious in October 2019, enjoys high approval ratings. The next election is scheduled for late 2023.

The country's euphoria of joining the eurozone gave way to despondency as the challenges of maintaining a common currency exposed economic weaknesses. The euro has brought both gain and pain.

Austerity brought sacrifice. Thousands of businesses failed, including the Espírito Santo Bank, the country's largest. Emigration increased dramatically to a quarter-million. Unemployment peaked at 17.6% and has fallen to 7%. The EU regards Portugal as a role model in dealing with one of Europe's longest recessions.

Portugal escaped the huge property bust that Spain experienced. Its exports are booming, including a 20% boost to countries outside the EU. The euro crisis that originated in Greece led to a scare that Portugal might follow. But Portugal is not Greece. The government acted quickly to introduce bold austerity measures.

The economy is in better shape than most observers had expected, but it has been battered by the European debt crisis and the Covid-19 pandemic. Rolling out the mass vaccination program will be the country's top priority. Germany gave a helping hand by sending planeloads of help from the German military. The budget deficit is coming down. A "clean exit" from its three-year rescue program in June 2014 was predictable.

In April 2019 Portuguese celebrated the 45th anniversary of the "Carnation Revolution." They can look with satisfaction on the legacies of that revolution: a stable parliamentary democracy, membership in the EU, and raised living standards. The year 2016 brought another occasion for celebration: victory in the European Soccer Championships.

Snake dance, Lisbon style

Andorra

The church Sant Cristòfol d'Anyós, high in the Andorran Pyrenees, dates from the 12th century.

Area: 188 sq. mi. (487 sq. km).

Population: 85,000 (2011). About 75% are foreigners.

Capital City: Andorra la Vella (pop., with adjoining Encamp, 22,000).

Climate: Cool, dry summer and snowy, mountain winter climate.

Neighboring Countries: France (north); Spain (south).

Official Language: Catalan; Spanish and French are also widely spoken.

Ethnic Background: Catalan stock; about 15% of residents are native Andorrans, 61% Spanish, 6% French.

Principal Religion: Roman Catholic.

Major Industries: Tourism, free port for consumer goods, tobacco products, hydroelectric power, timber.

Major Trading Partners: France, Spain, Germany, Japan.

Currency: Euro.

Year of Independence: 1278.

Government: Since 1993 a self-ruling sovereign state.

Chiefs of State: Figurehead Coprinces are the president of the French Republic (Emmanuel Macron) and the Spanish bishop of Seo de Urgel (Joan-Enric Vives i Sicilia), who are represented locally by officials called veguers.

Head of Government: Xavier Espot Zamora, Prime Minister (since May 2019).

National Flag: Three vertical bands of blue, yellow, and red, with the national coat of arms in the center.

Perched high in the Pyrenees Mountains is the largest of Europe's six microscopic

independent states: Andorra. Mountain peaks rising to 9,000 feet (2,743 meters) overlook six deep valleys on the southern slopes of the Pyrenees. Bordering on France to the north and on Spain to the south, Andorra, with its ruggedly beautiful landscape, is a geographic blend of glacial valleys, lakes, freshwater springs, and Alpine meadows. Abundant rainfall and snow give this tiny land a green, rich look half the year and a white mountain look the other half. In the 58 villages and hamlets in the highlands, with their typically granite, wood, and slate houses, live many of the native Andorrans, who now comprise only about 15% of the population.

They have a strong affinity with the region of Catalonia in northern Spain. They speak Catalan, a rich Romance language related to Provencal, spoken by approximately 6 million persons in the region that encompasses French and Spanish

Catalonia. In the age of the automobile, Andorra has been ripped from the Middle Ages, and its dizzying economic advancement has attracted thousands of Spaniards and French, who now comprise 61% and 6% of Andorra's residents, respectively. These developments have made Andorrans a minority in their own country, but they have also given the land a prosperous, international character.

There is evidence of human settlements in Andorra dating many thousands of years ago, and the first written records date from the 3rd century BC. It is a local legend that the mountain people in these valleys helped a grateful Charlemagne drive the Moors from the area in 806 AD. Charlemagne's son Louis the Pious granted the six valleys to the Spanish bishop of Seo de Urgel in 819 AD. In 1278 the French Count of Foix and the bishop recognized each other as coprinces of Andorra. Over the years, the Count of Foix's claims passed to the king of Navarre, then to the king of France, and finally to the president of the French Republic. Except for a brief period during the French Revolution, when the French occupied Andorra and declared it a republic, it has retained to the present day its coallegiance to France and the bishop of Seo de Urgel.

Until 1993 the coallegiance was formally acknowledged by a token annual tribute (*questia*) of 960 French francs (about $190) to France and 460 Spanish pesetas (about $15) to Spain in alternating years. Because of this tribute and because the country existed as a result of a feudal grant, Andorra was technically not a state, according either to international law or to its own statutes. It was a fief, a feudal carryover from the Middle Ages with no equivalence in modern Europe.

POLITICAL SYSTEM

In 1990 reformer Josep Maria Beal was elected sindic, pledging to modernize the country's institutions to enable it to survive in the new Europe. With the support of his successor, Jordi Farras, and other Andorran leaders, such as Oscar Ribas Reig, his pledge was fulfilled. In 1993 the tiny country adopted its first-ever constitution. With three-quarters of the eligible voters participating, 74.2% opted for sovereignty. By choosing self-rule, they acquired the right to have their own judicial system and foreign policy.

Andorrans are now completely free to establish political parties. Traditionally, all Andorran candidates ran as independents. In 1976 Andorra's first political party, the Andorran Democratic Association, was formed. Elections were held in April 2011 for the 28 seats in the General Council: 14 are elected by popular vote via proportional representation (PR), and 14 are elected by absolute majority vote.

In the April 2011 elections, the newly founded party Democrats for Andorra (DA), a coalition of center-right groups led by Antoni Martí, won big, capturing 55% of the votes and 20 out of 28 seats in the General Council. An architect and former mayor of one of Andorra's seven communities, Martí replaced Jaume Bartumeu as prime minister. The outgoing center-left Social Democrats (PS), led by Bartumeu, won 34.8% of the votes and 6 seats (down from 14). The Lauredian Union (UL) won two seats (up from zero). Andorra for Change (ApC) lost all three of its seats, after winning only 6.7% of the votes. The Greens of Andorra (Vd'A) got 3.35% of the votes, but they won no seats. Turnout was 74%.

Prime Minister Xavier Espot Zamora

THE COPRINCES OF ANDORRA

His Excellency the Honorable Emmanuel Macron, president of the French Republic

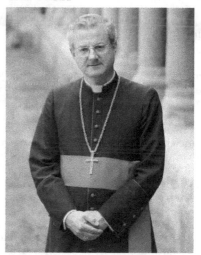

His Excellency the Most Reverend Joan-Enric Vives i Sicilia, bishop of Seo de Urgel

The right to vote is very restricted. Only the 22,000 Andorrans whose families have had Andorran citizenship for three generations are permitted to vote. This amounts to only a fourth of the population. Women citizens were granted suffrage in 1970. The new constitution affects every preexisting political institution in the country.

The president of France and the bishop of Seo de Urgel are figurehead coprinces of Andorra and until 1993 had full executive, legislative, and judicial power. In practice, veguers (their designated representatives) and battles (magistrates) represented them in the country. These feudal offices were combined with more modern elected offices.

The country had no constitution before 1993 but a Plan of Reform, adopted in 1866. It established the groundwork for a General Council of 28 members (at least 4 of whom are elected from each of the 6 parishes in

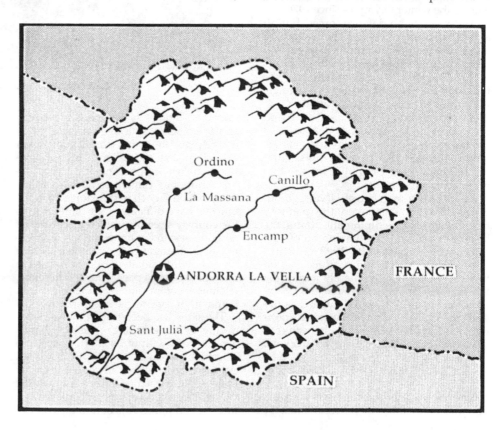

Andorra

the 6 valleys—Andorra, Canillo, Encamp, La Massana, Ordino, and Sant Julià). Each member is elected to a four-year term, and half the members were elected every two years. Before the new constitution was implemented, the General Council had no formal legislative power, but it was the supreme administrative body. It elected for three-year terms a sindic (manager) and subsindic to implement its decisions. There was usually tension within the General Council between the 4 representatives from the capital city, where two-thirds of the country's population lives, and the remaining 20 representatives from the more rural parishes. When the capital's four representatives request funds for facilities needed by the rapidly growing capital city, the remaining members are inclined to demand similar facilities for their parishes. This often created deadlocks on important issues.

The judicial system is now independent. It is based on French secular and Spanish ecclesiastical law. That such a hybrid legal system could function in Andorra is demonstrated by the fact that the entire country maintains only six jail cells, most of which usually are empty. The constitution emboldened the judiciary in 1993 to arrest the director of state security and president of the Olympic Committee in a new effort to fight corruption. Earlier, the country's main families had been powerful enough to suppress scandals through their dominance of the French and Spanish courts in Andorra. The tiny mountainous land has sent athletes to the winter Olympics since 1976.

Andorra has no defense forces, but all able-bodied men between the ages of 16 and 60 are required to arm themselves and be ready to serve without pay or uniforms in the People's Militia, which has not fought in a war for 700 years. This strange, unorganized army regards all its "soldiers" as officers. In practice, France and Spain provide for Andorra's defense, and the Barcelona police and French gendarmerie alternate year by year in assisting the 160-man Andorran police to maintain order within the country.

Andorra is a member of UNESCO, but until 1993 France played the primary role in handling its diplomatic affairs, the bishop of Seo de Urgel having no official international status. Its 1993 constitution permits Andorra to conduct its own foreign policy. It immediately joined the UN as a full member, entered the Council of Europe in 1994, and tightened its ties with the EU. The United States' relations with Andorra have traditionally been conducted through its consulate in Barcelona.

ECONOMY

Since only 4% of the country's land can be cultivated, most of its food must be

Statue in front of the main government building

imported. It owes its livelihood to tourism and to its status as a free port (duty-free marketplace) for manufactured goods from many industrialized nations. This duty-free status makes Andorra one of the most active smuggling centers of Europe, an activity which French and Spanish customs officials have difficulty controlling due to the country's remote and rugged frontier and due also to the impossibility of checking all the thousands of automobiles which cross its borders daily. Andorra refuses to make smuggling a penal offense. Therefore, dealing in contraband, by either organized criminals or legal merchants, thrives.

The same had been true of money laundering and the hiding of assets. Banks account for a fifth of its GDP. There is no central bank. In 2000 the OECD placed Andorra on a list of "uncooperative tax havens." It reached an agreement with the EU in 2003 to collect taxes for bank account interest and return 75% of it to the country

of residence without providing account holders' names. It got off the OECD's list. In 2015, the US Treasury Department issued a report accusing an Andorran bank (BPA) of laundering hundreds of millions for powerful criminal gangs, including ones from Russia, China, and Venezuela. In that year, assets under management were 17 times GDP. They made Andorra a rich country as measured by per-capita GDP.

In 2009 the government announced its willingness to enter into tax information exchange agreements and its intention to eliminate strict bank secrecy for tax purposes by the end of the year. It entered its first agreements with France and Spain, allowing the exchange of information on bank accounts. By 2011 much of its bank secrecy had been given up.

This tiny country absorbs 11 million visitors each year. Two-thirds of them are from Spain, mainly day-trippers. What awaits this throng of visitors is one huge mall with

444

good bargains at gaudy shops but also long traffic jams, tight parking, exhaust-filled air, shoulder-to-shoulder walking, and almost interminable waiting at the border. Commerce trumps charm. For export, it manufactures cigars and cigarettes, matches, anisette liqueur, and sandals. It also produces for sale that customary product of microstates: beautiful postage stamps, although no postage whatsoever is required for mail *within* the country. In January 2002 the euro became the official currency.

The principality faces economic problems. Foreign investors have withdrawn much of their money. There has been a fall in the real estate market, as well as many business closings and reductions in the income of hotels and restaurants. Prime Minister Martí, who took office in April 2011, must pull the former tax paradise out of its worst economic crisis in recent history.

Both France and Spain want to limit Andorra's duty-free business. For example, cigarettes are 60% cheaper than in neighboring France. Many Andorrans fear that the attractiveness of a shopping trip to their country will decline in the future. Andorra's favorable trade agreements with Spain and France give it legal trade outlets to the entire EU. In 1990, for the first time in 700 years, Andorra signed an international treaty, approving a trade agreement with the EU. It makes Andorra a member of the EU customs union. It

permits industrial goods to flow freely to and from the EU and obligates Andorra to apply the EU's external tariffs on such goods to third countries.

Full EU membership must wait. Spain insists that Andorra introduce adequate labor and social security laws for the 20,000 Spaniards who work in Andorra, mainly in tourism, before the tiny country is considered for EU membership. Andorra's 1993 constitution permits the establishment of labor unions, hitherto banned.

It has a hydroelectric plant at Escaldes, which provides electricity for Andorra and exports a modest amount of power to the northern part of Barcelona Province and to southern France. Residents of Andorra pay no personal income taxes.

The 1993 constitution grants freedom of religion, although Roman Catholicism remains the established church. That helps explain why Andorra's is among the strictest abortion laws in Europe. Andorra's school system is a cumbersome combination of French secular schools and Spanish parochial schools, financed and staffed by France and Spain and terminating educational possibilities within Andorra at age 14. Because there is no university, young Andorrans go to France or Spain for higher education. Only half of them return, in part because the exorbitant property prices, which had spiraled to Parisian levels before the bubble popped, kept them away.

Andorra has two daily newspapers, *Diari d'Andorra* and *El Periodic*, and one monthly, *Andorra Magazine*. Radio service is provided by Radio Nacional d'Andorra, which operates Radio Andorra and Andorra Musica. Andorrans can receive many Spanish and French television stations, as well as its own TVA, operated by Radio i Televiso d'Andorra. There are no railroad or airport facilities, but good roads tie the country to Spain and, except in the winter months, to France.

FUTURE

Andorra has undergone great social, economic, and political changes, from a traditional pastoral and farming fiefdom and economy to a sovereign ministate thriving on commerce and tourism. This process, which led to a quadrupling of Andorra's population in a quarter-century, brings both promise and problems to the future Andorra. Population density has become and will remain very high.

Economic problems have taken some of the shine off the principality's economy. There has been too little snow in recent years, which damages overnight tourism. Tourism can no longer be counted on to provide prosperity for years to come. It is uncertain anyway whether it will destroy Andorra's traditions and mountain tranquility. Nevertheless, Andorra can face the future with relative confidence.

Web Sites and Bibliography of Key English-Language Books

WEBSITES

The UN, EU, OECD, NATO, and Other

Aktion Euro. https://www.aktion-euro.de. Site for the euro currency.

Carnegie Endowment for International Peace. https://carnegieendowment.org/.

Central Intelligence Agency. https://www.cia.gov/index.html. Includes useful CIA publications, such as *The World Factbook* and maps.

Delegation of the European Union to the United States. https://eeas.europa.eu/delegations/united-states-america_en.

EUobserver. https://www.euobserver.com.

Euractiv. https://www.euractiv.com. Diverse new on EU and Europe.

European Commission. https://europa.eu/european-union/about-eu/institutions-bodies/european-commission_en.

European Council. https://europa.eu/european-union/about-eu/institutions-bodies/european-council_en.

European Parliament. http://www.europarl.europa.eu/portal/en.

European Sources Online. https://www.europeansources.info/. Search engine for all documents published by EU institutions, by subscription.

European Union. https://europa.eu/european-union/index_en.

Library of Congress, Collection: Country Studies. https://www.loc.gov/collections/country-studies/about-this-collection/. Coverage of more than 100 countries.

Link to Your Roots. https://www.hamburg.de/bkm/eculture/7361886/netzwerk bildung/. A database to help Americans trace their European roots.

North Atlantic Treaty Organization. https://www.nato.int/.

Organisation for Economic Co-operation and Development. https://www.oecd.org/about/.

Organization for Security and Co-operation in Europe. https://www.osce.org/.

United Nations. https://www.un.org.

United Nations System: Chief Executive Board for Coordination. https://www.unsystem.org.

US Department of State. https://www.state.gov/. Includes country reports.

The World Bank. https://www.worldbank.org/. News and publications with links to other financial institutions.

World Trade Organization. https://www.wto.org/.

XE Currency Converter. https://www.xe.com/currencyconverter/. The most up-to-date foreign currency values.

Newspapers, Journals, and Television with Good Coverage on European Affairs

BBC. https://www.bbc.com.

Chicago Tribune. https://www.chicagotribune.com/. Named best overall US newspaper online service for newspapers with circulation more than 100,000.

Christian Science Monitor. https://www.csmonitor.com/. Named best overall US newspaper online service for newspapers with circulation under 100,000.

CNN. https://www.cnn.com. Latest news with external links.

C-SPAN. https://www.c-span.org. Includes *C-SPAN International*.

Economist. https://www.economist.com. British weekly news magazine.

Financial Times. https://www.ft.com. Authoritative British newspaper.

Foreign Affairs. https://www.foreignaffairs.org. One of best-known international affairs journals.

Libertad Digital. https://www.libertaddigital.com. Spain's first online newspaper.

New York Times. https://www.nytimes.com. Respected US newspaper; now owns *International Herald Tribune*, published as *New York Times Global Edition*.

Politico. https://www.politico.eu/. Formerly *European Voice*; weekly news on EU and European affairs.

Time, World edition. https://time.com/section/world/. Includes stories on European news for *Time* magazine.

Washington Post. https://www.washingtonpost.com. Respected US newspaper.

Western Europe

Expatica. https://www.expatica.com/. "The complete guide to expat life."

Washington, DC, Embassies. https://www.embassy.org/embassies. A site with links to all embassy websites in Washington, DC.

Country Sites

Great Britain

European Health Defence. http://www.european-defence.co.uk.

Foreign and Commonwealth Office. https://www.gov.uk/government/organisations/foreign-commonwealth-office.

Prime Minister's Office. https://www.gov.uk/government/organisations/prime-ministers-office-10-downing-street.

Margaret Thatcher Foundation. https://www.margaretthatcher.org.

Ministry of Defence. https://www.gov.uk/government/organisations/ministry-of-defence.

UK Parliament. https://www.parliament.uk/.

Ireland

Government of Ireland. https://www.gov.ie/en/.

France

France in the United States: Unofficial Website. https://www.info-france-usa.org. French culture and government.

Netherlands

Eerste Kamer: Der Staten-Generaal. https://www.eerstekamer.nl/begrip/english_2.

Ministry of General Affairs. https://www.government.nl/ministries/ministry-of-general-affairs.

Royal House of the Netherlands. https://www.royal-house.nl/.

Tweede Kamer: Der Staten-Generaal. https://www.houseofrepresentatives.nl/.

Belgium

Belgian Federal Government. https://www.belgium.be/en.

Fédération Wallonie-Bruxelles. http://www.federation-wallonie-bruxelles.be/.

Flanders: State of the Art. https://www.vlaanderen.be/en.

Wallonie. https://www.wallonie.be/fr.

Switzerland

The Federal Council of the Swiss Government. https://www.admin.ch/gov/en/start.html.

Liechtenstein

Liechtenstein: Official Tourism Website. https://www.tourismus.li/en.

Italy

Government of Italy, Presidency of the Council of Ministers. http://www.governo.it/.

Ministry of Foreign Affairs and International Cooperation, Italy. https://www.esteri.it/mae/en/.

Portugal

Portugal-US Chamber of Commerce. http://portugal-us.com/.

Vatican City

The Holy See. http://w2.vatican.va/content/vatican/en.html.

Malta

Government of Malta. https://www.gov.mt/en/Pages/home.aspx.

Malta Independent Online. http://www.independent.com.mt/. Maltese newspaper in English.

Times of Malta. https://www.timesofmalta.com/.

Greece

Embassy of Greece in Washington, DC. https://www.mfa.gr/usa/en/the-embassy.

Greek Reporter. https://greece.greekreporter.com/category/greek-news/.

Hellenic Republic, General Secretariat for Media and Communication. http://www.greeknewsagenda.gr/.

Hellenic Republic, Ministry of Foreign Affairs. https://www.mfa.gr/en.

WESTERN EUROPE

Anderson, Stephanie B. *Crafting EU Security Policy: In the Pursuit of a European Identity.* Boulder, CO: Lynne Rienner, 2008.

Bale, Tim. *European Politics: A Comparative Introduction.* 2nd ed. New York: Palgrave Macmillan, 2008.

Balme, Richard, and Didier Chabanet. *European Governance and Democracy: Power and Protest in the EU.* Lanham, MD: Rowman and Littlefield, 2008.

Barzini, Luigi. *The Europeans.* New York: Simon and Schuster, 1983.

Bauman, Zugmunt. *Europe: An Unfinished Adventure.* Malden, MA: Polity Press, 2004.

Bell, David S. *Western European Communists and the Collapse of Communism.* Oxford, UK: Berg, 1993.

Benjamin, Daniel, ed. *Europe 2030.* Washington, DC: Brookings Institution Press, 2009.

Bindi, Federiga, ed. *The Foreign Policy of the European Union.* Washington, DC: Brookings Institution Press, 2009.

Biscop, Sven. *The European Security Strategy.* Abington, UK: Ashgate, 2005.

Bisco, Sven, and Johan Lembke, eds. *EU Enlargement and the Transatlantic Alliance: A Security Relationship in Flux.* Boulder, CO: Lynne Rienner, 2007.

Black, Cyril E., et al. *Rebirth: A History of Europe since World War II.* Boulder, CO: Westview Press, 1992.

Brimmer, Esther, ed. *The EU's Search for a Strategic Role.* Washington, DC: Brookings Institution Press, 2004.

Brunnermeier, Markus K., Harold James, and Jean-Pierre Landau. *The Euro and the Battle of Ideas.* Princeton, NJ: Princeton University Press, 2016.

Cafruny, Alan W., and J. Magnus Ryner. *Europe at Bay: In the Shadow of US Hegemony.* Boulder, CO: Lynne Rienner, 2007.

Calleo, David P. *Rethinking Europe's Future.* Princeton, NJ: Princeton University Press, 2001.

Carr, Matthew. *Fortress Europe: Dispatches from a Gated Continent.* New York: New Press, 2012. About immigration.

Cini, Michelle, and Nieves Pérez-Solórzano Borragá, eds. *European Union Politics.* 3rd ed. Oxford, UK: Oxford University Press, 2009.

Craig, Gordon A. *Europe since 1815.* 3rd ed. New York: Holt, Rinehart, Winston, 1971.

Curtis, Michael. *Western European Government and Politics.* New York: Longman, 1997.

De Grazia, Victoria. *America's Advance through Twentieth-Century Europe.* Cambridge, MA: Harvard University Press, 2005.

Dinan, Desmond, ed. *Encyclopedia of the European Union.* Updated ed. Boulder, CO: Lynne Rienner, 2000.

———. *Europe Recast: A History of European Union.* 2nd ed. Boulder, CO: Lynne Rienner, 2014.

———. *Ever Closer Union: An Introduction to European Integration.* 4th ed. Boulder, CO: Lynne Rienner, 2010.

Dragnich, Alex N., Jorgen S. Rasmussen, and Joel C. Moses. *Major European Governments.* 9th ed. Chicago: Dorsey Press, 1994.

Dunkerley, David, Lesley Hodgson, Stanislaw Konopacki, Tony Spybey, and Andrew Thompson. *Changing Europe: Identities, Nations and Citizens.* New York: Routledge, 2002.

Duroselle, Jean-Baptiste. *Europe: A History of Its Peoples.* New York: Viking, 1990.

Dyson, Kenneth, and Kevin Featherstone. *The Road to Maastricht: Negotiating Economic and Monetary Union.* New York: Oxford University Press, 2000.

Eichengreen, Barry. *The European Economy since 1945.* Princeton, NJ: Princeton University Press, 2007.

Gaddis, John Lewis. *The Cold War: A New History.* New York: Penguin Press, 2006.

Gallagher, Michael, Michael Laver, and Peter Mair. *Representative Government in Modern Europe.* 3rd ed. New York: McGraw Hill, 2001.

Gärtner, Heinz, Adrian Hyde-Price, and Erich Reiter. *Europe's New Security Challenges.* Boulder, CO: Lynne Rienner, 2001.

George, Stephen, and Ian Bache. *Politics in the European Union.* New York: Oxford, 2001.

Gillingham, John. *European Integration, 1950–2003.* Cambridge, UK: Cambridge University Press, 2003.

Ginsberg, Roy H. *Demystifying the European Union: The Enduring Logic of Regional Integration.* 2nd ed. Lanham, MD: Rowman and Littlefield, 2010.

Giustino, David de. *A Reader in European Integration: A Selection of Key Documents.* New York: Longman, 1996.

Givens, Terri E., and Rahsaan Maxwell. *Immigrant Politics: Race and Representation in Western Europe.* Boulder, CO: Lynne Rienner, 2012.

Goodby, James E., Petrus Buwalda, and Dmitri Trenin. *A Strategy for Stable Peace: Toward a Euroatlantic Security Community.* Washington, DC: United States Institute of Peace Press, 2002.

Gordon, Philip H., and Jeremy Shapiro. *Allies at War: America, Europe, and the Crisis over Iraq.* New York: McGraw Hill, 2004.

Green, David Michael. *The Europeans: Political Identity in an Emerging Polity.* Boulder, CO: Lynne Rienner, 2007.

Hamilton, Daniel S., ed. *Conflict and Cooperation in Transatlantic Relations.* Washington, DC: Brookings Institution Press, 2004.

———, ed. *Transatlantic Transformations: Equipping NATO for the 21st Century.* Washington, DC: Brookings Institution Press, 2004.

Hamilton, Daniel S., and Frances Burwell. *Shoulder to Shoulder: Forging a Strategic US-EU Partnership.* Washington, DC: Brookings Institution Press, 2010.

Hamilton, Daniel S., and Joseph P. Quinlan. *Globalization and Europe: Prospering in the New Whirled Order.* Washington, DC: Brookings Institution Press, 2008.

———. *Partners in Prosperity: The Changing Geography of the Transatlantic Economy.* Washington, DC: Brookings Institution Press, 2004.

Hancock, M. Donald, et al. *Politics in Europe.* 5th ed. Washington, DC: CQ Press, 2011.

Hitchcock, William I. *The Struggle for Europe: The Turbulent History of a Divided Continent 1945 to the Present.* New York: Anchor Books, 2004.

Hix, Simon. *The Political System of the European Union.* 2nd ed. New York: Palgrave Macmillan, 2005.

Hoffman, Stanley. *The Atlantic Alliance under Stress.* New York: Cambridge University Press, 2005.

Hogwood, Patricia, and Geoffrey K. Roberts. *European Politics Today.* 2nd ed. Manchester, UK: Manchester University Press, 2003.

Horowitz, Joseph. *Artists in Exile: How Refugees from Twentieth-Century War and Revolution Transformed the American Performing Arts.* New York: HarperCollins, 2008.

Hosli, Madeleine O. *The Euro: A Concise Introduction to Europe's Single Currency.* Boulder, CO: Lynne Rienner, 2005.

Hunter, Robert E. *The European Security and Defense Policy: NATO's Companion—or Competitor?* Santa Monica, CA: Rand, 2002.

Israeli, Raphael. *The Islamic Challenge in Europe.* New Brunswick, NJ: Transaction, 2008.

Jones, Robert A. *The Politics and Economics of the European Union.* Williston, VT: Edger Elgar, 1996.

Judt, Tony. *Postwar: A History of Europe since 1945.* New York: Penguin Press, 2005.

Kaelble, Hartmut, ed. *The European Way: The Societies of Europe in the 19th and 20th Centuries.* New York: Berghahn, 2004.

Bibliography

Kagan, Robert. *Of Paradise and Power: America and Europe in the New World Order*. New York: Alfred A. Knopf, 2003.

Kaplan, Lawrence S. *NATO Divided, NATO United: The Evolution of an Alliance*. Westport, CT: Praeger, 2004.

Kershaw, Ian. *To Hell and Back: Europe 1914–1949*. New York: Viking, 2015.

Kesselman, Mark, et al. *European Politics in Transition*. 4th ed. New York: Houghton Mifflin, 2002.

Kirchner, Emil, and James Sperling. *EU Security Governance*. Manchester, UK: Manchester University Press, 2008.

Klausen, Jytte. *The Islamic Challenge: Politics and Religion in Western Europe*. New York: Oxford University Press, 2005.

Kramer, Jane. *Europeans*. New York: Penguin Books, 1992.

Kupchan, Charles A. *The End of the American Era: US Foreign Policy and the Geopolitics of the Twenty-First Century*. New York: Knopf, 2003.

Lane, Jan-Erik, and Svante O. Ersson. *European Politics*. 4th ed. Beverly Hills, CA: Sage, 1998.

Laqueur, Walter. *Europe in Our Time: A History, 1945–1992*. New York: Viking, 1993.

Laurence, Jonathan. *The Emancipation of Europe's Muslims: The State's Role in Minority Integration*. Princeton, NJ: Princeton University Press, 2012.

Leach, Rodney. *Europe: A Concise Encyclopedia of the European Union*. 4th ed. London: Profile Books, 2004.

Leiken, Robert. *Europe's Angry Muslims: The Revolt of the Second Generation*. New York: Oxford University Press, 2012.

Mahncke, Dieter, Wayne C. Thompson, and Wyn Rees. *Redefining Transatlantic Relations: The Challenge of Change*. Manchester, UK: Manchester University Press, 2004.

Mair, Peter, ed. *The Western Europe Party System*. Oxford, UK: Oxford University Press, 1990.

Mak, Geert. *In Europe: Travels through the Twentieth Century*. New York: Pantheon, 2007.

Markovits, Andrei S. *Uncouth Nation: Why Europe Dislikes America*. Princeton, NJ: Princeton University Press, 2007.

Marks, Gary, and Marco R. Steenbergen, eds. *European Integration and Political Conflict*. Cambridge, UK: Cambridge University Press, 2003.

McCormick, John. *The European Union: Politics and Policies*. 3rd ed. Boulder, CO: Westview Press, 2004.

———. *Understanding the European Union: A Concise Introduction*. 4th ed. New York: Palgrave, 2008.

McGuire, Steven, and Michael Smith. *The European Union and the United States: Convergence and Competition in the Global Arena*. New York: Palgrave, 2008.

Menasse, Robert. *The Capital*. Translated by Jamie Bulloch. New York: Liveright, 2019. A novel about intrigue and bureaucracy in Brussels.

Merkl, Peter H. *The Rift between America and Old Europe: The Distracted Eagle*. New York: Routledge, 2005.

Merlingen, Michael. *EU Security Policy: What It Is, How It Works, Why It Matters*. Boulder, CO: Lynne Rienner, 2012.

Miller, Steven L., ed. *European Unification: A Conceptual Guide for Educators*. Bloomington, IN: ERIC Clearinghouse for Social Studies, 1995.

Murray, Douglas. *The Strange Death of Europe: Immigration, Identity, Islam*. New York: Bloomsbury, 2017.

Mushaben, Joyce Marie. *Becoming Madam Chancellor: Angela Merkel and the Berlin Republic*. New York: Cambridge, 2017.

Nelsen, Brent F., and Alexander Stubb, eds. *The European Union: Readings of the Theory and Practice of European Integration*. 4th ed. Boulder, CO: Lynne Rienner, 2014.

Nugent, Neill, ed. *European Union Enlargement*. New York: Palgrave Macmillan, 2004.

———. *The Government and Politics of the European Union*. 6th ed. New York: Palgrave Macmillan, 2006.

Occhipinti, John D. *The Politics of EU Police Cooperation: Toward a European FBI*. Boulder, CO: Lynne Rienner, 2003.

Olson, Lynne. *Those Angry Days: Roosevelt, Lindbergh, and America's Fight over World War II, 1939–1941*. New York: Random House, 2013.

Opello, Walter C., Jr., and Katherine A. R. Opello. *European Politics: The Making of Democratic States*. Boulder, CO: Lynne Rienner, 2009.

Patten, Chris. *Cousins and Strangers: America, Britain, and Europe in a New Century*. New York: Times Books, Henry Hold, 2006.

Pells, Richard. *Not Like Us: How Europeans Have Loved, Hated and Transformed American Culture since World War II*. New York: Basic Books, 1997.

Perry, Marvin. *An Intellectual History of Modern Europe*. Boston: Houghton Mifflin, 1993.

Peterson, John, and Mark A. Pollack. *Europe, America, Bush: Transatlantic Relations in the Twenty-First Century*. New York: Routledge, 2003.

Peterson, John, and Michael Shackleton. *The Institutions of the European Union*. New York: Oxford University Press, 2002.

Pinder, John. *European Community: The Building of a Union*. 3rd ed. Oxford, UK: Oxford University Press, 1998.

———. *The European Union: A Very Short Introduction*. Oxford, UK: Oxford University Press, 2001.

Pond, Elizabeth. *Friendly Fire: The Near-Death of the Transatlantic Alliance*. Washington, DC: Brookings Institution Press, 2003.

———. *The Rebirth of Europe*. 2nd ed. Washington, DC: Brookings Institution Press, 2002.

Roberts, Geoffrey, and Patricia Hogwood. *European Politics Today*. New York: St. Martin's Press, 1997.

Salmon, Trevor C., and Alistair Shepherd. *Toward a European Army: A Military Power in the Making?* Boulder, CO: Lynne Rienner, 2003.

Schain, Martin. *The Marshall Plan: Fifty Years After*. New York: Palgrave Macmillan, 2001.

———. *The Politics of Immigration in France, Britain, and the United States*. New York: Palgrave Macmillan, 2008.

Schimmelfennig, Frank. *The EU, NATO and the Integration of Europe: Rules and Rhetoric*. Cambridge, UK: Cambridge University Press, 2003.

Serfaty, Simon. *The Vital Partnership: Power and Order: America and Europe beyond Iraq*. Lanham, MD: Rowman and Littlefield, 2005.

Shawcross, William. *Allies: The US, Britain, Europe, and the War in Iraq*. New York: PublicAffairs, 2004.

Sloan, Stanley R. *NATO, the European Union, and the Atlantic Community: The Transatlantic Bargain Reconsidered*. Lanham, MD: Rowman and Littlefield, 2003.

Slomp, Hans. *European Politics into the Twenty-First Century: Integration and Division*. Westport, CT: Greenwood, 2000.

Smith, Michael E. *Europe's Foreign and Security Policy: The Institutionalization*. Cambridge, UK: Cambridge University Press, 2004.

Steiner, Josephine, and Lorna Woods. *EU Law*. 10th ed. New York: Oxford University Press, 2009.

Steiner, Jürg. *European Democracies*. 2nd ed. New York: Longman, 1991.

Stephan, Alexander, ed. *The Americanization of Europe: Culture, Diplomacy and Anti-Americanization after 1945*. New York: Berghahn, 2008.

Taras, Ray. *Europe Old and New*. Lanham, MD: Rowman and Littlefield, 2008.

Telò, Mario. *Europe: A Civilian Power? European Union, Global Governance, World Order*. London: Palgrave MacMillan, 2006.

Tiersky, Ronald, and Erik Jones. *Europe Today: A Twenty-First Century Introduction*. 3rd ed. Lanham, MD: Rowman and Littlefield, 2007.

Torbiörn, Kjell M. *Destination Europe: The Political and Economic Growth of a Continent*. Manchester, UK: Manchester University Press, 2003.

Tsoukalis, Loukas. *The New European Economy*. 3rd ed. New York: Oxford University Press, 1996.

Urwin, Derek W. *The Community of Europe: A History of European Integration since 1945*. 2nd. ed. New York: Longman, 1994.

———. *Dictionary of European History and Politics since 1945*. New York: Longman, 1996.

———. *Western Europe since 1945: A Political History*. 5th ed. New York: Longman, 1997.

Warmenhoven, Henri J. *Western Europe*. Guilford, CT: Dushkin, annually updated.

Weidenfeld, Werner, et al. *From Alliance to Coalitions: The Future of Transatlantic Relations*. Washington, DC: Brookings Institution Press, 2004.

Wood, Steve, and Wolfgang Quaisser. *The New European Union: Confronting the Challenges of Integration*. Boulder, CO: Lynne Rienner, 2008.

Young, John W. *Cold War Europe: 1945–1989*. New York: Routledge, 1991.

Youngs, Richard. *Europe and the Middle East: In the Shadow of September 11*. Boulder, CO: Lynne Rienner, 2006.

Zeff, Eleanor E., and Ellen B. Pirro, eds. *The European Union and the Member States*. 3rd ed. Boulder, CO: Lynne Rienner, 2015.

GREAT BRITAIN

Adolino, Jessica R. *Ethnic Minorities, Electoral Politics, and Political Integration in Britain*. Herndon, VA: Cassell, 1998.

Andrew, Christopher. *The Defence of the Realm: The Authorized History of MI5*. New York: Knopf, 2009.

Ascherson, Neal. *Stone Voices: The Search for Scotland*. New York: Hill and Wang, 2003.

Barr, Niall. *Eisenhower's Armies: The American-British Alliance during World War II*. New York: Pegasus Books, 2016.

Bartle, John, and Anthony King, eds. *Britain at the Polls 2005*. Washington, DC: CQ Press, 2005.

Bartlett, C. J. *The Special Relationship: A Political History of Anglo-American Relations since 1945*. New York: Longman, 1992.

Baylis, John. *Anglo-American Relations since the Second World War*. New York: St. Martin's Press, 1997.

Bennett, Gill. *Six Moments of Crisis: Inside British Foreign Policy*. Oxford, UK: Oxford University Press, 2013.

Birch, Anthony H. *The British System of Government*. 8th ed. New York: Routledge, 1990.

Blair, Cherie. *Speaking for Myself: The Autobiography*. Boston: Little, Brown, 2008.

Blair, Tony. *A Journey: My Political Life*. New York: Alfred A. Knopf, 2010.

———. *New Britain: My Vision of a Young Country*. Boulder, CO: Westview Press, 2004.

Bogdanor, Vernon. *The Coalition and the Constitution*. London: Hart, 2011.

———. *The New British Constitution*. London: Hart, 2009.

Bower, Tom. *Gordon Brown*. New York: HarperCollins, 2004.

Bradford, Sarah. *Queen Elizabeth II: Her Life in Our Times*. London: Viking, 2012.

Brendon, Piers. *The Decline and Fall of the British Empire: 1781–1997*. London: Jonathon Cape, 2007.

Briggs, Asa. *A Social History of England*. London: Weidenfeld Nicolson, 1983.

Brown, Gordon. *Beyond the Crash: Overcoming the First Crisis of Globalization*. London: Free Press, Simon and Schuster, 2011.

Budge, Ian, et al. *New British Politics*. 3rd ed. New York: Pearson Longman, 2004.

Butler, David, and Sloman, Anne, eds. *British Political Facts, 1900–1979*. 5th ed. New York: St. Martin's Press, 1980.

Campbell, Alastair. *The Blair Years*. New York: Alfred A. Knopf, 2007.

Campbell, John. *Roy Jenkins: A Well-Rounded Life*. London: Jonathan Cape, 2014.

Cashmore, E. Ellis. *United Kingdom? Class, Race, and Gender since the War*. London: Unwin Hyman, 1989.

Childs, David. *Britain since 1945: A Political History*. 6th ed. New York: Routledge, 2006.

Colley, Linda. *Acts of Union and Disunion*. London: Profile Books, 2013.

———. *Britons: Forging the Nation, 1707–1837*. New Haven, CT: Yale University Press, 1992.

Copus, Colin. *Party Politics and Local Government*. Manchester, UK: Manchester University Press, 2004.

Croft, Stuart. *British Security Policy: The Thatcher Years and the End of the Cold War*. New York: Routledge, 1992.

Crossman, R. H. S. *Introduction to Bagehot's English Constitution*. London: Fontana, 1963.

D'Ancona, Matthew. *The Inside Story of the Coalition Government*. London: Viking, 2013.

Darwin, John. *Unfinished Empire: The Global Expansion of Britain*. New York: Bloomsbury, 2013.

Davies, John. *A History of Wales*. New York: Penguin Books, 2000.

Davis, Charlotte. *Welsh Nationalism in the Twentieth Century*. Westport, CT: Praeger, 1989.

Devine, T. M. *The Scottish Nation: A History, 1700–2000*. New York: Viking, 2000.

Edgell, Stephen, and Vic Duke. *A Measure of Thatcherism: A Sociology of Britain in the 1980s*. New York: Routledge, 1991.

Evans, Eric J. *Thatcher and Thatcherism*. 2nd ed. New York: Routledge, 2002.

Evans, Geoffrey, and Anand Menon. *Brexit and British Politics*. Cambridge, UK: Polity Press, 2017.

Forman, F. N. *Constitutional Change in the United Kingdom*. New York: Routledge, 2002.

Forster, Anthony. *Euroscepticism in British Politics*. New York: Routledge, 2002.

Freedman, Lawrence. *Britain and the Falklands War*. Cambridge, MA: Basil Blackwell, 1988.

Garner, Robert, and Richard Kelly. *British Political Parties Today*. 2nd ed. Manchester, UK: Manchester University Press, 1998.

Gilbert, Martin. *Churchill and America*. New York: Free Press, 2006.

Goring, Rosemary. *Scotland: The Autobiography—2,000 Years of Scottish History by Those Who Saw It Happen*. London: Viking, 2007.

Hardie, Frank. *The Political Influence of the British Monarchy, 1868–1952*. London: Batsford, 1970.

Harvie, Christopher. *Scotland and Nationalism: Scottish Society and Politics 1707–Present*. 4th ed. New York: Routledge, 2004.

Hasan, Mehdi, and James Macintyre. *Ed: The Milibands and the Making of a Labour Leader*. London: Biteback, 2011.

Hattersley, Roy. *Borrowed Time: The Story of Britain between the Wars*. Boston: Little, Brown, 2007.

Havighurst, Alfred F. *Britain in Transition: The Twentieth Century*. Chicago: University of Chicago Press, 1979.

Hennessey, Thomas, and Claire Thomas. *Spooks: The Unofficial History of MI5*. London: Amerley, 2009.

Hennessy, Peter. *The Prime Minister: The Office and Its Holders since 1945*. London: Penguin Press, 2000.

Holland, James. *The Battle of Britain: Five Months That Changed History, May–October 1940*. London: Bantam Press, 2010.

Holliday, Ian, ed. *Fundamentals in British Politics*. New York: St. Martin's Press, 1999.

Hurd, Douglas. *Robert Peel: A Biography*. London: Weidenfeld and Nicolson, 2007.

Irwin, John. *Modern Britain: An Introduction*. 3rd ed. New York: Routledge, 1994.

James, Simon. *British Cabinet Government*. New York: Routledge, 1992.

Jeffery, Keith. *MI6: The History of the Secret Intelligence Service*. London: Bloomsbury, 2010.

Jenkins, Simon. *Thatcher and Sons: A Revolution in Three Acts*. London: Penguin Press, Allen Lane, 2006.

Jones, Bill, and Dennis Kavanagh. *British Politics*. 7th ed. Manchester, UK: Manchester University Press, 2003.

Jones, Bill, Dennis, Michael Moran, Philip Norton. *Politics UK*. 5th ed. NY: Pearson Longman, 2004.

Jones, R. Brinley, ed. *The Anatomy of Wales*. Peterston-super-Ely, UK: Gwerin, 1972.

Bibliography

Kavanagh, Dennis. *Thatcherism and British Politics: The End of Consensus?* 2nd ed. Oxford, UK: Oxford University Press, 1990.

Kellner, Peter. *Democracy: 1,000 Years in Pursuit of British Liberty.* London: Mainstream, 2009.

King, Anthony, et al. *New Labour Triumphs: Britain at the Polls.* Chatham, NJ: Chatham House, 1998.

Kirk, Russell. *America's British Culture.* New Brunswick, NJ: Transaction, 1992.

Korda, Michael. *With Wings Like Eagles: A History of the Battle of Britain.* New York: HarperCollins, 2008.

Krieger, Joel. *Reagan, Thatcher, and the Politics of Decline.* New York: Oxford University Press, 1986.

Laybourn, Keith, and Christine F. Collette. *Modern Britain since 1979: A Reader.* New York: Palgrave Macmillan, 2003.

Lynch, Peter. *SNP: The History of the Scottish National Party.* Cardiff, UK: Welsh Academic Press, 2002.

Magnusson, Magnus. *Scotland: The Story of a Nation.* Camp Hill, PA: History Book Club, 2004.

Major, John. *John Major: The Autobiography.* London: HarperCollins, 1999.

Mandelson, Peter. *The Third Man: Life at the Heart of New Labour.* London: Harper Press, 2010.

Mannin, Michael L. *British Government and Politics. Balancing Europeanization and Independence.* Lanham, MD: Rowman and Littlefield, 2009.

Marquand, David. *Britain since 1918: The Strange Career of British Democracy.* London: Weidenfeld and Nicolson, 2008.

Marr, Andrew. *A History of Modern Britain.* London: Macmillan, 2007.

———. *The Real Elizabeth: An Intimate Portrait of Queen Elizabeth II.* New York: Henry Holt, 2012.

Marwick, Arthur. *Culture in Britain since 1945.* Cambridge, MA: Basil Blackwell, 1991.

Massie, Allan. *The Thistle and the Rose: Six Centuries of Love and Hate between the Scots and the English.* London: John Murray, 2005.

McCormick, John. *Contemporary Britain.* New York: Palgrave Macmillan, 2003.

McCrone, David. *Understanding Scotland: The Sociology of a Nation.* New York: Routledge, 2001.

McNaughton, Neil. *Understanding British and European Political Issues.* Manchester, UK: Manchester University Press, 2003.

Mead, Walter Russell. *God and Gold: Britain, America and the Making of the Modern World.* New York: Knopf, 2007.

Meyer, Christopher. *DC Confidential: The Controversial Memoirs of Britain's Ambassador to the US at the Time of 9/11 and the Iraq War.* London: Weidenfeld and Nicolson, 2005.

Mitchell, James. *Governing Scotland: The Invention of Administrative Devolution.* New York: Palgrave Macmillan, 2003.

Mitchinson, John, and Merullo, Annabel. *British Greats.* London: Cassell, 2000.

Moore, Charles. *Margaret Thatcher: The Authorised Biography.* Vol. 1: *From Grantham to the Falklands.* London: Knopf, 2013.

Morgan, Kenneth O. *Labour People.* Oxford, UK: Oxford University Press, 1987.

———, ed. *The Oxford History of Britain.* Rev. ed. New York: Oxford University Press, 1999.

Murkens, Jo E., Peter Jones, and Michael Keating. *Scottish Independence: A Practical Guide.* Edinburgh, UK: Edinburgh University Press, 2002.

Naughtie, James. *The Best President We Never Had: The Political Tragedy of Tony Blair.* New York: PublicAffairs, 2004.

Nicholl, Katie. *William and Harry.* New York: Weinstein Books, 2010.

Norton, Bruce F. *Politics in Britain.* Washington, DC: CQ Press, 2007.

Norton, Philip. *The British Polity.* 3rd ed. New York: Longman, 1994.

Olson, Lynne. *Citizens of London: The Americans Who Stood with Britain in Its Darkest, Finest Hour.* New York: Random House, 2010.

Overy, Richard. *The Morbid Age: Britain between the Wars.* London: Allen Lane, 2009.

Paterson, Alan. *The Law Lords.* London: Macmillan, 1982.

Paxman, Jeremy. *The English: A Portrait of the People.* London: Penguin Press, 1999.

Pearce, Malcolm, and Geoff Stewart. *British Political History 1867–1990.* New York: Routledge, 1992.

Pilkington, Colin. *Britain in the European Union Today.* Manchester, UK: Manchester University Press, 2001.

———. *Devolution in Britain Today.* Manchester, UK: Manchester University Press, 2003.

———. *Representative Democracy in Britain Today.* Manchester, UK: Manchester University Press, 1997.

Prescott, John. *Prezza: My Story: Pulling No Punches.* London: Headline Review, 2008.

Rasmussen, Jorgen S. *British Politics.* Belmont, CA: Wadsworth, 1993.

Rawnsley, Andrew. *The End of the Party: The Rise and Fall of New Labour.* New York: Viking, 2010.

Reitan, Earl A. *Tory Radicalism: Margaret Thatcher, John Major, and the Transformation of Modern Britain.* Lanham, MD: Rowman and Littlefield, 1997.

Rentoul, John. *Tony Blair: Prime Minister.* Boston: Little, Brown, 2001.

Riddell, Peter. *Hug Them Close: Blair, Clinton, Bush and the "Special Relationship."* London: Politico's, 2003.

———. *The Thatcher Decade: How Britain Has Changed during the 1980s.* Cambridge, MA: Basil Blackwell, 1989.

Robbins, Keith. *Nineteenth-Century Britain: England, Scotland and Wales: The Making of a Nation.* Oxford, UK: Oxford University Press, 1988.

Rose, Richard. *Politics in England.* 5th ed. New York: HarperCollins, 1989.

Royle, Edward. *Modern Britain: A Social History, 1750–1997.* 2nd ed. New York: Oxford University Press, 1997.

Russell, Andrew, and Edward Fieldhouse. *Neither Left nor Right? The Liberal Democrats and the Electorate.* Manchester, UK: Manchester University Press, 2004.

Sampson, Anthony. *Who Runs This Place? The Anatomy of Britain in the 21st Century.* London: John Murray, 2004.

Sandbrook, Dominic. *State of Emergency: The Way We Were: Britain, 1970–1974.* London: Allen Lane, 2010.

Särlvik, Bo, and Ivor Crewe. *Decade of Dealignment: The Conservative Victory of 1979 and Electoral Trends in the 1970s.* Cambridge, UK: Cambridge University Press, 1983.

Seitz, Raymond. *Over Here.* London: Phoenix, 1998.

Seldon, Anthony, ed. *Conservative Century: The Conservative Party since 1900.* Oxford, UK: Oxford University Press, 1994.

Shaw, Eric. *The Labour Party since 1979: Crisis and Transformation.* New York: Routledge, 1994.

Shawcross, William. *Queen Elizabeth, the Queen Mother: The Official Biography.* New York: Knopf, 2009.

Shell, Donald, and Davide Beamish, eds. *The House of Lords at Work.* Oxford, UK: Oxford University Press, 1993.

Sked, Alan, and Chris Cook. *Post-War Britain: A Political History.* 2nd ed. New York: Penguin Books, 1990.

Skidelsky, Robert, ed. *Thatcherism.* Cambridge, MA: Basil Blackwell, 1990.

Smith, Julie, and Mariana Tsatsas. *The New Bilateralism: The UK's Relations within the EU.* Washington, DC: Brookings Institution Press, 2002.

Smith, Martin J., and Joanna Spear. *The Changing Labour Party.* New York: Routledge, 1992.

Smith, Michael. *The Spying Game: The Secret History of British Espionage.* Rev. ed. London: Politico's, 2003.

Soames, Mary. *A Daughter's Tale: The Memoir of Winston Churchill's Youngest Child.* New York: Random House, 2012.

Solomos, John. *Race and Racism in Britain.* New York: Palgrave Macmillan, 2003.

Stephens, Philip. *Tony Blair: The Making of a World Leader.* London: Viking, 2004.

Thatcher, Margaret. *The Path to Power and Downing Street Years.* 2 vols. New York: HarperCollins, 1993, 1995.

———. *Statecraft: Strategies for a Changing World.* New York: HarperCollins, 2002.

Thomas, Gordon. *Inside British Intelligence: 100 Years of MI5 and MI6.* London: J. R. Books, 2009.

Thompson, Juliet S., and Wayne C. Thompson. *Margaret Thatcher: Prime Minister Indomitable.* Boulder, CO: Westview Press, 1994.

Trevelyan, G. M. *History of England.* London: Longman, 1963.

Turner, Alwyn. *A Classless Society: Britain in the 1990s.* London: Aurum, 2013.

Twigge, Stephen, Edward Hampshire, and Graham Macklin. *British Intelligence: Secrets, Spies and Sources.* London: National Archives, 2009.

Underhill, William. *Britain: A New Kind of Union Trouble.* 2010. About Labour leader Ed Miliband.

Vinen, Richard. *Thatcher's Britain: The Politics and Social Upheaval of the Thatcher Era.* New York: Simon and Schuster, 2009.

Wall, Stephen. *A Stranger in Europe: Britain and the EU from Thatcher to Blair.* London: Oxford University Press, 2008.

Wapshott, Nicholas. *Ronald Reagan and Margaret Thatcher: A Political Marriage.* New York: Sentinel, 2007.

Williams, Glyn, and Ramsden, John. *Ruling Britannia: A Political History of Britain 1688–1988.* New York: Longman, 1990.

Wills, Clair. *Lovers and Strangers: An Immigrant History of Post-War Britain.* London: Allen Lane, 2017.

Young, Hugo. *The Iron Lady: A Biography of Margaret Thatcher.* New York: Farrar, Straus, and Giroux, 1989.

Young, John W. *Britain and the World in the Twentieth Century.* New York: Oxford University Press, 1997.

NORTHERN IRELAND

Adams, Gerry. *Hope and History: Making Peace in Ireland.* London: Brandon, 2004.

Arthur, Paul. *Government and Politics of Northern Ireland.* 2nd ed. New York: Longman, 1984.

Arthur, Paul, and Keith Jeffery. *Northern Ireland since 1968.* Cambridge, MA: Basil Blackwell, 1988.

Aughey, Arthur. *The Politics of Northern Ireland.* Abington, UK: Routledge, 2005.

Barton, Brian, and Patrick J. Roche. *The Northern Ireland Question.* Brookfield, VT: Ashgate, 1999.

Bower, Tom. *Boris Johnson: The Gambler.* London: WH Allen, 2020.

Boyle, Keven, and Tom Hadden. *Northern Ireland: The Choice.* New York: Praeger, 1998.

Bruce, Steve. *The Edge of the Union: The Ulster Loyalist Political Vision.* Oxford, UK: Oxford University Press, 1994.

———. *God Save Ulster! The Religion and Politics of Paisleyism.* Oxford, UK: Oxford University Press, 1989.

Burns, Anna. *Milkman.* New York: Graywolf Press, 2018. A novel set in Northern Ireland during "the Troubles."

Coogan, Tim Pat. *The IRA.* Rev. ed. London: HarperCollins, 2000.

Dixon, Paul. *The Northern Ireland Peace Process: Choreography and Theatrical Politics.* New York: Routledge, 2006.

Elliott, Marianne. *The Catholics of Ulster: A History.* New York: Basic Books, 2002.

———. *The Long Road to Peace in Northern Ireland.* Liverpool, UK: Liverpool University Press, 2002.

Farren, Sean, and Robert F. Mulvihill. *Paths to a Settlement in Northern Ireland.* New York: Oxford University Press, 2000.

Feeney, Brian. *Sinn Fein: A Hundred Turbulent Years.* Madison: University of Wisconsin Press, 2003.

Gaffikin, Frank, and Mike Morrissey. *Northern Ireland: The Thatcher Years.* Atlantic Highlands, NJ: Humanities Press, 1990.

Geraghty, Tony. *The Irish War: The Hidden Conflict between the IRA and British Intelligence.* Baltimore, MD: Johns Hopkins University Press, 2000.

Godson, Dean. *Himself Alone: David Trimble and the Ordeal of Unionism.* New York: HarperCollins, 2004.

Hull, Roger H. *Irish Triangle: Conflict in Northern Ireland.* Princeton, NJ: Princeton University Press, 1976.

Irvine, Maurice. *Northern Ireland: Faith and Faction.* New York: Routledge, 1991.

Maillot, Agnes. *New Sinn Fein: Irish Republicanism in the Twenty First Century.* New York: Routledge, 2006.

Maloney, Ed. *A Secret History of the IRA.* New York: Norton, 2002.

McDonald, Henry, and Jim Cusack. *UDA: Inside the Heart of Loyalist Terror.* Dublin: Penguin Ireland, 2004.

Mitchell, Paul, and Rick Wilford, eds. *Politics in Northern Ireland.* Boulder, CO: Westview Press, 1998.

Murray, Gerard, and Jonathan Tonge. *Sinn Fein and the SDLP: From Alienation to Participation.* London: Hurst, 2005.

O'Kane, Eamonn. *Anglo-Irish Relations and the Northern Ireland Conflict.* New York: Routledge, 2006.

Ruane, Joseph, and Jennifer Todd. *The Dynamics of Conflict in Northern Ireland.* New York: Cambridge University Press, 2003.

Tonge, Jonathan. *Northern Ireland.* London: Polity, 2005.

Whyte, John, and Garret Fitzgerald. *Interpreting Northern Ireland.* Oxford, UK: Oxford University Press, 1991.

Wichert, Sabine. *Northern Ireland since 1945.* New York: Longman, 1991.

REPUBLIC OF IRELAND

Ardagh, John. *Ireland and the Irish: Portrait of a Changing Society.* New York: Penguin, 1998.

Boyce, D. George. *Nationalism in Ireland.* 2nd ed. New York: Routledge, 1991.

Chubb, Basil. *The Government and Politics of Ireland.* 3rd ed. New York: Longman, 1992.

Coakley, John, and Michael Gallagher, eds. *Politics in the Republic of Ireland.* 4th ed. Abington, UK: Routledge, 2004.

Cobain, Ian. *Anatomy of a Killing.* Granta, 2021.

Collins, Neil, and Frank McCann. *Irish Politics Today.* 3rd. ed. New York: St. Martin's Press, 1997.

Coulter, Colin, and Steve Coleman, eds. *The End of Irish History? Critical Approaches to the Celtic Tiger.* Manchester, UK: Manchester University Press, 2003.

Curtis, Edmund. *A History of Ireland.* London: Methuen, 1961.

Fitzgerald, Garret. *All in a Life.* London: Macmillan, 1991.

———. *Reflections on the Irish State.* Dublin: Irish Academic Press, 2002.

Foster, Roy F., ed. *Luck and the Irish: A Brief History of Change 1970–2000.* Oxford, UK: Oxford University Press, 2007.

———. *The Oxford History of Ireland.* Oxford, UK: Oxford University Press, 1992.

Fulton, John. *The Tragedy of Belief: Division, Politics, and Religion in Ireland.* Oxford, UK: Oxford University Press, 1991.

Gallagher, Michael, Michael Marsh, and Paul Mitchell, eds. *How Ireland Voted 2002.* New York: Palgrave Macmillan, 2003.

Johnson, Nuala C. *Ireland, the Great War and the Geography of Remembrance.* Cambridge, UK: Cambridge University Press, 2003.

Lalor, Brian, ed. *The Encyclopedia of Ireland.* New Haven, CT: Yale University Press, 2003.

Llosa, Mario Vargas. *The Dream of the Celt.* New York: Farrar, Straus, and Giroux, 2013. About Roger Casement.

Lynch, David. *When the Luck of the Irish Ran Out: The World's Most Resilient Country and Its Struggle to Rise Again.* London: Palgrave Macmillan, 2010.

Macardle, Dorothy. *The Irish Republic.* Dublin: Irish Press, 1951.

Mallie, Eamonn, and David McKittrick. *Endgame in Ireland.* London: Hodder and Stoughton, 2001.

McCaffrey, Lawrence J. *Ireland from Colony to Nation-State.* Englewood Cliffs, NJ: Prentice-Hall, 1977.

McCourt, Malachy. *History of Ireland.* Philadelphia: Running Press, 2004.

Munck, Ronnie. *The Irish Economy.* Boulder, CO: Westview Press, 1993.

O'Toole, Fintan. *Enough Is Enough: How to Build a New Republic.* London: Faber, 2010.

Patterson, Henry. *Ireland since 1939: The Persistence of Conflict.* Dublin: Penguin Ireland, 2006.

Bibliography

Roy, James Charles. *The Back of Beyond: A Search for the Soul of Ireland*. Boulder, CO: Westview Press, 2004.

———. *The Fields of Athenry: A Journey through Ireland*. Boulder, CO: Westview Press, 2003.

Savage, Robert J., Jr., ed. *Ireland in the New Century: Politics, Culture, and Identity*. Dublin: Four Courts Press, 2003.

Sweeney, Eamonn. *Down, Down Deeper and Down: Ireland in the '70s and '80s*. Dublin: Gill and Macmillan, 2010.

Tanner, Marcus. *Ireland's Holy Wars: The Struggle for a Nation's Soul, 1500–2000*. New Haven, CT: Yale University Press, 2001.

Townshend, Charles. *Ireland: The 20th Century*. New York: Oxford University Press, 1999.

———. *Political Violence in Ireland*. Oxford, UK: Oxford University Press, 1985.

Uris, Leon. *Trinity*. New York: Doubleday, 1975.

FRANCE

Adams, William James. *Restructuring the French Economy: Government and the Rise of Market Competition since World War II*. Washington, DC: Brookings Institution Press, 1989.

Alexander, Martin S. *French History since Napoleon*. New York: Oxford University Press, 1999.

Ardagh, John. *France in the New Century: Portrait of a Changing Society*. Rev. ed. New York: Penguin, 2000.

Beevor, Antony. *D-Day: The Battle for Normandy*. New York: Viking, 2009.

Begley, Louis. *Why the Dreyfus Affair Matters*. New Haven, CT: Yale University Press, 2010.

Bell, David S. *French Politics Today*. Manchester, UK: Manchester University Press, 2002.

———. *The French Socialist Party*. Oxford, UK: Oxford University Press, 1988.

Bell, David S., and Byron Criddle. *The French Communist Party in the Fifth Republic*. Oxford, UK: Oxford University Press, 1994.

Bernstein, Richard. *Fragile Glory: A Portrait of France and the French*. New York: Alfred A. Knopf, 1990.

Blanchard, Jean-Vincent. *Eminence: Cardinal Richelieu and the Rise of France*. New York: Walker, 2011.

Bowen, John. *Can Islam Be French? Pluralism and Pragmatism in a Secularist State*. Princeton, NJ: Princeton University Press, 2009.

Bozo, Frederic. *Mitterrand: The End of the Cold War and German Reunification*. New York: Berhahn Books, 2009.

Braudel, Fernand. *The Identity of France: History and Environment*. New York: HarperCollins, 1989.

Brenner, Michael, and Guillaume Parmentier. *Reconcilable Differences: US-French Relations in the New Era*. Washington, DC: Brookings Institution Press, 2002.

Bridgford, Jeff. *The Politics of French Trade Unionism*. New York: St. Martin's Press, 1992.

Brogan, D. W. *France under the Republic (1870–1939)*. New York: Harper and Row, 1940.

Brogan, Hugh. *Alexis de Tocqueville: Prophet of Democracy in the Age of Revolution: A Biography*. New Haven, CT: Yale University Press, 2006.

Brown, Frederick. *For the Soul of France: Culture Wars in the Age of Dreyfus*. New York: Knopf, 2010.

Chapman, Herrick, and Laura Frader. *Race in France: Interdisciplinary Perspectives on the Politics of Difference*. New York: Berghahn, 2004.

Cogan, Charles. *French Negotiating Behavior: Dealing with La Grande Nation*. Herndon, VA: United States Institute of Peace Press, 2003.

Cole, Alistair. *François Mitterrand: A Study in Political Leadership*. New York: Routledge, 1994.

Cross, Maire, and Sheila Perry. *Population and Social Policy in France*. Herndon, VA: Cassell, 1997.

Davies, Peter. *The Extreme Right in France, 1789 to the Present: From De Maistre to Le Pen*. New York: Routledge, 2002.

De Gaulle, Charles. *Memoirs of Hope and Endeavor*. New York: Simon and Schuster, 1970.

———. *The War Memoirs of Charles de Gaulle*. 3 vols. New York: Simon and Schuster, 1960.

Doyle, William. *The Oxford History of the French Revolution*. Oxford, UK: Oxford University Press, 1990.

Ehrmann, Henry, and Martin A. Schain. *Politics in France*. 5th ed. New York: HarperCollins, 1992.

Esdaile, Charles. *Napoleon's Wars: An International History, 1803–1815*. London: Allen Lane, 2007.

Evans, Jocelyn, ed. *The French Party System*. Manchester, UK: Manchester University Press, 2003.

Evans, Martin. *Algeria: France's Undeclared War*. Oxford, UK: Oxford University Press, 2011.

Fenby, Jonathan. *France: A Modern History from the Revolution to the War with Terror*. New York: St. Martin's Press, 2016.

———. *The General: Charles De Gaulle and the France He Saved*. New York: Simon and Schuster, 2010.

Friend, Julius W. *The Long Presidency: France in the Mitterrand Years, 1981–1995*. Boulder, CO: Westview Press, 1999.

———. *Unequal Partners: French-German Relations, 1989–2000*. Washington, DC: CSIS Press, 2001.

Fysh, Peter, and Jim Wolfreys. *The Politics of Racism in France*. New York: Palgrave Macmillan, 2003.

Gaffney, John. *The French Left and the Fifth Republic: The Discourses of Communism and Socialism in Contemporary France*. New York: St. Martin's Press, 1989.

Gildea, Robert. *France since 1945*. Oxford, UK: Oxford University Press, 1996.

Glass, Charles. *Americans in Paris: Life and Death under Nazi Occupation 1940–44*. New York: HarperCollins, 2009.

Godin, Emmanuel, and Tony Chafer, eds. *The French Exception*. New York: Berghahn, 2005.

Gopnik, Adam. *Paris to the Moon*. New York: Random House, 2000.

———. *The Table Comes First: Family, France, and the Meaning of Food*. New York: Knopf, 2011.

Gordon, Philip H. *A Certain Idea of France: French Security Policy and the Gaullist Legacy*. Princeton, NJ: Princeton University Press, 1993.

Gordon, Philip, H., and Sophie Meunier. *The French Challenge: Adapting to Globalization*. Washington, DC: Brookings Institution Press, 2001.

Hanley, David. *Party, Society, Government: Republican Democracy in France*. New York: Berghahn, 2001.

Harris, Ruth. *The Man on Devil's Island: Alfred Dreyfus and the Affair That Divided France*. London: Allen Lane, 2010.

Hauss, Charles. *Politics in France*. Washington, DC: CQ Press, 2008.

Hazareesingh, Sudhir. *Political Traditions in Modern France*. Oxford, UK: Oxford University Press, 1994.

Higonnet, Patrice. *Paris: Capital of the World*. New York: Belknap, 2002.

Hill, Michael. *Elihu Washburne: The Diary and Letters of America's Minister to France during the Siege and Commune of Paris*. New York: Simon and Schuster, 2013.

Hirschfeld, Gerhard. *Collaboration in France: Politics and Culture during the Nazi Occupation, 1940–1944*. Oxford, UK: Berg, 1989.

Hoffmann, Stanley, and George Ross, eds. *Continuity and Change in Mitterrand's France*. New York: Oxford University Press, 1987.

Hollifield, James F., and George Ross, eds. *Searching for the New France*. New York: Routledge, 1992.

Holman, Valerie, ed. *France at War in the Twentieth Century: Propaganda, Myth and Metaphor*. New York: Berghahn, 2000.

Horne, Alistair. *La Belle France: A Short History*. New York: Vintage, 2004.

———. *Seven Ages of Paris: Portrait of a City*. New York: Alfred A. Knopf, 2002.

Hussey, Andrew. *The French Intifada: The Long War between France and Its Arabs*. New York: Faber and Faber, 2014.

Jackson, Julian. *Charles de Gaulle*. London: Haus, 2003.

——. *France: The Dark Years, 1940–1944*. Oxford, UK: Oxford University Press, 2001.

Jones, Colin. *The Great Nation: France from Louis XV to Napoleon, 1715–99*. New York: Allen Lane, Penguin Press, 2002.

Kedward, Rod. *La Vie en Bleu: France and the French since 1900*. New York: Overlook Press, 2006.

Keiger, John. *France and the World in the Twentieth Century*. New York: Oxford University Press, 2000.

Larkin, Maurice. *France since the Popular Front: Government and People, 1936–1986*. Oxford, UK: Oxford University Press, 1988.

Lawday, David. *Danton: The Gentle Giant of Terror*. New York: Grove, Atlantic, 2010.

Lewis-Beck, ed. *How France Votes*. Chatham, NJ: Chatham House, 1999.

May, Catherine. *The Black and the Red*. New York: Harcourt Brace Jovanovich, 1987. Biography of Mitterrand.

McCullough, David. *The Greater Journey: Americans in Paris*. New York: Simon and Schuster, 2011.

McMillan, James F. *Twentieth Century France. Politics and Society in France, 1898–1991*. New York: Routledge, 1992.

Mitchell, Allan. *Nazi Paris: The History of an Occupation, 1940–1944*. New York: Berghahn, 2010.

Morgan, Ted. *Valley of Death: The Tragedy at Dien Pien Phu That Led America into the Vietnam War*. New York: Random House, 2010.

Neiberg, Michael. *The Blood of Free Men: The Liberation of Paris, 1944*. New York: Basic Books, 2012.

Northcutt, Wayne. *Mitterrand: A Political Biography*. New York: Holmes and Meier, 1992.

Perry, Sheila. *Voices of France: Social, Political and Cultural Identity*. Herndon, VA: Cassell, 1997.

Riding, Alan. *And the Show Went On: Cultural Life in Nazi-Occupied Paris*. London: Gerald Duckworth, 2011.

Roger, Philippe. *The American Enemy: The History of French Anti-Americanism*. Chicago: University of Chicago Press, 2005.

Sarkozy, Nicolas. *Testimony: France in the Twenty-First Century*. New York: Pantheon Books, 2007.

Schoenbrun, David. *Soldiers of the Night: The Story of the French Resistance*. New York: New American Library, 1981.

Sciolino, Elaine. *La Seduction: How the French Play the Game of Life*. New York: Times Books, 2011.

Short, Philip. *A Taste for Intrigue: The Multiple Lives of François Mitterrand*. New York: Henry Holt, 2014.

Smith, Leonard V., and Stéphane Audoin-Rouzeau. *France and the Great War, 1914–1918*. Cambridge, UK: Cambridge University Press, 2003.

Soloman, John. *DSK: The Scandal That Brought Down Dominique Strauss-Kahn*. New York: St Martin's Press, 2012.

Stevens, Anne. *The Government and Politics of France*. 3rd ed. New York: Palgrave Macmillan, 2003.

Tilly, Charles. *The Contentious French: Four Centuries of Popular Struggle*. Cambridge, MA: Harvard University Press, 1986.

Tocqueville, Alexis de. *The Old Regime and the French Revolution*. New York: Doubleday Anchor, 1955.

Tombs, Robert, and Isabelle Tombs. *That Sweet Enemy: The French and the British from the Sun King to the Present*. London: William Heinemann, 2006.

Védrine, Hubert, with Dominique Moisi. *France in an Age of Globalization*. Washington, DC: Brookings Institution Press, 2001.

Wahl, Nicholas, ed. *De Gaulle and the United States, 1930–1970*. Oxford, UK: Berg, 1992.

Wall, Irwin M. *France, the United States, and the Algerian War*. Ithaca, NY: Cornell University Press, 2001.

Wawro, Geoffrey. *The Franco-Prussian War: The German Conquest of France in 1870–1871*. Cambridge, UK: Cambridge University Press, 2003.

Wells, Sherrill Brown. *Jean Monnet: Unconventional Statesman*. Boulder, CO: Lynne Rienner, 2011.

Wieviorka, Olivier. *Normandy: The Landings to the Liberation of Paris*. Cambridge, MA: Harvard University Press, 2008.

Williams, Charles. *The Last Great Frenchman: A Life of General De Gaulle*. New York: John Wiley and Sons, 1993.

——. *Pétain*. New York: Palgrave Macmillan, 2005.

Wright, Vincent. *The Government and Politics of France*. 4th ed. New York: Routledge, 1994.

Zeldin, Theodore. *The French*. New York: Pantheon Books, 1982.

THE BENELUX COUNTRIES

Eych, F. Gunther. *The Benelux Countries: An Historical Survey*. Princeton, NJ: Van Nostrand, 1959.

Kossman, E. H. *The Low Countries, 1780–1940*. Oxford, UK: Oxford University Press, 1978.

Stein, George J. *Benelux Security Cooperation*. Boulder, CO: Westview Press, 1990.

THE NETHERLANDS

Ali, Ayaan Hirsi. *Infidel—My Life: The Story of My Enlightenment*. New York: Free Press, 2007.

——. *Nomad: From Islam to America*. New York: Simon and Schuster, 2010.

Anderweg, Rudi B., and Galen A. Irwin. *Governance and Politics of the Netherlands*. New York: Palgrave Macmillan, 2002.

Bakvis, Herman. *Catholic Power in the Netherlands*. Toronto: McGill-Queen's University Press, 1981.

Beevor, Antony. *Arnhem: The Battle for the Bridges, 1944*. New York: Viking, 2018.

Buruma, Ian. *Murder in Amsterdam: The Death of Theo van Gogh and the Limits of Tolerance*. New York: Penguin Press, 2006.

Cox, Robert H. *The Development of the Dutch Welfare State*. Pittsburgh: University of Pittsburgh Press, 1993.

Daalder, Hans, and Galen A. Irwin. *Politics in the Netherlands: How Much Change?* Portland, OR: Frank Cass, 1989.

de Bruin, Ellen. *Dutch Women Don't Get Depressed: Hoe komen die vrouwen zo stoer?* Amsterdam: Uitgeverij Contact, 2008.

Gladdish, Ken. *Governing from the Center: Politics and Policy-Making in the Netherlands*. DeKalb: Northern Illinois University Press, 1992.

Israel, Jonathan I. *Dutch Primacy in World Trade, 1585–1740*. Oxford, UK: Oxford University Press, 1990.

Lijphart, Arend. *The Politics of Accommodation: Pluralism and Democracy in the Netherlands*. Berkeley: University of California Press, 1968.

Mak, Geert. *Amsterdam*. Cambridge, MA: Harvard University Press, 2000.

Shorto, Russell. *Amsterdam: A History of the World's Most Liberal City*. New York: Doubleday, 2013.

BELGIUM

Boudart, Marina, Michel Boudart, and René Bryssinck, eds. *Modern Belgium*. Palo Alto, CA: Society for the Promotion of Science and Scholarship, 1990.

Cowie, Donald. *Belgium: The Land and the People*. Cranbury, NJ: A. S. Barnes, 1977.

Fitzmaurice, John. *Politics of Belgium: Crisis and Compromise in a Plural Society*. New York: St. Martin's Press, 1983.

Fox, Renée C. *In the Belgian Chateau: The Spirit and Culture of a European Society in an Age of Change*. Chicago: Ivan R. Dee, 1994.

Hochschild, Adam. *King Leopold's Ghost: A Story of Greed, Terror, and Heroism in Colonial Africa*. New York: Houghton Mifflin, 1998.

Hooghe, Liesbet. *A Leap in the Dark: Nationalist Conflict and Federal Reform in Belgium*. Ithaca, NY: Cornell University Press, 1993.

Lijphart, Arend, ed. *Conflict and Coexistence in Belgium*. Berkeley: University of California Press, 1980.

Meeus, Adrien de. *History of the Belgians*. New York: Praeger, 1962.

Bibliography

Menasse, Robert. *The Capital*. MacLehose Press, 2019. A novel about intrigue and bureaucracy in Brussels.

Mouton, Olivier, Marie-Anne Wilssens, Frederic Antoine, and Marc Reynebeau. *Belgium: A State of Mind*. Tielt, Belgium: Uitgeverij Lannoo, 2001.

Schrijvers, Peter. *Liberators: The Allies and Belgian Society 1944–1945*. New York: Cambridge University Press, 2009.

Strikwerda, Carl. *A House Divided: Catholics, Socialists, and Flemish Nationalists in Nineteenth-Century Belgium*. Lanham, MD: Rowman and Littlefield, 1998.

LUXEMBOURG

Barteau, Harry C. *Historical Dictionary of Luxembourg*. Metuchen, NJ: Scarecrow Press, 1996.

Majerus, Pierre. *The Institutions of the Grand Duchy of Luxembourg*. Luxembourg: Ministry of State, Press, and Information Service, 1976.

Margue, Paul. *A Short History of Luxembourg*. Luxembourg: Ministry of State, Press, and Information Service, 1976.

SWITZERLAND

Bonjour, E., H. S. Offler, and G. R. Potter. *A Short History of Switzerland*. Oxford, UK: Clarendon Press, 1972.

Bradfield, B. *The Making of Switzerland: From Ice Age to Common Market*. Zurich: Schweizer Spiegel Verlag, 1964.

Church, Clive H. *Switzerland and the European Union*. New York: Routledge, 2006.

Craig, Gordon A. *The Triumph of Liberalism: Zurich in the Golden Age, 1830–1869*. New York: Collier, 1990.

Gabriel, Jürg Martin, and Thomas Fischer. *Swiss Foreign Policy, 1945–2002*. New York: Palgrave Macmillan, 2003.

Goetschel, Laurent, Magdalena Bernath, and Daniel Schwarz. *Swiss Foreign Policy: Foundations and Possibilities*. New York: Routledge, 2004.

Gstöhl, Sieglinde. *Reluctant Europeans: Norway, Sweden, and Switzerland in the Process of Integration*. Boulder, CO: Lynn Rienner, 2002.

Hilowitz, Janet Eve. *Switzerland in Perspective*. Westport, CT: Greenwood, 1990.

Kieser, Rolf, and Kurt R. Spillman, eds. *The New Switzerland: Problems and Policies*. Palo Alto, CA: Society for the Promotion of Science and Scholarship, 1996.

Linder, Wolf. *Swiss Democracy*. New York: St. Martin's Pres, 1994.

Luck, Murray J. *History of Switzerland: The First Hundred Thousand Years from Before the Beginning to the Days of the Present*. Palo Alto, CA: Society for the Promotions of Science and Scholarship, 1985.

McPhee, John. *La Place de la Concorde-Suisse*. New York: Farrar, Straus, Giroux, 1983.

Milivojevic, Marko, and Pierre Mauerer. *Swiss Neutrality and Security: Armed Forces, National Defence and Foreign Policy*. New York: St. Martin's Press, 1991.

Remak, Joachim. *A Very Civil War: The Swiss Sonderbund War of 1847*. Boulder, CO: Westview Press, 1993.

Sorell, Walter. *The Swiss*. New York: Bobbs-Merrill, 1972.

Steinberg, Jonathan. *Why Switzerland?* 2nd ed. Cambridge, UK: Cambridge University Press, 1996.

Steiner, Jürg. *Amicable Agreement versus Majority Rule: Conflict Resolution in Switzerland*. Chapel Hill: University of North Carolina Press, 1974.

——. *Conscience in Politics*. Levittown, PA: Garland, 1996.

LIECHTENSTEIN

Kranz, Walter, ed. *The Principality of Liechtenstein: A Documentary Handbook*. Schaan, Liechtenstein: Lingg, 1973.

Raton, Pierre. *Liechtenstein: History and Institutions of the Principality*. Vaduz, Liechtenstein: Liechtenstein Verlag, 1970.

Schlapp, Manfred. *This Is Liechtenstein: People and Places, Yesterday and Today, Monarchy and Democracy, Citizen and States, Culture, Art, and Sports, Economy and Society, Domestic and Foreign Policy*. Stuttgart, Germany: Seewald, 1980.

MEDITERRANEAN EUROPE

Abulafia, David. *The Great Sea: A Human History of the Mediterranean*. New York: Oxford University Press, 2011.

Aliboni, Roberto, ed. *Southern European Security in the 1990s*. New York: St. Martin's Press, 1992.

Chilcote, Ronald H., et al. *Transitions from Dictatorship to Democracy: Comparative Studies of Spain, Portugal and Greece*. Bristol, PA: Crane Russak, 1990.

Kurth, James, and James Petras. *Mediterranean Paradoxes: The Politics and Social Structure of Southern Europe*. Oxford, UK: Berg, 1992.

Liebert, Ulrike, and Maurizio Cotta, eds. *Parliament and Democratic Consolidation in Southern Europe: Italy, Spain, Portugal, Greece and Turkey in Comparison*. New York: Columbia University Press, 1990.

GREECE

Bahcheci, Tozun. *Greek-Turkish Relations since 1955*. Boulder, CO: Westview Press, 1989.

Beaton, Roderick. *Byron's War: Romantic Rebellion, Greek Revolution*. Cambridge, UK: Cambridge University Press, 2013.

Bryant, Ralph C., Nicholas C. Garganas, and George S. Tavlas. *Greece's Economic Performance and Prospects*. Washington, DC: Brookings Institution Press, 2002.

Clark, Bruce. *Twice a Stranger: The Mass Expulsions That Forged Modern Greece and Turkey*. Cambridge, MA: Harvard University Press, 2006.

Clogg, Richard. *A Concise History of Greece*. 2nd ed. Cambridge, UK: Cambridge University Press, 2002.

——, ed. *Greece in the 1980's*. London: Macmillan, 1983.

——, ed. *The Struggle for Greek Independence: Essays to Mark the 150th Anniversary of the Greek War of Independence*. London: Macmillan, 1973.

Constas, Dimitri, ed. *The Greek-Turkish Conflict in the 1990s: Domestic and External Influences*. New York: St. Martin's Press, 1991.

Couloumbis, Theodore A., Theodore Kariotis, and Fotini Bellou, eds. *Greece in the Twentieth Century*. London: Frank Cass, 2003.

Couloumbis, Theodore A., John A. Petropoulos, and Harry J. Psomiades. *Foreign Interference in Greek Politics: An Historical Perspective*. New York: Pella, 1976.

Featherstone, Kevin, ed. *The Challenge of Modernization: Politics and Policy in Greece*. Special issue, *West European Politics* 28, no. 2 (March 2005).

Featherstone, Kevin, and Dimitrios K. Katsoudas, eds. *Political Change in Greece: Before and After the Colonels*. Kent, UK: Croom Helm, 1988.

Fox, Robin Lane. *The Classical World: An Epic History from Homer to Hadrian*. New York: Basic Books, 2006.

Hadjiyannis, Stylianos. *Social Conflict and Change in Modern Greece*. Bristol, PA: Crane Russak, 1991.

Kazakos, Panos, and P. C. Ioakimidis, eds. *Greece and EC Membership Evaluated*. New York: St. Martin's Press, 1995.

Koliopoulos, J. S., and Thanos M. Veremis. *Greece: The Modern Sequel: From 1821 to the Present*. London: Hurst, 2002.

Kourvetaris, Yorgos A., and Betty A. Dobratz. *A Profile of Modern Greece: In Search of Identity*. Oxford, UK: Oxford University Press, 1988.

Lacey, Jim. *The First Clash: The Miraculous Greek Victory at Marathon and Its Impact on Western Civilization*. New York: Bantam Books, 2011.

Mazower, Mark. *Inside Hitler's Greece: The Experience of Occupation, 1941–44*. New Haven,, CT: Yale University Press, 2001.

Nachmani, Amikam. *International Intervention in the Greek Civil War*. Westport, CT: Praeger, 1990.

Pagoulatos, George. *Greece's New Political Economy.* New York: Palgrave Macmillan, 2003.

Pettifer, James. *The Greeks: The Land and People since the War.* 2nd ed. New York: Penguin, 2000.

Richard, Carl J. *Greeks and Romans Bearing Gifts: How the Ancients Inspired the Founding Fathers.* Lanham, MD: Rowman and Littlefield, 2008.

Spourdalakis, Michalis. *The Rise of the Greek Socialist Party.* New York: Routledge, 1988.

Stavrakis, Peter J. *Moscow and Greek Communism, 1944–1949.* Ithaca, NY: Cornell University Press, 1992.

Stearns, Monteagle. *Entangled Allies: US Policy toward Greece, Turkey, and Cyprus.* New York: Council on Foreign Relations Press, 1992.

Sullom, Simon Levis. *The Italian Executioners: The Genocide of the Jews of Italy.* Princeton: Princeton University Press, 2018.

Tzannatos, Zafiris. *Socialism in Greece.* Brookfield, VT: Gower, 1986.

Winnifrith, Tom and Penelope Murray, eds. *Greece Old and New.* New York: St. Martin's Press, 1982.

Woodhouse, C. M. *Karamanlis: The Restorer of Greek Democracy.* New York: Oxford University Press, 1982.

———. *Modern Greece: A Short History.* New York: Faber and Faber, 1977.

CYPRUS

Calotychos, Vangelis, ed. *Cyprus and Its People: Nation, Identity, and the Experience in an Unimaginable Community, 1955–1997.* Boulder, CO: Westview Press, 1998.

Diez, Thomas, ed. *The European Union and the Cyprus Conflict: Modern Conflict, Postmodern Union.* Manchester, UK: Manchester University Press, 2002.

Dodd, Clement H. *The Cyprus Imbroglio.* Concord, MA: Paul and Company Publishers Consortium, 1998.

Hart, Parker T. *Two NATO Allies at the Threshold of War: Cyprus, a Firsthand Account of Crisis Management, 1965–1968.* Durham, NC: Duke University Press, 1990.

Holland, Robert. *Britain and the Revolt in Cyprus, 1954–1959.* New York: Oxford University Press, 1998.

Joseph, Joseph S. *Cyprus: Ethnic Conflict and International Politics: From Independence to the Threshold of the European Union.* New York: Saint Martin's Press, 1997.

Kitromilides, Paschalis M. *Cyprus.* Rev. ed. Santa Barbara, CA: ABC-CLIO, 1995.

Lordos, Alexandros, Erol Kaymak, and Nathalie Tocci. *A People's Peace in Cyprus: Testing Public Opinion on the Options for a Comprehensive Settlement.* Washington, DC: Brookings Institution Press, 2009.

O'Malley, Brendan. *Cyprus Conspiracy.* New York: I. B. Tauris, 2000.

Pace, Roderick. *The European Union's Mediterranean Enlargement: Cyprus and Malta.* New York: Routledge, 2006.

Panteli, Stavros. *Historical Dictionary of Cyprus.* Lanham, MD: Scarecrow Press, 1995.

Salem, Norma, ed. *Cyprus: A Regional Conflict and its Resolution.* New York: St. Martin's Press, 1992.

Solstein, Eric, ed. *Cyprus: A Country Study.* 4th ed. Washington, DC: US Government Printing Office, 1993.

ITALY

Atkinson, Rick. *The Day of Battle: The War in Sicily and Italy, 1943–1944.* New York: Henry Holt, 2007.

Bailey, Roderick. *Target Italy: The Secret War against Mussolini, 1940–1943.* London: Faber and Faber, 2014.

Barkan, Joanne. *Visions of Emancipation: The Italian Workers' Movement since 1945.* New York: Praeger, 1984.

Barzini, Luigi. *The Italians.* New York: Atheneum, 1977.

Bosworth, R. J. B. *Italian Venice: A History.* New Haven, CT: Yale University Press, 2014.

———. *Mussolini's Italy: Life under the Dictatorship, 1915–1945.* New York: Penguin Books, 2005.

Bull, Martin, and Martin Rhodes, eds. *Crisis and Transition in Italian Politics.* Portland, OR: Frank Cass, 1997.

———, eds. *Italy: A Contested Polity.* Special issue, *West European Politics* 30, no. 4 (September 2007).

Burnett, Stanton H., and Luca Mantovani. *The Italian Guillotine: Operation Clean Hands and the Overthrow of Italy's First Republic.* Lanham, MD: Rowman and Littlefield, 1998.

Caesar, Michael, and Peter Hainsworth, eds. *Writers and Society in Contemporary Italy.* 2nd rev. ed. Oxford, UK: Berg, 1993.

Catanzaro, Raimondo, ed. *The Red Brigades and Left-Wing Terrorism in Italy.* New York: St. Martin's Press, 1991.

D'Alimonte, Roberto, and David Nelken, eds. *Italian Politics: The Center-Left in Power.* Boulder, CO: Westview Press, 1997.

DiScala, Spencer M. *Italy: From Revolution to Republic: 1700 to the Present.* 4th ed. Boulder, CO: Westview Press, 2008.

Duggan, Christopher. *Fascist Voices: An Intimate History of Mussolini's Italy.* London: Bodley Head, 2012.

Duggan, Christopher, and Christopher Wagstaff, eds. *Italy in the Cold War: Politics, Culture and Society 1948–1958.* Oxford, UK: Berg, 1993.

Ebner, Michael R. *Ordinary Violence in Mussolini's Italy.* London: Cambridge University Press, 2011.

Emmott, Bill. *Good Italy, Bad Italy: Why Italy Must Conquer Its Demons to Face the Future.* New Haven, CT: Yale University Press, 2012.

Farneti, Paolo. *The Italian Party System.* London: Frances Pinter, 1985.

Friedman, Alan. *My Way: Berlusconi in His Own Words.* London: Biteback, 2015.

Furlong, Paul. *Modern Italy: Representation and Reform.* New York: Routledge, 1994.

Giammanco, Rosanna Mulazzi. *The Catholic-Communist Dialogue in Italy: 1944 to the Present.* Westport, CT: Praeger, 1989.

Gilbert, Mark. *The Italian Revolution: The End of Politics, Italian Style?* Boulder, CO: Westview Press, 1995.

Gilmour, David. *The Pursuit of Italy: A History of a Land, Its Regions and Their Peoples.* New York: Farrar, Straus, and Giroux, 2011.

Ginsborg, Paul. *A History of Contemporary Italy: Society and Politics 1943–1988.* New York: Palgrave Macmillan, 2003.

———. *Italy and Its Discontents: Family, Civil Society, State, 1980–2001.* New York: Penguin, 2002.

Gold, Thomas. *The Lega Nord and Contemporary Politics in Italy.* New York: Palgrave Macmillan, 2003.

Hearder, Harry. *Italy: A Short History.* Cambridge, UK: Cambridge University Press, 1990.

Hibbert, Christopher. *Rome: The Biography of a City.* New York: Viking, 1985.

Hine, David. *Governing Italy: The Politics of Bargained Pluralism.* Oxford, UK: Oxford University Press, 1993.

Hooper, John. *The Italians.* London: Allen Lane, 2015.

Hughes, Robert. *Rome: A Cultural, Visual and Personal History.* London: Weidenfeld and Nicholson, 2011.

Italian Politics: A Review. New York: Columbia University Press, annual updated editions.

Jones, Tobias. *The Dark Heart of Italy: Travels through Space and Time across Italy.* New York: North Point Press, 2004. A critique of Silvio Berlusconi's government.

Kertzer, David I. *Comrades and Christians: Religion and Political Struggle in Communist Italy.* Prospect Heights, IL: Waveland, 1992.

Knox, Amanda. *Waiting to Be Heard: A Memoir.* New York: HarperCollins, 2013.

Kogan, Norman H. *Political History of Postwar Italy: From the Old to the New Center Left.* New York: Praeger, 1981.

Lane, David. *Into the Heart of the Mafia: A Journey through the Italian South.* London: Profile Books, 2009.

Leonardi, Robert, and Douglas A. Wertman. *Italian Christian Democracy.* New York: St. Martin's Press, 1989.

Levy, Carl, ed. *Italian Regionalism: History, Identity and Politics.* New York: Berg, 1996.

Bibliography

Locke, Richard M. *Remaking the Italian Economy*. Ithaca, NY: Cornell University Press, 1997.

Lorenzi, Paola, and Luisetta Chomel. *Italia: Civilta e Cultura*. Lanham, MD: University Press of America, 2009.

Lupo, Salvatore. *History of the Mafia*. New York: Columbia University Press, 2009.

McCarthy, Patrick. *The Crisis of the Italian State*. New York: St. Martin's Press, 1997.

Morgan, Philip. *The Fall of Mussolini*. Oxford, UK: Oxford University Press, 2007.

Moss, David. *The Politics of Left-Wing Violence in Italy, 1969–85*. New York: St. Martin's Press, 1990.

Mountjoy, Alan B. *The Mezzogiorno*. New York: Oxford University Press, 1973.

Newell, James, ed. *The Italian General Election of 2001: Berlusconi's Victory*. New York: Palgrave Macmillan, 2003.

Nuzzi, Gianluigi, and Claudio Antonelli. *Blood Ties: The 'Ndrangheta: Italy's New Mafia*. London: Pan Books, 2012.

Parker, Simon, and Paolo Natale. *Contemporary Italian Politics*. New York: Routledge, 2006.

Partridge, Hillary. *Italian Politics Today*. New York: St. Martin's Press, 1998.

Pridham, Geoffrey. *Political Parties and Coalitional Behavior in Italy*. New York: Routledge, 1988.

Procacci, Giuliano. *History of the Italian People*. Hammondsworth, UK: Penguin Books, 1973.

Putnam, Robert D. *Making Democracy Work: Civic Traditions in Modern Italy*. Princeton, NJ: Princeton University Press, 1993.

Reski, Petra. *The Honoured Society: The Secret History of Italy's Most Powerful Mafia*. London: Atlantic Books, 2012.

Riall, Lucy. *Garibaldi: Invention of a Hero*. New Haven, CT: Yale University Press, 2007.

Richards, Charles. *The New Italians*. New York: Penguin, 1995.

Saviano, Roberto. *Gomorrah: A Personal Journey into the Violent International Empire of Naples' Organized Crime System*. New York: Farrar, Straus, and Giroux, 2007.

Sciascia, Leonardo. *The Moro Affair*. London: Granta Books, 2002.

Sullam, Simon Levis. *The Italian Executioners: The Genocide of the Jews of Italy*. Princeton, NJ: Princeton University Press, 2018.

Trevelyan, J. O. *A Short History of the Italian People*. London: Allen and Unwin, 1956.

Viroli, Maurizio. *The Liberty of Servants: Berlusconi's Italy*. Translated by Antony Shugaar. Princeton, NJ: Princeton University Press, 2012.

Weinberg, Leonard. *The Transformation of Italian Communism*. New Brunswick, NJ: Transaction, 1995.

SAN MARINO

Bent, James T. *A Freak of Freedom or the Republic of San Marino*. Port Washington, NY: Kennikat, 1970.

Rossi, Giuseppe. *The Republic of San Marino, the Oldest and Smallest Republic of the World*. San Marino: Governmental Tourist Body, Sport and Spectacle, n.d.

———. *A Short History of the Republic of San Marino*. San Marino: Poligrafico Artioli-Modena, n.d.

San Marino. Milan: Ediz. Garami (Garanzini Milano), 1977.

VATICAN CITY

Bernstein, Carl, and Marco Politi. *His Holiness: John Paul II and the Hidden History of Our Time*. New York: Bantam Doubleday Dell, 1996.

Flamini, Roland. *Pope, Premier, President*. New York: Macmillan, 1980.

Franco, Massimo. *Parallel Empires: The Vatican and the United States: Two Centuries of Alliance and Conflict*. New York: Doubleday, 2009.

Ivereigh, Austen. *The Great Reformer: Francis and the Making of a Radical Pope*. New York: Henry Holt, 2014.

Kreutz, Andres. *Vatican Policy on the Palestinian-Israeli Conflict: The Struggle for the Holy Land*. Westport, CT: Greenwood, 1990.

Lo Bello, Nino. *Vatican Empire*. New York: Trident Press, 1969.

Nichols, Peter. *The Pope's Divisions*. New York: Holt, Rinehart, and Winston, 1981.

Partner, Peter. *The Lands of St. Peter: The Papal State in the Middle Ages and the Early Renaissance*. London: Methuen, 1972.

Vallely, Paul. *Pope Francis: Untying the Knots*. London: Bloomsbury, 2013.

Walsh, Michael J. *Vatican City State*. Santa Barbara, CA: ABC-CLIO, 1983.

MALTA

Berg, Warren G. *Historical Dictionary of Malta*. Metuchen, NJ: Scarecrow Press, 1995.

Blouet, Brian. *The Story of Malta*. Rev. ed. London: Faber and Faber, 1972.

Holland, James. *Fortress Malta: An Island under Siege 1940–1943*. London: Phoenix, 2003.

Pace, Roderick. *The European Union's Mediterranean Enlargement: Cyprus and Malta*. New York: Routledge, 2006.

Sire, H. J. A. *The Knights of Malta*. New Haven, CT: Yale University Press, 1996.

IBERIAN PENINSULA

Manuel, Paul C., and Sebastian Royo. *Spain and Portugal in the European Union:* *The First Fifteen Years*. New York: Routledge, 2004.

Mar-Molinero, Clare, and Angel Smith. *Nationalism and the Nation in the Iberian Peninsula: Competing and Conflicting Identities*. New York: Berg, 1996.

Michener, James. *Iberia*. New York: Random House, 1968.

Payne, Stanley G. *A History of Spain and Portugal*. 2 vols. Madison: University of Wisconsin Press, 1973.

Tovias, Alfred. *Foreign Economic Relations of the European Community: The Impact of Spain and Portugal*. Boulder, CO: Lynne Rienner, 1990.

Wiarda, Howard J. *Iberia and Latin America: New Democracies, New Policies*. Lanham, MD: Rowman and Littlefield, 1996.

———. *Politics in Iberia: The Political Systems of Spain and Portugal*. New York: HarperCollins, 1993.

SPAIN

Alba, Victor. *The Communist Party in Spain*. New Brunswick, NJ: Transaction, 1983.

———. *The Transition in Spain: From Franco to Democracy*. New Brunswick, NJ: Transaction, 1978.

Archer, E. G. *Gibraltar, Identity and Empire*. New York: Routledge, 2005.

Balfour, Sebastian. *The Politics of Contemporary Spain*. New York: Routledge, 2005.

Beevor, Antony. *The Battle for Spain: The Spanish Civil War 1936–1939*. New York: Penguin, 2006.

Bertrand, Louis, and Sir Charles Petrie. *The History of Spain: From the Musulmans to Franco*. New York: Collier Books, 1971.

Burns, Jimmy. *La Roja: How Soccer Conquered Spain and How Spanish Soccer Conquered the World*. New York: Nation Books, 2012.

Carr, Raymond, and Juan Pablo Fusi. *Spain: 1808–1975*. 2nd ed. New York: Oxford University Press, 1982.

———. *Spain: Dictatorship to Democracy*. 2nd ed. Winchester, MA: Allen and Unwin, 1981.

Castro, Americo. *The Spaniards: An Introduction to Their History*. Berkeley: University of California Press, 1985.

Cercas, Javier. *The Anatomy of a Moment: Thirty-Five Minutes in History and Imagination*. London: Bloomsbury, 2011. About the military capture of the Cortes in 1981.

Chislett, W. *Spain: Going Places*. Madrid: Telefónica, 2008.

———. *Spain and the United States: The Quest for Mutual Rediscovery*. Madrid: Real Instituto Elcano de estudios internacionales y estratégicos, 2005.

Collins, Roger. *The Basques*. London: Blackwell, 1987.

Conversi, Daniele. *Nationalist Mobilization in Catalonia and the Basque Country*. Reno: University of Nevada Press, 1995.

Eaton, Samuel D. *The Forces of Freedom in Spain, 1974–1979*. Palo Alto, CA: Hoover, 1981.

Fusi, J. P. *Franco: A Biography*. Translated by Felipe Fernández-Armesto. New York: Harper and Row, 1987.

Gil, Federico G., and Joseph S. Tulchin, eds. *Spain's Entry into NATO*. Boulder, CO: Lynne Rienner, 1988.

Gillespie, Richard. *The Spanish Socialist Party: A History of Factionalism*. Oxford, UK: Oxford University Press, 1989.

Gillespie, Richard, and Richard Youngs, eds. *Spain: The European and International Challenges*. Portland, OR: Frank Cass, 2003.

Gilmour, David. *Cities of Spain*. Chicago: Ivan R. Dee, 1992.

———. *The Transformation of Spain*. Topsfield, MA: Quartet, 1986.

Gold, Peter. *Gibraltar: British or Spanish?* New York: Routledge, 2005.

Graham, Helen. *The Spanish Republic at War 1936–1939*. Cambridge, UK: Cambridge University Press, 2003.

Grugel, Jean, and Tim Rees. *Franco's Spain*. New York: St. Martin's Press, 1997.

Gunther, Richard, ed. *Politics, Society, and Democracy: The Case of Spain*. Boulder, CO: Westview Press, 1993.

Gunther, Richard, José Ramón Montero, and Joan Botella. *Democracy in Modern Spain*. New Haven, CT: Yale University, 2004.

Gunther, Richard, Giacomo Sani, and Goldie Shabad. *Spain after Franco: The Making of a Competitive Party System*. Berkeley: University of California Press, 1988.

Holguin, Sandie. *Creating Spaniards: Culture and National Identity in Republican Spain*. Madison: University of Wisconsin Press, 2002.

Hooper, John. *The New Spaniards*. 2nd rev. ed. New York: Penguin, 2006.

Jackson, Gabriel. *The Spanish Republic and the Civil War, 1931–1939*. Princeton, NJ: Princeton University Press, 1965.

Kamen, Henry. *The Disinherited: The Exiles Who Created Spanish Culture*. London: Allen Lane, 2007.

Kenwood, Alun, ed. *The Spanish Civil War: A Cultural and Historical Reader*. Oxford, UK: Berg, 1992.

Kurlansky, Mark. *The Basque History of the World*. New York: Penguin, 1999.

Magone, José M. *Contemporary Spanish Politics*. New York: Routledge, 2002.

Maravall, José. *The Transition to Democracy in Spain*. New York: St. Martin's Press, 1983.

Maxwell, Kenneth, ed. *Spanish Foreign and Defense Policy*. Boulder, CO: Westview Press, 1991.

Maxwell, Kenneth, and Steven Spiegel. *The New Spain: From Isolation to Influence*. New York: Council on Foreign Relations, 1994.

McRoberts, Kenneth. *Catalonia*. New York: Oxford University Press, 2000.

Nadeau, Jean-Benoit, and Julie Barlow. *The Story of Spanish*. New York: St. Martin's Press, 2013.

Newton, Michael T. *Institutions of Modern Spain: A Political and Economic Guide*. New York: Cambridge University Press, 1997.

Parry, J. H. *The Spanish Seaborne Empire*. Berkeley: University of California Press, 1990.

Payne, Stanley G. *Basque Nationalism*. Reno: University of Nevada Press, 1975.

———. *Fascism in Spain, 1923–1977*. Madison: University of Wisconsin Press, 1999.

———. *The Franco Regime 1936–1975*. London: Phoenix Press, 2000.

———. *The Spanish Civil War, the Soviet Union, and Communism*. New Haven, CT: Yale University Press, 2004.

Pilar, Ortuño Anaya. *European Socialists and Spain: The Transition to Democracy, 1959–77*. New York: Palgrave Macmillan, 2002.

Preston, Paul. *The Last Stalinist: The Life of Santiago Carrillo*. London: William Collins, 2014.

———. *The Politics of Revenge: Fascism and the Military in 20th Century Spain*. New York: HarperCollins, 1990.

———, ed. *Spain in Crisis: The Evolution and Decline of the Franco Regime*. London: Harvester Press, 1976.

———. *The Spanish Holocaust: Inquisition and Extermination in Twentieth-Century Spain*. New York: W. W. Norton, 2012.

———. *The Triumph of Democracy in Spain*. London: Methuen, 1986.

———. *We Saw Spain Die: Foreign Correspondents in the Spanish Civil War*. London: Constable, 2008.

———. *A People Betrayed*. New York: Liveright, 2020.

Radosh, Ronald, Mary R. Habeck, and Grigory Sevostianov, eds. *Spain Betrayed: The Soviet Union in the Spanish Civil War*. New Haven, CT: Yale University Press, 2001.

Reinares, Fernando. *Al-Qaeda's Revenge: The 2004 Madrid Train Bombings*. New York: Columbia University Press, 2017.

Rhodes, Richard. *Hell and Good Company: The Spanish Civil War and the World It Made*. New York: Simon and Schuster, 2015.

Salmon, Keith. *The Modern Spanish Economy: Transformation and Integration into Europe*. New York: Columbia University Press, 1991.

Shubert, Adrian. *A Social History of Modern Spain*. New York: HarperCollins, 1990.

Sullivan, J. L. *ETA and Basque Nationalism: The Fight for Euskadi 1890–1986*. Kent, UK: Croom Helm, 1988.

Thomas, Hugh. *World without End: The Global Empire of Philip II*. London: Allen Lane, 2014.

Tortella, Gabriel. *The Development of Modern Spain: An Economic History of the Nineteenth and Twentieth Centuries*. Cambridge, MA: Harvard University Press, 2000.

EU institutions in Brussels   Courtesy: Central audiovisual Library, European Commision

Bibliography

Treglown, Jeremy. *Franco's Crypt: Spanish Culture and Memory since 1936*. New York: Farrar, Straus, and Giroux, 2014.

Tremlett, Giles. *Ghosts of Spain: Travels through a Country's Hidden Past*. Faber and Faber, 2007.

Vilar, Pierre. *Spain: A Brief History*. 2nd ed. New York: Pergamon, 1980.

Williams, Mark. *The Story of Spain*. 3rd ed. Fuengirola, Spain: Santana Books, 2000.

Woolard, Kathryn A. *Double Talk: Bilingualism and the Politics of Ethnicity in Catalonia*. Palo Alto, CA: Stanford University Press, 1989.

PORTUGAL

Birmingham, David. *A Concise History of Portugal*. Cambridge, UK: Cambridge University Press, 2003.

Bruce, N. *Portugal: The Last Empire*. New York: Wiley, 1975.

Bruneau, Thomas C. *Political Parties and Democracy in Portugal*. Boulder, CO: Westview Press, 1997.

———. *Politics and Nationhood: Post-Revolutionary Portugal*. New York: Praeger, 1984.

Bruneau, Thomas C., and Alex Macleod. *Politics in Contemporary Portugal: Parties and the Consolidation of Democracy*. Boulder, CO: Lynne Rienner, 1986.

Chilcote, Ronald H. *The Portuguese Revolution: State and Class in the Transition to Democracy*. Lanham, MD: Rowman and Littlefield, 2009.

dos Passos, John. *The Portugal Story: Three Centuries of Exploration and Discovery*. New York: Doubleday, 1969.

Figueiredo, Antonio de. *Portugal: 50 Years of Dictatorship*. London: Penguin, 1975.

Graham, Lawrence. *The Portuguese Military and the State*. Boulder, CO: Westview Press, 1993.

Graham, Lawrence, and Henry Makler, eds. *Contemporary Portugal: The Revolution and Its Antecedents*. Austin: University of Texas Press, 1979.

Hamilton, Kimberly A. *Lusophone Africa, Portugal, and the United States*. Boulder, CO: Westview Press, 1992.

Harsgor, Michael. *Portugal in Revolution: The Washington Papers* 3, no. 32. Beverly Hills, CA: Sage, 1976.

Harvey, Robert. *Portugal: Birth of Democracy*. New York: St. Martin's Press, 1978.

Janitschek, Hans. *Mario Soares: Portrait of a Hero*. New York: St. Martin's Press, 1986.

Livermore, H. V. *Portugal: A Short History*. Edinburgh, UK: Edinburgh University Press, 1973.

Lochery, Neill. *Lisbon: War in the Shadows of the City of Light, 1939–1945*. New York: PublicAffairs, 2012. About World War II.

MacDonald, Scott B. *European Destiny, Atlantic Transformations: Portuguese Foreign Policy under the Second Republic, 1974–1992*. New Brunswick, NJ: Transaction, 1993.

Magone, José M. *European Portugal: The Difficult Road to Sustainable Democracy*. New York: St. Martin's Press, 1997.

———. *Politics in Contemporary Portugal: Democracy Evolving*. Boulder, CO: Lynne Rienner, 2014.

Marques, Antonio H. *History of Portugal*. 2 vols. New York: Columbia University Press, 1972.

Maxwell, Kenneth. *The Making of Portuguese Democracy*. New York: Cambridge University Press, 1995.

Nataf, Daniel. *Democratization and Social Settlement: The Politics of Change in Contemporary Portugal*. Albany: State University of New York Press, 1995.

Opello, Walter C., Jr. *Portugal: From Monarchy to Pluralist Democracy*. Boulder, CO: Westview Press, 1991.

Pinto, António Costa, ed. *Introducing Modern Portugal*. Palo Alto, CA: Society for the Promotion of Science and Scholarship, 1998.

———. *Salazar's Dictatorship and European Fascism*. New York: Columbia University Press, 1996.

Porch, Douglas. *The Portuguese Armed Forces and the Revolution*. Palo Alto, CA: Hoover Institution, 1991.

Raby, D. L. *Fascism and Resistance in Portugal: Communists, Liberals and Military Dissidents in the Opposition to Salazar, 1941–1974*. New York: St. Martin's Press, 1988.

Schneidman, Witney W. *Engaging Africa. Washington and the Fall of Portugal's Colonial Empire*. Lanham, MD: University Press of America, 2004.

Silva Lopes, José de, ed. *Portugal and EC Membership Evaluated*. New York: St. Martin's Press, 1994.

Wheeler, Douglas L. *Historical Dictionary of Portugal*. Metuchen, NJ: Scarecrow Press, 1993.

ANDORRA

Cameron, Peter. *Andorra*. New York: Farrar, Straus, Giroux, 1997.

Carter, Youngman. *On to Andorra*. New York: Norton, 1964.

Deane, Shirley. *The Road to Andorra*. New York: Morrow, 1961.

Morgan, Bryan. *Andorra, the Country in Between*. Nottingham, UK: Palmer, 1964.

CPSIA information can be obtained
at www.ICGtesting.com
Printed in the USA
BVHW060549171021
618720BV00005B/19